P9-CKH-712

FUNDAMENTALS OF INVESTING

FUNDAMENTALS OF INVESTING

FIFTH EDITION

LAWRENCE J. GITMAN
San Diego State University

MICHAEL D. JOEHNK
Arizona State University

HarperCollins*CollegePublishers*

To our wives, Robin and Charlene

Acquisitions Editor: Kirsten D. Sandberg
Developmental Editor: Ann Torbert
Project Coordination, Text and Cover Design: York Production Services
Production/Manufacturing: Michael Weinstein/Paula Keller
Compositor: York Graphic Services, Inc.
Printer and Binder: R.R. Donnelley & Sons Company
Cover Printer: The Lehigh Press, Inc.

For permission to use copyrighted material, grateful acknowledgment is made to the copyright holders on pp. C-1–C-2, which are hereby made part of this copyright page.

FUNDAMENTALS OF INVESTING, Fifth Edition

Copyright © 1993 by Lawrence J. Gitman and Michael D. Joehnk

Library of Congress Cataloging-in-Publication Data

Gitman, Lawrence J.
    Fundamentals of investing / Lawrence J. Gitman, Michael D. Joehnk.
    —5th ed.
        p.   cm.
    Includes bibliographical references and index.
    ISBN 0-06-500615-1
    1. Investments.   I. Joehnk, Michael D.   II. Title.
HG4521.G547   1993
332.6'78—dc20   92-33410
                                                              CIP

    93 94 95 9 8 7 6 5 4 3 2

BRIEF CONTENTS

        11 Options: Rights, Warrants, Puts and Calls   442
        12 Commodities, Financial Futures, and Tangible Investments   486

PART FIVE   OTHER POPULAR INVESTMENT VEHICLES   533

        13 Mutual Funds: An Indirect Route to the Market   534
        14 Real Estate Investments   580
        15 Tax Shelters and Limited Partnerships   615

PART SIX   INVESTMENT ADMINISTRATION   655

        16 Planning and Building a Portfolio   656
        17 Portfolio Management and Control   699

            APPENDIXES   A-1

        A   Financial Tables   A-2
        B   Guide to Professional Certification Programs   A-15
        C   Guideline Answers to CFA Questions   A-19
        D   The Black-Scholes Option Pricing Model   A-26
        E   Key Equations and Disk Routines   A-32
            Selected Readings   S-1
            Glossary   G-1
            Credits   C-1
            Index   I-1

DETAILED CONTENTS

PREFACE

"Market Hits New High." "TWA Files for Bankruptcy Protection." "Michael Milken Sentenced." "Money Market Yields Fall Below 3%." "Real Estate Values Plummet." Readers of the financial press have become accustomed to such headlines in the past few years. These and numerous other events illustrate clearly that investors operate in a dynamic environment in which the only certainty is change itself. Such events add to the excitement of investing, creating both new challenges and opportunities for investors. This textbook, *Fundamentals of Investing,* fifth edition, reflects the realities of today's changing investment environment—from new investment techniques, vehicles, and strategies to regulations and taxes. The book serves investors who are, or will be, actively developing and monitoring their own investment portfolios. It meets the needs of professors and students in the first course in investments offered at colleges and universities, junior and community colleges, professional certification programs, and continuing education courses.

Focusing on portfolios, *Fundamentals of Investing* describes techniques, vehicles, and strategies for implementing investment goals in light of risk-return trade-offs. A conversational tone and liberal use of examples guide students through the material and demonstrate important points. Clearly, the benefits of the book's readability accrue not only to students but also to their instructors.

CHANGES IN THE FIFTH EDITION

The fifth edition reflects the numerous changes in the investment environment, yet appreciates the ever-present time constraints of instructors in investments courses. Using information gathered from both academicians and practicing investment professionals plus feedback from adopters, we developed a detailed revision plan for this edition. General changes, of a major nature, enhance the text's timeliness, breadth, and depth of coverage. Beyond that, we made important, but less sweeping, changes in every chapter.

Timely Topics

Various issues and developments are reshaping the financial markets and investment vehicles. To retain the text's state-of-the-art coverage, we included discussions of ethics and insider trading, wrap accounts, foreign investment products, bond duration and immunization, and asset allocation schemes. These discussions provide students with a realistic understanding of the investment arena, thereby allowing them to develop and implement effective investment strategies.

Globalization

As a result of the growing globalization of securities markets, this edition stresses the global aspects of investing. We look at the role of foreign securities in the investment portfolio, the global securities markets, and various ways to access them—foreign securities, dollar-denominated securities linked to foreign securities, and mutual funds composed of foreign securities. In addition, we assess international investment performance and discuss international investment risks. These changes should help students understand the importance of maintaining a global focus when planning, building, and managing an investment portfolio.

More Quantitative Emphasis and Problems

Instructors told us they wanted more quantitative material in certain areas. We have carefully accommodated their needs. While the book is more quantitative in spots, it still retains its readability and easy-to-understand presentation.

We added the following new quantitative material: calculating stock market averages and indexes; finding bond equivalent yields and bank discount yields on Treasury bills; the relationship between real, risk-free, and required returns; calculating the standard deviation of a single asset; graphic derivation of beta; the variable growth dividend valuation model; bond pricing and yields based on annual and semi-annual compounding; bond duration and immunization; finding portfolio returns, standard deviations, and betas; the efficient frontier; and calculating the Sharpe, Treynor, and Jensen measures of portfolio performance.

To support the increased quantitative emphasis, we have increased both the quality and quantity of end-of-chapter problems, and numbered and defined many of the equations using variable names as well as descriptive labels. Finally, we added an end-of-text appendix on the Black/Scholes option pricing model, with supporting problems.

New Bond Chapter and Improved Planning Focus

To cover all the necessary bond topics, we expanded coverage by adding a second chapter, Chapter 9, "Bond Valuation and Analysis." Whereas the first chapter on bonds (Chapter 8) is descriptive in nature, this new chapter is more analytical and deals extensively with issues of bond valuation. It begins with an expanded discussion of market interest rates and the term structure of interest rates and then proceeds to the pricing of bonds, using both annual and semi-annual compounding.

Bond yields and returns are also presented, using both approximate and precise measures, followed by a new section on bond duration and immunization. The chapter closes with a discussion of various bond investment/portfolio strategies.

In order to clarify the early planning discussions and to accommodate the new bond chapter, in this edition we distilled the material in Chapters 3 and 4 of the previous edition into a single chapter, Chapter 3, ''Investment Information and Plans.'' We believe that the resulting clearer planning focus and the expanded coverage of bonds will make the text even more useful.

Specific Content Changes by Chapter

- **Chapter 1** on the role and scope of investments now discusses derivative securities.
- **Chapter 2** on investment markets and transactions now includes: discussions of the registration of new security issues and the role of the investment banker; a major section on globalization of securities markets; and discussions of trading hours, ethical issues, and arbitration procedures in disputes with brokers.
- **Chapter 3** on investment information and plans, which resulted from merging and refining Chapters 3 and 4 of the fourth edition, includes: discussion of major government publications and comparative data sources; updated coverage of news/retrieval and databases; calculation, with examples and comparisons, of market averages and indexes; discussion, with equations, of bond equivalent yield (BEY) and bank discount yield (BDY) on short-term securities; and material on banker's acceptances.
- **Chapter 4** on measuring investment return and risk now includes: discussion of real, risk-free, and required returns; coverage of the procedure used to find growth rates; the formula for standard deviation and an example of its use to measure an asset's risk; an improved discussion of the approximate yield formula; a brief discussion of tax risk; and an expanded discussion of beta that demonstrates its graphic derivation.
- **Chapter 5** on common stock investments has a new section on investing in foreign stocks, including an extensive table of comparative annual returns in the world's major equity markets, and discussion of how to invest in foreign stocks and the impact of currency exchange rates on total returns.
- **Chapter 6** on common stock analysis now includes an illustrated discussion of how the financial ratios of a given firm can be evaluated not only in relation to the average performance of the industry, but also relative to the performance of two or three of its major competitors.
- **Chapter 7** on common stock valuation, technical analysis, and efficient markets has several major modifications: a new section on the variable growth dividend valuation model and expanded material on efficient markets, which includes discussion of the different forms of efficient markets and various types of market anomalies.
- **Chapter 8** on bond investments has been totally restructured so that it is now one of two chapters on bonds. This chapter focuses on bonds as an investment

vehicle, including the different types of risk to which these securities are exposed; the taxable equivalent yield on municipal bonds; and the growing role of stripped-Treasuries (zero-coupon bonds) and collateralized mortgage obligations (CMOs). There's also a new section on the globalization of the bond market and different ways to invest in foreign debt securities.

- **Chapter 9,** the new chapter on bond valuation and analysis, deals with the analytical side of bond investing. It includes material on the term structure of interest rates and the various explanations for the behavior of the term structure; measures bond prices and yields using both annual and semi-annual compounding; and examines with the concept of bond duration and immunization.

- **Chapter 10** on preferred stock and convertible securities now discusses why preferreds and convertibles are issued by companies in the first place and contains material on measuring the payback period on convertible instruments.

- **Chapter 11** on options now focuses mostly on puts and calls, the most popular types of options. The chapter emphasizes the derivative nature of these securities and distinguishes between European and American options; looks at the pricing of options; and expands coverage of covered calls and LEAPS (long-term options) and Caps (capped options). For the mathematically inclined, an appendix at the end of the text offers even more detail on the option pricing model.

- **Chapter 12** on commodities, financial futures, and tangible investments now has a greatly expanded section on how various kinds of financial futures can be used as hedging vehicles in conjunction with other investment outlets like stocks, bonds, and foreign securities. A new box describes how stock index futures can be used to play the January effect in the market.

- **Chapter 13** on mutual funds has new sections on how mutual funds are organized and operated and on socially responsible mutual funds and automatic investment plans.

- **Chapter 14** on real estate investment now focuses on investment property rather than on personal residences and includes improved discussion of real estate investment securities.

- **Chapter 15** on tax shelters and limited partnerships now reflects the most recent tax rates and procedures. It includes discussion of programs that defer tax liabilities to retirement—401(k) plans, Keogh plans, and individual retirement accounts (IRAs), and streamlined coverage of deferred annuities, single-premium life insurance, and limited partnerships.

- **Chapter 16** on planning and building a portfolio now includes: demonstration of the calculation of portfolio returns and standard deviations; coverage of correlation and diversification; an expanded discussion of modern portfolio theory (MPT) that includes the efficient frontier and portfolio betas; and a revised asset allocation discussion and demonstration that includes foreign securities.

- **Chapter 17** on portfolio management and control now distinguishes between active and passive portfolio management and discusses, demonstrates, and compares the Sharpe, Treynor, and Jensen measures of portfolio performance.

PEDAGOGICAL FEATURES

Numerous pedagogical features help students focus their study of investments. Among them are a comprehensive yet flexible organization, learning objectives, running glossary, high-interest boxes, varied end-of-chapter materials, a number of useful appendixes, and end-of-text materials.

Comprehensive Yet Flexible Organization

The text first describes the overall investment environment, including the concepts of risk and return. With that foundation, it then examines each popular investment vehicle—common stocks, fixed-income securities, speculative investments, and real estate, among others—followed by mutual funds and tax shelters. The final section of the book combines all the investment vehicles in two chapters on portfolio administration. Although the first and last parts of the text are best covered at the start and end of the course, respectively, instructors can cover particular investment vehicles in any sequence.

We organized each chapter according to a decision-making perspective, in which we point out the pros and cons of various strategies and vehicles. With this useful information individual investors can then select the investment actions that are consistent with their objectives. In addition, we've illustrated the vehicles and strategies so that the student senses the decision-making implications and consequences of each contemplated investment action. The comprehensive yet flexible nature of the book enables instructors to customize it to their own course structure and teaching objectives.

Learning Objectives

Each chapter begins with six numbered learning objectives which clearly state the concepts and materials to be covered. Each objective now corresponds directly to a similarly numbered summary entry. We have found that these objectives help guide students through the chapter's content.

Running Glossary

New terms are set in boldface type and defined when first introduced in the text. In addition, each term and its definition appears in the text margin to facilitate understanding and review. All of the running glossary terms also appear in a separate end-of-book glossary.

High-Interest Boxes

In each chapter, two boxed essays, called "Investor Insights," describe real-life situations or events. Although we have kept some of the favorite boxes from the previous edition, the majority are new. These high-interest boxes demonstrate text concepts and enliven student reading.

End-of-Chapter Materials

A number of important elements at the end of each chapter provide students with a mechanism for reviewing and reinforcing the concepts, tools, and techniques described within the chapter. They are:

Summary

Each summary lists the chapter's six key concepts and ideas, which correspond directly with the similarly numbered learning objective presented at the beginning of the chapter.

Questions

A comprehensive set of 15 to 20 review questions offers students opportunity to review and practice their grasp of chapter content.

Problems

New to this edition is a separate and greatly expanded set of 8 to 15 problems at the end of each chapter except Chapter 1. The problems, which vary in complexity and scope, assure professors a wide choice of assignable materials. A disk symbol ■ appears next to the problems that can be solved using the *Investment Management Disk (IMD),* described in detail on page xxi.

CFA Questions

Eleven of the 17 chapters now include an end-of-chapter question from a recent CFA (Chartered Financial Analyst) exam, marked by a special CFA symbol. (Some of these questions are slightly altered to conform better to the format of material as covered in the textbook.) While the CFA certification requires extensive understanding of a variety of investment topics, the CFA questions in this book are indicative of the kind of *basic* knowledge demanded of CFA candidates. Full Guideline Answers for these questions are included in Appendix C of the text; these are actual answers, or very close approximations thereof, used in the grading of CFA exams. (Like some of the questions themselves, some of the CFA answers have been slightly modified so they better accommodate the pedagogical approaches used in this book. The modifications were always minor in nature, and they never altered the underlying thrust of the original question.)

Case Problems

Each chapter ends with two distinct case problems. These brief accounts encourage students to apply techniques presented in the chapter and recommend how an investor might solve a specific problem. Students can solve some of these with the *Investment Management Disk (IMD),* as indicated by the disk symbol printed next to the question.

Useful Appendixes

In addition to its 17 chapters, the book includes five appendixes. Appendix A is a full set of financial tables for use in making investment calculations. Appendix B is a guide to professional certification programs. Appendix C offers guideline answers to the end-of-chapter CFA questions. Appendix D describes the Black/Scholes Option Pricing Model (OPM) and includes related problems which allow interested students to understand this important model. Appendix E lists all equations found in text and all routines on the *Investment Management Disk (IMD)*.

End-of-Text Materials

Following the appendixes, end of text materials consist of three important items—selected readings for each chapter, glossary, and index. The *glossary* offers a single place in which to find definitions of the key terms from the text's running glossary and the chapter number in which each definition appears. In this edition, a chapter-by-chapter listing of *selected readings* directs students to recent articles of further interest. These timely references, from such publications as *Barron's Financial World, Forbes, Kiplinger's Personal Financial Magazine, Money,* and *The Wall Street Journal,* give students greater investment insights from the popular financial press. Finally, a comprehensive *index* helps readers quickly find topics and equations in the text.

SUPPLEMENTAL MATERIALS

We recognize the key role of a complete and creative package of materials to supplement a basic textbook. We believe that the following materials, offered with this fifth edition, will enrich the investments course for both students and professors alike.

 ### The Investment Management Disk

Included with each new copy of the book is the *Investment Management Disk (IMD)*, which was revised and improved for this fifth edition by Donald G. Crawford of DGC Consulting, Phoenix, Arizona. The purpose of the disk is to perform the calculations of virtually all of the formulas, ratios, and valuation procedures presented in the book and listed in Appendix E for quick reference. The 3 1/2" disk is user-friendly and fully interactive. It is more than a problem solver: it also enhances the student's understanding of the investment process. The disk is keyed to all applicable text discussions and end-of-chapter and ancillary materials with a computer disk symbol. Detailed instructions for using the disk are printed on the back left endpapers.

Investor's Resource Manual (IRM)

Shrink-wrapped free with each new copy of the textbook, this supplement, prepared by Ann Torbert of St. Louis, Missouri, will further enrich the student's learning experience. The IRM has two elements: First is the "List of Sources of Financial Information," an updated version of Appendix A from the fourth edition of the book, which contains a detailed list of sources of financial information as well as a list of leading mutual funds. This material should help students obtain useful information about specific securities and track down mutual fund investment opportunities. The second element includes a variety of company, industry, and economic reports obtained from Moody's, Standard & Poor's, Value Line, brokerage firms, and others. These reports provide a real-world slant to the study of investments and give students the opportunity for some hands-on experience. Bookstores can order extra copies of this reference guide to sell alone or with used copies of the book.

Tootsie Roll Industries, Inc., Annual Report

Also shrink-wrapped with each new copy of the book is the latest annual report for Tootsie Roll Industries, Inc. The ready availability of this report enables students to review an actual annual report and offers the raw material for use in performing fundamental analysis of Tootsie Roll Industries, especially in Chapters 6 and 7 on common stock. A series of suggested classroom exercises/assignments, found in the *Instructor's Manual*, accompany the Tootsie Roll report. These show the different types of information contained in annual reports and the different ways such reports can be used.

Study Guide

The student review manual, *Study Guide to accompany Fundamentals of Investing*, fifth edition, prepared by William J. Ruckstuhl of The American College, has been completely revised. Each chapter of the study guide contains a chapter summary, a chapter outline, and a programmed self-test that consists of true-false and multiple-choice questions, and problems with detailed solutions, and, where appropriate, calculator key strokes. All elements are similar in form and content to those found in the book.

Investment Games

New to this edition are two investment games, available to adopters. Both games allow students to gain practical experience in a competitive investment environment. They are:

Stock-Trak Portfolio Management Simulation

Stock-Trak is a mock brokerage service through which students can gain realistic portfolio management experience. Each student who registers with Stock-Trak receives a Stock-Trak brokerage account, with $100,000 in imaginary cash and six weeks in which to buy, sell, buy on margin, sell short, and/or write options and trade any of the following: stocks, stock options, bonds, index options, index futures, interest rate options and futures, commodity futures, and foreign currency options and futures. Students receive periodic statements of their account activity and performance, and instructors receive a summary of class results. Students who participate in Stock-Trak simply call a toll-free number and speak with "brokers" to make trades. For its brokers, Stock-Trak employs and carefully trains mostly graduate and undergraduate finance students from universities in the Atlanta area so that all have a working knowledge of subject matter.

Principle Investment Challenge (PIC)

Developed by Thomas M. Krueger, University of Wisconsin at LaCrosse, and Stephan A. Sonderman, University of North Carolina at Charlotte, this IBM PC-compatible portfolio simulation features a programmed electronic spreadsheet (Lotus 1-2-3) to record buys and sells made by student investment teams. The simulation may run over an extended period of time and with any amount of "cash" chosen by the instructor. Since the learning goal is to analyze and choose investments, not to manipulate spreadsheets, the "market manager" or the instructor enters all data to preserve the integrity of the game. Student teams submit buy and sell forms found in the Investor's Resource Manual to the market manager who inputs all orders and tracks team progress. Students may trade stocks, bonds, options, futures, commodities, and foreign currencies and may buy long, sell short, and make margin transactions. PIC represents a flexible and inexpensive tool for allowing students to gain hands-on investment experience.

Instructor's Manual

Written by the text authors, with the assistance of Marlene G. Bellamy of Writeline Communication Associates and Mark Chockalingam of Arizona State University, the manual contains chapter outlines, a list of major topics discussed in each chapter, detailed chapter reviews, answers to all review questions and problems, solutions to the decision cases, and ideas for outside projects, including a series of assignments and exercises to accompany the Tootsie Roll Industries, Inc., annual report. Instructions for the outside projects are printed on separate sheets, for ease in duplicating them for classroom distribution. The manual also contains nearly 100 transparency masters, consisting of outlines, exhibits, and problem and case solutions.

Test Bank

The test bank underwent a major revision in this edition. Revised by William J. Ruckstuhl, the fifth edition test bank includes a substantial number of new questions. Each chapter now contains 15 (or more) true-false questions, 40 (or more) multiple-choice questions, and several problems and short essay questions. The Test Bank is available on Testmaster, a highly acclaimed microcomputerized test-generating system with word-processing capabilities. The system produces customized tests and allows instructors to scramble questions and add new ones. Testmaster is available in both IBM and MacIntosh versions.

Acetate Transparencies

A set of 80 transparency acetates developed with the assistance of Marlene G. Bellamy is available free to adopters. The acetates include key art, tables, and equations from the text, solutions to problems and cases, and, for additional classroom practice, problems and solutions not found in the text.

ACKNOWLEDGMENTS

Many people gave their generous assistance during the initial development and revisions of *Fundamentals of Investing*. The expertise, classroom experience, and general advice of both colleagues and practitioners were invaluable. Reactions and suggestions from students throughout the country—which we especially enjoy receiving—sustained our belief in the need for a fresh, informative, and teachable investments text.

A few individuals provided significant subject matter expertise in the initial development of the book. They are Terry S. Maness of Baylor University, Arthur L. Schwartz, Jr., of the University of South Florida at St. Petersburg, and Gary W. Eldred. Their contributions are greatly appreciated. In addition, HarperCollins obtained the experienced advice of a large group of reviewers. We appreciate their many suggestions and criticisms, which have had a strong influence on various aspects of this volume. Our special thanks go to the following people who reviewed all or part of the manuscripts for the previous four editions of the book.

M. Fall Ainina	Robert T. LeClair
Gary Baker	Weston A. McCormac
Harisha Batra	David J. McLaughlin
Cecil C. Bigelow	Keith Manko
Richard B. Bellinfante	Kathy Milligan
A. David Brummett	Warren E. Moeller
Gary P. Cain	Homer Mohr
Daniel J. Cartell	Joseph Newhouse
P.R. Chandy	Joseph F. Ollivier
David M. Cordell	John Park
Timothy Cowling	Ronald S. Pretekin
Robert M. Crowe	Stephen W. Pruitt
Clifford A. Diebold	William A. Richard
James Dunn	William A. Rini
Betty Marie Dyatt	Roy A. Roberson
Steven J. Elbert	Edward Rozalewicz
Frank J. Fabozzi	William J. Ruckstuhl
Robert A. Ford	Gary G. Schlarbaum
Harry P. Guenther	Keith V. Smith
Elizabeth Hennigar	Harold W. Stevenson
Robert D. Hollinger	Nancy E. Strickler
Roland Hudson, Jr.	Glenn T. Sweeny
A. James Ifflander	Phillip D. Taylor
Donald W. Johnson	Robert C. Tueting
Bill Kane	Allan J. Twark
Daniel J. Kaufmann, Jr.	John R. Weigel
David S. Kidwell	Glenn A. Wilt, Jr.
Sheri Kole	John C. Woods
Thomas M. Krueger	Richard H. Yanow

The following people provided extremely useful reviews and input to the fifth edition:

Gary Carman, *Southwest Texas State University*
Gay Hatfield, *University of Mississippi*
Sue Beck Howard, *University of North Florida*
Ravindra R. Kamath, *Cleveland State University*
Phillip T. Kolbe, *Memphis State University*
George Kutner, *Marquette University*
Linda R. Richardson, *Siena College*
Keith V. Smith, *Purdue University*
Howard E. Van Auken, *Iowa State University*
Peter M. Wichert, *University of New Mexico*

Because of the wide variety of topics covered in this edition, we called upon many experts for advice. We'd like to thank them and their firms for allowing us to draw on their insights and awareness of recent developments in order to ensure that the text is as current as possible. In particular, we want to mention Russell L. Block, *San Diego, Calif.*; George Ebenhack, *Oppenheimer & Co., Los Angeles, Calif.*; Richard Esposito, *Prana Investments, Inc., New York*; Bob Hauser and Rich Wilburn of *Valley National Bank, Phoenix, Ariz.*; N. Arthur Hulick, *Investment Planning and Management, Scottsdale, Ariz.*; Martin P. Klitzner, *Sunrise Commodities, Inc., Del Mar, Calif.*; Douglas R. Lempereur, *Templeton Global Bond Managers, Ft. Lauderdale, Fla.*; David M. Love, *Monmouth Capital Management, Inc., San Diego, Calif.*; Robert Luck, CFA, *Institute of Chartered Financial Analysts, Charlottesville, Va.*; David H. McLaughlin, *Chase Investment Counsel Corp., Charlottesville, Va.*; Donald R. Maescher, *Seidler Amdec Realty Advisors, Inc., San Diego, Calif.*; Edwin P. Morrow, *Confidential Planning Services, Inc., Middletown, Ohio*; Michael R. Murphy, *Sceptre Investment Counsel, Toronto, Ontario, Canada*; Mark Nussbaum, *Western Federal, Los Angeles, Calif.*; John E. Rains, *Wells Fargo Bank, San Diego, Calif.*; Pat Rupp, *IDS, Inc., Dayton, Ohio*; Marc Salem, *PaineWebber, Scottsdale, Ariz.*; Eric Sorensen, *Salomon Bros., Inc., New York*; Linda H. Taufen, *Northern Trust Bank, Tucson, Ariz.*; Jeanine K. Volinski, *LaJolla Insurance Services, La Jolla, Calif.*; and Fred Weaver, *Great Western Bank, Phoenix, Ariz.*

We greatly appreciate the support of our colleagues at San Diego State University and Arizona State University. Special thanks go to Robert J. Wright of Wright & Wright, CPAs, San Diego, for his help in revising and updating the many tax discussions, to Professor Frank Griggs of Grand Valley State University for his ideas on beefing up the material on efficient markets in Chapter 7 and in preparing the appendix on option pricing, and to Sue Beck Howard, Keith Smith, and Peter Wichert for their detailed final reviews and many helpful suggestions. We would also like to thank Bill Ruckstuhl for his useful feedback, as well as for authoring the *Study Guide* and the *Test Bank*. Special thanks are due Marlene Bellamy for her research, writing, and proofreading help as well as her assistance in preparing the

Instructor's Manual and transparency acetates. Our thanks also go to Don Crawford for developing and revising the *Investment Management Disk (IMD),* Tom Krueger for his numerous excellent suggestions, and to Steve Sonderman for his work with Tom to prepare the *Principle Investment Challenge (PIC).* Thanks is also due to Ann Torbert for preparing the *Investor's Resource Manual* and Mark T. Brookshire of Stock-Trak, Inc., for licensing our use of Stock-Trak, and to Tootsie Roll Industries, Inc., for allowing us to bundle Tootsie Roll's annual report with this edition. We are grateful, too, for the research assistance provided by Joe Alfrey and Jamey Stephenson and for the clerical assistance of Pam Hively, Francis Grieshaber, and Jade Pearce.

The staff of HarperCollins, particularly Kirsten Sandberg and Meg Holden, contributed their creativity, enthusiasm, and commitment to this text. Thanks to HarperCollins personnel Kathy Smeilis, permissions editor, and Arianne Weber, editorial assistant, who managed the important task of organizing, and clearing permissions, and to Storm Jeter, inventory manager, who masterminded the text and supplements packaging. Freelance developmental editor Ann Torbert, production coordinator Susan Bogle of York Production Services, and production manager Michael Weinstein of HarperCollins deserve special thanks for shepherding the manuscript through the development and production stages. Without their care and concern the text would not have evolved into the teachable and interesting text we believe it to be. A very special word of thanks is due Ann Torbert both for her outstanding development work and her work on the *Investor's Resource Manual.*

Finally, our wives, Robin and Charlene, and our children, Jessica and Zachary, and Chris and Terry and Sara, played important parts by providing support and understanding during the book's development, revision, and production. We are forever grateful to them, and hope that this edition will justify the sacrifices required during the many hours we were away from them working on this book.

Lawrence J. Gitman

Michael D. Joehnk

PART ONE

THE INVESTMENT ENVIRONMENT

THE INVESTMENT ENVIRONMENT

INVESTMENT ADMINISTRATION

INVESTING IN COMMON STOCK	INVESTING IN FIXED-INCOME SECURITIES
SPECULATIVE INVESTMENT VEHICLES	OTHER POPULAR INVESTMENT VEHICLES

1 The Role and Scope of Investments

After studying this chapter, you should be able to:

1. Grasp the meaning of the term *investments* and understand the factors commonly used to differentiate between various types of investments.

2. Describe the structure of and participants in the investment process, the types of investors, and the rewards from investing.

3. Gain an understanding of the steps involved in the process of investing.

4. Discuss the principal types of investment vehicles, including short-term vehicles, common stocks, and fixed-income securities.

5. Describe other kinds of popular investments, such as options, commodities and financial futures, tangibles, mutual funds, real estate, tax shelters, and limited partnerships.

6. Summarize the content and organizational model around which this text is structured.

What is your idea of financial success? Making a million dollars? Owning an expensive house and car? Establishing a scholarship at your alma mater? Traveling around the world? Providing for your family now and in the future? The odds are probably against your achieving *all* the items on that list. After all, few people are millionaires. However, studying this book can help you make the most of your available financial resources. Our text provides the understanding needed to establish and fulfill investment goals by creating a *portfolio* containing a variety of investment vehicles that will produce an acceptable return for an acceptable level of risk. Familiarity with various investment alternatives, plus a set of well-developed investment plans, should greatly increase your chance of achieving a reasonable degree of financial success. This chapter sets the stage for an in-depth look at the essential concepts, tools, and techniques of investing that are presented throughout the text.

THE ROLE OF INVESTMENTS

The word investments can be used in a variety of ways. It can mean stocks or bonds purchased to fulfill certain financial goals; it can also mean tangible assets such as machines acquired to produce and sell a product. In the broadest sense, investments provide the mechanism needed to finance the growth and development of our economy. To give you a general idea of the role of investments, we begin by defining investment and then looking at the structure of the investment process, the participants, and types of investors.

Investment Defined

investment
a vehicle for funds, expected to maintain or increase its value and/or generate positive returns.

Simply stated, an **investment** is any vehicle into which funds can be placed with the expectation that they will be preserved or increase in value and/or generate positive returns. Cash in a simple checking account is not an investment, since its value is likely to be eroded by inflation and since it fails to provide any type of return. The same cash placed in a bank savings account would be considered an investment, since the account provides a positive return. The various types of investment can be differentiated on the basis of a number of factors, described below.

Securities and Property

securities
investments that represent debt, business ownership, or the legal right to buy or sell a business ownership interest.

property
investments in real property or in tangible personal property.

Investments that represent evidence of debt, ownership of a business, or the legal right to acquire or sell an ownership interest in a business are called **securities.** The most common types of securities are bonds, stocks, and options. **Property,** on the other hand, is investments in real property or tangible personal property. *Real property* is land, buildings, and that which is permanently affixed to the land. *Tangible personal property* includes items such as gold, antiques, art, and other collectibles. Although security investments are quite popular, many people prefer property investments because they feel more comfortable owning something they can see and touch. But because of the existence of organized mechanisms for buying and selling securities and their widespread popularity, in this book we will focus primarily on securities rather than on property investments.

Direct and Indirect

direct investment
investment in which an investor directly acquires a claim on a security or property.

indirect investment
investment made in a portfolio or group of securities or properties.

A **direct investment** is one in which an investor directly acquires a claim on a security or property. For example, if you buy a stock, a bond, a rare coin, or a parcel of real estate in order to preserve value or earn income, you have made a direct investment. An **indirect investment** is an investment made in a portfolio or group of securities or properties. For example, you may purchase a share of a *mutual fund,* which is a diversified portfolio of securities issued by a variety of firms. By doing so, you will own a claim on a fraction of the entire portfolio rather than on the security of a single firm. It is also possible to invest indirectly in property—for example, by buying an interest in a limited partnership that deals in real estate, oil wells, and the like. Although direct investments are preferred by many investors, indirect investments have certain attributes that make them attractive as well.

Debt, Equity, or Derivative Securities

debt
funds loaned in exchange for the receipt of interest income and the promised repayment of the loan at a given future date.

equity
an ongoing ownership interest in a specific business or property.

derivative securities
securities structured to exhibit characteristics similar to those of an underlying security and as a result, derive their value from the securities that underlie them.

Usually, an investment will represent a debt or an equity interest. **Debt**—an intangible investment—represents funds loaned in exchange for the receipt of interest income and the promised repayment of the loan at a given future date. When you buy a debt instrument like a *bond,* you in effect lend money to the issuer, who agrees to pay you a stated rate of interest over a specified period of time, at the end of which the original sum will be returned. **Equity** represents an ongoing ownership interest in a specific business or property. An equity investment may be held as a security or by title to a specific property. An investor typically obtains an equity interest in a business by purchasing securities known collectively as *common stock.* **Derivative securities** are neither debt nor equity. They are structured to exhibit characteristics similar to those of an underlying security and as a result, derive their value from the securities that underlie them. *Options* are an example. They are neither debt nor equity; rather they provide the investor with an opportunity to sell or buy another security or asset at a specified price over a given period of time. You may, for example, pay $500 for an option to purchase a 2 percent interest in the Alex Company for $30,000 until December 31, 1996. If a 2 percent interest is currently valued at only $24,000, you would not now exercise this option. Option and other derivative security investments, although not as common as debt and equity investments, have grown rapidly in popularity during recent years.

Low and High Risk

Investments are sometimes differentiated on the basis of risk. As used in finance, *risk* refers to the chance that the value or return on an investment will differ unfavorably from its expected value. In other words, risk is the chance of something undesirable occurring. The broader the range of possible values or returns associated with an investment, the greater its risk, and vice versa. Investors are confronted with a continuum ranging from low-risk government securities to high-risk commodities. Although each type of investment vehicle has a basic risk characteristic, the actual level of risk depends on the specific vehicle. For example, stocks are generally believed to be more risky than bonds. However, it is not difficult to find high-risk bonds that are in fact more risky than the stock of a financially sound firm such as IBM or McDonald's. Of course, as noted in the Investor Insights box nearby, investors also unfortunately face the risk of becoming victims of an investment scam. **Low-risk investments** are those considered safe with regard to the receipt of a positive return. **High-risk investments** are considered speculative.

The terms *investment* and *speculation* are used to refer to different approaches to the investment process. As already stated, *investment* is viewed as the process of purchasing securities or property for which stability of value and level of expected return are not only positive but somewhat predictable. **Speculation** is the process of buying similar vehicles in which the future value and level of expected earnings are highly uncertain. Simply stated, speculation is on the high-risk end of the investment process. Of course, due to the greater risk, the returns associated with speculation are expected to be greater. In this book we will use the term "investment" for both processes. We will consider the issue of investment return and risk more closely in Chapter 4.

Short and Long Term

The life of an investment can be described as either short or long term. **Short-term investments** typically mature within one year. **Long-term investments** are those with longer maturities or perhaps, like common stock, with no maturity at all. For example, a six-month certificate of deposit (CD) would be a short-term investment, whereas a 20-year bond would be a long-term investment. Of course, by purchasing a long-term investment and selling it after a short period of time, say six months, an investor can use a long-term vehicle to meet a short-term goal. As will become clear later, it is not unusual to find investors matching the maturity of an investment to the period of time over which they wish to invest their funds. For instance, an investor with money that will not be needed for six months could purchase a six-month certificate of deposit, whereas a 40-year-old investor wishing to build a retirement fund may well purchase a 20-year corporate bond. The breakdown of short term and long term may also be useful for tax purposes. Currently the tax laws define short-term and long-term gains (and losses) in a similar fashion—short-term is one year or less and *long-term* is longer than one year. Tax considerations will be discussed in Chapter 3 and various types of tax-sheltered investments will be described in Chapter 15.

The Structure of the Investment Process

The overall investment process is the mechanism for bringing together suppliers (those having extra funds) with demanders (those who need funds). Suppliers and demanders are most often brought together through a financial institution or a financial market. Occasionally—especially in property transactions such as real estate—buyers and sellers deal directly with one another. **Financial institutions** are organizations, such as banks and insurance companies, that channel the savings of government, businesses, and individuals into loans or investments. **Financial markets** are

---

low-risk investments investments considered safe with regard to the receipt of a positive return.

high-risk investments investments considered speculative with regard to the receipt of a positive return.

speculation the process of buying investment vehicles in which the future value and level of expected earnings are highly uncertain.

short-term investments investments that typically mature within one year.

long-term investments investments with maturities of longer than a year or with no maturity at all.

financial institutions organizations that channel the savings of individuals, businesses, and the governments into loans or investments.

financial markets important forums in which suppliers and demanders of funds are brought together to make transactions.

■■■ I N V E S T O R   I N S I G H T S ■■■

Investment Scams Don't Always Offer Exorbitant Returns

It's not just people trying to make a killing who get caught in investment scams. Indeed, investors hungry for safety may be even more vulnerable these days.

"In the 1980s, we saw frauds advertising 40% returns," says Lori A. Richards, assistant regional administrator of the Securities and Exchange Commission in Los Angeles. "Today, investment scams aren't offering exorbitant returns—they are appealing to people's concerns about safety." . . .

That's certainly what Max Strauss wanted. Mr. Strauss, 77 years old, a retired building director for the city of Beverly Hills, Calif., describes himself "as probably the most suspicious and conservative person you've ever talked to."

Yet he is one of hundreds of investors the SEC says lost millions of dollars buying phony municipal bonds sold by FSG Financial Services Inc., in Beverly Hills. . . .

Some FSG Financial investors lost their life savings, the SEC says. Mr. Strauss, a veteran municipal bond investor, . . . says he is out $25,000. "I still have egg on my face," Mr. Strauss laments. . . .

How did these cautious, conservative investors get taken?

Mr. Strauss says he is usually suspicious of telephone pitches. But he says he relaxed his guard when an FSG Financial salesman called to offer some California Health Facilities municipal bonds. Mr. Strauss said he previously had purchased a similar bond. The salesman told him the bonds were offering an 8.125% tax-free yield, were rated Triple-A and were secured by U.S. Government bonds both for principal and interest, he says.

You can't beat that for safety.

Still, Mr. Strauss says he didn't want to buy the bonds over the telephone and went to the Beverly Hills office of FSG Financial. He says he asked for a prospectus, and was told it would take several days to get it but that the bonds were available for only a short time.

Mr. Strauss decided not to wait. He says he bought $75,000 of bonds. But after his purchase, Mr. Strauss says he began to get worried. . . .

Looking back, Mr. Strauss says his big mistake was not investigating before he invested. "The higher interest rate should have made me suspicious. Hopefully at the age of 77, I can learn not to do this again."

Source: Earl C. Gottschalk, Jr., "How Safety Can Mean Investment Disaster," *The Wall Street Journal*, September 9, 1991, p. C-1.

important forums in which suppliers and demanders of funds are brought together to make transactions, often through intermediaries such as organized securities exchanges.

There are a number of financial markets, such as stock markets, bond markets, and options markets. Similar markets exist in most major economies throughout the world. Their common feature is that the price of the investment vehicle at any point in time results from an equilibrium between the forces of supply and demand. As new information about returns, risk, inflation, world events, and so on, becomes available, the changes in the forces of supply and demand may result in a new equilibrium or *market price*. Financial markets streamline the process of bringing together suppliers and demanders of funds, and they allow transactions to be made quickly and at a fair price. These markets price securities so as to allocate funds to the most productive uses. They also publicize security prices.

Figure 1.1 diagrams the investment process. Note that the suppliers of funds may transfer their resources to demanders through a financial institution, through a financial market, or directly. As the illustration shows, financial institutions can participate in financial markets as either suppliers or demanders of funds. The short-term financial market is called the *money market;* the long-term sector is the *capital market,* which is dominated by various securities exchanges. The characteristics of these markets will be discussed in greater detail in Chapter 2.

Participants in the Investment Process

Government, business, and individuals are the three key participants in the investment process. Each may act as a supplier or demander of funds.

Government

Each level of government—federal, state, and local—requires vast sums of money. Some goes to finance capital expenditures. These are long-term projects related to the construction of public facilities such as schools, hospitals, housing, and highways. Usually the financing for such projects is obtained by issuing various types of

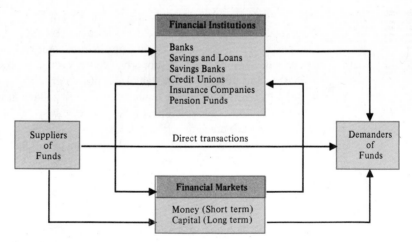

• F I G U R E   1 . 1   The Investment Process

Note that financial institutions participate in the financial markets as well as transfer funds between suppliers and demanders. Although the arrows go only from suppliers to demanders, for some transactions (such as the sale of a bond) the principal amount borrowed by the demander from the supplier (the lender) will eventually be returned.

long-term debt securities. Another demand for funds comes from operating needs, the money needed to keep the government running. The federal government, for example, in recent years has spent more than it collects in taxes. It therefore must obtain outside funds. Or a city might need operating funds when the tax money it will collect is not due for some time. Usually governments finance these operating needs with short-term debt securities.

Sometimes, governments are also suppliers of funds. If a state has temporarily idle cash, rather than hold these resources in a checking account, it may make a short-term investment to earn a positive return. The financial activities of governments, both as demanders and suppliers of funds, significantly affect the behavior of financial institutions and financial markets. In general, government is a *net demander* of funds: that is, it demands more funds than it supplies.

Business

Most business firms, no matter what the type, require large sums of money to support operations. Like government, the financial needs of business are both short- and long-term. On the long-term side, businesses seek funds to build plants, acquire equipment and facilities, and develop products. Short-term needs center around the need to finance inventory, accounts receivable, and other operating costs. Businesses issue a wide variety of debt and equity securities to finance these needs. They also supply funds when they have excess cash. In fact, many large business firms have active and sophisticated cash-management operations and are major purchasers of short-term securities. But, like government, business firms in general are *net demanders* of funds.

Individuals

Individuals supply funds through the investment process in a variety of ways. They may place funds in savings accounts, buy debt or equity instruments, buy insurance, or purchase various types of property. Depending upon personal goals and objectives, the choice of investment vehicles is often a difficult one. Individuals typically demand funds in the form of loans to finance the acquisition of property, usually automobiles and homes. Although the demand for such funds seems great, as a group individuals are *net suppliers* of funds: they put more funds into the investment process than they take out. Since both government and business are net demanders of funds, the individual investor's role in providing the funds needed to finance economic growth is significant.

Types of Investors

institutional investors
investment professionals paid to manage other people's money.

Investors can be either of two types—institutional or individual. **Institutional investors** are investment professionals who are paid to manage other people's money. They are employed by financial institutions (such as banks, life insurance companies, mutual funds, and pension funds), large nonfinancial corporations, and, in some cases, by individuals. Financial institutions invest large sums in order to earn a significant return for their customers. For example, a bank trust department must earn an acceptable return on the funds with which it is entrusted. Likewise, a life insurance company must invest its premium receipts in order to earn returns that will permit the payment of contractual cash values or death benefits to policyholders of beneficiaries. Nonfinancial businesses such as manufacturers and distributors often have sums of money which they invest in order to earn a return on idle funds or to meet future investment and operating needs.

individual investors
investors who manage their own funds.

Individual investors manage their personal funds in order to achieve their financial goals. The individual investor usually concentrates on earning a return on idle funds, building a source of retirement income, or providing security for one's family. The sole activity of many individual investors involves selecting the investment vehicles to be included in their employer retirement plan or individual portfolio. Individuals with large sums of money to invest, or those who lack the time or expertise to make investment decisions, often employ an institutional investor such as a bank trust department or a professional investment adviser.

The fundamental principles used by both institutional and individual investors are similar. However, institutional investors generally invest larger sums of money on behalf of others and therefore are often more sophisticated in both knowledge and methods than individual investors. Thus the information presented in this text represents only the first step toward developing the expertise needed to qualify as an *institutional* investor.

INVESTING

investing
the process of placing funds in selected investment vehicles with the expectation of increasing their value or earning a positive return.

The process of placing funds in selected investment vehicles with the expectation of increasing their value or earning a positive return is called **investing.** This activity has broad economic importance, provides rewards, and can be pursued by following a logical progression of steps.

The Economic Importance of Investing

The functioning and growth of our economy depend on the ready availability of funds. As we've seen, governments and businesses, as well as individuals, need funds to finance their activities. For example, without mortgage loans, very few homes would be purchased. A lack of mortgage money would result in fewer persons being employed to build homes as well as to manufacture the needed components (lumber, nails, glass, and so on). Likewise, manufacturers of goods such as furniture, carpeting, and major appliances suffer decreased sales. The net effect of decreased mortgage financing would thus contribute to a general slowdown in economic activity. The availability of funds to qualified individuals (as well as government and business) is needed to allow the economy to grow and prosper. Because individuals as a group are net suppliers of such funds while government and business are net demanders, the process of investing thus has a profound impact.

The Rewards from Investing

The rewards, or returns, from investing are received in either of two basic forms—current income or increased value. For example, money placed in a bank savings account would provide current income in the form of periodic interest payments. On the other hand, a raw land investment would be expected to offer an increase in value between the time of purchase and the time the land is sold. Those needing funds must provide a reward or return adequate to compensate the suppliers for the risk involved in supplying them. Simply stated, in order for the investment process to function smoothly, funds suppliers must be rewarded and funds demanders must provide these rewards. The magnitude and form of such rewards depends on factors such as the type of security or property transaction, the length of time involved, and the risks embedded in the transaction.

Steps in Investing

Investing can be conducted in various ways. One approach is to rely on plans carefully developed to achieve specific goals. Another, and diametrically opposite, approach is the haphazard, "seat-of-the-pants" method, in which actions are taken on a strictly intuitive basis. Evidence suggests that the more logical approach usually results in better returns. The serious investor should therefore try to develop and execute an investment program consistent with his or her overall financial goals. Such a program should result in a collection of investment vehicles that possesses the return and risk behavior desired. The following brief overview of the steps in investing will help to set the stage for the more detailed discussion of the concepts, tools, and techniques presented throughout the text.

Meeting Investment Prerequisites

Before investing, an individual must make certain that the necessities of life are adequately provided for. Investments are the mechanism for using current funds to satisfy future needs. In addition, a pool of easily accessible funds, typically held in some form of liquid, short-term investment vehicle, should be established for meeting emergency cash needs. Another prerequisite would be adequate protection against the losses that could result from loss of life, illness or disability, damage to property, or a negligent act. Protection against such risks can be acquired through life, health, property, and liability insurance. Although some types of insurance possess certain investment attributes, provision for adequate insurance protection is a necessary prerequisite to investing.

Planning for adequate retirement income may also be viewed as an investment prerequisite. The achievement of this goal may partially depend on the success of the investment program. At a minimum, the individual needs to establish certain retirement goals prior to setting specific investment goals. Considerations involved in establishing and satisfying investment prerequisites are discussed in Chapter 3.

Establishing Investment Goals

investment goals
statements of the timing, magnitude, form, and risks associated with a desired return.

Once the investor has satisfied the prerequisites and has clearly defined financial goals, he or she must establish **investment goals**—specific statements of the timing, magnitude, form, and risks associated with a desired return. For example, an investment goal might be to accumulate $15,000 for the down payment on a summer home to be purchased in 1997, or to accumulate $250,000 for use at retirement in 2009. These goals must be not only consistent with overall financial goals but also realistic. The investor must have adequate funds available for investment, and must use an attainable rate of return to achieve them. The development of investment goals as part of the overall personal financial planning process is discussed in Chapter 3.

Evaluating Investment Vehicles

valuation
procedure for estimating the perceived worth of an investment vehicle; uses measures of return and risk to estimate value.

Before selecting investment vehicles, the investor must evaluate them in terms of his or her investment goals. The evaluation process involves assessing the potential returns and risks offered by each vehicle. This process typically involves **valuation,** a procedure for estimating the perceived worth of an investment vehicle. The valuation process uses measures of return and risk to estimate the value of an investment vehicle. A general discussion of the procedures for measuring these key dimensions of potential investments is included in Chapter 4. Subsequent chapters focus on the valuation of specific vehicles.

Selecting Suitable Investments

The *selection* of investments determines a course of action and can significantly affect the investor's success in achieving planned goals. The best investments may not be those that simply maximize return; other requirements, such as risk and tax considerations, may also be relevant. For example, an investor wishing to receive maximum annual dividends may purchase the common stock with the highest expected earnings. However, if the firm whose stock was purchased goes bankrupt, the investor could lose the money instead. Careful selection of investment vehicles consistent with established goals and having acceptable levels of return, risk, and value is key to successful investing.

Constructing a Diversified Portfolio

portfolio
a collection of investment vehicles assembled to meet one or more investment goals.

An investment **portfolio** is a collection of investment vehicles assembled to meet one or more investment goals. Joan Smith's investment portfolio might contain 20 shares of IBM common stock, $20,000 in government bonds, and 10 shares of IDS Growth mutual fund. Using a variety of available tools and techniques, the investor can combine vehicles in such a way that investment goals can be achieved and return, risk, and investment values are optimized.

diversification
the inclusion of a number of different investment vehicles in a portfolio, in order to increase returns or be exposed to less risk.

Diversification, the inclusion of a number of different investment vehicles, is fundamental to constructing an effective portfolio. By diversifying, investors are able to earn higher returns or be exposed to less risk than if they limit their investments to just one or two vehicles. A portfolio has the surprising quality of possessing a different risk-return characteristic from those of the individual investment vehicles that comprise it. For example, the common stocks of young, high-tech companies are by themselves extremely risky investments—their prices fluctuate constantly and often dramatically. Yet when they are held with common stocks of large, established companies in a diversified portfolio, over time the portfolio exhibits lower risk or a higher return than if common stock of only one type (high-tech or established company) were held. Chapter 16 is devoted to planning and building a portfolio.

Managing the Portfolio

Once a portfolio has been constructed, the investor must measure and evaluate its actual behavior in relation to expected performance. If, for example, the investment return, risk, or value is not consistent with his or her objectives, the investor may need to take corrective action. Such action usually involves selling certain investments and using the proceeds to acquire other vehicles for the portfolio. Portfolio management therefore involves not only selecting a compatible group of investments that meet the investor's goals, but also monitoring and restructuring the portfolio as dictated by the actual behavior of the investments. Chapter 17 is devoted to portfolio management and control.

INVESTMENT VEHICLES

A broad range of investment vehicles is available to individual investors. Some vehicles are securities, others are not. And there are many different types of securities, each type having different lives, costs, return and risk characteristics, and tax considerations. The same is true of property investments. As noted in the nearby Investor Insights box the growing number of vehicles available to the individual investor makes investing in the 1990s challenging indeed. We will devote the bulk of this book—Chapters 5 through 15—to describing the characteristics, special features, returns and risks, and possible investment strategies that can be used with vehicles available to the individual investor. Here we will introduce the various investment outlets and give a brief description of each.

Short-Term Vehicles

short-term vehicles
savings instruments
that usually have lives
of one year or less.

Short-term vehicles include savings instruments that usually have lives of one year or less. The most important of these are savings and NOW accounts, money market deposit accounts and mutual funds, central asset accounts, certificates of deposit (CDs), commercial paper, banker's acceptances, U.S. Treasury bills (T-bills), and even Series EE U.S. savings bonds. Often such instruments are used to "warehouse" idle funds and earn a return while suitable long-term vehicles are being evaluated. That is, they serve as a liquid reserve. Because these vehicles generally carry little or no risk, they tend to be popular among those wishing to earn something on temporarily idle funds. They also are popular among conservative investors who may use short-term vehicles as a primary investment outlet.

In addition to the "warehousing" function served by short-term vehicles, they also round out an investor's portfolio by meeting liquidity needs. Such needs are an important part of any financial plan. As a rule of thumb, financial planners often suggest that anywhere from three to six months of after-tax income should be held in short-term vehicles to meet unexpected needs. A serious illness or loss of a job could create a need for immediate cash. Being forced to sell the long-term securities at a time when security prices are low can result in substantial losses. A closer look at meeting liquidity needs is provided in Chapter 3.

The Challenges of Investing in the '90s

Sophie Tucker, that grand old vaudevillian, once observed: "I've been rich, and I've been poor. Believe me, rich is better." For investors today, not only is rich better—it's almost a necessity. True, we wrestled inflation to the ground during the 1980s. But there is no guarantee it won't come surging back in the Nineties. Besides, despite a tamed CPI, many folks still seem to be losing ground.

The cost of life's main events, for example, have run well beyond the broad price indexes, and even outpaced most investments. The average tab for a normal hospital delivery jumped a spanking 14.4% annually over the past ten years, to $4,640. By comparison, the Standard & Poor's 500 stocks fell short, returning 13.9% a year on average over the same period. Feeling enriched by the 54% average appreciation in prices of homes over the past decade? Don't. The cost of a cemetery plot in Richmond, Virginia, rose faster—64%—over the same period, increasing the total price of dying to over $5,000.

The fight to stay ahead of rising costs will be tougher in the Nineties, even if inflation stays calm. Says Gary Brinson, president of Brinson Partners, a Chicago investment advisory firm: "We're not going to have the kind of investment returns that we had in the 1980s." The markets in stocks and bonds have cooled, and economies around the world are growing more slowly. But even if you cannot count on ever-rising markets to lift all your boats, you now have more investment vessels than ever to choose from. Take mutual funds: In 1980, Lipper Analytical Services, the Summit, New Jersey, financial research outfit, tracked 643 funds. Today Lipper follows over 3,000 of virtually every type and size.

In fact you can now invest in many ways that used to be open only to the pros. You can buy funds that invest in stocks just about anywhere in the world, or in a single sector of the economy—health care, say, or biotechnology. Some bond funds invest in the debt of countries all around the world; others confine themselves to municipals in a single state. Brokers and investment bankers now package and market nearly every kind of financial asset. You can buy a piece of your neighbor's mortgage or a contract that guarantees a future price for an ounce of gold or a quart of orange juice.

The task is to find your way through this financial marketplace. More than ever, investors need to devise a strategy that matches specific goals with the investments most likely to meet those goals. The challenge goes beyond choosing specific stocks, bonds, or mutual funds. You also need to combine your purchases so that you get the greatest return for your money at the least risk to your principal—and peace of mind....

You don't need an MBA to create an investment portfolio consistent with your goals. Nor will you need an oracle who can forecast the direction of interest rates. But following a little ancient advice is essential: Know thyself. That education begins with defining your financial goals.

Seems easy. With money, as with love, the point is to make lots of it, right? Not exactly, says Thomas Bailard, head of Bailard Biehl & Kaiser, a money management firm in San Mateo, California. You've got to specify what you will spend the money on. Says he: "Making 15% a year on your money isn't a goal. A goal is financing your son's college education in 2002 or taking a six-month sabbatical in Tanzania in 1995." . . .

Source: Terence P. Paré, "How to Maximize Your Profits," *Fortune 1992 Investor's Guide,* Fall 1991, pp. 38–46.

Common Stock

common stock
equity investment
representing owner-
ship in a corporation;
each share repre-
sents a fractional
ownership interest in
the firm.

dividends
periodic payments
made by firms to
their stockholders.

Common stock is an equity investment that represents ownership in a corporation. Each share of common stock represents a fractional ownership interest in the firm. For example, one share of common stock in a corporation that has 10,000 shares outstanding would represent 1/10,000 ownership interest. The return on common stock investment comes from either of two sources. One is the periodic receipt of **dividends,** which are payments made by the firm to its shareholders, and increases in value. The second source of return is *capital gains,* which result from selling the stock at a price above that originally paid. For example, imagine you purchased a single share of M and N Industries common stock for $40 per share. During the first year you owned it you received $2.50 per share in cash dividends; at the end of the year you sold the stock for $44 per share. If we ignore the costs associated with buying and selling the stock, you would have earned $2.50 in dividends and $4 in capital gains ($44 sale price − $40 purchase price). Next to short-term vehicles and home ownership, common stock, which offers a broad range of return-risk combinations, is the most popular form of investment vehicle. Because of the widespread popularity of common stock, three chapters—5, 6, and 7—are devoted to the study of this investment vehicle.

Fixed-Income Securities

**fixed-income securi-
ties**
investment vehicles
that offer a fixed
periodic return.

Fixed-income securities are a group of investment vehicles that offer a fixed periodic return. Some forms offer contractually guaranteed returns; others have specified, but not guaranteed, returns. Due to their fixed returns, fixed-income securities tend to experience their greatest popularity during periods of high interest rates, such as those during the late 1970s and early 1980s. The key forms of fixed-income securities are bonds, preferred stock, and convertible securities.

Bonds

bonds
long-term debt in-
struments (IOUs), is-
sued by corporations
and governments,
that offer a known
interest return plus
the return of the face
value at maturity.

Bonds are the long-term debt instruments (IOUs) of corporations and governments. A bondholder receives a known interest return, typically paid semiannually, plus the return of the face value of the bond at maturity (typically 20 to 40 years). If you purchased a $1,000 bond paying 9 percent interest in semiannual installments, you would expect to be paid $45 (that is, 9% × ½ year × $1,000) every six months; at maturity you would receive the $1,000 face value of the bond. An investor may be able to buy or sell a bond prior to maturity at a price different from its face value. As with common stock, a wide range of return-risk combinations is available to the bond investor. We will examine bond investments in detail in Chapters 8 and 9.

Preferred Stock

preferred stock
ownership interest in
a firm, giving a
stated dividend rate,
payment of which is
given preference
over dividends to
holders of the firm's
common stock.

Like common stock, **preferred stock** represents an ownership interest in a corporation. Unlike common stock, preferred has a stated dividend rate, payment of which is given preference over common stock dividends of the same firm. Preferred stock has no maturity date. Investors typically purchase it for the dividends, but it may also provide capital gains. The key aspects of preferred stock are described in Chapter 10.

Convertible Securities

convertible security
a fixed-income obligation (bond or preferred stock) with a feature permitting conversion into a specified number of shares of common stock.

A **convertible security** is a special type of fixed-income obligation (bond or preferred stock). It possesses a feature permitting the investor to convert it into a specified number of shares of common stock. Convertible bonds and convertible preferreds provide the fixed-income benefit of a bond (interest) or preferred stock (dividends), while offering the price-appreciation (capital gain) potential of common stock. A detailed discussion of convertibles appears in Chapter 10.

Speculative Investment Vehicles

speculative investment vehicles
investment vehicles with high levels of risk.

Speculative investment vehicles are those possessing high levels of risk. They usually have nonexistent or imperfect records of success, uncertain earnings, and unstable market values. Because of their above-average risk, these vehicles also have high levels of expected return. The key speculative vehicles are options, and commodities, financial futures, and tangibles.

Options

right
an option for a short period of time to buy a fraction of a share of an issue of common stock at a price below the current market price.

warrant
an option for a long period of time to buy one or more shares of common stock at a price initially above the market price.

put
an option to sell 100 shares of common stock at a specified price on or before some future date.

call
an option to buy 100 shares of common stock at a specified price on or before some future date.

As noted earlier, *options* are derivative securities that provide the investor with an opportunity to sell or buy another security or asset at a specified price over a given period of time. They are acquired and used by investors in a variety of ways and for a variety of reasons. Most often options are purchased in order to take advantage of an anticipated decrease or increase in the price of common stock. However, the purchaser of an option is not guaranteed any return and could lose the entire amount invested, either because the option never becomes attractive enough to use or because the life of the option expires. Aside from their speculative use, options are sometimes used to protect existing investment positions against losses.

Three common types of options are rights, warrants, and puts and calls (discussed in detail in Chapter 11). A **right** is an option to buy a *fraction of a share* of a new issue of common stock at a price *below* the current market price over a *short period* of time—generally one or two months. For example, one might obtain rights entitling the holder to buy one share of stock, with a current market price of $55 per share, at $50 per share for every 10 rights held (that is, each right is good for one-tenth of a share of common stock). A **warrant** is similar to a right but gives its holder an opportunity to purchase *one or more shares* of common stock at a price that is initially *above* the market price over a *long period* of time—typically 2 to 10 years or more. For example, a General Manufacturing warrant might allow its holder to purchase three shares of its stock currently selling for $70 per share at $80 per share at any time prior to December 31, 2000.

Puts and calls are types of options that have gained great popularity during the past 20 years. A **put** is an option to sell 100 shares of common stock on or before some future date at a specified price. A **call** is an option to buy 100 shares on or before some future date at a specified price. Most puts and calls have lives of 1 to 9 months and occasionally a year. The exercise or striking price of both puts and calls is set close to the market price at the time they are issued. An example of a call option might be a six-month call to buy 100 shares of Stable Industries at $30 per share. The holder of such an option could, at any time before its expiration, buy

100 shares of Stable at $30 per share regardless of the actual market price of the stock. Investors tend to purchase puts when they anticipate price declines and calls when they expect prices to rise. As we will see in Chapter 11, although put and call options are generally viewed as speculative investments, they can also be used to protect an investor's position against loss.

Commodities, Financial Futures, and Tangibles

commodities and financial futures contracts
obligations that the sellers of the contracts will make delivery and the buyers will take delivery of a specified commodity, foreign currency, or financial instrument at some specific date in the future.

Two other types of speculative investment vehicles are (1) commodities and financial futures and (2) tangibles. **Commodities and financial futures contracts** are legally binding obligations that the sellers of such contracts will *make delivery* and the buyers of the contracts will *take delivery* of a specified commodity, foreign currency, or financial instrument at some specific date in the future. Examples of commodities sold by contract include soybeans, pork bellies, and cocoa. Trading in commodities and financial futures is generally a highly specialized, high-risk proposition since the opportunity to make a profit depends on a variety of uncontrollable factors tied to world events and economic activity. **Tangibles,** in contrast, are investment assets, other than real estate, that can be seen or touched. They include gold and other precious metals, gems, and collectibles such as stamps, coins, art, and antiques. These speculative vehicles are purchased as investments in anticipation of price increases. During the ownership period some may also provide the investor with psychological or esthetic enjoyment. An expanded discussion of commodities, financial futures, and tangibles is presented in Chapter 12.

tangibles
investment assets, other than real estate, that can be seen or touched.

Mutual Funds

mutual fund
a company that invests in and professionally manages a diversified portfolio of securities and sells shares of the portfolio to investors.

A company that invests in and professionally manages a diversified portfolio of securities is called a **mutual fund.** The fund sells shares to investors, who thus obtain an interest in the portfolio of securities owned by the fund. Most mutual funds issue and repurchase shares as demanded at a price reflecting the value of the portfolio at the time the transaction is made. Chapter 13 is devoted to the study of this popular investment vehicle.

Other Popular Investment Vehicles

Various other investment vehicles are also widely used by investors. The most common are real estate, and tax shelters and limited partnerships.

Real Estate

real estate
property such as residential homes, raw land, and income property.

The term **real estate** includes investment in such entities as residential homes, raw land, and a variety of forms of income property, such as warehouses, office and apartment buildings, cooperatives (co-ops), and condominiums. As a result of generally increasing values and favorable tax treatments, real estate was a popular investment vehicle through the '70s and much of the '80s. Although its popularity has waned due to the recession and problems in many financial institutions, it is likely that real estate will experience a resurgence in popularity during the next few years. Historically, the appeal of real estate investment stemmed from the fact that it offered returns in the form of rental income, tax write-offs, and capital gains that were not available from alternative investment vehicles. A detailed look at the role real estate can play in the investment portfolio is presented in Chapter 14.

Tax Shelters and Limited Partnerships

Due to provisions in the federal tax law, some investment vehicles offer certain tax advantages over others. For example, interest received on most municipal bonds is not taxed at all, and income from Individual Retirement Accounts (IRAs) is deferred from taxes until the money is actually taken out of the account. Since the federal income tax rate for an individual can be as high as 31 percent, many investors look for **tax shelters**—investments structured to take advantage of existing tax laws. With these, they find that their after-tax rates of return can be far higher than with conventional investments. **Limited partnerships** may be attractive to those wishing to passively invest with limited liability; they receive the benefit of active professional management and apply the resulting profit or loss (under certain conditions) when calculating their tax liability. Various types of tax-sheltered investments, often structured as limited partnerships, were severely affected by the Tax Reform Act of 1986. A comprehensive review of the more common tax shelters and limited partnerships is presented in Chapter 15.

tax shelters
investments structured to take advantage of existing tax laws.

limited partnerships
a form of passive investment offering partners limited liability, active professional management, and the resulting profit or loss.

AN OVERVIEW OF THE TEXT

The text contains 17 chapters divided into six major parts listed below.

One: The Investment Environment
Two: Investing in Common Stock
Three: Investing in Fixed-Income Securities
Four: Speculative Investment Vehicles
Five: Other Popular Investment Vehicles
Six: Investment Administration

It begins with an overview of the investment environment (Part One), then describes the key aspects of the most popular investment vehicles (Parts Two through Five), and concludes with discussions of investment administration (Part Six). Each part, which is introduced with a listing of its chapters as well as its relationship to the overall investment process, explains an important aspect of investing. Figure 1.2 depicts the relationships among the six parts of the text. This plan of organization links the investor's activities in developing, implementing, and monitoring investment plans. It is intended to provide the understanding needed to establish an investment portfolio that provides an acceptable return for an acceptable level of risk.

To enhance the topical coverage and practical utility of the text, the computer has been introduced, where appropriate, as an investment decision-making aid. Keyed to various parts of the text is the *Investment Management Disk (IMD),* a menu-driven computer disk for use with IBM PCs and compatible microcomputers. The

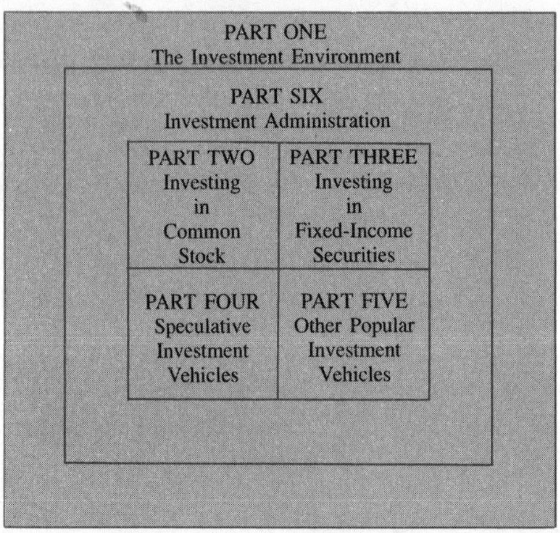

```
                        PART ONE
                  The Investment Environment

                        PART SIX
                  Investment Administration

                PART TWO          PART THREE
                Investing          Investing
                    in                in
                 Common         Fixed-Income
                  Stock           Securities

                PART FOUR         PART FIVE
                Speculative      Other Popular
                Investment        Investment
                 Vehicles          Vehicles
```

• FIGURE 1.2 An Overview of the Major Parts of the Text

The text approaches the individual investment process in a logical fashion, beginning with an overview of the investment environment (Part One). Next comes a description of the key aspects of the most popular investment vehicles (Parts Two through Five). The text concludes with a discussion of investment administration (Part Six).

disk can be used as an aid in performing many of the routine investment calculations and procedures presented. For convenience it is keyed to text discussions and end-of-chapter review questions, problems, and cases that can be solved with it. These items are clearly denoted by a disk symbol: ▪. Appendix E describes this tool in more detail.

SUMMARY

1. An investment is any vehicle into which funds can be placed in order to earn an expected positive return. Some vehicles are securities; other are forms of property. Some investments are made directly, others indirectly. An investment can be a debt, an equity, or a derivative security such as an option. It can possess risk ranging from very low to extremely high. An individual can invest in either short-term or long-term vehicles.

2. The investment process is structured around financial institutions and financial markets that bring together suppliers and demanders of funds. The participants are government, business, and individuals. Of these groups, only individuals are net funds suppliers. Investors can be either institutional investors or individual investors. Investing is important since it makes available funds needed to permit our economy to function and grow. The rewards for investing can be received either as current income or increased value.

3. The steps in investing involve the following: meeting investment prerequisites; establishing investment goals; evaluating investment vehicles; selecting suitable investments; constructing a diversified portfolio; and managing the portfolio.

4. A broad range of investment vehicles is available. Short-term vehicles have low risk. They are used to earn a return on temporarily idle funds or as a primary investment outlet of conservative investors. Common stocks offer dividends and capital gains. Fixed-income securities—bonds, preferred stock, and convertible securities—offer fixed periodic returns with some potential for gain in value.

5. Speculative investment outlets are high-risk vehicles such as options (rights, warrants, puts and calls), and commodities, financial futures, and tangibles that offer above-average expected returns. Mutual funds are popular investment vehicles that allow investors to conveniently buy or sell interests in a professionally managed diversified portfolio of securities. Other popular vehicles include real estate, and tax shelters and limited partnerships.

6. The text contains 17 chapters divided into six major parts. A simple model is used to link each part to the investment process.

QUESTIONS

1. Define the term *investment* and explain why individuals invest. What alternatives exist for investing idle funds?

2. Differentiate between securities and property investments. Which form of investment is more popular among individual investors?

3. What is the difference between direct and indirect investments? Cite an example of each.

4. Differentiate among debt, equity, and derivative securities. Give an example of each.

5. Describe how the term *risk* is used to depict the behavior of certain investments. Differentiate between low-risk and high-risk investments.

6. Describe the structure of the overall investment process. Define and explain the role played by financial institutions and financial markets.

7. Classify the role of: (a) government, (b) business, and (c) individuals as net suppliers or net demanders of funds. Discuss the impact of each on the investment process.

8. Define and differentiate between institutional investors and individual investors. Which group tends to be more sophisticated? Why?

9. Briefly discuss the economic importance of investing, and describe the rewards available to those placing funds in the investment process.

10. List and discuss the six steps involved in the personal investment process.

11. Discuss the role of short-term investment vehicles in an individual's investment plans and portfolio.

12. How much would an investor earn on a stock purchased one year ago for $63 if it paid an annual cash dividend of $3.75 and had just been sold for $67.50? Did the investor experience a capital gain? Explain.

13. Briefly define and differentiate the following fixed-income securities:

    a. Bonds.
    b. Preferred stocks.
    c. Convertible securities.

14. Explain the nature of an option and describe the opportunity for profit offered by this type of investment vehicle.

15. Describe the similarities and differences between a right and a warrant.

16. What is the difference between a put and a call? If you did not own shares of a company's stock but felt that its price would decline significantly in the near future, would you be likely to buy a put or a call? Explain.

17. Briefly describe each of the following types of investments, and indicate which factors are likely to affect the returns on each:

    a. Commodities and financial futures.
    b. Tangibles.

18. What is a mutual fund? Why is this form of investment popular among individual investors?

19. Briefly describe each of the following popular investment vehicles:

    a. Real estate.
    b. Tax shelters.
    c. Limited partnerships.

CASE PROBLEMS

1.1 Investments or Racquetball?

Judd Read and Judi Todd are senior accounting majors at a large midwestern university. They have been good friends since high school and look forward to their graduation at the end of next semester. Each has already found a job, which will begin upon graduation. Judd has accepted a position as an internal auditor in a medium-sized manufacturing firm. Judi will be working for one of the major public accounting firms. Each is looking forward to the challenge of a new career and to the prospect of achieving success both professionally and financially.

Judd and Judi are preparing to register for their final semester. Each has one free elective to select. Judd is considering taking a racquetball course offered by the physical education department; Judi is planning to take a basic investments course. Judi has been trying to convince Judd to take investments instead of racquetball. Judd believes he doesn't need to take investments, since he already knows what common stock is. He believes that whenever he has accumulated excess funds, he can invest in the stock of a company that is doing well. Judi argues that there is much more to it than simply choosing common stock. She feels an exposure to the field of investments would certainly be more beneficial than learning how to play racquetball.

Questions
1. Explain to Judd the structure of the investment process and the economic importance of investing.

2. Describe to Judd the steps in investing and emphasize the importance of this process to his overall financial success.
3. List and discuss the other types of investment vehicles with which Judd is apparently unfamiliar.
4. Assuming Judd is in good physical condition, what arguments would you give to convince Judd to take investments rather than racquetball?

1.2 Evaluating Molly Porter's Investment Plan

Molly Porter's husband, Vance, was recently killed in an airplane crash. Fortunately, he had a sizable amount of life insurance, the proceeds of which should provide Molly with adequate income for a number of years. Molly is 33 years old and has two children, David and Phyllis, who are 6 and 7 years old, respectively. Although Molly does not rule out the possibility of marrying again, she feels it is best not to consider this when making her financial plans. In order to provide adequate funds to finance her children's college education as well as her own retirement. Molly has estimated that she needs to accumulate $400,000 within the next 15 years. If she continues to teach school, she believes sufficient excess funds will be available each year (salary plus insurance proceeds minus expenses) to permit her to achieve this goal. She plans to make annual deposits of these excess funds into her money market deposit account, which currently pays 6 percent interest.

Questions
1. In view of Molly's long-term investment goals, assess her choice of a money market deposit account as the appropriate investment vehicle.
2. What alternative investment vehicles might Molly consider prior to committing her money to the money market deposit account?
3. If you were Molly, given your limited knowledge of investments, in what vehicles would you invest the excess funds? Explain.

2 Investment Markets and Transactions

After studying this chapter, you should be able to:

1. Describe the basic types of securities markets and the characteristics of both organized exchanges and the over-the-counter market.

2. Discuss globalization and regulation of the securities markets, ethical issues, and the general market conditions that have prevailed over the last fifty or so years.

3. Explain the role of the stockbroker and describe the basic types of orders and costs involved in making securities transactions.

4. Understand the economic motives and procedures for making margin transactions.

5. Summarize the various margin requirements and discuss the popular uses of margin trading.

6. Describe the motives for short selling, the procedures used by short sellers, and the popular applications of this trading technique.

In general, it would be difficult to drive cross country from one city to another without knowing how to read a map. In addition, an understanding of traffic regulations is needed to safely make such a trip. In spite of the fact that you may be able to drive a car, without these other skills you will probably be unable to complete the cross-country drive. The same logic applies to investing. Although investing is far more challenging than driving, it too involves a number of important procedures and rules that you need to know. Regardless of how well prepared you might be to select the best vehicle for achieving your particular investment goals, you must know other things as well: You need to understand the workings of the market in which that vehicle is bought and sold. You must know how to find and enter the market. And you should understand the basic types of transactions required. In this chapter we will look at key aspects of the investment environment so that you will know which market to enter for your purposes, how to enter it, and which basic types of transactions to make.

SECURITIES MARKETS

securities markets
markets allowing suppliers and demanders of funds to make transactions, in either money or capital.

Securities markets are the mechanism that allows suppliers and demanders of funds to make transactions. They also permit such transactions to be made *quickly* and at a fair price. Before describing the methods used to enter these markets, let us look at the various types of markets, their organization, their regulation, and their general behavior.

Types of Markets

money market
market in which short-term securities are bought and sold.

The securities markets may be classified as either money markets or capital markets. In the **money market** short-term securities are bought and sold. In the **capital market** transactions are made in longer-term securities such as stocks and bonds. In this book we will devote most of our attention to the capital market, through which stock, bond, options, and futures investments can be made. Capital markets can be classified as either primary or secondary.

capital market
market in which long-term securities such as stocks and bonds are bought and sold.

Primary Markets

primary market
market in which new issues of securities are sold to the public.

The market in which new issues of securities are sold to the public is the **primary market.** It is the market in which the proceeds of sales go to the issuer of the securities. The main vehicle in the primary market is the **initial public offering (IPO)**—the public sale of stock by a privately owned company. In order to better understand primary markets, it is helpful to consider the process of registering new securities and the role of the investment banker.

initial public offering (IPO)
the public sale of stock by a privately owned company.

shelf registration
securities registration procedure that allows a firm to sell securities during a two-year period under a "master registration statement" filed with the SEC.

Registration of New Securities. To offer its securities for public sale, the issuer must register them with and obtain approval from the *Securities and Exchange Commission (SEC),* a regulatory agency of the federal government. Since 1982, the SEC has allowed a streamlined registration procedure called **shelf registration** that allows issuers to better time their offerings. Under it, firms with more than $150 million in outstanding common stock can file a "master registration statement" that covers planned funding needs over a two-year period. Once the master statement is

public offering
the sale of a firm's
securities to the gen-
eral public.

rights offering
an offer of a new
issue of stock to ex-
isting stockholders
on a pro rata basis.

private placement
the sale of new se-
curities directly to
selected groups of
investors, without
SEC registration.

investment banker
financial intermediary
that purchases new
securities from the
issuing firm at an
agreed-upon price
and resells them to
the public.

underwriting
the role of the in-
vestment banker in
bearing the risk of
reselling at a profit
the securities pur-
chased from an issu-
ing corporation at an
agreed-upon price.

**underwriting syndi-
cate**
a group formed to
spread the financial
risk associated with
the selling of new
securities.

selling group
a large number of
brokerage firms that
join to accept re-
sponsibility for sell-
ing a certain portion
of the issue of a
new security.

secondary market
the market in which
securities are traded
after they have been
issued.

approved by the SEC, the firm can file a short statement and without further delay sell securities already approved under the master statement.

Role of the Investment Banker.   To market its securities, the firm has two choices: It can either make a **public offering,** in which it offers its shares for sale to the general public or a **rights offering,** in which it offers shares to existing stockholders on a pro rata basis. It can also make a **private placement,** in which new securities are sold directly, without SEC registration, to selected groups of investors such as insurance companies and pension funds. Most public offerings are made with the assistance of an **investment banker**—a financial intermediary (such as Goldman, Sachs, or Salomon Brothers) that specializes in selling new security issues. The main activity of the investment banker is **underwriting.** This process involves purchasing the security issue from the issuing firm at an agreed-upon price and bearing the risk of reselling it to other investors at a profit. The investment banker also provides issuers with advice about pricing and other important aspects of their issues. In the case of very large security issues, the investment banker will bring in other bankers as partners to form an **underwriting syndicate,** in order to spread the financial risk associated with the selling of the new securities. The originating investment banker and the syndicate members put together a **selling group,** normally made up of a large number of brokerage firms, each of which accepts the responsibility for selling a certain portion of the issue. The selling process for a new security issue is depicted in Figure 2.1. The relationships among the participants in this process can also be seen in the announcement of the offering of a new security issue, shown in Figure 2.2. The roles of the various participating firms can be identified from the layout of the announcement. Isolated firm names (or in many cases, a larger typeface) reflect the importance of the firm in the sale process. (In the figure, the key participants in the offering are labeled in the margin at the right.)

Compensation for underwriting and selling services typically comes in the form of a discount from the sale price of the securities. For example, an investment banker may pay the issuer $24 per share for stock to be sold for $25 per share. The investment banker may then sell the shares to members of the selling group for $24.75 per share. In this case, the original investment banker earns $0.75 per share ($24.75 sale price less $24 purchase price), and the members of the selling group earn $0.25 for each share they sell ($25 sale price less $24.75 purchase price). Although some primary security offerings are directly placed by the issuer, the majority of new issues are sold through public offering using the mechanism just described.

Secondary Markets

The market in which securities are traded after they have been issued is the **second-ary market,** or the *aftermarket*. The secondary market exists because after a security has been issued, some purchasers may wish to sell their shares, and others may wish to buy them. In the secondary market, unlike the primary market, the corporation whose securities are traded is not involved in the transaction. Instead, money

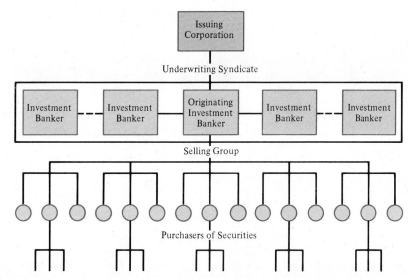

• FIGURE 2.1   The Selling Process for New Securities

The investment banker hired by the issuing corporation may form an underwriting syndicate, which then establishes a selling group to sell the new security issue in the primary market.

and securities are exchanged between investors—the seller exchanges securities for cash paid by the buyer. The secondary market gives security purchasers liquidity. It also provides a mechanism for continuous pricing of securities to reflect their value at each point in time based upon the best information then available.

Included among secondary markets are the various organized securities exchanges and the over-the-counter market. **Organized securities exchanges** are centralized institutions in which the forces of supply and demand for already outstanding securities are brought together. The **over-the-counter (OTC) market,** on the other hand, is a widely scattered telecommunications network through which buyers and sellers of certain securities can be brought together. Because popular investment vehicles are traded on both the organized exchanges and over-the-counter markets, the individual investor will probably make transactions in both of these markets.

organized securities exchanges centralized institutions in which transactions are made in already outstanding securities.

over-the-counter (OTC) market widely scattered telecommunications network through which buyers and sellers of certain securities can be brought together.

Organized Securities Exchanges

Securities traded on organized securities exchanges account for about 72 percent of the total *dollar volume* of domestic shares traded. All trading at a given exchange is carried out in one place (such as the New York Stock Exchange on Wall Street) and under a broad set of rules by persons who are members of that exchange. The best known exchanges on which stock and bond transactions are made are the New York Stock Exchange (NYSE) and the American Stock Exchange (AMEX), both located in New York City. They account for approximately 86 and 2 percent, respectively, of the total annual dollar volume of shares traded on organized U.S. exchanges.

This announcement is not an offer to sell or a solicitation of an offer to buy any of these securities. The offering is made only by the Prospectus, copies of which may be obtained in any State in which this announcement is circulated only from such of the several underwriters as may lawfully offer these securities in such State.

NEW ISSUE   January 7, 1992

2,587,500 Shares

 F&C International, Inc.

Common Stock

Price $13.50 Per Share

2,472,500 Shares

Investment
Banking
Syndicate

PaineWebber Incorporated

J. C. Bradford & Co.

The Chicago Corporation

Alex. Brown & Sons
Incorporated   The First Boston Corporation

A.G. Edwards & Sons, Inc.   Goldman, Sachs & Co.   Merrill Lynch & Co.

Morgan Stanley & Co.   Oppenheimer & Co., Inc.   Salomon Brothers Inc
Incorporated

Smith Barney, Harris Upham & Co.   Wertheim Schroder & Co.
Incorporated   Incorporated

William Blair & Company   Gruntal & Co., Incorporated

Selling
Group

Kemper Securities Group, Inc.   Ladenburg, Thalmann & Co. Inc.

McDonald & Company   Neuberger & Berman   Piper, Jaffray & Hopwood
Securities, Inc.   Incorporated

Sutro & Co. Incorporated   Tucker Anthony   Wheat First Butcher & Singer
Incorporated   Capital Markets

Brean Murray, Foster Securities Inc.   Fahnestock & Co. Inc.

First of Michigan Corporation   The Ohio Company   Roney & Co.

This tranche is being offered in the United States and Canada.

115,000 Shares

PaineWebber International

This tranche is being offered outside the United States and Canada.

• FIGURE 2.2 An Offering Announcement

This form of offering announcement is commonly referred to as a "tombstone." The participants in both the investment banking syndicate and the selling group established to sell the common stock of F&C International, Inc., are clearly noted on the tombstone. (*Source: The Wall Street Journal*, January 7, 1992, p. C20.)

Other domestic exchanges include *regional exchanges* such as the Midwest Stock Exchange and the Pacific Stock Exchange. Together, these exchanges, which deal primarily in securities with local or regional appeal, account for about 11 percent of the annual dollar share volume on organized U.S. exchanges. In addition, foreign stock exchanges list and trade shares of firms in their own foreign markets. Separate domestic exchanges exist for options trading and trading in commodities and financial futures. Here we will consider the basic structure, rules, and operations of each of these organized domestic securities exchanges. (Foreign exchanges are discussed later.)

The New York Stock Exchange

Most organized securities exchanges are modeled after the New York Stock Exchange (NYSE). In order to be a member, an individual or firm must own or lease a "seat" on the exchange. The word *seat* is used only figuratively, since members trade securities standing up. There are a total of 1,366 seats on the NYSE. During this century, seats on the exchange have sold for as much as $1,150,000 (in 1987) and as little as $17,000 (in 1947). Recently, seats have sold for around $400,000. The majority of seat holders are brokerage firms, each typically owning more than one seat. (The largest brokerage firm, Merrill Lynch Pierce Fenner & Smith, Inc., owns over 20 seats.) Firms such as Merrill Lynch designate officers to occupy seats. Only such designated individuals are permitted to make transactions on the floor of the exchange. Membership is often divided into broad classes based on the members' activities. Although the majority of members make purchase and sale transactions on behalf of their customers, some members specialize in making transactions for other members or for their own account. Table 2.1 classifies and briefly describes member activities. You can see that commission brokers and specialists perform the majority of the activities on the exchange.

Listing Policies. To become listed on an organized stock exchange, a firm must file an application. Some firms are listed on more than one exchange; they are said to have **dual listing.** The New York Stock Exchange has the most stringent listing requirements. Currently over 1,800 firms, accounting for about 2,300 stocks (common and preferred) and 2,900 bonds, are listed on the NYSE.

In order to be eligible for listing on the NYSE, a firm must have at least 2,000 stockholders owning 100 or more shares. It must have a minimum of 1.1 million shares of publicly held stock, a demonstrated earning power of $2.5 million before taxes at the time of the listing and $2 million before taxes for each of the preceding two years, net tangible assets of $18 million, and a total of $18 million in market value of publicly traded shares. It also must pay a listing fee. Once a firm's securities have been accepted for listing, it must meet the requirements of the federal Securities and Exchange Commission (SEC), which regulates certain aspects of listed securities. If listed firms do not continue to meet specified requirements, they may be **de-listed** from the exchange.

dual listing
a listing of a firm's shares on more than one exchange.

de-listed
to be removed from listing on an organized stock exchange.

TABLE 2.1 NYSE Member Activities

Type of Member	Approximate % Total Membership*	Primary Activities
A. Make Transactions for Customers		
Commission brokers	52%	Make purchase and sale transactions of stocks and bonds as requested by customers.
Bond brokers	2	Commission brokers who only make bond transactions for customers.
B. Make Transactions for Other Members		
Floor brokers ("Two-dollar brokers")	10	Execute orders for other brokers who are unable to do so due to excessive market activity.
Specialists	29	Make a continuous, fair, and orderly market in the 6 to 15 issues assigned to them. Also make purchase and sale transactions of less than 100 shares (odd lots) for members of the exchange.
C. Make Transactions for Their Own Account		
Registered traders	4	Purchase and sell securities for their own account. Must abide by certain regulations established to protect the public.

*Because approximately 3 percent of the members are inactive, the percentages given total to only 97 percent.

Trading Activity. Trading is carried out on the floor of an exchange. The floor of the NYSE is an area about the size of a football field. On the floor are 18 trading posts. Certain stocks are traded at each of the posts. Bonds and less active stocks are traded in an annex. All trades are made on the floor of the exchange by members of the exchange. Around the perimeter are telephones and telegraph equipment used to transmit buy-and-sell orders from brokers' offices to the exchange floor and back again once an order has been executed.

All transactions on the floor of the exchange are made through an auction process. The goal is to fill all buy orders at the lowest price and to fill all sell orders at the highest price. The actual auction takes place at the post where the particular security is traded. Members interested in purchasing a given security publicly negotiate a transaction with members interested in selling that security. The job of the **specialist**—exchange member who specializes in making transactions in one or more stocks—is to provide for a continuous and orderly market in that security. The specialist offers to buy or sell (at specified prices) whenever there is a lack of continuity or order in the market for the security.

specialist
stock exchange member who specializes in one or more stocks.

The American Stock Exchange

The American Stock Exchange (AMEX) is the second largest organized U.S. security exchange in terms of the number of listed companies. In terms of dollar volume of trading, the AMEX is actually smaller than the two largest regional exchanges—the Midwest and the Pacific. Its organization and procedures are similar to those of the NYSE, except that its listing requirements are not as stringent. In March of 1992 the AMEX initiated a new market, the *Emerging Company Marketplace (ECM)*, geared toward raising capital for smaller growth companies. Initially viewed as an experiment, this market may provide investors with an opportunity to conveniently invest in emerging company stocks. There are approximately 660 seats on the AMEX, with over 1,000 listed stocks and 260 (corporate) listed bonds.

Regional Stock Exchanges

The number of companies having securities listed on each of the regional exchanges is typically in the range of 100 to 500. As a group these exchanges handle about 12 percent of the dollar volume of all shares traded on organized U.S. exchanges. The best-known regional exchanges are the Midwest, Pacific, Philadelphia, Boston, and Cincinnati. Most are modeled after the NYSE, but their membership and listing requirements are considerably more lenient. It is not uncommon for the regional exchanges to list securities that are also listed on the NYSE or AMEX. This dual listing is often done to enhance a security's trading activity. In addition, a number of the regional exchanges, along with the NYSE, AMEX, and the over-the-counter market, are linked together through an electronic communications network—the *Intermarket Trading System (ITS)*—which allows brokers and other traders to make transactions at the best prices.

Options Exchanges

Options allow the holder to sell or purchase a financial asset at a specified price over a stated period of time. They are listed and traded on the Chicago Board Options Exchange (CBOE), as well as on the American Stock Exchange, the New York Stock Exchange, the Pacific Stock Exchange, and the Philadelphia Stock Exchange. The dominant options exchange is the CBOE. Usually an option for the sale (a *put*) or purchase (a *call*) of a given financial asset is listed on only one of the options exchanges, although dual listing does sometimes occur. Options exchanges deal only in security options; options to purchase or sell property are not traded in this marketplace.

Futures Exchanges

Futures contracts guarantee the future delivery of a specified commodity, foreign currency, or financial instrument at a given future date. The dominant exchange on which commodity and financial futures are traded is the Chicago Board of Trade (CBT). There are a number of other futures exchanges, some of which specialize in certain commodities rather than the broad spectrum listed on the CBT. The larger of these exchanges include the New York Mercantile Exchange, the Chicago Mercantile Exchange, the Commodity Exchange of New York, the New York Coffee, Sugar & Cocoa Exchange, the New York Cotton Exchange, the Kansas City Board of Trade, and the Minneapolis Grain Exchange.

The Over-the-Counter Market

The over-the-counter market is not a specific institution; rather, it is another way of trading securities. It accounts for about 28 percent of the total *dollar volume* of domestic shares traded. Securities traded in this market are sometimes called *unlisted securities*. The over-the-counter (OTC) market is the result of an intangible relationship among purchasers and sellers of securities, who are linked by a telecommunications network. The prices at which securities are traded are determined by both competitive bids and negotiation. The actual process depends on the general activity of the security. A numerical majority of stocks are traded over the counter, as are most government and corporate bonds. Of the over 35,000 issues traded over the counter, about 4,700 have an active market in which frequent transactions take place. A numerical majority of all corporate bonds, some of which are also listed on the NYSE, are traded in the OTC market.

New Issues and Secondary Distributions

secondary distributions
the public sales of large blocks of previously issued securities held by large investors.

In order to create a continuous market for unlisted securities, the OTC market also provides a forum in which initial public offerings (IPOs), both listed and unlisted, are sold. If they are listed, subsequent transactions will be made on the appropriate organized securities exchange; unlisted securities will continue to trade in the OTC market. **Secondary distributions**—the public sales of large blocks of previously issued securities held by large investors—are also made in the OTC market in order to minimize the potentially negative effects of such transactions on the price of listed securities. These transactions are forms of *third or fourth market* trades, which are described below.

dealers
traders who make markets by offering to buy or sell certain over-the-counter securities at stated prices.

The Role of Dealers

The market price of OTC securities results from a matching of the forces of supply and demand for the security by traders known as **dealers.** Each makes markets in certain securities by offering to buy or sell at stated prices. Thus, unlike the organized exchanges (where the buyer and seller of a security are brought together by a broker), dealers are always the second party to a transaction. For example, a dealer making a market in Raco Enterprises might offer to buy shares from investors at $29.50 and sell shares to other investors at $31. The **bid price** is the highest price offered by the dealer to purchase a given security; the **ask price** is the lowest price at which the dealer is willing to sell the security. As an investor, you could *sell* stock in Raco Enterprises at the (lower) bid price of $29.50; or you could *buy* it at the (higher) ask price of $31. The dealer makes a profit from the spread between the bid and the ask price.

bid price
the highest price offered by a dealer to purchase a given security.

ask price
the lowest price at which a dealer is willing to sell a given security.

National Association of Securities Dealers Automated Quotation (Nasdaq) System
an automated system that provides up-to-date bid and ask prices on certain selected, highly active OTC securities.

Nasdaq

OTC dealers are linked with the purchasers and sellers of securities through the **National Association of Securities Dealers Automated Quotation (Nasdaq) System.** Nasdaq is an automated system that provides up-to-date bid and ask prices on over 4,700 selected, highly active OTC securities. It enables buyers and sellers to locate one another easily. To trade in securities not quoted on Nasdaq, purchasers and sellers must find each other through references or through known dealers in the securities.

About 2,600 of the Nasdaq stocks meeting the qualification standards relative to financial size, performance, and trading activity are included in the **Nasdaq/ National Market System (Nasdaq/NMS).** Transactions in stocks on this list are carefully tracked, and their more detailed quotations are therefore isolated from other OTC stocks when published in the financial press.

Nasdaq/National Market System (Nasdaq/NMS)
a list of Nasdaq stocks meeting certain standards of financial size, performance, and trading activity.

Third and Fourth Markets

The **third market** is the name given to over-the-counter transactions made in securities listed on the NYSE, AMEX, or one of the other organized exchanges. It exists to serve the needs of large institutional investors, such as mutual funds, pension funds, and life insurance companies, by allowing them to make large transactions at a reduced cost. These transactions are typically handled by firms or dealers that are not members of an organized securities exchange. For bringing together large buyers and sellers, these firms charge commissions below those charged for making similar transactions on the associated securities exchange. Institutional investors are thus often able to realize sizable savings in brokerage commissions as well as to have minimal impact on the price of the transaction. Since the introduction of negotiated commissions on the organized exchanges in 1975, the importance of this market has been somewhat reduced.

third market
over-the-counter transactions made in securities listed on the NYSE, AMEX, or other organized exchanges.

The **fourth market** is the name given to transactions made directly between large institutional buyers and sellers. Unlike the third market, fourth-market transactions bypass the dealer. But in order to find a suitable seller or buyer, an institution may hire a firm to facilitate the transaction.

fourth market
transactions made directly between large institutional buyers and sellers.

Globalization of Securities Markets

Today, investors, issuers of securities, and securities firms look beyond the markets of their home countries to find the best returns, lowest costs, and best international business opportunities. Advances in technology and communications, together with the elimination of many political and regulatory barriers, allow investors to make cross-border securities transactions with relative ease. In short, we are experiencing a *globalization* of the securities markets, enabling investors to seek out opportunities to profit from rapidly expanding economies throughout the world.

The international equity markets currently have a combined market value of over $8.4 trillion, and the worldwide bond markets have a market value in excess of $10 trillion. In the U.S. alone, American investments in foreign assets exceed $650 billion. Foreign ownership of U.S. assets is more than $1 trillion. Clearly, as discussed in the nearby Investor Insights Box, global investing can represent a prudent strategy that reduces risk and enhances returns. To enter the international investment arena, today's investors need to understand how international securities markets operate, ways to invest in foreign securities, and the rewards and risks of international investing.

INVESTOR INSIGHTS

Global Investing: A Prudent Strategy

Prevalent among U.S. investors not so very long ago was the illusion that putting money into foreign securities was only for daring risk takers. But in recent years more and more Americans have come to understand that having part of your stake invested abroad is prudent, lessening risk rather than increasing it. . . .

Despite all the interconnectedness of national economies, some will be doing better than others at any given time, so having stakes in several countries spreads your risks. It is pretty certain, moreover, that some countries will grow more vigorously than the U.S. during the Nineties. Accordingly, there is a good chance that an American with well-chosen investments abroad will get larger overall returns than a stay-at-home investor.

While the U.S. stock market did very well for investors in the Eighties, quite a few stock markets abroad did even better. Morgan Stanley reports that over the decade, the U.S. stock market had a total return of 325%. Very nice, but eight markets abroad topped that by substantial margins, with returns ranging from 431% for Britain to more than 1,100% for Japan and Sweden.

Philippe Jorion, associate professor of international finance at Columbia's business school, advises American investors to commit 20% or more of their portfolios to a diverse mix of foreign securities. Those who did so during the years 1978 to 1988, a study by Jorion shows, would have fared significantly better than investors who stuck to the U.S.

But what do you do when confronted with a world of stocks—so many stocks, so little time to choose among them? To begin with, remember that when you buy a foreign stock you also buy into a foreign stock market. The markets where prices are rising the fastest are not always the best to invest in, and neither are those where stocks look extraordinarily

Growing Importance of International Markets

Although the U.S. equity market is still the world's largest, today it represents about 30 percent of total share value, compared to almost two-thirds of total share value in 1971. Japan is second largest at about 25 percent followed by Great Britain at about 9 percent. U.S. money and capital markets therefore face stiff competition for investment dollars from major stock exchanges around the world.

Foreign Securities Markets.   There are organized securities exchanges in more than 30 countries worldwide. They are located not only in the major industrialized nations such as Japan, Great Britain, Canada, and Germany, but also in emerging economies such as Brazil, Chile, Malaysia, Mexico, Taiwan, and Thailand. The top three securities markets worldwide are the New York, Tokyo, and London stock exchanges. Other important foreign exchanges include Frankfurt, Paris, Toronto, Montreal, Sydney, Hong Kong, Zurich, and Buenos Aires. The European stock markets are expected to take on additional importance with economic integration of the European Community (EC) during the 1990s. Among the EC's major goals are the development of a central capital market, a central bank, and a single currency cheap. Prices in torrid markets can overheat in a hurry, and low prices sometimes betray high risk. . . .

It is well to be aware also that returns from owning foreign securities can be wagged by the performance of the dollar in exchange markets. If you buy a Swiss stock and the dollar goes down relative to the Swiss franc, that increases the value of the stock in terms of dollars. If the dollar goes up instead, that decreases the dollar value of the stock.

The dollar's sustained skid against other currencies from 1985 to 1988 gave a big boost to Americans' returns on foreign securities. During that stretch, a Morgan Stanley index of stock markets outside the U.S. climbed a dazzling 210% when measured in dollars but only 76% when measured in local currencies.

A divergence that wide, or anything near it, is not in prospect for the Nineties. The dollar may sink some more, but it will hardly keep sinking as persistently as in the past several years. . . . A larger proportion of any returns will have to come from the performance of the securities themselves.

An investor who wants to go international has a choice between buying shares in a mutual fund that invests abroad or buying individual stocks. A personal portfolio of stocks might bring larger rewards, but most pros discourage that approach for anyone who has less than $200,000 to stake abroad. It takes at least that much to achieve a prudent degree of diversification. Says George Foot, a partner at Newgate Management, a New York investment adviser specializing in foreign markets: "The trick to international investing is not to hit the hot stock, but to diversify your risks." . . .

Source: David Carey, "Why Investors Should Go Global," *Fortune 1991 Investor's Guide,* Fall 1990, pp. 97–108.

unit for the 12 member countries. The current market capitalization of the combined EC markets represents a market competitive with New York and Tokyo.

Bond markets, too, are going global as investors are purchasing government and corporate fixed-income securities in foreign markets. The United States dominates the international government bond market, followed by Japan, Germany, and Great Britain.

**American Deposi-
tary Receipts (ADRs)
(ADRs)**
negotiable receipts
for company stock
held in trust in a for-
eign branch of a U.S.
bank

Yankee bonds
debt securities is-
sued by foreign gov-
ernments or corpora-
tions and traded in
U.S. securities mar-
kets.

Purchasing Foreign Securities.   There are several ways to invest in foreign securities. Investors can purchase dollar-denominated securities that are linked to foreign stocks and bonds, make direct purchases of foreign shares, or buy shares of mutual funds composed of foreign securities (discussed in Chapter 13). Two dollar-denominated securities are *American Depositary Receipts (ADRs)* and *Yankee bonds.* **American Depositary Receipts (ADRs)** are dollar-denominated negotiable receipts representing stock of a foreign company that is held in trust by foreign branches of U.S. banks. Currently about 900 ADRs representing 38 countries are listed in the United States; of these, about 200 trade actively. **Yankee bonds** are dollar-denominated debt securities issued by foreign governments or corporations and traded in U.S. securities markets. In addition, many investors choose to diversify their portfolios internationally by acquiring shares in U.S.–based multinationals with substantial foreign operations. For example, Exxon, IBM, Citicorp, Dow Chemical, Coca-Cola, Colgate-Palmolive, and Hewlett-Packard are among U.S. corporations receiving over 50 percent of their revenues from overseas operations.

Investments in dollar-denominated foreign securities are handled by the investor's broker in much the same way as U.S. securities transactions. Shares of a foreign company can also be purchased directly; however, doing so is complex and is not for the timid or inexperienced investor. The basic steps in investment transactions—placing the order to buy or sell, exchanging money and the securities, and holding the securities, paying taxes, and receiving dividends—occur no matter where you buy securities. However, each country's exchange has its own regulations and procedures with regard to these steps. Therefore, investors must be prepared to cope not only with varying degrees of market regulation and efficiency, but also with different stock exchange rules, settlement procedures, accounting standards, tax laws, and language barriers.

The best way for U.S. individual investors to buy foreign securities is through brokers at major U.S. Wall Street firms with large international operations. Such firms include Merrill Lynch, Dean Witter, PaineWebber, Lehman Brothers, and large discount broker Charles Schwab. In addition, major banks such as Bankers Trust and Citicorp have special brokerage units to handle foreign securities transactions. Brokers at any of these institutions can provide advice on transaction procedures and often have research on major foreign stocks. These institutions are governed by U.S. securities regulations and will execute orders for foreign securities in much the same way as for U.S. securities. They will deal with foreign currency conversion for purchase, sale, and dividend payments. The currency conversion is typically made at the exchange rate at the time of the trade or when dividends are received. Generally, foreign security certificates are held for the investor by a foreign correspondent bank.

It is also possible to deal directly with a foreign broker-dealer. In this case, the investor must comply with local securities regulations and customs and deal with the problems of currency conversion, possible delays in settlement, and risk of fraud or broker bankruptcy.

International Investment Performance

A primary motive for investing overseas is the lure of high returns. In fact, only once since 1980 did the United States finish number one among the major stock markets of the world. For example, in 1990, investors would have earned higher returns in such markets as Great Britain, Hong Kong, and Austria than in the United States. For the ten-year period 1981–1990, the London Stock Exchange outperformed the New York Stock Exchange with an average annual return of 18.26 percent, compared to 13.96 percent on the NYSE. Of course, foreign securities markets tend to be more risky than U.S. markets. A market with high returns in one year may not do so well the next year.

Investors can compare activity on U.S. and foreign exchanges by following market indexes that track the performance of those exchanges. (We'll discuss indexes in more detail in Chapter 3.) Most of the major indexes, trading activity in selected stocks on major foreign exchanges, and foreign exchange rates are reported daily in *The Wall Street Journal* and regularly in other financial publications such as *Barron's* and *Business Week*. Also, *The Wall Street Journal*'s Investor Insight section frequently compares performance of the U.S. and selected foreign markets.

Risks of Investing Internationally

Investing abroad is not without its pitfalls, however. In addition to the risks involved in making *any* security transaction, the international investor must consider the risks associated with doing business in a particular foreign country. Changes in government regulations such as trade policies, labor laws, and taxation may affect operating conditions for the country's firms. The government itself may not be stable.

U.S. securities markets are generally viewed as highly regulated, efficient, and reliable. This is not always the case in foreign markets, many of which lag substantially behind the U.S. in both operations and regulation. Some countries place various restrictions on foreign investment. In Korea, Brazil, and Thailand, for example, mutual funds are the only way for foreigners to invest; Mexico has a two-tier market with some securities restricted to foreigners. Some countries make it difficult for foreigners to get their funds out, and many impose taxes on dividends—Swiss taxes are about 20 percent on dividends paid to foreigners. Accounting standards vary from country to country. Other difficulties include illiquid markets and an inability to obtain reliable investment information due to a lack of reporting requirements.

Because international investing involves securities denominated in foreign currencies, trading profits and losses are affected not only by a security's price changes but also by changes in foreign exchange rates. The values of the world's major currencies fluctuate with respect to each other on a daily basis, and the relationship between two currencies is called the **foreign exchange rate.** On December 4, 1991, the foreign exchange rate for the French franc (Ff) and the U.S. dollar (US$) was expressed as follows:

foreign exchange rate
the relationship between two currencies at a specific date.

$$US\$1.00 = Ff\ 5.49$$

$$Ff\ 1.00 = US\$.182$$

On that day, you would have received 5.49 French francs for every $1. Conversely, each French franc was worth $.182.

Changes in the value of a particular foreign currency with respect to the US$—or any other currency—are called *appreciation* and *depreciation*. For example, on December 11, 1991, the Ff/US$ exchange rate was 5.40, indicating that in one week the French franc *appreciated* relative to the dollar (and the dollar depreciated relative to the franc). On December 11 it took *fewer* French francs to buy $1 (5.40 versus 5.49), so each franc was worth more in dollar terms ($.185 versus $.182).

However, compared to a year earlier, the value of the French franc *depreciated*. On December 11, 1990, the exchange rate was Ff/US$ = 5.03; on December 11, 1991, it took *more* French francs to buy $1 (5.40 versus 5.03) than it did on the same day in 1990, and each franc was worth $.199.

foreign exchange risk
the risk caused by varying exchange rates between two countries.

Foreign exchange risk is the risk caused by the varying exchange rates between the currencies of two countries. For example, assume that on December 11, 1990, you bought 100 shares of a French stock at 100 Ff per share, held it for one year, and then sold it for 105 French francs. The following table summarizes the transactions:

Date	Transaction	Number of Shares	Price in Ff	Value of Transaction, Ff	Exchange Rate Ff/US$	Value in US$
12/11/90	Purchase	100	100	10,000	5.03	$1,988.07
12/11/91	Sell	100	105	10,500	5.40	$1,944.44

Although you realized a *gain* of 500 French francs, in dollar terms the transaction resulted in a *loss*. The value of the stock in dollars decreased because the French franc was worth less (had depreciated) relative to the dollar. Therefore, investors in foreign securities must be aware that value of the foreign currency in relationship to the dollar can have a profound effect on their returns from foreign security transactions.

Trading Hours

To compete more effectively with foreign securities markets, in which investors can execute trades when U.S. markets are closed, both the organized U.S. exchanges and Nasdaq recently expanded trading hours beyond the traditional session (9:30 A.M.–4:00 P.M., Eastern time). In mid-1991, the NYSE added two short electronic trading sessions that begin after the 4 P.M. closing bell. The first, from 4:15 to 5 P.M., trades stocks at that day's closing prices via a computer-matching system. Transactions occur only if a match can be made and are handled on a first-come, first-served basis. The second session lasts from 4 to 5:15 P.M. and allows institutional investors to trade large blocks of stock valued at $1 million or more.

Nasdaq began its own expanded-hours electronic trading session in January 1992. Called Nasdaq International, it runs from 3:30 A.M. (when the London Exchange opens) to 9 A.M. Eastern time, one-half hour before the start of regular trading sessions in U.S. markets. Because it lists NYSE stocks as well as other U.S. equities and has less stringent disclosure requirements than other markets, Nasdaq International is designed to attract traders from both the New York and London exchanges. Unlike the NYSE and Nasdaq, the Pacific Stock Exchange conducts its after-hours trading session from 4 to 4:50 P.M., Eastern time, on an auction basis. It continues to make markets, rather than trading electronically at fixed prices. Other U.S. markets such as the American and Philadelphia Stock Exchanges are considering expanded hours as well.

These actions represent the first steps toward the development of 24-hour global trading of securities, both electronically and at auction through organized exchanges. Actually, investors are already able to trade securities after hours (from 4 P.M. to 9:30 A.M., Eastern time) through Instinet, a private electronic trading system owned by Reuters, the British communications conglomerate. This system lists 10,000 U.S. and European stocks. Many experts expect longer trading sessions to be used primarily by institutional investors but question their value for the average individual investor.

Regulation of Securities Markets

A number of state and federal laws provide for adequate and accurate disclosure of information to potential and existing investors. Such laws also regulate the activities of various participants in the securities markets. State laws, which regulate the sale of securities within state borders, are commonly called "blue sky laws" because they are intended to prevent investors from being sold nothing but "blue sky." These laws typically establish procedures for regulating both security issues and sellers of securities doing business within the state. As part of this process, most states have a regulatory body, such as a state securities commission, that is charged with the enforcement of the related state statutes. However, the most important securities laws are those enacted by the federal government.

Securities Act of 1933

This act was passed by Congress to ensure full disclosure of information with respect to new security issues and prevent a stock market collapse similar to that which occurred in 1929–1932. It requires the issuer of a new security to file with the Securities and Exchange Commission (SEC) a registration statement containing information with respect to the new issue. The firm cannot sell the security until the SEC approves the registration statement, a process that usually takes about 20 days.

prospectus
a portion of a security registration statement that details the key aspects of the issue, the issuer, and its management and financial position.

red herring
a preliminary prospectus made available to prospective investors after a registration statement has been filed but before its approval.

One portion of the registration statement, called the **prospectus,** details the key aspects of the issue, the issuer, and its management and financial position. During the waiting period between filing the statement and its approval, a **red herring,** which is a *preliminary prospectus* indicating the tentative nature of the offer, is made available to prospective investors. It is so named because, printed in red on the front of the prospectus, it states that the information contained therein is preliminary and subject to change. Once the statement has been approved, the new security issue can be offered for sale. If the registration statement is found to be fraudulent, the SEC will reject the issue and may also sue the directors and others responsible for the misrepresentation. *Approval of the registration statement by the SEC does not mean the security is a good investment; it merely indicates that the facts presented in the statement appear to reflect the firm's true position.*

Securities Exchange Act of 1934

This act formally established the SEC as the agency in charge of the administration of federal securities laws. The act established the SEC's power to regulate the organized securities exchanges and over-the-counter markets by extending disclosure requirements to outstanding securities. It required the stock exchanges as well as the stocks traded on them to be registered with the SEC.

As a result of this act, the SEC covered exchanges and the OTC market, their members, brokers and dealers, and the securities traded in these markets. Each of these participants must report with the SEC and must periodically update such data. The act has been instrumental in providing adequate disclosure of facts on outstanding issues that are traded in the secondary markets. The 1934 act, which has been amended several times over the years, and the Securities Act of 1933, remain the key pieces of legislation that protect participants in the securities markets.

Maloney Act of 1938

This act, an amendment to the Securities Exchange Act of 1934, provided for the establishment of trade associations for the purpose of self-regulation within the securities industry. Since its passage, only one such trade association, the National Association of Securities Dealers (NASD), has been formed. NASD members include nearly all of the nation's securities firms that do business with the public. Membership in NASD allows member firms to make transactions with other member firms at rates below those charged to non-members. Today any securities firms that are not members of NASD must agree to be supervised directly by the SEC. Because the SEC has the power to revoke NASD's registration, its power over this organization is the same as over the exchanges. In addition to its self-regulatory role, NASD has greatly streamlined the functioning of the over-the-counter market by creating Nasdaq.

Investment Company Act of 1940

This act was passed to protect those purchasing investment company shares. An *investment company* is one that obtains funds by selling its shares to numerous investors and uses the proceeds to purchase securities. (The dominant type of investment company, the mutual fund, is discussed in detail in Chapter 13.) The Investment Company Act of 1940 established rules and regulations for investment companies and formally authorized the SEC to regulate their practices and procedures. It required the investment companies to register with the SEC and to fulfill certain disclosure requirements. The act was amended in 1970 to prohibit investment companies from paying excessive fees to their advisors as well as from charging excessive commissions to purchasers of company shares.

Investment Advisers Act of 1940

This act was passed to protect investors against potential abuses by *investment advisers*—persons hired by investors to advise them about security investments. It requires the advisers disclose all relevant information about their backgrounds, conflicts of interest, and so on, as well as about any investments they recommend. The act requires advisers to register and file periodic reports with the SEC. A 1960 amendment extended the SEC's powers to permit inspection of the records of investment advisers and revocation of the registration of advisers who violate the act's provisions. *This act does not provide any guarantee of competence on the part of advisers; it merely helps to protect the investor against fraudulent and unethical practices by the adviser.*

Securities Acts Amendments of 1975

In 1975 Congress amended the securities acts to require the SEC and the securities industry to develop a competitive national system for trading securities. As a first step the SEC abolished fixed commission schedules, thereby providing for negotiated commissions. A second action was the establishment of the Intermarket Trading System (ITS). Today this electronic communications network links eight markets, including the NYSE, AMEX, major regional exchanges, and the Nasdaq market, and trades over 2,100 eligible issues. Unquestionably the Securities Acts Amendments have been highly effective in initiating a national market system. However, many institutional and organizational barriers remain to be overcome before a truly competitive national market system can be established.

Ethical Issues

The 1980s were a decade of general economic prosperity and rapidly rising stock prices. As typically happens during periods of excess in the financial markets, the decade also witnessed a takeover and buyout mania that spawned a host of greedy speculators intent on profiting from the values created by the market. Many times these speculators operated without regard for the legality of their actions. Although the tactics varied, many of the illegal gains were achieved through insider-trading practices. **Insider trading** involves using *inside information,* which is private (non-public) information about a company's plans or performance to make profitable securities transactions. Such information may have been obtained from a company's directors, officers, major shareholders, bankers, investment bankers, accountants, or attorneys. *Insider trading is both illegal and unethical.*

insider trading
the illegal use of non-public information about a company to make profitable securities transactions.

Of all the unethical players in the 1980s, none achieved the notoriety and wealth of Michael Milken, the ''junk bond king.'' Not content with over $1 billion in salary and bonuses he received from his employer Drexel Burnham Lambert in the late 1980's, Milken made hundreds of millions more through a variety of illegal and unethical means. Through his network of corporate raiders and investors, Milken profited significantly from an avalanche of inside information. He also created hundreds of private partnerships which received fees, stock warrants, and bargain-priced securities in connection with securities transactions arranged by Drexel. These fees and warrants were intended to go to investors buying securities from Drexel, but Milken used them for his personal gain and to reward favored clients. Some of these interests were given to bank officers to induce their banks to purchase junk bonds from Drexel. Though cleverly disguised, this practice would usually be called a ''kickback'' in non-financial circles.

Michael Milken was apprehended and punished for his crimes, including racketeering, insider trading, and fraud. He received a ten-year prison sentence and a $600 million fine as part of a plea bargain agreement. Many argue that this punishment was too lenient given the magnitude of his offenses. The conviction of Milken and others like him created a body of case law which more clearly defines illegal and unethical acts. The definition of ''insider,'' which originally referred only to a company's employees, directors, and their relatives, was expanded to include *any-*

one who obtains private information about a company. New legislation substantially increased the penalties for insider trading and gave the SEC greater power to investigate and prosecute claims of illegal insider trading activity.

Clearly, the many insider-trading cases of the 1980s have significantly heightened the public's awareness of **ethics**—standards of conduct or moral judgment—in business. Today the financial community is involved in developing and enforcing ethical standards that will motivate market participants to adhere to laws and regulations. Although it is indeed difficult to enforce ethical standards, it appears that opportunities for abuses in the financial markets will be reduced, thereby providing a more level playing field for market participants.

ethics
standards of conduct or moral judgment.

General Market Conditions: Bull or Bear

Conditions in the securities markets are commonly classified as "bull" or "bear," depending on whether securities prices are rising or falling over time. Changing market conditions generally stem from changes in investor attitudes, changes in economic activity, and government actions aimed at stimulating or slowing down the level of economic activity. **Bull markets** are favorable markets normally associated with rising prices, investor optimism, economic recovery, and governmental stimulus. **Bear markets** are unfavorable markets normally associated with falling prices, investor pessimism, economic slowdowns, and government restraint.

bull markets
favorable markets associated with rising prices, investor optimism, economic recovery, and governmental stimulus.

Over the past fifty or so years, the behavior of the stock market has been generally bullish, reflecting the growth and prosperity of the economy. Figure 2.3 shows the stock price movements from 1950 to 1991. Both the bull (downward lines) and bear (upward lines) can be seen. The most notorious bull market was surely the one that started in August of 1982 and peaked in August of 1987. It is the one that's associated with the big market crash of October 19, 1987. Actually, the market had started dropping in late August of 1987 and by mid-October, the market (averages) had already fallen about 15 percent. Then came "black Monday," when the market experienced its biggest and hardest crash in history: in *one day* the market fell nearly 23 percent, and the market lost roughly half a *trillion* dollars in value. The bear market initiated with this decline was the result of major federal budget deficits, unfavorable trade balances, and congressional discussions directed at regulating acquisitions and the issuance of junk bonds.

bear markets
unfavorable markets associated with falling prices, investor pessimism, economic slowdowns, and government restraint.

In general, investors experience higher (or positive) returns on common stock investments during a bull market. However, some securities are bullish in a bear market or bearish in a bull market. Of course, during bear markets many investors will invest in vehicles other than securities to obtain higher and less risky returns. Market conditions are difficult to predict and usually can be identified only after they exist. The actual assessment of market conditions and the use of this information by investors is described in Chapter 3.

MAKING SECURITY TRANSACTIONS

Understanding how the securities markets are structured and how they function is just the first step in developing a sound investment program. The individual investor

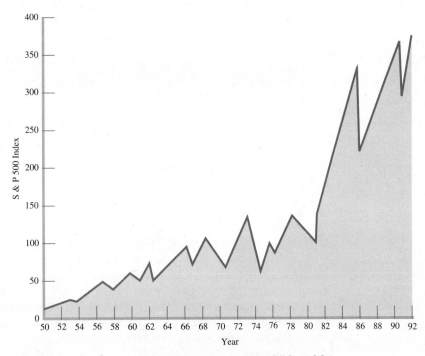

• FIGURE 2.3 Bull and Bear Markets, 1950–1991

Rising stock prices, shown here by increases in the Standard & Poor's 500 Composite Index (upward lines) are called *bull markets*. *Bear markets* are periods of falling prices (downward lines). (*Source:* Graph data for 1950–1989 from Manuel Schiffres, ''Investing in a Perilous Market,'' *Changing Times,* October 1990, pp. 40–41. Data for 1990 from ''Daily Action Stock Charts,'' *Trendline,* Standard & Poor's Corporation, November 22, 1991.)

must also understand the procedures required to make transactions, the various types of orders that can be placed, and the costs associated with making investment transactions.

Stockbrokers

stockbrokers
individuals licensed by stock exchanges to enable investors to buy and sell securities; also called *account executives.*

Stockbrokers, or *account executives,* as they are sometimes called, enable investors to buy and sell securities. They must be licensed by the exchanges on which they place orders and must abide by the ethical guidelines of the exchanges and the SEC. Stockbrokers work for the brokerage firms that own seats on the organized securities exchanges. Members of the securities exchange actually execute orders transmitted to them by the brokers in the various sales offices. For example, the largest U.S. brokerage firm, Merrill Lynch Pierce Fenner & Smith, has offices in most major cities throughout the country. Orders from these offices are transmitted to the main office of Merrill Lynch and then to the floor of the stock exchange (NYSE and AMEX) or to the OTC market, where they are executed. Confirmation of the order is sent back to the broker placing the order, who then relays it to the customer. This process can be carried out in a matter of minutes with the use of sophisticated telecommunications networks.

Orders for over-the-counter securities must be executed through *market makers,* who are dealers specializing in that security. The Nasdaq system, along with the available information on who makes markets in certain securities, enables brokers to execute orders in OTC securities. Normally, OTC transactions can be executed rapidly, since market makers maintain inventories of the securities in which they deal. Although the procedure for executing orders on organized exchanges may differ from that in the OTC market, an investor always places orders with his or her broker in the same manner, regardless of the market in which the security is traded.

Brokerage Services

The primary activity of stockbrokers involves making the purchase and sale transactions requested by clients. Account executives do not actually buy or sell securities; they only execute their clients' transactions at the best possible price. Brokerage firms will hold the client's security certificates for safekeeping. The stocks kept by the firm in this manner are said to be held in ''street name,'' since the broker can liquidate them for the client without having to obtain the latter's signature.

In addition, stockbrokers offer clients a variety of other services. For example, the stockbrokerage normally provides free information ranging from stock and bond guides that summarize the activity of securities to research reports on specific securities or industries. Quite often the firm will have a research staff that periodically issues analyses of economic, market, industry, or company behavior and makes recommendations to buy or sell certain securities. It is the job of the stockbroker to provide the client with relevant information. As a client of a large brokerage firm, you can expect to receive regular bulletins discussing market activity and possibly a recommended investment list. You will also receive a statement describing your transactions for the month and showing commission and interest charges, dividends and interest received, and your account balance.

Today, most brokerage firms will invest surplus cash left in a customer's account in a money market fund, allowing the customer to earn a reasonable rate of interest on these balances. Such arrangements help the investor manage cash effectively and earn as much as possible on temporarily idle funds. Most brokerage offices also have electronic equipment that provides up-to-the-minute stock price quotations and world news. Price information can be obtained from the quotation board (a large screen that electronically displays all NYSE and AMEX security transactions within minutes after they take place) or by keying into a computer system that provides a capsulized description of almost all securities and their prices. World news, which can significantly affect the stock market, is obtained from a wire service subscribed to by the brokerage office. Finally, most offices have a reference library available for use by the firm's clients.

Selecting a Stockbroker

It is of primary importance to select a stockbroker who understands your investment goals and who can effectively assist you in pursuing these goals. If you choose a broker whose own disposition toward investing is similar to yours, you should be able to establish a solid working relationship. In addition, when selecting a broker you should consider the cost and types of services available from the firm with which he or she is affiliated. Often, significant difference can be found among firms. The broker you select should be the person you believe best understands your investment goals and will provide the best service at the lowest possible cost to you. It is probably wise to ask friends or business associates to recommend a broker. However, it is not important—and often not even advisable—to know your stockbroker personally. A strictly business relationship eliminates the possibility that social concerns will interfere with the achievement of your investment goals. This does not mean that your broker's sole interest should be commissions. Responsible brokers do not engage in **churning**—that is, causing excessive trading of their clients' accounts in order to increase commissions, often leaving clients no better off than before. Churning is both illegal and unethical under SEC and exchange rules. However, it is often difficult to prove.

Investors who wish merely to make transactions and are not interested in obtaining the full array of brokerage services mentioned above should consider using a **discount broker.** These brokers merely make transactions for customers—they provide little or no research information or investment advice. Transactions are initiated by calling a toll-free number; the discount broker then confirms the transaction by return mail. Discount brokers that charge the lowest commissions and provide virtually no services are commonly referred to as *deep discounters*. The rapidly growing volume of business done by discount brokers attests to their success.

Today many banks and savings institutions are making discount brokerage services available to their depositors; some have set up investment centers where customers can buy stocks, bonds, and mutual funds. Brokerage services can also be obtained at a **financial supermarket,** which is a financial institution at which a customer can obtain a full array of financial services. Such services include checking, savings, brokerage, insurance, retirement, and estate planning. These one-stop financial centers appeared to be gaining in popularity during the 1980s and early 1990s. Sears, Roebuck and Company's ''Sears Financial Network'' offered a broad range of financial services and was widely touted as a model financial supermarket. But in late 1992 Sears began to dismantle its supermarket by selling its Dean Witter Financial Services unit, which included both stock brokerage and Discover card operations, most of its Coldwell Banker real estate holdings, and 20 percent of its Allstate insurance unit. At the same time, a number of other emerging financial supermarkets were rumored to be preparing to dismantle their operations. Apparently, the break-up of the one-stop financial supermarket resulted from an inability to achieve the expected benefits of combining a number of financial service firms. It appears that the financial supermarket, formerly touted as the financial services institution for the 1990s, may be on its way to extinction.

churning
an illegal and unethical act by a broker to increase commissions through excessive trading of clients' accounts.

discount broker
brokers who make transactions for customers but provide little or no research information or advice.

financial supermarket
a financial institution at which customers can obtain a full array of financial services.

Opening an Account

To open an account, the customer will be asked to fill out various documents that establish a legal relationship between the customer and the brokerage firm. By filling out and signing a signature card and a personal data card, the client provides the information needed to identify his or her account. The stockbroker must also have a reasonable understanding of a client's personal financial situation in order to assess his or her investment goals and also to be sure that the client can pay for the securities purchased. Instructions relating to the transfer and custody of securities must also be given to the broker. If the customer wishes to borrow money in order to make transactions, a *margin account* (described below) will have to be established. If the customer is acting as a trustee or an executor, or is a corporation, additional documents will be necessary to establish the account. No laws or rules prohibit an investor from establishing accounts with more than one stockbroker. Many investors establish accounts at different firms in order to obtain the benefit and opinions of a diverse group of brokers.

Types of Accounts

A number of different types of accounts can be established with a stockbroker. We will briefly consider several of the more popular types.

custodial account
the brokerage account of a minor, in which a parent or guardian must be part of all transactions.

Single or Joint.   A brokerage account may be either single or joint. Joint accounts are most common between husband and wife or parent and child. The account of a minor (a person less than 18 years of age) is a **custodial account,** in which a parent or guardian must be part of all transactions. Regardless of which form of account is maintained, the name(s) of the account holder(s), along with an account number, are used to identify the account.

cash account
a brokerage account in which a customer can make only cash transactions.

Cash or margin.   A **cash account,** the most common type, is one in which the customer can make only cash transactions. Customers can initiate transactions via the phone, even though they may not have sufficient cash in their account to cover the cost of the transaction. They are given five business days in which to get the cash to the brokerage firm. The firm is likewise given five business days in which to deposit the proceeds from the sale of securities in the customer's account.

margin account
a brokerage account in which the customer has borrowing privileges.

A **margin account** is an account in which the customer has been extended borrowing privileges by the brokerage firm. By leaving securities with the firm to be held as collateral, the customer is permitted to borrow a prespecified proportion of the purchase price. Prior to opening a margin account, the brokerage firm will assess the creditworthiness of the customer. It will of course charge the customer a specified rate of interest on borrowings. (A more detailed discussion of margin trading is included later in the chapter.)

wrap account
an account in which customers with large portfolios pay a brokerage firm a flat annual fee that covers the cost of a money manager's services and the cost of commissions.

Wrap.   The **wrap account** allows brokerage customers with large portfolios (generally $100,000 or more) to conveniently shift the burden of stock-selection decisions to a professional—either in-house or independent—money manager. In return for paying a flat annual fee equal to between 2 and 3 percent of the portfolio's total asset value, the brokerage firm helps the investor select a money manager, pays the manager's fee, and executes the money manager's trades. Of course the investor's overall goals are initially communicated to the manager. Wrap accounts are appealing for a number of reasons other than convenience. Because the annual fee in most cases covers commissions on *all* trades, the chance of the broker *churning* the account is virtually eliminated. In addition, the broker monitors the manager's performance and provides the investor with detailed reports, typically quarterly.

Odd-Lot or Round-Lot Transactions

odd lot
less than 100 shares of stock.

round lot
100 share units of stock or multiples thereof.

Stock transactions can be made in either odd or round lots. An **odd lot** consists of less than 100 shares of a stock, while a **round lot** is a 100-share unit or multiple thereof. Thus, you would be dealing in an odd lot if you bought, say, 25 shares of stock, but a round lot if you bought 200 shares. A trade of 225 shares would be a combination of an odd and two round lots. Because the purchase or sale of odd lots requires additional processing and the assistance of a specialist, an added fee—known as an *odd-lot differential*—is tacked on to the normal commission charge, driving up the costs of these small trades. Small investors in the early stages of their investment programs are primarily responsible for odd-lot transactions.

Basic Types of Orders

Different types of orders are used in making security transactions. The type placed normally depends on the investor's goals and expectations. The three basic types of orders are the market order, the limit order, and the stop-loss order.

Market Order

market order
an order to buy or sell stock at the best price available when the order is placed.

An order to buy or sell stock at the best price available when the order is placed is a **market order.** It is usually the quickest way to have orders filled, since market orders are usually executed as soon as they reach the exchange floor or are received by the dealer. Because of the speed with which market orders are executed, the buyer or seller of a security can be sure that the price at which the order is transacted will be very close to the market price prevailing at the time the order was placed.

Limit Order

limit order
an order to buy at or below a specified price or to sell at or above a specified price.

An order to buy at a specified price or lower, or sell at or above a specified price, is known as a **limit order.** When a limit order is placed, the broker transmits it to a specialist dealing in the security. The specialist makes a notation in his or her book, indicating the number of shares and price of the limit order. The order is executed as soon as the specified market price (or better) exists and all other orders with precedence (similar orders received earlier, or buy orders at a higher specified price, or sell orders at a lower specified price) have been satisfied. The order can be placed as: (1) a *fill-or-kill order* that if not immediately executed is cancelled; (2) a *day order* that if not executed is automatically cancelled at the end of the day; or (3) a *good-'til-cancelled (GTC) order* that generally remains in effect for six months unless executed, cancelled, or renewed.

Assume, by way of example, that you place a limit order to buy 100 shares of a stock currently selling at 30½ (security market terminology for $30.50) at a limit price of $30. Once the specialist has cleared all similar orders received before yours, and once the market price of the stock has fallen to $30 or less, the order is executed. It is possible, of course, that your order might expire (if it is not a GTC order) before the stock price drops to $30.

Although a limit order can be quite effective, it can also keep you from making a transaction. If, for instance, you wish to buy at $30 or less and the stock price moves from its current $30.50 price to $42 while you are waiting, your limit order has caused you to forgo the opportunity to make a profit of $11.50 per share ($42 − $30.50). Had you placed a market order to buy at the best available price ($30.50), the profit of $11.50 would have been yours. Limit orders for the sale of a stock are also disadvantageous when the stock price closely approaches but does not attain the minimum sale price limit before dropping substantially. Generally speaking, limit orders are most effective when the price of a stock is known to fluctuate greatly, since there is then a better chance that the order will be executed.

Stop-Loss Order

stop-loss order
an order to sell a stock when its market price reaches or drops below a specified level; also called a *stop order*.

An order to sell a stock when its market price reaches or drops below a specified level is called a **stop-loss** or **stop order.** Stop-loss orders are *suspended orders* that are placed on stocks when and if a certain price is reached. The stop-loss order is placed on the specialist's book and becomes active once the stop price has been reached. When activated, the stop order becomes a *market order* to sell the security at the best price available. Because of this, it is possible that the actual price at which the sale is made could be well below the price at which the stop was initiated. These orders are used to protect investors against the adverse effects of a rapid decline in share price. For example, assume you own 100 shares of Ballard Industries, which is currently selling for $35 per share. Because you believe the stock price could decline rapidly at any time, you place a stop order to sell at $30. If the stock price does in fact drop to $30, the specialist will sell the 100 shares of Ballard at the best price available at that time. But if the market price declines to $28 by the time your stop-loss order comes up, you will receive less than $30 per share. Of course, if the market price stays above $30 per share you will have lost nothing as a result of placing the order, since the stop order will never be initiated. Often investors will raise the level of the stop as the price of the stock rises; such action helps to lock in a higher profit when the price is increasing.

Stop orders can also be placed to *buy* a stock, although they are far less common than sell orders. For example, an investor may place a stop order to buy 100 shares of MJ Enterprises, currently selling for $70 per share, once its price rises to, say, $75—the stop price. These orders are commonly used to limit losses on short sales (discussed later) and to get into a stock as its price supposedly starts to rise.

To avoid the risk of the market moving against you when your stop order becomes a market order, you can place a *stop-limit* order, rather than a plain stop order. It is an order to buy or sell stock at a given price or better once a stipulated stop price has been met. For example, in the Ballard Industries illustration above, had a stop-limit order been in effect, once the market price of Ballard dropped to $30, the broker would have entered a limit order to sell your 100 shares at $30 a share, *or better*. Thus, there would be no risk of you getting less than $30 a share for your stock—*unless the price of the stock kept right on falling.* Then, like any limit order, you might miss the market altogether and end up with stock worth much less than $30. Even though the stop order to sell was triggered (at $30), the stock will *not* be sold, with a limit order, if it keeps falling in price.

Transaction Costs

Rather than going through the trouble of direct negotiation trying to find someone who wants to buy that which they want to sell (or vice versa), investors make transactions through brokers or dealers. Transaction costs are paid by the investor to compensate the broker for executing the transaction. Such costs are usually levied on both the purchase and the sale of securities. The structure and magnitude of transaction costs need to be considered when making investment decisions, since they affect returns.

With the passage of the Securities Acts Amendments of 1975, brokers have been permitted to charge whatever commission they deem appropriate. Most firms have established **fixed-commission schedules** that are applicable to small transactions, the ones most often made by individual investors. On large institutional transactions, **negotiated commissions**—commissions agreed upon by the client and broker as a result of their negotiations—are usually used. Brokerage firms can thus compete not only on the basis of services offered, but also on a cost basis. Negotiated commissions are also available to individual investors who maintain sizable accounts—typically in the range of $25,000 or more.

The commission structure varies depending upon the type of security and type of broker. The basic commission structures for various types of securities are described in subsequent chapters as part of the detailed discussion of given securities. The commissions charged on differing sizes of transactions in a $26 stock, shown (both in dollars and as a percentage of purchase cost) in Table 2.2, clearly demonstrate varying transactions costs among full-service, discount, and deep-discount brokers. Obviously, discount brokers charge substantially less than full-service brokers for the same transaction. Most discounters charge a minimum fee to discourage small orders. For example, Charles Schwab, the nation's largest discounter, charges

fixed-commission schedules
fixed brokerage charges applicable to small transactions.

negotiated commissions
commissions agreed upon by the client and the broker as a result of their negotiations.

TABLE 2.2 Comparative Brokerage Commissions on a $26 Stock (March 1991)

	Number of Shares Traded		
Brokerage Firm	**100**	**200**	**1,000**
Full Service:	**Commissions (Percent of Purchase Cost)**		
Merrill Lynch	$80 (3.1%)	$132 (2.6%)	$418 (1.6%)
Shearson Lehman	75 (2.9)	139 (2.7)	497 (1.9)
Discounter:			
Quick & Reilly	49 (1.9)	61 (1.2)	121 (0.5)
Charles Schwab	49 (1.9)	82 (1.6)	143 (0.6)
Deep Discounter:			
Waterhouse Securities	35 (1.4)	35 (0.7)	128 (0.5)
York Securities	35 (1.4)	35 (0.7)	75 (0.3)

Note: Many firms offer additional discounts or rebates for active traders, with the amount linked to trading activity.

Source: Tom Herman, ''Not All Discount Brokers Offer the Same Bargains,'' *The Wall Street Journal,* March 6, 1991, p. C1.

a minimum fee of about $40 for any stock transaction. Depending on the size and type of transaction, the discount broker can typically save investors between 30 and 80 percent of the commission charged by the full-service broker. The savings from the discounter are substantial. However, investors must weigh the added commissions they pay a full-service broker against the value of the advice they receive, since that is the only major difference between the discount and the full-service broker.

Investor Protection: SIPC and Arbitration

As a client, you are protected against the loss of the securities or cash held by your broker. The **Securities Investor Protection Corporation (SIPC),** a non-profit membership corporation, was authorized by the Securities Investor Protection Act of 1970 to protect customer accounts against the consequences of financial failure of the brokerage firm. Although subject to SEC and congressional oversight, SIPC is *not* an agency or establishment of the U.S. government. It insures each customer's account for up to $500,000, except that claims for cash are limited to $100,000 per customer. Note, however, that SIPC insurance *does not* guarantee that the dollar value of the securities will be recovered; it guarantees only that the securities themselves will be returned. Some brokerage firms insure certain customer accounts for amounts in excess of the required $500,000 of SIPC insurance. Certainly, in light of the diversity and quality of services available among brokerage houses, careful consideration should be given not only to the selection of an individual broker (the *person* you deal with), but also to the choice of a *firm*.

SIPC provides protection in case your brokerage firm fails. But what happens if your broker gave you bad advice and as a result, you lost a lot of money on an investment? SIPC won't help. It's not intended to insure you against bad investment advice. Instead, if you have a dispute with your broker, the first thing you should do is discuss the situation with the managing officer at the branch where you do your business. If that doesn't do any good, then write or talk to the firm's compliance officer, and contact the securities commission in your home state.

If you still don't get any satisfaction, you may have no choice but to take the case to **arbitration,** a process whereby you and your broker present the two sides of the argument before an arbitration panel. The panel then decides the case. Many brokerage firms *require* you to resolve disputes by binding arbitration; in this case, you don't have the option to sue. You must accept the arbitrator's decision, and you cannot go to court to appeal your case. Thus, before you open an account, check whether the brokerage agreement contains a binding arbitration clause.

Settling securities disputes through arbitration rather than litigation has advantages and disadvantages. Arbitration proceedings typically cost less and are resolved more quickly than litigation. However, until recently many brokerage agreements not only required investors to submit to binding arbitration but also specified the use of securities industry arbitration panels. There was considerable controversy as to whether these panels, which prior to 1989 were often composed entirely of persons who had relationships to the securities industry, were fair to investors. As a result of pressure from the SEC and a July 1990 court decision in New York State,

---

Securities Investor Protection Corporation (SIPC)
a nonprofit membership corporation authorized by the federal government that insures each brokerage customer's account for up to $500,000.

arbitration
a dispute process in which a broker and customer present their cases before a panel which then decides the case.

many investors now have the option of using either securities industry panels or independent arbitration panels such as those sponsored by the American Arbitration Association (AAA), which are considered more sympathetic toward investors. In addition, only one of the three arbitrators on a panel can be connected with the securities industry. Recently, the NASD and other securities organizations began encouraging investors to mediate disputes and voluntarily negotiate a settlement rather than immediately starting arbitration proceedings. Although mediation is not binding, it can further reduce costs and time for both investors and brokers. Even so, probably the best thing you can do to avoid such a situation is to use care when selecting a broker, understand the financial risks involved in the broker's recommendations, and carefully evaluate the advice he or she offers.

BASIC TYPES OF TRANSACTIONS

An investor can make a number of basic types of security transactions. Each type is available to those who meet certain requirements established by various government agencies as well as by brokerage firms. Although the various types of transactions can be used in a number of ways to meet investment objectives, only the most popular use of each transaction is described here. The three most common types of transaction are the long purchase, margin trading, and short selling.

Long Purchase

long purchase
a transaction in which investors buy securities in the hope that they will increase in value and can be sold at a later date for profit.

The **long purchase** is a transaction in which investors buy securities in the hope that they will increase in value and can be sold at a later date for profit. The object, then, is to buy low and sell high. A long purchase is the most common type of transaction. Each of the basic types of orders described above can be used with long transactions. Because investors generally expect the price of the security to rise over the period of time they plan to hold it, their return comes from any dividends or interest received during the ownership period, plus the difference between the price at which they sell the security and the price paid to purchase it (capital gains). This return, of course, is reduced by the brokerage fees paid to purchase and sell the securities.

Ignoring any dividends (or interest) and brokerage fees, the long purchase can be illustrated by a simple example. After studying various aspects of Varner Manufacturing, Inc., Fae Johnson is convinced that its common stock, which currently sells for $20 per share, will increase in value over the next few years. Based on her analysis, Fae expects the stock price to rise to $30 per share within two years. She places a limit order and buys a round lot (100 shares) of Varner for $20. If the stock price rises to, say, $40 per share, Fae will profit from her long purchase; if it drops below $20 per share, she will experience a loss on the transaction. Obviously, one of the major motivating factors in making a long transaction is an expected rise in the price of the security.

Margin Trading

margin trading
the use of borrowed funds to purchase securities; magnifies returns by reducing the amount of capital that must be put up by the investor.

Most security purchases do not have to be made on a cash basis; borrowed funds can be used instead. This activity is referred to as **margin trading,** and it is used for one basic reason: to magnify returns. This is possible because the use of borrowed funds reduces the amount of capital that must be put up by the investor. As peculiar as it may sound, the term *margin* itself refers to the amount of *equity* in an investment, or the amount that is not borrowed. If an investor uses 75 percent margin, for example, it means that 75 percent of the investment position is being financed with the person's own capital and the balance (25 percent) with borrowed money. The Federal Reserve Board (''the Fed''), which governs our banking system, sets the **margin requirement** that specifies the minimum amount of equity that must be the margin investor's own funds. By raising or lowering margin requirements, the Fed can depress or stimulate activity in the securities markets.

margin requirement
the minimum amount of equity (stated as a percentage) a margin investor must put up; established by the Federal Reserve Board.

Margin purchases must be approved by a broker. The brokerage firm then lends the purchaser the needed funds and retains the purchased securities as collateral. Margin requirements for stocks have been at 50 percent for some time. It is important to recognize that margin purchasers must pay a specified rate of interest on what they borrow. This rate is usually 1 to 3 percent above the **prime rate**—the lowest interest rate charged the best business borrowers—or at the prime rate for large accounts.

prime rate
the lowest interest rate charged the best business borrowers.

A simple example will help to clarify the basic margin transaction. Jeffrey Lawrence wishes to purchase 70 shares of Universal Fiber common stock, which is currently selling for $63.50 per share. Since the prevailing margin requirement is 50 percent, Jeffrey must put up only 50 percent of the total purchase price of $4,445 ($63.50 per share × 70 shares), or $2,222.50, in cash. The remaining $2,222.50 will be lent to Jeffrey by his brokerage firm. Jeffrey will, of course, have to pay interest on the $2,222.50 he borrows, along with the applicable brokerage fees. It should be clear that with the use of margin an investor can purchase more securities than he or she could afford on a strictly cash basis. In this way investors can magnify their returns.

Essentials of Margin Trading

Margin trading can be used with most kinds of securities. It is regularly used, for example, with both common and preferred stocks, most types of bonds, warrants, commodities, financial futures, and mutual funds. It is not normally used with tax-exempt municipal bonds since the interest paid on such margin loans is not deductible for income tax purposes. For simplicity we will use common stock as the vehicle in our discussion of margin trading, and assume that the securities have already been analyzed along the lines to be discussed in Chapters 6 and 7.

Although margin trading normally leads to increased returns, there are also some substantial risks. One of the biggest is that the issue may not perform as expected. If this in fact occurs, no amount of margin trading can correct matters. Margin trading can only *magnify* returns, not *produce* them. Because the security being margined is always the ultimate source of return, *the security selection process is critical to this trading strategy*.

Magnified Profits and Losses.   Using an investor's equity as a base, the idea of margin trading is to employ *financial leverage,* or debt, to magnify returns. Here is how it works: Suppose you have $5,000 to invest and are considering the purchase of 100 shares of stock (at $50 per share) because you feel the stock in question will go up in price. If you do not margin, you can buy outright (ignoring brokerage commissions) 100 shares of the stock. However, if you margin the transaction—for example, at 50 percent—you could acquire the same $5,000 position with only $2,500 of your own money. This would leave you with $2,500 to use for other investments, or to buy another 100 shares of the same stock. Either way, you will reap greater benefits from the stock's price appreciation by margining.

The concept of margin trading is more fully illustrated in Table 2.3. An unmargined (100 percent equity) transaction is depicted along with the same transaction using various margins. Remember that the margin rates (such as 65 percent) indicate the equity in the investment, or the amount of capital the investor must put up. When the investment is unmargined and the price of the stock goes up by $30 per share, the investor enjoys a very respectable 60 percent rate of return. However, observe what happens when margin is used: The rate of return shoots up to as high as 120 percent, depending on the amount of equity in the investment. This is so because the gain is the same ($3,000) *regardless of how the transaction is financed*. Clearly, as the investor's equity in the investment *declines* (with lower margins), rate of return *increases* accordingly.

TABLE 2.3 The Effect of Margin Trading on Security Returns

	Without Margin (100% Equity)	With Margins of		
		80%	65%	50%
Number of $50 shares purchased	100	100	100	100
Cost of investment	$5,000	$5,000	$5,000	$5,000
Less: Borrowed money	0	1,000	1,750	2,500
Equity in investment	$5,000	$4,000	$3,250	$2,500
A. Investor's Position if Price Rises by $30 to $80/Share				
Value of stock	$8,000	$8,000	$8,000	$8,000
Less: Cost of investment	5,000	5,000	5,000	5,000
Capital gain	$3,000	$3,000	$3,000	$3,000
Return on investor's equity (capital gain/equity in investment)	60%	75%	92.3%	120%
B. Investor's Position if Price Falls by $30 to $20/Share				
Value of stock	$2,000	$2,000	$2,000	$2,000
Less: Cost of investment	5,000	5,000	5,000	5,000
Capital *loss*	$3,000	$3,000	$3,000	$3,000
Return on investor's equity (capital loss/equity in investment)*	(60%)	(75%)	(92.3%)	(120%)

*With a capital loss, return on investor's equity is *negative*.

Three facets of margin trading become obvious from the table: (1) The price of the stock will move in whatever way it is going to regardless of how the position is financed. (2) The lower the amount of the investor's equity in the position, the greater the rate of return the investor will enjoy when the price of the security rises. (3) The risk of loss is also magnified (by the same rate) when the price of the security falls.

Advantages and Disadvantages.   As already stated, a magnified return is the major advantage of margin trading. The size of the magnified return will depend on both the price behavior of the security being margined and the amount of margin being used. Another, more modest benefit of margin trading is that it allows for greater diversification of security holdings, since investors can spread their capital over a greater number of investments.

The major disadvantage of margin trading, of course, is that the price of the security may fall rather than rise, resulting in magnified losses rather than gains. Another disadvantage is the cost of the margin loans themselves. A **margin loan** is the official vehicle through which the borrowed funds are made available in a margin transaction. Such loans are used with most types of margin transactions. All margin loans are made at a stated interest rate, which depends on prevailing market rates and the amount of money being borrowed. This cost, which must be absorbed by the investor, will mount daily, reducing the level of profits (or magnifying losses) accordingly.

margin loan
vehicle through which borrowed funds are made available, at a stated interest rate, in a margin transaction.

Making Margin Transactions

To execute a margin transaction, it is necessary to establish a *margin account*. It is opened with a minimum of $2,000 in equity, either in the form of cash or securities. Margin credit can be obtained from a broker or a banker, although nearly all margin trading is done through brokers. The broker will retain any securities purchased on margin as collateral for the loan.

The margin requirement established by the Federal Reserve Board set the minimum amount of equity for margin transactions. This does not mean, of course, that investors must execute all margin transactions by using exactly the minimum amount of margin; they can use more than the minimum if they wish. Moreover, it is not unusual for *brokerage houses* and the major exchanges to establish their own margin requirements, which are more restrictive than those of the Federal Reserve. There are basically two types of margin requirements: initial margin and maintenance margin.

initial margin
the minimum amount of money (or equity) that must be provided by a margin investor at the time of purchase.

Initial Margin.   Initial margin stipulates the minimum amount of equity that must be provided by the investor *at the time of purchase*. It is used to prevent overtrading and excessive speculation. Generally, it is this margin requirement that investors refer to when discussing margin trading. Any security that can be margined has a specific initial requirement, although these can be changed by the authorities from time to time. As Table 2.4 shows, initial margin requirements vary by type of

TABLE 2.4 Initial Margin Requirements for Various Types of Securities (December 1991)

Security	Minimum Initial Margin (Equity) Required
Listed common and preferred stock	50%
OTC stocks traded on Nasdaq/NMS	50
Convertible bonds	50
Corporate bonds	30
U.S. Treasury bills, notes, and bonds	8% of principal
Other federal government issues	10% of principal
Federal government guaranteed issues	15% of principal

security. The more stable investment vehicles, such as Treasury issues, generally enjoy substantially lower margin requirements and therefore offer greater magnification opportunities. Note in Table 2.4 that OTC stocks traded on the Nasdaq/NMS can be margined like listed securities. All other OTC stocks are considered to have *no* collateral value and therefore *cannot* be margined.

As long as the margin in an account remains at a level equal to or greater than prevailing initial requirements, the investor is free to use the account in any way he or she sees fit. If the value of the investor's holdings declines, the margin in his or her account will also drop. This situation can lead to what is known as a **restricted account,** one whose equity is less than the initial margin requirement. It does not mean that the investor must put up additional cash or equity, but it does require the investor to bring the margin back to the initial level when securities are sold while the account is restricted.

restricted account
a margin account whose equity is less than the initial margin requirement; the investor must bring the margin back to the initial level when securities are sold while the account is restricted.

maintenance margin
the minimum amount of margin (equity) that an investor must maintain in the margin account at all times.

margin call
notification of the need to bring the equity of an account whose margin is below the maintenance level up to the required level or have margined holdings sold to reach this point.

Maintenance Margin. **Maintenance margin** is the absolute minimum amount of margin (equity) that an investor must maintain in the margin account at all times. If the margin falls below the maintenance margin, the broker is authorized to sell enough of the securities to bring the account back up to standard. When an insufficient amount of maintenance margin exists, an investor will receive a **margin call** to remedy the situation. This call gives the investor a short period of time (perhaps 72 hours) to find some means of bringing the equity up to the required level. If this is not done, the broker has no alternative but to sell enough of the investor's margined holdings to bring the equity in the account up to this level. The maintenance margin protects both the brokerage house and investors: Brokers avoid having to absorb excessive investor losses, and investors avoid being wiped out. The maintenance margin on equity securities is currently at 25 percent. It rarely changes, although it is often set slightly higher by brokerage houses for the added protection of both brokers and their customers. For straight debt securities like Treasury bonds, there is no official maintenance margin except that set by the brokerage houses themselves.

The Basic Margin Formula

The amount of margin is always measured in terms of its relative amount of equity, which is considered the investor's collateral. A simple formula can be used with all types of *long purchases* to determine the amount of margin in the transaction (or account) at any given point. Basically, only two pieces of information are required: (1) the prevailing market value of the securities being margined, and (2) the amount of money being borrowed, or the size of the margin loan, which is known as the **debit balance.** Given this information, we can compute margin according to Equation 2.1:

debit balance
the amount of money being borrowed; the size of a margin loan.

Equation 2.1

$$\text{Margin} = \frac{\text{value of securities} - \text{debit balance}}{\text{value of securities}}$$

Equation 2.1a

$$= \frac{V - D}{V}$$

To illustrate its use, consider the following example. Assume you want to purchase 100 shares of stock at $40 per share, using a 70 percent initial margin. First we must determine how this $4,000 transaction will be financed. Since we know that 70 percent of it (the stated prevailing initial margin requirement) must be financed with equity, the balance (30 percent) can be financed with a margin loan. Therefore you will borrow $1,200 ($4,000 × .30 = $1,200); this, of course, is the debit balance. The remainder ($2,800) represents your equity in the transaction. This amount is measured as the difference between the value of the securities being margined ($4,000) and the amount being borrowed ($1,200). In other words, *equity* is represented by the numerator $(V - D)$ in the margin formula. If over time the price of the stock moves to $65, the margin would then be:

$$\text{Margin} = \frac{V - D}{V} = \frac{\$6,500 - \$1,200}{\$6,500} = .815 = \underline{\underline{81.5\%}}$$

Note that the margin (equity) in this investment position has now risen to 81.5 percent. When the price of the stock goes up, the investor's margin also increases. When the price of the security goes down, so does the amount of margin. For instance, if the price of the stock in our illustration drops to $30 per share, the new margin would equal only 60 percent. In that case we would be dealing with a restricted account, since the margin level has dropped below the prevailing initial margin. Finally, note that although our discussion has been couched mostly in terms of individual *transactions,* the same margin formula is used with margin *accounts.* The only difference is that we would be dealing with input that applies to the account as a whole—the value of all securities held in the account and the total amount of margin loans.

Return on Invested Capital

When assessing the return on margin transactions, we must take into account the fact that the individual puts up only part of the funds, the balance being borrowed. Therefore, we are concerned with the rate of profit earned *on only that portion of the funds provided by the investor.* Using both current income received from dividends or interest and total interest paid on the margin loan, we can use Equation 2.2 to determine the *return on invested capital* from margin transaction:

Equation 2.2

$$
\begin{array}{c}
\text{Return on} \\
\text{invested} \\
\text{capital from} \\
\text{a margin} \\
\text{transaction}
\end{array}
=
\frac{
\begin{array}{c}
\text{total current} \\
\text{income} \\
\text{received}
\end{array}
-
\begin{array}{c}
\text{total interest} \\
\text{paid on} \\
\text{margin loan}
\end{array}
+
\begin{array}{c}
\text{market value} \\
\text{of securities} \\
\text{at sale}
\end{array}
-
\begin{array}{c}
\text{market value} \\
\text{of securities} \\
\text{at purchase}
\end{array}
}{\text{amount of equity invested}}
$$

This equation can be used to compute either the expected or actual return from a margin transaction. To illustrate: consider an investor who wants to buy 100 shares of stock at $50 per share because she feels it will rise to $75 within six months. The stock pays $2 per share in annual dividends (though with the six-month holding period, the investor will receive only half of that amount, or $1 per share. The investor is going to buy the stock with 50 percent margin and pay 10 percent interest on the margin loan. Thus, she is going to put up $2,500 equity to buy $5,000 worth of stock that she hopes will increase to $7,500 in six months. Since the investor will have a $2,500 margin loan outstanding at 10 percent for six months, she will pay $125 in total interest costs ($2,500 × .10 × $^6/_{12}$ = $125). We can substitute this information into Equation 2.2 to find the expected return on invested capital for this transaction:

$$
\begin{array}{c}
\text{Return on} \\
\text{invested capital} \\
\text{from a margin} \\
\text{transaction}
\end{array}
= \frac{\$100 - \$125 + \$7,500 - \$5,000}{\$2,500} = \frac{\$2,475}{\$2,500} = .99 = \underline{\underline{99\%}}
$$

Keep in mind that the 99 percent figure represents the rate of return earned over a six-month holding period. If we wanted to compare this rate of return to other investment opportunities, we could determine the transaction's *annualized* rate of return by multiplying by 2 (the number of six-month periods in a year). This would amount to 198 percent (99% × 2 = 198%).

Uses of Margin Trading

pyramiding
the technique of using paper profits in margin accounts to partly or fully finance the acquisition of additional securities.

excess margin
more equity than is required in a margin account.

Margin trading is most often used in one of two ways. As we have seen, one of its uses is to magnify transaction returns. Another major margin tactic is called pyramiding, which takes the concept of magnified returns to its limits. **Pyramiding** uses the paper profits in margin accounts to partly or fully finance the acquisition of additional securities. This allows such transactions to be made at margins below prevailing initial margin levels, and sometimes substantially so. In fact, with this technique, it is even possible to buy securities with no new cash at all; rather, they can all be financed entirely with margin loans. The reason is that the paper profits in the account lead to **excess margin,** more equity in the account than necessary. For instance, if a margin account holds $60,000 worth of securities and has a debit balance of $20,000, it is at a margin level of 66⅔ percent [($60,000 − $20,000) ÷

■ INVESTOR INSIGHTS ■

Some Tips for Finding the Right Stockbroker

First-time investors often walk into a brokerage asking for any available stockbroker. They are likely to be introduced to the broker of the day, "the broker who, that day, gets all the walk-ins and phone-ins of new clients," said Bob Edwards, director of education for the American Association of Individual Investors, a non-profit educational group based in Chicago. . . .

If you walk into the brokerage office off the street, you will need to select the brokers in that office you would like to interview. Ask for the office manager, who oversees the brokers in the office, David H. Rambeau, a Florida stockbroker, said. Explain to the manager the types of investments you are interested in and ask to be introduced to a broker with an interest in those securities. If your interests are very broad, ask for a broker who is a generalist, he said.

Of course, you must decide—before interviewing brokers—what kind of investments you want. You may have to do some research beforehand if this is the first time you have opened an account. "You should not, in general, rely on the broker to perform a teaching function. They would rather be dealing with knowledgeable investors they don't have to hand hold through every step," Edwards said.

Once you are sitting across the desk from the candidates you have chosen, you should interview them extensively. Your questions should include:

- How long have you been in the business? Rambeau said investors should look for a broker with at least three years of experience. That is long enough, he said, to winnow out the brokers who find they don't like the job and those who find they can't do the job. . . .

$60,000]. This account would hold a substantial amount of excess margin if the prevailing initial margin requirement were only 50 percent.

The principle of pyramiding is to use the excess margin in the account to purchase additional securities. The only constraint, and the key to pyramiding, is that when the additional securities are purchased, the investor's margin account must be at or above the prevailing required initial margin level. Remember that it is the account, and not the individual transactions, that must meet the minimum standards. If the account has excess margin, the investor can use it to build up security holdings. Pyramiding can continue as long as there are additional paper profits in the margin account and as long as the margin level exceeds the prevailing initial requirement when purchases are made. The tactic is somewhat complex but also profitable, especially because it minimizes the amount of new capital required in the investor's account.

In general, margin trading is simple, but it is also risky. It should therefore be used only by investors who fully understand its operation and appreciate its pitfalls.

- What is your educational background? All stockbrokers must pass the so-called Series 7 exam, administered by the NASD, to earn a broker's license, but Edwards recommended that you look for a broker who has an economic and financial education. The Series 7 classes teach brokers the mechanics of the market, but not the theories behind the valuation of investments, Edwards said.

- What is your investment philosophy? Do you prefer to buy and hold investments or trade quickly as the value rises? What is your opinion about stocks (bonds, options, futures or other investments) as an investment? Why do you like or dislike that type of investment? . . . There are no right or wrong answers to these questions, the experts say, but their answers should agree with yours.

- May I have the names of three to five satisifed customers? Financial professionals differ on whether investors should ask prospective brokers about past performance, because, Edwards pointed out, past performance is no indicator of future performance. On the other hand, it may give you an idea of how that broker performs during bear markets. . . .

All brokers must register with the NASD to trade securities, and the NASD keeps a record of their conduct on the job. To learn if your prospective broker has ever been disciplined by the NASD, the SEC, one of the stock exchanges or a state government, or if he has ever been convicted on criminal charges, write or call the NASD. . . .

Finally, though, "it has to boil down to a gut reaction," Rambeau said. "You know when you sit down with somebody there's that chemistry."

Source: Lisa M. Keefe, of the *Orlando Sentinel,* "Going for Brokers: Check it Out," reprinted in *Dayton, Inc.* of the *Dayton Daily News,* February 9, 1989, p. 12.

Short Selling

Short selling is used when a decline in security prices is anticipated. This technique enables investors to profit from falling security prices. However, as we shall see, it can also be used to *protect* investors from falling security prices. Almost any type of security can be "shorted": Common and preferred stocks, all types of bonds, convertible securities, warrants, options, and listed mutual funds can all be sold short. Although the list is fairly extensive, the short-selling activities of most investors are limited almost exclusively to common stock and to put and call options. Because short sales, like long and margin transactions, require the investor to work through a broker, it is important to consider the tips for finding the right stockbroker given in the nearby Investor Insights box. The text that follows reviews the short-selling tactic and discusses some of the essential ingredients of this trading technique. We will then look at short-sale procedures, and examine some of the popular uses of short selling.

Essentials of Short Selling

Short selling is generally defined as the practice of selling borrowed securities. Short sales start when securities that have been borrowed from a broker are sold in the marketplace. Later, when the price of the issue has declined, the short seller buys back the securities, which are then returned to the lender. The lender's primary concern in a short-sale is that the securities being shorted are provided total and constant protection.

Making Money When Prices Fall.   Making money when security prices fall is what short selling is all about. Like their colleagues in the rest of the investment world, short sellers are also trying to make money by buying low and selling high. The only difference is that they reverse the investment process by starting the transaction with a sale and ending it with a purchase. Table 2.5 shows how a short sale works and how investors can profit from such transactions. In the illustration, we assume the investor has found a stock he feels will drop from its present level of $50 per share to about $25. As a result, it has all the ingredients of a profitable short sale. The amount of profit or loss generated in a short sale is dependent on the price at which the short seller can buy back the stock. Short sellers make money only when the proceeds from the sale of the stock are greater than the cost of buying it back.

High Risk, Limited Return.   A fact of many short-sale transactions is that the investor must settle for high-risk exposure in the face of limited return opportunities. The price of a security can fall only so far (to a value of or near zero), yet there is really no limit to how far such securities can rise in price. (Remember, when a security goes up in price, a short seller loses.) For example, notice in Table 2.5 that the stock in question cannot possibly fall by more than $50, yet who is to say how high its price can go?

Another less serious disadvantage is that short sellers never earn dividend (or interest) income. In fact, short sellers are responsible for making up the dividends (or interest) that are paid while the transaction is outstanding. That is, if a dividend is paid during the course of a short-sale transaction, the *short seller* must pay an equal amount to the lender of the stock (the mechanics of which are taken care of automatically by the short seller's broker).

The major *advantage* of selling short is, of course, the chance to profit from a price decline. In addition, the technique can be used by investors to protect profits

TABLE 2.5 The Mechanics of a Short Sale

1. 100 shares of stock are *sold* at $50/share:	
Proceeds from sale to investor	$5,000
2. Later, 100 shares of the stock are *purchased* at $25/share:	
Cost to investor	2,500
Net profit	$2,500

that have already been earned and to defer the taxes on such profits. And as we will see, when used in this manner, short selling becomes a highly conservative investment strategy.

Short-Sale Procedures

Short selling is a fairly popular trading technique. It accounted for about 9 percent of the total share value on the NYSE in 1990. In addition to NYSE stock, virtually any type of security (listed or OTC) can be shorted, and such transactions can be executed in both odd and round lots. Moreover, they are subject to the same commissions and transaction costs as any other type of transaction. In fact, about the only difference is that a short-sale transaction must be identified as such on the broker's order-execution form. The reason for this is that these transactions are stringently regulated by the SEC.

The Basic Rules. Extensive regulation of short selling was required in order to curb the many abuses and misuses of this tactic that occurred prior to the great crash of 1929. Today, a short sale can be executed only under the following two circumstances: when the last trade was a price increase, or when the last trade was unchanged and the prior price change was an increase. This is known as an **uptick** and indicates that the price of an issue has gone up since its last transaction. For example, a stock can be sold short if the prior transaction was at 51⅛, which was above the price of 51 for the transaction that immediately preceded it. The stock cannot be shorted if the prior transaction was at 50⅞, since it would be less than the immediately preceding price of 51. The latter situation is known as a **downtick.** It indicates that the price of the security is off from its prior transaction. As an investor, you can place a short-sell order at any time, but your broker will not be able to execute it until the issue undergoes an uptick. (*Note:* A short seller can avoid waiting for an uptick by offering to sell the stock at a price that if accepted is an uptick. If a purchaser accepts the stock at the uptick price, the transaction will comply with the uptick rule.)

Certain (minimal) amounts of equity capital must be put up by the short seller in order to initiate a short-sale transaction. The investment necessary to execute a short sale is defined by an initial margin requirement, which is currently 50 percent for equity securities like common stock. Thus if an investor wishes to short $5,000 worth of stock at a time when the prevailing short-sale margin requirement is 50 percent, he or she must deposit $2,500 with a broker.

Who Lends the Securities? Acting through their brokers, short sellers obtain securities from brokerage houses or from other investors. Of the two, brokers are the principle source of borrowed securities. As a service to their customers they lend securities held in the brokers' portfolios or in **street name** accounts. Street name securities are those held by brokers for their customers; the stock certificates are issued in the brokerage house's name but held in trust for their clients. This is actually a common way of buying securities, since many investors do not want to be bothered with handling and safeguarding stock certificates. In such cases, the certif-

---

uptick
the increase in the price of a stock issue since its last transaction.

downtick
the decrease in the price of a stock issue since its last transaction.

street name
stock certificates issued in the brokerage house's name but held in trust for their customers who actually own them.

icates are issued in the street name of the broker, who then records the details of the transaction and keeps track of these investments through a series of bookkeeping entries. When dividends, notices, and so on, are received by the broker, they are automatically forwarded to the proper owner of the securities. It is important to recognize that the broker lends the short seller the securities of other investors, and the short seller sells these borrowed securities with the expectation that she can later purchase them at a lower price and return them to the lender.

Uses of Short Selling

Investors short sell for one of two reasons: to seek speculative profits when the price of a security is expected to drop, or to protect a profit and defer taxes by "hedging" their position. The first use is the standard short-sale transaction. The hedge tactic, in contrast, is a conservative use of short selling, employed to lock in a given profit level. *All shorts are executed on margin,* so it seems appropriate to begin our discussion of uses of short selling by looking at how margin fits into a short sale and affects returns.

Shorting on Margin.   There are no borrowed funds with margined short sales. With short selling, the term "margin" simply indicates the size of the equity deposit the investor must make in order to initiate the transaction. Margined short sales are executed in the same margin account as margined long transactions. They are subject to initial margin requirements and have maintenance margin levels (currently 30 percent for short sales). In fact, the only thing that we do not have to be concerned about with a margined short sale is the account's debit balance. Margining a short sale, then, is much like margining a long transaction. Many of the investment principles, margin features, and behavioral characteristics we discussed previously apply equally here.

Of course, if the price of the security being shorted goes up, the investor loses money. If the price of the security being shorted goes up too much, the account can become restricted or subject to a margin call. To demonstrate, consider the following situation: Assume an investor wants to short 100 shares of stock at $60 per share by using 70 percent initial margin. In this instance, the value of the securities amounts to $6,000 (100 × $60). The sales proceeds would also be $6,000, as this is the amount of money that would be realized by selling 100 shares of stock at $60 per share. The margin (equity deposit) is $4,200—70 percent of the value of the transaction. Now see what happens when the price of the stock rises $10 to $70 per share: In this case a potential loss of $1,000 (100 × $10) results. The investor will have to pay $10 more per share ($70 rather than $60) to buy back the stock at today's price. This will lower the investor's equity position from $4,200 to $3,200. The investor would now have $3,200 equity on a $7,000 market value—a 46 percent ($3,200 ÷ $7,000) margin percentage. As the price of the stock goes up, the investor loses money and the amount of margin in the position drops. Because (at 46 percent) the amount of margin has dropped below the initial margin requirement (70 percent), the investor would be faced with a *restricted account*. But since it is above the 30 percent maintenance margin for short sales, a margin call would not be issued.

The reverse would happen if, instead of rising, the price of the stock were to fall $10, to $50 per share. In this case, the investor's equity would increase by $1,000 to $5,200, which would then represent 104 percent ($5,200 ÷ $5,000) of the then-prevailing market value. Clearly an excess of equity would exist in this case.

Return on Invested Capital. Because short sales are executed on margin, the amount of invested capital is limited to the investor's equity deposit. This amount therefore is the basis for figuring the rate of return. The only complication in this return measure is that any dividends paid by the short seller to the lender of the securities must be netted out of the profit. Other than that, no dividends are received by the short seller and no interest is paid, so the return formula in Equation 2.3 is fairly straightforward.

Equation 2.3

$$\begin{array}{c}\text{Return on}\\\text{invested capital}\\\text{from}\\\text{short sale}\end{array} = \frac{\begin{array}{c}\text{proceeds from sale} - \begin{array}{c}\text{purchase cost}\\\text{of securities}\end{array} - \begin{array}{c}\text{dividends paid}\\\text{by short seller}\end{array}\end{array}}{\text{equity deposit}}$$

To illustrate, assume an investor uses 70 percent initial margin to short a stock at $60 per share he feels will drop to $40 within a six-month period. Because the company pays annual dividends of $2 per share, the short seller estimates he will probably be liable for about $1 per share over the expected six-month holding period. Using Equation 2.3 to compute the return on a per-share basis, we see that the expected return on invested capital for this short sale is about 45 percent:

$$\frac{\text{Return on invested capital}}{\text{from short sale}} = \frac{\$60 - \$40 - \$1}{\$42} = \frac{\$19}{\$42} = .45 = \underline{\underline{45\%}}$$

This figure will be the same regardless of how many shares are actually involved in the transaction. This high rate of return results not only from the profit earned when the price of the stock drops, but also from the limited amount of capital provided by the investor (a margin of only 70 percent).

Speculating with Short Sales. Selling short for speculative purposes is perhaps the most common use of this technique. Because the short seller is betting against the market, this approach is highly speculative and subject to a considerable amount of risk exposure. It works like this: Assume an investor has uncovered a stock that she feels is about to tumble over the next eight months from its present level of $50 per share to somewhere around $30. She therefore decides to short sell 300 shares of the stock at $50 by using 50 percent margin (the prevailing initial margin requirement). Table 2.6 shows the basics of this hypothetical transaction. Note that the transaction generates a profit of $6,000 to the investor (ignoring dividends and brokerage commissions). Since it can be executed with an equity deposit of only $7,500, the transaction should yield a return on invested capital of 80 percent. However, if the market moves against the short seller, all or most of her $7,500 investment could be lost.

TABLE 2.6 Speculating with a Short Sale

Short sale initiated: 300 shares of the stock sold at $50/share	$15,000
Short sale covered: 300 shares of the stock bought back at $30/share	9,000
Net profit	$ 6,000
Equity deposit (.50 × $15,000)	$ 7,500

$$\text{Return on invested capital*} = \frac{\$15,000 - \$9,000}{\$7,500} = \frac{\$6,000}{\$7,500} = \underline{\underline{80\%}}$$

*Assume the stock pays no dividends and therefore the short seller has no dividend liability.

TABLE 2.7 Shorting-against-the-Box (Hedging with a Short Sale)

Transaction 1: Purchase 100 shares of stock at $20		$2,000
Price of Stock Rises to $50/Share		
Current profit in transaction:		
Current value of stock		$5,000
Cost of transaction		⟨2,000⟩
Net profit		$3,000
Transaction 2: Short sell 100 shares at $50		
A. Now Price of Stock Rises to $80/Share		
Current profit in *both* transactions:		
Value of stocks owned (trans. 1)		$8,000
Cost of transaction		⟨2,000⟩
Profit		$6,000
Less loss on short sale:		
Short sale initiated	$5,000	
Short sale covered	⟨8,000⟩	⟨3,000⟩
Net profit		$3,000
B. Price of Stock Falls to $30/Share		
Current profit in *both* transactions:		
Value of stocks owned (trans. 1)		$3,000
Cost of transaction		⟨2,000⟩
Profit		$1,000
Plus profit from short sale:		
Short sale initiated	$5,000	
Short sale covered	⟨3,000⟩	2,000
Net profit		$3,000

Shorting-against-the-Box. This exotic-sounding term describes a conservative technique used to protect existing security profits. Like insurance, the purpose of this hedge is to minimize or eliminate exposure to loss. **Shorting-against-the-box** is done after an investor has generated a profit through an earlier long transaction by following it with a short sale. An investor who already owns 100 shares of stock (the long transaction) would short an equal number of shares of stock in the same company. By doing this, he or she is able to protect the profit already made in the long transaction, and, as a by-product, can defer the taxes on this profit until the next taxable year.

shorting-against-the-box
a conservative technique used to protect existing security profits by following a profitable long transaction with a short sale.

Here is how it works: Suppose that early last year you bought 100 shares of NuLox, Inc., at $20 per share and have since watched the price of NuLox rise to $50. You presently have a $3,000 net profit. Although you do not want to sell the stock right now, you do not want to lose any of your profit either. In essence, you would like to ride things out for a while and still protect the profit you have earned up to now. A simple short sale against the box will allow you to do this. By shorting 100 shares of NuLox at $50 per share, and you have "locked in" your profit of $3,000. No matter what happens to the price of the stock, you are guaranteed a profit of $3,000. You now have two positions—one long and one short—both involving an equal number of shares. Table 2.7 summarizes this tactic and demonstrates how the profit becomes locked in. Note, however, that although this short-sale transaction is executed with borrowed securities, it is not necessary to put up an equity deposit, because your current holdings of the stock serve this purpose. Thus, the cost of shorting-against-the-box is reasonably low and involves only the brokerage commissions associated with initiating and covering the short sale.

SUMMARY

1. Short-term investment vehicles are traded in the money market, whereas longer-term securities, such as stocks and bonds, are traded in the capital market. The organized securities exchanges, which include the New York Stock Exchange (NYSE), the American Stock Exchange (AMEX), regional stock exchanges, foreign stock exchanges, and other specialized exchanges, act as secondary markets. The over-the-counter (OTC) market acts as a primary market and also handles secondary trading in unlisted securities. Today securities market must be viewed globally due to the growing importance of international markets and foreign security transactions.

2. The securities markets are regulated by the federal Securities and Exchange Commission (SEC) and by state commissions. The key federal laws regulating the securities industry are the Securities Act of 1933; Securities Exchange Act of 1934; Maloney Act of 1938; Investment Company Act of 1940; Investment Advisers Act of 1940; and the Securities Acts Amendments of 1975. During the 1980s the blatant violation of these laws, particularly with regard to insider trading, raised important ethical issues.

3. Stockbrokers provide the key link between the individual investor and the markets. A variety of types of brokerage accounts, such as single, joint, custodial, cash margin, and wrap, may be established. An investor can make odd-lot and round-lot transactions

using the market order, the limit order, or the stop-loss order. On small transactions most brokers have fixed-commission schedules; on larger transactions they will negotiate commissions. The Securities Investor Protection Corporation (SIPC) insures customers' accounts against the brokerage firm's failure. Arbitration procedures are frequently employed to resolve disputes between an investor and broker.

4. Most investors make long purchases in expectation of price increases. Many investors establish margin accounts in order to use borrowed funds to enhance their buying power. Short-scale transactions are much less common, although they provide opportunities for financial gain when a decline in share price is anticipated.

5. When stock is bought on margin, the investor puts up cash or securities equal to a portion of the purchase price and borrows the rest from a brokerage house or bank. If a stock purchased on margin increases in price, the investor's rate of return on funds is larger than it would have been on a straight cash purchase, and vice versa. The Fed sets the initial margin (equity) required to purchase securities and the minimum maintenance margin. If the price of the stock declines, the account can become restricted and possibly result in a margin call. Margin is commonly used to increase transaction returns, sometimes by pyramiding profits.

6. Short selling involves selling borrowed securities with the expectation of earning a profit by repurchasing them at a lower price in the future. To execute a short sale, the investor establishes a margin account and borrows the necessary shares through a broker or other investor. A short seller is exposed to potentially unlimited losses, while gains are limited to the amount of the short-sale price. Short selling may be used either to seek speculative profits from an anticipated share price decline or to protect earned profits and defer the associated taxes by shorting-against-the-box.

QUESTIONS

1. Define and differentiate between each of the following pairs of words:

   a. Money market and capital market.
   b. Primary market and secondary market.
   c. Organized securities exchanges and over-the-counter (OTC) market.

2. Briefly describe the following aspects of the New York Stock Exchange (NYSE):

   a. Membership.
   b. Listing policies.
   c. Trading activity.

3. For each of the items in the left-hand column match the most appropriate item in the right-hand column. Explain the relationship between the items matched.

a. AMEX.	1. Unlisted securities are traded.
b. CBT.	2. Futures exchange.
c. Boston Stock Exchange.	3. Options exchange.
d. CBOE.	4. Foreign securities are traded.
e. OTC.	5. Second largest security exchange.
f. ADR.	6. Regional stock exchange.

4. Describe the over-the-counter market, and explain how it works. Be sure to mention dealers, bid and ask prices, Nasdaq, and the Nasdaq/NMS. What role do initial public offerings (IPOs) and secondary distributions play in this market?

5. Why is globalization of securities markets an important issue today? How are foreign security transactions made? How do exchange rate changes affect foreign security prices?

6. Briefly describe the key rules and regulations resulting from each of the following securities acts:

   a. Securities Act of 1933.
   b. Securities Exchange Act of 1934.
   c. Maloney Act of 1938.
   d. Investment Company Act of 1940.
   e. Investment Advisers Act of 1940.
   f. Securities Acts Amendments of 1975.

7. What role does the stockbroker play in the overall investment process? Describe the types of services offered by brokerage firms, and discuss the criteria for selecting a suitable stockbroker.

8. What must one do in order to open a brokerage account? Briefly differentiate among the following types of brokerage accounts:

   a. Single or joint.   d. Margin.
   b. Custodial.   e. Wrap.
   c. Cash.

9. Differentiate between a market order, a limit order, and a stop-loss order. What is the rationale for using a stop-loss order rather than a limit order?

10. What protection does the Securities Investor Protection Corporation (SIPC) provide securities investors? How are arbitration procedures used to settle disputes between investors and their brokers?

11. Describe margin trading, and explain how profits (and losses) are magnified with margin trading.

12. What advantages and disadvantages does margin trading hold for the individual investor?

13. Describe the process of short selling; note how profits are made in such transactions. Be sure to explain how margin is used in a short-sale transaction.

14. What are the advantages and disadvantages of short selling? What is shorting-against-the-box, and how does it differ from a regular short sale?

PROBLEMS

1. In each of the following cases, calculate the price of one share of the foreign stock measured in US$.

   a. A Belgian stock priced at 9,000 Belgian francs (Bf) when the exchange rate is 35.3 Bf/US$.
   b. A French stock price at 700 French francs (Ff) when the exchange rate is 5.60 Ff/US$.
   c. A Japanese stock price at 1,350 yen (Y) when the exchange rate is 125 Y/US$.

2. Lola Paretti purchased 50 shares of BMW, a German stock traded on the Frankfurt Exchange, for 500 marks (DM) per share exactly one year ago, when the exchange rate was 1.60 DM/US$. Today the stock is trading at 530 DM per share and the exchange rate is 1.30 DM/US$.

a. Did the DM depreciate or appreciate relative to the US$ during the past year? Explain.

b. How much in US$ did Lola pay for her 50 shares of BMW when she purchased them a year ago?

c. How much in US$ can Lola sell her BMW shares for today?

d. Ignoring brokerage fees and taxes, how much profit (or loss) in US$ would Lola realize on her BMW stock if she sells it today?

3. Albert Cromwell places a market order to buy a round lot of Thomas, Inc., common stock, which is traded on the NYSE and is currently quoted at $50 per share. Ignoring brokerage commissions, how much money would Cromwell likely have to pay? If he had placed a market order to sell, how much money would he receive? Explain.

4. Imagine that you have placed a limit order to buy 100 shares of Sallisaw Tool at a price of $38, though the stock is currently selling for $41. Discuss the consequences, if any, of each of the following:

a. The stock price drops to $39 per share two months prior to cancellation of the limit order.

b. The stock price drops to $38 per share.

c. The minimum stock price achieved prior to cancellation of the limit order was $38.50, and when canceled the stock was selling for $47.50 per share.

5. If you place a stop-loss order to sell at $23 on a stock currently selling for $26.50 per share, what is likely to be the minimum loss you will experience on 50 shares if the stock price rapidly declines to $20.50 per share? Explain. What if you had placed a stop-limit order to sell at $23, and the stock price tumbles to $20.50?

6. Elmo Inc.'s stock is currently selling at $60 per share. For each of the following situations (ignoring brokerage commissions), calculate the gain or loss realized by Maureen Katz if she makes a round-lot transaction.

a. She sells short and repurchases the borrowed shares at $70 per share.

b. She takes a long position and sells the stock at $75 per share.

c. She sells short and repurchases the borrowed shares at $45 per share.

d. She takes a long position and sells the stock at $60 per share.

7. Assume an investor buys 100 shares of stock at $50 per share, putting up a 70 percent margin.

a. What would be the debit balance in this transaction?

b. How much equity capital would the investor have to provide in order to make this margin transaction?

c. If the stock rises to $80 per share, what would be the investor's new margin position?

8. Ms. Jerri Kingston bought 100 shares of stock at $80 per share using an initial margin of 60 percent. Given a maintenance margin of 25 percent, how far does the stock have to drop before Ms. Kingston faces a margin call? (Assume there are no other securities in the margin account.)

9. An investor buys 200 shares of stock selling for $80 per share, using a margin of 60 percent. If the stock pays *annual* dividends of $1 per share and a margin loan can be obtained at an annual interest cost of 8 percent, determine the return on invested capital the investor would realize if the price of the stock increases to $104 within six months. What is the annualized rate of return on this transaction?

10. Marlene Bellamy purchased 300 shares of Writeline Communications stock at $55 per share using the prevailing minimum initial margin requirement of 50 percent. She held the stock for

exactly four months and sold it without any brokerage costs at the end of that period. During the four-month holding period the stock paid $1.50 per share in cash dividends. Marlene was charged 9 percent annual interest on the margin loan. The minimum maintenance margin was 25 percent.

a. Calculate the initial value of the transaction, the debit balance, and the equity position on Marlene's transaction.

b. For each of the following share prices calculate the actual margin percentage and indicate whether Marlene's margin account would have excess equity, be restricted, or be subject to a margin call:
(1) $45
(2) $70
(3) $35

c. Calculate the dollar amount of (1) dividends received and (2) interest paid on the margin loan during the four-month holding period.

d. Use each of the following sale prices at the end of the four-month holding period to calculate Marlene's annualized rate of return on the Writeline Communications stock transaction:
(1) $50
(2) $60
(3) $70

11. Not long ago Dave Edwards bought 200 shares of Almost Anything, Inc., at $45 per share; he bought the stock on margin of 60 percent. The stock is now trading at $60 per share, and the Federal Reserve has recently lowered initial margin requirements to 50 percent. Dave now wants to do a little pyramiding and buy another 300 shares of the stock. What's the minimum amount of equity he'll have to put up in this transaction?

12. Assume an investor short sells 100 shares of stock at $50 per share, putting up a 70 percent margin.

a. How much cash will the investor have to deposit in order to execute this short-sale transaction?

b. What is the new margin for this transaction if the price of the stock falls to $20 per share?

13. Bob Barloe recently short sold 200 shares of stock at $72 per share, using 50 percent margin.

a. Determine the size of the initial margin deposit required to make this transaction.

b. What would the new margin (in percent) be if the stock price drops to $50 a share?

c. What kind of profit (in dollars) and return on invested capital would Bob realize if he covered this short sale at $50 a share?

d. What would the new margin position (in percent) be if, instead of dropping, the price of the stock *rose* to $86.50 a share? Given a 30 percent maintenance margin, would this account be subject to a margin call?

14. Susan Davidson strongly believed that the price of BBP, Inc., stock was about to experience a significant decline. As a result, she decided to short sell 400 shares at the current price of $35 per share. A 60 percent initial margin deposit is required, and the maintenance margin requirement is 30 percent.

a. How large an initial margin deposit must Susan make in order to short sell the BBP, Inc., shares?

b. For each of the following share prices, calculate the actual margin percentage and indicate whether Susan's margin deposit will be in excess, be restricted, or be subject to a margin call:
   (1) $80
   (2) $50
   (3) $30

c. If during the time Susan held this short position the shorted stock paid dividends of $1.15 per share, how much in total dividends would she have paid the owner of the shares that were shorted?

d. Use your findings in **c** and the data presented above to calculate Susan's return on invested capital if she buys back the shares of BBP, Inc., at the following share prices:
   (1) $20
   (2) $40
   (3) $60

15. A well-heeled investor, Mr. Oliver Stanley, recently purchased 1,000 shares of stock at $48 per share. They have since risen to $55 per share. Although Mr. Stanley wants to sell out, he hesitates to do so because it is so near the end of year and he wants to defer the tax liability until next year. As a result, he decides to short-against-the-box, by shorting 1,000 shares of the stock at its current price of $55.

   a. What total profit will Mr. Stanley make if the price of the stock continues to rise to $60 per share?

   b. How much of this will come from the long transaction and how much from the short sale?

CASE PROBLEMS

2.1 Dara's Dilemma: Hold, Sell, Or?

As a result of her recent divorce, Dara Simmons—a 40-year-old mother of two teenage children—received 400 shares of Casinos International common stock. The stock is currently selling for $54 per share. After a long discussion with a friend who is an economist with a major commercial bank, Dara believes that the economy is turning down and a bear market is likely. She has researched, with the aid of her stockbroker, Casinos International's current financial situation and finds that the future success of the company may hinge on the outcome of pending court proceedings on the firm's application to open a new gambling casino in Pacific City. If the permit is granted, it seems likely that the firm's stock will experience a rapid increase in value, regardless of economic conditions. On the other hand, if the permit is not granted, the stock value is likely to be adversely affected.

Dara felt that, based upon the available information, the price of Casinos was likely to fluctuate a great deal over the near future. Her first reaction was to sell the stock and invest the money in a safer security, such as a high-rated corporate bond. At the same time, she felt that she might be overly pessimistic due to her recent divorce. She realized that if Casinos had their Pacific City application granted, she would make a killing on the stock. As a final check before making any decision, Dara talked with her accountant, who suggested that for tax purposes it would be best to delay the sale of the stock for an additional four months. After making a variety of calculations, the accountant indicated that the consequences of selling the stock now at $54 per share would be approximately equivalent to receiving $48 per share anytime after the four-month period had elapsed.

Dara felt the following four alternatives were open to her:

Alternative 1. Sell now at $54 per share and use the proceeds to buy high-rated corporate bonds.

Alternative 2. Keep the stock and place a limit order to sell the stock at $60 per share.

Alternative 3. Keep the stock and place a stop-loss order to sell at $45 per share.

Alternative 4. Hold the stock for an additional four months prior to making any decision.

Questions

1. Evaluate each of these alternatives. Based on the limited information presented, recommend which you feel is best.

2. If the stock price rises to $60, what will happen under alternatives 2 and 3? Evaluate the pros and cons of these outcomes.

3. If the stock price drops to $45, what will happen under alternatives 2 and 3? Evaluate the pros and cons of these outcomes.

4. In light of the rapid fluctuations anticipated in the price of Casinos' stock, how might a stop-limit order to sell be used by Dara to reduce the risk associated with the stock? What is the cost of such a strategy? Explain.

2.2 Ravi Dumar's High-Flying Margin Account

Ravi Dumar is a stockbroker who lives with his wife Sasha and their five children in Milwaukee, Wisconsin. Ravi firmly believes that the only way to make money in the market is to follow an aggressive investment posture—for example, to use margin trading. In fact, Ravi himself has built a substantial margin account over the years. He presently holds $75,000 worth of stock in his margin account, though the debit balance in the account amounts to only $30,000. Recently Ravi uncovered a stock which, based on extensive analysis, he feels is about to take off. The stock, Running Shoes (RS), currently trades at $20 per share. Ravi feels it should soar to at least $50 within a year. RS pays no dividends, the prevailing initial margin requirement is 50 percent, and margin loans are now carrying an annual interest charge of 10 percent. Because Ravi feels so strongly about RS, he wants to do some pyramiding by using his margin account to purchase 1,000 shares of the stock.

Questions

1. Discuss the concept of pyramiding as it applies to this investment situation.

2. What is the present margin position (in percent) of Ravi's account?

3. Ravi buys the 1,000 shares of RS through his margin account (bear in mind that this is a $20,000 transaction). Now:

   a. What would the margin position of the account be *after* the RS transaction if Ravi followed the prevailing initial margin (50 percent) and used $10,000 of his money to buy the stock?

   b. What if he uses only $2,500 equity and obtains a margin loan for the balance ($17,500)?

   c. How do you explain the fact that the stock can be purchased with only 12.5 percent margin when the prevailing initial margin requirement equals 50 percent?

4. Assume that Ravi buys 1,000 shares of RS stock at $20 per share with a minimum cash investment of $2,500, and that the stock does take off by moving to $40 per share in a year.

   a. What is the return on invested capital for this transaction?

   b. What return would Ravi have earned had he bought the stock without margin—if he had used all of his own money?

5. What do you think of Ravi's idea to pyramid? What are the risks and rewards of this strategy?

3 Investment Information and Plans

After studying this chapter, you should be able to:

1. Identify the types and uses of investment information.

2. Discuss news retrieval and databases, the use of investment advisors, and the features of investment clubs.

3. Explain the characteristics, interpretation, and uses of the commonly cited market averages and indexes.

4. Describe common investment goals, the importance of meeting life insurance needs, and important personal tax considerations.

5. Discuss the methods used to establish an investment program and note how the process of investing changes in different economic environments and over the life cycle.

6. Understand the role, types, and features of the popular short-term investment vehicles available for meeting liquidity needs.

Generally speaking, *it takes more than money to be a successful investor!* Indeed, knowing where to find useful investment information and having a carefully developed investment plan are vital. Although there are people who have made a lot of money with neither investment information nor plans, an investor with good information and plans will normally be more effective than one who operates solely on the basis of intuition. Some individuals will buy a particular stock because they like the firm's product. Such criteria, while helpful, are clearly insufficient for decision-making purposes. They leave unanswered numerous relevant questions, such as: How will the economy change? What behavior is the stock market expected to exhibit over the near term? Is the company profitable, and will it continue so? Like a space vehicle that can be directed toward its desired destination only with appropriate navigational aids and expertise, the achievement of financial goals in life can be reached only through the use of carefully developed investment plans. In this chapter, we begin with an examination of the important aspects of investment information, and then look at investment plans.

TYPES AND SOURCES OF INVESTMENT INFORMATION

descriptive information
factual data on the past behavior of the economy, the stock market, or a given investment vehicle.

analytical information
available current data in conjunction with projections and recommendations about potential investments.

Investment information allows the investor to formulate expectations of the risk-return behaviors of potential investments. It can be considered either descriptive or analytical. **Descriptive information** presents factual data on the past behavior of the economy, the market, or a given investment vehicle. **Analytical information** presents available current data and includes projections and recommendations about potential investments. The sample page from *Value Line* included in Figure 3.1 provides both descriptive and analytical information on Pepsico, Inc. Items that are primarily descriptive are keyed with a *D;* analytical items are noted with an *A.*

Some forms of investment information are free; others must be purchased individually or by annual subscription. Free information can be obtained from newspapers, magazines, and brokerage firms, and more can be found in public, university, and brokerage firm libraries. Alternatively, an investor can subscribe to services that provide clients with periodic reports summarizing the investment outlook and recommending certain actions. Such services cost the investor money, but obtaining, reading, and analyzing free information all cost time. So it is necessary to evaluate the worth of potential information. For example, spending 15 hours locating or paying $40 for information that increases one's return by $27 would not be economically sound. The larger an individual's investment portfolio, the easier it is to justify information purchases, since their benefit can usually be applied to a number of investments.

Types of Information

Investment information can be classed into five types, each concerned with an important aspect of the investment process.

1. *Economic and current event information* provides background as well as forecast data related to economic, political, and social trends, on a domestic as well

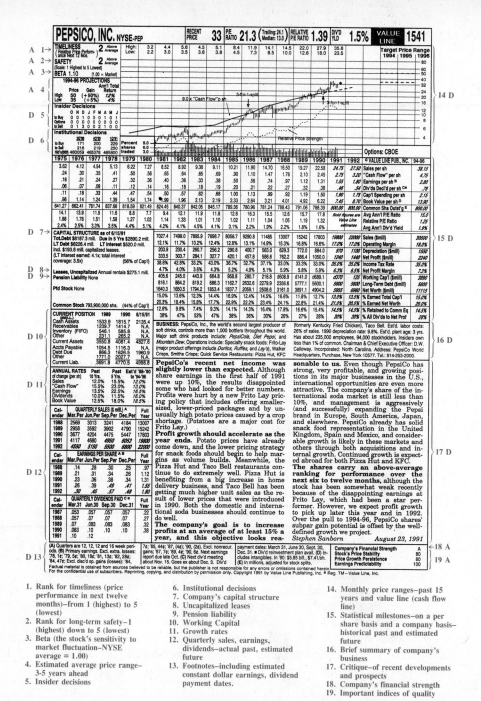

1. Rank for timeliness (price performance in next twelve months)--from 1 (highest) to 5 (lowest)

2. Rank for long-term safety--1 (highest) down to 5 (lowest)

3. Beta (the stock's sensitivity to market fluctuation--NYSE average = 1.00)

4. Estimated average price range--3-5 years ahead

5. Insider decisions

6. Institutional decisions

7. Company's capital structure

8. Uncapitalized leases

9. Pension liability

10. Working Capital

11. Growth rates

12. Quarterly sales, earnings, dividends--actual past, estimated future

13. Footnotes--including estimated constant dollar earnings, dividend payment dates.

14. Monthly price ranges--past 15 years and value line (cash flow line)

15. Statistical milestones--on a per share basis and a company basis--historical past and estimated future

16. Brief summary of company's business

17. Critique--of recent developments and prospects

18. Company's financial strength

19. Important indices of quality

• FIGURE 3.1 A Report Containing Descriptive and Analytic Information

This report—*Value Line*'s full page report on Pepsico, Inc., from August 23, 1991—contains both descriptive (marked D) and analytic (marked A) information. Examples of descriptive information are the company's capital structure and monthly price ranges for the past 15 years. Examples of analytic information are rank for timeliness and estimated average price range for the next 3 to 5 years. (*Source:* Adapted from Arnold Bernhard and Co., *The Value Line Investment Survey, Ratings and Reports,* Edition 1, August 23, 1991, page 1541. © Value Line, Inc.)

as global basis. Such information provides a basis for assessing the environment in which decisions are made.

2. *Industry and company information* provides background as well as forecast data on specific industries and companies. Investors use such information to assess the outlook in a given industry or specific company. Due to its company orientation, it is most relevant to stock, bond, or options investments.

3. *Information on alternative investment vehicles* provides background and predictive data for securities other than stocks, bonds, and options, as well as for various forms of property investment.

4. *Price information* contains current price quotations on certain investment vehicles, particularly securities. These quotations are commonly accompanied by statistics on the recent price behavior of the vehicle.

5. *Information on personal investment strategies* provides recommendations on investment strategies or specific purchase or sale actions. In general this information tends to be educational or analytical rather than descriptive.

Sources of Information

A complete listing of the sources of each type of investment information is beyond the scope of this book; we can consider only the basic forms of investment information here. For those desiring expanded source information, *The Investor's Resource Manual* that accompanies this textbook provides an annotated listing. The discussion here is concerned with the most common sources of information on economic and current events, industries and companies, and prices.

Economic and Current Event Information

It is clearly important for investors to stay abreast of major economic and current events. An awareness of such events should translate into better decisions. Popular sources of economic and current event information include the financial journals, general newspapers, institutional news, business periodicals, government publications, and special subscription services.

The Wall Street Journal
a daily newspaper, published regionally by Dow Jones; the most popular source of financial news.

Financial Journals. *The Wall Street Journal* is the most popular source of financial news. It is published daily, in a number of locations around the country; European and Asian editions are also published. In addition to giving daily price quotations on thousands of investment vehicles, it reports world, national, regional, and corporate news. The first page of the third section of the *Journal* usually contains a column "Your Money Matters," which addresses topics that deal directly with personal finance issues.

Barron's
a weekly publication by Dow Jones; the second most popular source of financial news.

A second popular source of financial news is *Barron's,* which is published weekly. Articles in *Barron's* tend to be directed more at strictly financial types of issues than those in the *Journal*. *Barron's* generally offers lengthier articles on a variety of topics of interest to individual investors. Probably the most popular column in *Barron's* is Alan Abelson's "Up and Down Wall Street," which provides a critical, and often humorous, assessment of major developments affecting the stock market and business. In addition, current price quotations and a summary of statistics on a range of investment vehicles are included.

Investor's Daily, a third national business newspaper, is published daily Monday through Friday. It is similar to *The Wall Street Journal* but contains more detailed price and market data. Other sources of financial news are the *Commercial and Financial Chronicle,* the *Media General Financial Weekly,* and the *Journal of Commerce.*

General Newspapers.   Another popular source of financial news is *USA Today*— the national newspaper published Monday through Friday. Each issue contains a "Money" section devoted to business and personal financial news in addition to current security price quotations and summary statistics.

Local newspapers provide still another convenient source of financial news. In most large cities the daily newspaper devotes two or more pages to financial and business news. Major metropolitan newspapers such as *The New York Times* and *The Los Angeles Times* provide investors with a wealth of financial information. Most major newspapers contain stock price quotations for major exchanges, price quotations on stocks of local interest, and a summary of the major stock market averages and indexes.

Institutional News.   The monthly economic letters of the nation's leading banks, such as Bank of America (San Francisco), Citibank (New York), and Harris Trust (Chicago), provide useful economic information. To keep customers abreast of important news developments, most brokerage firms subscribe to a number of wire services such as the Dow Jones, AP (Associated Press), and UPI (United Press International) services. Access to these services is best obtained through a stockbroker.

Business Periodicals.   Business periodicals range in scope. Some present general business and economic articles, others cover securities markets and related topics, still others focus solely on specific industries or property investments. Regardless of the subject matter, most financial periodicals present descriptive information, and some also include analytical information. However, they rarely offer recommendations.

General business and economic articles are presented in the business sections of periodicals such as *Newsweek, Time,* and *U.S. News and World Report.* A number of strictly business and finance-oriented periodicals are also available. These include *Business Week, Fortune, Business Month,* and *Nation's Business.*

Securities and marketplace articles can be found in a number of financial periodicals. The most basic, commonsense articles appear in *Forbes, Kiplinger's Personal Finance Magazine,* and *Money. Forbes,* published every two weeks, is the most investment oriented. Each January it publishes an "Annual Report on American Industry," which compares the growth and performance of key industries over the past five years. In August of each year *Forbes* also publishes a comparative evaluation of mutual funds. *Kiplinger's Personal Finance Magazine* and *Money* are published monthly and contain articles on managing personal finances and on investments.

Other periodicals aimed at the sophisticated investor are listed and described in *The Investor's Resource Manual* that accompanies this book.

Government Publications.   A number of government agencies publish economic data and articles useful to investors. A broad view of the current and expected state of the economy can be found in the annual *Economic Report of the President*. This document reviews and summarizes economic policy and conditions and includes data on important aspects of the economy. *The Federal Reserve Bulletin* published monthly by the Board of Governors of the Federal Reserve System and periodic reports published by each of the twelve Federal Reserve District Banks provide articles and data on various aspects of economic and business activity. Useful Department of Commerce publications include *Business Conditions Digest* and *Survey of Current Business*. Both are published monthly and include indicators and data relating to economic and business conditions. A good source of financial statement information on all manufacturers, broken down by industry and asset size, is the *Quarterly Financial Report for Manufacturing Corporations*, published jointly by the Federal Trade Commission and the Securities and Exchange Commission.

Special Subscription Services.   For those who want additional insights into business and economic conditions, special subscription services are available. These reports include business and economic forecasts and give notice of new government policies, union plans and tactics, taxes, prices, wages, and so on. One popular service is the *Kiplinger Washington Letter,* a weekly publication that provides a wealth of economic information and analyses.

Industry and Company Information

Of special interest to investors is information on particular industries and companies. Often, after choosing an industry in which to invest, the investor will analyze specific companies. General articles related to the activities of specific industries can be found in trade publications such as *Chemical Week, American Banker, Computer, Public Utilities Fortnightly,* and *Brewers Digest*. More specific popular sources are discussed below.

stockholder's (annual) report
a report published yearly by every publicly held firm; contains a wide range of information including financial statements for the most recent fiscal year.

Form 10-K
a statement filed with the SEC by all firms listed on a securities exchange or traded in the national OTC market.

Stockholder's Reports.   An excellent source of data on an individual firm is its **stockholder's** or **annual report,** published yearly by publicly held corporations. These reports contain a wide range of information, including financial statements for the most recent period of operation, along with summarized statements for several prior years. A sample page from Pepsico, Inc's 1990 Stockholder's Report is shown in Figure 3.2. These reports are free and may be obtained from the companies themselves or from brokers. In addition to the stockholder's report, many serious investors will review a company's **Form 10-K,** which is a statement that firms having securities listed on an organized exchange or traded in the national OTC market must file with the SEC.

Financial Highlights

PepsiCo Inc.

($ in millions except per share amounts)	1990	1989	Percent Change
Net sales	**$17,803**	15,242	+ 17
Soft drinks	**$ 6,523**	5,777	+ 13
Snack foods	**$ 5,054**	4,215	+ 20
Restaurants	**$ 6,226**	5,250	+ 19
Segment operating profits	**$ 2,224**	1,896	+ 17
Soft drinks	**$ 768**	676	+ 14
Snack foods	**$ 934**	805	+ 16
Restaurants	**$ 522**	415	+ 26
Income from continuing operations	**$ 1,091**	901	+ 21
Per Share	**$ 1.37**	1.13	+ 21
Net income	**$ 1,077**	901	+ 20
Per Share	**$ 1.35**	1.13	+ 19
Cash dividends declared	**$ 302**	253	+ 19
Per Share	**$ 0.383**	0.320	+ 20
Net cash generated by continuing operations	**$ 2,110**	1,886	+ 12
Purchases of property, plant and equipment for cash	**$ 1,180**	944	+ 25
Acquisitions and investments in affiliates for cash	**$ 631**	3,297	
Return on average shareholders' equity	**% 24.8**	25.6	

Per share information reflects the 1990 three-for-one stock split.
Return on average shareholders' equity was calculated using income from continuing operations.

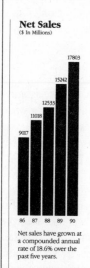

Net Sales
($ In Millions)

Net sales have grown at a compounded annual rate of 18.6% over the past five years.

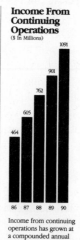

Income From Continuing Operations
($ In Millions)

Income from continuing operations has grown at a compounded annual rate of 20.7% over the past five years.

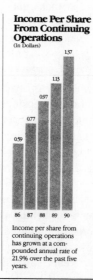

Income Per Share From Continuing Operations
(In Dollars)

Income per share from continuing operations has grown at a compounded annual rate of 21.9% over the past five years.

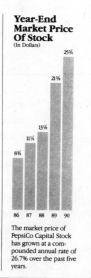

Year-End Market Price Of Stock
(In Dollars)

The market price of PepsiCo Capital Stock has grown at a compounded annual rate of 26.7% over the past five years.

● FIGURE 3.2 A Page from a Stockholder's Report

The inside of the front cover of Pepsico, Inc.'s report quickly acquaints the investor with the key financial data on the firm's operations over the past year, both in tabular and graphic form. (*Source:* Pepsico, Inc., 1990 Stockholder's Report. Purchase, New York: Pepsico, Inc., 1990.)

Comparative Data Sources. A number of useful sources of comparative data, typically broken down by industry and firm size, are available for use in analyzing the financial conditions of companies. Among these sources are Dun & Bradstreet's *Key Business Ratios,* Robert Morris and Associates' *Annual Statement Studies,* the *Quarterly Financial Report for Manufacturing Corporations* (cited above), and the *Almanac of Business and Industrial Financial Ratios.* The data provided by these sources is used as a baseline when evaluating the financial outcomes and conditions of a company.

Subscription Services. A variety of subscription services provide information on specific industries and companies. Generally, a subscriber pays a basic fee that entitles him or her to certain information published and periodically updated by the service. In addition to the basic service, a subscriber can purchase other services that provide information of greater depth or range. The major subscription services provide both descriptive and analytical information, but they generally do not make recommendations. Most investors, rather than subscribing to these services, gain access to them through their stockbroker or a large public or university library. The dominant subscription services are those offered by Standard & Poor's Corporation, Moody's Investor Services, and the *Value Line Investment Survey.*

Standard & Poor's
Corp. (S&P)
publisher of a variety of financial reports and services, including *Corporation Records* and *Stock Reports.*

Standard & Poor's Corporation (S&P) offers approximately 25 different financial reports and services. One major service, *Corporation Records,* provides detailed descriptions of publicly traded securities. A second major service, *Stock Reports,* contains up-to-date reports on firms. Each report presents a concise summary of the firm's financial history, its current finances, and its future prospects (for selected companies only). A sample of the first page of such a report is presented in Figure 6.4 on p. 257. Standard & Poor's Trade and Securities Service provides background information on business in general, as well as past, present, and future assessments of specific industries. The *Stock Guide* and *Bond Guide* are additional S&P publications. Published monthly, they contain statistical information on major stocks and bonds along with an analytical ranking of investment desirability. One other S&P publication worthy of note is its weekly magazine, *Outlook,* which includes analytical articles providing investment advice about the market and about specific industries and/or securities.

Moody's Investor
Services
publisher of a variety of financial reference manuals, including *Moody's Manuals.*

Moody's Investor Services publishes a variety of materials. Its key publications are reference manuals *(Moody's Manuals),* similar to S&P's *Corporation Records.* Each of the six reference manuals contains a wealth of historical and current financial, organizational, and operational data on all major firms within certain business groupings. Frequent supplements keep these manuals up to date. Other Moody's publications are the *Handbook of Common Stocks,* which provides much financial information on over 1,000 stocks; *Dividend Record,* which provides recent dividend announcements and payments by thousands of companies; *Bond Survey,* a weekly publication that assesses market conditions and new offerings; and *Bond Record,* a monthly publication reporting the price and interest rate behavior of thousands of bonds.

**Value Line Invest-
ment Survey**
a weekly subscrip-
tion service covering
about 1,700 of the
most widely held
stocks and their in-
dustries; popular
among individual
investors.

The **Value Line Investment Survey** is one of the most popular subscription services used by individual investors. It is published weekly and covers approximately 1,700 of the most widely held stocks and their industries. Ratings of "timeliness," "safety," and "financial strength" are included for each company. In exchange for an annual subscription fee of about $525, three basic services are provided subscribers. The "Summary and Index" is a weekly update showing the current ratings for each stock. "Ratings and Reports" is also updated weekly and contains a full-page analysis for each of about 130 stocks. (One example of such a report for Pepsico, Inc. was included earlier in Figure 3.1.) The third service, "Selection and Opinion," is a weekly section containing a detailed analysis of an especially recommended stock plus a large amount of investment background information.

**back-office research
reports**
analyses of and rec-
ommendations on
current and future
investment opportu-
nities; published by
and made available
to clients of broker-
age firms.

Brokerage Reports. In addition to making available reports from various subscription services, brokerage firms provide clients with prospectuses for new security issues and back-office research reports. As noted in Chapter 2, a *prospectus* is a document describing in detail the key aspects of the issue, the issuer, and its management and financial position. The cover of the 56-page prospectus describing the 1991 stock issue of F&C International, Inc., is shown in Figure 3.3. **Back-office research reports** are made available to clients of brokerage firms. They include analyses of and recommendations on prospects for the securities markets, specific industries, or specific securities. Usually a brokerage firm will publish lists of securities classified by their research staff as either "buy" or "sell." Brokerage research reports are available upon request at no cost to existing as well as potential customers.

investment letters
provide, on a sub-
scription basis, the
analyses, conclusions,
and recommenda-
tions of various ex-
perts in different
aspects of securities
investment.

Investment Letters. **Investment letters** provide, on a subscription basis, the analyses, conclusions, and recommendations of experts in different aspects of securities investment. Some letters concentrate on specific types of securities, whereas others are concerned solely with assessing the economy or security markets. Among the more popular investment letters are *Dick Davis Digest, The Dines Letter, Granville Market Letter, Growth Stock Outlook, Holt Investment Advisory, Prudent Speculator, Professional Tape Reader, Wellington Letter,* and *The Zweig Forecast.* The more popular ones, which are generally issued weekly or monthly, usually range in cost from $75 to $400 a year. Advertisements for many of these investment letters can be found in *Barron's.*

Price Information

quotations
price information
about various types
of securities, includ-
ing current price
data and statistics on
recent price behav-
ior.

Price information about various types of securities is contained in their **quotations,** which include current price data along with statistics on recent price behavior. Price quotations are readily available for actively traded securities. The most up-to-date quotations can be obtained from a stockbroker. Some brokerage offices have equipment that allows customers to key into a computer terminal to obtain quotations. Another automated quotation device found in most brokerage offices is the *ticker,* a

2,250,000 Shares

F&C International, Inc.

Common Stock

Of the 2,250,000 shares of Common Stock offered hereby, 1,750,000 shares are being sold by F & C International, Inc. and 500,000 shares are being sold by the Selling Shareholders. The Company will not receive any of the proceeds from the sale of shares of the Common Stock by the Selling Shareholders. See "Principal and Selling Shareholders." Of the 2,250,000 shares of Common Stock offered, 2,150,000 shares are being offered hereby in the United States (the "U.S. Shares") and 100,000 shares are being offered in a concurrent international offering outside the United States. The price to the public and aggregate underwriting discounts and commissions per share will be identical for both offerings. See "Underwriting."

Prior to this offering, there has been no public market for the Common Stock of the Company. See "Underwriting" for a discussion of the factors considered in determining the initial public offering price.

The Common Stock has been approved for quotation on the NASDAQ National Market System under the symbol "FCIN."

See "Investment Considerations" for information that should be considered by prospective investors.

THESE SECURITIES HAVE NOT BEEN APPROVED OR DISAPPROVED BY THE SECURITIES AND EXCHANGE COMMISSION OR ANY STATE SECURITIES COMMISSION NOR HAS THE SECURITIES AND EXCHANGE COMMISSION OR ANY STATE SECURITIES COMMISSION PASSED UPON THE ACCURACY OR ADEQUACY OF THIS PROSPECTUS. ANY REPRESENTATION TO THE CONTRARY IS A CRIMINAL OFFENSE.

	Price to Public	Underwriting Discounts and Commissions(1)	Proceeds to Company(2)	Proceeds to Selling Shareholders
Per Share	$13.50	$0.94	$12.56	$12.56
Total	$30,375,000	$2,115,000	$21,980,000	$6,280,000
Total Assuming Full Exercise of Over-Allotment Option(3)	$34,931,250	$2,432,250	$26,219,000	$6,280,000

(1) See "Underwriting."

(2) Before deducting expenses estimated at $1,100,000, which are payable by the Company.

(3) Assuming exercise in full of the 45-day option granted by the Company to the Underwriters to purchase up to 337,500 additional shares, on the same terms, solely to cover over-allotments. See "Underwriting."

The U.S. Shares are being offered by the U.S. Underwriters, subject to prior sale, when, as and if delivered to and accepted by the U.S. Underwriters, and subject to their right to reject orders in whole or in part. It is expected that delivery of the Common Stock will be made in New York City on or about December 20, 1991.

PaineWebber Incorporated

J. C. Bradford & Co.

The Chicago Corporation

The date of this Prospectus is December 13, 1991.

● FIGURE 3.3 Cover of a Prospectus for a Stock Issue

Some of the key factors relating to the 1991 stock issue by F&C International, Inc., are summarized on the cover of its 56-page prospectus. (*Source:* F&C International, Inc., December 13, 1991, p. 1.)

lighted screen on which stock transactions made on the floor of the exchange are reported as they occur. The ticker symbols for some well-known companies are listed in Table 3.1. Access to price information via personal computers is now available on a fee basis for use by professional and active individual investors. An investor can easily find security price quotations in the published news media, both nonfinancial and financial. The major source of security price quotations is *The Wall Street Journal,* which presents quotations for each previous business day's activities in all major markets. Actual price quotations will be demonstrated and discussed as part of the coverage of specific investment vehicles in later chapters.

News Retrieval and Databases

Given the widespread use of personal computers (PCs), many investors access up-to-the-minute information through news/retrieval systems and *databases,* which are organized collections of historical as well as current information. Investment analyses require considerable amounts of economic and financial information, and the more current it is, the better. The nearby Investor Insights box describes several ways PCs can be used when making investment decisions.

Professional investors are in constant contact with many news sources, and they buy and sell securities almost automatically when important events take place. The PC owner can use this same news to update his or her database. Currently, Dow Jones is the undisputed leader in investment news/retrieval software. Table 3.2 summarizes the key investor information services available on Dow Jones News/ Retrieval. The cost of using News/Retrieval depends on the time of day and the database used. Most of the financial databases cost $2.16 per minute in prime time and drop to $0.21 to $1.35 after 6 p.m. Additional charges are based on the amount of information accessed and type of report requested. For a flat fee of $25 per month, individual investors can get unlimited use of certain news and quotation

TABLE 3.1 Ticker Symbols for Some Well-Known Companies

Company	Symbol	Company	Symbol
Aluminum Co. of America	AA	Mobil Corporation	MOB
American Telephone & Telegraph	T	Occidental Petroleum	OXY
Coca-Cola	KO	Pepsico, Inc.	PEP
Disney (Walt)	DIS	Polaroid Corporation	PRD
Eastman Kodak	EK	Procter & Gamble	PG
Ford Motor	F	Quaker Oats	OAT
General Electric	GE	Sears, Roebuck	S
General Motors	GM	Sherwin-Williams	SHW
International Business Machines	IBM	Texas Instruments	TXN
McDonalds Corporation	MCD	Wendy's International	WEN
Minnesota Mining and Manufacturing	MMM	Xerox Corporation	XRX

INVESTOR INSIGHTS

Investing with Your PC

No longer is computerized investment analysis solely the province of professional money managers or sophisticated individual investors with large portfolios. With recent price reductions for powerful, sophisticated PCs and the proliferation of "user-friendly" investment software and financial databases, electronic investing is now available to the average investor. The PC allows investors to sort through vast numbers of statistics quickly and easily, to track the performance of many stocks, and to execute trades in a fraction of the time it would otherwise take.

First, consider what an investor can accomplish with one of the general computer information services (such as CompuServe or Prodigy) or a financial service (such as Dow/Jones News/Retrieval). Assume you are interested in finding out more about a certain stock. Using CompuServe, you can get current and historical stock quotes on a daily, weekly, or monthly basis, plus dividends for at least the past eight quarters. You can save this data so that portfolio management programs compatible with CompuServe can graph price movements. Next, you can request security analysts' opinions and earnings projections of the stock and also get information on the company's investments, stockholders, salaries of top executives, and management's opinions of the company's prospects. If what you learn convinces you to buy the stock, you can execute the transaction with one of three discount brokerages affiliated with CompuServe. And the best part? It would only take about 15 minutes to perform all these tasks, at a cost of about $15 to $20. (These broad-based services charge monthly or annual fees plus time-based on-line connect charges.)

The PC helps with other types of securities research as well. No longer do you have to spend hours searching through the *S&P Stock Guide* or *Value Line* to find stocks meeting certain investment criteria. Instead, you could ask a special stock-screening program to identify all stocks with a dividend yield of 7 percent priced under $30 per share. Two such programs are *Value Screen,* which tracks 49 variables on the 1,700 stocks in the *Value Line* service, and *Market Base,* with over 100 variables for a 4,700 stock database. The price for these services ranges from about $250 to $700, depending on the frequency of database updates and, in the case of *MarketBase,* the size of the database you wish to access.

Portfolio management is another area in which computers can save time and effort. Programs such as *Dow Jones Market Manager Plus* ($299) and Charles Schwab's *The Equalizer* ($99) allow you to track the stocks in your portfolio and to set up hypothetical portfolios to test various investment strategies. As you update prices periodically from published quotes or automatically from on-line databases, the program recalculates the value of your holdings. When you trade securities, the program figures out the profit or loss. Graphics and reporting features are also included.

With the help of your PC, all the information you need to make wise investment decisions is at your fingertips.

Sources: Kristin Davis, "Best of the Investment Software," *Changing Times,* June 1990, pp. 73–78; and Joel Dreyfuss, "How to Invest with Your PC," *Fortune 1991 Investor's Guide,* Fall 1990, pp. 211–14.

TABLE 3.2 Summary: Key Investor Services Available on Dow Jones
News/Retrieval

BUSINESS AND WORLD NEWSWIRES

Dow Jones Business Newswires: Searches seven leading newswire simultaneously. Provides up-to-the-second news and coverage that is held for 90 days.

*Dow Jones News: Company and industry news

*Dow Jones International News: International news

*Professional Investor Report: Unusual intra-day trading activity on more than 5,000 stocks traded on the New York and American exchanges and OTC.

*Dow Jones Capital Markets Report: Fixed income and financial futures market news

*Federal Filings: Real-time SEC filings.

Business Wire and PR Newswire: Business, financial, general, and government press releases.

DOW JONES TEXT LIBRARY

Text Search Services: Access full text of all or selected articles from *The Wall Street Journal* (U.S., European, and Asian editions), *Barron's, Business Week,* and more than 1,000 national regional, industry, and trade publications.

DowQuest: Retrieves current business articles from 350 publications.

COMPANY/INDUSTRY INFORMATION

Corporate Canada Online: Canadian corporate news and financial reports.

Duns Financial Records Plus: Dun & Bradstreet reports on 1.5 million companies.

Disclosure Database: SEC filings extracts.

Zacks Corporate Earnings Estimator: Earnings forecasts for 3,500 companies and 100 industries.

Investext: Analysts' research reports on companies, industries, and countries.

Media General Financial Services: Financial and statistical comparisons of companies and industries.

Dow Jones QuickSearch: Comprehensive company reports compiled from 8 News/Retrieval databases.

Standard & Poor's Online: Standard & Poor's profiles and earnings estimates.

Corporate Ownership Watch: Insider trading activity and tender offer filings.

Worldscope: Financial profiles and performance data on companies in 25 countries.

QUOTES, STATISTICS, AND COMMENTARY

Dow Jones Enhanced Current Quotes: Current stock quotes (15-minute delay).

Dow Jones Real-Time Quotes: Real-time stock quotes.

Dow Jones Historical Quotes: Historical stock quotes.

Tradeline: Screening and historical pricing on securities and indexes.

Dow Jones Futures and Index Quotes: Current and historical quotes for futures and indexes.

Municipal Funds Performance Report: Comprehensive data on more than 1,500 mutual funds.

Historical Dow Jones Averages: Daily data for Dow Jones averages.

Innovest Technical Analysis Reports: Technical analysis reports of more than 4,500 stocks.

MMS Weekly Market Analysis: U.S. money market and foreign exchange trends and commentary.

*Wall Street Week Online: Transcripts of the PBS program "Wall Street Week."

*Exclusive to Dow Jones.

Source: Dow Jones News/Retrieval, June 1991.

databases between specified non-prime-time hours. In addition, for individual sub-scribers there currently is a $30 one-time fee plus an annual service charge of $18, which is waived in the first year. Another less expensive source of price quotes, market activity, and current business and financial news is DowPhone, a voice-information service that costs $0.75 to $1.25 per minute with a $15 initial sign-up fee.

Using Investment Advisors

investment advisors individuals or firms that provide invest-ment advice, usually for a fee.

Although numerous sources of financial information are available, many investors have neither the time nor the expertise to analyze this information and make deci-sions on their own. Instead, they turn to an investment advisor. **Investment advisors** are individuals or firms that provide investment advice—typically for a fee.

The Advisor's Product

The "product" provided by investment advisors ranges from broad general advice to specific detailed analyses and recommendations. The most general form of ad-vice is a newsletter published by the advisor. These letters offer general advice on the economy, current events, market behavior, and specific securities. Investment advisors also provide complete investment evaluation, recommendation, and man-agement services.

Regulation of Advisors

As pointed out in Chapter 2, the Investment Advisors Act of 1940 ensures that investment advisors make full disclosure of information about their backgrounds, conflicts of interest, and so on. The act requires professional advisors to register and file periodic reports with the SEC. A 1960 amendment extended the SEC's powers to permit it to inspect the records of investment advisors and to revoke the registra-tion of those who violate the act's provisions. However, persons such as financial planners, stockbrokers, bankers, and accountants who provide investment advice *in addition to* their main professional activity are not regulated by the act. Many states have also passed similar legislation, requiring investment advisors to register and abide by the guidelines established by the state law.

The federal and state laws regulating the activities of professional investment advisors do not *guarantee competence*. Rather, they are intended to protect the investor against fraudulent and unethical practices. It is important to recognize that, at present, *no law or regulatory body controls entrance into the field*. Therefore investment advisors can range from the highly informed professional to the totally incompetent amateur. Advisors possessing a professional designation such as CFA (Chartered Financial Analyst), CIC (Chartered Investment Counselor), CFP (Certi-fied Financial Planner), ChFC (Chartered Financial Consultant), CLU (Chartered Life Underwriter), or CPA (Certified Public Accountant) are usually preferred be-cause they have completed academic courses in areas directly or peripherally related to the investment process. Appendix B provides a guide to these professional certifi-cation programs.

The Cost and Use of Investment Advice

Professional investment advice typically costs between ¼ of 1 percent and 2 percent annually of the amount of money being managed. For large portfolios, the fee is typically in the range of ¼ to ¾ percent. For small portfolios (less than $100,000), an annual fee ranging from 1 to 2 percent of the amount of funds managed would not be unusual. These fees generally cover complete management of a client's money, excluding, of course, any purchase or sale commissions. The cost of periodic investment advice not provided as part of a subscription service could be based on a fixed-fee schedule or quoted as an hourly charge for consultation.

Like most services, some investment advisory services are better than others. In many cases a less expensive service may provide better advice than a more expensive one. It is best to study carefully the "track record" and overall reputation of an investment advisor prior to purchasing its services. Not only should the advisor have a good performance record, but also he or she should be responsive to the investor's personal goals.

Investment Clubs

investment club
a legal partnership through which a group of investors is bound to an organizational structure, operating procedures, and purpose.

In order to gain both investment advice and experience, many investors—especially those of moderate means—join an investment club. The **investment club** is a legal partnership binding a group of investors (partners) to a specified organizational structure, operating procedures, and purpose. The goal of most clubs is making investments in vehicles of moderate risk to earn favorable long-run returns.

Investment clubs are usually formed by a group of individuals with similar goals who wish to pool their knowledge and money to create a jointly owned portfolio. Certain members are responsible for obtaining and analyzing data on a specific investment vehicle or strategy. At periodic meetings the members present their findings and recommendations, which are discussed and further analyzed by the membership. The group decides whether the proposed vehicle or strategy should be pursued. Most clubs require members to make scheduled contributions to the club's treasury, thereby providing for periodic increases in the pool of investable funds. Although most clubs concentrate on investments in stocks and bonds, they are occasionally formed to invest in options, commodities, and real estate.

Membership in an investment club provides an excellent way for the new investor to learn the key aspects of portfolio construction and investment management, while (one hopes) earning a favorable return on funds. The National Association of Investors Corporation (NAIC), which has about 7,500 affiliated clubs, publishes a variety of useful materials. It also sponsors regional and national meetings. (A free information package on how to start an investment club can be obtained by writing: NAIC, 1515 East Eleven Mile Rd., Royal Oak, MI 48067; or by calling 313-543-0616.)

MARKET AVERAGES AND INDEXES

Just as it is important to understand when the economy is moving up or down, it is also important to know whether *market behavior* is favorable or unfavorable. The ability to interpret various market measures should help an investor to select and *time* investment actions. Therefore it is important that the investor understand the general behavior of the market. A widely used way to assess the behavior of securities markets is to study the performance of market averages and indexes. These measures allow investors to conveniently (1) gauge general market conditions, (2) compare their portfolio's performance to that of a large diversified (market) portfolio, and (3) study market cycles, trends, and behaviors in order to forecast future market behavior. Key measures of stock and bond market activity and the small investor's portfolio are discussed here; discussion of averages and indexes associated with other forms of investments is deferred to the chapter devoted to each vehicle.

Stock Market Averages and Indexes

averages
numbers used to measure the general behavior of stock prices by reflecting the arithmetic average price behavior of a representative group of stocks at a given point in time.

indexes
numbers used to measure the general behavior of stock prices by measuring the current price behavior of a representative group of stocks in relation to a base value.

Dow Jones Industrial Average (DJIA)
a stock average made up of 30 high-quality industrial stocks selected for total market value and broad public ownership and believed to reflect overall market activity.

Stock market averages and indexes are used to measure the general behavior of stock prices over time. Although the terms "average" and "index" tend to be used interchangeably when discussing market behavior, technically they are different types of measures. **Averages** reflect the arithmetic average price behavior of a representative group of stocks at a given point in time. **Indexes** measure the current price behavior of a representative group of stocks in relation to a base value set at an earlier point in time. Many investors compare averages or indexes at differing points in time in order to assess the relative strength or weakness of the market.

Averages and indexes provide a convenient method of capturing the general mood of the market. Current and recent values of the key averages and indexes are quoted daily in the financial news; most local newspapers and many radio and television news programs also quote their prevailing values. Figure 3.4, published daily in *The Wall Street Journal*, provides a summary and statistics on the major stock market averages and indexes. Let us take a look at the key averages and indexes.

The Dow Jones Averages

Dow Jones, publisher of *The Wall Street Journal*, prepares four stock averages. The most popular is the **Dow Jones Industrial Average (DJIA),** which is made up of 30 stocks selected for total market value and broad public ownership. The group consists of high-quality industrial stocks whose activities are believed to reflect overall market activity. The box within Figure 3.5 lists the stocks currently included in the DJIA. Occasionally a merger, a bankruptcy, or extreme lack of activity causes a particular stock to be dropped from the average. In that case a new stock is added, and the average is readjusted so that it continues to behave in a way consistent with the immediate past.

The value of the DJIA is calculated each business day by substituting the closing prices of each of the 30 stocks in the average into the following equation:

Equation 3.1

$$\text{DJIA} = \frac{\substack{\text{closing price} \\ \text{of stock 1}} + \substack{\text{closing price} \\ \text{of stock 2}} + \cdots + \substack{\text{closing price} \\ \text{of stock 30}}}{\text{DJIA divisor}}$$

STOCK MARKET DATA BANK 1/7/92

MAJOR INDEXES

HIGH	LOW (†365 DAY)		CLOSE	NET CHG		% CHG	†365 DAY CHG		% CHG	FROM 12/31		% CHG
DOW JONES AVERAGES												
3204.83	2470.30	30 Industrials	3204.83	+	4.70	+ 0.15	+ 695.42	+27.71	+	36.00	+	1.14
1383.03	895.80	20 Transportation	1383.03	+	17.56	+ 1.29	+ 484.98	+54.00	+	25.03	+	1.84
226.15	195.17	15 Utilities	221.83	−	1.19	− 0.53	+ 14.90	+ 7.20	−	4.32	−	1.91
1167.25	880.82	65 Composite	1167.25	+	4.43	+ 0.38	+ 276.51	+31.04	+	10.43	+	0.90
393.90	288.96	Equity Mkt. Index	392.43	−	0.37	− 0.09	+ 100.53	+34.44	+	0.53	+	0.14
NEW YORK STOCK EXCHANGE												
230.35	170.97	Composite	229.69	−	0.16	− 0.07	+ 57.08	+33.07	+	0.25	+	0.11
287.33	210.80	Industrials	286.24	−	0.19	− 0.07	+ 73.10	+34.30	+	0.42	+	0.15
102.27	86.77	Utilities	101.39	−	0.38	− 0.37	+ 13.16	+14.92	−	0.74	−	0.72
201.87	137.54	Transportation	201.60	+	1.34	+ 0.67	+ 63.50	+45.98	−	0.27	−	0.13
174.16	116.11	Finance	174.16	+	0.25	+ 0.14	+ 56.89	+48.51	+	1.48	+	0.86
STANDARD & POOR'S INDEXES												
419.34	311.49	500 Index	417.40	−	0.56	− 0.13	+ 102.50	+32.55	+	0.31	+	0.07
495.78	364.90	Industrials	493.46	−	0.60	− 0.12	+ 124.30	+33.67	+	0.74	+	0.15
341.46	226.22	Transportation	341.12	+	2.77	+ 0.82	+ 111.94	+48.84	−	0.34	−	0.10
155.70	133.52	Utilities	153.58	−	0.78	− 0.51	+ 15.77	+11.44	−	1.58	−	1.02
34.40	21.97	Financials	34.40	unch		....	+ 12.28	+55.52	+	0.30	+	0.88
148.08	95.16	400 MidCap	148.08	+	0.45	+ 0.30	+ 52.21	+54.46	+	1.49	+	1.02
NASDAQ												
602.29	355.75	Composite	602.29	+	4.39	+ 0.73	+ 243.29	+67.77	+	15.95	+	2.72
690.39	387.47	Industrials	690.39	+	6.59	+ 0.96	+ 301.09	+77.34	+	21.44	+	3.21
605.61	434.23	Insurance	605.61	+	0.75	+ 0.12	+ 168.66	+38.60	+	4.52	+	0.75
363.84	246.07	Banks	363.84	+	5.60	+ 1.56	+ 114.96	+46.19	+	13.28	+	3.79
266.96	157.16	Nat. Mkt. Comp.	266.96	+	1.96	+ 0.74	+ 108.44	+68.41	+	7.22	+	2.78
276.61	154.97	Nat. Mkt. Indus.	276.61	+	2.70	+ 0.99	+ 121.05	+77.82	+	8.82	+	3.29
OTHERS												
401.71	296.72	Amex	401.71	+	2.44	+ 0.61	+ 101.93	+34.00	+	6.66	+	1.69
252.70	186.78	Value-Line (geom.)	252.70	+	0.59	+ 0.23	+ 63.11	+33.29	+	3.36	+	1.35
195.77	125.25	Russell 2000	195.77	+	1.40	+ 0.72	+ 68.19	+53.45	+	5.84	+	3.07
4060.97	2938.58	Wilshire 5000	4059.40	+	3.48	+ 0.09	+1094.29	+36.91	+	18.29	+	0.45

†-Based on comparable trading day in preceeding year.

• F I G U R E 3 . 4 Major Stock Market Averages and Indexes
The "Stock Market Data Bank" summarizes the key indexes and includes statistics showing the change from the previous day, the annual change, and the year-to-date change. (*Source: The Wall Street Journal,* January 8, 1992, p. C2.)

The value of the DJIA is merely the sum of the closing prices of the 30 stocks included in it, divided by a "divisor." For example, on January 7, 1992, the sum of the closing prices of the 30 industrials was 1791.50, which when divided by the divisor of 0.559 resulted in a DJIA value of 3204.83 (i.e., 1791.50 ÷ 0.559). The purpose of the divisor is to adjust for any stock splits, company changes, or other events that have occurred over time, thereby allowing the DJIA to be used to make useful time-series comparisons.

Because the DJIA results from summing the prices of the 30 stocks, higher-priced stocks tend to more greatly affect the index than do lower-priced stocks. For example, a 5 percent change in the price of a $50 stock (i.e., $2.50) will have less impact on the index than a 5 percent change in a $100 stock (i.e., $5.00). In spite of

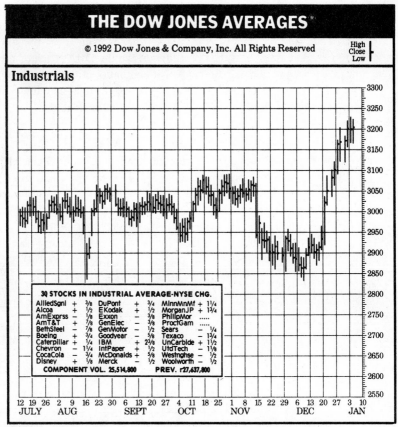

THE DOW JONES AVERAGES ®

© 1992 Dow Jones & Company, Inc. All Rights Reserved

High
Close
Low

Industrials

30 STOCKS IN INDUSTRIAL AVERAGE-NYSE CHG.

AlliedSgnl	+	³/₈	DuPont	+	³/₄	MInnMnMf	+	1¹/₄
Alcoa	+	¹/₂	EKodak	+	¹/₂	MorganJP	+	1³/₄
AmExprss	−	¹/₈	Exxon	−	³/₈	PhillpMor	.....	
AmT&T	+	⁷/₈	GenElec	−	³/₈	ProctGam	.....	
BethSteel	−	⁷/₈	GenMotor	−	¹/₂	Sears	−	¹/₄
Boeing	+	³/₄	Goodyear	−	⁵/₈	Texaco	−	1³/₄
Caterpillar	+	¹/₄	IBM	+	2³/₈	UnCarbide	+	1¹/₂
Chevron	−	1¹/₄	IntPaper	+	¹/₂	UtdTech	−	1¹/₈
CocaCola	−	³/₄	McDonalds	+	⁵/₈	Westnghse	−	¹/₂
Disney	+	¹/₈	Merck	−	¹/₂	Woolworth	−	¹/₂

COMPONENT VOL. 25,514,800   PREV. r27,637,800

12 19 26 2 9 16 23 30 6 13 20 27 4 11 18 25 1 8 15 22 29 6 13 20 27 3 10
JULY   AUG   SEPT   OCT   NOV   DEC   JAN

• F I G U R E 3 . 5 The DJIA from July 12, 1991 to January 7, 1992

In late 1991 through early 1992, the stock market was bullish. Indeed, as measured by the DJIA, it moved from 2900 to 3200, a gain of over 10 percent, within 30 days. (*Source: The Wall Street Journal,* January 1992, p. C3. Reprinted by permission of *The Wall Street Journal,* © Dow Jones & Company, Inc., 1992. All rights reserved.)

this and other criticisms levied against the DJIA, it remains the most widely cited stock market indicator.

The actual value of the DJIA is meaningful only when compared to earlier values. For example, the DJIA on January 7, 1992, closed at 3204.83. This value becomes meaningful only when compared to the previous day's closing value of 3200.13. Many people mistakenly believe that one DJIA ''point'' equals $1 in the value of an average share; actually one point currently translates into about 1.86 cents in share value. Figure 3.5 shows the DJIA over the 6-month period July 12, 1991, to January 7, 1992. Beginning in mid-December of 1991, the DJIA showed a rapid increase through January 7, 1992.

The three other Dow Jones averages are the transportation, the utilities, and the composite. The *Dow Jones Transportation Average* is based on 20 stocks, including railroads, airlines, freight forwarders, and mixed transportation companies. The *Dow Jones Utilities Average* is computed using 15 public utility stocks. The *Dow Jones 65 Stocks Composite Average* is made up of the 30 industrials, the 20 transportations, and the 15 utilities. Like the DJIA, each of the other Dow Jones averages is calculated to allow for continuity of the average over time. The transportation, utilities, and 65 stocks composite averages are often cited in the financial news along with the DJIA, as shown in Figure 3.4.

Standard & Poor's indexes
true indexes that measure the current price of a group of stocks relative to a base which has an index value of 10.

Standard & Poor's (S&P's) Indexes

Standard & Poor's Corporation, another major financial publisher, publishes six major common stock indexes. One commonly cited "S&P" index is the 500 stock composite index. Unlike the Dow Jones averages, **Standard & Poor's indexes** are true indexes. They are calculated each business day by substituting the closing *market value of each stock* (i.e., closing price × number of shares outstanding) into the following equation:

Equation 3.2

$$\frac{\text{S\&P}}{\text{index}} = \frac{\begin{array}{c}\text{current} \\ \text{closing market} \\ \text{value of} \\ \text{stock 1}\end{array} + \begin{array}{c}\text{current} \\ \text{closing market} \\ \text{value of} \\ \text{stock 2}\end{array} + \cdots + \begin{array}{c}\text{current} \\ \text{closing market} \\ \text{value of} \\ \text{last stock}\end{array}}{\begin{array}{c}\text{base period} \\ \text{closing market} \\ \text{value of} \\ \text{stock 1}\end{array} + \begin{array}{c}\text{base period} \\ \text{closing market} \\ \text{value of} \\ \text{stock 2}\end{array} + \cdots + \begin{array}{c}\text{base period} \\ \text{closing market} \\ \text{value of} \\ \text{last stock}\end{array}} \times 10$$

The value of the S&P index is found by dividing the sum of the market values of all stocks included in the index by the market value of the stocks in the base period and then multiplying the resulting quotient by 10—the base value of the S&P indexes. Most indexes are calculated in a fashion similar to this; the main difference lies in the stocks included in the index, the base period, and the base value of the index. For example, on January 7, 1992, the ratio of the closing market values of the S&P 500 composite stocks to the 1941–1943 base-period closing market values was 41.740, which when multiplied by the base value of the S&P index of 10 results in an index value of 417.40 (as shown in Figure 3.4).

Certain of the S&P indexes contain many more shares than do the Dow averages, and all of them are based upon market values rather than share prices. Therefore, many investors feel they provide a more broad-based and representative measure of general market conditions than do the Dow averages. Although some technical computational problems exist with these indexes, they are widely used—frequently as a basis for estimating the "market return," an important concept introduced in Chapter 4.

Like the Dow averages, the S&P indexes are meaningful only when compared to values in other time periods or the 1941–1943 base period value of 10. For example, the January 7, 1992, value of the S&P 500 stock composite index of 417.40 means that the market values of the stocks in the index increased by a factor of 41.74 (417.40 ÷ 10) since the 1941–1943 period. The January 7, 1992, market value of the stocks in the index was 1.34 times the lowest index value of 311.49 in the preceding 365-day period (417.40 ÷ 311.49), or an increase of 34 percent.

The six major common stock indexes published by Standard & Poor's are as follows: The *industrials index* is made up of the common stock of 400 industrial firms; the *transportation index* includes the stock of 20 transportation companies; the *utilities index* is made up of 40 public utility stocks; the *financials index* contains 40 financial stocks; the *composite index* (used above) consists of the total of 500 stocks included in the industrials, transportation, utilities, and financials indexes. The newest S&P index is the *midcap index,* which was launched in June 1991. It is made up of the stocks of 400 medium-sized companies—stock market values between $200 million and $5.5 billion with a median value of about $700 million. The popularity of this index results from growing investor interest in the stocks of medium-sized companies. Like the Dow, the S&P indexes are frequently quoted in the financial news, as shown in Figure 3.4.

Although the Dow Jones averages and S&P indexes tend to behave in a similar fashion over time, their day-to-day magnitude and even direction (up or down) can differ from one another significantly, since the Dows are averages and the S&P's are indexes.

NYSE, AMEX, and Nasdaq Indexes

NYSE index
measure of the current price behavior of the stocks listed on the NYSE.

Three exchange-based indexes are the New York Stock Exchange (NYSE), the American Stock Exchange (AMEX), and the National Association of Securities Dealers Automated Quotation (Nasdaq). Each reflects the movement of stocks listed on its exchange. The **NYSE index** includes all of the about 2,300 stocks listed on the "big board." The base of 50 reflects the December 31, 1965, value of stocks listed on the NYSE. In addition to the composite index, the NYSE also publishes indexes for industrials, utilities, transportation, and finance subgroups. The behavior of the NYSE industrial index will normally be similar to that of the DJIA and the S&P 500 indexes.

AMEX index
measure of the current price behavior of stocks listed on the AMEX.

The **AMEX index** reflects the price of all shares traded on the American Stock Exchange relative to a base of 100, set August 31, 1973. Although it may not always closely follow the S&P or NYSE indexes, the AMEX index tends to behave like those mentioned earlier.

Nasdaq indexes
measures of current price behavior of securities sold OTC.

The **Nasdaq indexes** reflect over-the-counter market activity. They are based on a value of 100, set February 5, 1971. The most comprehensive of the Nasdaq indexes is the *OTC composite index,* which is calculated using the about 4,700 domestic common stocks traded on the Nasdaq system. The other five commonly quoted Nasdaq indexes are the *industrials,* the *insurance,* the *banks,* the *national market composite,* and the *national market industrials.* Although their degrees of responsiveness may vary, the Nasdaq indexes tend to move in the same direction at the same time as the other major indexes.

Value Line Indexes

Value Line publishes a number of stock indexes constructed by equally weighting the price of each stock included. This is accomplished by considering only the percentage changes in stock prices. This approach eliminates the effects of differing market price and total market value on the relative importance of each stock included in the index. Instead the index captures only the effects of *changes* in share prices. The **Value Line composite index** includes the approximately 1,700 stocks in the *Value Line Investment Survey* that are traded on the NYSE, AMEX, and OTC market. The base of 100 reflects the June 30, 1961 stock prices. In addition to its composite index, Value Line publishes indexes for *industrials, rails,* and *utilities.* These indexes are especially appealing to individual investors because they include stocks that are likely to be held in their portfolios.

Value Line composite index
a stock index published by Value Line, that reflects the percentage changes in share price of about 1,700 stocks traded on the NYSE, AMEX, and OTC market relative to a base of 100.

Wilshire 5000 Index
measure of the total dollar value of 5,000 actively traded stocks, including all those on the NYSE and the AMEX, plus active OTC stocks.

Other Averages and Indexes

In addition to the major indexes just described, a number of others are available. The **Wilshire 5000 Index,** published by Wilshire Associates, Inc., is reported daily in *The Wall Street Journal.* It represents the total dollar value (in billions of dollars) of 5,000 actively traded stocks, including all those on the NYSE and AMEX in addition to active OTC stocks. *Barron's* publishes a 50-Stock Average and a Low-Price Stock Index. *The New York Times* publishes its own average, which is quite similar to the Dow Jones averages. And Moody's Investors Services prepares market indicators for a variety of groupings of common stock. In addition, a list of stock market indexes for 20 foreign stock markets, including the widely followed Tokyo *Nikkei Average* and Morgan Stanley Capital International's *Europe/Australia/Far East (EAFE)* index, are published daily in *The Wall Street Journal*'s ''World Markets'' column.

Bond Market Indicators

A number of bond market indicators are available for assessing the general behavior of these markets. However, there are not nearly as many indicators of overall bond market behavior. The key measures are bond yields, the Dow Jones bond averages, and the New York Stock Exchange bond statistics.

Bond Yields

bond yields
summary measures of the return an investor would receive on a bond if it were held to maturity; reported as an annual rate of return.

Bond yields represent a summary measure of the return an investor would receive on a bond if it were held to maturity. They are reported as an annual rate of return. For example, a bond with a yield of 8.50 percent will provide its owner with a return in the form of periodic interest *and* capital gain or loss that would be equivalent to an 8.50 percent annual rate of earnings on the amount invested, if held to maturity.

Typically, bond yields are quoted for a group of bonds that are similar with respect to type and quality. For example, *Barron's* quotes the average yields for the Dow Jones 10 utilities, 10 industrials, 20 bond composites, as well as for other groups of Treasury and municipal bonds. Similar bond yield data are also available from S&P, Moody's, and the Federal Reserve. Like stock market averages and indexes, bond yield data are especially useful when viewed over time.

Dow Jones Bond Averages

The **Dow Jones bond averages** include a utility, industrial, and a composite bond average. Each average reflects the simple mathematical average of the closing prices, rather than yields, for each group of bonds included. The utility bond average is based on the closing prices of 10 utility bonds; the industrial bond average is based on the closing prices of 10 industrial bonds; and the composite bond average is based on the closing prices of 10 utility and 10 industrial bonds. Like bond price quotations, the bond averages are presented in terms of the percentage of face value at which the bond sells. For example, the January 7, 1992, Dow Jones composite bond average of 99.46 indicates that, on average, bonds were, on the day reported, selling for 99.46 percent of their face or maturity value. For a $1,000 bond, the average price of an issue would equal about $994.60. The Dow Jones bond averages are published daily in *The Wall Street Journal* and summarized weekly in *Barron's*.

New York Stock Exchange Bond Statistics

The New York Stock Exchange is the dominant organized exchange on which bonds are traded, so certain summary statistics on daily bond-trading activity on the NYSE provide useful insight into the behavior of the bond markets in general. These statistics include the number of issues traded; the number that advanced, declined, or remained unchanged; the number of new highs and new lows; and total sales volume in dollars. For example, on January 7, 1992, 662 domestic issues were traded; 322 advanced; 200 declined; and 140 remained unchanged. Of the issues traded, 99 achieved new price highs for the year, and 4 fell to the new price lows. Total sales volume was $68,210,000. NYSE bond statistics are published daily in *The Wall Street Journal,* and summarized weekly in *Barron's*.

Small Investor's Portfolio Index

Money magazine's **Small Investor Index** measures the average investor's gains and losses. The index is based on a value of 100 set at the end of the immediately preceding year, and is reported weekly each Monday in *USA Today* and monthly as part of *Money's* "Investor's Scorecard." The Small Investor Index is based on a portfolio that includes ten types of investments held in proportions consistent with Federal Reserve data on what the average household owns. The investments included and their proportions in the small investor's portfolio are shown in Table 3.3. Although this index is not widely used on Wall Street, it does provide the individual investor with a standard against which he or she can assess both the composition and performance of his or her portfolio.

INVESTMENT GOALS AND PLANS

Establishing investment goals consistent with overall financial objectives is important. Once such goals have been established, an **investment plan,** a written document describing how funds will be invested, should be developed. For each goal, the target date for its achievement and the amount of tolerable risk must be speci-

TABLE 3.3 Investments Included in *Money's* Small Investor Index (December 1991)

Type of Investment	Percent of Portfolio
NYSE stocks	20.1%
AMEX/OTC stocks	6.3
Stock mutual funds	4.6
Taxable bonds	16.5
Municipal bonds	4.3
Bond mutual funds	5.0
Certificates of deposit	19.3
Cash and equivalents	22.5
Real estate (excludes residences)	.8
Gold	.6
Total Portfolio	100.0%

investment plan a written document describing investment goals, how funds will be invested, the target date for the accomplishments of goals, and the amount of tolerable risk.

investment goals the financial objectives one wishes to achieve by investing in potential investment vehicles.

fied. Generally the more important the financial objective, the less the risk that should be assumed. Investment plans must be developed in a manner that considers taxes, and with adequate provision for life insurance coverage and liquidity.

Investment Goals

Investment goals are the financial objectives that one wishes to achieve by investing in any of a wide range of potential investment vehicles. Clearly your investment goals will determine the types of investments you will make. Common investment goals include:

1. *Accumulating Funds.* Accumulating funds for retirement is *the single most important reason for investing*. Too often, however, retirement planning occupies only a small amount of a person's time; many people tend to rely heavily on Social Security and employers for this provision. It is of the utmost importance to review the amounts that can realistically be expected from these sources and decide, based on your retirement goals, *whether they will be adequate to meet your needs*. If they are not, such sources must be supplemented through your own investment program. The earlier in life an assessment of retirement needs is made, the greater the chance of success in accumulating the needed funds. (Retirement plans will be discussed in greater detail in Chapter 15.)

2. *Enhancing Current Income.* The ability of an investment to enhance current income depends on the amount of income, usually dividends or interest, that it can bring in. Retired individuals frequently choose investments offering *high current income at low risk*. The idea of a retired person "clipping coupons" from high-yield bonds is a fair description of what most senior citizens *should* be doing at that point in their lives.

3. *Saving for Major Expenditures.* Families often put aside money over the years in order to accumulate the funds necessary for making a few major expenditures. The most common of these are the down payment on a home, college education for one's children, a "once-in-a-lifetime" vacation, capital to start one's own business, and the purchase of a very special item (perhaps jewelry or an antique). Once the amount of money needed is known, the appropriate types of investment vehicles can be selected. For purposes such as the down payment on a home or a child's education, for example, much *less* risk should be tolerated than for other goals, since the attainment of such basic goals should not, if possible, be placed in jeopardy.

4. *Sheltering Income from Taxes.* As will be explained in Chapter 15, federal income tax law allows certain noncash charges to be deducted from certain other sources of income, thereby reducing the amount of final taxable income. Obviously if a person can avoid (or defer) paying taxes on the income from an investment, he or she will have more funds left for reinvestment.

A series of supporting investment goals can be developed for each long-run goal. Suppose, for example, one long-run goal is to accumulate $80,000 in cash at the end of 10 years. In this case one must specify the desired return and acceptable risk associated with this goal. Our example could be more precisely stated as an investment goal to accumulate $80,000 in cash by investing in a portfolio evenly divided between low-risk and speculative stocks providing a total return of 10 percent per year. The more specific you can be in the statement of investment goals, the easier it will be to establish an investment plan consistent with your goals.

Meeting Life Insurance Needs

Before undertaking an investment program, the would-be investor needs to make sure that his or her insurance needs are met. Insurance is an important prerequisite for two reasons: (1) It provides protection against consequences that can adversely affect finances. (2) It can provide certain long-term cash benefits. An **insurance policy** is a contract between the insured (you) and the insurer (an insurance company) that requires the insured to make periodic premium payments in exchange for the insurer's promise to pay for losses according to specified terms. Decisions regarding insurance purchases may affect the amount of funds available for investment. The many different types of insurance available can be broken down into three basic forms: life insurance, health insurance, and property and liability insurance. Although many types of health, property, and liability insurance are essential, here we focus on life insurance due to its investment attributes.

insurance policy
a contract between the insured and the insurer that requires the insured to make periodic premium payments in exchange for the insurer's promise to pay for losses according to specified terms.

Types of Life Insurance

Life insurance provides a mechanism that can be used to provide financial protection for a family if the primary breadwinner or any other family member dies prematurely. Some types of life insurance provide only death benefits; others also allow for the accumulation of savings. The four basic types of life insurance are term, whole life, universal life, and variable life.

life insurance
a mechanism that can provide financial protection for a family if the primary breadwinner or other family member dies prematurely.

term life insurance
form of life insurance in which the insurer agrees to pay a specified amount if the insured dies within the policy period.

Term Insurance.   A **term life insurance** policy is one that covers the insured for a specific period (typically 5 to 20 years). The insurance company is obligated to pay a specified amount if the insured dies within the policy period. *Term is the least expensive form of life insurance,* although its cost rises as the insured ages and can become quite expensive as an insured ages. It provides protection but does not contain a savings feature. Many employers offer free or low-cost *group term insurance* protection for their employees. Very frequently this benefit is the least expensive way to obtain life insurance. If you need to increase your term life insurance, you may be able to purchase additional amounts at low cost through group insurance. Keep in mind that many of these plans are not transportable, however. That means that you can't take your term protection with you if you leave your job.

whole life insurance
form of life insurance that provides coverage over the entire life of the insured; offers a savings benefit.

cash value
the amount of money set aside by an insurer to provide for the payment of a death benefit.

Whole Life.   As the name implies, **whole life insurance** provides insurance coverage over the entire life of an insured. The insured pays a premium each year until death or termination of the policy. Whole life also offers a savings benefit commonly called the **cash value.** The cash value is the amount of money set aside by the insurer to provide for the payment of the death benefit. Since the investment earnings that accrue to the insurer increase as its reserves against the policy rise over time, the cash value also increases. From the insurer's view, increased cash values are necessary since as the insured gets older the probability of death increases. Either the beneficiaries of the insured will receive the amount of the death benefit upon the death of the insured, or the policyholder at some predetermined time can terminate the policy and receive its cash value.

Whole life insurance is advantageous in that the premium payments contribute toward the tax-sheltered accumulation of value regardless of whether the insured lives or dies. It also provides insurance protection at a given premium rate over the whole life of the insured. However, the actual cash value accumulation of a whole life policy reflects an annual earnings rate generally *below* what could be earned on alternative investments. For this reason some financial advisors recommend purchasing the cheaper term insurance and investing the premium savings.

universal life insurance
form of life insurance that combines term insurance with a tax-sheltered savings/investment account that pays interest at competitive rates.

Universal Life.   **Universal life insurance** retains the savings features of whole life but provides a higher return on the cash value portion of the policy than most whole life policies. Basically, universal life combines *term* insurance, which provides the death benefits, with a tax-sheltered savings/investment account that pays interest at *competitive money market rates.*

A key advantage of universal life over whole life is that the purchaser is more aware of what he or she is buying than is the whole life policyholder. In contrast to whole life, universal life insurance carries a detailed breakdown of policy costs as well as all benefits. All charges for costs, such as sales commissions, insurance company service fees, and actual insurance protection, are explicitly listed. (Usually whole life sellers quote the premium amount and little else.) Another advantageous feature of universal life is that many policies allow a buyer under certain conditions to skip or reduce a premium payment.

variable life insurance
form of life insurance that offers insurance coverage with a savings feature that allows the insured to decide how the cash value is invested; the amount of insurance coverage varies with the policy's investment returns.

Variable Life. **Variable life insurance** is like whole life and universal life in that it combines insurance coverage with a savings account. It differs from them in two respects: (1) It allows the policyholder to decide how the money in the savings account (cash value account balance) is invested. (2) It does *not* specify a guaranteed minimum return. Variable life offers the highest and most attractive level of investment returns. And, as its name implies, the amount of insurance coverage provided will *vary* with the profit (*and losses*) being generated in the investment (savings) account. Thus, in variable life insurance, the amount of death benefit payable is, for the most part, related to the policy's investment returns. (*Note:* The level of insurance coverage can never fall below the policy's stated *minimum death benefit*.) Like all life insurance, the investment earnings can grow within the policy free of any current taxation, and the policy's death benefit passes tax-free to beneficiaries. Because variable life is really an *investment vehicle* wrapped in an insurance policy, it is *probably best used as a tax-sheltered investment vehicle* rather than a source of primary life insurance coverage.

Estimating Life Insurance Needs

Any of a number of possible techniques can be used to estimate a person's life insurance needs. One can assess the individual's financial situation to determine how much protection is required in order to leave his or her beneficiaries in a desired financial position. Or one can look at the individual's projected earnings and convert them into a present value that would represent the amount of needed insurance protection. The worksheet in the Investor Insights box demonstrates one way to estimate life insurance needs.

Considering Personal Taxes

The tax consequences associated with various investment vehicles and strategies must be considered when establishing an investment program. A knowledge of the tax laws should help you employ strategies that result in the reduction of taxes, thereby increasing the amount of after-tax dollars available for achieving your investment goals. Because tax laws are complicated and subject to frequent revision, here we will present only the key concepts and their applications to basic investment transactions.

Basic Sources of Taxation

The two major types of taxes are those levied by the federal government and by state and local governments. The major federal tax is the income tax, which is also the major source of personal taxation. Rates currently range from 15 to 31 percent of taxable income. Unlike federal taxes, state and local taxes vary from area to area. Some states have income taxes that may range as high as 15 percent or more of income. Some cities, especially large East Coast cities, also have local income taxes that typically range between 1 and 5 percent of income. In addition to income taxes, state and local governments rely heavily on sales and property taxes as a source of revenue. Although sales taxes vary from state to state, most are between 3 and 7

The Life-Insurance Quandary: How Much Is Really Enough?

How much life insurance do you need?

Many people have either too little or too much, financial advisers say. But the specialists frequently disagree on just how much is enough. . . .

The key is to accept that there isn't a magic number. "It's a bit naive to think there's one right answer. But there probably is a correct range" of coverage for each person, says George E.L. Barbee, executive director of personal financial services for accountants Price Waterhouse.

A reasonable game plan: Try a few methods to estimate insurance needs. Scrutinize and vary the assumptions used. Weigh the costs of different amounts of coverage. Then settle on a figure that feels right. Any thoughtful decision will probably be better than no decision at all.

The goal is to provide money your dependents can tap immediately and over the years if you should die tomorrow. Don't worry if you can't figure out what it will cost to send your daughter to college in 2003, or that your spouse's ideas about retirement could change several times before 2014.

Use the best information you have now. And keep in mind that insurance coverage can—and should—be modified as family circumstances change. "We see so often that even one year later so many things have changed," says Robert DeValle, a Palo Alto, Calif., insurance agent. . . .

Source: Adapted from Karen Slater, "The Life-Insurance Quandary: How Much Is Really Enough?" *The Wall Street Journal,* July 10, 1990, p. C1.

A LIFE-INSURANCE WORKSHEET

Completing this worksheet, using current dollar amounts, can help in estimating how much life insurance is needed. (*Note*: While this worksheet is useful in making a *rough estimate* of life insurance needs, it is not a substitute for careful and deliberate life insurance planning.)

FUNDS TO COVER:

		Example*
1. Funeral and other final expenses		$ 10,000
2. Estate taxes	+ _____	
3. Paying off mortgage (optional)	+ _____	150,000
4. Paying off other family debts (optional)	+ _____	10,000
5. College fund	+ _____	80,000
6. Special needs	+ _____	
7. Subtotal	= _____	**250,000**

FUNDS FOR SURVIVORS' LIVING EXPENSES:

8. Current household expenses		51,500
9. Target percentage	×	67%
10. Survivors' annual expenses	=	34,505
11. Social Security benefits	−	
12. Spouse's take-home pay	−	20,000
13. Annual need	=	14,505
14. Number of years needed	×	38
15. Subtotal	=	**551,190**
16. Total assets needed (7 + 15)		801,190
17. Existing insurance	−	150,000
18. Income-producing assets	−	65,000
19. Additional insurance needed	=	**586,190**

*Figures are for a 45-year-old man who earns $75,000 a year. His wife, age 42, earns $25,000 working part-time. Their two children are 15 and 12.

Based on a worksheet by Virginia Applegarth, TFC Financial Management, Boston, Mass.

INSTRUCTIONS AND EXPLANATIONS (BY LINE)

1. Several insurance specialists suggested figures between $5,000 and $20,000.

2. Federal estate taxes are imposed on estates of $600,000 or more, but sums left to a spouse are not subject to the levy. Some states also impose estate taxes, and their rules vary.

5. For the 1989–90 academic year, average costs for college tuition, fees, room and board were $4,597 at public schools and $10,778 at private schools, according to the College Board. The example uses a figure of $10,000 per year per child.

6. This might be a lump sum for one's elderly parents or for a favorite charity.

8. Employment income after taxes and savings (and minus mortgage expense if part of insurance proceeds will be used to pay off mortgage). In the example, the couple's $100,000 of wages is reduced by $25,000 of income tax, $7,000 in annual savings and $16,500 in mortgage payments.

9 and 11. Ms. Applegarth suggests a target percentage of 80%. But if there are minor children, and the calculation is simplified by not including their Social Security benefits as income, she suggests a target of two-thirds.

Note that Social Security benefits will vary over time with the survivor's ages. Under the current benefit schedule, the family in the example would get about $9,500 a year for each child while the children are under 18 and then nothing at all until the wife reaches retirement age.

14. The example assumes the wife will live to age 80 and the husband wants to provide for her for that whole time.

17. The example assumes the husband has group insurance at work of two times his salary.

18. Savings and investments plus any sums that would be paid at death from retirement plans.

percent. Property taxes are levied on real estate and personal property, such as furniture and automobiles. These taxes vary from community to community. Income taxes have the greatest impact on security investments, whereas property taxes could have a sizable impact on real estate and other forms of property investment.

Types of Income

The income of individuals used to be classified simply as either ordinary or capital gain (or loss). Under the Tax Reform Act of 1986, that's no longer the case. One of the major revisions of the sweeping 1986 tax legislation was the creation of *three basic categories of income*. Devised as a way to curtail the amount of write-offs that could be taken in tax-sheltered investments, they consist of the following:

1. *Active income* consists of everything from wages and salaries to bonuses, tips, pension income, and alimony. It is made up of income earned on the job as well as most other forms of *noninvestment* income.
2. *Portfolio income,* in contrast is comprised of the earnings generated from various types of investment holdings. In fact, this category of income covers *most* (but not all) types of investments, from stocks, bonds, savings accounts, and mutual funds to stock options and commodities. For the most part, portfolio income consists of interest, dividends, and capital gains (i.e., the profit on the sale of an investment).
3. *Passive income,* a special category of income, is comprised chiefly of income derived from real estate, limited partnerships, and other forms of tax shelters.

The key feature of these categories is that they limit the amount of deductions (write-offs) that can be taken, particularly with regard to portfolio and passive income. Specifically, the amount of allowable, deductible expenses associated with portfolio and passive income *is limited to the amount of income derived from these two sources*. For example, if you had a total of $380 in portfolio income for the year, you could write off no more than $380 in investment-related interest expense. It is important to understand that for deduction purposes, the portfolio and passive income categories cannot be mixed or combined with each other or with active income. *Investment-related expenses can be used only with portfolio income,* and with a few exceptions, *passive investment expenses can be used only to offset the income from passive investments*.

Ordinary Income.   Regardless of whether it's classified as active, portfolio, or passive, ordinary income—after certain computations—is taxed at one of three rates: either 15, 28, or 31 percent. There is one structure of tax rates for taxpayers who file *individual* returns and another for those who file *joint* returns. Table 3.4 shows the tax rates and income brackets for these two filing categories. Notice that the rates are *progressive*—individuals with taxable income above a specified amount are taxed at a higher rate.

TABLE 3.4 Tax Rates and Income Brackets for Individual and Joint Returns (1991)

	Taxable Income	
Tax Rates	**Individual Returns**	**Joint Returns**
15%	$0 to $20,350	$0 to $34,000
28%	$20,351 to $49,300	$34,001 to $82,150
31%	over $49,300	over $82,150

An example will demonstrate how ordinary income is taxed. Consider the Ellis sisters, Joni and Cara. Both are single. Joni's taxable income is $18,000; Cara's is $36,000. Using Table 3.4, we can calculate their taxes as follows:

Joni:

$$(.15 \times \$18,000) = \underline{\$2,700}$$

Cara:

$$(.15 \times \$20,350) + [.28 \times (\$36,000 - \$20,350)] = \$3,053 + \$4,382 = \underline{\$7,435}$$

The progressive nature of the federal income tax structure can be seen by the fact that although Cara's taxable income is twice that of Joni, her income tax is nearly three times Joni's.

Capital Gains and Losses. A *capital asset* is property owned and used by the taxpayer for personal reasons, pleasure, or investment. The most common types are securities and real estate, including one's home. A **capital gain** represents the amount by which the proceeds from the sale of a capital asset exceed its original purchase price. The amount of any capital gain realized is added to other sources of income and the total is taxed at the rates given in Table 3.4, but *the maximum tax rate on the capital gain is 28 percent.* For example, imagine that James McFail, a single person who has other taxable income totaling $40,000, sold at $12 per share 500 shares of stock originally puchased for $10 per share. The total capital gain on this transaction was $1,000 [500 shares × ($12/share − $10/share)]. Thus McFail's taxable income would total $41,000. His total tax would be $8,835 [(.15 × $20,350) + (.28 × ($41,000 − $20,350)]. Had McFail's other taxable income been, say, $60,000, all of his income over $49,300 would have been taxable at 31 percent (see Table 3.4). In spite of this, the $1,000 capital gain would be taxed at the maximum 28 percent rate for capital gains rather than at the 31 percent rate.

Capital gains are appealing since they are not taxed until actually realized. For example, if you own a stock originally purchased for $50 per share which at the end of the tax year has a market price of $60 per share, you have a "paper gain" of $10 per share. This paper or *unrealized gain* is not taxable since you still own the stock. Only *realized gains* are taxed. If you sold the stock for $60 per share during the tax year, you would have a realized—and therefore taxable—gain of $10 per share.

capital gain
the amount by which the proceeds from the sale of a capital asset exceed its original purchase price.

capital loss
the amount by which the proceeds from the sale of a capital asset are less than its original purchase price.

net losses
the amount by which capital losses exceed capital gains; up to $3,000 can be applied against ordinary income.

A **capital loss** results when a capital asset is sold for less than its original purchase price. Before taxes are calculated, all gains and losses must be netted out. Up to $3,000 of **net losses** can be applied against ordinary income in any year. Losses that cannot be applied in the current year may be carried forward and used to offset future income, subject to certain conditions.

Investments and Taxes

From an investor's point of view, the key dimensions of taxes revolve around current (ordinary) income, capital gains, tax shelters, and tax planning. Investors in vehicles providing current income tend to be those in the lower two tax brackets (15 and 28 percent)—especially retirees. The predominant form of current investment income is interest and dividends. To a lesser degree, another source of current income is rental income from various types of real estate investment. From a tax point of view, capital gains resulting from the appreciation in the value of an investment are very appealing to many investors. The fact that these gains are not taxed until actually realized allows the investor to defer as well as control the timing of the tax payments on them. In addition, because capital gains are taxed as ordinary income up to a maximum tax rate of 28 percent, they provide a small *tax-rate* advantage to taxpayers in the top (31 percent) tax bracket.

Due to the higher risk associated with capital gain income versus current investment income, the choice of investment vehicles cannot be made solely on the basis of the timing and possible reduction of tax payments. The levels of return and risk need to be viewed in the light of their tax effects. *It is the after-tax return and associated risk* that should be considered.

Tax shelters are certain forms of investment that capitalize on available "tax writeoffs." Some investments in real estate (income-generating property) and natural resources (oil and gas drilling) currently provide these desirable deductions, but only under very restrictive conditions. Such shelters can change at the whim of the Congressional writers of the tax code. Chapter 15 presents detailed discussions and illustrations of the basic mechanics of tax-sheltered investments.

tax planning
the formulation of strategies that will defer and minimize an individual's level of taxes.

Due to the opportunities and challenges created by the tax laws, tax planning is important in the investment process. **Tax planning** involves looking at an individual's earnings, both current and projected, and developing strategies that will defer and minimize the level of taxes. The tax plan should guide an investor's activities in such a way that over the long run he or she will achieve maximum after-tax returns for an acceptable level of risk.

Tax plans should also reflect the desired form in which returns are to be received—current income, capital gains, or tax-sheltered income. One common strategy is to claim losses as soon as they occur and to delay profit taking. Such an approach allows you to benefit from the tax deductibility of a loss and to delay having to claim income from gains. Although the use of tax planning, which is commonly done in coordination with an accountant, tax expert, or tax attorney, is most common among individuals with high levels of income ($75,000 or more annually), sizable savings can result for investors with lower incomes as well.

The Investment Program

Once investment goals have been specified, a program must be developed. The backbone of the program is the *investment plan*. The plan indicates the general strategy that will be used to achieve each goal. Since some portion of the goals may be achieved through government or employer pension programs outside the individual's control, any contribution of such plans toward goal achievement must be recognized. The overriding consideration in the plan is **diversification.** This concept emphasizes the need to hold a variety of investment vehicles in order to minimize the risk that one bad investment will hinder the goal of accumulating a specified amount. A well-balanced portfolio lessens such risk.

diversification
the use of a variety of investment vehicles in order to minimize risk.

As any investment program progresses, checkpoints should be established at various time intervals to allow for assessment of progress. Adjustments in both goals and plans may be required as new information is received; goals may be too lax or too restrictive, or plans unrealistic. By monitoring actual outcomes and making needed adjustments, an investor should be better able to establish and achieve realistic financial goals over the long run.

Investing in Different Economic Environments

The first rule of investing is to know *where* to put your money; the second is to know *when* to make your moves. The first question is easier to deal with because it basically involves matching your risk and return objectives with the available investment alternatives. For example, if you're a seasoned investor who can tolerate the risk, then speculative stocks may be right for you; on the other hand, if you're a novice who wants a fair return on your capital, perhaps you should consider a good growth-oriented mutual fund. Unfortunately, although stocks or growth funds may do well when the economy is expanding, they can turn out to be disasters at other times. This leads to our second, and more difficult question: What effect do economic/market conditions have on investment returns?

The question of when to invest is difficult because it deals with *market timing*. The fact is that most investors, even professional money managers, *cannot* predict the peaks and troughs in the market with much consistency. It's a lot easier to get a handle on the *current state* of the economy/market. That is, knowing whether the economy/market is in a state of expansion or decline is considerably different from being able to pinpoint when it's about to change course. Thus for our purposes we can define market timing as *the process through which we identify the current state of the economy/market and assess the likelihood of its continuing on its present course*.

As an investor, it's probably best to confine your assessment of the market to three distinct conditions: (1) the economy/market is in a state of *recovery/expansion;* (2) it's in a state of *decline/recession;* or (3) you're *uncertain* as to the direction in which it's going to move. These different stages are illustrated in Figure 3.6. It's easy to see when things are moving up (recovery/expansion) or when they're moving down (decline/recession). The difficulty comes with the peaks and troughs. That is why these are shown in the shaded areas, depicting *uncertainty*. How you

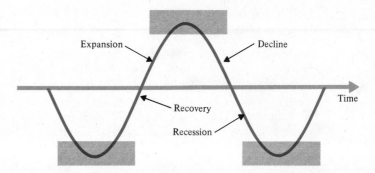

• FIGURE 3.6 Different Stages of an Economic/Market Cycle
The economic/market cycle shows three different conditions: (1) a state of recovery/expansion, (2) a state of decline/recession, and (3) uncertainty as to the direction in which the economy/market is going to move (shown by the shaded areas at peak and troughs).

will respond to these conditions depends on whether you're in stocks, bonds, or tangible investments.

Stocks and the Business Cycle

Common stocks and other equity-related securities (such as stock mutual funds, convertible securities, stock options, and stock index futures) are highly responsive to conditions in the economy, which are described generically as the *business cycle*. The business cycle reflects the current status of a variety of economic variables, including GDP (gross domestic product), industrial production, personal disposable income, unemployment rates, and more. When the economy is strong, it's reflected in a strong, expanding business cycle, and when business is good and profits are up, stocks react accordingly. Growth-oriented and speculative stocks tend to do especially well in such markets as, to a lesser extent, do low-risk and income-oriented stocks. In contrast, when the business cycle is declining, the returns on common stocks tend to be off as well.

Bonds and Interest Rates

Bonds and other forms of fixed-income securities (such as preferred stocks and bond funds) are highly sensitive to movements in interest rates. In fact, interest rates are the single most important variable in determining bond price behavior and returns to investors. Because interest rates and bond prices move in *opposite* directions (as will be explained in Chapter 8), it follows that rising interest rates are *unfavorable* for *outstanding bonds* already held in an investor's portfolio. Of course, high interest rates enhance the attractiveness of new bonds since they offer high returns.

Tangible Investments and Inflation

Tangible investments include things like real estate, commodities, and gold. These vehicles are generally responsive more to the *rate of inflation* than to anything else. The cost of housing, along with commodities like coffee, oil, meat, corn, and sugar, goes into making up the consumer price index (CPI). *When prices start rising, the returns on these tangible asset investments start going up as well.* Consider what happened over the 16-year period from 1977 to 1992. In the first five years of that period inflation was running high, hitting 13.5 percent. At the same time investments in real estate, commodities, and other tangible assets were generating correspondingly high rates of return and, indeed, outperforming all other forms of investments. But when inflation was brought back down to more normal levels (3 to 5 percent) beginning around 1982, returns on tangible instruments plummeted. Certainly the rate of inflation significantly affects the returns on tangible investments.

Investing Over the Life Cycle

Investors tend to follow different investment philosophies as they move through different stages of the life cycle. Generally speaking, most investors tend to be more aggressive when they're young and more conservative as they grow older. In general, investors tend to move through the following investment stages:

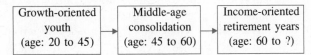

Most young investors, in their twenties and thirties, tend to prefer growth-oriented investments that stress *capital gains* rather than current income. Often young investors don't have much in the way of investable funds, so capital gains are viewed as the quickest (if not necessarily the surest) way to build up investment capital. Such investors are inclined to favor speculative and growth-oriented vehicles. As investors approach the middle-age consolidation stage of life (the mid-forties), family demands and responsibilities take a big change and so does the approach to investing. Thus the whole portfolio goes through a transition to higher-quality securities. Low-risk growth and income stocks, preferred stocks, convertibles, high-grade bonds, and mutual funds are all widely used at this point in life. Finally, investors move into their retirement years, wherein *preservation of capital and current income* are the principal concerns. A *secure, high level of income* is now paramount, and capital gains are viewed as merely a pleasant occasional by-product of investing. The investment portfolio now becomes *highly conservative,* consisting of low-risk income stocks, high-yielding government bonds, quality corporate bonds, bank certificates of deposit (CDs), and other money market investments. It's at this stage that you should be able to reap the rewards of a lifetime of saving and investing.

MEETING LIQUIDITY NEEDS: INVESTING IN SHORT-TERM SECURITIES

liquidity
the ability to convert
an investment into
cash quickly and
with little or no loss
in value.

Investment goals and plans should provide the investor with adequate liquidity. **Liquidity** as used here refers to the ability to convert an investment into cash quickly and with little or no loss in value. A checking account is highly liquid. Stocks and bonds are not liquid, because there is no definite assurance of being able to sell the securities at a price equal to or greater than their purchase price.

Role of Short-Term Securities

Short-term securities are an important part of most savings and investment programs. Although they do generate income—which can be quite high during periods of high interest rates—their primary function is to provide a pool of reserves that can be used for emergencies, or simply to accumulate funds for some specific purpose. When viewed as part of an investment portfolio, short-term securities are usually held as a temporary, highly liquid investment outlet until something better comes along, or as a form of investment by individuals who are more comfortable with these vehicles. In fact, this approach has had considerable merit during periods of economic (and investment) instability, such as those experienced during the 1970s and early 1980s. Whatever the reasons for holding them, short-term securities should be evaluated in terms of their risk and return.

Determining Interest on Short-Term Securities

Short-term investments earn interest in one of two ways. First, some investments, such as a savings account, pay a stated rate of interest. In this case the interest rate is easily obtained by the investor—it's the stated rate on the account. Another way interest is earned on short-term investments is on a **discount basis.** This means that the security is purchased at a price *below* its redemption value, the difference being the interest earned. Treasury bills (T-bills), for example, are issued on a discount basis. This return can be expressed as a **bond equivalent yield (BEY),** which is the annual percentage rate that would be earned by an investor in a short term security sold at a discount who purchases it today at its current price and holds it to its maturity. The following equation gives the BEY:

discount basis
a method of earning interest on short-term investments by purchasing a security at a price below its redemption value, the difference being the interest earned.

bond equivalent yield (BEY)
the annual rate of return that would be earned by an investor in a short-term security sold at a discount if it is purchased today at its current price and held to maturity.

Equation 3.3

$$\text{Bond equivalent yield on a discount security} = \left[\frac{365}{\text{number of days to maturity}}\right] \times \left[\frac{\text{redemption value} - \text{current price}}{\text{current price}}\right]$$

Equation 3.3a

$$BEY = [365/n] \times \left[\frac{R - P}{P}\right]$$

To illustrate, suppose you buy a T-bill for $9,905 that can be redeemed for $10,000 at the end of 91 days. The total interest on this security is $95 (redemption value − current price), and its bond equivalent yield (BEY) is:

$$BEY = (365/91) \times \left(\frac{\$10,000 - \$9,905}{\$9,905}\right)$$

$$= (4.011) \times (.0096) = \underline{.0385, \text{ or } 3.85\%}$$

Risk Characteristics

Short-term investments are generally considered low in risk. The primary risk results from the loss of potential purchasing power that occurs when the rate of return on these investments falls short of the inflation rate. Unfortunately this has often been the case with deposits such as passbook savings accounts. Most other short-term investments have averaged, over long periods of time, rates of return that are about equal to, or maybe even slightly higher than, the average inflation rate.

The risk of default (nonpayment) is virtually nonexistent with short-term investment vehicles. The principal reason is that the primary issuers of most money market securities are highly reputable institutions, such as the U.S. Treasury, large money center banks, and major corporations. Furthermore, deposits in commercial banks, savings banks, savings and loans, and credit unions are insured for up to $100,000 per account by government agencies. Finally, because the value of short-term investments does not change much in response to changing interest rates, exposure to capital loss is correspondingly low. These securities have short maturities (often measured in days and never exceeding a year), and the shorter the maturity of an issue, the less volatile its market price.

Advantages and Disadvantages of Short-Term Investments

As noted, the major advantages of short-term investments are their high liquidity and low risk. Most are available from local financial institutions and can be readily converted to cash with minimal inconvenience. Finally, since the returns on most short-term investments vary with inflation and market interest rates, investors can readily capture the higher returns as rates move up. Of course on the negative side, when interest rates go down, returns drop as well.

Although a decline in market rates has undesirable effects on most short-term vehicles, perhaps their biggest disadvantage is their relatively low return. Because these securities are generally so low in risk, you can expect the returns on short-term investments to generally average less than the returns on long-term investments.

Popular Short-Term Investment Vehicles

Over the past 15 to 20 years there has been a proliferation of savings and short-term investment vehicles, particularly for the individual investor of modest means. Saving and investing in short-term securities is no longer the easy task it once was, when the decision for most people amounted to whether funds should be placed in a passbook savings account or in Series E savings bonds. Today even some checking accounts pay interest on idle balances. Along with the dramatic increase in investment alternatives has come greater sophistication in short-term investment management. Short-term vehicles can be used as secure investment outlets for the long haul, or as a place to hold cash until the market becomes stronger and a more permanent outlet for the funds can be found. In the material that follows we will first examine each of the major short-term investment deposits and vehicles; then we will briefly look at several ways in which these deposits/securities can be used in an investment portfolio. (Note that all the *deposit* accounts discussed below are issued by commercial banks, savings and loans [S&Ls], savings banks, and credit unions; very often we will simply use the term ''bank'' to refer to any one or all of these financial institutions and not necessarily to commercial banks alone.)

Passbook Savings Accounts

passbook savings account
a savings vehicle, offered by banks and other thrift institutions, that generally pays a low rate of interest, has no minimum balance, and few or no restrictions on withdrawal.

The **passbook savings account** has been the traditional savings vehicle for many Americans. The term "passbook" arises from the fact that activity in the account was often recorded in a passbook, although bank statement report forms have generally replaced passbooks. Typically there are no minimum balances on these accounts, and you can make as many withdrawals as you choose, though there would be a slight fee for some of the withdrawals. These accounts are offered by banks and other thrift institutions. In spite of the fact that effective April 1, 1986, interest rate ceilings on these accounts were eliminated, these accounts continue to pay a relatively low rate of interest, typically between 3 and 6 percent. Passbook savings accounts are used primarily by depositors who like the convenience of maintaining a savings account at their local bank, who lack sufficient resources to invest in other short-term vehicles, or who are simply unaware of higher-yielding, equally safe outlets. Passbook accounts are generally viewed as a convenient savings vehicle but have little or no role in an investment program.

NOW Accounts

NOW (negotiated order of withdrawal) account
a checking account that pays interest; has no legal minimum balance but many banks impose their own.

A **NOW (negotiated order of withdrawal) account** is simply a checking account that pays interest at whatever rate the financial institution chooses. There is no legal minimum for a NOW, but many banks impose their own requirement, often between $500 and $1,000. Some banks have no minimum and pay interest on any balance in the account. Many banks pay interest at a higher rate on all balances over a specified amount, such as $2,500.

NOW accounts should be viewed primarily as checking accounts that are also potentially attractive savings vehicles. Since NOWs are in fact checking accounts, investors can earn interest on balances that must be kept for transaction purposes anyway; thus an individual can earn interest on what would otherwise be idle money. In most cases service charges on NOWs, if any, are no greater than those on regular checking accounts. However, despite the apparent appeal of NOWs, alternatives should be examined closely.

Money Market Deposit Accounts

money market deposit accounts (MMDAs)
a federally insured bank account with features similar to money market mutual funds; has no legal minimum balance but many banks impose their own.

Money market deposit accounts (MMDAs) were created to give banks and thrift institutions a vehicle with which to compete with money market mutual funds (discussed below). Although MMDAs do not legally require a minimum balance, banks commonly set a minimum of around $2,500. Most banks pay interest rates on these accounts that are 1 to 3 percent below those offered by money market mutual funds. MMDAs are popular with savers and investors due to their convenience and safety. The deposits, unlike those in money funds, are *federally insured*. Depositors have access to their MMDAs through checkwriting privileges or through automated teller machines; a total of six transfers (only three by check) is allowed each month, after which a penalty is charged for additional withdrawals. This feature reduces the flexibility of these accounts and makes them less attractive than NOWs. However, most banks offer higher rates on MMDAs than on NOWs, which enhances their appeal. And since most depositors apparently look upon MMDAs as a savings outlet rather than a convenience account, the limited-access feature has not been a serious obstacle.

Money Market Mutual Funds

money market mutual fund (MMMF)
a mutual fund that pools the capital of a large number of investors and uses it to invest in high-yielding, short-term securities.

A **money market mutual fund (MMMF)** is simply a mutual fund that pools the capital of a great number of investors and uses it to invest exclusively in high-yielding, short-term securities, such as Treasury bills, corporate commercial paper, jumbo certificates of deposit, and the like. Since such securities are sold in denominations of $10,000 to $1 million (or more), most small investors cannot purchase them individually, yet they very often offer the highest short-term yields. The MMMF makes these rates available to even small investors. Shares of MMMFs can be purchased (through brokers and investment dealers) with initial investments as low as $500 to $1,000 (although $1,000 to $5,000 is a more typical amount). Almost every major brokerage firm has a money fund of its own, and there are another 400 or so that are unaffiliated with a specific brokerage house.

The returns on money funds amount to what fund managers are able to earn from their investment activity in various short-term securities. Thus, the returns rise and fall with money market interest rates. As Figure 3.7 shows, these are *highly volatile rates* that cause investor yields to vary accordingly. The returns on MMMFs are closely followed in the financial media and, in fact, the current yields on about 450 of the largest funds are regularly reported in *The Wall Street Journal* and other major newspapers (see Figure 3.8). Note in this case that not only are yields reported, but so are average maturities. MMMFs provide convenient and easy access to funds through checkwriting privileges; the nice feature of this privilege is that you continue to earn interest while the check is being cleared through the banking system.

We will describe mutual funds more fully in Chapter 13; however, several characteristics of money funds should be noted here. One concern of many investors is the question of safety. One could argue that since they are not federally insured, MMMFs will always be less secure than deposits in federally insured institutions. However, the history of MMMFs has been virtually free of even the threat of failure. Default risk is almost zero, since the securities the funds purchase are very low in risk to begin with, and diversification by the funds lowers risk even more. Despite this remarkable record of safety, it is impossible to say with certainty that MMMFs are *as* risk-free as federally insured deposits. In the event of a massive financial crisis, they probably are not. On the other hand, the amount of extra risk might be viewed as so minimal as to be easily offset by a slightly higher yield. This is a choice the individual investor must make within his or her own risk-return framework.

tax-exempt money fund
a money market mutual fund that limits its investments to tax-exempt municipal securities with very short maturities.

In addition to the standard money market mutual fund, there are tax-exempt money funds and government securities money funds. The **tax-exempt money fund** limits its investments to tax-exempt municipal securities with very short (30 to 90 days) maturities. Except for this feature they are like the standard money market funds. Since their income is free from federal (and some state) income tax, they

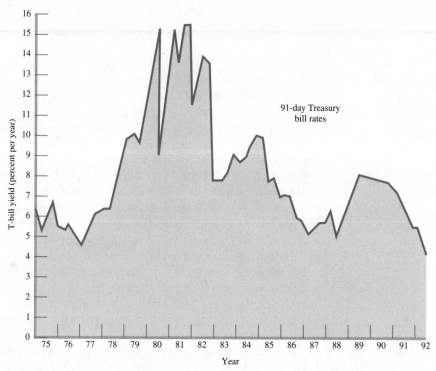

• FIGURE 3.7 The Behavior of Short-Term Market Rates over Time

The yields on marketable short-term securities (such as Treasury bills) are highly unstable. They therefore have a dramatic effect on returns to investors in money funds and other short-term vehicles (like MMDAs).

government securities money fund a money market mutual fund that limits its investments to Treasury bills and other short-term securities of the U.S. government and its agencies.

yield less than standard, fully taxable money funds. They appeal predominantly to investors in the higher tax bracket for whom the lower tax-free yield is better than the *after-tax* return they could earn on standard money funds. **Government securities money funds** were established as a way to meet investor concerns for safety. These funds effectively eliminate any risk of default by confining their investments to Treasury bills and other short-term securities of the U.S. government and its agencies. They are like standard MMMFs in all other respects except for slightly lower yields (which is the price you pay for the higher quality).

central asset account a comprehensive deposit account that combines checking, investing, and borrowing activities and automatically sweeps excess balances into short-term investments.

Central Asset Accounts

The **central asset account** is not a separate investment vehicle, but rather a comprehensive deposit account that combines checking, investing, and borrowing activities. These accounts are offered by banks, other depository institutions, brokerage houses, mutual funds, and insurance companies. Their distinguishing feature is that they automatically "sweep" excess balances into short-term investments. For example, a bank central asset account might be set up to combine a NOW and an

MONEY MARKET MUTUAL FUNDS

The following quotations, collected by the National Association of Securities Dealers Inc., represent the average of annualized yields and dollar-weighted portfolio maturities ending Wednesday, May 20, 1992. Yields don't include capital gains or losses.

Fund	Avg. Mat.	7Day Yld.	e7Day Yld.	Assets	Fund	Avg. Mat.	7Day Yld.	e7Day Yld.	Assets	Fund	Avg. Mat.	7Day Yld.	e7Day Yld.	Assets
AALMny	69	2.89	2.93	141	FlexFd	72	3.83	3.90	261	Natns FMM	69	3.65	3.72	519
AARP HQ	51	2.86	2.90	361	Fortis	32	3.16	3.21	117	NatwMM	43	3.36	3.41	538
AIM MM	25	3.09	3.14	139	Founders	39	2.93	2.98	136	NeubCsh	63	3.39	3.45	284
ASO Pr	63	3.48	3.54	451	FountSGv	60	3.52	3.58	84	NeubGvt	75	3.31	3.36	338
ASO US	74	3.54	3.60	336	FountUST Ob	40	3.49	3.55	36	Newton	47	3.63	3.71	247
ActAsGv	73	3.32	3.38	547	FountSCP	43	3.53	3.59	202	Nicholas	26	3.46	3.52	152
ActAsMny	64	3.57	3.63	3733	FountSTO	38	3.62	3.69	251	OldeMM	84	3.25	3.30	147
Aetna MM	52	4.20	4.20	27	FrnkIFT	64	3.88	3.95	186	OldePrPl	88	4.24	4.32	51
AlexBwn	48	3.44	3.50	1144	FrkUSTr	51	3.79	3.86	192	OldePrem	90	3.70	3.76	211
AlxBTr	52	3.34	3.40	721	FrkIFTGS	43	3.71	3.78	205	OppMoney	66	3.50	3.56	799
AlgerMM	65	3.98	4.06	147	FrkFdl b	20	3.06	3.11	152	OvldExMM	65	3.42	3.48	222
AlliaCpRs	74	3.42	3.48	1990	FrnkGvt	34	3.69	3.76	52	PFAMCo MM	31	3.53	3.59	13
AllaGvR	69	3.41	3.47	1687	FreeCsh	54	3.26	3.31	1118	PNC Gvt	52	3.54	3.60	182
AlliMny	76	3.41	3.47	1468	FreeGv	70	3.23	3.28	322	PNC Prm	56	3.61	3.67	625
AmAAdTr	86	3.82	3.89	65	FremntMM	78	3.48	3.54	29	PcHrzPr	79	3.82	3.88	7718
AmAAdMM	83	4.13	4.22	1824	FrkMny	32	3.11	3.16	1205	PcHrzTr	51	3.59	3.65	3094
AmCRes	66	2.95	2.99	329	FdTrMny	71	3.53	3.48	49	PacificGv	73	3.71	3.78	174
AmExDDIv	84	3.54	3.60	17600	GT Mny	77	3.01	3.05	70	Pacifica	78	3.76	3.83	129
AmExGv	83	3.61	3.67	3922	GW Glob	68	3.82	3.38	75	PW Cash	54	3.52	3.58	4069
AmNatl	15	3.09	3.17	7	GW Gv	69	3.43	3.49	46	PW MstrM b	61	1.80	1.82	29
AmPerCsh	87	3.72	3.79	144	Gab OC DP	29	3.65	3.72	172	PW RMA	69	3.59	3.66	4197
AmPerTrs	58	3.27	3.32	127	Gab OC Mgr	58	3.30	3.35	14	PW RM US	68	3.57	3.63	872
AmbMM	44	3.53	3.59	314	Gab OC UST	73	3.33	3.38	37	PW Retr	64	3.44	3.50	2258
AmbTreas	38	3.48	3.54	63	GalaxyGv	24	3.60	3.66	473	ParagTr	56	3.72	....	331
ArchUSTr	57	3.32	3.37	160	GalxyMM	47	3.62	3.69	615	ParkPr	65	3.53	3.59	741
ArchFd	55	3.22	3.27	614	GalaxTr	53	3.63	3.70	423	ParkUS	65	3.61	3.64	417
					GnGvSec	84	3.58	3.64	642	Phonix	81	3.47	3.53	176
					GnMMkt	87	3.54	3.60	712	PillarUST A	38	3.15	3.19	222
					GSILFd f	56	3.70	3.76	1944	PionrCs	47	3.31	3.36	68
					GSILGv f	65	3.67	3.74	2809	PionUS	46	3.35	3.40	26
					GSILMM f	73	3.82	3.89	1401	PIprMM	63	3.20	3.25	1203
					GSILTrsOblg f	56	3.64	3.71	1877	PIprUS	65	3.18	3.23	204
					GSILPO f	70	3.78	3.85	6172	PortgeGv	42	3.27	3.33	55
					GSILTrsInst	53	3.56	3.62	359	PortInstMn	43	3.71	3.77	720
					GvInvTr	52	2.88	2.93	109	PortMM	57	3.54	3.60	155

• FIGURE 3.8 Published Yield Information on Major Money Market Mutual Funds

Data on money funds is widely quoted in the financial press. Here we see that the information includes the portfolios' average maturity (in days), the 7-day average of the yield currently available, the 7-day effective yield (noted ''e7Day'') that would have been earned over the prior 7-day period, and the total assets in the portfolio measured in million of dollars. (Source: *The Wall Street Journal*, May 21, 1992, p. C21. Reprinted by permission of *The Wall Street Journal*. © Dow Jones & Company, Inc., 1992. All rights reserved.)

MMDA. At the end of each day, if the NOW account balance exceeds $500, the excess is automatically swept into the higher-yielding MMDA. Merrill Lynch's ''cash management account (CMA)'' automatically sweeps the account holder's funds into its money market mutual fund, and if securities are purchased for an amount greater than the current balance, the needed funds are supplied automatically through a loan. Central asset accounts are exceptionally popular with investors. However, stipulated minimum balance requirements ranging from $5,000 to $20,000 limit the use of central asset accounts.

Certificates of Deposit (CDs)

certificates of deposit (CDs) savings instruments in which funds must remain on deposit for a specified period; premature withdrawals incur interest penalties.

Certificates of deposit (CDs) differ from the savings instruments discussed above in that funds must remain on deposit for a specified period, which can range from seven days to a year or more. Although it is possible to withdraw funds prior to maturity, an interest penalty (of 31 to 90 days of interest, depending on the original maturity of the CD) usually makes withdrawal somewhat costly. Banks and S&Ls today are free to offer any rate and maturity on these securities. A wide variety of

CDs is offered by most banks and thrift institutions, and these go by an equally wide variety of names. CDs are convenient to buy and hold, and all offer attractive and highly competitive returns plus federal insurance protection. The decision whether to invest in one of these or in, say MMDAs or MMMFs, generally depends on the length of the holding period and interest rate expectations. Uncertain holding periods and expected interest rate increases would favor MMDAs and MMMFs; certain holding periods and expected interest rate declines would favor CDs.

brokered CDs
certificates of deposit sold by stockbrokers; offer slightly higher yields than other CDs and no penalty for sale prior to maturity.

CDs can also be purchased from stockbrokers, in the form of **brokered CDs.** The brokerage house looks around the country for the highest yield it can get, buys these CDs, and then sells them to its customers. In essence, a bank or S&L issues the CDs, and the brokerage house merely sells (or places) them with the investing public. The minimum denomination is usually $1,000, so they are affordable, and there's usually no commission to pay since the broker earns its commission from the issuing bank. Brokered CDs are attractive for two reasons: *First,* they can be sold prior to maturity without incurring a penalty, since the brokerage firms maintain active secondary markets. Of course, there are no guarantees—the market prevails. If rates go up, the relative value of a CD falls, and its return will decline when it is sold prior to maturity. *Second,* brokered CDs may provide higher yields— frequently ¼ to ¾ of a percent higher—than those available from a local bank or thrift institution. But because a broker can always get higher yields by selling CDs issued by troubled financial institutions, it is best to *buy only brokered CDs that are issued by a federally insured institution.*

Commercial Paper

commercial paper
short-term, unsecured promissory notes issued by corporations with very high credit standings.

Commercial paper is short-term, unsecured promissory notes (IOUs) issued by corporations with very high credit standings. These notes are typically sold by firms in need of short-term loans. Although sometimes issued in denominations as small as $25,000 or $50,000, most commercial paper is initially sold in multiples of $100,000. Typical maturities range from a few days up to 270 days, the maximum maturity that does not require registration with the Securities and Exchange Commission (SEC). Since the secondary market for commercial paper is very limited, most investors hold commercial paper to maturity. Commercial paper is rated as to its quality by independent agencies. Its yield is comparable to the rate of return earned on large-denomination CDs.

Due to its large denominations, typically only larger institutions deal directly in commercial paper. Most individual investors obtain commercial paper from a bank or broker, who will "break down" the paper and sell the investor a small portion. MMMFs, which generally buy large quantities of paper to be included in their portfolios, probably provide the best method for the small investor to invest in commercial paper. However, individual investors can generally earn returns competitive with commercial paper by purchasing CDs, which, like commercial paper, have a fixed maturity but in addition have federal insurance protection. A popular strategy is to buy high-rated paper with a maturity closely matched to the desired investment horizon.

Banker's Acceptances

banker's acceptances
short-term, low-risk investment vehicles arising from bank guarantees of business transactions; are sold at a discount from their face value and provide yields generally slightly below those of CDs and commercial paper.

Banker's acceptances arise from short-term credit arrangements used by business firms to finance transactions, most often involving firms in foreign countries or firms with unknown credit capacities. An acceptance represents the guarantee by a bank to make a future payment (typically within 3 to 6 months) on behalf of a purchaser (importer) to their supplier (exporter). The exporter may sell the acceptance at a discount in order to obtain immediate cash from an investor, who is promised payment of its face value by the issuing bank at the specified future date. As a result of its sale, the banker's acceptance becomes a marketable security. The initial maturities of banker's acceptances are typically between 30 and 180 days, 90 days being most common. Banker's acceptances, which typically have a minimum denomination of $100,000 are low-risk securities with good secondary markets. The yields on banker's acceptances are generally slightly below those of CDs and commercial paper; they can usually be purchased through a bank or stockbroker.

U.S. Treasury Bills

U.S. Treasury bills (T-bills)
obligations of the U.S. Treasury, sold on a discount basis, and having varying short-term maturities and virtually no risk.

Prior to the many changes that have taken place in the financial markets in recent years, **U.S. Treasury bills** were the key short-term investment for most people who had sufficient funds to meet their rather high minimum investment requirement. T-bills are obligations of the U.S. Treasury issued as part of its ongoing process of funding the national debt. T-bills are sold on a discount basis in minimum denominations of $10,000, with $5,000 increments above that. Treasury bills are issued with 3-month (13-week or 91-day), 6-month (26-week or 182-day), and 1-year maturities. The 3- and 6-month bills are auctioned off every Monday (for delivery on the following Thursday), and there is an auction for 1-year bills approximately every four weeks.

Purchasing T-Bills. An individual investor can purchase T-bills directly (through participation in the weekly Treasury auctions) or indirectly (through local commercial banks or security dealers who buy bills for investors on a commission basis). Outstanding Treasury bills can also be purchased in the secondary market through banks or brokers. The biggest advantage of this approach is that the investor has a much wider selection of maturities to choose from, ranging from less than a week to as long as a year.

It is actually relatively simple to buy T-bills directly. All one need do is submit a tender offer to the nearest Federal Reserve Bank, or branch, specifying both the amount and maturity desired. (Tender forms are short and can be obtained by writing the Bureau of Public Debt, Securities Transaction Branch; Main Treasury Building; Washington, D.C. 20239; or by calling 202-287-4113.) The Treasury tries to accommodate individual investors through its noncompetitive bidding system, which most individual investors use because of its simplicity. In essence, all noncompetitive tender offers are awarded T-bills at a price equal to the average of all the accepted competitive bids. Thus, the investor is assured of buying bills in the quantity desired, while obtaining the benefits of an open auction system—all with-

bank discount yield
(BDY)
the rate at which
T-bills are quoted in
*The Wall Street Jour-
nal* and other finan-
cial media; repre-
sents the annualized
percentage discount
(redemption value −
current value) at
which the bill can
be currently pur-
chased.

out going through the hassle of a competitive bid. But T-bills bought directly through noncompetitive bidding are meant to be held to maturity; they should *not* be purchased by investors who may want to trade them. It's a difficult and time-consuming process to sell them in the after-market.

T-Bill Yield Calculations.   Treasury bill rates are quoted in *The Wall Street Journal* and other major financial media at the **bank discount yield (BDY),** which is its annualized percentage discount (redemption value − current value). The formula for BDY is given by Equation 3.4:

Equation 3.4

$$\text{Bank discount yield} = \frac{\left(\begin{array}{c}\text{redemption}\\\text{value}\end{array} - \begin{array}{c}\text{current}\\\text{value}\end{array}\right) \times \dfrac{360}{\begin{array}{c}\text{number of}\\\text{days to}\\\text{maturity}\end{array}}}{\text{redemption value}}$$

Equation 3.4a

$$BDY = \frac{(R - P) \times \dfrac{360}{n}}{R}$$

Substituting the data for the T-bill discussed earlier into Equation 3.4, we get a bank discount yield of:

$$BDY = \frac{(\$10,000 - \$9,905) \times \dfrac{360}{91}}{\$10,000} = \frac{\$95 \times 3.96}{\$10,000}$$

$$= \frac{\$95 \times 3.96}{\$10,000} = \frac{\$376.20}{\$10,000} = .0376, \text{ or } 3.76\%$$

Equation 3.5 can be used to convert a bank discount yield (BDY) to the *bond equivalent yield (BEY),* which (as noted earlier) is the annual percentage rate earned by purchasing the T-bill at its current price and holding it to maturity:

Equation 3.5

$$\text{Bond equivalent yield} = \frac{365 \times \text{bank discount yield}}{360 - \left(\begin{array}{c}\text{bank discount}\\\text{yield}\end{array} \times \begin{array}{c}\text{number of days}\\\text{to maturity}\end{array}\right)}$$

Equation 3.5a

$$BEY = \frac{365 \times BDY}{360 - (BDY \times n)}$$

Substituting the T-bill data into Equation 3.5, we get a bond equivalent yield of:

$$BEY = \frac{365 \times .0376}{360 - (.0376 \times 91)} = \frac{13.72}{356.58} = .0385, \text{ or } 3.85\%$$

Note that the 3.85 percent BEY is the same value calculated for the T-bill in Equation 3.3, which calculated BEY using the bond's price data rather than its bank discount yield (BDY). In this case, the T-bill which is quoted at an annualized bank discount yield (BDY) of 3.76 percent will provide the investor with a bond equivalent yield (BEY), or annual percentage rate of return, of 3.85 percent.

Evaluating T-bills. A particularly attractive feature of T-bills is that they are *exempt from state and local income taxes,* which in some areas can be as high as 20 percent. Like CDs and commercial paper, there are *no* (federal) taxes due until the interest is actually received at maturity. Because they are issued by the U.S. Treasury, T-bills are regarded as the safest but generally lowest-yielding of all investments. Furthermore there is a highly active secondary market for Treasury bills, so they can easily be sold if the investor needs the cash.

Series EE Savings Bonds

Series EE savings bonds are the well-known savings bonds that have been available for decades. (First issued in 1941, they used to be called Series E bonds.) EE bonds are often purchased through payroll deduction plans. Although issued by the U.S. Treasury, they are quite different from T-bills. In fact, perhaps their only similarity to the latter is that they are sold on a discount basis and are also exempt from state and local income taxes. These bonds are **accrual-type securities,** which means that interest is paid when the bond is cashed, on or before maturity, rather than periodically over the life of the bond. (The government does make Series HH bonds available; these are issued at their full face value and pay interest semiannually at the current fixed rate of 6 percent. Series HH bonds can be obtained only through the exchange of Series E or Series EE bonds, have a 10-year maturity, and are available in denominations of $500 to $10,000.) Series EE bonds are backed by the full faith and credit of the U.S. government and can be replaced without charge in case of loss, theft, or destruction. They can be purchased at banks or other thrift institutions, or through payroll deduction plans. They are issued in denominations of $50 through $10,000. The purchase price of all denominations is 50 percent of the face amount. Thus a $100 bond will cost $50 and be worth $100 at maturity.

The actual maturity date on EE bonds is unspecified, since the issues pay a variable rate of interest. The higher the rate of interest being earned, the shorter the period of time it takes for the bond to accrue from its discounted purchase price to its maturity value. In an effort to make these securities more attractive to investors, all EE bonds held five years or longer currently receive interest at the higher of 6 percent or 85 percent of the average return on five-year Treasury securities, as calculated every six months in May and November. The yield, therefore, changes every six months in accordance with prevailing Treasury security yields, although it can never drop below a guaranteed minimum rate of 6 percent. The rate being quoted in early 1992 was 6.38 percent. Current rates on Series EE bonds can be obtained from your bank or simply by calling 1-800-487-2663 (1-800-4USBOND). EEs can be redeemed any time after the first six months. Those held for less than five years earn interest according to a fixed, graduated scale beginning at 4.16 percent for bonds held six months and rising gradually to not less than the 6 percent guaranteed minimum rate at five years.

Series EE savings bonds
savings bonds issued by the U.S. Treasury and sold at banks and through payroll deduction plans, in varying denominations, at 50% of face value; pay a variable rate of interest depending on the length of time held.

accrual-type securities
securities for which interest is paid when the bond is cashed, on or before maturity, rather than periodically over the life of the bond.

In addition to being exempt from state and local taxes, Series EE bonds provide their holders with an appealing tax twist. *Investors need not report the interest earned on federal tax returns until the bonds are redeemed.* Although interest can be reported annually (this might be done, for example, if the bonds are held in the name of a child who has limited interest income), most investors choose to defer it. In effect, this means the funds are being reinvested at an after-tax rate of no less than the guaranteed minimum rate of 6 percent. What's more, it is even possible to defer the tax shelter *beyond* the redemption date of your Series EE bond. You can extend your tax shelter if, instead of cashing in the bonds, you exchange them for Series HH bonds. The accumulated interest on the Series EE bonds remains free of federal income tax for a while longer, since you will not have to pay the tax on those interest earnings until the HH bonds reach maturity (10 years) or until you cash *them* in. Thus in contrast to their predecessors, not only do today's Series EE bonds represent a safe and secure form of investment, but also they provide highly competitive yields and offer attractive tax incentives. Another attractive tax feature allows complete tax avoidance of EE bond earnings when proceeds are used to pay education expenses, such as college, by married couples with less than $62,900 of adjusted gross income, $41,950 or less for single filers (in 1992).

Investment Suitability

The accounts and securities discussed above are widely used by individuals as both savings and investment vehicles. They are used to build up or maintain a desired level of *savings* to meet unforeseen emergencies or for major expenditures that will or are likely to occur in the future. Whatever the reason, savings are viewed chiefly as a means of accumulating funds that will be readily available when and if the need arises—in essence, to provide safety and security. In this case high yield is less important than safety, liquidity, and convenience. Passbook savings accounts, NOW accounts, and Series EE savings bonds are popular savings vehicles. To a lesser extent so are money market deposit accounts, money funds, central asset accounts, CDs, commercial paper, banker's acceptances, and T-bills.

Yield is often just as important as liquidity when these vehicles are used for *investment* purposes. However, because the objective is different, the securities tend to be used much more aggressively than in savings programs. Most investors will hold at least a part of their portfolio in short-term, highly liquid securities, if for no other reason than to be able to act on unanticipated investment opportunities. Some investors, in fact, may as a matter of practice devote all or most of their portfolios to such securities in the belief that these investments provide attractive rates of return for the risk, because they are unfamiliar with other investment vehicles, or simply because they do not wish to devote the time necessary to managing their portfolios. One of the most common uses of short-term securities as investment vehicles is to employ them as temporary outlets. This is done for two reasons: either until an attractive permanent investment can be found, or as a temporary holding place in times of unsettled or undesirable market conditions. For example, an investor who has just sold some stock but does not have a suitable long-term investment alternative might place the proceeds in a money fund until he finds a more permanent use for them. Or, an investor who feels that interest rates are about to rise sharply sells her long-term bonds and uses the proceeds to buy T-bills. The high-yielding securities—like MMDAs, money funds, CDs, commercial paper, and banker's acceptances—are generally preferred for use as part of an investment program, as are the central asset accounts at major brokerage houses.

Deciding which securities are most appropriate for a particular situation requires consideration of such issue characteristics as availability, safety, liquidity, and yield. Although all the investments we have discussed satisfy the basic liquidity demand, they do so to varying degrees. A NOW account is unquestionably the most liquid of all, since you can write as many checks as you wish and for any amount. A certificate of deposit, on the other hand, is not as liquid, since early redemption involves an interest penalty. Table 3.5 summarizes the key characteristics for most of the short-term investments discussed here. The letter grade assigned the investments for each characteristic reflects an estimate of the investment's quality in that area. For example, MMMFs received only a B+ on liquidity, since withdrawals usually require a minimum of $500. NOW accounts, on the other hand, are judged somewhat better in this respect, since a withdrawal can be for any amount. Yields are self-explanatory, although you should note that as an investment scores lower on availability, safety, or liquidity, it will generally offer a higher yield.

TABLE 3.5 A Scorecard for Short-Term Accounts and Securities

Savings or Investment Vehicle	Availability	Safety	Liquidity	Yield (Average Rate)*
Passbook savings account	A+	A+	A	F (3.0%)
NOW account	A−	A+	A+	C− (3.2%)
Money market deposit account (MMDA)	B	A+	A	B− (3.4%)
Money market mutual fund (MMMF): standard and government security funds	B	A/A+	B+	A (4.5%)
Central asset account	B−	A	A+	B− (3.4%)
Certificate of deposit (3-month, large denomination)	B	A+	C	A (4.0%)
Commercial paper (90-day)	B−	A−	C	A (4.1%)
Banker's acceptance (90-day)	B−	A	B	A− (3.9%)
U.S. Treasury Bill (91-day)	B−	A++	A−	A− (3.8%)
Series EE savings bond	A+	A++	C−	B+ (6.4%)

*The average rates reflect representative or typical rates that existed in early 1992.

SUMMARY

1. Investment information, descriptive or analytical, can be classified as economic and current events; industry and company; alternative investment vehicles; price information; and personal investment strategies. It can be obtained from financial journals, newspapers, business periodicals, special subscription services, stockholders' reports, brokerage firms, and expert advisors.

2. News/retrieval and databases provide PC-based access to both current and historical investment information. There are a variety of different types of investment advisors. They charge an annual fee ranging from .25 percent to 2 percent of the amount being managed and are often regulated by federal and state law. Investment clubs are used by individual investors to obtain investment advice and experience.

3. Investors commonly rely on stock market averages and indexes to stay abreast of market behavior. The most cited averages are the Dow Jones, which includes the Dow Jones Industrial Average (DJIA). Other popular averages and indexes are Standard & Poor's, the NYSE index, the AMEX index, the Nasdaq indexes, and the Value Line indexes.

     Bond market indicators are most often reported in terms of average bond yields and average prices. The Dow Jones bond averages are among the most popular. Both stock and bond market statistics are published daily in *The Wall Street Journal* and summarized weekly in *Barron's*. *Money* magazine's Small Investor Index provides the individual investor with a standard that can be used to assess his or her portfolio.

4. Investment goals determine the types of investments made. Common investment goals include (1) accumulating retirement funds; (2) enhancing current income; (3) saving for major expenditures; and (4) sheltering income from taxes.

     Provision for adequate life insurance is an important prerequisite to investment planning. Life insurance may be bought in any of four basic forms: term; whole life; universal; and variable life insurance. The tax consequences associated with various investment vehicles and strategies must also be considered. The key dimensions are ordinary income, capital gains and losses, and tax shelters and tax planning.

5. Investment plans should first consider any known benefits as well as available funds, to determine the level of annual investment required to meet each goal. The actual investment vehicles selected will be affected by both economic/market cycles and the investor's stage in the life cycle.

6. Investment goals and plans should provide adequate liquidity, which can be met by holding a variety of short-term securities. These securities can earn interest at a stated rate or on a discount basis. They carry a low risk; the primary risk results from a potential loss in purchasing power. Numerous short-term investment vehicles are available from banks, brokerage firms, and the government. Their suitability depends on the investor's attitude toward availability, safety, liquidity, and yield.

QUESTIONS

1. Define and differentiate between descriptive and analytical information. How might one logically assess whether the acquisition of investment information or advice is economically justified?

2. What popular financial business periodicals would you use to follow the financial news? General news? Business news?

3. Briefly describe the following sources of company information and indicate the types of information they provide:

    a. Stockholder's report.
    b. Comparative data sources.
    c. Standard & Poor's *Stock Reports*.
    d. Moody's *Handbook of Common Stocks*.

4. List and briefly describe the subscription services and types of information available from:

    a. Standard & Poor's Corporation.
    b. Moody's Investor Services.
    c. *Value Line Investment Survey*.

5. Briefly describe the content and source of each of the following types of information:

    a. Prospectuses.
    b. Back-office brokerage research.
    c. Investment letters.
    d. Price quotations.

6. What role do news/retrieval and databases play in the use of personal computers by many professional and individual investors?

7. Who are professional investment advisors? Describe the services they perform, how they are regulated, and the cost of investment advice.

8. What is an investment club? What benefits does it offer the small investor?

9. Describe the basic philosophy and use of stock market average and indexes. Explain how the behavior of an average or index can be used to classify general market conditions as bull or bear.

10. List each of the major averages or indexes prepared by (a) Dow Jones and Company and (b) Standard & Poor's Corporation. Indicate the number and source of the securities used in calculating each average or index.

11. Briefly describe the composition and general thrust of each of the following indexes:

    a. New York Stock Exchange indexes.
    b. American Stock Exchange index.
    c. Nasdaq indexes.
    d. Value Line composite index.
    e. *Money's* Small Investor Index.

12. Discuss each of the following as they relate to assessing bond market conditions:

    a. Bond yields.
    b. Dow Jones bond averages.
    c. New York Stock Exchange bond statistics.

13. What are investment goals? Briefly describe each of the following commonly cited investment goals:

   a. Accumulating retirement funds.
   b. Enhancing current income.
   c. Saving for major expenditures.
   d. Sheltering income from taxes.

14. Why is insurance an important prerequisite to investment planning? Briefly define and differentiate among the following types of life insurance. Describe the basic motives that should underlie the use of each of these forms.

   a. Term insurance.
   b. Whole life insurance.
   c. Universal life insurance.
   d. Variable life insurance.

15. Define, differentiate, and explain how the following items relate to federal income taxes.

   a. Active (ordinary "earned") income.
   b. Portfolio (investment) and passive income.
   c. Capital gains.
   d. Capital loss.
   e. Tax shelters.
   f. Tax planning.

16. Explain how one should go about preparing an investment plan that provides for achievement of a given investment goal. Be sure to explain how existing investments or retirement benefits and current investable balances can be important factors to consider when estimating the amount of annual income that must be invested to achieve the goal. Comment on the role that monitoring an investment plan plays in the total investment program.

17. Describe the four stages of the economic/market cycle, and discuss the impact of this cycle on each of the following forms of investment:

   a. Stocks.
   b. Bonds.

18. Describe the differing investment philosophies typically observed during each of the following stages of an investor's life cycle:

   a. Youth (age 20 to 45).
   b. Middle-age (age 45 to 60).
   c. Retirement years (age 60 on).

19. What makes an asset liquid? Why hold liquid assets? Would 100 shares of IBM stock be considered a liquid investment? Explain.

20. Explain the characteristics of short-term investments with respect to both purchasing power and default risk.

21. Complete the following table for the short-term investments listed. Find their yields in a current issue of *The Wall Street Journal*.

Investment	Insured	Yield	Minimum Balance	Method and Ease of Withdrawing Funds
a. Passbook savings account	Yes		None	In person or through teller machines; very easy
b. NOW account				Unlimited check-writing privileges
c. Money market deposit account (MMDA)				
d. Money market mutual fund (MMMF)				
e. Central asset account				
f. Certificate of deposit (CD)				
g. Commercial paper				
h. Banker's acceptance				
i. U.S. Treasury bill				
j. Series EE savings bond			Virtually none	

PROBLEMS

1. Bill Shaffer estimates that if he does 10 hours of research using data that will cost $75, there is a good chance that he can improve his expected return on a $10,000 one-year investment from 8 percent to 10 percent. Bill feels that he must earn at least $10 per hour on the time that he devotes to his research.

a. Find the cost of Bill's research.
b. By how much (in dollars) will Bill's return increase as a result of the research?
c. On a strict economic basis, should Bill perform the proposed research?

2. Imagine the Mini-Dow Average (MDA) is based on the closing prices of five stocks. The divisor used in the calculation of the MDA is currently .765. The closing prices for each of the five stocks in the MDA today and exactly one year ago when the divisor was .790 are as follows:

Stock	Closing Stock Price	
	Today	One Year Ago
Ace Computers	$ 65	$74
Coburn Motor Company	37	34
National Soap & Cosmetics	110	96
Ronto Foods	73	72
Wings Aircraft	96	87

a. Calculate the MDA both today and one year ago.

b. Compare the values of the MDA calculated in (a) and describe the apparent market behavior over the last year. Was it a *bull* or a *bear* market?

3. The SP-6 index (a fictitious index) is used by many investors to monitor the general behavior of the stock market. It has a base value set equal to 100 on January 1, 1970. The closing market values for each of the six stocks included in the index are given below for three dates.

Stock	Closing Market Value of Stock (Thousands)		
	June 30, 1993	**January 1, 1993**	**January 1, 1970**
1	$ 430	$ 460	$240
2	1,150	1,120	630
3	980	990	450
4	360	420	150
5	650	700	320
6	290	320	80

a. Calculate the value of the SP-6 index both on January 1, 1993, and June 30, 1993, using the data presented above.

b. Compare the values of the SP-6 index calculated in (a) and relate them to the base index value. Would you describe the general market condition during the six-month period January 1 to June 30, 1993, as a *bull* or a *bear* market?

4. Carla Sanchez wishes to develop an average or index that can be used to measure the general behavior of stock prices over time. In this regard she has decided to include six closely followed high-quality stocks in the average or index. She plans to use August 15, 1975, as the base, and is interested in measuring the value of the average or index on August 15, 1990, and August 15, 1993. She has found the closing prices for each of the six stocks, A through F, at each of the three dates and has calculated a divisor that can be used to adjust for any stock splits, company changes, etc., that have occurred since the base year, which has a divisor equal to 1.00.

Stock	Closing Stock Price		
	August 15, 1993	**August 15, 1990**	**August 15, 1975**
A	$46	$40	$50
B	37	36	10
C	20	23	7
D	59	61	26
E	82	70	45
F	32	30	32
Divisor	.70	.72	1.00

Note: The number of shares of each stock outstanding has remained unchanged at each of the three dates. Therefore the closing stock prices will behave identically to the closing market values.

a. Using the data given above, calculate the market average, using the same methodology used to calculate the Dow averages, at each of the three dates—the fifteenth of August 1975, 1990, and 1993.

b. Using the data given above and assuming a base index value of 10 on August 15, 1975, calculate the market index, using the same methodology used to calculate the S&P indexes, at each of the three dates.

c. Use your findings in (a) and (b) to describe the general market condition—bull or bear—that existed between August 15, 1990, and August 15, 1993.

d. Calculate the percentage changes in the average and index values between August 15, 1990, and August 15, 1993. Why do they differ?

5. During 1991 the Allens and the Zells both filed joint tax returns. The Allens' taxable income was $130,000, and the Zells had total taxable income of $65,000 for the tax year ended December 31, 1991.

a. Using the federal tax rates given in Table 3.4, calculate the taxes for both the Allens and the Zells.

b. Calculate and compare the ratio of the Allens'-to-the-Zells' taxable income and the ratio of the Allens'-to-the-Zells' taxes. What does this demonstrate about the federal income tax structure?

6. Sonia Gomez, a 45-year-old widow, wishes to accumulate $250,000 over the next 15 years in order to supplement her retirement programs that are being funded by her employer and the federal government. She expects to earn an average annual return of about 8 percent by investing in a low-risk portfolio containing about 20 percent short-term investments, 50 percent bonds, and 30 percent common stock.

Sonia currently has $31,500 that at an 8 percent annual rate of return will grow to about $100,000 at the end of 15 years (found using time-value techniques that will be described in Chapter 4). Her financial advisor indicated that for every $1,000 Sonia wishes to accumulate at the end of 15 years, she will have to make an annual investment of $36.83. (This amount is also calculated based upon an 8 percent annual rate of return using the time-value techniques that are described in Chapter 4.) Sonia plans to accumulate needed funds by making equal, annual, end-of-year investments over the next 15 years.

a. How much money does Sonia need to accumulate by making equal, annual, end-of-year investments in order to reach her goal of $250,000?

b. How much must Sonia deposit annually in order to accumulate at the end of year 15 the sum calculated in (a) above?

7. A short-term investment vehicle with a $10,000 redemption value and 182 days to maturity can be purchased at its current price of $9,700.

a. Use Equation 3.3 to find the security's bond equivalent yield (BEY).

b. What effect would a drop in the current price to $9,600 have on the BEY calculated in (a)? Why?

8. A Treasury bill (T-bill) with a $10,000 redemption value and 91 days to maturity can currently be purchased for $9,800.

a. Use Equation 3.4 to find the T-bill's bank discount yield (BDY).

b. What effect would the fact that the T-bill has 182 days to maturity have on the BDY calculated in (a)? Why?

9. Chaim Begin is considering the purchase of a Treasury bill that has a bank discount yield (BDY) of 5.74 percent and has 182 days until it matures to its $10,000 redemption value.

   a. Use Equation 3.5 to find the bond equivalent yield (BEY) of this T-bill.
   b. What effect would a drop in the BDY to 5.10 percent have on the BEY calculated in (a)? Why?

 10. The O'Sheas are considering a short-term investment that has a redemption value of $50,000 at the end of 120 days. The investment can be purchased at a current price of $48,700.

   a. Use Equation 3.3 to find the bond equivalent yield (BEY) on the O'Shea's proposed investment.
   b. Use Equation 3.4 to find the bank discount yield (BDY) on the proposed investment.
   c. Use Equation 3.5 to convert the bank discount yield (BDY) found in (a) to a bond equivalent yield (BEY).
   d. Compare the comment on the values for BEY found in (a) and (c).

CFA QUESTION   (This question is from the 1986 Level I Exam.)

CFA

The investment manager of a corporate pension fund has purchased a U.S. Treasury bill with 180 days to maturity at a price of $9,600 per $10,000 face value. He has computed the discount yield at 8%.

a. Calculate the bond equivalent yield for the Treasury bill. Show calculations.
b. Briefly state why a Treasury bill's bond equivalent yield differs from its discount yield.

(See Appendix C for Guideline Answer to this question.)

CASE PROBLEMS

3.1   A Rich Uncle—The Perezes' Good Fortune

Angel and Marie Perez own a small pool hall located in southern New Jersey. They enjoy running the business, which they have owned for nearly three years. Angel, a retired professional pool shooter, saved for nearly 10 years to buy this business, which he and his wife own free and clear. The income from the pool hall is adequate to allow Angel, Marie, and their two children, Mary (age 10) and José (age 4), to live comfortably. Although lacking any formal education beyond the tenth grade, Angel has become an avid reader. He enjoys reading about current events and consumer affairs. He especially likes *Consumer Reports,* from which he has gained numerous insights for making various purchase transactions. Because of the long hours required to run the business, Angel can devote three to four hours a day (on the job) to reading.

Recently Angel and Marie were notified that Marie's uncle had died and left them a portfolio of stocks and bonds having a current market value of $300,000. They were elated to learn of their good fortune, but decided it would be best not to change their life style as a result of this inheritance. Instead, they wanted their new-found wealth to provide for their children's college education as well as their own retirement. They decided that like their uncle, they would keep these funds invested in stocks and bonds. Angel felt that in view of this, he needed to acquaint himself with the securities currently in the portfolio. He knew that if he were to manage the portfolio himself, he would have to stay abreast of the securities markets as well as the economy in general. He also realized he would need to follow each security in the portfolio and continuously evaluate possible alternative securities which could be substituted as conditions warrant. Because Angel had plenty of time in which to follow the market, he strongly believed that with proper information, he could manage the portfolio. Because of the amount of money involved, Angel was not too concerned with the information costs; rather, he wanted the best information he could get at a reasonable price.

Questions

1. Explain what role *The Wall Street Journal* and/or *Barron's* might play in fulfilling Angel's needs. What other general sources of economic and current event information might you recommend to Angel? Explain.

2. How might Angel be able to use the services of Standard & Poor's Corporation, Moody's Investors Services, and *Value Line Investment Survey* in order to acquaint himself with securities in the portfolio? Indicate which, if any, of these services you would recommend, and why.

3. Explain to Angel the need to find a good stockbroker and the role the stockbroker could play in providing information and advice.

4. Describe the services and sources of investment advice available to Angel. Would you recommend that he hire an advisor to manage the portfolio? Explain the potential costs and benefits of such an alternative.

5. Give Angel a summary prescription for obtaining information and advice that will help to ensure the preservation and growth of their family's new-found wealth.

3.2 Preparing Carolyn Bowen's Investment Plan

Carolyn Bowen, who just turned 55, is a widow currently employed as a receptionist for the Xcon Corporation, where she has worked for the past 20 years. She is in good health, lives alone, and has two grown children. A few months ago her husband, who was an alcoholic, died of liver disease. Although at one time a highly successful automobile dealer, Carolyn's husband has left her with only their home and the proceeds from a $50,000 life insurance policy. After paying medical and funeral expenses, $30,000 of the life insurance proceeds remained. In addition to the life insurance proceeds, Carolyn has $25,000 in a savings account, which she had secretly built over the past ten years. Recognizing that she is within ten years of retirement, Carolyn wishes to use her limited resources to develop an investment program that will allow her to live comfortably once she retires.

Carolyn is quite superstitious. After consulting with a number of psychics and studying her family tree, she feels certain she will not live past 80. She plans to retire at either 62 or 65, whichever will better allow her to meet her long-run financial goals. After talking with a number of knowledgable individuals—including, of course, the psychics—Carolyn estimates that to live comfortably, she will need $30,000 per year before taxes once she retires. This amount will be required annually for each of 18 years if she retires at 62 or for each of 15 years if she retires at 65. As part of her financial plans, Carolyn intends to sell her home at retirement and rent an apartment. She has estimated that she will net $75,000 if she sells the house at 62 and $85,000 if she sells it at 65. Carolyn has no financial dependents and is not concerned about leaving a sizable estate to her heirs.

If Carolyn retires at age 62, she will receive from social security and an employer-sponsored pension plan a total of $906 per month ($10,872 annually); if she waits until age 65 to retire, her total retirement income would be $1,125 per month ($13,500 annually). For convenience, Carolyn has already decided that in order to convert all her assets at the time of retirement into a stream of annual income, she will at that time purchase an annuity by paying a single premium. The annuity will have a life just equal to the number of years remaining until her eightieth birthday. Because Carolyn is uncertain as to the actual age at which she will retire, she obtained the following interest factors from her insurance agent in order to estimate the annual annuity benefit provided for a given purchase price.

Life of Annuity	Interest Factor
15 years	11.118
18 years	12.659

By dividing the factors into the purchase price, the yearly annuity benefit can be calculated. Carolyn plans to place any funds currently available into a savings account paying 6 percent compounded annually until retirement. She does not expect to be able to save or invest any additional funds between now and retirement. In order to calculate the future value of her savings, she will need to multiply the amount of money currently available to her by one of the following factors, depending upon the retirement age being considered.

Retirement Age	Time to Retirement	Future-Value Interest Factor
62	7 years	1.504
65	10 years	1.791

Questions

1. By placing currently available funds in the savings account, determine the amount of money Carolyn will have available at retirement once she sells her house if she retires at (a) age 62 and (b) age 65.
2. Using the results from question 1 and the interest factors given above, determine the level of annual income that will be provided to Carolyn through purchase of an annuity at (a) age 62 and (b) age 65.
3. With the results found in the preceding questions, determine the total annual retirement income Carolyn will have if she retires at (a) age 62 and (b) age 65.
4. From your findings, do you think Carolyn will be able to achieve her long-run financial goal by retiring at (a) age 62 and (b) age 65? Explain.
5. Evaluate Carolyn's investment plan in terms of her use of a savings account and an annuity rather than some other investment vehicles. Comment on the risk and return characteristics of her plan. What recommendations might you offer Carolyn? Be specific.

4 Measuring Investment Return and Risk

After studying this chapter, you should be able to:

1. Understand the concept, components, and importance of return and the forces that affect the investor's level of return.

2. Discuss the time value of money and the calculations involved in finding the future value of various types of cash flows.

3. Explain the concept of present value, the procedures for calculating present values, and the use of present value in determining a satisfactory investment.

4. Describe real, risk-free, and required returns, and the computation and application of holding period return, yield (internal rate of return), approximate yield, and growth rates.

5. Discuss risk, its relationship to return, the basic types of risk, and the major sources of risk.

6. Gain an appreciation of beta and the capital asset pricing model (CAPM), and the structure they provide for evaluating the risk-return characteristics of alternative investment vehicles.

When buying goods and services, most people have preconceived notions of value. For relatively inexpensive goods and services they will pay the marked or quoted price if it falls within the range of their preconceived notion. For instance, most people are willing to pay $0.45 to $0.75, and possibly $1.00, for a cup of coffee. But at prices in excess of $1.00 they are likely to decide to either make their own coffee, forgo it altogether, or switch to another beverage. In the purchase of more expensive items, considerations of price and value become more important. For example, most people when shopping for a used car will be unwilling to pay more than its ''book value'' as reflected in a widely circulated and respected used car price guide. It is unlikely you would be willing to pay, say, $9,500 for a used car that for its age, mileage, and condition has a book value of $8,750. The value of a good or service to individuals largely depends on the satisfaction they expect to receive from it. Because price and value are not necessarily the same, an economically rational individual would endeavor never to pay a price in excess of value. When making investment decisions, the same logic should apply in an even stricter sense.

An investment can be viewed as a financial commodity. The price is determined by the interaction of supply and demand which result from two key characteristics—return and risk. Although an investment's lack of physical qualities tends to complicate the valuation process, keep in mind that just as a physical commodity, such as an automobile, has certain characteristics (age, mileage, condition), so does an investment vehicle. The key characteristics of an investment are return and risk; together they determine its value. An understanding of these dimensions, their measurement, and their linkage to value is an important prerequisite to making wise investment decisions. In this chapter we consider return and risk; in subsequent chapters we consider the use of these factors to value specific investment vehicles. Here we first look at the concept of return.

THE CONCEPT OF RETURN

return
the expected level of profit from an investment; the reward for investing.

Investors are motivated to invest in a given vehicle by its expected return. **Return** can be seen as the reward for investing. Suppose, for example, you have $1,000 in a savings account paying 5 percent annual interest, and a business associate has asked you to lend her that much money. If you lend her the money for one year, at the end of which she pays you back, your return would depend on the amount of interest you charged. If you made an interest-free loan, your return would be zero. If you charged 5 percent interest, your return would be $50 (.05 × $1,000). Since you were already earning a safe 5 percent on the $1,000, it seems clear that you should charge your associate a minimum of 5 percent interest.

Some investment vehicles guarantee a return; others do not. For example, the $1,000 deposited in a savings account at a large bank can be viewed as a certain return. The $1,000 loan to your business associate might be less certain: What is your return if she runs into financial difficulty? Assume that she can repay you only $850. In this case, your return would be minus $150 ($850 − $1,000) or minus 15 percent ($150 ÷ $1,000). Thus the size of the expected return is one important factor in choosing a suitable investment.

Components of Return

The return on an investment may come from more than one source. The most common source is periodic payments such as interest or dividends. The other source of return is appreciation in value—the ability to sell an investment vehicle for more than its original purchase price. We will call these two sources of return *current income* and *capital gains (or losses)*.

Current Income

current income
cash or near-cash that is periodically received as a result of owning an investment.

Current income may take the form of interest received on bonds, dividends from stocks, rent received from real estate, and so on. To be considered income, it must be received in the form of cash or be readily convertible into cash. For our purposes, **current income** is cash or near-cash that is periodically received as a result of owning an investment.

Using the data in Table 4.1, we can calculate the current income from investments A and B—both purchased for $1,000—over a one-year period of ownership. Investment A would provide current income of $80; investment B would provide a $120 return. On the basis of the current income received over the one-year period, investment B seems preferable. Of course, the market value of the invested funds may have changed, so it would be premature to declare now which investment is better.

Capital Gains (or Losses)

The second dimension of return is concerned with the change, if any, in the market value of an investment. Investors pay a certain amount for an investment, from which they expect to receive not only current income but also the return of the invested funds sometime in the future. As noted in Chapter 3, the amount by which the proceeds from the sale of an investment exceed the original purchase price is called a *capital gain*. If an investment is sold for less than its original purchase price, a *capital loss* results.

TABLE 4.1 Profiles of Two Investments

	Investment	
	A	**B**
Purchase price (beginning of year)	$1,000	$1,000
Cash received		
1st quarter	$ 10	$ 0
2nd quarter	20	0
3rd quarter	20	0
4th quarter	30	120
Total (for year)	$ 80	$ 120
Sale price (end of year)	$1,100	$ 960

Let's calculate the capital gain or loss of investments A and B in Table 4.1. For investment A, a capital gain of $100 ($1,100 sale price − $1,000 purchase price) is realized over the one-year period. In the case of investment B, a $40 capital loss ($960 sale price − $1,000 purchase price) results. Combining the capital gains with the current income (calculated in the preceding section) gives the **total return** on each investment:

total return
the sum of the current income and the capital gains (or losses) earned on an investment over a specified period of time.

| | Investment | |
	A	B
Current income	$ 80	$120
Capital gain (loss)	100	(40)
Total return	$180	$ 80

In terms of the total return earned on the $1,000 investment over the one-year period, investment A is superior to investment B. Stated as a *percentage* of the initial investment, an 18 percent return ($180 ÷ $1,000) was earned on investment A, whereas B yielded only an 8 percent return ($80 ÷ $1,000). (The use of percentage returns is generally preferred over the use of dollar returns because percentages allow direct comparison of different sizes and types of investments.) Although at this point investment A appears preferable, differences in risk as well as certain tax factors might cause some investors to prefer B. (We will see why later in the chapter.)

Why Return Is Important

Return is a key variable in the investment decision: It allows us to compare the actual or expected gains provided by various investments with the levels of return required to justify them. For example, an investor would be satisfied with an investment that earns 12 percent if he or she requires it to earn only 10 percent. Return can be measured in a historical sense, or it can be used to formulate future expectations.

Historical Performance

Although most people recognize that future performance is not guaranteed by past performance, they would agree that past data often provide a meaningful basis for formulating future expectations. A common practice in the investment world is to look closely at the historical performance of a given vehicle when formulating expectations about its future. Because interest rates and other financial return measures are most often cited on an annual basis, evaluation of past investment returns is typically done on the same basis. Consider the data for a hypothetical investment presented in Table 4.2. Two aspects of this data are important: First, we can determine the average level of return generated by this investment over the past 10 years. Second, we can analyze the trend in this return. As a percentage, the average total return (column 6) over the past 10 years was 8.10 percent. Looking at the yearly returns, we can see that after the negative return in 1984, four years of positive and generally increasing returns occurred before the negative return was repeated in 1989. From 1990 through 1993 positive and increasing returns were again realized.

TABLE 4.2 Historical Investment Data for a Hypothetical Investment

		Market Value (Price)			Total Return	
Year	(1) Income	(2) Beginning of the Year	(3) End of the Year	(4) (3) − (2) Capital Gain	(5) (1) + (4) ($)	(6) (5) ÷ (2) (%)*
1984	$4.00	$100	$ 95	−$ 5.00	−$ 1.00	− 1.00%
1985	3.00	95	99	4.00	7.00	7.37
1986	4.00	99	105	6.00	10.00	10.10
1987	5.00	105	115	10.00	15.00	14.29
1988	5.00	115	125	10.00	15.00	12.00
1989	3.00	125	120	− 5.00	− 2.00	− 1.60
1990	3.00	120	122	2.00	5.00	4.17
1991	4.00	122	130	8.00	12.00	9.84
1992	5.00	130	140	10.00	15.00	11.54
1993	5.00	140	155	15.00	20.00	14.29
Average	$4.10			$ 5.50	$ 9.60	8.10%

*Percent return on beginning-of-year market value of investment.

Expected Return

In the final analysis when making investment decisions, it's the *future* that matters; *expected return* is a vital measure of performance. It's what you think the stock or bonds will earn in the future (in terms of current income and capital gains) that determines what you should be willing to pay for a security. To see how, let's return to the data in Table 4.2. Looking at the historical return figures in the table, an investor would note the increasing trend in returns from 1990 through 1993. But to project future returns, we need insights into the investment's prospects. If the trend in returns seems likely to continue, an expected return in the range of 12 to 15 percent for 1994 or 1995 would seem reasonable. On the other hand, if future prospects seem poor, or if the investment is subject to cycles, an expected return of 8 to 9 percent may be a more reasonable estimate. Over the past 10 years, the investment's returns have cycled from one poor year (1984 and 1989) to four years of increasing return (1985–1988 and 1990–1993). We might therefore expect low returns in 1994 to be followed by increasing returns in the 1995–1998 period.

Level of Return

The level of return achieved or expected from an investment will depend on a variety of factors. The key forces are internal characteristics and external forces.

Internal Characteristics

Certain characteristics of an investment affect its level of return. Examples include the type of investment vehicle, the quality of management, the way the investment is financed, and the customer base of the issue. For example, the common stock of a large, well-managed, completely equity-financed plastics manufacturer whose major customer is Apple Computer would be expected to provide a level of return different from that of a small, poorly managed, largely debt-financed, clothing manufacturer whose customers are small specialty stores. As we will see in later chapters, an assessment of internal factors and their impact on return is one important step in the process of analyzing potential investments.

External Forces

External forces such as war, shortages, price controls, Federal Reserve actions, and political events may also affect the level of return. None of these are under the control of the issuer of the investment vehicle. Because different investment vehicles are affected differently by these forces, it is not unusual to find two vehicles with similar internal characteristics offering significantly different returns. As a result of the same external force, the expected return from one vehicle may increase, while that of another may decrease.

inflation
a period of generally rising prices.

deflation
a period of generally declining prices.

Another external force is the general level of price changes, either up **(inflation)** or down **(deflation).** Inflation tends to have a favorable impact on certain types of investment vehicles, such as real estate, and a negative one on others, such as stocks and fixed-income securities. Rising interest rates, which normally accompany increasing rates of inflation, can significantly affect returns. Depending upon which actions, if any, are taken by the federal government to control inflation, its presence can increase, decrease, or have no effect on investment returns. Furthermore, the return on each *type* of investment vehicle exhibits its own unique response to inflation.

THE TIME VALUE OF MONEY*

time value of money
the principle that as long as an opportunity exists to earn interest, the value of money is affected by the point in time when it is expected to be received.

Imagine that at age 25 you begin making annual cash deposits of $1,000 into a savings account that pays 5 percent annual interest. After 40 years, at age 65, you would have made deposits totaling $40,000 (40 years × $1,000 per year). Assuming you have made no withdrawals, what do you think your account balance would be—$50,000? $75,000? $100,000? The answer is none of the above; your $40,000 would have grown to nearly $121,000! Why? Because the time value of money allowed the deposits to earn interest that was compounded over the 40 years. **Time value of money** refers to the fact that as long as an opportunity exists to earn interest, the value of money is affected by the point in time when it is expected to be received.

Because opportunities to earn interest on funds are readily available, *the sooner one receives a return on a given investment the better*. For example, two investments each requiring a $1,000 outlay and each expected to return $100 over a two-year holding period are *not* necessarily equally desirable. Assuming the base value of each investment remains at $1,000, if the first investment returns $100 at

*This section presents the fundamental concepts and techniques of time value of money. Those who have already mastered these important materials may wish to skip this discussion and continue at the heading "Determining a Satisfactory Investment" on page 139.

the end of the first year and the second investment returns the $100 at the end of the second, the first investment is preferable. This is so because the $100 interest earned by investment number 1 could be *reinvested to earn more interest* while the initial $100 from investment number 2 is still accruing. Thus time-value concepts should be considered when making investment decisions.

Interest: The Basic Return to Savers

A savings account at a bank is one of the most basic forms of investment. The saver receives interest in exchange for placing idle funds in an account. The saver will experience neither a capital gain nor loss, since the value of the investment (the initial deposit) will change only by the amount of interest earned. For the saver the interest earned over a given time frame is that period's current income.

Simple Interest

simple interest
interest paid only on the actual balance for the amount of time it is on deposit.

The income paid on such vehicles as certificates of deposit (CDs), bonds, and other forms of investment that pay interest is most often calculated using the **simple interest** method. Interest is paid only on the actual balance for the amount of time it is on deposit. If you have $100 on deposit in an account paying 6 percent interest for 1½ years, you would earn $9 in interest (1½ × .06 × $100) over this period. Had you withdrawn $50 at the end of half a year, the total interest earned over the 1½ years would be $6, since you would earn $3 interest on $100 for the first half year (½ × .06 × $100) and $3 interest on $50 for the next full year (1 × .06 × $50).

Using the simple interest method, the stated rate of interest is the *true rate of interest (or return)*. In the example above, the true rate of interest would be 6 percent. Because the interest rate reflects the rate at which current income is earned regardless of the size of the deposit, it is a useful measure of current income.

Compound Interest

compound interest
interest paid not only on the initial deposit but also on any interest accumulated from one period to the next.

Compound interest is paid not only on the initial deposit but also on any interest accumulated from one period to the next. This is the method usually used by savings institutions. The nearby Investor Insights box emphasizes the magic of compound interest. When interest is compounded annually, compound and simple interest calculations provide similar results; in this case the stated interest rate and the true interest rate would be equal. The data in Table 4.3 illustrate compound interest. In

TABLE 4.3 Savings Account Balance Data

(5% Interest Compounded Annually)

Date	(1) Deposit or (Withdrawal)	(2) Beginning Account Balance	(3) .05 × (2) Interest for Year	(4) (2) + (3) Ending Account Balance
1/1/92	$1,000	$1,000.00	$50.00	$1,050.00
1/1/93	(300)	750.00	37.50	787.50
1/1/94	1,000	1,787.50	89.38	1,876.88

INVESTOR INSIGHTS

The Magic of Compound Interest

John Maynard Keynes supposedly called it magic. One of the Rothschilds is said to have proclaimed it the eighth wonder of the world. Today people continue to extol its wonder and its glory.

The object of their affection: compound interest, a subject that bores or confuses as many people as it impresses.

Yet understanding compound interest can help people calculate the return on savings and investments, as well as the cost of borrowing. These calculations apply to almost any financial decision, from the reinvestment of dividends to the purchase of a zero-coupon bond for an individual retirement account.

Simply stated, compound interest is "interest on interest." Interest earned after a given period, for example, a year, is added to the principal amount and included in the next period's interest calculation. . . .

"With all the time you spend working, saving, borrowing and investing," says Richard P. Brief, a New York University business professor, "one could argue that the calculations (of compound interest) ought to be understood by most people. And it is within reach of most people."

The power of compound interest has intrigued people for years. Early in the last century, an English astronomer, Francis Baily, figured that a British penny invested at an annual compound interest of 5% at the birth of Christ would have yielded enough gold by 1810 to fill 357 million earths. Benjamin Franklin was more practical. At his death in 1790, he left 1,000 pounds each to the cities of Boston and Philadelphia on the condition they wouldn't touch the money for 100 years. Boston's bequest, which was equivalent to about $4,600, ballooned to $332,000 by 1890.

But savers and investors don't have to live to 100 to reap its benefits.

Consider an investment with a current value of $10,000 earning annual interest of 8%. After a year the investment grows to $10,800 (1.08 times $10,000). After the second year it's worth $11,664 (1.08 times $10,800). After three more years, the investment grows to $14,693.

The same concept applies to consumer borrowing. A $10,000 loan, with an 8% interest charge compounded annually, would cost $14,693 to repay in a lump sum after five years. . . .

Investors and savers can also take a rule-of-thumb shortcut to determine how long it would take to double a sum of money at a given interest rate with annual compounding: Divide 72 by the rate. For example, the $10,000 investment yielding 8% a year would double in about nine years (72 divided by eight).

But people should be aware that inflation compounds, too. Unless inflation disappears, that projected $20,000 investment nine years from now will be worth something less than that in today's dollars.

Source: Adapted from Robert L. Rose, "Compounding: It's Boring but a Wonder," *The Wall Street Journal*, June 17, 1985, p. 21. Reprinted by permission of *The Wall Street Journal*, © Dow Jones & Company, 1985. All rights reserved.

this case the interest earned each year is left on deposit rather than withdrawn. The $50 of interest earned on the $1,000 on deposit during 1992 becomes part of the balance on which interest is paid in 1993, and so on. *Note that the simple interest method is used in the compounding process;* that is, interest is paid only on the actual balance for the amount of time it is on deposit.

When compound interest is used, the stated and true interest rates are equal *only* when interest is compounded annually. In general, *the more frequently interest is compounded at a stated rate, the higher will be the true rate of interest*. The interest calculations for the deposit data in Table 4.3, assuming that interest is compounded semiannually (twice a year), are shown in Table 4.4. The interest for each six-month period is found by multiplying the balance for the six months by half of the stated 5 percent interest rate (see column 3 of Table 4.4). We can see that larger returns are associated with more frequent compounding: Compare the end of 1994 account balance of $1,876.88 (calculated in Table 4.3) at 5 percent compounded annually with the end of 1994 account balance of $1,879.19 (calculated in Table 4.4) at 5 percent compounded semiannually. Clearly, with semiannual compounding the true rate of interest is greater than the 5 percent rate associated with annual compounding. A summary of the true rates of interest associated with a 5 percent stated rate and various compounding periods is given in Table 4.5.

continuous compounding
interest calculation in which interest is compounded over the smallest possible interval of time.

Continuous compounding, which is compounding over the smallest possible interval of time, results in the maximum rate of return that can be achieved with a stated rate of interest. The data in Table 4.5 show that the more frequently interest is compounded, the higher the true rate of interest. Due to the impact that differences in compounding periods have on return, an investor should evaluate the true rate of interest associated with various alternatives prior to making a deposit.

Future Value: An Extension of Compounding

future value
the amount to which a current deposit will grow over a period of time when it is placed in an account paying compound interest.

Future value is the amount to which a current deposit will grow over a period of time when it is placed in an account paying compound interest. Consider a deposit of $1,000 that is earning 8 percent compounded annually. In order to find the future

TABLE 4.4 Savings Account Balance Data
(5% Interest Compounded Semiannually)

Date	(1) Deposit or (Withdrawal)	(2) Beginning Account Balance	(3) .05 × ½ × (2) Interest for Period (6 mo.)	(4) (2) + (3) Ending Account Balance
1/1/89	$1,000	$1,000.00	$25.00	$1,025.00
7/1/89		1,025.00	25.63	1,050.63
1/1/90	(300)	750.63	18.77	769.40
7/1/90		769.40	19.24	788.64
1/1/91	1,000	1,788.64	44.72	1,833.36
7/1/91		1,833.36	45.83	1,879.19

TABLE 4.5 True Rate of Interest for Various Compounding Periods

(5% Stated Rate of Interest)

Compounding Period	True Rate of Interest
Annually	5.000%
Semiannually	5.063
Quarterly	5.094
Monthly	5.120
Weekly	5.125
Continuously	5.127

value of this deposit at the end of one year, the following calculation would be made:

Equation 4.1

$$\text{Future value at end of year 1} = \$1,000 \times (1 + .08)$$

$$= \underline{\$1,080}$$

If the money were left on deposit for another year, 8 percent interest would be paid on the account balance of $1,080. Thus at the end of the second year there would be $1,166.40 in the account. This $1,166.40 would represent the beginning-of-year balance of $1,080 plus 8 percent of the $1,080 ($86.40) in interest. The future value at the end of the second year would be calculated as follows:

Equation 4.2

$$\text{Future value at end of year 2} = \$1,080 \times (1 + .08)$$

$$= \underline{\$1,166.40}$$

In order to find the future value of the $1,000 at the end of year *n*, the procedures illustrated above would have to be repeated *n* times. Because this process can be quite tedious, tables of future-value interest factors are available. A complete set of these tables is included in Appendix A, Table A.1; a portion of Table A.1 is shown in Table 4.6. The factors in the table represent the amount to which an initial $1 deposit would grow for various combinations of years and interest rates. For example, a dollar deposited in an account paying 8 percent interest and left there for two years would accumulate to $1.166. Using the future-value interest factor for 8 percent and 2 years (1.166), the future value of an investment (deposit) that can earn 8 percent over 2 years is found by *multiplying* the amount invested (or deposited) by the appropriate interest factor. In the case of $1,000 left on deposit for 2 years at 8 percent, the resulting future value is $1,166 (1.166 × $1,000), which agrees (except for a slight rounding difference) with the value calculated earlier.

A few points with respect to the future-value table should be highlighted. First, values in the table represent factors for determining the future value of one dollar at the *end* of the given year. Second, as the interest rate increases for any given year, the future-value interest factor also increases. Thus the higher the interest rate, the greater the future value. Third, note that for a given interest rate the future value of

TABLE 4.6 Future-Value Interest Factors for One Dollar

	Interest Rate					
Year	5%	6%	7%	8% ↓	9%	10%
1	1.050	1.060	1.070	1.080	1.090	1.100
→2	1.102	1.124	1.145	1.166	1.188	1.210
3	1.158	1.191	1.225	1.260	1.295	1.331
4	1.216	1.262	1.311	1.360	1.412	1.464
5	1.276	1.338	1.403	1.469	1.539	1.611
6	1.340	1.419	1.501	1.587	1.677	1.772
7	1.407	1.504	1.606	1.714	1.828	1.949
8	1.477	1.594	1.718	1.851	1.993	2.144
9	1.551	1.689	1.838	1.999	2.172	2.358
10	1.629	1.791	1.967	2.159	2.367	2.594

Note: All table values have been rounded to the nearest one-thousandth; thus, calculated values may differ slightly from the table values.

a dollar increases with the passage of time. Finally, it is also important to recognize that the future-value interest factor is always greater than 1. Only if the interest rate were zero would this factor equal 1, and the future value would therefore equal the initial deposit.

Future Value of an Annuity

annuity
a stream of equal cash flows that occur in equal intervals over time.

An **annuity** is a stream of equal cash flows that occur in equal intervals over time. Receiving $1,000 per year at the end of each of the next 10 years is an example of an annuity. The cash flows can be *inflows* of returns earned from an investment or *outflows* of funds invested (deposited) in order to earn future returns. Investors are sometimes interested in finding the future value of an annuity. Their concern is typically with what's called an *ordinary annuity*—one for which the cash flows occur at the *end* of each year. (We will concern ourselves only with this type of annuity.) Future value can be determined mathematically, using a financial calculator or computer, or using appropriate financial tables. Here we use tables of future-value interest factors for an annuity. A complete set of future-value interest tables for an annuity is included in Appendix A, Table A.2; a sample part of Table A.2 is shown in Table 4.7. The factors in the table represent the amount to which annual end-of-year deposits of $1 would grow for various combinations of years and interest rates. For example, a dollar deposited at the end of each year for eight years into an account paying 6 percent interest would accumulate to $9.897. Using the future-value interest factor for an eight-year annuity earning 6 percent (9.897), we can find the future value of this cash flow by *multiplying* the annual investment (deposit) by the appropriate interest factor. In the case of $1,000 deposited at the end of each year for 8 years at 6 percent, the resulting future value is $9,897 (9.897 × $1,000).

TABLE 4.7 Future-Value Interest Factors for a One Dollar Annuity

Year	Interest Rate					
	5%	6% ↓	7%	8%	9%	10%
1	1.000	1.000	1.000	1.000	1.000	1.000
2	2.050	2.060	2.070	2.080	2.090	2.100
3	3.152	3.184	3.215	3.246	3.278	3.310
4	4.310	4.375	4.440	4.506	4.573	4.641
5	5.526	5.637	5.751	5.867	5.985	6.105
6	6.802	6.975	7.153	7.336	7.523	7.716
7	8.142	8.394	8.654	8.923	9.200	9.487
→8	9.549	9.897	10.260	10.637	11.028	11.436
9	11.027	11.491	11.978	12.488	13.021	13.579
10	12.578	13.181	13.816	14.487	15.193	15.937

Note: All table values have been rounded to the nearest one-thousandth; thus calculated values may differ slightly from the table values.

Present Value: An Extension of Future Value

present value
the current value of a future sum; the inverse of *future value.*

Present value is the inverse of future value. That is, rather than measuring the value of a present amount at some future date, **present value** finds the current value of a future sum. By applying present-value techniques, we can calculate the value today of a sum to be received at some future date.

discount rate
the annual rate of return that could be earned currently on a similar investment; used when finding present value; also called *opportunity cost.*

When determining the present value of a future sum, the basic question being answered is: How much would have to be deposited today into an account paying y percent interest in order to equal a specified sum to be received so many years in the future? The applicable interest rate when finding present value is commonly called the **discount rate** (or *opportunity cost*). It represents the annual rate of return that could be earned currently on a similar investment. The basic present-value calculation is best illustrated using a simple example. Imagine that you are offered an opportunity that will provide you with exactly $1,000 one year from today. If you could earn 8 percent on similar types of investments, how much is the most you would pay for this opportunity? In other words, what is the present value of $1,000 to be received one year from now discounted at 8 percent? Letting x equal the present value, Equation 4.3 can be used to describe this situation:

Equation 4.3

$$x \times (1 + .08) = \$1,000$$

Solving Equation 4.3 for x, we get:

Equation 4.4

$$x = \frac{\$1,000}{(1 + .08)} = \underline{\underline{\$925.93}}$$

Thus, the present value of $1,000 to be received one year from now, discounted at 8 percent, is $925.93. In other words, $925.93 deposited today into an account paying 8 percent interest will accumulate to $1,000 in one year. To check this conclusion, *multiply* the future-value interest factor for 8 percent and one year, or 1.080 (from Table 4.6), by $925.93. The result is a future value of $1,000 (1.080 × $925.93).

The calculations involved in finding the present value of sums to be received in the distant future are more complex than for a one-year investment. Therefore the use of present-value tables is highly recommended. A complete set of these tables is included in Appendix A, Table A.3; a sample portion is given in Table 4.8. The factors in the table represent the present value of $1 associated with various combinations of years and discount rates. For example, the present value of $1 to be received one year from now discounted at 8 percent is $.926. Using this factor (.926), the present value of $1,000 to be received one year from now at an 8 percent discount rate can be found by *multiplying* it by $1,000. The resulting present value of $926 (.926 × $1,000) agrees (except for a slight rounding difference) with the value calculated earlier.

Another example may help clarify the use of present-value tables. The present value of $500 to be received seven years from now, discounted at 6 percent, would be calculated as follows:

$$\text{Present value} = .665 \times \$550 = \underline{\$332.50}$$

The .665 represents the present-value interest factor for seven years discounted at 6 percent.

A few points with respect to present value tables should be highlighted: First, the present-value interest factor for a single sum is always less than 1; only if the discount rate were zero would this factor equal 1. Second, the higher the discount rate for a given year, the smaller the present-value interest factor. In other words, the greater your opportunity cost, the less you have to invest today in order to have a given amount in the future. Third, the further in the future a sum is to be received, the less it is worth presently. Finally, remember that given a discount rate of 0

TABLE 4.8 Present-Value Interest Factors for One Dollar

Year	Discount (Interest) Rate					
	5%	6% ↓	7%	8% ↓	9%	10%
→1	.952	.943	.935	.926	.917	.909
2	.907	.890	.873	.857	.842	.826
3	.864	.840	.816	.794	.772	.751
4	.823	.792	.763	.735	.708	.683
5	.784	.747	.713	.681	.650	.621
6	.746	.705	.666	.630	.596	.564
→7	.711	.665	.623	.583	.547	.513
8	.677	.627	.582	.540	.502	.467
9	.645	.592	.544	.500	.460	.424
10	.614	.558	.508	.463	.422	.386

percent the present-value interest factor always equals 1; therefore, in such a case the future value of a sum equals its present value.

 ## The Present Value of a Stream of Income

In the material above we illustrated the technique for finding the present value of a single sum to be received at some future date. Because the returns from a given investment are likely to be received at various future dates rather than as a single lump sum, we need to be able to find the present value of a stream of returns. A stream of returns can be viewed as a package of single-sum returns; it may be classified as a mixed stream or an annuity. A **mixed stream** of returns is one that exhibits no special pattern. As noted earlier, an *annuity* is a pattern of equal returns. Table 4.9 illustrates each of these types of return patterns. In order to find the present value of each of these streams (measured at the beginning of 1993), we must calculate the total of the present values of all component returns. Because shortcuts can be used for an annuity, the calculation of the present value of each type of return stream will be illustrated separately.

mixed stream
a stream of returns that, unlike an annuity, exhibits no special pattern.

Mixed Stream

In order to find the present value of the mixed stream of returns given in Table 4.9, the present value of all of the returns must be found and then totaled. Assuming a 9 percent discount rate, the calculation of the present value of the mixed stream is shown in Table 4.10. The resulting present value of $187.77 represents the amount today (beginning of 1993) invested at 9 percent that would provide the same cash flows as the stream of returns in column 1 of Table 4.10. Once the present value of each return is found, the values can be added, since each is measured at the same point in time.

Annuity

The present value of an annuity can be found in the same way as the present value of a mixed stream. Fortunately there is also a simpler approach. Financial tables of present-value interest factors for annuities are available. A complete set of present-value interest factors for an annuity is included in Appendix A, Table A.4; a sample

TABLE 4.9 Mixed and Annuity Return Streams

| Year | Returns | |
	Mixed Stream	Annuity
1993	$30	$50
1994	40	50
1995	50	50
1996	60	50
1997	70	50

TABLE 4.10 Mixed-Stream Present-Value Calculation

Year	(1) Return	(2) 9% Present-Value Interest Factor	(3) (1) × (2) Present Value
1993	$30	.917	$ 27.51
1994	40	.842	33.68
1995	50	.772	38.60
1996	60	.708	42.48
1997	70	.650	45.50
		Present value of stream	$187.77

Note: Column (1) values are from Table 4.9. Column (2) values are from Table 4.8 for 9 percent discount rate and 1 through 5 years.

portion is given in Table 4.11 The factors in the table represent the present value of a one-dollar annuity associated with various combinations of years and discount rates. For example, the present value of $1 to be received at the end of each year for the next five years discounted at 9 percent is $3.890. Using this factor, the present value of the $50, five-year annuity (given in Table 4.9) at a 9 percent discount rate can be found by *multiplying* the annual return by the appropriate interest factor. The resulting present value is $194.50 (3.890 × $50).

Determining a Satisfactory Investment

The time value of money concept can be used to determine an acceptable investment. Ignoring risk at this point, a satisfactory investment would be one in which the present value of benefits (discounted at the appropriate rate) equals or exceeds

TABLE 4.11 Present-Value Interest Factors for a One-Dollar Annuity

Year	\ Discount (Interest) Rate 5%	6%	7%	8%	9% ↓	10%
1	.952	.943	.935	.926	.917	.909
2	1.859	1.833	1.808	1.783	1.759	1.736
3	2.723	2.673	2.624	2.577	2.531	2.487
4	3.546	3.465	3.387	3.312	3.240	3.170
→5	4.329	4.212	4.100	3.993	3.890	3.791
6	5.076	4.917	4.767	4.623	4.486	4.355
7	5.786	5.582	5.389	5.206	5.033	4.868
8	6.463	6.210	5.971	5.747	5.535	5.335
9	7.108	6.802	6.515	6.247	5.995	5.759
10	7.722	7.360	7.024	6.710	6.418	6.145

the present value of costs. Since the cost (or purchase price) of the investment would be incurred initially (at time zero), the cost and its present value are viewed as one and the same. If the present value of the benefits *just equals the cost,* an investor would earn a rate of return equal to the discount rate. If the present value of benefits *exceeds the cost,* the investor would earn more than the discount rate. If the present value of benefits were *less than the cost,* the investor would earn less than the discount rate. It should be clear that *an investor would therefore prefer only those investments for which the present value of benefits equals or exceeds cost.* In these cases the return would be equal to or greater than the discount rate.

The information in Table 4.12 can be used to illustrate how to apply present value to investment decision making. Assuming an 8 percent discount rate to be appropriate, we can see that the present value of the income to be received over the assumed seven-year period (1993–1999) is $1,175.28. If the cost of the investment were any amount less than or equal to $1,175.28, it would be acceptable; at a cost above $1,175.28, the investment would not be acceptable. At a cost of less than or equal to the $1,175.28 present value of income, a return equal to at least 8 percent would be earned; at a cost greater than $1,175.28, the return would be less than 8 percent.

MEASURING RETURN

Thus far we have discussed the concept of return in terms of its two components (current income and capital gains), its importance, and the key forces affecting the level of return (internal characteristics and external forces). These discussions intentionally oversimplified the computations usually involved in determining the historical or expected return. In order to compare returns from different investment vehicles, we need to apply a consistent measure. Such a measure must somehow incorporate time value of money concepts that explicitly consider differences in the timing of investment income and capital gains (or losses). It must also allow us to place a current value on future benefits. Here we will look at several measures that

TABLE 4.12 Present Value Applied to an Investment

Year	(1) Income	(2) 8% Present-Value Interest Factor	(3) (1) × (2) Present Value
1993	$ 90	.926	$ 83.34
1994	100	.857	85.70
1995	110	.794	87.34
1996	120	.735	88.20
1997	100	.681	68.10
1998	100	.630	63.00
1999	1,200	.583	699.60
		Present value of income	$1,175.28

required return
the rate of return an investor must earn on an investment in order to be fully compensated for its risk.

allow us to assess alternative investment outlets effectively. First we will define and consider the relationships among various rates of return.

Real, Risk-Free, and Required Returns

The **required return** on an investment is the rate of return an investor must earn in order to be fully compensated for its risk. To better understand the required returns upon which investors focus, it is helpful to consider their makeup. The required return on any investment i consists of three basic components—the real rate of return, an expected inflation premium, and a risk premium, as noted in Equation 4.5:

real rate of return
the rate of return that could be earned in a perfect world where all outcomes are known and certain.

Equation 4.5

Equation 4.5a

$$\begin{matrix} \text{Required return} \\ \text{on investment } i \end{matrix} = \begin{matrix} \text{real rate} \\ \text{of return} \end{matrix} + \begin{matrix} \text{expected inflation} \\ \text{premium} \end{matrix} + \begin{matrix} \text{risk premium} \\ \text{for investment } i \end{matrix}$$

$$r_i = r^* + IP + RP_i$$

The **real rate of return** is the rate of return that could be earned in a perfect world where all outcomes are known and certain—where there is no risk. In such a world the real rate of return would create an equilibrium between the supply of savings and the demand for funds. The real rate of return changes with changing economic conditions, tastes, and preferences. Historically it has been relatively stable and in the range of 2 to 3 percent. For convenience, we'll assume a real rate return of 3 percent. The **expected inflation premium** represents the average rate of inflation expected in the future. By adding the expected inflation premium to the real rate of return, we get the **risk-free rate**—the rate of return that can be earned on a risk-free investment, most commonly a U.S. Treasury bill. This rate is shown in Equation 4.6:

expected inflation premium
the average rate of inflation expected in the future.

risk-free rate
the rate of return that can be earned on a virtually risk-free investment.

Equation 4.6

Equation 4.6a

$$\begin{matrix} \text{Risk-free} \\ \text{rate} \end{matrix} = \begin{matrix} \text{real rate} \\ \text{of return} \end{matrix} + \begin{matrix} \text{expected inflation} \\ \text{premium} \end{matrix}$$

$$R_F = r^* + IP$$

To demonstrate, a real rate of return of 3 percent and an expected inflation premium of 4 percent would result in a risk-free rate of return of 7 percent (3% + 4%).

The required return can be found by adding to the risk-free rate a **risk premium,** which reflects the issue and issuer characteristics. The risk premium varies depending upon the specific issue and issuer characteristics. *Issue characteristics* refer to the type of vehicle (bond, stock, etc.), its maturity (2 years, 5 years, infinity, etc.), and its features (voting/nonvoting, callable/noncallable, etc.). *Issuer characteristics* refer to industry and company factors such as the line of business and financial condition of the issuer. Together these factors cause investors to require a risk premium above the risk-free rate.

risk premium
a return premium that reflects the issue and issuer characteristics associated with a given investment vehicle.

Substituting the risk-free rate, R_F, from Equation 4.6a, into Equation 4.5a for the first two terms to the right of the equal sign ($r^* + IP$), we get Equation 4.7:

Equation 4.7

Equation 4.7a

$$\begin{matrix} \text{Required return} \\ \text{of investment } i \end{matrix} = \begin{matrix} \text{risk-free} \\ \text{rate} \end{matrix} + \begin{matrix} \text{risk premium} \\ \text{for investment } i \end{matrix}$$

$$r_i = R_F + RP_i$$

For example, if the required return on IBM common stock is 12 percent when the risk-free rate is 7 percent, investors require a 5 percent risk premium (12% − 7%) as compensation for the risk associated with common stock (the issue) and IBM (the issuer). Later in this chapter, the relationship between the risk premium and required returns is further developed. Next we consider the specifics of return measurement.

Holding Period Return

The returns to a saver relate to the amount of current income (interest) earned on a given deposit. However, the amount "invested" in a savings account is not subject to change in value, as it is for investments such as stocks, bonds, and real estate. Because we are concerned with a broad range of investment vehicles, most of which have some degree of marketability, we need a measure of return that captures *both* periodic benefits and changes in value. One such measure is *holding period return*. The **holding period** is the period of time over which one wishes to measure the return on an investment vehicle. When making return comparisons, investors should use holding periods of the same length of time. For example, comparing the return on a stock over a six-month period ended December 31, 1992, with the return on a bond over a one-year holding period ended June 30, 1992, could result in a poor investment decision. To avoid this problem, the holding period should be defined and consistently applied or annualized to create a standard, and similar periods in time should be used when comparing the returns from alternative investment vehicles.

holding period
the period of time over which one wishes to measure the return on an investment vehicle.

Understanding Return Components

Earlier in this chapter we identified the two components of investment return: current income and capital gains (or losses). The portion of current income received by the investor during the period is a **realized return.** Most, but not all, current income is realized. For example, accrued interest on taxable zero-coupon bonds is treated as current income for tax purposes but is *not* a realized return until the bond is sold or matures. Capital gains returns are realized only when the investment vehicle is actually sold at the end of the holding period. Until the vehicle is sold, the capital gain is merely a **paper return.** For example, the capital gain return on an investment that increases in market value from $50 to $70 during a year is $20. To be realized, the investor would had to have sold the investment for $70 at the end of that year. The investor who purchased the same investment but plans to hold it for another three years would also have experienced the $20 capital gain return during the year specified, although he or she would not have *realized* the gain in terms of cash flow. However, *in spite of the fact that the capital gains return may not be realized during the period over which the total return is measured, it must be included in the return calculation.*

realized return
return received by an investor during the period.

paper return
a return that has been achieved, but not yet realized, by an investor during the period.

A second point to recognize about returns is that *both* the current income and the capital gains component can have a negative value. Occasionally an investment may have negative current income, which means that the investor may be required to pay

holding period return (HPR)
the total return earned from holding an investment for a specified holding period (usually one year or less).

out cash in order to meet certain obligations. This situation is most likely to occur in various types of property investments. For example, an investor may purchase an apartment complex, whose rental income due to poor occupancy may be inadequate to meet the payments associated with its operation. In such a case the investor would have to pay the deficit in operating costs, and such a payment would represent negative current income. A capital loss can occur on *any* investment vehicle: Stocks, bonds, options, commodities, gold, mutual funds, and real estate all can decline in market value over a given holding period.

Computing the Holding Period Return (HPR)

The **holding period return (HPR)** is the total return earned from holding an investment for a specified period of time (the holding period). *It is customarily used with holding periods of one year or less.* It represents the sum of current income and capital gains (or losses) achieved over the holding period, divided by the beginning investment value. The equation for HPR is as follows:

Equation 4.8

$$\text{Holding period return} = \frac{\begin{array}{c}\text{current income}\\\text{during period}\end{array} + \begin{array}{c}\text{capital gain (or loss)}\\\text{during period}\end{array}}{\text{beginning investment value}}$$

Equation 4.8a

$$HPR = \frac{C + CG}{V_0}$$

where

Equation 4.9

$$\begin{array}{c}\text{Capital gain (or loss)}\\\text{during period}\end{array} = \text{ending investment value} - \text{beginning investment value}$$

Equation 4.9a

$$CG = V_n - V_0$$

The HPR equation provides a convenient method for either measuring the total return realized or estimating the total return expected on a given investment. Table 4.13 summarizes the key financial variables for four investment vehicles over the past year. The total current income and capital gain or loss for each during the holding period are given in the lines labeled (1) and (3), respectively. The total return over the year is calculated, as shown in line (4), by adding these two sources of return. Dividing the total return value [line (4)] by the beginning-of-year investment value [line (2)], we find the holding period return, given in line (5). Over the one-year holding period the common stock had the highest HPR, 7.25 percent, and the savings account had the lowest, 6 percent. As these calculations show, all that is needed to find the HPR are beginning- and end-of-period investment values, along with the value of current income received by the investor during the period. Note that had the current income and capital gain (or loss) values in lines (1) and (3) of Table 4.13 been drawn from a six-month rather than a one-year period, the HPR values calculated in line (5) would be the *same*.

Holding period return can be negative or positive. HPRs can be calculated using either historical data (as in the preceding example) or forecast data. Regardless of whether historical or forecast data are used, the HPR formula in Equation 4.8 still applies.

TABLE 4.13 Key Financial Variables for Four Investment
Vehicles

	Investment Vehicle			
	Savings Account	Common Stock	Bond	Real Estate
Cash received				
1st quarter	$15	$10	$ 0	$0
2nd quarter	15	10	50	0
3rd quarter	15	10	0	0
4th quarter	15	15	50	0
(1) Total current income	$60	$45	$100	$0
Investment value				
End-of-year	$1,000	$2,100	$ 970	$3,200
(2) Beginning-of-year	1,000	2,000	1,000	3,000
(3) Capital gain (loss)	$ 0	$ 100	($ 30)	$ 200
(4) Total return [(1) + (3)]	$ 60	$ 145	$ 70	$ 200
(5) Holding period return [(4) ÷ (2)]	6.00%	7.25%	7.00%	6.67%

Using the HPR in Investment Decisions

The holding period return is easy to use in making investment decisions. Because it
considers both current income and capital gains relative to the beginning investment
value, it tends to overcome any problems that might be associated with comparing
investments of different size. If we look only at the total returns calculated for each
of the four investments in Table 4.13 [line (4)], the real estate investment appears
best since it has the highest total return. However, the real estate investment would
require the largest dollar outlay ($3,000). The holding period return offers a relative
comparison, by dividing the total return by the amount of the investment. Comparing HPRs, we find the investment alternative with the highest return per invested
dollar: the common stock's HPR of 7.25 percent. Since the return per invested
dollar reflects the efficiency of the investment, the HPR provides a logical method
for evaluating and comparing the investment returns.

Yield: The Internal Rate of Return

An alternative way to define a satisfactory investment is in terms of the compounded annual rate of return it earns. Why is an alternative measure to the HPR

**yield (internal rate
of return)**
the compounded
annual rate of return
earned by a long-
term investment.

needed? Because HPR fails to consider the time value of money. While the holding
period return is useful with investments held for one year or less, it is generally
inappropriate for longer holding periods. Sophisticated investors typically do not
use HPR when the time period is greater than one year. Instead, they use a present-
value-based measure, called **yield** or **internal rate of return,** to determine the

compounded annual rate of return on investments held for more than a year. The yield on an investment can also be defined as the discount rate that produces a present value of benefits just equal to its cost.

Once the yield has been determined, acceptability can be decided. If the yield on an investment is equal to or greater than the required return, the investment would be acceptable. An investment with a yield below the required return would be unacceptable: it fails to adequately compensate the investor for the risk involved.

The yield on an investment providing a single future cash flow is relatively easy to calculate, whereas the yield on an investment providing a stream of future cash flows generally involves more time-consuming calculations. Note that many hand-held calculators as well as computer software programs are available for simplifying these calculations.

For a Single Cash Flow

Some investments such as U.S. savings bonds, zero-coupon bonds, stocks paying no dividends, and gold are made by paying a fixed amount up front to purchase them. The investor expects them to provide *no* periodic income, but rather a single— hopefully, large—future cash flow at maturity or when the investment is sold. The yield on investments expected to provide a single future cash flow can be estimated using either future-value or present-value interest factors. Here we will use the present-value interest factors given in Appendix A, Table A.3. To illustrate the yield calculations, assume an investor wishes to find the yield on an investment costing $1,000 today and expected to be worth $1,400 at the end of a five-year holding period. We can find the yield on this investment by solving for the discount rate that causes the $1,400 to be received five years from now to equal the initial investment of $1,000. The first step involves dividing the present value ($1,000) by the future value ($1,400), which results in a value of .714. The second step is to find in the table of present-value interest factors the *five-year factor* that is closest to .714. Referring to the abbreviated present-value table (see Table 4.8), we find that for five years the factor closest to .714 is .713, which occurs at a 7 percent discount rate. Therefore the yield on this investment is approximately 7 percent. (The precise value found using a financial calculator is 6.96 percent.) If the investor requires a 6 percent return, this investment would be acceptable.

For a Stream of Income

Investment vehicles such as bonds, income-oriented stock, and income properties generally provide the investor with a stream of income. The yield for a stream of income is generally more difficult to estimate. The most accurate approach is based on searching for the discount rate that produces a present value of income just equal to the cost of the investment. If we use the investment in Table 4.12 and assume that its cost is $1,100, we find that the yield must be greater than 8 percent, since at an 8 percent discount rate the present value of income is greater than the cost ($1,175.28 vs. $1,100). The present values at both 9 percent and 10 percent discount rates are calculated in Table 4.14. If we look at the present value of income

TABLE 4.14 Yield Calculation for a $1,100 Investment

Year	(1) Income	(2) 9% Present-Value Interest Factor	(3) (1) × (2) Present Value at 9%	(4) 10% Present-Value Interest Factor	(5) (1) × (4) Present Value at 10%
1993	$ 90	.917	$ 82.53	.909	$ 81.81
1994	100	.842	84.20	.826	82.60
1995	110	.772	84.92	.751	82.61
1996	120	.708	84.96	.683	81.96
1997	100	.650	65.00	.621	62.10
1998	100	.596	59.60	.564	56.40
1999	1,200	.547	656.40	.513	615.60
Present value of income			$1,117.61		$1,063.08

calculated at the 9 and 10 percent rates ($1,117.61 and $1,063.08, respectively), we see that the yield on the investment must be somewhere between 9 and 10 percent. At 9 percent, the present value is too high, and at 10 percent it's too low. Somewhere in between we'll end up with a present value of $1,100. The discount rate that causes the present value of income to be closer to the $1,100 cost is 9 percent, since it is only $17.61 away from $1,100. At the 10 percent rate the present value of income is $39.62 away from the $1,100. (The precise value found using a financial calculator is 9.32 percent.) Thus if the investor requires an 8 percent return on the investment, it is clearly acceptable.

Interest-on-Interest: The Critical Assumption

The critical assumption underlying the use of yield as a return measure is an ability to earn a return equal to the yield on all income received from the investment during the holding period. This concept can be best illustrated using a simple example. Suppose you buy a $1,000 U.S. Treasury bond that pays 8 percent annual interest ($80) over its 20-year maturity. Each year you receive $80, and at maturity the $1,000 in principal is repaid. There is no loss in capital, no default; all payments are made right on time. But if you are unable to reinvest the $80 annual interest receipts, you end up earning only 5 percent—rather than 8 percent—on this investment. Figure 4.1, which shows the elements of return on this investment, can be used to demonstrate. If you *don't reinvest* the interest income of $80 per year, you'll end up on the 5 percent line; you'll have $2,600—the $1,000 principal plus $1,600 interest income (i.e., $80/year × 20 years)—at the end of 20 years. (The yield on a single cash flow of $1,000 today that will be worth $2,600 in 20 years is 5 percent.) In order to move to the 8 percent line you have to earn 8 percent on the annual interest receipts. If you do, you'll have $4,661—the $1,000 principal plus the $3,661 future value of the 20-year $80 annuity of interest receipts invested at 8 percent [i.e., $80/year × 45.762 (the 8%, 20-year factor from Table A.2)]—at the end of 20 years. (The yield on a single cash flow of $1,000 today that will be worth $4,661 in 20 years is 8 percent.) The future value of the investment would be

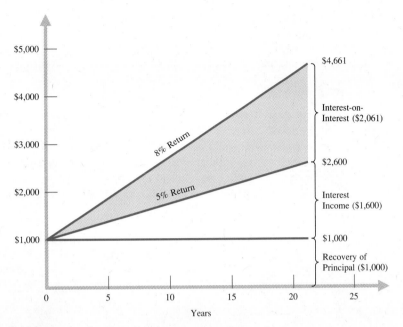

● FIGURE 4.1 Earning Interest-on-Interest

An investor in a $1,000, 20-year bond with an 8 percent coupon would have only $2,600 at the end of 20 years if he or she did not reinvest the $80 annual interest receipts—only a 5 percent rate of return. If the interest were reinvested at the 8 percent interest rate, the investor would have $4,661 at the end of 20 years—an 8 percent return. In order to achieve the calculated yield of 8 percent, the investor must therefore be able to earn interest-on-interest at that rate.

$2,061 greater (i.e., $4,661 − $2,600) by earning interest-on-interest than it would be without reinvestment of the interest receipts.

From this illustration it should be clear that since you started out with an 8 percent investment, you have to earn that same rate of return when reinvesting your income. The rate of return you start with, in effect, is the required, or minimum, reinvestment rate. By putting your current income to work at this rate you'll earn the rate of return you set out to. If you fail to do so, your return will decline accordingly. Even though a bond was used in this illustration, the same principle applies to any type of investment vehicle. It's just as relevant to common stocks, mutual funds, or T-bills as it is to long-term bonds. The notion of earning interest-on-interest is what the market refers to as a *fully compounded rate of return*. It's an important concept: You can't start reaping the full potential from your investments until you start earning a fully compounded return on your money.

As long as periodic investment income is involved, the reinvestment of that income and interest-on-interest are matters that have to be dealt with. In fact, *interest-on-interest is a particularly important element of return for investment programs that involve a lot of current income*. In contrast to capital gains, current income has to be reinvested by the individual investor. (With capital gains, the investment vehicle itself is automatically doing the reinvesting.) It follows, therefore, that for investment programs that lean toward income-oriented securities, interest-on-interest—and the continued reinvestment of income—plays an important role in defining the amount of investment success achieved.

Approximate Yield

For a given investment the *present value and the yield will provide the same conclusion with respect to acceptability.* It is clearly simpler to calculate present value as opposed to the yield, although many calculators provide the capability to find yields quickly. Even without a calculator it is possible to estimate the yield on an investment if the annual benefits are not radically different on a year-to-year basis. This estimate is made using the following *approximate yield formula:*

Equation 4.10

$$\text{Approximate yield} = \frac{\begin{array}{c}\text{average annual income} \\ \text{over investment horizon}\end{array} + \dfrac{\begin{array}{c}\text{ending} \\ \text{investment value}\end{array} - \begin{array}{c}\text{beginning} \\ \text{investment value}\end{array}}{\text{number of years in investment horizon}}}{\dfrac{\begin{array}{c}\text{ending} \\ \text{investment value}\end{array} + \begin{array}{c}\text{beginning} \\ \text{investment value}\end{array}}{2}}$$

Equation 4.10a

$$AY = \frac{\overline{C} + \dfrac{V_n - V_0}{n}}{\dfrac{V_n + V_0}{2}}$$

This formula can be applied to estimate the yield for both single cash flows and streams of income.

For a Single Cash Flow

Using our earlier example of the $1,000 investment that will be worth $1,400 in five years, we can demonstrate the approximate yield formula for a single cash flow. Since the investment involves a single future cash flow, the average annual income $(\overline{C})$ is zero. Substituting this value along with a future value (V_n) of $1,400, current cost (V_0) of $1,000, and an investment horizon (n) of 5 years into Equation 4.10a yield formula we get:

$$AY = \frac{\$0 + \dfrac{\$1,400 - \$1,000}{5}}{\dfrac{\$1,400 + \$1,000}{2}} = \frac{\$0 + \$80}{\$1,200} = \frac{\$80}{\$1,200}$$

$$= \underline{\underline{0.0667, \text{ or } 6.67\%}}$$

The approximate yield of 6.67 percent is reasonably close to the actual yield of 7 percent calculated earlier.

For a Stream of Income

We can use the data in Table 4.12 to illustrate the approximate yield formula for a stream of income. Suppose that in the year 1999 the $1,000 investment is sold for the future price of \$1,200 (V_n), shown in the table, and that it is the only income in that year. Assume further that the current price of the investment is \$1,175.28 (V_0). (*Note:* Setting up the investment this way should lead to an exact 8 percent yield, since that is the rate used to discount the income in Table 4.12 to obtain the \$1,175.28 value.) The average annual income is calculated by dividing the \$620 of total annual benefits from 1993 through 1998 (\$90 + \$100 + \$110 + \$120 + \$100 + \$100) by 7—the number of years in the investment horizon (n). Average annual income ($\overline{C}$) of \$88.57 (\$620 ÷ 7) results. [*Note:* To apply the approximate yield formula, Equation 4.10a, the income in the final year n is treated as the "ending investment value" (V_n) and the income in the n-1 prior years is averaged over the n-year period in order to find the "average annual income over investment horizon" ($\overline{C}$).] Substituting the data into Equation 4.10a results in the following calculations:

$$AY = \frac{\$88.57 + \dfrac{\$1,200 - \$1,175.28}{7}}{\dfrac{\$1,200 + \$1,175.28}{2}}$$

$$= \frac{\$88.57 + \$3.53}{\$1,187.64} = \frac{\$92.10}{\$1,187.64}$$

$$= \underline{0.0776, \text{ or } 7.76\%}$$

The approximate yield of 7.76 percent is reasonably close to the true yield of 8 percent. The approximate yield formula will be used at numerous points throughout the text to simplify what may otherwise be tedious yield calculations.

Finding Growth Rates

In addition to finding annual rates of return, we frequently need to find the *rate of growth* associated with a stream of dividends or earnings. Growth rates are often an important input to the common stock valuation process, which is presented in Chapter 7. Here we describe a simple technique for estimating growth rates that relies on the use of the present-value interest factors presented in Table A.3. The technique can best be demonstrated using an example.

Imagine that you wish to find the compound annual rate of growth for the dividends given in Table 4.15. The year numbers in the table show that 1984 is viewed

TABLE 4.15 Dividends Per Share

Year	Year Number	Dividends per Share	Year	Year Number	Dividends per Share
1984	0	\$2.45	1989	5	\$3.15
1985	1	2.60	1990	6	3.20
1986	2	2.80	1991	7	3.20
1987	3	3.00	1992	8	3.40
1988	4	3.20	1993	9	3.50

■ **INVESTOR INSIGHTS** ■

How Much Risk Can You Take?

Most of us know that we should consider our risk tolerance before making investment decisions. Yet few of us have any idea how to gauge the amount of risk we feel comfortable with. Several years ago, William Kuehl, a certified public accountant and financial planner in Richmond, Va., became frustrated about that. "All the rest of the financial planning process hinges on detecting the emotional and financial capacity for risk," Mr. Kuehl says, "and yet there was no way to do it." He decided to look for a solution.

The ability to handle risk is based on two things, according to Mr. Kuehl: a person's financial wherewithal and his or her emotional capacity to deal with volatility in the value of individual investments. Financial capacity depends on relatively measurable things like your age, occupation, number of dependents, health, investment knowledge, insurance coverage and, of course, your net worth.

In being able to take on risk, Mr. Kuehl says, "There's no substitute for wealth." But even having lots of money doesn't necessarily mean that you feel comfortable with risky investments. You must think about how you will feel if you invest $1,000 and it is suddenly worth only $750.

To help evaluate his clients' capacity for risk. Mr. Kuehl developed a risk tolerance quiz. Each question should be answered "yes" or "no." Mr. Kuehl warns that no one question can reveal your tolerance for risk. You must consider your overall score.

1. I would purchase a stock on the basis of a tip from a trusted friend.
2. I play poker, the lottery, or other games of chance for money.
3. I would be interested in starting my own business.
4. I would enjoy a job that requires lots of travel.
5. I enjoy driving fast.
6. I would invest in speculative stocks.
7. I am very independent minded.
8. I am highly energetic.
9. I would take a job on a strictly commission basis.
10. Security in an average-income job is more important than a higher-risk, higher-paid position.
11. I would invest in a profitable business.
12. I feel it's very important to be able to reasonably predict the outcome of an investment opportunity.
13. The stock market interests me.

as the base year (year 0) and the subsequent years, 1985–1993, are considered years 1 through 9, respectively. Although 10 years of data are presented in Table 4.15, they represent only 9 years of growth since the value for the earliest year must be viewed as the initial value at time zero. To find the growth rate, we first divide the dividend for the earliest year (1984) by the dividend for the latest year (1993). The resulting quotient is .700 ($2.45 ÷ $3.50); it represents the value of the present-value interest factor for 9 years. To find the compound annual dividend growth rate we find the discount rate in Table A.3 associated with the factor closest to .700 for 9 years. Looking across year 9 in Table A.3 shows that the factor for 4 percent is

14. I prefer a high interest rate from a certificate of deposit over appreciation on common stock.

15. I have a strong need for excitement.

16. I frequently offer new ideas at work.

17. I transact at least five security trades through my stockbroker each year.

18. I have a current will.

19. I own a vacation home at the beach.

20. I would buy stocks on margin, or on credit.

21. I would move to another city for a better paying job.

22. I enjoy trying new foods.

23. I have a private disability insurance policy.

24. I supervise others or make decisions in my job.

25. I have adequate liquidity—cash for three months of expenses.

26. I regularly participate or play in sports or competitive games like chess, bridge and board games.

27. I drive a sports car.

28. Real estate investments interest me.

29. I get nervous when the Dow Jones industrial average drops more than 30 points in a day.

30. I have an annual medical examination.

31. I usually need help in making investment decisions.

32. I smoke.

TO SCORE: If you answered yes to each of the following 19 questions, you have an extremely high tolerance for risk: 1, 2, 3, 4, 6, 7, 8, 9, 11, 13, 15, 16, 17, 19, 20, 21, 22, 24 and 26. If you answered yes to half of them, you have a low to moderate capacity for risk. (The other questions improve the accuracy of test results by disguising the pattern of answers that indicate risk-taking.) . . .

The capacity for physical risk appears to be unrelated to a willingness to take investment risks. When he began working on the quiz, Mr. Kuehl assumed that people who could handle physical risk, like test pilots and mountaineers, could also accept investment risk. His research, however, proved his theory wrong.

Source: Mary Rowland, "How Much Risk Can You Take?" *The New York Times,* April 8, 1990, Section 3, p. 17.

.703—very close to the .700 value. Therefore, the growth rate of the dividends in Table 4.15 is approximately 4 percent. (The precise value found using a financial calculator is 4.04 percent.)

RISK: THE OTHER SIDE OF THE COIN

Thus far the primary concern of this chapter has been return. However, we cannot consider return without also looking at **risk,** the chance that the actual return from an investment may differ from what is expected. In general, the more variable, or broader, the range of possible returns associated with a given investment, the

risk
the chance that the actual return from an investment may differ from what is expected.

risk-return tradeoff
the relationship between risk and return, in which investments with more risk should provide higher returns, and vice versa.

greater its risk, and vice versa. The risk associated with a given investment is directly related to its expected return. Put another way, riskier investments should provide higher levels of return. Otherwise, what incentive is there for an investor to risk his or her capital? In general, an investor will attempt to minimize risk for a given level of return or maximize return for a given level of risk. This relationship between risk and return, called the **risk-return tradeoff,** will be discussed later in this chapter. To get a feel for your own risk-taking orientation, you can take Kuehl's risk-tolerance quiz in the accompanying Investor Insights box.

In this part of the chapter we will examine various aspects of risk: the risk of a single asset; the basic types of risk; sources of risk; beta, a modern measure of risk; and the capital asset pricing model (CAPM), which uses beta to estimate return. Then we will discuss how to evaluate the risk associated with a potential investment.

Risk of a Single Asset

standard deviation
a statistic used to measure the dispersion around an asset's average or expected return, and the most common single indicator of an asset's risk.

Equation 4.11

The risk or variability of both single assets and portfolios of assets can be measured statistically. Here we focus solely on the risk of single assets. The most common single indicator of an asset's risk is the **standard deviation, s,** which measures the dispersion (variation of returns) around an asset's average or expected return. The formula is given in Equation 4.14:

$$\text{Standard} \atop \text{deviation} = \sqrt{\frac{\sum_{i=1}^{n}\left(\begin{array}{c}\text{return for} \\ \text{outcome } i\end{array} - \begin{array}{c}\text{average or} \\ \text{expected return}\end{array}\right)}{\begin{array}{c}\text{total number} \\ \text{of outcomes}\end{array} - 1}}$$

Equation 4.11a

$$S = \sqrt{\frac{\sum_{i=1}^{n}(r_i - \bar{r})^2}{n - 1}}$$

Consider two competing investments—A and B—described in Table 4.16. Notice that both investments earned an average return of 15 percent over the six-year

TABLE 4.16 Returns on Investments A and B

	Rate of Return	
Year	Investment A	Investment B
1988	15.6%	8.4%
1989	12.7	12.9
1990	15.3	19.6
1991	16.2	17.5
1992	16.5	10.3
1993	13.7	21.3
Average	15.0%	15.0%

period, 1988–1993. Reviewing the returns shown for each investment in light of their 15 percent averages, we can see that the returns for investment B vary more from this average than do the returns from investment A.

The standard deviation provides a more quantitative tool for use in assessing and comparing investment risk. Table 4.17 demonstrates the calculation of the standard deviations, s_A and s_B, for investments A and B, respectively.

TABLE 4.17 Calculation of Standard Deviations of Returns for Investments A and B

INVESTMENT A

Year (i)	(1) Return, r_i	(2) Average Return, $\bar{r}$	(3) (1) − (2) $r_i - \bar{r}$	(4) $(3)^2$ $(r_i - \bar{r})^2$
1988	15.6%	15.0%	.6%	0.36%
1989	12.7	15.0	−2.3	5.29
1990	15.3	15.0	.3	0.09
1991	16.2	15.0	1.2	1.44
1992	16.5	15.0	1.5	2.25
1993	13.7	15.0	−1.3	1.69

$$\sum_{i=1}^{6} (r_i - \bar{r})^2 = 11.12$$

$$s_A = \sqrt{\frac{\sum_{i=1}^{6} (r_i - \bar{r})^2}{n - 1}} = \sqrt{\frac{11.12}{6 - 1}} = \sqrt{2.224} = \underline{\underline{1.49\%}}$$

INVESTMENT B

Year (i)	(1) Return, r_i	(2) Average Return, $\bar{r}$	(3) (1) − (2) $r_i - \bar{r}$	(4) $(3)^2$ $(r_i - \bar{r})^2$
1988	8.4%	15.0%	−6.6%	43.56%
1989	12.9	15.0	−2.1	4.41
1990	19.6	15.0	4.6	21.16
1991	17.5	15.0	2.5	6.25
1992	10.3	15.0	−4.7	22.09
1993	21.3	15.0	6.3	39.69

$$\sum_{i=1}^{6} (r_i - \bar{r})^2 = 137.16$$

$$s_B = \sqrt{\frac{\sum_{i=1}^{6} (r_i - \bar{r})^2}{n - 1}} = \sqrt{\frac{137.16}{6 - 1}} = \sqrt{27.432} = \underline{\underline{5.24\%}}$$

diversifiable risk
the portion of an investment's risk resulting from uncontrollable or random events that can be eliminated through diversification; also called *unsystematic risk.*

nondiversifiable risk
risk attributable to forces affecting all investments and therefore not unique to any given vehicle; also called *systematic risk.*

total risk
the sum of an investment's diversifiable risk and nondiversifiable risk.

Equation 4.12

Evaluating the calculations in Table 4.17, we can see that the standard deviation of 1.49 percent for the returns on investment A is, as expected, considerably below the standard deviation of 5.24 percent for investment B. The greater dispersion of investment B's return reflected in its standard deviation indicates that it is the more risky investment. Of course, these values are based upon historical data. There is no assurance that the relative risk of these two investments will be the same in the future.

Basic Types of Risk

The risk of an investment consists of two components: diversifiable and nondiversifiable risk. **Diversifiable risk,** sometimes called *unsystematic risk,* results from uncontrollable or random events, such as labor strikes, lawsuits, and regulatory actions, and affects various investment vehicles differently. It represents the portion of an investment's risk that can be eliminated through diversification. **Nondiversifiable risk,** also called *systematic risk,* is attributed to forces, like war, inflation, and political events, that affect all investments and are therefore not unique to a given vehicle. The sum of the diversifiable risk and nondiversifiable risk is called **total risk,** as given by Equation 4.12:

$$\text{Total risk} = \text{diversifiable risk} + \text{nondiversifiable risk}$$

Because any intelligent investor can eliminate diversifiable risk by holding a diversified portfolio of securities, *the only relevant risk is nondiversifiable risk.* Studies have shown that by carefully selecting 8 to 15 securities for a portfolio, investors can almost completely eliminate diversifiable risk. Nondiversifiable risk is inescapable. Each security possesses its own unique level of nondiversifiable risk, which we can measure.

Sources of Risk

The risk associated with a given investment vehicle may result from a combination of any of a variety of possible sources. A prudent investor will consider how the major sources of risk—business risk, financial risk, purchasing power risk, interest rate risk, liquidity risk, tax risk, market risk, and event risk—might affect potential investment vehicles. Of course, as discussed in Chapter 2, *foreign exchange risk* should be considered when investing internationally.

Business Risk

business risk
the degree of uncertainty associated with an investment's earnings and the investment's ability to pay investors the returns owed them.

In general **business risk** is concerned with the degree of uncertainty associated with an investment's earnings and the investment's ability to pay investors interest, principal, dividends, and any other returns owed them. For example, a business firm may experience poor earnings and fail as a result. In this case, business owners might receive no return if earnings are not adequate to meet obligations. Debtholders, on the other hand, are likely to receive some—but not necessarily all—of the amount owed them, due to the preferential treatment they are legally afforded.

Much of the business risk associated with a given investment vehicle is related to its kind of business. For example, the business risk of a common stock of a public utility differs from that of a high-fashion clothing manufacturer or a parcel of commercial real estate. Generally, investments in similar types of firms or properties have similar business risk, although differences in management, costs, and location can cause varying levels of risk.

Financial Risk

financial risk
the degree of uncertainty associated with the mix of debt and equity used to finance a firm or property.

The risk associated with the mix of debt and equity used to finance a firm or property is **financial risk.** The larger the proportion of debt used to finance a firm or property, the greater its financial risk. Debt financing obligates the firm to make interest payments as well as to repay the debts, which increases the firm's risk. These fixed-payment obligations must be met prior to distributing any earnings to the owners of such firms or properties. Inability to meet obligations associated with the use of debt could result in business failure, and in losses for bondholders as well as stockholders and owners.

Purchasing Power Risk

purchasing power
the amount of some commodity that can be bought with a given amount of a currency, such as one dollar.

The possibility of changes in price levels within the economy also results in risk. In periods of generally rising prices, known as *inflation,* the **purchasing power** of the dollar declines. This means that a smaller quantity of some commodity can be purchased with a given number of dollars than could have been purchased in the past. For example, if last year a dollar would buy three candy bars, an increase in the price of a candy bar to 50 cents would mean that only two candy bars could be bought with the same dollar today. In periods of declining price levels, the purchasing power of the dollar will increase. In general, investments whose values move with general price levels are most profitable during periods of rising prices; those that provide fixed returns are preferred during periods of declining price levels or low inflation. The returns on property investments, for example, tend to move with the general price level, whereas returns from savings accounts and bonds do not.

Interest Rate Risk

interest rate risk
the degree of uncertainty in the prices of securities, associated with changes in interest rates.

Securities that offer purchasers a fixed periodic return are especially affected by **interest rate risk,** the uncertainty in the prices of securities, associated with changes in interest rates. As interest rates change, the prices of these securities fluctuate; they decrease with increasing interest rates and increase with decreasing interest rates. As we will see in greater detail in Chapters 8, 9, and 10, the prices of fixed-income securities drop when interest rates rise. They thus provide purchasers with the same rate of return that would be available at prevailing rates. The opposite occurs when interest rates fall: The return on a fixed-income security is adjusted downward to a competitive level by an upward adjustment in its market price. The interest rate changes themselves result from changes in the general relationship between the supply and demand for money.

A second more subtle aspect of interest rate risk is associated with *reinvestment* of income received from an investment. As noted in the earlier discussion of "interest-on-interest,'' only if the investor can earn the initial rate of return on income received from an investment can he or she achieve a fully compounded rate of return equal to the initial rate of return. In other words, if a bond pays 8 percent annual interest the investor must be able to earn 8 percent on the income received during the bond's holding period in order to earn a fully compounded 8 percent return over that period. This same aspect of interest rate risk applies to reinvestment of the proceeds received from a bond or other investment at its maturity or sale.

All investment vehicles are actually subject to interest rate risk. Although fixed-income securities are most directly affected by interest rate movements, other vehicles such as common stock and property are also influenced by them. Generally the higher the interest rate the lower the value, and vice versa.

Liquidity Risk

liquidity risk
the risk of not being able to liquidate an investment conveniently and at a reasonable price.

The risk of not being able to liquidate an investment conveniently and at a reasonable price is called **liquidity risk.** The liquidity of a given investment vehicle is an important consideration for an investor. In general, investment vehicles traded in *thin markets,* where demand and supply are small, tend to be less liquid than those traded in *broad markets*.

One can generally sell an investment vehicle merely by significantly cutting its price. However, to be liquid an investment must be easily sold at a reasonable price. For example, a security recently purchased for $1,000 would not be viewed as highly liquid if it can be quickly sold only at a greatly reduced price, such as $500. Vehicles such as bonds and stocks of major companies listed on the New York Stock Exchange are generally highly liquid; others, such as an isolated parcel of raw land located in rural Georgia, are not.

Tax Risk

tax risk
the chance that Congress will make unfavorable changes in the tax laws that make certain investments less attractive by driving down their after-tax returns and market values.

The chance that Congress will make unfavorable changes in tax laws is known as **tax risk.** The greater the chance that tax-law changes will occur to make certain investments less attractive by driving down their after-tax returns and market values, the greater the risk. Undesirable tax-law changes include elimination of tax-exempt items of income, limitation or elimination of deductions, and increases in tax rates. During recent years Congress has passed numerous tax-law changes. Probably most significant was the Tax Reform Act of 1986 which contained provisions that reduced the attractiveness of many investment vehicles, particularly real estate and tax-sheltered investments. By reducing the tax benefits of investments, the government can increase its tax revenues at the expense of investors who realize lower after-tax returns and investment values. While virtually all investments are vulnerable to tax-rate increases, certain tax-favored investments, such as municipal and other bonds, real estate, and natural resources, generally have greater risk.

Market Risk

market risk
risk of decline in investment returns due to market factors independent of the given security or property investment.

Market risk is the risk that investment returns will decline due to market factors independent of the given security or property investment. Examples include political, economic, and social events, or changes in investor tastes and preferences. It should be clear from this definition that market risk actually embodies a number of different risks: purchasing power, interest rate, and tax risks, described above, and event risk, which is described below. The impact of market factors on investment returns is not uniform; the degree as well as the direction of change in return differs among investment vehicles. For example, legislation placing restrictive import quotas on Japanese goods may result in a significant increase in the value (and therefore the return) of domestic automobile and electronics stocks. Essentially, market risk is reflected in the *price volatility* of a security—the more volatile the price of a security, the greater its perceived market risk.

Event Risk

event risk
risk that comes from a largely or totally unexpected event which has a significant and usually immediate effect on the underlying value of an investment.

More than just a buzz word used in the financial media, **event risk** occurs when something substantial happens to a company or property that has a sudden impact on its financial condition. Event risk goes beyond business and financial risk and can have a direct and dramatic impact on return. It does not necessarily mean the company or market is doing poorly. Instead, it involves an event that is largely (or totally) unexpected, and that has a significant and usually immediate effect on the underlying value of an investment. An example of event risk is the 1992 action by the Food and Drug Administration (FDA) to halt the use of silicone breast implants. The stock price of Dow Chemical—the dominant producer of this product—was quickly and negatively affected as a result. Event risk can take many forms and affect all types of investment vehicles. Fortunately, its impact tends to be isolated in most cases, affecting only certain companies or properties. For instance, as a result of the FDA's silicone breast implant actions, the stocks of only a small number of companies were affected.

Beta: A Modern Measure of Risk

beta
a measure of nondiversifiable risk, which shows how the price of a security responds to market forces; found by relating the historical returns on a security with the historical returns for the market.

Over approximately the past 30 years much theoretical work has been done on the measurement of risk and its use in assessing returns. The two key components of this theory are *beta,* which is a measure of risk, and the *capital asset pricing model (CAPM),* which relates the risk measured by beta to the level of required or expected return. First we will look at **beta,** a number that measures *nondiversifiable,* or *market, risk;* that is, beta indicates how the price of a security responds to market forces. The more responsive the price of a security is to changes in the market, the higher will be that security's beta. It is found by relating the historical returns on a security with the historical returns for the market.

market return
the average return on all, or a large sample of, stocks, such as those in the Standard & Poor's 500 stock composite index.

Market return is typically measured by the average return for all (or a large sample of) stocks. The average return on all stocks in the Standard & Poor's 500 stock composite index or some other broad stock index is commonly used to measure market return. Although betas for actively traded securities can be obtained from a variety of sources, it is important to understand their derivation, interpretation, and use.

Deriving Beta

The relationship between a security's return and the market return, and its use in deriving beta, can be demonstrated graphically. Figure 4.2 plots the relationship between the returns of two securities—C and D—and the market return. Note that the horizontal (*x*) axis measures the market returns and the vertical (*y*) axis measures the individual security's returns. The first step in deriving beta involves plotting the coordinates for the market return and security returns at various points in time. Such annual market-return–security-return coordinates are shown in Figure 4.2 for security D for the years 1986 through 1993 (with the years noted in parentheses). For example, in 1993 security D's return was 20 percent when the market return was 10 percent. By use of statistical techniques, the "characteristic line" that best explains the relationship between security-return and market-return coordinates is fit to the data points. *The slope of this line is beta*. The beta for security C is about .80 and for security D it is about 1.30. Security D's steeper

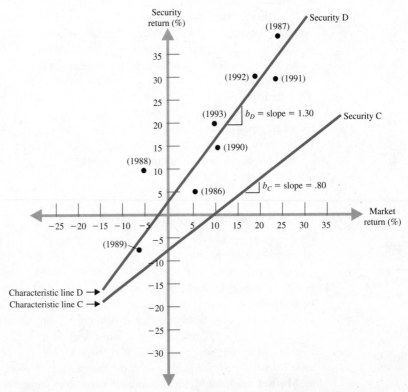

• FIGURE 4.2 Graphic Derivation of Beta for Securities C and D

Betas can be derived graphically by plotting the coordinates for the market return and security returns at various points in time and using statistical techniques to fit the "characteristic line" to the data points. The slope of the characteristic line is beta. For securities C and D, beta is found to be .80 and 1.30, respectively.

characteristic line slope indicates that D's return is more responsive to changing market returns: it has a higher beta and therefore is more risky.

Interpreting Beta

The beta for the overall market is considered to be equal to 1.0. All other betas are viewed in relation to this value. Table 4.18 shows some selected beta values and their associated interpretations. As can be seen, betas can be positive or negative, though nearly all betas are positive. The positive or negative sign preceding the beta number merely indicates whether the stock's return changes in the *same direction* as the general market (positive beta) or in the *opposite direction* (negative beta). Most stocks have betas that fall between 0.5 and 1.75. Listed below, for illustration purposes, are the actual betas for some popular stocks, as reported by *Value Line* in early 1992:

Stock	Beta	Stock	Beta
American Greetings	1.00	Eastman Kodak	1.00
Atlas Corporation	.70	Ford Motor	1.10
Bank of Boston	1.40	B.F. Goodrich	1.35
Briggs & Stratton	1.05	General Mills	1.00
Champion International	1.20	Hawaiian Electric	.65
Cincinnati Bell	.95	Lotus Development	1.45
Compaq Computer	1.40	Maytag Corporation	1.05
Digital Equipment	1.20	Quaker Oats	.90
Disney	1.25	United Telecom	.95
Dow Chemical	1.25	Winnebago Industries	1.20

Many large brokerage firms as well as subscription services like *Value Line* publish betas for a broad range of securities. The ready availability of security betas has enhanced their use in assessing investment risks. *In general the higher the beta,*

TABLE 4.18 Selected Betas and Associated Interpretations

Beta	Comment	Interpretation*
2.0	Move in same direction as market.	Twice as responsive as the market.
1.0		Same response or risk as the market.
0.5		Only half as responsive as the market.
0		Unaffected by market movement
−0.5	Move in opposite direction to market.	Only half as responsive as the market.
−1.0		Same response or risk as the market.
−2.0		Twice as responsive as the market.

*A stock that is twice as responsive as the market will experience a 2 percent change in its return for each 1 percent change in the return of the market portfolio. The return of a stock that is half as responsive as the market will change by ½ of 1 percent for each 1 percent change in the return of the market portfolio.

the riskier the security. The importance of beta in planning and building portfolios of securities will be discussed in greater detail in Chapter 16.

Using Beta

The individual investor will find beta useful in assessing market risk and understanding the impact the market can have on the return expected from a share of stock. Beta reveals how a security responds to market forces. For example, if the market is expected to experience a 10 percent *increase* in its rate of return over the next period, a stock having a beta of 1.50 would be expected to experience an increase in return of approximately 15 percent (1.50 × 10%) over the same period. Because the beta of this particular stock is greater than 1, it is more volatile than the market as a whole.

For stocks having positive betas, increases in market returns result in increases in security returns. Unfortunately decreases in market returns are likewise translated into decreasing security returns—and this is where the risk lies. In the preceding example, if the market is expected to experience a 10 percent *decline,* then the stock with a beta of 1.50 should experience a 15 percent decrease in its return. Because the stock has a beta of greater than 1, it is more responsive than the market, either way.

Stocks having betas of less than 1 will of course be less responsive to changing returns in the market. They therefore are considered less risky. For example, a stock having a beta of 0.50 will experience an increase or decrease in its return of about half that in the market as a whole. Thus, as the market goes down by 8 percent, such a stock will probably experience only about a 4 percent (0.50 × 8%) decline.

Here are some important points to remember about beta:

1. Beta measures the nondiversifiable, or market, risk of a security.
2. The beta for the market is 1.
3. Stocks may have positive or negative betas; nearly all are positive.
4. Stocks with betas of greater than 1 are more responsive to changes in market return—and therefore more risky—than the market. Stocks with betas of less than 1, are less risky than the market.
5. Due to its greater risk, the higher a stock's beta, the greater should be its level of expected return, and vice versa.

CAPM: Using Beta to Estimate Return

capital asset pricing model (CAPM)
model that uses beta and market return to help investors evaluate risk-return tradeoffs in investment decisions.

About 30 years ago, William F. Sharpe and John Lintner developed a model that uses beta to link together formally the notions of risk and return. Called the **capital asset pricing model (CAPM),** it was developed to explain the behavior of security prices and to provide a mechanism whereby investors can assess the impact of a proposed security investment on their portfolio's risk and return. We can use CAPM to understand the basic risk-return tradeoffs involved in various types of investment decisions. CAPM can be viewed both as an equation and as a graph.

The Equation

With beta, *b,* as the measure of nondiversifiable risk, the capital asset pricing model defines the required rate of return on an investment according to the following equation:

Equation 4.13

$$\frac{\text{Required return}}{\text{on investment } i} = \text{risk-free rate} + \left[\text{beta for investment } i \times \left(\frac{\text{market}}{\text{return}} - \frac{\text{risk-free}}{\text{rate}} \right) \right]$$

Equation 4.13a

$$r_i = R_F + [b_i \times (r_m - R_F)]$$

where

r_i = the required return on investment i given its risk as measured by beta

R_F = the risk-free rate of return; the return that can be earned on a risk-free investment

b_i = beta coefficient or index of nondiversifiable risk for investment i

r_m = the market return; the average return on all securities (typically measured by the average return on all securities in the Standard & Poor's 500 stock composite index or some other broad stock index)

The equation shows that as beta increases, the required return for a given investment increases.

Application of the CAPM can be demonstrated with the following example. Assume security Z with a beta (b_Z) of 1.25 is being considered at a time when the risk-free rate (R_F) is 6 percent and the market return (r_m) is 10 percent. Substituting these data into the CAPM equation, Equation 4.13a, we get:

$$r_Z = 6\% + [1.25 \times (10\% - 6\%)] = 6\% + [1.25 \times 4\%]$$
$$= 6\% + 5\% = \underline{\underline{11\%}}$$

The investor should therefore expect—indeed, require—an 11 percent return on this investment as compensation for the risk she has to assume, given the security's beta of 1.25. If the beta were lower, say 1.00, the required return would be lower:

$$r_Z = 6\% + [1.00 \times (10\% - 6\%)] = 6\% + 4\% = \underline{\underline{10\%}}$$

If the beta were higher, say 1.50, the required return would be higher:

$$r_Z = 6\% + [1.50 \times (10\% - 6\%)] = 6\% + 6\% = \underline{\underline{12\%}}$$

security market line (SML)
the graphic depiction of the capital asset pricing model; reflects the investor's required return for each level of nondiversifiable risk, measured by beta.

Clearly, CAPM reflects the positive mathematical relationship between risk and return, since the higher the risk (beta) the higher the required return.

The Graph: The Security Market Line (SML)

When the capital asset pricing model is depicted graphically, it is called the **security market line (SML).** Plotting CAPM, we would find that the SML will, in fact, be a straight line. For each level of nondiversifiable risk (beta), it reflects the required return the investor should earn in the marketplace. The CAPM at a given point in time can be plotted by simply calculating the required return for a variety of betas; of course, at the given point in time the risk-free rate and market return would be constant. For example, as we saw above, using a 6 percent risk-free rate and a 10 percent market return, the required return is 11 percent when beta is 1.25. Increase the beta to 2.0, and the required return equals 14 percent [6% + [2.0 × (10% − 6%)]]. Similarly we can find the required return for a number of betas and end up with the following combinations of risk (beta) and required return:

Risk (Beta)	Required Return (Percent)
0.0	6
0.5	8
1.0	10
1.5	12
2.0	14
2.5	16

Plotting these values on a graph (with beta on the horizontal axis and required returns on the vertical axis), we would have a straight line like the one in Figure 4.3. It is clear from the SML that as risk (beta) increases so does the required return, and vice versa.

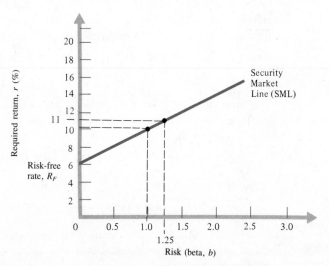

• **F I G U R E   4 . 3** The Security Market Line (SML)

The security market line (SML) clearly depicts the tradeoff between risk and return. At a beta of 0, the required return is the risk-free rate of 6 percent; at a beta of 1.0, the market return is 10 percent. Given this data, the required return on an investment with a beta of 1.25 is 11 percent.

Evaluating Risk

Techniques for quantifying the risk of a given investment vehicle will, however, be of little use to the investor who is unaware of his or her feelings toward risk. Investors must somehow relate the risk perceived in a given vehicle not only to the expected return but also to their own dispositions toward risk. The individual investor typically tends to seek answers to these questions: "Is the amount of perceived risk worth taking in order to get the expected return?" "Can I get a higher return for the same level of risk or a lower risk for the same level of return?" A look at the general risk-return characteristics of alternative investment vehicles, the question of an acceptable level of risk, and the decision process will help shed light on the nature of risk evaluations.

Risk-Return Characteristics of Alternative Investment Vehicles

A wide variety of risk-return behaviors is associated with each type of investment vehicle. Some common stocks offer low returns and low risk; others offer high returns and high risk. In general the risk-return characteristics of each of the major investment vehicles can be depicted on a set of risk-return axes, as shown in Figure 4.4. Of course, for each type of investment vehicle a broad range of risk-return behaviors exists for specific investments. In other words, once the appropriate type of vehicle has been selected, the decision as to which specific security or property to acquire must still be made.

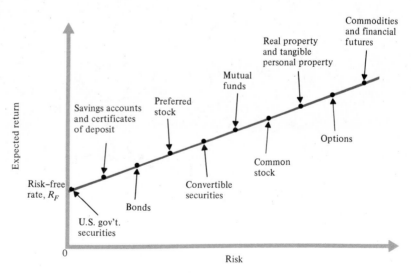

● F I G U R E 4 . 4 Risk-Return Tradeoffs for Various Investment Vehicles

A risk-return tradeoff exists such that for a higher risk one expects a higher return, and vice versa. Low-risk–low-return investment vehicles are U.S. government securities, savings accounts, and so on. High-risk–high-return vehicles include real property (real estate) and tangible personal property, options, and commodities and financial futures.

An Acceptable Level of Risk

Because of differing investor preferences, it is impossible to specify a general acceptable level of risk. The three basic risk-preference behaviors—risk-indifferent, risk-averse, and risk-taking—are depicted graphically in Figure 4.5. As risk goes from x_1 to x_2 on the graph, the required return does not change for the **risk-indifferent** investor: in essence, no change in return would be required as compensation for the increase in risk. For the **risk-averse** investor, the required return increases for an increase in risk. Because they shy away from risk, these investors require higher expected returns in order to compensate them for taking greater risk. And for the **risk-taking** investor, the required return decreases for an increase in risk. Theoretically, because they enjoy risk, these investors are willing to give up some return in order to take more risk.

Most investors are risk-averse, since for a given increase in risk they require an increase in return. Note that the security market line (SML) in Figure 4.3 clearly depicts the risk-averse behavior of investors who require increasing returns, r, for increased levels of nondiversifiable risk as measured by beta, b. The risk-averse behavior is also depicted in Figure 4.4. Of course, the amount of return required by each investor for a given increase in risk differs depending upon the investor's degree of risk aversion (reflected in the slope of the line). Investors generally tend to be conservative rather than aggressive when accepting risk.

The Decision Process

In the decision process investors should take the following steps when selecting from among alternative investments:

risk-indifferent
describes an investor who does not require greater return in exchange for greater risk

risk-averse
describes an investor who requires greater return in exchange for greater risk.

risk-taking
describes an investor who will accept a lower return in exchange for greater risk.

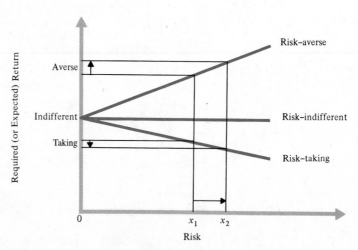

• FIGURE 4.5 Risk Preferences

The risk-indifferent investor requires no change in return for a given increase in risk, whereas the risk-averse investor requires an increase in return for a given risk increase, and the risk-taking investor gives up some return for more risk. The majority of investors are risk-averse.

1. Using historical or projected return data, estimate the expected return over a given holding period. Use yield (or present value) techniques to make sure that the time value of money is given adequate consideration.

2. Using historical or projected return data, assess the risk associated with the investment. The use of subjective risk assessment or the standard deviation of past returns and beta (for securities) are the primary approaches available to the individual investor.

3. Evaluate the risk-return behavior of each alternative investment to make sure that the return expected is ''reasonable'' given its level of risk. If other vehicles with equal or lower levels of risk provide equal or greater returns, the investment would not be acceptable.

4. Select the investment vehicles that offer the highest returns associated with the level of risk the investor is willing to take. Since most investors are risk-averse they will acquire lower-risk vehicles, thereby receiving lower investment returns. As long as they get the highest return for the acceptable level of risk, they have made a ''good investment.''

Probably the most difficult step in this process is assessing risk. Aside from risk and return considerations, other factors such as taxes, liquidity, and portfolio considerations will affect the investment decision. We will look at these in later chapters.

SUMMARY

1. Return is the reward for investing. The total return provided by an investment includes current income and capital gains (or losses). Return is commonly calculated on a historical basis and then used to project expected returns. The level of return depends on internal characteristics and external forces, which include the general level of price changes.

2. Because investors have opportunities to earn interest on idle funds, the time value of money must be considered when evaluating investment returns. Interest can be applied using either the simple interest method or the compound method. The more frequently interest is compounded at a stated rate, the higher the true rate of interest. The future value of a present sum or an annuity can be found using compound interest concepts.

3. The present value of a future sum is the amount deposited today, into an account earning interest at a given rate, that would accumulate to the specified future sum. The present value of streams of future returns can be found by adding the individual return present values. A satisfactory investment is one for which the present value of benefits exceeds the present value of costs.

4. The required return on an investment is the rate of return an investor must earn in order to be fully compensated for its risk. It represents the sum of the real rate of return and the inflation premium, which together represent the risk-free rate, and the risk premium for the investment. The risk premium varies depending upon issue and issuer characteristics. The holding period return (HPR) is the return earned over a specified period of time. It is frequently used to compare returns earned in period of one year or less.

Yield or internal rate of return is the actual compounded rate of return earned on a long-term investment. If the yield is greater than or equal to the required return, the investment would be acceptable. Implicit in the use of yield is an ability to earn a return equal to the calculated yield on all income received from the investment during the holding period. The yield on an investment can be estimated using the approximate yield formula. Present-value techniques can be used to find compound annual growth rates.

5. Risk is the chance that the actual investment return will differ from what is expected. The most common single indicator of an investment's risk is the standard deviation. There is a tradeoff between risk and return. The two basic types of risk are diversifiable and nondiversifiable; nondiversifiable risk is the relevant risk. Total risk derives from a variety of sources such as business risk, financial risk, purchasing power risk, interest rate risk, liquidity risk, tax risk, market risk, and event risk.

6. Beta can be used to measure the nondiversifiable, or market, risk associated with a security investment. It is derived from the historical relationship between a security's return and the market return. The capital asset pricing model (CAPM), which can be depicted graphically as the security market line (SML), relates risk (as measured by beta) to return. CAPM reflects increasing required returns for increasing risk.

Generally, each type of investment vehicle displays certain risk-return characteristics. Most investors are risk-averse: in exchange for a given increase in risk they require an increase in return. The investment decision will ultimately be made by combining the investor's risk preference with the expected return and risk data for a given investment.

QUESTIONS

1. Define what is meant by the return on an investment. Explain why a person wishing to invest should be able to earn a positive return.

2. Define, discuss, and contrast the following terms:

   a. Interest.
   b. Simple interest.
   c. Compound interest.

3. When interest is compounded more frequently than annually at a stated rate, what happens to the true rate of interest? Under what condition would the stated and true interest rates be equal? What is continuous compounding?

4. Describe, compare, and contrast the concepts of future value and present value. Explain the role of the discount rate (or opportunity cost) in the present-value calculation.

5. Define each of the following terms and describe how they are used to find the risk-free rate of return and the required rate of return for a given investment:

   a. Real rate of return.
   b. Expected inflation premium.
   c. Risk premium for a given investment.

6. Define what is meant by the holding period, and explain why it is advisable to use equal-length holding periods (covering the same period in time) when comparing alternative investment vehicles.

7. Define yield or internal rate of return and explain when it is appropriate to use yield rather than the holding period return (HPR) to measure the return on an investment.

8. Explain why you must earn 10 percent on all income received from an investment during its holding period in order for its yield actually to equal the 10 percent value you've calculated.

9. Explain how either the present value or the yield measure can be used to find a satisfactory investment. Given the following data, indicate which, if any, of the following investments is acceptable. Explain your findings.

	Investment		
	A	**B**	**C**
Cost	$200	$160	$500
Appropriate discount rate	7%	10%	9%
Present value of returns	—	$150	—
Yield	8%	—	8%

10. Define risk. What statistic can be used to measure risk? Explain what is meant by the risk-return tradeoff. What happens to the required return as risk increases? Explain.

11. Briefly define and give examples of each of the following components of total risk. Be sure to indicate which is the relevant risk and explain why.
    a. Diversifiable risk.
    b. Nondiversifiable risk.

12. Define and briefly discuss each of the following sources of risk:
    a. Business risk.   e. Liquidity risk.
    b. Financial risk.   f. Tax risk.
    c. Purchasing power risk.   g. Market risk.
    d. Interest rate risk.   h. Event risk.

13. Explain what is meant by beta. What is the relevant risk measured by beta?

14. What is meant by the market return? Where is it obtained? How is beta derived from data describing market returns and a security's returns at various points in time?

15. What range of values does beta typically exhibit? Are positive or negative betas more common? Explain.

16. Find the latest *Value Line* in your university or public library and use it to find and update the betas for the companies listed on page 159. Compare, contrast, and comment on the most recent betas in light of the early 1992 betas given in the text.

17. What is the capital asset pricing model (CAPM)? What role does beta play in it? How does the security market line (SML) relate to CAPM?

18. Differentiate among the three basic risk preferences—risk-indifferent, risk-averse, and risk-taking. Which of these behaviors best describes most investors? Explain. How does an investor's risk preference typically enter the investment decision process?

19. Describe the basic steps involved in the investment decision process. Be sure to mention how returns and risks can be measured and used to determine the group of acceptable or "reasonable" investments from which the final selection can be made.

PROBLEMS

1. Define and differentiate between current income and capital gains (or losses). If you purchased a share of stock for $50 one year ago and sold it today for $60, and during the year received three dividend payments totaling $2.70, calculate:

    a. Current income.
    b. Capital gain (or loss).
    c. Total return.
       (1) In dollars.
       (2) As a percentage of the initial investment.

2. Given the historical data below:

    a. Calculate the total return (in dollars) for each year.
    b. Indicate the level of return you would expect in 1994 and 1995.
    c. Comment on your forecast.

		Market Value (Price)	
Year	Income	Beginning	Ending
1989	$1.00	$30.00	$32.50
1990	1.20	32.50	35.00
1991	1.30	35.00	33.00
1992	1.60	33.00	40.00
1993	1.75	40.00	45.00

3. For the following savings account transactions, calculate:

    a. End-of-year account balance (assume that the account balance at December 31, 1992, is zero).
    b. Annual interest, using 6 percent simple interest and assuming all interest is withdrawn from the account as it is earned.
    c. True rate of interest, and compare it to the stated rate of interest. Discuss your finding.

Date	Deposit or (Withdrawal)
1/1/93	$5,000
1/1/94	(4,000)
1/1/95	2,000
1/1/96	3,000

4. Using the appropriate table of interest factors found in Appendix A, calculate:

    a. The future value of a $300 deposit left in an account paying 7 percent annual interest for 12 years.
    b. The future value at the end of 6 years of an $800 annual end-of-year deposit into an account paying 7 percent annual interest.

5. For each of the following initial investment amounts, calculate the future value at the end of the given investment period if interest is compounded annually at the specified rate of return given the investment period.

Investment	Investment Amount	Rate of Return	Investment Period
A	$ 200	5%	20 years
B	4,500	8	7
C	10,000	9	10
D	25,000	10	12
E	37,000	11	5

6. For each of the following annual deposits into an account paying the stated annual interest rate over the specified deposit period, calculate the future value of the annuity at the end of the given deposit period.

Deposit	Amount of Annual Deposit	Interest Rate	Deposit Period
A	$ 2,500	8%	10 years
B	500	12	6
C	1,000	20	5
D	12,000	6	8
E	4,000	14	30

7. If you could earn 9 percent on similar-risk investments, what is the least you would accept at the end of a six-year period given the following amounts and timing of your investment?

a. Invest $5,000 as a lump sum today.
b. Invest $2,000 at the end of each of the next five years.
c. Invest a lump sum of $3,000 today and $1,000 at the end of each of the next five years.
d. Invest $900 at the end of years 1, 3, and 5.

8. For each of the following investments, calculate the present value of the future sum using the specified discount rate and assuming the sum will be received at the end of the given year.

Investment	Future Sum	Discount Rate	End of Year
A	$ 7,000	12%	4
B	28,000	8	20
C	10,000	14	12
D	150,000	11	6
E	45,000	20	8

9. A Florida state savings bond can be converted to $1,000 at maturity eight years from purchase. If the state bonds are to be competitive with U.S. savings bonds, which pay 6 percent interest compounded annually, at what price will the state's bond sell, assuming they made no cash payments prior to maturity?

10. Find the present value of each of the following streams of income assuming a 12 percent discount rate.

A		B		C	
End of Year	Income	End of Year	Income	End of Year	Income
1	$2,200	1	$10,000	1–5	$10,000/yr
2	3,000	2–5	5,000/yr.	6–10	8,000/yr
3	4,000	6	7,000		
4	6,000				
5	8,000				

11. Given the following streams of income:

End of Year	Income Stream	
	A	B
1	$ 4,000	$ 1,000
2	3,000	2,000
3	2,000	3,000
4	1,000	4,000
Totals	$10,000	$10,000

a. Find the present value of each income stream using a 15 percent discount rate.

b. Compare the calculated present values and discuss them in light of the fact that the undiscounted total income amounts to $10,000 in each case.

12. For each of the following investments, calculate the present value of the annual end-of-year returns at the specified discount rate over the given period.

Investment	Annual Returns	Discount Rate	Period
A	$ 1,200	7%	3 years
B	5,500	12	15
C	700	20	9
D	14,000	5	7
E	2,200	10	5

13. Using the appropriate table of interest factors found in Appendix A, calculate:

a. The present value of $500 to be received four years from now, using an 11 percent discount rate.

b. The present value of the following end-of-year income streams, using a 9 percent discount rate and assuming it is now the beginning of 1994.

End of Year	Income Stream A	Income Stream B
1994	$80	$140
1995	80	120
1996	80	100
1997	80	80
1998	80	60
1999	80	40
2000	80	20

14. Terri Allessandro has an opportunity to make any of the following investments. The purchase price, the amount of its lump-sum value, and its year of receipt are given below for each investment. Evaluate each investment to determine if it is satisfactory and make an investment recommendation to Terri.

Investment	Purchase Price	Future Value	Year of Receipt
A	$18,000	$30,000	5
B	600	3,000	20
C	3,500	10,000	10
D	1,000	15,000	40

15. Kent Weitz wishes to assess whether or not the following two investments are satisfactory. Use his required return (discount rate) of 17 percent to evaluate each investment. Make an investment recommendation to Kent.

	Investment	
	A	B
Purchase price	$13,000	$8,500
End of Year	Income Stream	
1	$ 2,500	$4,000
2	3,500	3,500
3	4,500	3,000
4	5,000	1,000
5	5,500	500

16. Given a real rate of interest of 3 percent, an expected inflation premium of 5 percent, and risk premiums for investments A and B of 3 percent and 5 percent, respectively, find:

a. The risk-free rate of interest, R_F.

b. The required returns for investments A and B.

17. Calculate the holding period return (HPR) for the following two investment alternatives. Which, if any, of the return components is likely *not* to be realized if you continue to hold each of the investments beyond one year? Which vehicle would you prefer, assuming they are of equal risk? Explain.

	Investment Vehicle	
	X	Y
Cash received		
1st quarter	$ 1.00	$ 0
2nd quarter	1.20	0
3rd quarter	0	0
4th quarter	2.30	2.00
Investment value		
End-of-year	$29.00	$56.00
Beginning-of-year	30.00	50.00

18. Assume that you invest $5,000 today in an investment vehicle that promises to return to you $9,000 in exactly 10 years.

   a. Use the present-value technique to estimate the yield on this investment.
   b. Apply the approximate yield formula in order to estimate the yield on this investment.
   c. If a minimum return of 9 percent is required, would you recommend this investment?

19. Use the appropriate present-value interest factor table to estimate the yield to the nearest 1 percent for each of the following investments:

Investment	Initial Investment	Future Value	End of Year
A	$ 1,000	$ 1,200	5
B	10,000	20,000	7
C	400	2,000	20
D	3,000	4,000	6
E	5,500	25,000	30

20. Rosemary Santos must earn a return of 10 percent on an investment that requires an initial outlay of $2,500 and promises to return $6,000 eight years from now.

   a. Use present-value techniques to estimate the yield on this investment to the nearest 1 percent.
   b. Use the approximate yield formula to estimate the yield on this investment.
   c. Based on your findings in (a) and (b), should Rosemary make the proposed investment? Explain.

21. Use the appropriate present-value interest factors to estimate the yield to the nearest 1 percent for the two investments described below.

	Investment	
	A	B
Initial investment	$8,500	$9,500
End of Year	**Income**	
1	$2,500	$2,000
2	2,500	2,500
3	2,500	3,000
4	2,500	3,500
5	2,500	4,000

22. Elliott Dumjack must earn a minimum rate of return of 11 percent in order to be adequately compensated for the risk of the following investment:

Initial investment	$14,000
End of Year	**Income**
1	$6,000
2	3,000
3	5,000
4	2,000
5	1,000

a. Use present-value techniques to estimate the yield on this investment to the nearest 1 percent.

b. Use the approximate yield formula to estimate the yield on this investment.

c. Based on your findings in (a) and (b), should Elliott make the proposed investment? Explain.

23. Assume the investment-generating benefit stream B in question 13 can be purchased at the beginning of 1994 for $1,000 and sold at the end of 2000 for $1,200. Calculate the approximate yield for this investment. If a minimum return of 9 percent is required, would you recommend this investment? Explain.

24. For each of the following streams of dividends, estimate (to the nearest 1 percent) the compound annual rate of growth between the earliest year for which a value is given and 1993.

	Dividend Stream		
Year	**A**	**B**	**C**
1984		$1.50	
1985		1.55	
1986		1.61	
1987		1.68	$2.50
1988		1.76	2.60
1989	$5.00	1.85	2.65
1990	5.60	1.95	2.65
1991	6.40	2.06	2.80
1992	7.20	2.17	2.85
1993	8.00	2.28	2.90

25. The historic returns for two investments—A and B—are summarized below for the period 1989 to 1993. Use the data to answer the questions that follow it.

	Investment	
	A	**B**
Year	**Rate of Return**	
1989	19%	8%
1990	1	10
1991	10	12
1992	26	14
1993	4	16
Average	12%	12%

a. Based upon a review of the return data, which investment appears to be more risky? Why?

b. Calculate the standard deviation for each investment.

c. Based upon your calculations in (b), which investment is most risky? Compare the conclusion to your observation in (a).

26. Imagine you wish to estimate the betas for two investments, A and B. In this regard you have gathered the following return data for the market and each of the investments over the past 10 years, 1984–1993.

| | Historic Returns | | |
| | | Investment | |
Year	Market	A	B
1984	6%	11%	16%
1985	2	8	11
1986	−13	−4	−10
1987	−4	3	3
1988	−8	0	−3
1989	16	19	30
1990	10	14	22
1991	15	18	29
1992	8	12	19
1993	13	17	26

a. On a set of market return (x-axis)–investment return (y-axis) axes, use the data to draw the characteristic lines for investments A and B on the same set of axes.

b. Use the characteristic lines from (a) to estimate the betas from investments A and B.

c. Use the betas found in (b) to comment on the relative risks of investments A and B.

27. Assess the impact on the required return of a security with a beta of 1.20 in each of the following cases:

a. The market return increases by 15 percent.

b. The market return decreases by 8 percent.

c. The market return remains unchanged.

d. Is this security more or less risky than the market? Explain.

28. Assume the betas for securities A, B, and C are as given below:

Security	Beta
A	1.40
B	.80
C	− .90

a. Calculate the change in return for each security if the market experiences an increase in its rate of return of 13.2 percent over the next period.

b. Calculate the change in returns for each security if the market experiences a decrease in its rate of return of 10.8 percent over the next period.

c. Rank and discuss the relative risk of each security based on your findings. Which security might perform best during an economic downturn? Explain.

29. Use the capital asset pricing model (CAPM) to find the required return for each of the following securities in light of the data given below:

Security	Risk-free Rate	Market Return	Beta
A	5%	8%	1.30
B	8	13	.90
C	9	12	−.20
D	10	15	1.00
E	6	10	.60

30. The risk-free rate is currently 7 percent and the market return is 12 percent. Assume you are considering the following investment vehicles with the betas noted below:

Investment Vehicle	Beta
A	1.50
B	1.00
C	.75
D	0
E	2.00

a. Which vehicle is most risky? Least risky?
b. Use the capital asset pricing model (CAPM) to find the required return on each of the investment vehicles.
c. Draw the security market line (SML) using your findings above.
d. Based on your findings, what relationship exists between risk and return? Explain.

CFA QUESTION (This question is from the 1990 Level I Exam.)

 Fundamental to investing is the control of investment risk while maximizing total investment return. Identify *four* primary *sources* of risk faced by investors, and explain their possible impact on investment returns.
(See Appendix C for Guideline Answer to this question.)

CASE PROBLEMS

4.1 Solomon's Decision: A or B?

Dave Solomon, a 23-year-old mathematics teacher at Xavier High School, recently received a tax refund of $1,100. Because Dave doesn't currently have any need for this money, he decided to make a long-term investment. After surveying a large number of alternative investments costing no more than $1,100, Dave isolated two that seemed most suitable to his needs. Each of the investments cost $1,050 and was expected to provide income over a 10-year period. Investment A provided a relatively certain stream of income, while Dave was a little less certain of the income provided by investment B. From his search for suitable alternatives, Dave found that the appropriate discount rate for a relatively certain investment was 12 percent. Because he felt a bit uncomfortable with an investment such as B, he estimated that such an investment would have to provide a return at least 4 percent *higher* than investment A. Although Dave planned to reinvest funds returned from the investments in other vehicles providing similar returns, he wished to keep the extra $50 ($1,100 − $1,050) invested for the full 10 years in a savings account paying 5 percent interest compounded annually. In order to make his investment decision, Dave has asked for your help in answering the questions which follow the expected income data for each investment.

	Expected Returns	
Year	A	B
1994	$ 150	$100
1995	150	150
1996	150	200
1997	150	250
1998	150	300
1999	150	350
2000	150	300
2001	150	250
2002	150	200
2003	1,150	150

Questions

1. Assuming investments A and B are equally risky, using the 12 percent discount rate apply the present-value technique to assess the acceptability of each investment as well as the preferred investment. Explain your findings.

2. Recognizing the fact that investment B is more risky than investment A, reassess the two alternatives applying a 16 percent discount rate to investment B. Compare your findings relative to acceptability and preference to those found for question 1.

3. From your findings in questions 1 and 2, indicate whether the yield for investment A is above or below 12 percent and for investment B above or below 16 percent. Explain.

4. Use both the present-value technique and the approximate yield formula to find the yield on each investment. Compare your findings and contrast them with your response to question (3).

5. From the information given, which, if either, of the two investments would you recommend Dave make? Explain your answer.

6. Indicate to Dave how much money the extra $50 will have grown to by the end of 2003, given that he makes no withdrawals from the savings account.

4.2   The Risk-Return Tradeoff: Molly O'Rourke's Stock Purchase Decision

Over the past 10 years Molly O'Rourke has slowly built a diversified portfolio of common stock. Currently her portfolio includes 20 different common stock issues and has a total market value of $82,500. Molly is presently considering the addition of 50 shares of one of two common stock issues—X or Y. In order to assess the return and risk of each of these issues, she has gathered dividend income and share price data for both over each of the last 10 years (1984 through 1993). Molly's investigation of the outlook for these issues suggests that each will, on average, tend to behave in the future just as it has in the past. She therefore believes that the expected return can be estimated by finding the average holding period return (HPR) over the past 10 years for each of the stocks.

Molly plans to use betas to assess the risk and required return of each stock. Her broker, Jim McDaniel, indicated that the betas for stocks X and Y are 1.60 and 1.10, respectively. In addition, currently the risk-free rate is 7 percent and the market return is 10 percent. The historical dividend income and stock price data collected by Molly are given below.

	Stock X			Stock Y		
	Dividend	Share Price		Dividend	Share Price	
Year	Income	Beginning	Ending	Income	Beginning	Ending
1984	$1.00	$20.00	$22.00	$1.50	$20.00	$20.00
1985	1.50	22.00	21.00	1.60	20.00	20.00
1986	1.40	21.00	24.00	1.70	20.00	21.00
1987	1.70	24.00	22.00	1.80	21.00	21.00
1988	1.90	22.00	23.00	1.90	21.00	22.00
1989	1.60	23.00	26.00	2.00	22.00	23.00
1990	1.70	26.00	25.00	2.10	23.00	23.00
1991	2.00	25.00	24.00	2.20	23.00	24.00
1992	2.10	24.00	27.00	2.30	24.00	25.00
1993	2.20	27.00	30.00	2.40	25.00	25.00

Questions

1. Determine the holding period return (HPR) for each stock in each of the preceding 10 years. Find the expected return for each stock using the approach specified by Molly.

2. Use the HPRs and expected return calculated in question (1) to find the standard deviation of the HPRs for each stock over the 10-year period 1984 to 1993.

3. Use your findings above to evaluate and discuss the return and risk associated with stocks X and Y. Which stock seems preferable? Explain.

4. Use the capital asset pricing model (CAPM) to find the required return for each stock. Compare this value with the average HPRs calculated in question (1).

5. Compare and contrast your finding in questions (3) and (4). What recommendations would you give Molly in light of the investment decision currently under consideration? Explain why Molly is better off using beta rather than either a subjective approach or the standard deviation to assess investment risk.

PART TWO · INVESTING IN COMMON STOCK

THE INVESTMENT ENVIRONMENT

INVESTMENT ADMINISTRATION

| INVESTING IN COMMON STOCK | INVESTING IN FIXED-INCOME SECURITIES |
| SPECULATIVE INVESTMENT VEHICLES | OTHER POPULAR INVESTMENT VEHICLES |

·········· PART TWO INCLUDES ··········

5 | Common Stock Investments

After studying this chapter, you should be able to:

1. Explain the investment appeal of common stocks.

2. Describe stock returns from an historical perspective and in so doing, gain an appreciation of how current returns measure up to historical standards of performance.

3. Discuss the basic features of common stocks, including issue characteristics, stock quotations, and transaction costs.

4. Gain an understanding of the different kinds of common stock values and the ability of common stocks to serve as an inflation hedge.

5. Discuss common stock dividends, including how dividend decisions are made, types of dividends, and dividend reinvestment plans.

6. Describe various types of common stocks, including foreign stocks, and note the different ways that stocks can be used as investment vehicles.

Common stocks appeal to investors for a variety of reasons. To some, investing in stocks is a way to "hit it big" if the issues shoot up in price; to others, it's the level of current income they offer. But investing in stocks is, by no means, a one-way road to big returns. Losses can and often do occur, and even when the results are positive, the returns can be rather mediocre. There are no guarantees of success in this market. Therefore, it's in your best interest to learn as much as you can about these securities before investing in them. This is the first of three chapters on common stock investing. Here we will be concerned with some of the basic principles of investing in common stock. The next two chapters will look at how stocks can be valued and how to judge whether an issue might make an acceptable investment vehicle.

THE INVESTMENT APPEAL OF COMMON STOCKS

residual owners
owners/stockholders of a firm, who are entitled to dividend income and a pro-rated share of the firm's earnings only after all the firm's other obligations have been met.

The basic investment attribute of common stocks is that they enable investors to participate in the profits of the firm. Every shareholder, in effect, is a part owner of the firm and as such, is entitled to a piece of the firm's profit. But this claim on income is not without its limitations, for common stockholders are really the **residual owners** of the company. That is, they are entitled to dividend income and a share of the company's earnings only after all other corporate obligations have been met. Equally important, as residual owners, holders of common stock have *no* guarantee that they will ever receive any return on their investment. The challenge, of course, is to find stocks that will provide the kind of return you're looking for. And that's no easy task, given there are literally *thousands* of actively traded stocks to choose from.

What Stocks Have to Offer

Common stocks are a popular form of investing, used by literally millions of individual and institutional investors. Their popularity stems in large part from the fact that they offer investors the opportunity to tailor their investment programs to meet individual needs and preferences. In fact, given the size and diversity of the stock market, it's safe to say that no matter what the investment objective, there are common stocks to fit the bill. For retired people and others living off their investment holdings, stocks provide an excellent way of earning a steady stream of current income (from the dividends they produce). For investors less concerned about current income, common stocks can serve as the basis for long-run wealth accumulation. With this strategy, stocks are used very much like a savings account: Investors buy stock for the long haul as a way to earn not only dividends, but also a steady flow of capital gains. These investors recognize that stocks have a tendency to go up in price over time, and they simply position themselves to take advantage of that fact. Indeed, it is this potential for capital gains that is the real draw for most investors. For whereas dividends provide a steady stream of income, the big returns come from capital gains! And few securities can match common stocks when it comes to capital gains.

Putting Stock Returns into Perspective

Given the underlying nature of common stocks, when the market is strong, investors can generally expect to benefit in the form of steady price appreciation. When the market falters, so do investor returns. Put another way, the stock market can perform beautifully, or it can behave like a dog! A good example of the former is its performance in 1991: In spite of a war with Iraq and an attempted coup in the Soviet Union, the market still went up by some 20 percent. Figure 5.1 shows the market's performance for the year. As far as behaving badly, there's probably no better example than 1987: The year started off very nicely as stock prices shot up by almost 30 percent in the first six months, only to experience a terrible crash on October 19th. On that day, stock prices, as measured by the Dow Jones Industrial Average, fell 508 points on volume of over 600 million shares. October 19, 1987, was not just another bad day in the market—it was history. The 508-point drop easily set a record, as did the one-day volume of 600 million shares, and the percentage decline of 23 percent was almost twice the previous single-day record.

The reasons for the crash are still being debated today and likely will continue to be for years to come. Some argue that the cause was the government's inability to do anything about the enormous budget and trade deficits facing this country. Others say the crash was caused by inflation fears and sharply rising interest rates. And there are those who feel very strongly that while both of the above-noted causes probably played a role, the extent of the market drop was grossly magnified by a handful of institutional traders using fancy computer-driven techniques (like "pro-

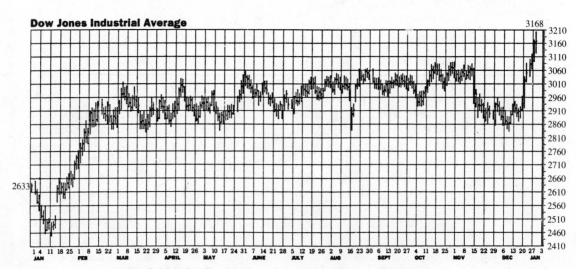

• FIGURE 5.1 The Stock Market in 1991

1991 was quite a year! It began with the U.S. about to go to war with Iraq and ended with the collapse of the U.S.S.R. In spite of all this turmoil, and a recession that just wouldn't go away, the stock market still turned in an impressive performance, as a strong year-end rally helped push the Dow up 20.3 percent. (*Source: The Wall Street Journal.*)

gram trading'' and ''portfolio insurance'') that ultimately drove prices down *much farther* than they would otherwise have gone.

Fortunately, the October 19ths of this world are the exceptions, rather than the rule. The stock market is not all risk and wild price volatility—it also offers some pretty attractive rewards. Consider the fact that even though the last quarter of 1987 was a wild one, the market still ended the year on the plus side—if up by only a meager 2 percent. And in 1988, the market went up another 12 percent, followed by an even better 27 percent jump in market prices during 1989. Indeed, if you look at the eight years from August 1982 (generally regarded as the beginning of the great bull market of the 1980s) through July 1990 (about the time Iraq invaded Kuwait), you'll find the market went up an impressive 280 percent—and that's *after* factoring in the impact of the 1987 crash and another smaller market plunge that occurred in October 1989. Clearly, it's this kind of resiliency and overall market performance that explain the appeal of common stocks.

A Look at the Record: 1950 to 1991

What would you consider to be an acceptable rate of return on common stocks? It's difficult to know what's good or bad, high or low, unless you have some understanding of the kind of returns common stocks are capable of producing. The best way to develop a feel for the market is to look at the market's past. Table 5.1 provides such a standard of performance, using the DJIA to show average market returns over the 42-year period from 1950 through 1991. In addition to total annual returns, note that market performance is also broken out between the two basic sources of return: dividends and capital gains. These figures, of course, are meant to reflect the *general behavior of the market as a whole,* and not necessarily that of *individual* stocks. Think of them as the return behavior on a well-balanced portfolio of common stocks.

The numbers show a market that has provided total returns ranging from a high of 48.28 percent (in 1954) to a low of −21.45 percent (in 1974). Breaking out the returns between dividends and capital gains, it's clear that the big returns (or losses) come from *capital gains.* And in that regard, note that prices went up far more often than they went down. (As a point of reference, the DJIA moved from just under 200 in January 1950 to nearly 3170 by the end of 1991). Overall, *stocks provided average annual returns of around 11 percent over the full forty-two year period.* And if you look at just the last 10 to 15 years, you'll find *average returns have been more like 13 to 15 percent.*

Keep in mind that these are market averages and that *individual stocks* can, and often do, perform a lot differently. But at least the averages provide us with a benchmark against which we can assess stock returns and our expectations. For example, if a return of 12 to 14 percent can be considered a good mid-point, then *sustained* returns of 18 to 20 percent, or more, should probably be viewed as fairly attractive, or even extraordinary. (These returns are possible, of course, but if you want the higher returns, you're going to have to take on more risk.) Likewise, long-run returns of only 6 to 8 percent should definitely be viewed as being on the low side. If that's the best you think you can do, then stick with bonds or CDs. Actually, returns of 12 percent or so are not all that bad, as Table 5.2 shows what a

TABLE 5.1 Annual Returns in the Stock Market, 1950–1991
(Returns Based on Performance of the DJIA)

Year	Rate of Return from Dividends	Rate of Return from Capital Gains	Total Rate of Return
1991	3.13%	20.32%	23.45%
1990	3.94	−4.34	−0.40
1989	3.74	26.96	30.70
1988	3.67	11.85	15.52
1987	3.67	2.26	5.93
1986	3.54	22.58	26.12
1985	4.01	27.66	31.67
1984	5.00	−3.74	1.26
1983	4.47	20.27	24.74
1982	5.17	19.60	24.77
1981	6.42	−9.23	−2.81
1980	5.64	14.93	20.57
1979	6.08	4.19	10.27
1978	6.03	−3.15	2.88
1977	5.51	−17.27	−11.76
1976	4.12	17.86	21.98
1975	4.39	38.32	42.71
1974	6.12	−27.57	−21.45
1973	4.15	−16.58	−12.43
1972	3.16	14.58	17.74
1971	3.47	6.11	9.58
1970	3.76	4.82	8.58
1969	4.24	−15.19	−10.95
1968	3.32	4.27	7.59
1967	3.33	15.20	18.53
1966	4.06	−18.94	−14.88
1965	2.95	10.88	13.83
1964	3.57	14.57	18.14
1963	3.07	17.00	20.07
1962	3.57	−10.81	−7.24
1961	3.11	18.71	21.82
1960	3.47	−9.34	−5.87
1959	3.05	16.40	19.45
1958	3.43	33.96	37.39
1957	4.96	−12.77	−7.81
1956	4.60	2.27	6.87
1955	4.42	20.77	25.19
1954	4.32	43.96	48.28
1953	5.73	−3.77	1.96
1952	5.29	8.42	13.71
1951	6.07	14.37	20.44
1950	6.85	17.63	24.48

Note: Total return figures are based on dividend income *and* capital gains (or losses); all figures are compiled from DJIA performance information, as obtained from *Barron's*.

TABLE 5.2 Holding Period Returns in the Stock Market, 1950–1991

Holding Periods	Average Annual Total Returns	Cumulative Total Returns	Amount to Which a $10,000 Investment Will Grow over Holding Period
5 yrs: 1987–91	14.48%	96.65%	$19,665
10 yrs: 1982–91	17.80	414.66	51,466
15 yrs: 1977–91	12.73	503.70	60,370
25 yrs: 1967–91	10.26	1,050.12	115,012
42 yrs: 1950–91	11.24	8,672.53	877,253

Note: Average annual total return figures are fully compounded returns and are based on dividend income *and* capital gains (or losses); all figures compiled from DJIA performance information, as obtained from *Barron's*.

$10,000 investment would have grown to over various holding periods within the 1950–91 time frame.

Advantages and Disadvantages of Stock Ownership

One reason stocks are so appealing to investors is the substantial return opportunities they offer. Indeed, as we just saw, stocks generally do provide attractive, highly competitive returns over the long haul. This is so because, with equity securities, stockholders are entitled to fully participate in the residual profits of the firm. The market price of a share of stock ordinarily reflects the profit potential of the firm; when the company prospers, so do investors. These increasing profits, in turn, translate into rising share prices (capital gains) and are a critical part of stock returns.

Investors are also drawn to common stocks for the current income they offer in the form of dividends, especially now that the Tax Reform Act of 1986 has effectively *lowered* taxes on dividends and *raised* them on capital gains. But stocks offer other benefits as well: Common stocks are easy to buy and sell, and the transaction costs are modest. Moreover, price and market information is widely disseminated in the news and financial media. A final advantage of stock ownership is that the unit cost of a share of common is usually well within the reach of most individual savers and investors. Unlike bonds, which carry minimum denominations of at least $1,000, and some mutual funds that have fairly hefty minimum requirements, common stocks present no such investment hurdles. Instead, most stocks today are priced at less than $75 a share—and any number of shares, no matter how few, can be bought or sold.

There are also some *disadvantages* to common stock. The risky nature of the security is perhaps the most significant disadvantage. Stocks are subject to a number of different types of risk, including business and financial risk, purchasing power risk, market risk and possibly even event risk. All of these can adversely affect a stock's earnings and dividends, its price appreciation, and, of course, the rate of return earned by an investor. Even the best of stocks possess elements of risk that are difficult to overcome. A major reason for this is that common stock represents residual ownership of a company whose earnings are subject to many factors, including government control and regulation, foreign competition, and the state of the economy. Because such factors can affect sales and profits, they can also affect the price behavior of the stock and possibly even dividends, all of which leads to another disadvantage: Since the earnings and general performance of stocks are subject to wide swings, it is difficult to value common stocks and consistently select top performers. The selection process is complex because so many elements go into formulating expectations of how the price of the stock will perform in the future. In other words, not only is the future outcome of the company and its stock uncertain, but the evaluation and selection process itself is far from perfect.

A final disadvantage is the sacrifice in current income. Several types of investments—bonds for instance—not only pay higher levels of income, but do so with much greater certainty. Figure 5.2, compares the dividend yield of common stocks with the coupon yield of bonds. It shows how the spread in current income has behaved over time and reveals the degree of sacrifice common stock investors make. Although the spread has improved lately, common stocks still have a long

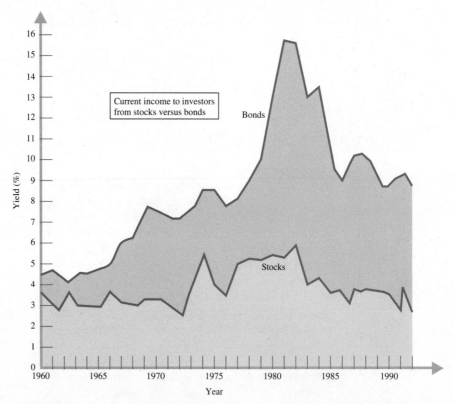

• FIGURE 5.2 The Current Income of Stocks versus Bonds

Clearly, the level of current income (dividends) paid to stockholders falls far short of the amount of interest income paid to bondholders.

way to go before they catch up with the current income levels available from other investment vehicles.

BASIC CHARACTERISTICS OF COMMON STOCK

Each share of common stock represents a part ownership (equity) position in a company. Indeed, it's this equity position which explains why common stocks are often referred to as *equity securities*. Every share entitles the holder to equal participation in the corporation's earnings and dividends, an equal vote, and an equal voice in management. The number of shares issued depends on the size of the company and its financial needs. Common stock has no maturity date and as a result, remains outstanding indefinitely.

Common Stock as a Corporate Security

equity capital
evidence of ownership position in a firm, in the form of shares of common stock.

Common stocks are a form of **equity capital,** such shares being evidence of an ownership position in a company. The shares of many corporations, however, are never traded because the firms are either too small or are family-controlled. The stocks of interest to us in this book are the so-called **publicly traded issues**—the shares that are readily available to the general public and that are bought and sold in the open market. The issuing firms of such shares range from giants like AT&T and IBM to much smaller regional or local firms, whose securities are traded either over-the-counter or on one of the regional exchanges. The market for publicly traded stocks is immense, as the market value of all actively traded listed and OTC stocks in early 1992 was roughly *$4 trillion*. Let's now look more closely at common stocks—at the basic nature and investment merits of this popular form of security.

publicly traded issues
shares of stock readily available to the general public, that are bought and sold in the open market.

public offering
an offering to sell to the investing public a set number of shares of a firm's stock at a specified price.

Ways of Issuing Stock

Shares of common stock can be issued in one of several ways. One popular method is a **public offering:** The corporation, working with an underwriter, offers the investing public a certain number of shares of its stock at a certain price. Figure 5.3 depicts an announcement for such an offering. Note in this instance that Black & Decker sold nearly 21 million shares of stock (in both the U.S. and in foreign markets) at a price of $23¼ a share. When issued, the new shares of stock will be co-mingled with the outstanding shares; the net result will be an increase in the number of shares outstanding.

rights offering
an offering of a new issue of stock to existing stockholders who may purchase new shares in proportion to their current ownership position.

A **rights offering** is another popular way of issuing common stock. Such offerings are compulsory in states which require that existing stockholders be given first crack at the new issue and be allowed to purchase new shares in proportion to their current ownership position. For instance, if a stockholder currently owns 1 percent of a firm's stock and the firm issues 10,000 additional shares, that stockholder will be given the opportunity, via a rights offering, to purchase 1 percent (or 100 shares) of the new issue.

deferred equity securities
securities initially issued in one form (warrants or convertibles) and later redeemed or converted into shares of common stock.

Still another way to issue common stock is through the use of **deferred equity securities.** Warrants and convertible securities enable holders to buy a stipulated

May 5, 1992

20,700,000 Shares

◆ BLACK&DECKER®

The Black & Decker Corporation

Common Stock

Price $23¼ Per Share

Copies of the Prospectus may be obtained in any State in which this announcement
is circulated only from such of the undersigned as may legally
offer these securities in such State.

This portion of the underwriting is being offered in the United States by the undersigned.

16,560,000 Shares

Number of shares being offered in the U.S.

Lehman Brothers

The First Boston Corporation

Goldman, Sachs & Co.

Bear, Stearns & Co. Inc.	Alex. Brown & Sons	Dillon, Read & Co. Inc.
	Incorporated	
A.G. Edwards & Sons, Inc.	Hambrecht & Quist Kemper Securities Group, Inc.	Kidder, Peabody & Co.
	Incorporated	Incorporated
Lazard Frères & Co.	Merrill Lynch & Co. Montgomery Securities	Morgan Stanley & Co.
		Incorporated
Oppenheimer & Co., Inc. PaineWebber Incorporated Prudential Securities Incorporated Robertson, Stephens & Company		
Salomon Brothers Inc	ScotiaMcLeod (USA) Inc.	Smith Barney, Harris Upham & Co.
		Incorporated
Wasserstein Perella Securities	Wertheim Schroder & Co.	Dean Witter Reynolds Inc.
a Division of Grantchester Securities, Inc.	Incorporated	
Advest, Inc. Robert W. Baird & Co. J. C. Bradford & Co. Dain Bosworth Ferris, Baker Watts Furman Selz		
Incorporated	Incorporated Incorporated	
Ladenburg, Thalmann & Co. Inc. Legg Mason Wood Walker McDonald & Company Piper Jaffray Inc.		
	Incorporated Securities, Inc.	
Raymond James & Associates, Inc. The Robinson-Humphrey Company, Inc. Wheat First Butcher & Singer		
		Capital Markets
Adams, Harkness & Hill, Inc. Baird, Patrick & Co., Inc. First Manhattan Co.		
Gerard Klauer Mattison & Co., Inc. Interstate/Johnson Lane Janney Montgomery Scott Inc. Mabon Securities Corp.		
	Corporation	
Parker/Hunter RAS Securities Corp. Ragen MacKenzie Roney & Co. Sutro & Co. Incorporated		
Incorporated	Incorporated	

This portion of the underwriting is being offered outside the United States by the undersigned.

4,140,000 Shares

Number of shares being offered in foreign markets

Lehman Brothers International

Credit Suisse First Boston Limited

Goldman Sachs International Limited

ABN AMRO Bank N.V. Banca Commerciale Italiana Commerzbank Credit Lyonnais Securities Credito Italiano		
	Aktiengesellschaft	
Daiwa Europe Limited Dresdner Bank Nomura International Salomon Brothers International Limited		
	Aktiengesellschaft	
Société Générale Swiss Bank Corporation S.G. Warburg Securities		

• FIGURE 5.3 An Announcement of a New Stock Issue

Here the company is issuing nearly 21 million shares of stock at a price of $23¼ a share. For Black & Decker, that will mean over $480 million in new capital. Note in this case that in addition to selling the stock in the United States, over 4 million shares are being sold outside the U.S. to foreign investors—which, by the way, is becoming increasingly common, as companies are going global in their search for capital. (*Source: The Wall Street Journal*, May 5, 1992.)

number of shares of common stock at a stipulated price within a stipulated time period (as in the case of warrants), or to exchange them for a certain number of shares of common stock (as in the case of convertibles). Either way, the securities are initially issued in one form and then later redeemed or converted into shares of common stock. The net result is the same as with a public offering or a rights offering: The firm ends up with more equity in its capital structure, and the number of shares outstanding increases.

Stock Splits

stock split
a maneuver in which a company increases the number of shares outstanding by exchanging a specified number of new shares of stock for each outstanding share.

Companies can also increase the number of shares outstanding by executing what is known as a **stock split.** In declaring a split, a firm merely announces its intention to increase the number of shares outstanding by exchanging a specified number of new shares for each outstanding share of stock. For example, in a 2-for-1 stock split, two new shares of stock are exchanged for each old share; in a 3-for-2 split, three new shares are exchanged for every two shares outstanding. Thus, a stockholder who owned 200 shares of stock before a 2-for-1 split automatically becomes the owner of 400 shares; the same investor would hold 300 shares if there had been a 3-for-2 split.

Stock splits are used whenever a firm wants to enhance its stock's trading appeal by lowering its market price. And normally, that's just what happens; for unless the stock split is accompanied by a big increase in the level of dividends, it is common market behavior for the price of the stock to fall in close relation to the terms of the split. Thus, using the ratio of the number of old shares to new, we can expect a $100 stock, for example, to trade at or close to $50 after a 2-for-1 split. Specifically, dividing the original price of $100 a share by the ratio of new shares to old (2/1), we have: $100 ÷ 2/1 = $100 ÷ 2 = $50. That same $100 stock would trade at about $67 with a 3-for-2 split ($100 ÷ 3/2 = $100 ÷ 1.5 = $67).

reverse stock split
a strategy in which a company reduces the number of shares outstanding by exchanging a fractional amount of a new share for each outstanding share of stock.

Most stock splits are executed in order to increase the number of shares outstanding. Sometimes, however, a **reverse stock split** is declared. Such splits reduce the number of shares outstanding and increase the share price of the stock by exchanging less than one share of new stock for each outstanding share. For example, in a 1-for-2 reverse split, one new share of stock is exchanged for two old shares. Reverse splits are also used to enhance the trading appeal of the stock by boosting the price of a stock to a more respectable range. (A variation of the stock split, known as a *stock dividend,* will be discussed later in this chapter.)

Treasury Stock

Corporations sometimes find it desirable to reduce the number of shares in the hands of the investing public by buying back their own stock. These *buy-backs,* as they're called, became very popular in the 1980s and contributed in large part to the whopping *35 percent* reduction in the number of common shares trading in the market. Generally speaking, firms repurchase their own stocks when they view them as undervalued (i.e., underpriced) in the marketplace. When that happens, the company's own stock becomes an attractive investment candidate. Those firms that can afford it will begin acquiring their stock in the open market by becoming an investor

treasury stock
shares of stock that
have been sold and
subsequently repur-
chased (and held)
by the issuing firm.

like any other individual or institution. When these shares are acquired, they become known as **treasury stock.** Technically, treasury stocks are simply shares of
stock that have been issued and subsequently repurchased by the issuing firm.
Treasury stocks are kept by the corporation and can be used by it for mergers and
acquisitions, to meet employee stock option plans, or as a means of paying stock
dividends—or they can simply be held in treasury for an indefinite period of time.
The impact of share repurchases from the investor's point of view will, of course,
vary with the number of shares repurchased. If the stock buy-back plan is substantial, the stockholder's equity position and claim on income will increase, which, in
turn, is likely to benefit stockholders to the extent that such action has a positive
effect on the market price of the stock.

Classified Common Stock

**classified common
stock**
common stock is-
sued in different
classes, each of
which offers different
privileges and bene-
fits to its holders.

For the most part, all the stockholders in a corporation enjoy the same benefits of
ownership. Occasionally, however, a company will issue different classes of common stock, each of which entitles the holder to different privileges and benefits.
These issues are known as **classified common stock.** Well over 300 publicly traded
firms have created such stock classes. Even though offered by the same company,
each class of common stock is different and has its own value. Classified common
stock is customarily used to denote either different voting rights and/or different
dividend obligations. For instance, class A could be used to designate nonvoting
shares, and class B would carry normal voting rights. Or the class A stock would
receive *no* dividends, whereas class B would receive regular cash dividends. Notable for its use of classified stock is the Ford Motor Company, which has two classes
of stock outstanding: Class A stock is owned by the investing public, and class B
stock is owned by the Ford family and their trusts or corporations. The two classes
of stock share equally in the dividends but whereas class A stock has one vote per
share, the voting rights of the class B stock are structured to give the Ford family a
40-percent absolute control of the company. Similar stock classes are used at the
Washington Post, Dillards Department Stores, General Media, Dow Jones & Co.,
and the Adolph Coors Company. Regardless of the specifics, whenever there is
more than one class of common stock outstanding, investors should always be sure
to determine the privileges, benefits, and limitations of each class *before* buying
stock in the company.

Buying and Selling Stocks

Whether buying or selling stocks, an investor should be familiar with the way stocks
are quoted and with the costs of executing common stock transactions. Certainly,
keeping track of current prices is an essential element in the buy-and-sell decisions
of investors. In essence, it's the link in the decision process that lets the investor
know when the time is right to buy or sell a stock; it also lets investors monitor the
market performance of their security holdings. Similarly, transaction costs are important because of the impact they can have on investment returns. Indeed, sometimes just the costs of executing stock transactions can consume most or all of the
profits from an investment; as a result, these costs should not be taken lightly.

Stock Quotes

Investors in the stock market have come to rely on a highly efficient information system that quickly disseminates market prices to the public. The stock quotes that appear daily in the financial press are a vital part of that information system. To see how price quotations work and what they mean, consider the quotes that appear daily (Monday through Friday) in *The Wall Street Journal*. As we'll see, these quotes give not only the most recent prices of each stock but also a great deal of additional information.

Some NYSE stock quotes are presented in Figure 5.4—let's use the *Disney* quotations for purposes of illustration. These quotes were published in *The Wall Street Journal* on Monday, October 7, 1991. They describe the trading activity that occurred the day before, which in this case, was Friday, October 4. A glance at the quotations shows that stock prices are expressed in eighths of a dollar; each eighth of a point is worth 12½ cents. The first two columns, labeled "Hi" and "Lo," contain the highest and lowest prices at which the stock sold during the past 52

	52 Weeks Hi	Lo	Stock	Sym	Div	Yld %	PE	Vol 100s	Hi	Lo	Close	Net Chg
	48½	27¾	DeluxeCp	DLX	1.28	2.8	21	363	46¼	45½	45⅞	+ ⅜
n	28⅝	18⅛	DestecEngy	ENG		...	21	403	20⅛	19¾	19¾	− ¼
	32¼	27	DetEd	DTE	1.88	5.9	9	1245	32	31½	31⅞	+ ¼
▲	174	155¼	DetEd pf		5.50	3.1	...	1	177½	177½	177½	+3½
	90¾	78	DetEd pf		7.68	8.5	...	z100	90¼	90¼	90¼	...
▲	87	75	DetEd pf		7.36	8.4	...	z70	87¼	87¼	87¼	+ ½
	26⅛	18	Dexter	DEX	.88	4.5	15	112	20	19¾	19¾	− ¼
	25¼	10½	Diagnstek	DXK		...	63	401	24½	23⅞	24⅛	+ ⅛
▲	43½	22¼	DiagnstPdt	DP	.32	.7	31	215	44¾	43¾	44¼	+1
	37½	19	DialCp	DL	1.40	3.8	12	237	36¾	36⅜	36⅜	− ½
	56	42½	DialCp pf		4.75	9.0	...	z100	52¾	52¾	52¾	−1
	16¼	9⅞	DialREIT	DR	1.68	13.6	13	182	12½	12⅜	12⅜	...
	26⅝	17¼	DiaSham	DRM	.48	2.4	6	345	20¼	19⅞	19⅞	...
	4⅜	2	DiaShamOff	DSP	.52e	13.9	10	21	3⅞	3¾	3¾	...
	4½	**1¾**	**DianaCp**	**DNA**		...	...	**19**	**2⅛**	**2**	**2**	− ⅛
s	29½	8⅜	Diasonic	DIA		...	...	297	28	27	27¾	+ ⅜
	47⅞	30	Diebold	DBD	1.60	3.4	26	672	47	46½	46⅞	+ ⅛
	21½	**8⅞**	**DigitalComm**	**DCA**		...	**10**	**1884**	**16½**	**15**	**15⅝**	**−1⅛**
	83	45½	DigitalEqp	DEC		...	...	4841	54⅛	53	53¾	+ ¼
	135¾	63⅜	DillardStrs	DDS	.24	.2	24	915	127¾	125	127	− ⅜
	6¾	1½	DimeSvgNY	DME		...	...	1450	3½	3⅛	3⅜	...
	13⅝	7⅛	DiscountNY	DCY	.40	4.0	...	34	10⅝	10⅛	10⅛	− ¼
	129¾	86	Disney	DIS	.70	.6	23	3762	114¾	112¾	113⅛	+ ⅝
	5	1⅝	Divrsind	DMC		...	...	26	2¼	2¼	2¼	...
	48	26¼	DoleFood	DOL	.30e	.7	18	2987	42⅛	41½	42⅛	+ ¼
▲	53½	42⅝	DominRes	D	3.44	6.4	13	1742	53⅝	53¼	53⅜	+ ¼
	9	6½	Domtar	DTC		...	...	14	6¾	6¾	6¾	...

- High and low prices for previous 52 weeks
- Company name
- Stock symbol used to identify company
- Annual dividends per share for past 12 months
- Dividend yield (dividends as percent of share price)
- Price/earnings ratio: $\left(\frac{\text{market price}}{\text{earnings per share}}\right)$
- Share volume, in hundreds
- High and low prices for the day
- Closing (final) price for the day
- Net change in price from previous day

Source: The Wall Street Journal, Oct. 7, 1991.

• FIGURE 5.4 Stock Quotations

Shown in this figure are the quotations for a small sample of stocks traded on the NYSE; these quotes provide a summary of the transactions that occurred on one day. (*Source: The Wall Street Journal,* October 7, 1991.)

weeks; note that Disney traded between 86 and 129¾ during the preceding 52-week period. Listed to the right of the company's name is its *stock symbol;* Disney goes by the three-letter abbreviation **DIS.** These stock symbols are the abbreviations used on the *market tapes* seen in brokerage offices and on CNBC/FNN television to identify specific companies. The figure listed right after the stock symbol is the annual cash dividend paid on each share of stock. This is followed by the stock's dividend yield and its price/earnings (P/E) ratio. The daily volume follows the P/E ratio: The sales numbers are listed in lots of 100 shares, so the figure 3762 means there were actually 376,200 shares of Disney stock traded on October 4. The next three entires, in the "Hi," "Lo," and "Close" columns, contain the highest, lowest, and last (closing) prices at which the stock sold on the day in question. Finally, as the last (Net Change) column shows, Disney closed up ⅝ of a point (62½ cents a share) on October 4, which means that the stock closed at 112½ the day before (October 3).

The same basic quotation system is used for AMEX stocks and for *some* OTC stocks. Actually, for quotation purposes, OTC stocks can be divided into two groups: Nasdaq National Market issues and other OTC stocks. The National Market stocks are those of major, actively traded companies; *they are quoted just like NYSE issues*. Other OTC stocks are either quoted in highly abbreviated form (as in the case of Nasdaq Small Cap issues) or they're listed on the basis of their *bid* and *ask* prices. (Recall that the bid price is what the investor can *sell* a stock for, whereas the ask price is what the investor would pay to *buy* the stock.) An example of a bid/ask quote is provided below:

Stock & Div.	Sales (100s)	Bid	Asked	Net Chg
CrownAm .40	115	12¼	13	−¼

The name of the company and the amount of cash dividends paid are indicated, as is the sales volume in round lots (115 = 11,500 shares of stock traded). Then, the *highest* bid price for the day is listed along with the *lowest* ask price. Finally, the change shown represents the change in the ask price of the stock.

A key part of the stock quotations are the footnotes that accompany the quotes. You'll notice in the NYSE quotes shown above that there are various symbols and initials that appear with some of the quotations. For example, looking down the first column, next to the stock's 52-week high, you'll see the following initials or symbols: n, ▲, and s. The "n" means *DestecEngy* is a *new* stock that's been issued some time in the past 12 months. The ▲ means the stock has just hit a new 52-week high. The "s" means *Diasonic* has recently gone through a *stock split* or paid a major stock *dividend*. In addition, look at the second *DialCp* stock, which is a preferred stock, as indicated by the letters "pf"; and notice the number of shares sold is shown as "z100." The "z" indicates that the sales volume shown is *the actual number of shares traded*—thus, there were only 100 shares of Dial preferred sold. The various symbols and footnotes that are sprinkled throughout the quotes are meant to provide investors with additional, valuable information about a particular security. In essence, these footnotes are added bits of information that help to put the quotes in proper perspective. Figure 5.5 spells out what many of these footnotes mean.

Although the quotation systems described above apply to major listed and OTC stocks, there's a big piece of the market that's not included in these quotes. Indeed, there are literally thousands of small, thinly traded stocks that never show up in the

---

EXPLANATORY NOTES

The following explanations apply to New York and American exchange-listed securities and the Nasdaq over-the-counter securities.

FOOTNOTES:

▲	New 52-week high.
▼	New 52-week low.
a	Extra dividend or extras in addition to the regular dividend.
b	Indicates annual rate of the cash dividend and that a stock dividend was paid.
c	Liquidating dividend.
e	Indicates a dividend was declared or paid in the preceding 12 months, but that there isn't a regular dividend rate.
g	Indicates the dividend and earnings are expressed in Canadian money. The stock trades in U.S. dollars. No yield or P/E ratio is shown.
h	Indicates a temporary exception to Nasdaq qualifications.
j	Indicates dividend was paid this year, and that at the last dividend meeting a dividend was omitted or deferred.
k	Indicates dividend declared or paid this year on cumulative issues with dividends in arrears.
n	Newly issued in the past 52 weeks. The high-low range begins with the start of trading and doesn't cover the entire period.
pf	Preferred stock.
pr	Preference stock.
r	Indicates a cash dividend declared or paid in the preceding 12 months, plus a stock dividend.
rt	Rights.
s	Stock split or stock dividend amounting to 25% or more in the past 52 weeks.
t	Dividends paid in stock in the preceding 12 months, estimated cash value on ex-dividend or ex-distribution date.
v	Trading halted on primary market.
vj	In bankruptcy or receivership or being reorganized under the Bankruptcy Code, or securities assumed by such companies.
wi	When issued.
wt	Warrants.
ww	With warrants.
x	Ex-dividend or ex-rights.
xw	Without warrants.
z	Sales in full, not in hundreds.

• FIGURE 5.5 Some Widely Used Stock Quotation Footnotes

Explained here are some of the more widely used stock quotation footnotes. You're likely to encounter these footnotes fairly regularly, as they pertain to major corporate developments or stock characteristics. (*Source: The Wall Street Journal.*)

INVESTOR INSIGHTS

Pink Sheets: The Hidden Stock Market

Looking for a stock that's not on the New York Stock Exchange or even the NASDAQ bid/ask quotes? Chances are you'll find it in the *pink sheets*. Described by some as ''the flea market of Wall Street,'' the pink-sheets list OTC stocks that are not widely traded—in effect, there's too little market activity in these stocks to justify including them in the mainline published quotes. The pink sheets are home to about 12,000 thinly traded stocks that, for one reason or another, are unable—or unwilling—to meet the financial reporting requirements of the SEC. Not surprisingly, you'll find a lot of trash here—namely, companies in or near bankruptcy and penny stocks being manipulated by crooked brokers. But you'll also find some tender young growth stocks, as well as a few obscure, yet very solid companies. There are even some well-known companies, like Rand McNally, Hoffmann-LaRoche, Manischewitz, and Churchill Downs. You might expect to find these businesses on the Big Board, but they prefer to remain ''in the pinks'' because they're closely held or don't want the publicity that comes with active stock trading.

Founded in 1913, the pink-sheets market is one of the oldest in the United States. Two Wall Street pioneers, Roger Babson and Arthur Elliott, saw the need to disseminate stock-price information and organized the National Quotation Bureau. Runners were sent to brokerage houses to collect sheets of paper on which traders listed prices for the stocks they were willing to buy or sell.

Babson and Elliott consolidated the information, and in the 1930s started printing it on pink sheets for hand-delivery to brokerage offices. That process has changed little in the half century since. Today a desk-thumping 400 pages thick and still printed on pink paper, the pink sheets are hand-carried five days a week to brokerages in the financial districts of major cities and shipped overnight to trading offices elsewhere.

---

published quotes; instead, the only place you will find them is in the so-called *pink sheets*. These sheets, so named because of the color of the paper the bid/ask quotes are printed on, are published daily and are available from brokers. The accompanying *Investor Insights* box sheds more light on this little-known and often overlooked segment of the market.

Transaction Costs

Common stock can be bought and sold in round or odd lots. A *round lot* is 100 shares of stock, or multiples thereof. An *odd lot* is a transaction involving less than 100 shares. The sale of 400 shares of stock would be considered a round lot transaction; the sale of 75 shares would be an odd lot transaction. Trading 250 shares of stock would involve a combination of two round lots and an odd lot. The cost of executing common stock transactions has risen dramatically since the introduction—on May 1, 1975—of negotiated commissions. **Negotiated commissions** mean, in effect, that brokerage fees are not fixed. In practice, however, most brokerage firms have fixed fee schedules that are applied to small transactions. Although negotiated

negotiated commissions
transactions costs for the sale and purchase of securities that are negotiated between brokers and institutional investors or individuals with large accounts.

One concession to the quickly changing nature of securities trading was made in 1986, when a pink-sheets database was offered over the Quotron computer network to which most brokerage firms subscribe. That means some OTC brokers can look up a pink-sheets stock by turning to a desktop terminal. The information your broker sees displayed may be out of date, however. Trades are not reported, and the bid and offering prices on the system are updated only at the request of traders who make the markets in pink-sheet stocks.

Most dealing is still done by telephone. If you ask your broker for a quote on a little-known pink, and the firm doesn't happen to own the stock at the time, your broker has to call a market maker—a broker who does hold the issue—to learn the latest price. Change is under way, however. On October 1, 1989, the NASD began publishing information resulting from a new SEC requirement that market makers report significant trading. For the first time, reports will indicate the volume of activity in the nonregulated pink sheets, notes Bob Ferri, a NASD spokesman.

In spite of all these changes, this is still a highly segmented market. Not surprisingly, therefore, bids and offers recorded on the pink sheets should be regarded as nothing more than indications of what the true prices might be. Spreads between them can be surprising. It's not unusual to see a pink sheet bid at 50 cents and offered at $1.50, and there's no such thing as an "inside" market, or best price. While your broker should be willing to sell you a pink-sheet stock at $1.50 if that's the offered price, he or she isn't obligated to. "Remember that you enjoy none of the safeguards that come with trading a stock listed on an exchange," notes Jacobson.

Source: Adapted from Dan Ruck, "The Hidden Stock Market," *Money Maker,* December/January 1989, pp. 46–48.

commissions have reduced the costs of trading for large institutional investors and individuals of substantial capital, they have not proved so beneficial for investors of more modest means.

Basically, an investor incurs two types of transaction costs when buying or selling stock. The major component is, of course, the brokerage fee paid at the time of transaction. As a rule, brokerage fees equal between 1 and 5 percent of most transactions—though they can go much higher, particularly for very small trades. Table 5.3 shows a commission schedule used by one major brokerage house. Not surprisingly, the amount of the commission increases as the number and price of the shares traded increases. Thus, the cost of selling 50 shares of stock trading at $10 per share amounts to $35, whereas the cost of trading 200 shares of a $10 stock is $66.77. However, although the dollar cost obviously increases with the size of the transaction, on a relative basis it actually declines. In the example above, the brokerage fee for the 50-share transaction amounts to 7 percent of the transaction, whereas that for the 200-share trade represents a cost of only 3.3 percent. Clearly, dealing in odd lots quickly adds to the cost of a stock transaction. This is so because

TABLE 5.3 A Schedule of Brokerage Commissions Paid in Common Stock Transactions

Share Price	Number of Shares						
	5	**10**	**25**	**50**	**100**	**200**	**500**
$ 1	$35.00	$35.00	$35.00	$35.00	$35.00	$ 35.00	$ 59.81
5	35.00	35.00	35.00	35.00	35.00	44.90	101.13
10	35.00	35.00	35.00	35.00	35.92	66.77	129.73
25	35.00	35.00	35.00	37.52	58.71	103.63	225.03
35	35.00	35.00	35.00	45.79	70.15	132.11	284.83
50	35.00	35.00	37.26	58.18	84.77	168.00	354.60
75	35.00	35.00	47.58	72.48	88.52	175.97	434.33
100	35.00	35.00	57.91	84.23	88.52	175.97	438.33
125	35.00	37.10	65.06	87.99	88.52	175.97	438.33
150	35.00	41.22	72.21	87.99	88.52	175.97	438.33

Source: A major full-service brokerage house. (*Note:* These commissions are, of course, subject to change; also, some brokers/dealers may charge more than the indicated commission, others less.)

all transactions made on the floors of major stock exchanges are in *round* lots and, as such, the purchase or sale of odd lots requires the assistance of a specialist, known as an odd-lot dealer. This usually results in an *odd-lot differential* of 12.5 to 25 cents per share, which is tacked on to the normal commission charge, driving up the costs of these small trades. Indeed, the relatively high cost of an odd-lot trade makes it better to deal in round lots whenever possible. The other components of the transaction cost are the transfer fees and taxes levied on the *seller* of the securities. Fortunately, these charges are modest compared to brokerage commissions.

The commission schedule in Table 5.3 is that used by a full-service brokerage firm. Security transactions can also be made through **discount brokers.** Discounters are basically in business to execute orders for their customers at *substantially reduced commissions.* Some of the major discount and full-service brokerage houses are:

discount brokers security brokers who execute orders for clients at substantially reduced commissions.

Discount Brokers:	Full-Service Brokers:
Brown & Company*	A.G. Edwards & Sons
Charles Schwab	Dean Witter Reynolds
Fidelity Brokerage Services	Kidder, Peabody
Muriel Siebert & Company*	Merill Lynch
Pacific Brokerage Services*	Paine Webber
Quick & Reilly	Prudential Securities
Rose & Company	Shearson Lehman
York Securities*	Smith Barney, Harris Upham

(Those companies marked with an * indicate bare-bones, deep-discount brokers.)

As a rule, discount brokers are best suited to active traders who deal in round lots and who are not all that interested in obtaining other broker services. Discount brokers tend to have low overhead operations and may offer little or nothing in the way of customer services. Transactions are initiated by calling a toll-free number and placing the desired buy or sell order. The order is then executed by the broker at the best possible price, with details of the transaction confirmed shortly thereafter by mail. In order to discourage small orders, most discounters charge a minimum transaction fee of $25 to $40. Depending on the size of the transaction, discount brokers can normally save investors from 30 to 80 percent of the commissions charged by full-service brokers. A brief comparison of full-service versus discount brokerage commissions is provided in Table 5.4.

Common Stock Values

The worth of a share of common stock can be described in a number of ways. Terms such as par value, book value, liquidation value, market value, and investment value are all found in the financial media. Each designates some accounting, investment, or monetary attribute of the stock in question.

Par Value

par value
the stated, or face, value of a stock.

The term **par value** refers to the stated, or face, value of a stock. It is not really a measure of anything, and except for accounting purposes, it is relatively useless. In many ways, it is a throwback to the early days of corporate law, when par value was used as a basis for assessing the extent of a stockholder's legal liability. Since the term holds little or no significance for investors, many stocks today are issued as no par or low par stocks (i.e., they may have par values of only a penny or two).

Book Value

book value
the amount of stock-holders' equity in a firm; equals the amount of the firm's assets minus the firm's liabilities and preferred stock.

Book value represents the amount of stockholders' equity in the firm. It is an accounting measure which, as we will see in the next chapter, is commonly used in security analysis and stock valuation. Book value is found by subtracting the firm's

TABLE 5.4 Comparative Commissions: Full-Service Brokers versus Discounters

	Size of Stock Transaction				
Type of Broker	**$3,000** (100 shs. at $30)	**$5,000** (500 shs. at $10)	**$10,000** (1,000 shs. at $10)	**$15,000** (300 shs. at $50)	**$25,000** (500 shs. at $50)
Typical full-service broker	$65	$130	$240	$235	$355
Typical discount broker	$40	$ 60	$ 80	$ 60	$ 80
Discount broker commissions as percent of full-service broker commissions	61%	46%	33%	25%	22%

liabilities and preferred stock from its assets. It indicates the amount of stockholder funds used to finance the firm. Let's assume that a corporation has $10 million in assets, owes $5 million in various forms of short- and long-term debt, and has $1 million worth of preferred stock outstanding. The book value of this firm would be $4 million. This amount can be converted to a per share basis—*book value per share*—by dividing it by the number of shares of common stock outstanding. For example, if this firm has 100,000 shares of common stock outstanding, then its book value per share would be $40. As a rule, you'd expect most stocks to have market prices that are above their book values.

Liquidation Value

Liquidation value is an indication of what a firm would bring on the auction block, were it to cease operations. After the assets are sold off at the best possible price, and the creditors and preferred stockholders paid off, the amount left is the **liquidation value** of the firm. Obviously, if and until liquidation actually occurs, this measure is no more than an estimate of what the firm would be worth under such circumstances. While this measure is vital to high stakes take-over artists, it is *very difficult* to arrive at and is generally of little interest to the typical individual investor who tends to view the firm as a "going concern."

liquidation value
the amount left if a firm's assets were sold or auctioned off and the creditors and preferred stockholders paid off.

Market Value

Market value is one of the easiest to determine, since it is simply the prevailing market price of an issue. In essence, market value is an indication of how the market participants as a whole have assessed the worth of a share of stock. By multiplying the market price of the stock by the number of shares outstanding, we can also find the market value of the firm itself—or what is known as the firm's *market capitalization*. For example, if a firm has 1 million shares outstanding and its stock is trading at $50 per share, the company has a market value (or "market cap") of $50 million. Because investors are always interested in an issue's market price, the market value of a share of stock is generally of considerable importance to most stockholders as they formulate their investment policies and programs.

market value
the prevailing market price of a security.

Investment Value

Investment value is probably the most important measure for a stockholder. It is an indication of the worth investors place on the stock—in effect, it is what they think the stock should be trading for. Determining a security's investment worth is a fairly complex process, but in essence it is based on expectations of the return and risk behavior of a stock. Any stock has two potential sources of return: annual dividend payments and the capital gains that arise from appreciation in market price. In establishing investment value, investors try to determine how much money they will make from these two sources, and then use such estimated information as the basis for formulating the return potential of the stock. At the same time, they try to assess the amount of risk to which they will be exposed by holding the stock. Together, such return and risk information helps them place an investment value on the stock.

investment value
the amount that investors believe a security should be trading for, or what they think it's worth.

This value represents a *maximum* price they would be willing to pay for the issue (and is the major topic of discussion in Chapter 7).

Stocks as an Inflation Hedge

For many years, conventional wisdom held that common stocks were the ideal inflation hedge. This line of reasoning followed from the belief that common stocks, on average, could provide rates of return that were large enough to cover the annual rate of inflation and still leave additional profits for the stockholder. Stated another way, stocks could be counted on to provide rates of return that consistently exceeded the annual inflation rate. Through the mid-1960s, stocks did indeed perform as inflationary hedges. But then inflation in this country rose alarmingly, and most stocks simply could not keep up. Instead, many other investment vehicles, such as fixed income securities and even short-term Treasury bills, began to outperform common stocks. With the quality of earnings declining in an inflationary economy, stock prices reacted predictably: They began to stagnate. The net result, as seen in Figure 5.6, was a market that literally went nowhere from 1965 to 1982. Even more alarming was the effect inflation had on the "real" value of stocks. Note that two lines appear in Figure 5.6: The upper line indicates the actual reported behavior of the Dow, and the other, lower, line shows what happens when the DJIA is adjusted for inflation. In real terms, *the Dow fell almost without interruption for 17 years.* Clearly, during this period, stocks were anything but an inflation hedge. However, in 1982 a major bull market began, and as inflation subsided, stocks were once again able to produce attractive inflation-adjusted returns. Indeed, stocks have done quite well against inflation during the past decade and it's very likely, so long as the annual rate of inflation remains at reasonably low levels of 3 to 4 percent, that stocks will continue to act as an inflation hedge.

COMMON STOCK DIVIDENDS

In 1991, American corporations paid out some $140 billion in dividends—nearly three times the amount paid in 1980. Yet, in spite of these numbers, dividends still don't seem to get any respect. That's unfortunate, since today's tax code tends to favor dividends as a form of income. The preferential treatment of long-term capital gains has pretty much been eliminated, so that capital gains are now taxed at almost the same rate as dividends. (Granted, there is a *slight* difference in the two, but it's really not that much: The maximum tax on dividends is 31 percent, while the maximum on capital gains is 28 percent.) Thus, for all practical purposes, dividends are more valuable, since not only is the amount you can keep *after taxes* about the same as capital gains, but dividends are far *less risky* than the capital gains that may or may not occur some time in the future. Although capital gains do represent the principal vehicle through which the really big returns are realized, the new tax code throws a whole new (and far more favorable) light on dividends. We will now look more closely at this important source of income and examine several procedural aspects of the corporate dividend decision.

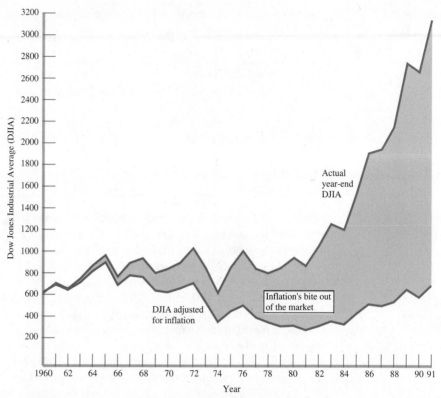

• FIGURE 5.6 Stocks in Real Terms

From 1965 through 1981, stocks were losing ground to inflation. Finally, in 1982, the returns from stocks again began to exceed the rate of inflation and the inflation-adjusted DJIA began to rise sharply.

The Dividend Decision

Companies often share the profits they earn with their stockholders by paying out dividends, typically on a quarterly basis. Actually, the question of how much to pay in dividends is decided by a firm's board of directors. The directors evaluate the firm's operating results and financial condition to determine whether, and in what amount, dividends should be paid. If dividends are to be paid, several important payment dates are also established by the board. But before dealing with those dates, let's take a look at the corporate and market factors that go into the decision to pay dividends, since this information is helpful in assessing the dividend potential of a stock.

Corporate versus Market Factors

When the board of directors assembles for a regular dividend meeting, it will weigh a variety of factors in determining the size of forthcoming dividends. First, the

**earnings per share
(EPS)**
the amount of annual
earnings available to
common stockhold-
ers, as stated on a
per share basis.

board will look at the firm's earnings. For even though a company doesn't have to show a profit to pay dividends, profits are still considered a vital link to the dividend decision. With stocks, the annual earnings of a firm are usually measured and reported in terms of **earnings per share (EPS).** Basically, EPS translates total corporate profits into profits on a per share basis and provides a convenient measure of the amount of earnings available to stockholders. Earnings per share is found by using the following simple formula:

Equation 5.1

$$EPS = \frac{\frac{net\ profit}{after\ taxes} - preferred\ dividends}{number\ of\ shares\ of\ common\ stock\ outstanding}$$

For example, if a firm reports a net profit of $1.25 million, pays $250,000 in dividends to preferred stockholders, and has 500,000 shares of common outstanding, it would have an EPS of $2 [($1,250,000 − $250,000)/500,000]. Note in Equation 5.1 that preferred dividends are *subtracted* from profits, since they have to be paid before any monies can be made available to common stockholders.

While profits are being assessed, the board will also look at the firm's growth prospects. Very likely, some of the firm's present earnings will be needed for investment purposes and to partly finance expected growth. Then the firm's cash position will be examined to make sure there is sufficient liquidity to meet a cash dividend of a given size. Finally, the board will want to assure itself that it is meeting all legal and contractual constraints. (For example, the firm may be subject to a loan agreement that legally limits the amount of dividends it can pay.) After having looked at internal matters, the board will consider certain market effects and responses. The market generally places a high value on dividends. Moreover, most investors feel that if a company is going to retain earnings rather than pay them out in dividends, it should exhibit proportionately higher growth and profit levels. The market's message is clear: If the firm is investing the money wisely and at a high rate of return, fine; otherwise, pay a larger portion of earnings out in the form of dividends. Moreover, to the extent that different types of investors tend to be attracted to certain types of firms, the board must make every effort to meet the dividend expectations of its shareholders. For example, income-oriented investors are attracted to firms that generally pay high dividends; failure to meet those expectations can lead to disastrous results in the marketplace.

Some Important Dates

date of record
the date on which
an investor must be
a registered share-
holder of a firm to
be entitled to re-
ceive a dividend.

When the directors declare a dividend, they indicate the payment times and other important dates associated with the dividend. Normally, the directors issue a statement to the press indicating their dividend decision, along with the pertinent dividend payment dates. These statements are widely quoted in the financial media; typical of such releases are the dividend news captions depicted in Figure 5.7. Three dates are particularly important to the stockholder: date of record, ex-dividend date, and payment date. The **date of record** is the date on which the investor must be a registered shareholder of the firm to be entitled to a dividend. These stockholders

CORPORATE DIVIDEND NEWS

BSN Corp, Dallas, said it will initiate a quarterly of 12.5 cents a share, to be paid in cash or, possibly, marketable securities owned by the company. The sporting goods concern owns 1.3 million shares of Sport Supply Group Inc. and about 2.1 million shares of Riddell Sports. It said payment of dividends in those securities would be subject to regulatory approval. A company spokesman said he believes the dividend probably would begin next year.

* * *

Dividends Reported November 4

Company	Period Amt.	Payable date	Record date
REGULAR			
BankAmerica Corp	Q .30	12–13–91	11–22
BankAmerica adjpfA	Q .81¼	11–30–91	11–14
BankAmerica adjpfB	Q 1.50	11–30–91	11–14
First Illinois	Q .13	12–3–91	11–15
1st Natl Bk Anchor	Q 5.00	12–16–91	12–2
Garan Inc	Q .25	12–6–91	11–20
General Motors	Q .40	12–10–91	11–14
Genl Motors clE	Q .16	12–10–91	11–14
Genl Motors clH	Q .18	12–10–91	11–14
GenlMotors $3.75pf	Q .93¾	2–1–92	1–6
GenlMotors $5pf	Q 1.25	2–1–92	1–6
Genl Motors prefE1	Q .71½	2–1–92	1–6
Jefferson-Pilot	Q .42	12–6–91	11–15
Jefferson-Pilot	Q .42	3–6–92	2–14
Lockheed Corp	Q .50	12–2–91	11–18
Manor Care Inc	Q .033	11–27–91	11–15
Mead Corp	Q .25	12–1–91	11–14
Miller Building Sys	Q .02½	12–2–91	11–15
Natl Semicon deppf	Q 1.00	12–1–91	11–15
Olsten Corp	Q .06	12–2–91	11–15
Owens & Minor	Q .05¼	12–31–91	12–16
Pittston Co	Q .05	12–2–91	11–15
Providence&Worc RR	S .05	11–29–91	11–14
Scurry Rainbow Oil	S b.25	1–1–92	12–6
Sthrn Calif Water	Q .55	12–1–91	11–15
Tribune Co	Q .24	12–12–91	11–27

STOCK			
BOK Financial	pp	12–3–91	12–3
pp-One-for-100 reverse stock split.			
Continental Tyre	vv	11–22–91	11–12
vv-Distribution of .258 shares of Export Tyre Holding Co. for each Contl Tyre share held.			
Customedix Corp	nn	11–4–91	11–4
nn-One-for-ten reverse stock split.			
Whittaker Corp	v	12–2–91	11–14
v-Distribution of one common share of Biowhittaker Inc for each share Whittaker held.			

INCREASED

		–Amounts– New	Old		
Golden West Finl	Q	.05½	.04½	12–10–91	11–15
Oregon Steel Mills	Q	.14	.12	11–29–91	r11–13
r-Revised record date.					

REDUCED

		–Amounts– New	Old		
Market Facts Inc	Q	.05	.08	11–27–91	11–20

INITIAL

Enquirer/Star Grp	–	.04	12–26–91	11–20
Sands Regent	–	.10	12–12–91	11–22

SPECIAL

Thermal Industries	–	.04	1–7–92	12–6

A-Annual; b-Payable in Canadian funds; h-From income; k-From capital gains; M-Monthly; Q-Quarterly; S-Semi-annual.

* * *

Stocks Ex-Dividend November 6

Company	Amount	Company	Amount
Amer Fructose clA	.12	Houghton Mifflin	.19½
Amer Fructose clB	.12	LeaRonal Inc	.12
Amer Home Prod	.65	Morrison-Knudsen	.37
AmerTrAmHomePrd pr.64⅜		NorcenEngyRes Mult	b.15
AmerTrAmHomePrd un.64⅜		NorcenEngyRes Sub	b.15
AmerTrAmoco pr	.54⅜	b-Canadian funds.	
AmerTrAmoco un	.54⅜	Oregon Steel Mills	.14
Amoco Corp	.55	Phila Electric	.32½
Church & Dwight	.09	Phila Suburban	.25
Consol Ed NY	.46½	Potlatch Corp	.35

• F I G U R E 5 . 7 Important Dates and Data about Dividends

The dividend actions of corporations are big news in the financial community. This news release, taken from *The Wall Street Journal*, provides timely information about cash and stock dividends, as well as stocks that have gone ex-dividend. (*Source: The Wall Street Journal*, November 5, 1991.)

are often referred to as *holders of record*. When the board specifies the date of record, all investors who are official stockholders of the firm as of the close of business on that date will receive the dividends that have just been declared.

Because of the time needed to make bookkeeping entries when a stock is traded, the stock will sell on an ex-dividend basis for four business days prior to the date of record. Thus, the **ex-dividend date** will dictate whether you were an official shareholder and therefore eligible to receive the declared dividend. If you sell a stock after the ex-dividend date, you receive the dividend. If you sell on or before this date, the new shareholder will receive the recently declared dividend. The *payment date* is also set by the board of directors and generally follows the date of record by a week or two. It is the actual date on which the company will mail dividend checks to holders of record.

ex-dividend date
the date four business days before the date of record, which determines whether one is an official shareholder of a firm and thus eligible to receive a declared dividend.

To see how this all works, consider the following sequence of events: On June 3, the board of directors of Cash Cow, Inc., declares a quarterly dividend of $0.50 a share to holders of record on June 18, with checks to be mailed on June 30. The calendar below shows these various dividend dates:

June

S	M	T	W	T	F	S	
	1	2	③——	—4——	—5——	—6———	—— Declaration date
7	8	9	10	11	⑫——	—13———	—— Ex-dividend date
14	15	16	17	⑱——	—19——	—20———	—— Date of record
21	22	23	24	25	26	27	
28	29	㉚——				———	—— Payment date

Thus, if you owned 200 shares of the stock on June 12, you'd receive a check in the mail sometime after June 30 in the amount of $100.

Types of Dividends

cash dividend
payment of a dividend in the form of cash.

stock dividend
payment of a dividend in the form of additional shares of stock.

Normally, companies pay dividends in the form of cash, though sometimes they do so by issuing additional shares of stock. The first type of distribution is known as a **cash dividend;** the latter is called a **stock dividend.** Occasionally dividends will be paid in still other forms. For example, the firm might pay what is known as a *spinoff dividend*. This is like a stock dividend, except that the company pays its stockholders in shares *other than its own*. Generally, these are shares in subsidiary companies that the corporation owns and which it is spinning off—i.e., for one reason or another, it is reducing (or eliminating) its investment in the subsidiary operation. But dividends in the form of either cash or stock remain by far the most popular, so let's take a closer look at them.

Cash or Stock

dividend yield
a measure that relates dividends to share price and in so doing, puts common stock dividends on a relative (percent) rather than absolute (dollar) basis.

More firms use cash dividends than any other type of dividend payment procedure. A nice by-product of cash dividends is that *they tend to increase over time, as companies' earnings grow*. In fact, the average annual increase in dividends is around 5 to 7 percent. Such a tendency appeals to investors since a steady stream of dividends—even better, a *steadily increasing* stream of dividends—acts to shore up stock returns in soft markets.

A convenient way of assessing the amount of dividends received is to measure the stock's **dividend yield.** Basically, dividend yield is a measure of common stock dividends on a relative (percent) rather than absolute (dollar) basis. That is, the dollar amount of dividends received is related to the market price of the stock.

Dividend yield, in effect, indicates the rate of current income earned on the investment dollar. It is computed as follows:

Equation 5.2

$$\text{Dividend yield} = \frac{\text{annual dividends received per share}}{\text{current market price of the stock}}$$

Thus, a company that annually pays $2 per share in dividends to its stockholders, and whose stock is trading at $25, has a dividend yield of 8 percent.

To put dividend yield into perspective, it's often helpful to look at a company's **dividend payout ratio.** By definition, the payout ratio describes that portion of earnings per share (EPS) that is paid out as dividends. It is computed as follows:

Equation 5.3

$$\text{Dividend payout ratio} = \frac{\text{dividends per share}}{\text{earnings per share}}$$

dividend payout ratio
that portion of earnings per share (EPS) that a firm pays out as dividends.

Thus, a company would have a payout ratio of 50% if it had earnings of $2 a share and paid annual dividends of $1 a share. Although stockholders like to receive dividends, they normally do not like to see excessively high payout ratios—say, over 60–70 percent. Payout ratios of that size are often taken as a sign that the company is going to have trouble maintaining such a payout level.

Occasionally, a firm may declare a stock dividend instead of a cash dividend. A stock dividend simply means that the dividend is paid in additional shares of stock. For instance, if the board declares a 10 percent stock dividend, each shareholder will receive 1 new share of stock for each 10 shares currently owned. If you own 200 shares of stock, you will receive 20 new shares under such an arrangement. Although they seem to satisfy the needs of some investors, *stock dividends really have no value* because they represent the receipt of something already owned. The market will respond to such dividends by adjusting share prices according to the terms of the stock dividend. Thus, in the example above, a 10 percent stock dividend will normally lead to a decline of around 10 percent in the share price of the stock. As a result, if the market value of your shareholdings amounted to, say, $10,000 before a stock dividend, it is likely that the same total market value will prevail after the stock dividend. You may have more shares, but each will carry a lower market price. There is, however, one bright spot in all this: Unlike cash dividends, at least you don't have to pay taxes on these dividends *until the stocks are actually sold.*

Dividend Reinvestment Plans

dividend reinvestment plans (DRPs)
plans in which shareholders have cash dividends automatically reinvested in additional shares of the firm's common stock.

In recent years, a growing number of firms have established **dividend reinvestment plans (DRPs),** whereby shareholders can have their cash dividends automatically reinvested into additional shares of the company's common stock. The basic investment philosophy at work here is that *if the company is good enough to invest in, it's good enough to reinvest in.* As Table 5.5 demonstrates, such an approach can have a tremendous impact on your investment position over time. Today, over 1,000 companies (including most major corporations) offer dividend reinvestment plans, and each one provides investors with a convenient and inexpensive way to accumulate capital. Stocks in most DRPs are acquired free of any brokerage commissions.

TABLE 5.5 Cash or Reinvested Dividends?

Situation: Buy 100 shares of stock at $25 a share (total investment $2,500); stock currently pays $1 a share in annual dividends. Price of the stock increases at 8% per year; dividends grow at 5% per year.

Investment Period	Number of Shares Held	Market Value of Stock Holdings	Total Cash Dividends Received
TAKE DIVIDENDS IN CASH			
5 years	100	$ 3,672	$ 552
10 years	100	5,397	1,258
15 years	100	7,930	2,158
20 years	100	11,652	3,307
PARTICIPATE IN DIVIDEND REINVESTMENT PLAN			
5 years	115.59	$ 4,245	$0
10 years	135.66	7,322	0
15 years	155.92	12,364	0
20 years	176.00	20,508	0

Some plans even sell stocks to their DRP investors at below-market prices—often at discounts of 3 to 5 percent. In addition, most plans will credit fractional shares to the investor's account.

Shareholders can join these plans by simply sending in a completed authorization form to the company. (Generally, it takes about 30–45 days for all the paperwork to be processed.) There's really only one requirement: In order to join a dividend reinvestment plan, *you must be a "shareholder of record."* This means you *cannot* hold your stock in "street name" (in the name of your broker); instead, the shares must actually be recorded in your name. Once you're enrolled in the plan, the number of shares you hold will begin to accumulate with each dividend date. There is a catch, however: Even though these dividends take the form of additional shares of stock, taxes must be paid on them as though they were cash dividends. Don't confuse these dividends with stock dividends—*reinvested dividends are taxable as ordinary income in the year they're received,* just as if they had been received in cash.

TYPES AND USES OF COMMON STOCK

Common stocks appeal to investors because they offer the potential for everything from current income and stability of capital to attractive capital gains. The market contains a wide range of stock, from the most conservative to the highly speculative. Generally, the kinds of stock sought by investors will depend on their investment objectives and their investment program. We will examine several of the more popular kinds of common stock here, as well as the various ways such securities can be used in different types of investment programs.

Kinds of Stock

It is helpful to understand the market system used to classify common stock, because a stock's general classification denotes not only its fundamental source of return, but also the quality of the company's earnings, the issue's susceptibility to market risks, the nature and stability of its earnings and dividends, and even the susceptibility of the stock to adverse economic conditions. Such insight is useful in selecting stocks that best fit one's overall investment objectives. Among the many different types of stock, blue chips, income stocks, growth stocks, speculative stocks, cyclical stocks, defensive stocks, and small cap stocks are the most common. We will now look at each of these to see not only what they are, but also how they might be used.

Blue Chips

Blue chips are the cream of the common stock crop; they are stocks that are unsurpassed in quality and have a long and stable record of earnings and dividends. They are issued by large, well-established firms that have impeccable financial credentials. The companies hold important, if not leading, positions in their industries and frequently determine the standards by which other firms are measured. Not all blue chips are alike, however. Some provide consistently high dividend yields; others are more growth oriented. Good examples of blue chip growth firms are Merck, Philip Morris, General Mills, Procter & Gamble, and Wal-Mart Stores (shown here). high-yielding blue chips include American Home Products, Exxon, Olin Corp., K Mart, and Pfizer. Blue chips are particularly attractive to investors who seek quality investment outlets that offer decent dividend yields and respectable growth potential. Many use them for long-term investment purposes, and because of their relatively low risk exposure, as a way of obtaining modest but dependable rates of return on their investment dollars. They are popular with a large segment of the investing public and as a result, are often relatively high priced, especially when the market is unsettled and investors become more quality-conscious.

Wal-Mart Stores

NYSE Symbol WMT   Options on CBOE (Mar-Jun-Sep-Dec)   In S&P 500

Price	Range	P-E Ratio	Dividend	Yield	S&P Ranking	Beta
Jun. 20'91	1991					
43	$44\frac{1}{4}$–$28\frac{1}{2}$	36	0.17	0.4%	A+	1.21

SUMMARY: Wal-Mart operates a chain of discount department stores primarily spanning the Sunbelt and the Midwest, with locations generally in smaller communities. Strong base expansion and an aggressive pricing posture should facilitate market share gains in the Wal-Mart division, while improving profitability of the wholesale clubs and contributions from larger-store formats enhance longer-term prospects.

Source: S&P's *NYSE Stock Reports,* June 28, 1991.

Income Stocks

Some stocks are appealing simply because of their dividend yields. This is the case with *income stocks*—issues that have a long and sustained record of regularly paying higher than average dividends. Income shares are ideally suited for those who seek a relatively safe and high level of current income from their investment capital. But there's more: Holders of income stocks (unlike bonds and preferred stocks) can expect the amount of dividends they receive to increase regularly over time. Take Potomac Electric Power, for example: It paid dividends of 79 cents a share in 1981; 10 years later, in 1991, it was paying $1.56 a share. That's a big jump in dividends— nearly 98 percent—and it's something that can have quite an impact on total return. The major disadvantage of these securities is that some of them may be paying high dividends because of limited growth potential. Indeed, it's not unusual for income shares to exhibit only low or modest rates of growth in earnings. This does not mean that such firms are unprofitable or lack future prospects. Quite the contrary: Most firms whose stocks qualify as income shares are highly profitable organizations with excellent future prospects. A number of income stocks are among the giants of American industry, and many are also classified as quality blue chips. Most public utilities, such as Consolidated Edison, Atlanta Gas Light, Duke Power, and PacifiCorp (shown here) are found in this group, as are phone stocks (like Ameritech and U.S. West) and selected industrial and financial issues, like Kimberly-Clark, Dow Chemical, PNC Financial, and Wells Fargo. By their nature, income stocks are not exposed to a great deal of business and market risk. They are, instead, subject to a fair amount of interest rate risk.

PacifiCorp

NYSE Symbol PPW   Options on Pacific (Feb-May-Aug-Nov)   In S&P 500

Price	Range	P-E Ratio	Dividend	Yield	S&P Ranking	Beta
Jun. 14'91	1991					
20⅞	23–20⅜	11	1.50	7.2%	A−	0.36

SUMMARY: This major utility holding company also has interests in mining and resource development, telecommunications, and financial services. Combined electric operations serve customers in Utah, Oregon, Wyoming, Washington, Idaho, California and Montana. On August 31, 1990, PPW and Pinnacle West Capital (PNW) announced an asset sale and power exchange agreement, subject to regulatory approval. PPW has agreed to terminate its efforts to purchase PNW if the transactions are closed.

Source: S&P's *NYSE Stock Reports,* June 24, 1991.

Growth Stocks

Shares that have experienced, and are expected to continue experiencing, consistently high rates of growth in operations and earnings are known as *growth stocks*. A good growth stock might exhibit a *sustained* rate of growth in earnings of 15 to 18 percent a year over a period when common stocks, on average, are experiencing growth rates of only 5 to 6 percent. Generally speaking, established growth companies combine steady earnings growth with high returns on equity. In addition, they have high operating margins and plenty of cash flow to service their debt. H & R Block (shown here), Newell Co., Stride Rite, Archer-Daniels-Midland, GATX Corp., and Schering-Plough are prime examples of growth stocks. As this list suggests, some growth stocks also rate as blue chips and provide quality growth, whereas others possess higher levels of speculation. Growth stocks normally pay little or no dividends, and their payout ratios seldom exceed 15 to 20 percent of earnings, as all or most of the profits are reinvested in the company and used to at least partially finance rapid growth. Thus the major source of return to investors is price appreciation. Growth shares generally appeal to investors who are looking for attractive capital gains rather than dividends and who are therefore willing to assume a higher element of risk. Most growth stock investors, however, view this added risk as acceptable in light of the relatively high potential return these securities offer.

Block (H & R)

NYSE Symbol HRB   Options on ASE (Jan-Apr-Jul-Oct)   In S&P 500

Price	Range	P-E Ratio	Dividend	Yield	S&P Ranking	Beta
May 31'91	1991					
53¾	55¾–39⅞	24	1.56	2.9%	A	0.93

SUMMARY: This company is the largest preparer of federal income tax returns for individuals, completing over 10% of returns filed in both the U.S. and Canada. Earnings have risen steadily for nearly two decades; long-term prospects are buoyed by growth in new services and businesses, gains in market share, and ongoing operating synergies. Cash dividends have been raised in each calendar year since 1962.

Source: S&P's *NYSE Stock Reports,* June 10, 1991.

Speculative Stocks

Shares that lack sustained records of success but still offer the potential for substantial price appreciation are known as *speculative stocks*. Perhaps it's a new management team taking over a troubled company or the introduction of a promising new product that spurs investors' hopes. Other times, it's the possibility that some new information, discovery, or production technique will come along, favorably affect the growth prospects of the firm, and inflate the price of the stock. Speculative stocks are a special breed of securities, and they enjoy a wide following, particularly when the market is bullish. Generally speaking, their earnings are uncertain and highly unstable; they are subject to wide swings in price; and they usually pay little or nothing in dividends. On the plus side, speculative stocks like Amgen (shown here), U.S. Bioscience, Flightsafety Int'l., Harley-Davidson, and Archive Corp. offer attractive growth prospects and the chance to ''hit it big'' in the market. But to be successful, an investor has to identify the big-money winners before the rest of the market does, and before the price of the stock is driven up. Speculative stocks, then, are highly risky. They require not only a strong stomach, but also considerable investor know-how. They are used to seek capital gains, and investors will often aggressively trade in and out of these securities as the situation demands.

Amgen

NASDAQ Symbol AMGN   (Incl. in Nat'l Market; marginable)

Price	Range	P-E Ratio	Dividend	Yield	S&P Ranking	Beta
May. 22'91	1991					
121¾	137–56½	NM	None	None	NR	1.12

SUMMARY: Amgen is a leading biotechnology firm developing products based on recombinant DNA technology and molecular biology. Results in fiscal 1991 were boosted by impressive sales of Amgen's initial product, Epogen, which stimulates the production of red blood cells, and were further aided by the successful February 1991 launch of Neupogen, a stimulator of white blood cell production in cancer patients.

Source: S&P's *OTC Stock Reports,* May 31, 1991.

Cyclical Stocks

Cyclical stocks are issued by companies whose earnings are closely linked to the general level of business activity. They tend to reflect the general state of the economy and move up and down as the business cycle moves through its peaks and troughs. Companies that serve markets tied to capital equipment spending on the part of business, or consumer spending for big-ticket durable items like houses and cars, typically head the list of cyclical stocks. These include companies like Caterpillar, Timken, Federal Paper Board, Reynolds Metals, and Georgia-Pacific (shown here). For obvious reasons, these stocks have the most appeal when the economic outlook is strong (i.e., when the country's about to come out of a recession). They are perhaps best avoided when the economy begins to weaken. Because their prices have a tendency to move with the level of economic activity, they are probably most suitable for investors who are willing to trade in and out of these issues as the economic outlook dictates and who can tolerate the accompanying exposure to risk.

Georgia-Pacific

NYSE Symbol GP   Options on Phila (Jan-Apr-Jul-Oct)   In S&P 500

Price	Range	P-E Ratio	Dividend	Yield	S&P Ranking	Beta
May. 2'91	1991					
47⅞	49⅛–36¼	16	1.60	3.3%	B+	1.25

SUMMARY: Through the March 1990 acquisition of Great Northern Nekoosa, Georgia-Pacific became one of the largest forest products company in the world. GP is a leading producer of softwood plywood, uncoated papers, market pulp and containerboard, and is the largest owner of timberlands in North America. The costly acquisition, however, will greatly increase GP's interest charges for the next several years. Earnings for 1991 will be hurt by weak homebuilding markets.

Source: S&P's *NYSE Stock Reports,* May 10, 1991.

Defensive Stocks

Sometimes it is possible to find stocks whose prices will remain stable, or even prosper, when general economic activity is tapering off. These securities are known as *defensive stocks*. They tend to be less affected by downswings in the business cycle than the average issue. Examples of defensive stocks include the shares of many public utilities, as well as industrial and consumer goods companies that produce or market such staples as beverages, foods, and drugs. An excellent example of a defensive stock is Bandag (shown here); this recession-resistant company is the world's leading manufacturer of rubber used to retread tires. Other examples include Loctite, the producers of super glue, Union Corp., a debt collection company, and Checkpoint Systems, a manufacturer of anti-theft clothing security clips. Perhaps the best known of all defensive stocks, particularly in inflationary periods, are gold mining shares; these stocks literally flourish when inflation becomes a serious problem. Defensive shares are commonly used by more aggressive investors. For the most part, such investors tend to "park" their funds temporarily in defensive stocks while the market and/or economy is off, and until the investment atmosphere improves.

Bandag, Inc.

NYSE Symbol BDG

Price	Range	P-E Ratio	Dividend	Yield	S&P Ranking	Beta
Jul. 19'91	1991					
102	105¼–81½	19	1.10	1.1%	A+	1.03

SUMMARY: Bandag is a leading manufacturer of tread rubber, equipment and supplies used in a patented "cold" bonding process for the recapping of truck and bus tires. Foreign operations account for a significant portion of sales and operating income. BDG's long record of rising earnings may be broken in 1991, but higher profits are likely in 1992. Dividends have been increased in each year since their initiation in 1976. The Carver family controls about 74% of the voting power.

Source: S&P's *NYSE Stock Reports*, July 29, 1991.

Small Cap Stocks

Some investors consider small companies to be in a class by themselves. They believe the stocks of these firms hold especially attractive return opportunities, which in many cases, has turned out to be true. Known as *small cap* stocks—due to their relatively low market capitalizations—these companies generally have annual sales of less than $250 million, and because of their size, spurts of growth can have dramatic effects on their earnings and stock prices. International Dairy Queen, Farr Co., Fiserve, WD–40, and Tootsie Roll (shown here) are just a few examples of some of the better-known small cap stocks. While firms like Dairy Queen and Tootsie Roll are solid companies with equally solid financials, that's not the case with a lot of small cap stocks. Indeed, because many of these companies are so small, they don't have a lot of stock outstanding, and their shares are not widely traded. In addition, small company stocks have a tendency to be ''here today and gone tomorrow.'' While some of these stocks may hold the potential for high returns, investors should also be aware of the very high-risk exposure that comes with many of them.

Tootsie Roll Industries

NYSE Symbol TR

Price	Range	P-E Ratio	Dividend	Yield	S&P Ranking	Beta
Jun. 28'91	1991					
50½	53–35⅝	21	0.26	0.5%	A	1.11

SUMMARY: This company is a manufacturer and distributor of candy, sold primarily under the Tootsie Roll brand name. It also manufactures and sells Cella's, Mason and Bonomo candies, and in September 1988, acquired Charms Co., the largest U.S. lollipop confectioner. Sales and profits reached record levels in 1990 for the 14th and ninth consecutive years, respectively, aided by record domestic and international sales. Successful sales promotions, expense reduction programs and increased interest income resulted in higher earnings in 1991's first quarter. The quarterly dividend was boosted 16% in May, 1991.

Source: S&P's *NYSE Stock Reports,* July 10, 1991.

initial public offering (IPO)
a special category of common stocks issued by (relatively) new firms going public for the first time.

A special category of small company stock is the so-called **initial public offering.** Most of these IPOs, as they are known, are small, relatively new companies that are going public for the first time. (Prior to their public offering, these stocks were privately held and *not* publicly traded.) Like other small cap stocks, IPOs are attractive because of the substantial—sometimes phenomenal—capital gains that can be earned by investors. But there's also a downside. The chances are *very high* that you won't make much at all on the investment. In fact, you may well end up with a loss. For proof, just look at how IPOs performed during the 1980s. Over the ten-year time span, there were nearly 3,200 companies that went public. Here's how they ended up as the decade came to a close (and remember, the 1980s were a good time to be in stocks):

- Only 33 percent of the stocks *rose* in price.
- Some 25 percent of the stocks *dropped* in price.
- The remaining 42 percent of the companies either failed, merged, or were liquidated.

Without a doubt, IPOs are extremely high-risk investments, with the odds stacked against the investor. Since there's no market record to rely on, these stocks should be used only by investors who know what to look for in the company and who can tolerate the substantial exposure to risk. If you are buying IPOs, by all means, diversify; don't put all your money on one long shot. Also, before you invest in an IPO, be sure to get a copy of the prospectus and study it carefully. Pay particular attention to how the proceeds from the stock issue will be used. If all or most of it is to be used to fund the ongoing growth of the company, that's fine. But if it's going to *cash out the current owners* (i.e., the current owners are selling all or a big chunk of their stock in the company), then you might want to reconsider the investment. IPOs tend to flourish when the market heats up, and they very definitely are faddish, often dominated by trendy retail outlets, food chains, and high-tech firms.

Investing in Foreign Stocks

The 1980s produced a number of changes in our financial markets system, one of the most dramatic of which was the trend towards globalization. Globalization has become the buzzword of the 1990s, and nowhere is that more evident than in the world equity markets. Consider, for example, that in 1970, the U.S. stock market accounted for fully *two-thirds of the world market*. In essence, our stock market was twice as big as all the rest of the world's stock markets, *combined*. That's no longer true: In 1991, the U.S. share of the world equity market had dropped to 30 percent.

Today, the world equity markets are dominated by six countries (which, together, account for about 80 percent of the total market):

	Approximate Market Value (1991)
U.S.	$4.1 trillion
Japan	$3.4 trillion
U.K./Britain	$850 billion
Germany	$400 billion
France	$360 billion
Canada	$250 billion

The United States is still the biggest player and along with Japan, is one of only two countries with trillion-dollar stock markets. In addition to these six, there are another half-dozen or so markets which are also regarded as major world players. Included in this second tier are: Switzerland, Australia, Italy, Netherlands, Hong Kong, Spain, and Singapore. Finally, there are a number of relatively small, emerging markets—like those in South Korea, Sweden, Austria, Denmark, Norway, and Mexico—that are beginning to make their presence felt. Clearly, the landscape has changed a lot in the last 20 years and there's every reason to believe—with the historic changes taking place in Eastern Europe and the Communist bloc—that even greater changes lie ahead.

But a question remains: How has the U.S. equity market performed in contrast to the rest of the world's major stock markets? Unfortunately, not too well. Table 5.6 provides a summary of total annual returns (in U.S. dollars) for the 15-year period from 1977 through 1991, for ten of the world's major equity markets. Note that the U.S. finished first only once (in 1982); indeed, more often than not—in 8 out of the 15 years—the U.S. equity markets finished in the bottom five! The message is clear: Investors who concentrate solely on U.S. stocks are overlooking more than two-thirds of the publicly traded equity markets; equally important, they're missing out on investment returns that often exceed those obtained on U.S securities.

TABLE 5.6 Comparative Annual Returns in the World's Major Equity Markets

ANNUAL TOTAL RETURNS (IN U.S. DOLLARS)

	Australia	Canada	France	Germany	Hong Kong	Japan	Singapore	Switzerland	U.K.	U.S. (Rank*)
1991	35.8%	12.1%	18.6%	8.7%	49.6%	9.0%	24.6%	16.8%	16.0%	23.5% (4th)
1990	-16.2	-12.2	-13.3	-8.8	9.2	-35.9	-11.5	-5.1	10.4	-0.4 (3rd)
1989	10.8	25.2	37.6	48.2	8.4	2.3	42.4	28.0	23.1	30.7 (4th)
1988	38.2	17.9	37.1	19.8	28.0	35.4	33.1	5.8	4.1	15.5 (8th)
1987	9.5	14.8	-13.9	-24.6	-4.0	41.0	2.3	-9.2	35.2	5.9 (5th)
1986	45.0	10.8	79.9	36.4	56.2	101.2	45.1	34.7	27.7	26.1 (10th)
1985	21.1	16.2	84.2	138.1	51.7	44.0	-22.2	109.2	53.4	31.7 (7th)
1984	-12.4	-7.1	4.8	-5.2	46.9	17.2	-26.8	-11.1	5.3	1.2 (5th)
1983	55.2	32.4	33.2	23.9	-3.1	24.8	31.3	19.9	17.3	24.7 (6th)
1982	-22.2	2.6	-4.2	10.5	-44.2	-0.6	-16.2	2.9	9.0	24.8 (1st)
1981	-23.8	-10.1	-28.5	-10.3	-16.2	15.7	18.0	-9.5	-10.2	-2.8 (3rd)
1980	54.7	21.6	-2.0	-10.7	73.8	30.4	62.4	-7.8	42.0	20.6 (7th)
1979	43.7	52.3	29.0	-4.1	82.8	-11.8	28.6	12.4	21.5	10.3 (8th)
1978	22.2	22.3	74.7	25.4	18.4	54.5	45.5	20.3	12.2	2.9 (10th)
1977	6.7	6.2	0.2	12.2	-12.4	-5.0	0.5	5.4	41.6	-11.8 (9th)

AVERAGE ANNUAL RETURNS OVER EXTENDED HOLDING PERIODS

	Australia	Canada	France	Germany	Hong Kong	Japan	Singapore	Switzerland	U.K.	U.S. (Rank*)
5 yrs: 1977–81	17.2%	16.7%	9.6%	1.6%	22.5%	14.3%	29.2%	3.5%	19.7%	3.2% (9th)
1982–86	13.2	10.2	34.7	33.3	13.5	33.3	-1.9	25.3	21.4	21.2 (5th)
1987–91	13.8	10.8	10.8	5.8	16.8	6.4	16.4	6.4	17.3	14.5 (4th)
10 yrs: 1982–91	13.5	10.5	22.2	18.8	15.1	19.1	6.9	15.5	19.3	17.8 (5th)
15 yrs: 1977–91	14.7	12.5	17.8	12.7	17.6	17.5	13.8	11.3	19.5	12.7 (7th)

Note: Total Return = Coupon Income + Capital Gain (or Loss) + Profit (or Loss) From Changes in Currency Exchange Rates.

*Parenthetical "Rank" shows how U.S. returns ranked among the listed major markets—e.g., in 1991, U.S. ranked 4th out of the 10 markets listed in the table.

Source: International returns obtained from Morgan Stanley Capital International and Templeton International; U.S. returns based on DJIA.

Going Global: Direct Investments versus ADRs

Basically, there are two ways to invest in foreign stocks. (There *is* a third way, and that's through international mutual funds, which we'll discuss in Chapter 13.) Without a doubt, the most adventuresome way is to *buy shares directly in foreign markets*. Investing directly is *not* for the uninitiated, however. You have to know what you're doing and be prepared to tolerate a good deal of market risk, for, with the possible exception of Canada, buying stocks in a foreign market can be challenging, to say the least. Although most major U.S. brokerage houses are set up to accommodate investors interested in buying foreign securities, there are still many *logistical* problems to be faced. To begin with, you have to cope with currency fluctuations and changing foreign exchange rates. As we'll see below, these can have a dramatic impact on investor returns. But that's just the start: You also have to deal with a different set of regulatory and accounting standards. The fact is that most foreign markets, even the bigger ones, are not as closely regulated as U.S. exchanges. Investors in foreign markets thus have to put up with insider trading and a lot of other practices that can cause wild swings in market prices. Further, accounting standards are often much looser, making detailed information about a company's financial condition and operating results a lot harder to come by. Finally there are the obvious language barriers, tax problems, and general "red tape" that all too often seem to be a part of international transactions. There's no doubt that the returns from direct foreign investments can, at times, be substantial, but so are many of the hurdles that are placed in your way.

Fortunately, there is an easier way to invest in foreign stocks and that is to buy *American Depositary Receipts (ADRs)*—or, American Depositary *Shares,* as they're sometimes called. As we saw in Chapter 2, ADRs are negotiable instruments, issued by American banks, with each ADR representing a specific number of shares in a specific foreign company. An ADR is treated like, and trades like, a share of American stock. ADRs are traded on the NYSE, AMEX, and Nasdaq/OTC markets. To see how ADRs are structured, take a look at Cadbury Schweppes, a British food and household products firm. Each Cadbury ADR represents ownership of 10 shares of Cadbury stock. These shares are held in a custodial account by a U.S. bank (or its foreign correspondent), which receives dividends, pays any foreign withholding taxes, then converts the net proceeds to U.S. dollars and passes them on to investors. ADRs are an interesting investment vehicle and hold a lot of appeal for U.S. investors. The accompanying *Investor Insights* box on pages 216 and 217 provides additional information about American depositary receipts.

Stock Returns in a Global Perspective

Whether an investor is buying foreign stocks directly or ADRs, the whole process of investing is a bit more complex and more risky than domestic investing. When investing globally, the investor not only has to pick the right stock but also the right market. Basically, foreign stocks are valued much the same way as American stocks. Indeed, the same variables that drive U.S. share prices (such as earnings, dividends, and the like) also drive stock values in foreign markets. On top of this, each market reacts to its own set of economic forces (like inflation, interest rates, the level of economic activity, and so forth), which set the tone of the market. At any given point in time, therefore, some markets are performing better than others. The challenge facing global investors is to be in the right market at the right time. As with American stocks, foreign shares produce the same two basic sources of stock returns: dividends and capital gains (or losses).

But with global investing, there's a third variable—*currency exchange rates*—that plays a very important role in defining returns to U.S. investors. For as the U.S. dollar becomes weaker or stronger relative to a foreign currency, the returns to U.S. investors, from foreign stocks, will increase or decrease accordingly. Essentially, in a global context, total return to U.S. investors in foreign securities is defined as follows:

Equation 5.4

$$\begin{array}{c}\text{Total return}\\\text{(in U.S. dollars)}\end{array} = \begin{array}{c}\text{current income}\\\text{(dividends)}\end{array} + \begin{array}{c}\text{capital gains}\\\text{(or loss)}\end{array} +/- \begin{array}{c}\text{changes in currency}\\\text{exchange rates}\end{array}$$

Since current income and capital gains are in "local currencies" (that is, the currency in which the foreign stock is denominated, such as the German mark or the Japanese yen), we can shorten the total return formula to:

Equation 5.5

$$\begin{array}{c}\text{Total return}\\\text{(in U.S. dollars)}\end{array} = \begin{array}{c}\text{returns from current}\\\text{income \& capital gains}\\\text{(in local currency)}\end{array} +/- \begin{array}{c}\text{returns from changes in currency}\\\text{exchange rates}\end{array}$$

Thus, *the two basic components of total return are those generated by the stocks themselves (dividends plus change in share prices) and those derived from movements in currency exchange rates.*

Exchange rates can have a dramatic impact on investor returns. Quite often, they can convert mediocre returns, or even losses, into very attractive returns—and vice versa. There's really only one thing that determines whether the impact is going to be positive or negative, and that's the behavior of the U.S. dollar relative to the currency in which the foreign security is denominated. In effect, *a stronger dollar has a negative impact on total returns to U.S. investors, and a weaker dollar has a positive impact.* Thus, other things being equal, the best time to be in foreign securities is when the dollar is *falling,* because that *adds* to returns to U.S. investors. Of course, the greater the amount of fluctuation in the currency exchange rate, the greater the impact on total returns. The challenge facing global investors, therefore, is to find not only the best performing foreign stock(s), but also the best performing foreign currencies. And this applies both to the direct investment in foreign stocks and to the purchase of ADRs (even though ADRs are denominated in dollars, their quoted prices vary with ongoing changes in currency exchange rates).

Alternative Investment Strategies

Basically, common stocks can be used (1) as a "warehouse" of value, (2) to accumulate capital, and (3) as a source of income. Storage of value is important to all investors, since nobody likes to lose money. However, some investors are more concerned about it than others and therefore put safety of principal first in their stock selection process. These investors are more quality-conscious and tend to

INVESTOR INSIGHTS

ADRs: Foreign Stocks for Stay-at-Home Investors

Spurred by the historic developments in Europe and the growth of Japan's economic muscle, more and more U.S. investors are eagerly looking for opportunities in foreign markets. Many of them are turning to mutual funds that specialize in foreign shares. Others who like to pick their own stocks are enduring the headaches and heavy fees involved in purchasing shares directly on foreign stock exchanges.

But more American investors are discovering that there is another way for them to jump on the international bandwagon: More than 800 companies from over 30 foreign countries are traded on U.S. exchanges as *American depositary receipts.*

ADRs "are great for Americans who want to take advantage of foreign stocks without the hassle of converting dollars into local currencies," says Jonathan S. Paris, a vice president at European Investors Inc. in New York. That's because ADRs are bought and sold, on American markets, just like stocks in U.S. companies—and their prices are quoted in dollars, not British pounds, Japanese yen or German marks. Furthermore, dividends are paid in dollars.

ADR investors also don't have to worry about the often considerable hassles involved in storing and transferring foreign stock certificates. They also avoid certain taxes and other fees associated with trading in some overseas markets. And they don't have to be concerned about delays in settling trades in foreign markets.

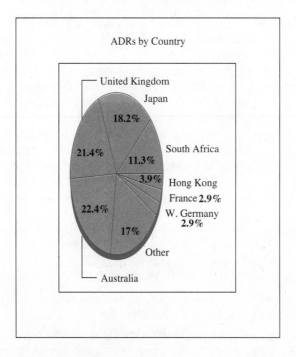

ADRs by Country

United Kingdom
Japan
18.2%
South Africa
21.4%
11.3%
3.9%
Hong Kong
France 2.9%
22.4%
W. Germany 2.9%
17%
Other
Australia

The securities are called "receipts," rather than "stocks," because they represent claims on foreign shares held in safekeeping for U.S. investors by financial institutions. "It's basically a warehouse receipt that you can trade," says Seth M. Lynn Jr., president of Axe Core Investors Inc., a money-management firm in Tarrytown, N.Y. Some ADRs represent a single share or a fraction of a share, while others represent multiple shares.

ADRs have been around since the late 1920s, but interest has surged in recent years as more investors have seen the rich rewards in overseas markets. Indeed, gains for U.S. investors in several foreign stock markets have been outpacing those available at home. Consider the fact that over the past 5 years (from 1985 to 1990), the U.S. stock market ranked a dismal 15th out of 18 international stock markets, as measured in total return in U.S. dollars. During that period, U.S. stocks returned 146.9%, including dividends—far below gains of 697% in Austria, 551.8% in Belgium, 510.7% in Spain and 465.7% in Japan.

However, investors tempted to take the plunge should beware: While ADRs make it easier for Americans to buy and sell interests in foreign companies, they by no means eliminate some of the special risks of international investing. For starters, investors who buy into foreign companies should be prepared for enormous volatility. Even the U.S. stock market's erratic mood swings look tame compared with the gyrations in many foreign markets. Foreign investing is also more complicated than just picking the right stock—or ADR. Investors not only need to worry about the prospects for a particular company or industry, *they also have to judge the foreign exchange markets correctly*. An unexpected blip in the dollar can suddenly transform a brilliant stock pick into a disaster. Another problem: investors who venture into foreign markets also need to be ready for tax complications. Much to their dismay, U.S. investors discover that foreign countries routinely withhold part of the dividend payments on ADRs and foreign stocks. How much is withheld depends on the home country of the company paying the dividend. To get that money back, U.S. citizens must file a "very complex" form, says Bob Decelles, a tax partner at KPMG Peat Marwick in New York.

Then there's the problem of keeping up with foreign news, as well as mastering the intricacies and eccentricities of foreign accounting practices that are vital in analyzing foreign companies. Several leading money managers say U.S. investors often don't hear about important foreign corporate news until too late, well after investors in that country already have acted on it. Thus, many U.S. investment managers still prefer to keep most of their money at home, where they have a keener understanding of markets.

While ADRs are appealing to American investors, keep in mind they represent only a small fraction of the total number of publicly traded foreign companies. As a result, investors who limit themselves to ADRs are greatly limiting their horizons, which is why several foreign stock experts recommend international mutual funds instead. Still, further expansion of the ADR market is likely. More international companies want to expand their investor base beyond their home country, and ADRs are a great way to do it.

Source: Adapted from Tom Herman and M.R. Sesit, "ADRs: Foreign Issues with U.S. Accents," *The Wall Street Journal,* February 8, 1990, p. C1.

gravitate toward blue chips and other nonspeculative shares. Accumulation of capital, in contrast, is generally an important goal to those with long-term investment horizons. These investors use the capital gains and/or dividends that stocks provide to build up their wealth. Some use growth stocks for such purposes; others do it with income shares; still others use a little of both. Finally, some investors use stocks as a source of income. To them, a dependable flow of dividends is essential. High-yield, good-quality income shares are usually the preferred investment vehicle for these people.

Investors can use a number of different *investment strategies* to reach one or more of their investment goals. These include buy-and-hold, high income, quality long-term growth, aggressive stock management, and speculation and short-term trading. The first three strategies would probably appeal to investors who consider storage of value important. Depending on the temperament of the investor and the time he or she has to devote to an investment program, any one of the strategies just mentioned might be used to accumulate capital. In contrast, the high-income strategy is the most logical choice for those using stocks as a source of income.

Buy-and-Hold

Buy-and-hold is the most basic, and certainly one of the most conservative, of all investment strategies. The objective is to place money in a secure investment outlet (safety of principal is vital) and watch it grow over time. High-quality stocks that offer attractive current income and/or capital gains are selected and held for extended periods—perhaps as long as 15 to 20 years. This strategy is often used to finance future retirement plans, to meet the educational needs of children, or simply as a convenient way of accumulating capital over the long haul. Generally, investors will pick out a few good stocks and then invest in them on a regular basis for long periods of time, until either the investment climate or corporate results change dramatically. Not only do investors regularly add fresh capital to their portfolios (many treat it like a savings plan), but most of the income from annual dividends is also plowed back into the portfolio and reinvested in additional shares (these investors often participate in dividend reinvestment plan). Long popular with so-called *value-oriented investors,* this approach is used by quality-conscious individuals who are looking for highly competitive returns over the long haul.

High Income

Investors often use common stocks to seek high levels of current income. Common stocks are viewed as desirable outlets for such purposes not only because of their current yields, but also because their *dividend levels tend to increase over time.* Safety of principal and stability of income are vital, and capital gains are of secondary importance. Quality income shares are the popular investment medium for this kind of strategy. Because of the high yields available from many income shares, some investors adopt this strategy simply as a way of earning high (and relatively safe) returns on their investment capital. More often than not, however, high-income strategies are used by those trying to supplement their income and who plan to use the added income for consumption purposes, such as a retired couple supplementing their social security benefits with income from stocks.

Quality Long-Term Growth

This strategy is *less* conservative than either of the first two in that it seeks capital gains as the primary source of return. There is a fair amount of trading with this approach, although most of it is confined to quality growth stocks offering attractive growth prospects and the chance for considerable price appreciation. Dividends are not ignored, however, as there are a number of growth stocks that also pay dividends, which many growth-oriented investors consider *an added source of return.* But even with dividend-paying growth stocks, this strategy still emphasizes capital gains as the principal way of earning the bigger returns. Because the approach involves a greater element of risk, a good deal of diversification is often used. Long-term accumulation of capital is the most common reason for using this approach, but compared to the buy-and-hold tactic, the investor aggressively seeks a bigger payoff by doing considerably more trading and assuming more market risk.

Aggressive Stock Management

Aggressive stock management also uses quality issues, but this time to seek attractive rates of return through a fully managed portfolio—that is, one in which the investor aggressively trades in and out of various stocks in order to achieve handsome yields from both current income (dividends) and capital gains. Blue chips, income shares, growth stocks, and cyclical issues are the primary investment vehicles; more aggressive investors might even consider foreign shares or ADRs. Income, cyclical, and/or growth stocks would probably be the major investments during bull markets; defensive securities, cash, or some short-term debt instrument would likely be used when the market is off. This approach is somewhat similar to the quality long-term growth strategy, but it involves considerably more trading, and the investment horizon is generally much shorter. For example, rather than waiting two or three years for a stock to move, an aggressive stock trader would go after the same investment payoff in six months to a year. Timing security transactions and turning investment capital over more rapidly are both key elements of this strategy. It has obvious and substantial risks, and it also places real demands on the individual's time and investment skills, but the rewards can be equally substantial.

Speculation and Short-Term Trading

Speculation and short-term trading is the least conservative of all investment strategies, especially when carried to its extreme. The sole investment objective is capital gains; and if it can be achieved in two weeks, all the better. Although such investors confine most of their attention to speculative or small cap common stocks, they are not averse to using other forms of common stock if they offer attractive short-term capital gains opportunities. Many speculators find that information about the industry or company is much less important in this kind of strategy than market psychology or the general tone of the market itself. It is a process of constantly switching from one position to another as new investment opportunities unfold. Because the strategy involves so much risk, many transactions end up with little or no profit, or even substantial losses. The hope is, of course, that when one does hit, it will be in a big way and returns will be more than sufficient to offset losses. This strategy obviously requires considerable knowledge, time, and—perhaps most important— the psychological and financial fortitude to withstand the shock of financial losses.

SUMMARY

1. Common stocks have long been popular because of the attractive return opportunities they provide investors. From current income to capital gains, there are common stocks available to fit just about any investment need.

2. Historically (over the past 40 years, or so), stocks have provided investors with annual returns of around 10 to 15 percent. These returns consist of both dividends and capital gains and are fairly reflective of what you can expect from stocks over the long haul. Of course, higher returns may be possible over shorter periods of time, or for those willing to assume a greater amount of risk.

3. Common stocks are a form of equity capital, each share being evidence of partial ownership of a company. Publicly traded stock can be issued by public offering, through a rights offering to existing stockholders, or through the use of deferred equity securities (warrants or convertible securities). Companies can increase the number of shares outstanding through a stock split. To reduce the number of shares of stock in circulation, companies can declare a reverse stock split or can buy back shares that then are held as treasury stock. Occasionally a company will issue different classes of common stock, known as classified common stock.

4. There are several ways to calculate the value of a share of stock, from book value, which represents accounting value, to market and investment values, which are most important to investors. These latter two represent what the stock is, or should be, worth.

     While common stocks are often referred to as the ideal inflation hedge, the fact is that when inflation really starts heating up, stocks generally do a rather unsatisfactory job of protecting the investor from inflation.

5. Companies often share their profits by paying out cash dividends to stockholders; such actions are normally taken only after carefully considering a variety of corporate and market factors. Sometimes, companies declare stock dividends rather than, or in addition to, cash dividends. Many firms that pay cash dividends have automatic dividend reinvestment plans, whereby shareholders can have their cash dividends automatically reinvested in the company's stock.

6. The type of stock selected depends on an investor's needs and preferences. In today's market the investor has a full range of stocks to choose from, including blue chips, income stocks, growth stocks, speculative issues, cyclicals, defensive shares, small cap stocks, and initial public offerings. In addition to stocks in U.S. companies, there's a growing interest in foreign securities. American investors can buy the common stocks of foreign companies in one of two ways: either on foreign exchanges, or on U.S. exchanges and OTC markets as American Depositary Receipts (ADRs).

Generally speaking, common stocks can be used as a storage of value, to accumulate capital, and as a source of income. Different investment strategies—buy-and-hold, high income, quality long-term growth, aggressive stock management, and speculation and short-term trading—can be followed to achieve these objectives.

QUESTIONS

1. What is a common stock? What is meant by the statement that holders of common stock are the residual owners of the firm?

2. What are two or three of the major investment attributes of common stocks?

3. What are some of the advantages *and* disadvantages of owning common stock? What are the major types of risk to which stockholders are exposed?

4. Explain the difference between a stock split and a stock dividend.

   a. Assume you hold 250 shares of Consolidated Everything, Inc. How many shares of stock would you hold after the firm declared a 2-for-1 stock split?
   b. What would happen if the firm declared a 200 percent stock dividend?

5. Discuss how a stock split can affect the market value of a share of stock; note both the immediate and long-term impact on share prices. Do you think it would make any difference (in price behavior) if the company also changed the dividend rate on the stock? Explain.

6. Look at the record of stock returns in Tables 5.1 and 5.2, particularly the return performance during the 1970s and '80s.

   a. How would you characterize the returns during the 1970s versus those produced in the '80s?
   b. How important are dividends as a source of return? What about capital gains? Which is more important to total return? Which causes wider swings in total return?
   c. Considering the average annual returns that have been generated over *holding periods* of 5 years or more, what rate of return do you feel is typical for the stock market in general? Is it unreasonable to expect this kind of return, on average, in the future? Does this mean that higher rates of return aren't possible? Explain.

7. Define and differentiate among each of the following pairs of terms:

   a. Treasury stock vs. classified stock.
   b. Par value vs. liquidation value.
   c. Cash dividends vs. stock dividends.
   d. Date of record vs. payment date.
   e. Growth stock vs. small cap stock.

8. Are stocks a good inflation hedge? Explain.

9. Define and briefly discuss the investment merits of each of the following:

   a. Blue chips.
   b. Income stocks.
   c. Defensive stocks.
   d. American Depositary Receipts.

    e. Growth stocks.

    f. IPOs.

10. Why do most income stocks offer only limited capital gains potential? Does this mean the outlook for continued profitability is also limited? Explain.

11. Assume that a wealthy individual comes to you looking for investment advice. He is in his early 40s and has $250,000 to put into stocks. He wants to build up as much capital as he can over a 15-year period and is willing to tolerate a "fair amount" of risk.

    a. What types of stocks do you think would be most suitable for this investor? Come up with at least three different types of stocks and briefly explain the rationale for each.

    b. Would your recommendations change if you were dealing with a smaller amount of money—say, only $50,000? What if the investor were more risk adverse? Explain.

12. With all the securities available in this country, why would a U.S. investor want to buy foreign stocks? Briefly describe the two ways that a U.S. investor can buy stocks in a foreign company. As an American investor, which approach would you prefer? Explain.

13. Identify and briefly describe the three sources of return to U.S. investors in foreign stocks. How important are currency exchange rates, and with regard to currency exchange rates, when's the best time to be in foreign securities? Since ADRs are denominated in U.S. dollars, are their returns affected by currency exchange rates? Explain.

14. Why is the ex-dividend date so important to stockholders? If a stock is sold *on* the ex-dividend date, who receives the dividends: the buyer or the seller? Explain.

15. Briefly define each of the following types of investment programs, and note the kinds of stock (blue chip, speculative stocks, and so on) that would best fit with each:

    a. A buy-and-hold strategy.

    b. A high income portfolio.

    c. Aggressive stock management.

16. Assume that the following quote for the Alpha Beta Corp. (a NYSE stock) was obtained from the Thursday, April 10, issue of *The Wall Street Journal:*

    254 150½   AlphaBet ALF 6.00 3.1 15 755 194¼ 189 189⅛ −3⅞

Given this information, answer the following questions:

    a. On what day did the trading activity occur?

    b. At what price did the stock sell at the end of the day on Wednesday, April 9?

    c. What are the highest and lowest prices at which the stock sold on the day quoted?

    d. What is the firm's price/earnings ratio? What does that indicate?

    e. What is the last price at which the stock traded on the day quoted?

    f. How large a dividend is expected in the current year?

    g. What is the highest and lowest price at which the stock traded during the latest 52-week period?

    h. How many shares of stock were traded on the day quoted?

    i. How much, if any, of a change in stock price took place between the day quoted and the immediately preceding day? What did the stock close at on the immediately preceding day?

17. Answer the questions below using the following quote for DEF, Inc. (a stock traded in the OTC market):

DEF 1.10 86 41⅝ 42⅛ +¼

a. At what price could you have purchased a share of DEF stock on the day quoted? What is this price called?
b. What is the annual dividend per share on DEF's stock?
c. How many shares of DEF were traded on the day reported above?
d. At what price could you have purchased a share of DEF on *the day preceding* that quoted above? Explain.
e. At what price could the stock be *sold* on the day quoted? What is this price called?

PROBLEMS

1. An investor owns some stock in General Refrigeration & Cooling. The stock recently underwent a 5-for-2 stock split. If the stock was trading at $50 per share just before the split, how much would each share likely be selling for right after the split? If the investor owned 200 shares of the stock before the split, how many shares would she own afterward?

2. The Kracked Pottery Company has total assets of $2.5 million, total short- and long-term debt of $1.8 million, and $200,000 worth of 8 percent preferred stock outstanding. What is the firm's total book value? What would its book value per share amount to if it had 50,000 shares of common stock outstanding?

3. The W.C. Fields Beverage Company recently reported net profits after taxes of $15.8 million. It has 2.5 million shares of common stock outstanding and pays preferred dividends of $1 million per year.

   a. Compute the firm's earnings per share (EPS).
   b. Assuming the stock currently trades at $60 per share, what would the firm's dividend yield be if it paid $2 per share to common stockholders?
   c. What would the firm's dividend payout ratio be if it paid $2 a share in dividends?

4. You're given the following information about Associated Industries, Inc.:

Total assets	$240 million
Total debt	$115 million
Preferred stock	$25 million
Common stockholders equity	$100 million
Net profits after taxes	$22.5 million
Number of preferred stock outstanding	1 million shares
Number of common stock outstanding	10 million shares
Preferred dividends paid per share	$2/share
Common dividends paid per share	$0.75/share
Market price of the preferred stock	$30.75/share
Market price of the common stock	$25.00/share

Use this information to find the following:

a. The company's book value.
b. Its book value per share.
c. The stock's earnings per share (EPS).
d. The dividend payout ratio.
e. The dividend yield on the common stock.
f. The dividend yield on the preferred stock.

5. Angus Hoffmeister owns 200 shares of Consolidated Glue. The company's board of directors recently declared a cash dividend of 50 cents a share payable April 18 (a Wednesday) to shareholders of record on March 22 (a Thursday).

a. How much in dividends, if any, will Angus receive if he *sells* his stock on March 20?
b. Assume Angus decides to hold on to the stock rather than sell it. If he belongs to the company's dividend reinvestment plan, how many new shares of stock will he receive if the stock is presently trading at 40 and the plan offers a 5 percent discount on the share price of the stock? (Assume all of Angus's dividends are diverted to the plan.) Will Angus have to pay any taxes on these dividends, since he's taking them in stock rather than cash?

6. Southwest Investments Corp. has the following five-year record of earnings per share:

Year	EPS
1990	$1.40
1991	2.10
1992	1.00
1993	3.25
1994	0.80

Which procedure would provide the greater amount of dividends to stockholders over this five-year period:

a. Paying out dividends at a fixed payout ratio of 40 percent? or
b. Paying out dividends at the fixed rate of $1 per share?

7. Using the resources available at your campus or public library, select *any three* common stocks you like and determine the latest book value per share, earnings per share, dividend payout ratio, and dividend yield for each. (*Note:* Show all your calculations.)

8. In January 1987, an investor purchased 800 shares of Engulf & Devour, a rapidly growing, high-tech conglomerate. Over the five-year period from 1987 through 1991, the stock turned in the following dividend and share price performance:

Year	Share Price at Beginning of the Year	Dividends Paid during the Year	Share Price at End of the Year
1987	$42.50*	$0.82	$ 54.00
1988	54.00	1.28	74.25
1989	74.25	1.64	81.00
1990	81.00	1.91	91.25
1991	91.25	2.30	128.75

Note: Investor purchased stock in 1987 at this price.

a. Based on this information, find the *annual* holding period returns for 1987 through 1991. (*Hint:* See Chapter 4 for the HPR formula).

b. Use the return information in Table 5.1 to evaluate the investment performance of this stock. How do you think Engulf & Devon stacks up against the market? Would you consider this a good investment? Explain.

CFA QUESTION (This question is from the 1989 Level I Exam.)

Mother Prewitt's Handmade Cookie Corporation (MPH), relying on forecasts of increasing cookie consumption by aging baby boomers, constructed a highly sophisticated manufacturing facility in the early 1980s. Unfortunately for MPH, recent medical findings have encouraged a swing in consumer preferences toward high-fiber bran products and resulted in lower cookie consumption. Following several years of losses, the company is being offered for sale. You have been instructed to consider the purchase of MPH.

The current balance sheet of the firm is as follows:

ASSETS	
Current assets	$14,000,000
Plant & equipment (net)	14,000,000
Total assets	$28,000,000

STOCKHOLDERS' EQUITY	
Preferred stock ($7.50 annual dividends)— authorized 200,000 shares, issued 100,000, cumulative, nonparticipating; liquidation value = $160/share	$15,000,000
Common stock—authorized 300,000 shares, issued 200,000, par value $75	15,000,000
Capital contributed in excess of par value	100,000
Retained earnings (deficit)	(2,100,000)
Total stockholders' equity	$28,000,000

Note: Preferred dividends are two years in arrears—meaning preferred dividends have *not* been paid in the past two years. (Since the preferred stock is cumulative, these dividends must be paid, eventually.)

Calculate the book value per share of MPH common stock. Show all calculations.
(See Appendix C for Guideline Answer to this question.)

CASE PROBLEMS

5.1 Sara Contemplates the Stock Market

Sara Thomas is a child psychologist who has built up a thriving practice in her hometown of Phoenix, Arizona. Her practice has been so lucrative, in fact, that over the past several years she has been able to accumulate a substantial sum of money. She has worked long and hard to be successful, but she never imagined anything like this. Fortunately, success has not spoiled

Sara. Still single, she keeps to her old circle of friends. One of her closest friends is Terry Jenkins, who happens to be a stockbroker. Sara sees a lot of Terry, who has acted as her financial advisor.

Not long ago, Sara attended a public seminar on investing in the stock market. Like a lot of other people, Sara was beginning to feel that holding all her money in low-yielding savings accounts was a serious mistake. One evening, Sara confided to Terry that she had been doing some reading lately about the stock market and had found several stocks she thought looked "sort of interesting." She described them as follows:

- *North Atlantic Swimsuit Company:* It's a highly speculative stock and pays no dividends. Although the earnings of NASS have been a bit erratic, Sara feels that its growth prospects have never been brighter—"what with more people than ever going to the beaches the way they are these days."
- *Town and Country Computers:* This is a long-established computer firm that pays a modest dividend yield (of about 3 percent). It's considered a quality growth stock. From one of the stock reports she'd read, Sara understands that it offers excellent long-term growth and capital gains potential.
- *Southeastern Public Utility Company:* An income stock, it pays a nice dividend yield of around 8 percent. Although it's a solid company, it has limited growth prospects because of its location.
- *International Gold Mines, Inc.:* This stock performed quite well several years ago. Sara feels that if it can do so well in inflationary times, it will do even better in a strong economy. Unfortunately, the stock has experienced wide price swings in the past and pays almost no dividends.

Questions
1. What do you think of the idea of Sara keeping "substantial sums" of money in savings accounts? Would common stocks make better investments than savings accounts?
2. What is your opinion of the four stocks Sara has described; do you think they are suitable for her investment needs?
3. What kind of common stock investment program would you recommend for Sara? What investment objectives do you think she should set for herself, and how can common stocks help her achieve her goals?

5.2   Dave Goes after Dividend Yield

Dave Peterson is a commercial artist who make a good living by doing free lance work—mostly layout and illustration work for local ad agencies and major institutional clients, like large department stores. Dave has been investing in the stock market for some time, buying mostly high-quality growth stocks. He has been seeking long-term growth and capital appreciation and feels that with the limited time he has to devote to his security holdings, high-quality issues are his best bet. He has become a bit perplexed lately with the market, disturbed that some of his growth stocks aren't doing even as well as many good-grade income shares. He therefore decides to have a chat with his broker, Al Fried.

During the course of their conversation, it becomes clear that both Al and Dave are thinking along the same lines. Al points out that dividend yields on income shares are, indeed, way up and, because of the state of the economy, the outlook for growth stocks is not particularly bright. He suggests that Dave seriously consider putting some of his money into income shares to capture some of the high dividend yields that are available—after all, as Al points out, "the bottom line is not so much where the payoff comes from, as how much it amounts to!'' They then talk about a high-yield public utility stock, Hydro-Electric Light and Power. Al digs up some forecast information about Hydro-Electric and presents it to Dave for his consideration.

Year	Expected EPS	Expected Dividend Payout Ratio
1993	$3.25	40%
1994	3.40	40
1995	3.90	45
1996	4.40	45
1997	5.00	45

The stock presently trades at $60 per share, and Al thinks that within five years it should be trading at a level of $75 to $80. Dave realizes that in order to buy the Hydro-Electric stock, he will have to sell his holdings of CapCo Industries—a highly regarded growth stock which Dave has become disenchanted with because of recent substandard performance.

Questions

1. How would you describe Dave's present investment program? How do you think it fits him and his investment objectives?

2. Looking at the Hydro-Electric stock:
   a. Determine the amount of annual dividends Hydro-Electric is expected to pay over the years 1993 to 1997.
   b. Compute the total dollar return Dave would make from Hydro-Electric if he invests $6,000 in the stock and all the dividend and price expectations are realized.
   c. If Dave participates in the company's dividend reinvestment plan, how many shares of stock would he have by the end of 1997, and what would they be worth, given the stock trades at $80 on 12/31/97? Assume the stock could have been purchased through the dividend reinvestment plan at a net price of $50 a share in 1993, $55 in '94, $60 in '95, $65 in '96, and $70 in '97. Use fractional shares, to 2 decimals, in your computations. Also, assume as in part (b) above that Dave starts with 100 shares of stock and all dividend expectations are realized.

3. Would Dave be going to a different investment strategy if he decided to buy shares in Hydro-Electric? If the switch is made, how would you describe his new investment program? What do you think of this new approach, and is it likely to lead to more trading on Dave's behalf? If so, how do you think that stacks up with the limited amount of time he has to devote to his portfolio?

6 Fundamental Analysis of Common Stock

After studying this chapter, you should be able to:

1. Discuss the security analysis process, including its goals and the functions it performs.

2. Gain an appreciation of the purpose and contribution of economic and industry analysis to the stock valuation process.

3. Describe the concept of fundamental analysis and note how it is used to assess a company's financial position and operating results.

4. Discuss why a firm's market position and competitive stature are important variables in the stock valuation process.

5. Calculate a variety of financial ratios and describe how financial statement analysis can be used to determine the financial vitality of a company.

6. Use various financial measures to compare a company's recent performance with its own past and with other companies in the same industry, and explain how the insights derived from such analysis form the basic input for the valuation process.

To many individuals, common stocks are synonymous with investments. Stories recounting shrewd market plays seem to fascinate people from all walks of life, as the prospect of seeing a small sum grow into a vast fortune has the same attraction for the homemaker, the service station attendant, or the college professor as it does for the Wall Street tycoon. Consider, for example, the case of Wal-Mart. An investor could have purchased 100 shares of Wal-Mart for $1,650 when it first went public in 1970. Adjusting for stock splits, the value of that investment would have skyrocketed to nearly $2.6 million by 1991. Not bad for a 21-year period of time— indeed, that's not bad for a lifetime!

Unfortunately, for every story of great success in the market there are dozens more that don't end so well. Most of the disasters can be traced to bad timing, greed, poor planning, or failure to use common sense in making investment decisions. In this, the first of two chapters dealing with security analysis, we will introduce some of the principles and techniques used to evaluate the investment suitability of common stocks. Although these chapters cannot offer the keys to sudden wealth, they do provide sound principles for formulating a successful long-range investment program. The techniques described are quite traditional; they are the same (proven) methods that have been used by millions of investors to achieve attractive rates of return on their capital.

PRINCIPLES OF SECURITY ANALYSIS

security analysis
the process of gathering and organizing information and then using it to determine the value of a share of common stock.

intrinsic value
the underlying or inherent value of a stock, as determined through fundamental analysis.

Security analysis consists of gathering information, organizing it into a logical framework, and then using the information to determine the intrinsic value of a common stock. That is, given a desired rate of return and an assessment of the amount of risk involved in a proposed transaction, **intrinsic value** provides a measure of the underlying worth of a share of stock. It provides a standard for helping an investor judge whether a particular stock is undervalued, fairly priced, or overvalued. This whole valuation concept is based on the belief that all securities possess an inherent or intrinsic value that their current market or trading values must approach over time. In investments, the question of value centers around return. In particular, a satisfactory investment candidate is one that offers *a level of expected return that's commensurate with the amount of risk involved*. That is, there's a *desired or minimum rate of return* that you should be able to earn on an investment, which varies with the amount of risk you have to assume. As a result, not only must an investment candidate be profitable, it must be *sufficiently profitable*—in the sense that you'd expect it to generate a return that's high enough to offset perceived exposure to risk.

If you could have your way, you'd probably like to invest in something that offers preservation of capital, along with a satisfactory level of current income or capital gains. The problem, of course, is finding such a security. One approach is to buy whatever strikes your fancy. A more rational approach is to use security analysis to seek out promising investment candidates. Security analysis addresses the question of *what to buy* by determining what a stock *ought to be worth*. Presumably an investor would buy a stock only so long as its prevailing market price does not exceed its worth—its intrinsic value. Ultimately, intrinsic value will depend on

(1) estimates of the stock's future cash flows (the amount of dividends the investor can expect to receive over the holding period, and the estimated price of the stock at time of sale); (2) the discount rate used to translate these future cash flows into a present value; and (3) the amount of risk embedded in achieving the forecasted level of performance.

Traditional security analysis usually takes a "top-down" approach: It begins with economic analysis, then moves to industry analysis, and finally to fundamental analysis. *Economic analysis* is concerned with assessing the general state of the economy and its potential effects on security returns. *Industry analysis* deals with the industry within which a particular company operates, how the company stacks up to the major competitors in the industry, and the general outlook for that industry. *Fundamental analysis* looks in depth at the financial condition and operating results of a specific company and the underlying behavior of its common stock. Fundamental analysis is closely linked to the notion of intrinsic value, as *it provides the basis for projecting a stock's future cash flows*. In essence, to understand the future prospects of the firm and its stock, an investor should have a good handle on the company's current condition and its ability to produce earnings. Fundamental analysis helps investors predict the future by looking at the past and determining how well the company is situated to meet challenges that lie ahead.

The Role of Security Analysis in an Efficient Market Environment

The concept of security analysis in general, and fundamental analysis in particular, is based on the assumption that investors are capable of formulating reliable estimates of a stock's future behavior. This, of course, is a pretty strong assumption, and there are many who, for one reason or another, just don't accept it. These are the so-called *efficient market* advocates. They believe that the market is so efficient in processing new information that securities trade very close to or at their proper prices at all times. Thus, argue efficient market advocates, it is virtually impossible to consistently outperform the market. In contrast, fundamental analysis operates on the broad premise that some securities may be miss-priced in the marketplace at any given time. Further, fundamental analysis explicitly assumes that it is possible to distinguish those securities that are correctly priced, from those that are not, by merely undertaking a careful analysis of the inherent characteristics of each of the firms in question. However reasonable these two assumptions might appear, they would be denounced by financial theorists as direct violations of the *efficient markets hypothesis*. Indeed, in its strongest form, the efficient markets hypothesis denies (1) that securities are ever substantially mispriced in the marketplace, and (2) that any security analysis, however detailed, is capable of identifying mispriced securities with a frequency greater than that which might be expected by random chance alone. Is the efficient markets hypothesis correct? Is there a place for fundamental analysis in modern investment theory? Interestingly, most financial theorists and practitioners would answer yes to *both* of these questions.

The solution to this apparent paradox is simple. Basically, fundamental analysis is of value in the selection of alternative investment vehicles for two important reasons: First, financial markets are as efficient as they are merely because a large number of people and powerful financial institutions invest a great deal of time and money in analyzing the fundamentals of most widely-held investments. In other words, markets tend to be efficient—and securities tend to trade at or near their intrinsic values—simply because a great many people have done the research necessary to determine just what their intrinsic values should be. A second reason fundamental analysis is of value in investment research is that although the financial markets are generally quite efficient, they are by no means perfect. Pricing errors are inevitable, and those individuals who have conducted the most thorough studies of the underlying fundamentals of a given security are the ones most likely to be able to profit when errors occur. We will study the ideas and implications of efficient markets in some detail in Chapter 7. For now, however, we will assume that traditional security analysis is useful in identifying attractive equity investments.

ECONOMIC ANALYSIS

If we lived in a world where economic activity had absolutely no effect on the stock market or security prices, we could avoid studying the economy altogether. The fact is, of course, that we do not live in such a world. Rather, stock prices are heavily influenced by the state of the economy and by economic events. As a rule, stock prices tend to move up when the economy is strong, and they retreat when the economy starts to soften. Of course, it's not a perfect relationship, but still, it is a powerful one. The reason the economy is so important to the market is simple: The overall performance of the economy has a significant bearing on the performance and profitability of the companies that issue common stock. As the fortunes of the issuing firms change with economic conditions, so will the prices of their stocks. But not all stocks are affected in the same way and to the same extent. Some sectors of the economy, like food retailing, may be only mildly affected; others, like the construction and auto industries, are often hard hit when times get rough.

It is important that an investor not only have a grasp of the *underlying nature of the economic environment,* but that he or she also be able to assess the *current state* of the economy and formulate expectations about its *future course.* **Economic analysis** may include a detailed examination of each sector of the economy, or it may be done on a very informal basis. Regardless of how it is performed, the purpose is always the same: to establish a sound foundation for the valuation of common stock. Let's briefly examine the economic analysis process to see how it can be carried out by investors.

economic analysis
a study of general economic conditions that is used in the valuation of common stock.

Economic Analysis and the Business Cycle

Economic analysis sets the tone for security analysis. If the future looks bleak, then you can probably expect most stock returns to be equally dismal. If the economy looks strong, stocks should do well. As we saw in Chapter 3, the behavior of the economy is captured in the **business cycle,** which reflects change in total economic activity over time. Two widely followed measures of the business cycle are gross domestic product and industrial production. *Gross domestic product* (or GDP as it

business cycle
an indication of the current state of the economy, reflecting change in total economic activity over time.

INVESTOR INSIGHTS

The Federal Reserve: It Walks Quietly But Carries a Big Economic Stick

America's central bank, the Federal Reserve is a powerful though little understood institution that's run by a seven-member board of governors who are appointed by the President to 14-year terms. One of the governors is designated by the President to serve a four-year term as chairman. Congress could pass legislation requiring the Fed to pursue policies to its liking, but it has never done so.

The discount rate is the only interest rate controlled directly by the Fed. Each regional Federal Reserve bank stands ready to make temporary loans to any deposit-taking institution that's in a bind and needs the money. The interest charged for such loans is called the *discount rate,* and it can be changed at the Fed's will. A high discount rate tends to discourage borrowing and thus slow the economy down; a low rate tends to encourage borrowing. By boosting this rate, the Fed signals its fear that an overheating economy is threatening to rekindle inflation.

But the Fed's main policy-making body is its Federal Open Market Committee, made up of the seven governors and presidents of five of the 12 regional Federal Reserve banks. Eight times a year it reviews the economy and decides whether to tighten or loosen credit. Usually the committee relies on subtle and indirect actions. Its favorite tactic is to manipulate the total level of reserves held by banks, s&l's and credit unions. In so doing, the Fed controls the supply of money that financial institutions have for making loans. A bank with more reserves than it needs can lend some to a bank that's temporarily short of reserves. Borrowing to boost their reserves allows banks to satisfy their customer's cravings for credit; lending out extra reserves lets banks that are flush earn money on their otherwise-idle excess. The interest charged for these overnight loans is called the *federal funds rate.*

is more commonly known) represents the market value of all goods and services produced in a country over the period of a year. *Industrial production,* in contrast, is a measure (actually it's an index) of the activity/output in the industrial or productive segment of the economy. Normally, GDP and the index of industrial production move up and down with the business cycle. One of the major players in this economic drama is a small, low-key, but *very powerful* organization known as the Federal Reserve. Even though the Fed, as it's called, is this country's *central bank,* it remains little known and largely misunderstood. The accompanying *Investor Insights* box sheds some light on this governmental body and briefly explains some of the things it does and why it does them.

Key Economic Factors

Several parts of the economy are especially important because of the impact they have on total economic activity. These include:

The Fed affects that rate by manipulating the level of reserves via huge purchases or sales of U.S. Treasury securities. The Fed buys from one or more of the 40 banks or brokerage firms that act as primary dealers. It pays by check, and therein lies its power to manipulate the level of reserves available to financial institutions. When the seller's bank presents the check to the Fed for payment, the Fed doesn't fork over any cash; instead, it credits that institution's reserve account at its Federal Reserve bank.

Presto—money has been created. The seller's bank gets additional reserves and increases its lending activity. Thus, with more money available to the economy, the federal funds rate should fall and other short-term interest rates should follow. The reverse occurs if the Fed sells Treasury securities. Reserves at the buyer's bank are marked down to pay for the transaction. The bank makes fewer loans, competition for the available money heats up and short-term rates should rise.

But the impact of the Fed's buying and selling doesn't stop there. In a financial emergency—such as occurred when banks were afraid to lend money to brokerage houses that were squeezed by the stock market's collapse—the Fed can inject almost unlimited amounts of new money into the banking system by buying securities and thus increasing banks' reserves. The mere announcement that it was willing to do so averted a panic last fall.

The Fed has one more weapon in its arsenal. It can raise or lower the amount of cash that deposit-taking institutions must hold in reserve in their vaults or at a regional Fed bank. When the Fed hikes those percentages, financial institutions have less money to lend and interest rates rise. Conversely, when the Fed lowers the reserve requirements, more money is available for loans and rates decline. But altering the *reserve requirement* is administratively awkward and is seldom done.

Source: Manual Schiffres. ''The Federal Reserve Walks Quietly, But it Affects the Economy With a Big Stick,'' *Changing Times,* October, 1988, p. 16.

Government fiscal policy:
   Taxes
   Government spending
   Debt management
Monetary policy (actions of the Federal Reserve Board):
   Money supply
   Interest rates
Other factors:
   Inflation
   Consumer spending
   Business investments
   Foreign trade and foreign exchange rates

Government fiscal policy tends to be *expansive* when it encourages spending—when the government reduces taxes and/or increases the size of the budget. Simi-

████████

TABLE 6.1 Keeping Track of the Economy

To sort out the confusing array of figures that flow almost daily from Washington, and to help you keep track of what's happening in the economy, here are some of the most important economic measures and reports to watch. . . .

• **Gross domestic product**—This is the broadest measure of the economy's performance, and replaces the old "GNP" measure. Issued every three months by the Commerce Department, it is an estimate of the total dollar value of all the goods and services produced in this country. Movements in many areas of the economy are closely related to changes in GDP, making it a good analytic tool. In particular, watch the annual rate of growth or decline in "real" or "constant" dollars. This number eliminates the effects of inflation, so that the actual volume of production is measured. Remember, though, that frequent revisions of GDP figures sometimes change the picture of the economy.

• **Industrial production**—Issued monthly by the Federal Reserve Board, this index shows changes in the physical output of America's factories, mines, and electric and gas utilities. The index tends to move in the same direction as the economy, making it a good guide to business conditions between reports on GDP. Detailed breakdowns of the index give a reading on how individual industries are faring.

• **Leading indicators**—This boils down to one number, the movement of a dozen statistics that tend to predict—or "lead"—changes in the GDP. The monthly index, issued by the Commerce Department, includes such things as layoffs of workers, new orders placed by manufacturers, changes in the money supply, and the prices of raw materials. If the index moves in the same direction for several months, it's a fair sign that total output will move the same way in the near future.

• **Personal income**—A monthly report from the Commerce Department, this shows the before-tax income received by people in the form of wages and salaries, interest and dividends, rents, and other payments such as Social Security, unemployment, and pensions. As a measure of individuals' spending power, the report helps explain trends in consumer buying habits, a major part of total GDP. When personal income rises, it often means that people will increase their buying. But note a big loophole: Excluded are the billions of dollars that change hands in the so-called underground economy—cash transactions that are never reported to tax or other officials.

• **Retail sales**—The Commerce Department's monthly estimate of total sales at the retail level includes everything from cars to bags of groceries. Based on a sample of retail establishments, the figure gives a rough clue to consumer attitudes. It can also indicate future conditions: A long slowdown in sales can lead to cuts in production.

larly, monetary policy is said to be expansive when money is readily available and interest rates are relatively low. An expansive economy also depends on a generous level of spending by consumers and business concerns. These same variables moving in a reverse direction can have a recessionary impact on the economy—for example, when taxes and interest rates increase, or when spending by consumers and businesses falls off.

The impact of these major forces filters through the system and affects several key dimensions of the economy, the most important of which are industrial production, corporate profits, retail sales, personal income, the unemployment rate, and inflation. For example, a strong economy exists when industrial production, corpo-

---

- **Money supply**—A measure of the amount of money in circulation as reported weekly by the Federal Reserve. Actually, there are *three* measures of the money supply: **M1,** which is basically currency, demand deposits and NOW accounts; **M2,** the most widely followed measure, which equals M1 plus savings deposits, money market deposit accounts, and money market mutual funds; and **M3,** which is M2 plus large CDs and a few other less significant types of deposits/transactions. It's felt that reasonable growth in the money supply, as measured by M2, is necessary to accommodate an expanding economy. Such growth should have a positive impact on the economy—*unless* the money supply is growing too rapidly. A rapid rate of growth in money is considered to be inflationary; in contrast, a sharp slowdown in the growth rate is viewed as recessionary.

- **Consumer prices**—Issued monthly by the Labor Department, this index shows changes in prices for a fixed market basket of goods and services. The most widely publicized figure is for all urban consumers. A second, used in labor contracts and some government programs, covers urban wage earners and clerical workers. Both are watched as a measure of inflation, but many economists believe that flaws cause them to be wide of the mark.

- **Producer prices**—This is a monthly indicator from the Labor Department showing price changes of goods at various stages of production, from crude materials such as raw cotton, to finished goods like clothing and furniture. An upward surge may mean higher consumer prices later. The index, however, can miss discounts and may exaggerate rising price trends. Watch particularly changes in the prices of finished goods. These do not fluctuate as widely as crude materials and thus are a better measure of inflationary pressures.

- **Employment**—The percentage of the work force that is involuntarily out of work is a broad indicator of economic health. But another monthly figure issued by the Labor Department—the number of payroll jobs—may be better for spotting changes in business. A decreasing number of jobs is a sign that firms are cutting production.

- **Housing starts**—A pickup in the pace of housing starts usually follows an easing of credit conditions—the availability and cost of money—and is an indicator of improvement in economic health. This monthly report from the Commerce Department also includes the number of new building permits issued across the country, an even earlier indicator of the pace of future construction.

---

rate profits, retail sales, and personal income are moving up and unemployment is down. Thus, when conducting economic analysis, an investor will want to keep an eye on fiscal and monetary policies, consumer and business spending, and foreign trade *for the potential impact they have on the economy*. At the same time, he or she must stay abreast of the level of industrial production, corporate profits, retail sales, personal income, unemployment, and inflation *in order to assess the state of the business cycle*.

To help you keep track of the economy, Table 6.1 provides a brief description of some key economic measures. These economic statistics are compiled by government agencies and are widely reported in the financial media (most of the reports are released monthly). Take the time to carefully read about the various economic measures and reports covered in Table 6.1. By keeping an eye on the behavior of these statistics, you can make your own educated guess as to the current state of the economy and where it's headed.

One final point: As noted in Chapter 5, inflation can have devastating effects on common stocks (and on many other investment vehicles as well). In an inflationary environment, many companies may report higher profits, but the quality of these earnings actually declines as profit margins are ''squeezed'' and the purchasing power of the dollar deteriorates. Furthermore, the high interest rates that accompany inflation not only contribute to rising costs but also reduce the competitive edge of common stocks. That is, as interest rates rise, the returns to bonds and preferred stock improve and make the investment merits of common stock look relatively less attractive. Because of the serious consequences inflation holds for stock prices, investors should devote special attention to this factor as they analyze the economy and its prospects. By the same token, as we saw in the early to mid-1980s, when inflation slows down, the stock market is often one of the major beneficiaries. Certainly, the great bull market that began in 1982 was fueled in large part by a dramatic drop in the rate of inflation, with the economy, corporate profits, and interest rates all benefiting.

Developing an Economic Outlook

Conducting an economic analysis involves studying fiscal and monetary policies, inflationary expectations, consumer and business spending, and the state of the business cycle. Often investors do this on a fairly informal basis. Many rely on one or more of the popular published sources (like *The Wall Street Journal, Barron's, Fortune,* and *Business Week*), as well as on periodic reports from major brokerage houses to form their economic judgments. As Figure 6.1 shows, such sources provide a convenient summary of economic activity and enable investors to develop a general feel for the condition of the economy.

Once you have developed a general economic outlook, you can use the information in one of two ways. One approach is to construct an economic outlook and then consider where it leads in terms of possible areas for further analysis. For example, suppose that as part of your economic analysis you uncovered information that strongly suggested the outlook for business spending is very positive. Based on such a perspective, you might want to look more closely at capital goods producers, such as machine tool manufacturers, as attractive investment candidates. Similarly, if you feel, because of the sweeping changes taking place in Eastern Europe and what used to be the U.S.S.R., that government defense spending is likely to drop off substantially, you might want to avoid the stocks of major defense contractors.

A second way to use information about the economy is to consider specific industries or companies and ask: How will they be affected by expected developments in the economy? *Consider, for example, an investor with an interest in apparel stocks.* Due to the nature of the business (durable fashion goods), these stocks are susceptible to changing economic conditions. Especially important here is the level of discretionary consumer spending: Normally such spending tends to

Tracking the Economy Jan. 27, 1992

President Bush suggested recently that the U.S. economy is in a "free fall." Economic data, however, point to growth, says Mickey Levy, chief economist at CRT Government Securities Ltd. in New York.

Mr. Levy says this week's release of fourth-quarter Gross Domestic Product will buttress his view. The broadest gauge of U.S. economic health, GDP will show an economy expanding 1.5% at an annual rate, he estimates. He contends, furthermore, that the economy is maintaining that pace, be it "ever so modest," in early 1992.

Mr. Levy acknowledges that retail and automobile sales were poor in the fourth quarter. But increased spending on services came close to offsetting that weakness, he says. And a narrower trade gap and improved investment in homes and durable-goods equipment also boosted growth.

December data due for release this week will highlight why annual economic growth has been held below 2%. Personal income, for example, probably rose 0.4%, but personal spending likely fell 0.2%, Mr. Levy says. While more people worked more hours for more pay last month, the increased

GDP: Slow Growth?
Annualized percentage change in real GDP

* Consensus forecast

income wasn't enough to lift consumer spending, he says.

Manufacturers may already be suffering from the end of the Cold War. Mr. Levy estimates new orders for durable goods last month fell 1%, as a drop in defense-related procurement defused a 4% gain in nondefense orders.—*Andrew Sobel*

Statistics to Be Released This Week

ECONOMIC INDICATOR	PERIOD	RELEASE DATE	PREVIOUS ACTUAL	MMS CONSENSUS FORECAST
Consumer Confidence	January	Jan. 28	52.4%	53.0%
Real GDP (ann. rate)	4th qtr. advance	Jan. 29	+1.8%	+0.5%
Durable Goods	December	Jan. 30	+1.0%	−1.0%
Personal Income	December	Jan. 30	−0.1%	+0.5%
Personal Spending	December	Jan. 30	+0.7%	No change
Initial Jobless Claims	Week to Jan. 18	Jan. 30	447,000	450,000
Money Supply: M1	Week to Jan. 20	Jan. 30	+$11.2 billion	+$4.5 billion
Money Supply: M2	Week to Jan. 20	Jan. 30	+$14.7 billion	+$8.0 billion
Money Supply: M3	Week to Jan. 20	Jan. 30	+$37.3 billion	+$10.0 billion
Leading Indicators	December	Jan. 31	−0.3%	+0.1%
New Home Sales	December	Jan. 31	No change	+2.0%

Statistics Released Last Week

Housing Starts (ann. rate)	1,103,000	N.A.=Not available	
December	+2.6%	*Source: MMS International; NY, NY*	

● FIGURE 6.1 An Economic Overview

News reports like this one, which appear every Monday in *The Wall Street Journal,* provide investors with a convenient overview of the current state of the economy and some observations on where it may be heading. (*Source: The Wall Street Journal,* January 27, 1992.)

pick up when the economy picks up steam and slackens when the economy slows down. In this instance, our imaginary investor would first want to assess the current state of the business cycle and then, using this insight, formulate some expectations about the future of the economy and the potential impact that it holds for apparel stocks. To see how this might be done, let's assume that the economy has just recently entered the recovery stage of the business cycle. Employment is starting to pick up, inflation and interest rates are at reasonably low levels, and Congress is putting the finishing touches on a major piece of legislation that would lead to reduced taxes. More important, because the economy now seems to be in the early stages of a recovery, it should be getting even stronger in the future, and personal income should increase. This should be good for apparel companies, since a good deal of their sales and an even larger portion of their profits depend on the level of consumer income and spending. In short, our investor sees an economy that appears to be in good shape and set to become even stronger, the consequences of which are all favorable for apparel stocks.

Note that these conclusions were reached by relying on sources no more sophisticated than *Barron's* and *Business Week*. In fact, about the only "special thing" the investor did was to *pay careful attention to those economic forces that are important to the apparel industry (like personal income)*. The economic portion of the analysis, in effect, has set the stage for further evaluation by indicating the type of economic environment to expect in the near future. The next step is to narrow the focus a bit and conduct the industry phase of the analysis.

However, before continuing with our analysis, it is vital to further clarify the relationship between the stock market and the economy. The economic outlook is used to direct investors to developing industry sectors for possible profit, but it is important to note that changes in stock prices normally occur *before* the actual forecasted changes become apparent in the economy. To go a bit further, the current trend of stock prices is frequently used to help *predict* the course of the economy itself. The apparent conflict here can be resolved somewhat by noting that because of this relationship, it is even more important to derive a reliable economic outlook and to be sensitive to underlying economic changes that may mean the current outlook is becoming dated. Investors in the stock market tend to look into the future in order to justify the purchase or sale of stock. If their perception of the future is changing, stock prices will most likely also be changing. Therefore, watching the course of stock prices as well as the course of the general economy can make for more accurate investment forecasting.

INDUSTRY ANALYSIS

An industry is made up of similar firms involved in producing similar goods and services. The oil industry, for example, is made up of firms that produce gasoline and other oil-related products. Companies in an industry may be different in size, manner of operation, and product lines, but they have similar operating characteristics and are subject to similar socioeconomic forces.

Key Issues

Have you ever thought about buying oil stocks, or autos, or chemicals? How about conglomerates or electric utility stocks? Looking at securities in terms of industry groupings is a popular way of viewing stocks and is widely used by both individual and professional investors. This is a sensible approach, too, because stock prices are influenced, at least in part, by industry conditions. The level of demand in an industry and other industry forces set the tone for individual companies. Clearly, if the outlook is good for an industry, then the prospects are likely to be strong for the companies that make up that industry.

industry analysis
study of industry groupings, by looking at the competitive position of a particular industry in relation to others and by identifying companies within an industry that hold particular promise.

The first step in **industry analysis** is to establish the competitive position of a particular industry *in relation to others,* for as Figure 6.2 suggests, not all industries perform alike. The next step is to identify companies within the industry that hold particular promise. This sets the stage for a more thorough analysis of individual companies and securities. Analyzing an industry means looking at such things as the makeup and basic characteristics of the industry, key economic and operating variables that are important in defining industry performance, and the outlook for the industry. The investor will also want to keep an eye out for specific companies that appear well situated to take advantage of industry conditions. Companies with strong market positions should be favored over those with more tentative positions. Such dominance provides the company with the ability to maintain pricing leadership and suggests that the firm will be in a position to enjoy economies of scale and low-cost production. Of course, market dominance will also enable a company to support a strong research and development effort, thereby helping it secure its leadership position for the future.

Normally, an investor can gain valuable insight about an industry by seeking answers to these questions:

1. *What is the nature of the industry?* Is it monopolistic, or are there many competitors; do a few set the trend for the rest?
2. *To what extent is the industry regulated?* Is it regulated (like public utilities) and if so, how "friendly" are the regulatory bodies?
3. *What role, if any, does labor play in the industry?* How important are labor unions? Are there good labor relations within the industry? When is the next round of contract talks?
4. *How important are technological developments?* Are there any taking place, and what is the likely impact of potential breakthroughs?
5. *Which economic forces are especially important to the industry?* Is demand for the industry's goods and services related to key economic variables? If so, what is the outlook for those variables? How important is foreign competition to the health of the industry?
6. *What are the important financial and operating considerations?* Is there an adequate supply of labor, material, and capital? What are the capital spending plans and needs of the industry?

Industry Group	Stock Price Index		Change in Index			1991 P/E
	12/31/81	12/31/91	10 Year	5 Year	1 Year	
S&P 400 Industrials	$137.12	$442.42	222.7%	63.9%	14.2%	22.8
Aerospace	$135.63	$388.69	186.6%	20.8%	7.1%	11.3
Airlines	$69.73	$253.94	264.2%	22.4%	8.0%	28.6
Automobiles	$43.23	$107.22	148.0%	−15.3%	−9.8%	15.3
Beverages (Alcoholic)	$252.38	$361.30	43.2%	10.3%	22.0%	15.8
Beverages	$111.50	$1,111.47	896.8%	249.7%	34.8%	26.6
Broadcast media	$600.98	$3,905.60	549.9%	73.2%	−7.9%	41.1
Building materials	$107.11	$185.35	73.0%	3.8%	16.8%	16.4
Chemicals	$56.26	$170.36	202.8%	37.0%	15.7%	15.3
Communication equip. mfgrs.	$25.34	$70.16	176.9%	151.6%	48.3%	28.1
Computer software & services	$17.46	$75.87	334.5%	10.3%	25.5%	20.6
Conglomerates	$25.51	$49.68	94.7%	9.7%	0.3%	41.4
Cosmetics	$47.53	$219.07	360.9%	148.1%	25.9%	19.9
Electric utilities	$29.33	$73.42	150.3%	25.9%	15.7%	14.3
Electrical equipment	$394.12	$923.90	134.4%	37.3%	9.9%	21.4
Electronics (Semiconductors)	$25.03	$62.79	150.9%	47.9%	8.1%	33.0
Entertainment	$294.70	$1,215.44	312.4%	119.0%	0.7%	22.3
Foods	$82.52	$763.74	825.5%	138.9%	24.6%	18.9
Homebuilding	$29.31	$55.61	89.7%	11.1%	41.8%	13.6
Hospital Management	$37.64	$65.20	73.2%	44.2%	−27.1%	9.0
Hotel-motel	$70.10	$126.72	80.8%	−27.8%	22.5%	43.4
Household furnishings	$159.35	$377.05	136.6%	−16.1%	23.9%	54.5
Leisure	$76.05	$122.32	60.8%	−34.1%	21.7%	24.0
Natural gas	$103.71	$346.56	234.2%	3.8%	−15.2%	12.1
Oil: domestic	$337.15	$583.77	73.1%	33.4%	−11.2%	33.5
Oil: International	$209.78	$340.25	62.2%	63.1%	4.2%	11.6
Pollution control	$45.21	$296.95	556.8%	87.9%	−0.6%	24.1
Publishing	$462.27	$1,364.34	195.1%	5.4%	6.0%	NM
Publishing newspapers	$37.19	$92.31	148.2%	−12.8%	0.3%	29.0
Restaurants	$42.12	$199.21	373.0%	56.2%	18.9%	15.1
Retail: drug chains	$33.40	$138.71	315.3%	62.2%	13.4%	17.7
Retail: food chains	$54.29	$390.56	619.4%	137.8%	−7.0%	13.6
Telephone	$27.50	$257.13	835.0%	36.0%	−7.1%	14.7
Textiles apparel mfgrs.	$41.54	$228.56	450.2%	31.4%	35.9%	18.3
Tobacco	$114.46	$1,208.18	955.5%	277.3%	26.7%	15.5
Toys	$14.31	$49.08	243.0%	105.8%	101.6%	35.3

• FIGURE 6.2 A Look at the Stock Performance of Key Industry Groups

In the search for value in the stock market, an early step is to look at the big picture: *industry group trends*. The data above present a broad overview of 35 key industries from Standard & Poor's list of 87 industry groups. Each of these industry groups has its own market index that measures the performance of stocks within that group. As is apparent, some industries have done much better than others. (*Source: 1991 Analyst's Handbook,* Standard & Poor's Corporation.)

growth cycle
a reflection of the amount of business vitality that occurs within a company or industry over time.

The above questions can sometimes be answered in terms of an industry's **growth cycle.** The first phase, that of *initial development,* is not one that is usually available to most investors. The industry is new and untried so the risks are very high. The second stage is *rapid expansion,* during which product acceptance is spreading and investors can foresee the industry's future more clearly. At this stage, economic variables have little to do with the industry's overall performance. Investors will be interested in investing almost regardless of the economic climate. This is the phase that is of considerable interest to investors, and a good deal of work is done to find such opportunities. Unfortunately, not all industries experience rapid growth for a very long period of time. Most eventually slip into the category of *mature growth,* which is the third stage and the one most influenced by economic developments. Expansion comes from growth of the economy. It is a slower source of overall growth than the growth in phase two. In stage three, the long-term nature of the industry becomes apparent. Industries in this category include defensive ones like food and apparel, and cyclical industries like autos and heavy equipment. The last phase is either *stability* or *decline.* In the decline phase, demand for the industry's products is diminishing, and companies are leaving the industry. Investment opportunities at this stage are almost nonexistent, unless the investor is seeking only dividend income. Avoidance of this stage is obviously a major concern to investors. However, few companies reach this stage because they try to introduce product changes that will help to continue mature growth.

Developing an Industry Outlook

Industry analysis can be conducted by investors themselves, or, as is more often the case, with the help of published industry reports such as the popular S&P *Industry Surveys.* These surveys cover all the important economic, market, and financial aspects of an industry, providing commentary as well as vital statistics. Other widely used sources of industry information include brokerage house reports and various writeups in the popular financial media. An example of a widely used industry report (in this case, an S&P *Industry Survey*) is provided in Figure 6.3.

Let's continue with our example of the investor who is interested in apparel stocks. Recall that his general economic analysis suggested a strong economy for the foreseeable future and one in which the level of personal disposable income would be expanding. Now he is ready to shift his attention to the apparel industry. A logical starting point is to assess the expected industry response to forecasted economic developments. Demand for the product and industry sales would be especially important. The industry is made up of many large and small competitors, and although it is an unregulated industry, it is labor-intensive and labor unions are an important force. Thus, our investor may want to look closely at these factors and especially at their potential effect on the industry's cost structure. Also important would be the outlook for imported fashion goods and foreign competition.

Industry analysis provides an understanding of the nature and operating characteristics of an industry, which can then be used to form judgments about the prospects for industry growth. Let's assume that our investor, by using various types of published reports, has examined the key elements of the apparel industry and has concluded that it is indeed well positioned to take advantage of the improving economy. Apparel demand should increase, and although profit margins may tighten a bit, the level of profits should move up smartly, providing a healthy growth outlook. Several companies within this industry stand out, but one looks particularly attractive: MarCor Industries, a moderately sized but rapidly growing

JUNE 13, 1991

OVERVIEW

Demand seen firming by late '91

In the early part of 1991, demand for textiles, apparel, furniture, and appliances remained weak, as had been expected. Preliminary numbers showed that in the first quarter of 1991, real consumer spending on nondurables (a category that includes textiles and apparel) declined 0.5% from the comparable year-earlier period, while real spending on durables, which includes furniture and appliances, decreased 10.7%.

· These unexciting numbers were in keeping with data reported over the past two years. In 1990, real nondurables spending was up only 0.2%, following a 1.8% rise in 1989; spending on durables declined 4.2%, following a 1.1% fall in 1989. A recession hit these consumer-oriented industries before the overall economic recession began in September 1990. Demand for textiles and apparel slackened in mid- to late 1989, while furniture and appliance sales dropped off in mid-1988 along with the softening housing market.

Buoyed by the U.S. victory in the Middle East war, however, consumer confidence levels are beginning to rise, although they remain constrained by the prevailing recession. Most economists, including those at S&P, expect a recovery to begin in the summer of 1991, led by lower interest rates and controlled inflation. At that time, consumers should begin shopping again. In fact, recently reported preliminary retail sales data from the Commerce Department for April 1991 (latest available) indicates that consumer spending may have bottomed out in March. Another positive development is lower mortgage rates, which should stimulate housing turnover and, thus, sales of home textiles, furniture, and appliances.

Results for full-year 1991, however, will be weighted down by a weak first half. S&P is currently forecasting a 2.2% decline in real consumer nondurables spending and a 7.2% dip in durables spending for the year. Nonetheless, upward trends established in the second half of this year should carry over into 1992. Furthermore, with 1992 being

an election year, the incumbent administration will do all in its power to encourage a stronger economy. S&P currently projects a 0.7% rise in nondurables spending and a 3.9% increase in durables spending for 1992.

TEXTILES

Mills see a long road to recovery

In a May 1991 survey taken by *The Daily News Record*, a daily newspaper covering the apparel and textile industries, to assess the state of the textile industry, most respondents were negative. The general opinion of textile executives was that, while the situation wasn't getting worse in their industries, it wasn't getting much better either. Most respondents said they didn't expect much improvement until the end of 1991 and that the climb out of this recession would be slow.

MILL SHIPMENTS, INVENTORIES AND PRODUCTION
(Seasonally Adjusted)

Elizabeth Vandeventer,
Textiles, Apparel & Home Furnishings Analyst

• FIGURE 6.3 A Popular Source of Industry Information
Reports like the one shown here provide easy-to-digest industry overviews, including the dynamics of an industry and what makes it tick, the outlook for the industry, and a wide array of vital industry statistics. (*Source: S&P Industry Surveys*, June 13, 1991.)

producer of medium- to high-priced apparel for men and women. Everything about the economy and the industry looks favorable, so our investor has decided to study MarCor more closely.

FUNDAMENTAL ANALYSIS

fundamental
analysis
the in-depth study of
the financial condi-
tion and operating
results of a firm.

Fundamental analysis is the study of the financial affairs of a business for the purpose of better understanding the nature and operating characteristics of the companies that issue common stocks. In this part of the chapter, we will deal with several aspects of fundamental analysis: We will examine the general concept of fundamental analysis, introduce the several types of financial statements that provide the raw material for this phase of the analytical process, describe the key financial ratios widely used in fundamental analysis, and conclude with an interpretation of financial ratios.

The Concept

Fundamental analysis rests on the belief that *the value of a stock is influenced by the performance of the company that issued the stock*. If a company's prospects look strong, we would expect the market price of its stock to reflect that and be bid up. However, the value of a security depends not only on the return it promises, but also on the amount of its risk exposure. Fundamental analysis captures these dimensions and conveniently incorporates them into the valuation process. It begins with an historical analysis of the financial strength of a firm. Using the insights obtained, along with economic and industry figures, an investor can then formulate expectations about the future growth and profitability of a company.

In the historical phase of the analysis, the investor would study the financial statements of the firm in order to learn the strengths and weaknesses of the company, identify any underlying trends and developments, evaluate operating efficiencies, and gain a general understanding of the nature and operating characteristics of the firm. The following points are of particular interest:

1. The competitive position of the company
2. Its composition and growth in sales
3. Profit margins and the dynamics of company earnings
4. The composition and liquidity of corporate resources (the company's asset mix)
5. The company's capital structure (its financing mix)

The historical phase of fundamental analysis is, in many respects, the most demanding and the most time-consuming. Most investors have neither the time nor the inclination to conduct such an extensive study and, thus, rely on published reports for the needed background material. Investors have many sources to choose from, including the reports and recommendations of major brokerage houses, the popular financial media, and/or various financial subscription services, like S&P and *Value Line*. These are all valuable sources of information, and the paragraphs that follow are not intended to replace them. Yet, to be an intelligent investor, it is important to fully understand the content and implications of such financial reports, and in the final analysis, to be able to use the information to develop one's own judgments about the company and its stock.

Financial Statements

Financial statements are a vital part of fundamental analysis, since they enable investors to develop an opinion about the operating results and financial condition of a firm. There are three types of financial statements that are used in fundamental analysis: (1) a balance sheet, (2) an income statement, and (3) a statement of cash flows. The first two statements are essential to carrying out fundamental analysis (in particular, to compute many of the financial ratios). The third statement—the cash flow report—is of critical importance because it is used to assess the cash/liquidity position of the firm. Company statements are prepared on a quarterly basis (these are *abbreviated* statements compiled for each three-month period of operation) and again at the end of each calendar year or *fiscal year* (a 12-month period the company has defined as its operating year, which may or may not end on December 31). Annual financial statements must be fully verified by independent certified public accountants (CPAs), filed with the U.S. Securities and Exchange Commission, and distributed on a timely basis to all stockholders in the form of annual reports. By themselves, corporate financial statements are a most important source of information to the investor; when used with financial ratios and in fundamental analysis, they become even more powerful.

The Balance Sheet

balance sheet
a financial summary of a firm's assets, liabilities, and shareholder's equity at a single point in time.

The **balance sheet** is a statement of the company's assets, liabilities, and shareholders' equity. The *assets* represent the resources of the company (the things the company owns), the *liabilities* are its debts, and *equity* is the amount of stockholders' capital in the firm. A balance sheet may be thought of as a summary of the firm's assets balanced against its debt and ownership positions *at a single point in time* (on the last day of the calendar or fiscal year, or at the end of the quarter). In order to balance, the total assets must equal the total amount of liabilities and equity. A typical balance sheet is illustrated in Table 6.2. It shows the comparative 1991–92 figures for MarCor Industries, the apparel firm our investor is interested in analyzing. Note that although the MarCor name is fictitious, the financial statements are not—*they are the real financial statements of an actual company*. While some of the entries have been slightly modified for pedagogical purposes, they are an accurate depiction of what real financial statements look like and how they're used in financial statement analysis.

The Income Statement

income statement
a financial summary of the operating results of a firm covering a specified period of time, usually one year.

The **income statement** provides a financial summary of the operating results of the firm. It is simply a summary of the amount of revenues (sales and income) generated over the period, the cost and expenses incurred over the same period, and the

TABLE 6.2 A Corporate Balance Sheet, MarCor Industries

($ Thousands, Fiscal Year Ended December 31)

	1992	1991	
Current assets	$ 7,846	$ 16,279	Cash and short-term investments
	105,400	102,889	Accounts receivable
	164,356	159,238	Inventories
	1,778	16,279	Prepaid expenses
	$279,380	$278,697	Total current assets
Long-term assets	$ 1,366	$ 1,317	Land
	13,873	13,889	Buildings
	75,717	73,199	Furniture, fixtures, and equipment
	49,412	50,209	Leasehold improvements
	$140,368	$138,614	Gross long-term assets
	(85,203)	(80,865)	Accumulated depreciation
	$ 55,165	$ 57,749	Net long-term assets
	$ 4,075	$ 4,108	Other assets
Total assets	$338,620	$340,554	
Current liabilities	$ 2,000	$ 11,500	Notes payable
	4,831	1,090	Current maturities
	68,849	69,696	Accounts payable and accrued expenses
	3,806	3,119	Taxes on earnings
	5,460	4,550	Other accrued taxes
	$84,946	$89,955	Total current liabilities
Long-term debt	$ 83,723	$ 91,807	Long-term debt, less current maturities
Stockholders' equity	$ 21,787	$ 21,777	Common shares, $2.50 par value
	10,068	10,028	Capital surplus
	138,096	126,987	Retained earnings
	$169,951	$158,792	Stockholders' equity
Total liabilities and stockholders' equity	$338,620	$340,554	

company's profits (which, of course, are obtained by subtracting all costs and expenses, including taxes, from revenues). Unlike the balance sheet, the income statement covers activities that have occurred over the course of time, or for a given operating period. Typically, this period extends no longer than a fiscal or calendar year. Table 6.3 shows MarCor Industries' income statements for 1991 and 1992. Note that these annual statements cover operations for a 12-month period ending on December 31, which corresponds to the date of the balance sheet. The income statement indicates how successful the firm has been in using the assets listed on the balance sheet. That is, the amount of success management has in operating the firm is reflected in the profit or loss the company generates during the year.

TABLE 6.3 A Corporate Income Statement, MarCor Industries

($ Thousands, Fiscal Year Ended December 31)

1992	1991	
$606,610	$567,986	Net sales
6,792	6,220	Other income
1,504	895	Interest income
$614,906	$575,101	Total revenues
$377,322	$354,424	Cost of goods sold
205,864	194,419	Selling, administrative, and other operating expenses
5,765	5,523	Interest expense
$588,951	$554,366	Total costs and expenses
$ 25,955	$ 20,735	Earnings before taxes
$ 7,950	$ 5,230	Taxes on earnings
$ 18,005	$ 15,505	Net earnings (Net profit after taxes)
$ 4.74	$ 4.08	Earnings per share
3,800	3,800	Number of common shares outstanding (in thousands)

Statement of Cash Flows

statement of cash flows
a financial summary of a firm's cash flow and other events that caused changes in the company's cash position.

The **statement of cash flows** provides a summary of the firm's cash flow and other events that caused changes in the cash position. A relatively new report, first required in 1988, it is also one of the most useful, as it shows how the company is doing in generating cash. The fact is, a company's reported earnings may have little resemblance to the firm's cash flow. Whereas profits are simply the difference between revenues and the accounting costs that have been charged against them, *cash flow is the amount of money a company takes in as a result of doing business.* Table 6.4 presents the 1991–92 statement of cash flows for MarCor Industries. Notice that this report brings together items from *both* the balance sheet and income statement to show how the company obtained its cash and how it used this valuable liquid resource. The statement is broken into three parts, the most important of which is the first one, labeled "Cash from Operations." It is important because it captures the *net cash flow from operations;* this is what is generally meant by the term *cash flow,* since it represents the amount of cash generated by the company and which was available for investment and financing activities. In the case of MarCor, its 1992 cash flow from operations was nearly $19 million—way up from the year before. However, because the company spent more on its investments and financing activities than it took in, its actual cash position declined by some $8.4 million. (Note near the bottom of the statement that the company had a net decrease in cash of some $8,433,000.) Ideally, you'd like to see a high (and preferably increasing) cash flow, since that would mean the company has plenty of money to pay dividends, service debt, and finance growth. In addition, you'd like to see the firm's cash position increase over time because of the positive impact that has on the

TABLE 6.4 A Statement of Cash Flows, MarCor Industries

($ Thousands, Fiscal Year Ended December 31)

1992	1991	
		Cash from Operations
$18,005	$15,505	Net earnings
8,792	8,202	Depreciation and amortization
560	54	Other non-cash charges
(7,296)	(21,696)	Increase in current assets
(1,268)	3,041	Increase (Decrease) in current liabilities
$18,793	$ 5,106	Net cash flow from operations
		Cash from Investment Activities
($ 6,685)	($ 4,686)	Acquisitions of property, plant, and equipment—net
($ 6,685)	($ 4,686)	Net cash flow from investing
		Cash from Financing Activities
—	$ 7,950	Proceeds from long-term borrowing
($11,825)	(1,240)	Reduction in long-term debt, including current maturities and early retirements
(8,626)	(7,287)	Payment of dividends to common stock
($20,451)	($ 577)	Net cash flow from financing
($ 8,433)	($ 157)	**Net Increase (Decrease) in Cash**
$16,279	$16,436	Cash & short-term investments at beginning of period
$ 7,846	$16,279	Cash & short-term investments at end of period

company's liquidity and its ability to meet operating needs in a prompt and timely fashion.

Key Financial Ratios

To see what accounting statements have to say about the financial condition and operating results of the firm, it's often necessary to turn to *financial ratios*. Such ratios are useful because they provide a different perspective of the financial affairs of the firm—particularly with regard to the balance sheet and income statement— and as such, expand the information content of the company's financial statements. Ratios lie at the very heart of company analysis. Indeed, fundamental analysis as a system of information would be incomplete without this key ingredient. **Ratio analysis** is the study of the relationships among and between various financial statement accounts. Each measure relates one item on the balance sheet (or income statement) to another; or as is more often the case, a balance sheet account is related to an operating (or income statement) element. In this way, attention is centered not on the absolute size of the financial statement accounts, but more importantly, on the liquidity, activity, and profitability of the firm. However, as the accompanying

ratio analysis
the study of the relationships among and between various financial statement accounts.

INVESTOR INSIGHTS

The Ten Commandments of Financial Statement Analysis

Individuals must pass a proficiency test before obtaining a driver's license. By contrast, investors need not pass any proficiency test before trying to use financial statements as part of their investment analysis. Investors are not required to have taken a course in accounting or financial statement analysis. They are not required even to have read or understood books written on the subject. Yet analyzing financial statements requires at least as much knowledge and skill as driving an automobile. Perhaps each financial statement should contain a warning to potential users, similar to those found on many products. The warning would include at least the following 10 commandments.

1. *Thou shalt not use financial statements in isolation, but only in the broader context of other available information.* The additional information includes data on economy-wide conditions and industry-wide conditions.

2. *Thou shalt not use financial statements as the only source of firm-specific information.* There are many other sources of information about the company. Consider, for example, the popular financial press and periodicals, as well as analysts' reports.

3. *Thou shalt not avoid reading footnotes, which are an integral part of financial statements.* Financial statements cannot be reasonably analyzed without reading and understanding the footnotes. By analogy, a temperature of 10 degrees is meaningless in isolation, unless one knows whether it is being measured on the Celsius or Fahrenheit scale. In a given country, a uniform temperature scale may be assumed. The same is not true of the accounting methods used under generally accepted accounting principles. GAAP, for example, permits a variety of inventory and depreciation methods. A description of a company's accounting policies is included as a part of the footnotes.

4. *Thou shalt not focus on a single number.* The investor should read and understand *all* the material presented in the financial statements. Financial statements are not designed to be reduced to a single number. Net income is not intended to be *the* number that summarizes *all* the information relevant to making an investment decision. A user must analyze growth and leverage, among other factors, as well as profitability.

Investor Insights box suggests, to get the most from ratio analysis, you must have a good understanding of the uses and limitations of the financial statements themselves.

The most significant contribution of financial ratios is that they enable an investor to assess the firm's past and present financial condition and operating results. Ratio mechanics are actually quite simple: Selected information is obtained from annual financial statements and used to compute a set of ratios, that are then compared to historical and/or industry standards to evaluate the financial condition and operating results of the company. When historical standards are used, the company's ratios are compared and studied from one year to the next. Industry standards, in contrast, involve a comparison of a particular company's ratios to the performance of other companies in the same line of business. And remember, the reason we're doing all this is to *develop information about the past that can be used to get a handle on the future*. For it's only from a thorough understanding of a company's past performance that an investor can be in a position to forecast its future with

5. *Thou shalt not overlook the implications of what is read.* It is not sufficient simply to know that a company is a high-growth firm or a highly leveraged firm; one must also know that such characteristics typically imply higher risk, as well.

6. *Thou shalt not ignore events subsequent to the financial statements.* Financial statements are not forecasts of the future. The annual financial statements report the financial condition of the company as of year-end. They do not purport to capture the effects of events that occur after year-end. They thus become increasingly out-of-date as the year progresses. The rate of deterioration in timeliness is related to many factors, including the growth rate of the firm.

7. *Thou shalt not overlook the limitations of financial statements.* Financial statements report on only a specified set of events, not all events or all possible financial effects of a single event. Financial statements do not generally represent estimates of the market values of the reported assets and liabilities, nor do they reflect changes in the market values of those assets and liabilities.

8. *Thou shalt not use financial statements without adequate knowledge.* Investors should be sufficiently competent to read, understand and analyze financial statements. Otherwise, the investor cannot be called a user of financial statements in any meaningful sense.

9. *Thou shalt not shun professional help.* If unwilling or unable to attain adequate knowledge, the investor should defer to someone who does have such ability, such as a financial analyst. If unwilling or unable to obtain help, the investor should hand over a portion of the investment process (hence a portion of the investment decision itself) to a professional manager.

10. *Thou shalt not take unnecessary risks.* If unwilling or unable to obtain professional help, the investor should undertake investments where investment risk is minimal, or where analysis of financial statements is not an issue. Investment in U.S. Treasury bills is one example. Of course, there may be more than 10 commandments for financial statement analysis, but these capture the primary issues.

Source: Adapted from William H. Beaver, "Ten Commandments of Financial Statement Analysis," *Financial Analysts Journal,* January/February 1991, pp. 9, 18.

---

liquidity measures financial ratios concerned with the firm's ability to meet its day-to-day operating expenses and satisfy its short-term obligations as they come due.

some degree of accuracy. For example, even if sales have been expanding rapidly over the past few years, an investor must carefully assess the reasons for the growth before naively assuming that past growth-rate trends will continue into the future. Such insights are obtained from financial ratios and financial statement analysis.

Financial ratios can be divided into five groups: (1) liquidity; (2) activity; (3) leverage; (4) profitability; and (5) common stock, or market measures. Using the 1992 figures from the MarCor financial statements (Tables 6.2 and 6.3), we will now identify and briefly discuss some of the more widely used measures in each of these five categories.

 ### *Measures of Liquidity*

Liquidity is concerned with the firm's ability to meet its day-to-day operating expenses and satisfy its short-term obligations as they come due. Of major concern is whether a company has adequate cash and other liquid assets on hand to service its debt and operating needs in a prompt and timely fashion. A general overview of a company's liquidity position can often be obtained from two simple measures: current ratio and net working capital.

Current Ratio.   The *current ratio* is one of the most commonly cited of all financial ratios. It is computed as follows:

Equation 6.1

$$\text{Current ratio} = \frac{\text{current assets}}{\text{current liabilities}}$$

In 1992, MarCor Industries had a current ratio of:

$$\text{Current ratio for MarCor} = \frac{\$279,380}{\$84,946} = \underline{\underline{3.29}}$$

This figure indicates that MarCor had $3.29 in short-term resources to service every dollar of current debt. This is a fairly high number, and by most standards, would be considered very strong.

Net Working Capital.   Though technically not a ratio in the formal sense of the word, net working capital is nonetheless often viewed as such. Actually, *net working capital* is an *absolute* measure of liquidity that indicates the dollar amount of equity in the working capital position of the firm. It is the difference between current assets and current liabilities. For 1992, the net working capital figure for MarCor Industries equaled:

Equation 6.2

$$\text{Net working capital} = \text{current assets} - \text{current liabilities}$$

$$\text{for MarCor} = \$279,380 - \$84,946 = \underline{\$194,434}$$

A net working capital figure that approaches the $200 million mark is substantial indeed and suggests that the liquidity position of this firm is good—so long as it is not made up of slow-moving and obsolete inventories and/or past due accounts receivable.

Activity Ratios

activity ratios
financial ratios that
are used to measure
how well a firm is
managing its assets.

Measuring general liquidity is only the beginning of the analysis, for we must also assess the composition and underlying liquidity of key current assets, and evaluate how effectively the company is managing its assets. **Activity ratios** compare company sales to various asset categories to measure how well the company is utilizing its assets. Three of the most widely used activity ratios deal with accounts receivable, inventory, and total assets.

Accounts Receivable Turnover.   A glance at most financial statements will reveal that the asset side of the balance sheet is dominated by just a few accounts that make up 80 to 90 percent, or even more, of total resources. Certainly, this is the case with MarCor where, as can be seen in Table 6.2, three entries (accounts receivable, inventory, and net long-term assets) accounted for about 95 percent of total assets in 1992. Most firms invest a significant amount of capital in accounts receivable, and for this reason they are viewed as a crucial corporate resource. *Accounts receivable turnover* is a measure of how these resources are being managed and is computed as follows:

Equation 6.3

$$\text{Accounts receivable turnover} = \frac{\text{annual sales}}{\text{accounts receivable}}$$

$$\text{for MarCor} = \frac{\$606,610}{\$105,400} = \underline{\underline{5.76}}$$

In essence, this turnover figure is an indication of the kind of return the company is getting from its investment in accounts receivable. Other things being equal, the higher the turnover figure, the more favorable it is. Observe that in 1992, MarCor turned its receivables over about 5.8 times; put another way, each dollar invested in receivables supported $5.76 in sales.

Inventory Turnover. Another important corporate resource, and one that requires a considerable amount of management attention, is inventory. Control of inventory is important to the well-being of a company and is commonly assessed with the *inventory turnover* measure:

Equation 6.4

$$\text{Inventory turnover} = \frac{\text{annual sales}}{\text{inventory}}$$

$$\text{for MarCor} = \frac{\$606,610}{\$164,356} = \underline{\underline{3.69}}$$

Again, the more mileage (sales) the company can get out of its inventory, the better the return on this vital resource. A figure of 3.69 for MarCor reveals its goods were bought and sold out of inventory about 3.7 times a year. Generally, the higher the turnover figure, the less time an item spends in inventory and, thus, the better the return the company is able to earn from funds tied up in inventory.

Total Asset Turnover. *Total asset turnover* indicates how efficiently assets are being used to support sales. It is calculated as follows:

Equation 6.5

$$\text{Total asset turnover} = \frac{\text{annual sales}}{\text{total assets}}$$

$$\text{for MarCor} = \frac{\$606,610}{\$338,620} = \underline{\underline{1.79}}$$

Note in this case that MarCor is generating about $1.80 in revenues from every dollar invested in assets. This is a fairly high number and is important because it has a direct bearing on corporate profitability. The principle at work here is much like the return to an individual investor: Earning $100 from a $1,000 investment is far more desirable than earning the same $100 from a $2,000 investment. A high total asset turnover figure suggests that corporate resources are being well managed and that the firm is able to realize a high level of sales (and ultimately, profits) from its asset investments.

Leverage Measures

leverage measures
financial ratios that
measure the amount
of debt being used
to support opera-
tions, and the ability
of the firm to service
its debt.

Leverage deals with different types of financing and indicates the amount of debt being used to support the resources and operations of the company. The amount of indebtedness within the financial structure and the ability of the firm to service its debt are major concerns in leverage analysis. There are two widely used leverage ratios: The first, the debt-equity ratio, measures the *amount of debt* being used by the company; the second, times interest earned, assesses how well the company can *service its debt.*

Debt-Equity Ratio.   A measure of leverage, or the *relative* amount of funds provided by lenders and owners, the *debt-equity ratio* is computed as follows:

Equation 6.6

$$\text{Debt-equity ratio} = \frac{\text{long-term debt}}{\text{stockholders' equity}}$$

$$\text{for MarCor} = \frac{\$83,723}{\$169,951} = \underline{\underline{.49}}$$

Since highly leveraged firms (those using large amounts of debt) run an increased risk of defaulting on their loans, this ratio is particularly helpful in assessing a stock's risk exposure. The 1992 debt-equity ratio for MarCor is reasonably low (at 49 percent), and shows that most of the company's capital comes from its owners. Stated another way, this figure means there was only 49 cents of debt in the capital structure for every dollar of equity.

Times Interest Earned.   *Times interest earned* is a so-called coverage ratio and measures the ability of the firm to meet its fixed interest payments. It is calculated as follows:

Equation 6.7

$$\text{Times interest earned} = \frac{\text{earnings before interest and taxes}}{\text{interest expense}}$$

$$\text{for MarCor} = \frac{\$25,955 + \$5,765}{\$5,765} = \underline{\underline{5.50}}$$

**profitability mea-
sures**
financial ratios that
measure the returns
of a company by re-
lating relative success
of a firm through
comparison of prof-
its to sales, assets, or
equity.

The ability of the company to meet its interest payments (which, with bonds, are fixed contractual obligations) in a timely and orderly fashion is an important consideration in evaluating risk exposure. In the case of MarCor Industries, there is about $5.50 available to cover every dollar of interest expense. As a rule, a coverage ratio of 6 to 7 times earnings is considered pretty strong. On the downside, there's usually little concern until the measure drops to something less than two or three times earnings.

Measures of Profitability

Profitability is a relative measure of success. Each of the various profitability measures relates the returns (profits) of a company to its sales, assets, or equity. There are three widely used profitability measures: net profit margin, return on assets, and return on equity.

Net Profit Margin. This is the "bottom line" of operations. *Net profit margin* indicates the *rate* of profit from sales and other revenues. The net profit margin is computed as follows:

Equation 6.8

$$\text{Net profit margin} = \frac{\text{net profit after taxes}}{\text{total revenues}}$$

$$\text{for MarCor} = \frac{\$18,005}{\$614,906} = \underline{\underline{2.9\%}}$$

The net profit margin looks at profits as a percentage of sales. Because it moves with costs, it also reveals the type of control management has over the cost structure of the firm. Note that MarCor had a net profit margin of 2.9 percent in 1992—that is, the company's return on sales was roughly 3 cents on the dollar. Although this is a bit below average for American corporations in general, a net profit margin of nearly 3 percent is good (i.e., *above* average) for a fashion apparel firm.

Return on Assets. As a profitability measure, *return on assets* looks at the amount of resources needed to support operations. Return on assets (ROA) reveals management's effectiveness in generating profits from the assets it has available, and *is perhaps the single most important measure of return*. It is computed as follows:

Equation 6.9

$$\text{ROA} = \frac{\text{net profit after taxes}}{\text{total assets}}$$

$$\text{for MarCor} = \frac{\$18,005}{\$338,620} = \underline{\underline{5.3\%}}$$

Because both return on sales (net profit margin) and asset productivity (total asset turnover) are embedded in ROA, it provides a clear picture of a company's managerial effectiveness, and the overall profitability of its resource allocation and investment decisions. In the case of MarCor Industries, the company earned 5.3 percent on its asset investments in 1992. ROA moves up (or down) over time as the net profit margin and total asset turnover move up (or down). As a rule, the higher the ROA, the more profitable a company. If the ROA is uncomfortably low, then the way to improve it is to shore up the net profit margin and/or total asset turnover.

Return on Equity. A measure of the overall profitability of the firm, *return on equity (ROE)* captures, in a single ratio, the amount of success the firm is having in managing its assets, operations, and capital structure. ROE is closely followed by seasoned investors because of its direct link to the profits, growth, and dividends of the company. Return on equity—or return on investment (ROI), as it's sometimes called—measures the return to the firm's stockholders by relating profits to shareholder equity:

Equation 6.10

$$\text{Return on equity (ROE)} = \frac{\text{net profit after taxes}}{\text{stockholders' equity}}$$

$$\text{for MarCor} = \frac{\$18,005}{\$169,951} = \underline{\underline{10.6\%}}$$

Essentially, ROE is an extension of ROA, as it introduces the company's financing decisions into the assessment of profitability. That is, it indicates the extent to which leverage can increase return to stockholders. ROE shows the annual payoff to investors, which in the case of MarCor amounts to nearly 11 cents for every dollar of equity. Generally speaking, look for a high or increasing ROE; in contrast, watch out for a falling ROE, as that could spell trouble later on.

Common Stock Ratios

There are a number of common stock, or so-called market, ratios that convert key bits of information about the company to a per share basis. They are used to assess the performance of a company for stock valuation purposes. These ratios tell the investor exactly what portion of total profits, dividends, and equity is allocated to each share of stock. Popular common stock ratios include earnings per share, price/earnings ratio, price-to-sales ratio, dividends per share, dividend yield, payout ratio, and book value per share. We have already examined two of these measures in Chapter 5 (earnings per share and dividend yield); let's look now at the other five.

Price/Earnings Ratio. This measure is an extension of the earnings per share ratio and is used to determine how the market is pricing the company's common stock. The *price/earnings (P/E) ratio* relates the company's earnings per share (EPS) to the market price of its stock:

Equation 6.11
$$P/E = \frac{\text{market price of common stock}}{\text{EPS}}$$

To compute the P/E ratio, it is necessary first to calculate the stock's EPS. Using the *earnings-per-share* equation from the previous chapter, we see that EPS for MarCor Industries in 1992 was:

Equation 6.11a
$$EPS = \frac{\text{net profit after taxes} - \text{preferred dividends}}{\text{number of common shares outstanding}}$$

$$\text{for MarCor} = \frac{\$18,005 - \$0}{3,800} = \underline{\$4.74}$$

In this case, the company's profits of $18 million translated into earnings of $4.74 for *each share* of outstanding common stock. Given this EPS figure and the stock's current market price (assume it is currently trading at 48½), we can now use Equation 6.11 to determine the P/E ratio for MarCor Industries:

$$P/E = \frac{\$48.50}{\$4.74} = \underline{10.2}$$

In effect, the stock is currently selling at a multiple of about 10 times its 1992 earnings. Price/earnings multiples are widely quoted in the financial press and are an essential part of many stock valuation models.

Price-to-Sales Ratio. Very simply, the *price-to-sales ratio (PSR)* relates sales per share to the market price of the company's stock. This measure is used by a lot of investors because it does a fairly good job of identifying *overpriced* stocks—stocks that should be *avoided*. The basic principle behind this ratio is that the *lower* the PSR, the *less* likely it is that the stock will be overpriced, or even fully priced. PSR is computed as follows:

Equation 6.12

$$PSR = \frac{\text{market price of common stock}}{\text{annual sales per share}}$$

To find the annual sales (or revenues) per share, just divide the company's annual sales by the number of common shares outstanding. That is:

Equation 6.13

$$\text{Annual sales/shares} = \frac{\text{annual sales}}{\text{number of common shares outstanding}}$$

$$\text{for MarCor} = \frac{\$606,610}{3,800} = \underline{\$159.63}$$

Thus, for each share of its common stock, the company is generating $159.63 in sales. We can use this figure, along with the latest market price of the stock, to calculate Equation 6.12, the price-to-sales ratio, as follows:

$$PSR = \frac{\$48.50}{\$159.63} = \underline{0.30}$$

At its current market price of $48.50, MarCor's stock is selling at a multiple of less than a third of its 1992 sales per share. Under most circumstances, this would be viewed as a fairly low price/sales ratio. Thus, the stock may have a lot more "play" left in it.

Dividends per Share. The principle here is the same as for EPS: to translate total common stock dividends paid by the company into a per share figure. (*Note:* If not on the income statement, the amount of dividends paid to common stock can be found on the statement of cash flows—Table 6.4.) *Dividends per share* is measured as follows:

Equation 6.14

$$\text{Dividends per share} = \frac{\text{annual dividends paid to common stock}}{\text{number of common shares outstanding}}$$

$$\text{for MarCor} = \frac{\$8,626}{3,800} = \underline{\$2.27}$$

For fiscal 1992, MarCor Industries paid out dividends of $2.27 per share—at a quarterly rate of about 57 cents per share. As we saw in the preceding chapter, we can relate dividends per share to the market price of the stock to determine its present *dividend yield:* $2.27 ÷ $48.50 = 4.7%.

Payout Ratio. Another important dividend measure is the dividend *payout ratio.* It provides an indication of the amount of earnings paid out to stockholders in the form of dividends. Well-managed companies have target payout ratios they try to maintain, so if earnings are going up, so will dividends. The payout ratio is calculated as follows:

Equation 6.15

$$\text{Payout ratio} = \frac{\text{dividends per share}}{\text{earnings per share}}$$

$$\text{for MarCor} = \frac{\$2.27}{\$4.74} = \underline{\underline{.48}}$$

For MarCor Industries in 1992, dividends accounted for about 48 percent of earnings. This is fairly typical. Most companies that pay dividends tend to pay out somewhere between 40 and 60 percent of earnings.

Book Value Per Share.   The last common stock ratio is *book value per share,* a measure that deals with stockholders' equity. Actually, book value is simply another term for equity (or net worth); it represents the difference between total assets and total liabilities. Book value per share is computed as follows:

Equation 6.16

$$\text{Book value per share} = \frac{\text{stockholders' equity}}{\text{number of common shares outstanding}}$$

$$\text{for MarCor} = \frac{\$169,951}{3,800} = \underline{\underline{\$44.72}}$$

Presumably, a stock should sell for *more* than its book value (as MarCor does). If not, it could be an indication that something is seriously wrong with the company's outlook and profitability. A convenient way to relate the book value of a company to the market price of its stock is to compute the *price-to-book-value ratio:*

Equation 6.17

$$\text{Price-to-book-value} = \frac{\text{market price of common stock}}{\text{book value per share}}$$

$$\text{for MarCor} = \frac{\$48.50}{\$44.72} = \underline{\underline{1.08}}$$

Widely used by investors, this ratio shows how aggressively the stock is being priced. As with MarCor, we'd expect most stocks to have a price-to-book-value of more than 1.0 (which simply indicates that the stock is selling for more than its book value). Indeed, in strong bull markets, it's not uncommon to find stocks trading at two or three times their book values. On the other hand, a price-to-book of only 1.08 is often viewed as a positive sign (especially by so-called "value investors") that the stock is reasonably priced relative to its underlying asset base.

Interpreting the Numbers

Rather than compute all the financial ratios themselves, most investors rely on published reports for such information. Many large brokerage houses and a variety of financial services publish such reports, an example of which is given in Figure 6.4. These reports provide a good deal of vital information in a convenient and easy-to-read format, and they relieve investors of the drudgery of computing the

Hartmarx Corp.

1105

NYSE Symbol HMX In S&P 500

Price	Range	P–E Ratio	Dividend	Yield	S&P Ranking	Beta
Jul. 10'91	1991					
9⁷/₈	13¹/₄–7⁵/₈	NM	0.60	6.1%	B+	1.05

Summary

This company manufacturers and retails of men's and women's brand name apparel. A substantial loss was incurred in fiscal 1990, partly reflecting a $51 million restructuring charge for losses associated with closing 65 stores and seven factories, and selling HMX's minority interest in its Mexican operation. The loss should narrow in fiscal 1991 and profitability is expected to resume in fiscal 1992. In May 1991, HMX filed a registration statement for a public offering of 4 million new common shares.

Current Outlook

A loss of $0.16 per share is projected for the fiscal year ending November 30, 1991, compared with fiscal 1990's loss of $3.11, which included a $2.59 restructuring charge. Earnings could recover to $0.50 a share in fiscal 1992.

The dividend should remain at $0.15 quarterly.

Sales for fiscal 1991 should be flat, reflecting the discontinuance of 65 retail locations in late 1990 and 1991, which will offset higher sales at Kuppenheimer's, particularly in the second half when the men's apparel business is expected to pick up (assuming an economic recovery), and higher wholesale men's apparel sales stemming from increased market share and new product introductions. Full-year margins should improve somewhat on lower wool prices, more centralized operations, and lower inventory levels and the absence of other expenses related to the closed stores, and other restructuring efforts. Interest charges should be lower, and the prior year's $51 million after-tax restructuring charge will be absent. The per share loss will be mitigated by more shares outstanding.

Net Sales (Million $)

Quarter:	1990-91	1989-90	1988-89	1987-88
Feb..............	319	342	327	302
May	293	304	304	273
Aug..............	---	313	317	290
Nov..............	---	336	348	310
	1,296	1,297	1,174

Sales for the six months ended May 31, 1991 declined 5.2%, year to year, reflecting lower retail sales. Margins narrowed, but in the absence of a $78 million restructuring charge, the pretax loss narrowed to $11.7 million from $80.7 million. After tax benefits of $4.5 million, versus $27.9 million, the net loss amounted to $7.2 million ($0.35 a share on 3.3% more shares), compared with $52.8 million ($2.68).

TRADING VOLUME
THOUSAND SHARES

1985 1986 1987 1988 1989 1990 1991

Common Share Earnings ($)

Quarter:	1990-91	1989-90	1988-89	1987-88
Feb................	d0.06	0.12	0.50	0.47
May	d0.29	d2.80	0.16	0.44
Aug................	E0.05	d0.24	0.02	0.30
Nov................	E0.14	d0.19	0.21	0.82
	Ed0.16	d3.11	0.89	2.03

Important Developments

May '91 — HMX filed a registration statement for a publicly offering of 4 million common shares, of which 3.2 million would be sold in the U.S. by First Boston Co. and Morgan Stanley & Co. and 800,000 internationally by Credit Suisse First Boston Ltd. and Morgan Stanley International. HMX granted the underwriters an over-allotment option for up to 600,000 additional shares. Proceeds would be used to pay down debt.

Next earnings report expected in early October.

Per Share Data ($)

Yr. End Nov. 30	1990	1989	1988	1987	1986	1985	1984	²1983	1982	²1981
Tangible Bk. Val.¹	14.60	18.37	19.21	18.26	17.59	17.60	16.24	14.80	13.44	12.56
Cash Flow	d1.33	2.48	3.37	3.11	2.22	3.29	3.16	2.85	2.41	2.01
Earnings	d3.11	0.89	2.03	2.01	1.20	2.25	2.24	2.03	1.68	1.40
Dividends	0.900	1.175	1.075	0.980	0.903	0.853	0.747	0.608	0.538	0.484
Payout Ratio	NM	132%	53%	45%	74%	38%	33%	30%	30%	34%
Prices—High³	19⁷/₈	28¹/₈	29³/₄	34³/₄	32	26³/₈	21⁷/₈	24¹/₄	18¹/₄	10³/₄
Low³	5¹/₂	18³/₄	20³/₄	18¹/₄	23¹/₂	18⁵/₈	15⁵/₈	14¹/₂	8	6¹/₄
P/E Ratio—	NM	32-21	15-10	17-9	27-20	12-8	10-7	12-7	11-5	8-4

Data as orig. reptd. Adj. for stk. div(s). of 50% May 1986, & 50% stk. exchange Apr. 1983. 1. Incl. intangibles. 2. Reflects merger or acquisition. 3. Cal. yr. NM-Not Meaningful. d-Deficit. E-Estimated.

Standard NYSE Stock Reports
Vol. 58/No. 137/Sec. 12

July 18, 1991
Copyright © 1991 Standard & Poor's Corp. All Rights Reserved

Standard & Poor's Corp.
25 Broadway, NY, NY 10004

• FIGURE 6.4 An Example of a Published Analytical Report with Financial Statistics

These and similar reports are widely available to investors and play an important part in the security analysis process. (*Source:* Standard & Poor's *NYSE Reports,* July 18, 1991.)

financial ratios themselves. Even so, investors still have to be able to evaluate this information. To do that, they need not only a basic understanding of financial ratios, but also some standard of performance, or benchmark, against which they can assess trends in company performance. Basically, there are two types of performance standards used in financial statement analysis: historical and industry. In the first case, various financial ratios and measures are run on the company for a period of three to five years (or longer) in order to assess developing trends in the company's operations and financial condition: That is, are they improving or deteriorating, and where do the company's strengths and weaknesses lie? Industry standards, in contrast, enable the investor to compare the financial ratios of the company with comparable firms, or the average results for the industry as a whole. Here, attention is centered on determining the relative strength of the firm with respect to its competitors. Using MarCor Industries, we'll see how both of these standards of performance can be used to evaluate and interpret financial ratios.

Take a look at Table 6.5. It provides a summary of historical data and average industry figures (for the latest year) for most of the ratios discussed above. To begin with, we can see a modest improvement in MarCor's already strong liquidity position, as the current ratio remains well above the industry standard. The activity

TABLE 6.5 Comparative Historical and Industry Ratios

	Historical Figures for MarCor Industries				Industry Averages for the Apparel Industry
	1989	1990	1991	1992	
Liquidity measures					
Current ratio	3.05	2.86	3.10	3.29	2.87
Activity measures					
Receivables turnover	5.22	4.87	5.52	5.76	8.00
Inventory turnover	3.10	2.98	3.57	3.69	3.75
Total asset turnover	1.75	1.65	1.67	1.79	1.42
Leverage measures					
Debt-equity ratio	.52	.56	.58	.49	.89
Times interest earned	4.65	4.50	4.75	5.50	3.35
Profitability measures					
Net profit margin	3.6%	3.0%	2.7%	2.9%	2.5%
Return on assets	6.3%	4.9%	4.6%	5.3%	3.9%
Return on equity	11.8%	8.6%	9.8%	10.6%	8.9%
Common stock measures					
Earnings per share	$4.67	$4.15	$4.08	$4.74	$2.86
Price/earnings ratio	9.50	10.90	11.20	10.20	10.10
Dividend yield	4.90%	4.20%	4.20%	4.70%	3.9%
Payout ratio	47.0%	46.0%	47.0%	48.0%	45.5%
Price-to-book-value	1.07	1.15	1.09	1.08	1.05

measures show that although receivables and inventory turnover are improving, they still remain below industry standards. Accounts receivable turnover appears to be especially out of line and is almost 40 percent below normal. Unless there is an operating or economic explanation for this, it would appear that a lot of excess (nonproductive) resources are being tied up in accounts receivable, which is costing the firm millions of dollars a year in profits. The inventory position, in contrast, has improved and although still a bit below average, it certainly does not appear to be much of a problem. Finally, note that total asset turnover is up from last year and continues well above average.

The leverage position of MarCor Industries seems well controlled: The company tends to use a lot less debt in its financial structure than the average firm in the apparel industry. The payoff for this judicious use of debt comes in the form of a coverage ratio that is well above average. The profitability picture for MarCor is equally attractive as the profit rate, return on assets, and ROE are all improving and remain well above the industry norm. In summary, our analysis suggests that this

TABLE 6.6 Comparative Financial Statistics: MarCor Industries and Its Major Competitors

(All Figures are for Year-End 1992, or for the 5-Year Period Ending in 1992, $ Millions)

Financial Measure	MarCor Industries	Regatta Group	Holbrook Industries	Bellwood, Inc.
Total assets	$338.6	$568.6	$231.9	$469.4
Long-term debt	$ 53.7	$124.8	$ 41.5	$128.1
Stockholders' equity	$170.0	$196.9	$103.7	$200.2
Stockholders' equity as a % of total assets	50.2%	34.6%	44.7%	42.6%
Total revenues	$614.9	$807.5	$505.9	$808.0
Net earnings	$ 18.0	$ 14.5	$ 10.6	$ 12.4
Net profit margin	2.9%	1.8%	2.1%	1.5%
5-year growth rates in:				
Total assets	8.9%	10.2%	8.6%	5.6%
Total revenues	8.8%	9.5%	9.0%	3.5%
Net earnings	32.0%	18.0%	7.5%	2.5%
Dividends	10.8%	N/A	8.0%	6.0%
Total asset turnover	1.79x	1.42x	2.18x	1.73x
Debt-equity ratio	0.49	0.74	0.60	0.84
Times interest earned	5.50x	2.65x	4.67x	2.26x
ROA	5.30%	4.10%	5.20%	4.50%
ROE	10.60%	6.70%	8.50%	9.20%
Price/earnings ratio	10.20x	10.20x	13.60x	12.90x
Payout ratio	48.00%	N/A	58.80%	67.00%
Dividend yield	4.70%	N/A	4.30%	6.25%
Price-to-book-value	1.08	1.07	0.95	1.17

firm is, with the possible exception of accounts receivable, fairly well managed and highly profitable. The results of this are reflected in common stock ratios that are consistently equal or superior to industry averages.

In addition to looking at a company historically and relative to *average performance* for the industry, it's also advisable to evaluate a firm relative to two or three of its major competitors. A lot can be gained by seeing how a company stacks up to its competitors, and by determining if the company is, in fact, a market leader and well-positioned to take advantage of unfolding developments. Table 6.6 does just that by providing an array of comparative financial statistics for MarCor and three of its major competitors. (This type of firm-specific data can generally be obtained from industry surveys similar to those put out by S&P, and others.)

As can be seen, MarCor Industries is fully capable of holding its own against the other leading producers in the industry. Indeed, in just about every category, Mar-Cor's numbers are about equal to or superior to any one of its three major competitors. It may be smaller than a couple of the firms, but it out-performs them in terms of profit margins and growth rates. Equally important, it's a lot less leveraged than the other manufacturers, which is a real plus in a highly volatile industry. Yet, even with its low financial leverage, it still is able to maintain a highly attractive ROE. In all, Tables 6.5 and 6.6 suggest that MarCor Industries is a solid, up-and-coming business that's been able to make a real name for itself in a highly competitive industry; the company has certainly done well in the past and appears to be well managed today. Our major concern at this point (and the topic of the first part of Chapter 8) is whether MarCor will continue to produce above-average returns to investors.

SUMMARY

1. While common stocks are popular investment vehicles, success in this market is largely a function of careful security selection and investment timing. Security analysis helps the investor make the crucial selection decision by determining the intrinsic value (or underlying worth) of a stock; security analysis consists of economic, industry, and fundamental (company) analyses.

2. Economic analysis deals with an evaluation of the general state of the economy and its potential effects on security returns. In essence, economic analysis tries to identify the kind of future economic environment the investor will be facing, and is used to set the tone for the security analysis process.

    In industry analysis, the investor narrows the focus a bit as attention is centered on the activities in one or more industries; it is the outlook for the industry that is important.

3. Fundamental analysis involves an in-depth study of the financial condition and operating results of the company. Once the historical position of the firm has been established, future expectations can be formulated about the company and its stock.

4. Fundamental analysis is conducted on the premise that the value of a share of stock is influenced in part by the performance of the company issuing the stock. Accordingly, the competitive position of the company, its sales and profit margins, asset mix, and capital structure are all important variables.

5. The company's balance sheet, income statement, and statement of cash flows are all used in fundamental analysis; an essential part of such analysis are financial ratios, which expand the perspective and information content of financial statements. There are five broad categories of financial ratios: liquidity; activity; leverage; profitability; and market (common stock) ratios, all of which involve the study of relationships among and between various financial accounts.

6. In order to properly evaluate financial ratios, it is necessary to base the analysis on historical and industry standards of performance. Whereas historical standards are used to assess developing trends in the company, industry benchmarks enable the investor to see how the firm stacks up to competitors.

QUESTIONS

1. Identify the three major parts of security analysis and discuss why security analysis is so important to the stock selection process. What is intrinsic value, and how does it fit into security analysis? Would there be any need for security analysis if we operated in an efficient market environment? Briefly explain.

2. What is a satisfactory investment vehicle? How does security analysis help in identifying such investment candidates?

3. Discuss the general concept of economic analysis. Is this type of analysis really necessary, and can it help the investor make a decision about a stock? Explain.

4. Why is the business cycle so important to economic analysis? Identify each of the following and note how each would probably behave in a strong economy:
   a. Fiscal policy.
   b. Interest rates.
   c. Industrial production.
   d. Retail sales.
   e. Consumer spending.

5. What is the Federal Reserve and how can it affect the general tone of the economy? What's the difference between the Federal Reserve discount rate and the federal funds rate?

6. Briefly describe each of the following:
   a. Gross domestic product.
   b. Leading indicators.
   c. Money supply.
   d. Producer prices.

7. What causes inflation? What effect does inflation have on common stocks?

8. Briefly describe the two ways that an economic forecast can be used to help select investments.

9. What is the relationship between the stock market and the economy? How does this relationship affect an economic outlook?

10. What is industry analysis and why is it important? Explain.

11. Identify and briefly discuss several aspects of an industry that are important to its behavior and operating characteristics; note especially how economic issues fit into industry analysis.

12. What are the four stages of an industry's growth cycle? Which of these stages is most influenced by the economic cycle?

13. What is fundamental analysis? Does the performance of a company have any bearing on the value of its stock? Explain.

14. Why do investors bother to look at the historical performance of a company when future behavior is what really counts? Explain.

15. What is ratio analysis? Describe the role and contribution of ratio analysis to the study of a company's financial condition and operating results.

16. Match the specific ratios from the left-hand column with the ratio categories listed in the right-hand column:

a. Inventory turnover.   1. Profitability ratios.
b. Debt-equity ratio.   2. Activity ratios.
c. Current ratio.   3. Liquidity ratios.
d. Net profit margin.   4. Leverage ratios.
e. Return on assets.   5. Common stock ratios.
f. Total asset turnover.
g. Price/earnings ratio.
h. Price-to-sales ratio.
i. Times interest earned.
j. Price-to-book-value.
k. Payout ratio.

17. Contrast historical standards of performance with industry standards. Briefly note the role of each in analyzing the financial conditon and operating results of a company.

PROBLEMS

 1. Assume you're given the following abbreviated financial statements:

	($ Millions)
Current assets	$150.0
Fixed & other assets	200.0
Total assets	$350.0
Current liabilities	$100.0
Long-term debt	50.0
Stockholders' equity	200.0
	$350.0
Common shares outstanding	10 million shares
Total revenues	$500.0
Total operating costs & expenses	435.0
Interest expense	10.0
Income taxes	20.0
Net profits	$ 35.0
Dividends paid to common stockholders	$10.0

Based on the above information, calculate as many liquidity, activity, leverage, profitability, and common stock measures as you can. (*Note:* Assume the current market price of the common stock is $75/share.)

2. The Amherst Company has net profits of $10 million, sales of $150 million, and 2.5 million shares of common stock outstanding. It pays $1 per share in common dividends and the stock trades at $20 per share. Given this information, determine:

    a. Amherst's earnings per share (EPS).
    b. Amherst's sales per share.
    c. The firm's price/earnings (P/E) ratio.
    d. Its price-to-sales ratio (PSR).
    e. Its dividend payout ratio.

3. Sunbelt Solar Products produces $2 million in profits from $28 million in·sales and has total assets of $15 million.

    a. Calculate SSP's total asset turnover and compute its net profit margin.
    b. Find the company's ROA, ROE, and book value per share, given that SSP has a total net worth of $6 million and 500,000 shares of common stock outstanding.

4. The Shasta Flower Farm has total assets of $10 million, an asset turnover of 2.0 times, and a net profit margin of 15 percent.

    a. What is Shasta's return on assets?
    b. Find Shasta's ROE, given 40 percent of the assets are financed with stockholders' equity.

5. Find the P/E ratio, PSR, and dividend yield of a company that has 5 million shares of common stock outstanding (the shares trade in the market at $25), earns 10 percent after taxes on annual sales of $150 million, and has a dividend payout ratio of 35 percent.

6. Using the resources available at your campus or public library, select *any* common stock you like and determine as many of the profitability, activity, liquidity, leverage, and market ratios as you can; compute the ratios for the latest available fiscal year. (*Note:* Show your work for all calculations.)

7. Listed below are 6 pairs of stocks:

    a. Wal-Mart vs. KMart.
    b. J.M. Smucker vs. Campbell Soup.
    c. I.B.M. vs. Intel.
    d. H&R Block vs. Crown Cork & Seal.
    e. Masco Corp. vs. Standard Brands Paint.
    f. General Dynamics vs. Weyerhaeuser.

    Pick *one of these pairs* and then, using the resources available at your campus or public library, comparatively analyze the two stocks to determine which one is fundamentally stronger and holds more promise for the future. Compute (or obtain) as many ratios as you see fit. As part of your analysis, obtain the latest S&P and/or *Value Line* reports on both stocks, and use them for added insights about the firms and their stocks.

8. Listed below are the 1989 and 1990 financial statements for Tootsie Roll Industries, the makers of those well-known chocolate treats:

Balance Sheets

ASSETS		
	December 31,	
	1990	**1989**
Current assets		
Cash and cash equivalents	$ 36,757,959	$ 18,491,700
Accounts receivable, less allowances of $748,000 and $744,000	16,206,648	12,060,954
Inventories	22,926,813	22,296,391
Prepaid expenses	2,037,710	1,358,694
Total current assets	77,929,130	54,207,739
Property, plant and equipment, at cost	67,974,610	63,146,514
Less: Accumulated depreciation and amortization	35,875,750	32,239,636
Net fixed assets	32,098,860	30,906,878
Other assets:	49,673,622	51,227,383
	$159,701,612	$136,342,000

LIABILITIES AND SHAREHOLDERS' EQUITY		
Current liabilities:		
Notes and accounts payable	$ 7,676,296	$ 7,006,477
Dividends payable	576,607	559,858
Accrued liabilities	14,297,963	13,155,263
Total current liabilities	22,550,866	20,721,598
Noncurrent liabilities:		
Long-term debt	7,305,779	6,058,150
Shareholders' equity		
Common stock	6,697,835	6,504,114
Capital in excess of par value	50,820,017	40,971,214
Retained earnings	72,327,115	62,086,924
Total shareholders' equity	129,844,967	109,562,252
	$159,701,612	$136,342,000
Average number of common shares outstanding	9,645,171	9,645,171

Income Statements

	For the Year Ended December 31,	
	1990	**1989**
Net sales	$194,299,018	$179,293,888
Cost of goods sold	103,204,922	93,999,176
Gross margin	91,094,096	85,294,712
Operating expenses:	54,328,598	51,386,641
Earnings from operations	36,765,498	33,908,071
Other income (expense), net	353,637	(701,659)
Earnings before income taxes	37,119,135	33,206,412
Provision for income taxes	14,563,000	12,994,000
Net earnings	22,556,135	20,212,412
Cash dividends ($.23 and $.22 per share)	$ 2,202,450	$ 2,138,762
Average price per share of common stock (in the 4th Qtr of the yr.)	$36.50	$34.25

a. Based on the information provided, calculate the following financial ratios for 1989 and 1990:

	Tootsie Roll		Industry Averages (for 1990)
	1989	**1990**	
Current ratio	————	————	2.37X
Total asset turnover	————	————	1.64X
Debt-equity ratio	————	————	0.42
Net profit margin	————	————	8.9%
ROA	————	————	13.4%
ROE	————	————	19.0%
EPS	————	————	N/A
P/E ratio	————	————	19.5X
Cash dividend yield	————	————	2.5%
Payout ratio	————	————	47.6%
Price-to-book-value	————	————	3.6X

b. Based on the financial ratios you computed, along with the industry averages, how would you characterize the financial condition of Tootsie Roll Industries? Explain.

CFA QUESTION   (This question is from the 1991 Level I Exam.)

The value of the components affecting the ROE of Merck & Co., Inc. for 1985 are indicated in Table 1 on page 266. Selected 1990 income statement and balance sheet information for Merck can be found in Table 2 on page 266.

a. Calculate *each* of the four ROE components for Merck in 1990. Using the four components, calculate ROE for Merck in 1990. (Also compute the 1990 ROE for Merck using
   Equation 6.10, as described in this chapter; notice any similarity?)

b. Based on your calculations, describe how *each* of the four ROE components contributed
   to the change in Merck's ROE between 1985 and 1990. Identify the major underlying
   reasons for the change in Merck's ROE.

Table 1
Merck & Co., Inc.
1985 ROE Components

1. Tax burden (net income/pretax income)	.621
2. Pretax profit margin (pretax income/sales)	.245
3. Total asset turnover (sales/assets)	.724
4. Financial leverage (assets/equity)	1.877
ROE (1 × 2 × 3 × 4)	.207

Table 2
Merck & Co., Inc.
1990 Selected Financial Data
($ Millions)

Income Statement Data

Sales revenue	$7,120
Depreciation	230
Interest expense	10
Pretax income	2,550
Income taxes	900
Net income	1,650

Balance Sheet Data

Current assets	$4,850
Net fixed assets	2,400
Total assets	7,250
Current liabilities	3,290
Long-term debt	100
Shareholders' equity	3,860
Total liabilities & shareholders' equity	7,250

Note: As discussed in this chapter, ROE captures, in a single
measure, the impact that asset productivity, profit margins, and
leverage have on the overall profitability of the firm. Mathematically, ROE can be broken into its component parts to see how
each contributes to the firm's overall profitability. In this CFA
problem, we can see how financial leverage, asset turnover,
profit margin, and tax burden directly effect Merck's ROE. (In
all 4 cases, the higher the component number, the better—i.e.,
the higher the ROE.) You can find ROE as described by Equation 6.10 in this chapter, or *you can multiply the 4 components
in Table 1 together*, as follows: tax burdens × pretax profit
margin × total asset turnover × financial leverage. Obviously,
with this latter approach, you can find out a lot more about what
causes ROE to change over time.

(See Appendix C for Guideline Answer to this question.)

CASE PROBLEMS

6.1 Some Financial Ratios Are Real Eye-Openers

Jack Simms is a resident of Brownfield, Texas, where he is a prosperous rancher and businessman. He has also built up a sizable portfolio of common stock which, he believes, is due to the fact that he thoroughly evaluates each stock he invests in. As Jack says, "Y'all can't be too careful about these things! Anytime I'm fixin' to invest in a stock, you can bet I'm gonna learn as much as I can about the company." Jack prefers to compute his own ratios even though he could easily obtain various types of analytical reports from his broker at no cost. (In fact, Billy Bob Smith, his broker, has been volunteering such services for years.)

Recently, Jack has been keeping an eye on a small chemical issue. This firm, South Plains Chemical Company, is big in the fertilizer business—which, not by coincidence, is something that Jack knows a lot about. Not long ago, he received a copy of the company's latest financial statements (summarized below) and decided to take a closer look at the company.

Balance Sheet
($ Thousands)

Cash	$ 1,250		
Accounts receivable	8,000	Current liabilities	$10,000
Inventory	12,000	Long-term debt	8,000
Current assets	$21,250	Stockholders' equity	12,000
Fixed and other assets	8,750		
Total	$30,000	Total	$30,000

Income Statement
($ Thousands)

Sales	$50,000
Cost of goods sold	25,000
Operating expenses	15,000
Operating profit	$10,000
Interest expense	2,500
Taxes	2,500
Net profit	$ 5,000

Notes: Dividends paid to common (dollars in thousands)	$1,250
Number of common shares outstanding	5 million
Recent market price of the common stock	$25

Questions

1. Compute the following ratios, using the South Plains Chemical Company figures:

	Latest Industry Averages
Liquidity	
a. Net working capital	N/A
b. Current ratio	1.95
Activity	
c. Receivables turnover	5.95
d. Inventory turnover	4.50
e. Total asset turnover	2.65
Leverage	
f. Debt-equity ratio	0.45
g. Times interest earned	6.75
Profitability	
h. Operating ratio	85.0%
i. Net profit margin	8.5%
j. Return on assets	22.5%
k. ROE	32.2%
Common Stock Ratios	
l. Earnings per share	$2.00
m. Price/earnings ratio	20.0
n. Price-to-sales ratio	3.0
o. Dividends per share	$1.00
p. Dividend yield	2.5%
q. Payout ratio	50.0%
r. Book value per share	$6.25
s. Price-to-book-value	6.4

2. Compare the company ratios you prepared to the industry figures. What are the company's strengths? What are its weaknesses?

3. What is your overall assessment of South Plains Chemical? Do you think Simms should continue with his evaluation of the stock? Explain.

6.2 Doris Looks at an Auto Issue

Doris Poure is a young career woman; she lives in Chicago, where she owns and operates a highly successful modeling agency. Doris manages her modest but rapidly growing investment portfolio, made up mostly of high-grade common stocks. Because she's young and single, and has no pressing family requirements, Doris has invested primarily in stocks that offer attractive capital gains potential. Her broker recently recommended one of the auto issues and sent her some literature and analytical reports to study. Among the reports was one prepared by the brokerage house she deals with; it provided an up-to-date look at the economy, an extensive study of the auto industry, and an equally extensive review of several auto companies (including the one her broker recommended). She feels very strongly about the merits of security analysis and feels it is important to spend some time studying a stock before making an investment decision.

Questions

1. Doris tries to stay abreast of the economy on a regular basis; at the present time, most economists agree that the economy, now well into the third year of a recovery, is healthy, with industrial activity remaining strong. What other information about the economy do you think Doris would find helpful in evaluating an auto stock? Prepare a list—be specific. Which three items of economic information (from your list) are especially important? Explain.

2. In relation to a study of the auto industry, briefly note the importance of each of the following:
   a. Auto imports.
   b. The United Auto Workers union.
   c. Interest rates.
   d. The price of a gallon of gas.

3. A variety of financial ratios and measures is provided about one of the auto companies and its stock; however, these are a bit incomplete, so some additional information will have to be computed. Specifically, we know that:

Net profit margin is	15%
Total assets are	$25 billion
Earnings per share are	$3.00
Total asset turnover is	1.5
Net working capital is	$3.4 billion
Payout ratio is	40%
Current liabilities are	$5 billion
Price/earnings ratio is	12.5

   Given this information, calculate the following:
   a. Sales.
   b. Net profits after taxes.
   c. Current ratio.
   d. Market price of the stock.
   e. Dividend yield.

7 Stock Valuation and Investment Decisions

After studying this chapter, you should be able to:

1. Explain the role that a company's future plays in the stock valuation process, and develop a forecast of a stock's expected cash flow, including future dividends and anticipated price behavior.

2. Discuss the concepts of intrinsic value and required rates of return, and note how they are used as standards of performance in judging the investment suitability of a share of common stock.

3. Gain an understanding of the importance that a stock's price-earnings ratio plays in defining price behavior, and the variables that affect this multiple.

4. Determine the underlying value of a stock using the dividend valuation model, as well as other stock valuation models that take into account both expected return and potential risk.

5. Describe the principle attributes of technical analysis, including some of the more popular measures and procedures used to assess the market, and the role that technical analysis plays in the stock selection process.

6. Discuss the idea of random walks and efficient markets, trace the development of the efficient market hypothesis, and note the challenges these theories hold for the entire stock valuation process.

How much would you be willing to pay for a share of stock? That's a tough question and one that investors have been wrestling with for about as long as common stocks have been traded. The answer, of course, depends on the kind of return you expect to receive and the amount of risk involved in the transaction. This chapter looks at the question of a stock's worth in detail as we continue our discussion of the stock valuation process.

In Chapter 6, we dealt with several preliminary aspects of security analysis: economic analysis, industry analysis, and the historical phase of fundamental (company) analysis. We now need to develop estimates for the future prospects of the company and the expected returns from its stock. Then we can complete the valuation process and finally decide whether a particular stock will make a potentially attractive investment vehicle. This chapter will also examine one of the most serious challenges traditional security analysis has ever faced: that is, as professed by the efficient market advocates, that security analysis and all its trappings are largely an exercise in futility.

VALUATION: OBTAINING A STANDARD OF PERFORMANCE

stock valuation
the process by which the underlying value of a stock is established, as based on future risk and return performance of the security.

Obtaining a standard of performance that can be used to judge the investment merits of a share of stock is the underlying purpose of **stock valuation.** A stock's intrinsic value furnishes such a standard since it provides an indication of the future risk and return performance of a security. The question of whether, and to what extent, a stock is undervalued or overvalued is resolved by comparing its current market price to its intrinsic value. At any given point in time, the price of a share of common stock depends on investor expectations about the future behavior of the security. If the outlook for the company and its stock is good, the price will probably be bid up. If conditions deteriorate, the price of the stock can be expected to go down. Let's look now at the single most important issue in the stock valuation process: *the future*.

The Company and Its Future

Thus far, we have examined the historical performance of the company and its stock. It should be clear, however, that it's *not the past* that's important, but rather *the future*. The primary reason for looking at past performance is to gain insight about the future direction of the firm and its profitability. Granted, past performance provides no guarantees about future returns, but it can give us a good idea of company strengths and weaknesses. For example, it can tell us how the company's products have done in the marketplace, how the company's fiscal health shapes up, and how management tends to respond to difficult situations. In short, it can reveal how well the company has done in the past and perhaps, more importantly, how well it's positioned to take advantage of the things that may occur in the future.

Because *the value of a stock is a function of its future returns,* the investor's task at hand is to use available historical data to project key financial variables into the future. In this way, the investor can assess the outlook for the company and thereby gain some idea about the benefits to be derived from investing in the stock. We are especially interested in dividends and price behavior.

Forecasted Sales and Profits

The key to our forecast is, of course, the future behavior of the *company,* and the most important aspects to consider in this regard are the outlook for sales and the trend in the net profit margin. One way to develop a sales forecast is to assume that the company will continue to perform as it has in the past, and simply extend the historical trend. For example, if a firm's sales have been growing at the rate of 10 percent per year, then assume they will continue at that rate of growth. Of course, if there is some evidence about the economy, industry, or company that suggests a faster or slower rate of growth, the forecast should be adjusted accordingly. More often than not, this "naive" approach will be just about as effective as other, more complex techniques.

Once the sales forecast has been generated, we can shift our attention to the net profit margin. We want to know what kind of return on sales we can expect from the company. A naive estimate can be obtained simply by using the average profit margin that has prevailed for the past few years; again, this should be adjusted to account for any unusual industry or company developments. For most investors, valuable insight about future revenues and earnings can be obtained from industry or company reports put out by brokerage houses, advisory services (like *Value Line*), and the financial media (such as *Forbes*).

Given a satisfactory sales forecast and estimate of the future net profit margin, we can combine these two pieces of information to arrive at future earnings:

Equation 7.1

$$\text{Future after-tax earnings in year } t = \text{estimated sales for year } t \times \text{net profit margin expected in year } t$$

The "year t" notation in equation 7.1 simply denotes a given calendar or fiscal year in the future. It can be next year, the year after that, or any other year in which we happen to be working. Let's say that in the year just completed, a company reported sales of $100 million, and it is estimated that revenues will grow at an 8 percent annual rate, while the net profit margin should amount to about 6 percent. Thus, estimated sales next year will equal $108 million ($100 million $\times$ 1.08), and with a 6 percent profit margin, we should see earnings next year of:

$$\text{Future after-tax earnings next year} = \$108 \text{ million} \times .06 = \underline{\underline{\$6.5 \text{ million}}}$$

Using this same process, we would then estimate sales and earnings for all other years in our forecast period.

Forecasted Dividends and Prices

At this point, we have an idea of the future earnings performance of the company—assuming, of course, that our expectations and assumptions hold up. We are now ready to evaluate the effects of this performance on returns to common stock investors. Given a corporate earnings forecast, we need three additional pieces of information:

1. An estimate of future dividend payout ratios.
2. The number of common shares that will be outstanding over the forecast period.
3. A future price/earnings (P/E) ratio.

For the first two variables, unless we have evidence to the contrary, we can simply project recent historical experience into the future and assume that these estimates will hold for the forecast period. Payout ratios are usually fairly stable, so there is little risk in using a recent average figure (or, if a company follows a fixed dividend policy, we could use the latest dividend rate in our forecast). At the same time, it is generally safe to assume that the number of common shares outstanding will hold at the latest level.

The only really thorny issue is defining the future P/E ratio. This is an important figure, since it has considerable bearing on the future price behavior of the stock. Generally speaking, the P/E ratio has been shown to be a function of several variables, including: (1) the growth rate in earnings; (2) the general state of the market; (3) the amount of debt in a company's capital structure; and (4) the level of dividends. As a rule, higher ratios can be expected with higher growth rates in earnings, an optimistic market outlook, and lower debt levels (since less debt means less financial risk). We can also argue that a high P/E ratio can be expected with high dividend payouts. In practice, however, most companies with high P/E ratios have *low* dividend payouts, due to the fact that earnings growth tends to be more valuable than dividends, especially in companies with high rates of return on equity.

A useful starting point in evaluating the P/E ratio is the *average market multiple,* which is simply the average P/E ratio of stocks in the marketplace. The average market multiple provides insight into the general state of the market and gives the investor an idea of how aggressively the market in general is pricing stocks. (Other things being equal, the higher the P/E, the more optimistic the market.) Table 7.1 lists S&P price/earnings multiples for the past 32 years and shows that market multiples do tend to move over a fairly wide range. With the market multiple as a benchmark, the investor can then evaluate a stock's P/E performance relative to the market. That is, a **relative P/E multiple** can be found by dividing a stock's P/E by the market multiple. For example, if a stock currently has a P/E of 25 while the market multiple is 15, the stock's relative P/E would be $25/15 = 1.67 \text{ times}$. Looking at this relative P/E, the investor can quickly get a feel for how aggressively the stock has been priced in the market and what kind of relative P/E is normal for the stock. Other things being equal, a high relative P/E is desirable, since the higher this measure, the higher the stock will be priced in the market. But watch out for the downside: High relative P/E multiples can also mean more price volatility. (In a similar fashion, we can also use average *industry* multiples to get a feel for the kind of P/E multiples that are standard for a given industry, and then use this information, along with market multiples, to assess or project the P/E for a particular stock.)

relative P/E multiple
the measure of how a stock's P/E behaves relative to the average market multiple.

TABLE 7.1 Average Market P/E Multiples 1960–1991

Year	Market Multiples (Avg. S&P P/E Ratio)	Year	Market Multiples (Avg. S&P P/E Ratio)
1960	17.8	1976	11.0
1961	22.4	1977	8.8
1962	17.2	1978	8.3
1963	18.7	1979	7.4
1964	18.6	1980	9.1
1965	17.8	1981	8.1
1966	14.8	1982	10.2
1967	17.7	1983	12.4
1968	18.1	1984	10.0
1969	15.1	1985	13.7
1970	16.7	1986	16.3
1971	18.3	1987	15.1
1972	19.1	1988	12.2
1973	12.2	1989	15.6
1974	7.3	1990	15.2
1975	11.7	1991	21.6

Source: Average year-end multiples derived from the S&P Index of 500 Stocks, Standard & Poor's *Statistical Service—Security Price Index Record,* various issues; listed P/Es are all year-end (December) figures.

Given the above, we can now generate a forecast of what the stock's *future* P/E will be over the anticipated *investment horizon,* the period of time over which we expect to hold the stock. For example, using the existing P/E multiple as a base, an *increase* might be justified if you believe the *market multiple* will increase (as the market tone becomes more bullish) and the *relative P/E* is likely to increase also. Armed with an estimate for the dividend payout ratio, the number of shares outstanding, and the price/earnings multiple, we can now forecast earnings per share:

Equation 7.2
$$\text{Estimated EPS in year } t = \frac{\text{future after-tax earnings in year } t}{\text{number of shares of common stock outstanding in year } t}$$

From here we can estimate dividends per share, as follows:

Equation 7.3
$$\frac{\text{Estimated dividends}}{\text{per share in year } t} = \frac{\text{estimated EPS}}{\text{in year } t} \times \frac{\text{estimated}}{\text{payout ratio}}$$

The last item is the future price of the stock, which can be determined as:

Equation 7.4
$$\frac{\text{Estimated share price}}{\text{at the end of year } t} = \frac{\text{estimated EPS}}{\text{in year } t} \times \frac{\text{estimated}}{\text{P/E ratio}}$$

For example, if the company had 2 million shares of common stock outstanding, and that number was expected to hold in the future, then given the estimated earnings of $6.5 million which we computed earlier, the firm should generate earnings per share (EPS) next year of:

$$\frac{\text{Estimated EPS}}{\text{next year}} = \frac{\$6.5 \text{ million}}{2 \text{ million}} = \underline{\underline{\$3.25}}$$

Using this EPS of $3.25, along with an estimated payout ratio of 40 percent, we see that dividends per share next year should equal:

$$\frac{\text{Estimated dividends}}{\text{per share next year}} = \$3.25 \times .40 = \underline{\underline{\$1.30}}$$

Of course, if the firm adheres to a *fixed dividend policy,* this estimate may have to be adjusted to reflect the level of dividends being paid. For example, if the company has been paying annual dividends at the rate of $1.25 per share, *and is expected to continue doing so for the near future,* then estimated dividends should be adjusted accordingly—that is, use $1.25/share. Finally, if it has been estimated that the stock should sell at 17.5 times earnings, then a share of stock in this company should be trading at a price of about 56⅞ by the *end* of next year:

$$\frac{\text{Estimated share price}}{\text{at the end of next year}} = \$3.25 \times 17.5 = \underline{\underline{\$56.88}}$$

Actually, we are interested in the price of the stock at the end of our anticipated investment horizon. Thus, if we had a one-year horizon, the 56⅞ figure would be appropriate. However, if we had a three-year holding period, we would have to extend the EPS figure for two more years and repeat our calculations with the new data. As we shall see, *estimated share price is important because it has embedded in it the capital gains portion of the stock's total return.*

Developing an Estimate of Future Behavior

Before illustrating the forecast procedure with a concrete example, let's quickly review the steps involved:

1. Estimate future sales.
2. Estimate a future net profit margin.
3. Derive future after-tax earnings (per Equation 7.1).
4. Estimate a future payout ratio (or fixed dividend rate).
5. Estimate the number of common shares outstanding in the future.
6. Estimate a future price/earnings (P/E) ratio.
7. Derive a future EPS figure (per Equation 7.2).
8. Derive future dividends per share (per Equation 7.3).
9. Derive a future share price (per Equation 7.4).
10. Repeat the process for each year in the forecast period.

Much of the required forecast data can be obtained from published sources (like *Value Line*) or analytical reports prepared by major brokerage firms. However, investors *cannot* rely solely on published reports: We still have to interject our own judgments and opinions about the future course of a company and its stock. We either agree or disagree with the published reports. If we agree, then we are inferring that our expectations are compatible with those embodied in the published reports; if we disagree, then we must adjust the forecasts to come up with our own figures.

Using MarCor Industries, we can now illustrate this forecasting process. Recall from Chapter 6 that an assessment of the economy and the apparel industry was positive, and that the company's operating results and financial condition looked strong, both historically and relative to industry standards. Because everything looks favorable for MarCor, we decide to take a look at the future of the company and its stock. Assume we have chosen a three-year investment horizon, based on our belief (formulated from earlier studies of economic and industry factors) that the economy and the market for apparel stocks should start running out of steam sometime near the end of 1995 or early 1996.

Selected historical financial data are provided in Table 7.2. They cover a six-year period (ending with the latest 1992 fiscal year) and will provide the basis for much of our forecast. An assessment of Table 7.2 reveals that except for 1987 (which was an "off" year for MarCor), the company has performed at a fairly steady pace and has been able to maintain a respectable rate of growth. Our economic analysis suggests that things are beginning to pick up. And based on earlier studies, we feel the industry and company are well situated to take advantage of the upswing. Therefore, we conclude that the rate of growth in sales should pick up in 1993 to about 9.5 percent; then, once a modest amount of pent-up demand is worked off, the rate

TABLE 7.2 Selected Historical Financial Data, MarCor Industries

	1987	1988	1989	1990	1991	1992
Total assets (millions)	$220.9	$240.7	$274.3	$318.2	$340.5	$338.6
Debt-equity ratio	53%	51%	52%	56%	58%	49%
Total asset turnover	1.72×	1.81×	1.75×	1.65×	1.67×	1.79×
Net sales (millions)	$397.9	$435.6	$480.0	$525.0	$568.0	$606.6
Annual rate of growth in sales*	−5.7%	9.5%	10.2%	9.4%	8.2%	6.8%
Interest and other income (millions)	$ 6.3	$ 6.0	$ 6.8	$ 7.7	$ 7.1	$ 8.3
Net profit margin	1.1%	2.0%	3.6%	3.0%	2.7%	2.9%
Payout ratio	97.0%	45.0%	47.0%	46.0%	47.0%	48.0%
Price/earnings ratio	8.3×	12.8×	9.5×	10.9×	11.2×	10.2×
Number of common shares outstanding (millions)	3.2	3.2	3.7	3.8	3.8	3.8

*Annual rate of growth in sales = change in sales from one year to the next divided by the level of sales in the base (or earliest) year; for 1988, the annual rate of growth in sales equaled 9.5% = (1988 sales − 1987 sales)/1987 sales = ($435.6 − $397.9)/$397.9 = .095.

of growth in sales should drop to about 9 percent in 1994 and stay there through 1995.

Since various published industry and company reports suggest a comfortable improvement in earnings, we decide to use a profit margin of 3.0 percent in 1993, followed by an even better 3.2 percent in 1994. Finally, because of some capacity problems prominently mentioned in one of the reports, we show a drop in the margin in 1995 back to 3.0 percent. Assume also that our assessment indicates the company will be able to handle the growth in assets and meet financing needs without issuing any new common stock. Moreover, assume the dividend payout ratio will hold at around 50 percent of earnings, as it has for most of the recent past—with the notable exception of 1987. The last element is the forecasted P/E ratio. Based primarily on expectations of improved growth in revenues and earnings, we are projecting a multiple that will gradually rise from its present level of 10 times earnings to roughly 11 times projected earnings in 1995. While this is a fairly conservative increase in the P/E, when coupled with the hefty growth in EPS the net effect will still be a big jump in the projected price of MarCor stock.

The essential elements of the financial forecast for 1993, 1994, and 1995 are provided in Table 7.3. Also included is the sequence involved in arriving at forecasted dividends and price behavior. Note that the company dimensions of the forecast are handled first, and that after-tax earnings are derived according to the procedure described earlier in this chapter. Then per-share data are estimated following the procedures established earlier. The bottom line of the forecast is, of course, the dividend and capital gains returns the investor can expect from a share of MarCor stock, given that the assumptions about net sales, profit margins, earnings per share, and so forth, hold up. We see in Table 7.3 that dividends should go up by about $1.21 per share over the next three years and that the price of a share of stock should undergo a better than 40 percent appreciation in value, rising from its latest price of $48.50 to $69.50 in 1995. We now have the figures on what the future cash flows of the investment are likely to be and are in a position to establish an intrinsic value for MarCor Industries stock.

The Valuation Process

valuation
process by which an investor determines the worth of a security using risk and return concepts.

Valuation is a process by which an investor determines the worth of a security using the risk and return concepts introduced in Chapter 4. It is a process that can be applied to any asset that produces a stream of cash flow, be it a share of stock, a bond, a piece of real estate, or an oil well. In order to establish the value of an asset, certain key inputs have to be determined, including the amount of future cash flows, the timing of these cash flows, and the rate of return required on the investment. In terms of common stock, the essence of valuation is to determine what the stock *ought to be worth,* given estimated returns to stockholders (future dividends and price behavior) and the amount of potential risk exposure. Toward this end, we employ various types of stock valuation models, the end product of which represents the elusive intrinsic value we have been seeking. That is, the stock valuation models determine either an expected rate of return or the intrinsic worth of a share of stock, which in effect represents the stock's "justified price." In this way, we

TABLE 7.3 Summary Forecast Statistics, MarCor Industries

	Latest Actual Figures (Fiscal 1992)	Average for the Past 5 Years (1988–1992)	Forecasted Figures		
			1993	1994	1995
Annual rate of growth in sales	6.8%	8.8%	9.5%	9.0%	9.0%
Net sales (millions)	$606.6	N/A*	$664.2**	$724.0**	$789.2**
+ Interest and other income (millions)	$ 8.3	$ 7.2	$ 7.2	$ 7.2	$ 7.2
= Total revenue (millions)	$614.9	N/A	$671.4	$731.2	$796.4
× Net profit margin	2.9%	2.8%	3.0%	3.2%	3.0%
= Net after-tax earnings (millions)	$ 18.0	N/A	$ 20.1	$ 23.4	$ 24.0
÷ Common shares outstanding (millions)	3.8	3.7	3.8	3.8	3.8
= Earnings per share	$ 4.74	N/A	$ 5.29	$ 6.16	$ 6.32
× Payout ratio	48.0%	39.0%	50.0%	50.0%	55.0%
= Dividends per share	$ 2.27	$ 1.75	$ 2.65	$ 3.08	$ 3.48
Earnings per share	$ 4.74	N/A	$ 5.29	$ 6.16	$ 6.32
× P/E ratio	10.20	10.92	10.50	10.75	11.00
= Share price at year end	$48.50	N/A	$ 55.50	$ 66.25	$ 69.50

*N/A = Not applicable.

**Forecasted sales figures: Sales from *preceding* year × growth rate in sales = growth in sales; then: growth in sales + sales from *preceding* year = forecast sales for the year. For example, for 1994: $664.2 × .09 = $59.5 + $664.2 = $724.0 million.

can obtain a standard of performance, based on *future* stock behavior, that can be used to judge the investment merits of a particular security.

If the computed rate of return equals or exceeds the yield the investor feels is warranted, or if the justified price (intrinsic worth) is equal to or greater than the current market price, the stock under consideration should be considered a worthwhile investment candidate. Note especially that a security is considered acceptable even if its yield simply *equals* the required rate of return or if its intrinsic value simply *equals* the current market price of the stock. There is nothing irrational about such behavior, since in either case, the security is meeting the minimum standards you've established (i.e., the security is giving you the required rate of return you wanted). But remember that although valuation plays an important part in the investment process, there is *absolutely no assurance* that the actual outcome will be even remotely similar to the forecasted behavior. The stock is still subject to economic, industry, company, and market risks that could well negate all the assumptions about the future. Security analysis and stock valuation models are used not to guarantee success, but to help investors better understand the return and risk dimensions of a proposed transaction.

Required Rate of Return

required rate of
return
the return necessary
to compensate an
investor for the risk
involved in an invest-
ment.

One of the key elements in the stock valuation process is the **required rate of return.** Generally speaking, the amount of return required by an investor should be related to the level of risk that must be assumed in order to generate that return. In essence, the required return provides the mechanism whereby the investor seeks compensation for the amount of risk involved in an investment. We need such a standard in order to determine whether the expected return on a stock (or any other security, for that matter) is satisfactory. Since we don't know for sure what the *future* cash flow of an investment will be, we should expect to earn a rate of return that reflects this uncertainty. Thus, the greater the perceived risk, the more return we should expect to earn. As we saw in Chapter 4, this is basically the notion behind the *capital asset pricing model* (CAPM).

Recall that using the CAPM, we can define a stock's required return as:

Equation 7.5

$$\text{Required rate of return} = \frac{\text{risk-free}}{\text{rate}} + \left[\frac{\text{stock's}}{\text{beta}} \times \left(\frac{\text{market}}{\text{return}} - \frac{\text{risk-free}}{\text{rate}} \right) \right]$$

The required input is readily available, as you can obtain a stock's beta from *Value Line* or S&P's *Stock Reports;* the risk-free rate is basically the average return on Treasury bills for the past year or so; and a good proxy for the market return is the average stock returns over the past 10 to 15 years (like the data reported in Table 5.1). In CAPM, it's felt that the risk of a stock is captured by its beta. For that reason, the required return on a stock will increase (or decrease) with increases (or decreases) in its beta. As an illustration of CAPM at work, consider a stock like MarCor that has a beta of 1.10; given the risk-free rate is, say, 5 percent and the market return is 13 percent, this stock would have a required return of:

$$\text{Required return} = 5\% + [1.10 \times (13\% - 5\%)] = \underline{\underline{13.8\%}}$$

This return (let's call it 14%) can now be used in a stock valuation model to assess the investment merits of a share of stock.

As an alternative, or in conjunction with CAPM, we could take a more subjective approach to finding required return. For example, if our assessment of the historical performance of the company had uncovered wide swings in sales and earnings, we could conclude that the stock is subject to a good deal of business risk. Also important is market risk, as measured by a stock's beta. A valuable reference point in arriving at a measure of risk is the rate of return available on less risky, but competitive, investment vehicles. For example, we can use the rate of return on long-term Treasury bonds or high-grade corporate issues as a starting point in defining our desired rate of return. That is, starting with yields on long-term, low-risk bonds, we can adjust such returns for the levels of business and market risk to which we believe the common stock is exposed.

To see how these elements make up the desired rate of return, consider once again the case of MarCor Industries. Assume it is now early 1993 and rates on Treasury bonds are hovering around 8 percent. Given that our analysis thus far has indicated that the apparel industry and MarCor Industries in particular are subject to a "fair" amount of business risk, we would want to adjust that figure upward—

■■■ INVESTOR INSIGHTS ■■■

Value Investing: No Guts, No Glory

During the fall of 1990, Warren E. Buffett, the legendary investor from Omaha, Nebraska, bought a 9.7 percent stake in Wells Fargo bank at $58 a share. At the time, bank stocks were in a free-fall. East Coast money managers believed that California real estate—the main collateral for the big California bank's loans—was going to plummet as it had in New York and Boston. By spring (1991), Wells Fargo hit $95. True, there was some luck involved. A war came and went, boosting the stock market with the euphoria that followed victory. But luck alone doesn't explain the huge rise.

Buffett is a "value" investor. Although all analysts on Wall Street claim to pick "undervalued" stocks, most aren't value analysts in the classic sense. Almost all of the Street's efforts go toward predicting earnings. If a company performs as anticipated, its stock rises, and money managers are heroes, at least for another quarter. If the company disappoints, they get egg on their faces. In contrast, value investors ignore projections and focus on the here and now. They compare the current stock price to a company's intrinsic value. Although the methods used by professionals like Buffet can get complex, investors can find many of the key indicators they use right in a company's annual report: the balance sheet, the footnotes, and financial ratios. Other information can often be found in the pages of the financial press.

Value investors put a lot of stock in such variables as price-to-book value, relative P/E multiples, return on assets and equity, free cash flow (generally defined as earnings plus depreciation minus capital expenditures and dividends), and stock betas. In essence, they search for value in a stock's fundamentals! But value investors do more than just comb through financial reports and generate a bunch of financial ratios. Rather, to them, *it's a way of investing*—an approach or philosophy that's adhered to almost religiously. They touch only stocks that, in their opinion, are severely "undervalued", i.e., stocks that are trading at prices a lot less than what their fundamentals say they should be selling for. In many respects, these investors are betting that they're right and the market is wrong.

probably by around 2 or 3 points. In addition, with its beta of 1.10, we can conclude that the stock carries some market risk. We should increase our base rate of return even more—say, by another 3 points. Given our base (Treasury bond) rate, along with our assessment of the stock's business and market risks, we conclude that an appropriate required rate of return should be around 14 percent for an investment in MarCor Industries common stock. That is, starting from a base of 8· percent, we tack on 3 percent for the company's added business risk and another 3 percent for the stock's market risk. Note that this figure of 14% is almost the same as what we would obtain from CAPM, using a beta of 1.1, a risk-free rate of 5%, and a market return of 13% (as in Equation 7.5). The fact that the two numbers are so close shouldn't be all that surprising. For if they're carefully (and honestly) done, you'd expect the two procedures—CAPM and the subjective approach—to yield similar results. Whichever procedure is used, the required rate of return stipulates the mini-

Accordingly, they *must* have the fortitude to be able to "sit it out" and wait for the market to reach a correct, true valuation. Generally speaking, value investors look for stocks that are trading well below historic highs, trading at or below book value, or that have "hidden" assets not reflected in the current price. If a stock passes one or more of these screens, value investors then look for reasons why the cloud depressing the stock should lift. Such factors might include prudent management, the sale of assets, the purchase of the company, or Wall Street's reevaluation of the company in a more reasonable light.

Last fall (1990), Wells Fargo was cheap: The stock was selling at a 50 percent discount to its 52-week high; it was selling right at book value, while the S&P 500 was selling at 2.5 times book; and it was selling at less than five times trailing earnings (that is, earnings already reported, as opposed to projected earnings), while the market was selling at a trailing price/earnings ratio of 15. And perhaps most impressive, the company's return on equity was 25 percent—double the average (which didn't come as a complete surprise, since Wells Fargo is known to attract top-quality management). Buffet believed that Wells Fargo was a well-managed, efficient bank—and that Wall Street had simply overreacted to the bank stock crisis. He bought the stock and waited, a move that can take a lot of guts when the crowd is running away.

Wells Fargo turned around fast. Usually, though, it takes longer—sometimes years— for the market to realize its mistake, or for an event to trigger that realization. Most money managers can't afford to wait: Their clients expect instant results. That's why most chase earnings instead of waiting for the market to recognize the value of a company's assets. "You have to be careful putting all of your money into these asset plays," says Mark Holloway of Bane Barham & Holloway Assets Management, an investment advisor in Portland, Oregon. "You could be staring at the wall for a long time."

Source: Adopted from Stuart Weiss, "Value Investing Revisited," *Investment Vision,* August/ September 1991, pp. 67–68.

mum return we would expect to receive from an investment. To accept anything less means we'll fail to be fully compensated for the amount of risk we must assume.

STOCK VALUATION MODELS

Certain stock valuation models emphasize appropriate price/earnings multiples as a key element in the valuation process. Others search for value in a company's financials—by keying in on such factors as book value, debt load, return on equity, cash flow, and so forth. These are the so-called *value investors,* who rely more on historical performance than on earnings projections to identify undervalued stocks; see the accompanying *Investor Insights* box for more discussion of value investing. There are still other models that use such variables as dividend yield, price/sales ratios, abnormally low P/E multiples, company size, and earnings momentum as key elements in the decision-making process. Our discussion here will center on several stock valuation models that are not only widely used by investment professionals, but are theoretically sound as well. In one form or another, these models use the required rate of return, along with expected cash flows from dividends and/or the future price of the stock, to derive the intrinsic value of an investment. Let's begin with a procedure known as the dividend valuation model.

The Dividend Valuation Model

In the valuation process, the intrinsic value of any investment equals the present value of the expected cash benefits. For common stock, this amounts to the cash dividends received each year plus the future sale price of the stock. Another way to view the cash flow benefits from common stock is to assume that the dividends will be received over an infinite time horizon—an assumption that is appropriate so long as the firm is considered a "going concern." Seen from this perspective, *the value of a share of stock is equal to the present value of all the future dividends it is expected to provide over an infinite time horizon.*

Although by selling stock at a price above that originally paid, a stockholder can earn capital gains in addition to dividends, from a strictly theoretical point of view, what is really sold is the right to all remaining future dividends. Thus, just as the *current* value of a share of stock is a function of future dividends, the *future* price of the stock is also a function of future dividends. In this framework, the future price of the stock will rise or fall as the outlook for dividends (and the required rate of return) changes.

dividend valuation model (DVM)
a model that values a share of stock on the basis of the future dividend stream it is expected to produce.

This approach, which holds that the value of a share of stock is a function of its future dividends, has come to be known as the **dividend valuation model (DVM).** There are three versions of the dividend valuation model, each based on different assumptions about the future rate of growth in dividends: (1) *the zero growth model,* which assumes that dividends will not grow over time; (2) *the constant growth model,* which is the basic version of the dividend valuation model and assumes that dividends will grow by a fixed/constant rate over time; and (3) *the variable growth model,* in which the rate of growth in dividends varies over time (and which is probably the most realistic version of the DVM).

Zero Growth

Perhaps the simplest way to picture the dividend valuation model is to assume that you're dealing with a stock that has a fixed stream of dividends. In other words, dividends stay the same year-in, year-out, and they're expected to stay that way in the future. Under such conditions, the value of a zero-growth stock is simply *the capitalized value of its annual dividends*. To find the capitalized value, just divide annual dividends by the required rate of return, which, in effect, acts as the capitalization rate; that is:

Equation 7.6

$$\text{Value of a share of stock} = \frac{\text{annual dividends}}{\text{required rate of return}}$$

For example, if a stock paid a (constant) dividend of $3 a share and you wanted to earn 10 percent on your investment, you would value the stock at $30 a share (i.e., $3/.10 = $30). As you can see, the only cash flow variable that's used in this valuation model is the fixed annual dividend. Since the annual dividend on this stock never changes, does that mean the price of the stock will never change? Absolutely not! For as the capitalization rate—i.e., the required rate of return— changes, so will the price of the stock. If the capitalization rate goes up (to, say, 15 percent), the price of the stock will fall to $20 ($3/.15). Although this may be a very simplified view of the valuation model, it's actually not as far-fetched as it may appear: As we'll see in Chapter 10, this is basically the procedure used to price *preferred stocks* in the marketplace.

Constant Growth

Rather than use no growth in dividends, the standard and more widely recognized version of the dividend valuation model assumes that dividends will grow over time at a specified rate. Under this variation of the model, the value of a share of stock is still considered to be a function of its future dividends, except that in this case, such dividends are expected to grow forever (to infinity) at a *constant* rate of growth, *g*. Accordingly, the value of a share of stock can be found as follows:

Equation 7.7

$$\frac{\text{Value of a share}}{\text{of stock}} = \frac{\text{next year's dividends}}{\text{required rate} - \text{constant rate of}}{\text{of return} \quad \text{growth in divs.}}$$

Equation 7.7a

$$= \frac{D_1}{k - g}$$

where:

D_1 = annual dividends expected to be paid *next* year (the first year in the forecast period).

k = the discount rate, or capitalization rate (which defines the required rate of return on the investment).

g = the annual rate of growth in dividends, which is expected to hold constant to infinity.

This model succinctly captures the essence of stock valuation: *Increase* the cash flow (through *D* or *g*) and/or *decrease* the required rate of return (*k*), and the value of the stock will *increase*. This is precisely what happened in the big bull market of 1982–87, as profits rose and the required rate of return dropped with lower inflation. As far as the cash flow is concerned, all that's required is some basic information about the stock's *current* level of dividends, and the expected rate of growth in dividends, *g*. Finding the dividend growth rate in practice is generally done by looking at the historical behavior of dividends and, if they're growing at a relatively constant rate, by assuming they'll continue to grow at (or near) that average rate into the future. You can find historical dividend data in a company's annual report, or it can be obtained from publications like *Value Line*. Given this stream of dividends, you can use basic present value arithmetic to find the average rate of growth. Here's how: Take the level of dividends, say, 10 years ago and divide that amount by the level of dividends paid today; you'll end up with a present value interest factor (PVIF). Look in Table A.3 for the discount rate that's linked to the interest factor you just computed. In this case, *the discount rate is the average rate of growth in dividends* (see Chapter 4 for a detailed discussion of how to use present value to find growth rates).

Now, once the dividend growth rate, g, has been determined, we can find next year's dividend, D_1, as: $D_0 (1 + g)$, where D_0 equals the actual (current) level of dividends. Let's say that in the latest year Sweatmore Industries paid $2.50 a share in dividends; if we expect these dividends to grow at the rate of 6 percent a year, we can find next year's dividends as follows: $D_1 = D_0(1 + g) = \$2.50(1 + .06) = \$2.50(1.06) = \$2.65$. The only other information we need is the capitalization rate, or required rate of return, k. (Note in the constant growth model that k must be greater than g in order for the model to be mathematically operative.)

To see this dividend valuation model at work, let's consider a stock that currently pays an annual dividend of $1.75 a share. Let's say that by using the present value approach described above, you find that dividends are growing at the rate of 8 percent a year and that they should continue to do so into the future. In addition, you feel that, because of the risks involved, the investment should carry a required rate of return of 12 percent. Given this information, we can use Equation 7.7 to price the stock. That is, given $D_0 = \$1.75$, $g = .08$, and $k = .12$, it follows that:

$$\text{Value of a share of stock} = \frac{D_0 (1 + g)}{k - g} = \frac{\$1.75 (1.08)}{.12 - .08} = \frac{\$1.89}{.04} = \underline{\underline{\$47.25}}$$

If the investor wants to earn 12 percent return on this investment, then according to the constant growth dividend valuation model, she should pay no more than $47.25 a share for the stock.

Note that with this version of the DVM, *the price of the stock will increase over time* so long as k and g don't change. This occurs because the cash flow from the investment will increase with time as dividends grow. To see how this can happen, let's carry our example further: Recall that $D_0 = \$1.75$, $g = 8\%$, $k = 12\%$, and based on this information we found the current value of the stock to be $47.25. Now look what happens to the price of this stock if k and g don't change:

Year	Dividend	Stock Price*
(Current Year) 0	$1.75	$47.25
1	1.89	51.00
2	2.04	55.00
3	2.20	59.50
4	2.38	64.25
5	2.57	69.50

*As determined by the dividend valuation model, given $g = .08$, $k = .12$, and $D_0 =$ dividend level for any given year.

As can be seen in the above illustration, the price of the stock *in the future* can also be found by using the standard dividend valuation model. To do this, we simply redefine the appropriate level of dividends. For example, to find the price of the stock in year 3, we use the expected dividend in the third year, $2.20, and increase it by the factor $(1 + g)$; thus, the stock price in year $3 = D_3(1 + g)/k - g = \$2.20(1 + .08)/.12 - .08 = \$2.38/.04 = \$59.50$. Of course, if future expectations about k and/or g do change, the *future price* of the stock will change accordingly. Should that occur, an investor could then use this new information to decide whether to continue to hold the stock.

Variable Growth

Although the constant growth dividend valuation model as presented above has many advantages, it also has some shortcomings, one of the most obvious of which is the fact that it does not allow for any changes in expected growth rates. To overcome this, there's a form of the DVM that allows for *variable rates of growth* over time. Essentially, the *variable growth dividend valuation model* uses two stages to derive a value based on future dividends and the future price of the stock (which price is a function of all future dividends to infinity). The variable growth version of the model finds the value of a share of stock as follows:

Equation 7.8

$$\begin{matrix} \text{Value of a} \\ \text{share of stock} \end{matrix} = \begin{matrix} \text{present value of} \\ \text{future dividends during} \\ \text{the initial variable} \\ \text{growth period} \end{matrix} + \begin{matrix} \text{present value of the price} \\ \text{of the stock at the end of} \\ \text{the variable growth period} \end{matrix}$$

Equation 7.8a

$$= (D_1 \times \text{PVIF}_1) + (D_2 \times \text{PVIF}_2) + \ldots$$
$$+ (D_v \times \text{PVIF}_v) + \left(\text{PVIF}_v \times \frac{D_v (1 + g)}{k - g} \right)$$

where:

D_1, D_2, etc. = future annual dividends

    PVIF = present value interest factor, as specified by the required rate of return for a given year t (use Table A.3 in the appendix).

       V = number of years in the initial variable growth period.

Note that the last element in this equation is the standard constant growth dividend valuation model, which is used to find the price of the stock at the end of the initial growth period.

This form of the DVM is appropriate for stocks/companies that are expected to experience variable rates of growth for the first few years—perhaps for the first three to five years, or more—and then settle down to a constant (average) growth rate thereafter. This, in fact, is the growth pattern of a lot of companies, and thus, the model does have real application in practice. Finding the value of a stock using Equation 7.8 is actually a lot easier than it looks. All you need do is follow these steps:

1. Estimate annual dividends during the initial variable growth period and then specify the constant rate, *g*, at which dividends will grow after the initial period.
2. Find the present value of the dividends expected during the initial variable growth period.
3. Using the constant growth DVM, find the price of the stock at the *end* of the initial growth period.
4. Find the present value of the price of the stock (as determined in step 3, above); note that the price of the stock is discounted at the *same PVIF* as the last dividend payment in the initial growth period, since the stock is being priced (per step 3) at the *end* of this initial period.
5. Add the two present value components (from steps 2 and 4, above) to find the value of a stock.

To see how this works, let's apply the variable growth model to MarCor Industries. Let's assume that dividends will grow at a variable rate for the first three years (1993, 1994, and 1995), after which time, the annual rate of growth in dividends is expected to settle down to 8 percent and stay there for the foreseeable future. We can use the dividend projections we prepared (for 1993–95) in Table 7.3, along with our required rate of return (formulated earlier) of 14 percent. Table 7.4 shows the variable growth DVM in action.

As we can see in the table, the value of MarCor stock, according to the variable growth DVM, is just under $49.25 a share. In essence, that's the maximum price an investor should be willing to pay for the stock if he or she wants to earn a 14 percent rate of return. Mechanically, this whole valuation process is really quite simple, as it relies on just three key pieces of input: future dividends, future growth in dividends, and a required rate of return. But there are some hazards: Certainly one of the most important (and most difficult) aspects of this model is *specifying the proper growth rate,* g, *over an extended period of time*. This not only has a bearing on the future price of the stock, but more important, on the intrinsic value that's being produced from the model. That is, the DVM is *very sensitive* to the growth rate being used; other things being equal, the higher the rate of growth in dividends, *g*, the higher the intrinsic value of the stock.

An Alternative to the DVM

The variable growth approach to stock valuation is fairly compatible with the way most people invest. That is, unlike the underlying assumptions in the standard dividend valuation model (which employs an infinite investment horizon), most investors have a *finite* holding period that seldom exceeds five to seven years. Under such circumstances, *the relevant cash flows are future dividends and the future selling price of the stock*. There is an alternative to the DVM that is also widely used in practice. It is similar to the variable growth DVM, to the extent that it's also present-value–based and its value is also derived from future dividends and the expected selling price of the stock. The big difference between the two procedures revolves around how the future price of the stock is determined. For rather

████████

TABLE 7.4 Using the Variable Growth DVM to Value MarCor Stock

Step

1. Projected annual dividends: 1993 $2.65
   (see Table 7.3)   1994 $3.08
                                      1995 $3.48

   Estimated annual rate of growth in dividends, g, for 1996 and beyond: 8%

2. Present value of dividends—using a required rate of return, k, of 14%—during the initial variable growth period:

Year	Dividends	×	PVIF $(k = 14\%)$	=	Present Value
1993	$2.65		.877		$2.32
1994	3.08		.769		2.37
1995	3.48		.675		2.35
				Total	$7.04 (to step 5)

3. Price of the stock at the end of the initial growth period:

$$P_{1995} = \frac{D_{1996}}{k - g} = \frac{D_{1995}\,(1 + g)}{k - g} = \frac{\$3.48\,(1.08)}{.14 - .08} = \frac{\$3.75}{.06} = \underline{\underline{\$62.50}}$$

4. Discount the price of the stock (as computed above) back to its present value, at $k = 14\%$:

$$PV(P_{1995}) = \$62.50 \times PVIF_{14\%,3\ yrs.} = \$62.50 \times .675 = \underline{\$42.19}\ (\text{to step 5})$$

5. Add the present value of the initial dividend stream (step 2) to the present value of the price of the stock at the end of the initial growth period (step 4):

$$\text{Value of MarCor Stock} = \$7.04 + \$42.19 = \underline{\$49.23}$$

than use future dividends to price the stock, this approach employs projected earnings per share and estimated P/E multiples—the same two variables that drive the price of the stock in the market.

Deriving a Justified Price

As we saw in the variable growth DVM, the value of a share of stock is a function of the amount and timing of future cash flows and the level of risk that must be taken on to generate that return. A stock valuation model has been developed that conveniently captures the essential elements of expected risk and return, and does so in a present value context. The model is as follows:

Equation 7.9

$$\begin{aligned}
\frac{\text{Present value}}{\text{of a share of stock}} &= \frac{\text{present value of}}{\text{future dividends}} + \frac{\text{present value of the price of}}{\text{the stock at date of sale}} \\
&= (D_1 \times PVIF_1) + (D_2 \times PVIF_2) + \cdots \\
&\quad + (D_N \times PVIF_N) + (SP_N \times PVIF_N)
\end{aligned}$$

where:

D_t = future annual dividend in year t.

PVIF_t = present-value interest factor, specified at the required rate of return (from Table A.3 in the appendix)

SP_N = estimated share price of the stock at date of sale, year N.

N = number of years in the investment horizon.

This is the so-called *present-value model*. Its major advantages are that it is not only a bit more flexible than the DVM, but it's also a lot easier to understand and apply. Using this valuation approach, the investor's attention is directed toward projecting future dividends and share price behavior over a defined, finite investment horizon, much as we did for MarCor in Table 7.3. Especially important here is finding a viable P/E multiple that can be used to project the future price of the stock. This is a critical part of this stock valuation process because of the major role that capital gains (and, therefore, the estimated share price of the stock at its projected date of sale) plays in defining the level of security returns. Using market and/or industry P/Es as benchmarks, the investor will try to establish a multiple that he or she feels the stock will trade at in the future. Couple this number with projected earnings per share and you have an estimate of what the stock should sell for in the future. Like the growth rate, g, in the DVM, the P/E multiple is the single most important (and most difficult) variable to project in the present-value model. Using this input, the present-value–based stock valuation model generates a *justified price* based on estimated returns to stockholders (future dividends and share-price behavior). Basically, this intrinsic value represents the price we should be willing to pay for the stock given its expected dividend and price behavior, and assuming we want to realize a return that is equal to or greater than our required rate of return, as found by using CAPM or some other more subjective approach.

To see how this procedure works, consider once again the case of MarCor Industries. Let's return to our original three-year investment horizon. Given the forecasted annual dividends and share price from Table 7.3, along with a 14 percent required rate of return, we can see from the computations below that the present value of MarCor is:

$$\begin{aligned}
\text{Present value of a share of MarCor stock} &= (\$2.65 \times .877) + (\$3.08 \times .769) + (\$3.48 \times .675) \\
&\quad + (\$69.50 \times .675) \\
&= \$2.32 + \$2.37 + \$2.35 + \$46.92 \\
&= \underline{\$53.96}
\end{aligned}$$

You'll note that, as compared to the variable growth DVM, this model produces a slightly higher intrinsic value ($53.96 vs. $49.23, as computed in Table 7.4). This difference, of course, is due to the higher share price we're projecting here ($69.50), compared to the one we ended up with in the DVM ($62.50). All the other variables are basically the same. In any event, the present-value figure computed here means that with the projected dividend and share price behavior, we would realize our desired rate of return *only* if we were able to buy the stock at around $54 a share. Because MarCor Industries is currently trading at $48.50, we can conclude that the stock presently *is* an attractive investment vehicle. That is, since we can buy the stock at something less than its computed intrinsic value, we'll be able to earn our required rate of return—so long as dividends, EPS, and P/E projections hold up.

Determining Approximate Yield

Sometimes investors find it more convenient to deal in terms of expected yield rather than present worth or justified price. Fortunately, this is no problem, nor is it necessary to sacrifice the present-value dimension of the stock valuation model to achieve such an end. For the *approximate yield* measure enables investors to find a present-value–based rate of return from long-term transactions. This version of the stock valuation model uses forecasted dividend and price behavior, along with the *current market price* of the stock, to arrive at an approximate yield. This measure of return, first introduced in Chapter 4 (as Equation 4.10), is determined as follows:

Equation 7.10

$$\text{Approximate yield} = \frac{\text{average} \atop \text{annual dividend} + \dfrac{\substack{\text{future sale} \\ \text{price of the stock}} - \substack{\text{current purchase} \\ \text{price of the stock}}}{\text{number of years in investment horizon}}}{\dfrac{\text{sales price of the stock} + \text{purchase price of the stock}}{2}}$$

The approximate yield formula is an indication of the fully compounded rate of return available from a long-term investment. To see how it works, let's look once more at MarCor Industries:

$$\text{Approximate yield} = \frac{\$3.07 + \dfrac{\$69.50 - \$48.50}{3}}{\dfrac{\$69.50 + \$48.50}{2}}$$

$$= \frac{\$3.07 + \$7.00}{\$59.00} = \underline{\underline{17.1\%}}$$

We see that MarCor can be expected to yield an annual return of around 17 percent, assuming the stock can be bought at $48.50, is held for three years (during which time annual dividends will average about $3.07 per share), and then sold for $69.50 per share. Note that in this version of the stock valuation model, it is the *average* annual dividend that is used rather than the specific dividends. For MarCor Industries, dividends will average $3.07 per share over each of the next three years— i.e., ($2.65 + $3.08 + $3.48)/3 = $3.07. When compared to the 14 percent required rate of return, the 17.1 percent yield this investment offers is clearly more than adequate!

Holding Period Returns

While approximate yield—as computed in Equation 7.10—is appropriate for long-term investment horizons, a different measure, *holding period return,* should be used with short investment periods. Holding period return (HPR), first introduced in Chapter 4 (Equation 4.8), is useful whenever the investment horizon is one year or less. It is computed as follows:

Equation 7.11

$$HPR = \frac{\text{future dividend receipts} + \text{future sale price of the stock} - \text{current purchase price of the stock}}{\text{current purchase price of the stock}}$$

Holding period return provides a measure of the yield that will be realized *if* the actual performance of the stock lives up to its expectations. Using the 1993 forecasted figures from Table 7.3 and assuming that the stock can be purchased at its current market price of $48.50, the (one year) holding period return for MarCor Industries would be as follows:

$$HPR\ (1993) = \frac{\$2.65 + (\$55.50 - \$48.50)}{\$48.50} = \frac{\$2.65 + \$7.00}{\$48.50} = \underline{\underline{19.9\%}}$$

Note that although we do not use capital gains specifically in this valuation model, it is embedded in the formula and appears as the difference between the future selling price of the stock and its current purchase price; as it turns out, MarCor Industries should provide a capital gain of $7.00 per share in the first year. When coupled with projected 1993 dividends, the net result is an HPR of nearly 20 percent, which exceeds the required rate of return by a wide margin. Thus, even over a short investment horizon, the stock of MarCor Industries remains a viable investment candidate.

TECHNICAL ANALYSIS

technical analysis
the study of the various forces at work in the marketplace and their effect on stock prices.

How many times have you turned on the TV and in the course of the day's news heard a reporter say, ''The market was up 17½ points today'' or ''The market remained sluggish in a light day of trading''? Such comments reflect the importance of the stock market itself. And rightly so, for as we will see, the market *is important* because of the role it plays in determining the price behavior of common stocks. In fact, some experts believe the market is so important that studying it should be the major, if not the only, ingredient in the stock selection process. These experts argue that much of what is done in security analysis is useless because it is the market that matters and not individual companies. Others would argue that studying the stock market is only one element in the security analysis process and is useful in helping the investor time decisions. Analyzing the stock market is known as **technical analysis,** and it involves a study of the various forces at work in the marketplace itself. For many investors, it's another piece of information to use when deciding whether to buy, hold, or sell a stock; for others, its the *only* input they use in their investment decisions; and for still others, technical analysis, like fundamental analysis, is just a big waste of time. Here, we will assume that technical analysis does have some role to play in the investment decision process. Accordingly, in the pages that follow, we will examine the major principles and components of technical analysis, as well as some of the techniques used to assess market behavior.

Principles of Market Analysis

Analyzing market behavior dates back to the 1800s, when there was no such thing as industry or company analysis. Detailed financial information simply was not made available to stockholders, let alone the general public. There were no industry figures, balance sheets, or income statements to study, no sales forecasts to make, and no earnings-per-share data or price/earnings multiples. About the only thing investors could study was the market itself. Some analysts used detailed charts in an attempt to monitor what large market operators were doing. These charts were intended to show when major buyers were moving into or out of particular stocks and to provide information that could be used to make profitable buy-and-sell decisions. The charts centered on stock price movements, because it was believed that these movements produced certain "formations" that indicated when the time was right to buy or sell a particular stock. The same principle is still applied today: Technical analysts argue that internal market factors, such as trading volume and price movements, often reveal the market's future direction long before the cause is evident in financial statistics.

If the behavior of stock prices were completely independent of movements in the market, then market studies and technical analysis would be useless. But we have ample evidence that this is simply not the case; in fact, stock prices do tend to move with the market. Studies of stock betas have shown that, as a rule, anywhere from 20 to 50 percent of the price behavior of a stock can be traced to market forces. When the market is bullish, stock prices in general can be expected to behave accordingly. When market participants turn bearish, most issues will feel the brunt to one extent or another. Stock prices, in essence, react to various supply and demand forces that are at work in the market: after all, it's the *demand* for securities and the *supply* of funds in the market that determine a bull or a bear market. So long as a given supply and demand relationship holds, the market will remain strong (or weak); when the balance begins to shift, however, future prices can be expected to change as the market itself changes. More than anything, technical analysis is intended to monitor the pulse of the supply and demand forces in the market, and to detect any shifts in this important relationship.

Measuring the Market

If assessing the market is a worthwhile endeavor, it follows that some sort of tool or measure is needed to do it. Charts are popular with some investors because they provide a convenient visual summary of the behavior of the market and the price movements of individual stocks. An alternative approach involves the use of various types of market statistics, such as moving averages, oacillators, and stochastic analysis. We will now examine some of the tools of technical analysis, by first considering some basic approaches to technical analysis, including technical indicators and the use of technical analysis, and then addressing the concept of charting.

Approaches to Technical Analysis

Technical analysis addresses those factors in the marketplace that have an effect on the price movements of stocks in general. Investment services, major brokerage houses, and popular financial media (like *Barron's*) provide technical information at little or no cost. Of the many approaches to technical analysis, several are particularly noteworthy: (1) the Dow theory, (2) trading action, (3) bellwether stocks, and (4) the technical condition of the market. We'll look at each in turn.

Dow theory
a technical approach that's based on the idea that the market's performance can be described by the long-term price trend in the DJIA, as confirmed by the Dow transportation average.

The Dow Theory.   The **Dow theory** is based on the idea that the market's performance can be described by the long-term price trend in the overall market. Named after Charles H. Dow, one of the founders of Dow Jones, this approach is supposed to signal the end of both bull and bear markets. Note that the theory does not indicate when a reversal will occur; rather, it is strictly an after-the-fact verification of what has already happened. It concentrates on the long-term trend in market behavior (known as the *primary trend*) and largely ignores day-to-day fluctuations or secondary movements. The Dow Jones industrial *and* transportation averages are used to assess the position of the market. Once a primary trend in the Dow Jones industrial average has been established, the market tends to move in that direction until the trend is canceled out by both the industrial and transportation averages. Known as *confirmation,* this crucial part of the Dow theory occurs when secondary movements in the industrial average are confirmed by secondary movements in the transportation average. When confirmation occurs, the market has changed from bull to bear, or vice versa, and a new primary trend is established. The key elements of the Dow theory are captured in Figure 7.1. Observe that in this case, the bull market comes to an end at the point of confirmation—when *both* the industrial and transportation averages are dropping. The biggest drawbacks of the Dow theory are that it is an after-the-fact measure with *no* predictive power, and that the investor really does not know at any given point whether an existing primary trend has a long way to go or is just about to end.

Trading Action.   This approach to technical analysis concentrates on minor trading characteristics in the market. Daily trading activity over long periods of time (sometimes extending back a quarter century or more) is examined in detail to determine whether or not certain characteristics occur with a high degree of frequency. The results of such statistical analysis are a series of trading rules, some of which may seem a bit bizarre. Some examples: If the year starts out strong (that is, if January is a good month for the market), the chances are that the whole year will be good; if the party in power wins the presidential election, it is also going to be a good year for the market; and it is best to buy air conditioning stocks in October and sell the following March (this buy-and-sell strategy was found to be significantly more profitable over the long haul than buy-and-hold). A most unusual but *highly successful* market adage holds that if a team from the National Football Conference (or one that was originally in the NFL, like Indianapolis or Pittsburgh) wins the Super Bowl, the market's in for a good year. Don't laugh; for whatever the reason— which no one seems to know—it's been correct for 22 of the first 25 Super Bowls! Clearly, the trading action approach is based on the simple assumption that the market moves in cycles and that these cycles have a tendency to repeat themselves. As a result, the contention is that what has happened in the past will probably happen repeatedly in the future.

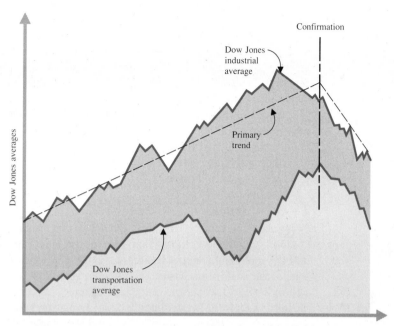

• FIGURE 7.1 The Dow Theory in Operation

Secondary movements (the sharp, short fluctuations in the Dow Jones industrial and transportation lines) are largely unimportant to the Dow theory. However, the primary trend in the DJIA, which is seen to remain on the upswing until a reversal is confirmed by the transportation average, is of key importance.

Bellwether Stocks.   There is a saying that "as GM goes, so goes the nation." Whether or not this is true today remains debatable, but to advocates of bellwether stocks, such an idea makes a lot of sense. That's because the stock of General Motors and a handful of others, like IBM, AT&T, and Procter & Gamble, are all considered **bellwether stocks**—stocks that are believed to consistently reflect the current state of the market. Actually, the list of stocks that qualify as bellwether issues tends to slowly change over time. Indeed, there's even a growing number of investors who feel IBM is no longer the bellwether issue it once was. Although the prices of bellwether stocks tend to move in a pattern that's close to the Dow or some other major market index, the bellwether procedure itself is much more than a simple reflection of the current state of affairs in the market: It is believed that bellwether stocks can also be used to determine shifts in market behavior. In particular, bellwether advocates hold that in a bull market, when a bellwether stock fails to hit a new yearly high for three or four months in a row, a market top is at hand; in a bear market, when the selected stock fails to hit a new low for three or four months, a market bottom is coming. Although there are many skeptics on Wall Street, the bellwether approach does seem to have some merit with respect to appraising the current state of the market.

bellwether stocks
stocks that are believed to consistently reflect the state of the market; watched by technical analysts for shifts in market behavior.

Technical Condition of the Market.   This approach is based on assessing several key elements of market behavior. For example, market prices are affected by such variables as the volume of trading, the amount of short selling, the buying and selling patterns of small investors (odd-lot transactions), and similar market forces. Normally, several of these indicators would be used together to assess the technical condition of the market. They may be used in an informal way, or more formally as a series of complex ratios and measures—like 200-day moving averages or buy-sell ratios. Assessing the technical condition of the market is one of the more popular approaches to technical analysis and is often used with some other approach, such as trading action and/or bellwether stocks. We'll now examine several of the more popular technical indicators.

Technical Indicators

Technical indicators are used to assess the current state of the market, as well as the possibility of changes in direction. The idea is to stay abreast of those aspects that reflect supply and demand conditions, underlying price pressures, and the general state of the market. In essence, the premise is that the forces of supply and demand will be reflected in various price and volume patterns. Although there are many technical indicators, we will confine our discussion to several of the more popular and closely followed measures: (1) market volume; (2) breadth of the market; (3) short interest; (4) odd-lot trading; (5) the confidence index; and (6) relative price levels.

Market Volume.   Market volume is an obvious reflection of the amount of investor interest. Volume is a function of the supply of and demand for stocks and indicates underlying market strengths and weaknesses. The market is considered to be *strong* when volume goes up in a rising market or drops off during market declines. In contrast, it is considered *weak* when volume rises during a decline or drops off during rallies. For instance, the market would be considered strong if the Dow Jones industrial average went up by, say, 48 points while market volume was very heavy. Investor eagerness to buy or sell is felt to be captured by market-volume figures. The financial press regularly publishes volume data, so investors can conveniently watch this important technical indicator. An example of this and other vital market information is given in Figure 7.2.

Breadth of the Market.   Each trading day, some stocks go up in price and others go down; in market terminology, some stocks *advance* and others *decline*. The breadth-of-the-market indicator deals with these advances and declines. The idea behind it is actually quite simple: So long as the number of stocks that advance in price on a given day exceeds the number that decline, the market is considered strong. Of course, the extent of that strength depends on the spread between the number of advances and declines. For example, if the spread narrows such that the number of declines starts to approach the number of advances, market strength is said to be deteriorating. Similarly, the market is considered weak when the number of declines repeatedly exceeds the number of advances. The principle behind this

STOCK MARKET DATA BANK 12/9/91

MAJOR INDEXES

HIGH	LOW (†365 DAY)		CLOSE	NET CHG	% CHG	†365 DAY CHG	% CHG	FROM 12/31	% CHG
DOW JONES AVERAGES									
3077.15	2470.30	30 Industrials	2871.65	− 14.75	− 0.51	+ 274.87	+10.59	+ 237.99	+ 9.04
1287.56	894.30	20 Transportation	1184.42	− 14.20	− 1.18	+ 274.75	+30.20	+ 274.19	+ 30.12
221.64	195.17	15 Utilities	220.77	− 0.37	− 0.17	+ 10.32	+ 4.90	+ 11.07	+ 5.28
1112.07	880.82	65 Composite	1048.58	− 6.83	− 0.65	+ 134.81	+14.75	+ 127.97	+ 13.90
372.98	288.96	Equity Mkt. Index	355.59	− 0.80	− 0.22	+ 50.95	+16.72	+ 50.00	+ 16.36
NEW YORK STOCK EXCHANGE									
219.37	170.97	Composite	209.21	− 0.53	− 0.25	+ 29.63	+16.50	+ 28.72	+ 15.91
273.32	210.80	Industrials	259.26	− 0.86	− 0.33	+ 37.44	+16.88	+ 35.66	+ 15.95
98.70	86.77	Utilities	96.89	unch		+ 5.34	+ 5.83	+ 5.59	+ 6.12
196.31	137.54	Transportation	180.90	− 3.26	− 1.77	+ 38.94	+27.43	+ 39.41	+ 27.85
165.48	116.11	Finance	155.84	+ 0.22	+ 0.14	+ 33.41	+27.29	+ 33.77	+ 27.66
STANDARD & POOR'S INDEXES									
397.41	311.49	500 Index	378.26	− 0.84	− 0.22	+ 49.37	+15.01	+ 48.04	+ 14.55
472.01	364.90	Industrials	445.36	− 1.39	− 0.31	+ 60.48	+15.71	+ 57.94	+ 14.96
329.05	226.22	Transportation	305.71	− 5.32	− 1.71	+ 72.71	+31.21	+ 71.04	+ 30.27
149.85	133.52	Utilities	146.74	+ 0.25	+ 0.17	+ 2.18	+ 1.51	+ 3.15	+ 2.19
32.54	21.97	Financials	30.16	+ 0.13	+ 0.43	+ 6.61	+28.07	+ 6.73	+ 28.72
139.07	95.16	400 MidCap	134.12	− 0.30	− 0.22	+ 35.60	+36.13	+ 34.12	+ 34.12
NASDAQ									
556.17	355.75	Composite	535.35	− 0.95	− 0.18	+ 163.88	+44.12	+ 161.51	+ 43.20
629.76	387.47	Industrials	606.91	− 1.77	− 0.29	+ 205.40	+51.16	+ 200.86	+ 49.47
585.08	434.23	Insurance	556.44	− 2.64	− 0.47	+ 106.21	+23.59	+ 104.60	+ 23.15
346.65	246.07	Banks	320.92	− 1.34	− 0.42	+ 63.57	+24.70	+ 66.01	+ 25.90
245.57	157.16	Nat. Mkt. Comp.	236.41	− 0.47	− 0.20	+ 72.51	+44.24	+ 71.24	+ 43.13
251.09	154.97	Nat. Mkt. Indus.	242.06	− 0.81	− 0.33	+ 81.87	+51.11	+ 79.72	+ 49.11
OTHERS									
392.37	296.72	Amex	370.59	− 2.04	− 0.55	+ 63.98	+20.87	+ 62.48	+ 20.28
246.89	186.78	Value-Line (geom.)	230.87	− 1.00	− 0.43	+ 34.44	+17.53	+ 34.88	+ 17.80
188.04	125.25	Russell 2000	176.69	− 0.86	− 0.48	+ 45.99	+35.19	+ 44.50	+ 33.66.
3862.46	2938.58	Wilshire 5000	3682.02	− 9.16	− 0.25	+ 597.31	+19.36	+ 580.66	+ 18.72

†-Based on comparable trading day in preceeding year.

MOST ACTIVE ISSUES

NYSE	VOLUME	CLOSE	CHANGE
IBM	3,895,100	85⅛	− 3⅞
RJR Nab Hldg	3,884,600	10¼	− ⅛
Gen Motors	2,538,800	27⅝	− 1⅜
British Tele.pf	2,402,400	22⅝	....
Glaxo Hldgs	2,024,700	29¾	+ ⅛
General Elec	1,735,800	64⅞	+ 1
Philip Morris	1,645,900	68⅝	+ ¾
Citicorp	1,632,900	10	− ¼
RJR Nabisco.pf	1,631,900	11	+ ⅛
Wal-Mart Str	1,568,000	51½	− ⅜
Limited Inc	1,497,800	27¾	+ 1
Amer Express	1,401,900	18⅝	− ¼
PepsiCo	1,381,400	x30½	+ ⅜
Toys R Us Inc	1,332,600	28	− 1⅛
Bristl-Myrs Sqb	1,197,300	78¾	− ⅛
NASDAQ NMS			
Sun Microsys	3,081,600	21¼	− 1⅞
M C I Comm	2,055,100	27	....
Novell Inc	1,991,000	53¼	− ¼
Intel Corp	1,752,700	42¼	+ ½
Tele-Comm A	1,585,200	14	+ ¼
Amgen	1,437,500	62¼	....
Quartrdeck Offc	1,255,300	18	− ¼
Microsoft Corp	1,202,500	102	− 2¼
Oracle Sys	1,178,400	12⅜	+ ⅜
Greater NY Sav	1,049,400	13/16	− ⅛
US Healthcare	1,022,500	39¼	− 1⅜
Softwr Tlwrk	938,800	5⅝	+ ⅜
CytRx Corp	914,500	4 9/16	+ 7/16
AMEX			
Enzo Biochem	1,125,200	5⅜	− 2½
Hanson Bwt.wi	630,200	¼	....
Contl Air Hldgs	454,000	½	− 1/16
Bergen Brunswg	367,300	16⅝	− ¼
Ivax Corp	342,000	28⅞	+ ⅜

DIARIES

NYSE	MON	FRI	WK AGO
Issues traded	2,176	2,178	2,167
Advances	699	874	927
Declines	941	775	781
Unchanged	536	529	459
New highs	69	72	44
New lows	70	72	67
zAdv vol (000)	62,030	93,474	125,680
zDecl vol (000)	86,834	73,220	41,430
zTotal vol (000)	174,700	198,170	188,050
Closing tick[1]	−215	+244	+483
Closing Arms[2] (trin)	1.03	.88	.39
zBlock trades	3,794	4,435	4,009
NASDAQ NMS			
Issues traded	4,181	4,188	4,183
Advances	891	993	941
Declines	1,132	932	1,087
Unchanged	2,158	2,263	2,155
New highs	72	68	46
New lows	61	51	66
Adv vol (000)	56,466	79,440	79,887
Decl vol (000)	60,019	55,470	41,648
Total vol (000)	155,387	171,831	145,913
Block trades	2,511	3,036	2,473
AMEX			
Issues traded	851	829	837
Advances	238	279	240
Declines	357	302	338
Unchanged	256	248	259
New highs	22	26	7
New lows	34	29	36
zAdv vol (000)	3,917	7,158	5,527
zDecl vol (000)	6,330	7,095	4,612
zTotal vol (000)	13,378	16,774	13,268
Comp vol (000)	16,416	19,797	15,782
zBlock trades	n.a.	225	203

← Arms Index

• FIGURE 7.2 Some Market Statistics

A variety of information is available about market volume, new highs and lows, number of advancing and declining stocks, and market averages. (*Source: The Wall Street Journal,* December 10, 1991.)

indicator is that the number of advances and declines reflects the underlying sentiment of investors; when the mood is optimistic, for example, look for advances to outnumber declines. Again, information on advances and declines is published daily in the financial press.

A market measure that attempts to capture both the *number* of advancing and declining stocks and the *volume* of shares rising or falling is the *Arms index,* named after the person who created the measure. The index is computed by relating the ratio of the number of advancing and declining issues to the ratio of the volume of shares going up and down. Sounds confusing, doesn't it? Nonetheless, this index is widely quoted in the financial media—it's reported in Figure 7.2—and is supposed to indicate the amount of buying or selling pressure in the market. An Arms index of less than 1.00 signals buying pressure.

Short Interest.   Investors will sometimes sell a stock short—that is, they will sell borrowed stock in anticipation of a market decline. The number of stocks sold short in the market at any given point in time is known as the **short interest.** The more stocks that are sold short, the higher the short interest. Since all short sales must eventually be ''covered'' (the borrowed shares must be returned), a short sale in effect ensures future demand for the stock. Thus, the market is viewed optimistically when the level of short interest becomes relatively high by historical standards. The logic is that as shares are bought back to cover outstanding short sales, the additional demand will push prices up. The amount of short interest on the NYSE, AMEX, and NASDAQ's National Market is published monthly in *The Wall Street Journal* and *Barron's;* see Figure 7.3 for a look at the type of information that's available.

Keeping track of the level of short interest can indicate future market demand, but it can also reveal *present* market optimism or pessimism. Short selling is usually done by knowledgeable investors, and it is felt that a significant buildup or decline in the level of short interest may reveal the sentiment of supposedly sophisticated investors about the current state of the market or a company. For example, a significant shift upward in short interest has pessimistic overtones concerning the *current* state of the market, even though it may be an optimistic signal with regard to *future* levels of demand.

Odd-Lot Trading.   There is a rather cynical saying on Wall Street that suggests that the best thing to do is just the opposite of whatever the small investor is doing. The reasoning behind this is that the small investor is notoriously wrong in its timing of investment decisions: The investing public usually does not come into the market in force until after a bull market has pretty much run its course, and does not get out until late in a bear market. Whether or not this view is valid is debatable, but it is the premise behind a widely followed technical indicator and is the basis for the **theory of contrary opinion.** This theory uses the amount and type of odd-lot trading as an indicator of the current state of the market and pending changes. Because many individual investors deal in transactions of less than 100 shares, the combined sentiments of this type of investor are supposedly captured in the odd-lot

short interest
the number of stocks sold short in the market at any given time; a technical indicator believed to indicate future market demand.

theory of contrary opinion
a technical indicator that uses the amount and type of odd-lot trading as an indicator of the current state of the market and pending changes.

SHORT INTEREST HIGHLIGHTS

Largest Short Positions

Rank	Dec. 13	Nov. 15	Change
NYSE			
1 RJR Nabisco	30,389,333	35,717,517	−5,328,184
2 NCNB	16,278,259	14,833,923	1,444,336
3 Blockbstr Ent	13,946,469	14,655,172	−708,703
4 Citicorp	12,877,109	11,144,431	1,732,678
5 Unisys	11,316,868	9,129,458	2,187,410
6 BankAmerica	10,599,615	12,378,819	−1,779,204
7 Tel Espana adr	9,336,521	8,962,878	373,643
8 AT&T	8,821,317	7,640,456	1,180,861
9 Marriott	8,136,726	9,144,568	−1,007,842
10 Chemical Bnkg	7,721,936	5,521,419	2,200,517
11 Chrysler	7,440,142	7,184,463	255,679
12 Wal-Mart Strs	5,984,198	5,572,303	411,895
13 Black & Dckr	5,926,259	5,876,897	49,362
14 News Corp adr	5,565,830	6,065,670	−499,840
15 CUC Intl	5,248,089	4,840,856	407,233
16 Chem Wst Mgt	4,650,625	4,393,895	256,730
17 Shoney's	4,415,584	4,464,823	−49,239
18 Glenfed	4,296,815	4,224,089	72,726
19 Home Depot	4,112,705	3,763,805	348,900
20 Conagra	4,052,194	1,379,647	2,672,547
AMEX			
1 Energy Svc	4,770,500	5,209,600	−439,100
2 Continentl Air	4,512,595	4,569,366	−56,771
3 Ivax	2,045,999	1,639,482	406,517
4 Alza wi	1,839,529	1,643,287	196,242
5 Jan Bell Mktg	1,799,753	1,705,953	93,800

Largest Changes

Rank	Dec. 13	Nov. 15	Change
NYSE			
1 ConAgra	4,052,194	1,379,647	2,672,547
2 Chemical Bkng	7,721,936	5,521,419	2,200,517
3 Unisys	11,316,868	9,129,458	2,187,410
4 Nuveen NYQlMn	2,139,830	0	2,139,830
5 Nuveen CA QlInc	2,048,231	0	2,048,231
6 Tyco Toys	1,940,126	0	1,940,126
7 First of Amr Bk	1,980,826	148,697	1,832,129
8 Citicorp	12,877,109	11,144,431	1,732,678
1 Panhandle Estrn	1,596,705	8,290,449	−6,693,744
2 RJR Nabisco	30,389,333	35,717,517	−5,328,184
3 BankAmerica	10,599,615	12,378,819	−1,779,204
4 Texas Util	680,344	2,238,541	−1,558,197
5 Conseco	643,073	1,683,739	−1,040,666
6 Marriott	8,136,726	9,144,568	−1,007,842
7 Wachovia	1,043,075	2,050,058	−1,006,983
8 McDonnell Dgls	2,802,432	3,765,504	−963,072
AMEX			
1 Enzo Biochem	684,075	227,374	456,701
2 Ivax	2,045,999	1,639,482	406,517
3 Amdahl	1,369,392	1,081,261	288,131
4 Response Tech	503,195	243,845	259,350
1 Bergen Brnswg	659,506	1,869,156	−1,209,650
2 Weatherfrd Intl	273,342	1,037,263	−763,921
3 Fruit of Loom	1,154,201	1,820,036	−665,835
4 IGI Inc	695,709	1,151,158	−455,449

NYSE Short Interest
(In millions of shares)

Short Interest Ratio
(NYSE)

D J F M A M J J A S O N D
1991

The short interest ratio is the number of days it would take to cover the short interest if trading continued at the average daily volume for the month.

Largest Short Interest Ratios

	Dec. 13 Short Int	Avg Dly Vol-a	Days to Cover
NYSE			
1 Nuveen CA Ql Inc	2,048,231	26,900	76
2 Nuveen NY Ql Mni	2,139,830	28,758	74
3 Cineplex Odeon	2,863,581	41,550	69
4 TCBY Entps	2,533,445	39,610	64
5 Tucson El Pwr	2,828,649	44,520	64
6 NRN Sts Pwr	2,417,265	39,990	60
7 USG Corp	1,974,078	34,040	58
8 Duff Phelps UtilTx	1,406,024	24,963	56
9 NCNB	16,278,259	322,030	51
10 Kansas Pwr&Lt	3,620,974	75,515	48
11 KU Energy	970,199	20,660	47
12 CUC Intl	5,248,089	116,540	45
13 Fairchild Cl A	1,032,238	22,925	45
14 Marriott	8,136,726	192,620	42
15 Tel Espana Adr	9,336,521	223,470	42
16 First of Amr Bk	1,980,826	48,350	41
17 Delmarva Pr&Lt	2,893,526	70,885	41
AMEX			
1 Energy Svc	4,770,500	133,745	36
2 Elan PLC	1,248,365	43,150	29
3 Continentl Air	4,512,595	156,850	29
4 O'Brien Enviro	542,939	22,145	25
5 Horn Hardart	668,435	28,415	24

a-Includes securities with average daily volume of 20,000 shares or more.

r-Revised. The largest percentage increase and decrease sections are limited to issues with previously established short positions in both months.

Largest % Increases

Rank	Dec. 13	Nov. 15	%
NYSE			
1 Nuveen Tx Ql Inc	189,673	538	35,155.2
2 Presley Cos	99,819	3,467	2,779.1
3 Bay State Gas Co	179,700	6,311	2,747.4
4 Newell Co	1,348,152	49,530	2,621.9
5 Value Cty Dpt Str	203,900	10,552	1,832.3
6 Homeplx Mtg Inv	74,200	4,400	1,586.4
7 Analog Devices	183,910	11,300	1,527.5
8 Fingerhut Cos	64,850	4,750	1,265.3
9 First of Amr Bk	1,980,826	148,697	1,232.1
10 Diasonics	67,865	5,265	1,189.0
11 Manpower	240,529	19,029	1,164.0
12 MCN Corp	177,273	14,305	1,139.2
13 Hanson PLC Wts	453,426	37,600	1,105.9
14 Attwoods Adr	692,393	59,099	1,071.6
15 Norsk Hydro Adr	750,225	75,000	900.3
16 Aegon (Ord)	68,496	7,709	788.5
17 Jones Apparel	88,930	10,925	714.0
18 Lilco	224,290	27,775	707.5
19 Atlanta Gas Light	133,659	17,817	650.2
20 Fansteel	64,040	8,940	616.3
AMEX			
1 AmrTr Arco Scr	175,989	32,403	443.1
2 Enzo Biochem	684,075	227,374	200.9
3 US Bioscience	243,578	97,017	151.1
4 Barr Labs Inc	121,526	53,500	127.2
5 Response Tech	503,195	243,845	106.4

Largest % Decreases

Rank	Dec. 13	Nov. 15	%
NYSE			
1 Latin Amr Equ	0	55,365	−100.0
2 Banco Cntl Adr	200	125,399	−99.8
3 Elf Aqtn	117	58,059	−99.8
4 Morgn StanEmMt	2,887	604,500	−99.5
5 Enquirer/Star	979	161,000	−99.4
6 Elscint Ltd	1,000	129,500	−99.2
7 Gallghr (ArthrJ)	852	51,104	−98.3
8 Wells Farg DS9%	6,302	282,831	−97.8
9 Fiat Ordadr	1,319	55,319	−97.6
10 Nuveen Ins MnOp	18,275	594,165	−96.9
11 Nuveen NJ QlInc	3,397	54,498	−93.8
12 Gabelli EquTrst	61,261	685,574	−91.1
13 Global Yield Fund	9,284	97,753	−90.5
14 Waban	82,903	760,903	−89.1
15 Bancorp Hawaii	65,116	543,910	−88.0
16 Oppen Mlti-Sctr	8,101	59,277	−86.3
17 Georgia Gulf Nw	93,097	607,900	−84.7
18 DPL Inc	68,900	430,944	−84.0
19 Repsol adr	18,553	115,225	−83.9
20 US Shoe	34,286	207,100	−83.4
AMEX			
1 AmrTr Gen El Pr	75	71,033	−99.9
2 Mountn Med Eq	33,971	138,759	−75.5
3 Weatherfrd Intl	273,342	1,037,263	−73.6
4 Bergen Brnswg	659,506	1,869,156	−64.7
5 Nrth Amer Vac	44,707	97,500	−54.1

• **FIGURE 7.3** Short Interest in the NYSE and AMEX

The amount of short selling being done in the market is closely watched by many investment professionals and individual investors. The summary report shown here provides an overview of the extent to which stocks are being shorted in the NYSE and the AMEX. In addition to summary statistics, this monthly report also lists all stocks that have been sold short and the number of shares shorted. (*Source: The Wall Street Journal,* December 20, 1991.)

figures. The idea is to see what odd-lot investors are doing ''on balance.'' So long as there is little or no difference in the spread between the volume of odd-lot purchases and sales, we can conclude that the market will probably continue pretty much along its current line (either up or down). But when the balance of odd-lot purchases and sales begins to change dramatically, it may be a signal that a bull or bear market is about to end. For example, if the amount of odd-lot purchases starts to exceed odd-lot sales by an ever-widening margin, it may suggest that speculation on the part of small investors is starting to get out of control—an ominous signal that the final stages of a bull market may be at hand.

confidence index
a ratio of the average yield on high-grade corporate bonds to the average yield on low-grade corporate bonds; a technical indicator based on the theory that market trends usually appear in the bond market before they do in the stock market.

Confidence Index.   Another measure that attempts to capture the sentiment of market participants is the **confidence index,** which, unlike other technical measures of the stock market, deals with *bond* returns. Computed and published weekly in *Barron's,* the confidence index is a ratio of the average yield on high-grade corporate bonds to the average yield on low-grade corporate bonds. The theory is that the trend of ''smart money'' is usually revealed in the bond market before it shows up in the stock market. Although low-rated bonds provide higher yields than high-grade issues, the logic is that the spread in yields between these two types of obligations will change over time as the amount of optimism or pessimism in the market outlook changes. Thus, a sustained rise in the confidence index suggests an increase in investor confidence and a stronger stock market; a drop in the index portends a softer tone.

Relative Price Levels.   While market volume, short-interest positions, and odd-lot trading are of interest to many investors, others are concerned more about market prices in general. To them, it's not so much a matter of what's driving the market, but rather, how pricey the market is getting. Many professional traders keep tabs of prices in the market by jointly monitoring three measures of overall market performance: (1) the *market P/E multiple;* (2) the *market's price-to-book-value ratio;* and (3) its *dividend yield*. In a sense, these measures provide yardsticks about the *relative value* of stocks and, as such, capture underlying price pressures in the market. For example, a large upward move in overall market prices will cause the market P/E and price-to-book ratios to move up, and the dividend yield down. The idea is that if prices are going up, they should be doing so because of a healthy growth in corporate earnings, stockholders' equity, and dividends—not because of unbridled investor speculation.

Using these three measures, technical analysts have developed historical standards of performance that are felt to reflect normal market behavior. These standards aren't designed to pinpoint market swings or indicate how deep or how long a bear (or bull) market will last. However, they do offer signals that historically have pointed up zones of extreme over- or under-valuation. That is, these relative price measures point out when the market is moving into danger zones (on the upside) or significant buying opportunities (on the downside). As a rule, it's felt that the market is starting to overheat and prices, in general, are getting too high when: the market P/E (on the S&P 500) moves above 18 to 20 times earnings, the market's average price-to-book goes over 2 to 2.5, and the average dividend yield drops below 3%. On the other hand, stocks have proven to be bargains when: the market P/E drops to 10 or less, the price-to-book starts getting close to 1.0, and dividend yield rises above 6%. Keeping track of the market's P/E, price-to-book, and dividend yield is fairly easy, since this information is regularly reported in *The Wall Street Journal, Barron's,* and a number of other sources.

Using Technical Analysis

Investors have a wide range of choices with respect to technical analysis. They can use the charts and complex ratios of the technical analysts or follow a more informal approach and use technical analysis just to get a general sense of the market. Presumably, in the latter case, it's not market behavior *per se* that is important as much as the implications such market behavior can have on the price performance of a particular common stock. Thus, technical analysis might be used in conjunction with fundamental analysis to determine the proper time to add a particular investment candidate to one's portfolio. Some investors and professional money managers, in fact, look at the technical side of a stock *before* doing any fundamental analysis. If the stock is found to be technically sound, then they'll spend the time to look at its fundamentals; if not, they'll look for another stock. For these investors, the concerns of technical analysis are still the same: *Do the technical factors indicate that this might be a good stock to buy?*

Most investors rely on published sources, such as those put out by brokerage firms, to obtain necessary technical insights, and they often find it helpful to use several different approaches. For example, an investor might follow a favorite bellwether stock, such as IBM or AT&T, and at the same time keep track of information on market volume and breadth of the market. This is information that is readily available and is a low-cost way of staying abreast of the market.

Charting

charting
the activity of charting price behavior and other market information, and then using the patterns that these charts form to make investment decisions.

Charting is perhaps the best-known activity of the technical analyst. Technicians— analysts who believe supply-and-demand forces establish stock prices—use various types of charts to plot the behavior of everything from the Dow Jones industrial average to the share-price movements of individual listed and OTC stocks. Also, just about every kind of technical indicator is charted in one form or another. Figure 7.4 shows a typical stock chart; in this case the price behavior of Hartmarx Corp. (formerly Hart Schaffner & Marx) has been plotted, along with a variety of supplementary information. Charts are popular because they provide a visual summary of activity over time, and perhaps more important, because, in the eyes of technicians at least, they contain valuable information about developing trends and the future behavior of the market and/or individual stocks. Chartists believe price patterns evolve into *chart formations* that provide signals about the future course of the market or a stock. We will now briefly review the practice of charting, including popular types of charts, chart formations, and investor uses of charts.

• FIGURE 7.4 A Stock Chart

This chart for Hartmarx Corporation contains information about the daily price behavior of the stock, along with the stock's relative strength, its trading volume, and several other pieces of supplementary data. (*Source:* "A Stock Chart—Hartmarx." Courtesy of Daily Graphs. Reprinted by permission of Daily Graphs, 12655 Beatrice Street, Los Angeles, CA. 90066, Phone 310 448 6893.)

Bar Charts

bar chart
the simplest kind of chart on which share price is plotted on the vertical axis and time on the horizontal axis; stock prices are recorded as vertical bars showing high, low, and closing prices.

The simplest and probably most widely used type of chart is the **bar chart.** Market or share prices are plotted on the vertical axis, and time on the horizontal axis. This type of chart derives its name from the fact that prices are recorded as vertical bars that depict high, low, and closing prices. A typical bar chart is illustrated in Figure 7.5; note that on 12/31, this particular stock had a high price of 29, a low of 27, and closed at 27½. Because these charts contain a time element, technicians will frequently plot a variety of other pertinent information on them. For example, volume is often put at the base of most bar charts (see the Hartmarx chart in Figure 7.4).

Point-and-Figure Charts

These charts are used strictly to keep track of emerging price patterns. Because there is no time dimension on **point-and-figure charts,** they are *not* used for plot-

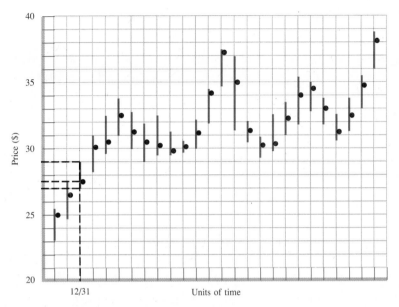

Key

◄— High price (for the day, week, month, or year).

● ◄— Closing price (for the day or other unit of time).

◄— Low price (for the day or other unit of time).

● FIGURE 7.5 A Bar Chart

Bar charts are widely used to track stock prices, market averages, and numerous other technical measures.

point-and-figure charts

charts used to keep track of emerging price patterns by plotting significant price changes with Xs and Os but with no time dimension used.

ting technical measures. In addition to the time feature, point-and-figure charts are unique in two other ways: First, only *significant* price changes are recorded on these charts; that is, prices have to move by a certain minimum amount—usually at least a point or two—before a new price level is recognized. Second, price reversals show up only after a predetermined change in direction occurs. Usually only closing prices are charted, though some point-and-figure charts use all price changes during the day. An *X* is used to denote an increase in price, and an *O* a decrease. Figure 7.6 shows a common point-and-figure chart. In this case, the chart employs a 2-point box, which means that the stock must move by a minimum of 2 points before any changes are recorded. The chart could cover a span of one year or less, if the stock is highly active. Or it could cover a number of years; if the stock is not very active, the chart could reflect price movements over, say, the past three to five years. As a rule, low-priced stocks will be charted with 1-point boxes, moderately priced shares will use increments of 2 to 3 points, and high-priced securities will appear on charts with 3- to 5-point boxes.

Here is how they work: Suppose we are at point A on the chart in Figure 7.6, where the stock has been hovering around the $40–$41 mark for some time. As-

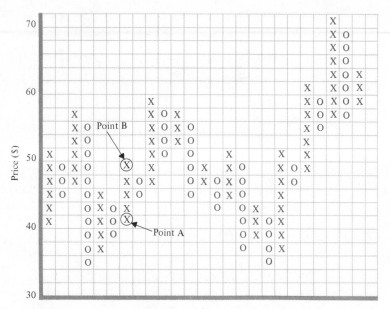

• FIGURE 7.6 A Point-and-Figure C

Point-and-figure charts are unusual because they have no time dimension. Rather, a column of *X*s is used to reflect a general upward drift in prices, and a column of *O*s is used when prices are drifting downward.

sume, however, that it just closed at 42⅛; because the minimum 2-point movement has been met, the chartist would place an *X* in the box immediately *above* point A. The chartist would remain with this new box as long as the price moved (up or down) within the 2-point range of 42 to 43⅞. Thus, although the chartist follows *daily* prices, a new entry is made on the chart only after the price has changed by a certain minimum amount and moved into a new 2-point box. We see that from point A, the price generally moved up over time to nearly $50 a share. At that point (indicated as point B on the chart), things began to change as a reversal set in. That is, the price of the stock began to drift downward and in time moved out of the 48–50 box. This reversal prompts the chartist to change columns and symbols: She moves one column to the right and records the new price level with an *O* in the 46–48 box. The chartist will continue to use the *O* as long as the stock continues to close on a generally lower note.

Chart Formations

The information that charts supposedly contain about the future course of the market (or a stock) is revealed in *chart formations*. That is, in response to certain supply and demand forces, chartists believe that emerging price patterns will result in various types of formations which historically have indicated that certain types of behavior are imminent. If you know how to interpret charts (which, by the way, is no easy task), you can see formations building and recognize buy and sell signals. As the following list reveals, chart formations are often given some pretty exotic names:

Head-and-shoulders	Broadening top
Double top	Dormant bottom
Triple bottom	Ascending triangle
Diamond	Exhaustion gap
Falling wedge	Island reversal
Pennant	Trend channel
Scallop and saucer	Complex top

Figure 7.7 shows six popular formations. The patterns form ''support levels'' and ''resistance lines'' that, when combined with the basic formations, yield buy and sell signals. Panel A is an example of a *buy* signal, which occurs when prices break out above a resistance line after a particular pattern has been formed. In contrast, when prices break out below a support level, as they do at the end of the formation in panel B, a *sell* signal is said to occur. Supposedly, a sell signal means everything is in place for a major drop in the market (or in the price of a share of stock), and a buy signal indicates that the opposite is about to occur. Unfortunately, one of the major problems of charting is that the formations rarely appear as neatly and cleanly as those in Figure 7.7. Rather, their identification and interpretation often require considerable imagination on the part of the chartist.

Investor Uses

Charts are nothing more than tools used by market analysts and technicians to assess conditions in the market and/or the price behavior of individual stocks. Unlike other types of technical measures, charting is seldom done on an informal basis; you either chart because you believe in its value, or you don't use it at all. A chart by itself tells you little more than where the market or a stock has been. But to a chartist, those price patterns yield formations that, along with things like resistance lines, support levels, and breakouts, tell what to expect in the future. Chartists believe that history repeats itself, so they study the historical reactions of stocks (or the market) to various formations and devise trading rules based on these observations. It makes no difference to chartists whether they are following the market or an individual stock, because it is the formation that matters, not the issue being plotted. The value of charts lies in knowing how to ''read'' them and how to respond to the signals they are said to give about the future. There is a long-standing debate on Wall Street (some would call it a feud) regarding the merits of charting. Although it may be scoffed at by a large segment of those following the market, to avid chartists, charting is no laughing matter.

Monitoring Performance

Keeping track of your investment holdings is an essential part of investing in stocks. Just as you need investment objectives to provide direction to your stock selections,

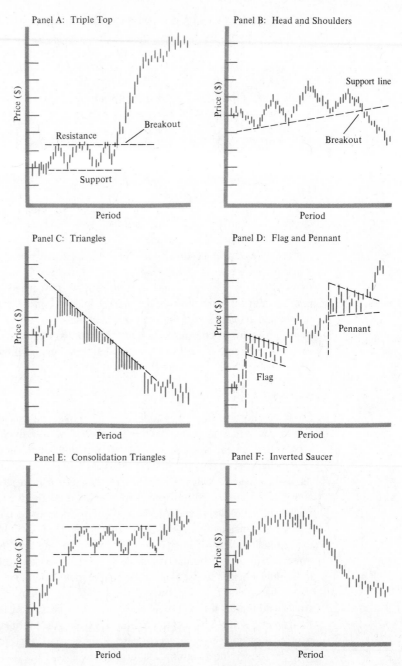

• FIGURE 7.7 Some Popular Chart Formations

To chartists, each of these formations has meaning about the future course of events.

so too do you need to keep track of your stock holdings in order to monitor their performance. We'll discuss the issue of monitoring your investments in detail in Chapter 17; suffice it to say at this point that you can't just buy stocks and then put everything on automatic pilot. Most equity investments are simply too risky for that sort of thing. Instead, you have to keep close tabs on how your investments have performed over time, and whether they've live up to expectations. After all, investments sometimes fail to perform the way you'd like them to, in which case, it may be time to *sell* the securities and put the money elsewhere. We have said a lot about *buying* stocks, about how fundamental and technical analysis can be used to find attractive investment candidates, but the fact is that knowing when to sell and when to hold can also have a significant impact on the amount of return you're able to generate from your capital. Indeed, with most securities, it's just as important to know when to say ''bye'' as it is to say ''buy.'' The accompanying *Investor Insights* box provides some suggestions on how to determine whether the time is right for selling a stock.

RANDOM WALKS AND EFFICIENT MARKETS

random walk hypothesis
the theory that stock price movements are unpredictable and, thus, there's really little way of knowing where future prices are headed.

If a drunk were abandoned in an open field at night, where would you begin to search for him the next morning? The answer, of course, is the spot where the drunk was left the night before, since there's no way to predict where the drunk will go. To some analysts, stock prices seem to wander about in a similar fashion. Observations of such erratic movements have led to a body of evidence called the **random walk hypothesis.** Its followers believe that price movements are unpredictable and as a result, security analysis will not help to predict future behavior. This obviously has serious implications for much of what we have discussed in the last two chapters.

A Brief Historical Overview

efficient markets
the theory that the market price of securities always-fully reflects available information, making it difficult, if not impossible, to consistently outperform the market by picking ''undervalued'' stocks.

To describe stock prices as a random walk suggests that price movements cannot be expected to follow any type of pattern, or put another way, that price movements are independent of one another. In order to find a theory for such behavior, researchers developed the concept of **efficient markets.** Basically, the idea behind an efficient market is that the market price of securities always fully reflects available information and therefore it is difficult, if not impossible, to consistently outperform the market by picking ''undervalued'' stocks.

Random Walks

The first evidence of random price movements dates back to the early 1900s. During that period, statisticians noticed that commodity prices seemed to follow a ''fair game'' pattern: That is, prices seemed to move up and down randomly, giving no advantage to any particular trading strategy. Although a few studies on the subject appeared in the 1930s, thorough examination of the randomness in stock prices did not begin until 1959. From that point on, particularly through the decade of the 1960s, the random walk issue became one of the most keenly debated topics in

▬▬▬ I N V E S T O R   I N S I G H T S ▬▬▬

When to Sell a Stock

Knowing when to sell a stock (or any other investment for that matter) is one of the toughest parts of investing. Too often an investor loses sight of the fact that what is bought will probably also have to be sold at some time in the future—and if things don't work out as planned, the time to sell might be sooner than expected. Sell too soon and you may miss profits; sell too late and you may watch your profits disappear. The decision to sell is seldom an easy one. In contrast, the refusal to sell—be it due to greed, stubbornness, fear, or inattention—is often the undoing of many an investor.

Obviously, you shouldn't cash in every time your stock moves a few points: Commissions and taxes can eat you alive. Nor should you panic in the face of a sharp market drop and sell everything. Rather, the best course of action is to pay attention to your stock and to the events that can affect it. Judge each company in which you *hold* stock just as carefully as you would judge a company in which you are considering investing. Ask yourself: Based on current prices, earnings, and prospects, would you buy the shares you now own? If the answer is no, you should probably consider selling! As a general rule, *you should continue to hold a stock as long as you can't earn a better risk-adjusted rate of return by putting your money somewhere else.*

Most investment professionals recommend preplanned strategies for taking profits and cutting losses. Unfortunately, the question of when to sell a stock often comes down to an investor's emotional stamina and investment horizon. Most individual investors just aren't disciplined enough to set up a strategy and stick with it in good *and* bad markets. To help you make that tough decision about when to sell a stock, you should keep track of the stock's fundamentals, watch dividends, and set a target.

stock market literature. The development of high-speed computers has helped researchers compile convincing evidence that stock prices do, in fact, come very close to a random walk.

Efficient Markets

Given the extensive random walk evidence, market researchers were faced with another question: What sort of market would produce prices that seem to fluctuate randomly? Such behavior could be the result of investors who are irrational and make investment decisions on whim. However, it has been argued much more convincingly that investors are not irrational at all; rather, random price movements are evidence of an efficient market.

An efficient market is one in which securities fully reflect all possible information quickly and accurately. The concept states that investors will incorporate all information into their decisions on the price at which they are willing to buy or sell. At any point in time, then, the current price of a security incorporates all information. Additionally, the current price not only reflects past information, such as

- *Follow the Fundamentals.* Whether you own a big name stock or an obscure over-the-counter venture, you need to follow the company's prospects, its earnings progress, and its business success as reflected in market share, sales growth, and profit margin. How do you keep track of such fundamentals? Easy! Just read the company reports you get and keep your eyes open for news stories about your company and research updates from brokerage houses. Your job is to pay close enough attention to be aware of developments that could bode ill for your investment. If the fundamentals start to weaken, it's time to review your position in the stock.

- *Watch the Dividend.* Whether or not you're investing in a company for current income, the security of its dividends is important to any stock's prospects. A dividend cut or signs that the dividend is "in trouble"—meaning that analysts or creditors are quoted somewhere as saying they don't think the company can maintain its payout to shareholders—can undermine the stock price. As a rule, dividend cuts spell double trouble for stockholders: less income and falling stock prices. So, a dividend cut should be a signal to take the first available exit!

- *Set a Target.* Many investors find it helpful to set specific price targets. Such guidelines can prompt you to clinch gains before they wither or to dump losers before the damage becomes unmanageable. If you're basically a buy-and-hold investor and your key concern is loss prevention, you don't have to get involved with the intricacies of the technicians' trade. You can take the simpler step of setting a "mental sell level." Once you've reached your objective, or hit your mental sell signal, take the money and run. If your price target is met, you ought to sell some or all of your stock. If the goals you've set for your stock are ultraconservative, you may miss some gains, but that's better than holding on too long and falling victim to the Wall Street axiom, "Bulls make money, bears make money, pigs get slaughtered."

might be found in company reports, financial newspapers, and magazine articles, but also includes information about events that have been announced but haven't actually occurred yet, like a forthcoming dividend payment. Furthermore, the current price also reflects predictions about future information: Investors, in their zeal to beat the competition, actively forecast important events and incorporate those forecasts into their estimate of the correct price. Obviously, because of the keen competition among investors, when new information becomes known, the price of the security adjusts very quickly. This adjustment is not always perfect: Sometimes it is too large and at other times too small, but on average it balances out and is correct. The new price, in effect, is set after investors have fully assessed the new information.

Why Should the Market Be Efficient?

Active markets such as the New York Stock Exchange, are efficient—they are made up of many rational, highly competitive investors who react quickly and objectively to new information. Investors, searching for stock market profits, compete vigorously for new information and do extremely thorough analysis. The **efficient markets hypothesis (EMH),** which is the basic theory describing the behavior of such a market, specifically states:

1. There are a large number of knowledgeable investors who are actively analyzing, valuing, and trading any particular security. No one of these individual traders alone can affect the price of any security.
2. Information is widely available to all investors at approximately the same time, and this information is practically "free."
3. Information on events, such as labor strikes, industrial accidents, and changes in product demand, tends to occur randomly.
4. Investors react quickly and accurately to new information, and this causes prices to adjust quickly, and on average, accurately.

For the most part, the securities markets do, in fact, exhibit these characteristics.

Levels of Market Efficiency

The EMH is concerned with information, meaning not only the type and source of information, but the quality and speed with which it is disseminated among investors. It is convenient to discuss the EMH in three cumulative categories or forms: *past prices only;* past prices *plus all other public data;* and finally, past prices and public data *plus private information.* Together, these three ways of looking at information flows in the market represent what are generally referred to as the weak, semi-strong, and strong forms of the EMH.

Weak Form

The *weak form of the EMH* holds that past data on stock prices are of no use in predicting future price changes. If prices follow a random walk, price changes over time are random. The price change today is unrelated to the price change yesterday, or any other day. If new information arrives randomly, then prices will change randomly. Each step by a drunkard is unrelated to previous steps.

A number of people have asserted that it is possible to profit from "runs" in a stock's price. They contend that when a stock price starts moving up, it will continue to move up for several consecutive days, developing a momentum. If you can spot a "run," then you could develop a trading strategy which would produce a profit, based on past prices alone. The results from much careful research suggest that indeed, momentum in stock prices does exist, and if investors *quickly* trade at the beginning of the "run," large profits can be made. But there's a problem: In addition to spotting a run right off the bat (no easy task), an investor would have to make many, many trades, and when commissions are factored in, the only person that makes a profit is the broker. Many other trading rules have been tested to determine if profits can be made by examining past stock price movements. There is very little, if any, evidence that a trading rule based solely on past price data can outperform a simple buy-and-hold strategy.

Semi-Strong Form

The *semi-strong form of the EMH* holds that abnormally large profits cannot be consistently earned using publicly available information. This includes not only past price and volume data, but also data such as corporate earnings, dividends, inflation, and stock splits. The semi-strong information set includes all of the information publicly considered in the weak form, *as well as all other information publicly available*. Tests of the semi-strong form of the EMH are basically concerned with the speed at which information is disseminated to investors. The overall conclusions support the position that stock prices adjust very rapidly to new information, and therefore support the semi-strong form of the EMH—but there are still some unanswered questions.

Most tests of semi-strong efficiency have examined how a stock price changes in response to an economic or financial event. A famous early study involved stock splits. A stock split does not change the value of a company, and so the value of the stock should not be affected by a stock split. Although the research indicated that there are sharp increases in the price of a stock *before* a stock split, the changes after the split are random. Investors cannot gain by purchasing stocks on or after the announcement of a split; they would have to purchase before the split to earn abnormal profits. By the time the stock split is announced, the market has already incorporated any favorable information associated with the split into the price. Other studies have examined the impact of major events on stock prices. The overwhelming evidence indicates that stock prices react within minutes, if not seconds, to any important new information. Certainly by the time an investor reads about the event in the newspaper, the stock price has almost completely adjusted to the news. Even hearing about the event on radio or television usually allows too little time to react and complete the transaction to make an abnormal profit!

Strong Form

The *strong form of the EMH* holds that there is no information, public or private, that allows investors to consistently earn abnormal profits. It states that stock prices immediately adjust to any information, even if it isn't available to every investor. This extreme form of the EMH has not received universal support.

One type of private information is the kind obtained by corporate insiders, such as officers, directors, or privileged individuals within a corporation. They have access to valuable information about major strategic and tactical decisions that are planned by the company. They also have detailed information about the true financial state of the firm that may not be available to other shareholders. While corporate insiders can legally trade shares of stock in their own company, they must report the transactions to the Securities and Exchange Commission (SEC) each month. This information is then made public, usually within several weeks. It should not be surprising to learn that most studies of corporate insiders find that they consistently earn abnormally large profits. They are able to position their stock holdings before major announcements are made to the public and can thereby profit from the stock price adjustment made after important news is released.

Other market participants occasionally have inside—nonpublic—information which they obtained *illegally*. With this information, they can gain an unfair advantage that permits them to earn an excess return. Since the mid-1980s, with the disclosure of the insider-trading activities of Ivan Boesky, Michael Milken, and others, major national attention has been focused on the "problem" of illegal insider trading and its resolution. Clearly those who trade securities based on illegal inside information have an unfair and illegal advantage. Empirical research has confirmed that those with inside information do indeed have an opportunity to earn an excess return.

Market Anomalies

market anomalies
irregularities or devia-
tions from the normal
behavior in an effi-
cient market.

Despite the overwhelming evidence in support of the EMH—especially the weak and semi-strong versions—there still exists some curious and as yet unexplained empirical results. These so-called **market anomalies** represent irregularities, or deviations from the norm. The studies, in effect, product results that are different from what we'd expect in a truly efficient market. These anomalies should not be viewed as a guaranteed way to outperform the market, as some stockbrokers and investment counselors would have you believe. Rather, they are areas that have yet to be fully explained—and may only exist because of the capability of computers to search through millions of pieces of data in search of interesting correlations and associations.

Calendar Effects.   One widely cited anomaly is the so-called *calendar effect,* which holds that stock returns may be closely tied to the time of the year or the time of the week. That is, certain months or days of the week may produce better investment results than others! For example, there is the *January effect,* which shows a seasonality in the stock market, with a tendency for small stock prices to go up during the month of January. Some explanations offer a tax-based reason for the phenomenon, but a completely satisfactory explanation has yet to be offered. The *weekend effect* is the result of evidence that stock returns, on average, are negative from the close of trading on Fridays until the close of trading on Mondays. The ability to consistently earn abnormal returns from using trading rules based on these results is still very questionable.

Small Firm Effect.   Another anomaly is the *small firm effect,* or firm-size effect, which states that the size of the firm has a bearing on the level of stock returns. Indeed, several studies have shown that small firms earn higher returns than large firms, even after adjusting for risk and other considerations. Whether this is an invalidation of the EMH or a problem with misspecification of the mathematical models remains to be seen.

Earnings Announcements.   Another market anomaly has to do with how stock prices react to *earnings announcements*. Obviously, earnings announcements contain important information that should, and does, affect stock prices. However, much of the information has already been anticipated by the market, and so—if the

EMH is correct—prices should only react to the "surprise" portion of the announcement. Studies have shown, in fact, that a substantial amount of the price adjustment does occur prior to the actual announcement, but there is also a surprisingly large adjustment for some time after the announcement. In an efficient market, the prices should adjust quickly to any surprises in the earnings announcement. The fact that it takes several days (or even months) to fully adjust remains something of a mystery. Additionally, there is some documentation that abnormally large profits can consistently be obtained by buying stocks after unusually good *quarterly* earnings reports, and selling stocks after unusually bad *quarterly* earnings reports. This suggests that the majority of market investors don't bother to read and evaluate quarterly reports, but instead only concentrate on annual reports. Such results remain puzzling.

P/E Effect.   According to the *P/E effect,* the best way to make money in the market is to stick with stocks that have relatively low P/E ratios. The P/E multiple is widely followed in the market and widely used in the stock valuation process. Studies have shown that, on average, low P/E stocks outperform high P/E stocks, even after adjusting for risk and other factors. The reason has not been determined, but it appears that the results have endured over a long period. Since the P/E ratio is public information, it should be fully reflected in the current price, and purchasing low P/E stocks should not produce larger profits, if the markets were truly efficient.

Possible Implications

The concept of an efficient market holds serious implications for investors. In particular, it could have considerable bearing on traditional security analysis and stock valuation procedures and on the way stocks are selected for investment. There are, in fact, some who contend that rather than trying to beat the market, investors should spend less time analyzing securities and more time on such matters as the reduction of taxes and transaction costs, the elimination of unnecessary risk, and the construction of a widely diversified portfolio that is compatible with the investor's risk temperament. Make no mistake about it, *even in an efficient market there are all sorts of return opportunities available*. But to proponents of efficient markets, the only way to increase returns is to invest in a portfolio of higher-risk securities.

For Technical Analysis

The most serious challenge the random walk evidence presents is to technical analysis. If price fluctuations are purely random, charts of past prices are not likely to produce significant trading profits. In a highly efficient market, shifts in supply and demand occur so rapidly that technical indicators simply measure after-the-fact events, with no implications for the future. If markets are less than perfectly efficient, however, information may be absorbed slowly, producing gradual shifts in supply and demand conditions—and profit opportunities for those who recognize the shifts early. Although the great bulk of evidence supports a random walk, many investors follow a technical approach because they believe it improves their investment results.

For Fundamental Analysis

Many strict fundamental analysts were at first pleased by the random walk attack on technical analysis. Further development of the efficient markets concept, however, was not so well received. For in an efficient market, it's argued that prices react so quickly to new information that not even security analysis will enable investors to realize consistently superior returns on their investments. Because of the extreme competition among investors, security prices are seldom far above or below their justified levels, and fundamental analysis thus loses much of its value. The problem is not that fundamental analysis is poorly done; on the contrary, it is done all too well! As a result, so many investors, competing so vigorously for profit opportunities, simply eliminate the opportunities before other investors can capitalize upon them.

So Who Is Right?

Some type of fundamental analysis probably has a role in the stock selection process. For even in an efficient market, there is no question that stock prices reflect a company's profit performance. Some companies are fundamentally strong while others are fundamentally weak, and investors must be able to distinguish between the two. Thus, some time can profitably be spent in evaluating a company and its stock to determine, not if it is undervalued, but whether it is fundamentally strong.

The level of investor return, however, is more than a function of the fundamental condition of the company; the level of risk exposure is also important. We saw earlier that fundamental analysis can help assess potential risk exposure and identify securities that possess risk commensurate with the return they offer. The extent to which the markets are efficient is still subject to considerable debate. At present, there seems to be a growing consensus that while the markets may not be *perfectly* efficient, the evidence seems to suggest that they are, at the least, *reasonably* efficient. In the final analysis, then, it is the individual investor who must decide on the merits of fundamental and technical analysis. Certainly, a large segment of the investing public believes in security analysis, even in a market that may be efficient. What is more, the principles of stock valuation—that promised return should be commensurate with exposure to risk—are valid in any type of market setting.

SUMMARY

1. The final phase of security analysis involves an assessment of the investment merits of a specific company and its stock, and is ultimately aimed at formulating expectations about the company's future prospects and the potential risk and return behavior of the stock.

2. Information such as projected sales, forecasted earnings, and estimated dividends is important in establishing the intrinsic worth of a stock—which is a measure of what the stock ought to be worth, based on expected return performance and risk exposure.

3. There are a number of stock valuation procedures in use today, including the dividend valuation model, which derives the value of a share of stock from the stock's future

growth in dividends and the appropriate market capitalization rate. Another popular valuation procedure is the present value approach, whereby an investor can determine the justified price of a security, or the fully compounded yield it offers, given expected security returns (dividends and future price behavior) over a specific investment horizon.

4. Using these valuation models, a stock is considered to be a viable investment candidate so long as its computed yield is equal to or greater than the required rate of return, or its computed justified price is equal to or greater than the stock's current market price.

5. Technical analysis is another phase of the analytical process; it deals with the behavior of the stock market and the various economic forces at work in the marketplace. Many investors use technical analysis to help them time their investment decisions.

6. In recent years, the whole notion of both technical and fundamental analysis has been seriously challenged by the random walk and efficient market hypotheses. Indeed, there is considerable evidence to indicate that stock prices do move in a random fashion.

    The efficient market hypothesis is an attempt to explain *why* prices behave randomly; the idea behind an efficient market is that available information about the company and/or its stock is always fully reflected in the price of securities, and therefore investors should *not* expect to consistently outperform the market. While few investors believe the market is *perfectly* efficient, there is a good deal of evidence to suggest that it is, at the very least, *reasonably* efficient.

QUESTIONS

1. What is the purpose of stock valuation? What role does intrinsic value play in the stock valuation process? Do you believe stock valuation serves a necessary purpose? Explain.

2. Are the expected future earnings of the firm important in determining a stock's investment suitability? Discuss how these and other future estimates fit into the stock valuation framework.

3. Briefly discuss some procedures that might be used by investors to forecast the following types of information about a company and its stock:

    a. Sales.
    b. Net profit margin.
    c. Price/earnings ratio.

4. Can the growth prospects of a company affect its price/earnings multiple? Explain. How about the amount of debt that a firm uses? Are there other variables that affect the level of a firm's P/E ratio? What is the market multiple, and how can it help in evaluating a stock's P/E? Is a stock's relative P/E the same thing as the market multiple? Explain.

5. In the stock valuation framework, how can you tell if a particular security is a worthwhile investment candidate? What role does the required rate of return play in this process? What difference does it make if you pick a stock whose return is less than the required rate of return?

6. Briefly describe the dividend valuation model. What is the difference between the constant growth model and the variable growth model? Explain how CAPM fits into the variable growth DVM.

7. What's the difference between the variable growth dividend valuation model, Equation 7.8, and the so-called present value model, Equation 7.9? Which of these two do *you* prefer? Explain.

8. Identify and briefly discuss at least three different ways of determining (or assessing) a stock's investment value. Note how such information is used in the investment decision-making process. What's the difference in finding the approximate yield on a stock versus its justified price?

9. Explain how risk fits into the stock valuation process. (Note especially its relationship to the investment return of a security.)

10. What is the purpose of technical analysis? Explain how and why it is used by technicians; note how it can be helpful in timing investment decisions.

11. Can the market really have a measurable effect on the price behavior of individual securities? Explain.

12. Briefly define each of the following, and note the conditions that would suggest the market is technically strong:

    a. Breadth of the market.
    b. Dow theory.
    c. The market's price-to-book ratio.
    d. Theory of contrary opinion.
    e. Head-and-shoulders.

13. What is a stock chart? What kind of information can be put on charts, and what is the purpose of charting?

    a. What is the difference between a bar chart and a point-and-figure chart?
    b. What are chart formations, and why are they important?

14. What is the random walk hypothesis, and how does it apply to stocks? What is an efficient market; how can a market be efficient if its prices behave in a random fashion? What are market anomalies and how do they relate to efficient markets?

15. Explain why it is difficult, if not impossible, to consistently outperform an efficient market.

    a. Does that mean that high rates of return are not available in the stock market?
    b. Explain how an investor can earn a high rate of return in an efficient market.

16. What are the implications of random walks and efficient markets for technical analysis? For fundamental analysis? Do random walks and efficient markets mean that technical and fundamental analysis are useless? Explain.

PROBLEMS

 1. An investor estimates that next year's sales for Gilt Edge Products should amount to about $75 million; the company has 2.5 million shares outstanding, generates a net profit margin of about 5 percent, and has a payout ratio of 50 percent. All figures are expected to hold for next year. Given this information, compute:

a. Estimated net earnings for next year.
b. Next year's dividends per share.
c. The expected price of the stock (assuming the P/E ratio is 12.5 times earnings).
d. The expected holding period return (latest stock price: $15/sh.).

2. Charlene Lewis is thinking about buying some shares of Education, Inc., at $50 per share; she expects the price of the stock to rise to $75 over the next three years, during which time she also expects to receive annual dividends of $5 per share.

a. What is the intrinsic worth of this stock, given a 10 percent required rate of return?
b. What is its approximate yield?

3. Amalgamated Something-or-Other, Inc., is expected to pay a dividend of $1.50 in the coming year. The required rate of return is 16 percent and dividends are expected to grow at 7 percent per year. Using the dividend valuation model, find the intrinsic value of the company's common shares.

4. Assume you've generated the following information about the stock of Bufford's Burger Barns: The company's latest dividends of $4 a share are expected to grow to $4.32 next year, $4.67 the year after that, and $5.04 in year 3. In addition, the price of the stock is expected to rise to $77.75 in three years.

a. Use the present value model and a required rate of return of 15 percent to find the value of the stock.
b. Given that dividends are expected to grow indefinitely at 8 percent, use a 15 percent required rate of return and the dividend valuation model to find the value of the stock.
c. Assume dividends in year 3 actually amount to $5.04, the dividend growth rate stays at 8 percent, and the required rate of return stays at 15 percent. Use the dividend valuation model to find the price of the stock at the end of year 3. [*Hint:* In this case, the value of the stock will depend on D_4, which equals $D_3 (1 + g)$.] Do you note any similarity between your answer here and the forecasted price of the stock ($77.75) given in the problem? Explain.

5. Let's assume that you're thinking about buying some stock in U.S. Electronics. So far in your analysis, you've uncovered the following information: The stock pays annual dividends of $2.50 a share (and that's not expected to change within the next few years—nor are any of the other variables); it trades at a P/E of 12 times earnings and has a beta of 1.15; in addition, you plan on using a risk-free rate of 7½ percent in the CAPM, along with a market return of 14 percent. You would like to hold the stock for three years, at the end of which time you think EPS will peak out at about $7 a share. Given that the stock presently trades at $55, use the approximate yield formula to find this security's expected return. Now use the present value model to put a price on this stock. Does this look like a good investment? Explain.

6. The price of Consolidated Everything is now $75; the company pays no dividends, and Ms. Bossard expects the price three years from now to be $100 per share. Should Ms. B. buy Consolidated E. if she desires a 10 percent rate of return? Explain.

7. This year, Southwest Light and Gas (SWL&G) paid its stockholders an annual dividend of $3 a share. A major brokerage firm recently put out a report on SWL&G which stated that, in their opinion, the company's annual dividends should grow at the rate of 10% per year for each of the next five years and then level off and grow at the rate of 6% a year thereafter.

a. Use the variable growth DVM and a required rate of return of 12% to find the maximum price you should be willing to pay for this stock.

b. Re-do the SWL&G problem in (a), except this time, assume that *after* year 5, dividends stop growing altogether (i.e., for year 6 and beyond, $g = 0$). Use all other information as given above to find the stock's intrinsic value.

c. Contrast your two answers and comment on your findings. How important is growth to this valuation model?

8. Assume there are three companies that in the past year paid exactly the same annual dividend of $2.25 a share. In addition, the future annual rate of growth in dividends for each of the three companies has been estimated as follows:

Buggies-Are-Us	Steady Freddie, Inc.	Gang Buster Group	
$g = 0\%$	$g = 6\%$	Yr. 1	$2.53
(i.e., dividends	(for the	2	$2.85
are expected	foreseeable	3	$3.20
to remain at	future)	4	$3.60
$2.25/share)		Yr. 5 and beyond: $g = 6\%$	

Assume also that due to a strange set of circumstances, these three companies all have the same required rate of return ($k = 10\%$).

a. Use the appropriate DVM to value each of these companies.

b. Comment briefly on the comparative values of these three companies. What's the major cause of the differences in these three valuations?

9. Drabble Company's stock sells at a P/E ratio of 14 times earnings; it is expected to pay dividends of $2 per share in each of the next five years and generate an EPS of $5 per share in year 5. Using the present value model and a 12 percent discount rate, compute the stock's justified price.

10. A particular company currently has sales of $250 million; these are expected to grow by 20 percent next year (year 1). For the year after next (year 2), the growth rate in sales is expected to equal 10 percent. Over each of the next two years the company is expected to have a net profit margin of 8 percent, a payout ratio of 50 percent, and to maintain the number of shares of common stock outstanding at 15 million shares. The stock always trades at a P/E ratio of 15 times earnings, and the investor has a required rate of return of 20 percent. Given this information:

a. Find the stock's intrinsic value (its justified price).

b. Determine its approximate yield, given that the stock is presently trading at $15 per share.

c. Find the holding period returns for year 1 and for year 2.

11. Using the resources available at your campus or public library, select a company from *Value Line* that would be of interest to you. (*Hint:* Pick a company that's been publicly traded for at least 10–15 years, and *avoid* public utilities, banks and other financial institutions.) Obtain a copy of the latest *Value Line* report on your chosen company. Using the historical and forecasted data reported in *Value Line,* along with one of the valuation techniques described in this chapter, calculate the maximum (i.e., justified) price you'd be willing to pay for this stock. Use CAPM to find the required rate of return on your stock. (For the purposes of this problem, use a market rate of return of, say, 12% and for the risk-free rate, use the latest 3-month Treasury bill rate).

a. How does the justified price you computed above compare to the latest market price of the stock?

b. Would you consider the stock you've valued to be a worthwhile investment candidate? Explain.

CFA QUESTION (This question is from the 1991 Level I Exam.)

 As a firm operating in a mature industry, Arbot Industries is expected to maintain a constant dividend payout ratio and constant rates of growth in earnings for the foreseeable future. Earnings were $4.50 per share in the recently completed fiscal year. The dividend payout ratio has been a constant 55% in recent years and is expected to remain so. Arbot's return on equity (ROE) is expected to remain at 10% in the future, and you require an 11% return on the stock. [*Note:* The following formula can be used to find the rate of growth, g: (ROE) × (1 − the dividend payout ratio).]

a. Using the constant growth dividend valuation model, calculate the current value of Arbot common stock. Show your calculations.

After an aggressive acquisition and marketing program, it now appears that Arbot's earnings per share and ROE will grow rapidly over the next two years. You are aware that the dividend valuation model can be useful in estimating the value of common stock even when the assumption of constant growth does not apply.

b. Calculate the current value of Arbot's common stock using the dividend valuation model assuming Arbot's dividend will grow at a 15% rate for the next two years, returning in the third year to the historical growth rate and continuing to grow at the historical rate for the foreseeable future. Show your calculations.

(See Appendix C for Guideline Answer to this question.)

CASE PROBLEMS

7.1 Chris Looks for a Way to Invest His New Found Wealth

Chris Norton is a young Hollywood writer who is well on his way to television superstardom. After writing several successful television specials, he was recently named the head writer for the top rated TV sitcom, "Muffy Green." Chris fully realizes that his business is a fickle one, and on the advice of his dad and manager, has decided to set up an investment program. Chris will earn about half a million dollars this year, and because of his age, income level, and desire to get as big a bang as possible from his investment dollars, he has decided to invest in speculative, high-growth stocks.

He's presently working with a respected and highly regarded Beverly Hills broker and is in the process of building up a diversified portfolio of speculative stocks. His broker recently sent him information on a hot new issue. She suggested Chris study the numbers and if he likes them, buy as many as 1,000 shares of the stock. In particular, the broker forecasts corporate sales for the next three years at:

Year	Sales (in millions)
1	$22.5
2	35.0
3	50.0

The firm has 1.2 million shares of common outstanding (they are currently being traded at 62½ and pay no dividends), it has been running a phenomenal net profit rate of 20 percent, and its stock has been trading at a P/E ratio of around 25 times earnings (which is a bit on the high side). All these operating characteristics are expected to hold in the future.

Questions

1. Looking first at the stock:
   a. Compute the company's net profits and EPS for each of the next three years.
   b. Compute the price of the stock three years from now.
   c. Assuming all expectations hold up and that Chris buys the stock at 62½, determine the approximate yield he can expect from this investment.
   d. What risks is he facing by buying this stock? Be specific.
   e. Should he consider the stock to be a worthwhile investment candidate? Explain.
2. Now, looking at his investment program in general:
   a. What do you think of his investment program? What do you see as its strengths and weaknesses?
   b. Are there any suggestions you would make?
   c. Do you think Chris should consider adding foreign stocks to his portfolio? Explain.

7.2 An Analysis of a High-Flying Stock

Glenn Wilt is a recent university graduate and a security analyst with the Kansas City brokerage firm of Lippman, Brickbats, and Shaft. Wilt has been following one of the hottest issues on Wall Street, C&I Construction Supplies, a company that has turned in an outstanding performance lately and, even more important, has exhibited excellent growth potential. It has 5 million shares outstanding and pays a nominal annual dividend of 25 cents per share. Wilt has decided to take a close look at C&I to see whether or not it still has any investment play left. Assume the company's sales for the *past* five years have been:

Year	Sales (in millions)
1988	$10.0
1989	12.5
1990	16.2
1991	22.0
1992	28.5

Wilt is concerned with the future prospects of the company, not its past. As a result, he pores over the numbers laboriously and generates the following estimates of future performance:

Expected net profit margin	12½%
Estimated annual dividends per share	25¢
Number of common shares outstanding	No change
P/E ratio at the end of 1993	35
P/E ratio at the end of 1994	50

Questions

1. Determine the average annual rate of growth in sales over the past five years.
   a. Use this average growth rate to forecast revenues for next year (1993) and the year after that (1994).
   b. Now determine the company's net earnings and EPS for each of the next two years (1993 and 1994).
   c. Finally, determine the expected future price of the stock at the end of this two-year period.

2. Because of several intrinsic and market factors, Wilt feels that 20 percent is a viable figure to use for a desired rate of return.
   a. Using the 20 percent rate of return and the forecasted figures you came up with above, compute the stock's justified price.
   b. If C&I is presently trading at $25 per share, should Wilt consider the stock a worthwhile investment candidate? Explain.

3. The stock is actively traded on the AMEX and enjoys considerable market interest. Recent closing prices are listed below.
   a. Prepare a point-and-figure chart of these prices (use a 1-point system—i.e., make each box worth $1).
   b. Discuss how these and similar charts are used by technical analysts.
   c. Cite several other types of technical indicators, and note how they might be used in the analysis of this stock.

Recent Price Behavior: C&I Construction Supplies

14 ← (8/15/92)	18½	20	17½
14¼	17½	20¼	18½
14⅞	17½	20¼	19¾
15½	17¼	20⅛	19½
16	17	20	19¼
16	16¾	20¼	20
16½	16½	20½	20⅞
17	16½	20¾	21
17¼	16⅛	20½	21¾
17½	16¾	20	22½
18	17⅛	20¼	23¼
18 ← (9/30/92)	17¼	20	24
18½	17¼	19½	24¼
18½	17¼14 ← (10/31/92)	19¼	24⅛
18¾	17¾	18¼ ← (11/30/92)	24¾
19	18¼	17½	25
19⅛	19¼	16¾	25½
18⅞	20½	17	25½ ← (12/31/92)

INVESTING IN FIXED-INCOME SECURITIES

```
THE INVESTMENT ENVIRONMENT

    INVESTMENT ADMINISTRATION

    INVESTING IN          INVESTING IN
    COMMON                FIXED-INCOME
    STOCK                 SECURITIES

    SPECULATIVE           OTHER POPULAR
    INVESTMENT            INVESTMENT
    VEHICLES              VEHICLES
```

PART THREE INCLUDES

8 Bond Investments

After studying this chapter, you should be able to:

1. Explain the basic investment attributes of bonds and discuss the appeal that these securities hold as investment vehicles.

2. Describe the essential features of a bond and be able to distinguish between different types of call, refunding, and sinking fund provisions.

3. Describe the relationship between bond prices and market interest rates and, in general, explain why some bonds are more volatile than others.

4. Identify the different types of bonds and the kinds of investment objectives these fixed-income securities can fulfill.

5. Gain an appreciation of how the market is becoming more global in nature, and discuss the difference between dollar-denominated and non-dollar-denominated foreign bonds.

6. Describe the role that bond ratings play in the market and how they're used by investors.

bonds
publicly traded long-term debt securities, whereby the issuer agrees to pay a fixed amount of interest over a specified period of time and to repay a fixed amount of principal at maturity.

For many years, bonds were viewed as rather dull investments that produced current income and little else. No longer is this true; instead, bonds today are viewed as highly competitive investment vehicles that offer the potential for attractive returns through current income and/or capital gains. **Bonds** are publicly traded long-term debt securities; they are issued in convenient denominations and by a variety of borrowing organizations, including the U.S. Treasury, various agencies of the U.S. government, state and local governments, and corporations. Bonds are often referred to as *fixed-income securities* because the debt-service obligations of the issuers are fixed. That is, the issuing organization agrees to pay a fixed amount of interest periodically and to repay a fixed amount of principal at maturity.

This is the first of three chapters dealing with various types of fixed-income securities. In this chapter we will examine bonds as an investment vehicle and look at some of the basic features of fixed income securities. In Chapter 9, our attention will shift to bond valuation and the various ways that these securities can be used by investors. Finally, in Chapter 10, we'll examine two hybrid types of fixed-income securities—preferred stocks and convertible bonds. Let's begin this chapter by looking at some important issue characteristics, including sources of return to investors, different types of bond features, and the underlying forces that drive bond price behavior.

WHY INVEST IN BONDS?

Most people would not buy an expensive piece of property sight unseen, because there are too many costly pitfalls to such a course of action. Similarly, we would not expect rational investors to spend money on securities they know nothing about. Bonds are no exception. In fact, it is especially important to know what you are getting into with bonds since, as we will see shortly, *many seemingly insignificant features can have dramatic effects on the behavior of an issue and its investment return.*

Like any other type of investment vehicle, bonds provide investors with two kinds of income: (1) They provide a generous amount of current income, and (2) they can often be used to generate substantial amounts of capital gains. The current income, of course, is derived from the interest payments received over the life of the issue. Capital gains, in contrast, are earned whenever market interest rates fall. A basic trading rule in the bond market is that *interest rates and bond prices move in opposite directions.* When interest rates rise, bond prices fall; when rates drop, bond prices move up. Thus, it is possible to buy bonds at one price and, if interest rate conditions are right, to sell them later at a higher price. Of course, it is also possible to incur a capital loss should market rates move against the investor. Taken together, the current income and capital gains earned from bonds can lead to attractive and highly competitive investor yields.

In addition to their yields, bonds are also a versatile investment outlet. They can be used conservatively by those who primarily (or exclusively) seek high current income. Alternatively, fixed-income securities can be used aggressively, by those who go after capital gains. While bonds have long been considered attractive investments for those seeking current income, it has only been since the advent of high and volatile interest rates that they have also been recognized as outstanding trading vehicles. This is so because, given the relation of bond prices to interest rates, investors found that the number of profitable trading opportunities increased substantially as wider and more frequent swings in interest rates began to occur. In addition, there are certain types of bonds that can be used for tax shelter: Municipal obligations are perhaps the best known in this regard, but as we'll see later in this chapter, there are also some tax advantages to Treasury and federal agency issues as well. And finally, due to the generally high quality of many bond issues, they can also be used for the preservation and long-term accumulation of capital. With quality issues, not only do investors have a high degree of assurance that they'll get their money back at maturity, but the stream of interest income is also highly dependable.

Putting Bond Market Performance in Perspective

The bond market is driven by interest rates. In fact, the *behavior of interest rates is the single most important force in the bond market*. These rates determine not only the amount of current income investors will make, but also the amount of capital gains (or losses) that bondholders will incur. It's not surprising, therefore, that interest rates are so closely followed by market participants, and that bond market performance is generally portrayed in terms of market interest rates. Figure 8.1 provides a look at bond interest rates over the 30-year period from 1961 to 1991. It shows that from a state of relative stability, interest rates took off in 1965, and over

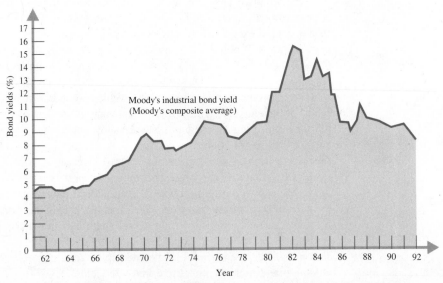

• FIGURE 8.1 The Behavior of Interest Rates Over Time

From an era of relative stability, bond interest rates rose dramatically and became far more volatile. The net result was that bond yields not only became highly competitive with the returns offered by other securities, they also provided investors with attractive capital gains opportunities.

the course of the next 15 years, the rates paid on high-grade bonds almost tripled. Indeed, interest rates rose from the 4 to 5 percent range in the early sixties to over 16 percent by 1982. But then things began to change, as rates dropped sharply, and by 1986 they were back to the single-digit range once again. Thus, after a protracted bear market (the bond market is considered *bearish* when market interest rates are high or rising), bonds abruptly reversed course, and we experienced the strongest bull market on record from 1982 to early 1987 (the bond market is considered *bullish* when rates are low or falling). Even though interest rates did move up again in 1987–88, they quickly retreated, so that by 1991, we were back to interest rate levels we hadn't seen in 20 years! Indeed, rates had come down so far that by late 1991, short-term securities, like Treasury bills and bank certificates of deposit, were yielding less than 4 percent, and long-term bonds were down to yields of only 7 or 8 percent.

Just like stocks, *total returns* in the bond market are also made up of current income and capital gains (or losses). Not surprisingly, because rising rates mean falling prices, the drawn-out bear market in bonds meant depressing returns for bondholders. Granted, for investors just entering the market, the higher market yields were welcomed, because they signified higher levels of interest income. *But for those already holding bonds,* the implications were much different, as returns fell way *below* expectations and in many cases, resulted in outright losses. Take a look at Table 8.1 on pages 326 and 327; it shows year-end market yields and total annual returns for high-grade corporate bonds for the 42-year period from 1950 through 1991. Note how bond returns started to slip in 1965, as market rates began to climb; in fact, from 1965 to 1981, there were no fewer than eight years when average returns were in the red. In contrast, look what happened over the ten-year period from 1982–91, when rates were in a general state of decline: A negative return occurred only once (in 1987), whereas double-digit returns (of 10.7% to 43.8%) occurred in no less than seven of the ten years. Clearly, the 1982–91 period was *not* a bad time for bonds! To see how market yields and bond returns have interacted over time, compare these two columns in Table 8.1. Note that when yields go one way, returns go the other. For example, in 1980, market yields went way up, but total returns fell to −2.62 percent. In contrast, two years later, in 1982, it was market yields that plunged, and total returns were a whopping 43.8 percent— providing a standard of performance that holds up well even against stocks!

Table 8.2 contains return performance over various *holding periods* of 5 to 42 years. These figures demonstrate the type of long-term returns possible from bonds, and they show that *average annual returns of around 8 to 10 percent on high-grade issues are not out of the question.* Although such performance may lag behind stocks (which it should in light of the reduced exposure to risk), it really isn't all that bad. For if you could earn, say, 10 percent on a $10,000 investment, in 15 years you'd end up with an investment worth more than $42,000.

Exposure to Risk

Like any other type of investment vehicle, fixed-income securities should also be viewed in terms of their risk and return. Generally speaking, there are five major

■■■■
TABLE 8.1 Historical Annual Yields and Returns in the Bond Market: 1950–1991

(Yields and Returns Based on Performance of High-grade Corporate Bonds)

Year	Year-end Bond Yields[a]	Total Rates of Return[b]
1991	8.34%	19.91%
1990	9.50	6.86
1989	9.18	15.59
1988	9.81	10.70
1987	10.33	− 0.27
1986	9.02	19.85
1985	10.63	30.90
1984	12.05	16.39
1983	12.76	4.70
1982	11.55	43.80
1981	14.98	− 0.96
1980	13.15	− 2.62
1979	10.87	− 4.18
1978	9.32	− 0.07
1977	8.50	1.71
1976	8.14	18.65
1975	8.97	14.64
1974	8.89	− 3.06
1973	7.79	1.14
1972	7.41	7.26
1971	6.48	11.01
1970	6.85	18.37

[a]Year-end bond yields are for (S&P) AA-rated corporate (industrial and utility) bonds.

[b]Total return and average annual holding period return figures are fully compounded returns and are based on interest income as well as capital gains (or losses).

types of risks to which bonds are exposed: interest rate risk, purchasing power risk, business/financial risk, liquidity risks, and call risk.

- **Interest Rate Risk**—this is the No. 1 source of risk to fixed-income investors, as *it's the major cause of price volatility in the bond market*. In the case of bonds, interest rate risk translates into market risk: the behavior of interest rates, in general, affects all bonds and cuts across *all* sectors of the market— even the U.S. Treasury market. When market interest rates rise, bond prices fall, and vice verse. And as interest rates become more volatile, so do bond prices.

- **Purchasing Power Risk**—this is what you get when you have inflation! During periods of mild inflation, bonds do pretty well, as their returns tend to outstrip inflation rates. Purchasing power risk really heats up when inflation

Year	Year-end Bond Yields[a]	Total Rates of Return[b]
1969	7.83	− 8.09
1968	6.62	2.57
1967	6.30	− 4.95
1966	5.55	0.20
1965	4.79	− 0.46
1964	4.46	4.77
1963	4.46	2.19
1962	4.34	7.95
1961	4.56	4.82
1960	4.52	9.07
1959	4.68	− 0.97
1958	4.19	− 2.22
1957	4.07	8.71
1956	3.90	− 6.81
1955	3.24	0.48
1954	2.95	5.39
1953	3.20	3.41
1952	3.05	3.52
1951	3.07	− 2.69
1950	2.73	2.12

Source: Annual yields derived from Standard & Poor's *S&P Trade and Security Statistics;* total return figures from Ibbotson and Sinquefield, *Stocks, Bonds, Bills, and Inflation: Historical Returns (1926–1992).*

takes off the way it did in the late 1970s; when that happened, bond yields started to lag behind inflation rates. The reason: you have a fixed coupon rate on your bond, so even though market yields are rising with inflation, your return is locked in for the long haul.

- **Business/Financial Risk**—this is basically the risk that *the issuer will default on interest and/or principal payments*. Business/financial risk has to do with the quality and financial integrity of the issuer; the stronger the issuer, the less business/financial risk there is to worry about. This is a risk that doesn't even exist for some securities (U.S. Treasuries, for example), while for others (like corporate and municipal bonds), it's a very important consideration.
- **Liquidity Risk**—this is the risk that a bond will be difficult to unload if you ever have to, or want to, sell it. Actually, this is a major problem in certain sectors of the market—far bigger than a lot of investors realize. For even

TABLE 8.2 Holding Period Returns in the Bond Market: 1950–1991

Holding Periods	Average Annual Total Returns[b]	Cumulative Total Returns	Amount to Which a $10,000 Investment Will Grow Over Holding Period
5 yrs: 1987–91	10.33%	63.52%	$ 16,352
10 yrs: 1982–91	16.22	349.53	44,953
15 yrs: 1977–91	10.08	322.24	42,224
25 yrs: 1967–91	8.16	611.12	71,115
42 yrs: 1950–91	5.72	935.71	103,570

[a]Year-end bond yields are for (S&P) AA-rated corporate (industrial and utility) bonds.

[b]Total return and average annual holding period return figures are fully compounded returns and are based on interest income as well as capital gains (or losses).

Source: Annual yields derived from Standard & Poor's *S&P Trade and Security Statistics;* total return figures from Ibbotson and Sinquefield, *Stocks, Bonds, and Inflation: Historical Returns (1926–1992).*

though the U.S. bond market is enormous, the market is chiefly over-the-counter in nature and much of the activity occurs in the primary/new issue market. As such, with the exception of the Treasury market and a good deal of the agency market, there just isn't much trading done in the secondary markets, particularly with corporates and municipals.

• **Call Risk**—this is the risk that a bond will be "called" (i.e., retired) long before its scheduled maturity date. Issuers are often given the opportunity to prepay their bonds and they do so by calling them in for prepayment (we'll examine call features later in this chapter). When they do that, the bondholders end up getting cashed out of the deal and have to find another place for their investment funds. And therein lies the rub. Because bonds are nearly always called for prepayment after interest rates have taken a big fall, comparable investment vehicles just aren't available! Thus, the investor has to replace a high yielding bond with a much lower yielding issue. Being able to prepay a bond might be great for the issuer, but from the bondholder's perspective, a called bond means not only a disruption in the investor's cash flow, but also a sharply reduced rate of return (yield).

Essential Features of a Bond

A *bond* is a negotiable, long-term debt instrument that carries certain obligations (including the payment of interest and repayment of principal) on the part of the issuer. Bondholders, unlike the holders of common stock, have no ownership or equity position in the organization that issues the bond. Because bonds are debt and because, in a roundabout way, bondholders are only lending money to the issuer, they are not entitled to an ownership position or any of the rights and privileges that go along with it.

Bond Interest and Principal

Bond issues are viewed as fixed-income securities because, in the absence of any trading, an investor's return is limited to fixed interest and principal payments. In essence, bonds involve a fixed claim on the issuer's income (as defined by the size of the periodic interest payments) and a fixed claim on the assets of the issuer (equal to the repayment of principal). As a rule, bonds pay interest every six months. There are exceptions, however; some issues carry interest payment intervals as short as a month, and a few as long as a year. The amount of interest due is a function of the **coupon,** which defines the annual interest income that will be paid by the issuer to the bondholder. For instance, a $1,000 bond with an 8 percent coupon would pay $80 in interest annually—generally in the form of two $40 semiannual payments. The **principal** amount of a bond, also known as an issue's *par value,* specifies the amount of capital that must be repaid at maturity. For example, there is $1,000 of principal in a $1,000 bond.

To facilitate the marketing of bonds, the issues are broken into standard principal amounts, known as **denominations.** Of course, debt securities regularly trade at market prices that differ from their principal (or par) values. This occurs whenever an issue's coupon differs from the prevailing market rate of interest. That is, the price of the issue will change inversely with interest rates until its yield is compatible with the prevailing market yield. Such behavior explains why a 7 percent issue will carry a market price of only $825 in a 9 percent market. The drop in price from its par value of $1,000 is necessary to raise the yield on this bond from 7 to 9 percent—in essence, the new, higher yield is produced in part from annual coupons and in part from capital gains, as the price of the issue moves from $825 back to $1,000 at maturity.

Maturity Date

Unlike common stock, all debt securities have limited lives and expire on a given date, the issue's **maturity date.** Although a bond carries a series of specific interest payment dates, the principal is repaid only once: on or before maturity. Because the maturity date is fixed (and never changes), it not only defines the life of a new issue, but also denotes the amount of time remaining for older, outstanding bonds. Such a life span is known as an issue's *term to maturity.* A new issue may come out as a 25-year bond; 5 years later, it'll have only 20 years remaining to maturity.

Two types of bonds can be distinguished on the basis of maturity: term and serial issues. A **term bond** has a single, fairly lengthy maturity date and is the most common type of issue. A **serial bond,** in contrast, has a series of different maturity dates, perhaps as many as 15 or 20, within a single issue. For example, a 20-year term bond issued in 1992 would have a single maturity date of 2012, but that same issue as a serial bond might have 20 annual maturity dates that extend from 1993 through 2012. At each of these annual maturity dates, a certain portion of the issue would come due and be paid off.

Maturity is also used to distinguish a *note* from a *bond.* That is, a debt security that's originally issued with a maturity of 2 to 10 years is known as a **note,** whereas

---

coupon
the feature on a bond that defines the amount of annual interest income.

principal
on a bond, the amount of capital that must be paid at maturity.

denominations
standard principal amounts into which a bond issue is broken to facilitate its sale to the public.

maturity date
the date on which a bond matures and the principal must be repaid.

term bond
a bond that has a single, fairly lengthy maturity date.

serial bond
a bond that has a series of different maturity dates.

note
a debt security originally issued with a maturity of from 2 to 10 years.

a *bond* technically has an initial term to maturity of *more than 10 years*. In practice, notes are often issued with maturities of 5 to 7 years, whereas bonds will normally carry maturities of 20 to 30 years, or more.

Call Features—Let the Buyer Beware!

Consider the following situation: you've just made an investment in a great, high-yielding, 25-year bond. Now all you have to do is sit back and let the cash flow in, right? Well, perhaps. Certainly, that will happen for the first several years. But if market interest rates drop off, it's also very likely that you'll be hit with a notice from the issuer that the bond is being *called*. This means that the issue is being retired before its maturity date, and there's really nothing you can do but turn in the bond and invest your money elsewhere. How can this happen? Well, so long as the bond is *callable,* it can be prematurely retired. It's all perfectly legal because every bond is issued with a **call feature,** which stipulates whether or not, and under what conditions a bond can be called in for retirement prior to maturity. Basically, there are three types of call features:

call feature
feature that specifies whether, and under what conditions, the issuer can retire a bond prior to maturity.

1. A bond can be *freely callable,* which means that the issuer can prematurely retire the bond at any time.
2. It can be *noncallable,* meaning that the issuer is prohibited from retiring the bond prior to maturity.
3. The issue could carry a *deferred call,* which means that the issue cannot be called until after a certain length of time has passed from the date of issue. In essence, the issue is noncallable during the deferment period and then becomes freely callable.

Obviously, in our illustration above, the high-yielding bond was either freely callable or, at best, it carried a relatively short deferred call provision.

call premium
the amount added to a bond's par value and paid to investors when a bond is retired prematurely.

call price
the price the issuer must pay to retire a bond prematurely; equal to par value plus the call premium.

Call features are placed on bonds for the benefit of the issuers. They're used most often to replace an issue with one that carries a lower coupon; the issuer benefits by being able to realize a reduction in annual interest cost. Thus, when market interest rates undergo a sharp decline, as they did in 1982–1986 and again in 1991 and 1992, bond issuers will retire their high-yielding bonds (by calling them in) and replace them with lower-yielding obligations. *The net result is that the investor is left with a much lower rate of return than anticipated*.

In a half-hearted attempt to compensate investors who find their bonds called out from under them, a **call premium** is tacked onto a bond and paid to investors, along with the issue's par value, at the time the bond is called. The sum of the par value plus call premium represents the issue's **call price** and is the price the issuer must pay to retire the bond prematurely. As a general rule, call premiums usually equal about one year's interest at the earliest date of call, and then become systematically smaller as the issue nears maturity. Using this rule, the initial call price of a 9 percent bond would be around $1,090, with $90 representing the call premium. In addition to call features, some bonds may also carry **refunding provisions,** which are much like call features except they prohibit just one thing: the premature retire-

refunding provisions
provisions similar to a call feature except that they prohibit the premature retirement of an issue from the proceeds of a lower-coupon refunding bond.

sinking fund
a provision that stipulates the amount of principal that will be retired annually over the life of a bond.

senior bonds
secured debt obligations, backed by a legal claim on specific property of the issuer.

mortgage bonds
senior bonds secured by real estate.

collateral trust bonds
senior bonds backed by securities owned by the issuer but held in trust by a third party.

equipment trust certificates
senior bonds secured by specific pieces of equipment; popular with railroads, airlines, and other transportation companies.

first and refunding bonds
a bond that's secured in part with both first and second mortgages.

junior bonds
debt obligations backed only by the promise of the issuer to pay interest and principal on a timely basis.

debenture
an unsecured (junior) bond.

subordinated debentures
unsecured bonds that have a claim that's secondary to other debentures.

ment of an issue from the proceeds of a lower-coupon refunding bond. For example, a bond could come out as freely callable but *nonrefundable* for five years; in this case, the bond would probably be sold by brokers as a deferred refunding issue, with little or nothing said about its call feature. The distinction is important, however, since it means that a nonrefunding or deferred refunding issue *can still be called and prematurely retired for any reason other than refunding.* Thus, an investor could face a call on a high-yielding (nonrefundable) issue if the issuer has the cash to prematurely retire the bond.

Sinking Funds

Another provision that's important to investors is the **sinking fund,** which stipulates how a bond will be paid off over time. This provision, of course, applies only to term bonds, since serial issues already have a predetermined method of repayment. Not all (term) bonds have sinking fund requirements, but for those that do, a sinking fund specifies the annual repayment schedule that will be used to pay off the issue; it indicates how much principal will be retired each year. Sinking fund requirements generally begin one to five years after the date of issue and continue annually thereafter until all or most of the issue is paid off. Any amount not repaid by maturity (which might equal 10 to 25 percent of the issue) would then be retired with a single "balloon" payment. Unlike a call or refunding provision, there's generally no call premium with sinking fund calls; instead, bonds are normally called for sinking fund purposes at par.

Secured or Unsecured Debt

A single issuer may have many different bonds outstanding at any given point in time. In addition to coupon and maturity, one bond can be differentiated from another by the type of collateral behind the issue. Issues can be either junior or senior. **Senior bonds** are secured obligations, since they are backed by a legal claim on some specific property of the issuer. Such issues would include **mortgage bonds,** which are secured by real estate; **collateral trust bonds,** which are backed by financial assets owned by the issuer but held in trust by a third party; **equipment trust certificates,** which are secured by specific pieces of equipment (like boxcars and airplanes) and are popular with railroads and airlines; and **first and refunding bonds,** which are basically a *combination* of first mortgage and junior lien bonds (i.e., the bonds are secured in part by a first mortgage on some of the issuer's property and in part by second, or third, mortgages on other properties—these issues are *less secure* than, and should *not* be confused with, straight first-mortgage bonds).

Junior bonds, on the other hand, are backed by only the promise of the issuer to pay interest and principal on a timely basis. There are several classes of unsecured bonds, the most popular of which is known as a **debenture.** Figure 8.2 shows the announcement of a debenture bond that was issued in 1992. Note that even though there was no collateral backing up this obligation, the issuer—Coca-Cola—was able to sell $1.5 *billion* worth of these securities. In addition, **subordinated deben-**

This announcement is neither an offer to sell nor a solicitation of an offer to buy these securities.
The offer is made only by the Prospectus Supplement and the related Prospectus.

New Issues/February 10, 1992

$1,500,000,000

Coca-Cola Enterprises Inc.

$500,000,000

7⅞% Notes Due February 1, 2002

Price 100% and accrued interest, if any, from February 11, 1992

$250,000,000

8½% Debentures Due February 1, 2012

Price 100% and accrued interest, if any, from February 11, 1992

$750,000,000

8½% Debentures Due February 1, 2022

Price 98.83% and accrued interest, if any, from February 11, 1992

Copies of the Prospectus Supplement and the related Prospectus may be obtained
in any State in which this announcement is circulated only from such of the
undersigned as may legally offer these securities in such State.

Salomon Brothers Inc

The First Boston Corporation	**Goldman, Sachs & Co.**	**Lehman Brothers**
J.P. Morgan Securities Inc.	**Morgan Stanley & Co.** Incorporated	**PaineWebber Incorporated**
Allen & Company Incorporated	**Bear, Stearns & Co. Inc.**	**Citicorp Securities Markets, Inc.**
Donaldson, Lufkin & Jenrette Securities Corporation		**Kidder, Peabody & Co.** Incorporated
Prudential Securities Incorporated		**SBCI Swiss Bank Corporation** Investment banking
Smith Barney, Harris Upham & Co. Incorporated	**UBS Securities Inc.**	**Dean Witter Reynolds Inc.**

● FIGURE 8.2 Announcement of a New Corporate Bond Issue
This three-part, $1.5 billion bond was issued by Coca-Cola and is secured with nothing more than the good name of the company. The last of the three bonds will not mature until 2022, and in *each* of the first 10 years of the life of this three-part issue, the company will pay nearly $125 million in interest. Indeed, by the time the last bond matures, Coke will have paid over $2.7 billion in interest on this issue. (Source: *The Wall Street Journal,* February 10, 1992.)

tures are also used; these issues have a claim on income secondary to other debenture bonds. **Income bonds,** the most junior of all, are unsecured debts which require that interest be paid only after a certain amount of income is earned; there is
no legally binding requirement to meet interest payments on a timely or regular
basis so long as a specified amount of income has not been earned. These issues are
similar in many respects to *revenue bonds* found in the municipal market.

income bonds
unsecured bonds
that require that in-
terest be paid only
after a specified
amount of income is
earned.

Registered or Bearer Bonds

Regardless of the type of collateral or kind of issue, a bond may be either registered
or issued in bearer form. **Registered bonds** are issued to specific owners, whose
names are formally registered with the issuer. The issuer keeps a running account of
ownership and automatically pays interest to the owners of record by check. In
contrast, the holders, or possessors, of **bearer bonds** are considered to be their
owners, and the issuing organization keeps no official record of ownership. Interest
is received by "clipping coupons" and sending them in for payment. Bearer bonds
were, at one time, the most prevalent type of issue, but they are destined to become
obsolete, as Congress has mandated that, effective July 1983, all bonds must be
issued in registered form. This was done to prevent bondholders from cheating on
their taxes (that is, since there's no record of ownership with bearer bonds, some
people simply would not report the interest income they received on their tax returns).

registered bonds
bonds issued to
specific owners,
whose names are
formally registered
with the issuer.

bearer bonds
bonds whose hold-
ers are considered to
be their owners;
there is no official
record of ownership
kept by the issuer.

PRINCIPLES OF BOND PRICE BEHAVIOR

The price of a bond is a function of its coupon, maturity, and the movement of
market interest rates. When interest rates go down, bond prices go up, and vice
versa. The relationship of bond prices to market rates is captured in Figure 8.3.
Basically, the graph reinforces the *inverse* relationship between bond prices and
market interest rates: Note that *lower* rates lead to *higher* bond prices. Figure 8.3
also shows the difference between premium and discount bonds. A **premium bond**
is one that sells for more than its par value, which occurs whenever market interest
rates drop below the coupon rate on the bond. A **discount bond,** in contrast, sells
for less than par and is the result of market rates being greater than the issue's
coupon rate. Thus, the 10 percent bond in our illustration traded as a premium bond
when market rates were at 8 percent, but as a discount bond when rates stood at 12
percent.

premium bond
a bond that has a
market value in ex-
cess of par; occurs
when interest rates
drop below the
coupon rate.

discount bond
a bond with a mar-
ket value lower than
par; occurs when
market rates are
greater than the cou-
pon rate.

When a bond is first issued, it is usually sold to the public at a price that equals,
or is very close to, its par value. Likewise, when the bond matures—some 15, 20,
or 30 years later—it will once again be priced at its par value. But what happens to
the price of the bond in between is of considerable concern to most bond investors.
In this regard, we know that the extent to which bond prices move depends not only
on the *direction* of change in interest rates but also on the *magnitude* of such
changes; for the greater the moves in interest rates, the greater the swings in bond
prices. However, bond prices are far more complex than that, for bond price volatility will also vary according to the coupon and maturity of an issue. That is, bonds

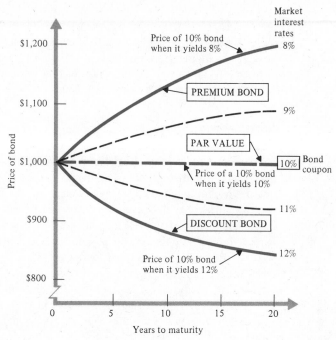

• FIGURE 8.3 Price Behavior of a Bond with a 10 Percent
                          Coupon

A bond will sell at its par value so long as the prevailing market interest rate remains the same as the bond's coupon (for example, when both coupon and market rates equal 10 percent). However, when market rates drop, bond prices rise; and as a bond approaches its maturity, the price of the issue will move toward its par value, *regardless* of the level of prevailing interest rates.

with lower coupons and/or longer maturities will respond more vigorously to changes in market rates and will therefore undergo sharper price swings. (Note in Figure 8.3 that for a given change in interest rates—for example, from 10 percent to 8 percent—the largest change in price occurs when the bond has the greatest number of years to maturity.) It should be obvious, therefore, that if a *decline* in interest rates is anticipated, an investor should seek lower coupons and longer maturities (since this would produce maximum amounts of capital gains). When interest rates move *up,* the investor should do just the opposite by seeking high coupons with short maturities; this will cause minimal price variation and act to preserve as much capital as possible.

Actually, of the two variables, the *maturity* of an issue has the bigger impact on price volatility. For example, look what happens to the price of an 8 percent bond when market interest rates rise by 1, 2, or 3 percentage points:

Bond Maturity	Change in the Price of an 8% Bond When Interest Rates Rise by:		
	1 Percentage Pt.	2 Percentage Pts.	3 Percentage Pts.
5 years	− 4.0%	− 7.7%	−12.5%
25 years	−10.9	−18.2	−33.7%

Clearly, the shorter (5-year) bond offers a lot more price stability. Such a behavioral trait is universal with all fixed-income securities. It is important because it means that if you want to reduce your exposure to capital loss or, more to the point, if you want to lower the amount of price volatility in your bond holdings, then just *shorten your maturities*.

THE MARKET FOR DEBT SECURITIES

Thus far, our discussion has dealt with basic bond features; we now shift our attention to a review of the market in which these securities are traded. The bond market is chiefly over-the-counter in nature, since listed bonds represent only a small portion of total outstanding obligations. In comparison to the stock market, the bond market is more price-stable. Granted, interest rates (and therefore bond prices) do move up and down and have become a bit volatile in recent times, but when bond price activity is measured on a daily basis, it is remarkably stable.

There are two things about the bond market that stand out—it's big and it has been growing at a rapid clip. From a $250 billion market in 1950, it has grown to the point where the amount of bonds outstanding in this country now (in early 1992) stands at some $5.3 *trillion*. That makes the bond market about 35 percent *bigger* than the U.S. stock market! Indeed, the bond market in this country has nearly quadrupled in the past 11 years. That's an incredible rate of growth and is just one indication of the extent to which America was hooked on debt during the decade of the 1980s.

Major Segments of the Market

There are issues available in today's bond market to meet almost any type of investment objective and to suit just about any investor. As a matter of convenience, the bond market is normally separated into four major segments, according to type of issuer: Treasury, agency, municipal, and corporate. As we will see below, each sector has developed its own issue and operating features, as well as trading characteristics.

Treasury Bonds

''Treasuries'' (or ''governments'' as they are sometimes called) are a dominant force in the fixed-income market, and if not the most popular type of bond, they certainly are the best known. The U.S. Treasury issues bonds, notes, and other types of debt securities (such as Treasury bills) as a way of meeting the ever-increasing needs of our federal government. All Treasury obligations are of the highest quality because they are backed by the full faith and credit of the U.S. government. This feature, along with their liquidity, makes them very popular with individual and institutional investors, both here and abroad. Indeed, the market for U.S. Treasury securities is the biggest and most active in the world. *Every day,* more than $100 billion worth of Treasury bonds change hands, as these securities are traded in all the major markets of the world, from New York to London to Tokyo. That's half a *trillion* dollars in bond trades every week. To put that number into perspective, in an average week, the NYSE trades only about $25 billion worth of stock. **Treasury notes** carry maturities of 2 to 10 years, whereas **Treasury bonds** have maturities of more than 10 years and up to 30 years. Treasury notes and bonds are sold in $1,000 denominations (except 2- to 3-year notes, which are sold in $5,000 minimums). Interest income is subject to normal federal income tax, but *is exempt from state and local taxes*.

The Treasury issues its notes and bonds at regularly scheduled auctions, the results of which are widely reported by the financial media (see Figure 8.4). It's through this auction process that the Treasury establishes the initial yields and coupons on the securities it issues. All government notes and bonds today are issued as *noncallable* securities. In fact, the last time the U.S. Treasury issued callable bonds was in 1984; up until then, most Treasury bonds carried long-term call deferments, where the bonds were not callable until the last five years of the life of the issue. There are about 20 deferred call Treasuries still outstanding, but they're easy to pick out since the deferred call features are a specific part of the bond listing

Treasury notes debt securities issued by the U.S. Treasury which are issued with maturities of 10 years or less.

Treasury bonds U.S. Treasury debt securities which are issued with maturities of more than 10 years—usually 20 years or more.

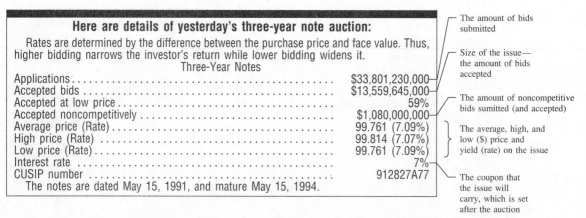

• FIGURE 8.4 The Reported Results of a Recent Treasury Note Auction

Treasury auctions are closely followed by the financial media; here, the results of a 3-year Treasury note auction are reported. These auctions are highly competitive; the amount of bids submitted generally far exceeds the size of the issue and as a result, the spread between the highest and lowest bid is quite small: here it amounts to just 2 basis points, or 2/100 of 1% (7.09% to 7.07%). (Source: *The Wall Street Journal.*)

system. For example, the 10 percent issue of 2005–10 signifies that this Treasury bond has a maturity date of 2010 and a deferred call feature that extends through 2005.

Agency Bonds

Agency bonds
debt securities issued by various agencies and organizations of the U.S. government, like the Tennessee Valley Authority.

Agency bonds are debt securities issued by various agencies and organizations of the U.S. government—like the Resolution Trust Corp., Federal Farm Credit Banks, and the Government National Mortgage Association. They are *not* obligations of the U.S. Treasury and, technically, should not be considered the same as a Treasury bond. An important feature of agency bonds is that they customarily provide yields that are comfortably above the market rates for Treasuries; as such, they offer investors a way to increase returns with little or no real difference in risk.

There are two types of agency issues: government-sponsored and federal agencies. Although there are only six government-sponsored organizations, the number of federal agencies exceeds two dozen. To overcome some of the problems in the marketing of many relatively small federal agency securities, Congress established the Federal Financing Bank to consolidate the financing activities of all federal agencies. (As a rule, the generic term "agency" is used to denote both government-sponsored and federal agency obligations.)

Selected characteristics of some of the more popular agency bonds are presented in Table 8.3. Most of the government agencies that exist today were created to support either agriculture or housing, which is pretty obvious from the list of issuers in Table 8.8. Although these issues are not direct liabilities of the U.S. government, a few of them actually do carry government guarantees and therefore effectively represent the full faith and credit of the U.S. Treasury. But even those issues that don't carry such guarantees are still highly regarded in the marketplace, since they're all viewed as *moral obligations* of the U.S. government—meaning that it's highly unlikely that Congress would ever allow one to default. Also, like Treasury securities, agency issues are normally noncallable or carry lengthy call deferment features. One final point: Since 1986 *all new agency (and Treasury) securities* have been issued in *book entry* form. This means that there is no certificate of ownership issued to the buyer of the bonds; rather, the buyer receives a "confirmation" of the transaction and then his or her name is entered on a computerized log book, where it remains as long as the security is owned. Many experts believe that in the not-too-distant future all security transactions will be handled in this way.

Municipal Bonds

municipal bonds
debt securities issued by states, counties, cities, and other political subdivisions, like school districts; most of these bonds are tax-exempt, meaning there's no federal income tax on interest income.

Municipal bonds are the issues of states, counties, cities, and other political subdivisions, such as school districts and water and sewer districts. This is an $850 billion market and it's the only segment of the bond market that's dominated by individual investors: about two-thirds of all municipal bonds are held by individuals. (There are few tax incentives for institutional investors to hold these securities.) These bonds are often issued as serial obligations, meaning that the issue is broken into a series of smaller bonds, each with its own maturity date and coupon. Munici-

TABLE 8.3 Characteristics of Popular Agency Issues

Type of Issue	Minimum Denomination	Initial Maturity	Tax Status* Federal	State	Local
Federal Farm Credit Banks	$ 1,000	13 months to 15 years	T	E	E
Federal Intermediate Credit Banks	5,000	9 months to 4 years	T	E	E
Federal Home Loan Bank	10,000	1 to 20 years	T	E	E
Federal Land Banks	1,000	1 to 10 years	T	E	E
Farmers Home Administration	25,000	1 to 25 years	T	T	T
Federal Housing Administration	50,000	1 to 40 years	T	T	T
Federal Home Loan Mortgage Corp.** ("Freddie Macs")	25,000	18 to 30 years	T	T	T
Federal National Mortgage Association** ("Fannie Maes")	25,000	1 to 30 years	T	T	T
Government National Mortgage Association** (GNMA— "Ginnie Maes")	25,000	12 to 40 years	T	T	T
Student Loan Marketing Association	10,000	3 to 10 years	T	E	E
Tennessee Valley Authority (TVA)	1,000	5 to 25 years	T	E	E
U.S. Postal Service	10,000	25 years	T	E	E
Federal Financing Bank	1,000	1 to 20 years	T	E	E

*T = taxable; E = tax-exempt

**Mortgage-backed securities.

general obligation bonds
municipal bonds backed by the full faith and credit, and taxing power, of the issuer.

revenue bonds
municipal bonds backed by the revenue-generating capacity of the issuer; requires that principal and interest be paid only if a sufficient level of revenue is generated.

pal bonds ("munis") are brought to the market as either general obligation or revenue bonds. **General obligation bonds** are backed by the full faith, credit, and taxing power of the issuer. **Revenue bonds,** in contrast, are serviced by the income generated from specific income-producing projects (for example, toll roads). Although general obligations dominated the municipal market prior to the mid-1970s, the vast majority of munis today come out as revenue bonds (accounting for about 65 to 70 percent of the new-issue volume).

The distinction between a general obligation and a revenue bond is an important one, since the issuer of a revenue bond is obligated to pay principal and interest *only if a sufficient level of revenue is generated*. (If the funds aren't there, the issuer does *not* have to make payment on the bond!) This is not the case with general obligation bonds, however. These issues are required to be serviced in a prompt and timely fashion irrespective of the level of tax income generated by the municipality. For reasons that should be fairly obvious, revenue bonds involve a lot more risk than general obligations, and because of that, they provide higher yields. Regardless of the type, municipal bonds are customarily issued in $5,000 denominations. Figure 8.5 shows a typical municipal bond issue and illustrates many of the characteristics customarily found with such obligations, including the serial nature of these issues.

This announcement appears as a matter of record only.

New Issue   Book-Entry Form Only

$142,895,000

CALIFORNIA EDUCATIONAL FACILITIES AUTHORITY
Revenue Bonds (Stanford University) Series J

Dated: December 15, 1991   Due: November 1, as shown below

The Bonds are limited obligations of the Authority payable only out of Revenues as defined in the Indenture and other amounts held in certain funds established by the Indenture. The Bonds are payable from funds to be paid by

STANFORD UNIVERSITY

The Bonds are issued for the purpose of refinancing all or a portion of certain outstanding debt of the Authority used for the acquisition, construction and completion of certain educational facilities for the benefit of the University.

PRINCIPAL AMOUNTS, MATURITIES, INTEREST RATES AND PRICES OR YIELDS

$50,090,000 Serial Bonds

Principal Amount	Maturity	Interest Rate	Price or Yield	Principal Amount	Maturity	Interest Rate	Yield
$ 970,000	1996	4.90 %	100 %	$5,590,000	2001	5.60 %	5.70 %
2,340,000	1997	5.10	100	5,940,000	2002	5.70	5.80
4,710,000	1998	5.30	100	6,315,000	2003	5.90	5.95
5,105,000	1999	5.40	5.45	6,505,000	2004	5.90	6.05
5,475,000	2000	5 1/2	5.60	7,140,000	2005	6	6.15

$33,205,000 6 % Term Bonds, due November 1, 2009 @ 95 1/2 %
$59,600,000 6 % Term Bonds, due November 1, 2016 @ 94 %

(plus accrued interest)

PRAGER, MCCARTHY & SEALY
Goldman, Sachs & Co.
Smith Barney, Harris Upham & Co. Inc.
Charles A. Bell Securities Corp.
M.R. Beal & Company
Smith, Mitchell & Associates, Inc.

December 19, 1991

• FIGURE 8.5 The Announcement for a New Municipal Bond Issue

This issue is a $142 million revenue bond that matures serially. Note that about 35 percent of the issue is retired annually from 1996 through 2005, and the balance (of about $93 million) is due in two large balloon payments some 18 to 25 years after the date of issue. Also note that, as is customary with municipal bonds, the coupon ("interest rate") increases with maturity. (Source: *The Wall Street Journal,* January 8, 1992.)

municipal bond guarantees
guarantees from a party other than the issuer that principal and interest payments will be made in a prompt and timely manner.

A somewhat unusual aspect of municipal bonds is the widespread use of **municipal bond guarantees.** These guarantees provide the bondholder with the assurance of a party other than the issuer that principal and interest payments will be made in a prompt and timely manner. As a result, bond quality is improved. The third party, in essence, provides an additional source of collateral in the form of insurance placed on the bond, at the date of issue, which is nonrevocable over the life of the obligation. Several states and four private organizations provide municipal bond guarantees. The four private insurers are the Municipal Bond Investors Assurance Corp. (MBIA), the American Municipal Bond Assurance Corporation (AMBAC), Financial Guaranty Insurance Co. (FGIC), and Financial Security Assurance, Inc. (FSA). All four of these private guarantors will insure any general obligation or revenue bond as long as it carries an S&P rating of triple-B or better. Municipal bond insurance results in higher ratings (usually triple-A) and improved liquidity, as these bonds are generally more actively traded in the secondary markets. About 30 percent of all municipal bonds issued today are insured. They're especially common in the revenue market and, as such, put a whole new light on these issues. That is, whereas an uninsured revenue bond lacks certainty of payment, a guaranteed issue is very much like a general obligation bond in that you know principal and interest payments will be made on time.

Without a doubt, the thing that makes municipal securities unique is the fact that in most cases, their interest income is immune from federal income taxes, which is why these issues are known as tax-free, or tax-exempt, bonds. Note, however, that in contrast to interest income, *capital gains on municipal bonds are subject to the usual federal taxes*. Normally, the obligations are also exempt from state and local taxes *in the state in which they were issued*. For example, a California issue would be free of California tax if the bondholder lived in California, but its interest income would be subject to state tax if the investor resided in Arizona.

Individual investors are the biggest buyers of municipal bonds, and tax-free yield is certainly a major draw. To put this yield in perspective, Table 8.4 shows what a taxable bond would have to yield to equal the net yield of a tax-free bond. *It demonstrates how the yield attractiveness of municipals varies with an investor's income level*. Clearly, the higher the individual's tax bracket, the more attractive municipal bonds become. Generally speaking, an investor has to be in one of the higher federal tax brackets (i.e., 28 or 31 percent) before municipal bonds offer yields that are competitive with fully taxable issues. This is because municipal yields are substantially lower than the returns available from fully taxable issues (such as corporates), and unless the *tax effect* is sufficient to raise the yield on a municipal to a figure that equals or surpasses taxable rates, it obviously doesn't make much sense to buy municipal bonds.

We can determine the kind of return a fully taxable bond would have to provide

TABLE 8.4 Taxable Equivalent Yields for Various Tax-Exempt Returns

Taxable Income*			Tax-Free Yield							
Joint Returns ($000)	Individual Returns ($000)	Federal Tax Bracket	5%	6%	7%	8%	9%	10%	12%	14%
$ 0–$35.8	$ 0–$21.4	15%	5.88	7.06	8.24	9.41	10.59	11.76	14.12	16.47
$35.8–$86.5	$21.4–$51.9	28	6.94	8.33	9.72	11.11	12.50	13.89	16.67	19.44
$86.5 and above	$51.9 and above	31	7.25	8.70	10.15	11.59	13.04	14.49	17.39	20.29

*Taxable income and federal tax rates effective January 1, 1992.

in order to match the after-tax return of a lower-yielding, tax-free issue by computing what is known as a municipal's **taxable equivalent yield.** This measure can be calculated according to the following simple formula:

Equation 8.1

$$\text{Taxable equivalent yield} = \frac{\text{yield of municipal bond}}{1 - \text{federal tax rate}}$$

taxable equivalent yield
the return a fully taxable bond would have to provide to match the after-tax return of a lower-yielding, tax-free municipal bond.

For example, if a certain municipal offered a yield of 6.5 percent, then an individual in the 31 percent tax bracket would have to find a fully taxable bond with a yield of 9.42 percent—i.e., 6.5%/.69 = 9.42%—in order to reap the same after-tax returns as the municipal.

Note, however, that Equation 8.1 considers *federal taxes only*. As a result, the computed taxable equivalent yield would apply only to states that have no state income tax, or to situations where you're comparing a municipal bond to a Treasury (or agency) bond—where *both* the Treasury and municipal bonds are free from state income tax. Under either of these conditions, the only tax that's relevant is federal income tax, and as such, use of Equation 8.1 is appropriate. But what if the investor is comparing an in-state bond to, say, a corporate bond? In this case, the in-state bond would be free from both federal and state taxes, whereas the corporate bond would not. As a result, Equation 8.1 could not be used. Instead, the investor should use an equivalent yield formula that considers *both* federal and state income taxes:

Equation 8.2

$$\begin{matrix}\text{Taxable equivalent yield} \\ \text{for both} \\ \text{federal \& state taxes}\end{matrix} = \frac{\text{municipal bond yield}}{1 - [\text{federal tax rate} + \text{state tax rate} (1 - \text{federal tax rate})]}$$

When both federal and state taxes are included in the calculations, the net effect is to *increase* the taxable equivalent yield. Of course, the size of the increase depends on the level of state income taxes; in a high tax state like California, for example, the impact can be quite substantial. Return to the 6.5 percent municipal bond introduced above: If a California resident in the maximum federal and state tax brackets (of 31 and 11 percent, respectively) were considering this corporate issue, she would have to get a yield of 10.59 percent on the corporate in order to match the 6.5 percent yield on the California bond:

$$\begin{matrix}\text{Taxable equivalent yield} \\ \text{for both} \\ \text{federal \& state taxes}\end{matrix} = \frac{6.5}{1 - [.31 + .11 (1 - .31)]} = \frac{6.5}{1 - [.31 + .076]} = \underline{\underline{10.59\%}}$$

This compares to a taxable equivalent yield of 9.42% when only federal taxes were included in the calculation. That's a difference of more than one full percentage point, certainly *not* an insignificant amount.

A word of caution regarding the tax-exempt status of municipal bonds: *Not all municipal bonds are exempt from federal income tax.* One of the provisions of the tax reform bill of 1986 was to restrict the types of bonds that qualify as tax-exempt issues. Specifically, if the bonds are used to finance projects considered "nonessential," the interest on such obligations is *not* tax exempt. Thus, a whole new breed of municipal bonds was created. Known as **taxable munis,** these issues are expected to eventually account for perhaps 20 to 25 percent of the municipal bond market. As

taxable munis
municipal bonds, used to finance projects considered non-essential, whose interest income is fully taxable by the federal government.

the name implies, the interest income on these bonds is *fully taxable* as far as federal income taxes are concerned. The after-tax yields of taxable municipals generally do *not* measure up to those on tax-free munies, but taxables do have some redeeming qualities of their own. For one thing, these issues offer yields that are considerably higher than those from Treasury bonds. Furthermore, taxable munies are usually *noncallable,* thereby allowing investors to lock in the high yields for a number of years.

Corporate Bonds

The major nongovernmental issuers of bonds are corporations. The market for *corporate bonds* is customarily subdivided into four segments: industrials (the most diverse of the groups), public utilities (the dominant group in terms of volume of new issues), rail and transportation bonds, and financial issues (banks, finance companies, and so forth). Not only is there a full range of bond quality available in the corporate market, but there's also a wide assortment of different types of bonds, ranging from first mortgage obligations to convertible bonds (which we'll examine in Chapter 10), debentures, subordinated debentures, senior subordinated issues, capital notes (a type of unsecured debt issued by banks and other financial institutions), and income bonds. Interest on corporate bonds is paid semiannually, and sinking funds are fairly common. The bonds usually come in $1,000 denominations and are issued on a term basis with a single maturity date. Maturities usually range from 25 to 40 years, and many corporates, especially the longer ones, carry call deferment provisions that prohibit prepayment for the first 5 to 10 years. Corporate issues are popular with individuals because of their relatively attractive yields.

Although most corporates fit the general description above, one that does not is the *equipment trust certificate,* which is a type of security issued by railroads, airlines, and other transportation concerns. The proceeds from equipment trust certificates are used to purchase equipment, such as jumbo jets and railroad engines, which in turn serve as the collateral for the issue. They are usually issued in *serial form* and carry uniform annual installments throughout. These bonds normally carry maturities that range from 1 year to a maximum that seldom exceeds 15 to 17 years. An attractive feature of equipment trust certificates is that in spite of a near-perfect payment record that dates back to predepression days, these issues offer above average yields to investors.

Specialty Issues

In addition to the basic bond vehicles described above, investors can also choose from a number of *specialty issues*—bonds that possess unusual issue characteristics. For the most part, these bonds have coupon or repayment provisions that are out-of-the-ordinary. Most are issued by corporations, although they are being used increasingly by other issuers as well. Probably the oldest type of specialty issue is the **variable-rate note.** First issued in this country in 1974, it has two unique features: (1) after the first 6 to 18 months of an issue's life, the coupon "floats" so that every 6 to 12 months it is pegged at a certain amount above prevailing Treasury

variable-rate note a specialty bond issue with two unique features: (1) after a specified period of time, the coupon "floats" at a certain amount above T-bill or T-note rates, and (2) every year or so the notes are redeemable at par, at the bondholder's option.

bill or Treasury note rates, and (2) every year or so, the notes are redeemable at par and at the *bondholder's* option. Thus, variable-rate notes represent long-term commitments on the part of borrowers (they're usually issued with 15- to 25-year maturities), yet they provide investors with all the advantages (especially price stability) of short-term obligations.

put bond
a type of specialty bond that gives the holder the right to redeem the bond at certain specified times before maturity.

extendable notes
a specialty issue, typically with short maturities (3–5 years), which can be redeemed or renewed for the same period at a new interest rate.

Another specialty issue, similar in some respects to a variable-rate note, is the **put bond.** Such an issue gives the holder the right to redeem the bonds before they mature—usually, 3 to 5 years after the date of issue, and then every 1 to 5 years thereafter. In return for the right to periodically ''put the bond'' for redemption, the investor receives a lower yield (which is usually fixed for the life of the issue). There are also **extendable notes,** which are actually short-term securities, typically with 3- to 5-year maturities, which can be redeemed or renewed for the same period at a new interest rate. For example, an issue might come out as a series of 3-year renewable notes, over a period of 15 years; every 3 years those notes are extendable for another 3 years, but at a new yield (coupon) comparable to the market interest rates that prevail at the time of renewal.

Three of the more actively traded specialty issues today are zero-coupon bonds, mortgage-backed securities (including CMOs, collateralized mortgage obligations), and high-yield junk bonds. A couple of these—including zero coupon bonds and mortgage-backed securities—rank as some of the more popular bonds on Wall Street. Let's now take a closer look at each of these specialty issues.

Zero-Coupon Bonds

zero-coupon bonds
a bond with no coupons that's sold at a deep discount from par value.

As the name implies, **zero-coupon bonds** have no coupons. Rather, these securities are sold at a deep discount from their par values, and then increase in value over time at a compound rate of return so that at maturity, they are worth much more than their initial investment. Other things being equal, the cheaper the bond, the greater the return you can earn: for example, whereas a 7 percent bond might cost $360, an issue with a 15 percent yield will cost only $123. Because they don't have coupons, these bonds do not pay interest semiannually; in fact they pay *nothing* to the investor until the issue matures. As strange as it might seem, this is the main attraction of zero-coupon bonds; that is, since there are no interest payments, investors do not have to worry about reinvesting coupon income twice a year. Instead, the fully compounded rate of return on a zero-coupon bond is virtually guaranteed at the stated rate that existed when the issue was purchased. For example, in early 1992, U.S. Treasury zero-coupon bonds with 20-year maturities were available at yields of around 8¼ percent; thus, for just $175 you could buy a bond that would be worth nearly six times that amount, or $1,000, at maturity in 20 years. Best of all, you would be *locking in* an 8¼ percent compound rate of return on your investment for the full 20-year life of the issue.

The foregoing advantages notwithstanding, there are also some serious disadvantages to zeros. One is that if rates do move up over time, you won't be able to participate in the higher return (since you'll have no coupon income to reinvest). In addition, zero-coupon bonds are subject to tremendous price volatility; thus, if market rates climb, you'll experience a sizable capital loss as the prices of zero-coupons plunge! (Of course, if interest rates *drop,* you'll reap enormous capital gains if you hold long-term zeros; indeed, such issues are unsurpassed in capital gains potential.) Finally, the IRS has ruled that zero-coupon bondholders must report interest as it is accrued, even though no interest is actually received. For this reason, most fully taxable zero-coupon bonds should either be used in tax-sheltered investments, like individual retirement accounts (IRAs), or be held by minor children, who are 14 or older and likely to be taxed the lowest rate, if at all.

Zeros are issued by corporations, municipalities, and federal agencies; you can even buy U.S. Treasury notes and bonds in the form of zero-coupon securities. Up until about 8 or 10 years ago, major brokerage houses used to package U.S. Treasury securities as zeros and sell them to the investing public in the form of investment trusts. These unit trusts were marketed under such names as TIGRS, CATS, and LIONS and became enormously popular with investors. Seeing this, the Treasury decided to eliminate the middleman and "issue" its own form of zero-coupon bond, known as **Treasury STRIPS,** or **STRIP-T's,** for short. When that happened, the market for CATS and other "felines" pretty much dried up; there are some old issues still available, but the new issue market for these securities has virtually disappeared.

> **Treasury STRIPS (STRIP-T's)**
> Zero-coupon bonds issued by the U.S. Treasury.

Actually, the Treasury does *not* issue zero-coupon bonds but, instead, *allows government securities dealers to take regular coupon-bearing notes and bonds in stripped form,* which can then be sold to the public as zero-coupon securities. Essentially, the coupons are *stripped* from the bond, repackaged, and then sold separately as zero-coupon bonds. For example, a 20-year Treasury bond has 40 semiannual coupon payments, plus one principal payment; each of these 41 cash flows can be repackaged and sold as 41 different zero-coupon securities, with maturities that range from 6 months to 20 years. Because they sell at such large discounts, Treasury STRIPS are often sold in minimum denominations (par values) of $10,000—but with their big discounts, that means you probably will pay only $1,700 or $1,800 for $10,000 worth of 20-year STRIP-T's, depending on their yields. There's an active secondary market for Treasury-STRIPS, so investors can get in and out of these securities, with ease, just about anytime they want. STRIP-T's offer the maximum in issue quality, a full array of different maturities, and an active secondary market—all of which goes to explain why these securities dominate the zero-coupon market today.

Mortgage-Backed Securities

> **mortgage-backed bond**
> a debt issue secured by a pool of home mortgages; issued primarily by federal agencies.

Simply put, a **mortgage-backed bond** is a debt issue that is secured by a pool of residential mortgages. An issuer, such as the Government National Mortgage Association (GNMA), puts together a pool of home mortgages and then issues securities in the amount of the total mortgage pool. These securities, known as *pass-through securities,* or *participation certificates,* are usually sold in minimum denominations of $25,000. Though their maturities can go out as far as 30 years, the average life of one of these issues is generally much shorter (perhaps as short as 8 to 10 years), because so many pooled mortgages are paid off early. (Technically, the *average life* of a mortgage-backed security (MBS) is the weighted-average time to full principal repayment. It does *not* mean the bond will be fully paid off in that period of time; indeed, only about half of the bond will have been paid off by the time it reaches its average life, so it will still have a number of years to go before it's fully retired.) As an investor in one of these securities, you hold an undivided interest in the pool of mortgages. Thus, when a homeowner makes a monthly mortgage payment, that payment is essentially passed through to you, the bondholder, to pay off the mortgage-backed bond that you hold. Although these securities come with normal coupons, the interest is paid monthly rather than semiannually. Actually, the monthly payments received by bondholders are, like mortgage payments, made up of *both* principal and interest. Since the principal portion of the payment represents return of capital, it is considered tax-free. Not so with interest income, however, which is subject to ordinary state and federal income taxes.

Mortgage-backed securities are issued primarily by three federal agencies. Although there are some state and private issuers—mainly big banks and S&Ls—agency issues dominate the market and account for 90 to 95 percent of the activity. The major agency issuers of mortgage-backed securities (MBSs) are:

- **Government National Mortgage Association (GNMA)**—known as "Ginnie Mae," the oldest and largest issuer of MBSs.
- **Federal Home Loan Mortgage Corporation (FHLMC)**—known as "Freddie Mac," was the first to issue pools containing conventional mortgages. Stock in FHLMC is publicly owned and traded on the NYSE.
- **Federal National Mortgage Association (FNMA)**—known as "Fannie Mae," it's the newest agency player and is the leader in the marketing of seasoned/older mortgages. Its stock also is publicly owned and traded on the NYSE.

One of the problems with mortgage-backed securities is that they are *self-liquidating,* since a portion of the monthly cash flow to the investor is the principal originally invested in the issue. Thus, the investor is always receiving back part of the original investment capital, so that at maturity there is *no* big principal payment that will be received. (Instead, the principal has been paid back in little chunks over the life of the bond.) Indeed, some uninformed investors are shocked to find there's

collateralized mortgage obligation (CMO)
a type of mortgage-backed bond whose holders are divided into classes based on the length of investment desired; then, principal is channeled to short-term investors first, intermediate-term investors next, and long-term investors last.

nothing (or very little) left of their original capital. To counter this problem, a number of *mutual funds* were formed that invest in mortgage-backed securities *but* which automatically and continually reinvest the capital/principal portion of the cash flows. Mutual fund investors, therefore, receive only the interest from their investments and as such, are able to preserve their capital.

Loan prepayments are another problem with mortgage-backed securities. In fact, it was in part an effort to defuse some of the prepayment uncertainty in standard mortgage-backed securities that led to the creation of **collateralized mortgage obligations,** or **CMOs.** Normally, as pooled mortgages are prepaid, *all* bondholders receive a prorated share of the prepayments, and as a result the net effect is to sharply reduce the life of the bond. A CMO, in contrast, divides investors into classes (formally called "tranches," which is French for "slice"), depending on whether they want a short-term, intermediate-term, or long-term investment. Now, while interest is paid to all bond-holders, *all principal payments* go first to the shortest class, until it is fully retired; then, the next class (tranche) in the sequence becomes the sole recipient of principal, and so on until the last tranche is retired. Thus in a CMO, only one class of bond at a time receives principal. Actually, most MBSs today are sold to the public as CMOs—or as REMICs (*Real Estate Mortgage Investment Conduits*), which are like CMOs except for some differences in the tax treatment accorded the issuers.

CMOs, in a sense, are *derivative* securities created from traditional mortgage-backed bonds, which are placed in a trust; participation in this trust is then sold to the investing public in the form of CMOs. The net effect of this transformation is that CMOs look and behave very much like any other bond: they offer predictable (monthly) interest payments and have predictable maturities. Unfortunately, while they carry the same triple-A ratings and implicit U.S. government backing as the mortgage-backed bonds that underlie them, CMOs represent a quantum leap in complexity. Some types of CMOs can be as simple and safe as Treasury bonds, but others can be far more volatile, and risky, than the standard MBS they're made from. That's because when putting CMOs together, Wall Street performs the financial equivalent of gene splicing: investment bankers isolate the interest and principal payments from the underlying MBSs and then rechannel them to a number of different tranches. It's not issue quality or risk of default that's the problem here, but rather prepayment, or call, risk—all the bonds will be paid off, it's just a matter of when. Different types of CMO tranches have different levels of prepayment risk. Since the overall risk in a CMO cannot exceed that of the underlying mortgage-backed bonds, it follows that in order to have some CMO tranches with very little (or no) prepayment risk, others have to endure a lot more. The net effect is that while some CMO tranches—like **PAC's** (*Planned Amortization Class* CMO's) or **Sequential Payers**—are low in risk, others—like "Inverse Floaters," "IO's/PO's," and "Z-bonds"—are extremely volatile.

Generally speaking (with the exception of those highly-volatile CMO tranches), MBSs are a safe form of investment, and they offer highly competitive, attractive returns. What's more, there's a well-developed after-market, so it's relatively easy to buy and sell these bonds in the open market. However, these are long-term debt securities and, like any long-term bond, they are subject to wide price swings when interest rates shoot up or down. Just because they're secured with a pool of mortgages doesn't make them immune to price volatility. These securities have been a big hit in the market: they have been enthusiastically received by institutional investors—and more recently, by individual investors as well.

asset-backed securities (ABS)
a type of security that's backed by a pool of bank loans, leases, and other assets; most ABS are backed by auto loans and credit cards—these issues are very similar to mortgage-backed securities.

The widespread acceptance of mortgage-backed securities and CMO's quickly led to the development of a new market technology—that is, the process of *securitization*, whereby various types of bank lending vehicles are transformed into marketable securities, much like a mortgage-backed security. Investment bankers are now selling billions of dollars worth of pass-through securities, known as **asset-backed securities** (or **ABS,** for short) which are backed by pools of auto loans, credit card bills, loans on mobile homes and recreational vehicles—even pools of home-equity loans. For example, GMAC, the financing arm of General Motors, is a regular issuer of collateralized auto loan securities; in a similar fashion, Master-Card and Visa receivables are regularly used as collateral on credit-card-backed securities. These obligations are just like mortgage-backed securities, except they have much shorter maturities (generally only about 3 to 5 years) and they're backed by a pool of auto loans or credit card receivables, rather than home mortgages. While ABS's are secured by everything from revolving lines of credit to equipment leases, the two principal types of collateral backing these securities are *car loans* and *credit card receivables;* together, these two types of securities account for about 85–90 percent of all ABS's.

Junk Bonds

junk bonds
high risk securities that have received low ratings and as such, produce high yields, so long as they don't go into default.

PIK-bond
a payment-in-kind junk bond, which makes some of the annual interest payments in new bonds rather than in cash.

Junk bonds, or "high-yield bonds" as they're also called, are highly speculative securities that have received low, sub–investment-grade, ratings (e.g., Ba or B) from such organizations as Moody's and Standard & Poor's. These bonds are issued primarily by corporations, and increasingly, by municipalities as well. Junk bonds generally take the form of *subordinated debentures*, meaning the debt is unsecured and has a very low claim on assets. These bonds are called "junk" because of the high risk of loss associated with them—they use excessive amounts of debt in their capital structures and their ability to service that debt is subject to a considerable amount of doubt. In other words, there's a high risk of default with these bonds. Probably the most unusual type of junk bond is something called a **PIK-bond.** The "PIK" stands for Payment In Kind, and means that rather than paying the bond's coupon in cash, annual interest payments can be made in the form of additional debt. This "financial printing press" usually goes on for five or six years, after which time the issuer is supposed to start making interest payments in real money.

Traditionally, the term *junk bond* was applied to the issues of *troubled companies;* these securities might have been well rated when first issued, only to slide to low ratings through corporate mismanagement, heavy competition, or other factors. That all changed during the past decade, as the vast majority of junk bonds originated *not* with troubled companies but with a growing number of mature (fairly well-known) firms that used *enormous* amounts of debt to finance takeovers and buy-outs. These companies would change overnight from investment-grade firms to junk as they piled on debt to finance a takeover—or the threat of one. (Wall Street refers to these firms as "Fallen Angels.")

Junk bonds were the hottest things on Wall Street through much of the 1980s. They provided the fuel that drove corporate takeovers and leveraged buyouts and by 1989 accounted for more than 20 percent of outstanding corporate debt. All that came to a screeching halt in early 1990 as the junk bond market and the main purveyors of junk bonds—Michael Milken and the brokerage firm of Drexel Burnham Lambert—came tumbling down. Many investors have found out first hand how much risk there is in junk bonds, as fully one-quarter of all junk bonds defaulted during the three-year period from 1989 through 1991. In dollar terms, that's over $50 *billion* worth of junk bonds that went under. As we can see in the accompanying *Investor Insights* box, the 1990s brought a new attitude about debt: whereas

INVESTOR INSIGHTS

The Drive to Dump Debt

Equity, largely ignored during the debt-driven '80s, is now in the driver's seat. In 1991, for the first time in eight years, the balance sheets of nonfinancial corporations ended the year with more equity relative to debt than they had when the year started. Most economists view this shift as healthy, for as new equity is used to retire debt, interest costs are reduced, operating restrictions are loosened, and credit-rating agencies cast a more favorable eye. Just as important, the retirement of debt may set the stage for a meaningful economic rebound as it frees up cash for companies to spend and puts them in position for another round of financing that can be plowed directly into capital spending.

Fueling this equity surge are some of the hard-learned lessons of the 1980s. During that time, few corporations could resist the allure of debt. Tax laws allowed deductions for interest payments but not for dividends. In addition, with debt, shareholders did not have to suffer dilution as they did through stock offerings. As the 1980s began, the typical broadly owned American corporation suffered from an agency problem. At the helm were not owners, but hired managers with a minuscule stake in the company. They were prone to squander surplus cash flow on perks and ill-conceived acquisitions that bolstered revenues and the case for high compensation at the top. Corporate raiders were the good guys who shook up this elite. Even when companies were forced into leveraged buyouts, or LBOs, to avoid takeover, the experience had its good side. LBOs chopped overhead, salaried employees, and capital expenditures. The mere appearance of raiders inspired a tighter financial regime at many companies that stayed independent.

If the tale had ended in mid-decade, the verdict on the decade might have been more favorable. But a kind of San Andreas fault separated the comparatively sane, often constructive, earlier half of the decade from the bizarre later years when most of the deals were done. New takeover ammunition changed everything. The new ammo: junk bonds, which originally were not used for hostile takeovers. But in 1984, Michael Milken, of Drexel Burnham Lambert, grabbed corporate America's attention with multibillion-dollar blind pools ready to be used for takeovers. Money from Drexel and from Wall Street imitators who crowded in, drove takeover prices beyond what could be justified by a company's earnings. By the mid-80s, it was not unusual for reasonably well-run billion-dollar companies to find themselves besieged by comparatively unknown speculators. Despite unproven management skills and an interest mainly in self-enrichment, these investors were able to line up enough financing for a credible threat. Often, the threat of a hostile takeover left managers little choice but to pile on debt in order to buy back stock if they were determined to remain independent.

The slice of corporate America that can tolerate a heavy debt burden is relatively

debt was "in" during the 1980s, it definitely is "out" in the 1990s, as companies are aggressively trying to "deleverage" themselves.

So, why would any rational investor be drawn to junk bonds? The answer is simple: they offer very high yields. Indeed, in a typical market, relative to investment-grade bonds, investors can expect to pick up anywhere from 2.5 to 5 percentage points in added yield. In early 1992, for example, investors were getting 11½ to small. Many companies were unable to handle the resulting debt. "Funny paper" devised to postpone interest expenses, such as deferred-interest bonds and payment-in-kind junk bonds (which pay interest in securities instead of money) softened the blow in the early years but gave no relief from tough repayment schedules demanded by banks, the senior lenders in the deals. The increasingly overpriced deals might still have worked out had the companies lived up to the promise of LBOs: that the discipline of huge debt forces managers to operate at undreamed-of efficiency. But by the late 1980s, it became clear that the hoped-for managerial miracle simply was not going to materialize. As a result, debt became a four-letter word that nobody wanted anything to do with.

Debt's fall from grace makes it an unattractive vehicle for future financing and is driving companies to dump what debt they've got. Junk bonds, creating perhaps the loudest thud in the fall, have lost their charm. And bankers have increasingly kept their wallets closed. In 1989, federal bank regulators started pressuring commercial banks to stop lending to companies whose bonds had fallen below investment grade because their balance sheets showed high debt-to-equity ratios. The result is that debt-to-equity ratios are improving as companies are shedding debt and generally *deleveraging* their balance sheets. The most common strategy for deleveraging seems to be a combination of maneuvers: unload some assets if you can, retire pricey old bonds by floating some new ones at a lower rate, and issue new equity. In 1991, companies trying to rebalance the scales *raised $61.1 billion in equity and unloaded $11.2 billion in debt.* RJR Nabisco, the biggest LBO ever done at $25 billion, is among those now dumping debt. The company, which had a debt-to-equity ratio as high as 25-to-1 at the time of the LBO in 1989, is considered a classic case of corporate deleveraging. Asset sales of $5.5 billion, a cash infusion from controlling shareholder Kohlberg Kravis Roberts, and proceeds from a series of huge common and preferred stock issues pushed RJR Nabisco's total debt down to $14 billion by December 1991. Acknowledging RJR's deleveraging drive, both Moody's Investors Service and Standard & Poor's elevated RJR bonds to the nonjunk elite in late 1991, the first time since the mammoth LBO.

But deleveraging can go only so far. The equity that vanished from balance sheets in the '80s may take quite a while to replace. Indeed, to restore equity to its former level, companies would have to keep issuing new stock at the record pace they set in 1991 *for the next 17 years!* No matter how hard they try to banish the ghosts of '80s excess, plenty of companies will be haunted by costly old liabilities for a long time to come.

Source: Adapted from Fred R. Bleakley, "A Decade of Debt Is Now Giving Way to the Age of Equity," *The Wall Street Journal,* December 16, 1991, p. A1; Edmund Faltermayer, "The Deal Decade: Verdict on the '80s," *Fortune,* August 26, 1991, pp. 58–70; and Anne B. Fisher, "The Big Drive to Reduce Debt," *Fortune,* February 10, 1992, pp. 118–24.

13 percent yields on junk bonds compared to 8½ to 9 percent on investment-grade corporates. Obviously, *such yields are available only because of the correspondingly higher exposure to risk.* But as we saw earlier in this chapter, there's more to bond returns than yield alone. The fact is, if it were just a matter of yield, the investment decision would be easy—pick the bonds with the high yields. But the *returns* you end up with don't always correspond to the *yields* you went in with.

That was particularly true with junk bonds during the decade of the '80s. Although the promised yields always looked attractively high, actual returns were another matter: the average annual return over the 10 years from 1980 through 1989 on junk bonds amounted to less than 10 percent—far under their promised yields and considerably less than the nearly 12 percent return generated by investment-grade corporate bonds!

Fortunately, the junk bond market has started to settle down and in 1991, the annual return to junk bond investors amounted to around 30 percent. Much of this improvement was due to the *less risky* end of the junk market—that is, to the performance of the stronger companies that have been able to maintain a decent cash flow and to replace their expensive debt with less expensive debt, or even equity capital. The junk bond market today has evolved into a two-tiered market made up of "good junk" and "bad junk." The good junk is made up of the less risky issues that are likely to survive, restructure, and avoid default. These are the higher rated (BB/BB+) issues, like RJR Nabisco and FMC Corp. They may not offer super-high yields, but that's because they're less likely to default. The bad junk, in contrast, are those bonds rated B and CCC that may find it very difficult to avoid default. Whether they're good junk or bad junk, these securities should be used only by investors who are thoroughly familiar with the risks involved and, equally important, who are comfortable with such risk exposure.

A Global View of the Market

Just like stocks, globalization has also hit the bond market, and investors—those who are taking advantage of it, anyway—are loving it. Foreign bonds are catching on with American investors because of their high yields and attractive returns. Indeed, as more and more of these securities find their way to the portfolios of U.S. investors, some market observers feel that foreign bonds will be to the '90s what junk bonds were to the '80s. There are risks, of course, but high risk of default (which is so prevalent with junk bonds) is *not* one of them. Instead, the big risk with foreign bonds has to do with currency exchange rates and the impact that currency fluctuations can have on returns in U.S. dollars.

By year-end 1990, the size (total value) of the world bond market reached approximately $12 trillion. This market is dominated by just eight countries, which together account for more than 90 percent of all bonds outstanding:

Country	Approximate Size of Market
U.S.	$5.3 trillion
Japan	2.2 trillion
Germany	1.1 trillion
Italy	800 billion
France	650 billion
U.K./Britain	400 billion
Canada	360 billion
Belgium	300 billion

While the U.S. today accounts for just under half of the available fixed-income securities, that percentage is sure to decline in the future as foreign markets continue to expand. Therefore, by investing solely in the U.S. fixed income markets, an investor is not only excluding half of the investment possibilities worldwide, but more importantly, the faster growing half. Not only that, but as Table 8.5 reveals, U.S. bond investors are missing out on some pretty attractive returns (here, the reported results are *total returns in U.S. dollars* and include coupon income, capital gains, or losses, and the effects of changes in currency exchange rates). In fact, over the 15-year period from 1977 through 1991, the U.S. market provided the highest annual return only once (in 1982), and generally, the returns in this country simply don't stack up very well to those available in other markets. A lot of this is due, of course, to the impact of currency exchange rates, but still, the fact remains that from an international perspective, better returns to U.S. investors are usually available to those willing to go off-shore.

U.S.-Pay versus Foreign-Pay Bonds

There are several different ways to invest in foreign bonds (*excluding* foreign bond mutual funds, which we'll examine in Chapter 13). From the perspective of a U.S. investor, foreign bonds can be divided into two broad categories on the basis of the currency in which the bond is denominated: *U.S.-pay* (or dollar-denominated) bonds and *foreign-pay* (or non-dollar-denominated) bonds. All the cash flows—including purchase price, maturity value, and coupon income—from dollar-denominated foreign bonds are in U.S. dollars, whereas the cash flows from non-dollar bonds are designated in a foreign currency or in a basket of foreign currencies, such as the European Currency Unit (ECU).

There are two types of dollar-denominated foreign bonds: Yankee bonds and Eurodollar bonds. **Yankee bonds** are issued by foreign governments or corporations or by so-called *supranational* agencies, like the World Bank and the Inter-American Bank. These bonds are issued and traded in the United States, they're registered with the SEC, and all transactions are in U.S. dollars. Buying a Yankee bond, then, is really no different from buying any other U.S. bond: these bonds are traded on U.S. exchanges and our OTC market, everything's in dollars, and there's no currency exchange risk to deal with. The bonds are generally very high in quality (which is not surprising given the quality of the issuers) and offer highly competitive yields to investors. **Eurodollar bonds,** in contrast, are issued and traded outside the U.S. They are demonimated in U.S. dollars, but they are *not* registered with the SEC, which means underwriters are legally prohibited from selling *new issues* to the U.S. public. (Only "seasoned" Eurodollar issues can be sold in this country.) The Eurodollar market today is dominated by foreign-based investors (though that is changing) and is primarily aimed at institutional investors.

From the standpoint of U.S. investors, foreign-pay international bonds encompass all those issues denominated in some currency other than dollars. These bonds are issued and traded overseas and are not registered with the SEC. Examples are the German bonds issued by German firms or the German government, which are payable in deutsche-marks, the Japanese bonds issued in yen, and so forth. When

Yankee bonds
bonds issued by foreign governments or corporations but denominated in dollars and registered with the SEC.

Eurodollar bonds
foreign bonds denominated in dollars but not registered with the SEC, thus restricting sales of new issues.

TABLE 8.5 Comparative Annual Returns in the World's Major Bond Markets

ANNUAL TOTAL RETURNS (IN U.S. DOLLARS)

	Australia	Belgium	Canada	France	Germany	Italy	Japan	Switzerland	U.K.	U.S. (Rank)*
1991	22.1%	12.8%	21.3%	15.4%	10.1%	22.0%	22.3%	3.0%	14.2%	19.9%(5th)
1990	17.7	24.3	5.3	18.8	12.5	22.2	6.3	20.3	28.0	6.9(8th)
1989	24.7	2.7	18.3	10.5	2.9	2.4	-17.3	-9.0	-6.2	15.6(3rd)
1988	33.6	-10.8	20.1	4.7	-8.7	0.5	1.7	-13.2	6.9	10.7(3rd)
1987	29.4	38.0	9.0	22.2	29.9	14.2	39.5	34.3	52.9	-0.3(10th)
1986	20.2	52.4	16.9	42.4	40.4	88.6	41.9	37.5	10.0	19.8(8th)
1985	-13.2	55.5	15.9	53.1	41.8	37.5	36.8	33.1	38.6	30.9(8th)
1984	4.9	0.7	8.7	6.6	1.4	21.9	2.3	-13.3	-12.4	16.4(2nd)
1983	0.5	0.8	8.6	-0.4	-7.7	15.1	12.3	-6.7	8.1	4.7(5th)
1982	15.0	-1.4	34.0	5.3	16.5	11.5	3.6	3.6	28.8	43.8(1st)
1981	-7.1	-12.7	1.1	-18.8	-8.8	-25.0	8.4	-1.7	-18.8	-0.9(3rd)
1980	-1.9	-8.9	1.9	-11.0	-10.3	-11.8	24.0	-11.2	31.2	-2.6(4th)
1979	-5.7	-2.6	1.4	-6.4	1.3	11.2	-23.7	-2.5	11.9	-4.2(7th)
1978	17.4	22.0	-4.7	33.9	16.5	25.1	32.2	35.9	3.3	-0.1(9th)
1977	26.2	26.1	-1.6	15.5	33.9	12.8	49.5	34.2	70.8	1.7(9th)
AVERAGE ANNUAL RETURNS OVER EXTENDED HOLDING PERIODS										
5 yrs: 1977–81	4.9%	3.6%	-0.1%	0.9%	5.3%	0.7%	15.2%	9.2%	16.0%	-1.2(10th)
1982–86	4.8	18.8	16.5	19.5	16.8	32.3	18.2	8.9	13.2	22.4(2nd)
1987–91	25.4	12.1	14.6	14.2	8.6	11.9	8.8	5.6	17.5	10.3(7th)
10 yrs: 1982–91	14.6	15.4	15.5	16.8	12.6	21.7	13.4	7.3	15.3	16.2(3rd)
15 yrs: 1977–91	11.3	11.3	10.0	11.2	10.1	14.2	14.0	7.9	15.6	10.1(7th)

Note: Total Return = Coupon Income + Capital Gain (or Loss) + Profit (or Loss) From Changes in Currency Exchange Rates.

*Parenthetical "Rank" shows how U.S. returns rank among the listed major markets—e.g., in 1991, U.S. ranked 5th out of the 10 markets listed in the table.

Source: International returns obtained from Ibbotson Associates and Templeton International; U.S. returns from Ibbotson and Sinquefield.

we speak of foreign bonds, it's this segment of the market that most investors are thinking of. *These bonds are subject to changes in currency exchange rates* which, in turn, can dramatically affect total returns to U.S. investors. Knowledgeable investors find foreign-pay bonds attractive because of their superior returns and the positive diversification effects they have on bond portfolios. Because the U.S. is the only country with a well-developed, actively traded corporate bond market, *the foreign-pay markets are dominated by foreign government issues*—it's estimated that about 80 percent, or more, of the non-dollar-denominated market is made up of foreign government bonds.

TRADING BONDS

Due in large part to the perceived safety and stability of bonds, many investors—particularly individual investors—view bond investing as a relatively simple process. Such thinking often leads to unsatisfactory results, even losses. The fact is that not all bonds are alike, and picking the right security for the time is just as important for bond investors as it is for stock investors. Indeed, success in the bond market demands a thorough understanding not only of the different types of bond vehicles, but of the many technical factors that drive bond yields, prices, and returns—things like call features, refunding provisions, and the impact that coupon and maturity have on bond price volatility. And because bond ratings are so important to a smooth running bond market, investors should also become thoroughly familiar with them. Let's now take a look at these ratings, as well as the quotation system used with bonds.

Bond Ratings

bond ratings
letter grades that designate investment quality, assigned to a bond issue on the basis of extensive financial analysis.

Bond ratings are like grades; a letter grade is assigned to a bond issue on the basis of extensive, professionally conducted, financial analysis that designates its investment quality. Ratings are widely used and are an important part of the municipal and corporate markets, where issues are regularly evaluated and rated by one or more of the rating agencies. Even some agency issues, like the Tennessee Valley Authority (TVA), are rated, although they always receive ratings that confirm the obvious—that the issues are prime grade. The two largest and best-known rating agencies are Moody's and Standard & Poor's; two other lesser-known, but still important, bond rating agencies are Fitch Investors Service and Duff & Phelps.

How Ratings Work

Every time a large new issue comes to the market, it is analyzed by a staff of professional bond analysts to determine default risk exposure and investment quality. (A fee that usually ranges from $1,000 to $15,000 is charged for rating each corporate bond and is paid by the issuer or the underwriter of the securities being rated.) The financial records of the issuing organization are thoroughly worked over and its future prospects assessed. Although the specifics of the actual credit analysis conducted by the rating agencies change with each issue, several major factors enter into most bond ratings. With a corporate issue, for example, these factors would include an analysis of the issue's indenture provisions, an in-depth study of the firm's earning power (including the stability of its earnings), a look at the company's liquidity and how it is managed, a study of the company's relative debt burden, and an in-depth exploration of its coverage ratios to determine how well it can service both existing debt and any new bonds that are being contemplated or proposed. As you might expect, the financial strength and stability of the firm is very important in determining the appropriate bond rating. Indeed, while there is far more to setting a rating than cranking out a few financial ratios, a strong relationship nevertheless does exist between the operating results and financial condition of the firm and the rating its bonds receive. Generally, the higher ratings are associated with the more profitable companies that rely *less* on debt as a form of financing, are more liquid and have stronger cash flows, and which have no trouble servicing their debt in a prompt and timely fashion.

Table 8.6 lists the various ratings assigned to bonds by each of the two major services. In addition to the standard rating categories noted in the table, Moody's

TABLE 8.6 Bond Ratings

Moody's	S&P	Definition
Aaa	AAA	*High-grade investment bonds.* The highest rating assigned, denoting extremely strong capacity to pay principal and interest. Often called "gilt edge" securities.
Aa	AA	*High-grade investment bonds.* High quality by all standards, but rated lower primarily because the margins of protection are not quite as strong.
A	A	*Medium-grade investment bonds.* Many favorable investment attributes, but elements may be present which suggest susceptibility to adverse economic changes.
Baa	BBB	*Medium-grade investment bonds.* Adequate capacity to pay principal and interest but possibly lacking certain protective elements against adverse economic conditions.
Ba	BB	*Speculative issues.* Only moderate protection of principal and interest in varied economic times. (This is one of the ratings carried by *junk bonds*.)
B	B	*Speculative issues.* Generally lacking desirable characteristics of investment bonds. Assurance of principal and interest may be small; this is another *junk bond* rating.
Caa	CCC	*Default.* Poor-quality issues that may be in default or in danger of default.
Ca	CC	*Default.* Highly speculative issues, often in default or possessing other market shortcomings.
C		*Default.* These issues may be regarded as extremely poor in investment quality.
	C	*Default.* Rating given to income bonds on which no interest is paid.
	D	*Default.* Issues actually in default, with principal or interest in arrears.

Source: Moody's *Bond Record* and Standard & Poor's *Bond Guide.*

uses numerical modifiers (1, 2, or 3) on bonds rated double A to B, and S&P uses plus (+) or minus (−) signs on the same rating classes to show relative standing within a major rating category. For example, an A+ (or A1) means a strong, high A rating, but an A− (or A3) indicates the issue is on the low end of the scale. Except for slight variations in designations (Aaa vs. AAA), the meanings and interpretations are basically the same. Note that the top four ratings (Aaa through Baa, or AAA through BBB) designate *investment-grade* bonds. Such ratings are highly coveted by issuers, since they indicate financially strong, well-run companies. The next two ratings (Ba/B, or BB/B) are reserved for *junk* bonds. These ratings mean that while the principal and interest payments on the bonds are still being met in a prompt and timely fashion, the *risk* of default is relatively high, as the issuers generally lack the financial strength found with investment-grade issues. (Sometimes the Caa1/CCC+ category will be counted as part of the junk category, although technically the C rating class is meant to designate bonds that are already in default, or getting very close to it.) Most of the time, Moody's and S&P assign identical ratings. Sometimes, however, an issue will carry two different ratings.

split ratings
different ratings given to a bond issue by the two major rating agencies.

These are known as **split ratings** and are viewed simply as ''shading'' the quality of an issue one way or another. For example, an issue might be Aa rated by Moody's, but A or A+ by S&P.

Also, just because a bond is given a certain rating at the time of issue doesn't mean it will keep that rating for the rest of its life. Ratings will change as the financial condition of the issuer changes. In fact, all rated issues are reviewed on a regular basis to ensure that the assigned rating is still valid. While many issues will carry a single rating to maturity, it is not uncommon for some ratings to be revised up or down during the life of the issue. As you might expect, the market responds to rating revisions by adjusting bond yields accordingly. For example, an upward revision (from, say, A to AA) will cause the market yield on the bond to drop, as a reflection of the bond's improved quality. Finally, although it may appear that the firm is receiving the rating, it is actually the *issue* that receives it. As a result, a firm can have different ratings assigned to different issues: the senior securities, for example, might carry one rating and the junior issues another, lower rating.

What Ratings Mean

Most bond investors pay careful attention to agency ratings since they can affect not only potential market behavior, but comparative market yields as well. Specifically, the higher the rating, the lower the yield of an obligation, other things being equal. Thus, whereas an A-rated bond might offer a 10 percent yield, a comparable triple-A issue would probably yield something like 9½ percent. Furthermore, investment-grade securities are far more interest-sensitive and tend to exhibit more uniform price behavior than junk bonds and other lower-rated issues. Bond ratings serve to relieve individual investors from the drudgery of evaluating the investment quality of an issue on their own. Large institutional investors often have their own staff of credit analysts who independently assess the creditworthiness of various corporate and municipal issuers; individual investors, in contrast, have very little if anything to gain from conducting their own credit analysis. After all, the credit analysis process is time-consuming, costly, and involves a good deal more expertise than the

███ **I N V E S T O R   I N S I G H T S** ███

Trading in the Dark: Real Bond Prices Are Hard to Come By

When market vibrations cause investors to worry about how their favorite stocks are holding up, all they have to do is check the closing prices in the business section of their newspaper. For those whose portfolios include fixed-income securities, however, particularly corporate or municipal bonds, keeping track isn't so simple. A scan of the financial pages produces little information on general bond market activity and even less on that of particular securities. Indeed, daily price quotes are widely available on only a handful of the hundreds of thousands of publicly traded corporate and muni bonds.

How come? One of the reasons is that bonds are overwhelmingly traded over the counter, and lack centralized exchanges. Bond people, noting that the institutions dominate the market for bonds, where buying a 100-share lot of securities with a face value of $1,000 each is outside the financial reach of most individual investors, imply that because they are presumably sophisticated the megabucks investors can always gain access to whatever information they need. And, they argue, an individual who wants a price quote or wishes to trade a bond can usually do so through his broker.

All of which is true as far as it goes. However, these apologists ignore a number of pertinent facts about the bond market and the motivations of its participants. While the price an individual gets through his broker for a corporate or municipal bond might reflect the current market, it likely is also influenced by how many of those bonds the brokerage has in its inventory and whether the firm regularly makes a market in the security. Those with an account at only one brokerage firm, which is the case with most individual investors, lack the means to confirm that the price they are quoted is the best one available to them. And while it is true that individuals generally don't trade the $1 million or larger lots of bonds that institutions routinely swap, the bond market has failed to adopt some of the most basic characteristics of equity markets, where the smallest of individuals' transactions take place side-by-side with large institutional trades.

---

average individual investor possesses. Most important, the ratings are closely adhered to by a large segment of the bond investment community, in large part because it's been shown that the rating agencies themselves do a remarkably good job of assessing bond quality. Thus, individual investors can depend on assigned agency ratings as a viable measure of the creditworthiness of the issuer and an issue's risk of default. A word of caution is in order, however: Bear in mind that bond ratings are intended as a measure of an issue's *default risk* only, all of which has no bearing whatsoever on an issue's exposure to *market risk*. Thus, if interest rates increase, even the highest-quality issues can (and will) go down in price, subjecting investors to capital loss and market risk.

Reading the Quotes

One thing you quickly learn in the bond market is that transactions are not always as easy to conduct as they may seem. In the first place, many bonds have relatively

Perhaps most significantly, the current framework motivates those with the information to keep it from those who don't have it. Because most bonds are traded over the counter, virtually every transaction takes place through a dealer, a firm that makes a market in a particular bond. The dealer, as middleman, makes a profit by buying from the seller at one price and selling to the buyer at a higher one. And therein lies the problem—for obviously, it's in the dealer's best interest to keep the playing field uneven by controlling the flow of information.

The fact is, the OTC market for most bonds is vastly different than that for stocks. There exists no unified system such as Nasdaq, through which quotes are posted and available to all market makers. Nor, as in the Nasdaq set-up, must a market maker in bonds post a verifiable price. Often a firm will find itself making a market simply because a customer has a large order he wishes to execute. The dilemma for individual investors is obvious. To determine where the market for a given bond is, an individual's broker usually cannot simply obtain a quote through one of the usual services. While several specialized outfits offer information on prices of the most active bonds, the broker usually must call his firm's bond trading desk to obtain that information. If the bond isn't one of that day's most active issues, the trader might have to call several other market makers to get the best available price. Of the three major bond markets—government (i.e., treasuries and agencies), corporate, and municipal—information is most widely available on prices of government securities. However, individuals wishing to buy or sell government bonds probably won't be able to trade at the prices quoted in the paper, because those prices are based on transactions of $1 million or more.

But for all its faults, when compared to publicly available information in the corporate and municipal bond markets, the government bond arena looks like the Library of Congress. In the corporate and muni markets, there are some services that offer trading data and prices on select bonds; however, quotes on the vast majority of issues simply aren't attainable. Thus, in these markets, individual investors truly are "trading in the dark!"

Source: Adapted from Edward A. Wyatt, "Trading in the Dark," *Barron's,* November 6, 1989, pp. 15, 43, 46, 47.

"thin" markets, meaning there's not a lot of trading being done. That is, some issues may trade only five or ten bonds a week, and many may have no secondary market at all. There are, of course, numerous high-volume issues, but even so, particularly close attention should be paid to an issue's trading volume—especially if an investor is looking for lots of price action and needs prompt order executions. In addition, there is the problem of the lack of market information: As the accompanying *Investor Insights* box reveals, it's not always easy to obtain current information on bond prices and other market developments. Finally, investors often have to look to both brokers and bankers to complete transactions. This is so because most brokerage houses tend to confine their activities to new issues and to secondary market transactions of listed Treasury obligations, agency issues, and corporate bonds; commercial banks, in contrast, are still the major dealers in municipal bonds and are active in Treasury and agency securities as well.

Except for municipal issues (which are usually quoted in terms of the yield they offer), all other bonds are quoted on the basis of their dollar prices. Such quotes are always interpreted as a *percent of par;* thus a quote of 97½ does not mean $97.50, but instead that the issue is trading at 97.5 percent of the par value of the obligation. In the bond market, it's assumed we're dealing with bonds that have par values of $1,000—or some multiple thereof. Accordingly, a quote of 97½ translates into a dollar price of $975. (In bond quotes, 1 point = $10, and ⅛ of a point = $1.25.) As can be seen in the bond quotes in Figure 8.6, there is one quotation system for corporate bonds and another for governments. (Treasuries and agencies are quoted the same.)

To understand the system used with corporate bonds, look at the Alabama Power (AlaP) issue in Figure 8.6. The group of numbers immediately following the abbreviated company name gives the coupon and the year in which the bond matures; the "10⅞ 05" means that this particular bond carries a 10⅞ percent annual coupon and will mature sometime in the year 2005. The next column, labeled "Curr Yld," provides the *current yield* being offered by the issue at its *current market price.* (Current yield is a measure of the amount of annual interest income a bond provides relative to its prevailing market price and is found by dividing annual coupon income by the closing price of the issue. In many respects, it is equivalent to the dividend yield measure used with stocks.) The "Vol" column shows the actual *number* of bonds traded—in this case, there were 20 bonds traded on the day of the quotes. The last two columns provide the bond's closing price for the day and the net change in the closing price. Note that corporate bonds are usually quoted in eighths of a point (106⅜). In contrast, government bonds (Treasuries and agencies) are listed in thirty-seconds of a point. With governments, the figures to the right of the colon (:) indicate the number of thirty-seconds in the fractional bid or ask price. For example, look at the bid price of the 10¾ percent Treasury issue; observe that it's being quoted at 122:29 (bid). Translated, that means the bond's being quoted at 122²⁹/₃₂, or 122.906 percent of par. Thus, an investor who wants to buy, say, $15,000 worth of this issue can expect to pay $18,436 (i.e., $15,000 × 1.22906). If the investor only has $15,000 to invest, he or she can buy only 12 of these bonds (since each bond is trading at $1,229, the number of bonds that can be purchased is $15,000 ÷ $1,229 = 12.2 bonds).

Treasury (and agency) bond quotes include not only the coupon (see the "rate" column of the Treasury quotes), but also the year and *month* of maturity. Note also when there's more than one date in the maturity column (see, for example, the 13⅞% Treasury bond, which shows a maturity of 2006-11), it's the *second* figure that indicates the issue's maturity date; the first one reveals when the bond becomes freely callable. Thus, the 13⅞ percent bond matures in May 2011, and carries a call deferment provision that extends through May 2006. In contrast, whenever a Treasury note or bond carries a single maturity date, such as the 10¾ percent bond of August 2005, it means that the issue is *non-callable.* Unlike corporates, these bonds are quoted in bid/ask terms, where the *bid* price signifies what the bond dealers are willing to pay for the securities (which is how much you can *sell* them for), and the *ask* price is what the dealers will sell the bonds for (which is what you have to pay to *buy* them). Finally, note that the "Yld" column with Treasuries is *not* the current yield of the issue, but instead, it's the bond's *promised yield-to-maturity,* which is

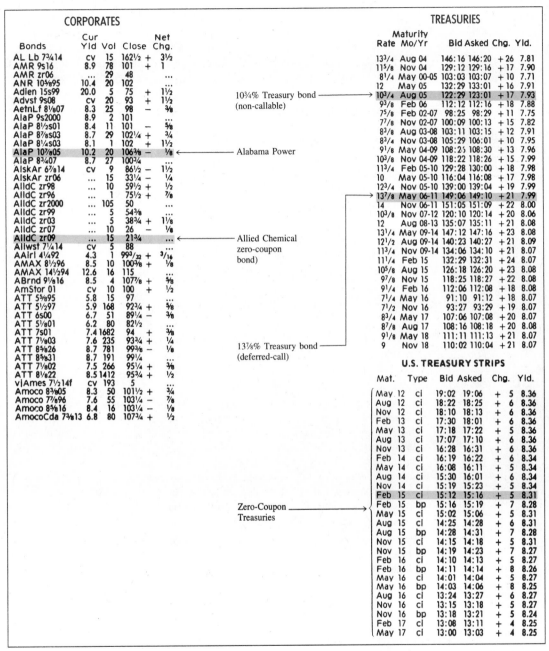

- **FIGURE 8.6** Price Quotations of Corporate and Government Bonds
While both corporate and Treasury bonds are quoted as a percent of their par values, note that corporate bonds are quoted in eighths of a point, whereas Treasuries are quoted in 32's. Also observe that both coupon and maturity play vital roles in the quotation system. (Source: *The Wall Street Journal,* March 18, 1992.)

basically a fully compounded measure of return that captures both current income and capital gains, or losses. (We'll examine yield-to maturity in Chapter 9.)

Also highlighted in both the corporate and Treasury quotes are some zero-coupon bonds. Look at Allied Chemical ("AlldC") in the corporate column; it has a number of zero-coupon bonds outstanding. Such bonds are identified by a "zr" in place of their coupons. For instance, with the Allied bonds, the "zr09" means that the issue is a zero-coupon bond that matures in 2009. Zeros are even easier to pick out in the Treasury quotes, as they're all listed under the heading *U.S. Treasury Strips*. As we discussed earlier in this chapter, the Treasury basically creates these securities by "stripping" the coupons from their bond issues and selling them separately from the principal. By doing so, the principal and interest *cash flows* can be sold on their own. (Look at the STRIPS quotes: a small "ci" behind the maturity date means the issue is made up of coupon/interest cash flow, whereas a small "bp" means it is made up of bond principal.) Regardless of whether they're corporates or stripped Treasuries, the prices of most zeros are quite low compared to regular coupon bonds; this is particularly true with longer maturities. Thus, the quoted price of 21¾ for the Allied Chemical issue is *not* a misprint; rather it means that you could buy this bond for $217.50 (21.75% of par) and in the year 2009 receive $1,000 in return. Likewise, you could buy the February-15 stripped Treasury for just $155.00 (15¹⁶/₃₂% of par) and in 2015 receive a payment of $1,000 on your investment.

SUMMARY

1. Bonds are publicly traded debt securities that provide investors with two types of income: (1) current income, and (2) capital gains. Current income, of course, is derived from the coupon (interest) payments received over the life of the issue, whereas capital gains can be earned whenever market interest rates fall. Investor interest in bonds has increased substantially in recent years as higher and more volatile interest rates have attracted both income- and capital-gains-oriented investors to the bond market. In addition to their yields and returns, bonds can also be used to shelter income from taxes, and for the preservation and long-term accumulation of capital.

2. All bonds carry some type of a coupon, which specifies the annual rate of interest to be paid by the issuer; most bonds carry coupon rates that remain fixed for the life of the issue. In addition, bonds have predetermined maturity dates—some bonds will carry a single maturity date (as is the case with term bonds), while others have a series of maturity dates (as in a serial issue).

   Every bond is issued with some type of call feature, be it freely callable, noncallable, or deferred callable; basically, call features spell out whether or not an issue can be prematurely retired, and if so, when. Some bonds will (temporarily) prohibit the issuer from paying off one bond with the proceeds from another by including a refunding provision, and others will be issued with sinking fund provisions, which actually specify how a bond will be paid off over time.

   The price behavior of a bond depends on the issue's coupon and maturity and on the movement in market interest rates. When interest rates go down, bond prices go up, and vice versa. However, the extent to which bond prices move up or down depends on the coupon and maturity of an issue. Bonds with lower coupons and/or longer maturities generate larger price swings.

3. Due to their senior position, bonds are relatively secure investments and are usually viewed as relatively default-free securities. There is price risk, however, as even the highest grade bonds will fall in price when interest rates begin to move up; in effect, since the provisions of a bond are fixed at the time of issue, changes in market conditions will cause the price of the bond to change.

4. Basically, the bond market is divided into four major segments: treasuries; agencies; municipals; and corporates. Treasury (or government) bonds are issued by the U.S. Treasury and are considered to be virtually default-free. Agency bonds are issued by various political subdivisions of the U.S. government and make up an increasingly important segment of the bond market. Municipal bonds are issued by state and local governments in the form of either general obligation or revenue bonds. (Most municipal bonds are tax exempt, but there's a growing market for taxable munis.) Corporate bonds make up the major nongovernment sector of the market and are backed by the assets and profitability of the issuing companies.

5. In addition to the securities issued in this country, there's a growing interest on the part of U.S. investors for foreign bonds—particularly foreign-pay securities—because of the highly competitive yields and returns they offer. Foreign-pay bonds cover all those issues that are denominated in some currency other than dollars (sometimes referred to as non-dollar denominated bonds); these are the German bonds denominated in German marks, etc. These bonds have an added source of return: currency exchange rates. In addition, there are also dollar-denominated foreign bonds: Yankee bonds and Eurodollar bonds; because these bonds are issued in U.S. dollars, there is no currency exchange risk.

6. Municipal and corporate issues are regularly rated for bond quality by independent rating agencies. A rating of Aaa indicates an impeccable record; lower ratings, such as A or Baa, indicate less protection for the investor; as with all investments, the returns required of lower-quality instruments generally are higher than those required of high-quality bonds.

QUESTIONS

1. Note some of the major advantages and disadvantages of investing in: (a) Treasury bonds, (b) agency issues, (c) municipal issues, (d) corporate bonds, and (e) foreign-debt securities.

2. Do issue characteristics (such as coupon and call features) affect the yield and price behavior of bonds? Explain.

3. Using Tables 8.1 and 8.2 as a basis of discussion, how would you describe the behavior of bond returns over the past 10 to 15 years? What do you think would be a fair rate of return to expect from an investment in bonds? Do swings in market interest rates have any bearing on bond returns? Explain.

4. What's the difference between a call feature and a sinking fund provision? Briefly describe the three different types of call features. Can a bond be freely callable but non-refundable? Explain.

5. Identify and briefly describe the five types of risks to which bonds are exposed. What is the most important source of risk for bonds in general? Explain. What are the major types of risk to which each of the following types of bonds are exposed?

    a. Treasury bonds   d. Corporate bonds
    b. Agency bonds   e. Foreign bonds
    c. Municipal bonds   f. CMOs

6. What three attributes are most important in determining an issue's price volatility? Explain.

7. Why should an aggressive bond trader be concerned with the trading volume of a particular issue?

8. "Treasury securities are guaranteed by the U.S. government; therefore, there is no risk in the ownership of such bonds." Briefly discuss the wisdom (or folly) of this statement.

9. Briefly define each of the following and note how they might be used by fixed-income investors: (a) zero-coupon bonds, (b) CMOs, (c) junk bonds, and (d) Yankee bonds.

10. What are the special tax features of (1) Treasury securities, (2) agency issues, (3) municipal bonds?

11. Select a security from the left column that best fits the investor needs described in the right column.

    a. 5-yr. Treasury note   1. Lock-in a high coupon yield.
    b. A bond with a low coupon and   2. Accumulate capital over a long
       long maturity   period of time.
    c. Yankee bond   3. Generate a monthly income.
    d. Insured revenue bond   4. Avoid a lot of price volatility.
    e. Long-term Treasury STRIPS   5. Generate tax-free income.
    f. Non-callable bond   6. Invest in a foreign bond.
    g. CMO   7. Go for the highest yield available.
    h. junk bond   8. Invest in a pool of credit card
    i. ABS   receivables.
                                        9. Go for maximum price appreciation.

12. Identify the six biggest bond markets in the world. How important is the U.S. bond market relative to the rest of the world? What's the difference between dollar-denominated and non-dollar-denominated foreign bonds? Briefly describe the two major types of U.S.-pay bonds. Can currency exchange rates effect the total return of U.S.-pay bonds? Of foreign-pay bonds? Explain.

13. What are bond ratings, and how can they affect investor returns? What are split ratings?

14. Using the quotes in Figure 8.6, answer the following questions:

    a. What's the dollar (bid) price of the May-'17 Treasury Strip bond and when does it mature?
    b. What's the current yield on that (May-'17 Treasury Strip) issue?
    c. Which is higher priced: the ATT 7⅛–03 or the 7½% U.S. Treasury of Nov-'16 (use ask price)?
    d. What's the dollar (ask) price of the 14% U.S. Treasury of Nov 06–11? Why is that issue priced so high? When does it mature?

e. Contrast the call feature on the 12½% Aug 09–14 Treasury bond with the 9¼% Feb-'16 Treasury issue.

f. Which bond was more actively traded: the ATT 8⅛–22, or the Alabama Power 8¼–03?

PROBLEMS

1. A 6 percent, 15-year bond has 3 years remaining on a deferred call feature (call premium is equal to one year's interest). The bond is currently priced in the market at $850. What is the issue's current yield?

2. An investor is in the 28 percent tax bracket and lives in a state with no income tax. He is trying to decide which of two bonds to purchase: one is a 7½ percent corporate bond which is selling at par, and the other is a municipal bond with a 5¼ percent coupon, which is also selling at par. If all other features of these two bonds are comparable, which should the investor select? Why? Would your answer change if this were an *in-state* municipal bond and the investor lived in a place with high state income taxes? Explain.

3. Sara Thomas is a wealthy investor who's looking for a tax shelter. And for good reason: Sara's in the maximum (31%) federal tax bracket, and she lives in a state with a very high state income tax (she pays the maximum of 11½% in state income tax). Sara is currently looking at two municipal bonds, both of which are selling at par: one's a double-A rated in-state bond that carries a coupon of 6⅜%, and the other is a double-A rated out-of-state bond that carries a 7⅛% coupon. Her broker has informed her that comparable fully-taxable corporate bonds are currently available with yields of 9¾%; alternatively, long Treasuries are now available at yields of 9%. She has $100,000 to invest, and since all the bonds are high-quality issues, she wants to select the one that will give her maximum after-tax returns.

a. Which one of the four bonds should she buy?

b. Rank the four bonds (from best to worst) in terms of their taxable equivalent yields.

4. Which of the following three bonds offers the highest current yield?

a. A 9½%, 20-year bond quoted at 97¾.

b. A 16%, 15-year bond quoted at 164⅝.

c. A 5¼%, 18-year bond quoted at 54.

5. Assume that an investor pays $850 for a long-term bond that carries a 7½% coupon. Over the course of the next 12 months, interest rates drop sharply and as a result, the investor sells the bond at a price of $962.50. Given this information:

a. Find the current yield that existed on this bond at the beginning of the year. What was it by the end of the one-year holding period?

b. Determine the holding period return on this investment. (*Hint:* See Chapter 4 for the HPR formula.)

6. In early January 1987, an investor purchased for her portfolio $30,000 worth of some single-A rated corporate bonds; the bonds carried a coupon of 8⅜% and mature in 2016. The investor paid 93¼ when she bought the bonds, and over the 5-year period from 1987 through 1991, the bonds were priced in the market as follows:

| Year | Quoted Prices | | Year-End Bond Yields |
	Beginning of the Year	End of the Year	
1987	93¼	81⅝	10.40%
1988	81⅝	83	10.23
1989	83	93¾	9.00
1990	93¾	90⅞	9.32
1991	90⅞	95	8.88

Coupon payments were made on schedule throughout the 5-year period.

a. Based on this information, find the *annual* holding period returns for 1987 through 1991. (*Hint:* See Chapter 4 for the HPR formula.)

b. Use the return information in Table 8.1 to evaluate the investment performance of this bond. How do you think it stacks up against the market? Explain.

CASE PROBLEMS

8.1 Lenny and Lucille Develop a Bond Investment Program

Lenny and Lucille Leadbetter, along with their two teenage sons, Lou and Lamar, live in Jenks, Oklahoma. Lenny works as an electronics salesman, and Lucille is a personnel officer at a local bank; together they earn an annual income of around $75,000. Lenny has just learned that his recently departed rich uncle has named him in his will to the tune of some $250,000, after taxes. Needless to say, the Leadbetters are elated. Lenny intends to spend $50,000 of his inheritance on a number of long-overdue family items (like some badly needed remodeling of their kitchen and family room, a new Nissan 300ZX, and braces to correct Lamar's overbite); he wants to invest the remaining $200,000 in various types of fixed-income securities. Lenny and Lucille have no unusual income requirements, health problems, or the like. Their only investment objectives are that they want to achieve some capital appreciation, and they want to keep their funds fully invested for a period of at least 20 years; they would rather not have to rely on their investments as a source of current income, but want to maintain some liquidity in their portfolio just in case.

Questions

1. Describe the type of bond investment program you think the Leadbetters should follow. In answering this question, give appropriate consideration to both return and risk factors.

2. List several different types of bonds that you would recommend for their portfolio, and briefly indicate why you would recommend each.

3. Using a recent issue of *The Wall Street Journal* or *Barron's,* construct a $200,000 bond portfolio for the Leadbetters. Use real securities and select *any* eight (8) bonds (or notes) you like, given the following ground rules:

   a. The portfolio must include at least one Treasury, one agency, and one corporate bond.

    b. No more than 5% of the portfolio can be in short-term U.S. Treasury bills.

    c. Ignore all transaction costs (so invest the full $200,000), and assume all securities have par values of $1,000 (of course, they can be trading in the market at something other than par).

    d. Use the latest available quotes to determine how many bonds/notes/bills you can buy.

4. Prepare a schedule listing all the securities in your recommended portfolio. Using a form like the one below, including the following information on each security in the portfolio:

Security		Latest Quoted Price	Number of Bonds Purchased	Amount Invested	Annual Coupon Income	Current Yield
Issuer-Coupon-Maturity						
1.	*Example:* U.S. Treas. - 8½%-'05	96⁸/₃₂	25	$24,062	$2,125	8.83%
2.						
3.						
4.						
5.						
6.						
7.						
8.						
	Totals	—	Total No.	$200,000	$	%

5. *In one brief paragraph,* note the key investment attributes of your recommended portfolio, and the investment objectives you hope to obtain with it.

8.2 The Case of the Missing Bond Ratings

While there's a lot that goes into a bond rating, it's probably safe to say that there's nothing more important in determining a bond's rating than the underlying financial condition and operating results of the company issuing the bonds. Generally speaking, a variety of financial ratios are used to assess the financial health of a firm, and just as financial ratios can be used in the analysis of common stocks, so can they also be used in the analysis of bonds, a process which we refer to as *credit analysis.* In credit analysis, attention is directed toward the basic liquidity and profitability of the firm, the extent to which the firm employs debt, and the ability of the firm to service its debt. The following financial ratios are often helpful in carrying out such analysis: (1) current ratio, (2) quick ratio, (3) net profit margin, (4) return on total capital, (5) long-term debt to total capital, (6) owners' equity ratio, (7) pre-tax interest converage, and (8) cash flow to total debt. The first two ratios measure the liquidity of the firm; the next two, its profitability; the following two, the debt load; and the final two, the ability of the firm to service its debt load. (For ratio 5, the *lower* the ratio, the better; for all the others, the *higher* the ratio, the better). The following table lists each of these ratios for six different companies.

A Table of Financial Ratios

(All Ratios are for the Calendar or Fiscal Year 1990)

Financial Ratio	Co. 1	Co. 2	Co. 3	Co. 4	Co. 5	Co. 6
1. Current ratio	1.13x	1.39x	1.78x	1.32x	1.03x	1.41x
2. Quick ratio	0.48x	0.84x	0.93x	0.33x	0.50x	0.75x
3. Net profit margin	4.6%	12.9%	14.5%	2.8%	5.9%	10.0%
4. Return on total capital	15.0%	25.9%	29.4%	11.5%	16.8%	28.4%
5. Long term debt to total capital	63.3%	52.7%	23.9%	97.0%	88.6%	42.1%
6. Owners' equity ratio	18.6%	18.9%	44.1%	1.5%	5.1%	21.2%
7. Pre-tax interest coverage	2.3x	4.5x	8.9x	1.7x	2.4x	6.4x
8. Cash flow to total debt	34.7%	48.8%	71.2%	20.4%	30.2%	42.7%

Notes: Ratio (2): Whereas the current ratio relates current assets to current liabilities, the quick ratio considers only the most liquid current assets (cash, short-term securities, and accounts receivable) and relates them to current liabilities.

Ratio (4): Relates pre-tax profit to the total capital structure (long-term debt + equity) of the firm.

Ratio (6): Shows the amount of stockholders' equity used to finance the firm (stockholders' equity ÷ total assets).

Ratio (8): Looks at the amount of corporate cash flow (from net profits + depreciation) relative to the total (current + long-term) debt of the firm.

The other four ratios are as described in Chapter 6.

Questions

1. Half (3) of these companies have bonds that carry *investment-grade ratings,* and the other half (3 companies) carry *junk-bond ratings.* Based on the information in the table, which three companies have the investment-grade bonds and which three the junk bonds? Briefly explain your selections.

2. One of these six companies is a AAA-rated firm and one is B-rated. Pick out those two companies. Briefly explain your selection.

3. Of the remaining four companies, one carries a AA rating, one an A rating, and two are BB rated. Which ones are they?

9 Bond Valuation and Analysis

After studying this chapter, you should be able to:

1. Explain the behavior of market interest rates and identify the forces that cause interest rates to move.

2. Describe the term structure of interest rates and note how these so-called yield curves can be used by investors.

3. Gain an understanding of how bonds are valued in the marketplace.

4. Describe the various measures of yield and return, and explain how these standards of performance are used in the bond valuation process.

5. Understand the basic concept of duration, how it can be measured, and its use in the management of bond portfolios.

6. Discuss various types of bond investment strategies and the different ways these securities can be used by investors.

When you get right down to it, a bond is pretty much like any other investment product: it provides a future cash flow to the investor, and depending on the amount and certainty of that cash flow, it has a given market value. The problem the investor faces is deciding whether the value as established in the marketplace will provide the kind of return he or she is looking for. This chapter addresses such concerns, as it deals with bond valuation and analysis. We pick up where we left off in Chapter 8, which was largely descriptive in nature, and which dealt with basic bond characteristics and features. Here, we will examine how bonds are valued and how they can be used to fulfill certain investor objectives. In particular, we'll look into the pricing of bonds and various measures of yield and return. In addition, we'll discuss a key measure of bond price volatility—duration—and see how it can be used to ''immunize'' bond portfolios from market and interest rate risks. We'll then close with a review of various investment strategies and bond management techniques. But first, because of the crucial role they play in the bond market, let's begin this discussion with a look at interest rates and the market forces that drive them.

THE BEHAVIOR OF MARKET INTEREST RATES

You will recall from Chapter 4 that rational investors will try to earn a return that fully compensates them for risk. In the case of bondholders, that required return (r_i), called the *market interest rate,* has three components—the real rate of return (r^*), an expected inflation premium (IP), and a risk premium (RP). It is expressed by the equation:

Equation 9.1
$$r_i = r^* + IP + RP$$

The real rate of return plus the inflation premium are external economic factors and together equal the risk-free rate (R_F). To get the required return, we must add to this the risk premium that relates to the particular bond issue and its issuer. Key issue and issuer characteristics include such variables as the type of bond (secured or unsecured, convertible, etc.), maturity, call features, and bond rating. These three components (r^*, IP, and RP) determine interest rate levels at a given point in time.

Because interest rates have such a significant bearing on bond prices and yields, they are closely monitored by both conservative and aggressive investors. Interest rates are important to conservative investors, since one of their major objectives is to lock in high yields. Aggressive traders also have a stake in interest rates because their investment programs are often built on the capital gains opportunities that accompany major swings in rates.

Keeping Tabs on Market Interest Rates

yield spreads
differences in interest rates that exist in various sectors of the market.

Just as there is no single bond market, but a series of different market sectors, so too there is no single interest rate applicable to all segments of the market. Rather, each segment has its own, somewhat unique level of interest rates. Granted, the various rates do tend to drift in the same direction over time and to follow the same general pattern of behavior, but it's also common for **yield spreads** (or interest-rate differentials) to exist in the various market sectors. We can summarize some of the more important market yields and yield spreads as follows:

1. Municipal bonds usually carry the lowest market rates because of the tax-exempt feature of these obligations. As a rule, their market yields are about two-thirds those of corporates. In the taxable sector, Treasuries have the lowest yields (because they have the least risk), followed by agencies and corporates, which provide the highest returns.
2. Those issues that normally carry bond ratings (such as municipals or corporates) generally display the same behavior: The lower the rating, the higher the yield.
3. There is generally a direct relationship between the coupon an issue carries and its yield: discount (low-coupon) bonds yield the least, and premium (high-coupon) bonds the most.
4. In the municipal sector, revenue bonds yield more than general obligation bonds.
5. Bonds that are freely callable generally provide the highest returns, at least at date of issue; these are followed by deferred call obligations, with noncallable bonds yielding the least.
6. As a rule, bonds with long maturities tend to yield more than short issues. However, this rule does not hold all the time, since there are periods, such as in early 1989, for example, when short-term yields exceeded the yields on long-term bonds.

The preceding list can be used as a general guide to the higher-yielding segments of the bond market. For example, income-oriented municipal bond investors might do well to consider certain high-quality revenue bonds as a way to increase yields; and agency bonds, rather than Treasuries, might be selected for the same reason by investors who like to stick to high-quality issues.

Investors should pay close attention to interest rates and yield spreads and try to stay abreast not only of the current state of the market, but also of *the future direction in market rates*. If a conservative (income-oriented) bond investor thinks, for example, that rates have just about peaked, that should be a clue to try to lock in the prevailing high yields with some form of call protection (such as buying bonds—like Treasuries or double-A–rated utilities—that are non-callable or still have lengthy call deferments). In contrast, if an aggressive bond trader thinks rates have peaked (and are about to drop), that should be a signal to buy bonds that offer maximum price appreciation potential—like low-coupon bonds that still have a long time to go before they mature. Clearly, in either case, *the future direction of interest rates is important!*

But how does a bond investor formulate such expectations? Unless the investor has considerable training in economics, he or she will have to rely on various published sources. Fortunately, there is a wealth of such information available. One's broker is an excellent source for such reports, as are investor services such as Moody's and Standard & Poor's. Finally, there are widely circulated business and financial publications—like *The Wall Street Journal, Forbes, Business Week,* and *Fortune*—that regularly address the current state and future direction of market interest rates. One of the best of these is illustrated in Figure 9.1. Make no mistake, predicting the future direction of interest rates is not an easy task. However, by taking the time to regularly and carefully read some of these publications and re-

---

CREDIT MARKETS

Long-Bond Prices Inch Higher; IBM Issues Slump As Company Loses Triple-A Rating From Moody's

By Tom Herman
And Terence Donnelly
Staff Reporters of The Wall Street Journal

NEW YORK—Long-term Treasury bond prices inched higher yesterday, snapping a two-day losing streak.

But intermediate-term bond prices drifted slightly lower, and most short-term interest rates were flat.

In another seesaw day, the Treasury's benchmark 30-year bonds recovered from an early-morning sinking spell and finished with a gain of ⅛ point, or $1.25 for each $1,000 face amount. The yield, which moves in the opposite direction as its price, slid to 7.91% from 7.92% Tuesday.

In the corporate bond arena, prices of investment-grade issues generally were little changed. But prices of International Business Machines Corp. debt issues slumped after news that the company had lost its coveted triple-A rating from Moody's Investors Service Inc.

Moody's, a leading credit-rating agency, reduced its rating on IBM's long-term debt to double-A-2, a decline of two notches. Traders said Moody's move didn't come as a major surprise because IBM's woes already have been heavily publicized. Nevertheless, prices of IBM's 8.375% debentures due 2019 were quoted late yesterday at 99 bid, down 1/2 point from late Tuesday.

IBM said it is "disappointed" by Moody's decision but expects "minimal" impact from the lower rating. The company said it has been a "consistent leader in earnings performance" with the exception of last year. It also said it has taken "significant actions that should result in improved financial performance and provide consistent earnings momentum."

Treasury Yield Curve

Yields as of 4:30 p.m. Eastern time

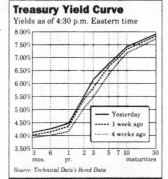

Source: Technical Data's Bond Data

YIELD COMPARISONS

Based on Merrill Lynch Bond Indexes, priced as of midafternoon Eastern time.

	3/4	3/3	−52 Week− High	Low
Corp.-Govt. Master	7.14%	7.14%	8.27%	6.53%
Treasury 1-10yr	6.22	6.20	7.61	5.44
10+ yr	7.97	7.97	8.69	7.43
Agencies 1-10yr	6.75	6.75	7.92	6.12
10+ yr	8.22	8.26	8.92	7.80
Corporate				
1-10 yr High Qlty	7.61	7.60	8.82	7.10
Med Qlty	8.12	8.13	9.68	7.70
10+yr High Qlty	8.65	8.66	9.45	8.30
Med Qlty	9.04	9.05	9.91	8.79
Yankee bonds(1)	8.28	8.29	9.32	7.79
Current-coupon mortgages				
GNMA 8.00%	8.31	8.30	9.13	8.31
FNMA 8.00%	8.37	8.37	9.35	8.37
FHLMC8.00%	8.30	8.29	9.28	8.30
High-yield corporates	11.91	11.90	16.09	11.90
New tax-exempts				
10-yr G.O. (AA)	5.95	5.95	6.50	5.60
20-yr G.O. (AA)	6.55	6.55	7.10	6.25
30-yr revenue (A)	6.83	6.85	7.55	6.52

Note: High quality rated AAA-AA; medium quality A-BBB/Baa; high yield, BB/Ba-C.
(1) Dollar-denominated, SEC-registered bonds of foreign issuers sold in the U.S.

ble bonds carry yields ranging from 8.50% in 1997 to 10.05% in 2010, 2015 and 2016.

Underwriters are expected to reprice the bulk of the offering to reduce yields on some maturities slightly.

Separately, Westchester County, N.Y., sold $52 million of general obligation bonds yesterday through competitive bidding. The bonds, won by a Roosevelt & Cross Inc. group, were offered to investors priced to yield from 3.25% on bonds due in 1993 to 6.25% in 2010-2012. An unsold balance of slightly more than $3 million was reported.

Underwriters led by Goldman, Sachs & Co. reported an unsold balance of about $283 million of bonds late yesterday on Georgia's offering of $567 million of general obligation bonds. The bonds, rated triple-A by Moody's and double-A-plus by Standard & Poor's Corp., were priced to yield from 2.75% in 1993 to 6.40% in 2011.

Corporate & Junk Bonds

About $575 million of new debt was sold yesterday.

Among issuers was Greyhound Financial Corp, which offered $125 million five-year notes to yield 8.362%. The non-callable notes were priced at a spread of 1.60 percentage points above the Treasury's five-year note.

Dial Corp., Greyhound Financial's parent, recently announced that shareholders had approved the spinoff of the financial services subsidiary. Greyhound will become a subsidiary of a newly formed New York Stock Exchange holding company to be named GFC Financial Corp.

In the wider investment-grade market, prices were little changed. In the market for high-yield, high-risk junk bonds, prices were firm.

• FIGURE 9.1 A Popular Source of Information About Interest Rates and the Credit Markets

The "Credit Markets" column appears every day in the *The Wall Street Journal* and provides a capsule view of current conditions and future prospects in the bond market. Note on this particular day that a good deal of the article was devoted to the downgrading of IBM bonds. (*Source: The Wall Street Journal*, March 5, 1992.)

ports, investors can readily keep track of the behavior of interest rates and at least get a handle on what is likely to occur in the near future—say, over the next 6 to 12 months, perhaps longer.

What Causes Interest Rates to Move?

Although the subject of interest rates is a complex economic issue, we do know that certain forces are especially important in influencing the general behavior of market rates. As bond investors, we should become familiar with the major determinants of interest rates and try to monitor those variables—at least in an informal fashion. Perhaps no variable is more important in this regard than *inflation*. Changes in the inflation rate (or even expectations about the future course of inflation) have a direct and pronounced effect on market interest rates, and they have been a leading cause of wide swings in interest rates. Clearly, if expectations are for inflation to slow down, then market interest rates should fall as well. To gain an appreciation of the extent to which interest rates are linked to inflation, refer to Figure 9.2. Note that as inflation drifts up, so too do interest rates; on the other hand, a drop in inflation is matched by a similar decline in interest rates.

In addition to inflation, there are at least five other important economic variables that can significantly affect the level of interest rates:

1. *Changes in the money supply:* An increase in the money supply pushes rates down (as it makes more funds available for loans), and vice versa.

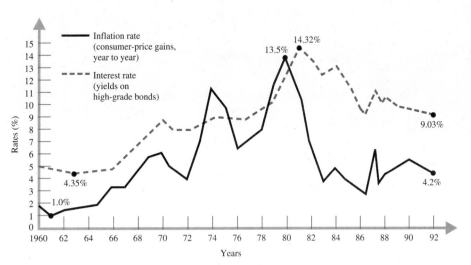

• FIGURE 9.2 The Impact of Inflation on the Behavior of Interest Rates

The behavior of interest rates has always been closely tied to movements in the rate of inflation. What changed in the early 1980s, however, was the spread between inflation and interest rates. Whereas a spread of roughly 3 points was common in the past, it has held at about 5 to 6 percentage points since 1982.

2. *The size of the federal budget deficit:* When the U.S. Treasury must borrow large amounts to cover the budget deficit, the increased demand for funds exerts an upward pressure on interest rates.

3. *The level of economic activity:* Businesses need more capital when the economy expands. This increases the demand for funds and rates tend to rise. During a recession, economic activity contracts and rates typically fall.

4. *Policies of the Federal Reserve:* Actions of the Federal Reserve to control the money supply through monetary policies, such as the level of the discount rate and open market operations (buying and selling Treasury securities), also have a major effect on interest rate levels. For example, the Fed's purchase of government bonds increases the money supply and lowers interest rates.

5. *The level of interest rates in major foreign markets:* Today investors look beyond national borders for investment opportunities. If rates in major foreign markets rise, rates in the U.S. will have to rise to attract investors—if not, investors will dump dollars, as they did in 1992, to buy high-yielding foreign securities.

The Term Structure of Interest Rates and Yield Curves

Although many factors affect the behavior of market interest rates, one of the most popular and widely studied is *bond maturity*. The relationship between the interest rate or rate of return (yield) and time to maturity for any class of similar-risk securities is called the **term structure of interest rates.** This relationship can be depicted graphically by a **yield curve,** which relates a bond's *term* to maturity to its *yield* to maturity at a given point in time. A particular yield curve exists for only a short period of time; as market conditions change, so does the yield curve's shape and location.

term structure of interest rates
The relationship between the interest rate or rate of return (yield) and time to maturity.

yield curve.
A graph that represents the relationship between a bond's term to maturity and its yield at a given point in time.

Types of Yield Curves

Two different kinds of yield curves are illustrated in Figure 9.3. By far, the most common type is curve 1, the *upward-sloping,* or normal, curve. It indicates that yields tend to increase with longer maturities. The longer a bond has to go to maturity, the greater the potential for price volatility and the risk of loss. Investors therefore require higher risk premiums to induce them to buy the longer, riskier bonds. Occasionally, the yield curve takes the inverted, or *downward-sloping,* shape shown in curve 2, where short-term rates are higher than long-term rates. This generally results from actions by the Federal Reserve to curtail inflation by raising short-term rates. Two other yield curves also appear from time to time: the *flat* yield curve, when rates for short- and long-term loans are essentially similar, and the *humped* yield curve, when intermediate-term rates are the highest.

Plotting Your Own Curves

Yield curves are constructed by plotting the yields for a group of bonds that are similar in all respects except maturity. Treasury securities (bills, notes, and bonds) are typically used to draw yield curves, for several reasons: Their yields are easily found in financial publications, they have no risk of default, and they are homoge-

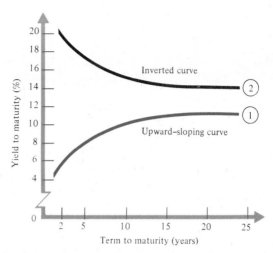

• **FIGURE 9.3** Two Kinds of Yield Curves

A yield curve relates term-to-maturity to yield-to-maturity at a given point in time. Although yield curves come in many shapes and forms, the most common is the upward-sloping curve, which shows that investor returns (yields) increase with the longer maturities.

neous with regard to quality and other issue characteristics. Investors can also construct yield curves for other classes of debt securities with similar characteristics, such as Aa-rated municipal bonds, Baa-rated corporate bonds, or certificates of deposit.

Figure 9.4 shows the yield curves for Treasury securities on two dates, one year apart: March 6, 1992 and March 7, 1991. To draw these curves, you need Treasury quotes from *The Wall Street Journal,* some of which are shown in the graph. Given the required quotes, select the yields for the Treasury bills, notes, and bonds maturing in approximately three months, six months, and one, two, five, 10, 20, and 30 years. The yields used for this curve are highlighted. (You could include more points, but they would not have much effect on the shape of the curve.) Next, plot the points on a graph whose horizontal (x) axis represents time to maturity in years and whose vertical (y) axis represents yield to maturity. Connect them to create the curves shown in Figure 9.4. Note in both cases, the pattern is upward sloping; this has historically been the "normal" pattern.

Explanations of the Term Structure of Interest Rates

As noted earlier, the shape of the yield curve changes over time. Three commonly-cited theories—the expectations hypothesis, liquidity preference theory, and market segmentation theory—explain more fully the reasons for the general shape of the yield curve.

expectations hypothesis
Theory that the shape of the yield curve reflects investor expectations of future interest rates.

Expectations Hypothesis. The **expectations hypothesis** suggests that the yield curve reflects investor expectations about future interest rates. The relationship

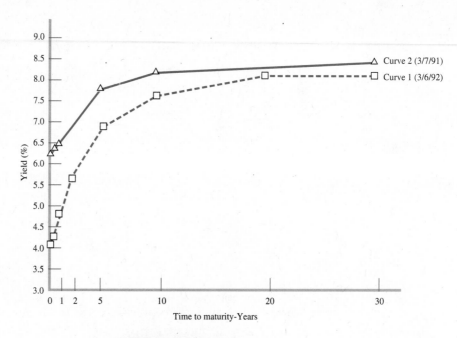

Yield Data for Curve #1
Treasury Issues—Bills, Notes, and Bonds and Notes
Friday, March 6, 1992

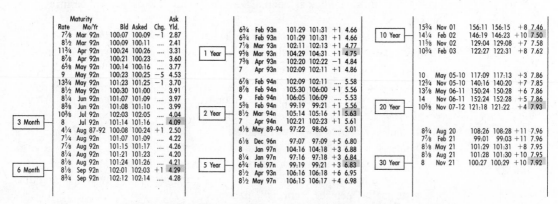

	Rate	Maturity Mo/Yr	Bld	Asked	Chg.	Ask Yld.
	$7\frac{7}{8}$	Mar 92n	100:07	100:09	−1	2.87
	$8\frac{1}{2}$	Mar 92n	100:09	100:11	....	2.41
	$11\frac{3}{4}$	Apr 92n	100:24	100:26	....	3.31
	$8\frac{7}{8}$	Apr 92n	100:21	100:23	....	3.60
	$6\frac{5}{8}$	May 92n	100:14	100:16	....	3.77
	9	May 92n	100:23	100:25	−5	4.53
	$13\frac{3}{4}$	May 92n	101:23	101:25	−1	3.70
	$8\frac{1}{2}$	May 92n	100:30	101:00	....	3.91
	$8\frac{1}{4}$	Jun 92n	101:07	101:09	....	3.97
	$8\frac{3}{8}$	Jun 92n	101:08	101:10	....	3.99
	$10\frac{3}{8}$	Jul 92n	102:03	102:05	....	4.04
3 Month	8	Jul 92n	101:14	101:16	....	4.09
	$4\frac{1}{4}$	Aug 87-92	100:08	100:24	+1	2.50
	$7\frac{1}{4}$	Aug 92n	101:07	101:09	....	4.22
	$7\frac{7}{8}$	Aug 92n	101:15	101:17	....	4.26
	$8\frac{1}{4}$	Aug 92n	101:21	101:23	....	4.20
	$8\frac{1}{8}$	Aug 92n	101:24	101:26	....	4.21
6 Month	$8\frac{1}{8}$	Sep 92n	102:01	102:03	+1	4.29
	$8\frac{3}{4}$	Sep 92n	102:12	102:14	....	4.28
	$6\frac{3}{4}$	Feb 93n	101:29	101:31	+1	4.66
	$6\frac{3}{4}$	Feb 93n	101:29	101:31	+1	4.66
	$7\frac{1}{8}$	Mar 93n	102:11	102:13	+1	4.77
1 Year	$9\frac{5}{8}$	Mar 93n	104:29	104:31	+1	4.75
	$7\frac{3}{8}$	Apr 93n	102:20	102:22	−1	4.84
	7	Apr 93n	102:09	102:11	+1	4.86
	$6\frac{7}{8}$	Feb 94n	102:09	102:11	....	5.58
	$8\frac{7}{8}$	Feb 94n	105:30	106:00	+1	5.56
	9	Feb 94n	106:05	106:09	....	5.53
	$5\frac{3}{8}$	Feb 94n	99:19	99:21	+1	5.56
2 Year	$8\frac{1}{2}$	Mar 94n	105:14	105:16	+1	5.63
	7	Apr 94n	102:21	102:23	+1	5.61
	$4\frac{1}{8}$	May 89-94	97:22	98:06	....	5.01
	$6\frac{1}{8}$	Dec 96n	97:07	97:09	+5	6.80
	8	Jan 97n	104:16	104:18	+3	6.88
	$8\frac{1}{4}$	Jan 97n	97:16	97:18	+3	6.84
5 Year	$6\frac{3}{4}$	Feb 97n	99:19	99:21	+3	6.83
	$8\frac{1}{2}$	Apr 93n	106:16	106:18	+6	6.95
	$8\frac{1}{2}$	May 97n	106:15	106:17	+4	6.98
	$15\frac{3}{4}$	Nov 01	156:11	156:15	+8	7.46
10 Year	$14\frac{1}{4}$	Feb 02	146:19	146:23	+10	7.50
	$11\frac{5}{8}$	Nov 02	129:04	129:08	+7	7.58
	$10\frac{3}{4}$	Feb 03	122:27	122:31	+8	7.62
	10	May 05-10	117:09	117:13	+3	7.86
	$12\frac{3}{4}$	Nov 05-10	140:16	140:20	+7	7.85
	$13\frac{7}{8}$	May 06-11	150:24	150:28	+6	7.86
	14	Nov 06-11	152:24	152:28	+5	7.86
20 Year	$10\frac{3}{8}$	Nov 07-12	121:18	121:22	+4	7.93
	$8\frac{3}{4}$	Aug 20	108:26	108:28	+11	7.96
	$7\frac{7}{8}$	Feb 21	99:01	99:03	+11	7.96
	$8\frac{1}{8}$	May 21	101:29	101:31	+8	7.95
	$8\frac{1}{8}$	Aug 21	101:28	101:30	+10	7.95
30 Year	8	Nov 21	100:27	100:29	+10	7.92

• FIGURE 9.4 Yield Curves on U.S. Treasury Issues

Here we see two yield curves constructed from actual market data (quotes). Note that although the general shape is unchanged, the steepness of curve 1 is much greater than that of curve 2, as short-term rates have fallen much more than long-term rates.

between rates today and rates expected in the future is due primarily to investor expectations regarding inflation: If investors anticipate higher future rates of inflation, they will require higher long-term interest rates, and vice versa. This widely-accepted explanation of the term structure of interest rates can be applied to the securities of a single issuer. For example, consider U.S. Treasury securities. Because they are considered essentially risk-free, there are only two components that determine the yield for Treasury securities: the real interest rate and inflation expectations. Since the real rate of interest is the same for all maturities, it is the differing inflation expectations associated with different maturities that causes yields to vary. This hypothesis can be illustrated using the March 6, 1992, yields for four maturities of the Treasury securities used in Figure 9.4. If we assume that the real rate of interest is 3 percent, the inflation expectation during the period to maturity can be calculated for each maturity and is shown in column 3 of the following table:

Maturity	(1) Yield	(2) Real Rate of Interest	(3) Inflation Expectation [(1) − (2)]
3 months	4.09%	3.00%	1.09%
1 year	4.75	3.00	1.75
5 years	6.83	3.00	3.83
30 years	7.92	3.00	4.92

Therefore, on March 6, 1992, investors expected that inflation would increase in the future, and the yield curve, as shown in Figure 9.4, was upward-sloping. Generally, under the expectations hypothesis, an increasing inflation expectation results in an upward-sloping yield curve, a decreasing inflation expectation results in a downward-sloping yield curve, and a stable inflation expectation results in a flat yield curve. Although, as we'll see below, other theories exist, the observed strong relationship between inflation and interest rates lends considerable credence to this widely accepted theory.

Liquidity Preference Theory. Another explanation for the frequency of the upward-sloping yield curve is the **liquidity preference theory.** This intuitively-appealing theory states that for a given issuer, long-term rates tend to be higher than short-term rates. It is based on two behavioral facts: First, investors perceive that short-term securities are inherently less risky than long-term securities, due to the greater certainty of near-term events, and as such, will accept lower yields for them. Short-term securities are preferred because they are more liquid (easily converted to cash) and less sensitive to changing market rates than long-term securities; there is less risk of loss of principal. For a given change in market rates, the prices of longer-term bonds will show a greater upward and downward movement than the prices of short-term bonds. Uncertainty increases over time, and investors therefore require a premium to invest in long-term maturities. Second, investors tend to require a premium for tying up funds for longer periods, while borrowers will pay a premium in order to obtain long-term funds. Borrowers thus assure themselves that funds will be available and can avoid having to roll over short-term debt at unknown, and possibly unfavorable, rates. Obviously, these preferences cause longer maturities to have higher interest rates than shorter maturities and result in an upward-sloping yield curve.

liquidity preference theory
Theory that investors tend to prefer the greater liquidity of short-term securities and therefore require a premium to invest in long-term securities.

Market Segmentation Theory.   Another often-cited theory, the **market segmentation theory,** suggests that the market for debt is segmented based on maturity preferences of different types of financial institutions and investors. The yield curve changes as the supply and demand for funds within each maturity segment determines its prevailing interest rate. The equilibrium between the financial institutions that supply short-term maturities, such as banks, and the borrowers of short-term funds, such as businesses with seasonal loan requirements, establishes interest rates in the short-term markets. Similarly, the equilibrium between suppliers and demanders in such long-term markets as life insurance and real estate determines the prevailing long-term interest rates. The shape of the yield curve would therefore be determined by the general relationship between rates in each market segment. It could be either upward- or downward-sloping. When supply outstrips demand for short-term loans, short-term rates will be relatively low. If at the same time the demand for long-term loans is higher than the available supply of funds, long-term rates will be high, and the yield curve will slope upward, Simply stated, low rates in the short-term segment and high rates in the long-term segment cause an upward-sloping yield curve, and vice versa.

Which Theory?   It is clear that all three theories of the term structure of interest rates have merit and explain the shape of the yield curve. From them we can conclude that at any time the slope of the yield curve is affected by (1) inflationary expectations, (2) liquidity preferences, and (3) the supply and demand conditions in the short- and long-term market segments. Upward-sloping yield curves results from higher future inflation expectations, lender preferences for shorter-maturity loans, and greater supply of short- as opposed to long-term loans relative to the respective demand in each market segment. The opposite behavior would, of course, result in a downward-sloping yield curve. At any point in time, it is the interaction of these forces that determine the prevailing slope of the yield curve.

Using the Yield Curve in Investment Decisions

Bond investors often use yield curves as part of their investment decision-making process. As noted earlier, yield curves change in accordance with market conditions. Analyzing the changes in yield curves over time provides investors with information about future interest rate movements and how they can affect price behavior and comparative returns. For example, if over a specific time period, the yield curve begins to rise sharply, it usually means that inflation is increasing; investors can expect that interest rates, too, will rise. Under these conditions, most seasoned bond investors turn to short or intermediate (3–5 years) maturities, which provide reasonable returns and at the same time minimize exposure to capital loss when rates go up (and prices therefore fall). A downward-sloping yield curve, though unusual, generally results from actions of the Federal Reserve to reduce inflation. As suggested by the expectations hypothesis, this would signal that rates have peaked and are about to fall.

Another factor to consider is the difference in yields on different maturities at a particular point in time, or the ''steepness'' of the curve. Comparing the two yield curves in Figure 9.4, we see that the difference between short- and long-term rates is much greater in March 1992 than it was a year earlier. This could be an indication that long-term rates are likely to fall somewhat to narrow the spread, providing an incentive to invest in longer-term securities. Steep yield curves are generally viewed as a bullish sign. Notice also that the yield spread on curve 2 between the 10- and 30-year maturities is basically flat; the difference is only 16 basis points. Investors would therefore tend to favor the 10-year security, because they would not gain enough (only 16 basis points) to justify the much greater risk of the 30-year maturity. However, if the spread were, say, 75 basis points, the investor would have to consider his or her own risk tolerance to determine whether this risk premium was sufficient for the additional risk of buying the longer-term security.

THE PRICING OF BONDS

If there's one common denominator in the bond market, it's the way bonds are priced. It doesn't make any difference who the issuer is, what kind of bond it is, whether it's fully taxable or tax-free, all bonds are priced pretty much the same: In particular, all bonds (including *notes* with maturities of more than a year) are priced according to the present value of their future cash flow streams. Indeed, once the prevailing or expected market yield is known, *the whole process becomes rather mechanical.* Even so, mechanical or not, this system is very effective, and it is the process through which the *market value* of a bond is established.

Bond prices are driven by market yields. That's because in the marketplace, *the appropriate yield at which the bond should sell is determined first, and then that yield is used to find the price (or market value) of the bond.* The appropriate yield on a bond is a function of certain market and economic forces (like the risk-free rate of return and inflation), as well as key issue and issuer characteristics, such as the number of years to maturity and the agency rating assigned to the bond. Together, these forces combine to form the *required rate of return*—which is the (expected) rate of return the investor would like to earn in order to justify an investment in a given fixed-income security. In the bond market, required return is *market driven* and is generally referred to as the issue's *market yield.* It defines the yield at which the bond should be trading and functions as the *discount rate* in the bond valuation process.

Basically, bond investors are entitled to two distinct types of cash flows: (1) the periodic receipt of coupon income over the life of the bond, and (2) the recovery of principal (or par value) at the end of the bond's life. Thus, in valuing a bond, you're dealing with an *annuity* of coupon payments plus a large *single cash flow,* as represented by the recovery of principal at maturity. These cash flows, along with the required rate of return on the investment, are then used in a present value–based bond valuation model to find the dollar price of a bond. We'll demonstrate the bond valuation process in two ways. First we'll use *annual compounding*—i.e., because of its computational simplicity, we'll assume we're dealing with annual coupons that are paid once a year. Second, we'll examine bond valuation under conditions of *semi-annual compounding,* which is more like the way most bonds actually pay their coupons.

Annual Compounding

Along with a table of present-value interest factors (see Appendix A, Tables A.3 and A.4), the following information is needed to value a bond: (1) the annual coupon payment, (2) the bond's par value, and (3) the number of years remaining to maturity. The prevailing market yield (or an estimate of future market rates) is then used as the discount rate to compute the price of a bond as follows:

Equation 9.2

Bond price = present value of the annuity of annual interest income + present value of the bond's par value

$$= (I \times PVIFA) + (PV \times PVIF)$$

where:

I = amount of annual interest income
$PVIFA$ = present-value interest factor for an *annuity* (Appendix A, Table A.4)
PV = par value of the bond, which is assumed to be $1,000
$PVIF$ = present-value interest factor for a *single cash flow* (Appendix A, Table A.3)

To illustrate the bond price formula in action, consider a 20-year, 9½ percent bond that's being priced to yield 10 percent. From this we know the bond pays an annual coupon of 9½ percent (or $95), has 20 years left to maturity, and should be priced to provide a market yield of 10 percent. As we saw in Chapter 4, the maturity and market yield information is used to find the appropriate present-value interest factors (in Appendix A, Tables A.3 and A.4). Given these interest factors, we can now use Equation 9.2 to find the price of our bond as follows:

Bond price = ($95 × *PVIFA* for 10% and 20 years)
+($1,000 × *PVIF* for 10% and 20 years)

= ($95 × 8.514) + ($1,000 × .149) = $957.83

Note that since this is a coupon-bearing bond, we have an annuity of coupon payments of $95 a year for 20 years, plus a single cash flow of $1,000 that occurs at the end of year 20. Thus, in bond valuation, we first find the present-value of the coupon annuity and then add that amount to the present value of the recovery of principal at maturity. In this particular case, around $958 is what we should be willing to pay for this bond so long as we're satisfied with earning 10% on our money.

Semi-Annual Compounding

In practice, most bonds pay interest every six months and as a result, semi-annual compounding is used in the valuation of bonds. Using annual compounding, as we did above, does simplify the valuation process a bit, but it's not the way bonds are actually valued in the marketplace. Fortunately, it's relatively easy to go from annual to semi-annual compounding: All you need do is cut the annual coupon payment in half, and make two minor modifications to the present-value interest factors. Given these changes, finding the price of a bond under conditions of semi-annual compounding is much like pricing a bond using annual compounding. That is:

Equation 9.3   Bond price (with semi- = present value of an annuity of *semi-annual* coupon payments
annual compounding)   + present value of the bond's par value

$$= (I/2 \times PVIFA^*) + (PV \times PVIF^*)$$

where:

PVIFA* = present-value interest factor for an annuity, *with required return and years-to-maturity adjusted for semi-annual compounding* (Appendix A, Table A.4)

PVIF* = present-value interest factor for a single cash flow, *with required return and years-to-maturity adjusted for semi-annual compounding* (Appendix A, Table A.3)

I, PV = as described above

Note that in equation 9.3, the present-value interest factors (*both PVIFA and PVIF*) are adjusted to accommodate semi-annual compounding. To do so, *simply cut the required return in half and double the number of years to maturity.* Thus, you're dealing with a semi-annual return and the number of 6-month periods to maturity (rather than *years* to maturity). For example, in our bond illustration above, we wanted to price a 20-year bond to yield 10 percent. With semi-annual compounding, we would be dealing with a semi-annual return of 10%/2 = 5%, and with 20 × 2 = 40 semi-annual periods to maturity. Thus, we'd find the present-value interest factors for 5% and 40 periods from Table A.4 (for *PVIFA**) and from Table A.3 (for *PVIF**). And note that we adjust the present-value interest factor for the $1,000 par value since that, too, will be subject to semi-annual compounding, even though the cash flow will be received in one lump sum. To see how this all fits together in the bond valuation process, consider once again the 20-year, 9½ percent bond, except this time, assume it's being priced to yield 10 percent, compounded semi-annually. Using Equation 9.3, we'd have:

Bond price (with semi- = ($95/2 × *PVIFA** for 5% and 40 periods)
annual compounding)   + ($1,000 × *PVIF** for 5% and 40 periods)

$$= (\$47.50 \times 17.159) + (\$1,000 \times .142) = \underline{\$957.02}$$

The price of the bond in this case ($957.02) is slightly less than the price we obtained with annual compounding ($957.83), so the use of annual vs. semi-annual compounding doesn't make all that much difference, though the differences do tend to increase a bit with lower coupons and shorter maturities.

MEASURES OF YIELD AND RETURN

Market yield is a vital part of the bond valuation process. Not only does yield affect the price at which a bond trades, it also serves as *an important measure of return*. To use yield as a measure of return, we simply reverse the bond valuation process described above and solve for the yield on a bond, rather than its price. Actually, there are two widely used measures of yield: current yield and yield-to-maturity. We'll look at both of them here, along with a variation of yield-to-maturity, known

current yield
return measure that indicates the amount of current income a bond provides relative to its market price.

as *expected return,* which measures expected (or actual) the rate of return earned over specific holding periods.

Current Yield

Current yield is the simplest of all return measures but has the most limited application. It indicates the amount of current income a bond provides relative to its prevailing market price. It is calculated as follows:

Equation 9.4

$$\text{Current yield} = \frac{\text{annual interest income}}{\text{current market price of the bond}}$$

For example, an 8 percent bond would pay $80 per year in interest for every $1,000 of principal. However, if the bond were currently priced at $800, it would have a current yield of 10 percent ($80/$800 = .10). Current yield is a measure of a bond's annual coupon income and as such, would be of interest to investors seeking high levels of current income.

Yield-to-Maturity

yield-to-maturity (YTM)
the fully compounded rate of return earned by an investor over the life of a bond, including interest income and price appreciation.

promised yield
same as yield-to-maturity.

Yield-to-maturity (YTM), the most important and widely used bond valuation measure, evaluates both interest income and price appreciation and considers total cash flow received over the life of an issue. Also known as **promised yield,** it indicates the fully compounded rate of return earned by an investor, given the bond is held to maturity and all principal and interest payments are made in a prompt and timely fashion. This measure of yield is used not only to gauge the return on a single issue but also to track the behavior of the market in general. That is, *market interest rates* are nothing more than a reflection of the average promised yields that exist in a given segment of the market. Promised yield provides valuable insight about an issue's investment merits and is used to assess the attractiveness of alternative investment vehicles. Other things being equal, the higher the promised yield of an issue, the more attractive it is.

Although there are several ways to compute promised yield, the simplest is to use a procedure first introduced in Chapter 4, known as the *approximate yield method:*

Equation 9.5

$$\text{Approximate yield-to-maturity} = \frac{\text{annual interest income} + \dfrac{\$1,000 - \text{current market price}}{\text{years remaining till maturity}}}{\dfrac{\$1,000 + \text{current market price}}{2}}$$

$$= \frac{I + \dfrac{\$1,000 - P}{N}}{\dfrac{\$1,000 + P}{2}}$$

As an example, consider the following hypothetical situation: Assume a 7½ percent bond with a par value of $1,000 has 15 years remaining to maturity and is currently priced at $809.50. Using this information, we see that the approximate yield-to-maturity on this bond is:

$$\text{Approximate yield-to-maturity} = \frac{\$75 + \dfrac{\$1,000 - \$809.50}{15}}{\dfrac{\$1,000 + 809.50}{2}} = \frac{\$75 + \$12.70}{\$904.75} = \underline{\underline{9.69\%}}$$

In this case, if an investor pays $809.50 for the bond and holds it to maturity, she can expect to earn an approximate yield of 9.69%. There's no doubt that promised yield is an important measure of performance, but as seen in the *Investor Insights* box on page 382, it provides only half the story.

A More Precise Measure of Yield

While approximate yield, as obtained from Equation 9.5, may be appropriate for many investment decisions, one big drawback of the procedure is its lack of precision. This could be a problem for some investors. If it is, then use a more precise measure—one that's derived directly from the bond valuation model described above. In particular, assuming annual compounding, we can use Equation 9.2 to find the yield-to-maturity on a bond. Expect in this case we know the current price of the bond and are trying to solve for the discount rate that equates the present value of the bond's cash flow (its coupon and principal payments) to its current market price. This procedure may sound familiar: it's just like the *internal rate of return* measure described in Chapter 4. Indeed, we're basically trying to find the internal rate of return on a bond, because if we find that, we have the bond's yield-to-maturity.

Unfortunately, unless you have a handheld calculator or computer software that will do the calculations for you, finding the precise yield-to-maturity is a matter of trial and error. Here's how it's done: Let's say we want to find the yield-to-maturity on the 7½ percent, 15-year bond we introduced above. With reference to Equation 9.2, we know that:

$$\text{Bond price} = (I \times PVIFA) + (PV \times PVIF)$$

As it now stands, we know the current market price of the bond ($809.50), the amount of annual interest/coupon income (7½% = $75), the par value of the bond ($1,000), and the number of years to maturity (15). To compute yield-to-maturity, we need to find the discount rate (in the present-value interest factors) that produces a bond price of $809.50.

Here's what we have so far:

$$\text{Bond price} = (I \times PVIFA) + (PV \times PVIF)$$

$$\$809.50 = (\$75 \times PVIFA \text{ for 15 years and a discount rate of ?\%})$$
$$+ (\$1,000 \times PVIF \text{ for 15 years and a discount rate of ?\%})$$

At this point, there's only one thing we know about the yield on this bond—it has to be more than 7½ (i.e., since this is a discount bond, the yield-to-maturity must exceed the coupon rate). To get even closer to the required solving rate, we can compute the approximate yield—recall this was found to be 9.69%. There are two properties of the approximate yield procedure that will prove helpful at this point.

████ INVESTOR INSIGHTS ████

There's More to Bond Returns Than Yield Alone

When individuals choose bond investments, they usually focus on yields, in the belief that higher yields generate better returns. But "yields" and "returns" are two different things, and investors who blindly chase higher yields can end up regretting it. The fact is, yield is only part of the story: it tells you what you can expect going into an investment, *not* what you'll actually end up earning on the deal. Indeed, yield is often a poor proxy for return, and confusing the two can be very damaging to your wealth.

Total return is much more consequential than yield because it's ultimately what determines future wealth. Institutions have long recognized this—they buy bonds as an investment like any other, which ultimately might be sold. "Total return" for fixed-income investments comprises not just the initial yield, but also interest on reinvested interest, and price change. In essence, *return* is a measure of *actual* performance over a given investment period. Only in the case of short-term investments, such as one-year CDs or Treasury bills, is yield a good gauge of total return. For long-term bonds, and bonds purchased at prices far above or below face value; other factors will often dwarf yield in determining total returns. That's true even when the bonds are of triple-A credit quality and are non-callable.

For instance, interest on interest easily becomes the biggest factor in returns for buy-and-hold investors in long-term bonds, especially if interest rates rise during the life of the bond. If you bought a 30-year Treasury bond yielding 7.9% today, and interest rates subsequently rose so that your average reinvestment rate was 9% over the life of the bond, almost 80% of your total return at maturity would come from income on reinvested interest, according to G.A.T. Integrated Financial Services, a fixed-income research firm. On the other hand, while interest on interest dominates bond returns for long holding periods, price change dominates total return for short-term investors. In either case, future interest-rate changes are the major concern for investors who want to safeguard their total returns.

The starting yield on a bond becomes a bigger boon or burden to investors the longer the bond's maturity—which makes total returns on longer-term bonds much more sensitive to interest rate swings. For instance, in the 1950s, 1960s and 1970s, long-term Treasury bonds actually had lower total returns than money-market funds, despite their persistently higher yields. Average yields on long-term Treasury bonds were roughly

They are: (1) *on a discount bond,* the approximate yield will always be less than the true yield, and (2) *on premium bonds,* the approximate yield will always be more than the true yield. Thus, since we're dealing with a discount bond, not only do we know the yield has to be more than the coupon, but more important, we also know the promised yield on this issue has to be more than its approximate yield of 9.69 percent. It's pretty obvious, therefore, that we should start our trial-and-error process with a discount rate of 10 percent:

$$\text{Bond price} = (\$75 \times PVIFA \text{ for 15 years and 10\%})$$
$$+ (\$1,000 \times PVIF \text{ for 15 years and 10\%})$$
$$= (\$75 \times 7.606) + (\$1,000 \times .239)$$
$$= \underline{\$809.45}$$

2.9% in the 1950s, 4.6% in the 1960s and 7.4% in the 1970s—compared with 1.9%, 3.9% and 6.3% for Treasury bills over the same three decades. Unfortunately, steadily rising interest rates erased an average of 2.5% a year from the value of long-term bond portfolios in the 1950–80 period—more than wiping out the bonds' yield advantage over T-bills. As a result, a $1,000 investment in a long-term Treasury bond fund would have grown to only $2,097 after the 30 years ending Dec. 31, 1979, compared with $3,243 for a like investment in a super-safe T-bill portfolio.

In the 1980s, by contrast, a steady decline in interest rates meant long-term bonds put on a much better showing than their yields would have indicated. While the average 10.4% yield on long term Treasurys was only 1.43 percentage points better than the average T-bill yield during the decade, rising bond prices (caused by falling market rates) pushed total returns on Treasurys up to an average of 12.6% a year—beating T-bill returns by a generous 3.7-percentage-point margin. And in 1991, long-term Treasury bonds racked up total returns of 19.3%—beating T-bills by a stunning 13.7 percentage points.

Of course, no one really knows where interest rates will go—and trying to predict them has proved a fruitless exercise, even for professionals. But investors can get a handle on the risks they face in the short run by considering how total returns on different investments might react to interest rate changes over, say, the next 12 months. For example, if interest rates were to fall one percentage point over the next 12 months, a typical portfolio of long-term bonds (maturing in more than 10 years) would generate an estimated total return of about 13%. But if interest rates were to *rise* by one percentage point, the total return would shrink to about 1%—making a money-fund return look good by comparison. Looking at the problem this way tells the investor how much rates would have to rise before the returns on long-term bonds are reduced to the level of, say, bank CDs or some other short-term benchmark. Clearly, the farther rates have to rise, the more cushion you have and the more secure are your investments. No matter how you look at it, however, the old adage "you can't tell a book by its cover" certainly does apply to the bond market: Just because a bond promises a *yield* of X percent doesn't mean that's the *return* you'll actually end up with.

Source: Adapted from Barbara Donnelly, "Bond Investors Who Fixate Too Much on Yields Risk Missing the Big Picture," *The Wall Street Journal,* March 13, 1992, p. C1.

Our computed price of $809.45 is reasonably close to the bond's current market price of $809.50. As a result, the solving rate of 10 percent is the true yield-to-maturity (or promised yield) on this bond.

Given some fairly simple modifications, it's also possible to find yield-to-maturity using semi-annual compounding. To do so, we cut the annual coupon in half, double the number of years (periods) to maturity, and use the bond valuation model in Equation 9.3. Returning to our 7½ percent, 15-year bond, let's see what happens when we try a discount rate of 10 percent. In this case, with semi-annual compounding, we'd use a discount rate of 5 percent (i.e., 10% ÷ 2); using this discount rate and 30 six-month periods to maturity (i.e., 15 × 2) to specify the present-value interest factor, we have:

$$\text{Bond price} = (\$75/2 \times PVIFA^* \text{ for 5\% and 30 periods})$$
$$+(\$1,000 \times PVIF \text{ for 5\% and 30 periods})$$

$$= (\$37.50 \times 15.373) + (\$1,000 \times .231) = \underline{\underline{\$807.49}}$$

As we can see, a semi-annual discount rate of 5 percent results in a computed bond value that's a bit short of our target price of $809.50. Given the inverse relationship between price and yield, it follows that if we need a higher price, we'll have to try a lower yield (discount rate). Thus, we know the semi-annual yield on this bond has to be something less than 5%. Through interpolation, we find that a semi-annual discount rate of 4.90% gives us a computed bond value of $809.50. *Now, the final step in the process is to double the solving rate in order to obtain an annual rate of return.* Doing so gives us a true yield-to-maturity (or promised yield) on this bond of 4.90% × 2 = 9.80%. That's the annual rate of return we'll earn on the bond if coupons are paid semi-annually and the issue is held to maturity.

Finding the Yield on a Zero

The same promised yield procedures as described above—Equation 9.2 with annual compounding or Equation 9.3 with semi-annual compounding—can also be used to find the yield-to-maturity on a zero coupon bond. The only difference is that the coupon portion of the equation can be ignored since it will, of course, equal zero. All you have to do to find the promised yield on a zero is to *divide the current market price of the bond by $1,000*; then, look for the computed interest factor in the present-value Table A.3 (in Appendix A). To illustrate, consider a 15-year zero-coupon issue that can be purchased today for $315. Dividing this amount by the bond's par value of $1,000, we obtain an interest factor of $315/$1,000 = .315. Now, using annual compounding, look in Appendix A, Table A.3 (the table of present-value interest factors for single cash flows): go down the first column to year 15 and then look across that row until you find an interest factor that equals (or is very close to) .315. Once you've found the factor, look up the column to the "interest rate" heading, and you've got the promised yield of the issue. Using this approach, we see the bond in our example has a promised yield of 8 percent, since that's the rate that gives us the interest factor we're looking for. Had we been using semi-annual compounding, we'd do exactly the same thing, excepts we'd go down to "year 30" and start the process there. (*Note:* Use of the approximate yield method is *not* recommended with zero coupon bonds since the margin of error is just too great.)

Expected Return

Rather than buying a bond and holding it to maturity (as presumed in the promised yield formulas), many investors will trade in and out of bonds long before they mature. These investors have short anticipated holding periods and certainly have no intention of holding the bonds to maturity. As a result, yield-to-maturity has relatively little meaning for them, other than providing an indication of the rate of return used to price the bond. These investors obviously need an alternative measure of return that can be used to assess the investment appeal of those bonds they intend

expected return
the rate of return an
investor can expect
to earn by holding a
bond over a period
of time less than the
life of the issue.

realized yield
same as expected
return

to trade in and out of. Such an alternative measure is **expected return,** which indicates the rate of return an investor can expect to earn by holding a bond over a period of time that's less (and in most cases, substantially less) than the life of the issue. (Expected return is also known as **realized yield** as it shows the return an investor would realize by trading in and out of bonds over short holding periods.) Expected return lacks the precision of yield-to-maturity, since the major cash flow variables are largely the product of investor expectations and estimates. In particular, going into the investment, both the length of the holding period and the future selling prices of the bond are pure estimates and as such, subject to varying degrees of uncertainty. For this reason, the approximate yield method is often used to measure expected return. With some modifications to the standard approximate yield formula, we can use the following equation to measure expected return:

Equation 9.6

$$\frac{\text{Expected}}{\text{return}} = \frac{\text{annual} \atop \text{interest income} + \dfrac{\text{expected future price} - \text{current market price}}{\text{years in holding period}}}{\dfrac{\text{expected future price} + \text{current market price}}{2}}$$

$$= \frac{I + \dfrac{FP - P}{n}}{\dfrac{FP + P}{2}}$$

Note that in this case the *expected future price* of the bond is used in place of par value ($1,000), and the *length of the holding period* is used in place of term to maturity. The *future price* of the bond has to be determined when computing expected realized yield; this is done by using the standard bond price formula, as described above. The most difficult part of deriving a reliable future price is, of course, coming up with future market interest rates that you feel will exist when the bond is sold. Based on an analysis of market interest rates, *the investor estimates a promised yield that the issue is expected to carry at the date of sale and then uses that yield to figure the bond's future price.*

To illustrate, take one more look at our 7½ percent, 15-year bond. This time, let's assume the bond is trading a discount, but the investor feels the price will rise sharply as interest rates fall over the next few years. In particular, assume the bond is presently priced at $810 (to yield 10%) and that the investor anticipates holding the bond for three years. Over that time she expects market rates to drop so that the price of the bond should rise to around $960 by the end of the three-year holding period. (Actually, we found the future price of the bond—$960—by assuming interest rates *will* fall to 8 percent in 3 years; we then used the standard bond price formula—in this case Equation 9.2—to find the value of a 7½ percent, 12-year obligation, which is how many years to maturity a 15-year bond will have at the end of a 3-year holding period.) Thus, we are assuming that an investor will buy the bond today at a market price of $810 and sell the issue 3 years later—after interest rates have declined to 8 percent—at a price of $960. Given these assumptions, the expected return (realized yield) on this bond would be:

$$\text{Expected return} = \frac{\$75 + \dfrac{\$960 - \$810}{3}}{\dfrac{\$960 + \$810}{2}} = \underline{\underline{14.12\%}}$$

The better-than-14 percent return on this investment is fairly substantial, but keep in mind that this is a measure of *expected* yield only. It is, of course, subject to variation if things do not turn out as anticipated, particularly with regard to the market yield expected to prevail at the end of the holding period. (*Note:* If the anticipated investment horizon is one year or less, Equation 9.6 could be used to measure expected return over such a short holding period. Alternatively, an investor could just as easily use a simple *holding period return* measure, like the one described in Chapter 4. There would be a slight difference in computed returns, but it wouldn't be all that much.)

Valuing a Bond

Depending on investor objectives, the value of a bond can be determined by either its promised yield or its expected return. Conservative, income-oriented investors will employ *promised yield* as the way to value bonds. Coupon income over extended periods of time is the principal objective of these investors, and promised yield provides a viable measure of return under these circumstances. More aggressive bond traders, on the other hand, will use *expected return* to value bonds. The capital gains that can be earned by buying and selling bonds over relatively short holding periods is a chief concern of these investors and as such, expected return is more important to them than the promised yield that exists at the time the bond is purchased.

In either case, promised or expected yield provides a *measure of return* that can be used to determine the relative attractiveness of fixed-income securities. But to do so, the appropriate measure of return should be evaluated in light of the amount of *risk* involved in the investment. Bonds are no different from stocks in that the amount of promised or expected return should be sufficient to cover the investor's exposure to risk. Thus, the greater the amount of perceived risk, the greater the amount of return that the bond should generate. If the bond meets this hurdle, it can then be compared to other potential investments outlets. If you find it difficult to do better in a risk-return sense, then the bond under evaluation should be given serious consideration as an investment outlet.

DURATION AND IMMUNIZATION

One of the problems with yield-to-maturity (YTM) is that it assumes you can reinvest the bond's periodic coupon payments at the same rate over time. But if you reinvest this interest income at a lower rate (or spend it), your real return will be much lower than that indicated by YTM. The assumption that interest rates will remain constant is a key weakness of YTM. Another flaw with YTM is that it assumes the issuer will make all payments on time and won't call the bonds before maturity, as often happens when interest rates drop. For bonds that aren't held to maturity, prices will reflect prevailing interest rates, which will likely differ from YTM. If rates have moved up since a bond was purchased, the bond will sell at a discount. If interest rates have dropped, it will sell at a premium. The sales price will obviously have a big impact on the total return earned.

The problem with yield-to-maturity, in effect, is that it fails to take into account the effects of reinvestment risk and price, or market, risk. To see how reinvestment and price risk behave relative to one another, consider a situation in which market interest rates have undergone a sharp decline. Under such conditions, a lot of investors might be tempted to cash out their holdings and take some gains (in other words, to do a little "profit taking"). The fact is that selling before maturity is the only way to take advantage of falling interest rates, since a bond will pay its par value at maturity, regardless of prevailing interest rates. The problem is that when interest rates fall, so too do opportunities to invest at high rates. Thus, whereas you gain on the price side, you lose on the reinvestment side. Even if you don't sell out, you are still faced with increased reinvestment risk, because in order to earn the YTM promised on your bonds, you have to be able to reinvest each coupon payment at the same YTM rate. Obviously, as rates fall, you'll find it increasingly difficult to reinvest the stream of coupon payments at or above the YTM rate. When market rates rise, just the opposite happens: The price of the bond falls, but your reinvestment opportunities improve.

What is needed is a yardstick or measure of performance that overcomes these deficiencies and takes into account both price and reinvestment risks. Such a yardstick is provided by something called **duration,** which captures in a single measure the extent to which the price of a bond will react to different interest rate environments. Because duration gauges the price volatility of a bond, it gives you a better idea of how likely you are to earn the return (YTM) you expect. That, in turn, will help you tailor your holdings to match your expectations of interest-rate movements.

duration
a measure of bond price volatility, it captures both price and reinvestment risks to indicate how a bond will react to different interest rate environments.

The Concept of Duration

The concept of duration was first outlined in 1938 by actuary Frederick Macaulay to help insurance companies match their cash inflows with payments. When applied to bonds, duration recognizes that the amount and frequency of the interest payments, yield-to-maturity, and time to maturity all affect the "time dimension" of a bond. The time to maturity is important because it influences how much a bond's price rises or falls as interest rates change. In general, bonds with longer maturities fluctuate more than shorter-term issues when rates move. However, maturity alone isn't a sufficient measure of the time dimension of bonds. Maturity tells you only when the last payment will be made. It doesn't say anything about interim payments. The amount of reinvestment risk is also directly related to the size of a bond's coupons: Bonds paying high coupons have greater reinvestment risk simply because there's more to reinvest.

Any change in interest rates will cause price risk and reinvestment risk to push and pull bonds in opposite directions. An increase in rates will produce a drop in price but will lessen reinvestment risk by making it easier to reinvest coupon payments at or above the YTM rate. Declining rates, in contrast, will boost prices but increase reinvestment risk. At some point in time, these two forces should exactly offset each other. *That point in time is the bond's duration.*

In general, bond duration possesses the following properties:

- Higher coupons result in shorter durations.
- Longer maturities mean longer durations.
- Higher yields (YTMs) lead to shorter durations.

Together, a bond's coupon, maturity, and yield interact with one another to produce the issue's measure of duration. Knowing a bond's duration is helpful because it combines price and reinvestment risks in such a way that it captures the underlying *volatility* of a bond. A *bond's duration and volatility are directly related:* the shorter the duration, the less volatility there is in the bond.

 ## Measuring Duration

Duration is a measure of the effective, as opposed to actual, maturity of a fixed-income security. As we will see, only those bonds promising a single payment to be received at maturity (i.e., no yearly coupons) have durations equal to their actual years to maturity. Zero-coupon bonds are such bonds. For all others, *duration measures are always less than their actual maturities.*

While a bond's term to maturity is certainly a useful concept, it falls short of being a reliable measure of a bond's effective life because it does not consider all the bond's cash flows or the time value of money. Duration is a far superior measure of the effective timing of a bond's cash flows since it explicitly considers both the time value of money and the bond's coupon and principal payments. Duration may be thought of as the *weighted-average life of a bond,* where the weights are the relative future cash flows of the bond, all of which are discounted to their present values. Mathematically, we can find the duration on a bond as follows:

Equation 9.7
$$\text{Duration} = \sum_{t=1}^{T}\left[\frac{PV(C_t)}{P_{\text{bond}}} \times t\right]$$

where

$PV(C_t)$ = present value of a future coupon or principal payment

P_{bond} = current market price of the bond

t = year in which the cash flow (coupon or principal) payment is received

T = the remaining life of the bond, in years

Note that in Equation 9.7, we are using *annual coupons and annual compounding,* to keep the discussion and calculations as simple as possible.

Although Equation 9.7 may appear formidable at first glance, it's really not as tough as it looks. Indeed, if you follow the steps as noted below, you'll find duration is relatively easy to calculate. Equation 9.7 can be "translated" into the following four steps:

Step 1.   Find the present value of each annual coupon or principal payment $[PV(C_t)]$. *Use the prevailing YTM on the bond as the discount rate.*

Step 2.   Divide this present value by the current market price of the bond (P_{bond}).

Step 3.   Multiply this relative value by the year in which the cash flow is to be received (t).

Step 4.   Repeat steps 1 through 3 for each year in the life of the bond, and then *add up* the values computed in step 3.

Table 9.1 illustrates this procedure, as it presents the duration calculation for a 7½ percent, 15-year bond priced (at $957) to yield 8 percent. Note that this particular 15-year bond has a duration of less than 9½ years—9.36 years, to be exact. Here's how we found that value: Along with the current market price of the bond ($957), the first 3 columns of Table 9.1 provide the basic input data: Column (1) is the year (t) of the cash flow; Column (2) is the amount of the annual cash flows (from coupons and principal); and Column (3) is the appropriate present value interest factors, given an 8% discount rate (which is equal to the prevailing YTM on the bond). The first thing we do—Step 1— is find the present value of each of the annual cash flows (Col. 4), and then—Step 2—divide each of these present values by the current market price of the bond (Col. 5). Finally, multiplying the relative

TABLE 9.1 Duration Calculation for a 7½%, 15-year Bond Priced to Yield 8%

(1)	(2)	(3)	(4)	(5)	(6)
Year (t)	Annual Cash Flow (C_t)	PVIF (@ 8%)	Present Value of Annual Cash Flows $[PV(C_t)]$ (2) × (3)	$PV(C_t)$ Divided by Current Market Price of the Bond* (4) ÷ $957	Time-Weighted Relative Cash Flow (1) × (5)
1	$75	.926	$69.45	.0726	.0726
2	75	.857	64.27	.0672	.1343
3	75	.794	59.55	.0622	.1867
4	75	.735	55.12	.0576	.2304
5	75	.681	51.08	.0534	.2668
6	75	.630	47.25	.0494	.2962
7	75	.583	43.72	.0457	.3198
8	75	.540	40.50	.0423	.3386
9	75	.500	37.50	0.392	.3527
10	75	.463	34.72	.0363	.3628
11	75	.429	32.18	.0336	.3698
12	75	.397	29.78	.0311	.3734
13	75	.368	27.60	.0288	.3749
14	75	.340	25.50	.0266	.3730
15	1075	.315	338.62	.3538	5.3076
				Duration	9.36 yrs.

*If this bond is priced to yield 8%, it would be quoted in the market at $957.

cash flows from Column (5) by the year *(t)* in which the cash flow occurs—Step 3—results in a time-weighted value for each of the annual cash flow streams (Col. 6). When we add up all the values in Column (6)—Step 4—we have the duration of the bond. As we can see, the duration of this bond is a lot less than its maturity—a condition that would exist with any coupon-bearing bond. In addition, keep in mind that *the duration on any bond will change over time* as YTM and term to maturity change. For example, the duration on this 7½ percent, 15-year bond will *fall* as the bond nears maturity and/or as the market yield (YTM) on the bond increases.

Duration is not merely a single security concept; rather, it also applies to whole portfolios of fixed-income securities. The duration of an entire portfolio is extremely easy to calculate—all that's required is the durations of the individual securities in the portfolio and the proportion that each security contributes to the overall value of the portfolio. Thus, *the duration of a portfolio is simply the weighted average of the durations of each security in the portfolio,* where the weights are the wealth proportions of each of the individual securities. For example, consider a five-bond portfolio made up as follows:

Bond	Amount Invested*	Weight	×	Bond Duration	=	Portfolio Duration
Government bonds	$ 270,000	0.15		6.25		0.9375
Aaa corporates	180,000	0.10		8.90		0.8900
Aa utilities	450,000	0.25		10.61		2.6525
Agency issues	360,000	0.20		11.03		2.2060
Baa industrials	540,000	0.30		12.55		3.7650
	$1,800,000	1.00				10.4510

*Amount invested = current market price times the par value of the bonds. That is, if the government bonds are quoted at 90 and the investor holds $300,000 in these bonds, then .90 × $300,000 = $270,000.

In this case, this $1.8 million bond *portfolio* has an average duration of approximately 10.5 years. Obviously, if you want to change the duration of the portfolio, you can do so by either changing the asset mix of the portfolio (shift the weight of the portfolio to longer- or shorter-duration bonds, as desired) and/or by adding new bonds to the portfolio with the desired duration characteristics. As we will see below, such information is used in a bond portfolio strategy known as *bond immunization.*

 ### Bond Duration and Price Volatility

A bond's price volatility is in part a function of its term to maturity and in part of its coupon yield. Unfortunately, there is no exact relationship between bond maturities and bond price volatilities with respect to interest rate changes. There is, however, a fairly close relationship between bond duration and price volatility—at least, so long as the market doesn't experience wide swings in yield. That is, duration can be used as a viable predictor of price volatility so long as the yield swings are relatively small (no more than 100 basis points or so). The problem is, because the price-yield relationship of a bond is convex in form (but duration is not), when the market (or bond) undergoes a big change in yield, duration will *understate* price appreciation when rates fall and will *overstate* the price decline when rates increase. Assuming that's not the case (i.e., that we're dealing with relatively small changes in market yield), then multiplying a bond's duration value by −1 results in its price elasticity with respect to interest rate changes. Thus, by calculating a bond's duration, it is possible to obtain a fairly accurate measure of how much its price will change relative to a given (reasonably small) change in market interest rates.

The mathematical link between bond price and interest rate changes involves the concept of *modified duration*. The formula for modified duration is provided below:

Equation 9.8
$$\text{Modified duration} = \frac{\text{duration in years}}{1 + \text{yield to maturity}}$$

Thus, the modified duration value for the 15-year bond discussed above is as follows:

$$\text{Modified duration} = \frac{9.36}{1 + 0.08} = \underline{\underline{8.67}}$$

To determine this bond's percentage price change resulting from an increase in market interest rates from, say, 8 to 8.5 percent, the modified duration value calculated above is first multiplied by −1 (due to the inverse relationship between bond prices and interest rates) and then by the change in the level of the market interest rates; that is:

Equation 9.9
$$\text{Percent change in bond price} = -1 \times \text{modified duration} \times \text{change in interest rates}$$
$$= -1 \times 8.67 \times 0.5\% = -4.33\%$$

Thus, a 50 basis point change in market interest rates will lead to almost a 4½ percent drop in the price of this 15-year bond. Such information is useful to bond investors seeking (or trying to avoid) high price volatility.

Uses of Bond Duration Measures

Bond investors have learned to use duration analysis in many ways. One use, for example, is to measure the potential price volatility of a particular issue, as we saw above with modified duration. Another, perhaps more important, use of duration is in the *structuring of bond portfolios*. For example, if a bond investor believes that interest rates are about to increase, he could calculate the expected percentage decrease in the value of his portfolio, given a certain change in market interest rates, and then reduce the overall duration of the portfolio by selling higher-duration bonds and buying those of shorter duration. Such a strategy would prove quite profitable since short-duration instruments do not decline in value to the same degree as longer bonds. Of course, if the investor believed that interest rates were about to decrease, the opposite strategy would be optimal.

Although active, short-term investors frequently use duration analysis in their day-to-day operations, longer-term investors have also employed duration analysis in planning their investment decisions. Indeed, a strategy known as *bond portfolio immunization* represents one of the most important uses of duration.

Bond Immunization

Some investors holding portfolios of bonds do not actively attempt to "beat the market" but, rather, seek to accumulate a specified level of wealth at the end of a given investment horizon. For these investors, bond portfolio immunization often proves to be of great value. Immunization allows an investor to derive a specified rate of return from bond investments over a given investment interval *regardless of what happens to market interest rates over the course of the holding period*. In essence, an investor is able to "immunize" his portfolio from the effects of changes in market interest rates over a given investment horizon.

To understand how and why bond portfolio immunization is possible, it is necessary to understand that changes in market interest rates lead to two distinct and opposite changes in bond valuation. The first effect, known as the *price effect,* results in portfolio valuation changes when interest rates change before the end of the desired investment horizon. This is true since interest rate decreases lead to bond price increases, and vice versa. The second effect, known as the *reinvestment effect,* arises because the yield-to-maturity calculation assumes that all of a bond's coupon payments will be reinvested at the prevailing yield to maturity on the bond when it was purchased. If interest rates increase, however, the forthcoming coupons may be reinvested at a higher rate than that expected by the investor, leading to increases in investor wealth. Of course, the opposite is true when interest rates decrease. Thus, whereas an increase in rates has a negative effect on a bond's price, it has a positive effect on the reinvestment of coupons: Taken together, when interest rate changes do occur, the price and reinvestment effects work against each other from the investor's wealth standpoint. When do these counteracting effects exactly offset each other and leave the investor's wealth position unchanged? You guessed it: when the average duration of the portfolio just equals the investment horizon of the investor. This should not come as much of a surprise, since such a property is already imbedded in and is fundamental to duration itself. Accordingly, if it applies to a single bond, it should also apply to the *weighted-average duration of a bond portfolio*. Such a condition (of offsetting price and reinvestment effects) is said to exist when a bond portfolio is immunized. More specifically, an investor's wealth position is immunized from the effects of interest rate changes when the *weighted-average duration of the bond portfolio is exactly equal to the desired investment horizon*. Table 9.2 provides an example of bond immunization using a 10-year, 8 percent coupon bond with a duration of eight years; here, we assume the investor's desired investment horizon is also eight years in length.

The example provided in Table 9.2 assumes that the investor originally purchased the 8 percent coupon bond when issued at par. It further assumes that market interest rates for bonds of this quality change from 8 percent to 6 percent at the end

TABLE 9.2 Bond Immunization

Year	Cash Flow from Bond						Terminal Value of Reinvested Cash Flow
1	$ 80	×	$(1.08)^4$	×	$(1.06)^3$	=	$ 129.63
2	80	×	$(1.08)^3$	×	$(1.06)^3$	=	120.03
3	80	×	$(1.08)^2$	×	$(1.06)^3$	=	111.14
4	80	×	(1.08)	×	$(1.06)^3$	=	102.90
5	80	×	$(1.06)^3$			=	95.28
6	80	×	$(1.06)^2$			=	89.89
7	80	×	(1.06)			=	84.80
8	80	×				=	80.00
8	1,036.64*					=	1,036.64
				Total			$1,850.31
				Investor's required wealth at 8%			$1,850.90
				Difference			$ 0.59

*The bond could be sold at a market price of $1,036.64, which is the value of an 8 percent bond with two years to maturity priced to yield 6 percent.

Note: Bond interest coupons are assumed to be paid at year-end. Therefore, there are four years of reinvestment at 8 percent and three years at 6 percent for the first year's $80 coupon.

of the fifth year. Since the investor had an investment horizon of exactly eight years and desires to lock in an interest rate return of exactly 8 percent, she expects to have a terminal wealth value of $1,850.90 [i.e., $1,000 invested at 8 percent for 8 years = $1,000 × $(1.08)^8$ = $1,850.90], regardless of interest rate changes in the interim. As can be seen from the bottom-line results presented in Table 9.2, the immunization strategy netted the investor a total of $1,850.31—which is just 59 *cents* short of the desired goal. This is a remarkable result and clearly demonstrates the power of bond immunization and the versatility of bond duration. Even though the table uses a single bond for purposes of illustration, the same results—i.e., the achievement of a desired terminal value/rate of return—could be obtained from a *bond portfolio* that is maintained at the *proper weighted-average duration.*

Although bond immunization is a powerful investment tool, it is clearly not a passive investment strategy as it *requires continual portfolio rebalancing on the part of the investor* in order to maintain a fully-immunized portfolio. Indeed, every time interest rates change, the duration of a portfolio will change. Since effective immunization requires that the portfolio have a duration value equal in length to the investor's (remaining investment) horizon, the composition of the investor's portfolio must be rebalanced each time interest rates change. Further, even in the absence of interest rate changes, a bond's duration declines more slowly than its term to maturity. This, of course, means that the mere passage of time will dictate changes in portfolio composition. Such changes will ensure that the duration of the portfolio continues to match the remaining time in the investment horizon. In summary, portfolio immunization strategies can be extremely effective bond management tools. At the same time, it is important to realize that immunization is not a totally passive strategy and is not without potential problems—the most notable of which are those associated with portfolio rebalancing.

BOND INVESTMENT STRATEGIES

Generally, bond investors tend to follow one of three kinds of investment programs. First, there are those who live off the income—the conservative, quality-conscious, income-oriented investors who seek to maximize current income. In contrast, speculators, or bond traders, have considerably different investment objective: to maximize capital gains, often within a short time span. This highly speculative investment approach requires considerable expertise, as it is based almost entirely on estimates of the future course of interest rates. Finally, there are serious long-term investors, whose objective is to maximize total income—from both current income and capital gains—over fairly long holding periods.

In order to achieve the objectives of any one of these three programs, an investor needs to adopt a strategy that will be compatible with his or her goals. Professional money managers use a variety of techniques to manage the multimillion-dollar bond portfolios under their direction. These vary from passive approaches, to semi-active strategies, to active fully managed strategies using interest-rate forecasting and yield-spread analysis. Most of these strategies are fairly complex and require substantial computer support. Even so, we can look briefly at some of the more basic strategies to at least gain an appreciation of the different ways that fixed-income securities can be used to reach different investment objectives.

Passive Strategies

The bond immunization strategies discussed above are considered to be primarily *passive* in nature; investors using these tools typically are *not* attempting to beat the market. Rather, these investors immunize their portfolios in an effort to lock in specified rates of return (or terminal values) that they deem acceptable, given the risks involved. Generally, passive investment strategies are characterized by a lack of input regarding investor expectations of interest rate and/or bond price changes. Further, these strategies typically do not generate significant transaction costs. A *buy-and-hold* trading strategy is perhaps the most passive of all investment strategies; all that is required is that the investor replace bonds that have deteriorating credit ratings, have matured, or have been called. Although buy-and-hold investors restrict their ability to earn above-average returns, they also minimize the dead-weight losses represented by transaction costs.

bond ladders
a bond investment strategy wherein an equal amount of money is invested in a series of bonds with staggered maturities.

One approach that's a bit more active than buy-and-hold, and which is popular with many individual and institutional investors, is the use of so-called **bond ladders,** wherein an equal amount is invested in a series of bonds with staggered maturities. Here's how a bond ladder works: Suppose an individual wants to confine her investing to fixed-income securities with maturities of 10 years or less; she could set up the *ladder* by investing in (roughly) equal amounts of, say, 3-, 5-, 7-, and 10-year issues. Then, when the 3-year issue matures, the money from it (along with any new capital) would be put into a *new* 10-year note. The process would continue rolling over like this so that eventually the investor would hold a full ladder of staggered 10-year notes. By rolling into new 10-year issues every two or three years, the investor can do a kind of dollar-cost averaging and thereby lessen the impact of swings in market rates. Actually, the laddered approach is a safe, simple, and almost automatic way of investing for the long haul—indeed, once the ladder is set up, it's followed in a fairly routine manner. A key ingredient of this or any other passive strategy is, of course, the use of high-quality investment vehicles that possess attractive features, maturities, and yields.

Trading on Forecasted Interest Rate Behavior

The *forecasted interest rate behavior* approach is highly risky, because it relies heavily on the imperfect forecast of future interest rates. It seeks attractive capital gains when interest rates are expected to decline and the preservation of capital when an increase in interest rates is anticipated. The idea is to increase the return on a bond portfolio by making strategic moves in anticipation of interest rate changes. Such a strategy is tantamount to *market timing* and as a result, carries with it some definite risks and costs. An unusual feature of this tactic is that most of the trading is done with *investment-grade securities,* since a high degree of interest rate sensitivity is required to capture the maximum amount of price behavior. Once interest rate expectations have been specified, this strategy rests largely on technical matters. For example, when a decline in rates is anticipated, aggressive bond investors will often seek to lengthen the maturity (or duration) of their bonds (or bond portfolios). The reason: longer-term bonds rise more in price in response to a given drop in rates than do their shorter-term counterparts. At the same time, investors look for low coupon and/or moderately discounted bonds as this adds to duration and increases the amount of potential price volatility. These interest swings are usually short-lived, so bond traders try to earn as much as possible in as short a time as possible. Margin trading (the use of borrowed money to buy bonds) is also used as a way of magnifying returns. When rates start to level off and move up, these investors begin to shift their money out of long, discounted bonds and into high-yielding issues with short maturities. In other words, they do a complete reversal. During these periods when bond prices are dropping, investors try to earn high yields and protect their money from capital losses. Thus, they tend to use such high-yield, short-term obligations as Treasury bills, money funds, short-term (2–5 year) notes, or even variable-rate notes.

As investors move from passive buy-and-hold postures to more actively managed positions, it's vital that they understand the full ramifications of trading in and out of bonds. Selling bonds to take out profits is fine, but it's usually done after interest rates have fallen. And that's the problem—once you sell the bonds, you have to find a place to reinvest the money. But as we see in the accompanying *Investor Insights* box, finding solid returns in an environment of low interest rates can be a challenge and, many times, can even lead to reduced realized yields.

■ I N V E S T O R   I N S I G H T S ■

Taking Early Profits on Bonds Can Be Costly

Ready to take profits on bonds you bought way back when? Before you do, take a hard look at the numbers. You may be surprised. With the sharp decline in interest rates over the recent past, bonds offered with double-digit yields in the 1980s are now selling at hefty premiums. That means fat profits for investors who sell. The problem is that once you have the profit, you need to reinvest. But where do you put the money to get equivalent return? Because of today's lower yields, taking profits on bonds means staying even at best for most investors. "I have rarely seen it work to the advantage of the seller," says Robert G. Levine, a vice president in the Winnetka, Ill., office of regional brokerage firm Robert W. Baird & Co., Milwaukee.

And if you are swapping municipal bonds, you can actually end up losing money. That's because you are trading tax-free income for a taxable capital gain. Here's how the numbers work. Let's say that in 1982 you bought $100,000 of non-callable, AA-rated, municipal bonds due in the year 2000 and yielding 11.25%. They would generate $11,250 a year of tax-free income. If you sold today, you would get a nice profit, since those bonds are now valued at $136,961. But your $36,961 gain would be taxed at 28%, cutting your profit to only $26,612. Moreover, if you reinvested that $126,612 in similar bonds, you would get a yield of only about 5.7%, dropping the annual tax-free income produced by your investment to $7,217. That's a loss of $4,033 in tax-free income a year. Over eight years, that comes to $32,264 in lost income. The bottom line? If you hold your original bonds until they mature in 2000, you will have your $100,000 of principal back plus eight years of interest, or $90,000, for a total of $190,000. But if you sold today and bought equivalent bonds, you would have only $184,348 in principal and interest, or $5,652 less.

It's the same story even if your bond is likely to be "called at par"—that is, redeemed at face value—before maturity. While it may seem like you will do better by selling the bond before it is called and reinvesting the money in a non-callable bond, the market has already priced your bond to its call date. Selling it early, you have to sell it at the market price. "For any bond swap to be successful, you have to give up something," says Mr. Levine. "You are either going to give up yield, give up quality or change the investment objective from, let's say, tax-exempt to taxable."

That means people who decide to sell their bonds need reasons other than just the desire to lock up profits. Some may need a profit to offset a loss on their income taxes. Others may want to shift their portfolio, changing maturities or trading yield for increased face value at maturity. Repositioning portfolios to improve credit quality can also make sense, given the large number of bond defaults and downgradings. By making the switch, an investor may be able to not only avoid losses in the future, but perhaps even lock in some profits. Of course, there are always those who are willing to bet that interest rates are going to head up, selling bonds at a profit with plans to invest for higher yield later. But if you take that approach, you are no longer an investor, but a speculator! And if you guess wrong, you may be left sitting on your profits for a long, long time.

Source: Lynn Asinof, "Taking Early Profits on Bonds May Add Up to Losses," *The Wall Street Journal,* February 13, 1992, p. C1.

Bond Swaps

bond swap
an investment strategy wherein an investor liquidates one of his current bond holdings and simultaneously buys a different issue in its place.

In a **bond swap,** an investor simply liquidates one position and simultaneously buys a different issue in its place. In essence, this is nothing more than swapping out of one bond into another. Swaps can be executed to increase current yield or yield to maturity, to take advantage of shifts in interest rates, to improve the quality of a portfolio, or for tax purposes. Although some swaps are highly sophisticated, most are fairly simple transactions. They go by a variety of colorful names, such as "profit takeout," "substitution swap," and "tax swap," but they are all used for one basic reason: *to seek portfolio improvement.* We will briefly review two types of bond swaps that are fairly simple and hold considerable appeal for investors: the yield pickup swap and the tax swap.

yield pickup swap
replacement of a low-coupon bond for a comparable higher-coupon bond in order to realize an increase in current yield and yield to maturity.

In a **yield pickup swap** an investor switches out of a low-coupon bond into a comparable higher-coupon issue in order to realize an automatic and instantaneous pickup of current yield and yield to maturity. For example, you would be executing a yield pickup swap if you sold the 20-year, A-rated 6½ percent bonds you held (which were yielding 8 percent at the time) and replaced them with an equal amount of 20-year, A-rated, 7 percent bonds that were priced to yield 8½ percent. By executing the swap, you would improve your current yield (by moving from coupon income of $65 a year to $70 a year), as well as your yield to maturity (from 8 percent to 8½ percent). Basically, such swap opportunities arise because of the *yield spreads* that normally exist between, say, industrial and public utility bonds. The mechanics are fairly simple, and any investor can execute such swaps by simply watching for swap candidates and/or by asking your broker to do so. In fact, the only thing you have to be careful of is that commissions and transaction costs do not eat up all the profits.

tax swap
replacement of a bond that has a capital loss for a similar security; used to offset a gain generated in another part of an investor's portfolio.

The other type of swap that's popular with many investors is the **tax swap,** which is also relatively simple and involves few risks. The technique would be used whenever an investor has a substantial tax liability that has come about as a result of selling some security holdings at a profit. The objective is to execute a bond swap in such a way that the tax liability which accompanies the capital gains *can be eliminated or substantially reduced.* This is done by selling an issue that has undergone a capital *loss* and replacing it with a comparable obligation. For example, assume that an investor had $10,000 worth of corporate bonds that she sold (in the current year) for $15,000, resulting in a capital gain of $5,000. The investor can eliminate the tax liability accompanying the capital gain by selling securities that have capital losses of $5,000. Let's assume the investor finds she holds a 20-year, 4¾ percent municipal bond that (strictly by coincidence of course) has undergone the needed $5,000 drop in value. The investor has the needed tax shield in her portfolio, so now all she has to do is find a viable swap candidate. Suppose she finds a comparable 20-year, 5 percent municipal issue currently trading at about the same price as the issue being sold. By selling the 4¾s and simultaneously buying a comparable amount of the 5s, the investor will not only increase her tax-free yield (from 4¾ to 5 percent), but she'll also eliminate the capital gains tax liability. The only caution that should be kept in mind is that *identical issues cannot be used* in such swap transactions, since the IRS would consider this a ''wash sale'' (see Chapter 3) and therefore disallow the loss. Moreover, it should be clear that the capital loss must occur in the same taxable year as the capital gain. These are the only limitations and explain why this technique is so popular with knowledgeable investors, particularly at year end, when tax loss sales (and tax swaps) multiply as investors hurry to establish capital losses.

SUMMARY

1. The behavior of *interest rates* is the single most important force in the bond market, as it determines not only the amount of current income an investor will receive but also the amount of capital gains (or losses) that an investor will earn. Indeed, changes in market interest rates can have a dramatic impact on the total annual returns actually obtained from bonds over time.

2. There are many forces that drive the behavior of interest rates over time, including inflation, the cost and availability of funds, the size of the federal deficit, and the level of interest rates in major foreign markets. One force that's particularly important, and is very closely followed, is the term structure of interest rates, which relates yield-to-maturity to term-to-maturity.

3. Bonds are valued (priced) in the marketplace on the basis of their required rates of return (or market yields). Indeed, the whole process of pricing a bond begins with the yield it should provide. Once that important piece of information is known (or estimated), the whole bond valuation process becomes rather mechanical: a standard, present-value–based model is used to find the dollar price of a bond.

4. There are basically three types of yields that are important to investors: current yield, promised yield, and expected yield. Promised yield (also known as yield-to-maturity) is the most important and widely used bond valuation measure and captures both the current income and price appreciation of an issue. Expected yield, in contrast, is a valuation measure that's used by aggressive bond traders to show the total return that can be earned from trading in and out of a bond long before it matures.

5. Bond duration is one of the most important concepts in bond valuation and investing. Basically, duration takes into account the effects of both reinvestment and price (or market) risks. It captures, in a single measure, the extent to which the price of a bond will react to different interest rate environments. Equally important, duration can be used to immunize whole bond portfolios from the often devastating forces of changing market interest rates.

6. As investment vehicles, bonds can be used as a source of income, as a way to seek capital gains by speculating on the movement in interest rates, or as a way of achieving attractive long-term returns. To achieve these objectives, investors will often employ one or more of the following bond investment strategies: various passive strategies (like buy-and-hold, bond ladders, and portfolio immunization), bond trading based on forecasted interest rate behavior, and bond swaps.

QUESTIONS

1. Is there a single market rate of interest applicable to all segments of the bond market, or is there a series of market yields that exists? Explain and note the investment implications of such a market environment.

2. Why is the reinvestment of interest income so important to bond investors?

3. Why is interest sensitivity important to bond speculators? Does the need for interest sensitivity explain why active bond traders tend to use high-grade issues? Explain.

4. Explain why interest rates are important to both conservative and aggressive bond investors. What causes interest rates to move, and how can individual investors monitor such movements?

5. What is the term structure of interest rates, and how does it relate to the yield curve? What information is required to plot a yield curve? For a given class of similar-risk securities, what does each of the following yield curve patterns reflect about interest rates?

    a. Upward-sloping
    b. Downward-sloping
    c. Flat

    Historically, which form has been dominant?

6. Describe briefly each of the following theories of the term structure of interest rates:

    a. Expectations hypothesis
    b. Liquidity preference theory
    c. Market segmentation theory

    According to these theories, what conditions would result in a downward-sloping yield curve? Which theory do you think is most valid, and why?

7. Using a recent copy of *The Wall Street Journal* or *Barron's,* find Treasury bond yields for securities with the following maturities: 3 months, six months, 1 year, 3 years, 5 years, 10 years, 15 years, 20 years, and 30 years. Construct a yield curve based on these reported yields, putting term-to-maturity on the horizontal *(x)* axis and yield-to-maturity on the vertical *(y)* axis. Briefly discuss the general shape of your yield curve. What conclusions might you draw about interest rate movements from this yield curve?

8. How might you, as a bond investor, use information on the term structure of interest rates and yield curves when making investment decisions?

9. Explain how market yield affects the price of a bond. Could you value (price) a bond without knowing its market yield? Explain.

10. Why are bonds usually priced using semi-annual compounding? Does it make all that much difference if you use annual compounding? Briefly explain how you'd go about pricing a zero-coupon bond.

11. What's the difference between current yield and yield-to-maturity? Between promised yield and realized yield?

12. What does the term *duration* mean to bond investors, and how does the duration on a bond differ from its maturity? What is modified duration and how is it used?

13. Describe the process of bond portfolio immunization, and note why an investor would want to immunize a portfolio. Would you consider portfolio immunization to be a passive investment strategy, comparable to, say, a buy-and-hold approach? Explain.

14. Briefly describe both of the following bond investment strategies, and note how and why they would be used by investors:

    a. Tax swaps
    b. Bond ladders

PROBLEMS

1. Two bonds have par values of $1,000; one is a 5 percent, 15-year bond priced to yield 8 percent, and the other is a 7½ percent, 20-year bond priced to yield 6 percent. Which of these two has the lower price? (Assume annual compounding in both cases.)

2. Using semi-annual compounding, find the prices of the following bonds:

    a. A 10½%, 15-year bond priced to yield 8%.
    b. A 7%, 10-year bond priced to yield 8%.
    c. A 12%, 20-year bond priced at 10%.

    Repeat the problem using annual compounding. Then comment on the differences you found in the prices of the bonds.

3. An investor is considering the purchase of an 8%, 18-year corporate bond that's being priced to yield 10%. She thinks that in a year, this same bond will be priced in the market to yield 9%. Using annual compounding, find the price of the bond today and in one year; next, find the holding period return on this investment, assuming the investor's expectations hold up.

4. Compute the current yield of a 10 percent, 25-year bond that is currently priced in the market at $1,200. Use the approximate method to find the promised yield on this bond. Repeat the promised yield calculation, but this time use semi-annual compounding to find the precise yield-to-maturity.

5. A 25-year, zero-coupon bond was recently being quoted at 11⅝. Find the current yield *and* promised yield of this issue, given the bond has a par value of $1,000. Using annual compounding, how much would an investor have to pay for this bond if it were priced to yield 12 percent?

6. Assume that an investor pays $800 for a long-term bond that carries an 8 percent coupon; in three years she hopes to sell the issue for $850. If her expectations come true, what realized yield would this investor earn? What would her holding period return be if she were able to sell the bond (at $850) after only six months?

7. Using annual compounding, find the yield-to-maturity for each of the following bonds:

    a. A 9½%, 20-year bond priced at $957.43.
    b. A 16%, 15-year bond priced at $1,684.76.
    c. A 5½%, 18-year bond priced at $510.65.

8. Find the duration and modified duration of a 20-year, 10% corporate bond that's being priced to yield 8%. According to the modified duration of this bond, how much of a price change would this bond incur if market yields rose to 9% in one year? Using annual compounding,

calculate the price of this bond in one year if rates do rise to 9%. How does this price change compare to that predicted by the modified duration? Explain the difference.

9. Which *one* of the following bonds would you select if you thought market interest rates were going to fall by 50 basis points over the next 6 months?

   a. A bond with a duration of 8.46 years that's currently being priced to yield 7½%.
   b. A bond with a duration of 9.30 years that's priced to yield 10%.
   c. A bond with a duration of 8.75 years that's priced to yield 5¾%.

10. Arlene Darling is an aggressive bond trader who likes to speculate on interest rate swings. Market interest rates are presently at 9 percent, but they're expected to fall to 7 percent within a year. As a result, Arlene is thinking about buying one of the following issues: *either* a 25-year, zero-coupon bond, or a 20-year, 7½ percent bond. (Both bonds have $1,000 par values and carry the same agency rating.) Assuming Arlene wants to maximize capital gains, which one of the two issues should she select? What if she wants to maximize the total return (interest income and capital gains) from her investment? Why did one issue provide better capital gains than the other? Based on the duration of each bond, which one should be more price volatile?

11. Bill Peters is a 35-year-old bank executive who's just inherited a large sum of money. Having spent several years in the bank's investment department, he's well aware of the concept of duration and decides to apply it to his bond portfolio. In particular, Bill intends to use $1 million of his inheritance to purchase four U.S. Treasury bonds:

    1. An 8¼%, 13-year bond that's priced at $1,045 to yield 7.47%.
    2. A 7⅞%, 15-year bond that's priced at $1,020 to yield 7.60%.
    3. A 20-year stripped Treasury that's priced at $202 to yield 8.22%.
    4. A 24-year, 7½% bond that's priced at $955 to yield 7.90%.

    a. Find the duration and modified duration of each bond.
    b. Find the duration of the whole bond portfolio if Bill puts $250,000 into each of the four U.S. Treasury bonds.
    c. Find the duration of the portfolio if Bill puts $360,000 each into bonds 1 and 3, and $140,000 each into bonds 2 and 4.
    d. Which portfolio (b or c) should Bill select if he thinks rates are about to head up and he wants to avoid as much price volatility as possible? Explain. From which portfolio does he stand to make more in annual interest income? Which portfolio would you recommend, and why?

12. Using the resources available at your campus or library, select any six bonds you like, consisting of *two* Treasury bonds, *two* corporate bonds, and *two* agency issues. Determine the latest current yield and promised yield for each. (*Note:* For promised yield, use the precise method, with annual compounding.) In addition, find the duration and modified duration for each bond. Be sure to show your work for all calculations.

CFA QUESTION (This question is from the 1990 Level I Exam.)

CFA — Duration may be calculated by *two* widely used methods. Identify these *two* methods, and briefly discuss the primary differences between them.

(See Appendix C for Guideline Answer to this question.)

CASE PROBLEMS

9.1 The Bond Investment Decisions of George and Penni Jock

George and Penelope Jock live in the Boston area, where he has a successful orthodontics practice. The Jocks have built up a sizable investment portfolio and have always had a major portion of their investments in fixed-income securities. They adhere to a fairly aggressive investment posture and actively go after both attractive current income and substantial capital gains. Assume that it is now 1993 and George is currently evaluating two investment decisions: one involves an addition to their portfolio, and the other a revision to it.

The Jocks' first investment decision involves a short-term trading opportunity. In particular, George has a chance to buy a 7½ percent, 25-year bond that is currently priced at $852 to yield 9 percent; he feels that in two years the promised yield of the issue should drop to 8 percent.

The second is a bond swap; the Jocks hold some Beta Corporation 7 percent, 2011 bonds that are currently priced at $785. They want to improve both current income and yield to maturity, and are considering one of three issues as a possible swap candidate: (a) Dental Floss, Inc., 7¼ percent, 2011, currently priced at $780; (b) Root Canal Products of America, 6½ percent, 2009, selling at $885; and (c) Kansas City Dental Insurance, 8 percent, 2013, priced at $950. All of the swap candidates are of comparable quality and have comparable issue characteristics.

Questions

1. Regarding the short-term trading opportunity:
   a. What basic trading principle is involved in this situation?
   b. If George's expectations are correct, what will the price of this bond be in two years?
   c. What is the expected yield of this investment?
   d. Should this investment be made? Why?
2. Regarding the bond swap opportunity:
   a. Compute the current yield and approximate promised yield of the bond the Jocks currently hold and each of the three swap candidates.
   b. Do any of the three swap candidates provide better current income and/or current yield than the Beta Corporation bond the Jocks currently hold? Which one(s)?
   c. Do you see any reason why George should switch from his present bond holding into one of the other three issues? If so, which swap candidate would be the best choice? Why?

9.2 Connie Decides to Immunize Her Portfolio

Connie Moore is the owner of an extremely successful dress boutique in mid-town Manhattan. Although high fashion is Connie's first love, she's also very interested in investments, particularly bonds and other fixed-income securities. She actively manages her own investments and over time has built up a substantial portfolio of securities. She's well-versed on the latest investment techniques and is not afraid to apply those procedures to her own investments. Connie's been playing with the idea of trying to immunize a big chunk of her bond portfolio. She'd like to cash out this part of her portfolio in seven years and use the proceeds to buy a vacation home along the South Carolina seashore. To do this, she intends to use the $200,000 she now has invested in the following four corporate bonds (she currently has $50,000 invested in each one):

1. A 12-year, 7½% bond that's currently priced at $895.
2. A 10-year, zero-coupon bond priced at $405.
3. A 10-year, 10% bond priced at $1,080.
4. A 15-year, 9¾% bond priced at $980.

(*Note:* These are all noncallable, investment-grade, nonconvertible/straight bonds.)

Questions

1. Given the information provided above, find the current yield and promised yield (use the precise method with annual compounding) for each bond in the portfolio.
2. Calculate the duration of each bond in the portfolio, and indicate how the price of each bond would change if interest rates were to rise (or fall) by 75 basis points.
3. Find the duration of the current four-bond portfolio. Given the seven-year target that Connie has, would you consider this to be an immunized portfolio? Explain.
4. How could you lengthen or shorten the duration of this portfolio? What's the *shortest* portfolio duration you can achieve? What's the *longest?*
5. Using one or more of the four bonds described above, is it possible to come up with a $200,000 bond portfolio that will exhibit the duration characteristics that Connie's looking for? Explain.
6. Using one or more of the four bonds, put together a $200,000 immunized portfolio for Connie. Since this portfolio will now be immunized, will Connie be able to treat it as a buy-and-hold portfolio—one she can put away and forget about? Explain.

10 Preferred Stock and Convertible Securities

After studying this chapter, you should be able to:

1. Describe the basic features of preferred stock, including sources of value and exposure to risk.

2. Discuss the rights and claims of preferred stockholders, and note some of the popular issue characteristics that are often found with these securities.

3. Develop an understanding of the various measures of investment worth, and identify several investment strategies that can be used with preferred stocks.

4. Identify the fundamental characteristics of convertible securities, and explain the nature of the underlying conversion privilege.

5. Describe the advantages and disadvantages of investing in convertible securities, including the risk and return attributes of these investment vehicles.

6. Measure the value of a convertible security, and explain how these securities can be used to meet different investment objectives.

What would you think of a stock that promised to pay you a fixed annual dividend for life—nothing more, nothing less? If you're an income-oriented investor, the offer might sound pretty good. But where do you find such an investment? The answer is: Right on the NYSE or AMEX, where hundreds of these securities trade everyday, in the form of *preferred stock*—a type of security that looks like a stock but doesn't behave like one. Well, if preferreds don't interest you, how about a bond that lets you participate in the price behavior of the company's stock? Does an investment that gives you the security of a bond, with the price behavior of a stock sound too good to be true? It's not—such securities actually do exist. They, too, are actively traded on the New York and American exchanges: They're called *convertible debentures,* and they truly are bonds that behave more like stocks.

Both preferreds and convertibles are corporate securities, and both are considered to be *fixed-income securities* (although preferreds are actually a form of equity ownership). Convertible securities, usually issued as bonds, are subsequently convertible into shares of the issuing firm's common stock. Indeed, the investment merits of these securities are based principally on the *equity kicker* they provide: That is, the tendency is for the market price of these issues to behave much like the common stock into which they can be converted. Preferred stocks, in contrast, are issued as equity and remain as equity. However, like bonds, they too produce a fixed-income. In fact, preferred stocks derive their name in part from the *preferred claim* on income they hold: All preferred dividends must be paid before any payment can be made to holders of common stock. In many respects, these two issues represent types of *hybrid securities* since there is a bit of debt and equity in both of them. Let's now take a closer look at each, starting with preferred stocks.

PREFERRED STOCKS

preferred stock
a stock that has a prior claim (ahead of common) on the income and assets of the issuing firm.

Preferred stocks carry fixed dividends that are paid quarterly and expressed either in dollar terms or as a percentage of the stock's par (or stated) value. They're used by companies that need the funds but don't want to raise debt to get it; in effect, preferred stocks are widely viewed by issuers as an alternative to debt. Companies like to issue preferreds because they don't count as common stock (and, therefore, don't effect EPS). Yet, being a form of equity, they don't count as debt either—and, therefore, don't add to the company's debt load. There are today about a thousand OTC and listed preferred stocks outstanding, most of which are issued by public utilities, although the number of industrial, financial, and insurance issues is rapidly increasing. Preferreds are available in a wide range of quality ratings, from investment-grade issues to highly speculative stocks. Table 10.1 provides a representative sample of some actively traded preferred stocks and illustrates the types of annual dividends and dividend yields these securities were producing in early 1992. Note especially the variety of different types of issuers, and how the market price of a preferred tends to vary with the size of the annual dividend.

Preferred Stocks as Investment Vehicles

Preferred stocks are considered hybrid securities because they possess features of both common stocks and corporate bonds. They are like common stock in that they

TABLE 10.1 A Sample of Some High-Yielding Preferred Stock

S&P Rating	Issuer	Annual Dividend	Market Price (early '92)	Dividend Yield
A	American Brands	$2.75	$32.50	8.5%
A	Capital Holdings	6.90	90.00	7.7
B	Citicorp	6.00	58.50	10.3
A	Dupont Chemical	3.50	51.75	6.8
A−	General Motors	3.75	47.90	7.8
A−	GTE	2.48	32.60	7.6
B	Illinois Power	3.62	46.00	7.9
B	Philadelphia Electric	3.80	47.50	8.0
B	Xerox	4.13	52.00	7.9
B+	Sears	2.22	26.25	8.5
B−	Tenneco	2.80	33.75	8.3
B	Litton	2.00	26.50	7.5
A−	KMart	3.41	47.75	7.1
A−	Comerica	4.32	50.00	8.6
NR	USX	4.52	48.50	9.3

Note: All of these issues are straight (nonconvertible) preferred stocks traded on the NYSE.

pay dividends, which may be suspended, or "passed," when corporate earnings fall below certain levels. Moreover, preferreds are a form of equity ownership and as such, are issued without stated maturity dates. On the other hand, preferreds are like bonds in that they provide investors with prior claims on income and assets; also, the level of current income is usually fixed for the life of the issue. Furthermore, preferred stocks can carry call features and sinking fund provisions, and a firm can have more than one issue of preferred outstanding at any point in time. Most important, perhaps, because these securities usually trade on the basis of their yield, they are in fact priced in the marketplace like fixed-income obligations. As a result, they are considered by many investors to be competitive with bonds. Preferred stocks have a lot to offer. And as you can see in the accompanying *Investor Insights* box, they have become increasingly popular with individual investors.

Advantages and Disadvantages

Investors are attracted to preferred stocks because of the current income they provide. Moreover, such dividend income is highly predictable, even though it lacks legal backing and can, under certain circumstances, be passed. Figure 10.1 illustrates the average yields on preferred stocks and shows how they compare to high-grade bond returns. Note the tendency for preferreds to yield returns that are slightly *less* than those on high-grade bonds. This is due to the fact that, as a rule, 70 percent of the preferred dividends *received by a corporation* are exempt from federal income taxes. (Actually, if 20% or more of the corporation paying the dividend is owned by the company receiving the dividends, then up to 100% of the dividend is tax free.) Regardless of the amount of the exemption, the net effect of this favorable

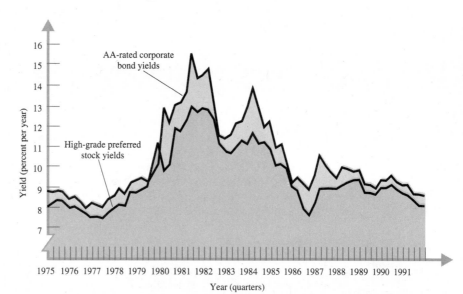

● FIGURE 10.1 Average High-Grade Preferred Stock Yields versus Average Market Yields on AA-Rated Corporate Bonds

Note how preferred stock yields tend to move in concert with the market behavior of bond returns—and how they tend to stay *below* bond yields. (*Source:* Standard & Poor's *Trade and Securities Statistics.*)

tax treatment is, of course, reduced preferred dividend yields. Safety is another desirable feature of preferreds. For despite a few well-publicized incidents, *high-grade* preferred stocks have an excellent record of meeting dividend payments in a prompt and timely manner. A final advantage of preferred stocks is the low unit cost of many of the issues, which gives even small investors the opportunity to participate actively in preferreds.

A major disadvantage of preferred stocks is their susceptibility to inflation and high interest rates. Like many fixed-income securities, preferred stocks simply have not proved to be satisfactory long-term hedges against inflation. Another disadvantage is that most preferreds lack substantial capital gains potential. Although it is possible to enjoy fairly attractive capital gains from preferred stocks when interest rates decline dramatically, these amounts generally do not match the price performances of common stocks. But perhaps the biggest disadvantage of preferreds is the *yield give-up* they incur relative to bonds. In essence, there is virtually nothing a preferred has to offer that can't be obtained from a comparably rated corporate bond—and *at less risk and more return than can be earned from a preferred.*

Sources of Value

With the exception of convertible preferreds, the value of high-grade preferred stocks is a function of the dividend yield they provide. More specifically, the value (or market price) of a preferred stock is closely related to prevailing market rates: As

██████████████████████ INVESTOR INSIGHTS ██████████

Preferreds: Perennial Wallflowers Start to Bloom for Investors

Yield-hungry investors are gobbling up new issues of preferred stock, turning a Wall Street wallflower into one of 1991's hottest financial products. But analysts warn that individual investors may be ignoring some of the pitfalls of preferreds. Corporations sold a record $16.5 billion of preferred stock in 1991, more than four times the prior year's total. Indeed, three of the year's five biggest stock offerings were preferred issues.

High-yielding preferred stocks are sizzling because investors are grabbing for preferreds' dividends of 8% or more. Those payouts look increasingly tempting with the dramatic fall-off in money-market fund yields, which have plummeted from 7.5% to 4.5% in the past year. Rushing to greet yield-starved investors have been scores of companies, concerned about their credit ratings and eager to raise equity by selling preferred stock, even if they have to pay hefty dividends to do it. Ford Motor Co. sold a record $2.3 billion preferred issue that offered a yield of 8.4%. And the dividend on a $1 billion preferred issue sold by General Motors, specifically aimed at individual investors, topped 9%.

This year's bumper crop of preferred issues has come in all shapes and sizes. Straight preferred stock offers a hefty dividend without any price gains tied to the company's underlying common stock. Other preferreds, like the Ford issue, are convertible into common, but at a price well above the common's stock price when the preferred is sold. Still other preferreds, including four of this year's five largest deals, have been a new security pioneered by Morgan Stanley & Co. called PERCs, for preference equity redemption convertible stock. Essentially, PERCs are convertible preferreds that let investors share in any price gains on a company's common stock, but only up to pre-set limits.

Eric Ryback, portfolio manager of the $224 million Lindner Dividend Fund, whose portfolio is 58% invested in preferred stock, endorses preferred issues for individuals, "particularly in a declining interest rate environment." Other experts note approvingly

the general level of interest rates moves up, so too do the yields of preferreds, and as such, their prices decline. When interest rates drift downward, so will the yields on preferreds, as their prices rise. Just like a bond, therefore, *the price behavior of a high-grade preferred stock is inversely related to market interest rates.* Moreover, its price is directly linked to the issue's level of income. That is, other things being equal, the higher the dividend payment, the higher the market price of an issue. As such, the price of a preferred can be defined as follows:

Equation 10.1
$$\text{Price of a preferred stock} = \frac{\text{annual dividend income}}{\text{prevailing market yield}}$$

This equation is simply a variation of the standard dividend yield formula, but here we solve for the price of the issue. (You might also detect a similarity between this formula and the zero growth dividend valuation model introduced in Chapter 7.)

that while preferred stocks don't go up as much as common in a rising stock market, they don't decline as drastically in a falling market.

But Kurt Brouwer, a San Francisco investment adviser, says, "I don't think preferreds are particularly good investments. They have the characteristics of bonds—fixed dividends—but they're not nearly as safe as a bond." Because equity ranks behind debt in any default or bankruptcy, preferred investors don't get as strong a promise of repayment as bondholders. Yet a company's preferred dividends may only slightly exceed—and could even be less than—the interest rate paid on its bonds.

Other drawbacks are less readily apparent. One is that many companies that issue preferred stock have reasons to be concerned about their debt levels or financial situation. "The companies that are doing this are all in some way or another trying to de-leverage or improve their situation with the rating agencies," says John Ward, a managing director in charge of marketing convertible securities at Kidder Peabody & Co. What's more, corporate investors, such as insurance companies, have a tax advantage in holding preferreds—a tax break that individual investors don't get. Since prices on preferred stock are often set by such institutional investors, this places individuals at a price disadvantage in buying preferred.

When Ford's preferred was sold, the preferred dividend was more than two percentage points higher than the dividend yield on Ford's common stock. Still, it would take investors 10 years of extra preferred dividends to equal just 20% of price appreciation in Ford's common stock. Also, whereas companies periodically boost the dividend on their common stock, their preferred dividends stay fixed at their original rate. At a minimum, most experts caution that individuals shouldn't put big chunks of their investments in a single preferred issue. Instead, they should diversify either by investing in at least a half dozen or more issues, preferably in safer utility or telecommunications preferreds, or through a mutual fund that holds preferreds.

Source: Adapted from Randall Smith, "Preferreds: Perennial Wallflower Blooms for Investors," *The Wall Street Journal,* December 6, 1991, C1.

Equation 10.1 is used to price preferred stocks and to compute the future price of a preferred, given an estimate of expected market interest rates. For example, a $2.50 preferred stock (which implies that the stock pays a dividend of $2.50 per year) would be priced at $20.83 if the prevailing market yield were 12 percent:

$$\text{Price} = \frac{\$2.50}{.12} = \underline{\underline{\$20.83}}$$

Note that higher prices are obtained with this formula by decreasing the market yield, thus giving us the inverse relationship between price and yield.

In addition to yield, the value of a preferred stock is also a function of the issue's quality: That is, the lower the quality of a preferred, the higher its yield. Such behavior is, of course, compatible with the risk-return tradeoffs that usually exist in the marketplace. Fortunately, the quality of preferred stocks is also rated, much like bonds, by Moody's and Standard & Poor's. Finally, the value of a preferred is affected by issue characteristics such as call features and sinking fund provisions. For example, freely callable preferreds will normally provide higher yields to investors than noncallable issues, due to the greater call risk inherent in the former type of security. Quality and issue features, however, have only slight effects on price behavior over time, and certainly do not compare in importance with the movement of market yields.

Risk Exposure

Preferred stock investors are exposed to both business and interest rate risks. Business risk is important with preferreds, since they are a form of equity ownership and lack many of the legal protections available with bonds. Annual operating costs and corporate financial strength, therefore, are of concern to preferred stockholders. Preferred stock ratings (discussed later in this chapter) can be used to assess the amount of business risk embedded in an issue; higher-quality/higher-rated issues are believed to possess less business risk. However, interest rate risk is generally viewed as the more important type of risk for preferred stocks because of their fixed income nature. Certainly it can be the most damaging, should interest rates move against the investor.

Transaction Costs

Preferred stocks are subject to the same transaction costs as shares of common stock: Their brokerage fees and transfer taxes are identical. In addition, preferred investors use the same types of orders (market, limit, or stop-loss) and operate under the same margin requirements. Even the quotes of preferred stock are co-mingled with those of common. Fortunately, preferreds are easy to pick out in the financial pages; simply look for the letters *pf* or *pr* after the name of the company. (Technically, the *pf* denotes *regular preferred* stock, and the *pr* stands for *prior preferred* stock—the differences will be explained below.)

The quotes are interpreted exactly like those for common stock, except that the price/earnings ratios are not listed. Note also that the preferreds are always listed right after the company's common stock. In the quotes in Figure 10.2, we see that there are five issues of preferred stocks listed for Pennsylvania Power & Light (PennP&L). Actually, the company could have other issues outstanding, but if they didn't trade on the day of the quotes, they wouldn't be listed. These preferreds pay annual dividends of anywhere from $4.40 per share to $8.60 (note that the higher the annual dividend, the higher the price of the stock). At quoted market prices, these preferreds were providing current yields of around 8 to 8½ percent. Observe also the relatively low unit cost of the stock, as two of the preferreds are priced at about $55 a share and the other three are moderately priced at around $100. As an aside, note the small letter *z* in the volume (or sales) column; this symbol has important meaning to serious preferred stock traders since it signifies *the actual number of shares traded,* rather than the normal round lot volume. For example, the *z150* listed with the $8.60 preferred doesn't mean there were 150 round lots traded; rather, it means *only 150 shares* of the $8.60 preferreds changed hands on this day.

| | 52 Weeks | | | | | Yld | | Vol | | | | Net |
	Hi	Lo	Stock	Sym	Div	%	Pe	100s	Hi	Lo	Close	Chg
	9⅞	7⅜	PatrDivFd	PDF	.80	8.5	...	192	9⅝	9⅜	9⅜	...
n	11⅛	8⅝	PatrDivFdII	PDT	.90	8.3	...	161	10⅞	10¾	10⅞	...
n▲	15⅞	12⅝	PatrSelDiv	DIV	1.65	10.4	...	301	16	15⅞	15⅞	...
	2¼	⅜	Patten	PAT		...	...	67	1⅛	1	1⅛	+ ⅛
	27	17¾	PennCentral	PC	.68	2.9	14	198	23¼	22⅞	23⅛	+ ¼
	58¼	42⅜	Penney JC	JCP	2.64	5.0	15	2055	52½	51½	52⅜	+ ⅞
	50⅝	41¾	PennP&L	PPL	3.10	6.3	12	798	49⅜	49⅛	49⅜	+ ⅛
	57½	48	PennP&L pf		4.40	7.9	...	z200	55½	55½	55½	...
	60½	49½	PennP&L pf		4.50	8.0	...	z250	57½	56½	56½	+ ½
	103	91½	PennP&L pf		8.60	8.4	...	z150	102	102	102	...
	102½	88	PennP&L pr		8.40	8.4	...	z100	100	100	100	...
▲	100	86	PennP&L pr		8.00	8.0	...	z100	100½	100½	100½	+ 1
	76½	54⅜	Pennzoil	PZL	3.00	5.4	23	537	55½	54⅜	55¼	+ ¾
	28¼	21¾	PeopEngy	PGL	1.72	6.4	13	284	27	26¾	26¾	− ¼

Penn P&L's preferred stocks { *(bracket spanning the five shaded PennP&L pf/pr rows)*

• **FIGURE 10.2** Published Quotes for Preferred Stocks
Preferred stock quotes are listed right along with the company's common stock, and they're identified by the 2-letter initials *pf* or *pr* that appear after the name of the company. (*Source: The Wall Street Journal,* December 13, 1991.)

Issue Characteristics

conversion feature allows the holder of a convertible preferred to convert to a specified number of shares of the issuing company's common stock.

Preferred stocks possess features that not only distinguish them from other types of securities but also help differentiate one preferred from another. For example, preferred stocks may be issued as convertible or nonconvertible, although the majority fall into the nonconvertible category. A **conversion feature** allows the holder to convert the preferred stock into a specified number of shares of the issuing company's common stock. Because convertible preferreds are, for all intents and purposes, very much like convertible bonds, a thorough examination of this vehicle will be deferred to later in the chapter. At this point we'll concentrate on *nonconvertible issues,* although many of the features we are about to discuss are equally applicable to convertible preferreds.

In addition to convertibility, there are several other important preferred stock features that investors should be aware of; they include the rights of preferred stockholders; the provision for cumulative dividends; call features; and sinking fund provisions.

Rights of Preferred Stockholders

The contractual agreement of a preferred stock specifies the rights and privileges of preferred stockholders. The most important of these deal with the level of annual dividends, the claim on income, voting rights, and the claim on assets. The issuing company agrees that it will pay preferred stockholders a (minimum) fixed level of quarterly dividends and that such payments *will take priority over common stock dividends.* The only condition is that the firm generate income sufficient to meet the preferred dividend requirements. The firm, however, is not legally bound to honor the dividend obligation. Of course, it cannot pass dividends on preferred stocks and then turn around and pay dividends on common stock, as that would clearly violate the preferreds' prior claim on income. Although most preferred stocks are issued with dividend rates that remain fixed for the life of the issue, in the early 1980s some preferreds began to appear with floating dividend rates. Known as **adjustable** (or **floating**) **rate preferreds,** the dividends on these issues are adjusted periodically in line with yields on specific Treasury issues, although minimum and maximum dividend rates are usually established as a safeguard.

Even though they hold an ownership position in the firm, preferred stockholders normally have no voting rights. If, however, conditions deteriorate to the point that the firm needs to pass one or more consecutive quarterly dividends, preferred shareholders are usually given the right to elect a certain number of corporate directors so that their views can be represented. *And if liquidation becomes necessary, the holders of preferreds are given a prior claim on assets.* These preferred claims, limited to the par or stated value of the stock, must be satisfied before those of the common stockholders. Of course, this does not always mean that the full par or stated value of the preferred will be recovered, since the claims of senior securities, like bonds, must be met first. That is, all bonds—including convertible bonds—have a higher claim on assets (and income) than preferred stock, whereas preferreds have a higher claim than common stock. Thus, preferred shareholders have a claim that's somewhere *between* that of bondholders and common stockholders.

Finally, when a company has more than one issue of preferred stock outstanding, it will sometimes issue **preference** (or **prior preferred**) **stocks.** Essentially, these stocks have seniority over other preferred stock in their right to receive dividends and in their claim on assets in the event of liquidation. As such, preference stocks should be viewed as *senior preferreds.* They're usually easy to pick out in the financial pages as they use the letters *pr* instead of *pf* in their quotes. For example, in Figure 10.2, you'll notice Pennsylvania P&L has two preference stocks listed along with their "regular" preferred stock issues.

Cumulative Provisions

Most preferred stocks are issued on a **cumulative** basis. This means that any preferred dividends that have been passed must be made up in full before dividends can be restored to common stockholders. Thus, as long as the dividends on preferred stocks remain **in arrears** (which denotes that there are outstanding unfulfilled preferred dividend obligations), a corporation will not be able to make dividend payments on common shares. Assume, for example, that a firm normally pays a $1 quarterly dividend on its preferred stock, but has missed the dividend for three quarters in a row. In this case, the firm has preferred dividends in arrears of $3 a share, which it is obligated to meet, along with the next quarterly dividend payment, before it can pay dividends to common shareholders. The firm could fulfill this obligation by paying, say, $2 per share to the preferred stockholders at the next quarterly dividend date, and $3 per share at the following one (with the $3 covering the remaining $2 arrears and the current $1 quarterly payment). If the preferred stock had carried a **noncumulative provision**—as some do—the issuing company would be under no obligation to make up any of the passed dividends. Of course,

adjustable (floating) rate preferreds
preferred stock whose dividends are adjusted periodically in line with yields on Treasury issues.

preference (prior preferred) stock
a type of preferred stock that has seniority over other preferred stock in its right to receive dividends and in its claim on assets.

cumulative provision
a provision requiring that any preferred dividends that have been passed must be paid in full before dividends can be restored to common stockholders.

in arrears
having outstanding unfulfilled preferred-dividend obligations.

noncumulative provision
a provision found on some preferred stocks excusing the issuing firm from having to make up any passed dividends.

the firm could not make dividend payments on common stock either, but all it would have to do to resume such payments would be to meet the next quarterly preferred dividend. Other things being equal, a cumulative preferred stock should be more highly valued than an issue without such a provision—that is, it should increase the price (and in so doing, lower the yield) of these issues.

Call Features

Since the early 1970s, it has become increasingly popular to issue preferred stocks with call features. Today, a large number of preferreds carry this provision, which gives the firm the right to call the preferred for retirement. Callable preferreds are usually issued on a *deferred-call basis,* meaning they cannot be retired for a certain number of years after the date of issue. After the deferral period, which often extends for five to seven years, the preferreds become freely callable. Of course, such issues are then susceptible to call if the market rate for preferreds declines dramatically, which explains why the yields on freely callable preferreds should be higher than those on noncallable issues. As with bonds, the call price of a preferred is made up of the par value of the issue and a call premium that may amount to as much as one year's dividends.

Sinking Fund Provisions

Another preferred stock feature that has become popular in the past 10 years or so is the *sinking fund provision,* which denotes how (all or a part of) an issue will be amortized, or paid off, over time. Such sinking fund preferreds actually have implied maturity dates. They are used by firms to reduce the cost of financing, since sinking fund issues generally have *lower* yields than nonsinking fund preferreds. A typical sinking fund preferred might require the firm to retire half the issue over a 10-year period by retiring, say, 5 percent of the issue each year. Unfortunately, the investor has no control over which shares are called for sinking fund purposes.

Putting a Value on Preferreds

Evaluating the investment suitability of preferreds involves an assessment of comparative return opportunities. Let's look now at some of the return measures that are important to preferred stockholders, and then at the role that agency ratings play in the valuation process.

Dividend Yield: A Critical Measure of Value

Dividend yield is the key variable in determining the price and return behavior of most preferred stocks. It is computed according to the following simple formula:

Equation 10.2

dividend yield
a measure of the amount of return earned on annual dividends.

$$\text{Dividend yield} = \frac{\text{annual dividend income}}{\text{current market price of the preferred stock}}$$

Dividend yield is a measure of the amount of return earned on annual dividends and is the basis upon which comparative preferred investment opportunities are evaluated. (It is basically the same as the *dividend yield* used in Chapter 6 with common stocks and is comparable to the *current yield* measure used with bonds, as described in Chapter 9.) Here is how it works: Suppose an 8 percent preferred stock has a par value of $25 and is currently trading at a price of $21 per share. The annual dividend on this stock is $2—for preferreds whose dividends are denoted as a percent of par (or stated) value, the dollar value of the annual dividend is found by multiplying the dividend rate (8 percent) by the par value ($25). The dividend yield in this example is

$$\text{Dividend yield} = \frac{\$2}{\$21} = \underline{\underline{9\tfrac{1}{2}\%}}$$

As we can see, at $21 a share, this particular preferred is yielding 9½ percent to investors. Should the price move up (to, say, $27 a share), the dividend yield would drop (in this case, to a little less than 7½ percent). In practice, we would expect investors to compute, or have available, a current dividend yield measure for each preferred under consideration, and then to make a choice by comparing the yields of the alternative preferreds—along with, of course, the risk and issue characteristics of each.

Long-term investors consider dividend yield to be a critical factor in their investment decisions. Short-term traders, in contrast, generally focus on anticipated price behavior and the expected return from buying and selling an issue over a short period of time. Thus, the expected future price of a preferred is important to short-term traders. It is found by first forecasting future market interest rates and then using that information to determine expected future price. To illustrate, suppose a preferred stock pays $3 in dividends, and its yield is expected to decline to 6 percent within the next two years. If such market rates prevail, then two years from now the issue would have a market price of $50 (using Equation 10.1, annual dividend ÷ yield = $3 ÷ .06 = $50). This forecasted price, along with the current market price and level of annual dividends, would then be used in either the approximate yield or holding period return (HRP) formula—both of which were first introduced in Chapter 4—to compute the expected yield from the transaction.

To continue the example, if the stock were currently priced at $28 a share, the expected yield on this stock (over the two-year investment horizon) would be a very attractive 35.9 percent:

Equation 10.3

$$\text{Expected yield} = \frac{\text{annual dividend} + \dfrac{\text{expected future selling price} - \text{current market price}}{\text{years in holding period}}}{\dfrac{\text{expected future selling price} + \text{current market price}}{2}}$$

$$= \frac{\$3 + \dfrac{\$50 - \$28}{2}}{\dfrac{\$50 + \$28}{2}} = \frac{\$3 + \$11}{\$39} = \underline{\underline{35.9\%}}$$

Such information is used to judge the relative attractiveness of preferred stock. In general, the higher the expected yield figure, the more appealing the investment.

Book Value

book value (net asset value)
a measure of the amount of debt-free assets supporting each share of preferred stock.

The **book value** (or **net asset value**) of a preferred stock is simply a measure of the amount of debt-free assets supporting each share of preferred stock. Book value per share is found by subtracting all the liabilities of the firm from its total assets and dividing the difference by the number of preferred shares outstanding. It reflects the quality of an issue with regard to the preferred's *claim on assets*. Obviously, a preferred with a book value of $150 per share enjoys generous asset support, and more than adequately secures a par value of, say, $25 a share. Net asset value is most relevant when it is used relative to an issue's par, or stated, value. Other things being equal, *the quality of an issue improves as the margin by which book value exceeds par value increases.*

Fixed Charge Coverage

fixed charge coverage
a measure of how well a firm is able to cover its preferred stock dividends.

Fixed charge coverage is a measure of how well a firm is able to cover its preferred dividends; attention centers on the firm's ability to service the dividends on its preferred stock and live up to the preferred's preferential *claim on income*. As such, fixed charge coverage is an important ingredient in determining the quality of a preferred issue. Fixed charge coverage is computed as follows:

Equation 10.4

$$\text{Fixed charge coverage} = \frac{\text{earnings before interest and taxes (or EBIT)}}{\text{interest expense} + \dfrac{\text{preferred dividends}}{.66}}$$

In this equation, the preferred dividends are adjusted by a factor of .66 (equivalent to multiplying dividends by 1.5) to take into account the (maximum) 34 percent corporate tax rate and to place preferred dividends on the same base as interest paid on bonds. (Recall that bond interest is tax deductible, whereas preferred dividends are not.) *Normally, the higher the fixed charge coverage, the greater the margin of safety.* A ratio of 1.0 means the company is generating just enough earnings to meet its preferred dividend payments—not a very healthy situation. A coverage ratio of 0.7 would suggest the potential for some real problems, whereas a coverage of, say, 7.0 would indicate that the preferred dividends are fairly secure.

Agency Ratings

Standard & Poor's has long rated the investment quality of preferred stocks, and since 1973, so has Moody's. S&P uses basically the same rating system as it does for bonds; Moody's uses a slightly different system. Figure 10.3 shows Moody's system and indicates why the various ratings are assigned. These two agencies assign ratings largely on the basis of their judgment regarding the relative safety of dividends. The greater the likelihood that the issuer will be able to service the preferred in a prompt and timely fashion, the higher the rating. Much like bonds, the top four ratings designate *investment-grade* (high quality) preferreds. Although preferreds come with a full range of agency ratings, most tend to fall in the medium-grade categories (a and baa), or lower; generally speaking, higher agency ratings reduce the market yield of an issue and increase its interest sensitivity. Agency

Rating Symbol	Definition
aaa	Indicates a "top quality" issue which provides good asset protection and the least risk of dividend impairment.
aa	A "high grade" issue with reasonable assurance that earnings will be relatively well-protected in the near future.
a	"Upper medium grade." Somewhat greater risk than *aa* and *aaa*, but dividends are still considered adequately protected.
baa	"Lower medium grade." Earnings protection adequate at present, but may be questionable in the future.
ba	A "speculative" type issue, its future earnings may be moderate and not well safeguarded. Uncertainty of position is common for this class.
b	Generally lacking in desirable investment quality, this class may have little assurance of future dividends.
caa–c	Likely to already be in arrears on dividend payments. These categories are reserved for securities that offer little or no likelihood of eventual payment.

Note: Preferred stock ratings should not be compared with bond ratings as they are not equivalent; preferreds occupy a position junior to the bonds.

• FIGURE 10.3 Moody's Preferred Stock Ratings

These agency ratings provide an indication of the quality of the issue and are based largely on an assessment of the firm's ability to pay preferred dividends in a prompt and timely fashion. (*Source:* Moody's Investor's Service, Inc.)

ratings are important to serious, long-term investors as well as to those who use preferreds for short-term trading. Not only do they eliminate much of the need for fundamental analysis, but they also help investors get a handle on the yield and potential price behavior of an issue.

Investment Strategies

There are several investment strategies that can be followed by preferred stockholders. Each is useful in meeting a different investment objective, and each one offers a different level of return and exposure to risk.

Using Preferreds to Obtain Attractive Yields

This strategy represents perhaps the most popular use of preferred stocks and is ideally suited for serious long-term investors. High current income is the objective, and the procedure basically involves seeking out those preferreds with the most attractive yields. Of course, consideration must also be given to such features as the quality of the issue, whether or not the dividends are cumulative, and the existence of any call or sinking fund provisions. This approach to investing got a big boost when Congress passed the Tax Reform Act of 1986, thereby sharply reducing tax rates. *The reason: investors gain more from income-oriented securities, like preferred stocks, at lower tax rates.*

Certainty of income and safety are important in this strategy, since yields are attractive only as long as dividends are paid. Some investors may never buy anything but the highest-quality preferreds. Others may sacrifice quality in return for higher yields when the economy is strong, and use higher-quality issues only during periods of economic distress. But whenever you leave one of the top four agency ratings, you should recognize the speculative position you are assuming and the implications it holds for your investment portfolio. This is especially so with preferreds, since their dividends lack legal enforcement. Individual investors should keep in mind, however, that this investment strategy often involves a *yield give-up* relative to what could be obtained from comparably rated corporate bonds: As we saw in Figure 10.1, preferreds usually generate somewhat lower yields than bonds, even though they are less secure and may be subject to a bit more risk.

Trading on Interest Rate Swings

Rather than assuming a ''safe'' buy-and-hold position, the investor who trades on movements in interest rates adopts an aggressive short-term trading posture. This is done for one major reason: *capital gains*. Of course, although a high level of return may be possible with this approach, it is not without the burden of higher risk exposure. Because preferreds are fixed-income securities, the market behavior of investment-grade issues is closely linked to the movements in interest rates. If market interest rates are expected to decline substantially, attractive capital gains opportunities may be realized from preferred stocks. Indeed, this is precisely what happened in the mid-1980s, when market interest rates dropped sharply. During this period, it was not uncommon to find preferreds generating *annual* returns of 20 to 30 percent, or more!

As is probably clear by now, this strategy is identical to that used by bond investors; in fact, many of the same principles used with bonds apply equally well to preferred stocks. For example, it is important to select high-grade preferred stocks, since interest sensitivity is an essential ingredient of this investment configuration. Moreover, margin trading is often used as a way of magnifying short-term holding period returns. A basic difference is that the very high leverage rates of bonds are not available with preferreds, since they fall under the same (less generous) margin requirements as common stocks. The investment selection process is simplified somewhat as well, since neither maturity nor the size of the annual preferred dividend (which is equivalent to a bond's coupon) has an effect on the *rate of price volatility*. That is, a $2 preferred will appreciate just as much (in percentage terms) as an $8 preferred for a given change in market yields.

Speculating on Turnarounds

This speculative investment strategy can prove profitable if you're nimble enough to catch the trading opportunity before everyone else does. The idea is to find preferred stocks whose dividends have gone into arrears and whose rating has tumbled to one of the speculative categories. The price of the issue, of course, would be depressed to reflect the corporate problems of the issuer. There is more to this strategy, however, than simply finding a speculative-grade preferred stock. The difficult part is to uncover a speculative issue whose fortunes, for one reason or another, are about to undergo a substantial *turnaround*. The tactic requires a good deal of fundamental analysis, and is in many respects akin to investing in specula-tive common stock. In essence, the investor is betting that the firm will undergo a turnaround and will once again be able to service its preferred dividend obligations easily—a set of conditions that obviously involves a fair amount of risk. Unfortu-nately, although the rewards from this kind of high-risk investing can be substantial, *they are somewhat limited*. For example, if the turnaround candidate is expected to recover to a single-a rating, we would expect its capital gains potential to be limited by the price level of other a-rated preferreds. This condition is depicted in Figure 10.4. As can be seen, while price performance may be somewhat limited, it is still substantial and can readily amount to holding period returns of 50 percent or more. However, in view of the substantial risks involved, such returns are certainly not out of line.

Investing in Convertible Preferreds

The investor following this strategy uses the conversion feature to go after specula-tive opportunities and the chance for attractive returns. The use of *convertible pre-*

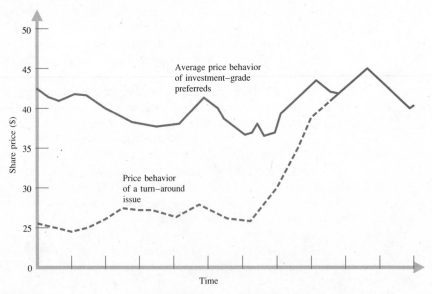

• F I G U R E   1 0 . 4   Price Pattern of a Hypothetical Preferred
"Turn-around" Candidate

Although a turn-around issue will seek the price level of other preferreds of comparable quality and dividend payout, this level also acts as a type of price cap and clearly limits capital appreciation.

ferreds is based on its link to the company's common stock and the belief that it will provide generous price appreciation. Convertibles will be reviewed in detail below; at this point, suffice it to say that as the price of the underlying common stock appreciates in value, so will the market price of a convertible preferred. This strategy can offer handsome returns, but remember that investors who employ it are actually speculating on the common stock dimension of the security. Therefore it is the equity position of the issue that should be subjected to scrutiny. In essence, the investor looks for equity situations that hold considerable promise for appreciation, and then, rather than buying the common stock of the firm, purchases its convertible preferred instead.

CONVERTIBLE SECURITIES

convertible securities
fixed-income obligations, with a feature permitting the holder to convert the security into a specified number of shares of the issuing company's common stock.

Convertible securities, more popularly known simply as "convertibles," represent still another type of fixed-income security. Usually issued as debenture bonds, these securities are subsequently convertible into shares of the issuing firm's common stock. Although it possesses the features and performance characteristics of both a fixed-income security and equity, a convertible should be viewed primarily as a form of equity. That's because most investors commit their capital to such obligations not for the attractive yields they provide. but rather for the potential price performance that the stock side of the issue offers. In fact, it is always a good idea *to determine whether a corporation has convertible issues outstanding whenever you are considering a common stock investment,* for there may well be circumstances in which the convertible will be a better investment than the firm's common stock.

Convertibles as Investment Outlets

equity kicker
another name for the conversion feature, giving the holder of a convertible security a deferred claim on the issuer's common stock.

Convertible securities are popular with investors because of their **equity kicker**— i.e., the tendency for the market price of the convertible to behave much like the price of the firm's common stock. They are issued by all types of corporations, and in 1992 there were over 1,000 convertible bonds and several hundred convertible preferreds outstanding. Companies like to issue convertibles principally because *they enable firms to raise equity capital at fairly attractive prices.* That is, when a company issues stock the normal way (by simply selling more shares in the company), it does so by setting a price on the stock that's *below* prevailing market prices (it might be able to get $25 for a stock that's currently priced in the market at, say, $30 a share). In contrast, when it issues the stock indirectly through a convertible issue, a firm can set a price that's *above* the prevailing market—i.e., they might be able to get $35 for the same stock. As a result, the company can raise the same amount of money by issuing a lot *less* stock through a convertible than by selling it directly in the market. Thus, companies issue convertibles *not* as a way of raising debt capital, but rather, as a way of raising equity. Because they are supposed to eventually be converted into shares of the issuing company's common stock, convertible securities are usually viewed as a form of **deferred equity.**

deferred equity
securities issued in one form and later redeemed or converted into shares of common stock.

Not surprisingly, whenever the stock market is strong, convertibles tend to be strong; when the market softens, so does interest in convertibles. Convertible bonds and convertible preferreds are both linked to the equity position of the firm and therefore are usually considered interchangeable for investment purposes. Except for a few peculiarities, such as the fact that preferreds pay dividends rather than interest, and do so on a quarterly basis rather than semiannually, convertible bonds and convertible preferreds are evaluated similarly. Our discussion therefore will be mostly in terms of bonds, but the information and implications apply equally well to convertible preferreds.

Convertible Bonds

Convertible bonds are usually issued as debentures (long-term, unsecured corporate debt), but carry the provision that within a stipulated time period *the bond may be converted into a certain number of shares of the issuing company's common stock.* Generally there is little or no cash involved at the time of conversion; the investor merely trades in the convertible bond for a stipulated number of shares of common stock. Figure 10.5 provides some specifics about a convertible bond recently issued by Wendy's International. Note that this obligation originally came out as a 7 percent subordinated debenture bond, but in time each $1,000 bond can be converted into Wendy's stock at $12.30 per share. Thus, *regardless of what happens to the market price of the stock,* the convertible bond investor can redeem each $1,000 bond for 81.30 shares of stock—that is, $1,000/$12.30 = 81.30 shares. If at the time of conversion the stocks are trading in the market at $30 a share, then the investor would have just converted a $1,000 bond into $2,439 worth of stocks (i.e., 81.30 × $30 = $2,439).

The *bondholder* is the one who has the right to convert the bond at any time, but more commonly, the issuing firm will initiate conversion by calling the bonds—a practice known as **forced conversion.** To provide the corporation with the flexibility to retire the debt and force conversion, most convertibles come out as freely callable issues, or they carry *very short* call deferment periods. To force conversion, the corporation would call for the retirement of the bond and give the bondholder one of two òptions: to convert the bond into common stock, or to redeem the bond for cash at the stipulated call price (which, in the case of convertibles, contains very little call premium). So long as the convertible is called when the market value of the stock exceeds the call price of the issue, seasoned investors would never choose the second option. Instead, they would opt to convert the bond, as the firm wants them to. After the conversion is complete, the bonds no longer exist; instead, there is additional common stock in their place.

forced conversion the calling in of convertible bonds by the issuing firm.

Conversion Privilege

The key element of any convertible is its **conversion privilege,** which stipulates the conditions and specific nature of the conversion feature. To begin with, it states exactly when the debenture can be converted. With some issues, there may be an initial waiting period of six months to perhaps two years after the date of issue, during which time the security cannot be converted. The **conversion period** then begins, after which the issue can be converted at any time. Although the conversion period typically extends for the remaining life of the debenture, it may exist for only a certain number of years. This is done to provide the issuing firm with more control over its capital structure. If the issue has not been converted by the end of its conversion period, it then reverts to a straight debt issue with *no* conversion privileges.

conversion privilege the conditions and specific nature of the conversion feature of convertible securities.

conversion period the time period during which a convertible issue can be converted.

April 9, 1991

$100,000,000

Wendy's International, Inc.

7% Convertible Subordinated Debentures Due 2006

Convertible into Common Shares at $12.30 per Share

Price 100%

(Plus accrued interest, if any, from date of issuance)

Smith Barney, Harris Upham & Co.
Incorporated

The First Boston Corporation

• FIGURE 10.5 A New Convertible Bond Issue

Holders of this Wendy's International bond can convert it into the company's common stock at the stated price of $12.30 per share. As a result, they would receive 81.30 shares of stock for each $1,000 convertible bond owned. Prior to conversion, the bondholder will receive annual interest income of $70.00 for each bond. (*Source: Institutional Investor,* April 1991.)

conversion ratio
the number of shares of common stock into which a convertible issue can be converted.

conversion price
the stated price per share at which common stock will be delivered to the investor in exchange for a convertible issue.

From the investor's point of view, the most important piece of information is the conversion price, or conversion ratio. These terms are used interchangeably and specify the number of shares into which the bond can be converted. **Conversion ratio** denotes the number of common shares into which the bond can be converted; **conversion price** indicates the stated value per share at which the common stock will be delivered to the investor in exchange for the bond. For example, a $1,000 convertible bond might stipulate a conversion ratio of 20, meaning that the bond can be converted into 20 shares of common stock. This same privilege could also be stated in terms of a conversion price—that the $1,000 bond may be used to acquire stock in the corporation at a ''price'' of $50 per share. Note that the Wendy's convertible depicted in Figure 10.5 uses conversion price (of $12.30 a share) to describe its conversion feature. (One basic difference between a convertible debenture and a convertible preferred is that whereas the conversion ratio of a debenture generally deals with large multiples of common stock, such as 15, 20, or 30 shares, the conversion ratio of a preferred is generally very small, often less than 1 share of common and seldom more than 2 or 3 shares.)

The conversion ratio is generally fixed over the conversion period, although some convertibles are issued with variable ratios/prices. In such cases, the conversion ratio decreases (while the conversion price increases) over the life of the conversion period to reflect the supposedly higher value of the equity. The conversion ratio is also normally adjusted for stock splits and significant stock dividends to maintain the conversion rights of the investor. As a result, if a firm declares, say, a 2-for-1 stock split, the conversion ratio of any of its outstanding convertible issues would also double. When the ratio includes a fraction, such as 33⅓ shares of common, the conversion privilege will specify how any fractional shares are to be handled. Usually, either the investor can put up the additional funds necessary to purchase another full share of stock at the conversion price, or receive the cash equivalent of the fractional share (at the conversion price). Table 10.2 lists some basic features for a number of actively traded convertible bonds and preferreds, and reveals a variety of conversion privileges.

Sources of Value

Because convertibles are fixed-income securities linked to the equity position of the firm, they are normally valued in terms of both the bond and the stock dimensions of the issue. In fact, it is ultimately the stock and the bond dimensions of the convertible that give the security its value. This, of course, explains why it is so important to analyze the underlying common stock *and* to formulate interest rate expectations when considering convertibles as an investment outlet. Let's look first at the stock dimension.

Convertible securities will trade much like common stock—in effect, they derive their value from the common stock—whenever the market price of the stock is equal to or greater than the stated conversion price. This means that whenever a convertible trades near its par value ($1,000) or above, it will exhibit price behavior that closely matches that of the underlying common stock: If the stock goes up in price, so will the convertible, and vice versa. In fact, the price change of the convertible will *exceed* that of the common, since the conversion ratio will define the convertible's rate of price change. For example, if a convertible carries a conversion ratio of, say, 20, then for every point the common stock goes up (or down) in price, the price of the convertible will move in the *same direction by a multiple of 20*. In essence, whenever a convertible trades as a stock, its market price will approximate a multiple of the share price of the common, with the size of the multiple being defined by the conversion ratio.

TABLE 10.2 Features of Some Actively Traded Convertible Securities

	S&P Rating	Conversion Ratio	Market Price of Convertible	Yield*	Conversion Premium
Convertible Bonds					
Champion Int'l 6½ (2011)	BBB−	28.78	$ 997.50	6.5%	22.2%
Chock Full O'Nuts 7 (2012)	B−	108.00	840.00	8.7	15.3
IBM 7⅞ (2004)	AA	6.51	1,020.00	7.6	77.4
Kerr-McGee 7¼ (2012)	BBB+	22.08	1,020.00	7.2	18.0
Mellon Bank 7¼ (1999)	BBB+	19.80	980.00	7.5	19.0
Noble Affiliates 7¼ (2012)	BBB−	50.96	1,010.00	7.2	31.1
Price Co. 5½ (2012)	BBB+	19.75	1,080.00	4.8	3.0
Union Carbide 7½ (2012)	BBB−	28.17	930.00	8.2	21.7
USLICO 8½ (2014)	BBB	31.90	960.00	8.9	43.0
Westinghouse Electric 9 (2009)	A−	64.52	1,280.00	6.3	8.0
WITCO Corp. 5½ (2012)	A−	18.33	950.00	5.9	13.0
Xerox 6 (1995)	A−	10.87	1,020.00	5.4	26.2
Convertible Preferreds					
BankAmerica $3.25 pfd.	BBB+	1.10	$ 56.00	5.8%	16.0%
Cooper Industries $1.60 pfd.	A	0.55	31.63	5.1	10.9
Cyprus Minerals $3.75 pfd.	BBB−	2.01	53.00	7.1	15.3
GATX $3.87 pfd.	BBB−	1.15	45.38	8.5	52.5
B.F. Goodrich $3.50 pfd.	BBB−	0.91	54.25	6.5	6.7
ITT $5.00 pfd.	A	1.45	94.25	5.3	2.8
James River $3.50 pfd.	BBB	1.25	40.00	8.8	48.0
National City $4.00 pfd.	BBB+	1.19	57.00	7.0	14.0
Norwest Corp. $3.50 pfd.	A−	1.37	58.00	6.0	12.0
Saralee $2.78 pfd.	A+	1.04	50.50	5.5	0.0
USF&G $5.00 pfd.	BB−	4.16	61.00	8.2	34.8
US Air $4.37 pfd.	B	2.49	45.00	9.7	35.1

*Yield-to-maturity for convertible bonds; current yield for convertible preferreds; all prices and yields as of May, 1992.

When the price of the common is depressed, so that its trading price is well below the conversion price, the convertible will lose its ties to the underlying common stock and begin to trade as a bond. The issue should then trade according to prevailing bond yields. At that point, an investor should focus attention on market rates of interest. However, because of the equity kicker and their relatively low agency ratings, convertibles generally do not possess high interest rate sensitivity. Gaining more than a rough idea of what the prevailing yield of the convertible obligation ought to be is often difficult. For example, if the issue is rated Baa by Moody's, and if the market rate for this quality range is 9 percent, the convertible should be priced to yield *something around* 9 percent, plus or minus perhaps as much as half a percentage point or so. The bond feature will also establish a *price floor* for the convertible. This price floor tends to parallel interest rates, and is independent of the behavior of common share prices. When convertible securities are viewed in this light, it's not surprising that the 1991 market was so good to convertible bondholders. For in 1991, investors were able to experience the best of both worlds: That is, not only did stock prices jump up, but bond interest rates dropped as well! Thus, *both* the stock values of convertibles and their bond price floors were going up together. In so doing, they provided investors not only with improved returns, but also with reduced exposure to risk.

Risk Exposure

The risk exposure of a convertible is a function of the issue's fixed-income and equity characteristics. Due to the vital role equity plays in defining the stock value of a convertible, the investor should evaluate the business, financial, and market risks to which the underlying common stock is exposed. Likewise, because of the fixed-income nature of convertibles, and because this aspect defines its price floor, purchasing power (inflation) risk and interest rate risk are also important.

Advantages and Disadvantages of Investing in Convertibles

The major advantage of a convertible issue is that it reduces downside risk (via the issue's bond value or price floor) and at the same time provides an upward price potential comparable to that of the firm's common stock. This two-sided feature is critical with convertibles and is impossible to match with straight common or straight debt. Another benefit is that the current income from bond interest normally exceeds the income from dividends that would be paid with a *comparable investment* in the underlying common stock. For example, let's say you had the choice of investing $1,000 in a new 8 percent convertible or the same amount in the company's common stock, presently trading at $42.50 a share. (As is customary with new convertibles, the stock price is a bit *under* the bond's conversion price—of $50 a share.) Under these circumstances, the investor could buy *one* convertible, or *23½ shares* of common stock (i.e., $1,000/$42.50 = 23.5). Now, if the stock paid $2 a share in annual dividends, a $1,000 investment in the stocks would yield $47 a year in dividends. In contrast, the investor could collect substantially more by putting the same amount into the company's convertible bond (where the investor would receive $80 a year in interest income). Thus, it is possible with convertibles to reap the advantages of common stock (in the form of potential upward price appreciation) and yet generate improved current income.

On the negative side, buying the convertible instead of directly owning the underlying common stock means the investor has to give up some potential profits. Consider the example in the preceding paragraph: Put $1,000 directly into the common stock and you can buy 23½ shares; put the same $1,000 into the company's convertible bond and you end up with a claim on only 20 shares of stock. Thus, the convertible bond investor is left with a *shortfall* of 3½ shares of stock—which, in turn, represent potential price appreciation that the convertible investor will never enjoy. In effect, its a *give-up* that the investor has to take in exchange for the

conversion premium
the amount by which the market price of a convertible exceeds its conversion value.

convertible's higher current income and safety. Looked at from another angle, this is basically what **conversion premium** is all about. That is, unless the market price of the stock is very high and exceeds the conversion price by a wide margin, a convertible will almost always trade at a price that is above its true value. The amount of this excess price is conversion premium, and it has the unfortunate side effect of diluting the price appreciation potential of a convertible. What is more, an investor who truly wants to hold bonds can almost certainly find better current and promised yields from straight debt obligations, and because of conversion premiums, he or she can probably realized greater capital gains by investing directly in the common stock.

So if improved returns are normally available from the direct investment in either straight debt and/or straight equity, why buy a convertible? The answer is simple: Convertibles provide a great way to achieve attractive risk-return tradeoffs. In particular, by combining the characteristics of both stocks and bonds into one security, convertibles offer some risk protection and at the same time considerable, although perhaps not maximum, upward price potential. Thus, although the return may not be the most in absolute terms, neither is the risk.

Transaction Costs

Convertible bonds are subject to the same brokerage fees and transfer taxes as straight corporate debt; and convertible preferreds trade at the same costs as straight preferreds and common stock. Any type of market or limit order that can be used with bonds or stocks can also be used with convertibles. Convertible debentures are listed along with corporate bonds; they are distinguished from straight debt issues by the "cv" in the "Cur Yld" column of the bond quotes, as illustrated in Figure 10.6. Note that it's not unusual for some convertibles (like the Harley Davidson 7¼ percent issue of 2015, for example) to trade at fairly high prices. These situations are justified by the correspondingly high values attained by the underlying common stock. Convertible preferreds, in contrast, normally are not isolated from other preferreds. They are listed with the "pf" markings, but they carry no other distinguishing symbols. As a result, the investor must turn to some other source to find out whether a preferred is convertible (one national business newspaper that *does* identify convertible preferreds is *Investor's Business Daily*—it provides a separate list of preferred stocks traded on the NYSE and AMEX and uses boldface type to highlight the convertible issues).

Measuring the Value of a Convertible

Evaluating the investment merits of convertible securities includes consideration of both the bond and stock dimensions of the issue. Fundamental security analysis of the equity position is, of course, especially important in light of the key role the equity kicker plays in defining the price behavior of a convertible. Agency ratings are helpful and are widely used in evaluating the bond side of the issue. And, just like other types of bonds, yield-to-maturity and current yield are important measures of return. But there's more; for in addition to analyzing the bond and stock dimensions of the issue, it is essential to evaluate the conversion feature itself. The

Bonds	Cur Yld	Vol	Close	Net Chg.
Gdyr 7.35s97	8.0	85	92¼ −	1¾
GrnTr dc8¼95	9.0	10	91½ +	1½
GreyF zr94	. . .	24	79	. . .
GrowGp 8½06	cv	50	92 +	1½
GtNoR 3⅛00	4.5	32	69½ +	1½
GtNoR 3⅛00r	4.6	3	67¾ −	¼
GtNoR 2⅝10	5.7	20	46 +	6
Gulfrd 6s12	cv	5	82 −	1
GlfRes 12½04	19.6	16	63⅞ +	⅜
HalwdGp 13½09	. . .	12	69	. . .
HarDav 7¼15	cv	20	118 +	2
Hartfd 8½96	10.0	10	85 −	1
Hellr 8½93	8.5	1	100¼	. . .
Hercul 8s10	cv	5	108 +	½
HmGrp 14⅞99	14.3	66	103⅞ +	⅜
Honey 9⅜09	9.3	15	100½ −	1
HousF 8½01	8.6	5	99¼ +	⅜
HousF 8.2s07	8.6	25	95 +	1½
HudFd 8s06	cv	5	80 +	½
HudFd 14s08	cv	27	108¼ +	¼
ICN 12⅞s98	13.8	439	93⅝ −	⅛

Harley Davidson convertible bond } (points to HarDav 7¼15 row)

conversion value
an indication of what a convertible issue should trade for if it were priced to sell on the basis of its stock value; equals the conversion ratio of the issue times the current market price of the underlying common stock.

• **FIGURE 10.6** Listed Quotes for Convertible Bonds

Convertible bonds (of which there are six in this figure) are listed right along with other corporate issues and are identified by the letters *cv* in the "Cur Yld" column. Except for this distinguishing feature, they are quoted like any other corporate bond. (*Source: The Wall Street Journal,* December 16, 1991.)

two critical areas in this regard are conversion value and investment value. These measures have a vital bearing on a convertible's price behavior and therefore can have a dramatic effect on an issue's holding period return.

Conversion Value

In essence, **conversion value** is an indication of what a convertible issue should trade for if it were priced to sell on the basis of its stock value. Conversion value is easy to find:

Equation 10.5

$$\frac{\text{Conversion}}{\text{value}} = \frac{\text{conversion}}{\text{ratio}} \times \frac{\text{current market}}{\text{price of the stock}}$$

conversion equivalent (conversion parity)
the price at which the common stock would have to sell in order to make the convertible security worth its present market price.

For example, a convertible that carries a conversion ratio of 20 would have a conversion value of $1,200 if the firm's stock traded at a current market price of $60 per share (20 × $60 = $1,200). Sometimes an alternative measure is used and the **conversion equivalent,** or what is also known as **conversion parity,** may be computed. The conversion equivalent indicates the price at which the common stock would have to sell in order to make the convertible security worth its present market price. Here's how to find the conversion equivalent:

Equation 10.6

$$\frac{\text{Conversion}}{\text{equivalent}} = \frac{\text{current market price of the convertible bond}}{\text{conversion ratio}}$$

Thus, if a convertible is trading at $1,400 and has a conversion ratio of 20, then the conversion equivalent of the common stock would equal $70 per share ($1,400 ÷ 20 = $70). In effect, we would expect the current market price of the common stock in this example to be at or near $70 per share in order to support a convertible trading at $1,400.

Unfortunately, convertible issues *seldom* trade precisely at their conversion values. Rather, as noted earlier, they trade at a conversion premium. The absolute size of an issue's conversion premium is determined by taking the difference between the convertible's market price and its conversion value (per equation 10.5, above). To place the premium on a relative basis, simply divide the dollar amount of the conversion premium by the issue's conversion value. That is:

Equation 10.7

$$\text{Conversion premium (in \$)} = \text{current market price of the convertible bond} - \text{conversion value}$$

where conversion value is found according to Equation 10.5. Then:

Equation 10.8

$$\text{Conversion premium (in \%)} = \frac{\text{conversion premium (in \$)}}{\text{conversion value}}$$

To illustrate, if a convertible trades at $1,400 and its conversion value equals $1,200, it would have a conversion premium of $200 ($1,400 − $1,200 = $200). In relation to what the convertible should be trading at, this $200 differential would amount to a conversion premium of 16.7 percent (i.e., $200/$1,200 = .167). Conversion premiums are common in the market (refer back to Table 10.2), and can often amount to as much as *25 to 30 percent* (or more) of an issue's true conversion value.

payback period
the length of time it takes for the buyer of a convertible to recover the conversion premium from the extra income earned on the convertible.

Investors are willing to pay a premium primarily because of the added current income that a convertible provides relative to the underlying common stock. An investor has two ways of recovering this premium: either through the added income the convertible provides, and/or by subsequently selling the issue at a premium equal to or greater than that which existed at the time of purchase. Unfortunately, the latter source of recovery is tough to come by, since conversion premiums tend to fade away as the price of the convertible goes up. Thus, if a convertible is bought for its potential price appreciation (which many are), all or a major portion of this price premium will probably disappear as the convertible appreciates and moves closer to its true conversion value. The size of the conversion premium can obviously have a big impact on investor return, so when picking convertibles, one of the major questions you should ask is whether the premium is justified. One way to assess conversion premium is to compute the issue's payback period. Basically, the **payback period** is a measure of the length of time it takes for the buyer to recover the conversion premium from the *extra* interest income earned on the convertible. Since this added income is a principle reason for the conversion premium, it makes sense to use it to assess the premium. The payback period can be found as follows:

Equation 10.9

$$\text{Payback period} = \frac{\text{conversion premium (in \$)}}{\begin{array}{c}\text{annual interest} \\ \text{income from convertible} \\ \text{bond}\end{array} - \begin{array}{c}\text{annual dividend} \\ \text{income from underlying} \\ \text{common stocks}\end{array}}$$

where *annual dividends are found by multiplying the stock's latest annual dividends per share by the bond's conversion ratio.*

For example, we saw in the illustration above that the bond has a conversion premium of $200; now, let's say this bond (which carries a conversion ratio of 20) has an 8½ percent coupon and the underlying stock paid dividends this past year of 50 cents a share. Given this information, we can use Equation 10.9 to find the payback period:

$$\frac{\text{Payback}}{\text{period}} = \frac{\$200.00}{\$85.00 - (20 \times \$0.50)}$$

$$= \frac{\$200.00}{\$85.00 - \$10.00} = \underline{2.7 \text{ years}}$$

In essence, the investor in this case will recover the premium in 2.7 years, which is a fairly decent payback period. As a rule, everything else being equal, *the shorter the payback period the better*. Also, watch out for excessively high premiums (of 50% or more), as you may have real difficulty ever recovering such astronomical premiums. Indeed, to avoid such premiums, most experts recommend that you stick to convertibles that have payback periods of 4 years or less! The bottom line is to get the most from these investments, take the time to *fully evaluate a bond's conversion premium before investing.*

Investment Value

investment value
the price at which a
convertible would
trade if it were non-
convertible and if it
were priced at or
near the prevailing
market yields of
comparable noncon-
vertible issues.

The price floor of a convertible is defined by its bond properties and is the object of the investment value measure. It's the point within the valuation process where attention is centered on current and expected market interest rates. **Investment value** is the price at which the bond would trade if it were nonconvertible and if it were priced at or near the prevailing market yields of comparable nonconvertible bonds. The same bond price formula given in Chapter 9 is used to compute investment value—see Equation 9.2. Since the coupon and maturity are known, the only additional piece of information needed is the market yield to maturity of comparably rated issues. For example, if comparable nonconvertible bonds are trading at 9 percent yields, and if a particular 20-year convertible carries a 6 percent coupon, its investment value would be $725. (*Note:* This value was calculated using techniques discussed in Chapter 9.) This figure indicates how far the convertible will have to fall before it hits its price floor and begins trading as a straight debt instrument. Other things being equal, the greater the distance between the current market price of a convertible and its investment value, the further the issue can fall in price before it hits its bond floor, and as a result, the greater the downside risk exposure.

Investment Strategies

Convertible securities offer some rewarding investment opportunities, as they can be used to meet several different investor objectives: Some investors buy them because of the underlying stock, others because of the attractive yields they offer as fixed-income securities. For the more savvy and adventuresome investors, there are

Look: It's a Bond, It's a Stock . . . No, It's a LYON

A sophisticated product in the convertible market is gaining popularity with long-term investors looking for protection of principal in their tax-deferred accounts. They carry the somewhat daunting name of "zero-coupon accreters." What's that mean? Zero-coupon debentures, convertible at a fixed ratio to common stock through the life of the issue. They can also be "put" back to the issuer, usually every three or five years, at specified values reflecting the accretion of the implied interest return. These put features reduce downside risk because they give *bondholders* the right (or option) to redeem their bonds at pre-specified prices. Thus, investors know that they can get out of these securities, at set prices, if things move against them. There are two types of put options: so-called "hard" puts, which are payable only in cash, and "soft" puts, which are the most common and may be paid in cash, common stock, notes, or some combination thereof. [*Note:* We'll examine put options in detail in Chapter 11.] Merrill Lynch created these zero-coupon convertibles six years ago and called them LYONs—liquid yield option notes. Now, most zero coupon convertibles come out with the features of a LYON, though they may be called something else.

What's their attraction? The conversion factor lets you participate in stock market gains while keeping a solid hedge against loss of principal through the put option. Issuers like them because they enhance cash flow: The implied interest is deducted from taxable income, but no cash is actually paid out. Of course, for the investor, the implied interest reflected in annual price accretion is subject to taxes, so these converts should be used only for tax-deferred accounts. Otherwise the investor will be paying cash out in taxes without getting any cash return. Remember, too, that convertibles can be as volatile as the common stock itself; so don't take the plunge unless you really plan to hold for a long time. Watch those conversion and put terms; they vary widely, and be sure you know what the issuer can use to pay off the put. This may be cash, but sometimes it can be stock or a new bond—not always what you might want. One other thing: because the conversion ratio is fixed while the underlying accreted value of the bond keeps increasing, the net effect is that the *conversion price on the stock will keep getting higher over time.* Thus, the market price of the stock had better go up by more than the rate of appreciation of the bond, or you'll never be able to convert your LYON.

For the investor who is more interested in the value of the underlying common stock than in yield, choose a zero convert with a low conversion premium, of no more than 15% over the common's market price. A zero-coupon convertible with a lower premium will go up in price faster than a high-premium security. When the conversion premium gets really high, so does the accretion "yield," and the bond becomes attractive on a yield basis, with conversion a remote kicker. Example: the Loews Corp. zeros of 2004, which trade at $407.50 to yield 6.75% to maturity but pay 8.9% to put in 1994. Conversion premium is 42%.

Sidney Fried, publisher of *R.H.M. Convertible Survey* in Glen Cove, N.Y., says zero-coupon convertibles are overlooked by many market participants who believe the securities are too complicated. But that shouldn't stop you from considering them as investments in the current market environment.

Source: Adapted from Ben Weberman, "Double-Edge Play in the Convert Market," *Forbes,* April 29, 1991, p. 343.

even *zero-coupon convertibles*. These securities, with their deep discounted prices, not only carry conversion features, but many of them also give holders the right to periodically cash in their bonds. An example of one such bond is the recent $1.3 billion AMR issue, shown in Figure 10.7. As more fully discussed in the accompanying *Investor Insights* box, these securities combine the steady appreciation of zero-coupon bonds with the capital gains potential of common stocks, and as such, truly do offer some unusual, yet highly attractive investment opportunities.

An Overview of Price and Investment Behavior

The price behavior of a convertible security is influenced by both the equity and fixed-income elements of the obligation. The variables that play key roles in defining the market value of a typical convertible therefore include: (1) the potential price behavior of the underlying common stock, and (2) expectations regarding the pattern of future market yields and interest rates. The typical price behavior of a convertible issue is depicted in Figure 10.8. In the top panel are the three market elements of a convertible bond: the bond value, or price floor; the stock (conversion) value of the issue; and the actual market price of the convertible. The figure reveals the customary relationship among these three important elements and shows that conversion premium is a common occurrence with these securities. Note especially that the conversion premium tends to diminish as the price of the stock increases. The top panel of Figure 10.8 is somewhat simplified, however, because of the steady price floor (which unrealistically assumes no variation in market interest rates) and the steady upswing in the stock's value. The lower panel of the figure relaxes these conditions, although for simplicity, we ignore conversion premium. The figure illustrates how the market value of a convertible will approximate the price behavior of the underlying stock so long as stock value is greater than bond value. When the stock value drops below the bond value floor, as it does in the shaded area of the illustration, the market value of the convertible becomes linked to the bond portion of the obligation, and it continues to move as a debt security until the price of the underlying stock picks up again and approaches, or equals, this price floor.

Convertibles as Deferred Equity Investments

Convertible securities—even zero-coupon convertibles—are purchased most often because of the *equity attributes* they offer to investors. Using convertibles as an alternative to a company's common stock, investors may be able to match (or possibly even exceed) the return from the common, but with less exposure to risk. Also, relative to stocks, convertibles generally offer improved current income. Convertibles can be profitably used as alternative equity investments whenever it is felt that the underlying stock offers desired capital gains opportunities. In order to achieve maximum price appreciation under such circumstances, the investor would want assurance that the convertible is trading in concert with its stock value, and that it does not have an inordinate amount of conversion premium. If these necessary conditions do in fact exist, investor attention should logically center on the

This announcement is under no circumstances to be construed as an offer to sell or as a solicitation of an offer to buy any of these securities. The offering is made only by the Prospectus.

New Issue   **March 8, 1991**

$1,300,000,000

AMR

AMR Corporation

Liquid Yield Option™ Notes due 2006

(Zero Coupon – Subordinated)

Price 39.727%

Copies of the Prospectus may be obtained in any State in which this announcement is circulated from the undersigned or other dealers or brokers as may lawfully offer these securities in such State.

Merrill Lynch & Co.

™Trademark of Merrill Lynch & Co., Inc.

• FIGURE 10.7 A Newly Issued Zero-Coupon Convertible Bond
AMR Corporation, which is the parent company of American Airlines, issued this LYON (zero-coupon convertible bond) at the deep discounted price of $397.27. If this bond is not converted or called between now and 2006, it will slowly appreciate over time to its full face value of $1,000. In the mean time, the bond can be converted into 5.769 shares of AMR stock (the conversion ratio), and it carries a ''put'' provision that gives holders the right to periodically redeem their notes (for cash, common stock, or a combination of the two). (*Source: The Wall Street Journal,* April 9, 1991, ''A Newly issued Zero Coupon Convertible Bond-AMR Corporation,'' March 8, 1991. Copyright © 1991 Merrill Lynch & Co. Reprinted by permission of Merrill Lynch, Pierce, Fenner & Smith Incorporated.)

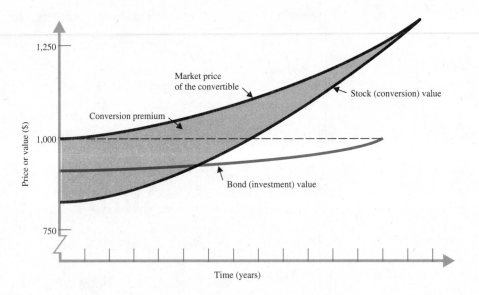

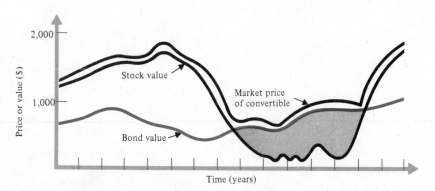

• FIGURE 10.8 Typical Price Behavior of a Convertible Bond

The price behavior of a convertible security is tied to the stock or the bond dimension of the issue: When the price of the underlying stock is up, the convertible will trade much like the stock, whereas the bond value will act as a price floor for the convertible when the price of the stock falls.

potential market behavior of the underlying stock. To assess such behavior, it is necessary to evaluate both current and expected conversion value.

For example, assume a 7 percent convertible bond carries a conversion ratio of 25 and is presently trading in the market at $900. In addition, assume the stock (which pays no dividends) is currently trading at $32 and the convertible is trading at a conversion premium of $100, or 12.5 percent. The formulation of future interest rates also comes into play with this trading strategy, as the investor will want to assess the bond price floor and the extent of downward risk exposure: Using the same approach as discussed in Chapter 9, future interest rates would be forecast and used to determine the possible bond price behavior of the issue. Generally speaking, a *drop* in interest rates would be viewed positively by convertible bond investors, since such behavior would signal a rise in the price floor of the convertible issue and therefore a reduction in downside risk exposure. That is, should the common stock not perform as expected, the price of the convertible could still go up as the (bond) price floor rises—or at the least, it would reduce any drop in the price of the convertible issue.

But most of the attention is centered not on the bond price floor; rather, it is directed toward the anticipated behavior of the common stock and the conversion premium. To continue our example, assume the investor expects the price of the stock to rise to $60 per share within the next two years. A conversion ratio of 25 would then yield a future conversion value of $1,500. If an expected conversion premium of 6 to 7 percent (or about $100) is added on, it means the market price of the convertible should rise to about $1,600 by the end of the two-year investment horizon. This expected future price of the convertible, along with its annual coupon payment and current market price, would then be used to determine the issue's expected yield. That is:

$$\text{Expected yield} = \frac{\$70 + \dfrac{\$1,600 - \$900}{2}}{\dfrac{\$1,600 + \$900}{2}} = \frac{\$70 + \$350}{\$1,250} = \underline{\underline{33.6\%}}$$

The expected yield equation above is identical to the one used with straight bonds and preferred stocks. It is really nothing more than the approximate yield formula first introduced in Chapter 4. Although this 33.6 percent rate of return may indeed appear attractive, the investor should be sure of several points before committing capital to this security—in particular, that this approach is in fact superior to a direct investment in the issuer's common stock (at least from a risk-return point of view) and that there is no better rate of return (with commensurate risk exposure) available from some other investment vehicle. To the extent that these conditions are met, investing in a convertible may be a suitable course of action, especially if (1) the price of the underlying common stock is under strong upward pressure, (2) bond interest rates are falling off sharply, and (3) there is little or no conversion premium in the price of the convertible. The first attribute means conversion value should move up, leading to appreciation in the price of the convertible. The second means that the bond value (price floor) should also move up, thereby reducing exposure to risk. And the third feature means the investor should be able to capture all or most of the price appreciation of the underlying common stock rather than lose a chunk of it to the inevitable drop in conversion premium. Although it would be nice if *all three* of these attributes were available with a single security, the fact is that very rarely is that the case. So investors normally have to settle for only one or two of these features and then assess the costs that the missing one(s) has on potential returns. Hopefully, the bottom line is that the convertible will still be an attractive investment vehicle.

Convertibles as High-Yield Fixed-Income Investments

Another common use of convertibles is to buy such issues for the attractive *fixed-income* returns they offer. The key element in this strategy is the issue's bond dimension. Many convertible securities provide current yields and yields to maturity that are safe and highly competitive with straight debt obligations. Investors should take care, however, to make certain that the high yields are not a function of low (speculative) ratings. Normally, such investors would seek discount issues, particularly those that are trading close to their bond price floor. Otherwise, the issue would be trading at a premium price, which would certainly involve a yield give-up, and perhaps a substantial one. Most of these investors view convertibles as ideal for locking in high rates of return. They are not widely used for speculating on interest rates, however, because even investment-grade convertibles often lack the needed interest sensitivity (due to the equity kicker of the issue). Yet for those who use convertibles to seek high, safe yields, the equity kicker can provide an added source of return if the underlying stock does indeed take off. The investor then has a bond that offers a handsome rate of return, plus an equity kicker to boot.

SUMMARY

1. Preferred stocks and convertible securities play an important role in many sound, well-balanced investment programs. They are hybrid securities (combining features of both debt and equity) that offer investors some interesting and potentially rewarding investment opportunities. Preferred stocks provide attractive dividend yields and, when interest rates decline, will produce capital gains as well.

2. Preferreds are considered less risky than common because their shareholders enjoy a senior position with regard to dividend payments and asset claims. Although failure to pay preferred dividends does not carry with it the same serious consequences as missing the interest payments on a bond, no common stock dividends can be paid until all preferred obligations are satisfied.

3. Except for convertible preferreds, the value of a preferred stock is generally linked to the dividend yield it provides to investors. Indeed, the price behavior of a preferred stock is inversely related to market interest rates.

   The principal purpose for holding preferreds is their yield. In addition, preferreds can be held for capital gains purposes by investors willing to trade on interest rate behavior or on turnaround situations.

4. Convertible securities are initially issued as bonds (or preferreds), but they can subsequently be converted into shares of common stock. As such, these securities are highly attractive because they offer investors a generous stream of fixed income (in the form of annual coupon payments) and an equity kicker to boot.

    Because convertible securities can be converted into common stock, the value of a convertible depends largely on the price behavior of the underlying common. This is captured in the security's conversion value, which represents the worth of a convertible if it were converted into common stock. (Conversion value rises in direct proportion to increases in share prices.)

5. From an investment perspective, convertibles provide a combination of both good upside potential (from the equity feature of the issue) and good downside protection (through the fixed-income characteristics of the issue). In fact, this risk-return tradeoff, combined with their relatively high current income, is unmatched by any other type of security.

6. Investors use convertible securities primarily as a form of deferred equity, where the investment is made as a way to capture the capital gains potential of the underlying common stock. In addition, convertibles are sometimes used as high-yielding fixed-income securities, when the investor principally goes after the higher current income of the bond (and the equity kicker is viewed as little more than a pleasant by-product). And today, a number of savvy investors are finding some unusual (and highly profitable) investment opportunities in zero-coupon convertible bonds.

QUESTIONS

1. Define a preferred stock. What types of prior claims do preferred stockholders enjoy?

2. In what ways is a preferred stock like equity? like a bond?

3. Distinguish a cumulative preferred from a callable preferred. Do cumulative dividend provisions and call features affect the investment merits of preferred issues? Explain.

4. Briefly describe each of the following, and note how each differs from a "regular" preferred stock:

    a. Convertible preferreds.
    b. Floating-rate preferreds.
    c. Prior preferred stocks.

5. What are the advantages and disadvantages of investing in preferreds?

6. Describe how high-grade preferred stocks are priced in the market. What role does dividend yield play in the valuation of preferred stocks? Could you use the zero growth dividend valuation model to value a preferred stock? Explain.

7. Discuss why dividend yield is critical in evaluating the investment merits of high-grade preferred stocks during periods when market yields are expected to decline.

8. Briefly discuss several investment uses of preferred stocks. Would preferreds be suitable for both conservative and aggressive investors? Explain.

9. Is it possible for a firm to pass dividends on preferred stocks, even if it earns enough to pay them? Explain. What usually happens when a company passes (misses) a dividend on a (cumulative) preferred stock? Are common stock dividends affected in any way?

10. What is a convertible debenture? How does a convertible bond differ from a convertible preferred?

11. Identify the equity kicker of a convertible security, and explain how it affects the value and price behavior of convertibles.

12. Why do companies like to issue convertible securities—i.e., what's in it for them? What about preferred stocks—why do companies like to issue them?

13. Explain why it is necessary to examine both the bond and stock properties of a convertible debenture when determining its investment appeal.

14. What are the investment attributes of convertible debentures? What are the disadvantages of such vehicles?

15. What is the difference between conversion parity and conversion value? How would you describe the payback period on a convertible? What is the bond investment value of a convertible and what does it reveal?

16. What is a LYON? Describe the key features of a LYON; note the similarities and differences between a LYON and a regular convertible debenture.

17. Discuss the various uses of convertible debentures. What are the three major attributes that make for an ideal investment outlet and that investors should look for when using convertibles as deferred equity investments?

PROBLEMS

1. An adjustable rate preferred is currently selling at a dividend yield of 9 percent; assume the dividend rate on the stock is adjusted once a year, and it's presently paying an annual dividend of $5.40 a share. Because of major changes that have occurred in the market, it's anticipated that annual dividends will drop to $4.50 a share on the next dividend adjustment date, which is just around the corner. What would the new dividend yield on this issue be if its market price does not change? What would the new market price on the issue be if the stock's dividend yield holds at 9%? What would it be if the yield drops to 7%?

2. The Danzer Company has 500,000 shares of $2 preferred stock outstanding; it generates an EBIT of $40,000,000 and has annual interest payments of $2,000,000. Given the above information, determine the fixed charge coverage of the preferred stock.

3. Select one of the preferred stocks listed in Table 10.1. Using the resources available at your campus or public library, determine the following:

    a. Latest market price.
    b. Dividend yield.
    c. Fixed charge coverage.
    d. Book value per share.
    e. The preferred's stated par value.

    Now, briefly comment on the issue's yield and the quality of its claim on income and assets.

4. DuPont has a preferred stock outstanding that pays annual dividends of $3.50 a share. At what price would this stock be trading if market yields were 7½ percent? Now, use one of the dividend valuation models (from Chapter 7) to price this same stock, assuming you have a 7½ percent required rate of return. Are there any similarities between the two prices? Explain.

5. Charlene Weaver likes to speculate with preferred stock by trading on movements in market interest rates. Right now, she thinks the market is poised for a big drop in rates. Accordingly, she is thinking seriously about investing in a certain preferred stock that pays $7 in annual dividends and is presently trading a $75 per share. What rate of return would she realize on this investment if the market yield on the preferred drops to 6½ percent within two years? How about if the drop in rates takes place in *one year?*

6. A certain 6 percent convertible bond (maturing in 20 years) is convertible at the holder's option into 20 shares of common stock. The bond is currently trading at $800, and the stock (which pays 75¢ a share in dividends) is currently priced in the market at $35 a share.

   a. What is the current yield of the convertible bond?
   b. What is the conversion price?
   c. What is the conversion ratio?
   d. What is the conversion value of this issue? What is its conversion parity?
   e. What is the conversion premium, in dollars and as a percentage?
   f. What is the bond's payback period?
   g. What is the approximate yield to maturity of the convertible bond?
   h. If comparably rated nonconvertible bonds sell to yield 8 percent, what is the investment value of the convertible?

7. An 8 percent convertible bond carries a par value of $1,000 and a conversion ratio of 20. Assume that an investor has $5,000 to invest and that the convertible sells at a price of $1,000 (which includes a 25 percent conversion premium). How much total income (coupon plus capital gains) would this investment offer if, over the course of the next 12 months, the price of the stock moves to $75 per share and the convertible trades at a price which includes a conversion premium of 10 percent? What is the holding period return on this investment? Finally, given the information in the problem, what is the underlying common stock currently selling for?

8. Assume you just paid $1,200 for a convertible bond that carries a 7½ percent coupon and has 15 years to maturity. The bond can be converted into 24 shares of stock, which are now trading at $50 a share. Find the bond investment value of this issue, given that comparable nonconvertible bonds are presently selling to yield 9 percent.

9. Find the conversion value of a *convertible preferred stock* that carries a conversion ratio of 1.8, given that the market price of the underlying common stock is $40 a share. Would there be any conversion premium if the convertible preferred were selling at $90 a share? If so, how much (in dollar and in percentage terms)? Also, explain the concept of conversion parity and then find the conversion parity of this issue, given that the preferred trades at $90 per share.

10. Using the resources available at your campus or public library, find the information requested below. (*Note:* Be sure to show your work for all calculations.)

   a. Select any two *convertible debentures* and determine the conversion ratio, conversion parity, conversion value, conversion premium, and payback period for each.

b. Select any two *convertible preferreds* and determine the conversion ratio, conversion parity, conversion value, conversion premium, and payback period of each.

CFA QUESTION (This question is from the 1988 Level II Exam.)

Bart Simons is a securities analyst specializing in the health care industry. Simons' analysis indicates that the common stock of Healthtronics, Inc., is attractive for purchase by long-term investors. Before recommending the stock, Simons consults with you about the Healthtronics convertible debentures.

You are given the following information about Healthtronics stock and convertible debenture:

Common Stock:
Current market price per share = $48.00
Current dividends per share = $1.44

Convertible Debenture:
Coupon rate = 8% (semi-annual payment)
Maturity = June 1, 1998
Conversion ratio = 18 shares
Current market price = $1,000
Call price = $1,080 (non-callable for the next three years)

Yield-to-maturity on comparable "nonconvertible" bonds = 10%

a. Calculate both the investment value and the conversion value for the Healthtronics convertible debenture as of June 1, 1988.
b. Recommend the Healthtronics security (either the common stock or the convertible debenture) that, in your opinion, would be more desirable for purchase by a long-term investor. Justify your recommendation (*Note:* Include conversion premium and payback period calculations in your answers).
c. Assume Healthtronics common stock appreciates to $65 per share and yields-to-maturity on comparable nonconvertible bonds increase 200 basis points to 12 percent. Under these assumptions, estimate the one-year holding period return on the Healthtronics convertible debentures.

(See Appendix C for Guideline Answer to this question.)

CASE PROBLEMS

10.1 Mary Beth Shows a Preference for Preferreds

Ms. Mary Beth Baugh is a young career woman who has built up a substantial investment portfolio. Most of her holdings are preferred stocks—a situation she does not want to change. Ms. Baugh is now considering the purchase of $4,800 worth of LaRamie Mine's $5 preferred, which is currently trading at $48 per share. Mary Beth's stockbroker has told her that he feels the market yield on preferreds like LaRamie should drop to 8 percent within the next two years, and that these preferreds would make a sound investment. Instead of buying the LaRamie preferred, Mary Beth has an alternate investment (with comparable risk exposure) which she is confident can produce earnings of about 10 percent over each of the next two years.

Questions

1. If preferred yields behave as Mary Beth's stockbroker thinks they will, what will be the price of the LaRamie $5 preferred in two years?
2. What realized yield would this investment offer over the two-year holding period if all the expectations about it come true (particularly with regard to the price it is supposed to reach)? How much profit (in dollars) will Mary Beth make from her investment?
3. Would you recommend that she buy the LaRamie preferred? Why?
4. What are the investment merits of this transaction? What are its risks?

10.2 Dave and Marlene Consider Convertibles

Dave and Marlene Jenkins live in Irvine, California, where she manages a bridal shop and he runs an industrial supply firm. Their annual income is usually in the mid to upper nineties; they have no children and maintain a "comfortable" life style. Recently, they came into a bit of money and are anxious to invest it in some high-yielding fixed-income security. Although not aggressive investors, they like to maximize the return on every investment dollar they have. For this reason, they like the high yields and added equity kicker of convertible bonds, and are presently looking at such an issue as a way to invest their recent windfall. In particular, they have their eyes on the convertible debentures of Maria Pottery, Inc. They have heard that the price of the stock is on the way up, and after some in-depth analysis of their own, they feel the company's prospects are indeed bright. They've also looked at market interest rates, and based on economic reports obtained from their broker, Dave and Marlene expect interest rates to decline sharply.

The details on the convertible they're looking at are as follows: It's a 20-year, $1,000 par value issue that carries a 7½ percent coupon and is presently trading at $800. The issue is convertible into 15 shares of stock, and the stock, which pays no dividends, was recently quoted at $49.50 per share.

Questions

1. Ignoring conversion premium, find the price of the convertible if the stock goes up to $66.67 per share. What if it goes up to $75 per share? To $100 per share? Repeat the computations, assuming the convertible will trade at a 5 percent conversion premium.

2. Find the approximate promised yield of the convertible. (*Hint:* Use the same approach as we did with straight bonds in Chapter 9.)
    a. Now find the bond value of the convertible if, within two years, interest rates drop to 8 percent. (Remember: In two years, the security will have only 18 years remaining to maturity.) What if they drop to 6 percent?
    b. What implication does the drop in interest rates hold as far as the investment appeal of the convertible is concerned?

3. Given expected future stock prices and interest rate levels (per above), find the minimum and maximum expected yield that this investment offers over the two-year holding period.
    a. What is the worst return (expected yield) Dave and Marlene can expect over their two-year holding period if the price of the stock drops to $40 per share and interest rates drop to only 9 percent? What if the price of the stock drops (to $40) and interest rates rise to 11 percent? (Assume a zero conversion premium in both cases.)
4. Should Dave and Marlene invest in the Maria convertibles? Discuss the pros and cons of the investment.

PART FOUR

SPECULATIVE INVESTMENT VEHICLES

THE INVESTMENT ENVIRONMENT

INVESTMENT ADMINISTRATION

INVESTING IN COMMON STOCK	INVESTING IN FIXED-INCOME SECURITIES
SPECULATIVE INVESTMENT VEHICLES	OTHER POPULAR INVESTMENT VEHICLES

11 Options: Rights, Warrants, Puts and Calls

After studying this chapter, you should be able to:

1. Describe the basic features and fundamental investment attributes of stock rights and stock warrants.

2. Explain the impact that leverage has on the speculative appeal of warrants, and discuss the trading strategies that can be used to gain maximum benefits from this investment vehicle.

3. Discuss the basic nature of puts and calls, how these investment vehicles work, and why they are so popular with individual and institutional investors.

4. Describe the different kinds of listed options, including puts and calls on stocks, stock indexes, and foreign currencies, as well as LEAPS and capped options.

5. Gain an understanding of how put and call options are valued, and the forces that drive options prices in the marketplace.

6. Explain the profit potential of puts and calls, as well as the risk and return behavior of various put and call investment strategies.

When investors buy shares of common or preferred stock, they become the registered owners of the securities and are entitled to all the rights and privileges of ownership. Investors who acquire bonds or convertible issues are also entitled to the benefits of ownership. However, options are another matter: Investors who buy options acquire nothing more than the right to subsequently buy or sell other, related securities. That is, an **option** gives the holder the right to buy or sell a certain amount of an underlying security at a specified price over a specified period of time.

The three basic kinds of options are: (1) rights, (2) warrants, and (3) puts and calls. The first type has little investment appeal for the average investor, but the latter two—and especially puts and calls—enjoy considerable popularity today as attractive trading vehicles. All of these securities are a bit unusual, and their use requires special investor know-how. The focus of the present chapter, therefore, is to learn what we can about the essential characteristics and investment merits of these securities, and to see how they can be used in various types of investment programs. After briefly looking at stock rights, we'll move on to warrants and examine them in some detail. *Most of the chapter, however, will be devoted to the study of puts and calls,* as these are, by far, the dominant type of options security and certainly the most actively traded.

option
a security that gives the holder the right to buy or sell a certain amount of an underlying financial asset at a specified price for a specified period of time.

RIGHTS

right
an option to buy shares of a new issue of common stock at a specified price, over a specified, fairly short, period of time.

A **right** is a special type of option that has a short market life; it usually exists for no more than a few weeks. Essentially, rights originate when corporations raise money by issuing new shares of common stock. From an investor's perspective, a right enables a stockholder to buy shares of the new issue at a specified price, over a specified, fairly short, time period. Although not specifically designed for speculation or for use as trading vehicles, *rights do have value,* and they should never be lightly discarded. Instead, unwanted rights should be sold in the open market.

Characteristics

Let's say a firm has 1 million shares of common stock outstanding and that it has decided to issue another 250,000 shares. This might well be done through a *rights offering:* the firm, rather than directly issuing the new shares of common, would issue stock rights instead. These rights could then be used by their holders to purchase the new issue of stock. Existing stockholders may be given the right to maintain their proportionate share of ownership in a firm, a privilege known as a **preemptive right.** Since each stockholder receives, without charge, one right for each share of stock currently owned, the company in our example would issue one million rights, and it would take *four rights plus the price of the stock,* to buy one new share of common.

preemptive right
the right of existing stockholders to maintain their proportionate share of ownership in a firm.

Rights and Privileges

Because most stock rights allow their holders to purchase only a fractional share of the new common stock, two or more rights are usually needed to buy a single new share. The price of the new stock is spelled out in the right, and is known as the

exercise price
with options, the
price at which a
new share of com-
mon stock will be
sold; also called
subscription price.

exercise (or **subscription**) **price.** It is always set below the prevailing market price of the stock. For each new share of common stock purchased, the investor has to *redeem a specified number of rights and pay the stipulated subscription price in cash.* Rights not used by their expiration date lose all value and simply cease to exist. Unfortunately, many investors allow their rights to expire and thereby lose money.

 ### The Value of a Right

Technically, the precise measure of a right's value depends on whether the security is trading rights-on or rights-off. **Rights-on** indicates that the common stock is trading with the right attached to it; an investor who buys a share of stock during such a period also receives the attached stock right. When issues are trading **rights-off,** or **ex-rights,** the company's stock and its rights are trading in separate markets and are distinct from one another. Regardless of how these securities are trading, we can use the following approximation formula to measure the value of a right:

rights-on
a condition when a
firm's common stock
is trading with a
stock right attached
to it.

Equation 11.1

$$\text{Value of a right} = \frac{\text{market price of old stock} - \text{subscription price of new stock}}{\text{number of rights needed to buy one new share}}$$

As an example of how Equation 11.1 works, let's continue with the illustration above. Assume the prevailing market price of the old stock is $50 and the new shares carry a subscription price of $40 per share. Remember that it takes four rights and $40 to buy one new share of stock. We thus find the approximate value of a right as follows:

rights-off
a condition when a
firm's common stock
and its rights are
trading in separate
markets, separate
from each other; also
called *ex-rights.*

$$\text{Value of a right} = \frac{\$50 - \$40}{4} = \frac{\$10}{4} = \$2.50$$

Each right in our hypothetical example will have a market value of about $2.50 (as long as the price of the stock remains at $50); if the investor is not going to exercise the rights, this is the price at which each right could be sold in the market.

Investment Merits

The major investment attribute of a stock right is that it lets the holder acquire stock at a reduced price. It also enables the holder to acquire additional shares of stock *without paying the customary commission fees.* Although the savings may not be enormous, the opportunity to execute commission-free transactions should not be overlooked. However, except for the commission savings, the cost of buying the stock will be the same whether the shares are bought outright or through the use of rights. That is, the cost of the rights plus the subscription price of the stock should just about equal the market price of the common. Unfortunately, stock rights hold little opportunity for profitable trading. The life of these securities is simply too short and the range of price activity too narrow to allow for any significant trading profits. Thus, the role of stock rights is limited in most individual investor portfolios to selling unwanted rights or to buying or using them to reduce the commissions on subsequent stock transactions.

WARRANTS

A *warrant* is also an option that enables the holder to acquire common stock and, like rights, is found in the corporate sector of the market. Occasionally, warrants can be used to purchase preferred stock or even bonds, but common stock is the leading redemption vehicle.

What Is a Warrant?

warrant
a long-lived option that gives the holder the right to buy stock in a company at a price specified in the warrant itself.

A **warrant** is a long-lived option. In fact, of the various types of options, warrants have the longest lives, with maturities that extend to 5, 10, or even 20 years or more. Indeed, some warrants have no maturity date at all. They have no voting rights, pay no dividends, and have no claim on the assets of the company. All the warrant offers is a chance to participate indirectly in the market behavior of the issuing firm's common stock and in so doing, to generate capital gains. With warrants, *price behavior and capital appreciation are the only dimensions of return.*

General Attributes

Warrants are created as "sweeteners" to bond issues. To make a bond more attractive, the issuing corporation will sometimes attach warrants, which give the holder the right to purchase a stipulated number of stocks at a stipulated price any time within a stipulated period of time. A single warrant usually allows the holder to buy one full share of stock, although some involve more than one share per warrant and a few involve fractional shares. The life of a warrant is specified by its *expiration date,* and the stock purchase price stipulated on the warrant is known as the *exercise price.*

Because warrants are a type of equity issue, they can be margined at the same rate as common stock. They are purchased through brokers and are subject to commission and transaction costs similar to those for common stock. Warrants are usually listed with the common stock of the issuer, but their quotes are easy to pick out, since the letters *wt* appear next to the name of the company. For example, the quote for the Tyco Toys warrant is highlighted in Figure 11.1. Notice that the

| 52 Weeks | | | | | Yld | | Vol | | | | Net |
Hi	Lo	Stock	Sym	Div	%	PE	100s	Hi	Lo	Close	Chg
9¾	3½	TucsonElec	TEP	...	...	...	1634	5¾	5½	5¾	+¼
s 25⅞	14⅞	20CentInd	TW	.42	1.9	9	232	22⅜	21¾	22	−⅝
22	13¾	TwinDisc	TDI	.70	3.5	88	1	20¼	20¼	20¼	+¼
52¼	28	TycoLabs	TYC	.36	.9	18	772	38¾	38⅛	38⅜	...
39½	12½	TycoToys	TTI		...	25	1875	38⅝	38½	38½	...
23¼	2⅞	TycoToys wt			...	...	43	22⅝	22½	22½	...
12¾	11⅛	TylerCabot	TMF	1.26	10.2	...	822	12⅜	12¼	12⅜	...
5	2½	TylerCp	TYL		...	71	157	4¼	4	4¼	...

• FIGURE 11.1 Stock Quotations Showing Market Information for a Warrant

Warrants are listed right along with common stocks, but they're easy to pick out—just look for the letters *wt* behind the company's name. *(Source: The Wall Street Journal.)*

market information for warrants is listed just like any other common stock except, of course, there's no dividend, dividend yield, or price/earnings ratio.

Advantages and Disadvantages

Warrants offer several advantages to investors, one of which is their tendency to exhibit price behavior much like the common stock to which they are linked. Warrants thus provide the investor with an alternative way of achieving capital gains from an equity issue; i.e., instead of buying the stock, the investor can purchase warrants on the stock. Indeed, such a tactic may even be more rewarding than investing directly in the stock. Another advantage is the relatively low unit cost of warrants and the attractive leverage potential that accompanies this low unit cost. The concept of **leverage** rests on the principle of reducing the level of required capital in a given investment position, without affecting the payoff or capital appreciation of that investment. Put another way, an investor can use warrants to obtain a given equity position at a substantially reduced capital investment. In so doing the investor can *magnify returns,* since the warrant provides basically the same capital appreciation as the more costly common stock. For example, note in Figure 11.1 that the Tyco warrants are trading at 22½ while Tyco common stocks are trading at a much higher price of 38½. Finally, the low unit cost of warrants also leads to reduced downside risk exposure. In essence, the lower unit cost simply means there is less to lose if the investment goes sour. For example, a $50 stock can drop to $25 if the market becomes depressed, but there is no way the same company's $10 warrants can drop by the same amount.

However, warrants do have some disadvantages. For one thing, warrants pay no dividends, which means that investors sacrifice current income. Second, because these issues usually carry an expiration date, there is only a certain period of time during which an investor can capture the type of price behavior sought. Although this may not be much of a problem with long-term warrants, it can prove to be a burden for those issues with fairly short lives (of perhaps one to two years, or less).

Characteristics of Warrants

There are three aspects of warrants that are particularly important to investors: (1) the issue's exercise price, (2) the value of a warrant, and (3) the amount of the premium. These features not only affect the price and return behavior of warrants but also have a bearing on choosing an investment strategy.

Exercise Price

The **exercise price** is the stated price the warrant holder will have to pay to acquire a share of the underlying common stock. It is the share price paid to the firm when the warrant is used to buy the stock—that is, when the option is "exercised." Usually, the exercise price remains fixed for the issue's full life, but some warrants may provide for an increase or decrease in exercise price as the security nears its expiration date. In addition, the exercise price will automatically be adjusted for stock splits or major stock dividends. The exercise price on a warrant can range anywhere

---

leverage
the ability to obtain a given equity position at a reduced capital investment, thereby magnifying returns.

exercise price
the price at which a share of stock can be purchased, as specified on a warrant.

from just a few dollars to $50 or more. But as we'll see below, the real significance of exercise price is when it's viewed in relation to the market price of the underlying common stock, for that's what drives value and propels the *market price of the warrant*.

Value

A warrant is a type of **derivative security.** That is, it derives its value from the price behavior of some other real or financial asset. Put and call options, as well as futures contracts (which we'll study in Chapter 12), are also derivative securities, since they too derive their value from underlying securities or assets. For example, the Tyco Toy warrants noted above are directly linked to the price behavior of Tyco common stock. Thus, under the right conditions, when Tyco stock goes up (or down) in price, the warrants will too. Actually, warrants possess value whenever the market price of the underlying common equals or exceeds the exercise price on the warrant. This so-called *fundamental value* is determined as follows:

derivative security
a security, such as puts, calls, and other options, whose value is derived from the price behavior of an underlying real or financial asset.

Equation 11.2

$$\text{Fundamental value of a warrant} = (M - E) \times N$$

where

M = prevailing market price of the common stock
E = exercise price
N = number of shares of stock that can be acquired with one warrant (if one warrant entitles the holder to buy one share of stock, $N = 1$; if, however, two warrants are required to buy one share of stock, $N = .5$, etc.)

The formula shows fundamental value, and therefore what the market value of a warrant *should be,* given the respective market and exercise prices of the common and the number of shares of stock that can be acquired with one warrant. As an example, consider a warrant that carries an exercise price of $40 per share and enables the holder to purchase one share of stock per warrant. If the common stock has a current market price of $50 a share, then the warrants would be valued at $10 each:

$$\text{Fundamental value of a warrant} = (\$50 - \$40) \times 1 = (\$10) \times 1 = \$10$$

Obviously the greater the spread between the market and exercise prices, the greater the fundamental value of a warrant. *So long as the market price of the stock equals or exceeds the exercise price of the warrant,* and the redemption provision carries a 1-to-1 ratio (meaning one share of common can be bought with each warrant), the value of a warrant will be directly linked to the price behavior of the common stock.

Premium

Equation 11.2 indicates how warrants should be valued, but they are seldom priced exactly that way in the marketplace. Instead, the market price of a warrant usually *exceeds* its fundamental value. This happens when warrants with negative values trade at prices greater than zero. It also occurs when warrants with positive values

warrant premium
the difference between the true value of a warrant and its market price.

trade at even higher market prices (as, for example, when a warrant that's valued at $10 trades at $15). This discrepancy is known as **warrant premium,** and it exists because warrants possess speculative value. As a rule, the amount of premium embedded in the market price of a warrant is directly related to the option's time to expiration and the volatility of the underlying common stock. That is, the longer the time to expiration and the more volatile the stock, the greater the size of the premium. On the other hand, the amount of premium does tend to diminish as the underlying (fundamental) value of a warrant increases. This can be seen in Figure 11.2, which shows the typical behavior of warrant premiums. Premium is easy to measure: Take the difference between the value of a warrant (as computed according to the formula above) and its market price. For instance, a warrant has $5 in premium if it has a value of $10 but is trading at $15. We can also put the amount of premium on a relative (percentage) basis by dividing the dollar premium by the warrant's fundamental value. For example, there is a 50 percent premium embedded in the price of our $15 warrant above: i.e., the dollar premium ÷ the value of the warrant = $5 ÷ $10 = .50. Premiums on warrants can at times become fairly substantial. Indeed, premiums of 20 to 30 percent, or more, are not all that uncommon.

Trading Strategies

Because their attraction to investors rests primarily with the capital gains opportunities they provide, warrants are used chiefly as alternatives to common stock investments. Let's now look at warrant trading strategies and the basic ways in which these securities can be profitably employed by investors.

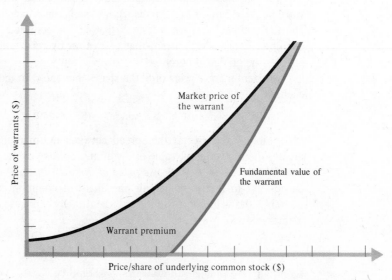

• FIGURE 11.2 The Normal Price Behavior of Warrant Premiums
Observe that as the price of the underlying common stock increases, the amount of premium in the market price of the warrant tends to decrease—though it never totally disappears.

The Basic Price Behavior of Warrants

Since warrants carry relatively low unit costs, they possess much greater price volatility and the potential for generating substantially higher *rates of return* than a direct investment in the underlying common stock. Consider the following illustration, which involves the common shares and warrants of the same company. Say the price of the common is now $50 per share and the warrant, which carries a one-to-one redemption provision, has a $40 exercise price. (We will ignore premium in this illustration.) Observe below what happens when the price of the stock increases by $10.

	Common Stock	Warrant
Issue price *before* increase	$50	$10
Increase in price of common	$10	—
Issue price *after* increase	$60	$20
Increase in market value	$10	$10
Holding period return (increase in value/beginning issue price)	20%	100%

The fact that the warrants provide a rate of return five times greater than the common is due to the fact that the two issues move parallel to one another, even though the warrant carries a lower unit cost.

As in our illustration above, holding period return would normally be used to assess the payoff when the investment horizon equals one year or less. Approximate yield would be used when the investment horizon amounts to more than a year. More specifically, we would measure holding period return (HPR) for warrants as:

Equation 11.3

$$HPR = \frac{\text{sale price of warrant} - \text{purchase price of warrant}}{\text{purchase price of warrant}}$$

The holding period return for the warrants in our illustration above, would be:

$$HPR = \frac{\$20 - \$10}{\$10} = \frac{\$10}{\$10} = 100\%$$

In contrast, if we assume a three-year investment horizon, we could find the return on the investment by using a slightly modified version of the approximate yield formula:

Equation 11.4

$$\text{Approximate yield} = \frac{\dfrac{\text{sale price of warrant} - \text{purchase price of warrant}}{\text{number of years in investment horizon}}}{\dfrac{\text{sale price} + \text{purchase price}}{2}}$$

$$= \frac{\dfrac{\$20 - \$10}{3}}{\dfrac{\$20 + \$10}{2}} = \frac{\$3.33}{\$15} = 22.2\%$$

Note in this case that we can ignore the dividend component of the standard approximate yield formula, since there are no dividends on warrants. Instead, the return in Equation 11.4 is based solely on the average annual capital gains produced from the investment.

Trading with Warrants

Warrant trading generally follows one of two approaches: (1) The leverage embedded in warrants is used to magnify dollar returns; or (2) their low unit cost is used to reduce the amount of invested capital and limit losses. The first approach is the more aggressive, whereas the second has considerable merit as a conservative strategy.

Our comparative illustration above can be used to demonstrate the first technique, which seeks to magnify returns. If an investor wishes to make a $5,000 equity investment and if price appreciation is the main objective, he or she would be better off by committing such a sum to the warrants. The reason is that a $5,000 investment in the common stock will buy 100 shares of stock ($5,000 ÷ $50 = 100 shares) which will generate only $1,000 in capital gains ($10 profits per share × 100 shares). That same $5,000 invested in the lower-priced warrants will buy 500 of these securities ($5,000 ÷ $10 = 500 warrants) and will result in $5,000 in profits ($10 in profits per warrant × 500 warrants). The common stock thus provides a 20 percent HPR, whereas the warrants yield 100 percent.

The major drawbacks to the aggressive approach are that the investor receives no dividends by buying warrants and that price appreciation has to occur before the warrant expires. The biggest risk in this investment is the potential loss exposure. Observe that if the price of the stock in our example decreases by $10, the warrant holder is virtually wiped out. In contrast, the price of the stock drops to "only" $40, and the stockholder would still have $4,000 in capital left.

One way to limit this exposure to loss is to follow the more conservative investment posture of the second trading approach. This can be done by buying only enough warrants to realize the same level of capital gains as available from the common stock. In our illustration, since we are dealing with options that carry one-to-one redemption provisions, the investor would need to acquire only 100 warrants to obtain the same price behavior as 100 shares of stock. Thus, rather than buying $5,000 worth of stock, the investor need purchase only $1,000 worth of the warrants to realize the same capital gains. If the stock performs as expected, the warrant investor will realize a 100 percent holding period return (as computed above) by generating the same amount of capital gains as the stock—$1,000. But since this will be done with substantially less capital, there will not only be greater yield with the warrants, but also less loss exposure. In this case, if the price of the stock drops by 10 points, the most the warrant holder can lose is $1,000. On the other hand, if the price of the stock drops by *more* than $10 a share, the warrant holder will still lose no more than $1,000, whereas the stockholder can lose a lot more, depending on the extent of the drop in share price.

Leverage and the Importance of Timing

Thus far we have assumed that the price behavior of a warrant is unaffected by outside variables. This assumption, although convenient, is not altogether true, for both leverage and downside risk protection are functions of the market price of the warrant. In particular, to realize maximum price appreciation, it is generally recommended that lower-priced issues be used. Other things being equal, *the lower the price of the warrant, the greater its leverage potential*. Not only does the amount of magnified return potential decrease as the price of the warrant increases, but the risk exposure of a subsequent drop in price also becomes greater. Generally speaking, as the market price of a warrant increases, *it begins to behave more like its underlying common stock*. And in so doing, a warrant's return potential drops off dramatically. Certainly, a low warrant price alone will not guarantee success, but it is obvious that a low warrant price is more desirable than a higher one since the *low unit price allows the investor to capture both increased price volatility and reduced downside risk*.

PUTS AND CALLS

The life span, or maturity, of puts and calls is generally a good deal *longer* than rights, but *shorter* than warrants. For the most part, you'll find put and call maturities typically range from about 30 days to eight months or so in duration.

Put and call options are much like warrants to the extent that they, too, provide attractive opportunities for speculation, offer appealing leverage potential, and can act as an alternative to the direct investment in common stock. Indeed, warrants differ from call options only in an institutional sense and *not* from an economic or market perspective. The fact is, for all practical purposes, the biggest difference in these two securities is that warrants normally last a lot longer than calls.

Definitions and Characteristics

One of the phenomena of the market of the 1970s was the remarkable performance and investment popularity of stock options—puts and calls on common stock. By the early 1980s, the interest in options spilled over to other kinds of financial assets. Thus, today, investors can trade puts and calls on:

- Common stock
- Stock indexes
- Debt instruments
- Foreign currencies
- Commodities and financial futures

As we will see, although the underlying financial assets may vary, the basic features and behavioral characteristics of these securities are much the same. Regardless of the type, much of the popularity of the options market stems from the fact that investors can buy a lot of price action with a limited amount of capital, while nearly always enjoying limited risk exposure.

A Negotiable Instrument

Puts and calls are negotiable instruments, issued in bearer form, that allow the holder to buy or sell a specified amount of a specified security at a specified price. For example, a put or a call on common stock covers 100 shares of stock in a specific company. A **put** enables the holder to sell the underlying security at a specified price over a set period of time. A **call,** in contrast, gives the holder the right to buy the securities at a stated price within a certain time period. Puts and calls possess value to the extend that they allow the holder to participate in the price behavior of the underlying financial asset. As with any option, there is no interest or dividend income, no voting rights, and no privileges of ownership.

Puts and calls are traded on listed exchanges and, on a *much smaller* scale, in the over-the-counter market. They provide attractive leverage opportunities because they carry low prices relative to the market price of the underlying financial assets. To illustrate, consider a call on a common stock that gives the holder the right to buy 100 shares of a $50 stock at a price of $45 a share. The stock would be priced at $50, but the call would trade at an effective price of only $5 a share (or the difference between the market price of the common and the price it can be purchased at as specified on the call). However, since a single stock option always involves 100 shares of stock, the actual market price of our $5 call would be $500; i.e., $5 × 100 shares = $500.

put
a negotiable instrument that enables the holder to sell the underlying security at a specified price over a set period of time.

call
a negotiable instrument that gives the holder the right to buy securities at a stated price within a certain time period.

American or European Options

Put and call options can be issued in either *American* or *European* form. Actually, this has absolutely nothing to do with where the options are traded, but rather, with when the options can be exercised. Specifically, an **American option** can be exercised on any business day that the option is traded, on or before the option's expiration date. In contrast, a **European option** can be exercised only on the date of expiration. Put another way, an American option can be exercised prior to expiration, a European option cannot. The vast majority of puts and calls traded in the U.S. are American options. For example, all listed stock options are of the American form; European options, on the other hand, are not as common, and are found mostly on stock index and foreign currency options. While it's true that, other things being equal, American options should be more valuable than European since they give you more exercise dates, the fact is that for all practical purposes, most investors couldn't care less whether an option is American or European. The reasons: First, only a tiny fraction of options are ever exercised, so it doesn't make much difference when they can be cashed in. Second, and more important, just because an option can't be exercised prior to maturity doesn't mean you have to hold it to expiration date. Any option—American or European—can be sold at any time. (For purposes of this and the next chapter, we'll assume that we're dealing with American options throughout.)

American option
an option that can be exercised on any business day that the option is traded, on or before the option's expiration date.

European option
an option that can be exercised only on the date of expiration.

Maker versus Buyer

Puts and calls are a unique type of security since they are *not* issued by the organizations that issue the underlying stocks. Instead, puts and calls *are created by inves-*

tors. It works like this: Suppose one individual wants to sell to another the right to buy 100 shares of common stock. This individual would *write* a call. The individual or institution writing the option is known as the **option maker** or **writer.** The maker who writes and sells an option is entitled to receive the price paid for the put or call (less modest commissions and other transaction costs). The put or call option is now a full-fledged financial asset and trades in the open market much like any other security. Puts and calls are both written (sold) and purchased through security brokers and dealers, and they are actively bought and sold in the secondary market. The writer stands behind the option, as it is the *writer* who must buy or deliver the stocks or other financial assets according to the terms of the option. Puts and calls are written for a variety of reasons, most of which we will explore below. At this point, suffice it to say that writing options can be a viable investment strategy and can be a profitable course of action since, more often than not, *options expire unexercised.*

option maker
the individual or in-stitution that writes put and call options; also called *option writer.*

How Puts and Calls Work

Using the buyer's point of view, let us now briefly examine how puts and calls work, and how they derive their value. To understand the mechanics of puts and calls, it is best to look at their profit-making potential. For example, using stock options as a basis of discussion, consider a stock currently priced at $50 a share. Assume we can buy a call on the stock for $500, which enables us to purchase 100 shares of the stock at a fixed price of $50 each. A *rise* in the price of the underlying security (in this case, common stock) is what we, as investors, hope for. With that in mind, what is the profit from this transaction if the price of the stock does indeed move up to, say, $75 by the expiration date on the call? The answer is that we will earn $25 ($75 − $50) on *each* of the 100 shares of stock in the call, or a total gross profit of some $2,500—and all from a $500 investment! This is so since we can buy 100 shares of the stock—from the option writer—at a price of $50 each and imme-diately turn around and sell them in the market for $75 a share. We could have made the same profit by investing directly in the common stock, but because we would have had to invest $5,000 (100 shares × $50 per share), our rate of return would have been much lower. Obviously, there is considerable difference between the profit potential of common stocks and calls, and it is this differential that attracts investors and speculators to calls whenever the price outlook for the underlying financial asset is *upward*. (Note that although our illustration is couched in terms of common stock, this same valuation principle applies to any of the other financial assets that may underlie call options, such as market indexes, foreign currencies, or futures contracts.)

A similar situation can also be worked out for puts. Assume that for the same $50 stock we could pay $500 and buy a put to sell 100 shares of the stock at $50 each. As the buyer of a put, we want the price of the stock to *drop*. Assume our expecta-tions are correct and the price of the stock does indeed drop, to $25 a share. Here again, we would realize a gross profit of $25 for each of the 100 shares in the put. We can do this by going to the market and buying 100 shares of the stock at a price of $25 a share, and immediately turning around and selling them to the writer of the put at a price of $50 per share.

Fortunately, put and call investors do *not* have to exercise these options and make simultaneous buy and sell transactions in order to receive their profit, *since options do have value and can be traded in the secondary market*. In fact, the value of both puts and calls is directly linked to the market price of the underlying financial asset. That is, the value of a *call* increases as the market price of the underlying security *rises,* whereas the value of a *put* increases as the price of the security *declines.* Thus, *investors can get their money out of options by selling them in the open market,* just as with any other security.

Advantages and Disadvantages

The major advantage of investing in puts and calls is the leverage they offer. This feature also carries the advantage of limiting the investor's exposure to risk, since there is only a set amount of money (the purchase price of the option) that can be lost. Also appealing is the fact that puts and calls can be used profitably when the price of the underlying security goes up *or* down.

A major disadvantage of puts and calls is that the holder enjoys no interest or dividend income, nor any other ownership benefit. Moreover, because the instruments have limited lives, the investor has a limited time frame in which to capture desired price behavior. Another disadvantage is the fact that puts and calls themselves are a bit unusual, and many of their trading strategies are complex. Thus investors must possess special knowledge and fully understand the subtleties of this trading vehicle.

Options Markets

Although the concept of options can be traced back to the writings of Aristotle, options trading in the United States did not begin until the late 1700s. Until the early 1970s, this market remained fairly small, largely unorganized, and the almost private domain of a handful of specialists and traders. All this changed, however, on April 26, 1973, when a new securities market was created with the launching of the Chicago Board Options Exchange (CBOE).

Conventional Options

conventional options
put and call options
sold over the
counter.

Prior to the creation of the CBOE, put and call options trading was conducted in the over-the-counter market through a handful of specialized dealers. Investors who wished to purchase puts and calls dealt with these options dealers via their own brokers, and the dealers would find individuals (or institutions) willing to write the options. If the buyer wished to exercise an option, he or she did so with the writer, and no one else—a system that largely prohibited any secondary trading. On the other hand, there were virtually no limits to what could be written, so long as the buyer was willing to pay the price. Put and call options were written on New York and American stocks as well as on regional and over-the-counter securities, for as short as 30 days and as long as a year. Over-the-counter options, known today as **conventional options,** were hard hit by the CBOE and other options exchanges. The conventional market still exists, although on a greatly reduced scale.

Listed Options

The creation of the CBOE signaled the birth of so-called **listed options,** a term used to denote put and call options traded on organized exchanges, rather than over-the-counter. The CBOE launched trading in calls on just 16 firms. From these rather humble beginnings, there evolved in a relatively short period of time a large and very active market for listed options. Today, trading in listed options is done in both puts and calls and takes place on five exchanges, the largest of which is the CBOE. Options are also traded on the AMEX, the NYSE, the Philadelphia Exchange, and the Pacific Stock Exchange. In total, *put and call options are now traded on over 700 different stocks.* Although most of these are NYSE issues, the list does include several dozen OTC stocks, such as Apple Computer, Intel, Liz Claiborne, and MCI. In addition to stocks, listed options are also available on stock indexes, debt securities, foreign currencies, and even commodities and financial futures.

Listed options provided not only a convenient market for the trading of puts and calls, but also standardized the expiration dates and the prices specified on the options. The listed options exchanges created a clearinghouse organization that eliminated direct ties between buyers and writers of options and reduced the cost of executing put and call transactions. They also developed an active secondary market, with wide distribution of price information. As a result, it is now as easy to trade a listed option as a listed stock. And like stocks, listed put and call options are not just an American phenomenon, as various types of puts and calls are actively traded on just about every major securities market in the world.

Stock Options

The advent of the CBOE and other listed option exchanges had a quick and dramatic impact on the trading volume of puts and calls. Indeed, the level of activity in listed stock options grew rapidly—so much so, in fact, that it took only eight years for the annual volume of contracts traded to pass the 100 million mark. And although contract volume has been off since 1987, it's still holding at over 100 million contracts a year. Normally, there's far more interest in calls than in puts—in fact, more than 70 percent of all stock option trading volume is in calls.

The creation and continued expansion of listed options exchanges has unquestionably given the field of investments a whole new dimension. However, in order to use these securities properly and avoid serious (and possibly expensive) mistakes, the investor must fully understand their basic features. In the sections that follow, we will look closely at the investment attributes and trading strategies that can be used with stock options. Later we'll explore stock index options and then briefly look at other types of puts and calls, including interest rate and currency options, long-term options, and capped options. (Futures options will be taken up in Chapter 12, after we study futures contracts.)

Stock Option Provisions

Because of their low unit cost, stock options (or *equity options* as they're also called) are very popular with individual investors. Except for the underlying financial asset, they are like any other type of put or call, subject to the same kinds of contract provisions and market forces. As far as options contracts are concerned, there are two provisions that are especially important and to which investors should pay particular attention: (1) the price, as specified on the option, at which the stock can be bought or sold—this is known as the *strike price;* and (2) the amount of time remaining until expiration. As we'll see below, both the strike price and the time remaining to expiration have a significant bearing on the valuation and pricing of options.

strike price
the price contract between the buyer of an option and the writer; it's the stated price at which you can buy a security with a call, or sell a security with a put.

Strike Price.   The **strike price** represents the price contract between the buyer of the option and the writer. For a call, the strike price specifies the price at which each of the 100 shares of stock can be bought. For a put, it represents the price at which the stock can be sold to the writer. (The strike price is also known as the exercise price.) With conventional (OTC) options, there are no constraints on strike price, although it is usually specified at or near the prevailing market price of the stock at the time the option is written. With listed options, however, strike prices are *standardized* such that stocks selling for less than $25 per share carry strike prices that are set in 2½ dollar increments (that is, $7½, $10, $12½, $15, and so on). The increment then jumps to $5 for stocks selling between $25 and $200 per share. Finally, for stocks that trade at prices in excess of $200 a share, the strike price is set in $10 increments. And of course, the strike price of both conventional and listed options is adjusted for substantial stock dividends and stock splits.

expiration date
the date at which the life of an option expires.

Expiration Date.   The **expiration date** is also an important provision because it specifies the life of the option in much the same way that the maturity date indicates the life of a bond. Expiration dates for options in the conventional market can fall on any working day of the month. In contrast, expiration dates are standardized in the listed options market. The exchanges initially created three expiration cycles for all listed options, and each issue was (and still is) assigned to one of these three cycles. One cycle is January, April, July, and October; another is February, May, August, and November; and the third is March, June, September, and December. This system has been modified a bit to include *both* the current month and the following month, *plus* the next two months in the regular expiration cycle. The exchanges still use *the same three expiration cycles,* but they've been altered so investors are always able to trade in the two near-term months plus the next two closest months in the option's regular expiration cycle. For reasons that are pretty obvious, this is sometimes referred to as a *''two-plus-two''* schedule. Take, for example, the January cycle—you'd find the following options available in January: January, February, April, and July. Thus, we'd have the two current months (January, February), plus the next two months in the cycle (April and July)—though prices are usually reported in the financial media for only the first *three* maturities. Then, in February, the available contracts would be: February, March, April, and July. Finally, come March, there would be across-the-board changes as follows: March, April, July, and October. And so on, as the expiration dates continue rolling-over like this during the course of the year. Given the month of expiration, the actual day of expiration is always the same: the Saturday following the third Friday of each expiration month. Thus, for all practical purposes, listed options always expire on the third Friday of the month of expiration.

The expiration date, in effect, specifies the length of the contract between the holder and the writer of the option. Thus, if you hold a six-month call on Sears, that option would give you the right to buy 100 shares of Sears common stock at a strike price of, say, $40 per share at any time over the next six months. Now, *no matter what happens to the market price of the stock,* you can use your call option to buy 100 shares of Sears at $40 a share for the next six months. If the price of the stock moves up, you stand to make money; if it goes down, you'll be out the cost of the option.

Put and Call Transactions

Option traders are subject to commission and transaction costs whenever they buy or sell an option, or when an option is written. The writing of puts and calls is subject to normal transaction costs, since it effectively represents remuneration to the broker or dealer for *selling* the option. In relation to the number of shares of common stock controlled (100 shares per option), the transaction costs for executing put and call trades are relatively low. However, that's not the case when costs are compared to the size of the transaction itself, particularly if there are only a few options involved in the trade. To see how expensive options transactions can get, consider the purchase of one $5 call: you can expect to pay a commission of $30, or more, on this (relatively small) $500 transaction. Although this may be low compared to what it would take to buy 100 shares of the underlying stock, simple arithmetic indicates that it involves a 6 percent sales charge ($30/$500 = .06). That's pretty steep, especially when you consider that this commission might have to be paid again if the option is sold prior to its expiration date. Fortunately, relative transaction costs *decline* fairly quickly as the number of contracts traded increases. For example, the cost to buy 10 $5 calls (in a single transaction) is around $150, which translates into a commission of only 3 percent. The same can be said of higher priced options: other things being equal, the higher the price of the option, the lower the relative (percentage) commission.

Listed options also have their own marketplace and quotation system. Finding the price (or premium, as it's called) of a listed stock option is fairly easy, as the options quotations in Figure 11.3 indicate. Note that quotes are provided for calls and puts separately, and for each option, there are three expiration dates (in this case, February, March, and June). Along with the striking price, such information is the basis for differentiating among various options. For example, there are numerous puts and calls outstanding on the Philip Morris stock, each with its own expiration date and striking price. The quotes are standardized and are read as follows: The name of the company and the closing price of the underlying stocks are listed first (note Philip Morris's stock closed at 75); the strike price is listed next; then closing prices are quoted relative to their expiration dates, with the three calls listed first followed by the three puts. Thus, we can see that a Philip Morris *call* with a $65 strike price and a March expiration date is quoted at 9½ (which translates

Option & NY Close	Strike Price	Calls-Last Feb	Calls-Last Mar	Calls-Last Jun	Puts-Last Feb	Puts-Last Mar	Puts-Last Jun
Pfizer	60	s	r	13 3/4	s	r	r
71 3/4	65	s	7 3/4	9 3/4	s	r	1 5/8
71 3/4	70	2 1/4	3 7/8	6 3/4	11/16	1 1/2	3 3/8
71 3/4	75	3/16	1 1/2	3 7/8	3 3/8	4 1/4	5 7/8
71 3/4	80	1/16	5/8	r	r	8 1/4	r
71 3/4	85	r	1/4	r	r	r	r
71 3/4	90	r	r	r	18	r	r
PhMor	60	s	r	r	s	r	3/8
75	65	r	9 1/2	r	r	3/16	1 1/8
75	70	r	5 5/8	r	3/16	5/8	2 5/16
75	75	13/16	2 2/16	4 1/4	7/8	2 1/4	4 1/4
75	80	1/16	9/16	2 7/16	4 7/8	6	7 1/4
75	85	r	3/16	1 3/8	r	r	r
75	90	r	r	5/8	r	r	r
PfdHlth	15	r	r	2 15/16	r	r	r
QuakSt	12 1/2	r	2 3/8	r	r	r	r
14 3/4	15	1/8	r	r	r	r	r
RJR Nb	7 1/2	r	3	r	r	r	r
10 3/8	10	1/2	3/4	1 3/16	r	1/4	5/8
10 3/8	12 1/2	r	1/16	3/8	r	r	r
SFePac	12 1/2	1/8	1/2	r	r	r	r
11 7/8	15	r	r	1/2	r	r	r

s: no options available; i.e., none have been written for this particular stock and strike price

Month of Expiration

Name of the company

Strike price on the option

Price of a March call with a strike price of 65

Latest price of the stock

Price of a June put that carries a strike price of 80

r: option not traded

FIGURE 11.3 Listed Options Quotations

As seen here, the quotes for puts and calls are listed side-by-side. In addition to the closing price of the option, the latest price of the underlying security is also shown along with the strike price on the option. *(Source: The Wall Street Journal.)*

into a dollar price of $950, because stock options trade in 100 share lots). In contrast, a Philip Morris *put* with an $80 strike price and June expiration date is trading at 7¼ (or $725).

Options Valuation and Pricing

The value of a put or call depends to a large extent on the market behavior of the common stock (or other financial asset) that underlies the option. Getting a firm grip on the current and expected future value of a put or call is extremely important to options traders and investors. Similarly, to get the most from any options trading program, it's imperative that investors have an understanding of how options are priced in the market. Continuing to use stock options as a basis of discussion, let's look now at the basic principles of options valuation and pricing, starting with a brief review of how profits are derived from puts and calls.

The Profit Potential of Puts and Calls

Although the quoted market price of a put or call is affected by such factors as time to expiration, stock volatility, market interest rates, and supply and demand conditions, by far the most important variable is *the market price behavior of the underlying common stock*. This is the variable that drives any significant moves in the price of the option and which in turn determines the option's profit (return) potential. Thus, when the underlying stock moves up in price, *calls do well;* when the price of the underlying stock drops, *puts do well*. Such performance also explains why it's so important to get a good handle on the expected future price behavior of a stock *before* an option is bought or sold (written).

The typical price behavior of an option is illustrated graphically in Figure 11.4. The diagram on the left depicts a call, and the one on the right shows a put. The *call* diagram is constructed assuming you pay $500 for a call that carries an exercise price of $50; likewise, the *put* diagram assumes you can buy a put for $500 and obtain the right to sell the underlying stock at $50 a share. With the call, the diagram shows what happens to the value of the option when the price of the stock increases; with the put, it shows what happens when the price of the stock falls. Observe that a call doesn't gain in value until the price of the stock advances past the stated *exercise price* ($50). Also, since it costs $500 to buy the call, the stock has to move up another 5 points (from $50 to $55) in order for the option investor to recover the premium and thereby reach a break-even situation. So long as the stock continues to rise in price, everything from there on out is profit. Once the premium

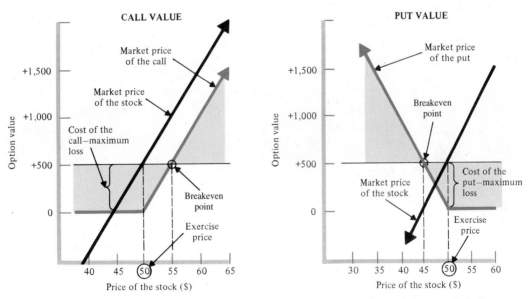

• FIGURE 11.4 The Valuation Properties of Put and Call Options

The value of a put or call is a reflection of the price behavior of its underlying common stock. As such, once the cost of the option has been recovered (which occurs when the option passes its breakeven point), the profit potential of a put or call is limited only by the price behavior of its underlying stock.

is recouped, the profit from the call position is limited only by the extent to which the stock price increases over the remaining life of the contract!

In a similar fashion, the value of a *put* is also derived from the price of the underlying stock, except their respective market prices move in opposite directions. We can see that the value of the put remains constant until the market price of the corresponding stock drops to the exercise price ($50) on the put. Then, as the price of the stock continues to fall, the value of the option increases accordingly. And again, note that since the put cost $500, you don't start making money on the investment until the price of the stock drops below the breakeven point of $45 a share. Beyond that point, the profit from the put is defined by the extent to which the price of the underlying stock continues to fall over the remaining life of the option.

Fundamental Value

As we saw above, the fundamental value of a put or call depends ultimately on the exercise price stated on the option, as well as on the prevailing market price of the underlying common stock. More specifically, *the value of a call* is determined according to the following simple formula:

Equation 11.5

$$\text{Fundamental value of a call} = \left(\begin{array}{c} \text{market price of} \\ \text{underlying} \\ \text{common stock} \end{array} - \begin{array}{c} \text{strike price} \\ \text{on} \\ \text{the call} \end{array} \right) \times 100$$

$$V = (MP - SPC) \times 100$$

In other words, the fundamental or underlying value of a call is nothing more than the difference between market price and strike price. As implied in Equation 11.5, a call has value whenever the market price of the underlying stock (or financial asset) *exceeds* the strike price stipulated on the call. A simple illustration will show that a call carrying a striking price of $50 on a stock presently trading at $60 has a value of $1,000 [($60 − $50) × 100 = $10 × 100].

A put, on the other hand, cannot be valued in the same way, since puts and calls allow the holder to do different things. To find *the value of a put,* simply reverse the order of the equation a bit, so that we have:

Equation 11.6

$$\text{Fundamental value of a put} = \left(\begin{array}{c} \text{strike price} \\ \text{on the} \\ \text{put} \end{array} - \begin{array}{c} \text{market price of} \\ \text{underlying} \\ \text{common stock} \end{array} \right) \times 100$$

$$V = (SPP - MP) \times 100$$

In this case, you can see that a put has value so long as the market price of the underlying stock (or financial asset) *is less than* the strike price stipulated on the put.

In-the-Money/Out-of-the-Money

When written, options do not necessarily have to carry strike prices at the prevailing market prices of the underlying common stocks. And as an option subsequently trades on the listed exchanges, the price of the option will move in response to moves in the price of the underlying common stock. When a call has a strike price that is less than the market price of the underlying common stock, it has a positive value and is known as an **in-the-money** option. A major portion of the option price in this case is based on (or derived from) the fundamental or intrinsic value of the call. When the strike price exceeds the market price of the stock, the call has no "real" value and is known as an **out-of-the-money** option. Since the option has no intrinsic value, its price is made up solely of investment premium. These terms are much more than convenient, exotic names given to options. As we will see below, they characterize the investment behavior of options and can affect return and risk. A put option, by the way, is in-the-money when its strike price is greater than the market price of the stock; it is out-of-the-money when the market price of the stock exceeds the strike price.

in-the-money
a call option with a strike price less than the market price of the underlying security; a put option with strike price greater than the market price of the underlying security.

out-of-the-money
a call option with no real value because the strike price exceeds the market price of the stock; a put option whose market price exceeds the strike price.

Option Prices and Premiums

Put and call values, as found according to Equations 11.5 and 11.6, denote what the options *should* be valued and trading at. This rarely occurs, however, as these securities almost always trade at prices that exceed their intrinsic or fundamental values, especially for options that still have a long time to run. That is to say, puts and calls nearly always trade at premium prices, which may explain why the term **option premium** is used to describe the market price of listed put and call options. Technically, option premium is the (quoted) price the buyer pays for the *right* to buy or sell a certain amount of the underlying common stock (or other financial asset) at a specified price for a specified period of time. The option seller, on the other hand, receives the premium and gets to keep it whether the option is exercised or not. To the option seller, it represents compensation for agreeing to fulfill certain *obligations* of the contract. As we'll see below, the term *premium* is also used to denote the extent to which the market price of an option exceeds its fundamental/intrinsic value. Thus, to avoid confusion and keep matters as simple as possible, we'll use the word *price* in the usual way: to describe the amount it takes to buy an option in the market.

option premium
the quoted price the investor pays to buy a listed put or call option.

What Drives Options Prices?

Option prices can be reduced to two separate components. The first is the *fundamental (or intrinsic) value* of the option, which is driven by the current market price of the underlying common stock. That is, as we saw in Equations 11.5 and 11.6, the greater the difference between the market price of the stock and the strike price on the option, the greater the value of the put or call. The second component of an option price is customarily referred to as the **time premium** and represents, in effect, the excess value imbedded in the option price. That is, time premium is the amount by which the option price exceeds the option's fundamental value. Table 11.1 lists some of the prices for Pfizer *calls* from the quotes shown in Figure 11.3. These quoted prices (Panel A) are then separated into fundamental value (Panel B) and time premium (Panel C). Note that there are three strike prices used—$65, $70, and $75. Relative to the market price of the stock ($71.75), one strike price ($65) is

time premium
the amount by which the option price exceeds the option's fundamental value.

TABLE 11.1 Option Price Components: Pfizer Calls

Stock Price	Strike Price	Expiration Months		
		Feb.	**Mar.**	**June**
Panel A: Quoted Options Prices				
71¾	65	s	7¾	9¾
71¾	70	2¼	3⅞	6¾
71¾	75	³⁄₁₆	1½	3⅞
Panel B: Underlying Fundamental Values				
71¾	65	—	6¾	6¾
71¾	70	1¾	1¾	1¾
71¾	75	neg.	neg.	neg.
Panel C: Time Premiums				
71¾	65	—	1	3
71¾	70	½	2⅛	5
71¾	75	³⁄₁₆	1½	3⅞

s: No option available at that strike price and expiration date.

neg.: Options have negative intrinsic/fundamental values.

well below market—this is an in-the-money call. One ($70) is fairly near the market. The third ($75) is well above the market—this is an out-of-the-money call. As such, you'll notice a considerable difference in the make-up of the options prices as we move from an in-the-money call to an out-of-the-money call.

Panel B in the table lists the fundamental values of the call options, as determined by Equation 11.5. For example, note that while the March 65 call (the call with the March expiration date and $65 strike price) is trading at 7¾, its intrinsic value is only 6¾. The difference, essentially, is how much the option is trading in-the-money. Thus, while most of the price of the March 65 call is made up of fundamental value, certainly not all of it is. Even better, look at the calls with the $75 strike price: None of these has any fundamental value; they're all out-of-the-money, as their prices are made up solely of time premium. Basically, the value of these options is determined entirely by the *belief* that the price of Pfizer stock could rise to over $75 a share before the options expire. Panel C shows the amount of premium imbedded in the call prices, which represents the difference in the quoted call prices (Panel A) and the call's fundamental value (Panel B). It shows that the price of every traded option contains at least some premium. Indeed, unless the options are about to expire, you'd expect them to be trading at a premium. And note with all three strike prices, the longer the time to expiration, the greater the size of the premium.

As you might expect, *time to expiration* is an important element in explaining the size of the price premium in Panel C. But there are a couple of other variables that also have a bearing on the behavior of this premium. One is *the price volatility of the underlying common stock.* Other things being equal, the more volatile the stock, the more it enhances the speculative appeal of the option—and, therefore, the bigger the time premium. In addition, the size of the premium is directly related to *the level of interest rates.* That is, the amount of premium imbedded in a call option will generally increase along with interest rates. In addition, other, less important variables include the dividend yield on the underlying common stock, the trading volume of the option, and the exchange on which the option is listed. For the most part, however, it should be clear that four major forces drive the price of an option. They are, in descending order of importance: (1) the price behavior of the underlying common stock (or other financial asset); (2) the amount of time remaining to expiration; (3) the amount of price volatility in the underlying common stock (or financial asset); and (4) the general level of interest rates.

Option Pricing Models

Financial economists, notably Professors Fisher Black and Myron Scholes, have developed option pricing formulas that are capable of valuing call options (and with minor modifications, put options) within a few cents of their fair values. Many active market traders use these formulas, which are most suitable for use with pre-programmed personal computers (or even some hand-held calculators), to identify and trade over- and undervalued options. It is not surprising that the parameter values required to implement these models follow directly from those variables identified above. For example, the five parameters used by the Black–Scholes Option Pricing Model are: (1) the risk-free rate of interest, (2) the price volatility of the underlying stock, (3) the current price of the underlying stock, (4) the strike price of the option, and (5) the option's time prior to expiration. After inputting these variables to a computer or pre-programmed calculator, fair market values for the options in question are produced within seconds. Options with market prices above those produced by the formula are considered overvalued and vice versa.

Trading Strategies

For the most part, stock options can be used in three types of trading strategies: (1) buying puts and calls for speculation; (2) hedging with puts and calls; and (3) option writing and spreading.

Buying for Speculation

Buying for speculation is the simplest and most straightforward use of puts and calls. Basically, it is just like buying stock ("buy low, sell high") and in fact represents an alternative to investing in stock. For example, if an investor feels the market price of a particular stock is going to move up, one way of capturing that price appreciation is to buy a call on the stock. In contrast, if an investor feels the stock is about to drop in price, a put could convert the price decline into a profitable situation. In essence, investors buy options rather than stock whenever the options are likely to yield a greater return. The principle here, of course, is to get the biggest return from one's investment dollar—something that can often be done with puts and calls, due to the added leverage they offer. Plus, as we saw in Figure 11.4 (page 459), options offer downside protection—the most you can lose is the cost of the option, which is less than the cost of the underlying stock. Thus, by using options as a vehicle for speculation, the investor can put a cap on losses and still get basically the same profit potential as the underlying common stock.

To illustrate the essentials of speculating with options, consider a situation in which you have uncovered a stock you feel will move up in price over the next six months. What you would like to find out at this point is what would happen if you were to buy a call on this stock rather than investing directly in the firm's common. To find out, let's see what the numbers show. Assume the price of the stock is now $49, and you anticipate that within six months it will rise to about $65. In order to determine the relative merits of your investment alternatives, you need to determine the expected return associated with each course of action. Because call options have short lives, holding period return can be used to measure yield. (Here we can measure HPR by using a formula similar to Equation 11.3, shown earlier in this chapter.) Thus, if your expectations about the *stock* are correct, it should go up by $16 and in so doing provide stockholders with a 33 percent holding period return [($65 − $49) ÷ $49 = $16 ÷ $49 = .33]. But there are also some listed options available on this stock, so let's see how they would do. We will use for illustrative purposes two six-month calls that carry $40 and $50 striking prices, respectively. A recap of these two call alternatives, relative to the behavior of the underlying common stock, is summarized in Table 11.2. Clearly either call option represents a superior investment to buying the stock itself. The dollar amount of profit may be a

TABLE 11.2 Speculating with Call Options

	100 Shares of Underlying Common Stock	Six-Month Call Options on the Stock	
		$40 Striking Price	$50 Striking Price
TODAY			
Market value of stock (at $49/sh.)	$4,900		
Market price of calls*		$1,100	$ 400
SIX MONTHS LATER			
Expected value of stock (at $65/sh.)	$6,500		
Expected price of calls*		$2,500	$1,500
Profit	$1,600	$1,400	$1,100
Holding period return	33%	127%	275%

*The price of the calls was computed according to Equation 11.5 and includes some investment premium in the purchase price of the calls, but *none* in the expected sales price.

bit more with the stock, but notice that the size of the required investment ($4,900) is *a lot* more, too.

Observe that one of the calls is an in-the-money option (the one with the $40 striking price) and the other is out-of-the-money. The difference in returns generated by these calls is rather typical: that is, investors are usually able to generate better rates of return with lower-priced (out-of-the-money) options and also enjoy less exposure to loss. Of course, the major drawback of out-of-the-money options is that their price is made up solely of investment premium—a sunk cost that will be lost if the stock does not move in price.

To see how investors can speculate in puts, consider the following situation: Assume that the price of your stock is now $51, but now you anticipate a drop in price to about $35 within the next six months. If that occurs, you could short sell the stock and make a profit of $16 per share. (See Chapter 2 for a discussion of short selling.) Alternatively, an out-of-the-money put (with a striking price of $50) can be purchased for, say, $300. Again, if the price of the underlying stock does indeed drop, investors will make money with the put. The profit and rate of return on the put are summarized below, along with the comparative returns from short selling the stock:

	Buy 1 Put	Short Sell 100 Shares of Stock
Purchase price (today)	$ 300	
Selling price (6 months later)	1,500	
Short sell (today)		$5,100
Cover (6 months later)		3,500
Profit	$1,200	$1,600
Holding period return	400%	63%*

*Assumes the short sale was made with a required margin deposit of 50 percent.

Once again, in terms of holding period return, the stock option is the superior investment vehicle by a wide margin. Of course, not all option investments perform as well as the ones in our examples; success in this strategy rests on picking the right underlying common stock. Thus, *security analysis and proper stock selection are critical dimensions of this technique*. It is a highly risky investment strategy, but it may be well suited for the more speculatively inclined investor.

Hedging

hedge
a combination of two or more securities into a single investment position for the purpose of reducing or eliminating risk.

A **hedge** is really nothing more than a combination of two or more securities into a single investment position for the purpose of reducing risk. This strategy might involve, for example, buying stock and simultaneously buying a put on that same stock; or it might consist of short selling some stock and then buying a call. There are many types of hedges, some of which are very sophisticated and others very simple. They are all used for the same basic reason: to earn or protect a profit without exposing the investor to excessive loss. For example, an options hedge may

be appropriate if you have generated a profit from an earlier common stock investment and wish to protect that profit, or if you are about to enter into a common stock
investment and wish to protect your money by limiting potential capital loss. If you
hold a stock that has gone up in price, the purchase of a put would provide the type
of downside protection you need; the purchase of a call, in contrast, would provide
protection to a short seller of common stock. Thus, option hedging always involves
two transactions—one, the initial common stock position (long or short), and the
other, the simultaneous or subsequent purchase of the option.

Let's examine a simple options hedge in which a put is used to limit capital loss
or protect profit. Consider an investor, Keith Gibson, who wants to buy 100 shares
of stock. Being a bit apprehensive about the stock's outlook, Keith decides to use an
option hedge to protect his capital against loss. He simultaneously buys the stock
and a put on the stock (which fully covers the 100 shares owned); this type of hedge
is known as a *protective put*. Preferably, the put would be a low-priced option with
a striking price at or near the current market price of the stock. Suppose Keith
purchases the common at $25 and pays $150 for a put with a $25 striking price.
Now, no matter what happens to the price of the stock over the life of the put, Keith
can lose no more than $150; at the same time, there's no limit on the gains. If the
stock does not move, he will be out the cost of a put. If it drops in price, then
whatever is lost on the stock will be made up with the put. However, if the price of
the stock goes up (as hoped), the put becomes useless, but Keith has earned capital
gains on the stock. The essentials of this option hedge are shown in Table 11.3. The

TABLE 11.3 Limiting Capital Loss with a Put Hedge

		Stock	Put*
TODAY			
Purchase price of the stock		$25	
Purchase price of the put			$1½
SOMETIME LATER			
A. Price of common goes *up* to:		$50	
Value of put			$0
Profit:			
100 shares of stock ($50 − $25)	$2,500		
Less: Cost of put	−150		
Profit:	$2,350		
B. Price of common goes *down* to:		$10	
Value of put (See Equation 11.6)			$15
Profit:			
100 shares of stock (loss: $10 − $25)	−$1,500		
Value of put (profit)	+ 1,500		
Less: Cost of put	− 500		
Loss:	$ 150		

*Put is purchased simultaneously and carries a striking price of $25

$150 paid for the put is sunk cost, and that's lost no matter what happens to the price of the stock; in effect, it is the price paid for the hedge. Moreover, this hedge is good only for the life of the put. When this put expires, Keith will have to replace it with another put or forget about hedging his capital.

The other basic use of an option hedge involves entering into the options position *after* a profit has already been made on the underlying stock. This could be done because of investment uncertainty, or for tax purposes (to carry over a profit to the next taxable year). For example, if Wendy Willson bought 100 shares of stock at $35 and it moved to $75, there would be a profit of $40 per share to protect. The profit could be protected with an option hedge by buying a put. Assume Wendy buys a three-month put with a $75 striking price at a cost of $250. Now, regardless of what happens to the stock over the life of the put, Ms. Willson is guaranteed a minimum profit of $3,750 (the $4,000 profit in the stock made so far, less the $250 cost of the put). This can be seen in Table 11.4. Notice that if the price of the stock should fall, the worst that can happen is a guaranteed minimum profit of $3,750. And there is still *no limit on how much profit can be made:* as long as the stock continues to go up, the investor will reap the benefits. (Note that although this

TABLE 11.4 Protecting Profits with a Put Hedge

		Stock	Three-Month Put with a $75 Striking Price
Purchase price of the stock (some time ago)		$35	
TODAY			
Market price of the stock		$75	
Market price of the put			$2½
THREE MONTHS LATER			
A. Price of common goes *up* to:		$100	
Value of put			$0
Profit:			
100 shares of stock ($100 − $35)	$6,500		
Less: Cost of put	−250		
Profit:	$6,250		
B. Price of common goes *down* to:		$50	
Value of put (See Equation 11.6)			$25
Profit:			
100 shares of stock ($50 − $35)	$1,500		
Value of put (profit)	2,500		
Less: Cost of put	− 250		
Profit:	$3,750		

■ INVESTOR INSIGHTS ■

Covered Strangles: A Way to Put Market Volatility to Work for You

Who says stock-market volatility is bad? Wild gyrations in stock prices often spark a rising chorus of complaints from individual investors, many market professionals and some members of Congress. But for shrewd investors, there's a way to make money on just about anything—and volatile stock prices are no exception. While all that jumping around may unnerve stock-market investors, it means fatter premiums and bigger potential profits for investors who dabble in the options market.

Investors who *buy* options pay a premium to the investors who *sell* options. And in times of stock-market volatility, options sellers demand higher premiums to compensate for the increased risk of being forced to sell their stock or compelled to purchase additional shares. Those bigger premiums can mean extra income for investors who follow a cautious approach. One strategy suggested by options-market professionals: a "covered strangle sale," sometimes referred to as a "combination write."

While it sounds arcane, *a covered strangle is simply the sale of both call and put options on a stock you already own*. Sellers of call options must be prepared to deliver the stock at the agreed strike price if the stock rises to that level and the owner of the call exercises the option. The premium paid for the option increases the effective price received for the shares. If the stock's price never exceeds the strike price of the option, the stock won't be called away. In that event, the call will expire worthless, and the premium is simply additional income.

Sellers of puts, on the other hand, must be prepared to buy additional stock at the strike price if the stock declines sufficiently in price and the put owner exercises the option. In this case, the premium income effectively reduces the cost of the additional shares the put seller must buy. If the stock doesn't drop below the put's strike price, the put won't be exercised. Again, the put will expire worthless, and the premium is simply additional income.

discussion pertains to put hedges, it should be clear that call hedges can also be set up to limit the loss or protect a profit on a short sale. For example, when a stock is sold short, a call can be purchased to protect the short seller against a rise in the price of the stock—with the same basic results as outlined above.)

Option Writing and Spreading

The advent of listed options has led to many intriguing options trading strategies. Yet, in spite of the apparent appeal of these exotic techniques, there is one important point that all the experts agree on: *Such specialized trading strategies should be left to experienced investors who fully understand their subtleties*. Our goal at this point is not to master these specialized strategies, but to learn in general terms what they are and how they operate. There are two types of specialized options strategies: (1) writing options and (2) spreading options.

A covered strangle is a particularly appealing strategy for investors who are interested in takeover stocks. For example, suppose an investor had bought NCR Corp. stock at $53 a share as an attractive investment and as a stock that has been mentioned in takeover rumors. Assume the stock is now selling for around $60. A covered strangle could be written on this stock by selling a March 65 call option for $238 per 100 shares, while simultaneously selling a March 55 put option for $125 per 100 shares. The total premium taken in would be $363. (Note that in this case the investor is writing/selling *both* a put and a call on the stock, whereas in a covered call, the investor writes/sells only a call on the stock.) With the covered strangle in place, if the stock rallies above the call option's $65 strike price, and stays there between now and the options' expiration in March, the stock will be called away from the investor. The effective price the investor receives will be $68.63 a share ($65 plus premium income of $3.63 a share). If the stock drops below the put option's $55 strike price, and remains there, the investor will be asked to purchase an additional 100 shares for each put sold. The effective purchase price would be the $55 strike price less the $3.63-a-share premium, or $51.37. Since the investor thought the stock a good buy at $53, he or she is likely to think it an even better investment at $51.37.

A danger with using a covered strangle is that investors who sell call options may not enjoy the full run-up in the price of a hot stock. That's because the shares will be called away before the stock's market price peaks, leaving call-option sellers with only part of the gain they would have realized if they hadn't been forced to sell. Another risk is that investors who sell puts have to purchase the additional shares at the agreed price, even if the stock's market price keeps falling after it declines below the strike price. Thus, investors could end up paying more for the shares than if they had waited and simply bought them in the market.

Source: Adopted from Stanley W. Angrist, ''Undaunted by the Wild Market? Try a Covered Strangle,'' *The Wall Street Journal,* November 6, 1989, p. C1.

Writing Options. Generally, investors write options because they feel the price of the underlying stock is going to move in their favor. That is, it is not going to rise as much as the buyer of a call expects, or fall as much as the buyer of a put hopes. *And more often than not, the option writer is right;* that is, he or she is going to make money far more often than the buyer of the put or call. Such favorable odds explain, in part, the underlying economic motivation for writing put and call options. Options writing represents an investment transaction to the writers, since they receive the full option premium (less normal transaction costs, of course) in exchange for agreeing to live up to the terms of the option.

Investors can write options in one of two ways. One is to write **naked options,** which are options on stock not owned by the writer. The investor simply writes the put or call, collects the option premium, and hopes that the price of the underlying stock does not move against him or her. If successful, naked writing can be highly

naked options
options written on securities not owned by the writer.

profitable due to the very modest amount of capital required. One thing that should be kept in mind, however, is that *the amount of return to the writer is always limited to the amount of option premium received*. On the other hand, there is really no limit to loss exposure. And that's the catch: The price of the underlying stock can rise or fall by just about any amount over the life of the option, and in so doing deal a real blow to the naked put or call writer.

Such risk exposure can be partially offset by writing **covered options,** which involves writing options against stocks which the investor (writer) already owns or has a position in. For example, an investor could write a call against stock she owns, or a put against stock she has short sold. In this way she can use the long or short position to meet the terms of the option. Such a strategy represents a fairly conservative way to generate attractive rates of return. The object is to write a slightly out-of-the-money option, pocket the option premium, and hope that the price of the underlying stock will move up or down to (but not exceed) the option's striking price. In effect, what an investor is doing is adding option premium to the other usual sources of return that accompany stock ownership or short sales (dividends and/or capital gains). But there's more: While the option premium adds to the return, it also reduces risk, since it can be used to cushion a loss if the price of the stock move against the investor. There is a hitch to all this, of course, and that is the amount of return the covered option investor can realize is limited. For once the price of the underlying common stock begins to exceed the striking price on the option, the option becomes valuable. And once that happens, the investor starts *losing* money on the options; from this point on, for every dollar the investor makes on the stock position, she loses an equal amount on the option position. That's a major risk of writing covered call options—if the price of the underlying stock takes off, you'll miss out on the added profits.

To illustrate the ins and outs of covered call writing, let's assume you own 100 shares of P/F/P, Inc.—an actively traded, high-yielding common stock. The stock is currently trading at 73½ and pays *quarterly* dividends of $1 a share. You decide to write a 3-month call on P/F/P giving the buyer the right to take the stock off your hands at $80 a share (i.e., the call carries a strike price of 80). Such options are trading in the market at 2½, so you receive $250 for writing the call. Now if you're like most covered call writers, you fully intend to hold on to the stock, so you'd like to see the price of P/F/P stock rise to no more than 80 by the expiration date on the call. If that happens, not only do you earn the dividends and capital gains on the stock, you also get to pocket the $250 you received when you wrote the call, since it (the call option) will expire worthless. Basically, you've just *added* $250 to the quarterly return on your stock.

Table 11.5 summarizes the profit and loss characteristics of this covered call position. Notice that the maximum profit on this transaction occurs *when the market price of the stock equals the strike price on the call*. That means if the price of the stock keeps going up, you miss out on the added profits. Even so, the $1,000 profit that's earned at a stock price of 80 or above translates into a (3-month) holding period return of a very respectable 13.6 percent (i.e., $1,000/$7,350)—which represents an *annualized* return of nearly 55 percent. With this kind of return potential,

TABLE 11.5 Covered Call Writing

	Stock	Three-Month Call with an $80 Strike Price
Current market price of the stock	$73½	
Current market price of the call		$2½
THREE MONTHS LATER		
A. Price of the stock is *unchanged:*	$73½	
Value of the call		$0
Profit:		
Quarterly dividends received	$100	
Proceeds from sale of call	$250	
Total profit:	$350	
		PRICE WHERE
B. Price of the stock goes *up* to:	$80 ⟵	**MAXIMUM PROFIT OCCURS**
Value of the call		$0
Profit:		
Quarterly dividends	$100	
Proceeds from sale of call	$250	
Capt. Gains on stock ($80 − 73½)	$650	
Total profit:	$1,000	
C. Price of the stock goes *up* to:	$90	
Value of the call (See Equation 11.5)		$10
Profit:		
Quarterly dividends	$100	
Proceeds from sale of call	$250	
Capt. Gains on stock ($90 − 73½)	$1,650	
Less: Loss on call	⟨$1,000⟩	
Net profit:	$1,000	
D. Price of the stock *drops* to:	$71 ⟵	**BREAKEVEN PRICE**
Value of the call		$0
Profit:		
Capital loss on stock (71 − 73½)	⟨$250⟩ ⎱ $0 profit or loss . . .	
Proceeds from sale of call	$250 ⎰	
Quarterly dividends	$100	
Net profit:	$100	

it's not difficult to see why covered call writing is so popular. Plus, as we see in situation D in the table, covered call writing also adds a little cushion to losses, as the price of the stock has to drop more than 2½ points (which is what you received when you wrote/sold the call) before you start losing money. There are a number of variations on the covered call theme; one of them is something called a *covered strangle,* and it's explained in the accompanying *Investor Insights* box.

option spreading
combining two or more options with different strike prices and/or expiration dates into a single transaction.

Spreading Options.   **Option spreading** is nothing more than combining two or more options into a single transaction. We could create an options spread, for example, by simultaneously buying and writing options on the same underlying stock. These cannot be identical options, however; they must differ with respect to striking price and/or expiration date. Spreads are a very popular use of listed options, and they account for a substantial amount of the trading activity on the listed options exchanges. These spreads go by a variety of exotic names, such as "bull spreads," "bear spreads," "money spreads," "vertical spreads," and "butterfly spreads." Each is different and is constructed to meet a certain type of investment goal. Consider, for example, a vertical spread; this particular type of spread would be set up by *buying* a call at one strike price and then *writing* a call (on the same stock and for the same expiration date) at a different—higher—strike price. A case in point: buy a February call on XYZ at a strike price of, say, 30 *and* simultaneously sell (write) a February call on XYZ at a strike price of 35. As bizarre as it may sound, such a position would generate a hefty return if the price of the underlying stock goes up by just a few points. Other spreads are used to profit from a falling market, and still others try to make money when the price of the underlying stock goes up *or* down. Whatever the objective, most spreads are created to take advantage of differences in prevailing option prices and premiums. The payoff from spreading is usually substantial, but so is the risk. In fact, some spreads that seem to involve almost no risk may end up with devastating results if the market and the "spread" (or difference) between option premiums move against the investor.

option straddle
the simultaneous purchase (or sale) of a put and a call on the same underlying common stock.

A variation of this theme involves an **option straddle,** the simultaneous purchase (or sale) of *both* a put *and* a call on the same underlying common stock. Unlike spreads, straddles will normally involve the same strike price and expiration date. Here, the object is to earn a profit from *either* an increase or decrease in the price of the underlying stock. Otherwise, the principles of straddles are much like those for spreads: to build an investment position with combinations of options that will enable an investor to capture the benefits of certain types of stock price behavior. But keep in mind that if the prices of the underlying stock and/or the option premiums do not behave in the anticipated manner, the investor loses. *Spreads and straddles are extremely tricky and should be used only by knowledgeable investors.*

Stock-Index Options

Imagine being able to buy or sell a major stock market index like the S&P 500—and at a reasonable cost. Think of what you could do: If you felt the market was heading up, you could invest in a security that tracks the price behavior of the S&P 500 index and make money when the market goes up. No longer would you have to go through the often haphazard process of selecting specific stocks that you *hope* will capture the market's performance. Rather, you could *play the market as a whole.* Well, that's exactly what investors can do with *stock-index options*—puts and calls that are written on major stock market indexes. Index options have been around for about ten years (since 1983) and have become immensely popular with both individual and institutional investors. In fact, the volume of trading in index options is equal to about 70 percent of all the trading done in stock options. That's quite a feat when you consider that nearly all of the trading in index options is confined to just *six* different contracts, compared to the more than *700* different stock option contracts. Let's now take a closer look at these popular and often highly profitable investment vehicles.

Contract Provisions

stock-index option
a put or call option written on a specific stock market index, such as the S&P 500.

Basically, a **stock-index option** is nothing more than a put or a call written on a specific stock market index, like the S&P 500. The underlying security in this case is the specific market index. Thus, when the market index moves in one direction or another, the value of the index option moves accordingly. Since there are no stocks or other financial assets backing these options, settlement is defined in terms of cash. Specifically the cash value of an *index option* is equal to 100 times the published market index that underlies the option. For example, if the S&P 500 is at 410, the cash value of an S&P 500 index option is: $\$100 \times 410 = \$41,000$; if the underlying index moves up or down in the market, so will the cash value of the option.

In early 1992, there were some 15 stock market index options available. Many of these, however, are very thinly traded and don't have much of a following. There are six indexes that dominate the market and account for the vast majority of trading activity. Those six are:

- S&P 500 Index (traded on the CBOE)
- S&P 100 Index (CBOE)
- Value Line Index (Philadelphia Exchange)
- Major Market Index (AMEX)
- Institutional Index (AMEX)
- S&P MidCap Index (AMEX)

The S&P 100 and S&P 500 are, by far, the most popular index options. In fact, these two are *the most actively traded of all listed options*. As the above list reveals, stock-index options are available not only on the popular S&P indexes (including its newest, the S&P MidCap, which tracks the market behavior of 400 mid-size companies), but also on the Value Line index (of the roughly 1,700 companies tracked by Value Line) and an index of the 75 stocks that are most favored by big institutional investors. And although the most popular index of them all—the Dow Jones Industrial Average—has refused to let itself be the basis of an index option, the AMEX has come up with an index (the Major Market index) designed to imitate the Dow; this index is made up of 20 stocks, 17 of which are part of the DJIA.

There are both puts and calls available on index options. They are valued and have issue characteristics like any other put or call. That is, a *put* lets a holder profit from a *drop* in the market (when the underlying market index goes down, the value of a put goes up); a *call* enables the holder to profit from a market that's going *up*. As seen in Figure 11.5, these options even have a quotation system that is virtually identical to puts and calls on stocks.

Chicago Board

S&P 100 INDEX-S100 times Index

Strike Price	Calls–Last			Puts–Last		
	Feb	Mar	Apr	Feb	Mar	Apr
330	...	...	...	$\frac{1}{16}$	...	...
335	...	...	...	...	$\frac{1}{4}$	...
340	...	$46\frac{1}{2}$	...	...	$\frac{5}{16}$	1
345	...	...	...	...	$\frac{7}{16}$	...
350	36	...	...	...	$\frac{5}{8}$	$1\frac{13}{16}$
355	32	$32\frac{1}{2}$	...	$\frac{1}{16}$	$\frac{13}{16}$	$2\frac{1}{8}$
360	27	$27\frac{1}{4}$	...	$\frac{1}{16}$	$1\frac{1}{16}$	$2\frac{5}{8}$
365	21	$22\frac{7}{8}$	$24\frac{1}{2}$	$\frac{1}{16}$	$1\frac{7}{16}$	$3\frac{1}{4}$
370	$16\frac{7}{8}$	18	$21\frac{1}{8}$	$\frac{1}{8}$	$1\frac{15}{16}$	$4\frac{1}{4}$
375	$11\frac{7}{8}$	$14\frac{3}{8}$	$14\frac{1}{2}$	$\frac{1}{8}$	$2\frac{3}{4}$	$5\frac{3}{8}$
380	$7\frac{1}{8}$	$10\frac{3}{4}$	14	$\frac{5}{16}$	$3\frac{7}{8}$	$7\frac{1}{8}$
385	$2\frac{5}{8}$	$7\frac{1}{2}$	$10\frac{3}{8}$	$\frac{15}{16}$	$5\frac{3}{4}$	$8\frac{1}{2}$
390	$\frac{1}{2}$	$4\frac{3}{4}$	$7\frac{3}{4}$	$3\frac{5}{8}$	$8\frac{1}{8}$	$10\frac{3}{4}$
395	$\frac{1}{16}$	$2\frac{3}{4}$	5	$8\frac{3}{8}$	$11\frac{1}{2}$	$14\frac{7}{8}$
400	$\frac{1}{16}$	$1\frac{9}{16}$	$3\frac{3}{8}$	...	$15\frac{1}{2}$	$17\frac{1}{4}$
405	$\frac{1}{16}$	$1\frac{3}{16}$	$2\frac{5}{16}$	$19\frac{1}{2}$	$19\frac{1}{4}$	$22\frac{1}{2}$
410	...	$\frac{7}{16}$	$1\frac{1}{2}$	...	$24\frac{1}{2}$	...

Total call volume 224,406　Total call open int. 420,423
Total put volume 203,680　Total put open int. 528,844
The index; High 386.90; Low 381.12; Close 386.78, +5.66

American Exchange

MAJOR MARKET INDEX

Strike Price	Calls–Last			Puts–Last		
	Feb	Mar	Apr	Feb	Mar	Apr
270	...	...	$1\frac{3}{16}$	...	$\frac{1}{8}$	...
275	...	$\frac{1}{4}$	...	...	...	$25\frac{1}{4}$
300	...	...	...	...	$\frac{1}{4}$	...
305	...	...	...	...	$\frac{3}{8}$	...
310	...	...	...	...	$\frac{3}{8}$	...
315	...	...	...	...	$\frac{9}{16}$	...
320	...	...	...	...	$\frac{5}{8}$	...
325	...	$24\frac{7}{8}$	...	...	1	$2\frac{1}{4}$
330	$20\frac{3}{4}$	$20\frac{1}{2}$	...	$\frac{1}{16}$	$1\frac{3}{16}$	$2\frac{11}{16}$
335	$15\frac{1}{4}$	$16\frac{3}{8}$	...	$\frac{1}{16}$	$1\frac{13}{16}$	...
340	$10\frac{1}{4}$	$12\frac{1}{2}$	15	$\frac{3}{16}$	$2\frac{9}{16}$	$4\frac{3}{4}$
345	$5\frac{7}{8}$	$9\frac{3}{8}$	...	$\frac{1}{4}$	1	$6\frac{1}{4}$
350	$1\frac{3}{4}$	6	...	$1\frac{3}{8}$	$5\frac{5}{8}$	$7\frac{3}{4}$
355	$\frac{3}{8}$	$3\frac{5}{8}$	...	$4\frac{5}{8}$	$7\frac{7}{8}$	...
360	$\frac{1}{16}$	$2\frac{1}{16}$	$3\frac{3}{4}$	$9\frac{3}{4}$	$14\frac{1}{4}$	$13\frac{1}{2}$
365	$\frac{1}{16}$	$1\frac{1}{8}$	$2\frac{1}{16}$	...	...	...

Total call volume 8.283　Total call open int. 40,818
Total put volume 8.635　Total put open int. 57,117
The Index: High 350.79; Low 343.90; Close 350.36, +6.46

● FIGURE 11.5 Quotations on Index Options

The quotation system used with index options is similar to that used with stock options. That is, the prices for puts and calls are listed relative to their expiration dates (February, March, or April), and to their strike prices; even the latest market value of the index itself is shown— see "index close." (*Source: The Wall Street Journal.*)

Putting a Value on Stock-Index Options

Like equity options, the market price of index options is a function of the difference in the strike price on the option (which is stated in terms of the underlying index) and the latest published stock market index. To illustrate, consider the highly popular S&P 100 Index, traded on the CBOE. As the index option quotes in Figure 11.5 reveal, this index recently closed at 386.78; at the same time, there was an April *call* on this index that carried striking price of 380. Given that a stock-index *call* will have a value so long as the underlying index exceeds the index striking price (just the opposite for *puts*), the intrinsic value of this call is 386.78 − 380 = 6.78. Now, as we can see in the quotes, this call was trading at 14, some 7.22 points above the call's underlying fundamental value; this difference, of course, was the *time premium*. Just like stock options, the amount of premium in an index option tends to *increase* with *longer* options (note the difference between February and April options) and with *more volatile* market conditions. Returning to our example, if the S&P 100 Index were to go up to 410 by late April (the expiration date on the call), this option would be quoted at 410 − 380 = 30; since all index options are valued in multiples of $100, this option would be worth $3,000. If an investor had purchased the option when it was trading at 14, it would have cost $1,400 and in a little over two months would have generated a profit of $3,000 − $1,400 = $1,600. From this example, it should be clear that because they're a form of derivative security, *index options are valued according to how the market (i.e., market index) performs*. Thus, calls should be more highly valued if the market is expected to go up in the future, whereas puts should be more highly valued in falling markets.

Investment Uses

Although they can be used in spreads and straddles, index options are used most often for speculating or for hedging. As a speculative vehicle, they provide investors with the opportunity to play the market with a relatively small amount of capital. Like any other put or call, *index options provide attractive leverage opportunities and at the same time, limit exposure to loss to the price paid for the option.*

Index options are equally effective as *hedging vehicles*. In fact, hedging is a *major use* of index options and accounts for a good deal of the trading in these securities. To see how these options can be used for hedging, consider an investor who holds a diversified portfolio of common stocks. One way to protect the whole portfolio against an adverse market is to buy *puts* on one of the market indexes. If you think the market's heading down and you hold a portfolio of, say, a dozen different stocks, you can protect your capital by selling all your stocks. However, that could become very expensive, especially if you plan to get back into the market after it drops. One way to "have your cake and eat it, too" is to hedge your stock portfolio with a stock index put. In this way, if the market does go down you'll make money on your puts, which can then be used to buy more stocks at the lower, "bargain" prices. On the other hand, if the market doesn't retreat but continues to go up, *you'll be out only the cost of the puts*—which could well be recovered from the increased value of your stock holdings. The principles of hedging with index

INVESTOR INSIGHTS

Using Index Options to Protect a Whole Portfolio of Stocks

When the stock market starts heading down, investors begin to worry about protecting the value of their portfolios. But simply liquidating their stock holdings and putting the proceeds into a money market fund is too drastic a step for most people. Not only would they incur substantial brokerage commissions and capital gains taxes; they also would risk being caught on the sidelines if the market rally regains its breath. There is, however, a far less drastic—and less costly—way for investors to shield their portfolios from the possibility of a sustained sell-off. Many market specialists say investors should consider buying ''insurance'' in the form of put options.

Put options based on a stock index offer a simple method of insuring the value of an entire portfolio with a single trade. That can be especially helpful because many issues in an investor's portfolio may not have individual put options traded on them. Such portfolio protection is in many ways no different from any other kind of insurance. The more protection investors want, and the less risk they are willing to bear, the more the insurance costs. For example, suppose an investor wants to hedge a $100,000 stock portfolio. Also suppose that after examining the characteristics of the major stock indexes, the investor concludes that the S&P 100 comes closest to matching the portfolio. With the S&P 100 index standing at, say, 372, the market value of the S&P 100 index would be $37,200. So the investor would have to buy three puts to approximate the total value of the $100,000 portfolio.

The investor might decide to buy three ''May 360'' puts, which are puts that expire in 3 months (i.e., in May) and have a strike price of 360. The price of these puts is about 4. To turn that into dollars, an investor multiplies by 100; the puts would cost about $400 each. That would mean $1,200 for all three—or 1.2% of the value of the $100,000 portfolio. Now suppose the market retreats about 15% from current levels, which would bring the S&P 100 down to about 318. Each of the May 360 puts would be worth a

options are exactly the same as those for hedging with stock options; the only difference is that with index options, your're trying to protect a *whole portfolio* of stocks rather than *individual* stocks.

There is one important consideration to keep in mind, however: The amount of profit you make, or protection you obtain, depends in large part on how closely the behavior of your stock portfolio is matched by the behavior of the index option you employ in the hedge. There is *no guarantee* that the two will behave in the same way. You should, therefore, select an index option that closely reflects the nature of the stocks in your portfolio. If, for example, you hold a number of OTC stocks, you might be well advised to select something like the National OTC Index as the hedging vehicle. If you hold mostly blue chips, you might choose the Major Market Index. While you probably can't get dollar-for-dollar portfolio protection, at least you should try to get as close a match as possible. After all, the closer the match, the minimum of 42 points (360 minus 318), or $4,200. After paying their cost, the investor would have a profit on the puts of: $11,400 (i.e., $4,200 − $400 = $3,800 × 3), which in turn would offset a substantial portion of the $15,000 the portfolio would have lost in a 15% decline.

By purchasing puts with strike prices that are 12 points below the current level of the S&P index, the investor is effectively insuring the portfolio against any losses that occur *after* the market has fallen 12 points, or 3.2%. In other words, the portfolio protection doesn't kick in until the index falls to 360. Had the investor been willing to bear more of the market risk, the cost of the insurance could have been reduced even more by purchasing puts with even lower strike prices. On the other hand, an investor who wanted to be fully insured might have bought puts with a higher strike price, but this would have raised the cost of the insurance. May 370 puts, for instance, would have cost 7¼, or $725 each. Harrison Roth, an options strategist, says the basic question for investors is: "Do you want to hedge against any and all declines, or do you simply want protection against catastrophic moves?" He believes that "most investors are in the second camp."

Even with relatively low-cost puts such as the May 360s, the cost of hedging with put options can add up if the insurance goes unused. Buying puts such as these with a three-month lifetime four times a year, for instance, would cost the investor the equivalent of 4.8% of a $100,000 portfolio. One way to reduce the cost is to sell the put options before they expire. Put options lose most of their value in the final six weeks before their expiration if they have strike prices below the current price of the underlying securities. For this reason, some market advisors recommend that investors hold their options only for a month before selling them and then buying the next month out. In that way they would recover most of the options' value, significantly reducing the cost of the hedge even after considering the higher commissions they would incur.

Source: Adapted from Stanley W. Angrist, "Put Options Can Help Protect Portfolios," *The Wall Street Journal,* February 28, 1989, p. C1.

greater your chances of offsetting any portfolio losses with gains from the index options. Another factor that's important in portfolio hedging is the cost of the underlying hedge vehicle itself. This and other considerations are discussed in the accompanying *Investor Insights* box, which deals with the use of index options in portfolio hedging.

Given their effectiveness for either speculating or hedging the entire market, it's little wonder that index options have become so popular with investors. But a word of caution is in order: Although trading index options appears simple and seems to provide high rates of return, they are in reality *high-risk* trading vehicles that are subject to considerable price volatility and should *not* be used by amateurs. True, there's only so much you can lose with these options; the trouble is, it's very easy to lose that amount. Attractive profits are indeed available from these securities, but they're not investments you can buy and then "forget about" until they expire.

With the wide market swings we're experiencing these days, *these securities must be closely monitored on a daily basis.*

Other Types of Options

Although options on stocks and stock indexes account for most of the market activity in listed options, put and call options can also be obtained on debt instruments and foreign currencies. In addition to these securities, puts and calls are now being sold with extended expiration dates (these options are known as *LEAPS*) and with ceilings on how high they can go up in value (these are known as *Caps*). Let's now take a brief look at these other kinds of options, starting with interest rate options.

Interest Rate Options

interest rate options
put and call options written on fixed-income (debt) securities.

Puts and calls on fixed-income (debt) securities are known as **interest rate options.** Specific Treasury securities (Treasury notes and bonds) underlie these options, and as their prices go up or down in the market, the puts and calls respond accordingly. A call, for example, enables the holder to buy a certain amount (usually $100,000) of a specific Treasury bond or note at a stipulated (striking) price for a specified period of time (as defined by the option's expiration date). A put, in contrast, gives the holder the right to sell the underlying financial assets under comparable provisions. One noteworthy feature of these options is that as a rule the securities will exist for *only one cycle.* That is, unless the debt security is considered to be a bellwether issue (one that's closely followed in the marketplace), once the initial three- and six-month options have expired, *there'll be no more puts and calls written on those Treasury securities.* The reason for this is that after the initial life of a T-bond or note, there's just not enough secondary trading in the securities to support an active options market. Thus, new options are constantly coming out on new government security issues. Unfortunately, the market for interest rate options never took hold and to this day remains very small. In an effort to beef up volume, the CBOE in mid-1989 introduced two new trading vehicles: an *option on short-term interest rates* and an *option on long-term rates.* But that didn't seem to help much, as trading volume continued to slide. Trading in interest rate options has all but dried up (and could well disappear altogether in the very near future) since most professional investors don't bother with these securities. Instead, they use interest rate futures contracts or options on these futures contracts (both of which will be examined in Chapter 12) for hedging or other investment purposes.

Currency Options

currency options
put and call options written on foreign currencies.

Foreign exchange options, or **currency options** as they're more commonly called, provide investors with a way to speculate on foreign exchange rates or to hedge foreign currency or foreign security holdings. Currency options are available on most of the countries we have strong trading ties with. These options are traded on the Philadelphia Exchange and include the following currencies:

- British pound
- Swiss franc

- German mark
- Canadian dollar
- Japanese yen
- Australian dollar

In essence, puts and calls on these currencies give the holders the right to sell or buy large amounts of the specified foreign currency. However, in contrast to the standardized contracts used with stock and stock index options, the specific unit of trading in this market varies with the particular underlying currency, the details of which are spelled out in Table 11.6. Currency options are traded in full or fractional cents per unit of the underlying currency, relative to the amount of foreign currency involved. Thus, if a put or call on the British pound were quoted at, say, 6.40 (which is read as "6.4 cents"), it would be valued at $2,000, since there are 31,250 British pounds that underlie this option—that is, 31,250 × .064 = $2,000.

The value of a currency option is linked to the exchange rate between the American dollar and the underlying foreign currency. For example, if the Canadian dollar becomes stronger *relative to the American dollar,* causing the exchange rates to go up, the price of a *call* option on the Canadian dollar will increase, and the price of a *put* will decline.

To understand how you can make money with currency options, consider a situation where an investor wants to *speculate* on exchange rates. The strike price of a currency option is stated in terms of *exchange rates*. Thus, a strike price of 150, for example, implies each unit of the foreign currency (such as one British pound) is worth 150 cents, or $1.50, in American money. If an investor held a (150) call on this foreign currency, he would make money if the foreign currency strengthened relative to the U.S. dollar so that the exchange rate rose (to, say, 155). In contrast, if he held a (150) put, he would profit from a decline in the exchange rate (to, say, 145). Success in forecasting movements in foreign exchange rates is obviously essential to a profitable foreign currency options program.

TABLE 11.6 Foreign Currency Option Contracts on the Philadelphia Exchange

Underlying Currency*	Size of Contracts
British pound	31,250 pounds
Swiss franc	62,500 francs
German mark	62,500 marks
Canadian dollar	50,000 dollars
Japanese yen	6,250,000 yen
Australian dollar	50,000 dollars

*The British pound, Swiss franc, German mark, Canadian dollar, and Australian dollar are all quoted in full cents; the Japanese yen is quoted in one-hundredths of a cent.

LEAPS and Caps

LEAPS
long-term options.

Although they may look like regular puts and calls, LEAPS and Caps each offer an important feature or characteristic that differentiates them from the pack. **LEAPS** are long-term options. Whereas standard options have maturities of eight months or less, LEAPS have expiration dates that extend out as far as two years. Known formally as *Long-term Equity AnticiPation Securities,* they are listed on all five of the major options exchanges. In early 1992, there were LEAPS available on some 100 different stocks and several stock indexes, including the S&P 100, S&P 500, and Major Market Index. Aside from the time frame, LEAPS work like any other equity or index option. For example, a single (equity) LEAPS contract gives the holder the right to buy or sell 100 shares of stock at a predetermined price on or before the specified expiration date. LEAPS give investors more time to be right about their bets on the direction of a stock or stock index, or hedgers more time to protect their positions. But there's a price for all this: You can expect to pay a lot more for a LEAPS than you would for a regular (short-term) option. For example, in early 1992, a 3-month call on IBM (with a strike price of 85) was trading at 7½; the same call with a 2-year expiration date was trading at 15¼. The difference should come as no surprise, since LEAPS, being nothing more than long-term options, are loaded with time premium. As we saw earlier in this chapter, other things being equal, *the more time an option has to go to expiration, the higher the quoted price.* That behavioral characteristic certainly applies to LEAPS.

**capped options
(Caps)**
index options, with cap prices that set a maximum value for the option, at which point the option is automatically exercised.

Capped options (known as **Caps,** for short) are also relatively new to the listed options market (they were first introduced in November 1991), and they, too, come with their own unique twist. At the present time, Caps are written only on *index options* (so far only on the S&P 100 and S&P 500) traded on the CBOE. Caps are so named because there's a cap, or ceiling, on the amount of profit an option holder can make. That is, in addition to strike prices, these options also have *cap prices,* which set the maximum value these options can attain. Cap prices are set 30 points above the strike prices on calls, and 30 points below for puts. For example, the cap price for the S&P 100 *call* option with a strike price of 360 is 390; a comparable 360 *put* option has a cap price of 330. So long as the underlying market index stays below the cap price on calls (or above it on puts), the value of the capped option will move like any other index option. The only time you'll notice a difference is when the index hits the cap price. Then, the capped options are automatically exercised, or closed out. That is, once the underlying market index closes at or above the cap price for calls (at or below for puts), the capped options automatically expire, and holders are paid the stipulated cap value two days later. As you might expect, because there's a cap on the capital gains potential of these securities, caps trade at slight discounts to regular (uncapped) index options. So far, caps haven't really caught on with investors; in early 1992, they had nowhere near the trading volume of LEAPS.

SUMMARY

1. A right is a short-lived financial instrument that enables the holder to purchase a new issue of common stock at a subscription price that's set below the prevailing market

price of existing stock. A warrant is similar to a right but its maturity is much longer. Attached to bond issues as "sweeteners," warrants allow the holder to purchase common stock at a set exercise price on or before a stipulated expiration date.

2. Trading in warrants is done primarily as a substitute for common stock investing and is based on the magnified capital gains they offer. The value of a warrant changes directly with and by approximately the same amount as the underlying common stock; but since a warrant's unit cost is often much lower than that of the common stock, the same dollar change in price represents a considerably larger percentage yield.

3. Puts and calls are by far the most popular and widely used type of option; these derivative securities offer attractive value and considerable leverage potential. They can be used for speculation, as a way to hedge a position, or in option writing and spreading programs.

   A put enables the holder to sell a certain amount of a specified security at a specified price over a specified time period. A call, in contrast, gives the holder the right to buy the same securities at a specified price over a specified period of time. The three basic features of puts and calls are (1) striking price, (2) the expiration date, and (3) the purchase price of the option itself.

4. Standardized listed put and call options are presently available on over 700 (mostly NYSE) common stocks (equity options); a dozen or so stock market indexes, like the S&P 500 (index options); and a number of debt securities and foreign currencies (interest rate and currency options). In addition, there are listed options that carry lengthy expiration dates (LEAPS) and options that set ceilings on the amount of capital appreciation that can be made (Caps).

5. The value of a call is measured by the market price of the underlying security less the strike price designated on the call; the value of a put is its strike price less the market price of the security. While the value of an option is driven by the current market price of the underlying asset, most puts and calls sell at premium prices, the amount of which depends on the length of the option contract (the so-called time premium), the speculative appeal and amount of price volatility in the underlying financial asset, and the general level of interest rates.

6. Aggressive investors will use puts and calls either for speculation or in highly specialized writing and spreading programs. Conservative investors, on the other hand, are attracted to puts and calls because of their low unit cost and the limited risk they offer in absolute dollar terms. Often, conservative investors will use options in covered call writing programs, or to form hedge positions in combination with other securities.

QUESTIONS

1. Describe a stock right and note how such rights are tied to the preemptive rights of investors. How would a stock right be used by an investor? Why does it have such limited investment appeal?

2. What is a warrant? What is the chief attraction of a warrant? Describe the leverage feature of a warrant and note why leverage is so attractive to investors.

3. What factors are important in determining the investment appeal of warrants? Why is the price of the warrant itself so important in the investment decision?

4. Describe put and call options. Are they issued like other corporate securities? Explain.

5. What are listed options, and how do they differ from conventional options? What's the difference between an American option and a European option? What's a derivative security? Give an example of one.

6. What are the main investment attractions of put and call options? What are the risks?

7. Briefly discuss the differences and similarities in stock index options and stock options; do the same for foreign currency options relative to stock options.

8. Using the stock or index option quotations in Figures 11.3 and 11.5, respectively, find the option premium, time premium, and the stock/index breakeven point for the following puts and calls:

    a. The June Pfizer *put*, with the $75 strike price.
    b. The March Quaker State *call*, with the $12½ strike price.
    c. The April S&P 100 *call*, with the strike price of 365.
    d. The March Major Market *put*, with the strike price of 360.

9. Name at least four variables that have an impact on the price behavior of listed options, and briefly explain how each affects prices. How important are fundamental (intrinsic) value and time value to in-the-money options? To out-of-the-money options?

10. Prepare a schedule similar to the one in Table 11.1 for the February, March, and April S&P 100 *calls* (use the ones with strike prices of 380, 385, and 390). Do the same for the February, March, and April Major Market *puts* (use strike prices of 350, 355, and 360). Briefly explain your findings.

11. Note the various ways stock options can be used by investors; do the same for index options and foreign currency options.

12. Assume an investor holds a well-balanced portfolio of common stocks. Under what conditions might he want to use a stock-index option to hedge his portfolio?

    a. Briefly explain how such options could be used to hedge a portfolio against a drop in the market.
    b. Discuss what would happen if the market does in fact go down.
    c. What happens if the market goes up instead?

13. Describe how writing a covered call option reduces the risk on the underlying common stock.

14. What are LEAPS and Caps? Why would an investor want to use a LEAPS option rather than a regular listed option? Give an example of how a LEAPS option might be used.

PROBLEMS

1. Assume a company has 1 million shares of common stock outstanding and intends to issue another 200,000 shares via a rights offering; the rights will carry a subscription price of $48. If the current market price of the stock is $53, what is the value of one right?

2. Assume that one warrant gives the holder the right to buy one share of stock at an exercise price of $40. What is the value of this warrant if the current market price of the stock is $44? At what premium ($ and %) would the warrants be trading if they were quoted in the market at a price of $5?

3. A warrant carries an exercise price of $20; assume it takes three warrants to buy one share of stock. At what price would the warrant be trading if it sold at a 20 percent premium, while the market price of the stock was $35 per share? What holding period return would an investor make if she buys these warrants (at a 20% peremium) when the stock is trading at $35, and sells them some time later when the stock is at $48½ and the premium on the warrants has dropped to 15%?

4. A six-month call on a certain common stock carries a striking price of $60; it can be purchased at a cost of $600. Assume that the underlying stock rises to $75 per share by the expiration date of the option. How much profit would this option generate over the six-month holding period, and what is its rate of return?

5. Dorothy Cappel does a lot of investing in the stock market and is a frequent user of stock index options. She is convinced that the market is about to undergo a broad retreat and has decided to buy a put on the S&P 100 Index. The put carries a striking price of 390 and is quoted in the financial press at 4½. Although the S&P Index of 100 stocks is presently at 386.45, Dorothy thinks it will drop to 365 by the expiration date on the option. How much profit will she make, *and* what will her holding period return be if she is right? How much will she lose if the S&P 100 goes up (rather than down) by 25 points, and reaches 415 by the date of expiration?

6. Bill Brickshooter holds 600 shares of Lubbock Gas and Light. He bought the stock several years ago at 48½, and shares are now trading at 75. Bill's a little concerned that the market's beginning to soften and while he doesn't want to sell the stock, he would like to be able to protect the profit that he's made. He decides to hedge his position by buying 6 puts on Lubbock G & L; the 3-month puts carry a strike price of 75 and are currently trading at 2½.

   a. How much profit or loss will Bill make on this deal if the price of Lubbock G & L does, indeed, drop—to $60 a share—by the expiration date on the puts?
   b. How would he do if the stock kept going up in price and reached $90 a share by the expiration date?
   c. What do you see as the major advantages to using puts as hedge vehicles?
   d. Would the investor have been better off using in-the-money puts—i.e., puts with an $85 strike price that are trading at 10½? How about using out-of-the-money puts—say, those with a $70 strike price, trading at 1? Explain.

7. Dave Benley just purchased 500 shares of AT&E at 61½ and he's decided to write covered calls against these stocks. Accordingly, he sells 5 AT&E calls at their current market price of 5¾; the calls have 3 months to expiration and carry a strike price of 65. Given the stock pays a quarterly dividend of 80 cents a share:

   a. Determine the total profit and holding period return Benley will generate if the stock rises to $65 a share by the expiration date on the calls.
   b. What happens to Benley's profit (and return) if the price of the stock rises to more than $65 a share?
   c. Does this covered call position offer any protection (or cushion) against a drop in the price of the stock? Explain.

CFA QUESTION (This question is from the 1992 Level II Exam.)

It has been decided to buy (stock-index) put options in order to protect one of your client's stock holdings from a potential price decline over the next 3 months. The following information has been assembled about three index options currently available in the market:

Index Option	Current Index Value	Underlining Value of One Put	Strike Price of Put	Put Premium	Average Daily Trading Volume of Puts
S&P 100	364.58	$100 times index	365	12.75	10,000
S&P 500	388.89	$100 times index	390	11.00	4,000
NYSE	214.73	$100 times index	215	6.25	1,000

Index	Amt. of Correlation With Client's Portfolio
S&P 100	0.86
S&P 500	0.95
NYSE	0.91

a. For each index option, determine the number of puts required to protect a $3,500,000 portfolio (hint: it'll take 96 of the S&P 100 puts . . .), and calculate the cost to set up each hedge.

b. Recommend and justify which index option to use in order to hedge the portfolio; include reference to factors other than cost in your answer.

(See Appendix C for Guideline Answer to this question.)

CASE PROBLEMS

11.1 The Slaters' Investment Options

Phil Slater is a highly successful businessman in Atlanta. The box manufacturing firm he and his wife Judy founded several years ago has prospered. Because he is self-employed, he is building his own retirement fund. So far he has accumulated a substantial sum in his investment account, mostly by following an aggressive investment posture; he does this because, as he puts it, "you never know when the bottom's gonna fall out in this business." Phil has been following the stock of Rembrandt Paper Products (RPP) and after conducting extensive analysis, feels the stock is about ready to move. Specifically, he believes that within the next six months, RPP could go to about $80 per share, from its current level of $57.50. The stock pays annual dividends of $2.40 per share, and Phil figures he would receive two quarterly dividend payments over his six-month investment horizon. In studying the company, Phil has learned that it has some warrants outstanding (they mature in eight years and carry an exercise price of $45); also, it has six-month call options (with $50 and $60 striking prices) listed on the CBOE. Each warrant is good for one share of stock, and they are currently trading at $15; the CBOE calls are quoted at $8 for the options with $50 striking prices, and $5 for the $60 options.

Questions
1. How many alternative investment vehicles does Phil have if he wants to invest in RPP for no more than six months? What if he has a two-year investment horizon?

 2. Using a six-month holding period and assuming the stock does indeed rise to $80 over this time frame:
   a. Find the market price of the warrants at the end of the holding period, given that they then trade at a premium of 10 percent.
   b. Find the value of both calls, given that at the end of the holding period neither contains any investment premium.
   c. Determine the holding period return for each of the four investment alternatives open to Mr. Slater.
3. Which course of action would you recommend if Phil simply wants to maximize profit? Would your answer change if other factors (like comparative risk exposure) were considered along with return? Explain.

11.2 Fred's Quandary—To Hedge or Not to Hedge

A little more than ten months ago, Fred Weaver, a mortgage banker in Phoenix, bought 300 shares of stock at $40 per share. Since then, the price of the stock has risen to $75 per share. It is now near the end of the year, and the market is starting to weaken; Fred feels there is still plenty of play left in the stock but is afraid the tone of the market will be detrimental to his position. His wife Denise is taking an extension course on the stock market and has just learned about put and call hedges. She suggests that he use puts to hedge his position. Fred is intrigued with the idea, which he discusses with his broker—who advises him that, indeed, the needed puts are available on his stock. Specifically, he can buy three-month puts, with $75 striking prices, at a cost of $550 each (quoted at 5½).

Questions
1. Given the circumstances surrounding Fred's current investment position, what benefits could be derived from using the puts as a hedge device? What would be the major drawback?
2. What would Fred's minimum profit be if he buys three puts at the indicated option price? How much would he make if he did not hedge but instead sold his stock immediately at a price of $75 per share?
3. Assuming Fred uses three puts to hedge his position, indicate the amount of profit he would generate if the stock moves to $100 by the expiration date of the puts. What if the stock drops to $50 per share?
4. Should he use the puts as a hedge? Explain. Under what conditions would you urge him *not* to use the puts as a hedge?

12 Commodities, Financial Futures, and Tangible Investments

After studying this chapter, you should be able to:

1. Describe the essential features of a futures contract, as well as the basic operating characteristics of the futures market.

2. Explain the role that hedgers and speculators play in the futures market, including how profits are made and lost.

3. Distinguish between a physical commodity and a financial future, and between a futures contract and an option on a futures contract.

4. Discuss the various investment strategies and trading techniques that investors can use with commodities and financial futures, and explain how investment returns can be measured.

5. Gain an appreciation of the growing role that financial futures play in the futures market today, and note how these securities can be used in conjunction with other investment vehicles, like stocks, bonds, and foreign securities.

6. Develop a basic understanding of the investment characteristics and suitability of gold and other tangible investments.

Psst, wanna buy some copper? How about some gold, or pork bellies, or plywood? Maybe the Japanese yen or Swiss franc strikes your fancy. Sound a bit unusual? Perhaps, but all these items have one thing in common: They represent investment vehicles that are popular with millions of investors. This is the more exotic side of investing—the market for commodities and financial futures—and it often involves a considerable amount of speculation. In fact, the risks are enormous, but the payoffs in these markets can at times be nothing short of phenomenal. For example, the purchase of a *single* S&P 500 futures contract in January 1991 would have produced an incredible $34,000 in profits by the end of May—a period of less than 5 months! A little bit of luck is obviously helpful in such situations, but equally important is the need for patience and know-how. *These are specialized investment vehicles that require specialized investor skills.* We will now look at these investment outlets to see not only what they are, but how they can be used in various types of investment programs. First, we will examine the futures market itself; then we will look at investing in commodities. After that, we'll focus on financial futures and how they can be used by investors. The chapter concludes with a brief look at still another type of specialized investment vehicle: so-called *tangible investments,* such as gold, precious metals and gemstones, stamps, coins, and other collectibles.

THE FUTURES MARKET

The amount of futures trading in the United States has mushroomed over the past two decades as an increasing number of investors have turned to futures trading as a way to earn attractive, highly competitive rates of return. But it's *not* the traditional commodities contracts that have drawn many of these investors; rather, it's the new investment vehicles being offered. Indeed, a major reason behind the growth in the volume of futures trading has been *the big jump in the number and variety of contracts available for trading.* Thus, today we find that in addition to the traditional primary commodities, such as grains and metals, markets also exist for live animals, processed commodities, crude oil and gasoline, foreign currencies, money market securities, U.S. Treasury notes and bonds, Eurodollar securities, and common stocks (via stock market indexes). In fact, you can even buy listed put and call *options* on just about any actively traded futures contract. All these commodities and financial assets are traded in what is known as the *futures market.*

cash market
a market where a product or commodity changes hands in exchange for a cash price paid at the time the transaction is completed.

futures market
the organized market for the trading of futures contracts.

Market Structure

When a bushel of wheat is sold, the transaction takes place in the **cash market;** in other words, the bushel changes hands in exchange for a cash price paid to the seller. The transaction occurs at that point in time and for all practical purposes is completed then and there. Most traditional securities are traded in this type of market. However, a bushel of wheat could also be sold in the **futures market,** the organized market for the trading of futures contracts. In this market, the seller would not actually deliver the wheat until some mutually agreed-upon date in the future. As a result, the transaction would not be completed for some time; the seller would receive partial payment for the bushel of wheat at the time the agreement was entered into, and the balance on delivery. The buyer, in turn, would own a highly liquid futures contract that could be held (and presented for delivery of the bushel of wheat) or traded in the futures market. No matter what the buyer does with the contract, as long as it is outstanding, the seller has a legally binding *obligation to make delivery* of the stated quantity of wheat on a specified date in the future, and the buyer/holder has a similar *obligation to take delivery* of the underlying commodity.

Futures Contracts

futures contract
a commitment to deliver a certain amount of some specified item at some specified date in the future.

A **futures contract** is a commitment to deliver a certain amount of a specified item at a specified date at a price agreed upon at the time the contract is sold. The seller of the contract agrees to make the specified future delivery, and the buyer agrees to accept it. Each exchange establishes its own contract specifications, which include not only the quantity and quality of the item, but the delivery procedure and delivery month as well. The **delivery month** for a futures contract is much like the expiration date used on put and call options; it specifies when the commodity or item must be delivered and thus defines the life of the contract. For example, the Chicago Board of Trade specifies that each of its soybean contracts will involve 5,000 bushels of USDA grade No. 2 yellow soybeans; delivery months are January, March, May, July, August, September, and November. In addition, *futures contracts have their own trading hours*. Unlike listed stocks and bonds, which begin and end trading at the same time, normal trading hours for commodities and financial futures vary widely. For example, oats trade from 9:30 A.M. to 1:15 P.M. (Central), silver from 7:25 A.M. to 1:40 P.M., live cattle from 9:05 A.M. to 1:15 P.M., U.S. Treasury bills from 7:20 A.M. to 2:15 P.M., S&P 500 stock index contracts from 8:30 A.M. to 3:15 P.M., and so forth. It may sound a bit confusing, but it seems to work.

delivery month
the time when a commodity must be delivered; defines the life of a futures contract.

The maximum life of a futures contract is about one year or less, although some (like silver and Treasury bonds) have lives as long as 2½ to 3 years. Table 12.1 lists a cross-section of 12 different commodities and financial futures and shows that the typical futures contract covers a large quantity of the underlying product or financial instrument. However, although the value of a single contract is normally quite large, the actual amount of investor capital required to deal in these vehicles is relatively small, because *all trading in this market is done on a margin basis*.

Options versus Futures Contracts.   In many respects futures contracts are closely related to the call options we studied in Chapter 11. Both involve the future delivery of an item at an agreed-upon price. But there is *a significant difference* between a futures contract and an options contract: A futures contract *obligates* a person to buy or sell a specified amount of a given commodity on or before a stated date, unless the contract is cancelled or liquidated before it expires; in contrast, an option gives the holder the *right* to buy or sell a specific amount of a real or financial asset at a specific price over a specified period of time. In addition, whereas *price* is one of the specified variables on a call option (i.e., strike price), it is *not* stated anywhere on a futures contract. Instead, the price on a futures contract is established through

TABLE 12.1 Futures Contract Dimensions

Contract	Size of a Contract*	Recent** Market Value of a Single Contract
Corn	5,000 bu	$ 13,750
Wheat	5,000 bu	21,500
Live cattle	40,000 lb	30,000
Pork bellies	40,000 lb	13,200
Coffee	37,500 lb	28,125
Cotton	50,000 lb	27,500
Gold	100 troy oz	36,000
Copper	25,000 lb	24,750
Japanese yen	12.5 million yen	98,750
Treasury bills	$1 million	960,000
Treasury bonds	$100,000	101,000
S&P 500 Stock Index	500 times the index	206,250

*The size of some contracts may vary by exchange.

**Contract values are representative of those that existed in early 1992.

trading on the floor of a commodities exchange—meaning the delivery price is set by supply and demand at whatever price the contract sells for. Equally important, the risk of loss with an option is limited to the price paid for it, whereas a futures contract has *no such limit on exposure to loss.*

Futures Contracts versus Forward Contracts. In addition to futures contracts, there are also **forward contracts.** Basically, a forward contract is an agreement whereby a seller agrees to deliver a specific commodity or product to a buyer sometime in the future, *at a price as specified in the contract itself.* Actually, forward contracts are widely used in practice and are common in real estate leases, fixed-rate loans, credit cards, mortgage loans, even magazine subscriptions. In all these cases, there's an agreement that a product or service will be delivered sometime in the future at some set price. For example, when home buyers apply for a mortgage, they can "lock in" an interest rate at the time they start the loan application process, rather than having to wait until the deal closes—which could be two or three months later. When they lock in the rate, they are effectively entering into a forward contract with the mortgage lender, with regard to the rate of interest that will be charged on the mortgage (assuming, of course, that the buyers qualify for the loan). Without forward contracts, it would be impossible for buyers and sellers to agree on anything, and prices would have to be constantly renegotiated.

Although they may appear to be the same, there are some real differences between futures and forward contracts. The most obvious, perhaps, has to do with price: Whereas price is specified on a forward contract, it is set through trading on a futures contract. Moreover, in contrast to futures contracts, prices and contract terms on forward contracts are *not standardized.* As a result, forward contracts are not actively traded on organized exchanges; there is a forward market for some

forward contract agreement whereby a seller agrees to deliver a specific commodity or product to a buyer sometime in the future, *at a price specified in the contract itself.*

types of contracts, but there are no organized exchanges. Since there are no exchanges, there are no central clearing houses in the forward market and as such, there is a risk that one, or both, of the parties won't be able to hold up their end of the bargain. In sharp contrast, there are certain financial constraints to prevent this type of thing from happening in the futures market.

Major Exchanges

Although futures contracts can be traced back to biblical times, their use on an organized basis in this country did not occur until the mid-1800s. They originated in the agricultural segment of the economy, where individuals who produced, owned, and/or processed foodstuffs sought a way to protect themselves against adverse price movements. Subsequently, futures contracts came to be traded by individuals who wanted to make money with commodities by speculating on their price swings. The first organized commodity exchange in the United States, the Chicago Board of Trade, opened in 1848. Over time additional exchanges came into existence, so that today futures trading is conducted on 12 U.S. exchanges:

- Chicago Board of Trade (CBOT)
- Chicago Mercantile Exchange (CME)
- Chicago Rice & Cotton Exchange (CRCE)
- Commodity Exchange of New York (COMEX)
- Kansas City Board of Trade (KCBT)
- MidAmerica Commodity Exchange (MidAm)
- Minneapolis Grain Exchange (MGE)
- New York Coffee, Sugar, and Cocoa Exchange (CSCE)
- New York Cotton Exchange (NYCE)
- New York Futures Exchange (NYFE)
- New York Mercantile Exchange (NYMEX)
- Philadelphia Board of Trade (PBOT)

The Chicago Board of Trade is the biggest exchange—in fact, it's the largest commodities exchange in the world—followed by the Chicago Mercantile Exchange, the NY Merc, and the Commodity Exchange of New York. These four exchanges account for more than 80 percent of all the trading volume conducted on American futures exchanges. All totalled, trading activity on the 12 major exchanges has reached the point where the futures market today is a *trillion-dollar* institution that, in many respects, rivals the stock market. In addition to these American exchanges, there's a growing number of futures markets found all over the globe. There are active commodities and financial futures exchanges in Canada, Great Britain, Germany, Japan, Australia, France, and Switzerland, among others. The United States is still the leading market, but its share of the world market is falling each year as these other markets become more active.

Returning to the American exchanges, each one deals in a variety of futures contracts, although some are more limited in their activities than others. For example, in contrast to the Minneapolis Grain Exchange, which deals in just three or four contracts, the CBOT lists corn, oats, soybeans, wheat, gold, and silver, as well as a variety of debt instruments and stock market indexes. In fact, most exchanges deal in a number of different commodities and/or financial assets, and many commodities and financial futures are traded on more than one exchange. Although the exchanges are highly efficient and annual volume has surpassed the trillion-dollar mark, futures trading is still conducted by **open outcry auction:** as shown in Figure 12.1, actual trading on the floors of these exchanges is conducted through a series of shouts, body motions, and hand signals.

Trading in the Futures Market

Basically, the futures market contains two types of traders: hedgers and speculators. The market simply could not exist and operate efficiently without either one. The **hedgers** are commodities producers and processors (which today include financial institutions and corporate money managers) who use futures contracts as a way to protect their interest in the underlying commodity or financial instrument. For example, if a rancher thinks the price of cattle will drop in the near future, he will hedge his position by selling a futures contract on cattle in the hope of locking in as high a price as possible for his herd. In effect, the hedgers provide the underlying strength of the futures market and represent the very reason for its existence. *Speculators,* in contrast, give the market liquidity; they are the ones who trade futures contracts not because of a need to protect a position in the underlying commodity, but simply to earn a profit on expected swings in the price of a futures contract. They are the risk takers, the investors who have no inherent interest in the commodity or financial future other than the price action and potential capital gains it can produce.

Trading Mechanics

Once the futures contracts are created by the hedgers and speculators, they can readily be traded in the market. Like common stocks and other traditional investment vehicles, futures contracts are bought and sold through local brokerage offices. Most firms have at least one or two people in each office (more in some cases) who specialize in futures contracts. In addition, a number of commodity firms that deal only in futures contracts stand ready to help individuals with their investment needs. Except for setting up a special commodity trading account, there is really no difference between trading futures and dealing in stocks or bonds. The same types of orders are used, and the use of margin is a standard way of trading futures. Any investor can buy or sell any contract, with any delivery month, at any time, so long as it is currently being traded on one of the exchanges.

Buying a contract is referred to as taking a *long position,* whereas selling one is termed taking a *short position*. It is exactly like going long or short with stocks and has the same connotation: The investor who is long wants the price to rise, and the short seller wants it to drop. Both long and short positions can be liquidated simply

open outcry auction
in futures trading, auction in which trading is done through a series of shouts, body motions, and hand signals.

hedgers
producers and processors who use futures contracts as a way to protect their interest in an underlying commodity or financial instrument.

• FIGURE 12.1   The Auction Market at Work on the Floor
of the Chicago Board of Trade

Traders employ a system of open outcry and hand signals to indicate whether they
wish to buy or sell and the price at which they wish to do so. Fingers held vertically
indicate the number of contracts a trader wants to buy or sell. Fingers held horizon-
tally indicate the fraction of a cent above or below the last traded full-cent price at
which the trader will buy or sell. (*Source:* Chicago Board of Trade, *Action in the
Marketplace: Commodity Futures Trading,* 1978.)

by executing an offsetting transaction. The short seller, for example, would cover his or her position by buying an equal amount of the contract. In general, less than 1 percent of all futures contracts are settled by delivery; the rest are offset prior to the delivery month. All trades are subject to normal transaction costs, which include **round trip commissions** of about $60 to $90 for each contract traded. (A round trip commission includes the commission costs on both ends of the transaction—to buy and sell a contract.) The exact size of the commission depends on the number and type of contracts being traded.

Margin Trading

Buying on margin means putting up only a fraction of the total price in cash; margin, in effect, is the amount of equity that goes into the deal. Margin trading plays a crucial role in futures transactions because *all futures contracts are traded on a margin basis*. The margin required usually ranges from about 2 to 10 percent of the value of the contract which, when compared to the margin required for stocks and most other types of securities, is very low. Furthermore, there is *no borrowing* required on the part of the investor to finance the balance of the contract; the margin, or **margin deposit** as it is called with futures, exists simply as a way to guarantee fulfillment of the contract. The margin deposit is not a partial payment for the commodity or financial instrument, nor is it in any way related to the value of the product or item underlying the contract. Rather, it represents security to cover any loss in the market value of the contract that may result from adverse price movements.

The size of the required margin deposit is specified as a dollar amount and varies according to the type of contract (i.e., the amount of price volatility in the underlying commodity or financial asset) and, in some cases, the exchange. Table 12.2 gives the margin requirements for the same 12 commodities and financial instruments listed in Table 12.1, above. In sharp contrast to the size and value of futures contracts, margin requirements are kept very low. The **initial deposit** noted in Table 12.2 is the amount of investor capital that must be deposited with the broker at the time the transaction is initiated and represents the amount of money required to make a given investment.

After the investment is made, the market value of a contract will, of course, rise and fall as the quoted price of the underlying commodity or financial instrument goes up or down. Such market behavior will cause the amount of margin on deposit to change. To be sure that an adequate margin is always on hand, investors are required to meet a second type of margin requirement, the **maintenance deposit.** This deposit is slightly less than the initial deposit and establishes the minimum amount of margin that must be kept in the account at all times. For instance, if the initial deposit on a commodity is $1,000 per contract, its maintenance margin might be $750. So long as the market value of the contract does not fall by more than $250 (the difference between the contract's initial and maintenance margins), the investor has no problem. But if the market moves against the investor and the value of the

---

round trip commissions
the commission costs on both ends (buying and selling) of a securities transaction.

margin deposit
amount deposited with a broker to cover any loss in the market value of a futures contract that may result from adverse price movements.

initial deposit
the amount of investor capital that must be deposited with a broker at the time of a commodity transaction.

maintenance deposit
the minimum amount of margin that must be kept in a margin account at all times.

TABLE 12.2 Margin Requirements for a Sample of Commodities and Financial Futures*

	Initial Margin Deposit	Maintenance Margin Deposit
Corn	$1,000	$ 750
Wheat	1,000	750
Live cattle	1,000	750
Pork bellies	1,000	750
Coffee	2,000	1,500
Cotton	1,000	750
Gold	1,300	1,000
Copper	1,000	800
Japanese yen	2,000	1,500
Treasury bills	1,000	750
Treasury bonds	2,700	2,000
S&P 500 Stock Index	9,000	6,000

*These margin requirements were specified by a major full-service brokerage firm in early 1992, and may exceed the minimums established by the various exchanges. They are meant to be typical of the on-going requirements that customers are expected to live up to. Depending upon the volatility of the market, exchange-minimum margin requirements are changed frequently, and thus the requirements in this table are also subject to change on short notice.

mark-to-the-market
a daily check of an investor's margin position; the gain or loss in a contract's value is determined at the end of each session, at which time the broker debits or credits the account as needed.

contract drops by more than the allowed amount, the investor will receive a *margin call*. He or she must then immediately deposit enough cash to bring the position back to the initial margin level. An investor's margin position is checked daily via a procedure known as **mark-to-the-market.** That is, the gain or loss in a contract's value is determined at the end of each session, at which time the broker debits or credits the trader's account accordingly. In a falling market, an investor may receive a number of margin calls and be required to make additional margin payments (perhaps on a daily basis) in order to keep the position above the maintenance margin level. Failure to do so will mean that the broker has no choice but to close out the position.

COMMODITIES

Physical commodities like grains, metals, wood, and meat make up a major portion of the futures market. They have been actively traded in this country for well over a century, and still account for a good deal of the trading activity. The material that follows focuses on *commodities trading* and begins with a review of the basic characteristics and investment merits of these vehicles.

Basic Characteristics

Various types of physical commodities are found on nearly all of the 12 U.S. futures exchanges (in fact, three of them deal only in commodities). The market for commodity contracts is divided into five major segments: grains and oilseeds, livestock and meat, food and fiber, metals and petroleum, and wood. Such segmentation does not affect trading mechanics and procedures but provides a convenient way of categorizing commodities into groups based on similar underlying characteristics. Table 12.3 shows the diversity of the commodities market and the variety of contracts available. While the list changes yearly, we can see from the table that investors had nearly 40 different commodities to choose from in 1992, and a number of these (like soybeans and wheat) are available in several different forms or grades.

A Commodities Contract

Every commodity has its own specifications regarding the amounts and quality of the product being traded. Figure 12.2 is an excerpt from the ''Futures Prices'' section of *The Wall Street Journal* and shows the contract and quotation system used with commodities. Each commodity quote is made up of the same five parts, and all prices are quoted in an identical fashion. In particular, every commodities contract (and quote) specifies: (1) the product, (2) the exchange on which the contract is traded, (3) the size of the contract (in bushels, pounds, tons, or whatever), (4) the

TABLE 12.3 Major Classes of Commodities

Grains and Oilseeds	Metals and Petroleum
Corn	Aluminum
Oats	Copper
Soybeans	Gold
Wheat	Platinum
Barley	Silver
Canola	Palladium
Flaxseed	Gasoline
Rapeseed	Heating oil
Sorghum	Crude oil
Rye	Gas oil
Rice	Propane
	Natural gas
Livestock and Meat	
Cattle	**Food and Fiber**
Hogs and pork bellies	Cocoa
Broilers	Coffee
	Cotton
Wood	Orange juice
Lumber	Sugar
Plywood	Potatoes
Stud lumber	Butter

FUTURES PRICES

Wednesday, January 29, 1992

Open Interest Reflects Previous Trading Day.

GRAINS AND OILSEEDS

	Open	High	Low	Settle	Change	Lifetime High	Lifetime Low	Open Interest
CORN (CBT) 5,000 bu.; cents per bu.								
Mar	264¾	265	263	263¼	- 1	277¼	228½	107,240
May	271	271¼	269¼	269½	- 1	279½	234¾	72,934
July	275½	276	274	274½	- ¾	282	239½	66,529
Sept	271½	272½	270¾	271¼	- ¼	272½	236½	7,793
Dec	268½	269¾	267½	268½	....	270	236½	26,153
Mr93	274¼	275¾	273½	274½	- ¼	275¾	258	1,810
Est vol 35,000; vol Tues 38,413; open int 282,545, +3,791.								
OATS (CBT) 5,000 bu.; cents per bu.								
Mar	142¾	145	142¼	144	+ 2	157	126½	5,853
May	147	149	146¾	148¼	+ 1¾	159½	132	2,752
July	151	153¼	151	152¼	+ 2¼	161½	138	1,079
Sept	153½	156	153½	155	+ 2¼	156	141½	145
Est vol 1,750; vol Tues 961; open int 9,903, +277.								
SOYBEANS (CBT) 5,000 bu.; cents per bu.								
Mar	583½	585¾	575	576¼	- 5¼	666	538	44,327
May	589	592¼	580½	582¼	- 6	668	547	26,005
July	597½	601	592½	593	- 3½	668	554	28,057
Aug	601½	604	595	596	- 4	660	565	3,352
Sept	604	605½	600	600	- 2½	628	557	1,955
Nov	612	614¾	607	607¾	- 3¼	620¾	552	15,299
Ja93	620	622½	618½	616½	- 2½	622½	578½	693
Mar	629	629	629	626½	- 2	629	590½	143
Est vol 43,000; vol Tues 26,869; open int 119,832, -690.								
SOYBEAN MEAL (CBT) 100 tons; $ per ton.								
Mar	179.10	180.30	176.70	176.80	- 2.30	197.00	163.50	28,815
May	180.50	181.50	178.00	178.10	- 2.10	194.00	164.50	14,115
July	181.00	183.30	180.10	180.30	- .80	196.00	166.00	12,742
Aug	181.20	183.80	180.50	180.70	- 1.10	188.50	170.90	2,577
Sept	182.50	184.60	182.00	182.00	- .50	186.00	171.30	3,123
Oct	196.50	198.00	196.50	196.60	+ .10	198.00	182.30	1,754
Dec	199.00	200.50	198.50	198.50	- .50	200.50	183.50	2,532
Est vol 19,000; vol Tues 12,445; open int 65,658, -851.								
SOYBEAN OIL (CBT) 60,000 lbs.; cents per lb.								
Mar	19.46	19.59	19.35	19.36	- .10	24.10	18.60	27,592
May	19.77	19.88	19.67	19.67	- .08	24.00	18.93	21,968
July	20.07	20.16	19.97	19.96	- .08	24.30	19.25	10,467
Aug	20.23	20.30	20.15	20.15	- .04	22.35	19.42	3,072
Sept	20.42	20.42	20.32	20.28	- .04	22.35	19.57	3,390
Oct	20.42	20.42	20.35	20.35	- .03	22.30	19.66	1,675
Dec	20.85	20.87	20.65	20.65	- .09	22.60	19.93	1,921
Est vol 13,000; vol Tues 7,463; open int 70,172, +200.								
WHEAT (CBT) 5,000 bu.; cents per bu.								
Mar	437¾	442	436½	441½	+ 4	442¾	279	24,071
May	421	422	418	421¼	+ 1¾	424	280½	14,19
July	388	388½	386¾	387½	- ½	388½	279	23,914
Sept	391	391½	390¼	391½	- ¼	391¾	292	2,823
Dec	400	400	398½	399¾	+ ¼	400	329½	3,073
Mr93	437¾	400	399	401	+ 1	400½	354	134
Est vol 16,000; vol Tues 14,182; open int 68,208, +154.								
WHEAT (KC) 5,000 bu.; cents per bu.								
Mar	438	439	436¼	437¾	+ ¼	439½	275½	17,442
May	418	419¼	416½	418½	+ 1	419¼	273	9,887
July	393	393½	391½	392¼	- 1	393½	272	7,077
Sept	395	395½	394	394¼	- ¾	395½	314	1,977
Dec	402	402	401	401¼	- ¾	403	354	856
Est vol 5,124; vol Tues 5,684; open int 37,239, +445.								
WHEAT (MPLS) 5,000 bu.; cents per bu.								
Mar	427	428¼	426	426¾	....	429	279½	7,274
May	415	417	415	416	+ 1¼	417	284	5,164
July	401½	402¾	401½	401½	....	402¾	308	891
Sept	390	390	388¼	389	- 1	391½	315	906
Dec	398	398	398	398	- 2	398	349	128
Est vol 1,788; vol Tues 2,398; open int 14,363, -4.								
BARLEY (WPG) 20 metric tons; Can. $ per ton								
Mar	88.70	89.00	88.30	88.50	+ .20	97.50	81.00	2,948
May	90.50	90.50	90.20	90.20	+ .10	96.00	85.70	1,469
July	92.00	92.50	92.00	92.30	+ .40	96.00	90.10	360
Oct	93.70	94.00	93.50	93.50	+ .60	94.80	74.70	407
Est vol 400; vol Tues 222; open int 5,184, -66.								
FLAXSEED (WPG) 20 metric tons; Can. $ per ton								
Mar	195.80	197.30	195.70	196.80	+ 1.20	234.50	186.40	1,726
May	200.00	202.00	200.00	201.00	+ 1.10	232.00	189.70	1,853
July	204.50	205.20	204.40	204.40	+ .90	221.50	194.80	1,239
Oct	211.50	212.10	211.40	211.40	+ .90	216.50	202.20	1,204
Est vol 1,175; vol Tues 1,236; open int 6,022, -378.								

	Open	High	Low	Settle	Change	Lifetime High	Lifetime Low	Open Interest
Sept	83.10	83.20	82.25	82.45	- .05	108.00	82.25	1,515
Dec	86.50	86.50	85.65	86.10	....	107.25	85.65	1,471
Mr93	89.50	89.50	89.50	89.20	+ .05	94.75	89.50	340
May	....	....		92.00	- .75	96.00	93.75	147
Est vol 9,003; vol Tues 11,100; open int 49,680, +954.								
SUGAR-WORLD (CSCE)-112,000 lbs.; cents per lb.								
Mar	8.33	8.39	8.26	8.34	- .01	10.14	7.56	36,024
May	8.41	8.45	8.34	8.44	+ .03	9.77	7.65	27,558
July	8.44	8.47	8.36	8.46	+ .02	9.16	7.80	14,196
Oct	8.49	8.50	8.39	8.48	- .01	9.06	7.93	17,345
Mr93	8.53	8.53	8.45	8.53	....	9.04	8.20	2,401
May	....	....		8.50	- .02	8.80	8.30	107
Est vol 15,320; vol Tues 17,747; open int 97,631, -463.								
SUGAR-DOMESTIC (CSCE)-112,000 lbs.; cents per lb.								
Mar	21.33	21.33	21.19	21.20	- .15	22.80	21.19	1,402
May	21.52	21.52	21.47	21.47	- .06	22.30	21.47	2,342
July	21.69	21.69	21.64	21.64	- .05	22.39	21.63	2,050
Sept	21.69	21.69	21.64	21.64	- .05	22.30	21.64	836
Nov	21.80	21.80	21.78	21.83	- .02	22.10	21.78	1,046
Ja93	....	....		21.78	- .07	22.00	21.80	168
Est vol 986; vol Tues 773; open int 7,881, +321.								
COTTON (CTN)-50,000 lbs.; cents per lb.								
Mar	53.75	54.05	53.36	53.95	+ .57	77.15	53.25	14,604
May	55.80	55.98	55.32	55.88	+ .51	77.30	55.20	9,821
July	57.10	57.40	56.81	57.30	+ .40	77.70	56.70	8,797
Oct	59.45	59.70	59.31	59.40	- .01	70.60	59.31	1,911
Dec	60.25	60.50	60.00	60.20	+ .03	69.00	60.00	5,155
Mr93	....	....		61.75	+ .05	67.30	62.00	1,187
Est vol 6,000; vol Tues 6,789; open int 41,564, -745.								
ORANGE JUICE (CTN)-15,000 lbs.; cents per lb.								
Mar	143.45	144.70	143.20	144.70	+ 1.25	178.40	113.60	4,893
May	144.00	145.30	143.85	145.30	+ 1.35	177.95	115.00	2,660
July	145.00	145.80	144.60	145.35	+ 1.35	175.50	115.25	813
Nov	....	....		133.60	+ 1.05	175.00	118.00	453
Ja93	132.90	133.85	132.90	133.50	+ 1.10	178.00	112.65	384
Mar	....	....		133.50	+ 1.10	164.00	126.00	268
Est vol 750; vol Tues 677; open int 9,482, +10.								

METALS AND PETROLEUM

	Open	High	Low	Settle	Change	Lifetime High	Lifetime Low	Open Interest
COPPER-HIGH (CMX)-25,000 lbs.; cents per lb.								
Jan	99.30	99.70	98.70	98.80	- .10	106.60	93.30	245
Feb	99.45	99.50	98.70	98.90	+ .10	105.70	93.60	894
Mar	99.65	99.95	98.55	99.10	+ .10	106.80	93.70	22,940
Apr	98.60	98.60	98.60	98.95	+ .05	103.00	93.50	606
May	99.25	99.70	98.40	98.85	....	106.20	93.30	8,262
June	98.50	98.50	98.50	98.85	....	102.00	94.80	425
July	99.30	99.40	98.50	98.80	....	103.80	92.80	4,262
Aug	....	....		98.85	- .05	101.00	95.70	278
Sept	98.80	98.90	98.50	98.90	- .05	103.45	92.80	2,709
Oct	....	....		98.90	- .05	99.80	95.90	247
Nov	....	....		99.00	- .05	99.30	96.00	232
Dec	99.70	99.70	99.00	99.10	- .05	101.10	91.60	2,858
Mr93	99.40	99.40	99.00	98.80	- .30	100.50	92.80	827
May	98.95	98.95	98.95	98.70	- .40	99.30	93.70	211
July	....	....		98.60	- .50	98.80	95.80	137
Sept	....	....		98.60	- .50	96.65	95.80	140
Est vol 11,000; vol Tues 7,337; open int 45,356, -326.								
GOLD (CMX)-100 troy oz.; $ per troy oz.								
Jan	....	....		356.10	+ .30	363.00	351.00	0
Feb	355.30	357.00	354.70	356.10	+ .20	456.50	348.50	19,030
Apr	357.30	359.10	356.80	358.20	+ .30	446.00	350.70	39,518
June	359.70	360.90	359.00	360.30	+ .30	467.00	353.80	14,895
Aug	363.00	363.00	363.00	362.50	+ .30	426.50	355.00	6,179
Oct	....	....		364.50	+ .20	410.80	358.50	2,279
Dec	....	....		366.70	+ .20	431.00	359.40	3,606
Fb93	....	....		369.00	+ .20	404.20	368.00	6,327
Apr	....	....		371.30	+ .10	410.00	368.50	5,372
June	....	....		373.80	+ .10	418.50	366.00	2,908
Aug	....	....		376.60	+ .10	395.50	374.50	1,134
Oct	....	....		379.50	+ .10	395.00	378.70	181
Dec	....	....		382.40	+ .10	402.80	374.50	926
Ju95	....	....		392.10	+ .10	....	....	100
Dec	....	....		402.30	+ .10	....	....	100
Est vol 42,000; vol Tues 27,567; open int 102,575, -1,893.								
PLATINUM (NYM)-50 troy oz.; $ per troy oz.								
Apr	346.50	352.50	346.50	349.40	- 2.00	438.50	329.50	10,477
July	346.50	350.50	346.50	349.40	- 2.00	427.50	331.00	1,762
Oct	353.00	353.00	353.00	352.40	- 1.50	404.00	336.00	1,529
Ja93	....	....		352.40	- 2.00	357.50	339.00	548
Est vol 2,679; vol Tues 919; open int 14,323, -227.								

• FIGURE 12.2 Quotations on Actively Traded Commodity Futures Contracts

These quotes reveal at a glance key information about the various commodities, including the latest high, low, and closing (''settle'') prices, as well as the lifetime high and low prices for each contract. (*Source: The Wall Street Journal,* January 31, 1992.)

method of valuing the contract, or pricing unit (like cents per pound, or dollars per ton), and (5) the delivery month. Using a corn contract as an illustration, we can see each of these parts in the illustration below:

KEY		Open	High	Low	Settle	Change	Lifetime High	Lifetime Low	Open Interest
① the *product*	① ② ③ ④								
② the *exchange*	Corn (CBT)—5,000 bu.; cents per bu.								
③ the *size of the contract*	May	253½	253¾	252¼	252½	−1¾	286½	230½	42,796
	July	258	258	256½	256¾	−1¾	288	233	60,477
④ the *pricing unit*	⑤ Sept.	260	260½	259	259	−1½	263	236	7,760
	Dec.	263½	264	262½	263	−1¼	267¼	244	41,638
⑤ the *delivery months*	Mar. 94	271¾	272	270¼	271	−1¼	276	254¾	11,098
	May	277¼	278	276¼	277	−1	281	273¼	1,326

The quotation system used for commodities is based on the size of the contract and the pricing unit. The financial media generally report the open, high, low, and closing prices for each delivery month. With commodities, the last price of the day, or the closing price, is known as the **settle price.** Also reported, at least by *The Wall Street Journal,* is the amount of **open interest** in each contract—that is, the number of contracts presently outstanding. Note in the above illustration that the settle price for May corn was quoted at 252½. Since the pricing system is cents per bushel, this means that the contract was being traded at $2.52½ per bushel, and that the market value of the contract was $12,625 (each contract involves 5,000 bushels and each bushel is worth $2.52½; thus, 5,000 × $2.525 = $12,625).

settle price
the closing price (last price of the day) for commodities and financial futures.

open interest
the number of contracts presently outstanding on a commodity or financial future.

Price Behavior

Commodity prices react to a unique set of economic, political, and international pressures—as well as the weather. Although the explanation of why commodity prices change is beyond the scope of this book, it should be clear that they do move up and down just like any other investment vehicle—which is precisely what speculators want. However, because we are dealing in such large trading units (5,000 bushels of this or 40,000 pounds of that), even a rather modest price change can have an enormous impact on the market value of a contract, and therefore on investor returns or losses. For example, if the price of corn goes up or down by just 20 cents per bushel, the value of a *single contract* will change by $1,000. Since a corn contract can be bought with a $750 initial margin deposit, it is easy to see the effect this kind of price behavior can have on investor return.

Do commodity prices really move all that much? Judge for yourself. If we examine the price change columns in Figure 12.2, we can uncover some excellent examples of sizable price changes that occur from one day to the next. Note, for example, that May soybeans fell $300, March wheat rose $200, and July orange juice contracts increased $202.50. Now, keep in mind that these are *daily* price swings that occurred on *single* contracts. These are sizable changes, even by themselves; but when you look at them relative to the (very small) original investment required, they add up to serious returns (or losses) in a hurry! And they occur not because the underlying prices are so volatile, but because of the sheer magnitude of the commodities contracts themselves.

Clearly, this kind of price behavior is one of the magnets that draws investors to commodities. The exchanges recognize the volatile nature of commodities contracts and try to put lids on price fluctuations by imposing daily price limits and maximum daily price ranges (similar limits are also put on financial futures). The **daily price limit** restricts the interday change in the price of the underlying commodity. For example, the price of corn can change by no more than 10 cents per bushel from one day to the next, and the daily limit on copper is 3 cents per pound. Such limits, however, still leave plenty of room to turn a quick profit. For example, the daily limits on corn and copper translate into per day changes of $500 for one corn contract and $750 for a copper contract. The **maximum daily price range,** in contrast, limits the amount the price can change *during* the day and is usually equal to twice the daily limit restrictions. Thus, the daily price limit on corn is 10 cents per bushel and its maximum daily range 20 cents per bushel.

daily price limit
restriction on the day-to-day change in the price of an underlying commodity.

maximum daily price range
the amount a commodity price can change during a day; usually equal to twice the daily price limit.

Return on Invested Capital

Futures contracts have only one source of return: the capital gains that can be earned when prices move in a favorable direction. There is no current income of any kind. The volatile price behavior of futures contracts is one reason high returns are possible; the other is leverage. That is, because all futures trading is done on margin, it takes only a small amount of money to control a large investment position and to participate in the large price swings that accompany many futures contracts. Of course, the use of leverage also means that it is possible for an investment to be wiped out with just one or two bad days.

return on invested capital
return to investors based on the amount of money actually invested in a security, rather than the value of the contract itself.

Investment return can be measured by calculating **return on invested capital.** This is simply a variation of the standard holding period return formula that bases return on *the amount of money actually invested in the contract,* rather than on the value of the contract itself. It is used because of the generous amount of leverage (margin) used in commodities trading. The return on invested capital for a commodities position can be determined according to the following simple formula:

Equation 12.1

$$\text{Return on invested capital} = \frac{\begin{array}{c}\text{selling price of} \\ \text{commodity contract}\end{array} - \begin{array}{c}\text{purchase price of} \\ \text{commodity contract}\end{array}}{\text{amount of margin deposit}}$$

Equation 12.1 can be used for both long and short transactions. To see how it works, assume you bought two September corn contracts at 245 ($2.45 per bushel) by depositing the required initial margin of $2,000 ($1,000 for each contract). Your investment amounts to only $2,000, but you control 10,000 bushels of corn worth $24,500 at the time they were purchased. Now assume September corn has just closed at 259, so you decide to sell out and take your profit. Your return on invested capital would be as follows:

$$\text{Return on invested capital} = \frac{\$25,900 - \$24,500}{\$2,000}$$

$$= \frac{\$1,400}{\$2,000} = \underline{\underline{70.0\%}}$$

Clearly this high rate of return was due not only to an increase in the price of the commodity, but also—and perhaps more important—to the fact that you were using very low margin. (The initial margin in this particular transaction equaled just 6 percent of the underlying value of the contract.)

Trading Commodities

Investing in commodities takes one of three forms. The first is *speculating,* which is popular with investors who use commodities as a way to generate capital gains. In essence, they try to capitalize on the wide price swings that are characteristic of so many commodities. Figure 12.3 provides the composite index of futures prices over the six-year period from 1986 through 1991, as compiled by the Commodity Research Bureau (CRB). It graphically illustrates the volatile behavior of commodity prices. Although such price movements may be appealing to speculators, they can frighten a lot of other investors. Some of these more cautious investors turn to *spreading,* the second form of commodities investing; they use sophisticated trading techniques intended to capture the benefits of volatile prices but at the same time limit their exposure to loss. Finally, producers and processors use various *hedging* strategies as a way to protect their interests in the underlying commodities. We will briefly examine each of these trading tactics not only to see what they are, but also to gain a better understanding of how commodities can be used as investment vehicles.

Speculating

Speculators are in the market for one reason: They expect the price of a commodity to go up or down, and they hope to capitalize on it by going long or short. To see why a speculator would go long when prices are expected to rise, consider an individual who buys a March silver contract at 533½ (i.e., $5.33½ an ounce) by depositing the required initial margin of $1,300. Since one silver contract involves 5,000 troy ounces, it has a market value of $26,675. If silver goes up, the investor makes money. Assume it does, and that by February (one month before the contract expires) the price of the contract rises to 552. The speculator then liquidates and makes a profit of 18½ cents per ounce (552 − 533½). That means $925 profit from an investment of just $1,300—which translates into a return on invested capital of 71.2 percent. Of course, instead of rising, the price of silver could have dropped by 18½ cents per ounce. In this case, our investor would have lost most of his original

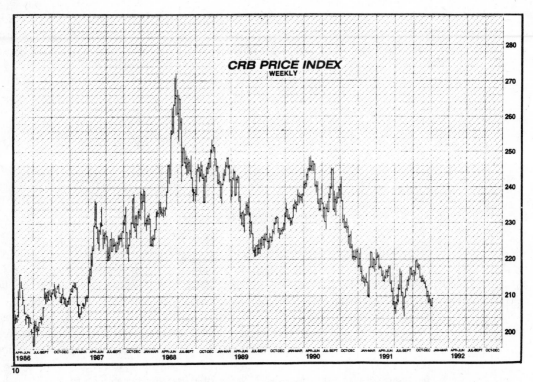

• FIGURE 12.3 The Behavior of Commodity Prices over Time
(1986–1991)

This graph shows the volatile nature of commodity prices and underscores the need for
investor know-how when dealing in commodities. (*Source:* Courtesy of *Commodity Price
Charts.*)

investment ($1,300 − $925 leaves only $375, out of which would have to come a
round trip commission of $60 or $70). But to a short seller, the drop in price would
be just what she was after, for she could profit from such a turn of events. Here's
how: She sells (shorts) the March silver at 533½ and buys it back sometime later at
515. Clearly, the difference between her selling price and purchase price is the same
18½ cents, but in this case it is *profit,* since the selling price exceeds the purchase
price (see Chapter 2 for a review of short selling).

Spreading

Instead of attempting to speculate on the price behavior of a futures contract, an
investor might choose to follow the more conservative tactic of spreading. (The
principles of spreading futures contracts are much the same as those we discussed
with put and call options.) The idea is to combine two or more different contracts
into one investment position that offers the potential for generating a modest amount
of profit while restricting exposure to loss. One very important reason for spreading

in the commodities market is that unlike stock options, *there is no limit to the amount of loss that can occur with a futures contract*. An investor will set up a spread by buying one contract and simultaneously selling another. Although one side of the transaction will lead to a loss, the investor obviously hopes that the profit earned from the other side will be more than enough compensation and that the net result will be at least a modest amount of profit. If the investor is wrong, the spread will serve to limit (but not eliminate) any losses.

Here is a simple version of how a spread might work: Suppose we buy contract A at 533½ and at the same time short sell contract B for 575½. Sometime later we close out our interest in contract A by selling it at 542 and simultaneously cover our short position in B by purchasing a contract at 579. Although we made a profit of 8½ points on the long position, contract A (542 − 533½), we lost 3½ points on the contract that we shorted, B (575½ − 579). The net effect, however, is a profit of 5 points, which, if we were dealing in cents per pound, would mean a profit of $250 on a 5,000-pound contract. All sorts of commodity spreads can be set up for almost any type of investment situation. Most are highly sophisticated and require specialized skills.

Hedging

A hedge is a "technical" approach to commodity trading used by producers and processors to protect a position in a product or commodity. For example, a producer or grower would use a commodity hedge to obtain as *high* a price for the goods he sells as possible; the processor or manufacturer who uses the commodity, however, would employ a hedge to obtain the goods at as *low* a price as possible. A successful hedge, in effect, means added income to producers and lower costs to processors. An example will show how hedging works and why it is done: Suppose a manufacturer uses platinum as a basic raw material in the production of catalytic converters. It is early in the year and platinum is selling for $380 per ounce, but it is expected to shoot up in price and be much more expensive by year-end. To protect against future price increases, our manufacturer decides to buy a platinum futures contract, now trading at $405 an ounce. Assume that eight months later, the price of platinum has indeed gone up (to $480 per ounce) but so has the price of the futures contract, which is now trading at, say, $525 an ounce. The manufacturer has made $120 per ounce on the 50-ounce futures contract and is $6,000 ahead on the transaction—a gain that will be used to offset the increase in the cost of platinum. As it turns out, the gain on the futures contract is $1,000 more than the increased cost of 50 ounces of platinum on the open market, since the cost of platinum rose by only $100 per ounce and the cost of 50 ounces of platinum in the cash market went up by only $5,000. This was a successful hedge for the manufacturer because it kept the cost of this raw material in check, at least for the time being. (Technically, the manufacturer could take delivery of the contracted platinum—at an *effective* cost of $405 per ounce, the price at which the futures contract was purchased—but that is unlikely in this case, since the manufacturer would have to forgo the $1,000 profit in order to do so.)

Commodities and the Individual Investor

For the most part, individuals use commodities in one of two ways: for speculation and/or spreading. Commodities appeal to investors because of the high rates of return they offer and their ability to act as inflation hedges during periods of rapidly rising consumer prices. When sustained high rates of inflation become a problem, traditional investment outlets just do not seem to be able to provide the type of return necessary to keep investors ahead of the game. That is, it seems that more often than not, in periods of high inflation, investors lose more in purchasing power than they gain from after-tax returns. Under such circumstances, investors can be expected to seek outlets that provide better protection against inflation, all of which explains why the interest in commodities tends to pick up with inflation.

Commodities can play an important role in a portfolio so long as *the investor understands the risks involved and is well versed in the principles and mechanics of commodities trading.* The quickest way to lose money in commodities is to jump in without knowing what you are doing. The fact is that over the long run the average return to commodities investors is *negative.* Because there is the potential for a lot of price volatility and because commodity trading is done on a very low margin, the potential for loss is enormous. Accordingly, most experts recommend that only a portion of an individual's investment capital be committed to commodities. The specific amount would, of course, be a function of investor aversion to risk and the amount of resources available. An investor has to be prepared mentally and should be in a position financially to absorb losses—perhaps a number of them. Not only should an adequate cash reserve be kept on hand (to absorb losses and/or meet margin calls), but it is also a good idea to maintain a diversified holding of commodities in order to spread your risks.

Individuals can invest directly in the commodities market, or they can buy put and call *options* on a number of the actively traded futures contracts. Alternatively, they can invest in limited-partnership *commodity pools.* These pools are a lot like mutual funds, and they might be used by individuals who wish to invest in the commodities market but who lack the time and/or expertise to manage their own investments. But remember that although these pools offer professional management, they by no means guarantee a profit. Instead, they only reduce some of the more obvious risks of commodity investing.

FINANCIAL FUTURES

Another dimension of the futures market is **financial futures,** a segment of the market where futures contracts are traded on a variety of financial instruments. Actually, financial futures are little more than an extension of the commodities concept. They were created for much the same reason as commodity futures; they are traded in the same market; their prices behave much like commodities; and they have similar investment merits. Yet, in spite of all these similarities, financial futures are a unique type of investment vehicle. Let's now look more closely at these instruments and how they can be used by investors.

The Financial Futures Market

financial futures
a type of futures contract where the underlying "commodity" consists of a certain amount of some type of financial asset, such as debt securities, foreign currencies, or market baskets of common stocks.

Even though the financial futures market has been around for only 20 years, it is today a dominant force in the whole futures market, and has reached a level of trading that far surpasses the traditional commodities market. The best-selling futures contracts today are, in fact, financial futures—like U.S. Treasury bonds, S&P 500, and Eurodollar contracts. Much of this interest in financial futures is due, of course, to hedgers and big institutional investors who use these futures contracts as portfolio- and debt-management tools. But there are still plenty of opportunities here for individual investors. For example, financial futures offer still another way to speculate on the behavior of interest rates. Or they can be used by investors who wish to speculate in the stock market. They even offer a convenient way to speculate in the highly specialized, and often highly profitable, foreign currency markets.

The financial futures market was established in response to the economic turmoil the United States had been experiencing during the 1970s. The dollar had become unstable on the world market and was causing serious problems for multinational firms. Closer to home, interest rates had begun to behave in a volatile manner, which caused severe difficulties for corporate treasurers, financial institutions, and money managers in general. All these parties needed a way to protect themselves from the ravages of wide fluctuations in the value of the dollar and interest rates, and so a market for financial futures was born. Hedging provided the economic rationale for the market in financial futures, but speculators were quick to respond as they found the price volatility of these instruments attractive and, at times, highly profitable. At present, financial futures are traded on seven exchanges: the New York Futures Exchange (NYFE), the Kansas City Board of Trade, the MidAmerica Commodity Exchange, the New York Cotton Exchange (through its FINEX subsidiary), the Chicago Board of Trade, the Chicago Merchantile Exchange (including a subsidiary of the CME set up to trade foreign currencies, the International Monetary Market), and the Philadelphia Board of Trade. The three basic types of financial futures include foreign currencies, debt securities, and stock indexes.

Foreign Currencies, Interest Rates, and Stock Indexes

currency futures
futures contracts on foreign currencies, traded much like commodities.

The financial futures market started rather inconspicuously in May 1972 with the listing of a handful of foreign currency contracts. Known as **currency futures,** they have become a major hedging vehicle as international trade (to and from this country) has mushroomed. Most of the currency trading today is conducted in the following six foreign currencies:

- British pound
- German mark
- Swiss franc
- Canadian dollar
- Japanese yen
- Australian dollar

All these currencies involve countries with which the United States has strong international trade and exchange ties. In October 1975, the first futures contract on debt securities, or **interest rate futures** as they are more commonly known, was established when trading started in GNMA pass-through certificates (a special type of mortgage-backed bond issued by an agency of the U.S. government). In time, other issues were added, so that today trading is carried out in the following kinds of debt securities and interest rates:

interest rate futures
futures contracts on debt securities, traded much like commodities.

- U.S. Treasury bills
- 30-day interest rates
- 90-day Eurodollar deposits
- U.S. Treasury notes
- U.S. Treasury bonds

All of these futures contracts, except the Eurodollar deposits, are based on *domestic* securities. Eurodollar deposits are dollars deposited in interest-bearing accounts in banks outside the United States. Interest rate futures were immediately successful, and their popularity has grown rapidly.

In February 1982, a new trading vehicle was introduced: the stock-index futures contract. **Stock-index futures,** as they are called, are contracts pegged to broad-based measures of stock market performance. At the present time, trading is done in four U.S. stock-index futures:

stock-index futures
futures contracts written on broad based measures of stock market performance like the S&P 500 Stock Index; traded much like commodities, allowing investors to participate in the general movements of the stock market.

- S&P 500 Stock Index
- NYSE Composite Stock Index
- Value Line Composite Stock Index
- Major Market Index (which is intended to track the DJIA)

(In addition to these U.S. stock indexes, there's also a Japanese index—the NIK-KEI 225 Stock index contract, traded on the Chicago Mercantile Exchange.) Stock-index futures—which are similar to the index options discussed in Chapter 11—allow investors to participate in the general movements of the entire stock market. These index futures (and other futures contracts) represent a type of *derivative security,* to the extent that they, like options, derive their value from the price behavior of the assets that underlie them. In the case of stock index futures, they are supposed to reflect the general performance of the stock market as a whole, as measured by a particular index like the S&P 500. Thus, when the market, as measured by the S&P 500 goes up, the value of an S&P 500 futures contract should go up as well. Such behavior enables investors to use stock-index futures as a way to buy the market—or a reasonable proxy thereof—and thereby participate in broad market moves. (Note that in addition to stock market indexes, there are several other types of index-based futures contracts available. For example, there's a futures contract available on an index of *municipal bonds;* another on an index that measures the value of the *U.S. dollar* against eight key foreign currencies; and even one based on an index of 21 *commodities* futures contracts.)

Program Trading

Stock-index futures contracts are widely used in **program trading**—a type of computer-assisted trading whereby brokerage houses and other institutional investors
simultaneously buy and sell *large* quantities of common stocks and stock-index
futures contracts. This particular type of program trading, known as an *index arbitrage,* has come under fire because it's felt that such trading leads to wide (and
largely unjustified) swings in stock prices. Indeed, some argue that, on far too many
occasions, it's the futures contracts that are driving stock prices, rather than the
other way around. (*Index options* are also used in program trading, in much the
same way as stock-index futures, but we'll confine our discussion here to the use of
futures contracts.)

Program trading originated as a means for brokerage firms to buy or sell large
baskets of stock for institutions without drastically disturbing share prices. But in
April 1982, the introduction of a futures contract linked to the S&P 500 stock index
created the opportunity for index arbitrage, the exploitation of minute differences
between the price of the futures contract and the prices of the underlying stocks.
Normally, the value of the stock-index futures closely tracks changes in the prices
of the underlying shares, but sometimes, differences do occur. When that happens,
the program trades kick in. That is, if the price difference widens enough, the
programs call for automatic placement of orders to sell the more expensive item and
buy the cheaper one. For example, if stock-index futures contracts were *purchased,*
a corresponding amount of stocks (those that underlie the stock index) would be
sold, and both of these transactions would occur simultaneously. Although this may
not sound like a big deal, the problem is the stock side of the transaction generally
involves huge amounts of stock—literally tens of thousands or even hundreds of
thousands of shares. Why is this done? Because by buying or selling *thousands* of
shares of stock simultaneously, index arbitrage can wring a substantial profit from
even the smallest price difference. When those buy or sell levels are reached and
program trading begins, the huge order flows that follow can heavily influence the
stock market's direction, at least temporarily.

Critics contend that index arbitrage program trading gives unfair advantage to
institutional users at the expense of individual investors, causes needless volatility
in stock prices, and creates opportunities for abuse. In response to these growing
criticisms, a number of so-called "collars" were placed on program traders to
temporarily prohibit or curtail such trading when the markets move sharply higher
or lower. For example, index arbitrage trading is "side-tracked"—effectively
halted—once the DJIA moves 50 points above or below the previous day's close.
These collars probably have curtailed market volatility caused by program trading.
But another very important development has also taken place. That is, more and
more big institutional traders have entered the index arbitrage game (for self-protec-
tion, if nothing else), and in so doing, they have kept the spreads between futures
and stock prices razor-thin. As you would expect in any efficient market, as more
players got into the game, profits became harder to come by. In spite of the shrink-
ing profit margins, index arbitrage is still around today, but not as a stand alone

money maker like it used to be. Rather, index arbitrage is now being used increasingly as a hedging technique for sophisticated, custom-designed equity options and swap contracts. And that's good news for the market, because this new brand of index arbitrage is far less likely to cause wide swings in stock prices.

Contract Specifications

In principle, financial futures contracts are like the commodities contracts that we examined above. They control large sums of the underlying financial instrument and are issued with a variety of delivery months. All this can be seen in Figure 12.4, which lists quotes for several foreign currency, interest rate, and stock-index futures contracts. Looking first at currency futures, we see that the contracts entitle the holders to a certain position in a specified foreign currency; in effect, the owner of a currency future holds a claim on a certain amount of foreign money. The precise amount ranges from 62,500 British pounds to 12.5 million Japanese yen. In a similar fashion, holders of interest rate futures have a claim on a certain amount of the underlying debt security. This claim is also quite large, as it amounts to $100,000 worth of Treasury notes and bonds, $1 million worth of Eurodollar deposits and Treasury bills, and $5 million in 30-day interest rate contracts.

Stock-index futures, however, are a bit different, as the seller of one of these contracts is *not* obligated to deliver the *underlying stocks* at expiration date. Instead, ultimate delivery is in the form of cash (which is fortunate, since it would indeed be a task to make delivery of the 1,700 stocks that make up the Value Line Index, or the 500 issues in the S&P index). The commodity underlying stock-index futures, therefore, is *cash*; basically, the amount of underlying cash is set at 500 times the value of the stock index. For example, if the S&P 500 Index stood at 410, the amount of cash underlying a single S&P 500 stock-index futures contract would be $500 \times 410 = \$205,000$. Again, the value is substantial. In terms of delivery months, the lives of financial futures contracts run from about 12 months or less for stock index and currency futures to about 3 years or less for interest rate instruments.

Prices and Profits

All currency futures are quoted in dollars or cents per unit of the underlying foreign currency (for instance, in dollars per British pound or cents per Japanese yen). Thus, according to the closing ("settle") prices in Figure 12.4, one June British pound contract was worth $109,762.50 (62,500 pounds $\times$ $1.7562) and a December Japanese yen was valued at $99,187.50 (since a quote of .7935 cents per yen amounts to less than a penny, we have 12,500,000 yen $\times$ $0.007935). Except for the quotes on Treasury bills and other short-term securities, which will be examined below, interest rate futures contracts are priced as a percentage of the par value of the underlying debt instrument (either Treasury notes or Treasury bonds). Since these instruments are quoted in increments of 1/32 of 1 percent, a quote of 99–31 for the settle price on the June Treasury bonds (in Figure 12.4) translates into $99^{31}/_{32}$—which, when you divide 31 by 32, converts finally into a quote of

CURRENCY

	Open	High	Low	Settle	Change	Lifetime High	Low	Open Interest
JAPAN YEN (IMM)—12.5 million yen; $ per yen (.00)								
Mar	.7975	.7988	.7934	.7944	+ .0014	.8139	.7000	58,709
June	.7964	.7977	.7928	.7933	+ .0016	.8125	.7015	4,586
Sept	....	....		.7930	+ .0018	.8080	.7265	1,709
Dec	....	....		.7935	+ .0021	.8045	.7512	1,623
Mr93	....	....		.7947	+ .0023	.8005	.7960	1,242
Est vol 24,751; vol Tues 20,990; open int 67,869, − 1,232.								
DEUTSCHEMARK (IMM)—125,000 marks; $ per mark								
Mar	.6252	.6275	.6166	.6196	− .0002	.6575	.5353	57,862
June	.6175	.6190	.6095	.6116	− .0004	.6490	.5322	3,953
Sept	....	....		.6048	− .0005	.6400	.5685	673
Dec				.5998	− .0002	.6106	.5645	1,146
Est vol 55,984; vol Tues 30,925; open int 63,636, +1,088.								
CANADIAN DOLLAR (IMM)—100,000 dlrs.; $ per Cdn $								
Mar	.8480	.8510	.8466	.8479	− .0001	.8857	.8253	20,441
June	.8425	.8450	.8413	.8425	− .0001	.8820	.8330	2,129
Sept	....	....		.8375	− .0001	.8774	.8348	150
Est vol 5,792; vol Tues 4,414; open int 22,817, +424.								
BRITISH POUND (IMM)—62,500 pds.; $ per pound								
Mar	1.7892	1.7974	1.7782	1.7822	+ .0072	1.8646	1.5560	22,382
June	1.7630	1.7710	1.7530	1.7562	+ .0068	1.8346	1.6410	2,535
Sept	1.7450	1.7470	1.7310	1.7330	+ .0070	1.8066	1.6740	116
Est vol 17,685; vol Tues 9,153; open int 25,033, +453.								

INTEREST RATE

	Open	High	Low	Settle	Chg	Yield Settle	Chg	Open Interest
TREASURY BONDS (CBT)—$100,000; pts. 32nds of 100%								
Mar	102-07	102-26	101-01	101-02	− 40	7.893	+ .123	298,778
June	101-05	101-23	99-30	99-31	− 40	8.003	+ .125	31,462
Sept	100-18	100-20	98-31	98-31	− 40	8.105	+ .127	8,460
Dec	99-20	99-20	98-01	98-01	− 41	8.202	+ .132	4,436
Mr93	98-26	98-27	97-07	97-07	− 41	8.287	+ .134	1,018
June	98-02	98-02	96-14	96-14	− 42	8.370	+ .039	155
Est vol 450,000; vol Tues 294,659; op int 344,428, −5,833.								
5 YR TREAS NOTES (CBT)—$100,000; pts. 32nds of 100%								
Mar	05-255	06-045	05-095	105-10	− 16	6.731	+ .115	110,118
June	104-28	105-06	104-11	04-115	− 17	6.953	+ .124	4,923
Est vol 28,888; vol Tues 25,364; open int 115,041, −1,678.								
2 YR TREAS NOTES (CBT)—$200,000, pts. 32nds of 100%								
Mar	104-19	04-255	104-15	04-165	− 30	5.582	+ .048	16,345
Est vol 1,200; vol Tues 1,359; open int 16,346, −465.								

	Open	High	Low	Settle	Chg	Discount Settle	Chg	Open Interest
TREASURY BILLS (IMM)—$1 mil.; pts. of 100%								
Mar	96.29	96.29	96.17	96.18	− .04	3.82	+ .04	31,155
June	96.18	96.18	96.03	96.04	− .06	3.96	+ .06	16,457
Sept	95.87	95.92	95.75	95.76	− .05	4.24	+ .05	2,834
Dec	95.39	95.39	95.20	95.20	− .07	4.80	+ .07	996
Est vol 13,450; vol Tues 7,114; open int 51,498, −34.								

INDEX

	Open	High	Low	Settle	Chg	High	Low	Open Interest
S&P 500 INDEX (CME) 500 times index								
Mar	414.60	418.85	408.60	410.90	− 4.55	422.85	372.90	142,484
June	416.00	420.35	410.80	412.35	− 4.55	424.40	374.50	5,076
Sept	418.45	421.50	412.00	413.75	− 4.65	425.50	376.25	419
Dec	419.40	423.50	413.80	415.20	− 4.80	427.25	391.40	345
Est vol 70,509; vol Tues 38,826; open int 148,324, +713.								
Indx prelim High 417.83; Low 409.17; Close 410.34 −4.62								
NYSE COMPOSITE INDEX (NYFE) 500 times index								
Mar	228.70	231.05	225.40	226.80	− 2.35	233.00	205.70	4,451
June	228.90	231.25	227.20	227.35	− 2.40	233.50	206.50	455
Sept	230.50	230.50	230.50	227.90	− 2.50	233.65	212.55	191
Est vol 9,024; vol Tues 3,856; open int 5,107, +349.								
The index: High 230.32; Low 226.17; Close 226.64 −2.31								
MAJOR MKT INDEX (CBT) $500 times index								
Feb	348.50	353.75	344.95	346.35	− 3.50	353.75	311.50	4,888
Mar	348.20	354.00	345.00	346.70	− 3.65	354.00	311.60	308
Apr	353.95	353.95	346.00	347.25	− 3.75	353.95	345.75	102
Est vol 3,000; vol Tues 1,757; open int 4,832, +212.								
The index: High 354.47; Low 345.20; Close 346.23 −4.56								

• FIGURE 12.4 Quotations on Selected Actively Traded Financial Futures

The trading exchange, size of the trading unit, pricing unit, and delivery months are all vital pieces of information included as part of the quotation system used with financial futures. (*Source: The Wall Street Journal,* January 30, 1992.)

99.96875 percent of par. Applying this rate to the par value of the underlying securities, we see that a June Treasury bond contract is worth $99,968.75 (i.e., $100,000 × 0.9996875). Stock index futures are quoted in terms of the actual underlying index, but, as noted above, they carry a face value of $500 times the index.

The value of an interest rate futures contract responds to interest rates exactly like the debt instrument that underlies the contract. That is, when interest rates go up, the value of an interest rate futures contract goes down, and vice versa. However, the quote system for interest rate as well as currency and stock-index futures is set up to reflect the market value of the contract itself. Thus, when the price or quote of a financial futures contract increases, the investor who is long makes money; in contrast, when the price decreases, the short seller makes money. Price behavior is the only source of return to speculators; for even though stocks and debt securities are involved in some financial futures, such contracts have no claim on the dividend and interest income of the underlying issues. Even so, huge profits (or losses) are possible with financial futures due to the equally large size of the contracts. For instance, if the price of Swiss francs goes up by just 2 cents against the dollar, the investor is ahead $2,500, since one futures contract covers 125,000 Swiss francs; likewise, a 3-point drop in the NYSE Composite Index means a $1,500 loss to an investor (3 × $500). When related to the relatively small initial margin deposit required to make transactions in the financial futures markets, such price activity can mean very high rates of return—or very high risk of a total wipeout.

Pricing Futures on Treasury Bills and Other Short-Term Securities

Because Treasury bills and other short-term securities are normally traded in the money market on what is known as a ''discount'' basis, it was necessary to devise a special pricing system that would reflect the actual price movements of these futures contracts. To accomplish this, an **index price** system was developed whereby the yield is subtracted from an index of 100. Thus, a Treasury bill or Eurodollar contract, for example, would be quoted at an index of 94.75 when the yield on the underlying security is 5.25 percent (100.00 − 5.25). Under such a system, when someone buys, say, a T-bill future and the index goes up, that individual has made money; when the index goes down, a short seller has made money. Note also that the 30-day interest rate futures, as well as 90-day T-bill and Eurodollar contracts are all quoted in *basis points,* where 1 basis point equals 1/100 of 1 percent. Thus, a quote of 95.20 (which was the settle price of the December T-bill contract) translates into a T-bill yield of 4.80 percent (100.00 − 95.20).

The index price system traces only the price behavior of the futures contract. To find the *actual price* or *value* of a 90-day T-bill or Eurodollar contract (the two most actively traded short-term contracts), we use the following formula:

index price
technique used to price T-bill (and other short-term securities) futures contracts, which reflects the actual price movements of these futures contracts.

Equation 12.2

$$\begin{array}{c}\text{Price of a 90-day} \\ \text{futures contract}\end{array} = \$1,000,000 - \left(\frac{\text{security's yield} \times 90 \times \$10,000}{360} \right)$$

(A similar formula would be used to find the price of a 30-day interest rate contract, except a value of 30 would be used in the formula's numerator, in place of the 90; everything else would be handled exactly the same as shown in Equation 12.2.)

Notice that this price formula is based not on the quoted price index, but on the *yield of the security itself,* which can be determined by subtracting the price index quote from 100.00. To see how it works, consider a 90-day T-bill futures contract quoted at 95.20; recall this T-bill futures contract is priced to yield 4.80 percent. Now, using Equation 12-2, we can see that the price (or value) of this futures contract is:

$$\begin{array}{rl} \text{Price of 90-day (CD)} & = \$1,000,000 - \left(\dfrac{4.80 \times 90 \times \$10,000}{360}\right) \\ \text{futures contract} & \\ & = \$1,000,000 - \$12,000 \\ & = \underline{\underline{\$988,000}} \end{array}$$

A handy shortcut for *tracking the price behavior* of T-bill or Eurodollar futures contracts is to remember that the price of a 90-day contract will change by $25 for every one basis point change in yield. Thus, when the yield on the underlying 90-day security moves from, say, 4.80 to 4.95 percent, it goes up by 15 basis points and causes the price of the futures contract to drop by $15 \times \$25 = \$375$.

Trading Techniques

Financial futures can be used for three purposes: hedging, spreading, and speculating. Multinational companies and firms that are active in international trade might consider *hedging* with currency or Eurodollar futures, whereas various types of financial institutions and corporate money managers often use interest rate futures for hedging purposes. In either case the objectives are the same: to lock in the best monetary exchange or interest rate possible. In addition, individual investors and portfolio managers use stock-index futures for hedging purposes in order to protect their security holdings against temporary market declines. Financial futures can also be used for *spreading*. This tactic is popular with investors who adopt strategies of simultaneously buying and selling combinations of two or more contracts to form a desired investment position. A type of futures spread is described in the *Investor Insights* box nearby—note in this case that the spread is set up to capture profits from the "January Effect" in the stock market. Finally, financial futures are widely used for *speculation*. As this brief review suggests, although the instruments may differ, the trading techniques used with financial futures are virtually identical to those used with commodities. While all three techniques are widely employed by investors, except for the *Investor Insights* box below, we will illustrate the use of financial futures by speculators and hedgers only. We will first examine speculating in currency and interest rate futures and then look at how these contracts can be used to hedge investments in stocks, bonds, and foreign securities.

Speculating in Financial Futures

Speculators are especially interested in financial futures because of the large size of the futures contracts. For instance, in early 1992, Canadian dollar contracts were worth over $84,000, Treasury notes were going for over $100,000, and Treasury bill contracts were being quoted at close to a million dollars. With contracts of this

Playing the "January Effect" with Stock Index Futures

In an efficient market, an investor should not be able to consistently out-perform the market. And yet we know that certain *market anomalies* do exist, such that knowledgeable investors can take advantage of unusual price patterns that seem to appear with some degree of regularity. One of the most widely-known market anomalies is the so-called *January effect,* in which small stocks typically begin to rally each December, outpacing big stocks, in a phenomenon that extends into January. This occurs after tax-related selling beats prices to bargain-basement levels. But trying to profit from the January effect is dicey at best. That's because playing this price pattern in the most obvious ways (buying and selling small stocks) isn't always so easy. For example, if investors buy just a few small stocks, they might select ones that perform poorly. And when they buy, they frequently pay the highest going price, the "asked price," and usually receive the lower "bid price" when they sell; obviously, this bid-ask penalty can put a real dent in January-effect profits. Then, throw in commissions, and investors are lucky if there's any profit left.

One way small investors can play the January effect *and* minimize transaction costs is to use the futures markets. The Value Line futures contract on the Kansas City Board of Trade is based on an index of 1,665 stocks; of these, 66% have a market value—the total shares outstanding times the market price—of less than $1 billion. Only about 30% of the stocks in the Standard & Poor's 500-stock index have market values below $1 billion. Other indexes top-weighted with big stocks are the New York Stock Exchange Composite Index and the Major Market Index. The difference in composition means the January effect can be exploited *by buying Value Line futures and simultaneously selling futures contracts based on an index with more big stocks, such as the S&P 500.* This kind of futures trade is known as a *spread*.

For instance, if the market really does rally and the January effect works, the Value Line contracts should move up more than the S&P 500 contracts do. If the market falls, the Value Line contracts should fall less than the big-stock index futures do. Either scenario would produce a profit for those holding a spread that consisted of long, or purchased, Value Line futures and short positions in futures based on a big-stock index.

Since 1982, when stock-index futures started trading, this futures strategy has produced a theoretical profit each year the Value Line contract was used as a proxy for small stocks and the S&P 500 represented big stocks. In each case, it was assumed that the trade was instituted on December 15 and closed out on the following January 15. All profit and

size, it obviously does not take much movement in the underlying asset to produce big price swings and therefore big profits. Currency or interest rate futures can be used for just about any speculative purpose. For example, if an investor expects the dollar to be devalued relative to the German mark, she would buy mark currency futures, since the contracts should go up in value. If a speculator anticipates a rise in interest rates, he might consider going short (selling) interest rate futures, since they should go down in value. Because margin is used and financial futures have the loss calculations were made using the prices for March futures contracts. (With a spread, if the market goes up, you'll make money on the long position but lose on the short—the object, of course, is to net out more profit than loss.) The accompanying table lists the track record of this particular futures spread. Note that the largest profit was $2,750 per spread (one contract purchased and one sold short) closed out in January 1991, and the smallest was $275 for a trade closed in 1989, and again in 1992. That's not bad—especially when you consider the minimum capital needed to execute this spread is only $9,500. And with commissions at a discount broker of only $30 to $50, there's still plenty of profit left. Of course, there's no guarantee that the January effect will occur each year. But it's clear that the futures spread described here puts you in a pretty good position to make a nice profit when it does—and, to make at least a little money even if the January effect doesn't occur!

Playing the "January Effect"

One way of playing the January effect involves buying the Value Line contract and simultaneously selling the S&P 500 contract. In this example, trades are entered on December 15 and closed out on January 15, or the first business day following if the 15th falls on a weekend. Calculations don't include commissions.

Entry Date	Exit Date	Profit Value Line vs. S&P 500
12/15/82	1/17/83	$2,275
12/15/83	1/16/84	1,725
12/17/84	1/15/85	2,325
12/16/85	1/15/86	1,800
12/15/86	1/15/87	1,225
12/15/87	1/15/88	2,700
12/15/88	1/16/89	275
12/15/89	1/15/90	675
12/17/90	1/15/91	2,750
12/16/91	1/15/92	275
Average		**$1,600**

Source: Adapted from Stanley W. Angrist, "Futures Offer Cheap Play on Small Stocks' Annual Rally," *The Wall Street Journal,* December 13, 1990, p. C1.

same source of return as commodities (appreciation in the price of the futures contract), return on invested capital is used to measure the profitability of financial futures.

Let's look at an example of a foreign currency contract. Suppose an individual investor feels that the Japanese yen is about to appreciate in value *relative to the dollar.* As a result, this investor decides to buy three September yen contracts at

.6195. Each contract is worth \$77,438 (12,500,000 × 0.006195), so the total market value of three contracts would be \$232,314. Even so, the investor has to deposit only \$6,000 to acquire this position. (Recall from Table 12.2 that the required initial margin for Japanese yen is \$2,000 per contract.) If the price of the yen moves up just a fraction (from .6195 to .6700), the value of the three contracts will rise to \$251,250, and the investor, in a matter of months, will have made a profit of \$18,936. Using Equation 12-1, for return on invested capital, such a profit translates into an enormous 316 percent rate of return. Of course, an even smaller fractional change in the other direction would have wiped out this investment, so it should be clear that *these high returns are not without their equally high risks*.

Now consider an investment in an interest rate future. Assume the investor is anticipating a sharp rise in long-term rates. Because a rise in rates means that interest rate futures will drop in value, the investor decides to short sell two December T-bond contracts at 87–22; this quote translates into a price of 87 22/32, or 87.6875 percent of par. The two contracts are worth \$175,375 (\$100,000 × .876875 × 2), but the amount of money required to make the investment is only \$5,400 (as the initial margin deposit is \$2,700 per contract). Assume that interest rates do in fact move up, and as a result the price on Treasury bond contracts drops to 80. Under such circumstances, the investor would buy back the two December T-bond contracts (in order to cover his short position) and in the process make a profit of \$15,375. (Recall that he originally sold the two contracts at \$175,375 and then bought them back some time later at \$160,000; like any investment, the difference between what you pay for a security and what you sell it for is profit.) In this case, the return on invested capital amounts to a whopping 285 percent. Again, however, this kind of return is due in no small part to the *enormous risk of loss* the investor assumes.

Trading Stock-Index Futures

Most investors use stock-index futures for speculation or hedging. (Stock-index futures are similar to the *index options* introduced in Chapter 11 and, as such, much of the discussion that follows also applies to index options.) Whether speculating or hedging, the key to success is *predicting the future course of the stock market*. Because investors are buying the market with stock-index futures, it is important to get a handle on the future direction of the market via technical analysis (as discussed in Chapter 7) or some other technique. Once an investor feels she has this, she can formulate a stock-index futures trading or hedging strategy. For example, if she feels strongly that the market is headed up, she would want to go long (buy stock-index futures); in contrast, if her analysis of the market suggests a sharp drop in equity values, she could make money by going short (selling stock-index futures). Speculating in this way would prove profitable so long as our investor's expectations about the market actually materialize.

Consider, for instance, an investor who believes the market is undervalued and therefore a move up is imminent. He can try to identify one or a handful of stocks that should go up with the market (and assume the stock selection risks that go along with this approach), or he can buy an S&P 500 stock-index future presently trading at, say, 424.45. To execute such a transaction the speculator need deposit an initial margin of only $9,000. Now, if his expectations are correct and the market does rise so that the S&P 500 Index moves to 440.95 by the expiration of the futures contract, the investor will earn a profit of $8,250: (440.95 − 424.45) × $500 = $8,250. Given that this amount was earned on a $9,000 investment, his return on invested capital would amount to a very respectable 92 percent. Of course, keep in mind that if the market drops by only 18 points (or just 4.2%), the investment will be a *total loss*.

Stock index futures also make excellent hedging vehicles in that they provide investors with a highly effective way of protecting stock holdings in a declining market. Although this tactic is not perfect, it does enable investors to obtain desired protection without disturbing their equity holdings. Here's how a so-called short hedge, which is used to protect an investor's stock portfolio against a decline in the market, would work. Assume an investor holds a total of 2,000 shares of stock in 15 different companies and that the market value of this portfolio is around $110,000. If the investor thinks the market is about to undergo a temporary sharp decline, he can do one of three things: sell his shares, short sell all his stock holdings against the box, or buy puts on each of his stocks. Clearly, these alternatives are cumbersome and/or costly and therefore undesirable for protecting a widely diversified portfolio. The desired results could be achieved, however, by short selling stock-index futures. (Note that basically the same protection can be obtained in this hedging situation by turning to options and buying a *stock index put*.)

Suppose the investor short sells one NYSE stock-index futures contract at 218.75. Such a contract would provide a close match to the current value of the investor's portfolio, as it would be valued at $109,375, and yet it would require an initial margin deposit of only $4,500. (Margin deposits are lower for hedgers than for speculators.) Now, if the NYSE Composite Index does drop to, say, 198.00, the investor will make a profit from the short sale transaction of some $10,000. That is, since the index fell 20.75 points (218.75 − 198.00), the total profit will be: 20.75 × $500 = $10,375. Ignoring taxes, this profit can be added to the portfolio (additional shares of stock can be purchased at their new lower prices), with the net result being a new portfolio position that will approximate the one that existed prior to the decline in the market. How well the "before" and "after" portfolio positions match will depend on how far the portfolio dropped in value. If the average price dropped about $5 per share in our example, the positions will closely match. However, this does not always happen; the price of some stocks will change more than others and therefore the amount of protection provided by this type of short hedge depends on how sensitive the stock portfolio is to movements in the market. Thus, the type of stocks held in the portfolio is an important consideration in structuring the stock-index short hedge. OTC and highly volatile stocks will probably require more protection than stocks that are relatively more price-stable or have betas closer to 1.0. In any event, hedging with stock-index futures can be a low-cost yet effective way of obtaining protection against loss in a declining stock market.

Hedging Other Securities

Just as stock-index futures can be used to hedge stock portfolios, so *interest rate futures* can be used to hedge bond portfolios and *foreign currency futures* can be used with foreign securities as a way to protect against foreign exchange risk. Consider an interest rate hedge: If an investor holds a substantial portfolio of bonds, the last thing he wants to see is a big jump in interest rates, as that could cause a sharp decline in the value of his portfolio. Assume this investor holds nearly $300,000 worth of Treasury and agency issues, with an average (approximate) maturity of 20 years. If he strongly believes that market rates are headed up, he could hedge his bond portfolio by short selling three U.S. Treasury bond futures contracts (since each T-bond futures contract is worth about $100,000, it would take three of them to cover a $300,000 portfolio). Now if rates do head up, his portfolio will be protected against loss—though as we noted with stocks above, the exact amount of protection will depend on how well the T-bond futures contracts parallel the price behavior of this particular bond portfolio.

There is, of course, a downside to all this: i.e., *if market interest rates go down, rather than up, the investor will miss out on potential profits as long as the short hedge position remains in place.* This is so because all or most of the profits being made in the portfolio will be offset by losses from the futures contracts. Actually, this will occur with any type of portfolio (stocks, bonds, or anything else) that's tied to an offsetting short hedge, because when the short hedge is created, it essentially *locks in a position at that point.* Although you don't lose anything when the market falls, you also don't make anything when the market goes up. In either case, the profits you make from one position are offset by losses from the other.

To see how futures contracts can be used to hedge foreign exchange risk, let's assume that an investor just purchased $150,000 worth of German government one-year notes (the investor did this because higher yields were available on the German notes than on comparable U.S. Treasury securities). Now, since these notes are denominated in *deutshe marks,* this investment is subject to loss if currency exchange rates move against the investor—i.e., if the value of the dollar rises relative to the mark. If all the investor wanted was the higher yield offered by the German note, she could basically *eliminate* the currency exchange risk by setting up a currency hedge. Here's how it's done: Let's say at the current exchange rate that one U.S. dollar will ''buy'' 1.65 marks, meaning marks are worth about 60 cents (i.e., $1/1.65 marks = 60¢). If currency contracts on German marks were trading at around $0.60 a mark, our investor would have to sell two contracts in order to protect her $150,000 investment: each German mark contract covers 125,000 marks, so if they're being quoted at .6000, then each contract is worth: $0.60 × 125,000 = $75,000.

Assume one year later the value of the dollar has, in fact, increased, relative to the mark, so that one U.S. dollar will now ''buy'' 1.725 marks. Under such conditions, a German mark futures contract would be quoted at around .5800 (i.e., $1/1.725 = $0.58). At this price, each futures contract would be worth $72,500 (125,000 × $0.58). Each contract, in effect, would be worth $2,500 *less* than it was a year ago, but since the contract was sold short when the hedge was set up, that means the hedger will make a profit of $2,500 per contract—a total profit of $5,000 on the two contracts. Unfortunately, that's *not* net profit, since all this profit will do is offset the loss the investor will incur on her German note investment. In very simple terms, when she sent her $150,000 overseas to buy the German notes, her money was worth 250,000 marks; however, when she brought the money back one year later, those 250,000 marks purchased only 145,000 American dollars. So the investor's out $5,000 on her original investment. Were it not for the currency hedge, this investor would be out the full $5,000, and the return on this investment would be a lot lower. But the hedge covered the loss and the net effect was that the investor was able to enjoy the added yield of the German note, without having to worry about any potential loss from currency exchange rates.

Financial Futures and the Individual Investor

Financial futures can play an important role in an investor's portfolio so long as: (1) the individual thoroughly understands these investment vehicles, (2) he or she clearly recognizes the tremendous risk exposure of such vehicles, and (3) he or she is fully prepared (financially and emotionally) to absorb some losses. Financial futures are highly volatile securities that have enormous profit and loss potential. For instance, in 1991, during an eight-month period of time, the March (1992) S&P 500 futures contract fluctuated in price from a low of 372.90 to a high of 422.85. This range of nearly 50 points for a single contract meant a potential profit, or loss, of nearly $25,000—and all from an initial investment of only $9,000. Investment diversification is obviously essential as a means of reducing the potentially devastating impact of price volatility. Financial futures are exotic investment vehicles, but if properly used they can provide generous returns.

Options on Futures

futures options
options that give the holders the right to buy or sell a single standardized futures contract for a specified period of time at a specified striking price.

The evolution that began with listed stock options and financial futures in time spread to interest rate options and stock-index futures. Eventually, it led to the merger of options and futures and to the creation of the ultimate leverage vehicle: options on futures contracts. Known as **futures options,** they represent listed puts and calls on actively traded futures contracts. In essence, they give the holders the right to buy (with calls) or sell (with puts) a single standardized futures contract for a specific period of time at a specified striking price. Table 12.4 provides a list of the futures options available in early 1992; note that such options are available on both commodities and financial futures. These puts and calls cover the same amount of assets as the underlying futures contracts—for example, 112,000 pounds of sugar, 100 ounces of gold, 62,500 British pounds, or $100,000 in Treasury bonds. Accordingly, they also involve the same amount of price activity as normally found with commodities and financial futures.

Futures options have the same standardized striking prices, expiration dates, and quotation system as other listed options. Depending on the striking price on the option and the market value of the underlying futures contract, these options can also be in-the-money and out-of-the-money. Futures options are valued like other puts and calls—by the difference between the option's striking price and the market price of the underlying futures contract (see Chapter 11). Moreover, they can also

TABLE 12.4 Futures Options: Puts and Calls on Futures Contracts

Commodities	Financial Futures
Corn	British pound
Soybeans	German mark
Soybean meal	Swiss franc
Soybean oil	Japanese yen
Heating oil	Canadian dollar
Gasoline	Australian dollar
Cotton	U.S. dollar index
Sugar	Municipal bond index
Live cattle	Eurodollar deposits
Live hogs	Treasury bills
Feeder cattle	Treasury notes
Pork bellies	Treasury bonds
Lumber	NYSE Composite Index
Orange juice	S&P 500 Stock Index
Cocoa	Major Market Index
Coffee	
Wheat	
Platinum	
Copper	
Gold	
Silver	
Crude oil	

be used like any other listed option, that is, for speculating or hedging, in writing programs, or for spreading.

The biggest difference between a futures option and a futures contract is that *the option limits the loss exposure* to the price of the option. The most you can lose is the price paid for the put or call, whereas there is no real limit to the amount of loss a futures investor can incur. To see how futures options work, consider an investor who wants to trade some gold contracts. She believes that the price of gold will increase over the next nine months from its present level of $355 an ounce to around $400 an ounce. She can buy a futures contract at 364.50 by depositing the required initial margin of $1,300, or she can buy a futures call option with a $350 per ounce strike price that is presently being quoted at, say, 10.75. (Since the underlying futures contract cover 100 ounces of gold, the total cost of this option would be: $10.75 × 100 = $1,075.) The call is an in-the-money option, since the market price of gold exceeds the exercise price on the option. The figures below summarize what happens to both investments if the price of gold reaches $400 per ounce by the expiration date, and in addition, what happens if the price of gold drops by $45 to $310 an ounce:

	Futures Contract		Futures Option	
	Dollar Profit (or Loss)	Return on Invested Capital	Dollar Profit (or Loss)	Return on Invested Capital
If price of gold *increases* by $45 an ounce	$3,550	273.1%	$3,925	365.1%
If price of gold *decreases* by $45 an ounce	($5,450)	—	($650)	—

Clearly, the futures option provides a much higher rate of return as well as a reduced exposure to loss. Futures options offer interesting investment opportunities, but they should be used only by knowledgeable commodities and financial futures investors.

TANGIBLE INVESTMENTS

tangible investment an investment that has an actual form or substance, such as precious metals, stamps, or works of art.

A **tangible investment** is one that can be seen and touched and that has an actual form or substance. Examples of tangible investments include real estate, precious metals and stones, stamps, coins, works of art, antiques, and other-so-called *hard assets*. A *financial asset,* in contrast, is a claim on paper evidencing ownership, debt, or an option to acquire an interest in some intangible or tangible asset. Many investors own tangibles because they can be seen and touched; others prefer them for their investment value. During the decade of the 1970s, particularly in 1978 and 1979, tangible investments soared in popularity. There were several reasons for this. First, the 1970s was a period of very high inflation. Double-digit inflation rates, unknown in the United States since the late 1940s, became commonplace. These high inflation rates made investors nervous about holding financial assets, like money, bank accounts, stocks, and bonds. Their nervousness was heightened by the poor returns financial assets offered in those years. As a result, they turned to investments that offered returns that exceeded the rate of inflation—in other words, to tangibles. The year 1979 in particular was a period of heavy tangibles investing. During that year, inflation soared, and the expectation was for even worse inflation in the future.

In 1981 and 1982, things began to change, however, as interest in tangibles waned and their prices underwent substantial declines. For example, in the 12-month period from June 1981 to June 1982 the price of gold dropped 34 percent, silver plunged 45 percent, and U.S. coins fell almost 30 percent in value. With a few exceptions, the investment returns on tangible investments continued at a substandard pace through the rest of the 1980s and into the 1990s. Such performance, of course, is precisely what you would have expected: These investment vehicles tend to perform very nicely during periods of high inflation, but they don't do nearly so well when inflation drops off—as it has since 1982. Indeed, as Table 12.5

TABLE 12.5 Comparative Rates of Return for Various Investment Vehicles

10 Years, 6/72–6/82	Return	10 Years, 6/82–6/92	Return
Stamps	21.9%	Stocks	18.4%
Gold	18.6	Bonds	15.2
Chinese ceramics	15.3	Old Master paintings	13.3
Silver	13.6	Chinese ceramics	8.5
Diamonds	13.3	3-month Treasury bills	7.6
Real estate	9.9	Diamonds	6.4
Old Master paintings	9.0	Foreign exchange	4.5
Stocks	3.8	Housing	4.0
Bonds	3.6	Gold	0.6

*Investment returns are measured in terms of *average annual* fully compounded rates of return. They represent the effective *annual* yields from these investments; annual returns do *not* include taxes or transaction costs.

Source: Salomon Bros., Inc.

reveals, the investment performance of tangibles from 1972 to 1982 stands in stark contrast to the returns on these same investments from 1981 to 1992. Note especially how stocks and bonds performed in the latest period compared to the decade of the seventies. There's no doubt financial assets are back and that such investments today are more lucrative than most tangible investments. Even so, since there's still a lot of interest in tangibles as investment vehicles, we'll take a brief look at this unusual, but at times highly profitable, form of investing.

Tangible Assets as Investment Outlets

Tangibles are real things: You can sit in an antique car, hold a gold coin, or look at a work of art. Some tangibles, such as gold and diamonds, are portable; others, such as land, are not. These differences can affect the price behavior of tangibles. Land, for example, tends to appreciate fairly rapidly during periods of high inflation and relatively stable international conditions. Gold, on the other hand, is preferred during periods of unstable international conditions, in part because it is portable. Investors appear to believe that if international conditions deteriorate past the crisis point, at least they can "take their gold and run." The market for tangibles varies widely and therefore so too does the *liquidity* of these investments. On one hand we have gold and silver, which can be purchased in a variety of forms and which are generally viewed as being fairly liquid to the extent that it's relatively easy to buy and sell these metals. (To a degree, platinum also falls into this category, since it's widely traded as a futures contract.) On the other hand, we have *all* the other forms of tangible investments, which are highly *illiquid:* They are bought and sold in rather fragmented markets, where transaction costs are very high and where selling an item is often a time-consuming and laborious process.

Alternative Investment Vehicles

One very popular way of investing in tangible assets is to buy *real estate*. Indeed, such investing dwarfs all other forms of tangible investing, and because of its importance, we examine real estate separately in Chapter 14. That still leaves a wide range of investment vehicles to choose from. Excluding real estate, the tangibles market is dominated by three forms of investments:

- Gold and other precious metals (silver and platinum)
- Gemstones (diamonds, rubies, emeralds, sapphires)
- Collectibles (everything from stamps and coins to artworks and antiques)

These are the tangibles that are likely to be of interest to so-called collector-investors.

Investment Merits

The only source of return from a tangible investment comes in the form of *appreciation in value*—capital gains, in other words. There's no current income (dividends or interest) from holding tangible investments. Instead, investors may be facing substantial *opportunity costs,* in the form of lost income that could have been earned on the capital, if their tangibles do not appreciate rapidly in value. Another factor to consider is that most tangibles have *storage* and/or *insurance costs* that require regular cash outlays.

The future prices, and therefore potential returns, on tangible investments tend to be affected by one or more of the following key factors:

- Rate of inflation
- Scarcity (or supply and demand) of the assets
- Domestic and international instability

Because future prices are linked to inflation as well as to the changing supply of these assets, such investments tend to be somewhat risky. A slowdown in inflation or a sizable increase in the supply of the asset can unfavorably affect its market price. On the other hand, increasing inflation and continued scarcity can favorably influence the return. Another factor that tends to affect the market value—and therefore the return—of tangible investments, especially precious metals and gemstones, is the domestic and/or international political environment. In favorable times, these forms of investing are not especially popular, whereas in times of turmoil, their demand tends to rise due to their tangible (and portable) nature.

Investing in Tangibles

Investing in tangibles is, to some extent, no different from investing in securities. Selection and timing are important in both cases and play a key role in determining the rate of return on invested capital. Yet, when investing in tangibles, you have to be careful to separate the economics of the decision from the pleasure of owning these assets. Let's face it, many people gain a lot of pleasure from wearing a diamond, driving a rare automobile, or owning a piece of fine art. There's certainly nothing wrong with that, but when you're buying tangible assets for their *investment merits,* there's only one thing that matters, and that's the economic payoff from the investment. Thus, as a serious investor you must consider expected price appreciation, anticipated holding period, and potential sources of risk. In addition, you should carefully weigh the insurance and storage costs of holding such assets, as well as the potential impact that a lack of a good resale market can have on return. Perhaps most important, *don't start a serious tangibles investment program until you really know what you're doing.* Know what to look for when buying a piece of fine art, a diamond, or a rare coin, and know what separates the good artworks (or diamonds or rare coins) from the rest. In the material that follows, we look at tangibles strictly as *investment vehicles.*

Gold and Other Precious Metals

precious metals
tangible assets, like
gold, silver, and plat-
inum, that concen-
trate a great deal of
value in a small
amount of weight
and volume.

Precious metals concentrate a great deal of value in a small amount of weight and volume. In other words, just a small piece of a precious metal is worth a lot of money. There are three kinds of **precious metals** that command the most investor attention: gold, silver, and platinum. Of these three, silver is the cheapest (far *less* expensive than either gold or platinum, which were about equally priced in early 1992); gold is, by far, the most popular. Thus, we'll use gold here as the principal vehicle to discuss precious metals. For thousands of years, people have been fascinated with gold. Records from the age of the pharaohs in Egypt show a desire to own gold. Today ownership of gold is still regarded as a necessity by many investors, although its price has dropped considerably since the January 1980 peak of $875 per ounce. Actually, Americans are relatively recent gold investors, due to the legal prohibition on gold ownership, except in jewelry form, that existed from the mid-1930s until January 1, 1975.

Like other forms of precious metals, gold is a highly speculative investment vehicle whose price has fluctuated widely in recent years (see Figure 12.5). Many investors hold at least a part—and at times, a substantial part—of their portfolios in gold as a hedge against inflation and/or a world economic or political disaster. Gold can be purchased as coins, bullion, or jewelry (all of which can be physically held); it can also be purchased though gold futures (and futures options), gold mining stocks, mutual funds, and gold certificates. Here's a brief run down of the different ways that gold can be held as a form of investing:

- **Gold Coins.** Gold coins have little or no collector value; rather, their value is determined primarily by the quality and amount of gold in the coins. Popular gold coins include the American Eagle, the Canadian Maple Leaf, the Mexican 50-Peso, and the Chinese Panda.
- **Gold Bullion.** Gold bullion is gold in its basic ingot (bar) form. Bullion ranges in weight from 5-gram to 400-gram bars; the kilo bar (which weighs 32.15 troy ounces) is probably the most popular size.

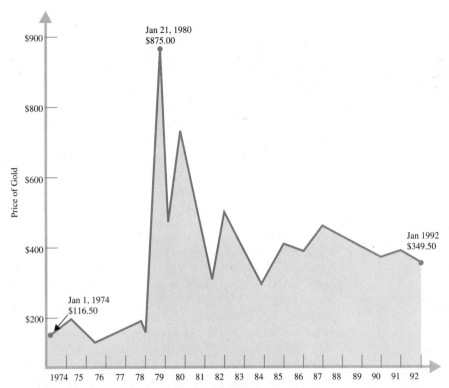

• FIGURE 12.5 The Price of Gold, 1974–1992

The price of gold is highly volatile and can pave the way to big profits or, just as easily, subject the investor to enormous losses.

- **Gold Jewelry.** Jewelry is a popular way to own gold, but it's not a very good way to *invest* in gold, because gold jewelry usually sells for a substantial premium over its underlying gold value (to reflect artisan costs, retail markups, and other factors). Moreover, most jewelry is not pure 24-carat gold but a 14- or 18-carat *blend* of gold and other nonprecious metals.
- **Gold Futures.** A popular way of investing in the short-term price volatility of gold is through futures contracts or futures options.
- **Gold Stocks and Mutual Funds.** Many investors prefer to purchase shares of gold-mining companies or mutual funds that invest in *gold stocks*. The prices of gold-mining stocks tend to move in direct relationship to the price of gold. Thus, if gold rises in value, these stocks usually move up too. It is also possible to purchase shares in mutual funds that invest primarily in gold-mining stocks. Gold funds offer not only professional management but a much higher level of portfolio diversification; the shares of gold-oriented mutual funds also tend to fluctuate along with the price of gold.
- **Gold Certificates.** A convenient and safe way to own gold is to purchase a gold certificate through a bank or broker. The certificate represents ownership

of a specific quantity of gold that is stored in a bank vault. In this way, investors do not have to be concerned about the safety that taking physical possession of gold entails; also, by purchasing gold certificates, investors can avoid state sales taxes (which may be imposed on coin or bullion purchases).

Like gold, silver and platinum can also be bought in a variety of forms. Silver can be purchased as bags of silver coins, bars or ingots, futures contracts, futures options, or stock shares. Similarly, platinum can be bought in the form of plates and ingots, coins, futures contracts, and platinum stocks.

Transaction costs in precious metals vary widely, depending on the investment form chosen. At one extreme, an investor buying one Canadian Maple Leaf coin might pay 5 percent commission, 7 percent dealer markup, and 4 percent gross excise tax (sales tax). In contrast, the purchase of a gold certificate would entail only a 2 percent total commission and markup, with no sales tax. Storage costs vary as well. Gold coins and bars can easily be stored in a safety deposit box that costs perhaps $20 per year. Gold purchased via gold certificates usually is subject to a storage fee of less than 1 percent per year. Gold coins, bullion, and jewelry can be easily stolen, so it is imperative that these items be safely stored. A safety deposit box at a bank or other depository can alleviate this worry. Except for transaction costs, the other expenses of buying and holding gold can be avoided when investments are made in gold futures and in gold mining stocks and mutual funds.

Gemstones

gemstones
diamonds and colored precious stones (rubies, sapphires, and emeralds).

By definition, **gemstones** consist of diamonds and the so-called colored precious stones (rubies, sapphires, and emeralds). Precious stones offer their owners beauty and are often purchased for psychic and aesthetic pleasure. However, diamonds and colored stones also serve as a viable form of investing. Along with gold, they are among the oldest of investment vehicles, providing a source of real wealth, as well as a hedge against political and economic uncertainties. However, diamonds and colored stones are very much a specialist's domain. Generally, standards of value are fully appreciated only by experienced personnel at fine stores, dealers, cutters, and an occasional connoisseur-collector. In diamonds, the value depends on the whiteness of the stone and the purity of crystallization. A key factor, therefore, is for the purchaser to understand the determinants of quality. Precious stones will vary enormously in price, depending on how close they come to gem color and purity.

Investment diamonds and colored stones can be purchased through registered gem dealers. Depending on quality and grade, commissions and dealer markups can range from 20 to 100 percent. Due to the difficulty in valuing gemstones, it is imperative to select only dealers with impeccable reputations. As investment vehicles, colored stones and diamonds offer no current income, but their prices are *highly* susceptible to changing market conditions. For example, the peak price of a one-carat flawless diamond, a popular investment diamond, was about $60,000 in early 1980. By late 1982, this stone was worth only about $20,000—a drop of 67 percent in just over two years. The big difficulty in precious stone investments, aside from the expertise needed in deciding what is in fact gem quality, is the relative *illiquidity* of the stones. As a rule gemstones should be purchased only by investors who can hold them for at least two years: High transaction costs usually prevent profitable resale after shorter periods. Furthermore, gemstones can be difficult to resell, and sellers often wait a month or more for a sale. Diamonds and colored stones also require secure storage, and there are no payoffs prior to sale.

Collectibles

collectibles
items that have value because of their attractiveness to collectors and because of their relative scarcity and historical significance.

Collectibles represent a broad range of items (from coins and stamps, to cars and posters) that are desirable for any number of reasons, such as beauty, scarcity, and age. A **collectible** has value because of its attractiveness to collectors. During the 1970s, many collectibles shot up in value, but since the early 1980s, most have either fallen in value or have appreciated at a much lower rate than inflation. There are some exceptions, of course, but they remain just that—the exception rather than the rule. Some examples of collectibles that did well in the 1980s are paintings, exotic automobiles and early muscle cars, cartoon celluloids, and baseball cards (as described in the accompanying *Investor Insights* box).

In general, collectibles are *not* very liquid. Their resale markets are poor, and transaction costs can be very high. Artwork, for example, commonly has a 100 percent dealer markup, and sales tax is added to the retail price. (Works sold on consignment to dealers have much lower costs—generally a commission of "only" 25 percent—but they can take months to sell.) In addition, investing in collectibles can be hazardous unless the investor understands the intricacies of the market. In this area of investing, *one is well advised to become a knowledgeable collector before even attempting to be a serious investor in collectibles*. Despite these obstacles, collectibles can provide highly competitive rates of return and can be good inflation hedges during periods of abnormally high inflation.

An investment-grade collectible is an item that is relatively scarce as well as historically significant within the context of the collectible genre itself, and, preferably, within the larger context of the culture that produced it. Further, it should be in excellent condition and attractive to display. Although there are almost no bounds to what can be collected (for example, beer cans, fishing tackle, magazines, and sheet music), the major categories of collectibles that tend to offer the greatest investment potential include:

- Rare coins (*numismatics*)
- Rare stamps (*philately*)
- Artwork (the paintings, prints, sculpture, and crafts of recognized artists)
- Antiques (cars, furniture, and so on)
- Baseball cards
- Books
- Games, toys, and comic books
- Posters
- Movie memorabilia
- Historical letters

INVESTOR INSIGHTS

There's More to Baseball Cards Than R.B.I.s and E.R.A.s

One of the most publicized tangible investments is baseball cards. Collectors of these cards can begin with little money and not much special expertise and still reap good results. A 1988 study in *The Wall Street Journal* reported a 43% compounded annual rate of return between 1980 and 1987 for baseball cards. Another study found card prices rose 32% a year from 1978 to 1988. No wonder the cards catch investor interest.

Perhaps the most famous baseball cards are those of Honus Wagner, a Pittsburgh Pirates shortstop in the early 1900s. A 1910 Honus Wagner card sold in 1987 for $110,000; its estimated worth in 1990 was $300,000. Although Wagner *is* in the Hall of Fame, the price of his cards is probably explained by scarcity: fewer than a hundred such cards are known to exist. Similarly, a rare 1932 Freddy Lindstrom card is valued at $1 million. Cards of more recent players are more affordable, yet highly prized: a 1952 rookie-year card of Mickey Mantle is valued at around $7,000; Nolan Ryan's 1968 rookie card sells for about $1,000; and the 1984 rookie card of Don Mattingly sells for about $80. As with any investment, the law of supply and demand applies. Some of the huge prices of older cards are determined by the fact that there just aren't many of them available.

Cards were first issued as promotions in the 1880s by U.S. cigarette companies. Production stopped during both World Wars and was started again in 1948 by gum and candy companies. Topps, now the market leader and the only company that still offers bubble gum along with its cards, began producing cards in 1951. Its first complete set was issued in 1952 with 407 cards, including the rookie cards of both Mickey Mantle and Willie Mays. Such a set today would be worth as much as $40,000. Baseball card companies no longer release information on the number of cards printed and distributed. Estimates of annual production range from 600,000 to 5 million per player and 5 billion total.

Baseball cards are traded by over one million serious collectors through some 3,500 retail card stores and 10,000 other dealers such as card shows and flea markets. There seem to be two main groups of card collectors: 25- to 45-year-old middle- to upper-income males and young traders, aged 6 to 16 years. The market for cards is largely driven by demand. For example, middle-aged collectors seldom sell their cards; when they do, it is typically to buy other cards.

Various forms of collecting often provide pleasure and satisfaction as well as attractive returns. However, although certain psychic income may be realized in the form of aesthetic pleasure, the financial return, if any, is realized only when the item is sold. While the acquisition of collectibles commonly stems from an individual's personal interest, on a strictly financial basis, items that have a good market and are likely to appreciate in value are the ones to collect. If an item under consideration is expensive, *its value and authenticity should always be confirmed by an expert prior to purchase* (there are many unscrupulous dealers in collectible items). And after purchase, one should make certain to store collectibles in a safe place and adequately insure them against all relevant perils.

A 1991 study by Dilip D. Kare and Kenneth M. Jennings sought to answer two key questions facing baseball card investors: (1) Which player's cards provide a maximum of return, and (2) which year in the sequence of that player's cards performs best? Kare and Jennings restricted their study to 28 well-known players in the major leagues. These players were divided into two groups: modern players (careers started in 1960s) and earlier players (late 1940s or early 1950s). All players in the study had name recognition through membership or likelihood of membership in the Hall of Fame.

Kare and Jennings plotted the price of individual cards against the age of the cards, using price data from the *Beckett Baseball Card Monthly,* the baseball collectors' bluebook. They found a clear relationship between the price and age of the card: as a card aged, it increased in price at a constant rate. They also found, for the 28 "blue chip" cards studied, that the group of earlier players had a lower average return than did the group of 17 modern players. The top performing card in the study was Tom Seaver's, with an average return of 45.5%. The lesson for collectors: The cards of "modern" players perform better, on average, than those of the players from the earlier generation. That finding appears to conflict with the actual returns cited earlier for rare cards but can perhaps be explained by the law of demand—as baby boomers move into the group of middle-aged collectors, they want the cards of players they remember from their childhood and youth, thus increasing demand. The year in which the card was printed—whether the rookie season or otherwise—was not found to be material to the card's return. Finally, the study found that, contrary to popular wisdom, an investment in non-mint cards (cards that may be tattered) of "blue-chip" players provided essentially the same rate of return as cards in mint condition.

An obvious conclusion to be drawn from the Kare/Jennings study is that the most important consideration in baseball card collecting is choosing the right player. This choice offers card collectors, whatever their age, the opportunity to display considerable fervor over the merits of various players and show off their baseball expertise. One other certain conclusion can be drawn: If she hasn't already done so, don't let your mom throw out your set of cards the next time she cleans out the attic!

Source: Based on Dilip D. Kare and Kenneth M. Jennings, "Avoiding the Strikeouts in Baseball Card Investing, *AAII Journal,* July 1991, pp. 7–10; and David R. Krause, "Baseball Cards Bat .425," *Money,* June 1988, pp. 140–47.

SUMMARY

1. Commodities and financial futures are traded in the futures market, a market that has its roots in the agricultural segment of our economy. Today there are 12 exchanges that deal in futures contracts, which are commitments to make (or take) delivery of a certain amount of some real or financial asset at a specified date in the future.

2. From the investor's point of view, the key fact about futures contracts is that they control large amounts of the underlying commodity or financial instrument and, as a result, can produce wide price swings and very attractive rates of return (or very unattractive losses); such returns (or losses) are further magnified since all trading in the futures market is done on margin. Whereas a speculator's profit is derived directly from the

wide price fluctuations that occur in the market, hedgers derive their profit from the protection they gain against adverse price moves.

3. Commodities like grains, metals, meat, and wood make up the traditional (commodities) segment of the futures market. Financial futures are the newcomers to the futures market. Trading in these vehicles did not begin until 1972, but even so, this segment of the market has grown to the point that the volume of trading in financial futures now exceeds that of commodities. In addition to the traditional futures contracts, there's also a growing interest in futures options: a type of trading vehicle that combines the features of both options and futures.

4. The same trading strategies are used with both commodities and financial futures; that is, they can be used for speculating, spreading, or hedging. Irrespective of whether investors are in a long or short position, they have only one source of return from commodities and financial futures: appreciation (or depreciation) in the price of the contract. Investors use the rate of return on invested capital to assess the actual or potential profitability of a futures transaction.

5. There are three types of financial futures: currency futures, interest rate futures, and stock-index futures. The first type deals in several different kinds of foreign currencies. Interest rate futures, in contrast, involve various types of short- and long-term debt instruments, like Treasury bonds and Treasury bills. Stock-index futures are contracts pegged to broad movements in the stock market, as measured by such indexes as the S&P 500 or the NYSE Composite Index. These securities are often used to hedge other security positions—for example, interest rate futures contracts are widely used to protect bond portfolios against a big jump in market interest rates, and currency futures are used to hedge the foreign currency exposure that accompanies investments in foreign securities.

6. Tangible assets represent a special type of investment vehicle, which can be seen and touched and have an actual form and substance. Excluding real estate, the three basic types of tangible investments include precious metals (gold, silver, and platinum); gemstones (diamonds and colored stones); and collectibles (coins, stamps, baseball cards, artwork, and so on). Although tangible investments were able to provide substantial returns in the 1970s, with few exceptions, they haven't done nearly so well in the past 10 or 12 years.

QUESTIONS

1. What is a futures contract? Briefly explain how it is used as an investment vehicle.

2. Discuss the difference between a cash market and a futures market.

   a. Note some of the reasons why the futures market has become so popular.
   b. What effect does inflation have on the futures market?
   c. What is the difference between a futures contract and a forward contract?

3. What is the major source of return to commodities speculators? How important are various types of current income like dividends and interest to these investors?

4. Using settle prices from Figure 12.2, find the value of the following commodity contracts:

   a. July barley.
   b. February ('93) gold.

    c. August soybeans.

    d. November orange juice.

5. Why are both hedgers and speculators so important to the efficient operation of a futures market.

6. Explain how margin trading is conducted in the futures market.

    a. What is the difference between an initial deposit and a maintenance deposit?

    b. Are investors ever required to put up additional margin? When?

    c. What is the effect of margin trading on an investor's rate of return?

7. Note and briefly define the five essential parts of a commodity contract. Which parts have a direct bearing on the price behavior of the contract?

8. Briefly define each of the following:

    a. Settle price.

    b. Daily price limit.

    c. Open interest.

    d. Maximum daily price range.

    e. Delivery month.

9. Note several approaches to investing in commodities and explain the investment objectives of each.

10. What is the difference between physical commodities and financial futures? What are their similarities?

11. Describe a currency future and contrast it with an interest rate future. What is a stock index future, and how can it be used by investors?

12. What is program trading? What kind of futures contracts are used in program trading? Does program trading have any impact on the price behavior of common stocks? Explain.

13. Explain why it is so important that an individual be well versed in the behavior and investment characteristics of commodities and financial futures. Why should futures holdings be well diversified?

14. Discuss how stock-index futures can be used for speculation and for hedging. What advantages are there to speculating with stock-index futures rather than specific issues of common stock?

15. What are futures options? Explain how they can be used by speculators. Why, for example, would an investor want to use an option on an interest rate futures contract rather than the futures contract itself?

16. Compare and contrast financial assets with tangible assets as investment vehicles. Explain the widespread popularity of tangible investments during the 1970s, and describe the conditions that tend to cause tangibles to rise in price and hence find favor with investors.

17. Identify and briefly discuss the three major classes of tangible investments. Note some of the popular forms of collectibles; what are the key variables that should be taken into account when investing in collectibles?

18. Suppose Eastman Kodak has just announced a new film that does not require silver in its manufacture or development. How do you suppose this development will affect silver bullion prices? Silver mining stock prices?

PROBLEMS

1. Using Figures 12.2 and 12.4, indicate how much profit or loss you would make in the following transactions:

   a. You buy three yen contracts at a quote of .7940 and sell them a few months later at .8125.
   b. The price of orange juice goes up 60 cents a pound, and you hold 3 contracts.
   c. You short sell two copper contracts at $1.30 a pound, and the price of copper drops to $1.05 a pound.
   d. You recently purchased a 90-day Treasury bill contract at 96.20, and T-bill interest rates rise to 4.50%.
   e. You short four Major Market contracts when the index is at 346.55 and cover when the index moves to 321.95.
   f. You short sell three cotton contracts at 54 cents a pound and the price of cotton goes up to 62½ cents a pound.

2. Kirk O'Malley considers himself to be a shrewd commodities investor. For instance, not long ago he bought one July cotton contract at 54 cents a pound and recently sold it at 58 cents a pound. How much profit did he make? What was his return on invested capital if he had to put up a $1,500 initial deposit?

3. Mrs. Shirley Ledbetter is a regular commodities speculator; she is presently considering a short position in July oats, which are now trading at 148. Her analysis suggests that July oats should be trading at about 140 in a couple of months. Assuming her expectations hold up, what kind of return on invested capital would she make if she shorts three July oats contracts (with each contract covering 5,000 bushels of oats) by depositing an initial margin of $500 per contract?

4. Explain the index price system used with Treasury bill futures contracts. Also, find the value of the following financial futures contracts:

   a. September German marks quoted at .5392.
   b. December Treasury bonds that settled at 87-22.
   c. March 90-day T-bills quoted at 93.55.
   d. June S&P 500 index that opened at 462.15.
   e. May 30-day interest rate contracts quoted at 96.25.

5. Walt Benaski is thinking about doing some speculating in interest rates; he thinks rates will fall and in so doing, the price of Treasury bond futures should move from 92-15, their present quote, to a level of about 98. Given a required margin deposit of $2,000 per contract, what would Walt's return on invested capital be if prices behave as he expects?

6. Judi Jordan has been an avid stock market investor for years; she manages her portfolio fairly aggressively and likes to short sell whenever the opportunity presents itself. Recently, she has become fascinated with stock-index futures, especially the idea of being able to play the market as a whole. At the present time, Judi thinks the market is headed down, and she decides to short sell some NYSE Composite stock-index futures. Assume she shorts three contracts at 287.95 and that she has to make a margin deposit of $6,000 for each contract. How much profit will she make, and what will her return on invested capital be if the market does indeed drop so that the NYSE contracts are trading at 265.00 by the time they expire?

7. A wealthy investor holds $500,000 worth of U.S. Treasury bonds; these bonds are currently being quoted at par (100). The investor is concerned, however, that rates are headed up over the next 6 months, and he would like to do something to protect this bond portfolio. His

broker advises him to set up a hedge using T-bond futures contracts; assume these contracts are presently trading at 101-06.

 a. Briefly describe how the investor would set up this hedge—would he go long or short, and how many contracts would he need?
 b. It's now 6 months later and rates have, indeed, gone up! The investor's Treasury bonds are now being quoted at 91½, and the T-bond futures contract used in the hedge are now trading at 94-00. Show what has happened to the value of the bond portfolio *and* the profit (or loss) made on the futures hedge.
 c. Was this a successful hedge? Explain.

8. Not long ago, Joan Atwood sold the company she founded for several million dollars (after taxes); she took some of that money and put it into the stock market. Today, Joan's portfolio of blue-chip stocks is worth $2.3 million. Joan wants to keep her portfolio intact, but she's concerned about a developing weakness in the market for blue chips. She decides, therefore, to hedge her position with 6-month futures contracts on the Major Market Index (MMI), which is currently trading at 460.

 a. Why would she choose to hedge her portfolio with the Major Market Index rather than the S&P 500?
 b. Given that Joan wants to cover the full $2.3 million in her portfolio, describe how she would go about setting up this hedge.
 c. If each contract required a margin deposit of $7,500, how much money would she need to set up this hedge?
 d. Assume that over the next 6 months stock prices do fall, and the value of Joan's portfolio drops to $2.0 million. If MMI futures contracts are trading at 391, how much will she make (or lose) on the futures hedge? Is it enough to offset the loss in her portfolio—i.e., what's her *net* profit or loss on the hedge?
 e. Will she now get her margin deposit back, or is that like a "sunk cost" and gone forever?

9. An American currency speculator feels strongly that the value of the Canadian dollar is going to fall relative to the U.S. dollar over the short-run. If he wants to profit from these expectations, what kind of a position (long or short) would he take in Canadian dollar futures contracts? How much money would he make from each contract if Canadian dollar futures contracts moved from an initial quote of .8775 to an ending quote of .8250?

10. With regard to *futures options,* how much profit would an investor make if she bought a call option on gold at 7.20 when gold was trading at $482 an ounce, given that the price of gold went up to $525 an ounce by the expiration date on the call? (*Note:* Assume the call carried a strike price of 480.)

CFA QUESTION (This question is from the 1991 Level II Exam.)

CFA

Robert Chen, CFA, is reviewing the characteristics of derivative securities and their use in portfolios. He is considering the addition of either a short position in stock index futures or a long position in stock index options to an existing well-diversified portfolio of equity securities. Contrast the way in which *each* of these *two* alternatives would affect the risk and return of the resulting combined portfolios.

(See Appendix C for Guideline Answer to this question.)

CASE PROBLEMS

12.1 T. J.'s Fast Track Investments: Interest Rate Futures

T. J. Patrick is a successful industrial designer who enjoys the excitement of commodities speculation. Although only 29 years old, T. J. has been dabbling in commodities since he was a teenager. He was introduced to it by his dad, who is a grain buyer for one of the leading food processors. T. J. recognizes the enormous risks involved in commodities speculating but feels that since he's still single, now is the perfect time to take chances. And he can well afford to, as this resident of Portland, Oregon, is a principal in a thriving industrial design firm. T. J.'s income ranges between $60,000 and $75,000 per year—enough to allow him to enjoy some of the finer things in life. Even so, he does follow a well-disciplined investment program and annually adds $10,000 to $15,000 to his portfolio.

Recently, T. J. has started playing with financial futures—interest rate futures, to be exact. He admits he is no expert in interest rates, but likes the price action these investment vehicles offer. This all started several months ago when T. J. was at a party and became acquainted with Vinnie Banano, a broker who specializes in financial futures. T. J. liked what Vinnie had to say (mostly how you couldn't go wrong with interest rate futures), and set up a trading account with Vinnie's firm: Banano's of Portland. The other day, Vinnie called T. J. and suggested he get into T-bill futures. As Vinnie saw it, interest rates were going to continue to head up at a brisk pace, and T. J. should short sell some 90-day T-bill futures. In particular, he thinks that rates on T-bills should go up by another half-point (moving from about 5½ up to 6 percent) and recommends that T. J. short four contracts. This would be a $4,000 investment, since each contract requires an initial margin deposit of $1,000.

Questions

1. Assume 90-day T-bill futures are now being quoted at 94.35.
   a. Determine the current price (underlying value) of this T-bill futures contract.
   b. What would this futures contract be quoted at if Vinnie is right and the yield goes up by ½ of 1 percent?

2. How much profit would T. J. make if he shorts four contracts at 94.35, and T-bill yields do go up by ½ of 1 percent—that is, if T. J. covers his short position when T-bill futures contracts are quoted at 93.85? Also, calculate the return on invested capital from this transaction.

3. What happens if rates go down? For example, how much would T. J. make if the yield on T-bill futures goes down by just ¼ of 1 percent?

4. What risks do you see in the recommended short sale transaction? What is your assessment of T. J.'s new interest in financial futures; how do you think it compares to his established commodities investment program.

12.2 Jim Parker Tries Hedging with Stock-Index Futures

Jim Parker and his wife, Polly, live in Birmingham, Alabama. Like many young couples today, the Parkers are a two-income family, as both are college graduates and hold well-paying jobs. Jim has been an avid investor in the stock market for a number of years and over time has built up a portfolio that is currently worth nearly $115,000. The Parker's portfolio is well balanced: it contains quality growth stocks, some high-income utilities, and a small amount of moderately speculative stock. The Parkers reinvest all dividends and regularly add investment capital to their portfolio; up to now, they have avoided short selling and do only a modest amount of margin trading.

Their portfolio has undergone a substantial amount of capital appreciation in the last 18 months or so, and Jim is anxious to protect the profit they have earned. And that's the problem! For Jim feels the market has pretty much run its course and is about to enter a period of decline. Parker has studied the market and economic news very carefully, and as a result does not believe the retreat will be of a major magnitude or cover an especially long period of time. He feels fairly certain, however, that most, if not all, of the stocks in his portfolio will be adversely affected by these market conditions—though they certainly won't all be affected to the same degree (some will drop more in price than others). Jim has been following stock index futures since they were first introduced in 1982. He's done some investing in them (with a moderate amount of success) and feels he knows the ins and outs of these securities pretty well. After careful deliberation, Jim decides to use stock-index futures—in particular, the NYSE Composite futures contract—as a way to protect (hedge) his portfolio of common stocks.

Questions

1. Explain why Parker would want to use stock-index futures to hedge his stock portfolio and note how he would go about setting up such a hedge; be specific.
   a. What alternatives does Jim have to protect the capital value of his portfolio?
   b. What are the benefits and risks of using stock-index futures for such purposes (as hedging vehicles)?

 2. Presume NYSE Composite futures contracts are presently being quoted at 225.60. How many contracts would Parker have to buy (or sell) to set up the hedge?
   a. If the value of the Parker portfolio dropped 12 percent over the course of the market retreat, to what price must the stock-index futures contract move in order to cover that loss?
   b. Given that a $6,000 margin deposit is required to buy or sell a single NYSE futures contract, what would be the Parkers' return on invested capital if the price of the futures contract changes by the amount computed in part 2(a)?

3. Assume the value of the Parker portfolio declined by $12,000, while the price of a NYSE Composite futures contract moved from 225.60 to 207.60 (assume Jim short sold one futures contract to set up the hedge).
   a. Add the profit from the hedge transaction to the new (depreciated) value of the stock portfolio; how does this compare to the $115,000 portfolio that existed just before the market started its retreat?
   b. Why did the stock-index futures hedge fail to give complete protection to the Parker portfolio? Is it possible to obtain *perfect* (dollar-for-dollar) protection from these types of hedges? Explain.

4. What if, instead of hedging with futures contracts, Parker decides to set up the hedge by using *futures options?* Suppose a put on a NYSE Composite futures contract (strike price = 225) is presently quoted at 5.80, while a comparable call is being quoted at 2.35. Use the same portfolio and futures price conditions as set out in question 3 (above) to determine how well the portfolio would be protected. (*Hint:* Add the net profit from the hedge to the new depreciated value of the stock portfolio.) What are the advantages and disadvantages of using futures options to hedge a stock portfolio, rather than the stock-index futures contract itself?

OTHER POPULAR INVESTMENT VEHICLES

THE INVESTMENT ENVIRONMENT

INVESTMENT ADMINISTRATION

INVESTING IN COMMON STOCK

INVESTING IN FIXED-INCOME SECURITIES

SPECULATIVE INVESTMENT VEHICLES

OTHER POPULAR INVESTMENT VEHICLES

P A R T   F I V E   I N C L U D E S

13 Mutual Funds: An Indirect Route to the Market

After studying this chapter, you should be able to:

1. Describe the features and basic characteristics of mutual funds, and explain how diversification and professional management are the cornerstones of the industry.

2. Explain the advantages and disadvantages of investing in mutual funds.

3. Discuss the types of funds available and the variety of investment objectives these funds seek to fulfill.

4. Identify and discuss the different kinds of investor services offered by mutual funds, and how these services can fit into an investment program.

5. Gain an appreciation of the investor uses of mutual funds, along with the variables that should be considered when assessing and selecting funds for investment purposes.

6. Identify the sources of return and compute the rate of return earned on an investment in a mutual fund.

Questions of which stock or bond to select, when to buy, and when to sell have plagued investors for as long as there have been organized capital markets. Such concerns lie at the very heart of the mutual fund concept and explain, in large part, the growth mutual funds have experienced. Many investors lack the time, the know-how, or the commitment to manage their own portfolios. As a result, they turn to others. More often than not, that means the professional portfolio management of mutual funds.

There are mutual funds available to meet just about any type of investment objective. These funds can be used to accumulate wealth, as a storehouse of value, or as a means of seeking high returns. Mutual funds are truly versatile investment vehicles with much to offer investors—not only those with limited resources but well-heeled, seasoned investors as well. We will now take a close look at the operating characteristics, sources of return, uses, and limitations of mutual funds. We begin by looking at the mutual fund concept, and some of the basic characteristics of mutual funds and mutual fund ownership.

THE MUTUAL FUND PHENOMENON

The first mutual fund in this country was started in Boston in 1924. By 1940 there were 68 funds with $448 million in assets and nearly 300,000 shareholder accounts. But that was only the beginning: By 1991, assets under management had grown to over $1.4 *trillion,* as more than 63 *million* investors held shares in over 3,200 publicly traded mutual funds. Actually, most of the growth in the mutual fund industry has occurred since the late 1970s, as fund assets mushroomed from just over $55 billion in 1978 to well over a trillion dollars in the early '90s. Three key developments took place to stimulate such growth: First, money market mutual funds experienced explosive growth. Second, there was the introduction of self-directed individual retirement accounts (IRAs), which in itself created a strong demand for mutual fund products. Third, the stock and bond markets benefited from a number of factors (including sharply reduced inflation) that led to record-breaking performances. Investors in unprecedented numbers began coming to the market, and the mutual fund industry responded by developing new products and new funds. So many new products were created, in fact, that *there are now more mutual funds in existence than there are stocks on the NYSE.*

Mutual fund investors come from all walks of life and all income levels. They range from highly inexperienced to highly experienced investors who all share a common view: Each has decided, for one reason or another, to turn over all or a part of their investment management activities to professionals. The widespread acceptance of the mutual fund concept has, in itself, been something of a phenomenon. From rather meager beginnings only a few decades ago, mutual funds have grown so that they are today a powerful force in the securities markets and a major financial institution in our economy. And, by the way, although we tend to think of mutual funds as an American phenomenon, the fact is that mutual funds, in one form or another, are found in all the major markets in the world. Indeed, in 1990, there was $1.1 trillion in assets under management in foreign funds, an amount nearly equivalent to the assets in U.S. funds.

An Overview of Mutual Funds

Mutual funds are popular because they offer not only a variety of interesting invest-ment opportunities but also a wide array of services that many investors find appeal-ing. Basically, a **mutual fund** is a type of financial service organization that re-ceives money from its shareholders and then invests those funds on their behalf in a diversified portfolio of securities. An investment in a mutual fund, therefore, repre-sents an *ownership position in a professionally managed portfolio of securities*. When you buy shares in a mutual fund, you become a part owner of a portfolio of securities.

mutual fund
an investment com-pany that invests its shareholders' money in a diversified port-folio of securities.

Pooled Diversification

The mutual fund concept is based on the simple idea of turning the problems of security selection and portfolio management over to professional money managers. In essence, a mutual fund is a type of **investment company** that combines the investment capital of many people with similar investment goals and invests the funds for those individuals in a wide variety of securities. (In an abstract sense, you might think of a mutual fund as the *financial product* that's sold to the public by an investment company. That is, the investment company builds and manages a portfo-lio of securities, and then sells ownership interests in that portfolio through a vehicle known as a mutual fund.) Investors receive shares of stock in the mutual fund and, through the fund, are able to enjoy much wider investment diversification than they could otherwise achieve. To appreciate the extent of such diversification, one need only look at Figure 13.1. It provides a partial list of the securities actually held in the portfolio of a major mutual fund (actually, just one page of a 15-page list of security holdings). Observe that in March 1991, the fund owned anywhere from 2,500 shares of one company (Energy Ventures, Inc.) to nearly 3.8 *million* shares of another (Reebok International). Furthermore, note that within each industry seg-ment, the fund diversified its holdings across a number of different stocks. Clearly, except for all but the super-rich, this is far more diversification than most investors could ever hope to attain. Yet each investor who owns shares in this fund is, in effect, a part owner of this diversified portfolio of securities.

investment com-pany
a firm, such as a mutual fund, that combines the capital of many people with similar investment goals and invests the money in a wide variety of securities.

Of course, not all funds are as big or as diversified as the one depicted in Figure 13.1. Even so, as the securities held by a fund move up and down in price, the market value of the mutual fund shares moves accordingly. When dividend and interest payments are received by the fund, they are passed on to the mutual fund shareholders and distributed on the basis of prorated ownership. For example, if you own 1,000 shares of stock in a mutual fund and that represents 10 percent of all shares outstanding, you would receive 10 percent of the dividends paid by the fund. When a security held by the fund is sold for a profit, the capital gain is also passed on to fund shareholders. The whole mutual fund idea, in fact, rests on the concept of **pooled diversification,** and it works very much like health insurance, whereby individuals pool their resources for the collective benefit of all the contributors.

pooled diversifica-tion
a process whereby investors buy into a diversified portfolio of securities for the collective benefit of the individual inves-tors.

Attractions and Drawbacks of Mutual Fund Ownership

The attractions of mutual fund ownership are numerous. One of the most important is *diversification*, which reduces the risk inherent in any one investment by spread-

	Shares	Value (Note 1)		Shares	Value (Note 1)
COMMON STOCKS – *continued*			Oceaneering International, Inc.*	502,900 $	5,909,075
			Petroleum Helicopters, Inc.	62,100	1,242,000
DURABLES – *continued*			Petroleum Helicopters, Inc.		
Furniture – 0.1%			(non vtg.)	183,300	3,574,350
Haverty Furniture Companies, Inc.	166,000 $	1,494,000	Rowan Companies, Inc.*	2,019,300	19,688,175
Heilig-Meyers Co.	142,900	4,090,513	Schlumberger Ltd.	380,000	22,135,000
LADD Furniture, Inc.	166,500	1,623,375	Smith International, Inc.*	1,380,600	19,673,550
La-Z Boy Chair Co.	23,700	485,850	Tidewater, Inc.*	823,200	11,421,900
		7,693,738	Varco International, Inc.*	397,600	4,075,400
			Weatherford International*	1,302,000	7,812,000
Household Products – 0.2%			Western Co. of North America*	371,900	5,067,138
First Brands Corp.	843,700	24,045,450			185,822,581
Newell Co.	40,000	1,280,000			
		25,325,450	**Oil and Gas – 6.6%**		
			Amerada Hess Corp.	443,000	20,710,250
Textiles and Apparel – 1.3%			Atlantic Richfield Co.	220,200	27,800,250
Crystal Brands, Inc.	309,600	8,630,100	Burlington Resources, Inc.	48,400	1,815,000
Delta Woodside Industries, Inc.	10,000	112,500	Cabot Oil & Gas Corp. Class A	119,200	1,788,000
Dominion Textile, Inc.	149,000	1,126,009	Cabre Exploration Ltd.*	413,580	3,214,766
Fruit of the Loom, Inc. Class A*	456,300	5,931,900	Canadian Natural Resources Ltd.*	663,400	2,435,069
Gitano Group, Inc.*	184,400	3,480,550	Coda Energy, Inc.*†	512,000	1,088,000
Guilford Mills, Inc.	40,800	918,000	Coho Resources, Inc.*	220,000	1,760,000
Hartmarx Corp.	92,500	1,110,000	Coho Resources Ltd. Class A*	724,300	2,033,052
Kellwood Co.	387,700	5,524,725	Edisto Resources Corp.*	386,000	3,088,000
Leslie Fay Companies, Inc.*†	1,076,400	21,931,650	Elf Aquitaine	2,673,150	160,393,625
Oshkosh B'Gosh, Inc. Class A	120,200	4,777,950	Encor, Inc.*	1,388,000	1,738,220
Phillips Van Heusen Corp.	123,200	2,633,400	Enron Oil & Gas Co.	289,200	5,820,150
Reebok International Ltd.	3,798,500	90,214,375	Exploration Company of Louisiana, Inc.* .	2,885,000	2,259,590
Russell Corp.	46,100	1,112,163	Exxon Corp.	433,600	25,474,000
Shaw Industries, Inc.	771,600	20,061,600	Freeport-McMoRan, Inc.	175,400	5,788,200
Springs Industries, Inc.	336,000	9,450,000	Hadson Energy Resources*	204,100	2,245,100
Texfi Industries, Inc.*†	598,000	3,289,000	Hamilton Oil Corp.	163,400	6,495,150
VF Corp.	653,600	17,483,800	Horsham Corp.*	3,585,300	32,126,332
		197,787,722	International Petroleum Corp.*	420,000	816,165
			International Petroleum Corp.		
TOTAL DURABLES		515,861,134	(warrants)*	150,000	90,684
			Kelley Oil & Gas Partners Ltd. †	631,100	11,359,800
ENERGY – 7.9%			Kerr-McGee Corp.	27,600	1,183,350
Coal – 0.0%			Louisiana Land & Exploration Co.	304,200	12,434,175
Westmoreland Coal Co. (Del.)	35,800	689,150	Maverick Tube Corp.*	165,900	2,612,925
Energy Services – 1.3%			Maxus Energy Corp.*	2,170,600	18,178,775
BJ Services Co.*	364,400	9,611,050	Mobil Corp.	348,100	22,452,450
Baker Hughes, Inc.	1,090,200	29,299,125	Morgan Hydrocarbons, Inc.*	970,000	5,340,713
Baroid Corp.	12,500	87,500	Morrison Petroleums Ltd.	520,000	4,715,636
CS Resources Ltd.*	588,000	2,361,443	Occidental Petroleum Corp.	50.000	937,500
Energy Ventures, Inc.*	2,500	47,500	Oryx Energy Co.	1,448,100	49,959,450
Enterra Corp.*	292,500	7,458,750	Pennzoil Co.	29,000	2,182,250
Global Marine, Inc.*	2,990,900	11,963,600	Phillips Petroleum Co.	3,021,800	84,988,125
Grant-Norpac, Inc.*†	612,000	4,131,000	Pogo Producing Co.*	449,300	2,920,450
Helmerich & Payne, Inc.	492,600	12,684,450			
Nabors Industries, Inc.*	1,122,900	7,579,575			

• FIGURE 13.1 A Partial List of Portfolio Holdings

The list of holdings in this one fund alone goes on for another 14 pages and includes stocks in several hundred different companies. Certainly, this is far more diversification than most individual investors could ever hope to achieve. (*Source:* Fidelity Investments.)

ing out holdings over a wide variety of industries and companies. Table 13.1 illustrates how the notion of diversification is applied to the equity holdings of the country's largest mutual funds, and it shows how security holdings will change over time as the market outlook changes. Another appeal of mutual funds is the full-time professional management that these funds offer, thereby removing much of the day-to-day management and recordkeeping chores from the shoulders of investors.

TABLE 13.1 Diversification in the Common Stock Holdings of Mutual Funds[*]

	Market Value 1983	Market Value 1990
Agricultural equipment	0.40%	0.80%
Aircraft mfg. & aerospace	2.16	1.49
Air transport	1.88	1.21
Auto & accessories (excl. tires)	3.21	2.76
Building materials & equipment	1.83	0.81
Chemicals	5.63	4.70
Communications (TV, radio, motion pictures)[a]	2.50	8.66
Computer services	0.72	2.84
Conglomerates	2.59	4.31
Containers	0.80	0.11
Drugs & cosmetics	5.87	6.06
Elec. equip. & electronics (excl. TV & radio)	13.15	5.87
Financial (incl. banks & insurance)	8.69	16.74
Foods and beverages	2.57	3.42
Hospital supplies & services	1.17	2.29
Leisure time	2.38	1.76
Machinery	1.85	2.01
Metals & mining	1.85	3.14
Office equipment	7.13	2.62
Oil	8.92	8.74
Paper	1.99	1.87
Printing & publishing	1.43	1.51
Public utilities (incl. natural gas)[b]	8.24	5.08
Railroads & railroad equipment	1.28	1.16
Retail trade	5.61	4.81
Rubber (incl. tires)	0.79	0.29
Steel	0.76	0.71
Textiles	0.72	0.74
Tobacco	1.00	0.29
Miscellaneous	2.88	3.20
Totals	100.00%	100.00%

[*]Composite industry investments drawn from the portfolios of the largest investment companies as of the end of calendar years 1983 and 1990.

[a]Includes telephone companies in 1990. [b]Includes telephone companies in 1983.

Source: Mutual Fund Fact Book, 1984 and 1991.

What's more, the fund may be able to offer better investment talents than individual investors can provide. Still another advantage is that most (but not all) mutual fund investments can be started with a modest capital outlay. Sometimes there is no minimum investment required at all; and after the initial investment has been made, additional shares can usually be purchased in small amounts. The services mutual funds offer also make them appealing to many investors: These include the automatic reinvestment of dividends, withdrawal plans, exchange privileges, and the like. Finally, mutual funds offer convenience. They are relatively easy to acquire, the funds handle the paperwork and recordkeeping, their prices are widely quoted, and it is possible to deal in fractional shares.

There are, of course, some major drawbacks to mutual fund ownership. One of the biggest disadvantages is that mutual funds in general can be very costly and involve substantial transaction costs. Many funds carry sizable commission charges (or what are known as "load charges"). In addition, a **management fee** is levied annually for the professional services provided, and it is deducted right off the top, regardless of whether it has been a good or bad year. Yet, even in spite of all the professional management and advice, it seems that mutual fund performance over the long haul is at best about equal to what you would expect from the market as a whole. There are some notable exceptions, of course, but most funds do little more than just keep up with the market—and in many cases can't even do that. Take a look at Figure 13.2; it shows the investment performance for 12 different types of equity funds over the five-year period from 1987 to 1991. (*Note:* These 12 categories represent more than 90% of assets under management by equity-oriented funds.) The reported returns are average, fully compounded, annual rates of return, and assume that all dividends and capital gains distributions are reinvested into additional shares of stock. Note that when compared to the S&P 500, there was only *one* fund category that outperformed the market, whereas a fair number fell far short of the mark. The message is clear: *Consistently beating the market is no easy task—not even for professional money managers*. Even though a handful of funds have given investors above-average, and even spectacular, rates of return, most mutual funds simply do not meet this level of performance. This is not to say that the long-term returns from mutual funds are substandard or that they fail to equal what you could achieve by putting your money in, say, a savings account or some similar risk-free investment outlet. Quite the contrary: The long-term returns from mutual funds have been substantial, but most of this return can be traced to strong market conditions and/or to the reinvestment of dividends and capital gains.

management fee
a fee levied annually for professional mutual fund services provided; paid regardless of the performance of the portfolio.

How Mutual Funds Are Organized and Run

Although it's tempting to think of a mutual fund as a single large entity, that's not really accurate. Various functions—investing, record keeping, safekeeping, and others—are split among two or more companies. Besides the fund itself, organized as a separate corporation or trust, there are several main players:

- The *management company* runs the fund's daily operations. These are the firms which we know as Fidelity, Kemper, IDS, Dreyfus, Oppenheimer, and so

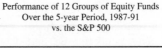

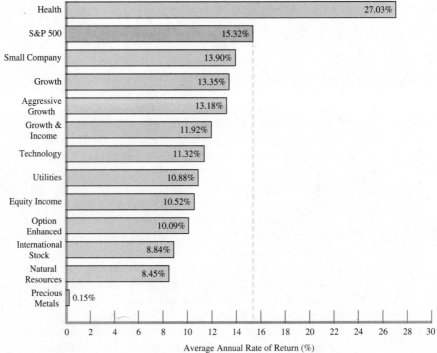

• FIGURE 13.2 The Comparative Performance of Mutual Funds versus the Market

As shown here, even with the services of professional money managers, it's tough to outperform the market. In this case, the average performance of 11 out of the 12 fund categories failed to meet the market's standard of return. (*Source:* Data developed from *Morningstar's Mutual Fund Performance Report,* September, 1991.)

forth, and which create the funds in the first place. Usually, the management firm also serves as investment adviser.

• The *investment adviser* buys and sells stocks or bonds and otherwise oversees the portfolio. Usually, there are three parties that participate in this phase of the operation: (1) the *money manager,* who actually runs the portfolio and makes the buy and sell decisions; (2) *security analysts,* who analyze securities and look for viable investment candidates; and (3) *traders,* who try to buy and sell big blocks of securities at the best possible price.

• The *distributor* sells fund shares, either directly to the public or through authorized dealers (like major brokerage houses and commercial banks). When you request a prospectus and sales literature, you deal with the distributor.

- The *custodian* physically safeguards the securities and other assets of a fund, without taking a role in the investment decisions. To discourage foul play, an independent party, usually a bank, serves in this capacity.
- The *transfer agent* keeps track of purchase and redemption requests from shareholders and maintains other shareholder records.

Each of these parties collects a fee for its services. However, actual ownership of a fund rests with the shareholders. With so many financial institutions wobbling and the economy hung over from a decade-long borrowing binge, one might be tempted to wonder if mutual funds are really all that safe. Well, as the accompanying *Investor Insights* box reveals, because of various safeguards, the chance of your losing any money from a mutual fund collapse is really quite low—almost nonexistent.

Mutual Fund Regulations

Although securities regulations were discussed in Chapter 2, it might be helpful to briefly review some of the major regulatory provisions that apply to mutual funds. To begin with, the *Securities Act of 1933* requires the filing of full information about the fund with the SEC. This act also requires the fund to provide potential investors with a current prospectus, disclosing the fund's management, its investment policies and objectives, and other essential data. In addition, the purchase and sale of mutual fund shares are subject to the anti-fraud provisions of the *Securities Exchange Act of 1934,* and the *Investment Advisors Act of 1940* regulates the activities of the investment advisors that work for mutual funds. Most important of all, in order to qualify for investment company status, a fund must comply with the provisions of the *Investment Company Act of 1940.* That comprehensive piece of legislation provides the foundation for the regulation of the mutual fund industry and, among other things, establishes standards of income distribution, fee structures, and diversification of assets. Finally, from a tax perspective, a mutual fund can be treated as an essentially tax-exempt organization (and thereby avoid the double taxation of dividends and income) so long as it qualifies under *Subchapter M* of the Internal Revenue Code of 1954. Briefly, to operate as a regulated investment company and enjoy the attending tax benefits, a fund must distribute all of its realized capital gains and at least 90 percent of its interest and dividend income each year to its shareholders. That way, the fund will pay *no* taxes on any of its earnings, irrespective of whether they're derived from current income or capital gains.

Essential Characteristics

Although investing in mutual funds has been made as simple and as painless as possible, investors still should have a clear understanding of what they're getting into. For not only are there many different types of mutual funds available, there are also some significant differences in organizational structure that you should be aware of, and there's a wide array of fees and charges that you should become familiar with.

Could Your Mutual Fund Go Under?

When historians look back at the 1990s, they'll remember it for traumatizing the nation's financial services industry. Savings and loans were already in trouble for fraud, mismanagement, and simply taking too many risks. The malaise also extended into the banking sector, and even some insurance companies found themselves in hot water, bogged down as they were with junk-bond–laden portfolios. One domino that didn't fall, however, was the mutual fund sector. The business remains generally healthy and, more to the point, offers a different set of protections for investors. Obviously, you can lose money if your fund's stock or bond holdings decline in price. But there's little chance of loss stemming from fraud, scandal or bankruptcy involving the management company itself. That's a key distinction: By transferring investment risk to shareholders, mutual fund companies have been able to sidestep many of the problems currently plaguing their financial cousins.

In addition, the legal structure and heavy regulation of mutual funds offer key safeguards. Many of these resulted from abuses that infected the fund industry back in the 1920s. At the time, closed-end portfolios were the rage, and managers were often guilty of self-dealing, inadequate disclosure, conflicts of interest and other practices that are illegal today. Also, many closed-end funds were heavily leveraged. When the market crashed in 1929, that wiped out a lot of fund shareholders and set the stage for subsequent regulation, including the Investment Company Act of 1940, which governs the fund industry today.

A regular, open-end mutual fund is a separate corporation or trust that's owned by its shareholders, not by the firm that runs it. The only formal link with the management company is through a contract that must be renewed on a regular basis. Consequently, the fund's assets—stocks, bonds, and cash in the portfolio—are not kept in the drawers of the management company. Rather, *they're placed in the custody of an independent third party, typically a trust or custodial bank.* "We do not have easy access to our shareholders' money," says Charles J. Tennes, a vice president with the GIT Investment Funds in Arlington, Va. "We have authority to buy and sell securities on their behalf, but the assets are held by someone else."

As another safeguard, each fund features a board of directors or trustees, who are

Open-End Investment Companies

open-end investment company
a type of investment company in which investors buy shares from, and sell them back to, the mutual fund itself, with no limit on the number of shares the fund can issue.

The term *mutual fund* is commonly used to denote an open-end investment company. Mutual funds are the dominant type of investment company and account for well over 90 percent of the assets under management. Many of these funds are fairly large, with some having portfolios that are measured in the *billions* of dollars. In an **open-end investment company,** investors actually buy their shares from, and sell them back to, the mutual fund itself. When the investor buys shares in an open-end fund, the fund issues new shares of stock and fills the purchase order with those new shares. There is no limit, other than investor demand, to the number of shares the fund can issue. (Occasionally, funds will *temporarily* close themselves to new investors—meaning they won't open any new accounts—in an attempt to keep fund charged with keeping tabs on the management company and renewing its contract. If the management firm was facing bankruptcy, the directors would liquidate or merge the fund, or find another outfit to run it. According to federal regulations, at least 40% of a fund's board members must be independent of the management company. The directors are elected by shareholders, are paid with shareholder money, and can be sued for ignoring their fiduciary duties. At GIT, for example, the independent board members have their own securities lawyer, who attends all meetings. Many independent directors are themselves shareholders in the fund.

As further protection, the management company and other affiliated parties can't engage in certain types of transactions with a fund. For example, the investment adviser can't dump its own stock and bond holdings by selling them to the fund. Nor can an adviser with a brokerage arm charge the fund excessive commissions for conducting trades. These conflict-of-interest provisions are often called the heart of the Investment Company Act of 1940.

Bob Pozen, general counsel and managing director of Fidelity Investments in Boston, believes there are some more fundamental reasons besides these structural safeguards for explaining the lack of scandal in the industry. First, he says, funds must stand ready to redeem investor shares upon demand. That forces them to stick with assets for which there's a liquid market. Second, funds must value their holdings every day, a process known as *marking-to-market*. "I feel one of the big problems with insurance companies is that they didn't mark-to-market their assets daily. They were able to go a long time before anybody realized they had a problem," Pozen says. "You can't do that with mutual funds. You know the problems immediately."

In 50 years and $1 trillion in fund assets, there has not been a major crisis or scandal like what has happened in other parts of the financial services industry. Tight regulations and structural firewalls have helped, as has the fact that shareholders bear the investment risks. The best thing you can say about mutual funds is that the federal government never promised to bail them out.

Source: Adapted from Russ Wiles, "Checks and Balances: How Funds Are Organized," *Personal Investor,* September 1991, pp. 28–30.

growth in check.) All open-end mutual funds stand behind their shares and buy them back when investors decide to sell. Thus, there is never any trading between individuals.

Both buy and sell transactions are carried out at prices based on the current value of all the securities held in the fund's portfolio (technically, this would also include the book value of any other assets, like cash and receivables from securities transactions, that the fund might hold at the time—though, for all practical purposes, these other assets generally account for only a tiny fraction of the fund's total portfolio). Known as the fund's **net asset value (NAV),** it is calculated at least once a day and represents the underlying value of a share of stock in a particular mutual fund. NAV is found by taking the total market value of all securities (and other assets) held by

net asset value (NAV)
the underlying value of a share of stock in a particular mutual fund.

the fund, less any liabilities, and dividing this amount by the number of fund shares outstanding. For example, if on a given day the market value of all the securities (and other assets) held by the XYZ mutual fund equaled some $10 million, and if XYZ on that particular day had 500,000 shares outstanding, the fund's net asset value per share would amount to $20 ($10,000,000/500,000 = $20). This figure, as we'll see below, is then used to derive the price at which the fund shares are bought and sold.

Closed-End Investment Companies

closed-end investment companies
a type of investment company that operates with a fixed number of shares outstanding.

Whereas the term *mutual fund* is supposed to be used only with open-end funds, it is, as a practical matter, regularly used with closed-end investment companies as well. Basically, **closed-end investment companies** operate with a fixed number of shares outstanding and do *not* regularly issue new shares of stock. In effect, they have a capital structure like that of any other corporation, except that the corporation's business happens to be investing in marketable securities. In early 1992, there were several hundred publicly traded closed-end funds; shares in these companies are actively traded in the secondary market, like any other common stock. Unlike open-end funds, *all trading is done between investors in the open market*. The fund itself plays no role in either buy or sell transactions; once the shares are issued, the fund is out of the picture. Most closed-end investment companies are traded on the New York Stock Exchange, several are on the American Exchange, and some are traded in the OTC market. As seen in Figure 13.3, the shares of closed-end companies are listed right along with other common stocks. In this case ASA Ltd. and Adams Express (two of the larger closed-end investment companies) are quoted on the NYSE.

The share prices of closed-end companies are determined not only by their net asset values, but also by general supply and demand conditions in the stock market. As a result, closed-end companies generally trade at a discount or premium to NAV. For example, if a fund has a net asset value of $10 per share and is trading at $9, it would be selling at a discount of $1. Similarly, it would be selling at a premium of $1 if it were quoted at a price of $11. Share price discounts and premiums can at times become quite large. For example, it's not unusual for such spreads to amount to as much as 25 to 30 percent of net asset value, occasionally more. Table 13.2 lists some actively traded closed-end funds, along with prevailing premiums (+) and discounts (−).

Unit Investment Trusts

unit investment trust
a type of investment vehicle whereby the trust sponsors put together a fixed/ unmanaged portfolio of securities and then sell ownership units in the portfolio to individual investors.

A **unit investment trust** represents little more than an interest in an *unmanaged* pool of investments. In essence, a portfolio of securities is simply held in safekeeping for investors under conditions set down in a trust agreement. The portfolios usually consist of corporate, government, or municipal bonds, with tax-free municipal bonds and mortgage-backed securities being the most popular type of investment vehicle. There is *no trading* in the portfolios, and as a result, the returns, or yields, are fixed and usually predictable—at least for the short run. Unit trusts are

52 Weeks Hi	Lo	Stock	Sym	Div	Yld %	PE	Vol 100s	Hi	Lo	Close	Net Chg
		-A-A-A-									
16⅞	9¼	AAR	AIR	.48	3.7	18	912	13¾	13	13	−⅜
11⅝	10⅜	ACM Gvt Fd	ACG	1.26	11.0	...	3877	11⅝	11¼	11½	+¼
9¾	8¾	ACM OppFd	AOF	1.01e	10.6	...	253	9⅝	9½	9½	−⅛
▲ 11	9⅜	ACM SecFd	GSF	1.26	11.5	...	4311	11⅛	10¾	11	+¼
9½	8¼	ACM SpctmFd	SI	1.01	11.1	...	1162	9¼	9	9⅛	+⅛
n 9⅛	7⅝	ACM MgdIncFd	AMF	1.01	11.1	...	339	9⅛	9	9⅛	...
12⅞	11½	ACM MgdMultFd	MMF	1.35	10.5	...	408	12⅞	12⅝	12⅞	+⅛
21½	5	ADT adr	ADTA	.32e	4.5	2	366	7¼	7	7⅛	−⅛
n 9½	5	ADT	ADT		...	...	1126	7⅜	7⅛	7¼	−⅛
24¾	14⅜	AL Labs A	BMD	.16	.7	26	359	23⅞	23¼	23¼	−¼
1⅞	¾	AM Int	AM		...	...	504	¹⁵⁄₁₆	⅞	¹⁵⁄₁₆	...
12	4⅛	AM Int pf		1.50j	...	...	14	5	4⅞	5	...
11¾	9⅛	AMEV Sec	AMV	1.05	9.3	...	74	11⅜	11¼	11¼	...
▲ 71⅛	44¼	AMR	aMR		...	...	6981	71⅞	69⅛	71⅝	+2⅛
25½	22¼	ANR pf		2.12	8.4	...	2	25⅜	25⅜	25⅜	−⅛
44¼	33⅛	ARCO Chm	RCM	2.50	6.4	20	27	39⅝	39¼	39¼	−⅜
2⅝	1	ARX	ARX		...	...	52	1½	1½	1½	...
56	41½	ASA	ASA	3.00	6.4	...	546	47⅛	46¾	47⅛	+⅜
6½	2⅛	ATT Cap yen wt			...	...	50	4⅝	4⅝	4⅝	+⅛
69½	39¼	AbbotLab	ABT	1.00	1.5	27	7057	68⅜	66½	67½	+¼
14⅝	9⅞	Abitibi g	ABY	.50	...	...	10	12¾	12½	12¾	+¼
6	3⅜	AcmeElec	ACE		...	...	32	5	4⅞	4⅞	+⅛
7½	4½	AcmeCleve	AMT	.40	5.5	...	91	7¼	7⅛	7¼	...
40	22¾	Acuson	ACN		...	22	1366	32¼	31⅛	31½	−⅝
20¼	14¼	AdamsExp	ADX	1.63e	8.6	...	462	19⅛	18¾	19	...
9⅜	3⅞	AdobeRes	ADB		...	...	150	5	4⅝	4¾	−⅜
20⅛	12⅞	AdobeRes pf			...	...	37	14¼	14	14	−½
18	10¾	AdobeRes pf			...	...	114	12⅛	11¾	12	...
▲ 18	4	AdvMicro	AMD		...	...	10862	18⅜	17⅞	18¼	+⅜

● F I G U R E   1 3 . 3   Stock Quotations for Closed-End Investment Companies

The quotes for closed-end investment companies are listed right along with those of other common stocks. Except for the lack of a P/E ratio, their quotes are pretty much the same as any other stock. (*Source: The Wall Street Journal,* January 6, 1992.)

like second cousins to mutual funds: Unlike conventional mutual funds, whose securities are actively traded, a trust sponsor simply puts together a portfolio of securities, and that's it. After the securities are deposited with a trustee, no new securities are added and, with rare exceptions, none are sold.

Various sponsoring brokerage houses put together these diversified pools of securities and then sell units of the pool to investors (each *unit* being like a share in a mutual fund). For example, a brokerage house might put together a diversified pool of corporate bonds that amounts to, say, $10 million. The sponsoring firm would then sell units in this pool to the investing public at a price of $1,000 per unit (a common price for these securities). The sponsoring organization does little more than routine recordkeeping, and it services the investments by collecting coupons and distributing the income (often on a monthly basis) to the holders of the trust

TABLE 13.2 Some Actively Traded Closed-End Mutual Funds

Fund Name	Stock Exch.	NAV	Stock Price	% Diff.
Diversified Common Stock Funds				
Adams Express	NYSE	20.36	19	− 6.68
Allmon Trust	NYSE	10.40	10	− 3.85
Baker Fentress	NYSE	21.57	17⅜	− 19.45
Blue Chip Value	NYSE	8.42	7⅞	− 6.47
Clemente Global Gro	NYSE	10.81	9¼	− 14.43
Gemini II Capital	NYSE	16.46	13	− 21.02
Gemini II Income	NYSE	9.35	13⅛	+ 40.37
General Amer Invest	NYSE	30.78	28⅜	− 7.81
Liberty All-Star Eqty	NYSE	11.24	10⅝	− 5.47
Niagara Share Corp.	NYSE	15.33	14½	− 5.41
Quest For Value Cap	NYSE	22.51	17⅜	− 22.81
Quest For Value Inco	NYSE	11.62	13⅜	+ 15.10
Royce Value Trust	NYSE	11.21	10⅜	− 7.45
Salomon Fd	NYSE	15.64	13⅞	− 11.29
Source Capital	NYSE	41.37	44½	+ 7.57
Tri-Continental Corp.	NYSE	28.78	27⅛	− 5.75
Worldwide Value	NYSE	15.39	12⅝	− 17.97
Zweig Fund	NYSE	12.41	13¾	+ 10.80
Closed End Bond Funds				
CIM High Yield Secs	AMEX	7.11	6½	− 8.58
Municipal High Inco	NYSE	9.49	9¼	− 2.53
Muni Yield Fd	NYSE	14.60	15⅜	+ 5.31
Zenix Income Fund	NYSE	6.07	6⅛	+ 0.91
Flexible Portfolio Funds				
America's All Seasn	OTC	5.90	4⁹⁄₁₆	− 22.67
European Warrant Fd	NYSE	7.11	6⅛	− 13.85
Zweig Total Return Fd	NYSE	9.77	10⅞	+ 11.31
Specialized Equity and Convertible Funds				
Alliance Global Env Fd	NYSE	13.37	11⅞	− 11.18
American Capital Conv	NYSE	22.29	19⅛	− 14.20
Argentina Fd	NYSE	11.16	14⅝	+ 31.05
ASA Ltd	NYSE	41.85	46¾	+ 11.71
Asia Pacific	NYSE	12.35	12½	+ 1.21
Austria Fund	NYSE	9.48	9	− 5.06
Bancroft Convertible	AMEX	21.31	18¾	− 12.01
Brazil	NYSE	15.10	15¾	+ 4.30
CNV Holdings Capital	NYSE	11.01	7	− 36.42

Source: *The Wall Street Journal*, January 6, 1992.

units. Trusts appeal primarily to income-oriented investors who are looking for monthly (rather than semiannual) income. But be careful, as these investments do have their dark sides. For one thing, they tend to be very costly and involve substantial up-front transactions costs. In addition, various strategies are used to artificially pump up yields and make returns look better than they really are; and contrary to what many investors believe (or are told), you *can* lose money on these things if premium-priced bonds in the trust are called for pre-payment.

Load and No-Load Funds

The question of whether a fund is "load" or "no-load" is a matter of concern only to investors in *open-end* funds. (Recall from our discussion above that closed-end funds trade on listed or OTC markets; thus they are subject to the same commission and transactions costs as any other share of common stock.) The load charge on an open-end fund is the commission the investor pays when buying shares in a fund. Generally speaking, the term **load fund** is used to describe a mutual fund that charges a commission when shares are bought (such charges are also known as *front-end loads*). A **no-load fund,** in contrast, means no sales charges are levied. Load charges can be fairly substantial and often range from 7 to 8.5 percent of the *purchase* price of the shares. Most mutual funds, however, offer quantity discounts (which usually start with single investments of 1,000 shares or more). Although there may be little or no difference in the performance of load and no-load funds, the cost savings with no-load funds tend to give investors a head start in achieving superior rates of return. Unfortunately, the true no-load fund may become extinct in the future, as more and more no-loads are becoming "12(b)-1 funds". Although such funds do not *directly* charge commissions at the time of purchase (so they can technically call themselves no-loads), they assess what are known as 12(b)-1 charges *annually* to make up for any lost commissions [12(b)-1 charges are more fully described below]. Overall, less than 30 percent of the funds sold today are pure no-loads; all the rest charge some type of load or fee.

Fortunately, it is possible to tell the players apart without a program: The quotation system used with mutual funds distinguishes the no-load from the load funds. That is, all open-end mutual funds are priced according to their net asset values, which—as you can see in Figure 13.4—are part of the standard mutual fund quotations. The NAV (net asset value) column is the price the mutual fund will pay to buy back the fund shares (or, from the investor's point of view, the price at which the shares can be sold). Next to the NAV is the Offer Price, the price the investor would have to pay in order to buy the shares. Note that the FPA Paramount Fund, for example, has a higher offer price ($13.65) than net asset value ($12.76); this difference of $0.89 per share represents the front-end load charge. For the FPA Paramount Fund, the load charge amounts to 6½ percent of the offer price. However, the load rate is actually *more* when the commission is related to a more appropriate base—the NAV of the fund. When stated as a percent of NAV, the load charge for this fund becomes 7.0 percent. Relative to what it costs to buy and sell common stocks, the cost of a load fund is fairly high even after taking into account the fact that you normally don't have to pay a commission on the *sale* of most funds.

load fund
a mutual fund that charges a commission when shares are bought; also known as *front-end load fund.*

no-load fund
a mutual fund that does not charge a commission when shares are bought.

The price you get when you **SELL** shares.		The price you pay when you **BUY** shares.

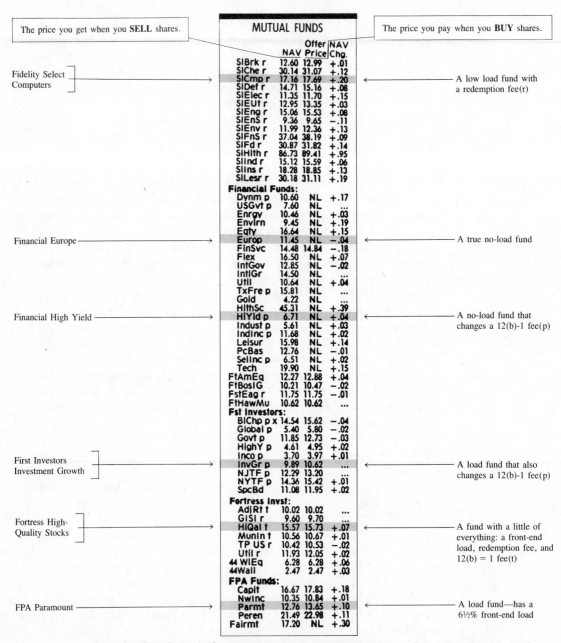

Fidelity Select Computers → A low load fund with a redemption fee(r)

Financial Europe → A true no-load fund

Financial High Yield → A no-load fund that changes a 12(b)-1 fee(p)

First Investors Investment Growth → A load fund that also changes a 12(b)-1 fee(p)

Fortress High-Quality Stocks → A fund with a little of everything: a front-end load, redemption fee, and 12(b) = 1 fee(t)

FPA Paramount → A load fund—has a 6½% front-end load

MUTUAL FUNDS

	NAV	Offer Price	NAV Chg.
SIBrk r	12.60	12.99	+.01
SIChe r	30.14	31.07	+.12
SICmp r	17.16	17.69	+.20
SIDef r	14.71	15.16	+.08
SIElec r	11.35	11.70	+.15
SIEUt r	12.95	13.35	+.03
SIEng r	15.06	15.53	+.08
SIEnS r	9.36	9.65	−.11
SIEnv r	11.99	12.36	+.13
SIFnS r	37.04	38.19	+.09
SIFd r	30.87	31.82	+.14
SIHlth r	86.73	89.41	+.95
SIInd r	15.12	15.59	+.06
SIIns r	18.28	18.85	+.13
SILesr r	30.18	31.11	+.19
Financial Funds:			
Dynm p	10.60	NL	+.17
USGvt p	7.60	NL	...
Enrgy	10.46	NL	+.03
Envirn	9.45	NL	+.19
Eqty	16.64	NL	+.15
Europ	11.45	NL	−.04
FinSvc	14.48	14.84	−.18
Flex	16.50	NL	+.07
IntGov	12.85	NL	−.02
IntlGr	14.50	NL	...
Util	10.64	NL	+.04
TxFre p	15.81	NL	...
Gold	4.22	NL	...
HlthSc	45.31	NL	+.39
HiYld p	6.71	NL	+.04
Indust p	5.61	NL	+.03
IndInc p	11.68	NL	+.02
Leisur	15.98	NL	+.14
PcBas	12.76	NL	−.01
SelInc p	6.51	NL	+.02
Tech	19.90	NL	+.15
FtAmEq	12.27	12.88	+.04
FtBosIG	10.21	10.47	−.02
FstEag r	11.75	11.75	−.01
FtHawMu	10.62	10.62	...
Fst Investors:			
BlChp p x	14.54	15.62	−.04
Global p	5.40	5.80	−.02
Govt p	11.85	12.73	−.03
HighY p	4.61	4.95	+.02
Inco p	3.70	3.97	+.01
InvGr p	9.89	10.62	...
NJTF p	12.29	13.20	...
NYTF p	14.36	15.42	+.01
SpcBd	11.08	11.95	+.02
Fortress Invst:			
AdjRt t	10.02	10.02	...
GISI r	9.60	9.70	...
HiQal t	15.57	15.73	+.07
MunIn t	10.56	10.67	+.01
TP US r	10.42	10.53	−.02
Util r	11.93	12.05	+.02
44 WIEq	6.28	6.28	+.06
44Wall	2.47	2.47	+.03
FPA Funds:			
Capit	16.67	17.83	+.18
NwInc	10.35	10.84	+.01
Parmt	12.76	13.65	+.10
Peren	21.49	22.98	+.11
Fairmt	17.20	NL	+.30

• FIGURE 13.4 Mutual Fund Quotations, Showing Load and No-Load Funds

Open-end mutual funds are listed separately from other securities, and they have their own quotation system. For one thing, these securities are quoted in dollars and cents (most other securities are listed in eighths or thirty-seconds). Also, the type of load charge, if any, is indicated as part of the quote. (*Source: The Wall Street Journal*, January 6, 1992.)

low-load fund
a mutual fund that charges a small commission (2 to 3 percent) when shares are bought.

back-end load
a commission charged on the sale of shares in a mutual fund.

12(b)-1 fee
a fee levied by some mutual funds to cover management and other operating costs; amounts to as much as 1¼ percent annually on the average net assets.

While the *maximum* load charge is 8½ percent of the purchase price, few funds charge the maximum. Rather, some funds, like Fidelity Select-Computers, charge commissions of only 2 or 3 percent—such funds are known as **low-load funds.** There is a commission to pay on low-load funds, and thus, there will still be a difference (albeit slight) in the fund's offer price and NAV; note that it amounted to only 53 cents in the case of Fidelity Select-Computers. In contrast, note the repeated use of the letters *N.L.* in the offer price column; for example, see the Financial European Fund in the quotes in Figure 13.4. Those letters indicate that the fund is a no-load, and as a result, the shares are bought *and* sold at the same NAV price of $11.45 a share.

Occasionally, a fund will have a **back-end load,** which means commissions are levied when shares are sold. These loads may amount to as much as 6 to 7 percent of the value of the shares sold, though back-end loads tend to decline over time and usually disappear all together after five to six years. The stated purpose of back-end loads is to enhance fund stability by discouraging investors from trading in and out of the funds over short investment horizons. In addition, a substantial (and growing) number of funds charge something called a **12(b)-1 fee**—a fee that's assessed annually for as long as you own the fund. Known appropriately as *hidden loads,* these fees have been allowed since 1980 and were originally designed to help funds (particularly the no-loads) cover their distribution and marketing costs. The 12(b)-1 fees can amount to as much as 1¼ percent *per year* of assets under management. In good markets and bad, they're paid, right off the top. And that can take its toll. Consider, for instance, $10,000 in a fund that charges a 1¼ percent 12(b)-1 fee: That translates into a charge of *$125 a year*. (*Note:* Mutual fund loads and fees may be coming down as the SEC in 1992 was looking into the idea of putting caps on many of these charges.)

Other Fees and Costs

Another cost of owning mutual funds is the *management fee,* the compensation paid to the professional managers who administer the fund's portfolio. It must be paid regardless of whether a fund is load or no-load, or whether it is open-end or closed. These fees generally amount to anywhere from .50 to as much as 2.50 percent of average assets under management. (These expense ratios bear watching, since high expenses will take their toll on performance.) Unlike load charges, which are one-time costs, management fees (and 12(b)-1 charges, if imposed) are levied *annually* and are paid *regardless of the performance of the portfolio*. In addition, there are the administrative costs of operating the fund; these are fairly modest and represent the normal cost of doing business (like the commissions paid when the fund buys and sells securities).

A final cost is the taxes paid on security transactions. In order to avoid double taxation, nearly all mutual funds operate as *regulated investment companies*. This means that all (or nearly all) of the dividend and interest income is passed on to the investor, as are any capital gains realized when securities are sold. The mutual fund thus pays no taxes, but instead passes the tax liability on to its shareholders. This holds true regardless of whether such distributions are reinvested in the company (in the form of additional mutual fund shares) or paid out in cash. Mutual funds annually provide each stockholder with a convenient summary report on the amount of dividends and capital gains received and the amount of taxable income earned (and to be reported) by the fund shareholder.

Keeping Track of Fund Fees and Loads

Critics of the mutual fund industry have come down hard on the proliferation of fund fees and charges. Indeed, some would argue that all the different kinds of charges and fees are really meant to do one thing: confuse the investor. The fact is that a lot of funds were going to great lengths—lower a cost here, tack on a fee there, hide a charge somewhere else—to make themselves look like something they weren't. The funds were following the letter of the law, and, indeed, they were fully disclosing all their expenses and fees. The trouble was that the funds were able to neatly hide all but the most conspicuous charges in a bunch of legalese. Fortunately, steps have been taken to bring fund fees and loads out into the open.

For one thing, fund charges are more fully reported by the financial press. You don't have to look any farther than the *mutual fund quotations* found in *The Wall Street Journal* and most other major papers. For example, refer back to the quotations in Figure 13.4; notice the use of the letters ''r,'' ''p,'' and ''t.'' If you see an ''r'' behind a fund's name, it means the fund charges some type of *redemption fee*, or back-end load, when you sell your shares; this is the case, for example, with Fidelity Select-Computers. The use of a ''p,'' in contrast, means the fund levies a *12(b)-1 fee*, which you'll have to pay, for example, if you invest in the Financial High Yield Fund. Finally, a ''t'' indicates funds that charge *both* redemption fees and 12(b)-1 fees; notice that's what you get with Fortress Investment's High Quality Stock Fund. In fact, if you look closely at the quotations, you'll see that Fortress High Quality not only levies redemption and 12(b)-1 fees *but also has a front-end load*—as indicated by the difference in its NAV and offer price. The point is: Don't be surprised to find load funds (like First Investor's Investment Growth) that also charge redemption and/or 12(b)-1 fees, and the same goes for no-load funds. The quotations, of course, tell you only the *kinds* of fees charged by the funds; they don't tell you how much is charged. To get the specifics on the amount charged, you'll have to turn to the fund itself.

All (open-end) mutual funds are required to *fully disclose* all their expenses in a standardized, easy-to-understand format. Every fund prospectus must contain, right up front, a fairly detailed *fee table*, much like the one illustrated in Table 13.3. Notice that this table has three parts. The first specifies all *shareholder transaction costs*. In effect, this tells you what it's going to cost to buy and sell shares in the mutual fund. The next section lists all the *annual operating expenses* of the fund. Showing these expenses as a percentage of average net assets, the fund must break out management fees, those elusive 12(b)-1 fees, and any other expenses. The third section provides a rundown of the *total cost over time* of buying, selling, and owning the fund. This part of the table contains both transaction and operating expenses and shows what the total costs would be over hypothetical 1-, 3-, 5-, and 10-year holding periods. To ensure consistency and comparability, the funds must follow a rigid set of guidelines when constructing the illustrative costs.

■■■■■

TABLE 13.3 Mutual Fund Expense Disclosure Table

Expenses and Costs of Investing in the Fund

The following information is provided in order to assist investors in understanding the transaction costs and annual expenses associated with investing in the Fund.

A. Shareholder Transaction Costs:

Sales load on purchases 2%
Sales load on reinvested dividends . . . . .None
Redemption fees or deferred sales charges . . . . .None
Exchange (or conversion) fees . . . . .None

B. Annual Fund Operating Expenses:
(as a percentage of average net assets)

Management fees 0.40%
12(b)-1 fees . . . . .None
Other expenses (estimated) 0.32%

C. Example of Fund Expenses over Time:

You would pay the following total expenses over time on a $1,000 investment assuming a 5% annual return, and a complete redemption of the investment at the end of each indicated time period:

1-year	3-years	5-years	10-years
$27	$43	$59	$108

It's obviously in your best interest to pay close attention to the fee table whenever you're considering an investment in a mutual fund. Other things being equal, look for low initial charges as well as low expense ratios over time. As a rule, the longer you intend to hold a fund, the more willing you should be to trade a higher load charge for lower annual management and 12(b)-1 fees. That will help you keep your total holding period costs down. In the final analysis, keep in mind that costs are only one element in the decision. Another very important variable is *performance*. There may be times when higher costs are justified; there may be other times when they're not. When it comes to costs, you might want to follow these guidelines:

- Consider a *more expensive* fund if it has a better performance record (and offers more return potential) than a less expensive fund. It's all a matter of whether you'd rather own a costly performer or a low-cost "dog".
- If there's little or no difference in performance records or return potential, go with the *less expensive* fund. In this case, lower expenses will make a difference in comparative returns.

TYPES OF FUNDS AND SERVICES

Some mutual funds specialize in stocks, others in bonds. Some have maximum capital gains as an investment objective, and some seek high current income. Some funds will thus appeal to speculators, whereas others will be of interest primarily to income-oriented investors. Every fund has a particular investment objective. Common objectives are growth (or capital gains), current income, tax-exempt income, preservation of capital, or some combination thereof. Disclosure of a fund's investment objective is required by the SEC, and each fund is expected to do its best to conform to its stated investment policy and objective. Categorizing funds according to their investment policies and objectives is widely practiced in the mutual fund industry, as it tends to reflect similarities not only in how the funds manage their money, but also in their risk and return characteristics. Some of the more popular types of mutual funds include growth, aggressive growth, equity-income, balanced, growth-and-income, bond, money market, specialty, sector, and international funds. Let's look now at the various types of mutual funds to see what they are and how they operate.

Types of Mutual Funds

Growth Funds

growth fund
a mutual fund whose primary goals are capital gains and long-term growth.

The objective of a **growth fund** is simple: capital appreciation. Long-term growth and capital gains are the primary goals of such funds and as a result, they invest principally in common stocks that have above-average growth potential but offer little (if anything) in the way of dividends and current income. Because of the uncertain nature of their investment income, growth funds may involve a fair amount of risk exposure. They are usually viewed as long-term investment vehicles most suitable for the more aggressive investor who wants to build up capital and has little interest in current income.

Aggressive Growth Funds

aggressive growth fund
a highly speculative mutual fund that seeks large profits from capital gains.

Aggressive growth funds are the so-called performance funds that tend to increase in popularity when markets heat up. **Aggressive growth funds** are highly speculative investment vehicles that seek large profits from capital gains. In many respects, they are an extension of the growth fund concept. Many are fairly small, and their portfolios consist mainly of high-flying common stocks. These funds often buy stocks of small, unseasoned companies, stocks with relatively high price/earnings multiples, and common stocks whose prices are highly volatile. They seem to be especially fond of turn-around situations and may even use leverage in their portfolios (that is, buy stocks on margin); they also use options very aggressively, various hedging techniques, and short selling. All this is designed, of course, to yield big returns. But aggressive funds are also highly speculative and are among the most volatile of all the types of funds. When the markets are good, aggressive growth funds do well; when the markets are bad, these funds often experience substantial losses.

Equity-Income Funds

equity-income fund
a mutual fund that emphasizes current income and capital preservation and which invests primarily in high-yielding common stocks.

Equity-income funds emphasize current income, and they do so by investing primarily in high-yielding common stocks. Capital preservation is also important and so is some capital gains, although capital appreciation is not a primary objective of equity-income funds. These funds invest heavily in high-grade common stocks, some convertible securities and preferred stocks, and occasionally even junk bonds or certain types of high-grade foreign bonds. As far as their stock holdings are concerned, they lean heavily toward blue chips, public utilities, and financial shares. They like securities that generate hefty dividend yields but also consider potential price appreciation over the longer haul. In general, because of their emphasis on dividends and current income, these funds tend to hold higher-quality securities that are subject to less price volatility than the market as a whole. They're generally viewed as a fairly low-risk way of investing in stocks.

Balanced Funds

balanced fund
a mutual fund whose objective is to generate a balanced return of both current income and long-term capital gains.

Balanced funds are so named because they tend to hold a balanced portfolio of both stocks and bonds, and they do so for the purpose of generating a well-balanced return of both current income and long-term capital gains. In many respects, they're a lot like equity-income funds, except that balanced funds usually put much more into fixed-income securities; generally, they keep at least 25 to 50 percent—and sometimes more—of their portfolios in bonds. The bonds are used principally to provide current income, and stocks are selected mainly for their long-term growth potential. The funds can, of course, shift the emphasis in their security holdings one way or the other. Clearly, the more the fund leans toward fixed-income securities, the more income-oriented it will be. For the most part, balanced funds tend to confine their investing to high-grade securities, including growth-oriented blue chip stocks, high-quality income shares, and high-yielding investment-grade bonds. As such, they're usually considered to be a relatively safe form of investing, one where you can earn a competitive rate of return without having to endure a lot of price volatility.

Growth-and-Income Funds

growth-and-income fund
a mutual fund that seeks both long-term growth and current income, with principal emphasis on capital gains.

Growth-and-income funds also seek a balanced return made up of both current income and long-term capital gains, but they place a greater emphasis on growth of capital. Moreover, unlike balanced funds, growth-and-income funds put most of their money into equities—indeed, it's not unusual for these funds to have 80 to 90 percent of their capital in common stocks. They tend to confine most of their investing to quality issues, so you can expect to find a lot of growth-oriented blue chip stocks in their portfolios, along with a fair amount of high-quality income stocks. One of the big appeals of these funds is the fairly substantial returns many of them have been able to generate over the long haul. But then, these funds do involve a fair amount of risk, if for no other reason than the emphasis they place on stocks and capital gains. As such, growth and income funds are most suitable for those investors who can tolerate the risk and price volatility.

Bond Funds

bond fund
a mutual fund that invests in various kinds and grades of bonds, with income as the primary objective.

As the name implies, **bond funds** invest exclusively in various kinds and grades of bonds—from Treasury and agency bonds to corporates and municipals. Income is the primary investment objective, although capital gains is not ignored. There are three important advantages to buying shares in bond funds, rather than investing directly in bonds. First, the bond funds are generally more liquid. Second, they offer a cost effective way of achieving a high degree of diversification in an otherwise expensive investment vehicle (most bonds carry minimum denominations of $1,000 to $5,000, or more). And third, bond funds will automatically reinvest interest and other income, thereby allowing the investor to earn fully compounded rates of return.

Although bond funds are generally considered to be a fairly conservative form of investment, they are not totally without risk, since the prices of the bonds held in the fund's portfolio will fluctuate with changing interest rates. While many bond funds may, indeed, be somewhat conservative, a growing number are becoming increasingly aggressive. In fact, much of the growth that bond funds have experienced recently can be attributed to this kind of investment attitude; as such, it's possible to find everything from high-grade government bond funds to highly speculative funds that invest in nothing but junk bonds. For many years, bond funds seemed to hold little appeal as investment vehicles. In the mid-1970s, however, fund managers became more aggressive and started managing their portfolios more fully. More recently, bond fund sales have been helped by the public's growing appetite for mortgage-backed securities. These funds invest primarily in government-backed mortgage securities (like GNMAs and CMOs) and in so doing, offer investors secure yet highly attractive rates of return. Mortgage-backed bond funds appeal to investors not only because they provide diversification and a more affordable way to get into these securities, but also because they have a provision that allows investors (if they so choose) to reinvest the *principal* portion of the monthly cash flow, thereby enabling them to preserve, rather than consume, their capital.

As indicated by the following list, there's a full range of different types of bond funds available today:

- *Government bond funds,* which invest in U.S. Treasury and agency securities.
- *Mortgage-backed bond funds,* which put their money into various types of mortgage-backed securities of the U.S. government (like GNMA issues).
- *High-grade corporate bond funds,* which invest chiefly in investment-grade securities rated triple-B or better.
- *High-yield corporate bond funds,* which are risky investments that buy *junk bonds* for the yields they offer.
- *Municipal bond funds,* which invest in tax-exempt securities and which are suitable for investors looking for tax-free income. Like their corporate counterparts, municipals can also come out as either high-grade or high-yield funds. A special type of municipal bond fund is the so-called *single-state* fund, which invests in the municipal issues of only one state, thus producing (for residents of that state) interest income that is *fully* exempt not only from federal taxes, but from state (and possibly even local/city) taxes as well.
- *Intermediate-term bond funds,* which invest in bonds with maturities of 7 to 10 years, or less, and offer not only attractive yields but relatively *low* price vola-

tility as well. The shorter (2- to 5-year) intermediate-term funds are often used as substitutes for money market investments by investors looking for higher returns on their money, especially when short-term rates are way down.

Clearly, no matter what you're looking for in a fixed-income security, you're likely to find a bond fund that fits the bill. The number and variety of such funds has skyrocketed in the past 10 years or so; the net result was that in early 1992, there were roughly 1,500 publicly traded bond funds that had more than $450 billion worth of bonds under management.

Money Market Funds

money market mutual fund (money fund)
a mutual fund that pools the capital of a number of investors and uses it to invest in short-term money market instruments.

The first **money market mutual fund,** or *money fund* for short, was set up in November 1972 with just $100,000 in total assets. It was a new idea that applied the mutual fund concept to the buying and selling of short-term money market instruments—such as bank certificates of deposit, U.S. Treasury bills, and the like. For the first time, investors with modest amounts of capital were given access to the high-yielding money market, where many instruments require minimum investments of $100,000 or more. (Money funds are discussed in greater detail in Chapter 3, along with other short-term investment vehicles.) The idea caught on quickly, and the growth in money funds was nothing short of phenomenal. That growth temporarily peaked in 1982, however, as the introduction of money market deposit accounts by banks and S&Ls caused money fund assets to level off and eventually decline. It didn't take long for the industry to recover, and by 1992, there were some 800 money funds that, together, held well over $500 billion in assets—which, by the way, *accounted for about 40 percent of all the assets held by mutual funds.*

Actually, there are several different kinds of money market mutual funds:

- *General purpose money funds,* which invest in any and all types of money market investment vehicles, from Treasury bills and bank CDs to corporate commercial paper. The vast majority of money funds are of this type. They invest their money wherever they can find attractive short-term yields.
- *Government securities money funds,* which were established as a way to meet investor concerns for safety. They effectively eliminate any risk of default by confining their investments to Treasury bills and other short-term securities of the U.S. government or its agencies.
- *Tax-exempt money funds,* which limit their investing to very short (30- to 90-day) tax-exempt municipal securities. Since their income is free from federal income tax, they appeal predominantly to investors in high tax brackets. The yields on these funds are about 25 to 35 percent *below* the returns on other types of money funds, so you need to be in a high enough tax bracket to produce a competitive after-tax return. Some tax-exempt funds confine their investing to the securities of a single state, so that residents of high-tax states can enjoy income that's free from *both* federal and state tax.

Just about every major brokerage firm has at least one or two money funds of its own, and hundreds more are sold by independent fund distributors. Most require minimum investments of $1,000 (although $2,500 to $5,000 minimum requirements are not uncommon). Because of the nature of the securities they hold (the maximum average maturity of fund holdings may not exceed 90 days, and at least 95 percent of the fund's assets must be invested in top-rated/prime-grade securities), money funds are highly liquid investment vehicles, and they're very low in risk since they are virtually immune to capital loss. However, the interest income produced by the funds is not so secure, as it tends to follow general interest rate conditions. As a result, the returns to shareholders are subject to the ups and downs of market interest rates. Even with their variability, the yields on money funds are highly competitive with other short-term securities, and with the checkwriting privileges they offer, they're just as liquid as checking or savings accounts. They are viewed by many investors as a convenient, safe, and profitable way to accumulate capital and temporarily store idle funds.

Specialty Funds

specialty fund
a mutual fund that strives to achieve attractive rates of return by adhering to unusual or unorthodox investment strategies.

Some funds seek to achieve their investment objectives by investing within a single industry or within a specified geographical area. Others confine their investments to certain types of small companies, or set up funds to invest in *other* mutual funds. These are all examples of **specialty funds** that strive to achieve fairly attractive (and sometimes even spectacular) rates of return by adhering to unusual and, at times, unorthodox investment strategies. Specialty funds make up about 15 to 20 percent of the total *number* of mutual funds. Due to their unusual approach to investing, most are relatively small in terms of assets under management.

In addition to those noted above, there are many other types of specialty funds, including *tax-managed funds,* which seek to minimize taxes by committing funds to tax-preferred investments; *index funds,* which buy and hold a portfolio of stocks (or bonds) equivalent to those in an index like the S&P 500, in order to do nothing more than match the performance of the stock market as a whole; *yield-enhanced* (or *hedge*) *funds,* which hedge their portfolios with futures and options; commodity funds; and others. Due to their unusual nature, specialty funds can involve substantial risk exposure and often require specialized knowledge on the part of investors. Two types of specialty funds that warrant more discussion are sector funds and socially responsible funds.

Sector Funds

sector fund
a mutual fund that restricts its investments to a particular segment of the market.

One of the hottest products on Wall Street is the so-called **sector fund,** a mutual fund that restricts its investments to a particular sector, or segment, of the market. In effect, these funds concentrate their investment holdings in one or more industries that make up the sector being aimed at. For example, a health care sector fund would confine its investments to those industries related to this segment of the market: drug companies, hospital management firms, medical suppliers, and biotech concerns. The portfolio of a sector fund would then consist of promising growth stocks from these particular industries. The underlying investment objective of a sector fund is *capital gains*. In many respects it is similar to a growth fund, and should be considered speculative in nature. The idea behind the sector fund concept is that the really attractive returns come from small segments of the market, so rather than diversifying your portfolio across the market, put your money where the action is! It's an interesting notion that certainly warrants consideration by the more aggressive investor willing to take on the added risks that often accompany these funds. Among the more popular sector funds are those that concentrate their investments in aerospace and defense; energy; financial services; gold and precious metals; leisure and entertainment; natural resources; electronics; chemicals; computers; telecommunications; utilities; and of course, health care—basically, all the "glamour" industries.

Socially Responsible Funds

socially responsible fund
a mutual fund that actively and directly incorporates ethics and morality into the investment decision.

For some, investing is far more than just cranking out financial ratios and calculating investment results. To these investors, the security selection process doesn't end with bottom lines, P/E ratios, growth rates, and betas; rather, it also includes the *active, explicit consideration of moral, ethical, and environmental issues*. The idea is that social concerns should play just as big a role in the investment decision as profits and other financial matters. Not surprisingly, there are a number of funds today that cater to such investors: Known as **socially responsible funds,** they actively and directly incorporate ethics and morality into the investment decision. These funds will consider only socially responsible companies for inclusion in their portfolios—if a company doesn't meet certain moral, ethical, or environmental tests, they simply won't consider buying the stock, no matter how good the bottom line looks. Generally speaking, these funds abstain from investing in companies that derive revenues from tobacco, alcohol or gambling; have dealings with South Africa (though this may change, if apartheid is abolished); are weapons contractors; or operate nuclear power plants. In addition, the funds tend to favor firms that produce "responsible" products or services, have strong employee relations and positive environmental records, and are socially responsive to the communities in which they operate. Although these screens may seem to eliminate a lot of stocks from consideration, these funds (most of which are fairly small) still have plenty of securities to choose from, so it's not all that difficult for them to keep their portfolios fully invested. As far as performance is concerned, the general perception is that there's a price to pay, in the form of lower average returns, for socially responsible investing. That's not too surprising, however, for as you add more investment hurdles, you're likely to reduce return potential. But those who truly believe in socially responsible investing apparently are willing to put their money where their mouths are!

International Funds

In their search for higher yields and better returns, American investors have shown a growing interest in foreign securities. Sensing an opportunity, the mutual fund

international fund
a mutual fund that
does all or most of
its investing in for-
eign securities.

industry was quick to respond with a proliferation of so-called **international funds**—a type of mutual fund that does all or most of its investing in foreign securities. Just look at the number of international funds around today versus a few years ago: In 1985, there were only about 40 of these funds; by 1991, the number had grown to over 200. The fact is that a lot of people would like to invest in foreign securities but simply don't have the experience or know-how to do so. International funds may be just the vehicle for such investors, *provided they have at least a basic appreciation of international economics.* Since these funds deal with the international economy, balance of trade positions, and currency valuations, investors should have a fundamental understanding of what these issues are and how they can affect fund returns.

Technically, the term *international fund* is used to describe a type of fund that *invests exclusively in foreign securities,* often confining their activities to specific geographic regions (like Mexico, Australia, Europe, or the Pacific Rim). In addition, there's a special class of international funds, known as *global funds,* which invest not only in foreign securities, *but also in U.S. companies*—usually multinational firms. As a rule, global funds provide more diversity and, with access to both foreign and domestic markets, can go where the action is. Regardless of whether they're global or international (from here on out, we'll use the term *international* to apply to both), you'll find just about any type of fund you could possibly want in the international sector. There are international *stock* funds, international *bond* funds, even international *money market* funds. In addition, there are aggressive growth funds, balanced funds, long-term growth funds, high-grade bond funds, and so forth. Thus, no matter what your investment philosophy or objective, you're likely to find what you're looking for in the international area.

Basically, these funds attempt to take advantage of international economic developments in two ways: (1) by capitalizing on changing market conditions, and (2) by positioning themselves to benefit from devaluation of the dollar. They do so because they can make money not only from rising share prices in a foreign market, but perhaps just as important, from a falling dollar (which, in itself, produces capital gains for American investors in international funds). Many of these funds, however, will attempt to protect their investors from currency exchange risks by using various types of *hedging strategies.* That is, by using foreign currency options and futures (or some other type of derivative product), the fund will try to eliminate (or reduce) the effects of currency exchange rates. Some funds, in fact, do this on a permanent basis: In essence, these funds hedge away exchange risk so they can concentrate on the higher returns that the foreign securities themselves offer. Most others are only occasional users of currency hedges and will employ them only if they feel there's a real chance of a substantial swing in currency values. But even with currency hedging, international funds are still considered to be fairly high-risk investments and should only be used by investors who understand and are able to tolerate such risks.

Investor Services

Ask most investors why they buy a particular mutual fund and they'll probably tell you that the fund provides the kind of income and return they're looking for. Now, no one would question the importance of return in the investment decision, but there are some other reasons for investing in mutual funds, not the least of which are the services they provide. Indeed, many investors find these services so valuable that they often buy the funds as much for their services as for their returns. Some of the most sought-after *mutual fund services* include automatic investment and reinvestment plans, regular income programs, conversion and phone-switching privileges, and retirement programs.

Automatic Investment Plans

automatic investment plan
a mutual fund service that allows shareholders to automatically send fixed amounts of money from their paychecks or bank accounts into the fund.

It takes money to make money, and for an investor, that means being able to accumulate the capital to put into the market. Unfortunately, that's not always the easiest thing in the world to do. Enter mutual funds, which have come up with a program that makes savings and capital accumulation as painless as possible. The program is the **automatic investment plan,** which allows fund shareholders to automatically funnel fixed amounts of money *from their paychecks or bank accounts* into a mutual fund. It's much like a payroll deduction plan, where investments to your mutual fund are automatically deducted from your paycheck or bank account. This fund service has become very popular, because it enables shareholders to invest without having to think about it. Just about every fund group offers some kind of automatic investment plan for virtually all of their stock and bond funds. To enroll, you simply fill out a form authorizing the fund to siphon a set amount (usually it has to be a minimum of $25 to $100 per period) from your bank account or paycheck at regular intervals—typically monthly or quarterly. Once enrolled, you'll be buying more shares in the fund(s) of your choice every month or quarter (most funds deal in fractional shares). Of course, if it's a load fund, you'll still have to pay normal sales charges on your periodic investments. To remain diversified, you can divide your money among as many funds (within a given fund family) as you like. Finally, you can get out of the program any time you like, without penalty, by simply calling the fund. Although convenience is perhaps the plans' chief advantage, they also make solid investment sense, as one of the best ways of building up a sizable amount of capital is to add funds to your investment program systematically over time. The importance of making regular contributions to your investment program cannot be overstated: it ranks right up there with compound interest.

Automatic Reinvestment Plans

automatic reinvestment plan
a mutual fund service that enables shareholders to automatically buy additional shares in the fund through reinvestment of dividends and capital gains income.

An automatic reinvestment plan is one of the real draws of mutual funds and is a service offered by just about every open-ended mutual fund. Whereas the automatic investment plans we discussed above deal with money that the shareholder is putting into a fund, automatic *re*investment plans deal with the dividends that the funds pay to their shareholders. A lot like the dividend reinvestment plans we looked at with stocks (in Chapter 5), the **automatic reinvestment plans** of mutual funds enable you to keep your capital fully employed. Through this service, dividend and/or capital gains income is *automatically used to buy additional shares in the* *fund*. Most funds deal in fractional shares, and such purchases are often commission-free. Keep in mind, however, that even though an investor may reinvest all dividends and capital gains distributions, the IRS will treat them as cash receipts and, as such, tax them as investment income in the year in which they were paid.

Automatic reinvestment plans are especially attractive since they enable investors to earn fully compounded rates of return. That is, by plowing back profits, the investor essentially can put his or her profits to work in generating even more earnings. Indeed, the effects of these plans on total accumulated capital over the long haul can be substantial. Figure 13.5 shows the long-term impact of one such plan. (These are the actual performance numbers for a *real* mutual fund—the Vanguard Windsor Fund.) In the illustration, we assume the investor starts with $10,000 and, except for the reinvestment of dividends and capital gains, *adds no*

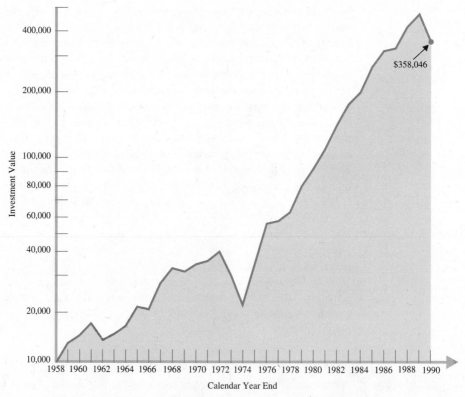

• FIGURE 13.5 The Effects of Reinvesting Income

Reinvesting dividends or capital gains can have tremendous impact on one's investment position. This graph shows the results of a hypothetical investor who initially invested $10,000 and for 32 years reinvested all dividends and capital gains distributions in additional fund shares. (No adjustment has been made for any income taxes payable by the shareholder—which would be appropriate so long as the fund was held in an IRA or Keogh account.) (*Source:* The Vanguard Windsor Fund.)

new capital over time. Even so, note that the initial investment of $10,000 grew to nearly $360,000 over a 32-year period (which, by the way, amounts to a compounded rate of return of 11.8 percent). Of course, not all periods will match this performance, nor will all mutual funds be able to perform as well even in strong markets. The point is, as long as care is taken in selecting an appropriate fund, *attractive benefits can be derived from the systematic accumulation of capital offered by automatic reinvestment plans.* Clearly, investors should consider very seriously the idea of incorporating these plans into their mutual fund investment program.

Regular Income

Although automatic investment and reinvestment plans are great for the long-term investor, what about the investor who's looking for a steady stream of income? Once again, mutual funds have a service to meet this kind of need. It's called a **systematic withdrawal plan,** and it's offered by most open-ended funds. Once enrolled in one of these plans, an investor will automatically receive a predetermined amount of money every month or quarter. Usually the funds require a minimum investment of $5,000 or more in order to participate in such plans, and the size of the minimum payment must normally be $50 or more per period (with no limit on the maximum). The funds will pay out the monthly or quarterly income first from dividends and realized capital gains. Should this source prove to be inadequate and should the shareholder so authorize, the fund can then tap the principal or original paid-in capital in the account to meet the required periodic payments.

systematic withdrawal plan
a mutual fund service that enables shareholders to automatically receive a predetermined amount of money every month or quarter.

Conversion Privileges and Phone Switching

Sometimes investors find it necessary, for one reason or another, to switch out of one fund and into another. The investor's investment objectives may change, or the investment climate itself may have changed. **Conversion** (or **exchange**) **privileges** were devised to meet the needs of such investors in a convenient and economical manner. Investment management companies that offer a number of different funds—known as **fund families**—often provide conversion privileges that enable shareholders to easily move from one fund to another, usually by phone. Indeed, with *phone switching,* an investor can simply pick up the phone to move money among funds—the only constraint being that the switches must be confined to the same *family* of funds. For example, an investor can switch from a Dreyfus growth fund to a Dreyfus money fund, or to its income fund, or to any other fund managed by Dreyfus. With some fund families, the alternatives open to investors seem almost without limit; indeed, some of the larger families offer 20 or 30 funds (or more). One investment company (Fidelity) has over 100 different funds in its family—everything from high-performance stock funds to bond funds, tax-exempt funds, a couple of dozen sector funds, and a couple dozen money funds.

conversion (exchange) privilege
feature of a mutual fund that allows shareholders to move money from one fund to another, within the same family of funds.

fund families
different kinds of mutual funds all offered by the same investment management company.

There are more than a hundred fund families in operation today. They all provide low-cost conversion/phone-switching privileges (some even *free*), although most families that offer free exchanges have limits on the number of times such switches can occur each year. Twenty of the largest fund families are listed in Table 13.4. Note that, together, these 20 families offer 928 different mutual funds to the investing public. Conversion privileges are usually considered beneficial from the shareholder's point of view, since they allow investors to meet their ever-changing long-term investment goals. In addition, they permit investors to manage their mutual fund holdings more aggressively by allowing them to move in and out of funds as the investment environment changes. Unfortunately there is one major drawback: For tax purposes, the exchange of shares from one fund to another is regarded as a sale transaction followed by a subsequent purchase of a new security. As a result, if any capital gains exist at the time of the exchange, the investor is liable for the taxes on that profit even though the holdings were not truly liquidated.

Retirement Programs

As a result of government legislation, self-employed individuals are permitted to divert a portion of their pre-tax income into self-directed *retirement plans*. Also, all working Americans, whether they are self-employed or not, are allowed to establish individual retirement accounts. (Even after the Tax Reform Act of 1986, IRAs can still be set up by anyone who is gainfully employed, although the tax deductibility

TABLE 13.4 Twenty of the Biggest Fund Families

Fund Families*	Number of Stock, Bond Funds	Number of Money Funds	Total Number of Funds
American Capital	21	1	22
Colonial Investment Services	26	1	27
Dean Witter Reynolds	29	5	34
Dreyfus Service Corp.	48	16	64
Federated Securities Corp.	15	4	19
Fidelity Distributors Corp.	113	29	142
Franklin Distributors	46	7	53
IDS Financial Services	34	3	37
Kemper Financial Services	36	3	39
Keystone Distributors	28	1	29
Mass. Financial Services	40	2	42
Merrill Lynch Funds	70	22	92
Oppenheimer Fund Mgmt	24	2	26
T. Rowe Price Assocs.	34	3	37
Prudential-Bache	56	13	69
Putnam Financial Services	46	4	50
Shearson Lehman Hutton	47	9	56
SteinRoe	12	3	15
Vanguard Group	48	8	56
Waddell & Reed (United Fds)	17	2	19

*Number of funds in existence in early 1992; all these fund families offer conversion privileges.

of IRA *contributions* is limited to certain individuals.) Today all mutual funds provide a special service that allows individuals to set up tax-deferred retirement programs as either IRA or Keogh accounts. The funds set up the plans and handle all the administrative details in such a way that the shareholder can easily take full advantage of available tax savings.

INVESTING IN MUTUAL FUNDS

Suppose you are confronted with the following situation: You have money to invest and are trying to select the right place to put it. You obviously want to pick a security that meets your idea of acceptable risk, but also one that will generate an attractive rate of return. The problem is you have to make the selection from a list of over 3,200 securities. Sound like a "mission impossible"? Well, that's basically what the investor is up against when trying to select a suitable mutual fund. But perhaps if the problem is approached systematically, it may not be so formidable a task. As we will see, it is possible to whittle down the list of alternatives by matching one's investment needs with the investment objectives of the funds. Before doing that, though, it might be helpful to examine more closely the various investor uses of mutual funds. With this background, we can then look at the selection process and at several measures of return that can be used to assess performance.

Investor Uses of Mutual Funds

Mutual funds can be used by individual investors in a variety of ways. For instance, performance funds can serve as a vehicle for capital appreciation, whereas bond funds can be used to provide current income. Regardless of the kind of income a fund provides, individuals tend to use these investment vehicles for one of three reasons: (1) as a way to accumulate wealth, (2) as a speculative vehicle for achieving high rates of return, and (3) as a storehouse of value.

Accumulation of Wealth

Accumulation of wealth is probably the most common reason for using mutual funds. Basically, it involves using mutual funds over the long haul for the purpose of building up investment capital. Depending upon the investor's personality, a modest amount of risk may be acceptable, but usually preservation of capital and capital stability are considered important. The whole idea is to form a "partnership" with the mutual fund in building up as big a capital pool as possible: You provide the capital by systematically investing and reinvesting in the fund, and the fund provides the return by doing its best to invest your resources wisely.

Speculation and Short-Term Trading

Speculation is not a common use of mutual funds; the reason, of course, is that most mutual funds are long-term in nature and as such, are not really meant to be used as aggressive trading vehicles. However, a growing number of funds (e.g., sector funds) now cater to speculators, and some investors find that mutual funds are indeed attractive outlets for speculation and short-term trading. One way to do this is to trade in and out of funds aggressively as the investment climate changes. Load charges can be avoided (or reduced) by dealing in "families" of funds offering low-cost conversion privileges and/or by dealing only in no-load funds. Some investors might choose to invest in funds for the long run but still seek extraordinarily high rates of return by investing in aggressive mutual funds. There are a number of funds that follow very aggressive trading strategies and that may well appeal to investors who are willing to accept substantial risk exposure. These are usually the fairly specialized smaller funds: Sophisticated hedge funds, leverage funds, option funds, and global funds are just a few examples, as are performance or sector funds. In essence, such investors are simply applying the basic mutual fund concept to their investment needs by letting professional money managers handle their accounts in a way they would like to see them handled: *aggressively*.

Storehouse of Value

Investors may also use mutual funds as a storehouse of value. The idea here is to find a place where investment capital can be fairly secure and relatively free from deterioration, yet still generate a relatively attractive rate of return. Short- and intermediate-term bond funds are logical choices for such purposes and so are money funds. Capital preservation and income over the long haul is very important to some investors. Still others might seek storage of value only for the short term, using money funds as a way to "sit it out" until a more attractive opportunity comes along.

The Selection Process

In many respects, the selection process is the critical dimension in defining the amount of success one will have with mutual funds. It means putting into action all you know about funds in order to gain as much return as possible from an acceptable level of risk. The selection process begins with an assessment of one's own investment needs; this sets the tone of the investment program. Obviously, what we want to do is select from those 3,200 funds the one or two (or three or four) that will best meet our total investment needs.

Objectives and Motives for Using Funds

Selecting the right investment means finding those funds that are most suitable to your total investment needs. *The place to start is with your own investment objectives.* In other words, why do you want to invest in a mutual fund, and what are you looking for in a fund? Obviously, an attractive rate of return would be desirable, but there is also the matter of a tolerable amount of risk exposure. Face it: Some investors are more willing to take risks than others, and this is certainly an important ingredient in the selection process. More than likely, when you look at your own risk temperament in relation to the various types of mutual funds available, you will discover that certain types of funds are more appealing to us than others. For instance, aggressive growth or sector funds will probably *not* be attractive to individuals who wish to avoid high exposure to risk.

Another important factor in the selection process is the intended use of the mutual fund. That is, do you want to invest in mutual funds as a means of accumulating wealth, to speculate for high rates of return, or as a storehouse of value? This is helpful information, since it puts into clearer focus the question of exactly what you are trying to do with your investment dollars. Finally, there is the matter of the types of services provided by the fund. If there are services you are particularly interested in, you should be sure to look for them in the funds you select. Having assessed what you are looking for in a fund, you now want to look at what the funds have to offer us.

What Funds Offer

The ideal mutual fund would achieve maximum capital growth when security prices rise, provide complete protection against capital loss when prices decline, and achieve high levels of current income at all times. Unfortunately, this fund does not exist. Instead, just as each individual has a set of investment needs, each fund has its own *investment objective,* its own *manner of operation,* and its own *range of services*. These three parameters are useful in helping us to assess investment alternatives. But where does the investor look for such information? One obvious place is the fund's *prospectus* (or its Statement of Additional Information), where detailed information on investment objectives, portfolio composition, management, and past performance can be obtained. The *Investor Insights* box below offers some suggestions on what to look for in a mutual fund prospectus. In addition, publications such as *The Wall Street Journal, Barron's, Financial World,* and *Forbes* provide useful data and information concerning mutual funds. These sources provide a wealth of operating and performance statistics in a convenient and easy-to-read format. For instance, each year, *Forbes* rates over 2,000 mutual funds, and every quarter, *Barron's* publishes an extensive mutual fund performance report. What's more, there are services available that provide background information and assessments on a wide variety of different kinds of funds. Among the best in this category are Morningstar's *Mutual Fund Values* (an excerpt of which is shown in Figure 13.6), Wiesenberger's *Investment Companies* (an annual publication with quarterly updates), and *Donoghue's Mutual Funds Almanac* (a low-cost, annual publication that provides a variety of operating and performance statistics). Using sources like these, investors can obtain information on such things as investment objectives, load charges and annual expense rates, summary portfolio analyses, services offered, historical statistics, and reviews of past performance.

Whittling Down the Alternatives

At this point, fund selection becomes a process of elimination as investor needs are weighed against the types of funds available. Large numbers of funds can be eliminated from consideration simply because they fail to meet these needs. Some may be too risky; others may be unsuitable as a storehouse of value. Thus, rather than trying to evaluate 3,200 different funds, you can use a process of elimination to

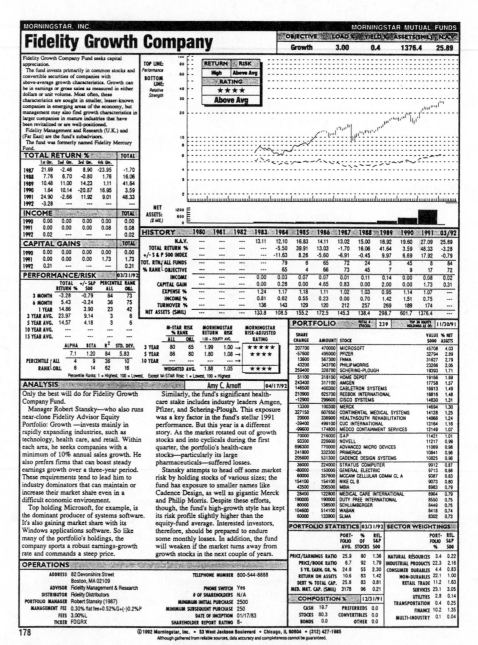

● FIGURE 13.6   Some Relevant Information about Specific Mutual Funds

Investors who want in-depth information about the operating characteristics, investment holdings, and market behavior of specific mutual funds, such as this one for Fidelity Growth Company, can usually find what they are looking for in periodicals like Morningstar Mutual Funds. (*Source:* Morningstar, Inc., Morningstar Mutual Funds, 1992.)

narrow the list down to two or three *types* of funds that best match your investment needs. From here, you can whittle the list down a bit more by introducing other constraints. For example, because of cost considerations, you may want to deal only in no-load or low-load funds, or you may be seeking certain services that are important to your investment goals. Now we introduce the final (but certainly not the least important) element in the selection process: *the fund's investment performance*. Useful information includes (1) how the fund has performed over the past five to seven years; (2) the type of return it has generated in good markets as well as bad; (3) the level of dividend and capital gains distributions; and (4) the type of investment stability the fund has enjoyed over time (or put another way, the amount of volatility/risk in the fund's return). By evaluating such information, it is possible to identify some of the more successful mutual funds—the ones that not only offer the investment objectives and services you seek but also provide the best payoffs as well. And while you're looking at performance, it probably wouldn't hurt to check out the fund's *fee structure*. Be on guard for funds that charge abnormally high management fees, as they can really hurt returns over time. As a point of reference, mutual funds experienced the following *average annual expense rates* in 1990: *stock funds* had median expense ratios of around 1½ percent of assets under management (of course, the larger the fund, the lower the expense rate); *bond funds* had expense rates of roughly 1 percent, across the board; and for *money funds,* the median was around ¾ of 1 percent.

Note that in this decision process considerable weight is given to *past performance*. As a rule, the past is given little or no attention in the investment decision—after all, it's the future that matters. Although the *future performance* of a mutual fund is still the variable that holds the key to success, a good deal of time is spent on past investment results in order to get a handle on how successful the fund's investment managers have been. In essence the success of a mutual fund rests in large part *on the investment skills of the fund managers*. Thus, when investing in a mutual fund, look for consistently good performance, in up as well as down markets, over *extended* periods of time (five years or more). Most important, check to see if the same key people are still running the fund. Although past success is certainly no guarantee of future performance, a strong team of money managers can have a significant bearing on the level of fund returns.

Measuring Performance

Like any investment decision, return performance is a major dimension in the mutual fund selection process. The level of dividends paid by the fund, its capital gains, and growth in capital are all important aspects of return. Such return information enables the investor to judge the investment behavior of the fund and to appraise its performance in relation to other funds and investment vehicles. Here, we will look at different measures that can be used by mutual fund investors to assess return; also, because risk is so important in defining the investment behavior of a fund, we will review it as well.

████ INVESTOR INSIGHTS ████

What to Look for in a Mutual Fund Prospectus

The Securities and Exchange Commission requires that a mutual fund's prospectus be in your hands before the fund can accept your investment. That might seem like a cruel joke, because the typical prospectus is about as readable as the Rosetta Stone. Yet if you don't plow through this document, you lay yourself open to nasty surprises later.

Investors often complain that a lot of funds go to great lengths to camouflage important information in the prospectus. Usually it's because prospectuses are written by lawyers, whose prose can be opaque. Fortunately, more sponsors are seeing benefits in sharper writing. T. Rowe Price, for example, has shifted its prospectus-writing largely to marketing people and has attorneys review the legal points. More good news: Funds must now include a table of all fees near the front of the prospectus, followed by a hypothetical total of all fees over several years, assuming the fund earns a 5% return. This feature should end disjointed disclosure of costs.

To help you get the most out of a mutual fund prospectus, here's a guided tour through this document:

- *Investment objective.* Certain words and phrases appear regularly. Bond funds all seem to aim for "highest level of current income" that's "consistent with preservation of capital." Stock funds tell their top and secondary priorities: capital growth, dividend income, a combination of the two and, possibly, a narrow strategy, such as hunting for "special situations" or "undervalued stocks." Strategies may or may not be well-defined. If they are, the prospectus is telling you about the riskiness of the fund. For example, Fidelity Special Situations explain, "We expect to be fully invested in stocks under most market conditions." So don't cry that its manager should have been in Treasury bills if stocks take a tumble. The Franklin Short-Inter-

Sources of Return

An open-end fund has three potential sources of return: (1) dividend income, (2) capital gains distribution, and (3) change in the price (or net asset value) of the fund. Depending on the type of fund, some mutual funds will derive more income from one source than another. For example, we would normally expect income-oriented funds to have much higher dividend income than capital gains distributions. Mutual funds regularly publish reports that recap investment performance. One such report is *The Summary of Income and Capital Changes,* an example of which is provided in Table 13.5. This statement, which is found in the fund's prospectus or annual report, gives a brief overview of the fund's investment activity, including expense ratios and portfolio turnover rates. Of interest here is the top part of the report (that runs from *Investment income to NAV at the end of the year*—lines 1 to 9); this is the part that reveals the amount of dividend income and capital gains distributed to the shareholders, along with change in the fund's net asset value.

mediate U.S. Government Securities Fund says it will maintain an average portfolio maturity of two to five years. That tells you that Franklin's investments will be subject to less price volatility than an "intermediate" fund empowered to stretch to perhaps 12 years' maturity.

- *Past performance*. Established funds include five years of results—if they are that old—in a table of *per-share income and capital changes*. These condensed financial statements reveal such facts as the ratio of expenses to average net assets (over 1% is high, unless it's an international or sector fund) and the portfolio turnover rate (100% means the manager trades every stock in the portfolio every year). Many, but by no means all, prospectuses compare the fund's results to the S&P 500 or another recognized index. Total return—the measurement of price gains or losses plus dividend and interest income—is still a voluntary feature in a prospectus. But you can estimate total return from the prospectus by taking the latest year-end share price, adding back all capital gains and dividends paid during the previous year and taking the percentage change from the previous year's ending price.

- *Management*. Funds don't have to tell the name and qualifications of the portfolio manager, though IDS even goes so far as to run color photos of its managers. Sometimes a fund will go out of its way to mention a resident celebrity.

- *Miscellaneous*. The back pages of the prospectus are the guts that describe such services as exchange privileges between funds in the family or signing up to a systematic withdrawal plan. If you're unfamiliar with these services, call shareholder services with questions. Ask the fund about anything you can't easily find in the prospectus. If enough investors tie up the phones to ask about what should be explained clearly in the prospectus, funds are apt to do a better job of writing them.

Source: Adapted from Jeff Kosnett, "What to Look for—and Look Out for—as You Read a Mutual Fund Prospectus," *Changing Times*, May 1988, p. 18.

---

dividend income
income derived from the dividend and interest income earned on the security holdings of a mutual fund.

capital gains distributions
payments made to mutual fund shareholders that come from the profits that a fund makes from the sale of its securities.

Dividend income is derived from the dividend and interest income earned on the security holdings of the mutual fund. It's paid out of the *net investment income* that's left after all operating expenses have been met. When the fund receives dividend or interest payments, it passes these on to shareholders in the form of dividend payments. The fund accumulates all the current income it has received for the period and then pays it out on a prorated basis. If a fund earned, say, $2 million in dividends and interest in a given year, and if that fund had 1 million shares outstanding, each share would receive an annual dividend payment of $2. **Capital gains distributions** work on the same principle, except that these payments are derived from the capital gains earned by the fund. It works like this: Suppose the fund bought some stock a year ago for $50 and sold that stock in the current period for $75 per share. Clearly the fund has achieved capital gains of $25 per share. If it held 50,000 shares of this stock, it would have realized a total capital gain of $1,250,000($25 × 50,000 = $1,250,000). Given that the fund has 1 million shares outstanding, each share is entitled to $1.25 in the form of a capital gains distribu-

TABLE 13.5 A Report of Mutual Fund Income and Capital Changes

(For a share outstanding throughout the year)

		1992	1991	1990
	INCOME AND EXPENSES			
	1. Investment income	$.76	$.88	$.67
	2. Less expenses	.16	.22	.17
	3. Net investment income	.60	.66	.50
Dividend Income⟶	4. Dividends from net investment income	(.55)	(.64)	(.50)
	CAPITAL CHANGES			
	5. Net realized and unrealized gains (or losses) on security transactions	6.37	(1.74)	3.79
Capital Gains Distribution⟶	6. Distributions from realized gains	(1.75)	(.84)	(1.02)
Change in NAV⟶	7. Net increase (decrease) in NAV[*]	4.67	(2.56)	2.77
	8. NAV at beginning of year	24.47	27.03	24.26
	9. NAV at end of year	$29.14	$24.47	$27.03
	10. Ratio of operating expenses to average net assets	1.04%	.85%	.94%
	11. Ratio of net investment income to average net assets	1.47%	2.56%	2.39%
	12. Portfolio turnover rate[**]	85%	144%	74%
	13. Shares outstanding at end of year (000s omitted)	10,568	6,268	4,029

[*]*Note: Net increase (decrease) in NAV,* line 7 = line 3 − line 4 + line 5 − line 6; for example, the 1992 net increase in NAV was found as $.60 − .55 + 6.37 − 1.75 = $4.67.

[**]*Portfolio turnover rate* relates the number of shares bought and sold by the fund to the total number of shares held in the fund's portfolio; a high turnover rate (for example, in excess of 100 percent) would mean the fund has been doing a lot of trading.

unrealized capital gains (paper profits)
a capital gain made only "on paper," that is, not realized until the fund's holdings are sold.

tion. Note that this capital gain distribution applies only to *realized* capital gains—that is, the security holdings were actually sold and the capital gains actually earned.

Unrealized capital gains (or **paper profits**) are what make up the third and final element in a mutual fund's return. When the fund's holdings go up or down in price, the net asset value of the fund moves accordingly. Suppose an investor buys into a fund at $10 per share, and some time later it is quoted at $12.50. The difference of $2.50 per share is the unrealized capital gains contained in the fund's security holdings. It represents the profit shareholders would receive (and are entitled to) if the fund were to sell its holdings. (Actually, as Table 13.5 shows, some of the change in net asset value can also be made up of *undistributed dividends*.)

The return on *closed-end* investment companies is derived from the same three sources as that of open-end funds, and from a fourth source as well: changes in price discounts or premiums. Because closed-end companies are traded like any common stock, they seldom trade exactly at their net asset value. Instead, they tend to trade below (at a discount) or above (at a premium) their NAV. As these discounts or premiums change over time, the return to shareholders is affected accordingly. The reason is that such changes in discount or premium affect the market price of the fund. Because discount or premium is already embedded in the share price of a fund, it follows that for a closed-end fund the third element of return (change in share price) is made up not only of change in net asset value, but also of change in price discount or premium.

What About Future Performance?

There's no doubt that a statement like the one in Table 13.5 provides a convenient recap of a fund's past behavior. Unfortunately, looking at past performance is one thing, but what about the future? Ideally, you want to evaluate the same three elements of return as noted above. The trouble is that when it comes to the future performance of a mutual fund, it's extremely difficult—if not impossible—to get a firm grip on what the future holds as far as dividends, capital gains, and NAV are concerned. The reason is that a mutual fund's future investment performance is directly linked to *the future makeup of the securities it holds in its portfolio,* which is something that is next to impossible to get a clear reading on. It's not like evaluating the expected performance of a share of stock, in which case you're keying in on one company. With mutual funds, investment performance depends on the behavior of many different stocks and bonds.

So, where do you look for insight on the future? Most market observers suggest the first place to look is the market itself. In particular, try to get a fix on the *future direction of the market as a whole.* This is important because the behavior of a well-diversified mutual fund tends to reflect the general tone of the market. Thus, if the feeling is that the market is going to be drifting generally up, so should the investment performance of mutual funds. Also spend some time evaluating the *track records* of potential investment candidates. As noted earlier, past performance has a lot to say about the investment skills of the fund's money managers. In essence, look for funds that you think will be able to capture the best of what the future market environment holds.

Measures of Return

A simple but effective measure of performance is to describe mutual fund return in terms of the three major sources noted above: dividends earned, capital gains distributions received, and change in price. These payoffs can then be converted to a convenient yield figure by using the standard holding period return formula. The computations necessary can be illustrated below using the 1992 figures from Table 13.5. Referring to the exhibit, we can see that in 1992 this hypothetical no-load fund paid 55 cents per share in dividends and another $1.75 in capital gains distributions; and it had a price at the beginning of the year of $24.47 that rose to $29.14 by the end of the year. Thus, summarizing this investment performance, we have:

Price (NAV) at the *beginning* of the year	$24.47
Price (NAV) at the *end* of the year	29.14
Net increase	$ 4.67
Return for the year:	
Dividends received	$ .55
Capital gains distributions	1.75
Net increase in price (NAV)	4.67
Total return	$ 6.97
Holding period return	28.5%
(Total return/beginning price)	

The measure is simple to calculate and follows the standard HPR format. It not only captures all the important elements of mutual fund return but also provides a handy indication of yield. Notice that we had a total dollar return of $6.97 and, based on a beginning investment of $24.47 (the initial share price of the fund), were able to realize an annual rate of return of 28.5 percent.

But what happens if dividends and capital gains distributions are reinvested into the fund? In that case, the investor receives additional shares of stock instead of cash. Holding period return can still be used to measure return, the only difference is that the investor has to keep track of the number of shares acquired through reinvestment. To illustrate, let's continue with the example above and assume that the investor initially bought 200 shares in the mutual fund. Assume also that the investor was able to acquire shares through the fund's reinvestment program at an average price of, say, $26.50 a share. Thus the $460 in dividends and capital gains distributions [($.55 + $1.75) × 200] provided the investor with another 17.36 shares in the fund ($460/$26.50). Holding period return under these circumstances would relate the market value of the stock holdings at the beginning of the period with holdings at the end, or:

Equation 13.1

$$\text{Holding period return} = \frac{\left(\begin{array}{c}\text{number of shares} \times \\ \text{ending price}\end{array}\right) - \left(\begin{array}{c}\text{number of shares} \times \\ \text{initial price}\end{array}\right)}{(\text{number of shares} \times \text{initial price})}$$

Thus, the holding period return for our hypothetical investor would be:

$$\text{Holding period return} = \frac{(217.36 \times \$29.14) - (200 \times \$24.47)}{(200 \times \$24.47)}$$

$$= \frac{(\$6,333.87) - (\$4,894.00)}{(\$4,894.00)} = 29.4\%$$

This holding period yield, like the preceding one, provides a rate of return measure that can now be used to compare the performance of this fund to that of other funds and other investment vehicles.

Rather than using one-year holding periods, it is sometimes necessary to assess the performance of mutual funds over extended periods of time. Under such circumstances, it would be *inappropriate* to employ holding period return as a measure of performance. Preferably, when faced with multiple-year investment horizons, the standard *approximate yield* measure should be used to determine the fund's average annual compound rate of return. This can be done by following established approximate yield procedures except for one slight modification: That is, *capital gains distributions should be added to dividends received to find total average annual income.* To illustrate, refer back to Table 13.5; assume that this time we want to find the annual rate of return over the full three-year period (1990 through 1992). In this case, we see that the mutual fund had *average* annual dividends of 56 cents a share [(.55 + 64 + .50)/3], *average* annual capital gains distributions of $1.20 a share [(1.75 + .84 + 1.02)/3], and total *average* annual income of $1.76 a share (1.20 + .56). Given that it had a price of $24.26 at the beginning of 1990 and a price of $29.14 at the end of 1992 (some 3 years later), we can find the fund's approximate yield as follows:

Equation 13.2

$$\frac{\text{Approximate}}{\text{yield}} = \frac{\text{total average} \atop \text{annual income} + \dfrac{\text{ending} \atop \text{share price} - \text{beginning} \atop \text{share price}}{\text{number of years held}}}{\dfrac{\text{ending} \atop \text{share price} + \text{beginning} \atop \text{share price}}{2}}$$

$$= \frac{\$1.76 + \dfrac{\$29.14 - \$24.26}{3}}{\dfrac{\$29.14 + \$24.26}{2}} = \underline{\underline{12.7\%}}$$

Thus, the mutual fund in Table 13.5 provided its investors with an average annual rate of return of approximately 12.7 percent over the three-year period in question. Such information is helpful in assessing fund performance and in comparing the return performance of one fund to other funds and to other investment vehicles. (According to SEC regulations, mutual funds must report historical return behavior in a standardized format that employs fully compounded, total return figures similar to ones obtained from the approximate yield measure. Although the funds are *not* required to report such information, if they do cite performance in their promotional material, they must follow a *full-disclosure* manner of presentation that takes into account not only dividends and capital gains distributions but also any increases or decreases in the fund's NAV that have occurred over the past 1-, 5-, and 10-year periods.)

The Matter of Risk

Because most mutual funds are so diversified, their investors, for the most part, are immune to the business and financial risks normally present with individual securities. Even with extensive diversification, however, the investment behavior of most funds is still exposed to a considerable amount of *market risk*. In fact, because mutual fund portfolios are so well diversified, they often reflect the behavior of the marketplace itself and as noted above tend to perform very much like the market. A few funds, like gold funds, tend to be defensive (or countercyclical), but for the most part, market risk is an important behavioral ingredient in a large number of mutual funds, both open- and closed-end. Investors should be aware of the effect the general market has on the investment performance of a fund and try to use such insight when formulating a mutual fund investment program. For example, if the market is trending downward and you see a continuation of such a trend, it might be best to place any new investment capital into something like a money fund until the market reverses itself. At that time, you can make a more permanent commitment.

Another important risk consideration revolves around the management practices of the fund itself. If the portfolio is managed conservatively, the risk of a loss in capital is likely to be much less than for aggressively managed funds. Obviously, the more speculative the investment goals of the fund, the greater the risk of instability in the net asset value. On the other hand, a conservatively managed portfolio does not necessarily eliminate all price volatility, since the securities in the portfolio are still subject to inflation, interest rate, and general market risks. However, these risks will generally be reduced or minimized as the investment objectives and portfolio management practices of the fund become more conservative.

SUMMARY

1. Mutual fund shares represent ownership in a diversified, managed portfolio of securities; many investors who lack the time, know-how, or commitment to manage their own portfolios turn to mutual funds as an investment outlet.

2. By investing in mutual funds, shareholders benefit from a level of diversification and investment performance they might otherwise find difficult to achieve; in addition, they can establish an investment program with a limited amount of capital and obtain a variety of investor services not available elsewhere.

    On the negative side, mutual fund investors may be faced with hefty load charges (commissions) as well as costly management fees and operating expenses that are paid annually, regardless of the level of investment income.

3. Investors can buy either open-end funds, which have no limit on the number of shares they may issue, or closed-end funds, which have a fixed number of shares outstanding and which trade in the secondary markets like any other share of common stock. Also available are unit investment trusts, which consist of unmanaged pools of securities that often pay income on a monthly basis.

    Each fund has an established investment objective that determines its investment policy and identifies it as a certain type of fund. Some of the more popular types of funds include growth funds, aggressive growth funds, equity-income funds, balanced funds, growth-and-income funds, bond funds, money funds, sector funds, socially responsible funds, and international funds. The different categories of funds have different risk-return characteristics and are important variables in the fund selection process.

4. In addition to the investment returns they offer, many investors buy mutual funds to take advantage of special services, such as automatic investment and reinvestment plans, systematic withdrawal programs, low-cost conversion and phone-switching privileges, and retirement programs.

5. The payoff from investing in a mutual fund includes dividend income, distribution of realized capital gains, and growth in capital (unrealized capital gains). Holding period returns and approximate yields recognize these three elements and provide simple yet effective ways of measuring the annual rate of return from a mutual fund.

6. While return is important to mutual fund investors, so is risk; and although a fund's extensive diversification may protect investors from business and financial risks, considerable market risk still remains because most funds tend to perform much like the market, or at least that segment of the market they specialize in.

QUESTIONS

1. What is a mutual fund? Discuss the mutual fund concept; why are diversification and professional management so important?

2. Briefly describe how a mutual fund is organized. Who are the key players in a typical mutual fund organization?

3. Briefly define each of the following:

   a. Closed-end investment company.
   b. Open-end investment company.
   c. Unit investment trust.

4. What is the difference between a load fund and no-load fund? Are there some advantages to either type? What is a 12(b)-1 fund? Can such a fund operate as a no-load fund? Briefly describe a back-end load; a low load; a hidden load. How can you tell what kind of fees and charges a fund has?

5. What are the attractions and drawbacks of mutual fund ownership?

6. Contrast mutual fund ownership with the direct investment in common stocks and bonds. Who should own mutual funds and why?

7. Using the mutual fund quotes in Figure 13.4, how much would you have to pay to buy each of the following funds, and how much would you pay (in dollars and percentage) in front-end load charges with each of these funds?

   a. Fidelity Select-Financial Services (SIFnS).
   b. Fairmont Fund (Fairmt).
   c. Financial Fund's U.S. Government Bonds (USGvt).
   d. FPA Capital Fund (Capit).
   e. Financial Fund's Industrial Income (IndInc).

   How much would you receive if you sold these funds? Which of the five funds listed above have 12(b)-1 fees? Which ones have redemption fees? Are any of them no-loads?

8. Briefly discuss each of the following types of mutual funds:

    a. Aggressive growth funds.
    b. Equity-income funds.
    c. Growth-and-income funds.
    d. Bond funds.
    e. Sector funds.
    f. Socially responsible funds.

9. What is so special about specialty funds? How do their investments differ from those of other types of mutual funds?

10. For each pair of funds listed below, select the one that would likely be *less* risky. Briefly explain your answer.

    a. Growth vs. growth-and-income.
    b. Equity-income vs. high-grade corporate bonds.
    c. Balanced vs. sector.
    d. Global vs. aggressive growth.
    e. Intermediate-term bonds vs. high-yield municipals.

11. What are fund families? What advantages do these families offer investors? Are there any disadvantages?

12. If growth, income, and capital preservation are the primary objectives of mutual funds, why do we bother to categorize them by type? Are such classifications helpful in the fund selection process?

13. List and briefly describe several services provided by mutual funds. How important should these services be in the mutual fund selection process? How do automatic reinvestment plans work? What is phone switching, and why would an investor want to use this type of service?

14. How important is the general behavior of the market in affecting the price performance of mutual funds? Explain. Why is a fund's *past* performance so important to the mutual fund selection process? Does the *future* behavior of the market matter any in the selection process? Explain.

15. Identify three potential sources of return to mutual fund investors and briefly discuss how each could affect total return to shareholders. Explain how the discount or premium of a closed-end fund can also be treated as a return to investors.

16. Discuss the various types of risk to which mutual fund shareholders are exposed. What is the major risk exposure of mutual funds? Are all funds subject to the same level of risk? Explain.

PROBLEMS

 1. A year ago, an investor bought 200 shares of a mutual fund at $8.50 per share; over the past year the fund has paid dividends of 90 cents per share and had a capital gains distribution of 75 cents per share. Find the investor's holding period return given that this no-load fund now has a net asset value of $9.10. Find the holding period return assuming all the dividends and capital gains distributions are reinvested into additional shares of the fund at an average price of $8.75 per share.

2. A year ago, the Really Big Growth Fund was being quoted at an NAV of $21.50 and an offer price of $23.35; today it's being quoted at $23.04 (NAV) and $25.04 (offer). What is the holding period return on this load fund, given that it was purchased a year ago and its dividends and capital gains distributions over the year have totaled $1.05 per share?

3. The All State Mutual Fund has the following five-year record of performance:

	1992	1991	1990	1989	1988
Net investment income	$ .98	$ .85	$ .84	$ .75	$ .64
Dividends from net investment income	(.95)	(.85)	(.85)	(.75)	(.60)
Net realized and unrealized gains (or losses) on security transactions	4.22	5.08	(2.18)	2.65	(1.05)
Distributions from realized gains	(1.05)	(1.00)	—	(1.00)	—
Net increase (decrease) in NAV	3.20	4.08	(2.19)	1.65	(1.01)
NAV at beginning of year	12.53	8.45	10.64	8.99	10.00
NAV at end of year	15.73	12.53	8.45	10.64	8.99

Find this no-load fund's five-year (1988–92) average annual compound rate of return; also find its three-year (1990–92) average annual compound rate of return. If an investor bought the fund in 1988 at $10.00 a share and sold it five years later (in 1992) at $15.73, how much total profit per share would she have made over the five-year holding period?

4. You've uncovered the following per-share information about a certain mutual fund:

	1990	1991	1992
Ending share prices:			
Offer	$46.20	$64.68	$61.78
NAV	43.20	60.47	57.75
Dividend income	2.10	2.84	2.61
Capital gains distribution	1.83	6.26	4.32
Beginning share prices:			
Offer	55.00	46.20	64.68
NAV	51.42	43.20	60.47

Based on this information, find the fund's holding period return for 1990, 1991, and 1992 (in all three cases, assume you buy the fund at the beginning of the year and sell it at the end each year). In addition, find the fund's average annual compound rate of return over the 3-year period, 1990–1992. What would the 1991 holding period return have been if the investor initially bought 500 shares of stock, and reinvested both dividends and capital gains distributions into additional shares of the fund, at an average price of $52.50 per share?

5. Listed below is the 10-year, per-share performance record of *Fidelity Magellan,* as obtained from the fund's May 30, 1991, prospectus:

	Years Ended March 31									
	1991	**1990**	**1989**	**1988**	**1987**	**1986**	**1985**	**1984**	**1983**	**1982**
1. Investment income	$ 1.98	$ 1.90	$ 1.64	$ 1.17	$ 81	$ .76	$ 1.11	$ .63	$ .44	$ .61
2. Expenses	.59	.55	.55	.54	.39	.27	.32	.26	.11	.23
3. Investment income—net	1.39	1.35	1.09	.63	.42	.49	.79	.37	.33	.38
4. Dividends from investment income—net	(.83)	(1.24)	(.90)	(.72)	(.46)	(.65)	(.37)	(.26)	(.33)	(.58)
5. Realized and unrealized gain (loss) on investments—net	8.10	9.39	8.63	(6.64)	11.39	19.59	5.75	2.73	15.80	(.02)
6. Distributions from realized gain on investments—net	(2.42)	(3.82)	—	(9.02)	(6.84)	(1.78)	(3.69)	(1.88)	(1.23)	(9.92)
7. Net increase (decrease) in net asset value	6.24	5.68	8.82	(15.75)	4.51	17.65	2.48	.96	14.57	(10.14)
Net asset value:										
8. Beginning of year	58.60	52.92	44.10	59.85	55.34	37.69	35.21	34.25	19.68	29.82
9. End of year	$64.84	$58.60	$52.92	$44.10	$59.85	$55.34	$37.69	$35.21	$34.25	$19.68

Use the information above to find Magellan's holding period return in 1991 and 1988. Also, find the fund's average annual rate of return over the 5-year period from 1987 through 1991, and the 10-year period, 1982–91. Finally, rework the four return figures assuming Fidelity Magellan has a front-end load charge of 3% (of NAV). Comment on the impact that load charges have on the return behavior of mutual funds.

6. Using the resources available at your campus or public library, select five mutual funds—a growth fund, an equity-income fund, an international (stock) fund, a sector fund, and a high-yield corporate bond fund—that you feel would make good investments. Briefly explain why you selected these funds; include the funds' holding period returns for the past year and their annual compound rates of return for the past three years. (Use a schedule like the one in Table 13.5 to show relevant performance figures.)

CASE PROBLEMS

13.1 Reverend Robin Ponders Mutual Funds

Reverend Robin is the minister of a church in the San Antonio area. He is married with one young child, and he earns what could best be described as a "modest income." Since religious organizations are not notorious for their generous retirement programs, the Reverend has decided it would be best for him to do a little investing on his own. He would like to set up a program that enables him to supplement the church's retirement program and at the same time, provide some funds for his child's college education (which is still some 12 years away). He is not out to break any investment records, but feels that he needs some backup in order to provide for the long-run needs of his family. Although his income is meager, Reverend Robin feels that with careful planning, he could probably invest about $250 a quarter (and, with luck, maybe increase this amount over time). He presently has about $15,000 in a passbook savings account which he would be willing to use to kick off this program. In view of his investment objectives, he is not interested in taking a lot of risk. Because his knowledge of investments extends to savings accounts, series EE bonds, and a little bit about mutual funds, he approaches you for some investment advice.

Questions

1. In view of the Reverend Robin's long-term investment goals, do you think mutual funds are an appropriate investment vehicle for him?
2. Do you think he should use his $15,000 savings to start off a mutual fund investment program?
3. What type of mutual fund investment program would you set up for the Reverend? Include in your answer some discussion of the types of funds you would consider, the investment objectives you would set, and any investment services (like withdrawal plans) you would seek. Would taxes be an important consideration in your investment advice? Explain.

13.2 Tom Lasnicka Seeks the Good Life

Tom Lasnicka is a widower who recently retired after a long career with a major midwestern manufacturer. Beginning as a skilled craftsman, he worked his way up to the level of shop supervisor over a period of more than 30 years with the firm. Tom receives Social Security benefits and a generous company pension—in all, these two sources amount to over $2,500 per month (part of which is tax free). The Lasnickas had no children, so he lives alone. Tom owns a two-bedroom rental house that is next to his home, with the rental income from it covering the mortgage payments for both the rental and his house. Over the years, Tom and his late wife, Camille, always tried to put a little money aside each month. The results have been nothing short of phenomenal, as the value of Tom's liquid investments (all held in bank CDs and passbook savings accounts) runs well into the six figures. Up to now, Tom has just let his money grow and has not used any of his savings to supplement his Social Security, pension, and rental income. But things are about to change. Tom has decided, "What the heck, it's high time I start living the good life!" Tom wants to travel and do some exciting things with his life—in effect, he is determined to start reaping the benefits of his labors. He has therefore decided to move $75,000 from one of his savings accounts to one or two high-yielding mutual funds. He would like to receive $1,000 a month from the fund(s) for as long as possible, since he plans to be around for a long time.

Questions

1. Given Tom's financial resources and investment objectives, what kind of mutual funds do you think he should consider?
2. Are there any factors in Tom's situation that should be taken into consideration in the fund selection process, and if so, how might these affect Tom's course of action?
3. What types of services do you think he should look for in a mutual fund?
4. Assume Tom invests in a mutual fund that earns about 10 percent annually from dividend income and capital gains. Given that Tom wants to receive $1,000 a month from his mutual fund, what would be the size of his investment account five years from now? How large would the account be if the fund could earn 16 percent on average and everything else remains the same? How important is the fund's rate of return to Tom's investment situation? Explain.

14 Real Estate Investments

After studying this chapter, you should be able to:

1. Describe the procedures for setting real estate investment objectives, including consideration of investment characteristics, constraints and goals, and analysis of important features.

2. Explain the key determinants of value in real estate: demand, supply, the property, and the property transfer process.

3. Discuss the valuation techniques commonly used to estimate the market value of real estate.

4. Gain an understanding of the procedures involved in forecasting real estate investment returns.

5. Apply real estate valuation techniques to a prospective real estate investment, and analyze its investment merits.

6. Describe real estate investment trusts (REITs) and real estate limited partnerships (RELPs), and explain the appeal they hold for investors.

Real estate offers an attractive way to diversify an investment portfolio. In addition, it offers favorable risk-return tradeoffs due to the uniqueness of properties and the localized and relatively inefficient market in which they are traded. Real estate differs from security investments in two ways: (1) it involves ownership of a tangible asset—*real property* rather than a financial claim—and (2) managerial decisions about real estate greatly affect the returns earned from investment in it. In real estate you must answer questions such as: What rents should be charged? How much should be spent on maintenance and repairs? What advertising media should be selected? What purchase, lease, or sales contract provisions should be used? Along with market forces, it is the answers to such questions that determine whether or not you will earn the desired return on a real estate investment. Like other investment markets, the real estate market changes over time. It also differs from region to region. Real estate investment today is very different than it was in earlier decades, as discussed in the accompanying *Investor Insights* box.

income property
leased-out residential or commercial real estate, that is expected to provide returns primarily from periodic rental income.

Thus investing in real estate means more than just "buying right" or "selling right." It also means managing the property right! The analytical framework presented here has two purposes: (1) to help you decide what price to pay for a property and (2) to guide you through the many operating decisions you will need to make. You can maximize returns only when you consider both types of decisions. We now take up the process of real estate investment analysis, beginning with objectives.

SETTING REAL ESTATE INVESTMENT OBJECTIVES

Setting objectives involves three steps. First, you should consider how the investment characteristics of real estate differ. Second, you should establish investment constraints and goals. Third, you should analyze important features.

residential property
a *single-family* or *multi-family* income property that is occupied by tenants who use it as a residence for living purposes.

Investment Characteristics

Individual real estate investments differ in their characteristics even more than individual people differ in theirs. So, just as you wouldn't marry without thinking long and hard about the type of person you'd be happy with, you shouldn't select an investment property without some feeling for whether or not it is the right one for you. To select wisely, you need to consider the available types of properties and whether you want an equity or a debt position.

commercial property
an income property that is used by the tenant for business rather than living purposes.

We can classify real estate into two investment categories: income properties and speculative properties. **Income properties** are residential and commercial properties that are leased out and expected to provide returns primarily from periodic rental income. **Residential properties** include *single-family* properties (houses, condominiums, cooperatives, and townhouses) and *multi-family* properties (apartment complexes and buildings). **Commercial properties** include office buildings, shopping centers, warehouses, and factories. **Speculative properties** typically include raw land and investment properties that are expected to provide returns primarily from appreciation in value due to location, scarcity, etc., rather than from periodic rental income.

speculative property
type of real estate investment property that is expected to provide returns primarily from appreciation in value.

Income properties are subject to a number of sources of risk and return. Losses can result from tenant carelessness, excessive supply of competing rental units, or

INVESTOR INSIGHTS

New Lessons for Real Estate Investors

Real estate investors today have a considerably different perspective than they had in the 1970s. During the period from about 1970 to 1989, real estate was a relatively low-risk, prestige investment. The potential for large profits from increases in both rental income and property values attracted investors. Tax considerations were another major factor until 1986; transactions were often made because of the tax savings the investor would receive from the project rather than the profit it would generate. (In fact, many tax-shelter projects were never profitable.) Credit for real estate loans was readily available; banks were willing and eager to finance projects. Many major office buildings were built on speculation. Though no tenants were lined up prior to the start of construction, as long as the economy was growing rapidly and businesses were expanding, many of these projects were successfully rented.

The 1986 Tax Reform Act brought an end to tax-oriented real estate deals. However, commercial building continued at a rapid pace because developers and bankers were caught up in the economic good times of the 1980s. As a result, they often did not adequately analyze new projects to determine whether there would be enough tenants to fill these "spec" buildings.

Finally, the supply of office space outstripped the demand. The problem was further compounded by the slowdown in economic growth that began in the late 1980s and developed into a recession in the early 1990s. With the recession came the biggest real estate crash since the Great Depression of the 1930s. The crash started in the "oil patch" areas—particularly Houston, Denver, and New Orleans—in the early- to mid-1980s. By 1990, it had spread to Boston, Hartford, and most of New England; within a year, it affected the rest of the country. Even California, which many analysts thought to be immune from real estate problems, suffered from declining property values. In response to the slowing economy, businesses downsized, laying off large numbers of employees,

poor management. On the profit side, however, income properties can provide increasing rental incomes, appreciation in the value of the property, and possibly even some shelter from taxes. Speculative properties, as the name implies, give their owners a chance to make a financial killing, but also the chance for heavy loss due to high uncertainty. For instance, rumors may start that a new multimillion dollar plant is going to be built on the edge of town. Land buyers would jump into the market, and prices soon would be bid up. The right buy-sell timing could yield returns of several hundred percent or more. But people who bought into the market late, or those who failed to sell before the market turned, might lose the major part of their investment. Before investing in real estate, you should determine the risks various types of properties present and then decide which risks you can afford.

In this chapter we discuss real estate investment primarily from the standpoint of equity. Individuals also can invest in instruments of real estate debt, such as mortgages and deeds of trust. Usually these instruments provide a fairly safe rate of return if the borrowers are required to maintain at least a 20 percent equity position and the overall demand for space decreased. Also, more people worked at home, further reducing the need for office and industrial space. With too few tenants and too much space, building owners were forced to reduce rents sharply, sometimes by 50 percent or more. Because a building's value is determined by its ability to generate rental income as well as its potential for price appreciation, by the early 1990s many commercial buildings were worth less than half what they had cost to build.

The lessons are clear for today's real estate investors and lenders: Macro issues such as the economic outlook, the demand for new space, the current supply of space, and regional considerations are of major importance. For example, in 1992 many metropolitan areas had a 10-year supply of vacant office space. Real estate no longer provides an inflation hedge and may not even keep pace with the current low inflation rates. Banks are taking enormous losses on their real estate loan portfolios and are reluctant to finance even very sound projects, let alone any that are remotely speculative.

The new emphasis is on the cash-on-cash yield—the cash return on cash invested—rather than on total return—cash return plus price appreciation. Investors now look at real estate as they would any other business and focus on a project's cash-generating ability—the bottom line— rather than price appreciation. They compare real estate with other investment opportunities on a yield basis and are looking for about 10 percent cash return. However, in recent years the average cash return has been about 7 percent, creating an imbalance between supply and demand. Because owners cannot increase cash flow by raising rents, the only way to increase the yield is by lowering the price. These depressed prices create a buyers' market, with good investment opportunities for experienced real estate investors but a very bleak outlook for property owners and banks holding real estate as loan collateral. As discussed later in the chapter and in the second *Investor Insights* box, real estate investment trusts (REITs) are the best way for the individual investor to take advantage of the current situation in the real estate market.

in the mortgaged property (no more than an 80 percent loan-to-value ratio). This owner equity position gives the real estate lender a margin of safety should foreclosure have to be initiated.

Constraints and Goals

When you decide to invest in real estate, you face a number of choices. In light of these options, you need to set both financial and nonfinancial constraints and goals. One financial constraint is the risk-return relationship you find acceptable. In addition, you must consider how much money you want to allocate to the real estate portion of your portfolio. Furthermore, you should define a quantifiable financial objective. Often this financial goal is stated in terms of *net present value* (also referred to as *discounted cash flow*) or approximate yield. Later in the chapter we will show how various constraints and goals can be applied to real estate investing.

Although you will probably want to invest in real estate for its financial rewards, you also need to consider how your technical skills, temperament, repair skills, and managerial talents fit a potential investment. Do you want a prestige, trouble-free property? Or would you prefer a fix-up special on which you can release your imagination and workmanship? Would you enjoy living in the same building as your tenants (as in a fourplex investment) or would you like as little contact with them as possible? Just as you wouldn't choose a career solely on the basis of money, neither should you buy a property just for the money.

Analysis of Important Features

The analytical framework suggested in this chapter can guide you in estimating a property's investment potential. Yet first you must consider four general features relating to real estate investment:

1. *Physical Property.* When buying real estate, make sure you are getting both the quantity and quality of property you think you are. Problems can arise if you fail to obtain a site survey, an accurate square-footage measurement of the buildings, or an inspection for building or site defects. When signing a contract to buy a property, make sure it accurately identifies the real estate and lists all items of personal property (such as refrigerator and curtains) that you expect to receive.

2. *Property Rights.* Strange as it may seem, when buying real estate what you buy is a bundle of legal rights that fall under concepts in law such as deeds, titles, easements, liens, and encumbrances. When investing in real estate make sure that along with various physical inspections, you also get a legal inspection from a qualified attorney. Real estate sale and lease agreements should not be the work of amateurs.

3. *Time Horizon.* Like a roller coaster, real estate prices go up and down. Sometimes market forces pull them up slowly but surely; in other periods prices can fall so fast they take an investor's breath away. Before judging whether a prospective real estate investment will appreciate or depreciate, you must decide what time period is relevant. The short-term investor might count on a quick drop in mortgage interest rates and buoyant market expectations, whereas the long-term investor might look more closely at population-growth potential.

4. *Geographic Area.* Real estate is a spatial commodity, which means that its value is directly linked to what is going on around it. With some properties, the area of greatest concern consists of a few square blocks; in other instances an area of hundreds or even thousands of miles serves as the relevant market area. As a result of these spatial differences, you must delineate boundaries before you can productively analyze real estate demand and supply.

DETERMINANTS OF VALUE

When analyzing real estate investment, value generally serves as the central concept. Will a property increase in value? Will it produce increasing amounts of cash flows? To address these questions, you should evaluate the four major determinants of real estate value: demand, supply, the property, and the property transfer process.

Demand

Demand refers to people's willingness and ability to buy or rent a given property. In part demand stems from a market area's economic base. In most real estate markets, the source of buying power comes from jobs. Property values follow an upward path when employment is increasing, and values typically fall when employers begin to lay off personnel. Therefore, the first question you should ask about demand is "What is the outlook for jobs in the relevant market area?" Are schools, colleges, and universities gaining enrollment? Are major companies planning expansion? And are wholesalers, retailers, and financial institutions increasing their sales and services? Upward trends in these indicators often signal a rising demand for real estate.

Population characteristics also influence demand. To analyze demand for a specific property, you should look at an area's population demographics and psychographics. **Demographics** refers to such things as household size, age structure, occupation, sex, and marital status. **Psychographics** are those characteristics that describe people's mental dispositions, such as personality, lifestyle, and self-concept. By comparing demographic and psychographic trends to the features of a property, you can judge whether it is likely to gain or lose favor among potential buyers or tenants.

Mortgage financing is also a key factor. Tight money can choke off the demand for real estate. As investors saw in the early 1980s, rising interest rates and the relative unavailability of mortgages caused inventories of unsold properties to grow and real estate prices to fall. Conversely, as mortgage interest rates fell, beginning in late 1982 and early 1983 and continuing through 1988, real estate sales activity in many cities throughout the United States rapidly expanded. Although interest rates rose slightly in 1989 and 1990, their steady decline in 1991 and 1992 failed to stimulate real estate activity due to generally poor economic conditions, a lack of attractive tax incentives, and most importantly, the low expected returns caused by a large surplus of investment properties.

Supply

Supply analysis really means sizing up the competition. Nobody wants to pay you more for a property than the price they can pay your competitor; nor when you're buying (or renting), should you pay more than the prices asked for other similar properties. As a result, an integral part of value analysis requires that you identify sources of potential competition and then inventory them by price and features.

In general, people in real estate think of competitors in terms of similar properties. If you are trying to sell a house, then it seems natural to see your competition as the other houses for sale in the same neighborhood. For longer-term investment decisions, however, you should expand your concept of supply. That is, you should identify competitors through the **principle of substitution.** This principle holds that people do not really buy or rent real estate per se. Instead, they judge properties as different sets of benefits and costs. Properties fill people's needs, and it is really these needs that create demand. Thus an analysis of supply should not limit potential competitors to geographically and physically similar properties. In some markets, for example, low-priced single-family houses might compete with condominium units, manufactured homes (formerly called mobile homes), and even with rental apartments. So before investing in any property, you should decide what market that property appeals to, and then define its competitors as other properties that its buyers or tenants might also typically choose from.

Real estate investment analysis requires that, after identifying all relevant competitors, you inventory these properties in terms of features and respective prices. In other words, look for the relative pros and cons of each property. Many large real estate investors hire professional market consultants to do the research that the analysis of demand and supply requires.

The Property

Up to now we have shown that a property's value is influenced by demand and supply. The price that people will pay is governed by their needs and the relative prices of the properties available to meet those needs. For example, a parent can buy a house on its college student child's campus for several students to share and hire their child to act as live-in rental manager. This strategy can create tax-deductible college housing for a child while acting as a real estate investment for the parents. Yet in real estate the property itself is also a key ingredient. To try to develop a property's competitive edge, an investor should consider five items: (1) restrictions on use; (2) location; (3) site characteristics; (4) improvements; and (5) property management.

Restrictions on Use

In today's highly regulated society, both state and local laws and private contracts limit the rights of all property owners. Government restrictions derive from zoning laws, building and occupancy codes, and health and sanitation requirements. Private restrictions include deeds, leases, and condominium bylaws and operating rules. Because of all these restrictions, you should not invest in a property until you or your lawyer determines that what you want to do with the property *fits within* applicable laws, rules, and contract provisions.

Location Analysis

You may have heard the adage, "The three most important determinants of real estate value are location, location, and location." Of course, location is not the only factor that affects value: yet a good location unquestionably increases a property's investment potential. With that said, how can you tell a bad location from a good one? A good location rates highly on two key dimensions: convenience and environment.

convenience
in real estate, the accessibility of a property to the places the people in a target market frequently need to go.

Convenience refers to how accessible a property is to the places the people in a target market frequently need to go. Any selected residential or commercial market segment will have a set of preferred places its tenants or buyers will want to be close to. Another element of convenience is transportation facilities. Availability of buses, taxis, subways, and commuter trains is of concern to both tenants and buyers of commercial and residential property. Commercial properties need to be readily accessible to their customers and vice versa.

In the analysis of real estate, the term **environment** has broader meaning than trees, rivers, lakes, and air quality. When you invest in real estate, you should really consider not only the natural environment, but also the esthetic, socioeconomic, legal, and fiscal environments. Neighborhoods with an *esthetic environment* are those where buildings and landscaping are well executed and well maintained. There is no intrusion of noise, sight, or air pollution, and encroaching unharmonious land uses are not evident. The *socioeconomic environment* refers to the demographics and lifestyles of the people who live or work in nearby properties. The *legal environment* relates to the restrictions on use that apply to nearby properties. And last, you need to consider a property's *fiscal environment:* the amount of property taxes and municipal assessments you will be required to pay, and the government services you will be entitled to receive (police, fire, schools, parks, waters, sewers, trash collection, libraries). Property taxes are a two-sided coin. On the one side they pose a cost, but on the other they give a property's users the right to services that may be of substantial benefit.

environment
in real estate, the natural as well as esthetic, socioeconomic, legal, and fiscal surroundings of a property.

Site Characteristics

One of the most important features of a property site is its size. For residential properties, such as houses, condominiums, and apartments, some people want a large yard for children to play in or for a garden. Others may prefer virtually no yard at all. For commercial properties, such as office buildings and shopping centers, adequate parking space is necessary. Also, with respect to site size, if you are planning a later addition of space, make sure the site is large enough to accommodate it, both physically and legally. Site quality such as soil fertility, topography, elevation, and drainage capacity is also important. For example, sites with relatively low elevation may be subject to flooding.

Improvements

In real estate, the term **improvements** refers to the man-made additions to a site, such as buildings, sidewalks, and various on-site amenities. Typically building size is measured and expressed in terms of square footage. Because square footage is so important in building and unit comparison, you should get accurate square footage measures on any properties you consider investing in.

improvements
in real estate, the man-made additions to a site, such as buildings, sidewalks, and various on-site amenities.

Another measure of building size is room count and floor plan. For example, a well-designed 750-square-foot apartment unit might in fact be more livable, and therefore easier to rent and at a higher price, than one of 850 square feet. You should make sure that floor plans are logical, that traffic flows throughout a building will pose no inconveniences, that there is sufficient closet, cabinet, and other storage space, and that the right mix of rooms exists. For example, in an office building you should not have to cross through other offices to get to the building's only bathroom, or as an exclusive access to any other room; small merchants in a shopping center should not be placed in locations where they do not receive the pedestrian traffic generated by the larger (anchor) tenants.

Attention should also be given to amenities, style, and construction quality. Amenities such as air conditioning, swimming pools, and elevators can significantly impact the value of investment property. In addition, the architectural style and quality of construction materials and workmanship are important factors influencing property value.

Property Management

In recent years real estate owners and investors have increasingly recognized that investment properties (apartments, office buildings, shopping centers, and so on) do not earn maximum cash flows by themselves. They need to be guided toward that objective, and skilled property management can help. Without effective property management, no real estate investment can produce maximum benefits for its users and owners. Today property management requires you (or a hired manager) to run the entire operation as well as to perform day-to-day chores. The property manager will segment buyers, improve a property's site and structure, keep tabs on competitors, and develop a marketing campaign. Management also assumes responsibility for the maintenance and repair of buildings and their physical systems (electrical, heating, air conditioning, and plumbing) and for keeping revenue and expense records. In addition, property managers decide the best ways to protect properties against loss from perils such as fire, flood, theft, storms, and negligence. In its broadest sense **property management** means finding the optimal level of benefits for a property, and then providing them at the lowest costs. Of course, for speculative investments such as raw land, the managerial task is not so pronounced and the manager has less control over the profit picture.

property management
in real estate, finding the optimal level of benefits for a property and then providing them at the lowest costs.

The Property Transfer Process

In Chapter 7 we introduced the concept of efficient markets, in which information flows so quickly among buyers and sellers that it is virtually impossible for an investor to outperform the average systematically. As soon as something good (an exciting new product) or something bad (a multimillion-dollar product liability suit) occurs, the price of the affected company's stock adjusts to reflect its current potential for earnings or losses. Some people accept the premise that securities markets are efficient, while others do not. But one thing is sure: *No one believes real estate markets are efficient.* What this means is that real estate market research pays off. Skillfully conducted analysis can help you beat the averages. The reasons real estate markets differ from securities markets is that no good system exists for complete information exchange among buyers and sellers, and among tenants and lessors. There is no central marketplace, like the NYSE, where transactions are conveniently made by equally well-informed investors who share similar objectives. Instead, real estate is traded in generally *illiquid markets* that are regional or local in nature and where transactions are made by investors, using information they have gathered and developed, in order to achieve their often unique investment objec-

property transfer process
the process of promotion and negotiation of real estate, which can significantly influence the cash flows a property can earn in the real estate market.

tives. In the **property transfer process** itself, the inefficiency of the market means that how you collect and disseminate information will affect your results. The cash flows a property will earn can be influenced significantly through promotion and negotiation.

Promotion refers to the task of getting information about a property to its buyer segment. You can't sell or rent a property quickly and for top dollar unless you can reach the people you want to reach in a cost-effective way. Among the major ways to promote a property are advertising, publicity, sales gimmicks, and personal selling.

Both advertising and publicity involve media coverage for your property. In the case of advertising, you pay for this coverage; with publicity, you create a newsworthy event. A sales gimmick often relies on some type of contest or perhaps a gift of some sort. A Houston office building developer, for example, perked up demand for his project when he offered a new Mercedes to new tenants who signed a five-year lease. This sales gimmick also got the developer's project a great deal of publicity. Personal selling is often the most costly, but also the most effective way to attract buyers or tenants to a property. It places you or your sales agent in a one-on-one customer relationship. In most instances property owners use two or more ways to promote their property. At the least, you should realize that maximizing a real estate investment's cash flows through promotion entails more than dashing off a classified newspaper advertisement.

Seldom does the minimum price a seller is willing to accept just equal the maximum price a buyer is willing to pay; often some overlap occurs. Also, in real estate the asking price for a property may be anywhere from 5 to 60 percent *above* the price that a seller (or lessor) will accept. Therefore the negotiating skills of each party determine the final transaction price.

REAL ESTATE VALUATION

market value
in real estate, the prevailing market price of a property, indicating how the market as a whole has assessed the property's worth.

In real estate the concept of **market value,** or actual worth, must be interpreted differently from its meaning in stocks and bonds. This difference arises for a number of reasons: (1) each property is unique; (2) terms and conditions of sale may vary widely; (3) market information is imperfect; (4) properties may need substantial time for market exposure, time that may not be available to any given seller; and (5) buyers, too, sometimes need to act quickly. All these factors mean that no one can tell for sure what a property's "true" market value is. As a result, many properties sell for prices significantly above or below their estimated (or appraised) market values. To offset such inequities, many real estate investors forecast investment returns in order to evaluate potential property investments. Here we look first at procedures for estimating the market value of a piece of real estate, and then describe methods for forecasting real estate investment returns.

Estimating Market Value

appraisal
a process for estimating the current market value of a piece of property.

In real estate, estimating the current market value of a piece of property is done through a process known as a real estate **appraisal.** Using certain techniques, an appraiser will set the value on a piece of property that he or she feels represents the current market value of the property. Even so, if you are told that a property has an appraised market value of, say, $150,000, you should interpret that value a little skeptically. Because of both technical and informational shortcomings, this estimate can be subject to substantial error. Although you can arrive at the market values of frequently traded stocks simply by looking at current quotes, in real estate, appraisers and investors typically must use three complex techniques and then correlate results to come up with one best estimate. These three imperfect approaches to real estate market value are (1) the cost approach, (2) the comparative sales approach, and (3) the income approach. Due to the complexity of this process, it is often helpful to use an expert.

The Cost Approach

cost approach
a real estate valuation approach based on the idea that a buyer should not pay more for a property than it would cost to rebuild it at today's prices.

The **cost approach** is based on the notion that an investor should not pay more for a property than it would cost to rebuild it at today's prices for land, labor, and construction materials. This approach to estimating value generally works well for new or relatively new buildings. Older properties, however, often suffer from wear and tear and outdated materials or design, making the cost approach more difficult to apply. To value these older properties, you would have to subtract some amount for physical and functional depreciation from the replacement cost estimates. Most experts agree that the cost approach is a good method to use as a check against a price estimate, but rarely should it be used exclusively.

The Comparative Sales Approach

comparative sales approach
a real estate valuation approach that uses as the basic input variable sales prices of properties that are similar to the subject property.

income approach
a real estate valuation approach that calculates a property's value as the present value of all its future income.

The **comparative sales approach** uses as the basic input variable the sales prices of properties that are similar to a subject property. This method is based on the idea that the value of a given property is about the same as the prices for which other similar properties have recently sold. Of course, the catch here is that all properties are unique in some respect. Therefore the price that a subject property could be expected to bring must be adjusted upward or downward to reflect its superiority or inferiority to comparable properties. Nevertheless, because the comparable sales approach is based on *selling* prices, not asking prices, it can give you a good feel for the market. As a practical matter, if you can find at least one sold property slightly better than the one you're looking at, and one slightly worse, their recent sales prices can serve to bracket an estimated market value for a subject property.

The Income Approach

Under the **income approach** a property's value is viewed as the present value of all its future income. The most popular income approach is called *direct capitalization*. This approach is represented by the formula in Equation 14.1.

Equation 14.1

$$\text{Market value} = \frac{\text{annual net operating income}}{\text{market capitalization rate}}$$

Equation 14.1a

$$V = \frac{\text{NOI}}{R}$$

net operating income (NOI)
the amount left after subtracting vacancy and collection losses and property operating expenses from an income property's *gross potential* rental income.

capitalization rate
the rate used to convert an income stream to a present value, which can be used to estimate the value of real estate under the income approach to value.

Annual **net operating income (NOI)** is calculated by subtracting vacancy and collection losses and property operating expenses, including property insurance and property taxes, from an income property's *gross potential* rental income. An estimated **capitalization rate**—which technically means the rate used to convert an income stream to a present value—is obtained by looking at recent market sales figures and seeing what rate of return investors currently require. Then, by dividing the annual net operating income by the appropriate capitalization rate, you get an income property's estimated market value. An example of the application of the income approach is given in Table 14.1

Using an Expert

Real estate valuation is a complex and technical procedure that requires reliable information about the features of comparable properties, their selling prices, and applicable terms of financing. As a result, rather than relying exclusively on their own judgment, many investors hire a real estate agent or a professional real estate appraiser to advise them about the market value of a property. As a form of insurance against overpaying, the use of an expert can be well worth the cost.

Forecasting Investment Returns

Estimates of market value play an integral role in real estate decision making. Yet today more and more investors supplement their market value appraisals with in-

TABLE 14.1 Applying the Income Approach

Comparable Property	(1) NOI	(2) Sale Price	(3) (1) ÷ (2) Capitalization Rate *(R)*
2301 Maple Ave.	$16,250	$182,500	.0890
4037 Armstrong St.	15,400	167,600	.0919
8240 Ludwell St.	19,200	198,430	.0968
7392 Grant Blvd.	17,930	189,750	.0945
Subject property	$18,480	?	?

From this market-derived information, an appraiser would work through Equation 14.1a:

$$V = \frac{NOI}{R}$$

$$V = \frac{\$18,480}{R}$$

$$V = \frac{\$18,480}{.093*}$$

$$V = \$198,710$$

*Based on an analysis of the relative similarities of the comparables and the subject property, the appraiser decided the appropriate *R* equals .093.

vestment analysis. This extension of the traditional approaches to value (cost, comparative sales, and income) gives investors a better picture of whether a selected property is likely to satisfy their investment objectives.

Market Value versus Investment Analysis

The concept of market value differs from investment analysis in four important ways: (1) retrospective versus prospective; (2) impersonal versus personal; (3) unleveraged versus leveraged; and (4) net operating income (NOI) versus after-tax cash flows.

Retrospective versus Prospective.   Market value appraisals look backward; they attempt to estimate the price a property will sell for by looking at the sales prices of similar properties in the recent past. Under static market conditions such a technique can be reasonable. But if, say, interest rates, population, or buyer expectations are changing rapidly, past sales prices may not accurately indicate the current value or the future value of a subject property. In contrast, an **investment analysis** not only considers what similar properties have sold for, but also looks at the underlying determinants of value that we have discussed. An investment analysis tries to forecast such factors as economic base, population demographics and psychographics, availability and cost of mortgage financing, and potential sources of competition.

Impersonal versus Personal.   As defined by professional appraisers, a market value estimate represents the price a property will sell for under certain specified conditions—in other words, a sort of market average. But in fact each buyer and seller has a unique set of needs, and each real estate transaction can be structured to meet those needs. So an investment analysis looks beyond what may constitute a "typical" transaction and attempts to evaluate a subject property's terms and conditions of sale (or rent) as they correspond to a given investor's constraints and goals.

For example, a market value appraisal might show that with normal financing and conditions of sale, a property is worth $180,000. Yet because of personal tax consequences, it might be better for a seller to ask a higher price for the property and offer owner financing at a below-market interest rate.

Unleveraged versus Leveraged.   The returns a real estate investment offers will be influenced by the amount of the purchase price that is financed. But simple income capitalization $[V = (NOI/R)]$ does not incorporate alternative financing plans that might be available. It assumes either a cash or an unleveraged purchase.

The use of financing, or **leverage,** gives differing risk-return parameters to a real estate investment. Leverage automatically increases investment risk because borrowed funds must be repaid. Failure to repay a mortgage loan results in foreclosure and possible property loss. Alternatively, leverage may also increase return. If a property can earn a return in excess of the cost of the borrowed funds, the investor's return will be increased to a level well above what could have been earned from an all-cash deal. This is known as **positive leverage.** Conversely, if return is below debt cost, the return on invested equity will be less than from an all-cash deal. This

---

investment analysis real estate analysis that considers not only what similar properties have sold for, but also looks at the underlying determinants of value.

leverage in real estate, the use of financing to purchase a piece of property and thereby affect its risk-return parameters.

positive leverage a position in which, if a property's return is in excess of its debt cost, the investor's return will be increased to a level well above what could have been earned from an all-cash deal.

is called **negative leverage.** The following example shows how leverage affects return and provides insight into the possible associated risks.

Assume an investor purchases a parcel of land for $20,000. The investor has two financing choices. Choice A is all cash; that is, no leverage is employed. Choice B involves 80 percent financing (20 percent down payment) at 12 percent interest. With leverage (choice B), the investor signs a $16,000 note (.80 × $20,000) at 12 percent interest with the entire principal balance due and payable at the end of one year. Now suppose the land appreciates during the year to $30,000. (A comparative analysis of this occurrence is presented in Table 14.2.) Had the investor chosen the all-cash deal, the one-year return on the investor's initial equity is 50 percent. The use of leverage would have magnified that return, no matter how much the property appreciated. The leveraged alternative (choice B) involved only a $4,000 investment in personal initial equity, with the balance financed by borrowing at 12 percent interest. The property sells for $30,000, of which $4,000 represents the recovery of the initial equity investment, $16,000 goes to repay the principal balance on the debt, and another $1,920 of gain is used to pay interest ($16,000 × .12). The balance of the proceeds, $8,080, represents the investor's return. The return on the investor's initial equity is 202 percent—over four times that provided by the no-leverage alternative, choice A.

We used 12 percent in the above example, but it is important to understand that the cost of money has surprisingly little effect on comparative (leveraged versus unleveraged) returns; for example, using 6 percent interest, the return on investor's equity rises to 226 percent, still way above the unleveraged alternative. Granted, using a lower interest cost does improve return, but, other things being equal, the thing that's really driving return on equity is the *amount* of leverage being used.

TABLE 14.2 The Effect of Positive Leverage on Return: An Example*

Purchase price: $20,000
Sale price: $30,000
Holding period: one year

Item Number	Item	Choice A No Leverage	Choice B 80% Financing
1	Initial equity	$20,000	$ 4,000
2	Loan principal	0	16,000
3	Sale price	30,000	30,000
4	Capital gain [(3) − (1) − (2)]	10,000	10,000
5	Interest cost [.12 × (2)]	0	1,920
6	Net return [(4) − (5)]	10,000	8,080
	Return on investor's equity [(6) ÷ (1)]	$\frac{\$10,000}{\$20,000} = +50\%$	$\frac{\$ 8,080}{\$ 4,000} = +202\%$

*To simplify this example, all value are presented on a *before-tax* basis. To get the true return, taxes on the capital gain and the interest expense would be considered.

There is another side to the coin, however. For no matter what the eventual outcome, risk is *always* inherent in leverage; it can easily turn a bad deal into a disaster. Suppose the $20,000 property discussed above dropped in value by 25 percent during the one-year holding period. The comparative results are presented in Table 14.3. The unleveraged investment has resulted in a negative return of 25 percent. This is not large, however, compared to the leveraged position in which the investor loses not only the entire initial investment of $4,000, but an additional $2,920 ($1,000 additional principal on the debt + $1,920 interest). The total loss of $6,920 on the original $4,000 of equity results in a (negative) return of 173 percent. Thus the loss in the leverage case is nearly seven times the loss experienced in the unleveraged situation.

NOI versus After-Tax Cash Flows.   Recall that to estimate market value, the income approach capitalizes net operating income (NOI). To most investors, though, the NOI figure holds little meaning. The reason is that, as discussed above, the majority of real estate investors finance their purchases. In addition, few investors today can ignore the effect of federal income tax law on their investment decisions. Investors want to know how much cash they will be required to put into a transaction, and how much cash they are likely to get out. The concept of NOI does not address these equations. Thus in real estate the familiar finance measure of investment return—discounted cash flow—is a prime criterion for selecting real estate investments. (Sometimes approximate yield is used instead to assess the suitability of a prospective real estate investment.)

TABLE 14.3 The Effect of Negative Leverage on Return: An Example*

Purchase price: $20,000
Sale price: $15,000
Holding period: one year

Item Number	Item	Choice A No Leverage	Choice B 80% Financing
1	Initial equity	$20,000	$ 4,000
2	Loan principal	0	16,000
3	Sale price	15,000	15,000
4	Capital loss [(3) − (1) − (2)]	5,000	5,000
5	Interest cost [.12 × (2)]	0	1,920
6	Net loss [(4) − (5)]	5,000	6,920
	Return on investor's equity [(6) ÷ (1)]	$\frac{\$5,000}{\$20,000} = -25\%$	$\frac{\$6,920}{\$4,000} = -173\%$

*To simplify this example, all value are presented on a *before-tax* basis. To get the true return, taxes on the capital loss and the interest expense would be considered.

Calculating Discounted Cash Flow

Calculating **discounted cash flow** involves the techniques of present value as discussed in Chapter 4; in addition, you need to learn how to calculate annual after-tax cash flows and the after-tax net proceeds of sale. With this knowledge you can discount the cash flows an investment is expected to earn over a specified holding period. This figure in turn gives you the present value of the cash flows. Next, you find the **net present value (NPV)**—the difference between the present value of the cash flows and the amount of equity required to make the investment. The resulting difference tells you whether the proposed investment looks good (a positive net present value) or bad (a negative net present value).

This process of discounting cash flows to calculate the net present value (NPV) of an investment can be represented by the following equation:

$$NPV = \left[\frac{CF_1}{(1+r)^1} + \frac{CF_2}{(1+r)^2} + \cdots + \frac{CF_{n-1}}{(1+r)^{n-1}} + \frac{CF_n + CF_{R_n}}{(1+r)^n} \right] - I_0$$

where

I_0 = the original required investment

CF_i = annual after-tax cash flow for year i

CF_{R_n} = the after-tax net proceeds from sale (reversionary after-tax cash flow) occurring in year n

r = the discount rate and $[1/(1+r)^i]$ is the present-value interest factor for \$1 received in year i using an r percent discount rate.

In this equation the annual after-tax cash flows, *CF*s, may be either inflows to investors or outflows from them. Inflows would be preceded by a plus (+) sign, and outflows by a minus (−) sign.

Calculating Approximate Yield

An alternate way of assessing investment suitability would be to calculate the **approximate yield,** which was first presented as Equation 4.11 in Chapter 4. Restating the formula in terms of the variables defined above, we have:

$$\text{Approximate yield} = \frac{\overline{CF} + \dfrac{CF_{R_n} - I_0}{n}}{\dfrac{CF_{R_n} + I_0}{2}}$$

where

$$\overline{CF} = \begin{array}{c}\text{average annual}\\\text{after-tax cash}\\\text{flow}\end{array} = \frac{CF_1 + CF_2 + \cdots + CF_{n-1} + CF_n}{n}$$

If the calculated approximate yield is greater than the discount rate appropriate for the given investment, the investment would be acceptable. In that case, the net present value would be positive.

When consistently applied, the net present value and approximate yield approaches will always give the same recommendation for accepting or rejecting a proposed real estate investment. Now, to show how all of the elements discussed in this chapter can be applied to a real estate investment decision, let's look at an example.

AN EXAMPLE OF REAL ESTATE VALUATION: THE ACADEMIC ARMS APARTMENTS

We will assume that Jack Wilson is deciding whether or not to buy the Academic Arms Apartments. Jack believes he can improve his real estate investment decision making if he follows a systematic procedure. He designs a schematic framework of analysis that corresponds closely to the topics we've discussed. Following this framework (Figure 14.1), Jack (1) sets out his investment objectives, (2) analyzes important features of the property, (3) investigates the determinants of the property's value, (4) calculates investment returns, and (5) synthesizes and interprets the results of his analysis.

Investor Objectives

Jack is a tenured associate professor of management at Finley College. He's single, age 40, and earns an income of $75,000 per year from salary, consulting fees, stock dividends, and book royalties. His applicable tax rate on ordinary income is 31 percent. Jack wants to further diversify his investment portfolio. He would like to add a real estate investment that has good appreciation potential and also provides a positive yearly after-tax cash flow. For convenience Jack requires the property to be close to his office, and he feels his talents and personality suit him for ownership of apartments. Jack has $60,000 cash to invest. On this amount he would like to earn a 13 percent rate of return; toward this end, he has his eye on a small apartment building, the Academic Arms Apartments.

Analysis of Important Features

The Academic Arms building is located six blocks from the Finley College student union. The building contains eight 2-bedroom, 2-bath units of 1,100 square feet each. It was built in 1975, and all systems and building components appear to be in good condition. The present owner gave Jack an income statement reflecting the property's 1992 income and expenses. The owner has further assured Jack that no adverse easements or encumbrances affect the building's title. Of course, if Jack decides to buy Academic Arms, he would have a lawyer verify the quality of the property rights associated with the property. For now, though, he accepts the owner's word.

In this instance Jack considers a five-year holding period reasonable. At present he's happy at Finley and thinks he will stay there at least until age 45. Jack defines the market for the property as a one-mile radius from campus. He reasons that students who walk to campus (the target market) would limit their choice of apartments to those that fall within that geographic area.

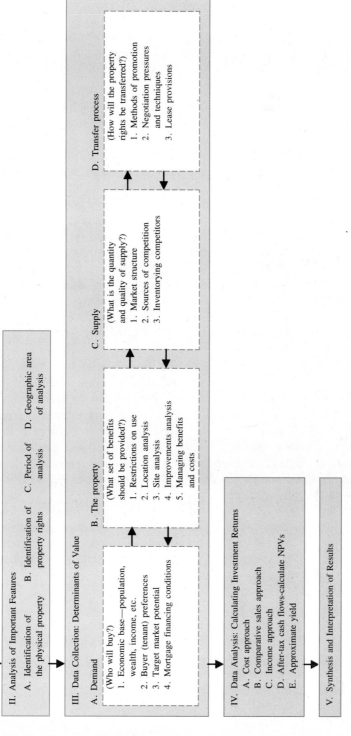

• FIGURE 14.1 Framework for Real Estate Investment Analysis

This framework depicts a logical approach for analyzing potential investment properties in order to assess whether or not they are acceptable investments that might be included in one's investment portfolio. (*Source:* Adapted from Gary W. Elred, *Real Estate: Analysis and Strategy*, New York: Harper & Row, 1987, p. 18.)

Determinants of Value

Once Jack has analyzed the important features, he next thinks about the factors that will determine the property's investment potential. As noted, these factors include: (1) demand, (2) the property, (3) supply, and (4) the transfer process.

Demand

The major institution, indeed the lifeblood institution in the market area, is Finley College. The base of demand for the Academic Arms Apartments will grow (or decline) with the size of the college's employment and student enrollment. On this basis, Jack judges the prospects for the area to be in the range of good to excellent. During the coming five years, major funding (due to a $25 million gift) will increase Finley's faculty by 35 percent, and expected along with faculty growth is a rise in the student population from 3,200 full-time students to 4,600 full-time students. Through further investigation Jack learns that 70 percent of the *new* students will live away from home. In the past Finley largely served the local market, but with its new affluence—and the resources this affluence can buy—the college will draw students from a wider geographic area. Furthermore, because Finley is a private college with relatively high tuition, the majority of students come from upper-middle-income families. Parental support can thus be expected to heighten students' ability to pay. Overall, then, Jack believes the major indicators of demand for the market area look promising.

The Property

Now the question becomes, Will the Academic Arms Apartments appeal to the desired market segment? On this issue Jack concludes the answer is yes. The property already is zoned multifamily, and its present (and intended) use complies with all pertinent ordinances and housing codes. Of major importance, though, is the property's location. Not only does the site have good accessibility to the campus, but it is also three blocks from the Campus Town shopping district. In addition, the esthetic, socioeconomic, legal, and fiscal environments of the property are compatible with student preferences.

On the negative side, the on-site parking has space for only six cars. Still, the building itself is attractive, and the relatively large 2-bedroom, 2-bath units are ideal for roommates. And although Jack has no experience managing apartments, he feels that if he studies several books on property management and applies his formal business education, he can succeed.

Supply

Jack realizes that even strong demand and a good property cannot yield profits if a market suffers from oversupply. Too much competition has pushed many property owners and real estate developers into bankruptcy. Fortunately Jack thinks that Academic Arms is well insulated from competing units. Most important is the fact that the designated market area is fully built up, and as much as 80 percent of the area is zoned single-family residential. Any efforts to change the zoning would be strongly opposed by neighborhood residents. The only potential problem that Jack sees is that the college might build more student housing on campus. There has been some administrative talk about it, but as yet no funds have been allocated to such a project. In sum, Jack concludes that the risk of oversupply in the Academic Arms market area is low.

The Transfer Process

As noted earlier, real estate markets are *not efficient*. Thus before a property's sales price or rental income can reach its potential, an effective means to get information to buyers or tenants must be developed. Here, of course, Jack has great advantage. Notices on campus bulletin boards and announcements to his classes should be all he needs to keep the property rented. Although he might experience some vacancy during the summer months, Jack feels he could overcome this problem by requiring students to sign 12-month leases, but then grant them the right to sublet as long as the sublessees meet the tenant-selection criteria.

Calculating Investment Returns

Real estate cash flows depend on the underlying characteristics of the property and the market. That is why we have devoted so much attention to analyzing the determinants of value. Often real estate investors lose money because they "run the numbers" without doing their homework. So as we go through our investment calculations, remember that the numbers coming out will be no better than the numbers going in.

The Numbers

At present Mrs. Bowker, the owner of Academic Arms Apartments, is asking $260,000 for the property. To assist in the sale, she is willing to offer owner financing to a qualified buyer. The terms would be 20 percent down, 11.5 percent interest, and full amortization of the outstanding mortgage balance over 30 years. The owner's income statement for 1992 is shown in Table 14.4. After talking with Mrs. Bowker, Jack believes she would probably accept an offer of $60,000 down, a price of $245,000, and a 30-year mortgage at 11 percent. On this basis Jack prepares his investment calculations.

Cash Flow Analysis

As a first step in cash flow analysis, Jack reconstructs the owner's income statement (as shown in Table 14.5). This reconstruction reflects higher rent levels, higher expenses, and a lower net operating income. Jack believes that due to poor owner management and deferred maintenance, the present owner is not getting as much in rents as the market could support. In addition, however, her expenses understate those he is likely to incur. For one thing, a management expense should be deducted. Jack wants to separate what is rightfully a return on labor from his return on capital. Also, once the property is sold, a higher property tax assessment will be levied against it. Except for promotion and advertising, other expenses have been

TABLE 14.4 Income Statement, Academic
Arms Apartments, 1992

Gross rental income		
(8 × $335 × 12)		$32,160
Operating expenses:		
Utilities	$2,830	
Trash collection	675	
Repairs and maintenance	500	
Promotion and advertising	150	
Property insurance	840	
Property taxes	3,200	
Less: Total operating expenses		8,195
Net operating income (NOI)		$23,965

increased to adjust for inflation and a more extensive maintenance program. With these adjustments, the expected NOI for Academic Arms during 1993 is estimated at $22,822.

To move from NOI to **after-tax cash flows (ATCFs),** we need to perform the calculations shown in Table 14.6. From this table you can see that to calculate ATCF, you must first compute the income taxes or income tax savings Jack would incur as a result of property ownership. In this case potential tax savings accrue during the first three years because the allowable tax deductions of interest and depreciation exceed the property's net operating income; in the final two years, income exceeds deductions and as such, taxes are due. The "magic" of simultane-

after-cash tax flows (ATCFs)
the annual cash flow earned on a real estate investment, net of all expenses, taxes, and debt service.

TABLE 14.5 Reconstructed Income Statement,
Academic Arms Apartments, 1993

Gross potential rental income	$37,800	
Less: Vacancy and collection losses at 4%	1,512	
Effective gross income (EGI)		$36,288
Operating expenses:		
Management at 5% of EGI	$ 1,814	
Utilities	3,100	
Trash collection	750	
Repairs and maintenance	2,400	
Promotion and advertising	150	
Property insurance	960	
Property taxes	4,292	
Less: Total operating expenses		13,466
Net operating income (NOI)		$22,822

TABLE 14.6 Cash Flow Analysis, Academic Arms Apartments, 1993–1997

	1993	1994	1995	1996	1997
INCOME TAX COMPUTATIONS					
NOI	$22,822	$24,419	$26,128	$27,957	$29,914
− Interest*	20,350	20,259	20,146	20,022	19,877
− Depreciation**	6,545	6,545	6,545	6,545	6,545
Taxable income (loss)	($ 4,073)	($ 2,385)	($ 563)	$ 1,390	$ 3,492
Marginal tax rate	.31	.31	.31	.31	.31
Taxes (−) or tax savings (+)	+$ 1,263	+$ 739	+$ 175	−$ 431	−$ 1,083
AFTER-TAX CASH FLOW (ATCF) COMPUTATIONS					
NOI	$22,822	$24,419	$26,128	$27,957	$29,914
− Mortgage payment	21,280	21,280	21,280	21,280	21,280
Before-tax cash flow	$ 1,542	$ 3,139	$ 4,848	$ 6,677	$ 8,634
+ Tax savings or − taxes	+ 1,263	+ 739	+ 175	− 431	− 1,083
After-tax cash flow (ATCF)	$ 2,805	$ 3,878	$ 5,023	$ 6,246	$ 7,551

$$\text{Average annual after-tax cash flow } (\overline{CF})*** = \frac{\$2,805 + \$3,878 + \$5,023 + \$6,246 + \$7,551}{5} = \$5,101$$

*Based on a $185,000 mortgage at 11 percent compounded annually. Some rounding has been used.

**Based on straight-line depreciation over 27.5 years and a depreciable basis of $180,000. Land value is assumed to equal $65,000.

***Found by substituting values for ATCF into Equation 14.4

depreciation
in real estate investing, a tax deduction based upon the original cost of a building and used to reflect its declining economic life.

ously losing and making money is caused by **depreciation.** Tax statutes incorporate this tax deduction, which is based on the original cost of the building, to reflect its declining economic life. However, since this deduction does not actually require a current cash outflow by the property owner, it acts as a *noncash expenditure* which reduces taxes and increases cash flow. In other words, in the 1993–1995 period the property ownership provides Jack with a *tax shelter;* that is, Jack uses the income tax losses sustained on the property to offset the taxable income he receives from salary, consulting fees, stock dividends, and book royalties. (We'll consider tax shelters in more detail in Chapter 15.)

Once the amount of taxes (or tax savings) is known, this amount is subtracted (or added) to the before-tax cash flow. Because Jack qualifies as an "active manager" of the property (an important provision of the Tax Reform Act of 1986 discussed more fully in Chapter 15), and since his income is low enough (also discussed in Chapter 15), he can use the real estate losses to reduce his other income. It is important to recognize that under the Tax Reform Act of 1986 the amount of tax losses that can be applied to other taxable income is limited. It is therefore important to consult a tax expert about the tax consequences of expected income tax losses when calculating ATCFs from real estate investments.

Proceeds from Sale

In this next step in his evaluation of the Academic Arms Apartments, Jack must estimate the net proceeds he will receive when he sells the property. For purposes of this analysis Jack has assumed a five-year holding period. Now he must forecast a selling price for the property. From that amount he must subtract selling expenses, the outstanding balance on the mortgage, and applicable federal income taxes. The remainder equals Jack's after-tax net proceeds from sale. These calculations are shown in Table 14.7. (Note that although Jack's ordinary income is subject to a 31 percent tax rate, the maximum rate of 28 percent is applicable to the capital gain expected on sale of the property.)

Jack wants to estimate his net proceeds from sale conservatively. He believes that at a minimum, market forces will push up the selling price of the property at the rate of 5 percent per year beyond his assumed purchase price of $245,000. Thus he estimates the selling price in 5 years will be $312,620; he does this by multiplying the $245,000 by the future-value interest factor of 1.276 from Appendix A, Table A.1, for 5 percent and 5 years (that is, $245,000 × 1.276 = $312,620). Making the indicated deductions from the forecasted selling price, Jack computes an after-tax net proceeds from the sale equal to $89,514.

Discounted Cash Flow

In this step Jack discounts the projected cash flows to their present value. In making this calculation (see Table 14.8) Jack finds that at his required rate of return of 13

TABLE 14.7 Estimated After-Tax Net Proceeds from Sale, Academic Arms Apartments, 1997

INCOME TAX COMPUTATIONS	
Forecasted selling price (at 5% annual appreciation)	$312,620
− Selling expenses at 7%	21,883
− Book value (purchase price less accumulated depreciation)	212,275
Gain on sale	$ 78,462
× Tax rate on gain*	28%
Taxes payable	$ 21,969

COMPUTATION OF AFTER-TAX NET PROCEEDS	
Forecasted selling price	$312,620
− Selling expenses	21,883
− Mortgage balance outstanding	179,254
Net proceeds before taxes	$111,483
− Taxes payable (calculated above)	21,969
After-tax net proceeds from sale ($CF_{R_{1994}}$)	$ 89,514

*Although Jack's ordinary income is taxed at a 31 percent rate, under the Tax Reform Act of 1986 this gain would be taxed at the 28 percent maximum rate applicable to capital gains.

TABLE 14.8 Net Present Value, Academic Arms Apartments*

$$NPV = \left[\frac{CF_1}{(1+r)^1} + \frac{CF_2}{(1+r)^2} + \frac{CF_3}{(1+r)^3} + \frac{CF_4}{(1+r)^4} + \frac{CF_5 + CF_{R_5}}{(1+r)^5} \right] - I_0$$

$$NPV = \left[\frac{\$2,805}{(1+.13)^1} + \frac{\$3,878}{(1+.13)^2} + \frac{\$5,023}{(1+.13)^3} + \frac{\$6,246}{(1+.13)^4} + \frac{\$97,065^{**}}{(1+.13)^5} \right] - \$60,000$$

$$NPV = \$2,483 + \$3,037 + \$3,481 + \$3,829 + \$52,707 - \$60,000^{***}$$

$$NPV = \$65,537 - \$60,000$$

$$NPV = +\underline{\$5,537}$$

*All inflows are assumed to be end-of-period receipts.

**Includes both the fifth year annual after-tax cash flow of $7,551 and the after-tax net proceeds from sale of $89,514.

***Calculated using present-value interest factors from Appendix A, Table A.3.

percent the net present value of these flows equals $5,537. Looked at another way, the present value of the amounts Jack forecasts he will receive exceeds the amount of his initial investment by about $5,500. The investment therefore meets (and exceeds) his acceptance criterion.

Approximate Yield

Alternatively, the approximate yield formula could be applied using the initial equity, I_0, of $60,000, along with the average annual after-tax cash flow, $\overline{CF}$, of $5,101 (calculated at the bottom of Table 14.6), and the after-tax net proceeds from sale, $CF_{R_{1997}}$, of $89,514 (calculated in Table 14.7). Substituting these values into the approximate yield formula presented in Equation 14.3 gives:

$$\text{Approximate yield} = \frac{\$5,101 + \dfrac{\$89,514 - \$60,000}{5}}{\dfrac{\$89,514 + \$60,000}{2}} = \frac{\$5,101 + \$5,903}{\$74,757}$$

$$= \frac{\$11,004}{\$74,757} = \underline{14.7\%}$$

Since the approximate yield of 14.7 percent is in excess of Jack's required rate of return of 13 percent, the investment meets (and exceeds) his acceptance criterion. Although we have merely approximated his return here, this technique, when consistently applied, should always result in the same conclusion as to acceptability as that obtained using net present value.

Synthesis and Interpretation

Now comes the time for Jack to review his work. He evaluates his market analysis, checks all the facts and figures in the investment return calculations, and then evaluates the results in light of his stated financial and nonfinancial objectives. He must ask himself: All things considered, is the expected payoff worth the risk? In this case, he decides it is. The property looks good. Even a positive finding, however, does not necessarily mean Jack should buy this property. He might still want to shop around to see if he can locate an even better investment. Furthermore, he might be wise to hire a real estate appraiser to confirm that the price he is willing to pay seems reasonable with respect to the recent sales prices of similar properties in the market area. Nevertheless, being an academic, Jack realizes that any problem can be studied to death; no one ever can obtain all the information that will bear on a decision. He gives himself a week to investigate other properties and talk to a professional appraiser. If nothing turns up to cause him second thoughts, he decides that he will offer to buy the Academic Arms Apartments. On the terms presented, he is willing to pay up to a maximum price of $245,000.

REAL ESTATE INVESTMENT SECURITIES

The most popular ways to invest in real estate are through individual ownership, real estate investment trusts (REITs), and real estate limited partnerships (RELPs). (Due to adverse tax consequences, real estate investors typically have avoided the corporate form of ownership.) Individual ownership of investment real estate is most common among wealthy individuals, professional real estate investors, and financial institutions. The strongest advantage of individual ownership is personal control, and the strongest drawback is that it requires a relatively large amount of capital. Although thus far we have emphasized active real estate investment, it is likely that most individuals will invest in real estate by purchasing shares of either a real estate investment trust or a limited partnership. Here we will examine each of these investment alternatives.

Real Estate Investment Trusts (REITs)

**real estate invest-
ment trust (REIT)**
a type of closed-end
investment company
that invests money,
obtained through the
sale of shares to in-
vestors, in various
types of real estate
and/or real estate
mortgages.

A **real estate investment trust (REIT)** is a type of closed-end investment company (see Chapter 13) that invests money, obtained through the sale of its shares to investors, in various types of real estate and/or real estate mortgages. REITs were established with the passage in 1960 of the Real Estate Investment Trust Act of 1960, which set forth requirements for forming a REIT as well as rules and procedures for making investments and distributing income. The appeal of REITs lies in their ability to allow the small investor to receive both the capital appreciation and income returns of real estate ownership without the headaches of property management. REITs were quite popular until the mid-1970s, when the bottom fell out of the real estate market as a result of many bad loans and an excess supply of property. In the early 1980s, however, both the real estate market and REITs began to make a comeback. Indeed, by 1992 there were about 210 such investment companies. Revived interest in REITs has been attributed to lower mortgage interest rates and the greatly diminished appeal of real estate limited partnerships (described later) resulting from the efforts of the IRS to reduce their tax advantages. (The efforts of the IRS in fact culminated in passage of the Tax Reform Act of 1986.) As a result,

REITs are popular forms of real estate investment that have been known to earn attractive annual rates of return of 10 to 20 percent, or more. Of course, REIT returns vary over time. For example, the average rate of return on publicly traded REITs was −17.5 percent in 1990 and 35.2 percent in 1991.

Basic Structure

REITs sell shares of stock to the investing public and use the proceeds, along with borrowed funds, to invest in a portfolio of real estate investments. The investor, therefore, owns part of the real estate portfolio held by the real estate investment trust. Typically REITs yield a return at least 1 to 2 percentage points above money market funds and about the same return as high-grade corporate bonds. REITs are required by law to pay out 95 percent of their income as dividends, which leaves little to invest in new acquisitions. Furthermore, they must keep at least 75 percent of their assets in real estate investments, earn at least 75 percent of their income from real estate, and hold each investment for at least four years.

Like any investment fund, each REIT has certain stated investment objectives, which should be carefully considered before acquiring shares. Actually, there are three basic types of REITs:

- **Equity REITs:** These invest in properties such as apartments, office buildings, shopping centers, and hotels.
- **Mortgage REITs:** These make both construction and mortgage loans to real estate investors.
- **Hybrid REITs:** These invest in both properties (like equity REITs) and construction and real estate mortgage loans (like mortgage REITs).

The shares of REITs are traded on organized exchanges such as the NYSE and AMEX as well as in the over-the-counter (OTC) market. Some of the better-known REITs include Continental Mortgage Equity Trust, Federal Realty Investment Trust, MGI Properties, New Plan Realty Trust, Rockefeller Center Properties, and Washington REIT.

Investing in REITs

REITs provide an attractive mechanism whereby an investor can make real estate property, mortgage, or both property and mortgage investments. They also provide professional management, thereby allowing the investor to assume a passive role. In addition, because their shares can be traded in the securities markets, investors can—unlike in most limited partnerships—conveniently purchase and sell shares with the assistance of a retail or discount broker. Investors in REITs can reap tax benefits by placing their shares in a Keogh plan, an individual retirement account (IRA), or some other tax-deferring vehicle.

The most direct way to investigate before you buy is to get the names of REITs that interest you and then call or write the headquarters of each REIT for information on the properties and/or mortgages it holds, its management, its future plans,

■ INVESTOR INSIGHTS ■

How to Buy a REIT

Real estate investment trusts (REITs), out of fashion for several years, are making a comeback. Evaluating a REIT involves different factors than those considered in analyzing stock and bond investments. Noted real estate and economic consultant Stephen E. Roulac provides the following advice to investors about selecting a REIT.

I anticipate that many insurance companies and other institutions that find themselves burdened with too much unwanted real estate will bundle their property holdings into REITS and attempt to sell parts of them to the public. Various existing partnerships and pension vehicles may be converted to REIT status, thereby creating new public investing opportunities. Seminars on how to organize new REITS are proliferating, a sure sign that a new product is about to hit the market.

My advice: Be highly selective and then be very careful.

What's a REIT? Basically, it's an investment fund that buys properties or mortgages. A REIT distributes nearly all of its earnings to its shareholders, and a REIT does not pay taxes at the entity level.

REITS have been around for decades, but like other investment concepts they tend to go in and out of fashion. Today cash is king in real estate, and investors demand liquidity so REITS make good sense. The extraordinary need to recapitalize several hundred billion dollars of real estate creates the opportunity for a REIT renaissance.

What should you look for as the new REITS begin to hit the market? My minimum requirements include scale, investment focus, geographic concentration, in-house management and insider ownership.

Scale

Most REITS have total capital (debt plus equity) of less than $250 million and portfolios of undistinguished properties. This means they lack the requisite size and quality to be major players. Look for REITS of substantial size, with capital of at least $500 million—and preferably $1 billion—invested in significant, institutional-grade properties.

Investment Focus

The smart REIT managements will specialize in particular types of investment. Some will buy apartment buildings, others hotels, others office buildings and so on. Focusing their

and its track record. Additional information on REIT investments can be obtained from the National Association of Real Estate Investment Trusts, 1129 20th Street NW, Suite 705, Washington, DC 20036 (202-785-8717).

The evaluation process will of course depend upon the type of REIT being considered. Equity REITs tend to be most popular since they share directly in real estate growth. If a property's rent goes up so will the dividend distribution, and share prices may also rise to reflect property appreciation. These REITs can be analyzed by applying the same basic procedures described in Chapters 6 and 7 for knowledge will enable them to get the best returns for their investors. Too many existing real estate portfolios are characterized by random collections of properties lacking any consistent theme.

Geographic Concentration

Carrying specialization a step further, the best REIT managers will focus on particular types of properties in specific parts of the country. There will be trusts specializing in apartment houses in Texas, shopping malls in the Northeast, hotels in the Northwest. The idea is to get the most bang for every dollar spent on buying and managing properties. Obviously, it is more cost effective to manage a portfolio of apartment buildings in a few neighboring cities than it is to worry about buildings spread out all over the country.

In-House Management

In the past, an advisory company controlled the REIT through an agency relationship and then contracted with outside suppliers for various real estate services. In contrast, the better REITS will be integrated investment organizations, whose own managers will finance, manage, develop and trade the properties. This strategy can save the trusts money.

Insider Ownership

I wouldn't consider a trust unless its management owns a big chunk of the equity. Like other companies I invest in, I want to feel that by looking out for themselves, the managers are also looking out for me.

Few of the REITS now on the market meet these criteria. But a handful come pretty close, and investors can find large, well managed, focused REITS, all of which stand to benefit as huge chunks of American real estate are recapitalized in the years ahead.

Source: Stephen E. Roulac, "Property Strategy: Renaissance," *Forbes,* May 25, 1992, p. 306.

common stock valuation. Since mortgage REITs earn most of their income as interest on real estate loans, they tend to trade like bonds; therefore many of the techniques for analyzing bond investments presented in Chapters 8 and 9 can be used to evaluate them. Hybrid REITs have the characteristics of both property and mortgages and should therefore be evaluated accordingly. Regardless of type, you should review the REIT's investment objective and performance in a fashion similar to that used in mutual fund investing (see Chapter 13). Carefully check the types of properties and/or mortgages held by the REIT. Be sure to look at the REIT's dividend yield and capital gain potential. And above all, as with any investment, the REIT selected should be consistent with your investment risk and return objectives. The accompanying *Investor Insights* box offers other guidelines for selecting a REIT.

Real Estate Limited Partnerships (RELPs)

real estate limited partnership (RELP)
a professionally managed real estate syndicate that invests in various types of real estate; the managers assume the role of general partner, whose liability is unlimited, and other investors are limited partners, whose liability is limited to the amount of their initial investment.

A **real estate limited partnership (RELP)** is a professionally managed real estate syndicate that invests in various types of real estate. Some RELPs are set up to speculate in raw land, others invest in income-producing properties like apartments, office buildings, and shopping centers, and still others invest in various types of mortgages (the so-called *debt partnerships* as opposed to the *equity partnerships* that own land and buildings). Managers of RELPs assume the role of general partner, which means their liability is unlimited, while other investors are limited partners, meaning they are legally liable for only the amount of their initial investment. Most limited partnerships require a minimum investment of between $2,500 and $10,000. Because of the limited liability, along with the potentially high returns provided by these arrangements, they often appeal to the individual investor wishing to buy real estate. (A detailed discussion of the structure and operation of limited partnerships is presented in Chapter 15). Investment in a limited partnership can be made directly through ads in the financial news, through stockbrokers or financial planners, or with the assistance of a commercial real estate broker.

Types of Syndicates

single property syndicate
a type of real estate limited partnership established to raise money to purchase a specific property.

blind pool syndicate
a type of real estate limited partnership formed by a syndicator to raise money to be invested at the syndicator's discretion.

There are two basic types of real estate limited partnerships: single property and blind pool syndicates. The **single property syndicate** is established to raise money to purchase a specific piece (or pieces) or property. For example, 50 units of a partnership can be sold at $7,500 each to buy a piece of property for $1 million. (A "unit" in a limited partnership is like a share of stock in a company and represents an ownership position in the partnership.) In this case a total of $375,000 (50 units × $7,500) would come from the partners, and the remaining $625,000 would be borrowed. The **blind pool syndicate,** on the other hand, is formed by a syndicator—often well-known—in order to raise a given amount of money to be invested at his or her discretion, though the general partner often has some or all of the properties already picked out. The blind pool syndicator takes a specified percentage of all income generated as a management fee. Large real estate brokerage firms commonly arrange these types of syndicates.

Investing in RELPs

Prior to the Tax Reform Act of 1986 much of the appeal of real estate limited partnerships came from the tax-sheltered income that these investments provided. However, that is no longer the case. Instead, like other forms of real estate, these limited partnerships are considered to be *passive* investments; as such, the amount of write-offs that can be taken on them is limited to the amount of income they generate. This means that such write-offs cannot be used to shelter ordinary income from taxes. Although limited partnerships have lost some of their appeal, they remain a popular way to invest in real estate, especially for those with limited investment capital. The big difference is that rather than emphasizing the tax-sheltered nature of their income, many of the real estate limited partnerships of today are less leveraged (some use *no* debt at all) and are structured to provide attractive current income (from rents, and so on) and/or capital gains. In essence, they are now being promoted for their underlying investment merits and not on the basis of some artificial tax motive. Certainly for an individual with as little as $1,000 to $5,000 to invest, a carefully selected limited partnership may be a sensible way to invest in real estate.

The annual return on RELPs *in the past* typically ranged between 5 and 15 percent of the amount invested. (There is, of course, *no* insurance that such returns will continue to be generated in the future.) The emphasis with respect to the type of return generated differs from one syndicate to another. Most real estate limited partnerships today place major emphasis on producing attractive levels of current income for their investors; some, however, still emphasize capital gains. Of course, the goals of the syndicate, the quality of its management, and the specific properties involved should be carefully evaluated *before* purchasing in order to estimate the expected risk and return. Information useful in analyzing RELPs can be obtained from the syndicator in the form of a *prospectus*. One of the key drawbacks of RELPs is that it's always been difficult to get out of them since there is no organized market for limited partnership units. Although a few years ago it appeared that **master limited partnerships (MLP)**—partnerships that are publicly traded on major stock exchanges—would improve partnership liquidity, recent tax law changes have greatly reduced their attractiveness. Before purchasing a RELP, make sure that it is the best vehicle for meeting your investment objectives.

master limited partnership (MLP)
a limited partnership that is publicly traded on a major stock exchange.

SUMMARY

1. The starting point for real estate investment analysis is setting objectives. This includes considering investment characteristics, setting both financial and nonfinancial constraints and goals, and analyzing important features such as the physical property, its associated legal rights, the relevant time period, and the geographic area of concern.

   Investment real estate includes income properties and speculative properties. Income properties can be residential, which includes single-family and multi-family properties, or commercial, which includes office buildings, shopping centers, etc. Speculative properties, such as raw land, are expected to provide returns from appreciation in value rather than from periodic rental income as is the case for income properties.

2. The four determinants of real estate value are demand, supply, the property, and the transfer process. *Demand* refers to people's willingness and ability to buy or rent, and *supply* includes all those properties from which potential buyers or tenants can choose. To analyze a property, applicable restrictions on its use, its location, site characteristics, improvements, and property management should be evaluated. The transfer process involves promotion and negotiation of a property.

3. A market value appraisal can be used to estimate real estate value. It relies on the cost approach, the comparative sales approach, and the income approach. An expert can be hired to give advice with regard to a property's market value.

4. Investment returns can be estimated by forecasting cash flows and calculating either the net present value or the approximate yield. Risk and return parameters vary depending on the degree of leverage employed in financing a real estate investment. Of course, any quantitative analysis of real estate value and returns must be integrated with various subjective and market considerations prior to making the investment decision.

5. The real estate investment trust (REIT) allows the investor to buy publicly traded ownership shares in a professionally managed portfolio of real estate properties, mortgages, and/or both. REITs can be analyzed in light of the investor's risk-return objective in a fashion similar to that used for stocks, bonds, and mutual funds.

6. Real estate limited partnerships (RELPs) provide a vehicle for buying shares in professionally managed real estate syndicates that invest in specified types of properties and/or mortgages. Their appeal today centers on the provision of attractive current income and/or capital gains rather than on tax-shelter advantages. A major drawback of RELPs is their general lack of liquidity.

QUESTIONS

1. Why should real estate investment analysis start with a definition of objectives?

2. How can adding real estate to your investment portfolio decrease your overall risk? Explain.

3. Define and differentiate between income properties and speculative properties. Differentiate between and give examples of residential and commercial income properties.

4. Which are more important when considering real estate investments, financial or nonfinancial considerations?

5. Briefly describe the following important factors to consider when making a real estate investment:
   a. Physical property
   b. Property rights
   c. Time horizon
   d. Geographic area

6. Demand is often shown on a graph as a downward-sloping curve. For purposes of real estate analysis, what does such a curve actually reflect?

7. Supply is often shown on a graph as an upward-sloping curve. For purposes of real estate analysis, what does such a curve actually reflect?

8. Why is property management important to a real estate investor?

9. Are real estate markets efficient? Why or why not?

10. Comment on the following: Market value is always the price at which a property sells.

11. Briefly describe each of the three approaches commonly used by real estate appraisers to estimate the market value of investment properties.

12. Real estate investments can be structured to meet a variety of investment goals. Explain various investment needs and the types of properties that best meet them.

13. What is leverage and what role does it play in real estate investment? How does it effect the risk-return parameters of a real estate investment?

14. Define tax depreciation. Explain why it is said to offer tax shelter potential. What real estate investments provide this benefit? Explain.

15. Define: (a) net operating income (NOI) and (b) after-tax cash flow (ATCF) as they apply to income from rental properties.

16. Explain why, in spite of being acceptable based on NPV or approximate yield, a real estate investment might still not be acceptable to a given investor.

17. Briefly describe the basic structure and investment considerations associated with the following passive forms of real estate investment:

 a. Real estate investment trust (REITs).
 b. Real estate limited partnerships (RELPs).

PROBLEMS

1. Charles Cook, an investor, is considering two alternative financing plans for purchasing a parcel of real estate costing $50,000. Alternative X involves paying cash; alternative Y involves obtaining 80 percent financing at 10.5 percent interest. If the parcel of real estate appreciates in value by $7,500 in one year, calculate: (a) Charles's net return and (b) his return on equity for each alternative. If the value dropped by $7,500, what effect would this have on your answers to (a) and (b)?

2. In the coming year, the Sandbergs expect a potential rental property investment costing $120,000 to have gross potential rental income of $20,000, vacancy and collection losses equalling 5 percent of gross income, and operating expenses of $10,000. The mortgage on the property is expected to require annual payments of $8,500. The interest portion of the mortgage payments as well as depreciation is given below for each of the next three years. The Sandbergs are in the 28-percent marginal tax bracket.

Year	Interest	Depreciation
1	$8,300	$4,500
2	8,200	4,500
3	8,100	4,500

The net operating income is expected to increase by 6 percent each year beyond the first year.

 a. Calculate the net operating income (NOI) for each of the next three years.
 b. Calculate the after-tax cash flow (ATCF) for each of the next three years.

3. Walt Hubble is contemplating selling rental property originally costing $200,000. He believes that it has appreciated in value at an annual rate of 6 percent over its four-year holding period. He will have to pay a commission equal to 5 percent of the sale price to sell the property. Currently the property has a book value of $137,000. The mortgage balance out-

standing at the time of sale currently is $155,000. Walt will have to pay a 28 percent tax on any capital gains.

a. Calculate the tax payable on the proposed sale.
b. Calculate the after-tax net proceeds associated with the proposed sale, CF_R.

 4. Bezie Foster has estimated the annual after-tax cash flows (ATCFs) and after-tax net proceeds from sale (CF_R) of a proposed real estate investment as noted below for the planned four-year ownership period.

Year	ATCF	CF_R
1	$6,200	
2	8,000	
3	8,300	
4	8,500	
4		$59,000

The initial required investment in the property is $55,000. Bezie, at minimum, must earn 14 percent on the investment.

a. Calculate the net present value (NPV) of the proposed investment.
b. Calculate the approximate yield from the investment.
c. From your findings in a and b what recommendations would your give Bezie? Explain.

CASE PROBLEMS

14.1 Gary Sofer's Appraisal of the Wabash Oaks Apartments

Gary Sofer wants to estimate the market value of the Wabash Oaks Apartments, an 18-unit building with nine 1-bedroom units and nine 2-bedroom units. The present owner of Wabash Oaks provided Gary with the following annual income statement. Today's date is March 1, 1993.

OWNER'S INCOME STATEMENT,
WABASH OAKS APARTMENTS, 1992

Gross income		$65,880
Less: Expenses		
Utilities	$14,260	
Property insurance	2,730	
Repairs and maintenance	1,390	
Property taxes	4,790	
Mortgage payments	18,380	
Total expenses		41,550
Net income		$24,330

Current rental rates of properties similar to Wabash Oaks typically run from $300 to $315 per month for 1-bedroom units and $340 to $360 per month for 2-bedroom units. From a study of the market, Gary determined that a reasonable required rate of return for Wabash

Oaks would be 9.62 percent and that vacancy rates for comparable apartment buildings are running around 4 percent.

Questions

1. Using Figure 14.1 as a guide, discuss how you might go about evaluating the features of this property.
2. Gary has studied economics and knows all about demand and supply, yet he doesn't understand how to apply it. Advise Gary in a practical way how he might incorporate demand and supply into an investment analysis of the Wabash Oaks Apartments.
3. Should Gary accept the owner's income statement as the basis for an income appraisal of Wabash Oaks? Why or why not?
4. In your opinion, what is a reasonable estimate of the market value for the Wabash Oaks?
5. If Gary could buy Wabash Oaks for $10,000 less than its market value, would it be a good investment for him? Explain.

14.2 Analyzing Dr. Davis's Proposed Real Estate Investment

Dr. Marilyn Davis, a single, 34-year-old heart specialist, is considering the purchase of a small office building. She wants to add some diversity to her investment portfolio, which now contains only corporate bonds and preferred stocks. In addition, because of her high federal tax bracket of 31 percent, Marilyn wants an investment that produces a good after-tax rate of return.

A real estate market and financial consultant has estimated that Marilyn could buy the office building for $200,000. In addition, this consultant analyzed the property's rental potential with respect to trends in demand and supply. He discussed the following items with Marilyn. (1) The office building was occupied by two tenants who each had three years remaining on their leases. (2) It was only four years old, was in excellent condition, and was located near a number of major thoroughfares. For her purposes, Marilyn decided the building should be analyzed on the basis of a three-year holding period. The gross rents in the most recent year were $32,000, and operating expenses were $15,000. The consultant pointed out that the leases had built-in 10 percent per year rent escalation clauses and that he expected operating expenses to increase by 8 percent per year. He further expected no vacancy or collection loss because both tenants were excellent credit risks.

Marilyn's accountant estimated that annual tax depreciation would be $5,100 in each of the next three years. To finance the purchase of the building Marilyn has considered a variety of alternatives, one of which would involve assuming the existing $120,000 mortgage. Upon the advice of a close friend, a finance professor at the local university, Marilyn decided to arrange a $150,000, 10.5 percent, 25-year mortgage from the bank at which she maintains her business account. The annual loan payment would total $17,000. Of this, the following breakdown between interest and principal would apply in each of the first three years:

Year	Interest	Principal	Total
1	$15,750	$1,250	$17,000
2	15,620	1,380	17,000
3	15,470	1,530	17,000

The loan balance at the end of the three years would be $145,840. The consultant expects the property to appreciate by about 9 percent per year to $260,000 at the end of three years.

Marilyn will incur a 5 percent sales commission expense on this assumed sale price. The building's book value at the end of three years would be $184,700. The net proceeds on the sale would be taxed at Marilyn's capital gains tax rate of 28 percent.

Questions

1. What is the expected annual after-tax cash flow (ATCF) for each of the three years (assuming Marilyn has other passive income that can be used to offset any losses from this property)?
2. At a 15 percent required rate of return, will this investment produce a positive net present value?
3. What rate of return does the approximate yield formula show for this proposed investment?
4. Could Marilyn increase her returns by assuming the existing mortgage at a 9.75 percent interest rate, rather than arranging a new loan? What measure of return do you believe Marilyn should use to make this comparison?
5. Do you believe Marilyn has thought about her real estate investment objectives enough? Why or why not?

15 Tax Shelters and Limited Partnerships

After studying this chapter, you should be able to:

1. Understand what is meant by taxable income and the basic procedures involved in its calculation.

2. Define tax avoidance and tax deferral and the characteristics of tax shelters.

3. Explain how investors can earn tax-favored income, with particular emphasis on income excluded from taxation, strategies that defer tax liabilities to the next year, programs that defer tax liabilities to retirement, strategies that trade current income for capital gains, and tax swaps.

4. Summarize the characteristics of deferred annuities, and of fixed versus variable annuities, their appeal as investment vehicles, and understand the potential tax shelter benefits of single-premium life insurance.

5. Describe the tax status of limited partnerships and how they work.

6. Discuss popular forms of limited partnerships available to investors and their essential investment considerations—use of leverage, risk and return, and investment suitability.

tax planning
the formation of
strategies that will
exclude, reduce, or
defer the level of
taxes to be paid.

It is often said that the necessities of life include food, clothing, and shelter. Shelter is important because it protects us from the elements—rain, wind, snow, extreme heat, or cold—in the physical environment. In a similar fashion investors need shelter from the taxes charged on income. Without adequate protection, the returns earned by an investor can be greatly reduced by the ravages of the tax code. Thus in making investment decisions we must assess not only risk and return, but also the tax effects associated with a given investment vehicle or strategy. Since the tax effects depend on one's "tax bracket," it is important to choose investment vehicles that provide the maximum after-tax return for a given risk. Making such choices is part of **tax planning,** which involves the formation of strategies that will exclude, reduce, or defer the taxes to be paid. An awareness of the various vehicles and strategies available for legally reducing one's tax liability and an understanding of the role they can play in a portfolio are fundamental to obtaining the highest after-tax returns for a given level of risk. Let us begin by looking at tax fundamentals.

TAX FUNDAMENTALS

As currently structured, federal income tax law imposes a higher tax burden on higher taxable income. This is done through a progressive rate structure that taxes income at one of three rates—either 15, 28, or 31 percent. There is one structure of rates for taxpayers filing *individual* returns and another for those filing *joint* returns. Table 15.1 shows the tax rates and income brackets for these two major filing categories. Notice that you pay not only more taxes as your taxable income increases, but you pay *progressively* more if your taxable income rises into a higher bracket. For example, as noted in Chapter 3, a single taxpayer with $18,000 of taxable income would pay $2,700 (15% × $18,000). If that same taxpayer had *double* that amount of taxable income—$36,000—he or she would pay about *2.75 times more tax,* computed as follows:

$$(.15 \times \$20,350) + [.28 \times (\$36,000 - \$20,350)] = \$3,053 + \$4,382 = \$7,435$$

Taxable Income

taxable income
the income to which
tax rates are applied;
equals adjusted
gross income minus
itemized deductions
and exemptions.

Taxable income, as its name implies, is the income to which tax rates are applied. From an investments perspective, this includes such items as cash dividends, interest, profits from a sole proprietorship or share in a partnership, and gains from the sale of securities or other assets. As we saw in Chapter 3, federal tax law retains an important distinction between ordinary income and capital gains (and losses).

TABLE 15.1 Tax Rates and Income Brackets for Individual and Joint Returns (1991)

Tax Rates	Taxable Income	
	Individual Returns	**Joint Returns**
15%	$ 0 to $20,350	$ 0 to $34,000
28%	$20,351 to $49,300	$34,001 to $82,150
31%	over $49,301	over $82,151

To review, broadly, *ordinary income* refers to any compensation received for labor services (active income) or from invested capital (portfolio or passive income). The form in which the income is received is immaterial. For example, if you owe a debt to someone and that person forgives (excuses you from repaying) the debt, the amount could wind up as income taxable to you, depending on how the debt was initially created and treated for tax purposes in previous periods. Situations such as this sometimes arise in real estate tax shelters. As a general rule *any event that increases your net worth is income, and unless it is specifically excluded from taxable income or considered a capital gain, it is ordinary income.*

The tax law as revised by the Tax Reform Act of 1986 treats gains or losses resulting from the sale of capital assets as ordinary income. A *capital asset* is defined as anything you own and use for personal purposes, pleasure, or investment. A house and a car are capital assets; so are stamp collections, bonds, and shares of common stock. Your **basis** in a capital asset usually means what you paid for it, including commissions and other costs related to the purchase. If an asset is sold for a price greater than its basis, a *capital gain* is the result; if the reverse is true, then you have a *capital loss*. All capital gains are included in full as a part of ordinary income. As for capital losses, a maximum of $3,000 of losses in excess of capital gains can be claimed in any one year. Any losses that cannot be applied in the current year can be carried forward to future years and then deducted. (Timing the sale of securities to optimize the tax treatment of capital losses is an important part of tax planning and is treated more thoroughly later in the chapter.)

basis
the amount paid for a capital asset, including commissions and other costs related to the purchase.

Determining Taxable Income

Determining taxable income involves a series of steps. Since these are illustrated more clearly with an example, let us consider the 1991 income tax situation of the Edward and Martha Meyer family, a family of three. In 1991 the family had the following income items:

1.	Wages and salaries	
	Edward	$26,000
	Martha	12,000
2.	Interest on tax-free municipal bonds	400
3.	Interest on savings accounts	900
4.	Dividends on common stock (owned jointly)	600
5.	Capital gains on securities	1,500

The family also had the following deductions in 1991:

1.	Deductible contribution to IRA account	$1,800
2.	Charitable contributions	1,000
3.	Interest on home mortgage	7,500

The Meyers' income tax due for 1991 was $3,638, as determined in Table 15.2 and explained below.

TABLE 15.2 Determining 1991 Federal Income Tax Due for the Edward and Martha Meyer Family

I.	**GROSS INCOME**	
	1. Wages and salaries ($26,000 + $12,000)	$38,000
	2. Interest on savings accounts	900
	3. Dividends	600
	4. Capital gains	1,500
	Gross income	$41,000
II.	**ADJUSTMENTS TO GROSS INCOME** Deductible IRA contribution	$ 1,800
III.	**ADJUSTED GROSS INCOME** (I − II) = ($41,000 − $1,800)	$39,200
IV.	**ITEMIZED DEDUCTIONS**	
	1. Charitable contributions	$ 1,000
	2. Mortgage interest	7,500
	Total itemized deductions	$ 8,500
V.	**EXEMPTIONS** Edward, Martha, and one child (3 × $2,150)	$ 6,450
VI.	**TAXABLE INCOME** (III − IV − V) = ($39,200 − $8,500 − $6,450)	$24,250
VII.	**FEDERAL INCOME TAX** (per rate schedule, Table 15.1) (.15 × $24,250)	$ 3,638
VIII.	**TAX CREDITS**	$ 0
IX.	**TAX DUE** (VII − VIII) = ($3,638 − $0)	$ 3,638

Gross Income

Gross income begins with all includable income but then allows certain exclusions that are provided in the tax law. Table 15.2 shows that in the Meyers' case, all income is included except interest on the tax-free municipal bonds, which is not subject to federal income tax. Notice that interest on savings accounts and dividend income is included. In addition, all capital gains are included in gross income, although the maximum tax rate applied to certain capital gains is 28 percent.

Adjustments to Gross Income

Adjustments to gross income reflect the intent of Congress to favor certain activities. The only one shown for the Meyers (there are others) is their allowable IRA contribution (discussed later) of $1,800, which was determined using a formula provided under the prevailing tax law. You should note the tax-sheltering quality of the IRA; without it, the Meyers would have paid taxes on an additional $1,800 of income in 1991.

Adjusted Gross Income

adjusted gross income
gross income less the total allowable adjustments for tax purposes.

Subtracting the adjustments from gross income provides **adjusted gross income.** This figure is necessary in calculating certain deductions (such as medical and dental expenses, charitable contributions, job and other expenses, and the amount of allowable real estate losses) not illustrated in our example. The Meyers' adjusted gross income is $39,200.

Itemized Deductions

standard deduction
an amount, indexed to the cost of living, that taxpayers can elect to deduct from adjusted gross income without itemizing.

Taxpayers can elect to take a **standard deduction** which is indexed to the cost of living. The standard deduction amounts for 1991 ranged from $3,400 to $8,300 depending on filing status, age, and vision. (There are specific deductions for blind taxpayers.) The standard deduction for the Meyers would have been $5,700. If they don't wish to take the standard deduction, taxpayers can choose to itemize deductions. Taxpayers with itemized deductions in excess of the applicable standard deduction will prefer to itemize. This group will typically include those individuals who own a mortgaged primary and/or second home. Such was the case for the Meyers, since their itemized deductions of $8,500 exceeded the $5,700 standard deduction.

itemized deductions
personal living and family expenses which can be deducted from adjusted gross income.

A number of items qualify as **itemized deductions,** the most common of which are residential mortgage interest and charitable contributions. All other things being equal, there is a tax advantage to ownership of a principal (as well as a second) residence, because interest on the associated mortgage loans is tax-deductible. Consumer interest is *not* tax-deductible, whereas investment interest—interest paid on funds borrowed for personal investment purposes—is deductible, subject to certain limitations. Clearly, allowable interest deductions are less expensive on an after-tax basis.

Exemptions

exemption
a deduction for each qualifying dependent of a federal taxpayer.

The tax law allows a deduction, called an **exemption,** for each qualifying dependent. It was $2,150 in 1991 ($2,300 in 1992, and an amount indexed to the cost of living after 1992). There are specific rules for determining who qualifies as a dependent. These should be reviewed if the potential dependent is not your child or an immediate member of your family residing in your home. Table 15.2 shows that the Meyers claimed three exemptions.

Taxable Income

Deducting itemized deductions and exemptions from adjusted gross income leaves *taxable income;* in the Meyers' case, this amount is $24,250. Although the Meyers have none, certain *miscellaneous expenses,* which include union dues, safe-deposit box rental, investment advice, membership dues for professional organizations, and the cost of business publications generally can be deducted only to the extent that they exceed 2 percent of adjusted gross income. In addition, certain *unreimbursed employee expenses* such as 80 percent of entertainment bills and 100 percent of travel expenses are deductible if substantiated by receipts.

marginal tax rate
the tax rate on additional income.

You can use Table 15.1 to calculate the tax due for the Meyers. Their taxable income of $24,250 puts them in the 15 percent income bracket. Thus their tax, as calculated in the table, is $3,638. The Meyers pay a 15 percent **marginal tax rate,** which means the tax rate on additional income up to $34,000 is 15 percent. *It is the marginal tax rate that should be considered when evaluating the tax implications of an investment strategy.*

average tax rate
taxes due divided by taxable income; different from the *marginal tax rate.*

By all means, do not confuse the marginal rate with the average rate. The **average tax rate** is simply taxes due divided by taxable income. In the Meyers' case, since they are in the lower tax bracket, this rate also equals 15.0 percent ($3,638/$24,250). Of course, for taxpayers in the 28 or 31 percent tax bracket, the marginal rate will exceed the average tax rate. The average tax rate has absolutely no relevance to the Meyers' investment decision making.

Tax Credits

tax credits
tax reductions allowed by the IRS on a dollar-for-dollar basis under certain specified conditions.

A number of **tax credits** are available. These are particularly attractive since they reduce taxes on a dollar-for-dollar basis in contrast to a *deduction,* which reduces taxes only by an amount determined by the marginal tax rate. A frequently used tax credit is for child- and dependent-care expenses. Other common credits include the credit for the elderly or disabled, foreign tax credit, minimum tax credit, mortgage interest credit, and nonconventional fuel credit. The Meyers, as is true for most taxpayers under the Tax Reform Act of 1986, were not eligible for any tax credits.

Taxes Due or Refundable

The final amount of tax due is determined by subtracting any tax credits from the income tax. The Meyers' tax due is $3,638. They now compare this amount to the total of tax withheld (indicated on their year-end withholding statements) and any estimated taxes they may have paid during 1991. If these two add up to *more* than $3,638, then they are entitled to a refund of the difference; if the total is *less* than $3,638, they must pay the difference when they file their 1991 federal income tax return.

The Alternative Minimum Tax

alternative minimum tax (AMT)
a tax passed by Congress to ensure that all individuals pay at least some federal income tax.

As a result of many taxpayers effectively using tax shelters (tax-favored investments) to reduce their taxable incomes to near zero, Congress in 1978 introduced the **alternative minimum tax (AMT).** The purpose of this measure is to raise additional revenue by making sure that all individuals pay at least some tax. The AMT rate is 24 percent of the alternative minimum tax base. This tax base is determined beginning with the individual's regular taxable income and then making a variety of adjustments. The procedures for determining the alternative minimum tax base and the alternative minimum tax are quite complicated. A tax expert should be consulted if you feel the alternative minimum tax might apply in your situation.

TAX STRATEGIES

A comprehensive tax strategy attempts to maximize the total after-tax income of an investor over his or her lifetime. This objective is accomplished by either avoiding taxable income altogether or by deferring it to another period when it may receive more favorable tax treatment as a result of a lower tax rate. Even when there is no tax reduction by deferral, it still offers the advantage of having the use of saved tax dollars over the deferral period.

Tax Avoidance and Tax Deferral

tax evasion
illegal activities designed to avoid paying taxes by omitting income or overstating deductions.

tax avoidance
reducing or eliminating taxes in legal ways that comply with the intent of Congress.

Tax avoidance should not be confused with **tax evasion,** which consists of illegal activities such as omitting income or overstating deductions. **Tax avoidance** is concerned with reducing or eliminating taxes *in legal ways* that comply with the intent of Congress, which wrote the special provisions into the tax law. As we have already noted in the Meyers' example, the most popular form of tax avoidance is investing in securities offering tax-favored income (to be explained in greater detail in the next section). Another broad approach to avoiding taxes is to distribute income-producing assets to family members (usually children) who either pay no taxes at all or pay them at much lower rates. Since this is also a highly specialized area of the tax law, we do not pursue it further in this text. Again, you should seek professional counsel whenever a tax strategy of this type is contemplated.

tax deferral
the strategy of delaying taxes by shifting income subject to tax into a later period.

   Tax deferral deals with means of delaying taxes and can be accomplished in a number of ways. Frequently, taxes are deferred for only one year as part of a year-end tax strategy to shift income from one year to the next when it is known that taxable income or tax rates will be lower then. A simple way to defer taxes is to use vehicles specifically designed to accomplish this objective. Included would be certain retirement plans—401(k)s, Keoghs, and IRAs—and annuities. The role of each of these vehicles is described later in this chapter.

Tax Shelters

tax shelter
an investment vehicle that offers potential reductions of taxable income.

A **tax shelter** is any investment vehicle that offers potential reductions of taxable income. Usually you must own the vehicle directly—rather than indirectly. For example, if the Meyers had a tax-deductible loss of $1,000 on investment property directly owned by them, it could have provided tax shelter. Had they, instead, set up a corporation to own this property, the net loss of $1,000 would have been the corporation's, not theirs. Thus they would have lost that tax deduction and the related tax savings. Similarly, when publicly owned corporations show huge losses, those losses are of no immediate tax benefit to the shareholders. Although the market price of the stock probably falls, which means you could sell it at a tax loss, such a capital loss is limited to only $3,000 a year (in excess of capital gains). If you owned a large amount of stock your loss might be many times that figure, and yet it may be of no immediate use in reducing your taxes.

   Thus there is a tax advantage in organizing certain activities as sole proprietorships or partnerships, and even more specifically, as limited partnerships. The majority of these tax shelters are designed primarily to pass on losses resulting from certain deductions—depreciation, depletion, and amortization—directly to individuals. The amount, if any, of such losses that can be deducted when calculating taxable income is currently limited by law. The few remaining tax shelters and the structure of the limited partnerships that makes them feasible are explained later in this chapter. Now, however, let us turn our attention to those vehicles that offer tax-favored income.

TAX-FAVORED INCOME

tax-favored income
an investment return
that is not taxable, is
taxed at a rate less
than that on other
similar investments,
defers the payment
of tax to a later pe-
riod, or trades cur-
rent income for capi-
tal gains.

An investment is said to offer **tax-favored income** if it has any of the following results: if it (1) offers a return that is not taxable, (2) if it offers a return that is taxed at a rate less than that on other similar investments, (3) if it defers the payment of tax to the next year or to retirement, or (4) if it trades current for capital gain income. These tax "favors" have been written into the tax law to foster or promote certain activities as well as to provide convenient tax-reporting procedures. So far in this book we have examined in detail how real estate can provide shelter from taxes for certain investors. Below we will briefly examine a number of other noteworthy tax-sheltered vehicles and strategies; later in this chapter we'll look at two other vehicles—deferred annuities and single-premium life insurance.

Income Excluded from Taxation

Some items are simply excluded from taxation, either totally or partially. These include interest earned on tax-free municipals and on Treasury and government agency issues, and certain proceeds from the sale of a personal residence. Because of the tax advantages they offer, these sources of income are particularly attractive investment vehicles.

Tax-Free Municipal Bond Interest

Municipal bonds were described in Chapter 8. All interest received from the most common form—tax-free municipals—is free of federal income tax. In fact, this income is not even reported on the return. However, any gains or losses resulting from the sale of municipal bonds must be included as capital gains or losses. In addition, interest paid on money borrowed to purchase municipal bonds is *not* tax-deductible.

Treasury and Government Agency Issues

Treasury and government agency issues were also discussed in Chapter 8. Although interest on these securities is included on the federal tax return, it is excluded for state and local income tax purposes. Since these combined income tax rates can be as high as 20 percent in some parts of the country, individuals in high tax brackets may find such exclusions worthwhile.

Sale of a Personal Residence

A capital gain results if you sell your personal residence for a price greater than its basis (the price originally paid for it). However, provisions in the tax law soften the tax impact and actually make investment in a home an excellent tax shelter. First, if a gain exists from the sale of your home, it can be deferred from taxation if you purchase another home at a price equal to or greater than the price of the home you sold—as long as you buy the other home within 24 months. The second, and more important, tax implication is that you have a one-time exclusion of $125,000 of gain from gross income from the sale of a personal residence. On a joint return, both spouses must be age 55 or older and must meet certain other conditions to be eligible for this exclusion. This is a major tax break for most people and certainly enhances the investment appeal of the personal residence.

Strategies that Defer Tax Liabilities to the Next Year

Very often an investor may purchase securities and enjoy sizable gains within a relatively short period of time. Suppose you bought 100 shares of XYZ common stock in mid-1992; by year-end 1993 your investment would have increased in value by 50 percent, since the price of this stock increased from $30 a share to around $45 over that period. Assume that at year-end 1993 you believe the stock is fully valued in the market and wish to sell it and invest the $4,500 elsewhere. In such a case, you would be taxed on a capital gain of $1,500 ($4,500 sale price − $3,000 cost). Assuming a 28 percent tax bracket, this would lead to income taxes for 1993 of $420 on the sale. Because tax rates may be lower next year or merely to benefit from the time value of money it may be advantageous to defer the tax on this transaction to the following year (1994). Three available strategies for preserving a gain while deferring tax to the following year are (1) the short sale against the box, (2) the put hedge, and (3) the deep-in-the-money call option.

Short Sale Against the Box

shorting-against-the-box
a technique used to lock in a security profit and defer the taxes on it to the following tax year by short-selling a number of shares equal to those already owned.

The short sale against the box technique can be used to lock in a profit and defer the taxes on a profit to the next taxable year. By **shorting-against-the-box**— short-selling a number of shares equal to what you already own—you lock in an existing profit, and thus eliminate any risk of a price decline. You also give up any future increases in price, but this should not be of concern since you believe that the current price is relatively high. For example, to lock in and defer the $1,500 capital gain on the XYZ transaction you would, prior to year-end, sell short 100 shares of XYZ. No matter what happens to the price of the stock, you are guaranteed $1,500. You would then have two positions—one long and one short—both involving an equal number (100) of XYZ shares. After year-end you would use the 100 shares held long to close out the short position, thereby realizing the $1,500 capital gain.

Put Hedge

put hedge
the purchase of a put option on shares currently owned in order to lock in a profit and defer taxes on the profit to the next taxable year.

The put hedge approach was covered in Chapter 11, where its use in locking in a profit and deferring the taxes on the profit to the next taxable year was discussed. It can be used as a technique to accomplish the same objectives as the short sale against the box without losing the potential for additional price appreciation. Essentially a **put hedge** involves buying a put option on shares currently owned. If the price of the stock falls, your losses on the shares are offset by the profit on the put option. For example, suppose when XYZ was trading at $45 you purchased a six-month put option with a striking price of $45 for $150. By doing this you locked in a price of $45: if the price fell, say, to $40 a share your $500 loss on the stock would be offset exactly by a $500 profit on the option. However, you would still be out the $150 cost of the option. At a closing price of $40, this would be your ending after-tax position:

1.	Initial cost of 100 shares		$3,000
2.	Profit on 100 shares [100 × ($40 − $30)]		1,000
3.	Profit on the put option	$ 500	
4.	Cost of the put option	−150	
5.	Taxable gain on put option [(3) − (4)]		350
6.	Total tax on transaction		
	Profit on stock (2)	$1,000	
	Plus taxable gain on put (5)	+ 350	
	Total gain	$1,350	
	Times tax rate	× .28	
	Total tax		378
7.	After-tax position [(1) + (2) + (5) − (6)]		$3,972

The final after-tax position here is about the same as if you had simply held the stock while its price declined to around $43.50 a share, but there are two important considerations: First, the put hedge locks in this position regardless of how low the price might fall, whereas simply holding the stock does not. Second, any price appreciation will be enjoyed with either approach. (Notice you do not give up this advantage as you do when shorting-against-the-box.)

Deep-in-the-Money Call Option

deep-in-the-money call option
a tax-deferral strategy that involves selling a call option on shares currently owned, locking in a price to the extent of the amount received from the sale of the call option but giving up potential future price appreciation.

Selling a **deep-in-the-money call option** is a strategy similar to the put hedge, but there are important differences: In this case you give up any potential future price increases, and you lock in a price only to the extent of the amount you receive from the sale of the call option.

To illustrate, suppose call options on XYZ with a $40 striking price and six-month maturity were traded at $600 ($6 per share) when XYZ was selling for $45. If six months later XYZ closed at $40, it would result in this ending after-tax position:

1.	Initial cost of 100 shares		$3,000
2.	Profit on 100 shares [100 × ($40 − $30)]		1,000
3.	Profit on the sale of the option; since it closed at the striking price, profit is the total amount received		600
4.	Total tax on transaction		
	Profit on stock (2)	$1,000	
	Plus profit on option (3)	+ 600	
	Total gain	$1,600	
	Times tax rate	× .28	
	Total tax		448
5.	After-tax position [(1) + (2) + (3) − (4)]		$4,152

This final after-tax position is better than with the put hedge, but it closes off any price appreciation. In effect, when you sell the call option you are agreeing to deliver your shares at the option's striking price. If the price of XYZ increases to, say, $50 or beyond, you do not benefit because you have agreed to sell your shares at $40. Furthermore, your downside protection extends only to the amount received for the option—$6 per share. Therefore, if XYZ's price went to $35 you would lose $4 a share before taxes ($45 − ($35 + $6)].

Summary of the Strategies

As you can see, deferring tax liabilities to the next year is a potentially rewarding activity requiring the analysis of a number of available techniques. The choice can be simplified by considering which method works best given one's expectation of the future price behavior of the stock. Table 15.3 summarizes how each strategy performs under different expectations of future price behavior. To complete the analysis you would have to consider commission costs—something we have omitted. Although these costs can be somewhat high in absolute dollars, they are usually a minor part of the total dollars involved if the potential savings is as large as the ones we have been considering in our examples. However, if the savings is relatively small—say, under $500—then commissions may be disproportionately large in relation to the tax savings and/or deferral. Clearly you need to work out the specific figures for each situation.

Programs that Defer Tax Liabilities to Retirement

As noted in Chapter 3, accumulating funds for retirement is *the single most important reason for investing*. A large part of the retirement income of many people comes from Social Security and basic employer-sponsored programs, which are part of employees' total compensation packages. Such programs may be totally funded by the employer, may require employee contributions, or may involve a combination of employer and employee contributions. Here we focus on retirement pro-

TABLE 15.3 Ranking of Strategies to Defer Tax Liabilities to the Next Year Given Different Expectations About the Future Price of the Stock*

Strategy	Price Will Vary by a Small Amount Above or Below Current Price	Price Will Vary by a Large Amount Above or Below Current Price	Future Price Will Be Higher than Current Price	Future Price Will Be Lower than Current Price
Do nothing—hold into next tax year	2	4	1	4
Short sale against the box	3+	2+	4	1
Put hedge	3+	1	2	2
Sell deep-in-the-money call option	1	2+	3	3

*Ranking: 1, best; 4 worst.

grams that give the employee (or self-employed person) an option to contribute to a retirement program that provides tax shelter by deferring taxes to retirement. The three programs are 401(k) plans, Keogh plans, and individual retirement accounts (IRAs).

401(k) Plans

401(k) plan
a retirement plan that allows employees to divert a portion of salary to a company-sponsored tax-sheltered savings account, thus deferring taxes until retirement.

Many employers offer their employees *salary reduction plans,* known as **401(k) plans.** While our discussion here will center on 401(k) plans, similar programs are also available for employees of public, nonprofit organizations; known as 403(b) plans, they offer many of the same features and tax shelter provisions as 401(k) plans. Basically, a 401(k) plan gives you, as an employee, the option to divert a portion of your salary or wages to a company-sponsored tax-sheltered savings account. The salary (wages) placed in the savings plan accumulate tax-free. Generally, participants in 401(k) plans are offered several options for investing their contributions—typically a money-market fund, company stock, one or more equity funds, or a *guaranteed investment contract (GIC).* About 60 percent of all 401(k) plan investments are made in **guaranteed investment contracts (GICs),** which are portfolios of fixed-income securities with guaranteed competitive rates of return that are backed and sold by insurance companies. A firm's pension plan manager buys large GIC contracts and invests employees' 401(k) contributions in them. Of course, *taxes will have to be paid on 401(k) funds eventually, but not until you start drawing down the account at retirement.* At that point, presumably, you are in a lower tax bracket. A special attraction of most 401(k) plans is that the firms offering them often "sweeten the pot" by matching all or part of an employee's contribution (up to a set limit). Presently, about 85 percent of the companies that offer 401(k) plans have some type of matching contribution program, often putting up 50 cents (or more) for each dollar contributed by the employee. Such matching programs provide both tax and savings incentives to individuals and clearly enhance the appeal of 401(k) plans.

guaranteed investment contract (GIC)
a portfolio of fixed-income securities with a guaranteed competitive rate of return that is backed and sold by an insurance company to pension plan managers.

In 1992, an individual employee could put as much as $8,728 (depending on his or her salary) into a tax-deferred 401(k) plan. The annual dollar cap increases yearly, since it is indexed to the rate of inflation. (The contribution limits for 403(b) plans are currently set at a maximum of $9,500 per year, and that amount won't be indexed to inflation until 401(k) contributions attain parity.) To encourage savings for retirement, such contributions are "locked up" until the employee turns 59½ or leaves the company. A major exception to this rule lets employees tap their accounts, without penalty, in the event of any of a number of clearly defined "financial hardships."

To see how such tax-deferred plans work, consider an individual who earned, say, $45,000 in 1992 and who would like to contribute the maximum allowable ($8,728) to the 401(k) plan where she works. Doing so would reduce her taxable income to $36,272 and enable her to lower her federal tax bill by nearly $2,444 (i.e., .28 × $8,728). Such tax savings will offset a good portion of her contribution. In effect, she will add $8,278 to her retirement program with only $6,284 of her own money; the rest will come from the IRS via a reduced tax bill. What's

INVESTOR INSIGHTS

Getting the Most from Your 401(k) Plan

To score the highest possible return in your company's 401(k) retirement program, position your portfolio for growth. Specifically, you should consider adding to your 401(k) mix small- and large-company stock growth funds. To determine just how much of your retirement plan you should devote to such investments, try this rule of thumb: subtract your age from 100 and allocate at least that percentage of your holdings to stocks. So if you're 25 years old, you would keep 75% of your account in equities.

If you're like most 401(k) participants, however, you're probably low on stocks right now. According to Greenwich Associates, a company-benefits consulting firm, some 60% of the $290 billion in 401(k)s is held in fixed-income accounts such as bond funds or the guaranteed investment contracts (GICs) issued by insurance companies. Fact is, these choices simply can't compete with the wealth-building power of equity investments.

As you fine-tune your account, keep in mind that financial planners caution against too much 401(k) tinkering. In your retirement plans, after all, your first concern should be assuring steady growth, not outsmarting the market. Still, if your employer's plan gives you the flexibility to switch in and out of various funds monthly or even more frequently, you might use any stock market corrections as opportunities to move more of your retirement money into equity investments at bargain prices. But if your plan, like most, strictly limits switching to, say, once every quarter, you're better off picking an allocation that makes sense for you and sticking with it through market ups and downs. Other tips for '92 and beyond:

- Coordinate your 401(k) with your overall portfolio. "Too many people consider their 401(k) holdings in isolation," says financial planner David Bugen of Individual Asset Planning in Morristown, N.J. "As a result, they can become dangerously overweighted in some assets." To guard against the possibility of winding up heavy in stocks, bonds, or cash, be sure you factor in both your 401(k) and your nonretirement holdings to achieve your overall allocation mix.

- Double-check the safety of your GIC. The lure of a fixed interest rate and guaranteed repayment of principal have made GICs the most popular 401(k) choices by far, drawing 50¢ out of each dollar invested. But the failure of insurers such as Executive Life has shaken the faith in these guarantees. If no more than 20% of your GIC is invested with a single insurance company, and no insurer receives less than an AA or equivalent rating from credit watchdogs such as Standard & Poor's, you probably don't need to worry. Otherwise, consider moving some of your money to a money-market account or short-term fund if your plan offers one.

- Lighten up on your own company's stock. A worrisome 30% of all 401(k) assets are held in employer stock. Warns Bugen: "A reversal in your company's fortunes could wipe you out financially." No matter how dazzling your employer tells you the company's future is, you should devote no more than 10% of your holdings to company stock.

Source: Penelope Wang, "Your Smartest 401(k) Moves Now," *Money,* Year-end 1991, p. 82.

more, all the *earnings* on her savings account will accumulate tax-free as well. Remember, the taxes on both the earnings placed in the 401(k) plan and the earnings accumulated on them are deferred until retirement. The accompanying *Investor Insights* box offers suggestions for maximizing 401(k) returns.

Keogh Plans

Keogh plans allow *self-employed individuals* to establish tax-deferred retirement plans for themselves and their employees. Like contributions to 401(k) plans, payments to Keogh accounts may be taken as deductions from taxable income. As a result they reduce the tax bill of self-employed individuals. The maximum contribution to this tax-deferred retirement plan is $30,000 per year or 20 percent of earned income, whichever is less. Any individual who is self-employed, either full- or part-time, is eligible to set up a Keogh account. Keoghs can be used not only by the self-employed business person or professional but also by individuals who hold full-time jobs *and* who "moon-light" on a part-time basis—for example, the engineer who has a small consulting business on the side or the accountant who does tax returns in the evenings and on weekends. Take the engineer for example: if he earns $10,000 a year from his part-time consulting business, he can contribute 20 percent of that income ($2,000) to his Keogh account and in so doing reduce both his taxable income and the amount he pays in taxes. And he is still eligible to receive full retirement benefits from his full-time job.

Keogh accounts can be opened at banks, insurance companies, brokerage houses, mutual funds, and other financial institutions. Annual contributions must be made at the time the respective tax return is filed, or by April 15 of the following calendar year (e.g., you have until April 15, 1993, to make the contribution to your Keogh for 1992). While a designated financial institution acts as custodian of all the funds held in a Keogh account, *the actual investments held in the account are under the complete direction of the individual contributor*. Unlike 401(k) plans, these are self-directed retirement programs, and thus the *individual* decides which investments to buy and sell (subject to a few basic restrictions). The income earned from the investments must be plowed back into the account, and it, too, accrues tax-free. All Keogh contributions and investment earnings must remain in the account until the individual turns 59½, unless the individual becomes seriously ill or disabled. However, you are not *required* to start withdrawing the funds at age 59½; rather, they can stay in the account and continue to earn tax-free income until you turn 70½, at which time you have your life expectancy over which to liquidate the account. In fact, as long as the self-employment income continues, an individual can continue to make tax-deferred contributions to a Keogh account, up to the maximum age of 70½. Of course once an individual starts withdrawing funds from a Keogh account (at age 59½ or after), all such withdrawals are treated as active income and are subject to the payment of ordinary income taxes. *Thus the taxes on all contributions to and earnings from a Keogh account are deferred to retirement when they will have to be paid.* [*Note:* A program that's similar in many respects to the Keogh account is something called a *Simplified Employee Pension Plan (SEP–IRA)*. It's aimed at small business owners, particularly those with *no employees*, who want a plan that is simple to set up and administer. SEP–IRAs *can be used in place of Keoghs*. Although they are simpler to administer and have the same annual dollar contribution cap ($30,000), their contribution *rate* is less generous: you can put in only 15% of earned income for a SEP–IRA, versus 20% for a Keogh.]

Individual Retirement Accounts (IRAs)

individual retirement account (IRA) a self-directed, tax-deferred retirement plan, in which employed persons may contribute annually.

An **individual retirement account (IRA)** is virtually the same as any other investment account you open with a bank, savings and loan, credit union, stockbroker, mutual fund, or insurance company—except that an IRA is a tax-deferred retirement program that is *available to any gainfully employed individual*. The form you complete to open the account designates the account as an IRA and makes the institution its trustee. The maximum annual IRA contribution is $2,000 for an individual and $2,250 for an individual and a nonworking spouse. If both spouses work, each can contribute up to $2,000 to his or her own IRA. In order to be able to use your annual IRA contributions as a tax deduction, *one* of the following two conditions has to be met: (1) neither you nor your spouse (if filing a joint return) can be covered by a company-sponsored pension plan, or (2) your adjusted gross income has to be less than $40,000 (for married couples) or $25,000 (for singles). Translated, this means your IRA contributions *would fully qualify* as a tax deduction if you were covered by a company-sponsored pension plan but your adjusted gross income fell below the specified amounts (of $40,000 for joint filers or $25,000 for singles), *or* if you (or your spouse) weren't covered by a company-sponsored pension plan, no matter how much your adjusted gross income was. [Note that the income ceilings are phased out, so that people with adjusted gross incomes of $40,000 to $50,000 (or $25,000 to $35,000) who are covered by employer pension plans, are still entitled to prorated *partial deductions*.] If the contributions qualify as tax deductions (as per the two conditions noted above), then the amount of the IRA contributions can be shown on the tax return as a deduction from taxable income—which, of course, will also reduce the amount of taxes that have to be paid. As with 401(k) and Keogh programs, the taxes on all the *earnings* from an IRA account are deferred until you start drawing down the funds.

Even if you don't qualify for a tax deduction, you can *still contribute up to the maximum of $2,000 a year to an IRA account;* the big difference is that these nondeductible contributions will have to be made with after-tax income. *The earnings you generate from the investments you hold in your IRA account are tax sheltered in that they can accumulate tax-free*. This provision applies regardless of your income or whether you're already covered by a pension plan at your place of employment. You can deposit as much or as little as you want up to the applicable limit, and there are no percentage-of-income contribution limitations. For example, if your earned income is only $1,800 then you can contribute *all* of it to your IRA.

IRAs are *self-directed accounts*—that is, you are free, within limits, to make whatever investment decisions you wish with the capital held or deposited in your IRA. Of course, your investment options are limited by the types of products offered by competing financial institutions. Banks and thrift institutions push their savings vehicles, insurance companies have their annuities, and brokerage houses offer everything from mutual funds to stocks, bonds, and annuities. Except for serious illness, any withdrawals from an IRA prior to age 59½ are subject to a 10 percent penalty on top of the regular tax on the withdrawal itself.

Bear in mind that IRAs, along with all other retirement plans permitting contributions on a pretax basis, *defer* but do not *eliminate* taxes. When you receive the income (contributions and investment earnings) in retirement, it is then taxed, at the then-prevailing tax rates. Even so, the impact of tax deferral is substantial. As Table 15.4 indicates, after about 25 years accumulated funds in an IRA are about twice as great as for a non-IRA; after 45 years the funds are nearly 2.6 times as great ($417,417 versus $159,502). This example assumes that you invest $1,000 of earned income each year. If you choose an IRA, you shelter from taxes both the $1,000 initial investment and its subsequent earnings, so that at the end of the first year, for example, you have accumulated $1,080. If you select the same investment vehicle but do not make it an IRA, you must first pay $280 in taxes (assuming a 28 percent tax rate), leaving only $720 to invest; the subsequent earnings of $58 (0.08 × $720) are also taxed at 28 percent, leaving after-tax income of only $42 [$58 − 0.28($58)] = $58 − $16 = $42). Thus the first-year accumulation is just $762.

Funding Keoghs and IRAs

As with any investment, an individual can be conservative or aggressive when choosing securities for a Keogh or IRA, though the nature of these retirement programs generally favors a more conservative approach. In fact, conventional wisdom favors funding your Keogh and IRA with *income-producing assets*. This strat-

TABLE 15.4 Accumulated Funds from a $1,000-a-Year Investment in an IRA and from a Fully Taxable (Non-IRA) Account*

Years Held	IRA	Non-IRA
1	$ 1,080	$ 762
5	6,335	4,272
10	15,645	9,926
15	29,323	17,405
20	49,421	27,359
25	78,951	40,471
30	122,341	57,821
35	186,097	80,778
40	279,774	111,153
45	417,417	159,502

*Contributions and earnings are taxed at 28 percent in the non-IRA account but are tax-free in the IRA; a rate of return of 8 percent is assumed in both cases.

egy would also suggest that if you are looking for capital gains, it is best to do so *outside* of your retirement account. The reasons for this are twofold: (1) Growth-oriented securities are by nature *more risky,* and (2) you cannot write off losses from the sale of securities held in a Keogh or IRA account. This does *not* mean it would be altogether inappropriate to place a good-quality growth stock or mutual fund in a Keogh or IRA—in fact, many advisors contend that growth investments should *always* have a place in your retirement account. The reason is their *performance:* Such investments may pay off handsomely, since they can appreciate totally free of taxes. In the end, *it is how much you have in your retirement account that matters rather than how your earnings were made along the way*.

Although very few types of investment are prohibited outright, there are some that should be avoided simply because they are inappropriate for such accounts. (For example, with tax-free municipal securities, the tax shelter from a Keogh or IRA would be redundant since their income is tax exempt anyway). In addition to most long-term securities, money market accounts—both bank deposits (MMDAs) and mutual funds (MMMFs)—also appeal to Keogh and IRA investors, especially to those who view short-term securities as one way to capture volatile market rates. Not surprisingly, as the size of an account begins to build up an investor will often use more than one kind of security, which makes sense from a portfolio-diversification point of view. Remember that although Keoghs and IRAs offer attractive tax shelter incentives, they in no way affect the underlying risks of the securities held in these accounts. Also, regardless of what types of investment vehicles are used, keep in mind that once money is put into a Keogh or IRA, it's meant to stay there for the long haul.

Strategies that Trade Current Income for Capital Gains

Whereas ordinary income is taxed in the year it's received, capital gains are not taxed until they are actually realized. This means that *unrealized* capital gains are not taxed. For example, the receipt of $100 in cash dividends on a stock in the current year would be taxed at the assumed 28 percent rate, leaving $72 of after-tax income. On the other hand, if the price of a stock that pays no dividend rises by $100 during the current year, no tax would be due *until the stock is actually sold*. Sooner or later you'll pay taxes on your income, but at least with capital gains they are deferred until the profit is actually realized, which could be years away. Therefore if the market price of the stock is stable or increasing, earning capital gains may be an attractive strategy for achieving a tax-deferred buildup of funds. From a strict tax viewpoint, investment vehicles that provide a tax-deferred buildup of value through unrealized capital gains may be more attractive than those that provide annual taxable income. Some of the more common methods for trading current income for capital gains are described below.

Growth versus Income Stocks

Choosing growth rather than income stocks is a simple yet basic way to earn capital gains income. Companies that pay out a low percentage of earnings as dividends usually reinvest the retained earnings to take advantage of growth opportunities. If you select a company that pays dividends amounting to a 10 percent current return on your investment, your after-tax return will be only 7.2 percent, assuming you are in the 28 percent tax bracket. In comparison, a company that pays no dividends but is expected to experience 10 percent annual growth in its share price from reinvestment of earnings will also offer an after-tax rate of return of 7.2 percent [(1.0 − 0.28) × .10], but in this case the taxes will not have to be paid until the stock is actually sold and the gain realized. This deferral of tax payment is of course appealing as long as the stock price continues to increase in value.

Deep Discount Bonds

deep discount
bond
a bond selling at a
price far below its
par value.

Purchasing a **deep discount bond**—one that is selling at a price far below its par value—also offers a capital gain opportunity. To illustrate, suppose you have the choice of buying ABC's bond, which has a coupon rate of 5 percent and is selling for $700 in the market. Or you could buy a DEF bond with a coupon of 10 percent selling at par. Which would you prefer if both mature to a $1,000 par value at the end of 10 years? With the ABC bond, you will earn interest of $50 a year taxed as ordinary income. At the end of 10 years you will have a $300 capital gain, which will also be taxed as ordinary income. With the DEF bond, all of your return—that is, the $100 you receive each year—is ordinary income. From a strict tax perspective, the ABC bond is clearly the better of the two, since *the portion of the return represented by the capital gain is not taxed until it's realized at maturity*. (Remember, though, that the higher-coupon bond is giving you a higher return earlier, and that adds to its attractiveness.)

To choose between the two bonds, a rate of return analysis could be performed, assuming an equal number of dollars is invested in each bond. For example, an investment of $7,000 would purchase 10 ABC bonds or 7 DEF bonds. Total annual interest on the ABC bonds would be $500; on the DEF bonds it would be $700. To an investor in the 28 percent tax bracket, the after-tax advantage of the DEF bonds is $144 (.72 × $200) a year. But the ABC bonds will be worth $10,000 at maturity, whereas the DEF bonds will be worth only their current value of $7,000. On an after-tax basis, the additional $3,000 is worth $2,160 [$3,000 − (.28 × $3,000)]. The choice boils down to whether you prefer $144 of additional income each year for the next 10 years or an additional $2,160 at the end of 10 years. Using the future value techniques developed in Chapter 4, you would arrive at the conclusion that it would take about a 9 percent rate of return to make you indifferent between the two bonds. That is, if you invest $144 a year for 10 years at 9 percent, it accumulates to around $2,160 at the end of 10 years. Interpreting this answer, if you can invest at an after-tax rate greater than 9 percent, you should select the DEF bonds; if you feel your after-tax reinvestment rate will be lower, then you should select the ABC bonds.

Income Property Depreciation

Federal tax law, as noted in Chapter 14, permits the *depreciation* of income property such as apartment houses and similar structures. Essentially, a specified amount of annual depreciation can be deducted from ordinary pretax income. The

Tax Reform Act of 1986 established depreciable lives of 27.5 years for residential rental property (apartment buildings) and 31.5 years for nonresidential property (office buildings and shopping centers). In both cases straight-line depreciation is used. When a property is sold, any amount received in excess of its book value is treated as a capital gain and is taxed at the same rate as ordinary income. For example, assume you buy a 4-unit apartment building for $100,000 and hold it for three years, taking $2,900 in depreciation each year. Now suppose at the end of the third year you sell it for its original $100,000 purchase price. The depreciation you took reduced ordinary income each year by $2,900 and was worth, assuming a 28 percent tax bracket, $812 (.28 × $2,900). Your gain on the sale is $8,700 (3 years × $2,900 per year), which results in a tax of $2,436 (.28 × $8,700). There is no tax savings in this situation; however, the benefit results from the tax deferral which results because the tax savings of $812 in each of the first three years does not have to be paid back until the property is sold at the end of the third year. (Of course, if the property were sold for less than its original purchase price, full repayment would not occur.)

The ability to use the depreciation deduction (which does not actually involve any cash payment) to reduce taxes during the property's holding period and delay the repayment of those taxes until the property is sold, represents a type of interest-free loan. *This tax deferral is the primary tax benefit provided by depreciation*. In our example, the tax deferral of $812 in each of the first three years, which is repaid as $2,436 of taxes at the end of the third year, represents a loan at a zero-percent rate of interest (that is, 3 × $812 = $2,436). However, very restrictive limits on the use of tax losses resulting from real estate investments established by the Tax Reform Act of 1986 may severely limit an investor's ability to take advantage of these depreciation tax benefits. As a result, as noted in Chapter 14, the appeal of real estate investment no longer lies in its potential tax shelter value, but rather in its ability to earn a profit from annual rents and/or price appreciation.

Tax Swaps: A Strategy that Reduces or Eliminates a Tax Liability

Thus far we have considered several short-term strategies aimed at affecting an investor's tax liability in one way or another: (1) ways to exclude income from taxation, (2) ways to defer taxes from one tax year to the next, (3) programs that defer tax liabilities to retirement, and (4) techniques that trade current income for capital gains. We will now look at a strategy that essentially reduces or eliminates a tax liability altogether. This procedure, a so-called tax swap, is extremely popular at year-end with knowledgeable stock and bond investors. Basically, a **tax swap** is nothing more than the replacement of one security with another in order to partially or fully offset a capital gain that has been *realized* in another part of the portfolio. Of course, since we are trying to offset a gain, the security that is sold in the tax swap would be one that has performed poorly to date and has *lost* money for the investor. Since we are selling one security that has experienced a capital loss and replacing it with another similar security, the investor's stock or bond position remains essentially unchanged, although his or her tax liability has been reduced—and perhaps substantially so.

tax swap
selling one security that has experienced a capital loss and replacing it with another similar security in order to partially or fully offset a capital gain that has been realized in another part of the investor's portfolio.

A tax swap works like this. Suppose that during the current year you realized a capital gain of $1,100 on the sale of bonds. Assume that in your portfolio you held 100 shares of International Oil Corporation common stock, purchased 20 months earlier for $38 per share and currently selling for $28 per share. Although you wish to maintain an oil stock in your portfolio, it does not matter to you whether you hold International Oil or one of the other multinational oils. To realize the $10-per-share capital loss on International Oil while not altering your portfolio, you sell the 100 shares of International Oil and buy 100 shares of World Petroleum, which is also selling for $28 per share. The result is a *realized* capital loss of $1,000 [100 × ($28 − $38)], which can be used to offset all but $100 of the $1,100 capital gain realized on the earlier bond sale. Clearly the tax swap is an effective way of reducing and possibly eliminating a tax liability without altering one's portfolio.

Swaps of common stock, such as the one illustrated above, are an important part of year-end tax planning. Even more popular are bond swaps, because it is usually far easier to find a substitute bond for the one held. Most full-service brokerage houses publish a list of recommended year-end swaps for both stocks and bonds. You might be wondering why it wouldn't make more sense just to sell the security for tax purposes and then immediately buy it back. This procedure is called a **wash sale** and is disallowed under the tax law. A sold security cannot be repurchased within 30 days before or after its sale without losing the tax deduction.

wash sale
the procedure, disallowed under the tax law, of selling securities on which capital losses can be realized and then immediately buying them back.

DEFERRED ANNUITIES AND SINGLE-PREMIUM LIFE INSURANCE

annuity
a series of payments guaranteed for a number of years or over a lifetime.

As noted in the discussions of tax-favored income, effective tax strategy seeks to defer taxable income for extended periods of time. Although such a strategy may not reduce total taxes, the earnings on investment are not taxed when earned and are therefore available for reinvestment during the period of deferment. The additional earnings resulting from investment of pretax rather than after-tax dollars over long periods of time can be large. Put in proper perspective, a tax-deferred annuity may be worth more to an individual investor than any other single tax strategy. That is why it is important to understand the topic thoroughly. In addition, a somewhat similar, but generally less attractive, product is single-premium life insurance.

single-premium annuity
a contract purchased with a single lump-sum payment.

installment annuity
an annuity contract acquired by making payments over time; at a specified future date the installment payments, plus interest earned on them, are used to purchase an annuity contract.

Annuities: An Overview

An **annuity** is a series of payments guaranteed for a number of years or over a lifetime. The two types of annuities are classified by their purchase provisions. The **single-premium annuity** is a contract purchased with a single lump-sum payment. The purchaser pays a certain amount and receives a series of future payments that begins either immediately or at some future date. The second type of contract, the **installment annuity,** is acquired by making payments over time; at a specified future date the installment payments, plus interest earned on them, are used to purchase an annuity contract. The person to whom the future payments are directed is called the **annuitant.** Annuities of many types are issued by hundreds of insurance companies.

annuitant
the person to whom the future payments on an annuity contract are directed.

immediate annuity
an annuity contract under which payments to the annuitant begin as soon as it is purchased.

deferred annuity
an annuity contract in which the payments to the annuitant begin at some future date.

accumulation period
under an annuity contract, the period of time between when payments are made to the insurance company and when the insurance company begins to pay the annuitant.

distribution period
under an annuity contract, the period of time over which payments are made to an annuitant.

current interest rate
for an annuity contract, the yearly return the insurance company is currently paying on accumulated deposits.

minimum guaranteed interest rate
for an annuity contract, the minimum interest rate on contributions that the insurance company will guarantee over the full accumulation period.

An **immediate annuity** is a contract under which payments to the annuitant begin as soon as it is purchased. The amount of the payment is based on statistical analyses performed by the insurance company and depends on the annuitant's sex and age; and the payment is a function of how long the insurance company expects the annuitant to live. A **deferred annuity,** in contrast, is one in which the payments to the annuitant begin at some future date. The date is specified in the contract or at the annuitant's option. The amount the annuitant will periodically receive depends on his or her contributions, the interest earned on them, the annuitant's sex, and the annuitant's age when payments begin. The period of time between when payments are made to the insurance company and when the insurance company begins to pay the annuitant is the **accumulation period.** All interest earned on the accumulated payments during this period is tax-deferred: It stays in the account, and because it is not paid out to the purchaser no tax liability is created. The period of time over which payments are made to the annuitant is the **distribution period.** Earnings on the annuity during the accumulation and distribution periods become taxable to the annuitant when received.

Characteristics of Deferred Annuities

The growth in popularity of deferred annuities stems from the competitive interest rates paid on these contracts. An annuity contract's **current interest rate** is the yearly return the insurance company is paying now on accumulated deposits. The current interest rate fluctuates with market rates over time and is not guaranteed by the insurance company. However, some contracts have a ''bailout'' provision that allows an annuity holder to withdraw the contract value—principal and all earned interest—if the insurance company fails to pay a minimum return—typically a return that is 1 percent or more below the initial rate.

The deferred annuity purchase contract specifies a **minimum guaranteed interest rate** on contributions. The insurance company will guarantee this rate over the full accumulation period. The minimum rate is usually substantially less than the current interest rate. However, you should study a prospectus or contract and remember that *the minimum rate is all you are guaranteed*. (Very often the promotional literature provided by the company emphasizes the high *current* interest rate.)

Special Tax Features

Deferred annuities, both single-premium and installment, have several advantageous tax-shelter features. First, interest earned on the purchaser's contributions is not subject to income tax until it is actually paid to the investor by the insurance company. Suppose that $10,000 is invested in a 7 percent single-premium deferred annuity. During the first year the contract is in effect the account earns $700 in interest. If none of this interest is withdrawn, no income tax is due. Thus for an investor in the 28 percent tax bracket the first year's tax savings is $196. The tax-deferral privilege permits the accumulation of substantial sums of compound interest that can be used to help provide a comfortable retirement income. However, it is important to note that the Tax Reform Act of 1986 provides that this tax-favored treatment is available only on annuity contracts held by individuals or trusts or other entities such as a decedent's estate, a qualified employer plan, a qualified annuity plan, or an IRA. In all other cases the income on the annuity is taxed when earned.

Certain employees of institutions such as schools, universities, governments, and not-for-profit organizations may qualify for the **tax-sheltered annuity.** A special provision in the income tax laws allow these employees to make a *tax-free contribution* from current income to purchase a deferred annuity. The interest on these contributions is tax-deferred as well. The maximum amount that can be contributed is limited and can be determined by formula. Purchasers of these annuities do not have to pay any income tax on contributions or interest earnings until they actually receive annuity payments in future years. The expectation is that, if timed to coincide with retirement, the deferred income will be taxed at a lower rate than current income would be. Thus the tax-sheltered annuity is attractive because it can save income taxes today as well as provide a higher level of retirement income later.

tax-sheltered annuity
an annuity contract available that allows employees of certain institutions and organizations to make a tax-free contribution from current income to purchase a deferred annuity.

Investment Payout

The investment return or **payout** provided by an annuity contract is realized when the distribution period begins. The annuitant can choose a **straight annuity,** which is a series of payments for the rest of his or her life. Most companies also offer a variety of other payout options, including a contract specifying payments for both annuitant and spouse for the rest of both their lives, as well as a contract specifying rapid payout of accumulated payments with interest over a short period of time. The amount an annuitant receives depends on the amount accumulated in the account and the payout plan chosen. It is important to choose the program that provides the highest return for the desired payout plan. Such a plan will probably have a relatively high interest rate and relatively low (or no) sales charges and administration fees.

payout
the investment return provided by an annuity contract, realized when the distribution period begins.

straight annuity
an annuity contract that provides for a series of payments for the rest of the annuitant's life.

Sales Charge and Administration Fees

Many annuities are sold by salespersons who must be compensated for their services. Some annuities, called "no-load," have no sales charges paid by the purchaser; in this case the insurance company pays the salesperson directly. Other annuities require the purchaser to pay commissions of up to 10 percent. Administration fees for management, yearly maintenance fees, and one-time "setup charges" may also be levied. The key item for a prospective purchaser to analyze is the *actual return on investment after all sales charges and administration fees are deducted.*

Deferred Annuities and Retirement Plans

Many investors tie the purchase of deferred annuities to their overall retirement plans. Because Keogh plans and individual retirement accounts (IRAs) are somewhat similar to deferred annuities, they should be evaluated with them. If you are not fully using any allowable IRA exclusion each year, you may prefer adding to it as a part of your retirement plan rather than purchasing a tax-deferred annuity. Far greater benefit results from deducting from taxable income the full amount of the allowable payment into an IRA. With an annuity, unless you're in one of the qualified professional fields noted above, you cannot deduct its purchase price but can only defer earned income.

While both IRA and deferred annuity withdrawals prior to age 59½ are subject to a 10 percent additional tax, it is important to recognize that income withdrawn from a deferred annuity will be taxed in the year it is withdrawn. Moreover, any annuity withdrawal is first viewed for tax purposes as income; once all income is withdrawn, subsequent withdrawals are treated as a return of principal, so any partial withdrawal will most likely be fully taxable.

Fixed versus Variable Annuity

fixed annuity
an annuity contract with a monthly payment amount that does not change.

The annuity payout during the distribution period can be either fixed or variable. Most contracts are written as **fixed annuities.** This means that once a payment schedule is selected, the amount of monthly income does not change. In contrast, a growing number of annuity plans adjust the monthly income according to the actual investment experience (and sometimes the mortality experience) of the insurer. These latter contracts are called **variable annuities.** The advantage of a fixed annuity is that the dollar amount of monthly income is guaranteed to the annuitant regardless of how poorly or well the insurer's investments perform. A major disadvantage, however, is that in periods of inflation the purchasing power of the dollar erodes. For example, with a 5 percent annual inflation rate, $1 of purchasing power is reduced to 78 cents in just five years.

variable annuity
an annuity contract that adjusts the monthly payment according to the investment experience (and sometimes the mortality experience) of the insurer.

To overcome the lack of inflation protection provided by fixed-dollar annuities, the variable annuity was developed. With this plan annuitants face a different risk, however. They cannot be certain how well the insurer's investments—which may consist of common stocks, bonds, or money market funds—will do. Annuitants therefore take a chance that they will receive an even lower monthly income, in absolute dollars, than a fixed-dollar contract would provide. Most people who participate in variable annuity plans of course anticipate that they will be able to at least keep up with the cost of living. Unfortunately variable annuity values and inflation, often measured by the consumer price index (CPI), do not always perform the same.

Some people invest in a variable annuity during the accumulation period and then switch to a fixed annuity at retirement. In this manner they participate in the growth of the economy over their working careers but guard against short-term recessions that may occur during retirement years.

Annuities as Investment Vehicles

Annuities have several potential uses in an investment program. An immediate annuity can provide a safe and predictable source of income for the balance of one's life. A deferred annuity offers tax shelter and safety features and in addition can provide a convenient method for accumulating funds. When considering the purchase of a deferred annuity, the investor needs to assess its investment suitability and understand the purchase procedures.

Investment Suitability

The principal positive feature of deferred annuities is that they allow an investor to accumulate tax-deferred earnings as a source of future income. The tax-deferral feature allows interest to accumulate more quickly than would be the case if earnings were taxed. For those qualifying for a tax-sheltered annuity, current income tax on premium payments can be deferred as well. Furthermore, annuities are a low-risk type of investment.

On the negative side, deferred annuities can be faulted for two reasons: (1) lack of inflation protection and (2) high sales charges and administration fees. Most variable annuities, in spite of providing a fluctuating interest rate during the accumulation period, do not provide an annual interest rate in excess of the rate of inflation. Thus they are not an inflation hedge. The second negative aspect of annuities—relatively high sales charges and administration fees—is due largely to the fact that sales commissions, whether paid by the purchaser or the insurance company, are generous and tend to lower the purchaser's return. In addition, insurance companies have high overheads that must be met from annuity proceeds. In general, then, although annuities can play an important role in an investment portfolio, they should not be the only vehicle held. Other vehicles providing higher returns (and probably carrying higher risk) are available.

Buying Annuities

Annuities are sold by licensed salespersons and many stockbrokers. There are probably 50 or more annuity plans available through these outlets in a given community. Prior to investing in a particular annuity, you should obtain a prospectus and any other available literature on a number of them. Then carefully compare these materials. The annuity you choose should be one that contains features consistent with your investment objectives and also offers the highest actual return on investment after all charges and fees are deducted. Just as important, since *the annuity is only as good as the insurance company that stands behind it,* check to see how the company is rated in *Best's Insurance Reports*. These ratings are much like those found in the bond market and are meant to reflect the *financial strength* of the firm. Letter grades (ranging from A+ down to C) are assigned on the principle that the stronger the company, the lower the risk of loss. Accordingly, if security is important to you, stick with insurers that carry A+ or A ratings. And if you're considering a *variable annuity,* go over it much the same way you would a traditional mutual fund: Look for superior past performance, proven management talents, moderate expenses, and the availability of attractive investment alternatives that you can switch in and out of.

Single-Premium Life Insurance (SPLI)

Since 1982, tax legislation has reduced the tax shelter appeal of single-premium deferred annuities (SPDAs). Currently a 10 percent federal tax penalty is charged on withdrawals made prior to age 59½, regardless of how long the annuity has been held. In addition, most insurers charge withdrawal penalties—typically on with-

single-premium life insurance policy (SPLI)
an insurance investment vehicle for which the policyholder pays a large premium to purchase a whole life policy that provides a stated death benefit and earns interest on the cash value buildup, which occurs over time on a tax-free basis.

drawals of 10 percent or more during the first 7 to 10 years. Clearly these restrictions limit the tax-shelter appeal of SPDAs.

As a result of the limitations placed on single-premium deferred annuities by the Tax Reform Act of 1986, the **single-premium life insurance policy (SPLI)** emerged as a popular alternative investment vehicle. These policies, in addition to offering the features of SPDAs, provided a mechanism for making tax-sheltered withdrawals prior to age 59½. Generally the policyholder paid a large premium, often $15,000 or more, to purchase *whole life insurance* (see Chapter 3) that provided a stated death benefit (that passed tax-free to beneficiaries) and earned a competitive interest rate on the cash value buildup, which occurred over time on a tax-free basis. As with any whole life policy, the policyholder could cancel the policy and withdraw its cash value. In such a case taxes would be due on any gains above the amount originally invested.

The most attractive feature of SPLI policies was the ability they afforded the policyholder to *make tax-free cash withdrawals at any time using a policy loan*. Unfortunately, in 1988 Congress closed the loophole in the tax law that allowed tax-free policy loans. As a result, investors can no longer conveniently use policy loans to withdraw tax-free earnings from single premium policies. Today's SPLI policies preserve the principal and usually guarantee returns for the first year or so. After that, rates of return are changed periodically to reflect prevailing money market rates; however, rates normally cannot fall below a certain minimum level (usually around 4 to 6 percent) as specified in the policy. Single premium *variable life* policies (see Chapter 3) let policyholders put their money in a number of investment choices, ranging from stocks and bonds to mutual funds and money market instruments. However these policies *do not* guarantee preservation of principal or a minimum return. Substantial investment losses can result in these policies.

The rate of return on investment in SPLI policies is frequently below the return on tax-exempt municipal bonds, and the value of SPLI as life insurance is not as great as that available from term insurance. Like all forms of whole life insurance, SPLI's only tax shelter appeals are the tax-free buildup of value and the tax-free passage of death benefits to beneficiaries. Because SPDAs are vehicles for retirement, whereas SPLI policies provide greatest benefits when held until death, interest rates on SPDAs are usually one-half percent point higher than on SPLIs (Universal and variable life insurance, as discussed in Chapter 3, also enable policyholders to accumulate earnings on a tax-free basis; as such, they are also viewed—by some at least—as viable tax shelter investments. But it should be understood that these vehicles, too, often suffer from relatively low earnings rates over the long haul.). Despite the aggressive and often tempting sales pitches, today most experts agree that this product is *not* well suited for young, moderate-income families since it is neither a very effective form of life insurance nor an especially attractive tax shelter.

limited partnership (LP)
a vehicle in which the investor can passively invest with limited liability, receive the benefit of active professional management, and apply the resulting profit or loss (subject to limits) to his or her tax liability.

USING LIMITED PARTNERSHIPS (LPS)

The **limited partnership (LP)** is a vehicle in which you can passively invest with limited liability, receive the benefit of active professional management, and apply the resulting profit or loss (subject to limits) to your tax liability. The Tax Reform

Act of 1986 effectively eliminated the tax-sheltering appeal of LPs. It limited the tax deductions for net losses generated by passive activities to the amount of net income earned by the taxpayer on all passive activities. Generally a **passive activity** is one in which the investor does not "materially participate" in its management or activity. Rental investments involving real estate, equipment, and other property are treated as passive activities regardless of whether or not the taxpayer materially participates. An important exception exists for taxpayers actively participating in real estate rental activities; in a given year they can apply up to $25,000 of net losses to other forms of income if their adjusted gross income (AGI) is less than $100,000. This exception is gradually phased out for AGI between $100,000 and $150,000; taxpayers with AGI above $150,000 cannot apply such losses. An exception to the material participation rule occurs for taxpayers experiencing losses from oil and gas properties, if the form of ownership does *not* limit their liability.

While the value of LPs for tax shelters is no longer significant, this form of ownership is widely used to structure profit-making, cash-flow-generating investments. Like any investment, limited partnerships should be purchased *on their investment merits* only after considering both risk and return. It is therefore important to first understand why LPs are used and how they work.

passive activity
an investment in which the investor does not "materially participate" in its management or activity.

Pooling of Capital and Sharing of Risks

In an effort to obtain economies of scale and diversify risk, investors often pool their resources and form joint ventures. These joint ventures, frequently called **syndicates,** can take several forms: general partnerships, corporations, or limited partnerships. In a **general partnership** all partners have management rights and all assume unlimited liability for any debts or obligations the partnership incurs. Obviously the unlimited liability feature can be disadvantageous to passive investors (those who do not wish to participate actively in the partnership's operation).

The corporate form of syndication—that is, a **corporation**—provides a limited liability benefit to shareholder investors. Additionally, corporations have an indefinite life and do not cease to exist if a stockholder dies (whereas a partnership could end if a general partner dies). However, the corporate form of syndication has a significant disadvantage: its profits and losses cannot be passed directly to its stockholders. The partnership form of syndication, on the other hand, provides for the flow-through of profits and losses. The *limited partnership* combines the favorable investment features of both the corporation and the general partnership to provide an investor with a limited-liability vehicle that allows profits and losses to flow through to each partner's tax return.

syndicate
a joint venture— general partnership, corporation, or limited partnership—in which investors pool their resources.

general partnership
a joint venture in which all partners have management rights and all assume unlimited liability for any debts or obligations the partnership incurs.

corporation
a form of organization that provides limited liability benefits to shareholder investors and that has an indefinite life.

How Limited Partnerships Work

Legal Structure

Limited partnership (LP) is a legal arrangement governed principally by state law. State laws vary, of course, but typically they require that various written documents be filed with a county or state official prior to the commencement of the limited partnership's business. Additionally, the structure of the limited partnership is normally established to conform to IRS regulations; this is done to ensure that any tax benefits generated can be used by the partners. Limited partnerships can be utilized to invest in many things, and their size and scope vary widely. However, all have one common characteristic: They must have at least one general partner and at least one limited partner.

Figure 15.1 illustrates a typical limited partnership arrangement. The **general partner,** the active manager of the operation, runs the business and, in addition, assumes unlimited liability. (Often, to mitigate their unlimited liability, the general partners are corporations.) The general partner's major contribution to the enterprise is frequently in the form of management expertise, not capital. Most of the capital is usually supplied by the limited partners, who do little else. The latter cannot participate in the management of the enterprise, or they will lose their limited liability protection. Furthermore, a limited partner's liability normally does not exceed his or her capital contribution, an amount specified in the partnership agreement. **Limited partners,** then, are the suppliers of capital whose role in the venture is passive. Usually the only power limited partners have is to fire the general partner and/or to sell their partnership investment. A person considering investment in a limited partnership should carefully analyze the general partner's management capabilities because the success of the partnership is literally "riding on" them.

> **general partner**
> the managing partner who accepts unlimited liability and makes all decisions in a partnership.

> **limited partners**
> the passive investors in a partnership, who supply most of the capital and have liability limited to the amount of their capital contributions.

Return to Investors

An investor can realize a return from a limited partnership investment in two basic ways—through cash flow and price appreciation. Investors in a successful limited partnership receive periodic cash payments as the investment generates income. These periodic returns are a project's *cash flow.* Limited partners receive a prorated share of the partnership's cash flow, depending on the size of their investment in the operation. Cash distributions may be made monthly, quarterly, or yearly, and these returns are taxable to the partners as ordinary income. The general partner's management fee is normally paid prior to the distribution of cash flow. However, fre-

• FIGURE 15.1 The Limited Partnership Structure

In a limited partnership, the general partner typically provides management expertise and accepts all liability. The limited partners are passive investors who supply most of the capital and accept liability limited only to the amount of their investment.

quently the general partner will take only a small fee until the limited partners have fully recovered their initial investment. Once this has occurred, the general partner's share of additional cash distributions will become commensurately larger.

The other source of investment return for limited partners is *price appreciation* resulting from an increase in the value of the investment. The general partner may earn a portion of the realized price appreciation as well. Investments, such as real estate, that increase in value due to inflation and other factors are often sources of appreciated value for limited partnership investors. Like the appreciation experienced on any investment vehicle, this form of return may be realized or unrealized (as an actual return of dollars or as a ''paper'' return). And of course realized capital gains are taxable to the partners.

Popular Forms of Limited Partnerships

Limited partnerships have been used to invest in many different types of assets. They are most often formed to invest in opportunities requiring sizable outlays and professional management that are expected to offer attractive returns. Limited partnerships vary in risk, from a conservative one formed to own a fully rented office building with long-term leases to a risky one formed to own the sperm bank of a famous thoroughbred horse that has never sired a winning offspring. Here we focus on three principal areas: real estate, energy resources, and equipment leasing. Other popular areas include livestock feeding or breeding programs, research and development programs, major movie or play production programs, cable TV programs, and real estate mortgage programs.

Real Estate

Depending upon property type, a periodic cash flow, price appreciation, and/or tax shelter can be realized from investing in real estate. As noted earlier, limited tax shelter may be available only to those *actively* participating in real estate investment. Raw land is normally purchased for its price appreciation potential. Apartment buildings, shopping centers, office buildings, and the like can provide cash flow as well as price appreciation. Very often, these types of properties are syndicated and bought by limited partnerships. The typical real estate limited partnership consists of a general partner who manages the investment and the limited partners who provide most or all of the capital.

There are two major types of real estate syndicates. The *blind pool syndicate* is formed by a syndicator—often well known—in order to raise a given amount of money to be invested at his or her discretion, though the general partner often has some or all of the properties already picked out. The *single property syndicate,* on the other hand, is established to raise money to purchase specific properties. Very often the large, multiproperty limited partnership syndicates with many investors are blind pools. Single property syndicates are generally smaller in scope, although many valuable parcels of property are owned by single property syndicates.

Energy Resources

The United States is heavily dependent on energy for its economic well-being, so the federal government has provided various tax incentives for those who invest in the search for energy. Utilizing the limited-partnership investment vehicle, capital is pooled to finance exploration for oil, natural gas, coal, and geothermal steam. The most popular energy-related limited partnerships are oil and gas investments.

There are three basic types of oil and gas limited partnerships. *Exploratory programs,* also known as ''wildcats,'' drill in areas where oil or gas is believed to exist but has not yet been discovered. *Developmental programs* finance the drilling of wells in areas of known and proved oil and gas reserves. (They often drill wells that are near already-producing oil or gas finds.) *Income programs* buy existing wells with proven reserves.

The oil and gas business is risky due to the high degree of uncertainty associated with it. Even the most knowledgeable geologists and petroleum engineers are never quite sure how much oil or gas is in a particular well or field. Oil and gas limited-partnership investments therefore contain risk elements as well. The degree of risk of course depends on the type of program an investor purchases. Exploratory programs carry the highest risk of the three types, and correspondingly offer the highest potential return.

Equipment Leasing

Another popular limited partnership investment is the kind that deals with various types of leasable property—airplanes, railroad cars, machinery, computers, trucks, automobiles. In these types of investments the limited partnership buys the equipment, such as a computer, and then leases it to another party. As the lessor of the equipment, the partnership can depreciate the item. Additionally, the partnership may use borrowed capital to increase potential return. The business of leasing property requires a great deal of knowledge and skill. The key to investment success in leasing is a competent general partner. Computers and various types of industrial machinery, for example, often have a high obsolescence risk. For very wealthy investors, limited partnerships involving giant oil tankers are available. The tanker is leased to an oil company for a number of years, and the tanker's owners (the partners) benefit from the cash flow generated by its rental income.

private partnership
a limited partnership that has a limited number of investors and is not registered with a public agency.

public partnership
a limited partnership that is registered with state and/or federal regulators and usually has 35 or more limited partners.

Partnership Structure: Private or Public

The size and scope of limited partnerships vary considerably. For example, three friends might establish a limited partnership to buy a six-unit apartment building. In contrast, large partnerships involving thousands of investors and tens of millions of dollars are frequently formed to acquire producing oil and gas properties. There are two distinct types of limited partnerships. The **private partnership** has a limited number of investors and is not registered with a public agency such as a state securities commission or the SEC. The **public partnership** is registered with the appropriate state and/or federal regulators and usually has 35 or more investors. State and federal laws regulate offerings of all limited partnership programs.

Private Partnerships

Private limited partnerships are often assembled by a local real estate broker or an attorney; they tend to be more for the well-to-do and to *take more risks* than public partnerships. Often the investors know one another personally. Potential investors in the partnership are commonly given a *private placement memorandum*, a document describing the property to be purchased, management fees, and other financial details. It usually also contains the limited partnership agreement. There are several advantages to private partnerships. First, since they do not have to be registered with a public agency they usually carry lower transaction and legal costs than public partnerships. Legal fees in connection with registration of securities are costly and are paid indirectly by the limited partners. Another advantage of the private partnership is that it may be easier to obtain first-hand knowledge about the general partner. A good source of information on a general partner is other limited partners who have previously invested in his or her partnerships.

Public Partnerships

Public limited partnership syndications must be registered with state and sometimes federal regulatory authorities. Interstate sales of limited-partnership interests must comply with federal as well as state laws. Offerings sold only within one state, however, need comply only with that state's laws. Public partnerships are sold by stockbrokers and other licensed securities dealers, and transaction costs are high. The brokerage commission on a typical oil and gas limited partnership is about 8 percent. Limited-partnership interests, both private and public, are relatively illiquid, and sometimes the interest cannot be sold without the approval of the state authority. A potential buyer of a public limited partnership must be given a *prospectus,* which is a detailed statement containing the financial data, management information, and transaction and legal costs associated with the offering. Most public partnerships are large in scope and usually contain over $1 million in assets. An investor in a public partnership may find that his or her shares represent an investment in a *diversified* portfolio of real estate or energy resource properties. Geographical diversity may be easier to obtain by investing in public partnerships.

Essential Investment Considerations

Limited-partnership promoters sometimes concoct unbelievable schemes for earning significant returns. They advertise that you can earn a sizable return on an investment as a result of the general partner's unique situation or expertise. Although this is possible, it is certainly not without risk, and generally the actual amount earned, if any, is far less than the amount suggested. For each potential investment in a limited partnership you should review its degree of leverage, its risk and return, and its investment suitability. The *Investor Insights* box on pages 646 and 647 discusses some of the major concerns facing limited partnership investors.

Leverage

In limited partnerships the presence of *leverage* indicates that the underlying business activity utilizes borrowed funds—perhaps in substantial amounts. An equipment-leasing venture, for example, might involve 80 to 90 percent of debt financing. This means your initial investment dollar buys more assets than would be the case if leverage were not used. For example, suppose a limited partnership raises $100,000, borrows $900,000 for which the partners have shared liability, and then buys computer equipment for $1,000,000 to lease to a business over a 10-year period. Suppose further that the partnership earns $50,000 in the first year. If you own 5 percent of the partnership (you invested $5,000), in the first year your earnings are $2,500. Your total first-year recovery is therefore equal to 50 percent of your total investment. Had the partnership not used leverage you would have had to invest $50,000 in order to own 5 percent (.05 × $1,000,000) of the investment. In such a case, your return would have only been 5 percent on your initial investment ($2,500 ÷ $50,000). Clearly, the use of leverage enhances your return. However, you must bear in mind that you are legally liable for your share of the loan, which is $45,000 or (.05 × $90,000). If the loan is with some type of captive finance company that is willing to forgive the debt if the partnership goes under, or if you do not have legal liability for your portion of the debt, the whole deal may (except in the case of real estate partnerships) be considered a sham by the Internal Revenue Service. In such a case, you could be subject to tax penalties. Remember that leverage can increase returns, but in order to do so it almost always carries more risk.

Risk and Return

Evaluating the risk and return of a limited partnership investment depends on the property involved, although there are two general factors to consider. First, the general partner must be carefully studied. Again, read the offering circular or prospectus carefully. Find out how much the promoters (general partner and associates) are taking off the top in commissions, legal fees, and management fees. The more they take, the less of your money is invested in the project and the less likely it is that you will receive a high return.

A second factor to recognize is that most limited partnerships are not very liquid. In fact, depending on state law, they may not be salable prior to their disbandment. In other words, your interest may be difficult, or perhaps impossible, to resell. Recently two vehicles for enhancing the marketability of LP shares have emerged. One is the *master limited partnership (MLP)*, which is a limited partnership that is publicly traded on a major stock exchange. The stock represents a marketable claim on a group of limited partnership interests that are acquired by the MLP in any of a number of ways. Although when they were first introduced it appeared that the MLPs would indeed improve partnership liquidity, subsequent tax law changes have greatly diminished their attractiveness. The second outlet for LP shares is the emerging secondary market for them. For better-known public limited partnerships, established market makers provide quotes. Private deals and smaller public deals

■■■ INVESTOR INSIGHTS ■■■

Key Questions Partnership Investors Ask

Brokerage industry officials have estimated that $5 to $10 billion, and probably much more, of the $100 billion of limited-partnership investments marketed publicly during the 1980s are in trouble. . . .

Bailing out of some partnership investments can be costly and have nasty tax consequences besides, financial advisers and partnership specialists say. Still, it may be worth investigating the informal resale market for partnership interests. Replacing a troubled general partner may also be an option. Yet another may be taking a sponsor or broker to securities arbitration or to court.

Here are answers to some of the major questions on partnership investors' minds:

How widespread are the problems of partnership sponsors?

While many real estate syndicators are struggling because that market is weak, not all of them by any means are in danger. Most syndicators with serious problems started out as big tax-shelter sellers, then failed to adapt to an investment landscape vastly changed by the 1986 tax overhaul. . . .

Will I lose my investment?

Not necessarily. Investors aren't always affected even when a troubled sponsor files for protection from its creditors.

Moreover, a partnership that is under-performing now, because it isn't delivering promised income, could still pay off handsomely in a few years when it is dissolved and its real estate holdings or other investments are sold off.

One risk, however, is that a bankrupt sponsor may no longer be able to devote the necessary attention to managing the partnership's investments. And if it has been keeping a troubled partnership afloat with its own cash, it may well have to suspend those payments.

If I'm worried, why not just get out?

Although you may sleep better, it will probably be expensive.

A number of small investment firms make a secondary market in limited partnerships, buying interests either for their own accounts or for resale to new investors. But the prices paid for interests in "used" partnerships are usually low, often 30% to 40% less (and sometimes 50% to 80% less) than the original investors paid to buy them. . . .

Other investors may find it impossible to even get a bid for their interests. Out of roughly 3,000 public partnerships in existence, interests in about 900 trade on the National Partnership Exchange in Tampa, Fla., the largest independent listing service.

George Hamilton, NAPEX president, says maybe 30% of those interests offered by investors for sale through the exchange's member brokers trade actively, meaning at least

remain quite illiquid, however. (*Note:* In early 1992 the Securities Industry Association (SIA) was actively engaged in discussions about the possibility of developing a central facility through which certain partnership units could be listed and then sold through competitive bidding. The first step in developing a central facility is once every three months. "Every day people call us up wanting to sell stuff we've never heard of," he says.

The sale of a partnership interest can also trigger the recapture of past tax write-offs. In the case of private syndications, it is almost certain to do so.

I'm still making payments on a private partnership that has soured. What happens if I stop?

Although tax overhaul killed the shelter in these deals, investors can't simply walk away from them. Doing so would almost certainly lead to a big tax bill, because of prior write-offs. Defaulting on a promise to pay could also entail legal problems and hurt an investor's credit standing.

What if my partnership follows the general partner into bankruptcy?

Investors should organize. "You need a bankruptcy lawyer sitting in court telling the judge, 'We want to be treated in the best possible way,'" says David M. Greenberg, a San Francisco lawyer formerly with the Securities and Exchange Commission.

If a partnership fails, investors may also need tax advice. Again, they may be hit with large tax bills because of earlier deductions and credits.

What about replacing the general partner?

That isn't easy in a public partnership, where it might take a two-thirds vote of thousands of investors. Just getting their names from an embattled sponsor or securities regulators in some states can be difficult.

But if the general partner is in bankruptcy, the limited partners can "ask the judge to force the sponsor to produce the list of other investors," says Mr. Greenberg.

A growing number of "work-out" specialists will take over. While they have performed some rescues, they may demand as much as 50% of the profits when a partnership liquidates in addition to annual management fees.

Do I have any recourse against the person who sold me a lousy partnership or the sponsor?

If the partnership wasn't purchased through a registered securities broker, you'll probably have to sue. But if you did buy it through a registered representative, take heart: Some investors have received money back by taking complaints to arbitration. . . .

Finally, a class-action suit against the sponsor is a possibility. Some lawyers take such cases on a contingency basis. Be prepared to wait years for a settlement, however, that might not amount to much if the sponsor is bankrupt.

Source: Excerpted from Jill Bettner, "Some Answers for Partnership Investors," *The Wall Street Journal,* February 16, 1990, p. C1.

expected to be a computerized, small-scale operation that would handle no more than half a dozen large partnerships from major firms.) Of course, sizable commissions must be paid on these LP transactions, and the general lack of LP liquidity tends to increase the risk associated with investment in them.

Investment Suitability

As you have probably concluded by now, limited partnerships are not for everyone. They tend to be risky and illiquid and thus are usually not suitable for conservative investors primarily interested in the preservation of capital. A private placement memorandum or prospectus will often contain a statement limiting purchase to investors of at least a certain net worth (say, $100,000) and in the 28 or 31 percent tax bracket. This rule excluding certain types of investors is called a **suitability rule.** Its purpose is to allow only investors who can bear a high amount of risk to participate. Additionally, there is usually a statement in the prospectus that says: "The securities offered herewith are very high risk." Believe this statement: If the regulatory authorities require it, it must be a high-risk investment. Suitability rules vary, depending on applicable state and federal laws. The rules are intended to prevent the sale of high-risk projects to investors who cannot sustain the loss financially. Suitability requirements are also usually fairly rigid for public limited partnerships (offerings registered with securities regulators).

suitability rule
a rule excluding investors who cannot bear a high amount of risk from buying limited partnership interests.

SUMMARY

1. As taxable income increases, so do tax burdens imposed by federal tax law. Taxable income can be either ordinary income—active ("earned"), portfolio, or passive—or capital gains or losses. Both ordinary income and capital gains are subject to the same schedule of tax rates. It is calculated first by finding gross income, which includes all forms of income with some exceptions. After subtracting certain adjustments to gross income, adjusted gross income results. Subtracting itemized deductions and exemptions results in taxable income from which federal income taxes are calculated. Taxes due are found by subtracting any eligible tax credits from the federal income tax.

2. Tax-avoidance strategies attempt to earn tax-favored income, which is essentially income not subject to taxes. Tax-deferral strategies attempt to defer taxes from current periods to later periods. A tax shelter is an investment vehicle that earns a portion of its return by offering potential offsets to the investor's other taxable income.

3. Tax-favored income excluded from taxation includes tax-free municipal bond interest, Treasury and government agency issues (free of state and local income taxes), and the sale of a personal residence. Strategies that defer tax liabilities to the next year include a short sale against the box, a put hedge, and selling a deep-in-the-money call option. Each strategy has relative advantages and disadvantages, depending on the assumed future movement of the stock's price.

   Programs that defer tax liabilities to retirement include 401(k) plans, Keogh plans, and individual retirement accounts (IRAs). Popular strategies that trade current for capital gains income include buying growth rather than income stocks, buying deep discount bonds, and investing in income property. Tax swaps are a strategy that can be used to reduce or eliminate a tax liability without altering the basic portfolio.

4. Because they pay relatively high market rates of interest and allow for tax-free reinvestment, deferred annuities have some appeal as a tax-deferral vehicle. Tax-sheltered annuities can be purchased by employees of certain institutions by making limited tax-free contributions from current income. Annuity payouts can be either fixed or variable; the payouts on variable annuities depend on the insurer's actual investment performance.

Deferred annuities are relatively low-risk vehicles that may not produce earnings on a par with inflation rates; therefore investors should determine by analysis whether they are suitable. The single-premium life insurance policy, in the past a popular alternative to the deferred annuity, has diminished in popularity during recent years due to tax law changes that virtually eliminated the ability to use policy loans to make tax-free withdrawals.

5. A limited partnership is an organizational form that allows an individual to invest passively with limited liability, receiving the benefit of professional management, and apply the resulting profit or loss (subject to limits) when calculating his or her tax liability. The return from a limited partnership comes from either cash flow or price appreciation. Limited partnerships have been formed to acquire many different kinds of assets; the most common are real estate, energy resources, and equipment for leasing purposes.

6. Limited partnerships can be structured as private or public partnerships. Leverage can increase the potential earnings as well as the risk in a limited partnership. Potential investors should study the private placement memorandum or prospectus for a limited partnership in order to carefully examine the investment's risk-return characteristics and hence its suitability. Often investors themselves must meet certain suitability rules prior to investing in a limited partnership.

QUESTIONS

1. What is *tax planning?* Describe the current tax rate structure and explain why it is considered *progressive*.

2. What is a capital asset? Explain how capital asset transactions are taxed, and compare their treatment to that of ordinary income.

3. Describe the steps involved in calculating a person's taxable income. How do any *tax credits* differ from *tax deductions?*

4. How does *tax avoidance* differ from *tax deferral?* Explain if either of these is a form of tax evasion. Is either the same thing as a *tax shelter?*

5. What is tax-favored income? Briefly describe the following forms of income excluded from taxation:

   a. Tax-free municipal bond interest.
   b. Treasury and government agency issues.
   c. Sale of a personal residence.

6. Explain conditions that favor the following strategies for deferring tax liabilities to the next year:

   a. A short sale against the box.
   b. A put hedge.
   c. Selling a deep-in-the-money call option.

   When is it best simply to hold the stock and do nothing?

7. Briefly describe each of the following programs for deferring taxes to retirement:

   a. 401(k) plans.
   b. Keogh plans.
   c. Individual retirement accounts (IRAs).

8. What are guaranteed investment contracts (GICs) and what role do they play in 401(k) plans? What investment vehicles might be suitable for funding a Keogh or IRA?

9. Briefly describe each of the following strategies that trade current for capital gains income:

   a. Growth stocks.
   b. Deep discount bonds.
   c. Income property depreciation.

10. Describe how a tax swap can be used to reduce or eliminate a tax liability without significantly altering the composition of one's portfolio.

11. Define an annuity, explain the role it might play in an investment portfolio, and differentiate between:

    a. Single-premium and installment annuities.
    b. Immediate and deferred annuities.
    c. Fixed and variable annuities.

12. Define the following terms as they relate to deferred annuities:

    a. Current interest rate.
    b. Minimum guaranteed interest rate.
    c. Payout.

13. Explain how a deferred annuity works as a tax shelter. How does a tax-sheltered annuity work, and who is eligible to purchase one? Discuss whether a deferred annuity is a better tax shelter than an IRA.

14. What is single-premium life insurance (SPLI)? Describe the basic features of SPLI, compare it to the single-premium deferred annuity (SPDA), and explain why the popularity of SPLI has recently diminished.

15. How does a limited partnership (LP) differ from a general partnership and a corporation? What are the functions of the general and limited partners? How did the Tax Reform Act of 1986 affect the popularity of LPs as tax shelters? Explain.

16. In which two ways can an investor earn a return from a limited partnership? Explain.

17. What are the popular forms of limited partnerships? Differentiate between private partnerships and public partnerships.

18. How does leverage affect the risk and return of a limited partnership? What are suitability rules, and why must they be met by limited-partnership investors.

19. A friend of yours wants you and several other individuals to invest in an equipment-leasing partnership. You and the other partners will buy a computer and then lease it to a local concern. Explain the potential risk-return factors you would consider in your analysis of this proposed investment.

PROBLEMS

1. Using Table 15.1, calculate Ed Robinson's income tax due on his $35,000 taxable income, assuming he files as a single taxpayer. After you make the calculation, explain to Ed what his marginal tax rate is and why it is important in making investment decisions.

2. During the year just ended, Jean Sanchez's taxable income of $48,000 was twice as large as her younger sister Rachel's taxable income of $24,000. Use the tax rate schedule in Table 15.1 to answer the following questions with regard to the Sanchez sisters, who are both single.

   a. Calculate each sister's tax liability.
   b. Determine the (1) marginal tax rate and (2) average tax rate for each sister.
   c. Do your findings in **b** demonstrate the progressive nature of income taxes? Explain.

3. Sheila and Jim Mendez reported the following income tax items in 1993:

Salaries and wages	$30,000
Interest on bonds	1,100*
Dividends (jointly owned stocks)	1,000
Capital gains on securities	1,500
Deductible IRA contribution	2,000
Itemized deductions	8,000

   *$400 of this total was received from tax-free municipal bonds.

   If Sheila and Jim claim three dependents and file a joint return for 1993, calculate their income tax due. (Use Table 15.1 and assume an exemption of $2,150 for each qualifying dependent.)

4. The Akais just finished calculating their taxable income for their 1993 joint federal income tax return. It totaled $58,750 and showed no tax credits. Just prior to filing their return, the Akais realized that they had treated a $1,000 outlay as an itemized deduction rather than correctly treating it as a $1,000 tax credit.

   a. Use the tax rate schedule in Table 15.1 to calculate the Akais' tax liability and tax due based on their original $58,750 estimate of taxable income.
   b. How much taxable income would the Akais have if they correctly treat the $1,000 as a tax credit rather than a tax deduction?
   c. Use your finding in **a** to calculate the Akais' tax liability and tax due after converting the $1,000 tax deduction to a tax credit.
   d. Compare and contrast your findings in **a** and **c**. Which would you prefer—a tax deduction or an equal-dollar-amount tax credit? Why?

5. Shawn Healy bought 300 shares of Apple Computer common stock at $32 a share. Fifteen months later, in December, Apple was up to $47 a share and Shawn was considering selling her shares since she believed Apple's price could drop as low as $42 within the next several months. What advice would you offer Shawn for locking in the gain and deferring the tax to the following year? Explain.

6. Karen Jones purchased 200 shares of Mex Inc. common stock for $10 per share exactly two years ago, in December 1991. Today, December 15, 1993, the stock is selling for $18 per

share. Because Karen strongly believes that the stock is fully valued in the market, she wishes to sell it and invest the proceeds in the stock of an attractive emerging company. Karen, who is in the 28 percent tax bracket, realizes that if she sells the stock prior to year-end the capital gain of $1,600 [200 shares × ($18 sale price − $10 purchase price)] would result in taxes for 1993 of $448 (.28 × $1,600). Because Karen would like to lock in her $1,600 profit but defer the tax on it until 1994, she plans to investigate the strategies available for accomplishing this objective.

a. How can Karen use shorting-against-the-box to accomplish her objective? Will she be able to benefit from any future increases in Mex Inc.'s stock price if she uses the shorting-against-the-box strategy?

b. If Karen can purchase two put options on Mex Inc.'s stock at a striking price of $18 for a total cost of $180 ($90 per 100-share option), what would be her after-tax position if the stock price declined to $16 per share? Will Karen be able to benefit from any future increases in Mex Inc.'s stock price using this put hedge strategy?

c. If Karen can sell two call options on Mex Inc.'s stock with a $16 striking price and 6-month maturity for $480 ($240 per 100-share option) when the stock is selling for $18 per share, what would be her after-tax position if the stock price declined to $16 per share? Will Karen be able to benefit from any future increases in Mex Inc.'s stock price using this deep-in-the-money call option strategy? Is the price of $18 fully locked in using this strategy?

d. Use your findings in **a, b,** and **c** to compare and contrast the three strategies, and recommend a strategy to Karen assuming the stock price does drop below the current price.

7. Juan Gonzalez, an employee of Harla, Inc., earned $48,000 in 1993 and is considering contributing $7,000 to the firm's 401(k) plan. If Juan is in the 28 percent tax bracket, what will this taxable income be? How much tax savings will result, and how much did it cost Juan on an after-tax basis to make the $7,000 contribution?

CASE PROBLEMS

15.1 Tax Planning for the Wilsons

Hal and Terri Wilson had most of their funds invested in common stock in the spring of 1992. The Wilsons didn't really do very much investment planning, and they had practically no background or understanding of how income taxes might affect their investment decisions. Their holdings consisted exclusively of common stocks selected primarily on the advice of their stockbroker, Sid Nichols. In spite of a relatively lackluster market they did experience some nice capital gains, even though several of their holdings showed losses from their original purchase prices. A summary of their holdings on December 20, 1992, appears below.

Stock	Date Purchased	Original Cost	Current Market Value
Consolidated Power and Light	2/10/90	$10,000	$16,000
Cargon Industries	7/7/92	3,000	8,000
PYT Corporation	6/29/92	7,000	6,000
Amalgamated Iron & Steel	8/9/91	8,000	5,000
Jones Building Supplies	3/6/88	4,500	4,700

Hal feels this might be a good time to revise their portfolio. He favors selling all their holdings and reinvesting the funds in several growth-oriented mutual funds and perhaps several real estate limited partnerships. Terri agrees their portfolio could use some revision, but she is reluctant to sell everything. For one thing, she is concerned that federal income taxes might take a sizable share of their profits. In addition, she strongly believes Amalgamated Iron & Steel will make a significant recovery, as will all steel stocks, in 1993.

After some discussion, the Wilsons decided to consult their friend, Elaine Byer, who was a CPA for a major public accounting firm. Byer indicated that she was not an expert in the investment field and therefore couldn't tell the Wilsons which securities to buy or sell from that perspective. From a tax point of view, however, she did not recommend selling everything in the 1992 tax year. Instead, she said that Consolidated Power and Light, PYT Corporation, Amalgamated Iron & Steel, and Jones Building Supplies should be sold in December of 1992, but that Cargon Industries should be carried into 1993 and sold then—if that was what the Wilsons wanted to do.

Hal and Terri were grateful for Byer's advice, but they had two major concerns. First, they were concerned about waiting to sell Cargon Industries, since it had showed such a sizable gain and they were afraid its price might decline sharply in a stock market selloff. Secondly, they were reluctant to sell Amalgamated Iron & Steel in spite of the benefit of its tax loss, since they wanted to remain invested in the steel industry over the long run. As a final step they contacted Nichols, their stockbroker, who agreed with Byer's advice; he said not to worry about the Cargon situation. The stock was selling at $80 a share, and he would put in a short-against-the-box for them, which would enable them to deliver the shares whenever they wanted. He also explained that they could use a tax swap in order to get the tax benefit of the loss on Amalgamated Iron & Steel while staying invested in the steel industry. He suggested United States Iron as a swap candidate since it was selling for about the same price as Amalgamated.

Questions

1. Assuming the Wilsons are in the 28 percent tax bracket, calculate the resulting federal income tax: (a) If they sold all their securities in 1992 at their current market values, and (b) if they sold Consolidated Power and Light, PYT Corporation, Amalgamated Iron & Steel, and Jones Building Supplies at their respective market values in 1992, and then sold Cargon Industries at its current market value on January 2, 1993. What do you conclude from your calculations?

2. As noted, Nichols suggested a short sale against the box for Cargon. Explain his reasoning about the future price of this stock.

3. Suppose you thought Cargon had a good possibility for further price increases in 1993, but you were equally concerned that its price could fall sharply. Would you then agree with the strategy Nichols recommended, or would you prefer a different strategy? Explain your answer.

4. Discuss the tax swap suggested by Nichols. Does this strategy allow the Wilsons to minimize taxes while retaining their position in the steel industry? Explain.

5. What overall strategies would you recommend to the Wilsons, given their investment objectives and tax status? Explain.

15.2 Do Oil and Fred Cranston Mix?

Fred Cranston, age 36, is the West Coast marketing manager and vice-president of a major auto parts supply firm. His salary reflects his success in his job: $90,000 per year. Additionally his firm provides him with a car, an excellent pension and profit-sharing plan, superior life and medical insurance coverage, and company stock options. Fred owns his home, which is located in the exclusive Marin County, California, area.

In addition to Fred's house and his pension and profit-sharing plans, he has a stock portfolio worth about $75,000, a tax-free municipal bond portfolio valued at $150,000, and about $100,000 in a highly liquid money market mutual fund. Fred would like to make some more risky investments in order to increase his returns. He is considering taking $50,000 out of the money market mutual fund and investing in some limited partnerships. His broker, Marie Bell, has proposed that he invest $50,000 divided among five oil and gas limited partnerships. Marie's specific recommendation is to buy two developmental and three income programs, each for $10,000. She explained to Fred that this $50,000 investment could potentially increase his income by $20,000 per year. Marie has also pointed out that if the expected rise in oil prices occurs, Fred could expect to receive even larger cash returns in future years. Fred meets the suitability rules required for such investments as prescribed by the securities commission of California. Being a relatively conservative individual, he is trying to justify in his mind the reasonableness of his broker's recommendations.

Questions

1. What do you think of Marie Bell's investment recommendations for Fred? Are developmental programs too risky? Should Fred buy five different oil and gas programs, or should he invest the entire $50,000 in one program? Explain.

2. How would you describe the legal structure of a limited partnership to Fred? What should Fred know about the general partner in each of these programs?

3. In general, does investment in oil and gas development and income programs make sense to you? Why, or why not?

4. What other forms of limited partnerships might you suggest that Fred consider? Discuss the leverage and risk-return tradeoffs involved in them.

PART SIX · INVESTMENT ADMINISTRATION

THE INVESTMENT ENVIRONMENT

INVESTMENT ADMINISTRATION

| INVESTING IN COMMON STOCK | INVESTING IN FIXED-INCOME SECURITIES |
| SPECULATIVE INVESTMENT VEHICLES | OTHER POPULAR INVESTMENT VEHICLES |

16 Planning and Building a Portfolio

After studying this chapter, you should be able to:

1. Understand the objectives of portfolio management and the procedures used to calculate the return and standard deviation of a portfolio.

2. Discuss the concepts of correlation and diversification and their impact on portfolio risk and return.

3. Review the two basic approaches to portfolio management—traditional management versus the modern approach—and reconcile them.

4. Describe the role of investor characteristics, investor objectives, and portfolio objectives and policies in planning and building an investment portfolio.

5. Summarize the motives and various approaches involved in using an asset allocation scheme to build an investment portfolio consistent with the investor's objectives.

6. Relate investor objectives to the asset allocations and risk-return profiles reflected in various types of portfolios.

Investors benefit from holding portfolios of investments rather than single invest-ment vehicles. *Without sacrificing returns, investors who hold portfolios can re-duce risk, often to a level below that of any of the investments held in isolation.* In other words, when it comes to risk, $1 + 1 < 1$.

In order to achieve his or her investment objectives, an investor needs to plan and build a portfolio that exhibits the desired risk-return behavior. The input to the portfolio is the risk-return characteristics of the individual investment vehicles; its output is the portfolio's risk and return. Selecting investment vehicles for a portfolio is best accomplished using certain analytical procedures. The body of knowledge on how to create portfolios that provide the best risk-return tradeoffs is based on com-plex mathematical concepts. Much of this knowledge is beyond the scope of the introductory investments course. In this chapter we will emphasize only general principles and simple approaches that will allow an investor to plan and build a portfolio consistent with his or her objectives. To demonstrate, four typical portfo-lios are analyzed.

PRINCIPLES OF PORTFOLIO PLANNING

growth-oriented portfolio
a portfolio whose primary objective is long-term price ap-preciation.

As defined in Chapter 1, a *portfolio* is a collection of investment vehicles assembled to meet a common investment goal. Of course, different investors will have differ-ent objectives for their portfolios. A **growth-oriented portfolio's** primary goal is long-term price appreciation. An **income-oriented portfolio** stresses current divi-dend and interest returns.

income-oriented portfolio
a portfolio that stresses current divi-dend and interest returns.

Portfolio Objectives

Setting portfolio objectives involves definite tradeoffs: tradeoffs between risk and return, between potential price appreciation and current income, and between vary-ing risk levels in the portfolio. These will depend on the investor's income tax bracket, current income needs, and ability to bear risk. The key point is that the portfolio objectives must be established *before* beginning to invest. The ultimate goal of an investor is the creation of an **efficient portfolio,** one that provides the highest return for a given level of risk, or has the lowest risk for a given level of return. Although it may be difficult to create such a portfolio, an investor should at least search out reasonable investment alternatives to get the best combinations of risk and return. Thus, when given the choice between two equally risky investments offering different returns, the investor would be expected to choose the alternative with the highest return. Likewise, given two investment vehicles offering the same returns but differing in risk, the *risk-averse* investor would prefer the vehicle with the lower risk. In pursuing the creation of an efficient portfolio, the investor should be able to create the best portfolio possible given his or her disposition toward risk and the alternative investment vehicles available.

efficient portfolio
a portfolio that pro-vides the highest re-turn for a given level of risk, or that has the lowest risk for a given level of return.

Portfolio Return and Standard Deviation

The *return* on a portfolio is calculated as a weighted average of returns on the assets (investment vehicles) from which it is formed. We can use Equation 16.1 to find the portfolio return, r_p:

Equation 16.1

$$\text{Return on portfolio} = \begin{pmatrix} \text{proportion of} \\ \text{portfolio's total} \\ \text{dollar value} \\ \text{represented by} \\ \text{asset 1} \end{pmatrix} \times \begin{matrix} \text{return} \\ \text{on assset} \\ 1 \end{matrix} + \begin{pmatrix} \text{proportion of} \\ \text{portfolio's total} \\ \text{dollar value} \\ \text{represented by} \\ \text{asset 2} \end{pmatrix} \times \begin{matrix} \text{return} \\ \text{on asset} \\ 2 \end{matrix} + \cdots +$$

$$\begin{pmatrix} \text{proportion of} \\ \text{portfolio's total} \\ \text{dollar value} \\ \text{represented by} \\ \text{asset } n \end{pmatrix} \times \begin{matrix} \text{return} \\ \text{on assset} \\ n \end{matrix} = \sum_{j=1}^{n} \begin{pmatrix} \text{proportion of} \\ \text{portfolio's total} \\ \text{dollar value} \\ \text{represented by} \\ \text{asset } j \end{pmatrix} \times \begin{matrix} \text{return} \\ \text{on asset} \\ j \end{matrix}$$

Equation 16.1a

$$r_p = (w_1 \times r_1) + (w_2 \times r_2) + \cdots + (w_n \times r_n) = \sum_{j=1}^{n} w_j \times r_j$$

Of course $\sum_{j=1}^{n} w_j = 1$, which means that 100 percent of the portfolio's assets must be included in this computation.

The *standard deviation* of a portfolio's returns is found by applying Equation 4.11, the formula used in Chapter 4 to find the standard deviation of a single asset. Assume that we wish to determine the return and standard deviation of returns for portfolio XY, created by combining equal portions (50 percent) of assets X and Y. The expected returns of assets X and Y for each of the next five years (1994–1998) are given in columns 1 and 2, respectively, in part A of Table 16.1. In columns 3 and 4, the weights of 50 percent for both assets X and Y, along with their respective returns from columns 1 and 2, are substituted in Equation 16.1 to get an expected portfolio return of 12 percent for each year, 1994 to 1998. Furthermore, as shown in part B of Table 16.1, the average expected portfolio return, $\bar{r}_p$, over the five-year period is also 12 percent. Substituting into Equation 4.11, portfolio XY's standard deviation, s_p, of 0 percent is calculated in part C of Table 16.1. This value should not be surprising since the expected return each year is the same—12 percent—and therefore no variability is exhibited in the expected returns from year to year shown in column 4 of part A of the table.

Correlation and Diversification

Diversification, as noted in Chapter 1, involves the inclusion of a number of different investment vehicles in a portfolio. It is an important aspect of creating an efficient portfolio. Underlying the intuitive appeal of diversification is the statistical concept of *correlation*. An understanding of the concepts of correlation and diversification and their relationship to a portfolio's total risk and return is an important part of effective portfolio planning. Here we take a closer look at these important concepts and their interrelationships.

Correlation

correlation
a statistical measure of the relationship, if any, between series of numbers representing data of any kind.

Correlation is a statistical measure of the relationship, if any, between series of numbers representing data of any kind. If two series move in the same direction,

TABLE 16.1 Expected Return, Average Return, and Standard Deviation of Returns for Portfolio XY

A. EXPECTED PORTFOLIO RETURNS

Year	(1) Expected return Asset X	(2) Asset Y	(3) Portfolio return calculation[a]	(4) Expected portfolio return, r_p
1994	8%	16%	$(.50 \times 8\%) + (.50 \times 16\%) =$	12%
1995	10	14	$(.50 \times 10) + (.50 \times 14) =$	12
1996	12	12	$(.50 \times 12) + (.50 \times 12) =$	12
1997	14	10	$(.50 \times 14) + (.50 \times 10) =$	12
1998	16	8	$(.50 \times 16) + (.50 \times 8) =$	12

B. AVERAGE EXPECTED PORTFOLIO RETURN, 1994–1998

$$\bar{r}_p = \frac{12\% + 12\% + 12\% + 12\% + 12\%}{5} = \frac{60\%}{5} = \underline{\underline{12\%}}$$

C. STANDARD DEVIATION OF EXPECTED PORTFOLIO RETURNS[b]

$$s_p =$$

$$\sqrt{\frac{(12\% - 12\%)^2 + (12\% - 12\%)^2 + (12\% - 12\%)^2 + (12\% - 12\%)^2 + (12\% - 12\%)^2}{5 - 1}}$$

$$= \sqrt{\frac{0\% + 0\% + 0\% + 0\% + 0\%}{4}} = \sqrt{\frac{0\%}{4}} = \underline{\underline{0\%}}$$

[a]Using Equation 16.1.
[b]Using Equation 4.11 presented in Chapter 4.

---

positively correlated
describes two series that move in the same direction.

negatively correlated
describes two series that move in opposite directions.

correlation coefficient
a measure of the degree of correlation between two series.

they are **positively correlated.** If the series move in opposite directions, they are **negatively correlated.** The degree of correlation is measured by the **correlation coefficient,** which ranges from +1 for **perfectly positively correlated** series to −1 for **perfectly negatively correlated** series. These two extremes are depicted in Figure 16.1 for series M and N. The perfectly positively correlated series move exactly together, while the perfectly negatively correlated series move in exactly opposite directions.

Diversification

To reduce overall risk in a portfolio, it is best to combine assets that have a negative (or a low positive) correlation. Combining negatively correlated assets can reduce the overall variability of returns, or risk, s. Figure 16.2 shows that a portfolio containing the negatively correlated assets F and G, both having the same average expected return, $\bar{r}$, also has the same return, $\bar{r}$, but has less risk (variability) than either of the individual assets. Even if assets are not negatively correlated, the lower the positive correlation between them, the lower the resulting risk.

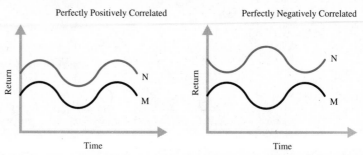

• FIGURE 16.1 The Correlation between Series M and N

The perfectly positively correlated series M and N in the left graph move exactly together. The perfectly negatively correlated series M and N in the right graph move in exactly opposite directions.

perfectly positively correlated
describes two positively correlated series that have a *correlation coefficient* of +1.

perfectly negatively correlated
describes two negatively correlated series that have a *correlation coefficient* of −1.

uncorrelated
Describes two series that lack any relationship or interaction and therefore have a *correlation coefficient* close to zero.

Some assets are **uncorrelated:** they are completely unrelated, with no interaction between their returns. Combining uncorrelated assets can reduce risk—not as effectively as combining negatively correlated assets, but more effectively than combining positively correlated assets. The correlation coefficient for uncorrelated assets is close to zero and acts as the midpoint between perfect positive and perfect negative correlation.

Correlation is important to reducing risk, but it can do only so much: A portfolio of two assets having perfectly positively correlated returns *cannot* reduce the portfolio's overall risk below the risk of the least risky asset. However, a portfolio combining two assets with less-than-perfectly-positive correlation *can* reduce total risk to a level below that of either of the components, which in certain situations may be zero. For example, assume you own the stock of a machine-tool manufacturer which is very *cyclical,* having high earnings when the economy is expanding and low earnings during a recession. If you bought stock in another machine-tool company, which would have earnings positively correlated with those of the stock you already own, the combined earnings would continue to be cyclical. As a result, risk would remain the same. As an alternative, however, you could buy stock in a sewing machine manufacturer which is *countercyclical,* having low earnings during economic expansion and high earnings during recession (since consumers are more likely to make their own clothes and clothing repairs at such a time). Combining the machine-tool stock and the sewing machine stock, which have negatively correlated earnings, should reduce risk: the low machine tool earnings during a recession would be balanced out by high sewing machine earnings, and vice versa.

A numeric example will provide a better understanding of the role of correlation in the diversification process. Table 16.2 presents the expected returns from three different assets—X, Y, and Z—over the next five years, along with their average returns and standard deviations. Each of the assets has an expected value of return of 12 percent and a standard deviation of 3.16 percent. The assets therefore have equal return and equal risk, although their return patterns are not necessarily identical. Comparing the return patterns of assets X and Y, we see that they are perfectly

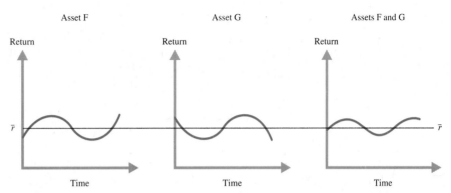

• **FIGURE 16.2** Combining Negatively Correlated Assets to Diversify Risk

The risks or variability of returns, resulting from combining negatively correlated assets F and G, both having the same expected return, $\bar{r}$, results in a portfolio (shown in the right-hand graph) with the same level of expected return but less risk.

TABLE 16.2 Expected Returns, Average Returns, and Standard Deviations for Assets X, Y, and Z and Portfolios XY and XZ

	Assets			Portfolios	
Year	X	Y	Z	XY[a] (50%X + 50%Y)	XZ[b] (50%X + 50%Z)
1994	8%	16%	8%	12%	8%
1995	10	14	10	12	10
1996	12	12	12	12	12
1997	14	10	14	12	14
1998	16	8	16	12	16
Statistics:					
Average returns[c]	12%	12%	12%	12%	12%
Standard deviation[d]	3.16%	3.16%	3.16%	0%	3.16%

[a]Portfolio XY, which consists of 50 percent of asset X and 50 percent of asset Y, illustrates *perfect negative correlation,* since these two return streams behave in completely opposite fashion over the five-year period. The return values shown here were calculated in part A of Table 16.1.

[b]Portfolio XZ, which consists of 50 percent of asset X and 50 percent of asset Z, illustrates *perfect positive correlation,* since these two return streams behave identically over the five-year period. These return values were calculated using the same method demonstrated for portfolio XY in part A of Table 16.1.

[c]The average return for each asset is calculated as the arithmetic average found by dividing the sum of the returns for the years 1994–1998 by 5—the number of years considered.

[d]Equation 4.11 was used to calculate the standard deviation. Calculation of the average return and standard deviation for portfolio XY is demonstrated in parts B and C, respectively, of Table 16.1. The portfolio standard deviation can be directly calculated from the standard deviation of the component assets using the following formula:

$$s_p = \sqrt{w_1{}^2 s_1{}^2 + w_2{}^2 s_2{}^2 + 2w_1 w_2 p_{1,2} s_1 s_2}$$

where w_1 and w_2 are the proportions of the component assets 1 and 2; s_1 and s_2 are the standard deviations of the component securities 1 and 2; and $p_{1,2}$ is the correlation coefficient between the returns of component assets 1 and 2.

negatively correlated; since they move in exactly opposite directions over time. A comparison of assets X and Z shows that they are perfectly positively correlated: they move in precisely the same direction. (Note that the returns for X and Z are identical, although it is *not* necessary for return streams to be identical in order for them to be perfectly positively correlated).

By combining equal portions of assets X and Y—the perfectly negatively correlated assets—portfolio XY (shown in Table 16.2) is created. Calculation of portfolio XY's annual expected returns, their average return, and the standard deviation of expected portfolio returns is demonstrated in Table 16.1. The risk in the portfolio created by this combination, as reflected in the standard deviation, is reduced to 0 percent, while its average return remains at 12 percent. Since both assets have the same average return, are combined in equal parts, and are perfectly negatively correlated, the combination results in the complete elimination of risk. Whenever assets are perfectly negatively correlated, an optimum combination (similar to the 50–50 mix in the case of assets X and Y) exists for which the resulting standard deviation will equal 0.

By combining equal portions of assets X and Z—the perfectly positively correlated assets—portfolio XZ (shown in Table 16.2) is created. The risk in this portfolio, reflected by its standard deviation which remains at 3.16 percent, is unaffected by this combination, and the average return remains at 12 percent. Whenever perfectly positively correlated assets such as X and Z are combined, the standard deviation of the resulting portfolio cannot be reduced below that of the least risky asset; the maximum portfolio standard deviation will be that of the riskiest asset. Since assets X and Z have the same standard deviation (3.16 percent), the minimum and maximum standard deviations are both 3.16 percent, which is the only value that could be taken on by a combination of these assets.

Effect on Risk and Return

In general, the lower (less positive and more negative) the correlation between asset returns, the greater the potential diversification of risk. For each pair of assets there is a combination that will result in the lowest risk (standard deviation) possible. The amount of potential risk reduction for this combination depends on the degree of correlation of the two assets. This concept is a bit difficult to grasp since many potential combinations could be made, given the expected return for each of two assets, the standard deviation for each asset, and the correlation coefficient. However, only one combination of the infinite number of possibilities will minimize risk.

Three possible correlations—perfect positive, uncorrelated, and perfect negative—illustrate the effect of correlation on the diversification of risk and return. Table 16.3 summarizes the impact of correlation on the range of return and risk for various two-asset portfolio combinations. The table shows that as we move from perfect positive correlation to uncorrelated assets to perfect negative correlation, the ability to reduce risk is improved. Note that in no case will creating portfolios of assets result in greater risk than that of the riskiest asset included in the portfolio. To

▬▬▬▬▬

TABLE 16.3 Correlation, Return, and Risk for Various Two-Asset Portfolio Combinations

Correlation coefficient	Range of return	Range of risk
+1 (perfect positive)	Between returns of two assets held in isolation	Between risk of two assets held in isolation
0 (uncorrelated)	Between returns of two assets held in isolation	Between risk of most risky asset and less than risk of least risky asset, but greater than 0
−1 (perfect negative)	Between returns of two assets held in isolation	Between risk of most risky asset and 0

demonstrate, assume that a firm has carefully calculated the average return, $\bar{r}$, and risk, s, for each of two assets—A and B—as summarized below:

Asset	Average return, $\bar{r}$	Risk (standard deviation), s
A	6%	3%
B	8%	8%

From these data we can see that asset A is clearly a lower-risk, lower-return asset than asset B.

To evaluate possible combinations, we consider three possible correlations—perfect positive, uncorrelated, and perfect negative. The results of the analysis are shown in Fig. 16.3. The ranges of return and risk exhibited are consistent with those noted in Table 16.3. In all cases the return will range between the 6 percent return of A and the 8 percent return of B. The risk, on the other hand, ranges between the individual risks of A and B (from 3 percent to 8 percent) in the case of perfect positive correlation, from below 3 percent (the risk of R), but greater than 0, to 8 percent (the risk of B) in the uncorrelated case, and between 0 percent and 8 percent (the risk of B) in the perfectly negatively correlated case. Note that *only in the case of perfect negative correlation can the risk be reduced to 0*. As the correlation becomes less positive and more negative (moving from the top of the figure down), the ability to reduce risk improves. Keep in mind that the amount of risk reduction achieved also depends on the proportions in which the assets are combined. While determination of the risk-minimizing combination is beyond the scope of this discussion, it is an important issue in developing portfolios of assets.

TRADITIONAL VERSUS MODERN PORTFOLIO THEORY

Two approaches are currently used by portfolio managers to plan and build their portfolios. The *traditional approach* refers to the methods money managers have

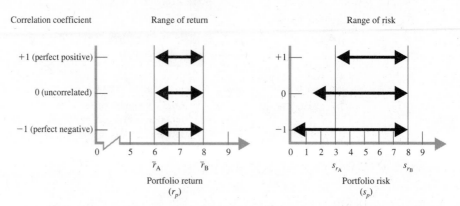

● F I G U R E   1 6 . 3 Range of Portfolio Return (r_p) and Risk (s_p) for
Combinations of Assets A and B for Various
Correlation Coefficients

The range of a portfolio's return is between that of the lowest and highest component asset
returns and is unaffected by the degree of asset correlations. Portfolio risk, on the other hand,
can be reduced below the risk of the least risky asset as the asset correlation moves from
perfectly positive to uncorrelated to perfectly negative, where it can be reduced to zero by
combining assets in the proper proportion.

been using since the evolution of the public securities markets. *Modern portfolio
theory (MPT)* is a more recent development. The theory behind it has been refined
over the past 25 or so years, and it continues to grow in popularity and acceptance.
Some MPT concepts are indirectly used by practitioners of the traditional approach,
yet there are major differences between the two.

The Traditional Approach

**traditional portfolio
management**
an approach to port-
folio management
that emphasizes bal-
ancing the portfolio
with a variety of
stocks and/or bonds
from a broad cross-
section of industries.

Traditional portfolio management emphasizes ''balancing'' the portfolio. The
traditional portfolio manager assembles a wide variety of stocks and/or bonds
within the portfolio. The typical emphasis is interindustry diversification, which
means that the portfolio contains securities of companies from a broad cross-section
of American industry. Most institutional portfolio managers utilize the security
analysis techniques discussed in Chapters 6 and 7 when they select individual securities for the traditional portfolio. Table 16.4 presents the industry groupings and
percent invested in them of a typical mutual fund that is managed by professionals
using the traditional approach. This fund, the Fidelity Blue Chip Growth Fund, is an
open-end mutual fund with a 3 percent initial load. The portfolio's value at January
31, 1992, was approximately $361 million. Its objective is to provide investors with
long-term capital growth by investing primarily in a diversified portfolio of the
common stock of well-known and established companies that have above average
potential for long-term earnings growth. The Blue Chip Growth Fund holds shares
of 127 different stocks from 36 industries, as well as two convertible bonds and
short-term obligations through investments in repurchase agreements.

███████

TABLE 16.4 Portfolio of Fidelity Blue Chip Growth Fund, January 31, 1992

The Fidelity Blue Chip Growth Fund appears to adhere to the traditional approach to portfolio management. Its portfolio value is about $341.6 million in common stock, including 127 different stocks in 36 industry groupings, plus about $1.6 million in convertible bonds and $17.7 million in short-term repurchase obligations.

Fidelity Blue Chip Growth Fund
Investments by Industry Group
as of January 31, 1992

Industry Group	Percent	Industry Group	Percent
COMMON STOCK—94.9%		**Nondurables**	**14.6**
		Beverages	2.6
Basic Industries	**4.8**	Foods	2.8
Chemicals and plastics	3.6	Household products	3.2
Paper and forest products	1.2	Tobacco	6.0
Durables	**0.4**	**Retail and Wholesale**	**8.4**
Textiles and apparel	0.4	General merchandise stores	4.5
		Grocery stores	0.6
Energy	**5.1**	Retail, miscellaneous	3.3
Energy services	1.0		
Oil and gas	4.1	**Services**	**2.1**
		Advertising	0.6
Finance	**11.9**	Leasing and rental	0.8
Banks	3.7	Services	0.7
Credit and other finance	0.1		
Federally sponsored credit	5.8	**Technology**	**9.9**
Insurance	2.2	Communications equipment	0.5
Securities industry	0.1	Computer systems and software	8.4
		Computers and office equipment	1.0
Health	**24.5**		
Drugs and pharmaceuticals	11.4	**Transportation**	**0.3**
Medical equipment and supplies	5.2	Railroads	0.3
Medical facilities management	7.9		
		Utilities	**3.4**
		Cellular	0.2
Industrial Machinery and Equipment	**6.4**	Telephone services	3.2
Electrical equipment	3.9		
Industrial machinery and equipment	0.9	**CONVERTIBLE BONDS—0.5%**	
Pollution control	1.6	Medical equipment and supplies	0.2
		Retail, miscellaneous	0.3
Media and Leisure	**2.8**		
Entertainment	1.5	**SHORT-TERM OBLIGATIONS—4.9%**	
Publishing	0.3	Investments in U.S. Treasury	
Restaurants	1.0	repurchase agreements	4.9

(*Source:* Annual Report, Fidelity Blue Chip Growth Fund, January 31, 1992.)

■ INVESTOR INSIGHTS ■

How to Build a Stock Portfolio Even If You Aren't a Moneybags

You don't need a mountain of cash to buy individual stocks.

Would-be investors are often told that unless they have more than $100,000 to put into stocks, they should stick with mutual funds.

"People espousing this are worried that you won't get enough diversification and that transaction costs on small portfolios are too high," says Arthur Micheletti, chief economist at Bailard, Biehl & Kaiser, a money-management firm in San Mateo, Calif.

But he and other investment advisers and portfolio managers say individuals can build an adequately diversified, high quality portfolio of individual stocks with as little as $25,000.

People who buy even as few as 10 stocks can be adequately diversified, if they buy securities in different industries and use a variety of selection criteria. And they can keep transaction costs low by buying round lots, using discount brokers, and keeping trading to a minimum.

It takes more work than buying mutual funds, and it requires discipline. Only investors who can hold their securities long-term should consider buying individual stocks, financial advisers say. They also have to be able to restrain themselves when they're tempted to chase the latest hot stock. . . .

How do you build a small portfolio?

First, consider the number of stocks needed. Academic research on diversification suggests that individuals need 10 to 20 securities. "So if you assume an average stock price of $20, you could buy 15 stocks in round lots of 100 shares for $30,000," says Elliot Lipson, president of Horizons Financial Advisors in Atlanta.

The number of stocks might be limited by the amount of time an individual has to devote to the portfolio. Peter Behuniak, 42 years old, an educational administrator in South Glastonbury, Conn., holds 10 to 20 stocks at any one time, and says he spends five to seven hours a week monitoring his portfolio.

To increase diversification, advisers recommend choosing securities in different industries.

"You don't want more than one company in an industry, and you don't want companies in related industries," says Mr. Lipson. For example, an auto manufacturer and a steel company that supplies auto manufacturers will move together. Further, "you also don't want industries that respond to the economic cycle the same way, such as trucking and basic manufacturing," he says.

Investors should also diversify by choosing both large companies and small companies (those under, roughly, $100 million in capitalization).

Analyzing the stock portion of the Blue Chip Growth Fund, which accounts for about 95 percent of the fund's total assets, we can observe the traditional approach to portfolio management at work. This fund holds a variety of stocks from a diverse cross-section of the total universe of available stocks, although its stocks represent only major American companies. The largest industry group is drugs and pharma-

Advisers suggest choosing from two or three broad categories—growth stocks (those with above-average earnings prospects), value stocks (which look inexpensive relative to their sales, earnings and other fundamentals) and yield stocks (those with high dividends). "If you really want to diversify, choose some from each," says Mr. Lipson.

While Mr. Lipson believes that investors need at least 15 stocks to be adequately diversified, other advisers are comfortable with a smaller number. "It's not so much the number of names that makes you diversified, but how you spread them out," says George Vanderheiden, who heads the equity growth group for Fidelity Investments.

Investors can add to their diversification by including some international exposure. "To be really well diversified, you need 10% of your portfolio in international stocks," says John Markese, president of the American Association of Individual Investors, an investor-education group based in Chicago.

But because brokerage costs for foreign stocks can be high, and getting information can be difficult, some advisers say it makes sense to buy an international mutual fund that invests in both Europe and Asia. . . .

Advisers say investors don't have to jump in all at once. Rather, they can buy the securities over a period of months. . . .

The focus should be on quality, not quantity. "A good four [stocks] is better than a bad 10," he says. . . .

In general, though, advisers say that it makes more sense to start with enough assets to buy at least six securities over a period of months. . . .

"Don't look at what the media's touting," cautions Mr. Markese of the Individual Investors association. And be cautious about tips from brokers, he says. "They're probably recommending stocks their firm wants peddled at the moment."

While it makes sense to buy only the kinds of stocks you understand, beware of the familiarity factor. "People tend to buy McDonald's, Toys 'R' Us and drug companies," says Michael Stolper, president of Stolper & Co., a San Diego firm that evaluates money managers. As a result, investors miss out on promising stocks in more arcane areas, like biotechnology.

Once a portfolio is in place, resist the urge to trade. "People have a pathological impulse to interact with their portfolio," says Mr. Stolper. "Action junkies are the ones who get killed." Not only is it tough to time the market successfully, but transaction costs and taxes can wipe out the 20% they may have picked up on a stock.

Source: Excerpted from: Ellen E. Schultz, "How to Build a Stock Portfolio, Even If You Aren't a Moneybags," *The Wall Street Journal,* April 14, 1992, p. C1.

ceuticals, with 11.4 percent of the total portfolio. Its largest individual holding is Philip Morris, a tobacco and food products conglomerate, which accounts for 4.7 percent of the total portfolio. Wal-Mart, a chain of discount department stores, ranks second, at 3.8 percent. The third largest holding—2.9 percent—is General Electric, whose many businesses include appliances and financial services. Federal

National Mortgage Association, a financial services organization, is fourth at 2.7 percent of the portfolio.

Traditional portfolio managers want to invest in well-known companies for three reasons: First, these companies have been and probably will continue to be successful business enterprises. Investing in securities of large, well-known companies is perceived as less risky than investing in lesser-known firms. Second, professional managers prefer to invest in large companies because the securities of these firms are more liquid and are available in large quantities. Managers of large portfolios invest substantial sums of money and need to acquire securities in large quantities to achieve an efficient order size. Third, traditional portfolio managers also prefer well-known companies because it is easier to convince clients to invest in well-known corporations. "Window dressing," a Wall Street cliché, refers to the practice of many investment managers to load up portfolios with well-known stocks, thus making it easier to sell their services to clients. Individual investors can also apply traditional portfolio management principles to any size portfolio, as described in the nearby Investor Insights box.

Modern Portfolio Theory

modern portfolio theory
an approach to portfolio management that uses statistical measures to develop a portfolio plan.

During the 1950s Harry Markowitz first developed the theories that form the basis of modern portfolio theory, and many other scholars and investment experts have contributed to it since. **Modern portfolio theory (MPT)** utilizes several basic statistical measures to develop a portfolio plan. Included are *expected returns* and *standard deviations* of returns for both securities and portfolios and the *correlation* between returns. According to MPT, diversification is achieved by combining securities in a portfolio so that individual securities have negative (or low positive) correlations between each other's rates of return. Thus the statistical diversification is the deciding factor in choosing securities for an MPT portfolio. Two important aspects of MPT are the *efficient frontier* and *beta*. As we'll see below, the efficient frontier is a more theoretical and less practical tool than is beta.

The Efficient Frontier

At any point in time an investor is faced with virtually hundreds of investment vehicles from which to choose. Using some or all of these vehicles, an investor can form a very large number of possible portfolios. In fact, using only, say, ten of the vehicles, hundreds of portfolios could be created by changing the weights, w_j, which represent the proportion of the portfolio's dollar value represented by each asset j. As noted earlier, each portfolio formed would have an expected return, r_p, and risk as measured by its standard deviation, s_p. Clearly, unless the securities included in a given portfolio are *perfectly positively correlated,* some risk reduction would result from the diversification achieved by the portfolio.

If we were to create all possible portfolios, calculate the return (r_p) and risk (s_p) of each, and plot each risk-return combination on a set of risk-return (r_p-s_p) axes, we would have the *feasible or attainable set* of all possible portfolios. This set is represented by the shaded area in Figure 16.4. It is the area bounded by

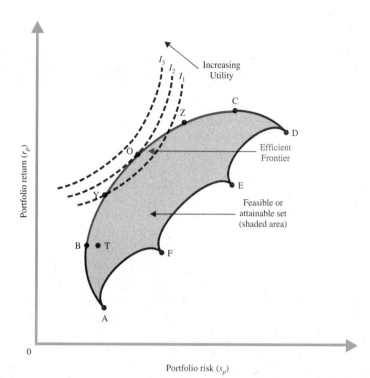

● **FIGURE 16.4** The Feasible or Attainable Set and the Efficient Frontier

The *feasible or attainable set* (shaded area) represents the risk-return combinations attainable with all possible portfolios; the *efficient frontier* is the locus of all *efficient portfolios*. The point O where the investor's highest possible indifference curve is tangent to the efficient frontier is the optimal portfolio. It represents the highest level of satisfaction the investor can achieve given the available set of portfolios.

ABYOZCDEF. As defined earlier, an *efficient portfolio* is a portfolio that provides the highest return for a given level of risk or provides minimum risk for a given level of return. For example, let's compare portfolio T to portfolios B and Y depicted in Figure 16.4. It appears that portfolio Y clearly dominates portfolio B since it has a higher return for the same level of risk. Portfolio B also dominates portfolio T because it has lower risk for the same level of return. The boundary BYOZC of the feasible or attainable set of portfolios, called the **efficient frontier,** represents all efficient portfolios—those that provide the best tradeoff between risk and return. All portfolios on the efficient frontier dominate all other portfolios in the feasible or attainable set. Any portfolios that would fall to the left of the efficient frontier are *not available* for investment, since they fall outside of the feasible or attainable set. Portfolios that fall to the right of the efficient frontier are *not desirable* since they are dominated by portfolios on the efficient frontier.

The efficient frontier can in theory be used with an *investor's utility function or*

efficient frontier
the left-most boundary of the feasible or attainable set of portfolios that includes all efficient portfolios—those providing the best attainable tradeoff between risk (measured by the standard deviation) and return.

risk-indifference curves, which indicate for a given level of utility (satisfaction) the set of risk-return combinations for which an investor would be indifferent. These curves, labeled I_1, I_2, and I_3 in Figure 16.4, reflect increasing utility as we move from I_1 to I_2 to I_3. The optimal portfolio, O, is the point at which indifference curve I_2 meets the efficient frontier. This portfolio reflects the highest level of satisfaction the investor can achieve given the available set of portfolios. The higher utility provided by I_3 cannot be achieved given the best available portfolios represented by the efficient frontier.

The efficient frontier when coupled with a risk-free asset can be used to develop the *capital asset pricing model* (introduced in Chapter 4) in terms of portfolio risk (measured by the standard deviation, s_p) and return (r_p). Rather than focus on further theoretical development, we shift our focus to the more practical aspects of the efficient frontier and its extensions. In this regard we revisit *beta,* the risk measure introduced in Chapter 4, and consider its use in a portfolio context.

Portfolio Betas

As noted above, portfolios strive for diversification by including a variety of non-complementary investment vehicles for the purpose of reducing the risk of loss while meeting the investor's return objective. Remember from Chapter 4 that any investment vehicle possesses two basic types of risk: *Diversifiable risk* is the risk unique to a particular investment vehicle, and *nondiversifiable risk* is the risk possessed by every investment vehicle.

A great deal of research has been conducted on the topic of risk as it relates to security investments. As noted in Chapter 4, the results show that in general *investors earn higher rates of return by buying riskier investments;* that is, *to earn more return, one must bear more risk.* More startling, however, are research results that show that only with nondiversifiable risk is there a positive risk-return relationship. High levels of diversifiable risk do not result in correspondingly high levels of return. Because there is no reward for bearing diversifiable risk, an investor should minimize this form of risk in the portfolio. This can be done by diversifying the portfolio so that the only type of risk remaining is nondiversifiable.

Risk Diversification. As we've seen, diversification minimizes diversifiable risk because of a balancing effort that tends to cause the poor return of one vehicle to be offset by the good return on another. Minimizing diversifiable risk through careful selection of investment vehicles requires that the vehicles chosen for the portfolio come from a wide range of industries.

To understand better the effect of diversification on the basic types of risk, consider what happens when we begin with a single asset (security) in a portfolio. Then we expand the portfolio by randomly selecting additional securities from, say, the population of all actively traded securities. Using the standard deviation, s, to measure the portfolio's *total risk,* we can depict the behavior of the total portfolio risk (y-axis) as more securities are added (x-axis), as done in Figure 16.5. With the addition of securities, the total portfolio risk declines, due to the effects of diversification (as explained earlier), and tends to approach a limit. Research has shown that

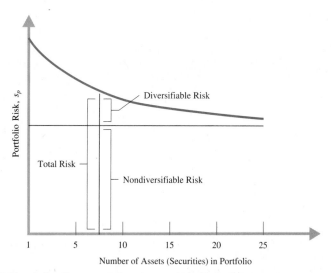

• FIGURE 16.5 Portfolio Risk and Diversification

As randomly selected assets (securities) are combined to create a portfolio, the total risk of the portfolio (measured by its standard deviation, s_p) declines. The portion of the risk eliminated is *diversifiable risk,* and the remaining portion is the *nondiversifiable* or *relevant risk.* Most of the benefits of diversification result from forming portfolios containing 8 to 15 randomly selected securities.

most of the benefits of diversification, in terms of risk reduction, can be gained by forming portfolios containing 8 to 15 randomly selected securities.

    Because any investor can create a portfolio of assets that will eliminate all, or virtually all, diversifiable risk, the only **relevant risk** is that which is nondiversifiable. Any investor must therefore be concerned solely with nondiversifiable risk, which reflects the contribution of an asset to the risk of the portfolio. The measurement of nondiversifiable risk is thus of primary importance in selecting those assets possessing the most desired risk-return characteristics.

relevant risk
risk that is nondiversifiable.

Calculating Portfolio Betas. The *nondiversifiable or relevant risk* of a security can be measured using *beta,* a measure that was defined, derived, and demonstrated in Chapter 4. Betas can be positive (return changes in same direction as market) or negative (return changes in opposite direction as market). Most betas are positive. The beta for the market is equal to 1.0. Securities with betas greater than 1.0 are more risky than the market, and those with betas below 1.0 are less risky than the market. The beta for the risk-free asset is 0.0. Betas for a broad range of securities can be readily obtained from brokerage firms and subscription services such as Value Line.

portfolio beta
the beta of a portfolio; calculated as the weighted average of the betas of the individual assets that it includes.

    The **portfolio beta, b_p,** is merely the weighted average of the betas of the individual assets that it includes. It can be easily estimated using the betas of the component assets. We can use Equation 16.2 to find the portfolio beta, b_p:

Equation 16.2

$$\text{Portfolio beta} = \begin{pmatrix} \text{proportion of} \\ \text{portfolio's total} \\ \text{dollar value} \\ \text{represented by} \\ \text{asset 1} \end{pmatrix} \times \begin{matrix} \text{beta} \\ \text{for} \\ \text{asset 1} \end{matrix} + \begin{pmatrix} \text{proportion of} \\ \text{portfolio's total} \\ \text{dollar value} \\ \text{represented by} \\ \text{asset 2} \end{pmatrix} \times \begin{matrix} \text{beta} \\ \text{for} \\ \text{asset 2} \end{matrix} + \cdots +$$

$$\begin{pmatrix} \text{proportion of} \\ \text{portfolio's total} \\ \text{dollar value} \\ \text{represented by} \\ \text{asset } n \end{pmatrix} \times \begin{matrix} \text{beta} \\ \text{for} \\ \text{asset } n \end{matrix} = \sum_{j=1}^{n} \begin{pmatrix} \text{proportion of} \\ \text{portfolio's total} \\ \text{dollar value} \\ \text{represented by} \\ \text{asset } j \end{pmatrix} \times \begin{matrix} \text{beta} \\ \text{for} \\ \text{asset } j \end{matrix}$$

Equation 16.2a

$$b_p = (w_1 \times b_1) + (w_2 \times b_2) + \cdots + (w_n \times b_n) = \sum_{j=1}^{n} w_j \times b_j$$

Of course, $\sum_{j=1}^{n} w_j = 1$, which means that 100 percent of the portfolio's assets must be included in this computation.

Portfolio betas are interpreted in exactly the same fashion as individual asset betas. They indicate the degree of responsiveness of the portfolio's return to changes in the market return. For example, when the market return increases by 10 percent, a portfolio with a beta of .75 will experience a 7.5 percent increase in its return (.75 × 10%), whereas a portfolio with a beta of 1.25 will experience a 12.5 percent increase in its return (1.25 × 10%). Low-beta portfolios are less responsive and therefore less risky than high-beta portfolios. Clearly, a portfolio containing mostly low-beta assets will have a low beta, and vice versa.

To demonstrate, consider the Austin Fund, a large investment company, that wishes to assess the risk of two portfolios—V and W. Both portfolios contain five assets, with the proportions and betas shown in Table 16.5. The betas for portfolios V and W, b_v and b_w, can be calculated by substituting the appropriate data from the table into Equation 16.2 as follows:

$$b_v = (.10 \times 1.65) + (.30 \times 1.00) + (.20 \times 1.30)$$
$$+ (.20 \times 1.10) + (.20 \times 1.25)$$
$$= .165 + .300 + .260 + .220 + .250 = 1.195 \approx \underline{\underline{1.20}}$$

$$b_w = (.10 \times .80) + (.10 \times 1.00) + (.20 \times .65)$$
$$+ (.10 \times .75) + (.50 \times 1.05)$$
$$= .080 + .100 + .130 + .075 + .525 = \underline{\underline{.91}}$$

Portfolio V's beta is 1.20 and portfolio W's is .91. These values make sense since portfolio V contains relatively high-beta assets and portfolio W contains relatively low-beta assets. Clearly portfolio V's returns are more responsive to changes in market returns and therefore more risky than portfolio W's.

Using Portfolio Betas. The usefulness of beta depends on how well it explains relative return fluctuations. The coefficient of determination (R^2) can be used to

TABLE 16.5 Austin Fund's Portfolios V and W

	Portfolio V		Portfolio W	
Asset	Proportion	Beta	Proportion	Beta
1	.10	1.65	.10	.80
2	.30	1.00	.10	1.00
3	.20	1.30	.20	.65
4	.20	1.10	.10	.75
5	.20	1.25	.50	1.05
Totals	1.00		1.00	

statistically derive a beta coefficient. That is, it indicates the percentage of the change in the return on an individual security that is explained by its relationship with the market return. R^2 can range from 0 to 1.0. If a regression equation has an R^2 of 0, this means none (0 percent) of the variation in the security's return is explained by its relationship with the market. An R^2 of 1.0 indicates the existence of perfect correlation (100 percent) between a security and the market.

Beta is much more useful in explaining a portfolio's return fluctuations than a security's return fluctuations. A well-diversified stock portfolio will have a beta equation R^2 of around .90. This means that 90 percent of the stock portfolio's fluctuations are related to changes in the stock market as a whole. Individual security betas have a wide range of R^2s, but tend to be in the .20 to .50 range. Other factors (diversifiable risk, in particular) also cause individual security prices to fluctuate. When securities are combined in a well-diversified portfolio, most of the fluctuation in that portfolio's return is caused by the movement of the entire stock market.

Interpreting Portfolio Betas. If a portfolio has a beta of $+1.0$, the portfolio experiences changes in its rate of return equal to changes in the market's rate of return. This means the $+1.0$ beta portfolio would tend to experience a 10 percent increase in return if the stock market as a whole experienced a 10 percent increase in return. Conversely, if the market return fell by 6 percent, the return on the $+1.0$ beta portfolio would also fall by 6 percent.

Table 16.6 lists the expected returns for three portfolio betas in two situations: when the market experiences an increase in return of 10 percent and a decrease in return of 10 percent. The 2.0 beta portfolio is twice as volatile as the market. When the market return increases by 10 percent, the portfolio return increases by 20 percent. Conversely, the portfolio's return will fall by 20 percent when the market has a decline in return of 10 percent. This portfolio would be considered a relatively high-risk, high-return portfolio. A .5 beta portfolio is considered a relatively low-risk, low-return portfolio—a conservative portfolio for investors who wish to maintain a low-risk investment posture. The .5 beta portfolio is half as volatile as the

TABLE 16.6 Portfolio Betas and Associated Changes in Returns

Portfolio Beta	Change in Return on Market	Change in Expected Return on Portfolio
+2.0	+10.0%	+20.0%
	−10.0	−20.0
+ .5	+10.0	+ 5.0
	−10.0	− 5.0
−1.0	+10.0	−10.0
	−10.0	+10.0

market. A beta of −1.0 indicates that the portfolio moves opposite the direction of the market. A bearish investor would probably want to own a negative beta portfolio, because this type of investment tends to rise in value when the stock market declines, and vice versa. Finding securities with negative betas is difficult, however. Most securities have positive betas, since they tend to experience return movements in the same direction as changes in the stock market.

The Risk-Return Tradeoff: Some Closing Comments

Another valuable outgrowth of modern portfolio theory is the specific delineation between nondiversifiable risk and investment return. The basic premise is that an investor must have a portfolio of relatively risky investments to earn a relatively high rate of return. That relationship is illustrated in Figure 16.6. The upward-sloping line shows the **risk-return tradeoff.** The point where the risk-return line crosses the return axis (R_F) is called the **risk-free rate.** This is the return an investor can earn on a risk-free investment such as a U.S. Treasury bill or an insured money market account. As we proceed upward along the line, portfolios of risky investments appear. For example, four investment portfolios, A through D, are depicted in Figure 16.6. Portfolios A and B are investment opportunities that provide a level of return commensurate with their respective risk levels. Portfolio C would be an excellent investment as it provides a high return at a relatively low risk level. Portfolio D, in contrast, is an investment situation that one should avoid, as it offers high risk but low return.

risk-return tradeoff
the inverse relationship between the risk associated with a given investment and its expected return.

risk-free rate (R_F)
the return an investor can earn on a risk-free investment such as a T-bill or an insured money market account.

Reconciling the Traditional Approach and MPT

We have reviewed two fairly different approaches to portfolio management—the traditional approach and MPT. The question that naturally arises is, Which technique should be used by the individual investor? There is no definite answer; the question must be resolved by the judgment of the investor. However, a few useful ideas can be offered. The average individual investor does not have the resources, computers, and mathematical acumen to implement an MPT portfolio strategy.

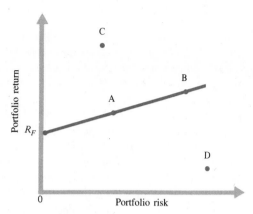

• F I G U R E 1 6 . 6 The Portfolio Risk-Return Tradeoff

As the risk of an investment portfolio increases from zero, the return provided should increase above the risk-free rate, R_F. Portfolios A and B offer returns commensurate with their risk, portfolio C provides a high return at a low-risk level, and portfolio D provides a low return for high risk. Portfolio C is highly desirable; portfolio D should be avoided.

Given that total MPT portfolio management is impractical for most individual investors, it follows that ideas should be drawn from *both* MPT and the traditional approach. The traditional approach stresses security selection using fundamental and technical analysis. It also emphasizes diversification of the portfolio across industry lines. MPT stresses negative correlations between securities' rates of return for the issues within the portfolio. This approach calls for diversification to minimize diversifiable risk. So, following either strategy, diversification must be accomplished in order to ensure satisfactory performance.

Beta is a useful tool for determining the level of a portfolio's nondiversifiable risk and should be part of the decision-making process. We recommend the following portfolio management policy:

• Determine how much risk you are willing to bear.
• Seek diversification among different types of securities and across industry lines, and pay attention to how the return from one security is related to another.
• Consider how a security responds to the market, and use beta in diversifying your portfolio as a way to keep the portfolio in line with your acceptable level of risk.
• Evaluate alternative portfolios to make sure that the portfolio selected provides the highest return for the given level of acceptable risk.

BUILDING A PORTFOLIO USING AN ASSET ALLOCATION SCHEME

In this section we will examine the criteria that can be used to build a portfolio. We will look at investor characteristics, and objectives and at portfolio objectives and policies. These factors will then be used to develop a plan for allocating assets in various investment categories. This plan provides the basic framework for selecting individual investment vehicles for the portfolio. In attempting to weave the concepts of risk and diversification into a solid portfolio policy, we will rely on both traditional and modern approaches to plan and build an investment portfolio.

Investor Characteristics and Objectives

An investor's personal financial and family situation are important inputs in determining portfolio policy. The following are vital determinants: level and stability of income, family factors, net worth, investor experience and age, and investor disposition toward risk. The portfolio strategy of an individual investor obviously must be tailored to meet that person's needs. The types of investments in the portfolio depend upon relative income needs and ability to bear risk. A relatively young investor may have an aggressive investment policy, particularly if that person's family obligations are well met. A married investor with young children would not be seeking high-risk investments until some measure of financial security has been provided for the family. Once financial security has been provided for, more risky ventures can be undertaken. Simply stated, *an investor's risk exposure should not exceed that person's ability to bear risk.*

The size of income and certainty of an investor's employment also bear on portfolio strategy. An investor with a secure job is more likely to embark on a risk-oriented investment program than one who has a less secure position. Income taxes bear on the investment decision as well. The higher an investor's income, the more important the tax ramifications of an investment program become. An individual's investment experience also influences the appropriate investment strategy. Normally investors assume higher levels of investment risk gradually over time. It is best to "get one's feet wet" in the investment market by slipping into it gradually rather than leaping in head first. Very often investors who make risky initial investments suffer heavy losses, damaging the long-run potential of their entire investment program. A cautiously developed investment program will likely provide more favorable long-run results than an impulsive, risky one.

Once an investor has developed a personal financial profile, the next question is, "What do I want from my portfolio?" There is generally a tradeoff between earning a high current income from an investment portfolio or obtaining significant capital appreciation from it. An investor must usually choose one or the other; it is difficult to have both. The price of having high appreciation potential in the portfolio is often low current income potential.

The investor's needs may determine which avenue is chosen. For instance, a retired investor whose income depends on his or her portfolio will probably choose a lower-risk, current-income-oriented approach out of the need for financial survival. In contrast, a high-income, financially secure investor (a physician, for instance) may be much more willing to take on risky investments in the hope of improving net worth. Thus it should be clear that a portfolio must be built around the individual's needs, which depend on income, responsibilities, financial resources, age, retirement plans, and ability to bear risk.

Portfolio Objectives and Policies

Building a portfolio is a logical activity and is best done after careful analysis of the investor's needs and of the investment vehicles available for inclusion in the portfolio. The following objectives should be considered when planning and building a portfolio: current income needs, capital preservation, capital growth, tax considerations, and risk.

Any one or more of these factors will play an influential role in defining the desirable type of portfolio for an investor. For convenience, these factors can be tied together as follows: The first two items, current income and capital preservation, are portfolio objectives synonymous with a low-risk, conservative investment strategy. Normally a portfolio with this orientation contains low-beta (low-risk) securities. A capital growth objective (the third item) implies increased risk and a reduced level of current income. Higher-risk growth stocks, options, commodities and financial futures, gold, real estate, and other more speculative investments may be suitable for this investor. An investor's tax bracket (the fourth item) will influence investment strategy. A high-income investor probably wishes to defer taxes and earn investment returns in the form of capital gains. This implies a strategy of higher-risk investments and a longer holding period. Lower-bracket investors are less concerned with how they earn the income, and they may wish to invest in higher current income vehicles. The most important item an investor must decide upon is *risk* (the final item). The risk-return tradeoff should be considered in all investment decisions.

Developing an Asset Allocation Scheme

asset allocation
a scheme that involves dividing one's portfolio into various asset classes in order to preserve capital by protecting against negative developments while still taking advantage of positive developments.

Once an investor's needs are converted into specific portfolio objectives, a portfolio designed to achieve these goals can be constructed. Before buying any stocks, bonds, short-term securities, or other vehicles, however, the investor must develop an *asset allocation scheme*. **Asset allocation** involves dividing one's portfolio into various asset classes such as U.S. stocks, U.S. bonds, foreign securities, short-term securities, and other vehicles such as tangibles (especially gold) and real estate. The emphasis of asset allocation is on *preservation of capital*—protecting against negative developments while still taking advantage of positive developments. Asset allocation, although similar to *diversification* in its objective, is a bit different: its focus is on *investment in various asset classes,* whereas diversification tends to focus more on investing in various vehicles *within* an asset class.

Asset allocation is based upon the belief that the total return of a portfolio is influenced more by the division of investments into asset classes than by the actual investments. In fact, studies have shown that as much as 90 percent or more of a portfolio's *return* comes from asset allocation. Therefore, less than 10 percent can be attributed to the actual security selection. Furthermore researchers have found that asset allocation has a much greater impact on reducing total *risk* than does selecting the best investment vehicle in any single asset category. Clearly asset allocation is an important aspect of portfolio management.

Approaches to Asset Allocation

There are three basic approaches to asset allocation. The first two—fixed weightings and flexible weightings—differ with respect to the nature of the proportions of each asset category maintained in the portfolio. The third—tactical asset allocation—is a more exotic technique frequently utilized by sophisticated institutional portfolio managers.

Fixed Weightings.   Under this approach, a fixed percentage of the portfolio is allocated to each of the asset categories, of which there typically are three to five. Assuming four categories—common stocks, bonds, foreign securities, and short-term securities—a fixed allocation might be:

Category	Allocation
Common stock	30%
Bonds	50
Foreign securities	15
Short-term securities	5
Total portfolio	100%

Generally with fixed weightings the weights do not change over time. Because of shifting market values, the portfolio may have to be adjusted annually or after major market moves in order to maintain the desired fixed percentage allocations. Fixed weights may or may not represent equal percentage allocations to each category. One could, for example, allocate 25 percent to each of the four categories above. Research has shown that over the 1967–1988 period, equal (20%) allocations to U.S. stocks, foreign stocks, long-term bonds, cash, and real estate resulted in a portfolio that outperformed the S&P 500 both in terms of return and risk. These findings add further support to the importance of even a somewhat naive "buy and hold" asset allocation strategy.

Flexible Weightings.   This approach involves the periodic adjustment of the weights for each asset category based either on market analysis or technical analysis (i.e., market timing). The use of a flexible weighting scheme is often called *strategic asset allocation*. For example the initial and new allocation based on a flexible weighting scheme may be:

Category	Initial Allocation	New Allocation
Common stock	30%	45%
Bonds	40	40
Foreign securities	15	10
Short-term securities	15	5
Total portfolio	100%	100%

The new allocation resulted from an expectation of lower inflation which was expected to result in increased domestic stock and bond prices and a decline in foreign and short-term security returns. The weightings were therefore changed to capture greater returns in a changing market.

Tactical Asset Allocation.   Tactical asset allocation is a sophisticated approach that uses stock index futures and bond futures (see Chapter 12) to change a portfolio's asset allocation. When stocks seem less attractive than bonds, this strategy involves selling stock index futures and buying bond futures. Conversely, when bonds seem less attractive than stocks, the strategy results in buying stock index futures and selling bond futures. Because, to be effective, this technique relies on a large portfolio and the use of quantitative models for cues, it is generally appropriate only for large institutional investors.

Asset Allocation Alternatives

Assuming the use of a fixed-weight asset allocation plan and using, say, four asset categories—common stock, bonds, foreign securities, and short-term securities, we can demonstrate three asset allocations. Table 16.7 shows allocations in each of the categories for a conservative (low-return—low-risk), moderate (average-return—average-risk), and an aggressive (high-return—high-risk) portfolio. The conservative allocation heavily relies on bonds and short-term securities to provide predictable returns. The moderate allocation includes mostly bonds and common stock, and more foreign securities and fewer short-term securities than the conservative allocation. Its moderate return-risk behavior reflects a move away from safe short-term securities to a larger dose of common stock and foreign securities than under the conservative allocation. Finally as we move to the aggressive portfolio, more dollars are allocated to common stock, fewer to bonds, and more to foreign securities, thereby generally increasing the expected portfolio return and risk.

Applying Asset Allocation

An asset allocation plan should consider the individual's investments, savings and spending patterns, the economic outlook, tax situation, return expectations, risk

TABLE 16.7 Alternative Asset Allocations

	Allocation Alternative		
Category	**Conservative (low-return– low-risk)**	**Moderate (average-return– average-risk)**	**Aggressive (high-return– high-risk)**
Common stock	15%	30%	40%
Bonds	45	40	30
Foreign securities	5	15	25
Short-term securities	35	15	5
Total portfolio	100%	100%	100%

Asset Allocation Advice from the Pros

Investment advisers have fretted for years that individual investors don't take enough risk—at least when it comes to moving out of "cash equivalents," like certificates of deposit, and into riskier assets like stocks and bonds.

Now, a growing number of Wall Street firms are clamoring to fix the problem, by offering services to small investors that purport to divine the "right" asset mix for them. In exchange for baring the intimate details of their personal finances, individuals get a free, customized "asset-allocation" blueprint.

But while the results may look precise and scientific, there's a lot of room for interpretation. And different services can come up with widely different advice for the same person. Asked to make recommendations for a 39-year-old single parent, for example, four firms came up with stock-market allocations that ranged from 18% to 66.3%.

Still, there's no denying that many people should be paying a great deal more attention than they are to how their investments are allocated.

A wealth of academic research shows that stocks offer the best chance for investors to stay ahead of inflation over the long run. But individuals on average have a meager 18% of their financial assets in stocks and stock funds, according to estimates from First Boston Corp. and the Federal Reserve. Nearly a quarter of their total financial assets is CDs and other cash investments, which are generally the least appealing assets long term.

Investor reaction to the asset-allocation services indicates that many individuals are eager for all the advice they can get.

When Dreyfus Corp. unveiled its new "investment allocation" service last month the giant mutual fund group got a stunning response. . . .

Shearson Lehman Brothers Inc. expects its "strategic asset allocation" service to handle "more than 100,000" applications in the first 12 months from its start-up in the spring of 1991, says Shelley Freeman, director of financial planning. Other firms, including PaineWebber Group Inc. and Prudential Securities Inc., are seeing a similar boom in interest for their allocation services.

"There's a resurgence of interest in asset-allocation advice," says Bruce Ventimiglia, senior vice president at Prudential. "A large portion of the general populace is under-invested" in stocks, bonds and other risky assets, he says, and "as interest rates fall, more people are looking for alternatives."

The asset-allocation services are clearly good marketing tools for the firms, whose main business is selling stocks, bonds and other investments to individuals. Besides directing how much money an individual should devote to broad asset classes, such as growth, fixed-income and cash, these services also are designed to push specific funds and securities that may meet those specifications.

. . .

What about results?

The accompanying table shows recommendations prepared by four firms, with the results summarized in three major asset categories: cash, fixed income (bonds) and "growth" (including not only stocks, but also options, commodities, partnerships and other investments). Each firm used information on the same four individual investors.

What's the "Right" Mix?

Recommendations from different asset-allocation services may vary, as shown by these suggestions from some major investment firms for four individual investors.

The Breadwinner

Early-30s, nonearner spouse, two kids; "moderate" risk taker, with investment assets of $726,200 (41.6% cash, 6.8% fixed income, 51.6% growth).

	Shearson	Prudential	PaineWebber	Dreyfus
CASH	5.8%	11.5%	12.6%	6–25%
FIXED INCOME	32.5	39.7	25.0	19–37
GROWTH	61.7	48.8	62.4	61–84

The Dinks

Double income, no kids, late-20s, "moderate" risk takers with investment assets of $182,000 (11.5% cash, 66.5% fixed income, 22% growth).

	Shearson	Prudential	PaineWebber	Dreyfus
CASH	7.5%	12.4%	27.0%	18–34%
FIXED INCOME	33.0	47.2	25.4	33–53
GROWTH	59.5	40.4	47.6	25–41

The Single Parent

Late-30s, one child; "moderate to aggressive" risk taker; investment assets of $95,300 (10.8% cash, 20.7% fixed income, 68.5% growth).

	Shearson	Prudential	PaineWebber	Dreyfus
CASH	3.8%	14.9%	29.0%	39–51%
FIXED INCOME	29.9	36.4	37.4	24–40
GROWTH	66.3	48.7	33.6	18–31

The Young Achiever

Single, mid-20s; "aggressive" risk taker; investment assets of $14,000 (60.7% cash, 39.3% growth).

	Shearson	Prudential	PaineWebber	Dreyfus
CASH	2.7%*	17.2%	45.4%	100%
FIXED INCOME	10.9*	26.4	23.0	0
GROWTH	86.4*	56.4	31.6	0

*Broker would override allocation model to put this investor 45.5% in cash, 54.5% in growth.

In reality, the asset-allocation recommendations individuals get from Shearson and Dreyfus pretty much stick with traditional stock, bond and cash investments. Other firms are willing to highlight more esoteric areas. Tangibles, such as gold, silver and collectibles, rate special treatment in Prudential's and PaineWebber's allocations. PaineWebber also puts special emphasis on illiquid "private" investments, such as outright ownership of real estate and limited partnerships.

International stock and bond funds figure only marginally—if at all—in all the firms' recommendations.

While the brokerage firms' allocation services specify very precise percentages of

INVESTOR INSIGHTS *(continued)*

wealth that the investor should put in each asset class, those firms expect the individual to consult with a broker to see what's really appropriate. Dreyfus, on the other hand, presents a wide range of allocations as "correct" for a given asset class, leaving more room for individuals to interpret the results themselves. "They can operate within that range according to what they feel fits," says Mr. Hoey.

On average, the PaineWebber and Dreyfus models show a more conservative bias than those of other firms by favoring more generous allocations to cash investments. Shearson brokers, however, may increase cash allocations beyond those recommended by the firm's model, to make sure individuals always keep three to six months of living expenses as an emergency cash reserve.

Source: Excerpted from Barbara Donnelly, "Now Wall Street Asks: Stocks, Bonds, or Cash?" *The Wall Street Journal,* November 25, 1991, p. C1.

asset allocation fund
a mutual fund that seeks to reduce volatility by investing in the right assets at the right time; emphasizes diversification and relatively consistent performance rather than spectacular gains.

tolerance, and so forth. Such plans must be formulated for the long run, stress capital preservation, and provide for periodic revision in order to maintain consistency with changing investment goals.

Generally, to decide on the appropriate asset mix, investors must evaluate each asset category relative to: current return, growth potential, safety, liquidity, transactions costs (brokerage fees), and potential tax savings. Many investors use mutual funds (see Chapter 13) as part of their asset allocation activities, in order to diversify within each asset category. As an alternative to building your own portfolio you can buy shares in an **asset allocation fund**—a mutual fund that seeks to reduce volatility by investing in the right assets at the right time. These funds, like all asset allocation schemes, emphasize diversification and perform at a relatively consistent level by passing up the potential for spectacular gains in favor of predictability. Some asset allocation funds such as Vanguard's STAR Fund, USAA's Cornerstone, and The Permanent Portfolio use fixed weightings, whereas others such as Blanchard's Strategic Growth, Fidelity's Asset Manager, and Oppenheimer's Asset Allocation have flexible weights that change within prescribed limits. As a rule, investors with more than about $50,000 to invest and adequate time can justify do-it-yourself asset allocation. Those with between $5,000 and $50,000 and adequate time can use mutual funds to create a workable asset allocation, and those with less than $5,000 and/or limited time may find asset allocation funds most attractive. Major Wall Street firms now offer individual investors asset allocation advice. Their approaches and recommendations may differ, however, as discussed in the Investor Insights box.

Most important, you should recognize that to be effective an asset allocation scheme *must be designed for the long haul*. Develop an asset allocation scheme you can live with for at least 7 to 10 years, and perhaps longer. Once you have it set, stick with it. The key to success involves remaining faithful to your asset allocation. That means fighting the temptation to wander.

PORTFOLIO PLANNING IN ACTION

In this section, we will analyze four portfolios that have been developed to meet four different investment objectives. The principles and ideas that have been developed throughout the book will be applied to these four situations.

In each of the analyses that follow, the objectives and the portfolios are real though the investors' and securities' names are fictitious. When possible, asset allocation weights are given. The specific reasons why a stock and/or bond is included in the portfolio are also given (the portfolios include only stocks and bonds). As a useful exercise the reader might want to consider each situation and develop his or her own recommendations utilizing current investment information.

The four cases have different risk-return profiles because the investors for whom the portfolios are designed have different incomes and lifestyles. Each portfolio is constructed using the traditional approach, with the following exceptions. First, the number of securities in each portfolio is *below the normal number* the traditional portfolio manager would likely recommend. In line with MPT, it is assumed that the proper interindustry diversification can be achieved with the careful selection of 8 to 12 securities in a $100,000 portfolio. A larger portfolio might have slightly more securities, but it would also probably have fewer securities than a traditionalist might recommend. Second, beta is utilized to quantify risk in the all-equity portfolios. Thus these examples blend elements of modern portfolio theory (MPT) with the traditional approach to portfolio management.

Dara Yasakawa: Woman Wonder

At 28 Dara Yasakawa has done well for herself. She has built a $300,000 investment portfolio consisting of investment real estate in Honolulu, Hawaii, with a current market value of $240,000, and $60,000 in short-term investments. Her current asset allocation is therefore 80 percent real estate ($240,000 ÷ $300,000) and 20 percent short-term investments. ($60,000 ÷ $300,000). Ms. Yasakawa is currently employed as the controller of Kamehameha Management, a real estate management firm in Honolulu. She is a CPA, and her income from salary and property rentals is $65,000 per year, putting her in a 35 percent marginal income tax bracket (federal and Hawaii state income tax combined). Ms. Yasakawa is single, and her only debts are secured by her properties.

Dara Yasakawa has decided to diversify her portfolio. Most of her net worth consists of rental condominiums located in the Waikiki area of Honolulu. Clearly, diversification is needed to reduce her risk exposure and to increase her overall investment return. The Hawaii real estate market is somewhat unpredictable, and Ms. Yasakawa wishes to lessen her risk exposure in that market. She asked her investment advisor, Marjorie Wong, to help her diversify into common stock. Marjorie recommended selling one of Dara's properties for $60,000 and selling $15,000 in short-term securities to obtain $75,000 to invest in common stock. The resulting asset allocation would be 60 percent real estate ($180,000 ÷ $300,000), 25 percent common stock ($75,000 ÷ $300,000), and 15 percent short-term securities

($45,000 ÷ $300,000). Because of her relatively young age and her strong future earning capacity, Ms. Yasakawa can bear the risks of a speculative investment program. Her portfolio of stocks will emphasize issues that have a strong price appreciation potential.

Ms. Yasakawa's common stock portfolio is presented in Table 16.8. It consists of eight stocks, all of which have above-average risk-return potential. The betas of the issues range from 1.13 to 2.31; the portfolio's beta (calculated using Equation 16.2) is approximately 1.59, indicating an above-average risk exposure. The portfolio is diversified across industry lines, with a fairly wide mix of securities. All are selected for their above-average price appreciation potential. Altuna Airlines, an inter-island carrier in Hawaii, was chosen because of the expected increase in the number of visitors to Hawaii. Betta Computer is a fast-growing personal computer manufacturer. Easy Work, Inc., is a growing retailer that services the do-it-yourself home improvement market. Gomez Industries is a rapidly expanding glass manufacturer and photo processor. Hercules is a growing brewer. Jama Motor, based in Japan, provides a measure of international diversification for the portfolio. Karl Lewis Enterprises is an expanding fast-food operator based in California. Ranch Petroleum is a small oil company with refining and oil-production interests.

Most of the securities Ms. Wong selected for Ms. Yasakawa are not "household names." Rather, they are firms with exciting growth potential. Given the portfolio's beta, Dara's holdings should fluctuate in value at a rate approximately 1.6 times greater than the stock market as a whole. The dividend yield on the portfolio is a relatively low 0.6 percent. Most of the return Ms. Yasakawa anticipates from this portfolio is in the form of price appreciation. She plans to hold the stocks for at least one to two years in order to realize this anticipated appreciation. Given Ms. Yasakawa's high marginal income tax bracket, it seems preferable for her to defer taxes and earn returns in the form of capital gains.

TABLE 16.8 Dara Yasakawa's Common Stock Portfolio

OBJECTIVE: SPECULATIVE GROWTH (HIGH-RISK, HIGH-RETURN POTENTIAL)

Number of Shares	Company	Dividend per Share	Dividend Income	Price per Share	Total Cost (including commission)	Beta	Dividend Yield
1,200	Altuna Airlines	$__	$__	$ 7	$ 8,480	1.75	__%
300	Betta Computer	—	—	30	9,090	1.87	—
400	Easy Work, Inc.	—	—	25	10,090	1.59	—
300	Gomez Industries	0.36	108	30	9,090	1.19	1.2
300	Hercules Brewing	0.80	240	32	9,700	1.27	2.5
300	Jama Motor ADR	0.35	105	33	10,000	1.13	1.1
500	Karl Lewis Enterprises	—	—	20	10,100	1.79	—
1,300	Ranch Petroleum	—	—	6	7,880	2.31	—
	Total		$453		$74,430		0.6%

Portfolio beta = 1.59

Bob and Gail Weiss: Lottery Winners

Bob Weiss, a professor of political science at the University of West Bay City in Michigan, and his wife, Gail, are lucky people. After buying a $1 Michigan State Lottery ticket, Professor Weiss won the $275,000 prize. After paying income taxes on the prize and after spending a small amount for personal needs, Bob and Gail had $210,000 remaining. Because of their philosophy of saving any windfalls and not spending accumulated capital on day-to-day living expenses, they chose to invest these funds (in contrast with many lottery winners, who simply blow their winnings on fast living).

The Weisses have two young children. Bob Weiss is 37 years of age and has a secure teaching position. His salary is approximately $50,000 per year. In addition, he earns approximately $15,000 per year from his book-publishing royalties and from several other small sources. Professor Weiss's tax bracket (federal and state) is approximately 30 percent. His life insurance protection of approximately $75,000 is provided by the university. Bob's wife, Gail, is a librarian. She currently is at home with the children and is not expected to be a source of steady income for another several years. The Weiss family owns (free and clear) their home in the Banks area of Bay City. In addition, they have about $40,000 in a money market mutual fund. Therefore their asset allocation prior to the lottery windfall was 100 percent money funds ($40,000 ÷ $40,000). They have no outstanding debts.

Professor Weiss asked his investment advisor, Gene Bowles, to develop an investment portfolio for them. Together, they decided on the following strategy. First, the professor and his wife tend to be somewhat risk-averse; that is, they do not wish to bear inordinate amounts of risk of loss. In addition, the Weisses indicated that they would welcome some increase in spendable income. Given these facts, Mr. Bowles suggested the portfolio presented in Table 16.9. With this portfolio

TABLE 16.9 Bob and Gail Weiss's Common Stock Portfolio

OBJECTIVE: LONG-TERM GROWTH (AVERAGE RISK, MODERATE DIVIDENDS)							
Number of Shares	Company	Dividend per Share	Dividend Income	Price per Share	Total Cost (including commission)	Beta	Dividend Yield
1,000	Bancorp West, Inc.	$1.20	$ 1,200	$22	$ 22,200	.86	5.4%
600	BST, Inc.	2.80	1,680	40	24,200	1.00	6.9
1,000	Florida Southcoast Banks	1.20	1,200	23	23,200	.84	5.2
1,000	Kings	1.60	1,600	25	25,300	.88	6.3
500	Light Newspapers	0.92	460	46	23,200	1.12	2.0
600	Miller Foods	1.88	1,128	37	22,400	1.07	5.0
800	State Oil of California	1.00	800	27	21,800	1.30	3.7
600	Vornox	2.28	1,368	40	24,200	1.04	5.7
600	Woodstock	1.30	780	36	21,800	1.32	3.6
	Total		$10,216		$208,300		4.9%

Portfolio beta = 1.04

their asset allocation would become about 84 percent common stock ($210,000 ÷ $250,000) and 16 percent money funds ($40,000 ÷ $250,000). The emphasis in the portfolio is long-term growth at an average risk level, with a moderate dividend return. The portfolio consists of nine issues, which appears to be sufficient diversification. The portfolio's beta is 1.04, indicating a level of nondiversifiable risk that approximately equals that of the stock market as a whole. The portfolio's dividend yield is about 4.9 percent, which approximates the average dividend return for the entire stock market. The betas of individual securities in the portfolio vary somewhat. However, the portfolio's overall risk is moderate.

The Weiss portfolio consists of stocks from a wide range of American business. All the companies had above-average growth potential, and none was engaged in high-risk businesses that could face technological obsolescence or heavy foreign competition. Two banking stocks were selected, Bancorp West, Inc., and Florida Southcoast Banks. The former is a well-managed bank holding company that owns the largest bank in California. The latter is a growing bank holding company located on the south coast of Florida. Both regions are experiencing rapid population and economic growth. BST, Inc., appears to be well positioned in the growing communications industry. Kings is a food processor with a solid future. Light Newspapers is a large chain with many Sunbelt papers. Miller Foods is expanding as well, helped by the 1992 acquisition of Denton Companies, a superbly managed supermarket chain. The portfolio has two natural resource stocks, State Oil and Woodstock. These companies are well positioned in their respective industries. Vornox is a major drug firm that should benefit from the aging demographic mix of America. All the stocks in the Weisses' portfolio are securities of well-managed companies. With this portfolio, the Weisses will have potential price appreciation coupled with a steady dividend income.

Julio and Gina Vitello: Retirees

Having just sold their family business and liquidated their real estate investment property, the Vitellos are eager to begin their retirement. At age 60, both have worked hard for 35 years building the successful business they recently sold. In addition, they had made some successful real estate investments over the years. The sale of their business and real estate holdings netted them $600,000 after taxes. They wish to invest these funds and have asked their investment advisor, Jane Tuttle, to develop a portfolio for them. The relevant financial information about the Vitellos is as follows: They own their home free and clear and have a $300,000 bond portfolio that yields yearly income of $30,000. In addition, they have $100,000 in short-term securities which they wish to hold as a ready cash reserve. Their most recent asset allocation is therefore 60 percent business and real estate investments ($600,000 ÷ $1,000,000), 30 percent bonds ($300,000 ÷ $1,000,000), and 10 percent short-term securities ($100,000 ÷ $1,000,000). Mr. Vitello has a $200,000 whole life insurance policy on his life, with Mrs. Vitello the designated beneficiary.

Now that they are retired, neither of the Vitellos plans to seek employment. They do have a small pension plan that will begin paying an income of $4,000 per year in five years. However, their main source of income will be their investment portfolio. During their last few working years, their combined yearly income was approximately $90,000. Their standard of living is rather high, and they do not wish to significantly change their lifestyle. They do not plan to spend any of their investment capital on living expenses, since they wish to keep their estate intact for their two children. Thus the Vitellos' basic investment objective is current income with some capital appreciation potential. The Vitellos do not wish to reinvest in real estate, but rather have asked Ms. Tuttle to develop a $600,000 securities portfolio for them. (They will leave their $300,000 bond portfolio and $100,000 in short-term securities undisturbed.) Their resulting asset allocation would shift to 60 percent common stock, 30 percent bonds, and 10 percent short-term securities.

The portfolio developed for the Vitellos is shown in Table 16.10. It contains nine stocks with approximately $65,000 invested in each issue. The emphasis is on quality, with low-risk, high-yield issues, and diversification. The portfolio's beta is approximately .80—a risk level that is below that of the general stock market. It is expected that a large portion of the portfolio's total return (dividends plus price appreciation) will be in the form of dividend income. The portfolio has a current dividend yield of approximately 8.7 percent, an above-average dividend yield. Dividend income totals over $52,000, which added to the bond income and the short-term securities' interest will provide the Vitellos with a gross income of about $90,000. The Vitellos' after-tax income will equal their working years' income; thus they will not have to alter their lifestyle.

Analyzing the individual issues in the Vitellos' portfolio, we can see that four public utility stocks are included. Utility stocks are often suitable for low-risk, current-income–oriented portfolios. High-quality electric and natural gas concerns tend to have moderate growth in earnings and dividends. The four issues in the

TABLE 16.10 Julio and Gina Vitello's Common Stock Portfolio

OBJECTIVE: CURRENT INCOME (LOW-RISK, HIGH-YIELD)

Number of Shares	Company	Dividend per Share	Dividend Income	Price per Share	Total Cost (Including Commission)	Beta	Dividend Yield
3,000	Alaska Bancorp, Inc.	$1.20	$ 3,600	$22	$ 66,600	.86	5.4%
2,000	Dallas National Corporation	2.40	4,800	30	60,600	.81	7.9
2,500	Energon	3.00	7,500	27	68,100	1.01	11.0
2,000	Findly Power and Light	3.36	6,720	32	64,600	.63	10.4
2,000	Geoco	2.80	5,600	35	70,700	1.13	7.9
2,500	Gulf Gas and Electric	3.00	7,500	28	70,700	.53	10.6
4,000	Public Power Company	1.76	7,040	16	64,600	.72	10.9
2,500	Smith, Roberts and Company	1.36	3,400	27	68,100	.92	5.0
3,000	Southwest Utilities	2.04	6,120	21	63,600	.60	9.6
	Total		$52,280		$597,600		8.7%

Portfolio beta = .80

portfolio, Findly Power and Light, Gulf Gas and Electric, Public Power Company, and Southwest Utilities, have growing service areas and records of profit and dividend increases. The stocks of two very large American companies, Energon and Smith, Roberts and Company, are included in the portfolio. Energon is a large U.S. energy company that offers a high dividend yield. Smith, Roberts is one of the largest retailers, and the company is now diversifying into financial services. Two bank holding company stocks were also selected, Alaska Bancorp and Dallas National. Alaska Bancorp offers a top-quality vehicle to participate in Alaska's growth. Dallas National was selected for its above-average dividend yield and because the firm is well positioned in the Dallas market. Additionally, the company has raised its dividend several times in recent years, and future dividend increases are expected. Geoco is a large company with chemical and other diversified operations. All the issues in the Vitello's portfolio are well-known, relatively large corporations. Stability, low risk, and a relatively high dividend yield with some potential for increase characterize the stocks in this portfolio.

Lucille Hatch: Widow

Most retirees are less fortunate than the Vitellos in the preceding example; most have less money to invest. Lucille Hatch, age 70, was recently widowed. Between the estate of her late husband, her personal assets, and their jointly owned assets, Lucille has approximately $350,000 in liquid assets, all of it in savings and money market accounts (short-term investments). Her current asset allocation is therefore 100 percent short-term investments ($350,000 ÷ $350,000). Lucille owns her home free and clear. Other than the interest on her savings, her income consists of $600 per month from Social Security. Unfortunately, her husband's employer did not have a pension plan. She has turned to her investment advisor, Charles Puckett, to discuss strategy and to develop an investment policy.

Between Social Security and interest earned on her short-term investments, Mrs. Hatch's current income is approximately $35,000 annually. She wishes to increase that income, if possible, while only minimally raising her risk exposure. Mr. Puckett recommended the investment portfolio presented in Table 16.11. The portfolio's objective is to maximize current income while keeping risk at a low level. As seen, all the money was invested in fixed-income securities, with approximately $296,000 going to high-quality corporate bonds and the balance (of $54,000) retained in short-term investments in order to provide a substantial contingency reserve. The resulting asset allocation is about 85 percent bonds ($296,000 ÷ $350,000) and 15 percent short-term investments ($54,000 ÷ $350,000). By investing in the bond portfolio, Mrs. Hatch's yearly income will rise from approximately $35,000 to about $47,800 ($7,200 Social Security, $4,000 earnings on short-term investments, and $36,600 bond interest). This puts Mrs. Hatch in a 30 percent marginal tax bracket (federal and state tax combined). Taxable corporate bonds were recommended over tax-free municipal bonds because her after-tax rate of return would be greater with the former.

TABLE 16.11 Lucille Hatch's Bond Portfolio

OBJECTIVE: MAXIMIZE CURRENT INCOME (MINIMAL RISK)

Par Value	Issue	Standard & Poor's Bond Rating	Interest Income	Price	Total Cost	Yield to Maturity	Current Yield
$50,000	Boise Northern 12⅞% due 2014	A	$ 6,437.50	100	$ 50,000	12.875%	12.875%
50,000	Dalston Company 11½% due 1998	A	5,750.00	98	49,000	11.900	11.700
50,000	Maryland-Pacific 10.70% due 1996	A	5,350.00	97	48,500	11.600	11.000
50,000	Pacific Utilities 12⅞% due 2022	AA	6,437.50	100	50,000	12.875	12.875
50,000	Trans-States Telephone 12.70% due 2028	A	6,350.00	97	48,500	13.200	13.100
50,000	Urban Life 12½% due 1999	AA	6,250.00	100	50,000	12.500	12.500
	Total		$36,575.00		$296,000	12.500%	12.400%

Turning to the portfolio, we see that there are six corporate bond issues that cost about $50,000 each. Each issuer is a high-quality company with a very low risk of default. Mrs. Hatch's portfolio is diversified in several ways. First, it contains a mix of industrial, utility, railroad, and financial issues. The two utility bond issues are Pacific Utilities and Trans-States Telephone. Both companies are quite large and financially secure. The two industrial concerns, Dalston and Maryland-Pacific, are very large as well. Boise Northern is a financially solid railroad, and Urban Life is a large, secure insurance company. A second added measure of diversification is attained by staggering the bonds' maturities. They mature in six different years: 1996, 1998, 1999, 2014, 2022, and 2028. The shorter-term bonds will provide ready cash when they mature, and they generally will fluctuate less in price than the longer-term ones. The portfolio has been diversified to keep the risk of loss very low. By switching funds out of her short-term investments into bonds, Mrs. Hatch was able to increase her current income substantially while experiencing only a minimal increase in risk.

SUMMARY

1. A portfolio is a collection of investment vehicles assembled to achieve a common investment goal. It involves a tradeoff between risk and return, potential price appreciation and current income, and varying risk levels in the portfolio. The return on a portfolio is calculated as a weighted average of the returns of the assets from which it is formed. The standard deviation of a portfolio's returns is found by applying the same formula that is used to find the standard deviation of a single asset.

2. Correlation is a statistic used to measure the relationship, if any, between the returns on assets. To diversify, it is best to add assets with negatively correlated returns. In general, the less positive and more negative the correlation between asset returns, the more effectively a portfolio can be diversified in order to reduce its risk. Through diversification the risk (standard deviation) of a portfolio can be reduced below the risk of the least risky asset (and sometimes to zero); however, the return of the resulting portfolio will be no lower than the smallest return of its component assets.

3. Under the traditional approach, portfolios are constructed by combining a large number of securities issued by companies from a broad cross-section of industries. Modern portfolio theory (MPT) uses statistical diversification to develop efficient portfolios. Theoretically, to determine the optimal portfolio, MPT finds the efficient frontier and couples it with an investor's utility function or risk-indifference curves. In practice, portfolio betas can be used to develop efficient portfolios consistent with the investor's risk-return preferences. Generally investors use elements of both the traditional approach and MPT to create portfolios.

4. To build a portfolio, the investor should consider characteristics such as level and stability of income, family factors, net worth, experience and age, and disposition toward risk. After an investor has developed a personal financial profile, he or she should specify objectives and plan and build a portfolio consistent with them. Commonly considered portfolio objectives include: current income, capital preservation, capital growth, tax considerations, and level of risk.

5. Asset allocation involves dividing one's portfolio into various asset classes such as U.S. stocks, U.S. bonds, foreign securities, short-term securities, and other vehicles in order to preserve capital. Similar to diversification, the objective of asset allocation is to protect against negative developments while taking advantage of positive developments. The basic approaches to asset allocation involve the use of fixed weightings, flexible weightings, or tactical asset allocation—a sophisticated approach that uses futures contracts. Asset allocation can be achieved on a do-it-yourself basis, with the use of mutual funds, or by merely buying shares in an asset allocation fund.

6. An investor's objectives determine the asset allocations and risk-return profile reflected in his or her portfolio. A single investor who wants to build wealth quickly will tend to allocate funds to more risky assets that have high growth potential; a retired couple that needs income to meet their living expenses will allocate funds to conservative, low-risk investment vehicles that provide periodic income in the form of dividends and/or interest. The asset classes, their weightings, and the specific vehicles included in an investor's portfolio should be consistent with his or her personal financial and family characteristics and investment and portfolio objectives.

QUESTIONS

1. What is a portfolio? What is an efficient portfolio, and what role should such a portfolio play in investing?

2. How can the return and standard deviation of a portfolio be determined? Compare the standard deviation calculation to that used for a single asset.

3. What is correlation, and why is it important with respect to asset returns? Describe the characteristics of returns that are (a) positively correlated, (b) negatively correlated, (c) and uncorrelated. Define and differentiate between perfect positive and perfect negative correlation.

4. What is diversification? How does the diversification of risk in the asset selection process allow the investor to combine risky assets so that the risk of the portfolio is less than that of the individual assets it contains?

5. Discuss how the amount of correlation between asset returns affects the risk and return behavior of the resulting portfolio. Describe the potential range of risk and return when the correlation between two assets is (a) perfectly positive, (b) uncorrelated, and (c) perfectly negative.

6. Describe the traditional approach to portfolio management. Give three reasons why traditional portfolio managers like to invest in well-established companies. Explain each reason.

7. What is modern portfolio theory (MPT)? What is the feasible or attainable set of all possible portfolios? How is it derived for a given group of investment vehicles?

8. What is the efficient frontier? How does it relate to the feasible or attainable set of all possible portfolios? How can it be used with an investor's utility function or risk-indifference curves to find the optimal portfolio?

9. Define and differentiate between the diversifiable, nondiversifiable, and total risk of a portfolio. Which is considered the relevant risk? How is it measured?

10. Define beta. How can you find the beta of a portfolio when you know the betas for each of the assets included within it?

11. What does the coefficient of determination (R^2) for the regression equation used to derive a beta coefficient indicate? Would this statistic indicate that beta is more useful in explaining the return fluctuations of individual assets or of portfolios?

12. Are there any particular techniques an investor can use as part of a portfolio strategy? Explain how traditional and modern portfolio approaches can be reconciled.

13. What role, if any, do an investor's personal characteristics play in determining portfolio policy? Explain.

14. What role do an investor's portfolio objectives play in building a portfolio?

15. What is an asset allocation scheme? How does it differ from diversification? What role does asset allocation play in building an investment portfolio?

16. Briefly describe the three approaches to asset allocation: (a) fixed weightings, (b) flexible weightings, and (c) tactical asset allocation.

17. Describe the procedures used to apply asset allocation. What role could an asset allocation fund play in this process?

18. Compare and contrast the expected portfolios of (a) a retired investor in need of income, (b) a high-income, financially secure investor, and (c) a young investor with a secure job and no dependents.

PROBLEMS

1. Assume you are considering a portfolio containing two assets, L and M. Asset L will represent 40 percent of the dollar value of the portfolio and asset M will account for the other 60 percent. The expected returns over the next six years, 1994–1999, for each of these assets, are summarized in the following table.

	Expected Return (%)	
Year	Asset L	Asset M
1994	14	20
1995	14	18
1996	16	16
1997	17	14
1998	17	12
1999	19	10

a. Calculate the portfolio return, r_p, for *each* of the six years.
b. Calculate the average portfolio return, $\bar{r}_p$, over the six-year period.
c. Calculate the standard deviation of expected portfolio returns, s_p, over the six-year period.
d. How would you characterize the correlation of returns of the two assets L and M?
e. Discuss any benefits of diversification achieved through creation of the portfolio.

2. You have been given the following return data on three assets—F, G, and H—over the period 1994–1997:

	Expected return (%)		
Year	Asset F	Asset G	Asset H
1994	16	17	14
1995	17	16	15
1996	18	15	16
1997	19	14	17

Using these assets you have isolated three investment alternatives:

Alternative	Investment
1	100% of asset F
2	50% of asset F and 50% of asset G
3	50% of asset F and 50% of asset H

a. Calculate the portfolio return over the four-year period for each of the three alternatives.
b. Calculate the standard deviation of returns over the four-year period for each of the three alternatives.

    c. Based on your findings above, which of the three investment alternatives would you recommend? Why?

3.   You have been asked for your advice in selecting a portfolio of assets and have been supplied with the following data:

Year	Expected Return (%)		
	Asset A	Asset B	Asset C
1994	12	16	12
1995	14	14	14
1996	16	12	16

You have been told that you can create two portfolios—one consisting of assets A and B and the other consisting of assets A and C—by investing equal proportions (i.e., 50 percent) in each of the two component assets.

    a. What is the average return, $\bar{r}$, for each asset over the three-year period?
    b. What is the standard deviation, s, for each asset's return?
    c. What is the average return, $\bar{r}_p$, for each of the two portfolios?
    d. How would you characterize the correlations of returns of the two assets making up each of the two portfolios identified in c?
    e. What is the standard deviation, s_p, for each portfolio?
    f. Which portfolio do you recommend? Why?

4.   Assume you wish to evaluate the risk and return behaviors associated with various combinations of assets V and W under three assumed degrees of correlation—perfect positive, uncorrelated, and perfect negative. The following average return and risk values were calculated for each of the assets.

Asset	Average Return, $\bar{r}$ (%)	Risk (Standard Deviation), s (%)
V	8	5
W	13	10

    a. If the returns of assets V and W are *perfectly positively correlated* (correlation coefficient = +1), describe the *range* of (1) return and (2) risk associated with all possible portfolio combinations.
    b. If the returns of assets V and W are *uncorrelated* (correlation coefficient = 0), describe the *approximate range* of (1) return and (2) risk associated with all possible portfolio combinations.
    c. If the returns of assets V and W are *perfectly negatively correlated* (correlation coefficient = −1), describe the *range* of (1) return and (2) risk associated with all possible portfolio combinations.

5.   Portfolios A through J listed in the following table along with their returns (r_p) and risk (measured by the standard deviation, s_p) represent all currently available portfolios in the feasible or attainable set:

Portfolio	Return (r_p)	Risk (s_p)
A	9%	8%
B	3	3
C	14	10
D	12	14
E	7	11
F	11	6
G	10	12
H	16	16
I	5	7
J	8	4

a. Plot the feasible or attainable set represented by the data above on a set of portfolio risk, s_p (x-axis)–portfolio return, r_p (y-axis) axes.

b. Draw the efficient frontier on the graph in (a).

c. Which portfolios lie on the efficient frontier? Why do these portfolios dominate all others in the feasible or attainable set?

d. How would an investor's utility function or risk-indifference curves be used with the efficient frontier to find the optimal portfolio?

6. David Finney randomly selected securities from all those listed on the New York Stock Exchange for his portfolio. He began with one security and added securities one by one until a total of 20 securities were held in the portfolio. After each security was added, David calculated the portfolio standard deviation, s_p. The calculated values are given below:

Number of Securities	Portfolio Risk, s_p (%)	Number of Securities	Portfolio Risk, s_p (%)
1	14.50	11	7.00
2	13.30	12	6.80
3	12.20	13	6.70
4	11.20	14	6.65
5	10.30	15	6.60
6	9.50	16	6.56
7	8.80	17	6.52
8	8.20	18	6.50
9	7.70	19	6.48
10	7.30	20	6.47

a. On a set of number of securities in portfolio (x-axis)–portfolio risk, s_p (y-axis) axes, plot the portfolio risk data given in the preceding table.

b. Divide the total portfolio risk in the graph into its *nondiversifiable* and *diversifiable* risk components and label each of these on the graph.

c. Describe which of the two risk components is the *relevant risk* and explain why it is relevant. How much of this risk exists in David Finney's portfolio?

7. If portfolio A has a beta of +1.5 and portfolio Z has a beta of −1.5, what do the two values indicate? If the return on the market rises by 20 percent, what impact, if any, would this have on the return from portfolios A and Z? Explain.

8. Stock A has a beta of 0.80, stock B has a beta of 1.40, and stock C has a beta of −0.30.
   a. Rank these stocks from the most risky to the least risky.
   b. If the return on the market portfolio increases by 12 percent, what change in the return for each of the stocks would you expect?
   c. If the return on the market portfolio declines by 5 percent, what change in the return for each of the stocks would you expect?
   d. If you felt the stock market was just ready to experience a significant decline, which stock would you likely add to your portfolio? Why?
   e. If you anticipated a major stock market rally, which stock would you add to your portfolio? Why?

9. Rose Berry is attempting to evaluate two possible portfolios—both consisting of the same five assets but held in different proportions. She is particularly interested in using beta to compare the risk of the portfolios and in this regard has gathered the following data.

		Portfolio Weights (%)	
Asset	Asset Beta	Portfolio A	Portfolio B
1	1.30	10	30
2	.70	30	10
3	1.25	10	20
4	1.10	10	20
5	.90	40	20
	Total	100	100

   a. Calculate the betas for portfolios A and B.
   b. Compare the risk of each portfolio to the market as well as to each other. Which portfolio is more risky?

CFA QUESTION (**This question is from the 1990 Level I Exam.**)

 You are being interviewed for a junior portfolio manager's job at Progressive Counselors, Inc., and are eager to demonstrate your grasp of portfolio management basics. Portfolio management is a process which involves *four* key steps that are applicable in all investment management situations. List these *four* key steps.

(See Appendix C for Guideline Answer to this question.)

CASE PROBLEMS

16.1 Traditional versus Modern Portfolio Theory: Who's Right?

Walt Davies and Shane O'Brien are district managers for Lee, Inc. Over the years as they moved through the firm's sales organization they became, and still remain, close friends. Walt, who is 33 years old, currently lives in Newark, New Jersey; Shane, who is 35, lives in Houston, Texas. Recently at the national sales meeting they were discussing various company matters, as well as bringing each other up to date on their families, when the subject of investments came up. Each of them had always been fascinated by the stock market and now that they had achieved some degree of financial success, they had begun actively investing. As they discussed their investments, Walt indicated that he felt the only way an individual who did not have hundreds of thousands of dollars can invest safely is to buy mutual fund shares. He emphasized that in order to be safe, a person needs to hold a broadly diversified portfolio and that only those with a lot of money and time can achieve the needed diversification that can be readily obtained by purchasing mutual fund shares.

Shane totally disagreed. He said, "Diversification! Who needs it?" He felt that what you must do is to look carefully at stocks possessing desired risk-return characteristics and then invest all your money in that one best stock. Walt told him he was crazy. He said, "There is no way to conveniently measure risk—you're just gambling." Shane disagreed. He explained how his stockbroker had acquainted him with beta, which is a measure of risk. Shane said that the higher the beta, the more risky the stock, and therefore the higher its return. By looking up the betas for potential stock investments in his broker's beta book, he can pick stocks having an acceptable risk level for him. Shane explained that with beta one does not need to diversify; one merely needs to be willing to accept the risk reflected by beta and then hope for the best. The conversation continued, with Walt indicating that although he knew nothing about beta, he didn't believe you could safely invest in a single stock. Shane continued to argue that his broker had explained to him that betas can be calculated not just for a single stock, but also for a portfolio of stocks such as a mutual fund. He said, "What's the difference between a stock with a beta, of say, 1.20 and a mutual fund with a beta of 1.20? They both have the same risk and should therefore provide similar returns."

As Walt and Shane continued to discuss their differing opinions relative to investment strategy, they began to get angry with each other. Neither was able to convince the other that he was right. The level of their voices now raised, they attracted the attention of the company vice-president of finance, Elmer Green, who was standing nearby. He came over and indicated he had overheard their argument about investments and thought that, given his expertise on financial matters, he might be able to resolve their disagreement. He asked them to explain the crux of their disagreement, and each reviewed his own viewpoint. After hearing their views, Elmer responded: "I have some good news and some bad news for each of you. There is some validity to what each of you says, but there also are some errors in each of your explanations. Walt tends to support the traditional approach to portfolio management; Shane's views are more supportive of modern portfolio theory." Just then, the company president interrupted them, needing to talk to Elmer immediately. Elmer apologized for having to leave and made an arrangement to continue their discussion later that evening.

Questions

1. Analyze Walt's argument and explain to him why a mutual fund investment may be over-diversified. Also explain why one does not necessarily have to have hundreds of thousands of dollars in order to diversify adequately.
2. Analyze Shane's argument and explain the major error in his logic relative to the use of beta as a substitute for diversification. Explain the key assumption underlying the use of beta as a risk measure.
3. Briefly describe the traditional approach to portfolio management and relate it to the approaches supported by Walt and Shane.
4. Briefly describe modern portfolio theory (MPT) and relate it to the approaches supported by Walt and Shane. Be sure to mention diversifiable, nondiversifiable, and total risk along with the role of beta.
5. Explain how the traditional approach and modern portfolio theory can be blended into an approach to portfolio management that might prove useful to the individual investor. Relate this to reconciling Walt's and Shane's differing points of view.

16.2 Susan Lussier's Inherited Portfolio: Does It Meet Her Needs?

Susan Lussier is a 35-year-old divorcee currently employed as a tax attorney for a major oil and gas exploration company. She has no children and earns nearly $90,000 per year from her salary as well as through participation in the company's drilling activities. Divorced only one year, Susan has found being single quite exciting. An expert on oil and gas taxation, Susan does not concern herself with job security—she is content with her income and finds it adequate to allow her to buy and do whatever she wishes. Her current philosophy is to live each day to its fullest, not concerning herself with retirement, which is too far in the future to require her current attention.

A month ago Susan's only surviving parent, her father, was killed in a sailing accident. He had retired in La Jolla, California, two years earlier and had spent most of his time sailing. Prior to retirement he owned a children's clothing manufacturing firm in South Carolina, which he sold. He invested the proceeds in a security portfolio that provided him with

CASE 16.2 Susan Lussier's Inherited Securities Portfolio

BONDS

Par Value	Issue	S&P Rating	Interest Income	Price	Total Cost	Current Yield
$40,000	Delta Power and Light 10⅛% due 2011	AA	$4,050	$ 98	$39,200	10.33%
30,000	Mountain Water 9¾% due 2003	A	2,925	102	30,600	9.56
50,000	California Gas 9½% due 1998	AAA	4,750	97	48,500	9.79
20,000	Trans-Pacific Gas 10% due 2009	AAA	2,000	99	19,800	10.10
20,000	Public Service 9⅞% due 1999	AA	1,975	100	20,000	9.88

COMMON STOCKS

Number of Shares	Company	Dividend per Share	Dividend Income	Price per Share	Total Cost	Beta	Dividend Yield
2,000	International Supply	$2.40	$4,800	$22	$44,900	.97	10.91%
3,000	Black Motor	1.50	4,500	17	52,000	.85	8.82

MUTUAL FUNDS

Number of Shares	Issue	Dividend per Share	Dividend Income	Price per Share	Total Cost	Beta	Dividend Yield
2,000	International Capital Income A Fund	$ .80	$ 1,600	$10	$ 20,000	1.02	8.00%
1,000	Grimner Special Income Fund	2.00	2,000	15	15,000	1.10	7.50
4,000	Ellis Diversified Income Fund	1.20	4,800	12	48,000	.90	10.00
	Total annual income:		$33,400	Portfolio value:	$338,000	Portfolio current yield:	9.88%

retirement income of over $30,000 per year. In his will, which incidentally had been drafted by Susan a number of years earlier, he left his entire estate to her. The estate had been structured in such a way that, in addition to a few family heirlooms, Susan received a security portfolio having a market value of nearly $350,000 and about $10,000 in cash. The portfolio contained 10 securities—5 bonds, 2 common stocks, and 3 mutual funds. A table listing the securities and key characteristics is given on page 697. The two common stocks were issued by large, mature, well-known firms that had exhibited continuing patterns of dividend payment over the past five years. The stocks offered only moderate growth potential—probably no more than 2 to 3 percent appreciation per year. The three mutual funds in the portfolio were income funds invested in diversified portfolios of income-oriented stocks and bonds. They provided stable streams of dividend income but little opportunity for capital appreciation.

Now that Susan owns the portfolio, she wishes to determine whether it is suitable for her situation. She realizes that the high level of income provided by the portfolio will be taxed at a rate (federal plus state) in excess of 35 percent. Since she does not currently need it, Susan plans to invest the after-tax income in tax-deferred real estate, oil and gas partnerships, and/or in common stocks offering high capital gain potential. She clearly needs to shelter taxable income. (Susan is already paying out a sizable portion of her current income in taxes.) She feels fortunate to have received the portfolio and wants to make certain that it provides her the maximum benefits, given her financial situation. The $10,000 cash left to her will be especially useful in paying broker's commissions associated with making portfolio adjustments.

Questions

1. Briefly assess Susan's financial situation, and develop a portfolio objective for her that's consistent with her needs.
2. Evaluate the portfolio left to Susan by her father. Assess its apparent objective, and evaluate how well it may be doing in fulfilling this objective. Use the total cost values to describe the asset allocation scheme reflected in the portfolio. Comment on the risk, return, and tax impact of this portfolio.
3. If Susan decided to invest in a security portfolio consistent with her needs (indicated in response to question 1), describe the nature and mix, if any, of securities you would recommend she purchase. What asset allocation scheme would result from your recommendation? Discuss the risk, return, and tax implications of such a portfolio.
4. Compare the nature of the security portfolio inherited by Susan (from the response to question 2) with what you believe would be an appropriate security portfolio for her (from the response to question 3).
5. What recommendations would you give Susan about the inherited portfolio? Explain the steps she should take to adjust the portfolio to her needs.

17 Portfolio Management and Control

After studying this chapter, you should be able to:

1. Discuss sources of needed data and common indexes used to evaluate the performance of investments.

2. Describe the techniques used to measure the performance of individual investment vehicles, and compare it to investment goals.

3. Understand the techniques used to measure current income, capital gains, and total portfolio return relative to the amount of money invested in a portfolio.

4. Use the Sharpe, Treynor, and Jensen measures to compare a portfolio's return with a risk-adjusted, market-adjusted rate of return, and discuss portfolio revision.

5. Describe the role of formula plans and the logic of dollar cost averaging, constant dollar plans, constant ratio plans, and variable ratio plans.

6. Explain the role of limit and stop-loss orders in investment timing, the warehousing of liquidity, and the key factors in timing investment sales in order to achieve maximum benefits.

Imagine that one of your most important personal goals is to accumulate savings of $15,000 three years from now in order to have enough money to purchase your first home. Based on your projections, the desired home will cost $100,000, and the $15,000 will be sufficient to make a 10 percent down payment and pay the associated closing costs. Your calculations indicate that this goal can be achieved by investing existing savings plus an additional $200 per month over the next three years in a vehicle earning 12 percent per year. Projections of your earnings over the three-year period indicate that you should just be able to set aside the needed $200 per month. Consultation with an investment advisor, Cliff Orbit, leads you to believe that under his management the 12 percent return can be achieved.

It seems simple: Give Cliff your existing savings, send him $200 each month over the next 36 months, and at the end of that period you will have the $15,000 needed to purchase the home. Of course, there are many uncertainties involved in this decision. For example, What if your income proves inadequate to set aside $200 each month? What if Cliff fails to earn the needed 12 percent annual return? What if the desired house costs more than $100,000 in three years? Clearly you must do more than simply devise what appears to be a feasible plan for achieving a future goal. By periodically assessing progress toward the goal, you can improve the chances that it will be met. For example, had you found that your earnings were not adequate to permit the $200 per month investment, you might have found a new, higher-paying job. Or if the required 12 percent return was not being earned on your funds, you might have sought a new investment advisor. As *actual* outcomes occur, one must compare them to the *planned* outcomes in order to make any necessary alterations in one's plans. If such changes do not permit goal achievement, the goal and/or its timing may have to be adjusted.

The final, and most important, aspect of the personal investment process involves continuously managing and controlling the portfolio as needed in order to keep moving toward the achievement of financial goals. This process involves assessing actual performance, comparing it to planned performance, revising and making needed adjustments, and timing these adjustments to achieve maximum benefit. Let us see how this is done.

EVALUATING THE PERFORMANCE OF INDIVIDUAL INVESTMENTS

Investment vehicles are typically selected for a portfolio on the basis of expected returns, associated risks, and certain tax considerations that may affect the returns. Since the actual outcomes may not coincide with those expected, investors must measure and compare actual performance with anticipated performance. Here we will emphasize developing measures suitable for analyzing investment performance. We begin with sources of data.

Obtaining Needed Data

The first step in analyzing investment returns is gathering data that reflect the actual performance of each investment. As pointed out in Chapter 3, a broad range of sources of investment information is available. *The Wall Street Journal* and *Bar-*

ron's, for example, contain numerous items of information useful in assessing the performance of securities. The same type of information used when making an investment decision is used to manage and control the performance of investments held as part of an investment portfolio. Two key areas one must keep abreast of are returns on owned investments, and economic and market activity.

Return Data

The basic ingredient in analyzing investment returns is current market information. Many publications provide daily price quotations for securities such as stocks and bonds. Investors often maintain logs that contain the cost of each investment, as well as dividends, interest, and other sources of income received. By regularly recording price and return data, an investor can create an ongoing record of price fluctuations and cumulative returns that can be used in managing and controlling performance. The investor should also monitor corporate earnings and dividends, since a company's earnings and dividends will affect its stock price. The two sources of investment return—current income and capital gains—of course must be combined to determine total return. The combination of components using the techniques presented in Chapter 4 will be illustrated for some of the more popular investment vehicles later in this chapter.

Economic and Market Activity

Changes in the economy and market will affect returns—both the level of current income and the market value of an investment vehicle. The astute investor will keep abreast of international, national, and local economic and market developments. By following economic and market changes, an investor should be able to assess their potential impact on individual investment returns and on the portfolio's return.

Stock prices, for example, are affected by the world economy. As we pointed out in Chapter 3, economic information is available from a variety of publications and special subscription services. An investor should relate macroeconomic developments to the returns on securities held in a portfolio. As economic and market conditions change, an investor must be prepared to make revisions in the portfolio to respond to new developments. In essence, a knowledgeable investor improves his or her chances of generating a profit (or avoiding a loss).

Indexes of Investment Performance

In measuring investment performance, it is often worthwhile to compare the investor's returns with appropriate broad-based market measures. Indexes useful for the analysis of common stock include the Dow Jones industrial average (DJIA), the Standard & Poor's 500 stock composite index (S&P 500), and the New York Stock Exchange composite index (NYSE index). (Detailed discussions of these averages and indexes were included in Chapter 3). Although the DJIA is widely cited by the news media, it is *not* considered the most appropriate comparative gauge of stock price movement because of its narrow coverage and because it excludes many types of stocks. For example, companies like CBS, Dow Chemical, K-Mart, and Quaker

Oats are not included. If an investor's portfolio is composed of a broad range of common stocks, the NYSE composite index is probably a more appropriate tool. This index consists of stocks that constitute more than 50 percent of all publicly traded stocks, based upon dollar market value. The scope of coverage as measured by market value is three times that of the DJIA.

A number of bond market indicators are also available for assessing the general behavior of these markets. These indicators consider either bond price behavior or bond yield. The Dow Jones composite bond average, based on the closing prices of 10 utility and 10 industrial bonds, is a popular measure of bond price behavior. Like bond quotations, this average reflects the average percentage of face value at which the bonds sell. Other sources of bond yield data, which reflect the rate of return one would earn on a bond purchased today and held to maturity, are also available. *Barron's,* Standard & Poor's, Moody's Investor Services, and the Federal Reserve are examples. Indexes of bond price and bond yield performance can be obtained for specific types of bonds (industrial, utility, and municipal), as well as on a composite basis. In addition, these and other indexes are sometimes reported in terms of *total returns*—that is, dividend/interest income is combined with price behavior (capital gain or loss) to reflect total return. Such indexes are available for both stocks and bonds.

There are a few other indexes that cover listed options and futures; there are no widely publicized indexes/averages for tangibles or mutual funds. Nor is there a broad index of real estate returns. Such returns tend to be localized; that is, they vary widely from area to area. And different types of property investments yield widely varying returns. For example, farmland moves in value in relation to farm product prices and to foreign investment in farmland. Thus real estate investors should compare their returns with those earned by other local real estate investors. In addition, it might be wise to compare the investor's real estate returns with the Consumer Price Index and with the NYSE composite index. The former will serve as a useful comparative measure of its effectiveness as an inflation hedge. The latter is useful in comparing the relative return on a diversified stock portfolio with that from real estate investment. Similar approaches can be used in assessing other forms of property investment.

Measuring the Performance of Investment Vehicles

Reliable techniques for consistently measuring the performance of each investment vehicle are needed to monitor an investment portfolio. In particular, the holding period return (HPR) measure first presented in Chapter 4 is also used to determine *actual* return performance from stocks, bonds, tangibles, mutual funds, real estate, and other investments. Investment holdings need to be evaluated periodically over time—at least once a year. HPR is an excellent way to assess actual return behavior, since it captures *total return* performance and is most appropriate for holding or assessment periods of one year or less. Total return, in this context, includes the periodic cash income from the investment as well as price appreciation or loss, whether realized or unrealized. Clearly the calculation of returns for periods of more than a year should, as noted in Chapter 4, be made using *yield* (internal rate of return) since it recognizes the time value of money; yield can easily be estimated with the *approximate yield formula*. Since the following discussions center on the annual assessment of return, HPR will be used as the measure of return. The formula for HPR, presented in Chapter 4 (Equation 4.8) and applied throughout this chapter, is restated in Equation 17.1:

Equation 17.1

$$\text{Holding period return} = \frac{\begin{array}{c}\text{current income} \\ \text{during period}\end{array} + \begin{array}{c}\text{capital gain (or loss)} \\ \text{during period}\end{array}}{\text{beginning investment value}}$$

Equation 17.1a

$$\text{HPR} = \frac{C + CG}{V_0}$$

where

Equation 17.2

$$\frac{\text{Capital gain (or loss)}}{\text{during period}} = \text{ending investment value} - \text{beginning investment value}$$

Equation 17.2a

$$CG = V_n - V_0$$

Stocks and Bonds

There are several measures of investment return for stocks and bonds. The dividend yield, for instance, measures the current yearly dividend return earned from a stock investment. It is calculated by dividing a stock's yearly cash dividend by its price. This measure of investment return was discussed in Chapter 5. The current yield and promised yield (yield to maturity) for bonds were analyzed in Chapter 8. These measures of investment return capture various components of an investor's return but do not reflect actual total return. To provide a measure of total return, the holding period return method is applied. The total return on an investment in stocks or bonds consists of two components: current income (dividends or interest), plus any capital gain or loss. *Holding period return (HPR) measures the total return (income plus change in value) actually earned on an investment over a given investment period*. We will use a holding period of approximately one year in the illustrations that follow.

Stocks. The HPR for common and preferred stocks includes both cash dividends received as well as any price change in the security during the period of ownership. Table 17.1 illustrates the HPR calculation as applied to the actual performance of a common stock. This investor purchased 1,000 shares of Dallas National Corporation in May 1992 at a cost of $27,312 (including commissions). After holding the stock for just over one year, the stock was sold with proceeds to the investor of $32,040. The investor received $2,000 in cash dividends during the period of ownership. In addition, a $4,728 capital gain was realized on the sale. Thus the calculated HPR is 24.63 percent.

The HPR found above was calculated without consideration for income taxes paid on the dividends and capital gain. Because many investors are concerned with both pretax and after-tax rates of return, it is useful to calculate an after-tax HPR. We assume, for simplicity, that the investor in this example is in the 30 percent tax

TABLE 17.1 Calculation of Pretax HPR
on a Common Stock

Security: Dallas National Corporation common stock
Date of purchase: May 1, 1992
Purchase cost: $27,312
Date of sale: May 7, 1993
Sale proceeds: $32,040
Dividends received (May 1992 to May 1993): $2,000

$$\text{Holding period return} = \frac{\$2,000 + (\$32,040 - \$27,312)}{\$27,312}$$

$$= \underline{\underline{+24.63\%}}$$

bracket (federal and state combined); we also assume that for federal and state tax purposes, capital gains are taxed at the full marginal tax rate. Thus, dividend and capital gain income to this investor is taxed at a 30 percent rate. Income taxes reduce the after-tax dividend income to $1,400 [(1 − .30) × $2,000] and the after-tax capital gain to $3,310 [(1 − .30) × ($32,040 − $27,312)]. The after-tax HPR, therefore, is 17.25 percent, a reduction of 7.38 percent. It should be clear that both the pretax and after-tax HPR are useful gauges of return.

Bonds.   The HPR for a bond investment is similar to that for stocks. The calculation holds for both straight debt and convertible issues. It includes the two components of a bond investor's return: interest income and capital gain or loss. Calculation of the HPR on a bond investment is illustrated in Table 17.2. The investor purchased the Phoenix Brewing Company bonds for $10,000, held them for just over one year, and then realized $9,704 at sale. In addition, the investor earned $1,000 in interest during the period of ownership. Thus the HPR of this investment

TABLE 17.2 Calculation of Pretax HPR
on a Bond

Security: Phoenix Brewing Company 10% bonds
Date of Purchase: June 2, 1992
Purchase cost: $10,000
Date of sale: June 5, 1993
Sale proceeds: $9,704
Interest earned (June 1992 to June 1993): $1,000

$$\text{Holding period return} = \frac{\$1,000 + (\$9,704 - \$10,000)}{\$10,000}$$

$$= \underline{\underline{+7.04\%}}$$

is 7.04 percent. The HPR is lower than the bond's current yield of 10 percent ($1,000 interest ÷ $10,000 purchase price) because the bonds were sold at a capital loss. Assuming a 30 percent tax bracket, the after-tax HPR is 4.93 percent: $\{[(1 - .30) \times \$1,000] + [(1 - .30) \times (\$9,704 - \$10,000)]\} \div \$10,000$—about 2 percent less than the pretax HPR.

Mutual Funds

There are two basic components of return from a mutual fund investment: dividend income (including any capital gains distribution) plus any change in value. The basic HPR equation for mutual funds is identical to that for stocks. Table 17.3 presents a holding period return calculation for a no-load mutual fund. The investor purchased 1,000 shares of the fund in July 1992 at an NAV of $10.40 per share. Because it is a no-load fund, no commission was charged, so the investor's cost was $10,400. During the one-year period of ownership, the Pebble Falls Mutual Fund distributed investment income dividends totaling $270 and capital gains dividends of $320. The investor redeemed (sold) this fund at an NAV of $10.79 per share, thereby realizing $10,790. As seen in Table 17.3, the pretax holding period return on this investment is 9.42 percent. Assuming a 30 percent tax bracket, the after-tax HPR for the fund is 6.60 percent $\{[(1 - .30) \times (\$270 + \$320)] + [(1 - .30) \times (\$10,790 - \$10,400)]\} \div \$10,400$—nearly 3 percent below the pretax return.

Real Estate

The two basic components of an investor's return from real estate are the yearly after-tax cash flow and the change in property value that is likely to occur. (For a more expanded analysis of real estate investments, see Chapter 14.)

An investor who purchases raw land is interested only in capital appreciation because there is normally no positive cash flow from such an investment. Carrying

---

TABLE 17.3 Calculation of Pretax HPR on a Mutual Fund

Security: Pebble Falls Mutual Fund
Date of purchase: July 1, 1992
Purchase cost: $10,400
Date of redemption: July 3, 1993
Sale proceeds: $10,790
Distributions received (July 1992 to July 1993):
  Investment income dividends: $270
  Capital gains dividends: $320

Holding period return =
$$\frac{(\$270 + \$320) + (\$10,790 - \$10,400)}{\$10,400}$$
$$= +9.42\%$$

reversion
the after-tax net pro-
ceeds received upon
disposition of real
property.

costs associated with a raw land investment may include property taxes, special assessments, and interest costs if financing is used. An investor's return from a raw land investment is normally realized on its disposition. **Reversion,** the after-tax net proceeds received upon disposition of property, is calculated by subtracting from the property's realized selling price all selling costs (commissions plus closing costs), plus any mortgage principal balances that are paid upon sale, and income taxes paid on realized capital gains from the sale. Reversion, then, represents the after-tax dollars an investor puts in his or her pocket when the property is sold.

An income property investment provides return in two forms: yearly after-tax cash flow and reversion. A property's yearly after-tax cash flow is basically its rental income minus operating expenses, mortgage payments, and income taxes. In other words, after-tax cash flow is the yearly net cash return an investor receives from rental properties. When calculating an investor's total return from a rental property, both yearly after-tax cash flow and reversion are included.

To provide some insight into the calculation of real estate investment returns, the calculation of the after-tax holding period return on an apartment property is demonstrated in Table 17.4 on page 707. (Note: Due to the more complex nature of real estate taxation, only the after-tax HPR calculation is illustrated.) The Maitland Apartments were acquired one year ago with a $100,000 equity investment by Prudence Zwick, who is in the 30 percent tax bracket. If Prudence sold the property today she would realize reversion of $110,000 after all sales expenses, mortgage repayments, and taxes. The holding period return analysis in Table 17.4 contains the proper real estate cash flow statement, owner's tax statement for the past year of ownership, and the HPR calculation. Ms. Zwick received $6,750 in after-tax cash flow plus $10,000 ($110,000 − $100,000) in after-tax capital appreciation, resulting in an after-tax HPR of 16.75 percent. An investor seeking to compare a security's return with real estate or other property investments' return should find the HPR calculation illustrated above a useful analytical tool.

Other Investment Vehicles

The only source of return on other investment vehicles (like options, commodities, financial futures, and tangibles) is capital gains. To calculate a holding period return for an investment in gold, for instance, the basic HPR formula is used (excluding current income, of course). If an investor purchased 10 ounces of gold for $425 per ounce and sold the gold one year later for $500 per ounce, the pretax holding period return would be 17.65 percent. This is simply sales proceeds ($5,000) minus cost ($4,250) divided by cost. Assuming a 30 percent tax rate, the after-tax HPR would be 12.35 percent, which is the after-tax gain of $525 [$750 − (.30 × $750)] divided by cost ($4,250). The HPRs of options, commodities, and financial futures are calculated in a similar fashion. Because the return is in the form of capital gains only, the HPR analysis can be applied to any investment on a pretax or an after-tax basis. (The same basic procedure would be used for securities that are sold short.)

TABLE 17.4 Cash Flow, Tax Statement, and After-Tax HPR Calculation for Maitland Apartments (Past Year)

REAL ESTATE CASH FLOW STATEMENT

Gross potential rental income	$51,000
Less: Vacancy and collection losses	− 1,500
Effective gross income (EGI)	$49,500
Less: Total operating expenses	− 20,000
Net operating income (NOI)	$29,500
Less: Mortgage payment	− 20,500
Before-tax cash flow	$ 9,000
Less: Owner's income tax (from below)	− 2,250
After-tax cash flow (ATCF)	$ 6,750

OWNER'S INCOME TAX STATEMENT

Net operating income	$29,500
Less: Interest	− 17,000
Less: Depreciation	− 5,000
Taxable income	$ 7500
Owner's income tax (tax rate = .30)	$ 2250

AFTER-TAX HPR CALCULATION

$$\text{After-tax HPR} = \frac{\$6,750 + (\$110,000 - \$100,000)}{\$100,000}$$

$$= +16.75\%$$

Comparing Performance to Investment Goals

After computing an HPR (or yield) on an investment, the investor must compare it to his or her investment goal. Keeping track of an investment's performance by periodically computing its return will help you decide which investments you should continue to hold and which have become possible candidates for sale. Clearly an investment holding would be a candidate for sale if: (1) it failed to perform up to expectations and no real change in performance is anticipated; (2) it has met the original investment objective; or (3) more attractive uses of your funds (better investment outlets) are currently available.

Comparing Risk and Return

In this book, we have frequently discussed the basic tradeoff between investment risk and return. The relationship is fundamentally as follows: To earn more return, you must take more risk. Risk is the chance that the actual investment return will be less than expected. In analyzing an investment, the key question is, "Am I getting the proper return for the amount of investment risk that I am taking?"

Nongovernment security and property investments are by nature riskier than U.S. government bonds or insured money market deposit accounts. This implies that a rational investor should invest in risky situations *only when the expected rate of return is well in excess of what could have been earned from a low-risk investment*. Thus, one benchmark against which to compare investment returns is the rate of return on low-risk investments. If an investor's risky investments failed to outperform low-risk investments, a careful examination of the investment strategy is in order. The fact that one's investments are outperforming low-risk investments is an indication that they are obtaining extra return for taking extra risk.

Isolating Problem Investments

problem investment
an investment that
has not lived up to
expectations.

A **problem investment** is one that has not lived up to expectations. It may be a loss situation or an investment that has provided a return less than the investor expected. Many investors try to forget about problem investments, hoping the problem will go away or the investment will turn around by itself. This is obviously a mistake. Problem investments require immediate attention, not neglect. In studying a problem investment, an investor must decide whether to continue to hold it. "Should I take my loss and get out, or should I hang on and hope it turns around?" is the key question. Some investors do not like to realize losses on their investments. They hold on to mediocre ones in hope that they will turn around and can eventually be sold for a profit. Such a strategy can result in a portfolio of poorly performing investments.

It is best to periodically analyze each investment in a portfolio. For each, two questions should be considered. First, has it performed in a manner that could reasonably be expected? Second, if the investment were not currently in the portfolio, would you buy it for the portfolio today? If the answers to both are negative, then the investment probably should be sold. A negative answer to one of the questions qualifies the investment for the "problem list." It should be watched closely. In general, maintaining a portfolio of investments requires constant attention and analysis to ensure the best chance of satisfactory returns. Problem investments need special attention and work.

ASSESSING PORTFOLIO PERFORMANCE

A portfolio can be either passively or actively built and managed. A *passive portfolio* results from random selection of securities that are held over the given investment horizon. An *active portfolio* is built using the traditional and modern approaches presented in Chapter 16; it is managed and controlled in order to, at minimum, achieve its stated objectives. While passive portfolios may outperform equally risky active portfolios, evidence suggests that in spite of *efficient market* arguments (see Chapter 7), **active portfolio management** is a worthwhile activity that can result in superior (excess) returns. Many of the ideas presented in this text are consistent with the belief that active portfolio management will improve the investor's chance of earning superior (excess) returns.

**active portfolio
management**
building a portfolio
using traditional and
modern approaches
and managing and
controlling it to meet
its objectives.

Once a portfolio is built, the first step in active portfolio management is to assess performance on a regular basis and use that information to revise the portfolio. Calculating the portfolio return can be tricky, as discussed in the accompanying Investor Insights box. The procedures used to assess portfolio performance are based on many of the concepts presented earlier in the chapter. Here we will look at the process of portfolio performance assessment, using a hypothetical securities portfolio over a one-year holding period. We will examine each of three measures that can be used to compare a portfolio's return with a risk-adjusted, market-adjusted rate of return.

Measuring Portfolio Return

Table 17.5 presents the investment portfolio of Robert K. Hathaway, as of January 1, 1993. Mr. Hathaway is 50 years old, a widower, and his children are married. His income is $60,000 per year. His primary investment objective is long-term growth with a moderate dividend return. He selects stocks with two criteria in mind: quality and growth potential. On January 1, 1993, his portfolio consisted of 10 issues, all of good quality. Mr. Hathaway has been fortunate in his selection process in that he has approximately $74,000 in unrealized price appreciation in his portfolio. During 1993 he decided to make a change in his portfolio. On May 7, he sold 1,000 shares of Dallas National for $32,040. Mr. Hathaway's holding period return for that issue was discussed earlier in this chapter (see Table 17.1). Using funds from the Dallas National sale, he acquired an additional 1,000 shares of Florida Southcoast Banks on May 10. He decided to make the switch because he believed the prospects for the Florida bank holding company were better than those of Dallas National, a Texas-based bank holding company. Florida Southcoast is based in one of the fastest-growing counties in the country.

TABLE 17.5 Robert K. Hathaway's Portfolio (January 1, 1993)

Number of Shares	Company	Date Acquired	Cost (Including Commissions)	Cost per Share	Current Price per Share	Current Value
1,000	Bancorp West, Inc.	1/16/91	$ 21,610	$21.61	$30	$ 30,000
1,000	Dallas National Corporation	5/ 1/92	27,312	27.31	29	29,000
1,000	Dator Companies, Inc.	4/13/87	13,704	13.70	27	27,000
500	Excelsior Industries	8/16/90	40,571	81.14	54	27,000
1,000	Florida Southcoast Banks	12/16/90	17,460	17.46	30	30,000
1,000	Maryland-Pacific	9/27/90	22,540	22.54	26	26,000
1,000	Moronson	2/27/90	19,100	19.10	47	47,000
500	Northwest Mining and Mfg.	4/17/91	25,504	51.00	62	31,000
1,000	Rawland Petroleum	3/12/91	24,903	24.90	30	30,000
1,000	Vornox	4/16/91	37,120	37.12	47	47,000
	Total		$249,824			$324,000

Portfolio Return is a Tough Figure to Find

Most investors have a pretty good idea how major market benchmarks like Standard & Poor's 500-stock index did in 1989. Even if the exact figures aren't on the tips of their tongues, they can easily look them up.

But when it comes to the return on their own portfolios, most people have only the roughest notion. And there aren't any easy answers in the year-end brokerage and mutual-fund statements that outnumber the bills in some investors' mailboxes these days.

Securities firms have added more information to their statements in recent years. But they still don't show an overall performance figure that can be compared with, say, last year's 31.7% total return on the S&P 500. Unless investors do the frequently daunting calculations for themselves, they generally have no way of knowing how their invest-ments stack up.

Mutual-fund investors don't have it much better. Fund companies do report total return figures for each fund, but that's often only part of the answer. People who moved their money around—say, shifting some dollars between a money-market fund and a stock fund—are still left groping in the dark.

A stock fund's annual return "doesn't tell you how you did if you bought at the highs and sold at the lows," or the reverse, says Lynn Hopewell, a Falls Church, Va., financial planner. . . .

Investors can calculate their own portfolio returns, of course. But unless they have only a few investment accounts and don't add or subtract money over the course of the year, they'll need lots of records and a strong stomach for math.

Take a simple case first. Say a family has a single brokerage account valued at $50,000 at the beginning of 1989, and no funds were added or withdrawn during the year. All income—including stock dividends, bond interest and mutual-fund distributions—was reinvested within the account.

The total return for 1989 would simply be the percentage difference between the value at year-end 1989 and the value at year-end 1988. That would tell the family the average return for 1989, including both price change and income, on dollars invested as of the beginning of the year.

Note that it doesn't matter how many or how few trades the family made. "It's all

Measuring the Amount Invested

Every investor would be well advised to periodically list his or her holdings, as done in Table 17.5. The table lists number of shares, acquisition date, cost, and current value for each issue. These data aid in continually formulating strategy decisions; the cost data, for example, are used to determine the amount invested. Mr. Hatha-way's portfolio does not utilize the leverage of a margin account. If leverage were present, all return calculations would be based on the investor's *equity* in the ac-count. (Recall from Chapter 2 that an investor's equity in a margin account equals the total value of all the securities in the account minus any margin debt.)

To measure Mr. Hathaway's return on his invested capital we need to perform a one-year holding period return analysis. His invested capital as of January 1, 1993, reflected in the ending market value, as long as there were no real cash flows in or out,'' says Robert Moseson, president of Performance Analytics Inc., a Chicago firm that advises institutional investors.

The equation gets tricky, however, if the family added money or subtracted money at some time during the year.

Say they added $15,000 from an inheritance. Depending on when the new money came in, it may have contributed in a big way or not at all to the gains or losses in the portfolio. So, contrary to first impressions, you can't just add the net inflow of new funds to the original balance and measure the percentage change over the year.

Instead, Mr. Moseson says, investors should add up asset values periodically, calculate average returns for short time periods and then combine them for an annual figure.

''You need to calculate those returns at least quarterly and ideally—or close to ideally—monthly. Mutual funds do it daily,'' says Mr. Moseson.

Limited information may force investors to restrict their calculations to holdings whose market values are readily determined. That would mean excluding things such as rarely traded limited-partnership interests, many of which have fallen in value as real-estate prices have fallen in value as real-estate prices have declined and tax laws have changed.

Investors should also take care in selecting appropriate benchmarks to measure their portfolios against. Mr. Moseson suggests constructing a customized index that represents a hypothetical portfolio with an investment mix similar to that of the investor.

Say, for instance, that in 1989 a family had about 50% of its investment dollars in common stocks, 30% in corporate and government bonds and 20% in money-market funds. Take the total return each category of investment produced last year: for instance, 31.7% for the S&P 500 index, 14.1% for Merrill Lynch & Co.'s corporate and government bond master index and 8.9% for the average taxable money fund, according to the Donoghue Organization, Holliston, Mass.

Then multiply each of those return percentages by the percentage of the portfolio they represent. Add up the results for a weighted average return. In this case the benchmark would be 21.9% (0.5 times 31.7%, plus 0.3 times 14.1%, plus 0.2 times 8.9%).

Source: Excerpted from Karen Slater, ''Portfolio Return Is Tough Figure to Find,'' *The Wall Street Journal,* January 22, 1990, p. C1.

---

is $324,000. No new additions of capital were made in the portfolio during 1993, although he sold one stock, Dallas National, and used the proceeds to buy another, Florida Southcoast Banks.

Measuring Income

There are two sources of return from a portfolio of common stocks: income and capital gains. Current income is realized from dividends. Current income from a portfolio of bonds is earned in the form of interest. Investors must report taxable dividends and interest on federal and state income tax returns. Companies are required to furnish income reports (Form 1099-DIV for dividends and Form 1099-INT for interest) to stockholders and bondholders. Many investors maintain logs to

TABLE 17.6 Dividend Income on Hathaway's Portfolio
(Calendar Year 1990)

Number of Shares	Company	Annual Dividend per Share	Dividends Received
1,000	Bancorp West, Inc.	$1.20	$ 1,200
1,000	Dallas National Corporation*	1.80	900
1,000	Dator Companies, Inc.	1.12	1,120
500	Excelsior Industries	2.00	1,000
2,000	Florida Southcoast Banks**	1.28	1,920
1,000	Maryland-Pacific	1.10	1,100
1,000	Moronson	—	—
500	Northwest Mining and Mfg.	2.05	1,025
1,000	Rawland Petroleum	1.20	1,200
1,000	Vornox	1.47	1,470
	Total		$10,935

*Sold May 7, 1993.

**1,000 shares acquired on May 10, 1993.

keep track of dividend and interest income as received. Table 17.6 lists Mr. Hathaway's dividends for 1993. He received two quarterly dividends of $.45 per share before he sold the Dallas stock, and he received two $.32 per share quarterly dividends on the additional Florida Southcoast Banks shares he acquired. His total dividend income for 1993 was $10,935.

Measuring Capital Gains

Table 17.7 shows the unrealized gains in value for each of the issues in the Hathaway portfolio. The January 1, 1993, and December 31, 1993, values are listed for each issue except the additional shares of Florida Southcoast Banks. The amounts listed for Florida Southcoast Banks reflect the fact that 1,000 additional shares of the stock were acquired on May 10, 1993, at a cost of $32,040. Mr. Hathaway's current holdings had beginning-of-the-year values of $327,040 (including the additional Florida Southcoast Banks shares at the date of purchase) and are worth $356,000 at year-end. During 1993 the portfolio increased in value by 8.9 percent, or $28,960, in unrealized capital gains. In addition, Mr. Hathaway realized a capital gain in 1993 by selling his Dallas National holding. From January 1, 1993, until its sale on May 7, 1993, the Dallas holding rose in value from $29,000 to $32,040. This was the only sale in 1993; thus total *realized* gain was $3,040. During 1993 the portfolio had both a realized gain of $3,040 and an unrealized gain of $28,960. The total gain in value equals the sum of the two: $32,000. Put another way, since no capital was added to or withdrawn from the portfolio over the year, the total capital gain is simply the difference between the year-end market value (of $356,000, from Table 17.7) and the value on January 1 (of $324,000, from Table 17.5). This, of course, amounts to $32,000, of which only $3,040 is considered realized for tax purposes.

■■■■■■

TABLE 17.7 Unrealized Gains in Value of Hathaway's Portfolio (January 1, 1993, to December 31, 1993)

Number of Shares	Company	Market Value (1/1/93)	Market Price (12/31/93)	Market Value (12/31/93)	Unrealized Gain (Loss)	Percentage Change
1,000	Bancorp West, Inc.	$ 30,000	$27	$ 27,000	$(3,000)	−10.0%
1,000	Dator Companies, Inc.	27,000	36	36,000	9,000	+33.3
500	Excelsior Industries	27,000	66	33,000	6,000	+22.2
2,000	Florida Southcoast Banks*	62,040	35	70,000	7,960	+12.8
1,000	Maryland-Pacific	26,000	26	26,000	—	—
1,000	Moronson	47,000	55	55,000	8,000	+17.0
500	Northwest Mining and Mfg.	31,000	60	30,000	(1,000)	− 3.2
1,000	Rawland Petroleum	30,000	36	36,000	6,000	+20.0
1,000	Vornox	47,000	43	43,000	(4,000)	− 8.5
	Total	$327,040**		$356,000	$28,960	+ 8.9%

*1,000 additional shares acquired on May 10, 1993, at a cost of $32,040. The value listed is the cost plus the market value of the previously owned shares as of January 1, 1993.

**This total includes the $324,000 market value of the portfolio on January 1, 1993 (from Table 17.5) plus the $3,040 *realized* gain on the sale of the Dallas National Corporation Stock on May 7, 1993. The inclusion of the realized gain in this total is necessary in order to calculate the *unrealized* gain on the portfolio during 1993.

Measuring the Portfolio's Holding Period Return

We use the HPR measurement to measure the total return on the Hathaway portfolio during 1993. The basic one-year HPR formula for portfolios is:

Equation 17.3

$$\text{Holding period return for a portfolio} = \frac{\text{dividends and interest received} + \text{realized gain} + \text{unrealized gain}}{\text{initial equity investment} + \left(\text{new funds} \times \dfrac{\text{number of months in portfolio}}{12}\right) - \left(\text{withdrawn funds} \times \dfrac{\text{number of months withdrawn from portfolio}}{12}\right)}$$

Equation 17.3a

$$HPR_p = \frac{C + RG + UG}{E_0 + \left(NF \times \dfrac{ip}{12}\right) - \left(WF \times \dfrac{wp}{12}\right)}$$

This formula includes both the realized return (income plus gains) and unrealized yearly gains of the portfolio. Portfolio additions and deletions are time-weighted for the number of months they are in the portfolio.

Table 17.7 analyzes in detail the portfolio's change in value: All the issues that are in the portfolio as of December 31, 1993, are listed and the unrealized gain during the year is calculated. The beginning and year-end values are included for comparison purposes. The crux of the analysis is the HPR calculation for the year, presented in Table 17.8. All the elements of a portfolio's return are included. Dividends total $10,935 (from Table 17.6). The realized gain of $3,040 represents

TABLE 17.8 Holding Period Return Calculation on Hathaway's Portfolio (January 1, 1993, to December 31, 1993, Holding Period)

DATA

Portfolio value (1/1/93): $324,000
Portfolio value (12/31/93): $356,000
Realized appreciation: $3,040 (1/1/93 to 5/7/93 when Dallas National was sold)
Unrealized appreciation (1/1/90 to 12/31/93): $28,960
Dividends received: $10,935
New funds invested or withdrawn: None

PORTFOLIO HPR CALCULATION

$$\text{HPR} = \frac{\$10,935 + \$3,040 + \$28,960}{\$324,000}$$

$$= \underline{\underline{+13.25\%}}$$

the increment in value of the Dallas National holding from January 1, 1993, until its sale. During 1993 the portfolio had a $28,960 unrealized gain (from Table 17.7). There were no additions of new funds and no funds were withdrawn. Utilizing Equation 17.3 for HPR, we find that the portfolio had a total return of 13.25 percent in 1993.

Comparison of Return with Overall Market Measures

The HPR figure derived from the calculation above should be utilized in a risk-adjusted, market-adjusted rate of return comparison. This type of comparative study is useful because it can provide some idea of how the portfolio is doing in comparison to the stock market as a whole. The S&P 500 stock composite index or the NYSE composite index are acceptable indexes for this type of analysis because they are broadly based and appear to represent the stock market as a whole. Assume that during 1993 the return on the S&P 500 index was +10.75 percent; this return includes both dividends and capital gains. The return from Mr. Hathaway's portfolio, as calculated above, was +13.25 percent. This compares very favorably with the broadly based index: The Hathaway portfolio performed about 23 percent better than this broad indicator of stock market return.

While such a comparison tends to factor out the influences of general market movements, it fails to consider risk. Clearly, a raw return figure, like the +13.25 percent above, requires further analysis because an investor needs to know how the portfolio has performed *in relation to other portfolios and in relation to the market in general*. A number of risk-adjusted, market-adjusted rate of return measures are

Sharpe's measure
a measure of portfolio performance, developed by William F. Sharpe, that measures the risk premium of a portfolio per unit of total risk, which is measured by the portfolio's standard deviation of return.

available for use in assessing portfolio performance. Here we'll discuss three of the most popular—Sharpe's measure, Treynor's measure, and Jensen's measure—and demonstrate their application to Hathaway's portfolio.

Sharpe's Measure

Sharpe's measure of portfolio performance, developed by William F. Sharpe, compares the risk premium on a portfolio to the portfolio's standard deviation of return. The risk premium on a portfolio is the total portfolio return minus the risk-free rate. Sharpe's measure can be expressed as the following formula:

Equation 17.4

$$\text{Sharpe's measure} = \frac{\text{total portfolio return} - \text{risk-free rate}}{\text{portfolio standard deviation}}$$

Equation 17.4a

$$SM = \frac{r_p - R_F}{s_p}$$

This measure allows the investor to assess the risk premium per unit of total risk, which is measured by the portfolio standard deviation. Assuming the risk-free rate, R_F, is 7.50 percent, the standard deviation of Hathaway's portfolio, s_p, is 16 percent. The total portfolio return, r_p, which is the HPR for Hathaway's portfolio calculated in Table 17.8, is 13.25 percent. Substituting those values into Equation 17.4, we get Sharpe's measure, SM:

$$SM = \frac{13.25\% - 7.50\%}{16\%} = \frac{5.75\%}{16\%} = \underline{\underline{.36}}$$

Sharpe's measure is meaningful when compared either to other portfolios or to the market. In general, the higher Sharpe's measure, the better—the higher the risk premium per unit of risk. If we assume the market return, r_m, is currently 10.75 percent and the standard deviation for the market portfolio, s_{p_m}, is 11.25 percent, Sharpe's measure for the market, SM_m, would be:

$$SM_m = \frac{10.75\% - 7.50\%}{11.25\%} = \frac{3.25\%}{11.25\%} = \underline{\underline{.29}}$$

Because Sharpe's measure for Hathaway's portfolio of .36 is greater than the measure of .29 for the market portfolio, Hathaway's portfolio exhibits superior performance—its risk premium per unit of risk is above that of the market. Of course, had Sharpe's measure for Hathaway's portfolio been below that of the market (i.e., below .29), the portfolio's performance would be considered inferior to the market performance.

Treynor's measure
a measure of portfolio performance, developed by Jack L. Treynor, that measures the risk premium of a portfolio per unit of diversifiable risk, which is measured by the portfolio's beta.

Treynor's Measure

Jack L. Treynor developed a portfolio performance measure that is similar to Sharpe's measure. Like Sharpe's, **Treynor's measure** measures the risk premium per unit of risk, but it differs in its portfolio risk measure. Treynor's measure uses the portfolio beta to measure risk; Sharpe's uses the portfolio standard deviation. Treynor therefore focuses only on nondiversifiable risk, assuming that the portfolio has been built in a fashion that diversifies away all diversifiable risk; Sharpe on the other hand uses total risk. Treynor's measure is calculated as shown in Equation 17.5:

Equation 17.5

$$\text{Treynor's measure} = \frac{\text{total portfolio return} - \text{risk-free rate}}{\text{portfolio beta}}$$

Equation 17.5a

$$TM = \frac{r_p - R_F}{b_p}$$

This measure gives the risk premium per unit of nondiversifiable risk, which is measured by the portfolio beta. Using the data for the Hathaway portfolio presented earlier and assuming that the beta for Hathaway's portfolio, b_p, is 1.20, we can substitute into Equation 17.5 to get Treynor's measure, TM, for Hathaway's portfolio:

$$TM = \frac{13.25\% - 7.50\%}{1.20} = \frac{5.75\%}{1.20} = \underline{\underline{4.79\%}}$$

Treynor's measure, like Sharpe's, is useful when compared either to other portfolios or to the market. Generally, the higher the value of Treynor's measure, the better—the greater the risk premium per unit of nondiversifiable risk. Again assuming the market return, r_m, is 10.75 percent, and recognizing that by definition (see Chapter 4) the beta for the market portfolio, bp, is 1.00, we can use Equation 17.5 to find Treynor's measure for the market, TM_m:

$$TM_m = \frac{10.75\% - 7.50\%}{1.00} = \frac{3.25\%}{1.00} = \underline{\underline{3.25\%}}$$

The fact that Treynor's measure of 4.79 percent for Hathaway's portfolio is greater than that measure of 3.25 percent for the market portfolio indicates that Hathaway's portfolio exhibits superior performance—its risk premium per unit of nondiversifiable risk is above that of the market. Conversely, had Treynor's measure for Hathaway's portfolio been below that of the market (i.e., below 3.25 percent), the portfolio's performance would be viewed as inferior to that of the market.

Jensen's Measure (Alpha)

Jensen's measure (alpha)
a measure of portfolio performance, developed by Michael C. Jensen, that uses the portfolio's beta and CAPM to calculate its excess return, which can be positive, zero, or negative.

Michael C. Jensen developed a portfolio performance measure that seems quite different from the measures of Sharpe and Treynor yet is theoretically consistent with Treynor's measure. **Jensen's measure,** also called **Jensen's alpha,** is based on the *capital asset pricing model (CAPM)*, which was developed in Chapter 4 (see Equation 4.13). It calculates the portfolio's *excess return*—the amount by which the portfolio's actual return deviates from its *required return*, which is determined using its beta and CAPM. The value of the excess return may be positive, zero, or negative. Like Treynor's measure, Jensen's measure focuses on only the nondiversifiable or relevant risk, by using beta and CAPM; it assumes that the portfolio has been adequately diversified. Jensen's measure is calculated as shown in Equation 17.6:

Equation 17.6

Jensen's measure = (total portfolio return − risk-free rate) − [portfolio beta ×

(market return − risk-free rate)]

Equation 17.6a

$$JM = (r_p - R_F) - [b_p \times (r_m - R_F)]$$

Jensen's measure indicates the difference between the portfolio's actual return and its required return. Positive values are preferred: they indicate that the portfolio earned a return in excess of its risk-adjusted, market-adjusted required return. A value of zero indicates the portfolio earned exactly its required return; negative values indicate that the portfolio failed to earn its required return.

Using the data for Hathaway's portfolio presented earlier, we can substitute into Equation 17.6 to get Jensen's measure, *JM*, for Hathaway's portfolio:

$$JM = (13.25\% - 7.50\%) - [1.20 \times (10.75\% - 7.50\%)]$$
$$= 5.75\% - (1.20 \times 3.25\%) = 5.75\% - 3.90\% = \underline{1.85\%}$$

The 1.85 percent value for Jensen's measure indicates that Hathaway's portfolio earned an excess return 1.85 percent above its required return, given its nondiversifiable risk as measured by beta. Clearly Hathaway's portfolio has outperformed the market on a risk-adjusted basis. Note that unlike the Sharpe and Treynor measures, Jensen's measure, through its use of CAPM, automatically adjusts for the market return. Therefore there is no need to make a separate market comparison. In general, the higher Jensen's measure, the better the portfolio has performed; only those portfolios with positive Jensen measures have outperformed the market on a risk-adjusted basis. Because of its computational simplicity, its reliance only on nondiversifiable risk, and the fact that it contains both risk and market adjustments, Jensen's measure (alpha) tends to be preferred over those of Sharpe and Treynor when assessing portfolio performance.

Portfolio Revision

In the Hathaway portfolio discussed above, one transaction occurred during 1993. The reason for this transaction was that Mr. Hathaway believed the Florida South-coast Banks stock had more return potential than the Dallas National stock. An investor should periodically analyze the portfolio with one basic question in mind: "Does this portfolio continue to meet my needs?" In other words, does the portfolio contain those issues that are best suited to the investor's risk-return needs? Investors who systematically study the issues in their portfolios will find an occasional need to sell certain issues and to purchase new securities. This process is

portfolio revision
the process of selling certain issues in a portfolio and of purchasing new ones.

commonly called **portfolio revision.** As the economy evolves, certain industries and stocks become either more or less attractive as investments. In today's stock market, timeliness is the essence of profitability.

Given the dynamics of the investment world, periodic reallocation and rebalancing of the portfolio are a necessity. Many circumstances require such changes. In Chapter 16 we noted that as an investor nears retirement, the portfolio's emphasis normally evolves from a strategy that emphasizes growth/capital appreciation to one that seeks to preserve capital. For an investor approaching retirement, an appropriate strategy might be to switch gradually from growth issues into low-risk, high-yield securities. Changing a portfolio's emphasis normally involves an evolutionary process rather than an overnight switch. Individual issues in the portfolio often change in risk-return characteristics. As this occurs, an investor would be wise to eliminate those issues that do not meet his or her objectives. In addition, the need for diversification is a constant one. As issues rise or fall in value, their diversification effect may be lessened. Thus portfolio revision may be needed to maintain diversification in the portfolio.

TIMING TRANSACTIONS

The essence of timing is to "buy low and sell high." This is the dream of all investors. Although there is no tried and true way for achieving such a goal, there are several methods you can utilize to time purchase and sale actions. For one thing, there are formula plans, discussed below. Investors can also use limit and stop-loss orders as a timing aid, follow procedures for warehousing liquidity, and take into consideration other aspects of timing when selling investments.

Formula Plans

formula plans
mechanical methods of portfolio management that try to take advantage of price changes in securities which result from cyclical price movements.

Formula plans are mechanical methods of portfolio management that try to take advantage of price changes in securities which result from cyclical price movements. Formula plans are not set up to provide unusually high returns; rather, they are conservative strategies that are primarily oriented toward investors who do not wish to bear a high level of risk. Four formula plans are discussed here: dollar cost averaging; the constant dollar plan; the constant ratio plan; and the variable ratio plan.

Dollar Cost Averaging

dollar cost averaging
a formula plan for timing investment transactions, in which a fixed dollar amount is invested in a security at fixed intervals.

Dollar cost averaging is a formula plan in which a fixed dollar amount is invested in a security at fixed intervals. In this passive buy-and-hold strategy, a periodic dollar investment is held constant. The investor must have the discipline to invest on a regular basis in order to make the plan work. The hoped-for outcome of a dollar cost averaging program is growth in the value of the security to which the funds are allocated. The price of the investment security will probably fluctuate over time. If the price declines, more shares are purchased per period; conversely, if the price rises, fewer shares are purchased per period.

In the example of dollar cost averaging shown in Table 17.9, the investor is investing $500 per month in the Wolverine Mutual Fund, a growth-oriented, no-load mutual fund. During one year's time the investor has placed $6,000 in the mutual fund shares. This is a no-load fund, so shares are purchased at net asset value. Purchases were made at NAVs ranging from a low of $24.16 to a high of $30.19. At year-end, the investor's holdings in the fund were valued at slightly less than $6,900. Whereas dollar cost averaging is a passive strategy, other formula plans are more active.

TABLE 17.9 Dollar Cost Averaging ($500 per Month, Wolverine Mutual Fund Shares)

	TRANSACTIONS	
Month	Net Asset Value (NAV), Month End	Number of Shares Purchased
January	$26.00	19.23
February	27.46	18.21
March	27.02	18.50
April	24.19	20.67
May	26.99	18.53
June	25.63	19.51
July	24.70	20.24
August	24.16	20.70
September	25.27	19.79
October	26.15	19.12
November	29.60	16.89
December	30.19	16.56

ANNUAL SUMMARY

Total investment: $6,000.00
Total number of shares purchased: 227.95
Average cost per share: $26.32
Year-end portfolio value: $6,881.81

Constant Dollar Plan

constant dollar plan a formula plan for timing investment transactions, in which the investor establishes a target dollar amount for the speculative portion of the portfolio and transfers funds to or from the conservative portion as needed to maintain the target dollar amount.

A **constant dollar plan** consists of a portfolio that is divided into two parts, speculative and conservative. The speculative portion is invested in securities having high promise of capital gains. The conservative portion consists of low-risk investments such as bonds or a money market account. The target dollar amount for the speculative portion is constant, and the investor establishes trigger points (upward or downward movement in the speculative portion) at which funds are removed from or added to that portion. The constant dollar plan basically skims off profits from the speculative portion of the portfolio if it rises a certain percentage or amount in value. These funds are then added to the conservative portion of the portfolio. If the speculative portion of the portfolio declines by a specific percentage or amount, funds are added to it from the conservative portion.

Table 17.10 is an illustration of a constant dollar plan over time. The beginning $20,000 portfolio consists of $10,000 invested in a high-beta no-load mutual fund and $10,000 deposited in a money market account. The investor has decided to rebalance the portfolio every time the speculative portion is worth $2,000 more or $2,000 less than its initial value of $10,000. If the speculative portion of the portfo-

TABLE 17.10 Constant Dollar Plan

Mutual Fund NAV	Value of Speculative Portion	Value of Conservative Portion	Total Portfolio Value	Transactions	Number of Shares in Speculative Portion
$10.00	$10,000.00	$10,000.00	$20,000.00		1,000
11.00	11,000.00	10,000.00	21,000.00		1,000
12.00	12,000.00	10,000.00	22,000.00		1,000
→12.00	10,000.00	12,000.00	22,000.00	Sold 166.67 shares	833.33
11.00	9,166.63	12,000.00	21,166.63		833.33
9.50	7,916.64	12,000.00	19,916.64		833.33
→ 9.50	10,000.00	9,916.64	19,916.64	Purchased 219.30 shares	1,052.63
10.00	10,526.30	9,916.64	20,442.94		1,052.63

lio equals or exceeds $12,000, sufficient shares of the fund are sold to bring its value down to $10,000. The proceeds from the sale are added to the conservative portion. If the speculative portion declines in value to $8,000 or less, funds are taken from the conservative portion and used to purchase sufficient shares to raise the value of the speculative portion to $10,000.

Two portfolio rebalancing actions are taken in the time sequence illustrated in Table 17.10. Initially $10,000 is allocated to each portion of the portfolio. Then, when the mutual fund's NAV rises to $12.00, so that the speculative portion is worth $12,000, the investor sells 166.67 shares valued at $2,000 and the proceeds are added to the money market account. Later the mutual fund's NAV declines to $9.50 per share, causing the value of the speculative portion to drop below $8,000. This triggers the purchase of sufficient shares to raise the value of the speculative portion to $10,000. Over the long run, if the speculative investment of the constant dollar plan rises in value, the conservative component of the portfolio will increase in dollar value as profits are transferred into it.

Constant Ratio Plan

constant ratio plan
a formula plan for timing investment transactions, in which a desired fixed ratio of the speculative to the conservative portion of the portfolio is established; when the actual ratio differs by a predetermined amount from the desired ratio, transactions are made to rebalance the portfolio.

The **constant ratio plan** is similar to the constant dollar plan except that it establishes a desired fixed *ratio* of the speculative to the conservative portion of the portfolio. When the actual ratio of the two differs by a predetermined amount from the desired ratio, rebalancing occurs. At that point transactions are made in order to bring the actual ratio back to the desired amount. An investor using the constant ratio plan must decide on the appropriate apportionment of the portfolio between speculative and conservative investments. Then, a decision must be made regarding the ratio trigger point at which transactions occur.

A constant ratio plan for an initial portfolio of $20,000 is illustrated in Table 17.11. The investor has decided to allocate 50 percent of the portfolio to the speculative high-beta mutual fund and 50 percent to a money market account. Rebalancing will occur when the ratio of the speculative portion to the conservative portion is greater than or equal to 1.20 or less than or equal to .80. A sequence of net asset

TABLE 17.11 Constant Ratio Plan

Mutual Fund NAV	Value of Speculative Portion	Value of Conservative Portion	Total Portfolio Value	Ratio of Speculative Portion to Conservative Portion	Transactions	Number of Shares in Speculative Portion
$10.00	$10,000.00	$10,000.00	$20,000.00	1.000		1,000
11.00	11,000.00	10,000.00	21,000.00	1.100		1,000
12.00	12,000.00	10,000.00	22,000.00	1.200		1,000
→12.00	11,000.00	11,000.00	22,000.00	1.000	Sold 83.33 shares	916.67
11.00	10,083.00	11,000.00	21,083.00	0.917		916.67
10.00	9,166.70	11,000.00	20,166.70	0.833		916.67
9.00	8,250.00	11,000.00	19,250.00	0.750		916.67
→ 9.00	9,625.00	9,625.00	19,250.00	1.000	Purchased 152.78 shares	1,069.44
10.00	10,694.40	9,625.00	20,319.40	1.110		1,069.44

value changes is listed in Table 17.11. Initially $10,000 is allocated to each portion of the portfolio. When the fund NAV reaches $12, the 1.20 ratio triggers the sale of 83.33 shares. Then, the portfolio is back to its desired 50–50 ratio. Later, the fund NAV declines to $9, lowering the value of the speculative portion to $8,250. The ratio of the speculative portion to the conservative portion is then .75, which is below the .80 trigger point. A total of 152.78 shares is purchased to bring the desired ratio back up to the 50–50 level.

The long-run expectation under a constant ratio plan is that the speculative securities will rise in value. When this occurs, sales of the securities will be undertaken to reapportion the portfolio and increase the value of the conservative portion. This philosophy is similar to the constant dollar plan, except that a *ratio* is utilized as a trigger point.

Variable Ratio Plan

variable ratio plan a formula plan for timing investment transactions, in which the ratio of the speculative portion to the total portfolio varies depending on the movement in the value of the speculative securities; when the ratio rises or falls by a predetermined amount, the amount committed to the speculative portion of the portfolio is reduced or increased, respectively.

The **variable ratio plan** is the most aggressive of these four fairly passive investment strategies. It attempts to capture stock market movements to the investor's advantage by timing the market; that is, it tries to "buy low and sell high." The ratio of the speculative portion to the total portfolio varies depending upon the movement in value of the speculative securities. When the ratio rises a certain predetermined amount, the amount committed to the speculative segment of the portfolio is reduced. Conversely, if the value of the speculative portion declines such that it drops significantly in proportion to the whole portfolio, the percentage of commitment in the speculative vehicle is increased. In implementing the variable ratio plan, an investor has several decisions to make. First, one has to determine the initial allocation between the speculative and conservative portions of the portfolio. Next, trigger points to initiate buy or sell activity are chosen. These points are a function of the ratio between the value of the speculative portion and the value of the *total* portfolio. Finally, the adjustments in that ratio at each trigger point are set.

TABLE 17.12 Variable Ratio Plan

Mutual Fund NAV	Value of Speculative Portion	Value of Conservative Portion	Total Portfolio Value	Ratio of Speculative Portion to Total Portfolio	Transactions	Number of Shares in Speculative Portion
$10.00	$10,000.00	$10,000.00	$20,000.00	0.50		1,000
15.00	15,000.00	10,000.00	25,000.00	0.60		1,000
→15.00	11,250.00	13,750.00	25,000.00	0.45	Sold 250 shares	750
10.00	7,500.00	13,750.00	21,250.00	0.35		750
→10.00	11,687.50	9,562.50	21,250.00	0.55	Purchased 418.75 shares	1,168.75
12.00	14,025.00	9,562.50	23,587.50	0.41		1,168.75

An example of a variable ratio plan is shown in Table 17.12. Initially the portfolio is divided equally between the speculative and the conservative portions. The former consists of a high-beta (around 2.0) mutual fund, and the latter is a money market account. It was decided that when the speculative portion is 60 percent of the total portfolio, its proportion would be reduced to 45 percent. If the speculative portion of the portfolio dropped to 40 percent of the total portfolio, then its proportion would be raised to 55 percent. The theory behind this strategy is an attempt to time the cyclical movements in the mutual fund's value. When the fund moves up in value, profits are taken and the proportion invested in the no-risk money market account is increased. When the fund declines markedly in value, the proportion of capital committed to it is increased.

A sequence of transactions is depicted in Table 17.12. When the fund NAV climbs to $15, the 60 percent ratio trigger point is reached and 250 shares of the fund are sold. The proceeds are placed in the money market account, which causes the speculative portion to then represent 45 percent of the value of the portfolio. Later the fund NAV declines to $10, causing the speculative portion of the portfolio to drop to 35 percent. This triggers a portfolio rebalancing, and 418.75 shares are purchased, moving the speculative portion to 55 percent. When the fund NAV then moves to $12, the total portfolio is worth in excess of $23,500. In comparison, if the initial investment of $20,000 had been allocated equally and no rebalancing had been done between the mutual fund and the money market account, the portfolio's value at this time would be only $22,000 ($12 × 1,000 = $12,000 in the speculative portion plus $10,000 in a money market account).

Using Limit and Stop-Loss Orders

In Chapter 2 we discussed the market order, the limit order, and the stop-loss order. Here we will see how the limit and stop-loss orders can be employed to rebalance a portfolio. These types of security orders, if properly used, can increase an investor's return by lowering transaction costs.

Limit Order

In review, there are two basic types of security transaction orders. The *market order* instructs the broker to buy or sell securities at the best price available. This often means that buy orders are executed at the market maker's "ask" price and sell orders at the market maker's "bid" price. Limit orders constrain the broker as to the price and the time limit until canceled if unexecuted. A *limit order* specifies the investor's minimum sell price or the maximum price he or she will pay to buy a security. For example, if an order to sell 100 shares of Full Curve Contact Lens at 18 was placed with a broker, the broker would sell those shares only if a price of $18 per share or higher was obtained. Conversely, if a buy order for that security was placed at that price, the order would be executed only if the broker could buy the stock for the customer at $18 per share or less. In addition to the price constraint, a limit order can have a time duration of one day or longer or can be **good 'til canceled (GTC).** A GTC order, often called an "open order," generally remains in effect for six months unless executed, canceled, or renewed. In contrast, a **day order** expires at the end of the trading day it was entered, if it was not executed that day.

There are many ways an investor can use limit orders when securities are bought or sold. For instance, if an investor has decided to add a stock to the portfolio, a limit buy order will ensure that the investor buys only at the desired purchase price or below. An investor using a limit GTC order to buy has the broker trying to buy stock until the entire order is filled. The primary risk in using limit instead of market orders is that the order may not be executed. For example, if an investor placed a GTC order to buy 100 shares of State Oil of California at $27 per share and the stock never traded at $27 per share or less, the order would never be executed. Thus an investor must weigh the need for immediate execution (market order) versus the possibility of a better price with a limit order. Limit orders, of course, can increase an investor's return if they enable the investor to buy a security at a lower cost or sell at a higher price. During a typical trading day a stock will fluctuate up and down over a normal trading range. For example, suppose the common shares of Jama Motor traded ten times in the following sequence: 36, 35⅞, 35¾, 35⅞, 35½, 35⅝, 35¾, 36, 36⅛, 36. A market order to sell could have been executed at somewhere between 35½ (the low) and 36⅛ (the high). A limit order to sell at 36 would have been executed at 36. Thus, a half-point per share (50 cents) might have been gained by using a limit order.

good 'til canceled (GTC)
an order to buy or sell securities that generally remains in effect for six months unless executed, canceled, or renewed.

day order
an order to buy or sell securities that expires at the end of the trading day it was entered, if not executed that day.

Stop-Loss Order

The *stop-loss order* is a type of suspended order that requests the broker to sell a security at the best available price only if it trades at a specific price or lower. In essence a stop-loss order becomes a market order to sell if a stock trades at the trigger price or lower. The order can be used to limit the downside loss exposure of an investment. For example, an investor purchases 500 shares of Easy Work at 26. The investor has set a specific goal to sell the stock if it reaches 32 or drops to 23.

INVESTOR INSIGHTS

Successful Selling Strategies Protect Profits

Figuring out what stock to buy is hard enough, but after you've got it, how do you know when to sell?

That's a question that befuddles many individual investors.

Too often, they answer it by selling their winners and keeping their losers. "That's the worst thing an investor can do," says Michael Metz, chief market strategist for Oppenheimer & Co.

Sometimes, it's simply a matter of not wanting to acknowledge that they made a mistake. Sometimes it's a case of trying to "get even"—waiting until the stock's price comes back up to what they paid for it.

Either way, investors end up with a portfolio of dogs. The sad fact, says Roger Newell, chairman of Newell Associates, a Palo Alto, Calif., investment-management firm, is that "some losing stocks go bankrupt; some get down to a dollar. Then it's impossible to do anything."

Market pros say investors owe it to themselves to be savvy sellers. Decide on some sensible "sell rules," they say, and stick with them. Over time, investors who follow a disciplined selling strategy will be better off than those who try to decide emotionally on each stock case by case, says William J. Breen, a Northwestern University finance professor.

But what rules should you follow?

Sell the losers, says Oppenheimer's Mr. Metz. Not only does it make sense financially, it also can bring emotional satisfaction. "I always feel it's cathartic to sell my losers," he says. If he leaves them in his portfolio, "they keep reproaching me for my stupidity."

Others say there are reasons for getting rid of stocks that haven't clearly fallen into the "losers" category.

One approach is to get rid of a stock when the reason why you purchased it is no longer valid. "When you bought the stock, you had some idea of growth in mind," says John Markese, research director of the American Association of Individual Investors. But in time, he says, maybe you see that the company didn't come through with an expected new product, a merger or spinoff didn't work, or the company's competitive position in its industry has deteriorated.

A.C. Moore, market analyst at Argus Investment Co., says this rule also applies to changes in a "thesis" that compelled you to buy a stock. Say you purchased a construction company stock on the thesis that federal and state governments would spend billions in the near future to repair the crumbling infrastructure. Then the recession comes along, and funds won't be available. That's a disruption in a thesis, he says, and a reason to sell.

Ralph Wanger, portfolio manager of Acorn Fund, a small-stock mutual fund, suggests that whenever you buy a stock, you write down the reason you bought it. "It can be just a

To implement this goal, a GTC stop order to sell is entered with a price limit of 32, and another stop order is entered at a price of 23. If the issue trades at 23 or less, the stop-loss order becomes a market order, and the stock is sold at the best price couple of lines,'' he says. ''Then when you review your portfolio, check if the reason you bought the stock still holds true. If it doesn't, sell.''

Mr. Breen and Eugene Lerner, another Northwestern finance professor, have tested dozens of sell rules in computer simulations. The one that has worked best over the long run: sell a stock if a company's earnings for any 12-month period decline, compared with the previous 12 months.

''No management likes to report a fall in earnings,'' says Prof. Breen. ''And there are lots of ways to make earnings come out the way management wants them to. But when management reports a fall in earnings, they are telling us that they have run out of options.'' A serious warning indeed.

The Northwestern professors say the earnings-decline rule has worked better than such other mechanical sell rules as selling when a stock's price declines more than 10%, and selling when a stock's price-earnings ratio—the stock price divided by the company's per share profit—rises above the company's annual growth rate.

A more aggressive version of the earnings-decline strategy is to sell a stock when its earnings don't live up to analysts' estimates. Thus, a sale can be triggered if a company shows a 20% increase in quarterly earnings instead of the 30% that Wall Street analysts were counting on.

''When a company reports a negative earnings surprise, that tends to be a good sell signal,'' says Melissa Brown, director of quantitative research for Prudential Securities Inc. Research has shown that it's likely that company will have another negative surprise, says Ms. Brown.

Studies in the mid-1980s by Richard L. Rendleman Jr. and colleagues at the University of North Carolina found that if investors sold stocks based on this rule, they could avoid taking significant losses.

Several Wall Street firms applied the earnings-surprise theory and use it today. ''Earnings estimate revisions [downward] are by far the best variable for picking out stocks that will underperform,'' says Easton Ragsdale, chief quantitative analyst for Kidder, Peabody & Co.

But Prof. Rendleman says the popularity of the earnings-surprise approach may be watering down its effect. ''A number of Wall Street houses and lots of institutional and individual investors use this technique,'' he says.

In light of the attention paid to earnings surprises, Prof. Rendleman says individuals ''should take these numbers seriously but not necessarily build an entire investment strategy around them.'' However, they remain one factor to consider when deciding to sell a stock, he says.

Source: Earl C. Gottschalk, Jr. ''If It's Hard to Decide When to Sell, Here Are a Few Rules of Thumb,'' *The Wall Street Journal,* July 24, 1991, p. C1.

available. Conversely, if the issue trades at 32 or higher, the broker will sell the stock. In the first situation, the investor is trying to reduce his losses, and in the second, he's trying to protect a profit.

whipsawing
the situation in which
a stock drops in
price and then
bounces back up-
ward.

The principal risk in using stop-loss orders is **whipsawing,** which refers to a situation where a stock temporarily drops in price and then bounces back upward. If Easy Work dropped to 23, then 22½, and then rallied back to 26, the investor who placed the stop-loss at 23 would have been sold out at 22½. For this reason limit orders, including stop-loss orders, require careful analysis before they are placed. An investor must consider the stock's probable fluctuations as well as the need to purchase or sell the stock when choosing between a market, a limit, and a stop-loss order.

Warehousing Liquidity

One recommendation for an efficient portfolio is to keep a portion of it in a low-risk, highly liquid investment. Let us see why and how this works.

A Buffer

Investing in risky stocks or in property offers probable returns in excess of money market accounts or bonds. However, stocks and property are risky investments. So, one reason to invest a portion of a portfolio in a low-risk asset is to protect against total loss. The low-risk asset acts as a buffer against possible investment adversity. A second reason for maintaining funds in a low-risk asset is the possibility of future opportunities. When opportunity strikes, an investor who has the extra cash available will be able to take advantage of the situation. A sudden market dip, a valuable painting available at a low price, or an attractive real estate deal are all examples of situations in which an investor with cash to invest immediately may benefit. An investor who has set aside funds in a highly liquid investment need not disturb the existing portfolio.

Choosing a Liquid Investment

There are two primary media for warehousing liquidity: money market accounts at financial institutions and money market mutual funds. The money market as well as some NOW accounts at banks and savings and loan associations provide relatively easy access to funds and provide returns competitive with (but somewhat lower than) money market mutual funds. Over time, the products offered by financial institutions are expected to become more competitive with those offered by mutual funds and stock brokerage firms. (See Chapter 3 for a detailed discussion of the role and vehicles available for warehousing liquidity.)

Timing Investment Sales

One of the more difficult decisions an investor must make concerns the appropriate time to sell an investment. Knowing when to sell a stock is as important as deciding which stock to buy. The nearby Investor Insights box offers several strategies for timing stock sales. Periodically an investor must review the portfolio and consider possible sales and new purchases. Two items relevant to the sales decision are discussed here: tax consequences and achieving investment goals.

Tax Consequences

Taxes affect nearly all investment actions. There are certain basics that all investors can and should understand. The treatment of capital losses is important: *a maximum of $3,000 of losses in excess of capital gains can be applied in any one year*. If an investor has a loss position in an investment and has concluded it would be wise to sell it, the best time to sell is when a capital gain is available against which the loss can be applied. Clearly, the tax consequences of investment sales should be carefully considered prior to taking action.

Achieving Investment Goals

Every investor would enjoy buying an investment at its lowest price and selling it at its top price. At a more practical level, an investment should be sold when it no longer meets the needs of the portfolio's owner. In particular, if an investment has become either more or less risky than is desired, or if it has not met its return objective, it should be sold. The tax consequences mentioned above help to determine the appropriate time to sell. However, taxes are not the foremost consideration in a sale decision: the dual concepts of risk and return should be the overriding concerns.

Each investment should be examined periodically in light of its return performance and relative risk. If the investment no longer belongs in the portfolio, the investor should sell it and buy vehicles that are more suitable. Finally, an investor should not hold out for every nickel of profit. Very often, those who hold out for the top price watch the value of their holdings plummet downward. If an investment looks ripe to sell, an investor should sell it, take the profit, reinvest it in an appropriate vehicle, and enjoy his or her good fortune. An investor, in sum, should set realistic goals and criteria, and stick with them.

SUMMARY

1. To analyze the performance of individual investments, the investor must gather current market information and stay abreast of international, national, and local economic and market events. Indexes of investment performance such as the Dow Jones Industrial Average (DJIA) and bond market indicators are available for use in assessing market behavior.

2. The performance of individual investment vehicles including stocks, bonds, mutual funds, real estate, and other investment vehicles (options, futures, tangibles) can be measured on both a pretax and an after-tax basis using the holding period return (HPR). HPR measures the total return (income plus change in value) actually earned on the investment during the investment period.

3. To measure portfolio return, the investor must estimate the amount invested, the income earned, and any capital gains—both realized and unrealized—over the relevant current time period. Using these values, along with information about any new funds added or funds withdrawn during the period, the investor can calculate the portfolio's holding period return (HPR) by dividing the total returns by the amount of investment during the period. Comparison of the portfolio's HPR to overall market measures can provide some insight with regard to the portfolio's performance relative to the market.

4. A risk-adjusted, market-adjusted comparison of a portfolio's return can be made using Sharpe's measure, Treynor's measure, or Jensen's measure. Sharpe's and Treynor's measures find the risk premium per unit of risk, which can be compared to similar market measures to assess the portfolio's performance relative to the market. Jensen's measure, which is theoretically consistent with Treynor's, calculates the portfolio's excess return using beta and CAPM. Because it is relatively easy to calculate and directly makes both risk and market adjustments, Jensen's measure tends to be preferred over Sharpe's and Treynor's. Portfolio revision—reallocation and rebalancing—should take place when returns are unacceptable or when the portfolio fails to meet the investor's objectives.

5. Formula plans are used to time purchase and sale decisions in order to take advantage of price changes that result from cyclical price movements. The four commonly used formula plans are dollar cost averaging, the constant dollar plan, the constant ratio plan, and the variable ratio plan.

6. Limit and stop-loss orders can be used to trigger the rebalancing of a portfolio to contribute toward improved portfolio returns. Low-risk, highly liquid investment vehicles such as money market accounts (and some NOWs) and money market mutual funds can warehouse liquidity. Such liquidity can protect against total loss and allow the investor to quickly seize attractive future investment opportunities. Investment sales should be timed to obtain maximum tax benefits (or minimum tax consequences) and to contribute to the achievement of the investor's goals.

QUESTIONS

1. Why is it important for an investor to continuously manage and control his or her portfolio? Explain.

2. What role does current market information play in analyzing investment returns? How do changes in economic and market activity affect investment returns? Explain.

3. Which indexes can an investor use to compare his or her investment performance to general market returns? Briefly explain each of these indexes.

4. What are bond market indicators and how are they different from stock market indicators? Name three sources of bond yield data.

5. Aside from comparing returns on real estate investment with those of local real estate investors, why would a real estate investor also compare returns with the Consumer Price Index and with the New York Stock Exchange composite index? Explain.

6. Briefly discuss dividend yield and holding period return (HPR) as measures of investment return. Are they equivalent? Explain.

7. Distinguish between the types of dividend distributions mutual funds make. Are these dividends the only source of return from a mutual fund? Explain.

8. What are the two basic components of an investor's return from real estate investment? What is meant by reversion, and how is it calculated? Explain.

9. Under what three conditions would an investment holding be a candidate for sale? What must be true about the expected return on a risky investment when compared with the return on a low-risk investment in order to cause a rational investor to acquire the risky investment? Explain.

10. What is a problem investment? What two questions should be considered when analyzing an investment portfolio? Explain.

11. What is active portfolio management? How does evidence with regard to it conflict with efficient-market arguments? Explain.

12. Describe the steps involved in measuring portfolio return. Explain the role of the portfolio's HPR in this process, and explain why one must differentiate between realized and unrealized gains.

13. Why is it important to utilize a portfolio's HPR in a risk-adjusted, market-adjusted rate of return comparison? Why is comparing a portfolio's return to the return on a broad market index generally inadequate? Explain.

14. Briefly describe each of the following risk-adjusted, market-adjusted return measures available for assessing portfolio performance, and explain how they are used.

    a. Sharpe's measure.
    b. Treynor's measure.
    c. Jensen's measure.

15. How is Jensen's measure similar to Treynor's measure? Why is Jensen's measure (alpha) generally preferred over the measures of Sharpe and Treynor when assessing portfolio performance? Explain.

16. Briefly define and discuss portfolio revision. Explain its role in the process of managing and controlling a portfolio.

17. Explain the role formula plans can play in timing security transactions. Describe the logic underlying the use of these plans.

18. Briefly describe and differentiate among each of the following plans.

    a. Dollar cost averaging.
    b. Constant dollar plan.
    c. Constant ratio plan.
    d. Variable ratio plan.

19. Define and differentiate among each of the following types of orders.

    a. Market order.
    b. Limit order.
    c. Good 'til canceled (GTC).
    d. Day order.
    e. Stop-loss order.

20. Give two reasons why an investor might want to maintain funds in a low-risk, highly liquid investment.

21. Describe the two items an investor should consider before reaching a decision to sell an investment vehicle.

PROBLEMS

 1. Mark Smith purchased 100 shares of the Tomco Corporation in December 1992, at a total cost of $1,762. He held the shares for 15 months and then sold them, netting $2,500. During the period he held the stock, the company paid him $200 in cash dividends. How much, if any, was the capital gain realized upon the sale of stock? Calculate Mark's pretax HPR.

2. Jill Clark invested $25,000 in the bonds of Industrial Aromatics, Inc. She held them for 13 months, at the end of which she sold them for $26,746. During the period of ownership she earned $2,000 interest. Calculate the pretax and after-tax HPR on Jill's investment. Assume she is in the 31 percent tax bracket.

3. Charlotte Smidt bought 2,000 shares of the balanced no-load LaJolla Fund exactly one year ago for a NAV of $8.60 per share. During the year the fund distributed investment income dividends of $.32 per share and capital gains dividends of $.38 per share. At the end of the year Charlotte, who is in the 35 percent tax bracket (federal and state combined), realized $8.75 per share on the sale of all 2,000 shares. Calculate Charlotte's pretax and after-tax HPR on this transaction.

4. Peter Hancock bought a parcel of land in Red Woods one year ago for $55,000. He sold the property this year for $63,000, and his reversion from the sale was $61,000 after deducting $2,000 in closing costs and income taxes. Estimate Peter's after-tax holding period return on the investment.

5. Marilyn Gore, who is in a 33 percent tax bracket (federal and state combined), purchased 10 ounces of gold for $4,000 exactly one year ago. Due to the release of a large amount of gold onto the market by the Commonwealth of Independent States, Marilyn netted only $370 per ounce upon the sale of her 10 ounces of gold today. What are Marilyn's pretax and after-tax HPRs on this transaction?

6. On January 1, 1993, Simon Love's portfolio of 15 common stocks, completely equity financed, had a market value of $264,000. At the end of May 1993 Simon sold one of the stocks, which had a beginning-of-year value of $26,300, for $31,500. He did not reinvest those or any other funds in the portfolio during the year. He received total dividends from stocks in his portfolio of $12,500 during the year. On December 31, 1993, Simon's portfolio had a market value of $250,000. Find the HPR on Simon's portfolio during the year ended December 31, 1993. (*Hint:* Measure the amount of withdrawn funds at their beginning-of-year value.)

7. Niki Malone's portfolio earned a return of 11.8 percent during the year just ended. The portfolio's standard deviation of return was 14.1 percent. The risk-free rate is currently 6.2 percent. During the year the return on the market portfolio was 9.0 percent, and its standard deviation was 9.4 percent.

   a. Calculate Sharpe's measure for Niki Malone's portfolio for the year just ended.
   b. Compare the performance of Niki's portfolio found in (a) to that of Hector Smith's portfolio, which has Sharpe's measure of .43. Which portfolio performed better? Why?
   c. Calculate Sharpe's measure for the market portfolio for the year just ended.
   d. Use your findings in (c) to discuss the performance of Niki's portfolio relative to the market during the year just ended.

8. During the year just ended, Anna Schultz's portfolio, which has a beta of .90, earned a return of 8.6 percent. The risk-free rate is currently 7.3 percent, and the return on the market portfolio during the year just ended was 9.2 percent.

   a. Calculate Treynor's measure for Anna's portfolio for the year just ended.
   b. Compare the performance of Anna's portfolio found in (a) to that of Stacey Quant's portfolio which has Treynor's measure of 1.25 percent. Which portfolio performed better? Explain.
   c. Calculate Treynor's measure for the market portfolio for the year just ended.

d. Use your findings in (c) to discuss the performance of Anna's portfolio relative to the market during the year just ended.

9. Chee Chew's portfolio has a beta of 1.3 and earned a return of 12.9 percent during the year just ended. The risk-free rate is currently 7.8 percent, and the return on the market portfolio during the year just ended was 11.0 percent.

   a. Calculate Jensen's measure (alpha) for Chee's portfolio for the year just ended.
   b. Compare the performance of Chee's portfolio found in (a) to that of Carri Uhl's portfolio which has Jensen's measure of −0.24. Which portfolio performed better? Explain.
   c. Use your findings in (a) to discuss the performance of Chee's portfolio relative to the market during the period just ended.

10. The risk-free rate is currently 8.1 percent. Use the data in the following table for the Fio family's portfolio and the market portfolio during the year just ended to answer the questions below.

Data Item	Fio's Portfolio	Market Portfolio
Rate of return	12.8%	11.2%
Standard deviation of return	13.5%	9.6%
Beta	1.10	1.00

   a. Calculate Sharpe's measure for the portfolio and the market, compare them, and assess the performance of the Fio's portfolio during the year just ended.
   b. Calculate Treynor's measure for the portfolio and the market, compare them, and assess the performance of the Fio's portfolio during the year just ended.
   c. Calculate Jensen's measure (alpha), and use it to assess the performance of the Fio's portfolio during the year just ended.
   d. Based on your findings in (a), (b), and (c), assess the performance of the Fio's portfolio during the year just ended.

11. Over the past two years Jonas Cone has used a dollar cost averaging formula to purchase $300 worth of FCI common stock each month. The price per share paid each month over the two years is given in the following table. Assume Jonas paid no brokerage commissions on these transactions.

	Price per Share of FCI	
Month	**Year 1**	**Year 2**
January	11⅝	11⅜
February	11½	11¾
March	11½	12
April	11	12
May	11¾	12⅛
June	12	12½
July	12⅜	12¾
August	12½	13
September	12¼	13¼
October	12½	13
November	11⅞	13⅜
December	11½	13½

a. How much was Jonas's total investment over the two-year period?
b. How many shares did Jonas purchase over the two-year period?
c. Use your findings in **a** and **b** to calculate Jonas's average cost per share of FCI.
d. What was the value of Jonas's holdings in FCI at the end of the second year?

CFA QUESTION (**This question is from the 1986 Level III Exam.**)

Assume that a portfolio of randomly-selected, low-P/E stocks will produce superior risk-adjusted returns over time. List *four* reasons why, even if this assumption is true, a portfolio manager might *not* wish to hold a portfolio of only low-P/E stocks.

(See Appendix C for Guideline Answer to this question.)

CASE PROBLEMS

17.1 Assessing the Stalchecks' Portfolio Performance

The Stalchecks, Mary and Nick, have an investment portfolio containing four vehicles. It was developed to provide them with a balance between current income and capital appreciation. Rather than acquire mutual fund shares or diversify within a given class of investment vehicle, they developed their portfolio with the idea of diversifying across various types of vehicles. The portfolio currently contains common stock, industrial bonds, mutual fund shares, and a real estate investment. They acquired each of these vehicles during the past three years, and they plan to invest in gold and other vehicles sometime in the future.

Currently the Stalchecks are interested in measuring the return on their investment and assessing how well they have done relative to the market. They hope that the return earned over the past calendar year is in excess of what they would have earned by investing in a portfolio consisting of the S&P 500 stock composite index. Their investigation indicates that the risk-free rate was 7.2 percent and the (before-tax) return on the S&P stock portfolio was 10.1 percent during the past year. With the aid of a friend, they were able to estimate the beta of their portfolio, which was 1.20. In their analysis they planned to ignore taxes, since they felt their earnings were adequately sheltered. Since they did not make any portfolio transactions during the past year, the Stalchecks would have to consider only unrealized capital gains, if any. In order to make the necessary calculations, the Stalchecks gathered the following information on each of the four vehicles in their portfolio:

Common stock. They own 400 shares of KJ Enterprises common stock. KJ is a diversified manufacturer of metal pipe and is known for its unbroken stream of dividends. Over the past few years it has entered new markets and as a result has offered moderate capital appreciation potential. Its share price has risen from 17¼ at the start of last calendar year to 18¾ at the end of the year. During the year, quarterly cash dividends of $.20, $.20, $.25, and $.25 were paid.

Industrial bonds. The Stalchecks own 8 Cal Industries bonds. The bonds have a $1,000 par value, a 9¾ percent coupon, and are due in 2003. They are A-rated by Moody's. The bond was quoted at 97 at the beginning of the year and ended the calendar year at 96⅜.

Mutual fund. They hold 500 shares in the Holt Fund, a balanced, no-load mutual fund. The dividend distributions on the fund during the year consisted of $.60 in investment income and $.50 in capital gains. The fund's NAV at the beginning of the calendar year was $19.45, and it ended the year at $20.02.

Real estate. They own a parcel of raw land that had an appraised value of $26,000 at the beginning of the calendar year. Although they did not have it appraised at year-end, they were offered $30,500 for it at that time. Since the offer was made through a realtor, they would have had to pay nearly $1,500 in sales commissions and fees in order to make the sale at that price.

Questions

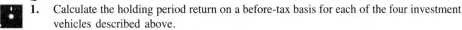 **1.** Calculate the holding period return on a before-tax basis for each of the four investment vehicles described above.

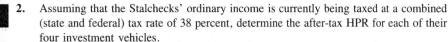 **2.** Assuming that the Stalchecks' ordinary income is currently being taxed at a combined (state and federal) tax rate of 38 percent, determine the after-tax HPR for each of their four investment vehicles.

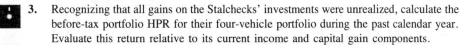 **3.** Recognizing that all gains on the Stalchecks' investments were unrealized, calculate the before-tax portfolio HPR for their four-vehicle portfolio during the past calendar year. Evaluate this return relative to its current income and capital gain components.

4. Use the HPR calculated in question 3 to calculate Jensen's measure (alpha) in order to analyze the performance of the Stalcheck's portfolio on a risk-adjusted, market-adjusted basis. Comment on your finding. Is it reasonable to use Jensen's measure to evaluate a four-vehicle portfolio? Why or why not?

5. Based upon your analysis in questions 1, 3, and 4, what, if any, recommendations might you offer the Stalchecks relative to the revision of their portfolio? Explain your recommendations.

17.2 Evaluating Formula Plans: Charles Schultz's Approach

Charles Schultz, a mathematician with Ansco Petroleum Company, wishes to develop a rational basis for timing his portfolio transactions. He currently holds a security portfolio with a market value of nearly $100,000, divided equally between a very conservative low-beta common stock, ConCam United, and a highly speculative high-beta stock, Fleck Enterprises. Based upon his reading of the investments literature, Charles does not believe it is necessary to diversity one's portfolio across 8 to 20 securities. His own feeling, based on his independent mathematical analysis, is that one can achieve the same results by holding a two-security portfolio in which one security is very conservative and the other is highly speculative. His feelings on this point will not be altered; he plans to continue to hold such a two-security portfolio until he finds that his theory does not work. During the past couple of years, he has earned a rate of return in excess of the risk-adjusted, market-adjusted rate expected on such a portfolio.

Charles's current interest centers on investigating and possibly developing his own formula plan for timing portfolio transactions. The current stage of his analysis centers on the evaluation of four commonly used formula plans in order to isolate the desirable features of each. The four plans being considered are (1) dollar cost averaging, (2) the constant dollar plan, (3) the constant ratio plan, and (4) the variable ratio plan. Charles's analysis of the plans will involve the use of two types of data. Since dollar cost averaging is a passive buy-and-hold strategy in which the periodic investment is held constant, whereas the other plans are more active in that they involve periodic purchases and sales within the portfolio, differing data are needed to evaluate each of them.

For evaluating the dollar cost averaging plan, Charles decided he would assume the investment of $500 at the end of each 45-day period. He chose to use 45-day time intervals in order to achieve certain brokerage fee savings that would be available by making larger transactions. The $500 per 45 days totaled $4,000 for the year and equaled the total amount Charles invested during the past year. (*Note:* For convenience, the returns earned on the portions of the $4,000 that remain uninvested during the year are ignored.) In evaluating this plan, he would assume that half ($250) was invested in the conservative stock (ConCam United) and the other half in the speculative stock (Fleck Enterprises). The share prices for each of the stocks at the end of the eight 45-day periods when purchases were to be made are given below.

	Price per Share	
Period	ConCam	Fleck
1	22⅛	22⅛
2	21⅞	24½
3	21⅞	25⅜
4	22	28½
5	22¼	21⅞
6	22⅛	19¼
7	22	21½
8	22¼	23⅝

In order to evaluate the other three plans, Charles planned to begin with a $4,000 portfolio evenly split between the two stocks. He chose to use $4,000, since that amount would correspond to the total amount invested in the two stocks over one year using dollar cost averaging. He planned to use the same eight points in time given earlier in order to assess and make, if required, transfers within the portfolio. For each of the three plans evaluated using these data, he established the triggering points given below.

Constant dollar plan. Each time the speculative portion of the portfolio is worth 13 percent more or less than its initial value of $2,000, the portfolio is rebalanced in order to bring the speculative portion back to its initial $2,000 value.

Constant ratio plan. Each time the ratio of the value of the speculative portion of the portfolio to the value of the conservative portion is greater than or equal to 1.15 or less than or equal to .84, the portfolio is rebalanced through sale or purchase, respectively, in order to bring the ratio back to its initial value of 1.0.

Variable ratio plan. Each time the value of the speculative portion of the portfolio rises above 54 percent of the total value of the portfolio, its proportion would be reduced to 46 percent. Each time the value of the speculative portion of the portfolio drops below 38 percent of the total value of the portfolio, its proportion would be raised to 50 percent of the portfolio value.

Questions

1. Under the dollar cost averaging plan, determine (a) the total number of shares purchased, (b) the average cost per share, and (c) the year-end portfolio value expressed both in dollars and as a percentage of the amount invested for (1) the conservative stock, (2) the speculative stock, and (3) the total portfolio.
2. Using the constant dollar plan, determine the year-end portfolio value expressed both in dollars and as a percentage of the amount initially invested for (1) the conservative portion, (2) the speculative portion, and (3) the total portfolio.
3. Repeat question 2 for the constant ratio plan. Be sure to answer all parts.
4. Repeat question 2 for the variable ratio plan. Be sure to answer all parts.
5. Compare and contrast your results from questions 1 through 4. You may want to summarize them in tabular form. Which plan would appear to have been most beneficial in timing Charles's portfolio activities during the past year? Explain.

APPENDIXES

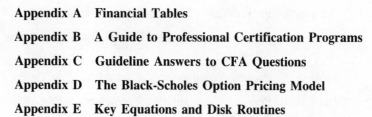

APPENDIX A

FINANCIAL TABLES

TABLE A.1 Future-Value Interest Factors for One Dollar, FVIF

| | INTEREST RATE | | | | | | | | | |
PERIOD	1%	2%	3%	4%	5%	6%	7%	8%	9%	10%
1	1.010	1.020	1.030	1.040	1.050	1.060	1.070	1.080	1.090	1.100
2	1.020	1.040	1.061	1.082	1.102	1.124	1.145	1.166	1.188	1.210
3	1.030	1.061	1.093	1.125	1.158	1.191	1.225	1.260	1.295	1.331
4	1.041	1.082	1.126	1.170	1.216	1.262	1.311	1.360	1.412	1.464
5	1.051	1.104	1.159	1.217	1.276	1.338	1.403	1.469	1.539	1.611
6	1.062	1.126	1.194	1.265	1.340	1.419	1.501	1.587	1.677	1.772
7	1.072	1.149	1.230	1.316	1.407	1.504	1.606	1.714	1.828	1.949
8	1.083	1.172	1.267	1.369	1.477	1.594	1.718	1.851	1.993	2.144
9	1.094	1.195	1.305	1.423	1.551	1.689	1.838	1.999	2.172	2.358
10	1.105	1.219	1.344	1.480	1.629	1.791	1.967	2.159	2.367	2.594
11	1.116	1.243	1.384	1.539	1.710	1.898	2.105	2.332	2.580	2.853
12	1.127	1.268	1.426	1.601	1.796	2.012	2.252	2.518	2.813	3.138
13	1.138	1.294	1.469	1.665	1.886	2.133	2.410	2.720	3.066	3.452
14	1.149	1.319	1.513	1.732	1.980	2.261	2.579	2.937	3.342	3.797
15	1.161	1.346	1.558	1.801	2.079	2.397	2.759	3.172	3.642	4.177
16	1.173	1.373	1.605	1.873	2.183	2.540	2.952	3.426	3.970	4.595
17	1.184	1.400	1.653	1.948	2.292	2.693	3.159	3.700	4.328	5.054
18	1.196	1.428	1.702	2.026	2.407	2.854	3.380	3.996	4.717	5.560
19	1.208	1.457	1.753	2.107	2.527	3.026	3.616	4.316	5.142	6.116
20	1.220	1.486	1.806	2.191	2.653	3.207	3.870	4.661	5.604	6.727
21	1.232	1.516	1.860	2.279	2.786	3.399	4.140	5.034	6.109	7.400
22	1.245	1.546	1.916	2.370	2.925	3.603	4.430	5.436	6.658	8.140
23	1.257	1.577	1.974	2.465	3.071	3.820	4.740	5.871	7.258	8.954
24	1.270	1.608	2.033	2.563	3.225	4.049	5.072	6.341	7.911	9.850
25	1.282	1.641	2.094	2.666	3.386	4.292	5.427	6.848	8.623	10.834
30	1.348	1.811	2.427	3.243	4.322	5.743	7.612	10.062	13.267	17.449
35	1.417	2.000	2.814	3.946	5.516	7.686	10.676	14.785	20.413	28.102
40	1.489	2.208	3.262	4.801	7.040	10.285	14.974	21.724	31.408	45.258
45	1.565	2.438	3.781	5.841	8.985	13.764	21.002	31.920	48.325	72.888
50	1.645	2.691	4.384	7.106	11.467	18.419	29.456	46.900	74.354	117.386

T A B L E   A . 1   Future-Value Interest Factors for One Dollar, FVIF *(Continued)*

INTEREST RATE

PERIOD	11%	12%	13%	14%	15%	16%	17%	18%	19%	20%
1	1.110	1.120	1.130	1.140	1.150	1.160	1.170	1.180	1.190	1.200
2	1.232	1.254	1.277	1.300	1.322	1.346	1.369	1.392	1.416	1.440
3	1.368	1.405	1.443	1.482	1.521	1.561	1.602	1.643	1.685	1.728
4	1.518	1.574	1.630	1.689	1.749	1.811	1.874	1.939	2.005	2.074
5	1.685	1.762	1.842	1.925	2.011	2.100	2.192	2.288	2.386	2.488
6	1.870	1.974	2.082	2.195	2.313	2.436	2.565	2.700	2.840	2.986
7	2.076	2.211	2.353	2.502	2.660	2.826	3.001	3.185	3.379	3.583
8	2.305	2.476	2.658	2.853	3.059	3.278	3.511	3.759	4.021	4.300
9	2.558	2.773	3.004	3.252	3.518	3.803	4.108	4.435	4.785	5.160
10	2.839	3.106	3.395	3.707	4.046	4.411	4.807	5.234	5.695	6.192
11	3.152	3.479	3.836	4.226	4.652	5.117	5.624	6.176	6.777	7.430
12	3.498	3.896	4.334	4.818	5.350	5.936	6.580	7.288	8.064	8.916
13	3.883	4.363	4.898	5.492	6.153	6.886	7.699	8.599	9.596	10.699
14	4.310	4.887	5.535	6.261	7.076	7.987	9.007	10.147	11.420	12.839
15	4.785	5.474	6.254	7.138	8.137	9.265	10.539	11.974	13.589	15.407
16	5.311	6.130	7.067	8.137	9.358	10.748	12.330	14.129	16.171	18.488
17	5.895	6.866	7.986	9.276	10.761	12.468	14.426	16.672	19.244	22.186
18	6.543	7.690	9.024	10.575	12.375	14.462	16.879	19.673	22.900	26.623
19	7.263	8.613	10.197	12.055	14.232	16.776	19.748	23.214	27.251	31.948
20	8.062	9.646	11.523	13.743	16.366	19.461	23.105	27.393	32.429	38.337
21	8.949	10.804	13.021	15.667	18.821	22.574	27.033	32.323	38.591	46.005
22	9.933	12.100	14.713	17.861	21.644	26.186	31.629	38.141	45.923	55.205
23	11.026	13.552	16.626	20.361	24.891	30.376	37.005	45.007	54.648	66.247
24	12.239	15.178	18.788	23.212	28.625	35.236	43.296	53.108	65.031	79.496
25	13.585	17.000	21.230	26.461	32.918	40.874	50.656	62.667	77.387	95.395
30	22.892	29.960	39.115	50.949	66.210	85.849	111.061	143.367	184.672	237.373
35	38.574	52.799	72.066	98.097	133.172	180.311	243.495	327.988	440.691	590.657
40	64.999	93.049	132.776	188.876	267.856	378.715	533.846	750.353	1051.642	1469.740
45	109.527	163.985	244.629	363.662	538.752	795.429	1170.425	1716.619	2509.583	3657.176
50	184.559	288.996	450.711	700.197	1083.619	1670.669	2566.080	3927.189	5988.730	9100.191

TABLE A.1 Future-Value Interest Factors for One Dollar, FVIF (Continued)

PERIOD	21%	22%	23%	24%	25%	30%	35%	40%	45%	50%
					INTEREST RATE					
1	1.210	1.220	1.230	1.240	1.250	1.300	1.350	1.400	1.450	1.500
2	1.464	1.488	1.513	1.538	1.562	1.690	1.822	1.960	2.102	2.250
3	1.772	1.816	1.861	1.907	1.953	2.197	2.460	2.744	3.049	3.375
4	2.144	2.215	2.289	2.364	2.441	2.856	3.321	3.842	4.421	5.063
5	2.594	2.703	2.815	2.932	3.052	3.713	4.484	5.378	6.410	7.594
6	3.138	3.297	3.463	3.635	3.815	4.827	6.053	7.530	9.294	11.391
7	3.797	4.023	4.259	4.508	4.768	6.275	8.172	10.541	13.476	17.086
8	4.595	4.908	5.239	5.589	5.960	8.157	11.032	14.758	19.541	25.629
9	5.560	5.987	6.444	6.931	7.451	10.604	14.894	20.661	28.334	38.443
10	6.727	7.305	7.926	8.594	9.313	13.786	20.106	28.925	41.085	57.665
11	8.140	8.912	9.749	10.657	11.642	17.921	27.144	40.495	59.573	86.498
12	9.850	10.872	11.991	13.215	14.552	23.298	36.644	56.694	86.380	129.746
13	11.918	13.264	14.749	16.386	18.190	30.287	49.469	79.371	125.251	194.620
14	14.421	16.182	18.141	20.319	22.737	39.373	66.784	111.119	181.614	291.929
15	17.449	19.742	22.314	25.195	28.422	51.185	90.158	155.567	263.341	437.894
16	21.113	24.085	27.446	31.242	35.527	66.541	121.713	217.793	381.844	656.841
17	25.547	29.384	33.758	38.740	44.409	86.503	164.312	304.911	553.674	985.261
18	30.912	35.848	41.523	48.038	55.511	112.454	221.822	426.875	802.826	1477.892
19	37.404	43.735	51.073	59.567	69.389	146.190	299.459	597.625	1164.098	2216.838
20	45.258	53.357	62.820	73.863	86.736	190.047	404.270	836.674	1687.942	3325.257
21	54.762	65.095	77.268	91.591	108.420	247.061	545.764	1171.343	2447.515	4987.883
22	66.262	79.416	95.040	113.572	135.525	321.178	736.781	1639.878	3548.896	7481.824
23	80.178	96.887	116.899	140.829	169.407	417.531	994.653	2295.829	5145.898	11222.738
24	97.015	118.203	143.786	174.628	211.758	542.791	1342.781	3214.158	7461.547	16834.109
25	117.388	144.207	176.857	216.539	264.698	705.627	1812.754	4499.816	10819.242	25251.164
30	304.471	389.748	497.904	634.810	807.793	2619.936	8128.426	24201.043	69348.375	*
35	789.716	1053.370	1401.749	1861.020	2465.189	9727.598	36448.051	*	*	*
40	2048.309	2846.941	3946.340	5455.797	7523.156	36117.754	*	*	*	*
45	5312.758	7694.418	11110.121	15994.316	22958.844	*	*	*	*	*
50	13779.844	20795.680	31278.301	46889.207	70064.812	*	*	*	*	*

*FVIF > 99,999.

TABLE A.2 Future-Value Interest Factors for a One-Dollar Annuity, FVIFA

PERIOD	1%	2%	3%	4%	5%	6%	7%	8%	9%	10%
1	1.000	1.000	1.000	1.000	1.000	1.000	1.000	1.000	1.000	1.000
2	2.010	2.020	2.030	2.040	2.050	2.060	2.070	2.080	2.090	2.100
3	3.030	3.060	3.091	3.122	3.152	3.184	3.215	3.246	3.278	3.310
4	4.060	4.122	4.184	4.246	4.310	4.375	4.440	4.506	4.573	4.641
5	5.101	5.204	5.309	5.416	5.526	5.637	5.751	5.867	5.985	6.105
6	6.152	6.308	6.468	6.633	6.802	6.975	7.153	7.336	7.523	7.716
7	7.214	7.434	7.662	7.898	8.142	8.394	8.654	8.923	9.200	9.487
8	8.286	8.583	8.892	9.214	9.549	9.897	10.260	10.637	11.028	11.436
9	9.368	9.755	10.159	10.583	11.027	11.491	11.978	12.488	13.021	13.579
10	10.462	10.950	11.464	12.006	12.578	13.181	13.816	14.487	15.193	15.937
11	11.567	12.169	12.808	13.486	14.207	14.972	15.784	16.645	17.560	18.531
12	12.682	13.412	14.192	15.026	15.917	16.870	17.888	18.977	20.141	21.384
13	13.809	14.680	15.618	16.627	17.713	18.882	20.141	21.495	22.953	24.523
14	14.947	15.974	17.086	18.292	19.598	21.015	22.550	24.215	26.019	27.975
15	16.097	17.293	18.599	20.023	21.578	23.276	25.129	27.152	29.361	31.772
16	17.258	18.639	20.157	21.824	23.657	25.672	27.888	30.324	33.003	35.949
17	18.430	20.012	21.761	23.697	25.840	28.213	30.840	33.750	36.973	40.544
18	19.614	21.412	23.414	25.645	28.132	30.905	33.999	37.450	41.301	45.599
19	20.811	22.840	25.117	27.671	30.539	33.760	37.379	41.446	46.018	51.158
20	22.019	24.297	26.870	29.778	33.066	36.785	40.995	45.762	51.159	57.274
21	23.239	25.783	28.676	31.969	35.719	39.992	44.865	50.422	56.764	64.002
22	24.471	27.299	30.536	34.248	38.505	43.392	49.005	55.456	62.872	71.402
23	25.716	28.845	32.452	36.618	41.430	46.995	53.435	60.893	69.531	79.542
24	26.973	30.421	34.426	39.082	44.501	50.815	58.176	66.764	76.789	88.496
25	28.243	32.030	36.459	41.645	47.726	54.864	63.248	73.105	84.699	98.346
30	34.784	40.567	47.575	56.084	66.438	79.057	94.459	113.282	136.305	164.491
35	41.659	49.994	60.461	73.651	90.318	111.432	138.234	172.314	215.705	271.018
40	48.885	60.401	75.400	95.024	120.797	154.758	199.630	259.052	337.872	442.580
45	56.479	71.891	92.718	121.027	159.695	212.737	285.741	386.497	525.840	718.881
50	64.461	84.577	112.794	152.664	209.341	290.325	406.516	573.756	815.051	1163.865

INTEREST RATE

TABLE A.2 Future-Value Interest Factors for a One-Dollar Annuity, FVIFA (Continued)

					INTEREST RATE					
PERIOD	11%	12%	13%	14%	15%	16%	17%	18%	19%	20%
1	1.000	1.000	1.000	1.000	1.000	1.000	1.000	1.000	1.000	1.000
2	2.110	2.120	2.130	2.140	2.150	2.160	2.170	2.180	2.190	2.200
3	3.342	3.374	3.407	3.440	3.472	3.506	3.539	3.572	3.606	3.640
4	4.710	4.779	4.850	4.921	4.993	5.066	5.141	5.215	5.291	5.368
5	6.228	6.353	6.480	6.610	6.742	6.877	7.014	7.154	7.297	7.442
6	7.913	8.115	8.323	8.535	8.754	8.977	9.207	9.442	9.683	9.930
7	9.783	10.089	10.405	10.730	11.067	11.414	11.772	12.141	12.523	12.916
8	11.859	12.300	12.757	13.233	13.727	14.240	14.773	15.327	15.902	16.499
9	14.164	14.776	15.416	16.085	16.786	17.518	18.285	19.086	19.923	20.799
10	16.722	17.549	18.420	19.337	20.304	21.321	22.393	23.521	24.709	25.959
11	19.561	20.655	21.814	23.044	24.349	25.733	27.200	28.755	30.403	32.150
12	22.713	24.133	25.650	27.271	29.001	30.850	32.824	34.931	37.180	39.580
13	26.211	28.029	29.984	32.088	34.352	36.786	39.404	42.218	45.244	48.496
14	30.095	32.392	34.882	37.581	40.504	43.672	47.102	50.818	54.841	59.196
15	34.405	37.280	40.417	43.842	47.580	51.659	56.109	60.965	66.260	72.035
16	39.190	42.753	46.671	50.980	55.717	60.925	66.648	72.938	79.850	87.442
17	44.500	48.883	53.738	59.117	65.075	71.673	78.978	87.067	96.021	105.930
18	50.396	55.749	61.724	68.393	75.836	84.140	93.404	103.739	115.265	128.116
19	56.939	63.439	70.748	78.968	88.211	98.603	110.283	123.412	138.165	154.739
20	64.202	72.052	80.946	91.024	102.443	115.379	130.031	146.626	165.417	186.687
21	72.264	81.698	92.468	104.767	118.809	134.840	153.136	174.019	197.846	225.024
22	81.213	92.502	105.489	120.434	137.630	157.414	180.169	206.342	236.436	271.028
23	91.147	104.602	120.203	138.295	159.274	183.600	211.798	244.483	282.359	326.234
24	102.173	118.154	136.829	158.656	184.166	213.976	248.803	289.490	337.007	392.480
25	114.412	133.333	155.616	181.867	212.790	249.212	292.099	342.598	402.038	471.976
30	199.018	241.330	293.192	356.778	434.738	530.306	647.423	790.932	966.698	1181.865
35	341.583	431.658	546.663	693.552	881.152	1120.699	1426.448	1816.607	2314.173	2948.294
40	581.812	767.080	1013.667	1341.979	1779.048	2360.724	3134.412	4163.094	5529.711	7343.715
45	986.613	1358.208	1874.086	2590.464	3585.031	4965.191	6879.008	9531.258	13203.105	18280.914
50	1668.723	2399.975	3459.344	4994.301	7217.488	10435.449	15088.805	21812.273	31514.492	45496.094

TABLE A.2 Future-Value Interest Factors for a One-Dollar Annuity, FVIFA (Continued)

INTEREST RATE

PERIOD	21%	22%	23%	24%	25%	30%	35%	40%	45%	50%
1	1.000	1.000	1.000	1.000	1.000	1.000	1.000	1.000	1.000	1.000
2	2.210	2.220	2.230	2.240	2.250	2.300	2.350	2.400	2.450	2.500
3	3.674	3.708	3.743	3.778	3.813	3.990	4.172	4.360	4.552	4.750
4	5.446	5.524	5.604	5.684	5.766	6.187	6.633	7.104	7.601	8.125
5	7.589	7.740	7.893	8.048	8.207	9.043	9.954	10.946	12.022	13.188
6	10.183	10.442	10.708	10.980	11.259	12.756	14.438	16.324	18.431	20.781
7	13.321	13.740	14.171	14.615	15.073	17.583	20.492	23.853	27.725	32.172
8	17.119	17.762	18.430	19.123	19.842	23.858	28.664	34.395	41.202	49.258
9	21.714	22.670	23.669	24.712	25.802	32.015	39.696	49.152	60.743	74.887
10	27.274	28.657	30.113	31.643	33.253	42.619	54.590	69.813	89.077	113.330
11	34.001	35.962	38.039	40.238	42.566	56.405	74.696	98.739	130.161	170.995
12	42.141	44.873	47.787	50.895	54.208	74.326	101.840	139.234	189.734	257.493
13	51.991	55.745	59.778	64.109	68.760	97.624	138.484	195.928	276.114	387.239
14	63.909	69.009	74.528	80.496	86.949	127.912	187.953	275.299	401.365	581.858
15	78.330	85.191	92.669	100.815	109.687	167.285	254.737	386.418	582.980	873.788
16	95.779	104.933	114.983	126.010	138.109	218.470	344.895	541.985	846.321	1311.681
17	116.892	129.019	142.428	157.252	173.636	285.011	466.608	759.778	1228.165	1968.522
18	142.439	158.403	176.187	195.993	218.045	371.514	630.920	1064.689	1781.838	2953.783
19	173.351	194.251	217.710	244.031	273.556	483.968	852.741	1491.563	2584.665	4431.672
20	210.755	237.986	268.783	303.598	342.945	630.157	1152.200	2089.188	3748.763	6648.508
21	256.013	291.343	331.603	377.461	429.681	820.204	1556.470	2925.862	5436.703	9973.762
22	310.775	356.438	408.871	469.052	538.101	1067.265	2102.234	4097.203	7884.215	14961.645
23	377.038	435.854	503.911	582.624	673.626	1388.443	2839.014	5737.078	11433.109	22443.469
24	457.215	532.741	620.810	723.453	843.032	1805.975	3833.667	8032.906	16579.008	33666.207
25	554.230	650.944	764.596	898.082	1054.791	2348.765	5176.445	11247.062	24040.555	50500.316
30	1445.111	1767.044	2160.459	2640.881	3227.172	8729.805	23221.258	60500.207	*	*
35	3755.814	4783.520	6090.227	7750.094	9856.746	32422.090	*	*	*	*
40	9749.141	12936.141	17153.691	22728.367	30088.621	*	*	*	*	*
45	25294.223	34970.230	48300.660	66638.937	91831.312	*	*	*	*	*
50	65617.202	94525.279	*	*	*	*	*	*	*	*

*FVIFA > 99,999.

TABLE A.3 Present-Value Interest Factors for One Dollar, PVIF

PERIOD	DISCOUNT (INTEREST) RATE									
	1%	2%	3%	4%	5%	6%	7%	8%	9%	10%
1	.990	.980	.971	.962	.952	.943	.935	.926	.917	.909
2	.980	.961	.943	.925	.907	.890	.873	.857	.842	.826
3	.971	.942	.915	.889	.864	.840	.816	.794	.772	.751
4	.961	.924	.888	.855	.823	.792	.763	.735	.708	.683
5	.951	.906	.863	.822	.784	.747	.713	.681	.650	.621
6	.942	.888	.837	.790	.746	.705	.666	.630	.596	.564
7	.933	.871	.813	.760	.711	.665	.623	.583	.547	.513
8	.923	.853	.789	.731	.677	.627	.582	.540	.502	.467
9	.914	.837	.766	.703	.645	.592	.544	.500	.460	.424
10	.905	.820	.744	.676	.614	.558	.508	.463	.422	.386
11	.896	.804	.722	.650	.585	.527	.475	.429	.388	.350
12	.887	.789	.701	.625	.557	.497	.444	.397	.356	.319
13	.879	.773	.681	.601	.530	.469	.415	.368	.326	.290
14	.870	.758	.661	.577	.505	.442	.388	.340	.299	.263
15	.861	.743	.642	.555	.481	.417	.362	.315	.275	.239
16	.853	.728	.623	.534	.458	.394	.339	.292	.252	.218
17	.844	.714	.605	.513	.436	.371	.317	.270	.231	.198
18	.836	.700	.587	.494	.416	.350	.296	.250	.212	.180
19	.828	.686	.570	.475	.396	.331	.277	.232	.194	.164
20	.820	.673	.554	.456	.377	.312	.258	.215	.178	.149
21	.811	.660	.538	.439	.359	.294	.242	.199	.164	.135
22	.803	.647	.522	.422	.342	.278	.226	.184	.150	.123
23	.795	.634	.507	.406	.326	.262	.211	.170	.138	.112
24	.788	.622	.492	.390	.310	.247	.197	.158	.126	.102
25	.780	.610	.478	.375	.295	.233	.184	.146	.116	.092
30	.742	.552	.412	.308	.231	.174	.131	.099	.075	.057
35	.706	.500	.355	.253	.181	.130	.094	.068	.049	.036
40	.672	.453	.307	.208	.142	.097	.067	.046	.032	.022
45	.639	.410	.264	.171	.111	.073	.048	.031	.021	.014
50	.608	.372	.228	.141	.087	.054	.034	.021	.013	.009

TABLE A.3 Present-Value Interest Factors for One Dollar, PFVIF (Continued)

DISCOUNT (INTEREST) RATE

PERIOD	11%	12%	13%	14%	15%	16%	17%	18%	19%	20%
1	.901	.893	.885	.877	.870	.862	.855	.847	.840	.833
2	.812	.797	.783	.769	.756	.743	.731	.718	.706	.694
3	.731	.712	.693	.675	.658	.641	.624	.609	.593	.579
4	.659	.636	.613	.592	.572	.552	.534	.516	.499	.482
5	.593	.567	.543	.519	.497	.476	.456	.437	.419	.402
6	.535	.507	.480	.456	.432	.410	.390	.370	.352	.335
7	.482	.452	.425	.400	.376	.354	.333	.314	.296	.279
8	.434	.404	.376	.351	.327	.305	.285	.266	.249	.233
9	.391	.361	.333	.308	.284	.263	.243	.225	.209	.194
10	.352	.322	.295	.270	.247	.227	.208	.191	.176	.162
11	.317	.287	.261	.237	.215	.195	.178	.162	.148	.135
12	.286	.257	.231	.208	.187	.168	.152	.137	.124	.112
13	.258	.229	.204	.182	.163	.145	.130	.116	.104	.093
14	.232	.205	.181	.160	.141	.125	.111	.099	.088	.078
15	.209	.183	.160	.140	.123	.108	.095	.084	.074	.065
16	.188	.163	.141	.123	.107	.093	.081	.071	.062	.054
17	.170	.146	.125	.108	.093	.080	.069	.060	.052	.045
18	.153	.130	.111	.095	.081	.069	.059	.051	.044	.038
19	.138	.116	.098	.083	.070	.060	.051	.043	.037	.031
20	.124	.104	.087	.073	.061	.051	.043	.037	.031	.026
21	.112	.093	.077	.064	.053	.044	.037	.031	.026	.022
22	.101	.083	.068	.056	.046	.038	.032	.026	.022	.018
23	.091	.074	.060	.049	.040	.033	.027	.022	.018	.015
24	.082	.066	.053	.043	.035	.028	.023	.019	.015	.013
25	.074	.059	.047	.038	.030	.024	.020	.016	.013	.010
30	.044	.033	.026	.020	.015	.012	.009	.007	.005	.004
35	.026	.019	.014	.010	.008	.006	.004	.003	.002	.002
40	.015	.011	.008	.005	.004	.003	.002	.001	.001	.001
45	.009	.006	.004	.003	.002	.001	.001	.001	*	*
50	.005	.003	.002	.001	.001	.001	*	*	*	*

*PVIF = .000 when rounded to three decimal places.

TABLE A.3 Present-Value Interest Factors for One Dollar, PVIF *(Continued)*

PERIOD	|	DISCOUNT (INTEREST) RATE								
		21%	22%	23%	24%	25%	30%	35%	40%	45%	50%
1		.826	.820	.813	.806	.800	.769	.741	.714	.690	.667
2		.683	.672	.661	.650	.640	.592	.549	.510	.476	.444
3		.564	.551	.537	.524	.512	.455	.406	.364	.328	.296
4		.467	.451	.437	.423	.410	.350	.301	.260	.226	.198
5		.386	.370	.355	.341	.328	.269	.223	.186	.156	.132
6		.319	.303	.289	.275	.262	.207	.165	.133	.108	.088
7		.263	.249	.235	.222	.210	.159	.122	.095	.074	.059
8		.218	.204	.191	.179	.168	.123	.091	.068	.051	.039
9		.180	.167	.155	.144	.134	.094	.067	.048	.035	.026
10		.149	.137	.126	.116	.107	.073	.050	.035	.024	.017
11		.123	.112	.103	.094	.086	.056	.037	.025	.017	.012
12		.102	.092	.083	.076	.069	.043	.027	.018	.012	.008
13		.084	.075	.068	.061	.055	.033	.020	.013	.008	.005
14		.069	.062	.055	.049	.044	.025	.015	.009	.006	.003
15		.057	.051	.045	.040	.035	.020	.011	.006	.004	.002
16		.047	.042	.036	.032	.028	.015	.008	.005	.003	.002
17		.039	.034	.030	.026	.023	.012	.006	.003	.002	.001
18		.032	.028	.024	.021	.018	.009	.005	.002	.001	.001
19		.027	.023	.020	.017	.014	.007	.003	.002	.001	*
20		.022	.019	.016	.014	.012	.005	.002	.001	.001	*
21		.018	.015	.013	.011	.009	.004	.002	.001	*	*
22		.015	.013	.011	.009	.007	.003	.001	.001	*	*
23		.012	.010	.009	.007	.006	.002	.001	*	*	*
24		.010	.008	.007	.006	.005	.002	.001	*	*	*
25		.009	.007	.006	.005	.004	.001	.001	*	*	*
30		.003	.003	.002	.002	.001	*	*	*	*	*
35		.001	.001	.001	.001	*	*	*	*	*	*
40		*	*	*	*	*	*	*	*	*	*
45		*	*	*	*	*	*	*	*	*	*
50		*	*	*	*	*	*	*	*	*	*

*PVIF = .000 when rounded to three decimal places.

TABLE A.4 Present-Value Interest Factors for a One-Dollar Annuity, PVIFA

PERIOD	1%	2%	3%	4%	5%	6%	7%	8%	9%	10%
					DISCOUNT (INTEREST) RATE					
1	.990	.980	.971	.962	.952	.943	.935	.926	.917	.909
2	1.970	1.942	1.913	1.886	1.859	1.833	1.808	1.783	1.759	1.736
3	2.941	2.884	2.829	2.775	2.723	2.673	2.624	2.577	2.531	2.487
4	3.902	3.808	3.717	3.630	3.546	3.465	3.387	3.312	3.240	3.170
5	4.853	4.713	4.580	4.452	4.329	4.212	4.100	3.993	3.890	3.791
6	5.795	5.601	5.417	5.242	5.076	4.917	4.767	4.623	4.486	4.355
7	6.728	6.472	6.230	6.002	5.786	5.582	5.389	5.206	5.033	4.868
8	7.652	7.326	7.020	6.733	6.463	6.210	5.971	5.747	5.535	5.335
9	8.566	8.162	7.786	7.435	7.108	6.802	6.515	6.247	5.995	5.759
10	9.471	8.983	8.530	8.111	7.722	7.360	7.024	6.710	6.418	6.145
11	10.368	9.787	9.253	8.760	8.306	7.887	7.499	7.139	6.805	6.495
12	11.255	10.575	9.954	9.385	8.863	8.384	7.943	7.536	7.161	6.814
13	12.134	11.348	10.635	9.986	9.394	8.853	8.358	7.904	7.487	7.103
14	13.004	12.106	11.296	10.563	9.899	9.295	8.746	8.244	7.786	7.367
15	13.865	12.849	11.938	11.118	10.380	9.712	9.108	8.560	8.061	7.606
16	14.718	13.578	12.561	11.652	10.838	10.106	9.447	8.851	8.313	7.824
17	15.562	14.292	13.166	12.166	11.274	10.477	9.763	9.122	8.544	8.022
18	16.398	14.992	13.754	12.659	11.690	10.828	10.059	9.372	8.756	8.201
19	17.226	15.679	14.324	13.134	12.085	11.158	10.336	9.604	8.950	8.365
20	18.046	16.352	14.878	13.590	12.462	11.470	10.594	9.818	9.129	8.514
21	18.857	17.011	15.415	14.029	12.821	11.764	10.836	10.017	9.292	8.649
22	19.661	17.658	15.937	14.451	13.163	12.042	11.061	10.201	9.442	8.772
23	20.456	18.292	16.444	14.857	13.489	12.303	11.272	10.371	9.580	8.883
24	21.244	18.914	16.936	15.247	13.799	12.550	11.469	10.529	9.707	8.985
25	22.023	19.524	17.413	15.622	14.094	12.783	11.654	10.675	9.823	9.077
30	25.808	22.397	19.601	17.292	15.373	13.765	12.409	11.258	10.274	9.427
35	29.409	24.999	21.487	18.665	16.374	14.498	12.948	11.655	10.567	9.644
40	32.835	27.356	23.115	19.793	17.159	15.046	13.332	11.925	10.757	9.779
45	36.095	29.490	24.519	20.720	17.774	15.456	13.606	12.108	10.881	9.863
50	39.197	31.424	25.730	21.482	18.256	15.762	13.801	12.234	10.962	9.915

TABLE A.4 Present-Value Interest Factors for a One-Dollar Annuity, PVIFA *(Continued)*

PERIOD	DISCOUNT (INTEREST) RATE									
	11%	12%	13%	14%	15%	16%	17%	18%	19%	20%
1	.901	.893	.885	.877	.870	.862	.855	.847	.840	.833
2	1.713	1.690	1.668	1.647	1.626	1.605	1.585	1.566	1.547	1.528
3	2.444	2.402	2.361	2.322	2.283	2.246	2.210	2.174	2.140	2.106
4	3.102	3.037	2.974	2.914	2.855	2.798	2.743	2.690	2.639	2.589
5	3.696	3.605	3.517	3.433	3.352	3.274	3.199	3.127	3.058	2.991
6	4.231	4.111	3.998	3.889	3.784	3.685	3.589	3.498	3.410	3.326
7	4.712	4.564	4.423	4.288	4.160	4.039	3.922	3.812	3.706	3.605
8	5.146	4.968	4.799	4.639	4.487	4.344	4.207	4.078	3.954	3.837
9	5.537	5.328	5.132	4.946	4.772	4.607	4.451	4.303	4.163	4.031
10	5.889	5.650	5.426	5.216	5.019	4.833	4.659	4.494	4.339	4.192
11	6.207	5.938	5.687	5.453	5.234	5.029	4.836	4.656	4.487	4.327
12	6.492	6.194	5.918	5.660	5.421	5.197	4.988	4.793	4.611	4.439
13	6.750	6.424	6.122	5.842	5.583	5.342	5.118	4.910	4.715	4.533
14	6.982	6.628	6.303	6.002	5.724	5.468	5.229	5.008	4.802	4.611
15	7.191	6.811	6.462	6.142	5.847	5.575	5.324	5.092	4.876	4.675
16	7.379	6.974	6.604	6.265	5.954	5.669	5.405	5.162	4.938	4.730
17	7.549	7.120	6.729	6.373	6.047	5.749	5.475	5.222	4.990	4.775
18	7.702	7.250	6.840	6.467	6.128	5.818	5.534	5.273	5.033	4.812
19	7.839	7.366	6.938	6.550	6.198	5.877	5.585	5.316	5.070	4.843
20	7.963	7.469	7.025	6.623	6.259	5.929	5.628	5.353	5.101	4.870
21	8.075	7.562	7.102	6.687	6.312	5.973	5.665	5.384	5.127	4.891
22	8.176	7.645	7.170	6.743	6.359	6.011	5.696	5.410	5.149	4.909
23	8.266	7.718	7.230	6.792	6.399	6.044	5.723	5.432	5.167	4.925
24	8.348	7.784	7.283	6.835	6.434	6.073	5.747	5.451	5.182	4.937
25	8.422	7.843	7.330	6.873	6.464	6.097	5.766	5.467	5.195	4.948
30	8.694	8.055	7.496	7.003	6.566	6.177	5.829	5.517	5.235	4.979
35	8.855	8.176	7.586	7.070	6.617	6.215	5.858	5.539	5.251	4.992
40	8.951	8.244	7.634	7.105	6.642	6.233	5.871	5.548	5.258	4.997
45	9.008	8.283	7.661	7.123	6.654	6.242	5.877	5.552	5.261	4.999
50	9.042	8.305	7.675	7.133	6.661	6.246	5.880	5.554	5.262	4.999

TABLE A.4 Present-Value Interest Factors for a One-Dollar Annuity, PVIFA (Continued)

PERIOD	\multicolumn{10}{c}{DISCOUNT (INTEREST) RATE}

PERIOD	21%	22%	23%	24%	25%	30%	35%	40%	45%	50%
1	.826	.820	.813	.806	.800	.769	.741	.714	.690	.667
2	1.509	1.492	1.474	1.457	1.440	1.361	1.289	1.224	1.165	1.111
3	2.074	2.042	2.011	1.981	1.952	1.816	1.696	1.589	1.493	1.407
4	2.540	2.494	2.448	2.404	2.362	2.166	1.997	1.849	1.720	1.605
5	2.926	2.864	2.803	2.745	2.689	2.436	2.220	2.035	1.876	1.737
6	3.245	3.167	3.092	3.020	2.951	2.643	2.385	2.168	1.983	1.824
7	3.508	3.416	3.327	3.242	3.161	2.802	2.508	2.263	2.057	1.883
8	3.726	3.619	3.518	3.421	3.329	2.925	2.598	2.331	2.109	1.922
9	3.905	3.786	3.673	3.566	3.463	3.019	2.665	2.379	2.144	1.948
10	4.054	3.923	3.799	3.682	3.570	3.092	2.715	2.414	2.168	1.965
11	4.177	4.035	3.902	3.776	3.656	3.147	2.752	2.438	2.185	1.977
12	4.278	4.127	3.985	3.851	3.725	3.190	2.779	2.456	2.196	1.985
13	4.362	4.203	4.053	3.912	3.780	3.223	2.799	2.469	2.204	1.990
14	4.432	4.265	4.108	3.962	3.824	3.249	2.814	2.477	2.210	1.993
15	4.489	4.315	4.153	4.001	3.859	3.268	2.825	2.484	2.214	1.995
16	4.536	4.357	4.189	4.033	3.887	3.283	2.834	2.489	2.216	1.997
17	4.576	4.391	4.219	4.059	3.910	3.295	2.840	2.492	2.218	1.998
18	4.608	4.419	4.243	4.080	3.928	3.304	2.844	2.494	2.219	1.999
19	4.635	4.442	4.263	4.097	3.942	3.311	2.848	2.496	2.220	1.999
20	4.657	4.460	4.279	4.110	3.954	3.316	2.850	2.497	2.221	1.999
21	4.675	4.476	4.292	4.121	3.963	3.320	2.852	2.498	2.221	2.000
22	4.690	4.488	4.302	4.130	3.970	3.323	2.853	2.498	2.222	2.000
23	4.703	4.499	4.311	4.137	3.976	3.325	2.854	2.499	2.222	2.000
24	4.713	4.507	4.318	4.143	3.981	3.327	2.855	2.499	2.222	2.000
25	4.721	4.514	4.323	4.147	3.985	3.329	2.856	2.499	2.222	2.000
30	4.746	4.534	4.339	4.160	3.995	3.332	2.857	2.500	2.222	2.000
35	4.756	4.541	4.345	4.164	3.998	3.333	2.857	2.500	2.222	2.000
40	4.760	4.544	4.347	4.166	3.999	3.333	2.857	2.500	2.222	2.000
45	4.761	4.545	4.347	4.166	4.000	3.333	2.857	2.500	2.222	2.000
50	4.762	4.545	4.348	4.167	4.000	3.333	2.857	2.500	2.222	2.000

APPENDIX B

A GUIDE TO PROFESSIONAL CERTIFICATION PROGRAMS

The financial services industry has in recent years undergone rapid and dynamic growth. More people, with greater incomes and a more sophisticated demand for financial security, currently participate in the financial markets than ever before. Opportunities for the financial services sector have been tremendous, and the need for well-educated, knowledgeable, and qualified professionals who possess high standards of personal integrity has increased. As a result, there has been more emphasis on the importance of professional associations or societies and the certifications they offer. Candidates for the various designations not only must meet certain academic qualifications but also must possess specified professional experience and conform to standards of performance and ethics. This appendix provides a brief overview of the major professional certification programs.

CHARTERED FINANCIAL ANALYST—CFA

The Chartered Financial Analyst (CFA) designation is conferred by the Association of Investment Management and Research (AIMR). The Association, formed in 1959 as the Institute of Chartered Financial Analysts, was organized on the principle that investors would receive maximum service from financial analysts who continuously work to meet reasonable professional and personal standards. These standards are set through the consensus and conscientious efforts of the Association's membership, and they are met by completion of several programs designed and implemented by the Association.

A financial analyst seeking membership in the AIMR must (1) meet eligibility requirements, including a bachelor's degree or the equivalent in professional work experience; (2) fully comply with the AIMR Code of Ethics and Standards of Professional Conduct; (3) study books, journal articles, and other readings chosen by the Association; and (4) successfully pass three examinations administered by the Association, each approximately six hours in length. The candidate for the CFA designation must have at least three years of experience in the investment decision-making process; the charter will not be awarded until this requirement is met although the candidate may take the exams before it is.

Once an applicant has been accepted for candidacy, he or she is sent a detailed reading list reflecting the latest in analytical theory and techniques. The entire CFA program is based on independent home study. No formal classroom instruction is presented by the Association, although it does organize study groups in cooperation with CFA educational coordinators of local analyst societies or colleges and universities. Study guides, textbooks, and reading lists published periodically by the Association also assist candidates in their study. On average, candidates spend an estimated 160 hours of individual study time preparing for each of the three exams.

The CFA Charter is awarded to candidates who pass the three examinations in sequence and meet the other requirements. The exams are given each year on the first Saturday in June at 125 locations around the world. Candidates may take only one exam per year, as all three exams are offered at the same time. The exams are:

- Level I: Investment Principles
- Level II: Applied Financial Analysis
- Level III: Investment Management

To register, the applicant must submit a detailed application form and supporting documents. Applications are due by August 31 of the year preceding the date on which the exam is to be taken. Late registrations are accepted between September 1 and February 1 but are charged a late fee. No applications are accepted after February 1. Fees for admission to take the examinations vary and depend on the time of registration and the examination for the which the candidate registers.

For more information about the CFA program, contact:

A.I.M.R. (Association of Investment Management and Research)
P.O. Box 3668
Charlottesville, VA 22903
Phone: (804) 977-6600

CHARTERED INVESTMENT COUNSELOR—CIC

The CIC designation is a specialized credential, given only to individuals who have earned the CFA Charter and who specifically work as investment counselors. The person can be employed by a financial services organization or by a private or public corporation or institution, or be an independent consultant, but he or she must be functioning as an investment counselor.

The Investment Counsel Association of America (ICAA) significantly upgraded the Chartered Investment Counselor program in 1975 in order to honor excellence in the investment counsel profession. The Charter recognizes the special qualifications of investment counselors within ICAA member firms who carry out the investment counsel function as defined in the ICAA Standards of Practice:

The responsibility of investment counsel is to render professional, unbiased and continuous advice to clients regarding their investments.

The CIC program was developed in cooperation with the Institute of Chartered Financial Analysts. To qualify, candidates must (1) hold the designation Chartered Financial Analyst (CFA); (2) be employed by a member firm of the ICAA at the time the charter is awarded; (3) meet the ethical and professional standards of the ICAA; (4) have completed three years in an eligible occupational position; and (5) demonstrate that their primary responsibility is the counseling function, i.e., the rendering of continuous person-to-person advice to clients regarding their investments. No ancillary course of study nor examination is required. If a Chartered Investment Counselor becomes disassociated from a member firm, the designation may be taken along, if certain conditions are met, the most important of which is that the individual be actively engaged in investment counseling.

For more information about the CIC designation, contact:

Investment Counsel Association of America, Inc.
20 Exchange Place
New York, NY 10005
Phone: (212) 344-0999

CHARTERED FINANCIAL CONSULTANT—ChFC

The Chartered Financial Consultant (ChFC) is a designation developed to expand the knowledge and professional skills of financial planners and life insurance agents. It is conferred upon successful completion of a 10-part course of study covering the fundamentals of financial planning, investments, life insurance, estate planning, income taxation, and retirement planning. The course of study can be completed through home study or by attending classes offered by either a local chapter of the American Society of Chartered Financial Consultants or an affiliated college or university.

Award of the ChFC designation requires three years of professional experience in the insurance, financial planning, or financial services environments. No specific academic degree is required, but a high school diploma is strongly suggested. Once awarded the ChFC designation, an individual must meet specific continuing education requirements.

The course of study consists of 10 college-level courses, each lasting approximately 15 weeks. A two-hour examination taken at the conclusion of each course must be passed to successfully complete the program. Computer tests can be taken year-round in testing centers in many cities.

For more information about the ChFC program, contact:

The American College
270 S. Bryn Mawr Avenue
Bryn Mawr, PA 19010
Telephone No.: (215) 526-1000

CHARTERED LIFE UNDERWRITER—CLU

The Chartered Life Underwriter (CLU) credential is specifically designed to enhance the knowledge of people employed in the life insurance industry. Most, but not all, individuals who seek or have earned this designation are also licensed insurance agents or brokers. The CLU is conferred only upon successful completion of a 10-part course of study which covers the fundamentals of estate planning, retirement planning, income taxation, investments, and other areas of risk management as they apply to life insurance. The course of study can be completed through home study or by attending courses offered by either a local chapter of the American Society of Chartered Life Underwriters or an affiliated college or university.

Award of the CLU designation requires that an individual have at least three years of professional experience in the insurance industry, preferably in life insurance. There are no degree requirements, although a high school diploma is strongly suggested. Once awarded the CLU designation, an individual must meet specific continuing education requirements.

The course of study consists of 10 college-level courses, each lasting approximately 15 weeks. A two-hour examination taken at the conclusion of each course must be passed to successfully complete the program. Computer tests can be taken year-round in testing centers in many cities.

For more information about the CLU program, contact:

The American College
270 S. Bryn Mawr Avenue
Bryn Mawr, PA 19010
Telephone No.: (215) 526-1000

CERTIFIED FINANCIAL PLANNER—CFP

Although the CFP designation was established 20 years ago by the College for Financial Planning, since 1986 it has been granted by the International Board of Standards and Practices for Certified Financial Planners, Inc. (IBCFP) in Denver, Colorado. The Certified Financial Planner designation is awarded after a candidate successfully meets four requirements: (1) completion of an IBCFP-approved course of study covering a six-part financial planning curriculum; (2) passing a two-day, 10-hour comprehensive examination; (3) providing proof of financial planning-related work experience; and (4) disclosing any legal proceedings and agreeing to uphold the IBCFP Code of Ethics.

For more information about the CFP designation, contact:

International Board of Standards and Practices for Certified Financial Planners, Inc.
1660 Lincoln Street, Suite 3050
Denver, CO 80264
Phone: (303) 830-7543

APPENDIX C

GUIDELINE ANSWERS
TO CFA QUESTIONS

Chapter 1

No CFA question.

Chapter 2

No CFA question.

Chapter 3

a. Using Eq. 3.3, the BEY for the T-bill is:

$$\text{BEY} = [365/n] \times \left[\frac{R-P}{P}\right]$$

$$= [365/180] \times \left[\frac{\$10,000 - \$9,600}{\$9,600}\right] = \underline{\underline{8.45\%}}$$

b. (1) The bond equivalent price of the instrument is used as the denominator instead of the redemption value.
   (2) The bond equivalent yield is based upon a 365-day year, whereas the bill's discount is based on a 360-day year.

Chapter 4

Four primary risks faced by investors are:

- *Purchasing power risk:* the risk of inflation reducing the returns on various investments. One should look at the total return of equities on a price-level–adjusted basis.
- *Interest rate risk:* a rise in the level of interest rates that depresses the prices of fixed income instruments and frequently causes lower prices for equities. Interest rate volatility and uncertainty are both relevant.
- *Business risk:* the risks associated with the business cycle. Stock prices tend to go down in anticipation of a downturn in the business cycle. Factors affecting the business cycle include the impact of monetary policy, changes in technology, and changes in supply of raw materials. Attempting to correctly forecast the turning point in a business cycle and the factors that affect a business cycle can reduce the business risk.

- *Market risk:* the general risk associated with fluctuations in the stock market. When the stock market declines, most stocks go down in price. While a low beta for a stock or a defensive stock position may reduce the volatility, the stock market has a pervasive influence on individual stocks.

Other sources of risk include:

- *Exchange rate risk:* the potential decline in investment value due to a decline in the currency in which the shares or bonds are held.
- *Regulatory risk:* the risk of an unanticipated change in the regulation of factors that affect investments such as changes in tax policy.
- *Political risk:* the unanticipated change in investment environment due to a change in political parties or a change of view of the current political party.

Chapter 5

[*Note:* This questions looks simpler than it actually is! The difficulty lies in coming up with the *net deficit*—which is no easy task. Once that's done, however, the problem becomes relatively straightforward, as it involves little more than finding the book value per share. While finding the net book deficit is a technical accounting matter and this text doesn't spend a great deal of time on these sorts of technical accounting issues, the guideline answer to this CFA question does provide some insight into how such matters could affect measures like book value and book value per share.]

First, find the *net deficit* as follows:

Retained earnings (deficit)*	($2,100,000)
Capital in excess of par*	100,000
Preferred dividends in arrears**	(1,500,000)
Preferred stock liquidation premium***	(1,000,000)
Net deficit	($4,500,000)

*See balance sheet (Stockholders' equity).

**Dividends in arrears = $7.50/share × 2 years × 100,000 shares = $1,500,000.

***Calculation of liquidation premium:
  Par value of stock (from balance sheet) = $15,000,000 ÷ 100,000 shares = $150 share
  Liquidation value = $160/share (from balance sheet)
  Liquidation premium = ($160 − $150) × 100,000 shares = $1,000,000.

Now, to find *book value per share:*

Par value (from balance sheet)	$15,000,000
Less: Net deficit	(4,500,000)
Net book value	$10,500,000
Number of preferred shares outstanding	100,000
Book value per share = $10,500,000/100,000 = $105	

Chapter 6

a. 1990 ROE component values for Merck are as follows:

$$\text{Tax burden} = \text{net income/pretax income}$$
$$= \$1,650/\$2,550 = \underline{.647}$$

$$\text{Pretax profit margin} = \text{pretax income/sales}$$
$$= \$2,550/\$7,120 = \underline{.358}$$

$$\text{Total asset turnover} = \text{sales/assets}$$
$$= \$7,120/\$7,250 = \underline{.982}$$

$$\text{Financial leverage} = \text{assets/equity}$$
$$= \$7,250/\$3,860 = \underline{1.878}$$

$$\text{ROE} = .647 \times .358 \times .982 \times 1.878 = \underline{.427}, \text{ or } \underline{42.7\%}$$

(Using Eq. 6.10 from the text:

$$\text{ROE} = \frac{\text{net income}}{\text{stockholders' equity}} = \frac{\$1,650}{\$3,860} = \underline{42.7\%}$$

Not surprisingly, the answers are the same.)

b.

COMPONENT	1985	1990	IMPACT
Tax burden	.621	.647	Favorable
Pretax profit margin	.245	.358	Big improvement
Total asset turnover	.724	.982	Big improvement
Financial leverage	1.877	1.878	No change
ROE	.207	.427	

The ROE for Merck more than doubled from 20.7% in 1985 to 42.7% in 1990. The two primary factors behind this improvement were an increase in the profit margin and an increase in the asset turnover. Merck was able to increase selling prices or reduce operating costs, or some combination of both. The higher asset turnover is indicative of greater efficiency because Merck was able to produce more sales revenue per dollar of assets.

Chapter 7

a. Current dividends per share:

$$\text{EPS} \times \text{dividend payout ratio} = \$4.50 \times .55 = \underline{\$2.48}$$

Rate of growth, g:

$$\text{ROE} \times (1 - \text{dividend payout ratio}) = .10 \times (1 - .55) = \underline{4.5\%}$$

Now, using the *constant growth dividend valuation model:*

$$P_0 = \frac{D_1}{k - g} = \frac{(D_0(1 + g)}{k - g} = \frac{\$2.48(1.045)}{.11 - .045} = \underline{\$39.87}$$

b. Use the *variable growth dividend valuation model,* with growth equal to 15% for the first two years, then 4½% thereafter:

$$D_1 = \$2.48(1 + .15) = \$2.85$$

$$D_2 = \$2.85(1 + .15) = \$3.27$$

$$D_3 = \$3.27(1 + .045) = \$3.42$$

$$P_2 = \frac{D_3}{k - g} = \frac{\$3.42}{.11 - .045} = \$52.62$$

Now, using a k (present-value discount rate) of 11% in the variable growth DVM, we have:

$$P_0 = \$2.85(.901) + \$3.27(.812) + \$52.62(.812)$$
$$= \$2.56 + \$2.65 + \$42.72 = \underline{\$47.93}$$

Chapter 8

No CFA question.

Chapter 9

The two methods are *modified* and *Macaulay* duration.

- Macaulay duration measures the average life of a bond, ignoring any options embedded in the security. Modified duration measures the price sensitivity of a bond to the change in yield to maturity.
- Modified duration is the more widely used method, particularly for corporate and mortgage-backed issues.

Chapter 10

a. Using a 10-year (1988–1998) investment period and semi-annual compounding, with a 10% required return, the *investment value* of the convertible is:

$$IV = [\$80/2 \times PVIFA_{5\%, \, 20 \, \text{periods}}] + [\$1,000 \times PVIF_{5\%, \, 20 \, \text{periods}}]$$

$$= (\$40 \times 12.462) + (\$1,000 \times .377)$$

$$= \$498.48 + \$377 = \underline{\$875.48}$$

Conversion value is:

$$CV = \text{conversion ratio} \times \text{market price of common}$$

$$= 18 \times \$48 = \underline{\$864.00}$$

b. Conversion premium (at a current market price of $1,000 on the convertible) is:

$$CP = \frac{\$1,000 - CV}{CV} = \frac{\$1,000 - \$864}{\$864} = \underline{15.7\%}$$

Payback period (see Eq. 10.9 in text) is:

$$P/B = \frac{\text{conversion premium (in \$)}}{\text{interest income} - \text{dividend income}}$$

$$= \frac{\$1,000 - \$864}{\$80 - (18 \times \$1.44)} = \frac{\$136}{\$80 - \$25.92} = \underline{2.5 \text{ yrs.}}$$

Given that the Heathtronics convertible has a "reasonable" conversion premium and a fairly low payback period, it should be viewed as the more desirable investment.

c. The convertible bond's new *conversion value* will be:

$$CV = \$65 \text{ (common stock price)} \times 18 \text{ shares (conversion ratio)}$$
$$= \underline{\$1,170.00}$$

The convertible bond's new *investment value* will be:

$$IV = \$40 \times 10.8276 \text{ (present value of coupon payments at}$$
$$6\% \text{ for 18 periods)} + \$1,000 \times .3503 \text{ (present value}$$
$$\text{of redemption payment at } 6\% \text{ for 18 periods)} = \underline{\$783.40}.$$

The new conversion value of $1,170.00 exceeds the new investment value of $796.62 and therefore will dominate in determining the convertible bond's new market price. Because the conversion value exceeds the bond's call price of $1,080, the convertible is not likely to have a large premium over conversion value (if the bond is called, the bondholders would lose this premium). Therefore, the market price of the convertible bond is expected to be only slightly above the bond's conversion value.

The one-year percentage return (assuming a $1,170 price) is as follows:

$$\frac{\$1,170 \text{ (current price)} - \$1,000 \text{ (original price)} + \$80 \text{ (annual coupon)}}{\$1,000 \text{ (original price)}}$$

$$= \frac{\$250}{\$1,000} = \underline{\underline{25\%}}$$

Chapter 11

a. A single put will hedge an amount equal to the current market value of the put times $100. For the three index puts in this question, each will hedge the following amounts:

S&P 100	364.58 × $100 = $36,458
S&P 500	388.89 × $100 = $38,889
NYSE	214.73 × $100 = $21,473

Therefore, the number of puts required to hedge a $3,500,000 portfolio are as follows:

S&P 100	$3,500,000/$36,458 =	96 puts
S&P 500	$3,500,000/$38,889 =	90 puts
NYSE	$3,500,000/$21,473 =	163 puts

And the total cost of setting up the hedge is:

	NO. PUTS	× PUT PREMIUM	= TOTAL COST
S&P 100	96	× ($12.75 × 100) =	$122,400
S&P 500	90	× ($11.00 × 100) =	$ 99,000
NYSE	163	× ($ 6.25 × 100) =	$101,875

b. The costs of the S&P 500 and NYSE puts are about the same, and both are substantially cheaper than the S&P 100; that fact alone would rule out the S&P 100. Of the remaining two, the S&P 500 has a higher correlation with the portfolio (meaning it would do a much better job in tracking the behavior of—i.e., in protecting—the target portfolio). Also, it is much more actively traded than the NYSE put. Therefore, *the purchase of 90 S&P 500 puts is recommended*.

Chapter 12

Because Chen is considering adding either short index futures or long index options (a form of protective put) to an existing well-diversified equity portfolio, he evidently intends to create a hedged position for the existing portfolio. Both the *short futures* and the *long options* positions will reduce the risk of the resulting combined portfolios, but in different ways.

Assuming that the short futures contract is perfectly negatively correlated with the existing equity portfolio, and that the size of the futures position is sufficient to hedge the risk of the entire equity portfolio, any movement up or down in the level of stock market prices will result in offsetting gains and losses in the combined portfolio's two segments (the equity portfolio itself and the short futures position). Thus, Chen is effectively removing the portfolio from exposure to market movements by eliminating all systematic (market) risk; unsystematic (specific) risk has already been minimized because the equity portfolio is a well-diversified one. Once the equity portfolio has been perfectly hedged, no risk remains, and Chen can expect to receive the risk-free rate of return on the combined portfolio. If the hedge is less than perfect, some risk and some potential for return beyond the risk-free rate are present, but only in proportion to the completeness of the hedge.

If, on the other hand, Chen hedges the portfolio by purchasing stock index puts, he will be placing a floor price on the equity portfolio. If the market declines and the index value drops below the strike price of the puts, the value of the puts increases, offsetting the loss in the equity portfolio. Conversely, if the stock market rises, the value of the put options will decline, and they may expire worthless; however, the potential return to the combined portfolio is unlimited and reduced only by the cost of the puts. As with the short futures, if the long options hedge is less than perfect, down-side risk remains in the combined portfolio in proportion to the amount not covered by the puts.

In summary, either short futures or long options (puts) can be used to reduce or eliminate risk in the equity portfolio. Use of the options (put) strategy, however, permits unlimited potential returns to be realized (less the cost of the options), while use of the short futures strategy effectively guarantees the risk-free rate but reduces or eliminates potential returns above that level. Neither strategy dominates the other; each offers a different risk/return profile and involves different costs. Arbitrage ensures that, on a risk-adjusted basis, neither approach is superior.

Chapter 13

No CFA question.

Chapter 14

No CFA question.

Chapter 15

No CFA question.

Chapter 16

The investment process itself is common to all managers everywhere, whether in a one-manager shop where a hand-held calculator is used or in the offices of an industry giant employing the latest in real-time, on-line, interactive computer systems.

The four key steps in the portfolio management process are:

1. Identify and specify the *investor's objectives, preferences, and constraints,* in order to develop explicit investment policies.
2. Develop and implement *strategies* through the choice of optimal combinations of financial and real assets in the marketplace.
3. Monitor market *conditions,* relative *asset values,* and the investor's *circumstances.*
4. Make *portfolio adjustments* as appropriate to reflect significant changes in any or all of the relevant variables.

Portfolio management is a dynamic and continuous process in which these four steps are repeated again and again.

Chapter 17

Here are four reasons that a portfolio manager may *not* want to hold such a concentrated portfolio:

1. Diversification.
2. Portfolio liquidity.
3. Tax considerations of yield and capital gains.
4. The desire to tilt the portfolio toward characteristics deemed desirable by the portfolio manager (quality, beta, price/book, dividend requirements, factor sensitivity).

APPENDIX D

▐ THE BLACK-SCHOLES OPTION PRICING MODEL

One of the best-known and most widely used formulas in finance is the Black-Scholes option pricing model (OPM). It was originally developed in 1973 by two professors, Fischer Black and Myron Scholes. They designed the model to calculate the price of a European-style call option on non-dividend-paying stocks. (Recall that a European option is one that can be exercised only on the expiration date, not before, as opposed to an American option, which can be executed any time before the expiration date.) Options traders and others who make their living in the market quickly learned to use the Black-Scholes model to determine the correct price for options and to help them adjust their complicated stock and options combinations. The model can be modified to make it applicable to American options, puts, and options on stocks that pay dividends, as well as to options on other underlying securities such as futures and indexes.

Understanding the basic Black-Scholes model is fundamental to understanding both the theory of option pricing and the strategies of profitable trading. The mathematical concepts that underlie the model are advanced and complex, but the application of the model is relatively simple, especially with calculators or computers. For the first course in investments, rather than try to derive the option pricing model, it's probably more beneficial simply to explain the concept and show how to use the model to price options.

The foundation of the model rests on the construction of a hypothetical risk-free portfolio, consisting of long call options and short positions in the underlying stock. With proper selection of the number of call options held and the number of stocks sold, the investor can lock in a certain amount of profit. Since this profit is certain, or risk-free, the investor earns the risk-free rate on the portfolio. The model uses four directly observable variables (the market price of the stock, the exercise price on the call, the time remaining until expiration on the call, and the risk-free interest rate) and one variable that is fairly easy to estimate (the standard deviation of the stock's returns). With the five variables, the basic Black-Scholes option pricing model calculates the *price of a call option* as follows:

Equation D.1

$$C = (S)[N(d_1)] - (X)(\exp^{-rt})[N(d_2)]$$

where

C is the price of the call, or the call premium

S is the price of the underlying asset, such as a stock price

X is the exercise price or the strike price of the call

r is the continuously compounded annual risk-free interest rate

t is the time (in fractions of 1 year) to the option's maturity

exp equals approximately 2.718292; it is included as a function key (sometimes labeled e^x) on most financial calculators

$N(d_1)$ and $N(d_2)$ are probabilities from the cumulative standard normal distribution (see Table D.1)

Let's look at this equation before we try to use it. It begins by stating that in calculating the price of a call, the difference between the stock price and the exercise price is very important. In fact, at expiration, either the price of a call will be zero, if it is out-of-the-money (i.e., if the stock price is less than the strike price), or it will be equal to the difference between the stock price and the strike price, if it is in-the-money. Because we are trying to price the call at a point in time before expiration, we explicitly capture the time value of money by finding the present value of the exercise price. This continuous discounting process is performed by $\exp^{-rt}$. Also, since we do not know what the stock price will be by the expiration date, we must use a probability distribution to adjust the call premium for the uncertainty involved. The variables $N(d_1)$ and $N(d_2)$ are probabilities of the stock price being at a certain price relative to where it is now. The values for d_1 and d_2 are used to calculate the probabilities that the stock price at expiration will be a certain number of standard deviations above or below the standardized mean (i.e., 0). Their formulas are:

Equation D.2
$$d_1 = \frac{\ln(S/X) + (r + .5\sigma^2)t}{\sigma\sqrt{t}}$$

Equation D.3
$$d_2 = d_1 - \sigma\sqrt{t}$$

Notice that in the calculation of d_1, *ln* refers to the natural logarithm of the ratio of the stock price and exercise price. This function, too, is included on most financial calculators. Also note that the equation uses both the standard deviation, σ, and the variance, σ^2, of the stock's returns. The variable t is included as a fraction of a 365-day year, and r is the risk-free interest rate in decimal form.

Although you will most often want to use the Black-Scholes option pricing formula on a preprogrammed calculator or computer, it is useful to work through an application to see how the model works. Assume that you want to earn income by writing a call option on Gogol MegaCorp stock, which you think will decrease in value. The current stock price is $32 5/8, and you want to write a call with a strike price of $30, to expire in 85 days. The risk-free rate is currently 7%, and you estimate that the volatility of the stock's returns has a standard deviation of .32.

TABLE D.1 Standard Normal Distribution Function

t	0	1	2	3	4	5	6	7	8	9
−3	.0013									
−2.9	.0019	.0018	.0018	.0017	.0017	.0016	.0015	.0015	.0014	.0014
−2.8	.0026	.0025	.0024	.0023	.0023	.0022	.0021	.0021	.0020	.0019
−2.7	.0035	.0034	.0033	.0032	.0031	.0030	.0029	.0028	.0027	.0026
−2.6	.0047	.0045	.0044	.0043	.0041	.0040	.0039	.0038	.0037	.0036
−2.5	.0062	.0060	.0059	.0057	.0055	.0054	.0052	.0051	.0049	.0048
−2.4	.0082	.0080	.0078	.0075	.0073	.0071	.0069	.0068	.0066	.0064
−2.3	.0107	.0104	.0102	.0099	.0096	.0094	.0091	.0089	.0087	.0084
−2.2	.0139	.0136	.0132	.0129	.0125	.0122	.0119	.0116	.0113	.0110
−2.1	.0179	.0174	.0170	.0166	.0162	.0158	.0154	.0150	.0146	.0143
−2.0	.0228	.0222	.0217	.0212	.0207	.0202	.0197	.0192	.0188	.0183
−1.9	.0287	.0281	.0275	.0268	.0262	.0256	.0250	.0244	.0239	.0233
−1.8	.0359	.0351	.0344	.0336	.0329	.0322	.0314	.0307	.0300	.0294
−1.7	.0446	.0436	.0427	.0418	.0409	.0401	.0392	.0384	.0375	.0367
−1.6	.0548	.0537	.0526	.0516	.0505	.0495	.0485	.0475	.0465	.0455
−1.5	.0668	.0655	.0643	.0630	.0618	.0606	.0594	.0582	.0571	.0560
−1.4	.0808	.0793	.0778	.0764	.0750	.0735	.0721	.0708	.0694	.0681
−1.3	.0968	.0951	.0934	.0918	.0901	.0885	.0869	.0853	.0838	.0823
−1.2	.1151	.1131	.1112	.1093	.1075	.1056	.1038	.1020	.1003	.0985
−1.1	.1357	.1335	.1314	.1292	.1271	.1251	.1230	.1210	.1190	.1170
−1.0	.1587	.1562	.1539	.1515	.1492	.1469	.1446	.1423	.1401	.1379
− .9	.1841	.1814	.1788	.1762	.1736	.1711	.1685	.1660	.1635	.1611
− .8	.2119	.2090	.2061	.2033	.2005	.1977	.1949	.1921	.1894	.1867
− .7	.2420	.2389	.2358	.2327	.2296	.2266	.2236	.2206	.2177	.2148
− .6	.2743	.2709	.2676	.2643	.2611	.2578	.2546	.2514	.2483	.2451
− .5	.3085	.3050	.3015	.2981	.2946	.2912	.2877	.2843	.2810	.2776
− .4	.3446	.3400	.3372	.3336	.3300	.3264	.3228	.3192	.3156	.3121
− .3	.3821	.3783	.3745	.3707	.3669	.3632	.3594	.3557	.3520	.3483
− .2	.4207	.4168	.4129	.4090	.4052	.4013	.3974	.3936	.3897	.3859
− .1	.4602	.4562	.4522	.4483	.4443	.4404	.4364	.4325	.4286	.4247
− .0	.5000	.4960	.4920	.4880	.4840	.4801	.4761	.4721	.4681	.4641

To value this call, we must first compute d_1 and d_2; that is:

$$d_1 = \frac{ln(S/X) + (r + .5\sigma^2)t}{\sigma\sqrt{t}}$$

$$= \frac{ln\left(\frac{32.625}{30}\right) + (.07 + .5[.32^2])\left(\frac{85}{365}\right)}{.32\sqrt{\frac{85}{365}}}$$

$$= \frac{ln(1.0875) + (.1212)(.2329)}{.32\sqrt{.2329}} = \frac{.0839 + .0282}{.1544} = \underline{\underline{.7260}}$$

TABLE D.1 Standard Normal Distribution Function *(Continued)*

t	0	1	2	3	4	5	6	7	8	9
.0	.5000	.5040	.5080	.5120	.5160	.5199	.5239	.5279	.5319	.5359
.1	.5398	.5438	.5478	.5517	.5557	.5596	.5636	.5675	.5714	.5753
.2	.5793	.5832	.5871	.5910	.5948	.5987	.6026	.6064	.6103	.6141
.3	.6179	.6217	.6255	.6293	.6331	.6368	.6406	.6443	.6480	.6517
.4	.6554	.6592	.6628	.6664	.6700	.6736	.6772	.6808	.6844	.6880
.5	.6915	.6950	.6985	.7019	.7054	.7088	.7123	.7157	.7190	.7224
.6	.7257	.7291	.7324	.7357	.7389	.7422	.7454	.7486	.7517	.7549
.7	.7580	.7611	.7642	.7673	.7704	.7734	.7764	.7794	.7823	.7852
.8	.7881	.7910	.7939	.7967	.7995	.8023	.8051	.8078	.8106	.8133
.9	.8159	.8186	.8212	.8238	.8264	.8289	.8315	.8340	.8365	.8389
1.0	.8413	.8438	.8461	.8485	.8508	.8531	.8554	.8577	.8599	.8621
1.1	.8643	.8665	.8686	.8708	.8729	.8749	.8770	.8790	.8810	.8830
1.2	.8849	.8870	.8888	.8907	.8925	.8944	.8962	.8980	.8997	.9015
1.3	.9032	.9049	.9066	.9082	.9099	.9115	.9131	.9147	.9162	.9177
1.4	.9192	.9207	.9222	.9236	.9251	.9265	.9279	.9292	.9306	.9319
1.5	.9332	.9345	.9357	.9370	.9382	.9394	.9406	.9418	.9429	.9441
1.6	.9452	.9463	.9474	.9484	.9495	.9505	.9515	.9525	.9535	.9545
1.7	.9554	.9564	.9573	.9582	.9591	.9599	.9608	.9616	.9625	.9633
1.8	.9641	.9649	.9656	.9664	.9671	.9678	.9686	.9693	.9700	.9706
1.9	.9713	.9719	.9726	.9732	.9738	.9744	.9750	.9756	.9761	.9767
2.0	.9772	.9778	.9783	.9788	.9793	.9798	.9803	.9808	.9812	.9817
2.1	.9821	.9826	.9830	.9834	.9838	.9842	.9846	.9850	.9854	.9857
2.2	.9861	.9864	.9868	.9871	.9875	.9878	.9881	.9884	.9887	.9890
2.3	.9893	.9896	.9898	.9901	.9904	.9906	.9909	.9911	.9913	.9916
2.4	.9918	.9920	.9922	.9925	.9927	.9929	.9931	.9932	.9934	.9936
2.5	.9938	.9940	.9941	.9943	.9945	.9946	.9948	.9949	.9951	.9952
2.6	.9953	.9955	.9956	.9957	.9959	.9960	.9961	.9962	.9963	.9964
2.7	.9965	.9966	.9967	.9968	.9969	.9970	.9971	.9972	.9973	.9974
2.8	.9974	.9975	.9976	.9977	.9977	.9978	.9979	.9979	.9980	.9981
2.9	.9981	.9982	.9982	.9983	.9984	.9984	.9985	.9985	.9986	.9987
3.	.9987									

Value for $d_1(.73)$ → .7

Value for $d_2(.57)$ ← .7224

Now for d_2:

$$d_2 = d_1 - \sigma\sqrt{t}$$
$$= .7260 - .1544 = \underline{.5716}$$

Next, we take these numbers to the cumulative standard normal table to find the associated probabilities. These values are given in Table D.1. To use it, we need to first round d_1 and d_2 to two decimal places. This gives $d_1 = .73$ and $d_2 = .57$. Looking these values up in the table, we find the respective probabilities of $N(d_1) = .7673$ and $N(d_2) = .7157$.

We can now complete the OPM by calculating the call price:

TABLE D.2 Determinants of the Call Premium

AN INCREASE IN . . .	WILL CAUSE THE CALL PREMIUM TO . . .
stock price	increase
exercise price	decrease
time to expiration	increase
volatility of returns	increase
risk-free rate	increase

$$C = (S)[N(d_1)] - (X)(\exp^{-rt})[N(d_2)]$$
$$= 32.625(.7673) - 30\exp^{(-0.07)(.2329)}(.7157)$$
$$= 25.03 - 30(.9838)(.7157)$$
$$= 25.03 - 21.12$$
$$= \underline{\$3.91}$$

Computer solutions may give slightly different answers, due to rounding and the accuracy involved in using the standard normal table. Also, the solution provided by the Black-Scholes model will not always exactly equal the price at which the option is trading. This basic model ignores the fact that the stock could pay a dividend and that the option is American, not European. Even so, the option price provided by the model (especially by the more complicated extensions of the model) is usually very close to the actual price; if it is not, then a trading opportunity may exist. A number of empirical studies have attempted to test the accuracy of various versions of the option pricing model. Most find that the model gives fairly accurate results.

A change in any of the five variables of the option pricing model will result in a change in the call premium—i.e., in the price of the option. A summary of the direction of change is given in Table D.2. Most of these changes can be observed by looking at a quotation of options prices and observing the option premiums over a period of time.

A simple extension of the Black-Scholes model can be made to incorporate dividend information. The annual dividend yield of the stock is the expected annual dividend divided by the current stock price. Instead of using the stock price directly in the formulas, the following substitution should be made:

Equation D.4

$$S' = S(\exp^{-Dt})$$

where D is the annual dividend yield. For example, suppose Gogal MegaCorp is expected to pay \$2 per share in dividends in the coming year. This means that the dividend yield is about 6.13% ($2 \div 32.625$). If we use $S' = 32.16$ instead of $S = 32.625$, we get an option price of about \$3.50. This result makes intuitive sense: the lower the stock price (S), the lower will be the price of the call (C).

The option pricing model also gives another useful number besides the option price. The variable $N(d_1)$ is called the **hedge ratio**, or the **delta**, for the call option. The hedge ratio tells how much the option price will change when the underlying stock price changes by some small amount. For example, our option for Gogal MegaCorp had a hedge ratio of about .77. This means that if the price of Gogal increased (or decreased) by one dollar per share, the price of the call option would increase (or decrease) by about \$0.77. This information is very useful for option traders who are trying to combine stocks and options into portfolios that will

hedge ratio (delta) the amount an option price will change when the underlying stock price changes by some small amount.

have offsetting movements. The number of call contracts or stocks held can be adjusted using the hedge ratio to produce protected portfolios. Remember, though, that the hedge ratio will change whenever the stock price changes and also as the time to maturity decreases. Thus, the information provided by the hedge ratio is good for only small stock price changes, and for only a short period of time.

PROBLEMS

1. Using the Black-Scholes option pricing formula, calculate the value of a call option given the following information:

   Stock price = $50
   Exercise price = $45
   Interest rate = 6%
   Time to expiration = 90 days
   Standard deviation = 0.4

2. Using the above information, re-calculate the call price if the stock paid a $1.50 annual dividend.

3. Using the information in Problem 1, determine how much the call price changes if all values stay the same except:

   a. The interest rate doubles to 12%.
   b. The standard deviation doubles to 0.8.
   c. What do your answers tell you about the relative importance of the interest rate and the standard deviation?

APPENDIX E

KEY EQUATIONS AND DISK ROUTINES

Topic	Equation number	On disk	Page number
Risk-free rate	4.6		141
Holding period return (HPR)	4.8	∎	143
Capital gain (or loss) during period	4.9		143
Yield (internal rate of return) for a single cash flow		∎	145
Yield (internal rate of return) for a stream of income		∎	145–146
Yield (internal rate of return) for an annuity		∎	
Approximate yield	4.10	∎	148–149
Finding growth rates		∎	149–151
Standard deviation, single asset	4.11	∎	152–154
Capital asset pricing model (CAPM)	4.13	∎	161

STOCKS

Chapter 5

Topic	Equation number	On disk	Page number
Book value per share		∎	197
Earnings per share (EPS)	5.1	∎	201
Dividend yield	5.2	∎	204
Dividend payout ratio	5.3	∎	204
Total return from foreign investment, in U.S. dollars	5.4, 5.5		215

Chapter 6

Topic	Equation number	On disk	Page number
Current ratio	6.1	∎	250
Net working capital	6.2	∎	250
Accounts receivable turnover	6.3	∎	251
Inventory turnover	6.4	∎	251
Total asset turnover	6.5	∎	251
Debt-equity ratio	6.6	∎	252
Times interest earned	6.7	∎	252
Net profit margin	6.8	∎	253
Return on assets (ROA)	6.9	∎	253
Return on equity (ROE)	6.10	∎	253
Price/earnings (P/E) ratio	6.11	∎	254
Earnings per share	6.11a	∎	254
Price-to-sales ratio	6.12	∎	255
Dividends per share	6.14	∎	255
Dividend yield		∎	
Dividend payout ratio	6.15	∎	256
Book value per share	6.16	∎	256

SELECTED READINGS

Chapter 1

Bodner, Janet. "Rethinking the American Dream." *Changing Times,* March 1991, pp. 27–30.

"Complete Guide to Financial Services." *Consumers Digest,* September/October 1991, pp. 49–62.

Giese, William. "Do Your Investments Fit Your Goals?" *Changing Times,* February 1991, pp. 51–55.

Harris, Diane. "How You Can Live Better." *Money,* October 1991, pp. 132–46.

Lynch, Peter. *One Up on Wall Street.* New York: Simon & Schuster, 1989.

Schiffres, Manuel. "Getting Started in Stocks." *Kiplinger's Personal Finance Magazine,* July 1991, pp. 51–56.

Special Investment Guides published at least annually by major periodicals:
Forbes Annual Money Guide, published in June
Fortune Investor's Guide, published each fall
Money Magazine Year-End Issue
U.S. News & World Report, Money Guide, published in July, and *Investment Guide,* published in December

Chapter 2

Davis, Kirsten. "Battle Your Broker and Win." *Changing Times,* May 1991, pp. 41–43.

Egan, Jack. "Does Your Broker Have a Hidden Agenda?" *U.S. News & World Report,* January 22, 1990, p. 71.

Markese, John. "Placing Your Stock Order: A Long Menu to Choose From." *AAII Journal,* February 1990, pp. 32–34.

Mendes, Joshua. "Getting the Most from Brokers." *Fortune 1992 Investor's Guide,* Fall 1991, pp. 183–186.

Pike, Elizabeth. "That Personal Touch." *Personal Investing,* November 1991, pp. 38–43.

Schiffres, Manuel. "Best Brokers for Small Investors." *Kiplinger's Personal Finance Magazine,* November 1991, pp. 54–58.

———. "Great Ways to Go Global." *Changing Times,* February 1991, pp. 37–40.

Schultz, Ellen E. "Can Strangers Easily Trade Your Stocks?" *The Wall Street Journal,* October 16, 1991, p. C1.

———. "Failing to Consider Commissions Can Be A Costly Error." *The Wall Street Journal,* June 25, 1991, p. C1.

Weiss, Gary. "The Long and Short of Short-Selling." *Business Week,* June 10, 1991, pp. 106–8.

Chapter 3

Asinoff, Lynn. "Old Standby: The Investment Club Approach Finds a 'New' Popularity." *The Wall Street Journal,* July 17, 1991, p. C1.

Giese, William. "Do Your Investments Fit Your Goals?" *Changing Times,* February 1991, pp. 51–55.

Herman, Tom. "Buying Treasuries Without a Middleman." *The Wall Street Journal,* May 1, 1991, p. C1.

Kosnett, Jeff. "Life Insurance Choices that Save You Money." *Changing Times,* February 1991, pp. 45–48.

_____. "What a Money Manager Can Do for You." _Changing Times,_ June 1991, pp. 39–43.

Kuhn, Susan E. "Newsletters That Pick Winning Portfolios." _Fortune,_ September 23, 1991, p. 32.

Leahy, Tad. "Research Reports: Just the Facts." _Personal Investor,_ March 1991, pp. 22–27.

O'Reilly, Brian. "Picking the Right Financial Planner." _Fortune,_ February 25, 1991, pp. 144–47.

Pike, Elizabeth. "Bucks of the Month." _Personal Investing,_ September 1990, pp. 50–52, 56–58.

Schultz, Ellen E. "Detective Work: Checking Out a Financial Advisor." _The Wall Street Journal,_ September 13, 1990, p. C1.

Smith, Anne Kates. "Advice for Do-It-Yourself Investors." _U.S. News & World Report,_ August 27/ September 3, 1990, pp. 82–84.

Spiro, Leah Nathan. "Accounts That Do It All." _Business Week,_ February 3, 1992, pp. 82–83.

Chapter 4

Hoffman, Paul. "The Use of Statistics in Making Investment Decisions." _AAII Journal,_ September 1991, pp. 11–13.

Kritzman, Mark P. "What Practitioners Need to Know About Uncertainty." _Financial Analysts Journal,_ March/April 1991, pp. 17–21.

Laderman, Jeffrey M. "The Yield Trap." _Business Week,_ January 20, 1992, pp. 72–77.

Main, Jeremy. "Is Anything Safe Anymore?" _Fortune 1992 Investor's Guide,_ Fall 1991, pp. 49–56.

Pring, Martin. "It's a Risk vs. Return Balancing Act." _Investment Vision,_ February/March 1991, pp. 40–43.

Rock, Andrea. "Winning Investors Know Their Returns." _Money,_ September 1989, pp. 149–50.

Shukla, Ravi, and Charles Trzcinka. "Research on Risk and Return: Can Measures of Risk Explain Anything?" _Journal of Portfolio Management,_ Spring 1991, pp. 15–21.

White, James A. "When Figuring the Rate of Return . . . Don't Be Confused by the Sales Hype." _The Wall Street Journal,_ March 13, 1990, pp. C1.

Winkler, Matthew. "No Risk, No Reward." _Forbes,_ December 23, 1991, p. 185.

Chapter 5

Albers, Robert. "What to Expect From a Dividend Reinvestment Plan." _AAII Journal,_ April 1991, pp. 17–19.

Baldwin, William. "Prowling the Pink Sheets." _Forbes,_ June 25, 1990, pp. 264–68.

Barrett, Amy. "Foreign Pastures." _Financial World,_ January 9, 1990, pp. 58–59.

Baskin, J. "Dividend Policy and the Volatility of Common Stocks." _Journal of Portfolio Management,_ Spring 1989, pp. 19–25.

Coler, Mark. "The Individual Investor's Guide to Selecting a Discount Broker," _AAII Journal,_ January 1991, pp. 8–11.

Edgerton, Jerry, and Baie Netzer. "The Hunt for the Best High Yields." _Money,_ May 1991, pp. 102–6.

"Foreign Investing Made a Little Easier." _Forbes,_ July 22, 1991, pp. 290–92.

Fredman, Albert J. "Sizing Up Small Stocks," _Personal Investor,_ September 1989, pp. 22–27.

Jones, Charles P., and Jack W. Wilson. "Is Stock Price Volatility Increasing?" _Financial Analysts Journal,_ November/December 1989, pp. 20–26.

Poole, Claire. "There's an IPO Buyer Born Every Minute." _Forbes,_ June 24, 1991, pp. 222–25.

Schultz, Ellen. "Climbing High With Discount Brokers." _Fortune,_ 1990 Investor's Guide, pp. 219–23.

Solt, Michael E., and Meir Statman. "Good Companies, Bad Stocks." _Journal of Portfolio Management,_ Summer 1989, pp. 39–44.

Chapter 6

Cutler, David M., James Poterba, and Lawrence H. Summers. "What Moves Stock Prices?" _Journal of Portfolio Management,_ Spring 1989, pp. 4–12.

DeBondt, Werner F.M. "What Do Economists Know About the Stock Market?" _Journal of Portfolio Management,_ Winter 1991, pp. 84–88.

Hector, Gary. "Cute Tricks on the Bottom Line." _Fortune,_ April 24, 1989, pp. 193–200.

Hoeper, Paul J. "What Investors Should Know About Financial Statements." _AAII Journal,_ April 1991, pp. 7–12.

Jasen, Georgette. ''Red Flags: Putting a Company in Its Proper Prospectus.'' *The Wall Street Journal,* September 7, 1989, p. C1.

Laderman, Jeffrey M. ''Earnings, Schmernings—Look at The Cash.'' *Business Week,* July 24, 1989, pp. 56–57.

Lynch, Peter. ''Some Famous Numbers From 'One Up on Wall Street'.'' *AAII Journal,* April 1989, pp. 8–12.

Markese, John. ''Common Stock Analysis: Examining Cash Flow.'' *AAII Journal,* May 1990, pp. 32–37.

Pring, Martin J. ''Gearing Your Investments to the Business Cycle.'' *Investment Vision,* July/August 1990, pp. 31–35.

Renshaw, Edward, and David Molnar. ''Recessions and Recoveries: How the Stock Market Behaves.'' *AAII Journal,* February 1991, pp. 7–9.

Updegrave, Walter L. ''To Keep Profits on a Roll, Stay Tuned to the Business Cycle.'' *Money,* May 1989, pp. 169–72.

Wechsler, Dana, and Katarzyna Wandycz. ''An Innate Fear of Disclosure.'' *Forbes,* February 5, 1990, pp. 126–28.

Chapter 7

Ettredge, Michael, and Russell J. Fuller. ''The Negative Earnings Effect.'' *Journal of Portfolio Management,* Spring 1991, pp. 27–34.

Evans, Michael K. ''Taking the Measure of the Market.'' *Investment Vision,* March/April 1990, pp. 18–21, 62.

Fasciocco, Leo. ''Recognize Bear Tracks to Avoid a Mauling.'' *Barron's,* April 1, 1991, p. 1.

Fromson, Brett D. ''The Pros Share Their Secrets.'' *Fortune 1991 Investor's Guide,* pp. 75–82.

Jacobs, Bruce I., and Kenneth N. Levy. ''Calendar Anomalies: Abnormal Returns at Calendar Turning Points.'' *Financial Analysts Journal,* November/December 1988, pp. 28–39.

Leahy, Tad. ''Picking the Perfect 10.'' *Personal Investor,* May 1990, pp. 33–34.

Leibowitz, Martin L., and Stanley Kagelman. ''Inside the P/E Ratio: The Franchise Factor.'' *Financial Analysts Journal,* November/December 1990, pp. 17–35.

Mann, Charles C. ''Fama's Market.'' *Investment Vision,* October/November 1991, pp. 53–55.

Markese, John. ''Investing in Growth: Earnings and Price Momentum.'' *AAII Journal,* June 1990, pp. 35–37.

McGough, Robert. ''Putting a Value on Tomorrow's Stocks.'' *Financial World,* September 19, 1989, pp. 26–29.

Peters, Donald J. ''Valuing a Growth Stock.'' *Journal of Portfolio Management,* Spring 1991, pp. 49–51.

Zweig, Martin, and Ned Davis. ''Cash on the Sidelines.'' *Investment Vision,* September/October 1990, pp. 64–66.

Chapter 8

Asinof, Lynn. ''Bond Insurance Offers Layer of Protection.'' *The Wall Street Journal,* May 8, 1991, p. C1.

Barrett, Amy. ''Scanning the Globe for High Yields.'' *Financial World,* September 18, 1990, pp. 48–51.

DeMuth, Jerry. ''CMO's: A Better Way to Invest in Mortgages.'' *Kiplinger's Personal Finance Magazine,* August 1991, pp. 65–68.

Donnelly, Barbara. ''Zero-Coupon Bonds: Simple Appeal But Not Zero Risk.'' *The Wall Street Journal,* June 26, 1989, p. C1.

———. ''CMOs May Promise Big Fat Yields, But Investors Should Know the Risks.'' *The Wall Street Journal,* November 12, 1991, p. C1.

Fabozzi, Frank J. *The Handbook of Fixed Income Securities,* 3rd ed. Homewood, Ill.: Business One Irwin, 1991.

Fredman, Albert J. ''All About Bonds.'' *Personal Investor,* March 1990, pp. 48–52.

''How Good Is Corporate America's Credit?'' *Institutional Investor,* March 1992, pp. 29–30.

Lamb, Robert B. ''Municipal Bonds.'' *Investment Vision,* February/March 1991, pp. 53–56.

Smith, Melanie. ''Junk Bonds.'' *Investment Vision,* September/October 1989, pp. 44–46.

Wyatt, Edward A. ''Trading in the Dark: Real Bond Prices Are Hard to Come By.'' *Barron's,* November 6, 1989, pp. 15, 43–47.

Chapter 9

Abken, Peter A. "Innovations in Modeling the Term Structure of Interest Rates." *Federal Reserve Bank of Atlanta, Economic Review,* July/August 1990, pp. 2–27.

Bierwag, G.O., and George G. Kaufman. "Expected Bond Returns and Duration: A General Model." *Financial Analysts Journal,* January/February 1991, pp. 82–84.

Choie, Kenneth S. "A Simplified Approach to Bond Portfolio Management." *Journal of Portfolio Management,* Spring 1990, pp. 40–45.

Dattatreya, Ravi E., and Frank J. Fabozzi. "A Framework for Analyzing Bonds: Horizon Return, Duration, and Convexity." In Fabozzi, Frank J. and Fabozzi, T. Dessa, *Current Topics in Investment Management* (New York: HarperCollins, 1990), pp. 173–94.

Fabozzi, F.J. and T.D. Fabozzi. *Bond Markets, Analysis and Strategies.* (Englewood Cliffs, N.J.: Prentice Hall, 1989).

Fong, Gifford, and O.A. Vasicek. "Fixed-Income Volatility Management." *Journal of Portfolio Management,* Summer 1991, pp. 41–46

Dialynas, Chris P. "Bond Yield Spreads Revisited." *Journal of Portfolio Management,* Winter 1988, pp. 57–62.

Grantier, Bruce J. "Convexity and Bond Performance: The Benter the Better." *Financial Analysts Journal,* November/December 1988, pp. 79–81.

Litterman, Robert and J. Scheinkman. "Common Factors Affecting Bond Returns." *The Journal of Fixed-Income,* June 1991, pp. 54–61.

McEnally, Richard W. "Portfolio Objectives and Management Policies for Fixed-Income Investors." In Fabozzi, Frank J. and Fabozzi, T. Dessa, *Current Topics in Investment Management* (New York: Harper Collins, 1990), pp. 163–72.

Markese, John. "An Investor's Guide to Spreads in Bond Yields." *AAII Journal,* September 1989, pp. 32–34.

Taylor, Richard W. "Bond Duration Analysis: A Pedagogical Note." *Financial Analysts Journal,* July/August 1987, pp. 69–72.

Chapter 10

Altman, Edward I. "The Convertible Debt Market: Are Returns Worth the Risk?" *Financial Analysts Journal,* July–August 1989, pp. 23–31.

Hardy, Eric, and Warren Midgett. "Caution on Converts." *Forbes,* March 18, 1991, p. 147.

Hetherington, Norriss. "High Return and Low Risk in Called Preferreds." *Journal of Portfolio Management,* Spring 1987, pp. 81–83.

Herman, Tom. "Preferreds' Rich Yields Blind Some Investors to Risks." *The Wall Street Journal,* March 24, 1992, pp. C1, 21.

Kuhn, Susan E. "Cutting Bull Market Risk with Convertible Bonds." *Fortune,* April 22, 1991, pp. 44, 48.

Liscio, John. "Best of All Worlds: Convertibles Never Had It So Good." *Barron's,* August 7, 1989, pp. 16, 25.

Mitchell, Constance. "Zero-Coupon Convertibles Find a Market." *The Wall Street Journal,* December 11, 1989, p. C1.

Ourusoff, Alexandra. "Double Play: Convertibles Can Give Both High Yield and Price Appreciation." *Financial World,* October 2, 1990, p. 43.

Scharf, Jeffrey R. "Question of Preference: How Preferreds Stack Up vs. Bonds." *Barron's,* September 8, 1986, p. 71.

Stovall, Robert H. "Percing Up Equities." *Financial World,* October 15, 1991, p. 68.

Weberman, Ben, and Jason Zweig. "The Mixed Bag— Convertible Bonds and Preferred." *Forbes,* June 27, 1988, pp. 222–23.

Wilson, Richard S. "Convertible Bonds." *Financial World,* December 10, 1991, p. 118.

Chapter 11

Angrist, Stanley W. "Capped Stock-Index Options May Help Calm Jittery Investors." *The Wall Street Journal,* November 21, 1991, p. C1.

————. "Long-Term Options Can Cut Stock Risk." *The Wall Street Journal,* January 4, 1991, p. C1.

————. "How Being 'Married' Can Protect Stocks." *The Wall Street Journal,* October 18, 1989, p. C1.

Bosold, Patrick D. "Options: A Walk on the Safe Side." *Personal Investor,* January 1991, pp. 48–53.

Burghardt, Galen, and Morton Lane. "How To Tell If Options Are Cheap." *Journal of Portfolio Management,* Winter 1990, pp. 72–78.

Chance, Don. "Option Volume and Stock Market Performance." *Journal of Portfolio Management,* Summer 1990, pp. 42–51.

Figlewski, S. "What Does An Option Pricing Model Tell Us About Option Prices?" *Financial Analyst Journal,* September–October 1989, pp. 12–13.

Greising, David. "Putting A Little More Punch Into Your Portfolio." *Business Week,* December 25, 1989, p. 138.

Hopewell, Lynn. "The Downside Defense." *Investment Vision,* August/September 1991, pp. 73–74.

Moscovitz, Steven D. "They Warrant a Look—How Warrants Work as Hedging Devices." *Barrow's,* December 21, 1987, pp. 28–29.

Chapter 12

Angrist, Stanley, W. "Futures Shock: Investors Cope With 'Slippage'." *The Wall Street Journal,* April 30, 1991, p. C1.

———. "Taming the Risks of Commodity Trading." *The Wall Street Journal,* August 11, 1989, p. C1.

Brown, Christie. "Mickey Mania." *Forbes,* October 30, 1989, pp. 230–32.

Dobrzynski, Judy. "The Art of the Bid." *Business Week,* April 22, 1991, pp. 112–113.

Finnerty, Joseph E., and Hun Y. Park. "How to Profit from Program Trading." *Journal of Portfolio Management,* Winter 1988, pp. 40–46.

Gastineau, Gary L. "A Short History of Program Trading." *Financial Analyst Journal,* September/October 1991, pp. 4–7.

Irwin, Scott H., and Diego Landa. "Real Estate, Futures, and Gold as Portfolio Assets." *Journal of Portfolio Management,* Fall 1987, pp. 29–34.

Kawaller, Ira G. "To Hedge or Not to Hedge." *Financial Analysts Journal,* March/April 1989, pp. 4–5.

Myers, David W. "Building a Coin Portfolio." *Personal Investor,* November 1989, pp. 16–22.

Samorajski, Gregory S., and Bruce D. Phelps. "Using Treasury Bond Futures to Enhance Total Returns." *Financial Analysts Journal,* January/February 1990, pp. 58–65.

Chapter 13

Clements, Jonathan. "Selecting a Fund: Expenses Can Be Crucial." *The Wall Street Journal,* July 24, 1991, p. C1.

Fredman, Albert J., and George Scott. "Analyzing and Finding Data on Closed-End Funds." *AAII Journal,* September 1991, pp. 15–19.

Giese, William. "When Your Fund Manager Bails Out." *Changing Times,* June 1990, pp. 35–38.

Granito, Michael R. "The Problem with Bond Index Funds." *Journal of Portfolio Management,* Summer 1987, pp. 41–48.

Herman, Tom. "A Primer for Fund Investors at Tax Time." *The Wall Street Journal,* March 15, 1991, p. C1.

"How to Buy a Bond Fund." *Consumer Reports,* June 1990, pp. 428–35.

Marcus, Alan J. "The Magellan Fund and Market Efficiency." *Journal of Portfolio Management,* Fall 1990, pp. 85–88.

Schiffres, Manuel. "How to Spot Tomorrow's Great Funds Today." *Kiplinger's Personal Finance Magazine,* September 1991, pp. 29–34.

Scott, Maria Crawford. "Social Investing: Another Variable in the Investment Equation?" *AAII Journal,* October 1991, pp. 16–19.

White, James A. "The Index Boom: It's No Longer Just the S&P 500 Stock Index." *The Wall Street Journal,* May 29, 1991, p. C1.

Wiles, Russ. "Mutual Fund Risk and Return: Facing Up to Reality." *Personal Investor,* July 1990, pp. 50–52.

———. "The Prospectus: Reading between the Lines." *Personal Investor,* July 1990, pp. 40–45.

Chapter 14

Banning, Kent. "Gunslingers, Bottom Fishers: How to Spot a Turnaround." *Barron's,* November 11, 1991, pp. 66–67.

de Gannon, Victoria Eve. "Commercial Real Estate Lending from Appraisal to Bankruptcy." *Real Estate Law Journal,* Spring 1992, pp. 321–46.

De Muth, Jerry. "A Better Way to Invest in Mortgages?" *Kiplinger's Personal Finance Magazine,* August 1991, pp. 65–68.

Hall, Randall M. "The Role of Leverage in Real Estate Portfolios." *Real Estate Review*, Spring 1992, pp. 23–27.

Kuhn, Susan E. "Real Estate: Riding the REIT Rebound." *Fortune 1992 Investor's Guide*, Fall 1991, p. 31.

Light, Larry. "Real Estate Needn't Be Scary If You Find the Right REIT." *Business Week*, March 2, 1992, pp. 108–9.

Loomis, Carol J. "Victims of the Real Estate Crash." *Fortune*, May 18, 1992, pp. 70–83.

Marks, Andrew. "A Falling Out of Partners." *Institutional Investor*, December 1991, p. 163.

Norwell, William. "The Real Estate Decision Process." *Journal of Property Management*, March–April 1992, pp. 58–60.

Randle, Paul A., and Richard I. Johnson. "Do Real Estate Investments Meet Your Rate of Return Expectations?" *Real Estate Finance*, Winter 1992, pp. 63–70.

Roulac, Stephan E. "Bottom, Bottom, Where's the Bottom?" *Forbes*, March 16, 1992, p. 169.

Roulac, Stephan E., Lloyd Linford, and Gilbert H. Castle III. "Real Estate Decision Making in an Information Era." *Real Estate Finance Journal*, Summer 1990, pp. 8–15.

Vinocur, Barry. "How Much Is Your Partnership Really Worth?" *Barron's*, August 26, 1991, p. 53.

Chapter 15

Angrist, Stanley. "Software Can Help Plan Your Retirement." *The Wall Street Journal*, June 9, 1991 p. C1.

Brenner, Lynn. "Retirement Planning: Three Case Studies." *Working Woman*, May 1992, pp. 48–52.

Building Your Future with Annuities, Booklet #891. Consumer Information Catalog, Pueblo, Co. 81009.

Fierman, Jaclyn. "How Safe Is Your Nest Egg?" *Fortune*, August 12, 1991, pp. 48–54.

Hardy, Eric. "How Well Did Your Annuity Do?" *Forbes*, April 13, 1992, pp. 134–35.

Marks, Andrew. "A Falling Out of Partners." *Institutional Investor*, December 1991, p. 163.

"1992 Retirement Guide." *U.S. News & World Report*, May 25, 1992, pp. 66–92.

O'Reilly, Brian. "How to Make the Most of Annuities." *Fortune 1992 Investor's Guide*, Fall 1991, pp. 109–12.

Pearson, Kim. "What You Should Know about Your 401(k) Plan." *Black Enterprise*, August 1991, pp. 99–105.

Schiffres, Manuel. "Winning Big with Variable Annuities." *Kiplinger's Personal Finance Magazine*, April 1992, p. 49–54.

Schultz, Ellen E., "In New Pension Plans, Companies are Putting the Onus on Workers." *The Wall Street Journal*, July 7, 1992, p. A1.

———. "The Need to Check Performance of Funds Is a Constant with Variable Annuities." *The Wall Street Journal*, April 21, 1992, p. C1.

Slater, Karen. "Market Isn't Kind to Sellers of Units in Partnerships." *The Wall Street Journal*, February 18, 1992, p. C1.

Tritch, Teresa. "Six Shelters to Trim Your Federal Taxes. *Money*, January 1992, pp. 90–93.

Updegrave, Walter L. "Getting Past the Hype of Annuities." *Money*, September 1991, pp. 118–28.

Willis, Clint. "Starting Out Right." *Money*, June 1991, pp. 84–97.

———. "Getting Set for Life." *Money*, June 1991, pp. 106–15.

Chapter 16

Brealey, Richard A. "Portfolio Theory versus Portfolio Practice." *Journal of Portfolio Management*, Summer 1990, pp. 6–10.

Brinson, Gary P., and Brian D. Singer. "Determinants of Portfolio Performance II: An Update." *Financial Analysts Journal*, May–June 1991, pp. 40–48.

Clements, Jonathan. "Why It's Risky Not to Invest More in Stocks." *The Wall Street Journal*, February 11, 1992, p. C1.

Clowes, Michael J. "Study Puts Beta on Back Shelf." *Pensions & Investments*, March 2, 1992, pp. 3, 35.

Dorfman, John R. "Frequent Fiddling with Investment Results Isn't Necessary to Achieve Strong Results." *The Wall Street Journal*, November 1, 1991, p. C1.

Dumaine, Brian, et al. "Strategies for the Stages of Life." *Fortune 1992 Investor's Guide*, Fall 1991, pp. 123–44.

Ford, John K. "Diversification: How Many Stocks Will Suffice?" *AAII Journal,* January 1990, pp. 14–16.

Harvey, Sharon. "Portfolio Strategy: Can You Catch a Falling Dow?" *Institutional Investor,* May 1991, pp. 139–40.

Hulbert, Mark. "Spreading the Risks." *Forbes,* May 11, 1992, p. 215.

Leibowitz, Martin L., and Stanley Kogelman. "Asset Allocation under Shortfall Constraints." *Journal of Portfolio Management.,* Winter 1991, pp. 18–23.

Markese, John. "All Eggs in One Basket, or a Basket for Each Egg?" *AAII Journal,* August 1990, pp. 31–33.

Nawrocki, David. "Tailoring Asset Allocation to the Individual Investor." *International Review of Economics and Business,* October/November 1990, pp. 977–90.

Paré, Terence P. "Investing for Hard Times." *Fortune,* December 30, 1991, pp. 74–76.

———. "Investment Strategy and Vehicles: How to Maximize Your Profits." *Fortune 1992 Investor's Guide,* Fall 1991, pp. 38–46.

Updegrave, Walter L. "Protect Your Wealth Against Risks." *Money,* April 1992, pp. 142–58.

Willis, Clint. "How You Can Still Earn 10% Safely." *Money,* July 1991, pp. 64–72.

Chapter 17

Beebower, G. L., and A. P. Varikooty. "Measuring Market Timing Strategies." *Financial Analysts Journal,* November–December 1991, pp. 78–84, 92.

Brinson, Gary P., and Brian D. Singer. "Determinants of Portfolio Performance II: An Update." *Financial Analysts Journal,* May–June 1991, pp. 40–48.

Clements, Jonathan. "Knowing the Right Time to Bail Out of Mutual Fund." *The Wall Street Journal,* May 30, 1991, p. C1.

Edgerton, Jerry. "Today's Best Way to Invest." *Money,* December 1991, pp. 98–99.

Ferson, Wayne E., and Campbell R. Harvey. "Sources of Predictability in Portfolio Returns." *Financial Analysts Journal,* May–June 1991, pp. 49–56.

Gelband, Joseph. "Long and Short: A Painless Way to End an Investment Dilemma." *Barron's,* January 6, 1992, p. 24.

Manners, John. "Size Up Your Portfolio Like a Professional." *Money,* May 1992, pp. 88–93.

Niederman, Derrick. "When to Sell." *Worth,* February/March 1992, pp. 148–52.

Paré, Terence. "Smart Investing Is Tax-Wise, Too." *Fortune,* March 9, 1992, pp. 127–36.

Renberg, Walter. "Second Opinion—Market Timing, Study Says, Does Boost Returns." *Barron's,* February 10, 1992, pp. M10–M12.

Zimmerman, Heinz, and Claudia Zogg-Wetter. "On Detecting Selection and Timing Ability: The Case of Stock Market Indexes." *Financial Analysts Journal,* January–February 1992, pp. 80–83.

Zinn, Laura. "Buy? Sell? Think Fast—or Use a Market Timer." *Business Week,* February 12, 1990, pp. 98–99.

GLOSSARY

Numbers in parentheses indicate the chapter in which the term is discussed in detail.

12(b)-1 fee (13)   a fee levied by some mutual funds to cover management and other operating costs; amounts to as much as 1¼ percent annually on the average net assets.

401(k) plan (15)   a retirement plan that allows employees to divert a portion of salary to a company-sponsored tax-sheltered savings account, thus deferring taxes until retirement.

accrual-type securities (3)   securities for which interest is paid when the bond is cashed, on or before maturity, rather than periodically over the life of the bond.

accumulation period (15)   under an annuity contract, the period of time between when payments are made to the insurance company and when the insurance company begins to pay the annuitant.

active portfolio management (17)   building a portfolio using traditional and modern approaches and managing and controlling it to meet its objectives.

activity ratios (6)   financial ratios that are used to measure how well a firm is managing its assets.

adjustable (floating) rate preferreds (10)   preferred stock whose dividends are adjusted periodically in line with yields on Treasury issues.

adjusted gross income (15)   gross income less the total allowable adjustments for tax purposes.

after-cash tax flows (ATCFs) (14)   the annual cash flow earned on a real estate investment, net of all expenses, taxes, and debt service.

Agency bonds (8)   debt securities issued by various agencies and organizations of the U.S. government, like the Tennessee Valley Authority.

aggressive growth fund (13)   a highly speculative mutual fund that seeks large profits from capital gains.

alternative minimum tax (AMT) (15)   a tax passed by Congress to ensure that all individuals pay at least some federal income tax.

American Depositary Receipts (ADRs) (2, 5)   negotiable receipts for company stock held in trust in a foreign branch of a U.S. bank

American option (11)   an option that can be exercised on any business day that the option is traded, on or before the option's expiration date.

AMEX index (3)   measure of the current price behavior of stocks listed on the AMEX.

analytical information (3)   available current data in conjunction with projections and recommendations about potential investments.

annuitant (15)   the person to whom the future payments on an annuity contract are directed.

annuity (4, 15)   a stream of equal cash flows that occur in equal intervals over time; also, a series of payments guaranteed for a number of years or over a lifetime.

appraisal (14)   a process for estimating the current market value of a piece of property.

approximate yield (4)   procedure for assessing investment suitability that recognizes the time value of money in its calculation of the rate of return (yield) on an investment.

arbitration (2)   a dispute process in which a broker and customer present their cases before a panel which then decides the case.

ask price (2)   the lowest price at which a dealer is willing to sell a given security.

asset allocation (16)   a scheme that involves dividing one's portfolio into various asset classes in order to preserve capital by protecting against negative developments while still taking advantage of positive developments.

asset allocation fund (16)   a mutual fund that seeks to reduce volatility by investing in the right assets at the right time; emphasizes diversification and relatively consistent performance rather than spectacular gains.

asset-backed securities (ABS) (8)   a type of security that's backed by a pool of bank loans, leases, and other assets; most ABS are backed by auto loans and credit cards—these issues are very similar to mortgage-backed securities.

automatic investment plan (13)   a mutual fund service that allows shareholders to automatically send fixed amounts of money from their paychecks or bank accounts into the fund.

automatic reinvestment plan (13)   a mutual fund service that enables shareholders to automatically buy additional shares in the fund through reinvestment of dividends and capital gains income.

average tax rate (15)   taxes due divided by taxable income; different from the *marginal tax rate*.

averages (3)   numbers used to measure the general behavior of stock prices by reflecting the arithmetic average price behavior of a representative group of stocks at a given point in time.

back-end load (13)   a commission charged on the sale of shares in a mutual fund.

back-office research reports (3)   analyses of and recommendations on current and future investment opportunities; published by and made available to clients of brokerage firms.

balance sheet (6)   a financial summary of a firm's assets, liabilities, and shareholder's equity at a single point in time.

balanced fund (13)   a mutual fund whose objective is to generate a balanced return of both current income and long-term capital gains.

bank discount yield (BDY) (3)   the rate at which T-bills are quoted in *The Wall Street Journal* and other financial media; represents the annualized percentage discount (redemption value − current value) at which the bill can be currently purchased.

banker's acceptances (3)   short-term, low-risk investment vehicles arising from bank guarantees of business transactions; are sold at a discount from their face value and provide yields generally slightly below those of CDs and commercial paper.

bar chart (7)   the simplest kind of chart on which share price is plotted on the vertical axis and time on the horizontal axis; stock prices are recorded as vertical bars showing high, low, and closing prices.

***Barron's* (3)**   a weekly publication by Dow Jones; the second most popular source of financial news.

basis (15) the amount paid for a capital asset, including commissions and other costs related to the purchase.

bear markets (2) unfavorable markets associated with falling prices, investor pessimism, economic slowdowns, and government restraint.

bearer bonds (8) bonds whose holders are considered to be their owners; there is no official record of ownership kept by the issuer.

bellwether stocks (7) stocks that are believed to consistently reflect the state of the market; watched by technical analysts for shifts in market behavior.

beta (4) a measure of nondiversifiable risk, which shows how the price of a security responds to market forces; found by relating the historical returns on a security with the historical returns for the market.

bid price (2) the highest price offered by a dealer to purchase a given security.

blind pool syndicate (14) a type of real estate limited partnership formed by a syndicator to raise money to be invested at the syndicator's discretion.

bond equivalent yield (BEY) (3) the annual rate of return that would be earned by an investor in a short-term security sold at a discount if it is purchased today at its current price and held to maturity.

bond fund (13) a mutual fund that invests in various kinds and grades of bonds, with income as the primary objective.

bond ladders (9) a bond investment strategy wherein an equal amount of money is invested in a series of bonds with staggered maturities.

bond ratings (8) letter grades that designate investment quality, assigned to a bond issue on the basis of extensive financial analysis.

bond swap (9) an investment strategy wherein an investor liquidates one of his current bond holdings and simultaneously buys a different issue in its place.

bond yields (3) summary measures of the return an investor would receive on a bond if it were held to maturity; reported as an annual rate of return.

bonds (1, 8) publicly traded long-term debt securities, issued by corporations and governments, whereby the issuer agrees to pay a fixed amount of interest over a specified period of time and to repay a fixed amount of principal at maturity.

book value (5) the amount of stockholders' equity in a firm; equals the amount of the firm's assets minus the firm's liabilities and preferred stock.

book value (net asset value) (10) a measure of the amount of debt-free assets supporting each share of preferred stock.

brokered CDs (3) certificates of deposit sold by stockbrokers; offer slightly higher yields than other CDs and no penalty for sale prior to maturity.

bull markets (2) favorable markets associated with rising prices, investor optimism, economic recovery, and governmental stimulus.

business cycle (6) an indication of the current state of the economy, reflecting change in total economic activity over time.

business risk (4) the degree of uncertainty associated with an investment's earnings and the investment's ability to pay investors the returns owed them.

call (1, 11) a negotiable instrument that gives the holder the option to buy 100 shares of common stock at a stated price within a certain time period.

call feature (8) feature that specifies whether, and under what conditions, the issuer can retire a bond prior to maturity.

call premium (8) the amount added to a bond's par value and paid to investors when a bond is retired prematurely.

call price (8) the price the issuer must pay to retire a bond prematurely; equal to par value plus the call premium.

capital asset pricing model (CAPM) (4) model that uses beta and market return to help investors evaluate risk-return tradeoffs in investment decisions.

capital gain (3) the amount by which the proceeds from the sale of a capital asset exceed its original purchase price.

capital gains distributions (13) payments made to mutual fund shareholders that come from the profits that a fund makes from the sale of its securities.

capital loss (3) the amount by which the proceeds from the sale of a capital asset are less than its original purchase price.

capital market (2) market in which long-term securities such as stocks and bonds are bought and sold.

capitalization rate (14) the rate used to convert an income stream to a present value, which can be used to estimate the value of real estate under the income approach to value.

capped options (Caps) (11) index options, with cap prices that set a maximum value for the option, at which point the option is automatically exercised.

cash account (2) a brokerage account in which a customer can make only cash transactions.

cash dividend (5) payment of a dividend in the form of cash.

cash market (12) a market where a product or commodity changes hands in exchange for a cash price paid at the time the transaction is completed.

cash value (3) the amount of money set aside by an insurer to provide for the payment of a death benefit.

central asset account (3) a comprehensive deposit account that combines checking, investing, and borrowing activities and automatically sweeps excess balances into short-term investments.

certificates of deposit (CDs) (3) savings instruments in which funds must remain on deposit for a specified period; premature withdrawals incur interest penalties.

charting (7) the activity of charting price behavior and other market information, and then using the patterns that these charts form to make investment decisions.

churning (2) an illegal and unethical act by a broker to increase commissions through excessive trading of clients' accounts.

classified common stock (5) common stock issued in different classes, each of which offers different privileges and benefits to its holders.

closed-end investment companies (13) a type of investment company that operates with a fixed number of shares outstanding.

collateral trustbonds (8) senior bonds backed by securities owned by the issuer but held in trust by a third party.

collateralized mortgage obligation (CMO) (8) a type of mortgage-backed bond whose holders are divided into classes based on the length of investment desired; then, principal is channeled to short-term investors first, intermediate-term investors next, and long-term investors last.

collectibles (12) items that have value because of their attractiveness to collectors and because of their relative scarcity and historical significance.

commercial paper (3) short-term, unsecured promissory notes issued by corporations with very high credit standings.

commercial property (14) an income property that is used by the tenant for business rather than living purposes.

commodities and financial futures contracts (1) obligations that the sellers of the contracts will make delivery and the buyers will take delivery of a specified commodity, foreign currency, or financial instrument at some specific date in the future.

common stock (1) equity investment representing ownership in a corporation; each share represents a fractional ownership interest in the firm.

comparative sales approach (14) a real estate valuation approach that uses as the basic input variable sales prices of properties that are similar to the subject property.

compound interest (4) interest paid not only on the initial deposit but also on any interest accumulated from one period to the next.

confidence index (7) a ratio of the average yield on high-grade corporate bonds to the average yield on low-grade corporate bonds; a technical indicator based on the theory that market trends usually appear in the bond market before they do in the stock market.

constant dollar plan (17) a formula plan for timing investment transactions, in which the investor establishes a target dollar amount for the speculative portion of the portfolio and transfers funds to or from the conservative portion as needed to maintain the target dollar amount.

constant ratio plan (17) a formula plan for timing investment transactions, in which a desired fixed ratio of the speculative to the conservative portion of the portfolio is established; when the actual ratio differs by a predetermined amount from the desired ratio, transactions are made to rebalance the portfolio.

continuous compounding (4) interest calculation in which interest is compounded over the smallest possible interval of time.

convenience (14) in real estate, the accessibility of a property to the places the people in a target market frequently need to go.

conventional options (11) put and call options sold over the counter.

conversion equivalent (conversion parity) (10) the price at which the common stock would have to sell in order to make the convertible security worth its present market price.

conversion (exchange) privilege (13) feature of a mutual fund that allows shareholders to move money from one fund to another, within the same family of funds.

conversion feature (10) allows the holder of a convertible preferred to convert to a specified number of shares of the issuing company's common stock.

conversion period (10) the time period during which a convertible issue can be converted.

conversion premium (10) the amount by which the market price of a convertible exceeds its conversion value.

conversion price (10) the stated price per share at which common stock will be delivered to the investor in exchange for a convertible issue.

conversion privilege (10) the conditions and specific nature of the conversion feature of convertible securities.

conversion ratio (10) the number of shares of common stock into which a convertible issue can be converted.

conversion value (10) an indication of what a convertible issue should trade for if it were priced to sell on the basis of its stock value; equals the conversion ratio of the issue times the current market price of the underlying common stock.

convertible securities (1, 10) fixed-income obligations, with a feature permitting the holder to convert the security into a specified number of shares of the issuing company's common stock.

corporation (15) a form of organization that provides limited liability benefits to shareholder investors and that has an indefinite life.

correlation (16) a statistical measure of the relationship, if any, between series of numbers representing data of any kind.

correlation coefficient (16) a measure of the degree of correlation between two series.

cost approach (14)   a real estate valuation approach based on the idea that a buyer should not pay more for a property than it would cost to rebuild it at today's prices.

coupon (8)   the feature on a bond that defines the amount of annual interest income.

covered options (11)   options written against stock owned (or short sold) by the writer.

cumulative provision (10)   a provision requiring that any preferred dividends that have been passed must be paid in full before dividends can be restored to common stockholders.

currency futures (12)   futures contracts on foreign currencies, traded much like commodities.

currency options (11)   put and call options written on foreign currencies.

current income (4)   cash or near-cash that is periodically received as a result of owning an investment.

current interest rate (15)   for an annuity contract, the yearly return the insurance company is currently paying on accumulated deposits.

current yield (9)   return measure that indicates the amount of current income a bond provides relative to its market price.

custodial account (2)   the brokerage account of a minor, in which a parent or guardian must be part of all transactions.

daily price limit (12)   restriction on the day-to-day change in the price of an underlying commodity.

date of record (5)   the date on which an investor must be a registered shareholder of a firm to be entitled to receive a dividend.

day order (17)   an order to buy or sell securities that expires at the end of the trading day it was entered, if not executed that day.

dealers (2)   traders who make markets by offering to buy or sell certain over-the-counter securities at stated prices.

debenture (8)   an unsecured (junior) bond.

debit balance (2)   the amount of money being borrowed; the size of a margin loan.

debt (1)   funds loaned in exchange for the receipt of interest income and the promised repayment of the loan at a given future date.

deep discount bond (15)   a bond selling at a price far below its par value.

deep-in-the-money call option (15)   a tax-deferral strategy that involves selling a call option on shares currently owned, locking in a price to the extent of the amount received from the sale of the call option but giving up potential future price appreciation.

deferred annuity (15)   an annuity contract in which the payments to the annuitant begin at some future date.

deferred equity securities (5, 10)   securities initially issued in one form (warrants or convertibles) and later redeemed or converted into shares of common stock.

deflation (4)   a period of generally declining prices.

de-listed (2)   to be removed from listing on an organized stock exchange.

delivery month (12)   the time when a commodity must be delivered; defines the life of a futures contract.

demand (14)   in real estate, people's willingness and ability to buy or rent a given property.

demographics (14)   characteristics of an area's population, such as household size, age structure, occupation, sex, and marital status.

denominations (8)   standard principal amounts into which a bond issue is broken to facilitate its sale to the public.

depreciation (14)   in real estate investing, a tax deduction based upon the original cost of a building and used to reflect its declining economic life.

derivative securities (1, 11)   securities such as puts, calls, and other options, structured to exhibit characteristics similar to those of an underlying security and as a result, derive their value from the securities that underlie them.

descriptive information (3)   factual data on the past behavior of the economy, the stock market, or a given investment vehicle.

direct investment (1)   investment in which an investor directly acquires a claim on a security or property.

discount basis (3)   a method of earning interest on short-term investments by purchasing a security at a price below its redemption value, the difference being the interest earned.

discount bond (8)   a bond with a market value lower than par; occurs when market rates are greater than the coupon rate.

discount broker (2, 5)   brokers who make transactions for customers at substantially reduced commissions, but provide little or no research information or advice.

discount rate (4)   the annual rate of return that could be earned currently on a similar investment; used when finding present value; also called *opportunity cost.*

discounted cash flow (14)   a measure of investment return, commonly used in real estate investment analysis; calculated by subtracting the original required investment from the present value of cash flows to find *net present value (NPV).*

distribution period (15)   under an annuity contract, the period of time over which payments are made to an annuitant.

diversifiable risk (4)   the portion of an investment's risk resulting from uncontrollable or random events that can be eliminated through diversification; also called *unsystematic risk.*

diversification (1, 3)   the inclusion of a number of different investment vehicles in a portfolio, in order to increase returns or be exposed to less risk.

dividend income (13)   income derived from the dividend and interest income earned on the security holdings of a mutual fund.

dividend payout ratio (5)   that portion of earnings per share (EPS) that a firm pays out as dividends.

dividend reinvestment plans (DRPs) (5)   plans in which shareholders have cash dividends automatically reinvested in additional shares of the firm's common stock.

dividend valuation model (DVM) (7)   a model that values a share of stock on the basis of the future dividend stream it is expected to produce.

dividend yield (5)   a measure that relates dividends to share price and in so doing, puts common stock dividends on a relative (percent) rather than absolute (dollar) basis.

dividends (1)   periodic payments made by firms to their stockholders.

dollar cost averaging (17)   a formula plan for timing investment transactions, in which a fixed dollar amount is invested in a security at fixed intervals.

Dow Jones bond averages (3)   mathematical averages of closing prices for groups of utility, industrial, and composite bonds.

Dow Jones Industrial Average (DJIA) (3)   a stock average made up of 30 high-quality industrial stocks selected for total market value and broad public ownership and believed to reflect overall market activity.

Dow theory (7) a technical approach that's based on the idea that the market's performance can be described by the long-term price trend in the DJIA, as confirmed by the Dow transportation average.

downtick (2) the decrease in the price of a stock issue since its last transaction.

dual listing (2) a listing of a firm's shares on more than one exchange.

duration (9) a measure of bond price volatility, it captures both price and reinvestment risks to indicate how a bond will react to different interest rate environments.

earnings per share (EPS) (5) the amount of annual earnings available to common stockholders, as stated on a per share basis.

economic analysis (6) a study of general economic conditions that is used in the valuation of common stock.

efficient frontier (16) the left-most boundary of the feasible or attainable set of portfolios that includes all efficient portfolios—those providing the best attainable tradeoff between risk (measured by the standard deviation) and return.

efficient markets (7) the theory that the market price of securities always-fully reflects available information, making it difficult, if not impossible, to consistently outperform the market by picking "undervalued" stocks.

efficient markets hypothesis (EMH) (7) basic theory of the behavior of efficient markets, in which information is widely available to investors and they react quickly to new information, causing securities prices to adjust quickly and accurately.

efficient portfolio (16) a portfolio that provides the highest return for a given level of risk, or that has the lowest risk for a given level of return.

environment (14) in real estate, the natural as well as esthetic, socio-economic, legal, and fiscal surroundings of a property.

equipment trust certificates (8) senior bonds secured by specific pieces of equipment; popular with railroads, airlines, and other transportation companies.

equity capital (1, 5) evidence of ownership position in a firm, in the form of shares of common stock.

equity kicker (10) another name for the conversion feature, giving the holder of a convertible security a deferred claim on the issuer's common stock.

equity-income fund (13) a mutual fund that emphasizes current income and capital preservation and which invests primarily in high-yielding common stocks.

ethics (2) standards of conduct or moral judgment.

Eurodollar bonds (8) foreign bonds denominated in dollars but not registered with the SEC, thus restricting sales of new issues.

European option (11) an option that can be exercised only on the date of expiration.

event risk (4) risk that comes from a largely or totally unexpected event which has a significant and usually immediate effect on the underlying value of an investment.

excess margin (2) more equity than is required in a margin account.

ex-dividend date (5) the date four business days before the date of record, which determines whether one is an official shareholder of a firm and thus eligible to receive a declared dividend.

exemption (15) a deduction for each qualifying dependent of a federal taxpayer.

exercise price (11) with options, the price at which a new share of common stock will be sold; also called *subscription price*.

expectations hypothesis (9) Theory that the shape of the yield curve reflects investor expectations of future interest rates.

expected inflation premium (4) the average rate of inflation expected in the future.

expected return (9) the rate of return an investor can expect to earn by holding a bond over a period of time less than the life of the issue.

expiration date (11) the date at which the life of an option expires.

extendable notes (8) a specialty issue, typically with short maturities (3–5 years), which can be redeemed or renewed for the same period at a new interest rate.

financial futures (12) a type of futures contract where the underlying ''commodity'' consists of a certain amount of some type of financial asset, such as debt securities, foreign currencies, or market baskets of common stocks.

financial institutions (1) organizations that channel the savings of individuals, businesses, and the governments into loans or investments.

financial markets (1) important forums in which suppliers and demanders of funds are brought together to make transactions.

financial risk (4) the degree of uncertainty associated with the mix of debt and equity used to finance a firm or property.

financial supermarket (2) a financial institution at which customers can obtain a full array of financial services.

first and refunding bonds (8) a bond that's secured in part with both first and second mortgages.

fixed annuity (15) an annuity contract with a monthly payment amount that does not change.

fixed charge coverage (10) a measure of how well a firm is able to cover its preferred stock dividends.

fixed-commission schedules (2) fixed brokerage charges applicable to small transactions.

fixed-income securities (1) investment vehicles that offer a fixed periodic return.

forced conversion (10) the calling in of convertible bonds by the issuing firm.

foreign exchange rate (2) the relationship between two currencies at a specific date.

foreign exchange risk (2) the risk caused by varying exchange rates between two countries.

Form 10-K (3) a statement filed with the SEC by all firms listed on a securities exchange or traded in the national OTC market.

formula plans (17) mechanical methods of portfolio management that try to take advantage of price changes in securities which result from cyclical price movements.

forward contract (12) agreement whereby a seller agrees to deliver a specific commodity or product to a buyer sometime in the future, *at a price specified in the contract itself*.

fourth market (2) transactions made directly between large institutional buyers and sellers.

fund families (13) different kinds of mutual funds all offered by the same investment management company.

fundamental analysis (6) the in-depth study of the financial condition and operating results of a firm.

future value (4) the amount to which a current deposit will grow over a period of time when it is placed in an account paying compound interest.

futures contract (12) a commitment to deliver a certain amount of some specified item at some specified date in the future.

futures market (12) the organized market for the trading of futures contracts.

futures options (12) options that give the holders the right to buy or sell a single standardized futures contract for a specified period of time at a specified striking price.

gemstones (12) diamonds and colored precious stones (rubies, sapphires, and emeralds).

general obligation bonds (8)   municipal bonds backed by the full faith and credit, and taxing power, of the issuer.

general partner (15)   the managing partner who accepts unlimited liability and makes all decisions in a partnership.

general partnership (15)   a joint venture in which all partners have management rights and all assume unlimited liability for any debts or obligations the partnership incurs.

good 'til canceled (GTC) (17)   an order to buy or sell securities that generally remains in effect for six months unless executed, canceled, or renewed.

government securities money fund (3)   a money market mutual fund that limits its investments to Treasury bills and other short-term securities of the U.S. government and its agencies.

gross income (15)   all includable income for federal income-tax purposes.

growth cycle (6)   a reflection of the amount of business vitality that occurs within a company or industry over time.

growth fund (13)   a mutual fund whose primary goals are capital gains and long-term growth.

growth-and-income fund (13)   a mutual fund that seeks both long-term growth and current income, with principal emphasis on capital gains.

growth-oriented portfolio (16)   a portfolio whose primary objective is long-term price appreciation.

guaranteed investment contract (GIC) (15)   a portfolio of fixed-income securities with a guaranteed competitive rate of return that is backed and sold by an insurance company to pension plan managers.

hedge (11)   a combination of two or more securities into a single investment position for the purpose of reducing or eliminating risk.

hedgers (12)   producers and processors who use futures contracts as a way to protect their interest in an underlying commodity or financial instrument.

high-risk investments (1)   investments considered speculative with regard to the receipt of a positive return.

holding period (4)   the period of time over which one wishes to measure the return on an investment vehicle.

holding period return (HPR) (4)   the total return earned from holding an investment for a specified holding period (usually one year or less).

immediate annuity (15)   an annuity contract under which payments to the annuitant begin as soon as it is purchased.

improvements (14)   in real estate, the man-made additions to a site, such as buildings, sidewalks, and various on-site amenities.

in arrears (10)   having outstanding unfulfilled preferred-dividend obligations.

income approach (14)   a real estate valuation approach that calculates a property's value as the present value of all its future income.

income bonds (8)   unsecured bonds that require that interest be paid only after a specified amount of income is earned.

income property (14)   leased-out residential or commercial real estate, that is expected to provide returns primarily from periodic rental income.

income statement (6)   a financial summary of the operating results of a firm covering a specified period of time, usually one year.

income-oriented portfolio (16)   a portfolio that stresses current dividend and interest returns.

index price (12)   technique used to price T-bill (and other short-term securities) futures contracts, which reflects the actual price movements of these futures contracts.

indexes (3)   numbers used to measure the general behavior of stock prices by measuring the current price behavior of a representative group of stocks in relation to a base value.

indirect investment (1)   investment made in a portfolio or group of securities or properties.

individual investors (1)   investors who manage their own funds.

individual retirement account (IRA) (15)   a self-directed, tax-deferred retirement plan, in which employed persons may contribute annually.

industry analysis (6)   study of industry groupings, by looking at the competitive position of a particular industry in relation to others and by identifying companies within an industry that hold particular promise.

inflation (4)   a period of generally rising prices.

initial deposit (12)   the amount of investor capital that must be deposited with a broker at the time of a commodity transaction.

initial margin (2)   the minimum amount of money (or equity) that must be provided by a margin investor at the time of purchase.

initial public offering (IPO) (2, 5)   a special category of common stocks issued by (relatively) new firms going public for the first time.

insider trading (2)   the illegal use of non-public information about a company to make profitable securities transactions.

installment annuity (15)   an annuity contract acquired by making payments over time; at a specified future date the installment payments, plus interest earned on them, are used to purchase an annuity contract.

institutional investors (1)   investment professionals paid to manage other people's money.

insurance policy (3)   a contract between the insured and the insurer that requires the insured to make periodic premium payments in exchange for the insurer's promise to pay for losses according to specified terms.

interest rate futures (12)   futures contracts on debt securities, traded much like commodities.

interest rate options (11)   put and call options written on fixed-income (debt) securities.

interest rate risk (4)   the degree of uncertainty in the prices of securities, associated with changes in interest rates.

international fund (13)   a mutual fund that does all or most of its investing in foreign securities.

in-the-money (11)   a call option with a strike price less than the market price of the underlying security; a put option with strike price greater than the market price of the underlying security.

intrinsic value (6)   the underlying or inherent value of a stock, as determined through fundamental analysis.

investing (1)   the process of placing funds in selected investment vehicles with the expectation of increasing their value or earning a positive return.

investment (1)   a vehicle for funds, expected to maintain or increase its value and/or generate positive returns.

investment advisors (3)   individuals or firms that provide investment advice, usually for a fee.

investment analysis (14)   real estate analysis that considers not only what similar properties have sold for, but also looks at the underlying determinants of value.

investment banker (2) financial intermediary that purchases new securities from the issuing firm at an agreed-upon price and resells them to the public.

investment club (3) a legal partnership through which a group of investors is bound to an organizational structure, operating procedures, and purpose.

investment company (13) a firm, such as a mutual fund, that combines the capital of many people with similar investment goals and invests the money in a wide variety of securities.

investment goals (1, 3) the financial objectives one wishes to achieve by investing in potential investment vehicles; specify the timing, magnitude, form, and risks associated with a desired return.

investment letters (3) provide, on a subscription basis, the analyses, conclusions, and recommendations of various experts in different aspects of securities investment.

investment plan (3) a written document describing investment goals, how funds will be invested, the target date for the accomplishments of goals, and the amount of tolerable risk.

investment value; convertibles (10) the price at which a convertible would trade if it were nonconvertible and if it were priced at or near the prevailing market yields of comparable nonconvertible issues.

investment value (5) the amount that investors believe a security should be trading for, or what they think it's worth.

itemized deductions (15) personal living and family expenses which can be deducted from adjusted gross income.

Jensen's measure (alpha) (17) a measure of portfolio performance, developed by Michael C. Jensen, that uses the portfolio's beta and CAPM to calculate its excess return, which can be positive, zero, or negative.

junior bonds (8) debt obligations backed only by the promise of the issuer to pay interest and principal on a timely basis.

junk bonds (8) high risk securities that have received low ratings and as such, produce high yields, so long as they don't go into default.

Keogh plan (15) a retirement plan that allows self-employed individuals to establish tax-deferred retirement plans for themselves and their employees.

LEAPS (11) long-term options.

leverage (11, 14) the ability to obtain a given equity position at a reduced capital investment, thereby magnifying returns.

leverage measures (6) financial ratios that measure the amount of debt being used to support operations, and the ability of the firm to service its debt.

life insurance (3) a mechanism that can provide financial protection for a family if the primary breadwinner or other family member dies prematurely.

limit order (2) an order to buy at or below a specified price or to sell at or above a specified price.

limited partners (15) the passive investors in a partnership, who supply most of the capital and have liability limited to the amount of their capital contributions.

limited partnership (LP) (1, 15) a vehicle in which the investor can passively invest with limited liability, receive the benefit of active professional management, and apply the resulting profit or loss (subject to limits) to his or her tax liability.

liquidation value (5) the amount left if a firm's assets were sold or auctioned off and the creditors and preferred stockholders paid off.

liquidity (3) the ability to convert an investment into cash quickly and with little or no loss in value.

liquidity measures (6) financial ratios concerned with the firm's ability to meet its day-to-day operating expenses and satisfy its short-term obligations as they come due.

liquidity preference theory (9) Theory that investors tend to prefer the greater liquidity of short-term securities and therefore require a premium to invest in long-term securities.

liquidity risk (4) the risk of not being able to liquidate an investment conveniently and at a reasonable price.

listed options (11) put and call options listed and traded on organized securities exchanges, such as the CBOE.

load fund (13) a mutual fund that charges a commission when shares are bought; also known as *front-end load fund*.

long purchase (2) a transaction in which investors buy securities in the hope that they will increase in value and can be sold at a later date for profit.

long-term investments (1) investments with maturities of longer than a year or with no maturity at all.

low-load fund (13) a mutual fund that charges a small commission (2 to 3 percent) when shares are bought.

low-risk investments (1) investments considered safe with regard to the receipt of a positive return.

maintenance deposit margin (2, 12) the minimum amount of margin that must be kept in a margin account at all times.

management fee (13) a fee levied annually for professional mutual fund services provided; paid regardless of the performance of the portfolio.

margin account (2) a brokerage account in which the customer has borrowing privileges.

margin call (2) notification of the need to bring the equity of an account whose margin is below the maintenance level up to the required level or have margined holdings sold to reach this point.

margin deposit (12) amount deposited with a broker to cover any loss in the market value of a futures contract that may result from adverse price movements.

margin loan (2) vehicle through which borrowed funds are made available, at a stated interest rate, in a margin transaction.

margin requirement (2) the minimum amount of equity (stated as a percentage) a margin investor must put up; established by the Federal Reserve Board.

margin trading (2) the use of borrowed funds to purchase securities; magnifies returns by reducing the amount of capital that must be put up by the investor.

marginal tax rate (15) the tax rate on additional income.

market anomalies (7) irregularities or deviations from the normal behavior in an efficient market.

market order (2) an order to buy or sell stock at the best price available when the order is placed.

market return (4) the average return on all, or a large sample of, stocks, such as those in the Standard & Poor's 500 stock composite index.

market risk (4) risk of decline in investment returns due to market factors independent of the given security or property investment.

market segmentation theory (9) Theory that the market for debt is segmented based on maturity, that supply and demand within each segment determines the prevailing interest rate, and that the slope of the yield curve depends on the relationship between the prevailing rates in each segment.

market value (5, 14) the prevailing market price of a security; in real estate, the prevailing market price of a property, indicating how the market as a whole has assessed the property's worth.

mark-to-the-market (12) a daily check of an investor's margin position; the gain or loss in a contract's value is determined at the end of each session, at which time the broker debits or credits the account as needed.

master limited partnership (MLP) (14) a limited partnership that is publicly traded on a major stock exchange.

maturity date (8) the date on which a bond matures and the principal must be repaid.

maximum daily price range (12) the amount a commodity price can change during a day; usually equal to twice the daily price limit.

minimum guaranteed interest rate (15) for an annuity contract, the minimum interest rate on contributions that the insurance company will guarantee over the full accumulation period.

mixed stream (4) a stream of returns that, unlike an annuity, exhibits no special pattern.

modern portfolio theory (16) an approach to portfolio management that uses statistical measures to develop a portfolio plan.

money market (2) market in which short-term securities are bought and sold.

money market deposit accounts(MMDAs) (3) a federally insured bank account with features similar to money market mutual funds; has no legal minimum balance but many banks impose their own.

money market mutual fund (money fund) (3, 13) a mutual fund that pools the capital of a number of investors and uses it to invest in short-term money market instruments.

Moody's Investor Services (3) publisher of a variety of financial reference manuals, including *Moody's Manuals*.

mortgage bonds (8) senior bonds secured by real estate.

mortgage-backed bond (8) a debt issue secured by a pool of home mortgages; issued primarily by federal agencies.

municipal bond guarantees (8) guarantees from a party other than the issuer that principal and interest payments will be made in a prompt and timely manner.

municipal bonds (8) debt securities issued by states, counties, cities, and other political subdivisions, like school districts; most of these bonds are tax-exempt, meaning there's no federal income tax on interest income.

mutual fund (1, 13) a company that invests in and professionally manages a diversified portfolio of securities and sells shares of the portfolio to investors.

naked options (11) options written on securities not owned by the writer.

Nasdaq indexes (3) measures of current price behavior of securities sold OTC.

Nasdaq/National Market System (Nasdaq/NMS) (2) a list of Nasdaq stocks meeting certain standards of financial size, performance, and trading activity.

National Association of Securities Dealers Automated Quotation (Nasdaq) System (2) an automated system that provides up-to-date bid and ask prices on certain selected, highly active OTC securities.

negative leverage (14) a position in which, if a property's return is below its debt cost, the investor's return will be less than from an all-cash deal.

negatively correlated (16) describes two series that move in opposite directions.

negotiated commissions (2, 5) commissions agreed upon by the client and the broker as a result of their negotiations.

net asset value (NAV) (10, 13) the underlying value of a share of stock in a particular mutual fund; also used with preferred stock.

net losses (3) the amount by which capital losses exceed capital gains; up to $3,000 can be applied against ordinary income.

net operating income (NOI) (14) the amount left after subtracting vacancy and collection losses and property operating expenses from an income property's *gross potential* rental income.

net present value (NPV) (14) the difference between the present value of the cash flows and the amount of equity required to make an investment.

no-load fund (13) a mutual fund that does not charge a commission when shares are bought.

noncumulative provision (10) a provision found on some preferred stocks excusing the issuing firm from having to make up any passed dividends.

nondiversifiable risk (4) risk attributable to forces affecting all investments and therefore not unique to any given vehicle; also called *systematic risk*.

note (8) a debt security originally issued with a maturity of from 2 to 10 years.

NOW (negotiatedorder of withdrawal) account (3) a checking account that pays interest; has no legal minimum balance but many banks impose their own.

NYSE index (3) measure of the current price behavior of the stocks listed on the NYSE.

odd lot (2) less than 100 shares of stock.

open interest (12) the number of contracts presently outstanding on a commodity or financial future.

open outcry auction (12) in futures trading, auction in which trading is done through a series of shouts, body motions, and hand signals.

open-end investment company (13) a type of investment company in which investors buy shares from, and sell them back to, the mutual fund itself, with no limit on the number of shares the fund can issue.

option (11) a security that gives the holder the right to buy or sell a certain amount of an underlying financial asset at a specified price for a specified period of time.

option maker (11) the individual or institution that writes put and call options; also called *option writer*.

option premium (11) the quoted price the investor pays to buy a listed put or call option.

option spreading (11) combining two or more options with different strike prices and/or expiration dates into a single transaction.

option straddle (11) the simultaneous purchase (or sale) of a put and a call on the same underlying common stock.

organized securities exchanges (2) centralized institutions in which transactions are made in already outstanding securities.

out-of-the-money (11) a call option with no real value because the strike price exceeds the market price of the stock; a put option whose market price exceeds the strike price.

over-the-counter (OTC) market (2) widely scattered telecommunications network through which buyers and sellers of certain securities can be brought together.

paper return (4) a return that has been achieved, but not yet realized, by an investor during the period.

par value (5) the stated, or face, value of a stock.

passbook savings account (3) a savings vehicle, offered by banks and other thrift institutions, that generally pays a low rate of interest, has no minimum balance, and few or no restrictions on withdrawal.

passive activity (15) an investment in which the investor does not "materially participate" in its management or activity.

payback period (10) the length of time it takes for the buyer of a convertible to recover the conversion premium from the extra income earned on the convertible.

payout (15) the investment return provided by an annuity contract, realized when the distribution period begins.

perfectly negatively correlated (16) describes two negatively correlated series that have a *correlation coefficient* of −1.

perfectly positively correlated (16) describes two positively correlated series that have a *correlation coefficient* of +1.

PIK-bond (8) a payment-in-kind junk bond, which makes some of the annual interest payments in new bonds rather than in cash.

point-and-figure charts (7) charts used to keep track of emerging price patterns by plotting significant price changes with Xs and Os but with no time dimension used.

pooled diversification (13) a process whereby investors buy into a diversified portfolio of securities for the collective benefit of the individual investors.

portfolio (1) a collection of investment vehicles assembled to meet one or more investment goals.

portfolio beta (16) the beta of a portfolio; calculated as the weighted average of the betas of the individual assets that it includes.

portfolio revision (17) the process of selling certain issues in a portfolio and of purchasing new ones.

positive leverage (14) a position in which, if a property's return is in excess of its debt cost, the investor's return will be increased to a level well above what could have been earned from an all-cash deal.

positively correlated (16) describes two series that move in the same direction.

precious metals (12) tangible assets, like gold, silver, and platinum, that concentrate a great deal of value in a small amount of weight and volume.

preemptive right (11) the right of existing stockholders to maintain their proportionate share of ownership in a firm.

preference (prior preferred) stock (10) a type of preferred stock that has seniority over other preferred stock in its right to receive dividends and in its claim on assets.

preferred stock (1, 10) a stock that has a prior claim (ahead of common) on the income and assets of the issuing firm.

premium bond (8) a bond that has a market value in excess of par; occurs when interest rates drop below the coupon rate.

present value (4) the current value of a future sum; the inverse of *future value*.

primary market (2) market in which new issues of securities are sold to the public.

prime rate (2) the lowest interest rate charged the best business borrowers.

principal (8) on a bond, the amount of capital that must be paid at maturity.

principle of substitution (14) the principle that people do not buy or rent real estate per se but rather that they judge properties as different sets of benefits and costs.

private partnership (15) a limited partnership that has a limited number of investors and is not registered with a public agency.

private placement (2) the sale of new securities directly to selected groups of investors, without SEC registration.

problem investment (17) an investment that has not lived up to expectations.

profitability measures (6) financial ratios that measure the returns of a company by relating relative success of a firm through comparison of profits to sales, assets, or equity.

program trading (12) a type of computer-assisted trading whereby brokerage houses and other institutional investors simultaneously buy and sell large quantities of common stocks and stock-index futures contracts; also known as *index arbitrage*.

promised yield (9) same as yield-to-maturity.

property (1) investments in real property or in tangible personal property.

property management (14) in real estate, finding the optimal level of benefits for a property and then providing them at the lowest costs.

property transfer process (14) the process of promotion and negotiation of real estate, which can significantly influence the cash flows a property can earn in the real estate market.

prospectus (2) a portion of a security registration statement that details the key aspects of the issue, the issuer, and its management and financial position.

psychographics (14) characteristics that describe people's mental dispositions, such as personality, lifestyle, and self-concept.

public offering (2, 5) an offering to sell to the investing public a set number of shares of a firm's stock at a specified price.

public partnership (15) a limited partnership that is registered with state and/or federal regulators and usually has 35 or more limited partners.

publicly traded issues (5) shares of stock readily available to the general public, that are bought and sold in the open market.

purchasing power (4) the amount of some commodity that can be bought with a given amount of a currency, such as one dollar.

put (1, 11) a negotiable instrument that enables the holder to sell the underlying security at a specified price over a set period of time.

put bond (8) a type of specialty bond that gives the holder the right to redeem the bond at certain specified times before maturity.

put hedge (15) the purchase of a put option on shares currently owned in order to lock in a profit and defer taxes on the profit to the next taxable year.

pyramiding (2) the technique of using paper profits in margin accounts to partly or fully finance the acquisition of additional securities.

quotations (3) price information about various types of securities, including current price data and statistics on recent price behavior.

random walk hypothesis (7) the theory that stock price movements are unpredictable and, thus, there's really little way of knowing where future prices are headed.

ratio analysis (6) the study of the relationships among and between various financial statement accounts.

real estate (1) property such as residential homes, raw land, and income property.

real estate investment trust (REIT) (14) a type of closed-end investment company that invests money, obtained through the sale of shares to investors, in various types of real estate and/or real estate mortgages.

real estate limited partnership (RELP) (14) a professionally managed real estate syndicate that invests in various types of real estate; the managers assume the role of general partner, whose liability is unlimited, and other investors are limited partners, whose liability is limited to the amount of their initial investment.

real rate of return (4) the rate of return that could be earned in a perfect world where all outcomes are known and certain.

realized return (4) return received by an investor during the period.

realized yield (9) same as expected return

red herring (2) a preliminary prospectus made available to prospective investors after a registration statement has been filed but before its approval.

refunding provisions (8) provisions similar to a call feature except that they prohibit the premature retirement of an issue from the proceeds of a lower-coupon refunding bond.

registered bonds (8) bonds issued to specific owners, whose names are formally registered with the issuer.

relative P/E multiple (7) the measure of how a stock's P/E behaves relative to the average market multiple.

relevant risk (16) risk that is nondiversifiable.

required (rate of) return (4, 7) the return necessary to compensate an investor for the risk involved in an investment.

residential property (14) a *single-family* or *multi-family* income property that is occupied by tenants who use it as a residence for living purposes.

residual owners (5) owners/stockholders of a firm, who are entitled to dividend income and a prorated share of the firm's earnings only after all the firm's other obligations have been met.

restricted account (2) a margin account whose equity is less than the initial margin requirement; the investor must bring the margin back to the initial level when securities are sold while the account is restricted.

return (4) the expected level of profit from an investment; the reward for investing.

return on invested capital (12) return to investors based on the amount of money actually invested in a security, rather than the value of the contract itself.

revenue bonds (8) municipal bonds backed by the revenue-generating capacity of the issuer; requires that principal and interest be paid only if a sufficient level of revenue is generated.

reverse stock split (5) a strategy in which a company reduces the number of shares outstanding by exchanging a fractional amount of a new share for each outstanding share of stock.

reversion (17) the after-tax net proceeds received upon disposition of real property.

right (1, 11) an option to buy shares of a new issue of common stock at a specified price, over a specified, fairly short, period of time.

rights offering (2, 5) an offer of a new issue of stock to existing stockholders on a pro rata basis.

rights-off (11) a condition when a firm's common stock and its rights are trading in separate markets, separate from each other; also called *ex-rights*.

rights-on (11) a condition when a firm's common stock is trading with a stock right attached to it.

risk (4) the chance that the actual return from an investment may differ from what is expected.

risk premium (4) a return premium that reflects the issue and issuer characteristics associated with a given investment vehicle.

risk-averse (4) describes an investor who requires greater return in exchange for greater risk.

risk-free rate (R_F) (4, 16) the return an investor can earn on a risk-free investment such as a T-bill or an insured money market account.

risk-indifferent (4) describes an investor who does not require greater return in exchange for greater risk

risk-return tradeoff (4, 16) the inverse relationship between the risk associated with a given investment and its expected return; investments with more risk should provide higher returns, and vice versa.

risk-taking (4) describes an investor who will accept a lower return in exchange for greater risk.

round lot (2) 100 share units of stock or multiples thereof.

round trip commissions (12) the commission costs on both ends (buying and selling) of a securities transaction.

secondary distributions (2) the public sales of large blocks of previously issued securities held by large investors.

secondary market (2) the market in which securities are traded after they have been issued.

sector fund (13) a mutual fund that restricts its investments to a particular segment of the market.

securities (1) investments that represent debt, business ownership, or the legal right to buy or sell a business ownership interest.

Securities Investor Protection Corporation (SIPC) (2) a nonprofit membership corporation authorized by the federal government that insures each brokerage customer's account for up to $500,000.

securities markets (2) markets allowing suppliers and demanders of funds to make transactions, in either money or capital.

security analysis (6) the process of gathering and organizing information and then using it to determine the value of a share of common stock.

security market line (SML) (4) the graphic depiction of the capital asset pricing model; reflects the investor's required return for each level of nondiversifiable risk, measured by beta.

selling group (2) a large number of brokerage firms that join to accept responsibility for selling a certain portion of the issue of a new security.

senior bonds (8) secured debt obligations, backed by a legal claim on specific property of the issuer.

serial bond (8) a bond that has a series of different maturity dates.

Series EE savings bonds (3) savings bonds issued by the U.S. Treasury and sold at banks and through payroll deduction plans, in varying denominations, at 50% of face value; pay a variable rate of interest depending on the length of time held.

settle price (12) the closing price (last price of the day) for commodities and financial futures.

Sharpe's measure (17) a measure of portfolio performance, developed by William F. Sharpe, that measures the risk premium of a portfolio per unit of total risk, which is measured by the portfolio's standard deviation of return.

shelf registration (2) securities registration procedure that allows a firm to sell securities during a two-year period under a "master registration statement" filed with the SEC.

short interest (7) the number of stocks sold short in the market at any given time; a technical indicator believed to indicate future market demand.

short selling (2) the sale of borrowed securities, their eventual repurchase by the short seller at a lower price, and their return to the lender.

shorting-against-the-box (2, 15) a conservative technique used to lock in a security profit and defer the taxes on it to the following tax year by short-selling a number of shares equal to those already owned.

short-term investments (1) investments that typically mature within one year.

short-term vehicles (1) savings instruments that usually have lives of one year or less.

simple interest (4) interest paid only on the actual balance for the amount of time it is on deposit.

single property syndicate (14) a type of real estate limited partnership established to raise money to purchase a specific property.

single-premium annuity (15) a contract purchased with a single lump-sum payment.

single-premium life insurance policy (SPLI) (15) an insurance investment vehicle for which the policyholder pays a large premium to purchase a whole life policy that provides a stated death benefit and earns interest on the cash value buildup, which occurs over time on a tax-free basis.

sinking fund (8) a provision that stipulates the amount of principal that will be retired annually over the life of a bond.

Small Investor Index (3) an index that measures gains and losses of the average investor relative to a base of 100; based on a portfolio including types of investments held by average small investors.

socially responsible fund (13) a mutual fund that actively and directly incorporates ethics and morality into the investment decision.

specialist (2) stock exchange member who specializes in one or more stocks.

specialty fund (13) a mutual fund that strives to achieve attractive rates of return by adhering to unusual or unorthodox investment strategies.

speculation (1) the process of buying investment vehicles in which the future value and level of expected earnings are highly uncertain.

speculative investment vehicles (1) investment vehicles with high levels of risk.

speculative property (14) type of real estate investment property that is expected to provide returns primarily from appreciation in value.

split ratings (8) different ratings given to a bond issue by the two major rating agencies.

Standard & Poor's Corp. (S&P) (3) publisher of a variety of financial reports and services, including *Corporation Records* and *Stock Reports*.

Standard & Poor's indexes (3) true indexes that measure the current price of a group of stocks relative to a base which has an index value of 10.

standard deduction (15) an amount, indexed to the cost of living, that taxpayers can elect to deduct from adjusted gross income without itemizing.

standard deviation (4) a statistic used to measure the dispersion around an asset's average or expected return, and the most common single indicator of an asset's risk.

statement of cash flows (6) a financial summary of a firm's cash flow and other events that caused changes in the company's cash position.

stock dividend (5) payment of a dividend in the form of additional shares of stock.

stock split (5) a maneuver in which a company increases the number of shares outstanding by exchanging a specified number of new shares of stock for each outstanding share.

stock valuation (7) the process by which the underlying value of a stock is established, as based on future risk and return performance of the security.

stockbrokers (2) individuals licensed by stock exchanges to enable investors to buy and sell securities; also called *account executives*.

stockholder's (annual) report (3) a report published yearly by every publicly held firm; contains a wide range of information including financial statements for the most recent fiscal year.

stock-index futures (12)   futures contracts written on broad based measures of stock market performance like the S&P 500 Stock Index; traded much like commodities, allowing investors to participate in the general movements of the stock market.

stock-index option (11)   a put or call option written on a specific stock market index, such as the S&P 500.

stop-loss order (2)   an order to sell a stock when its market price reaches or drops below a specified level; also called a *stop order*.

straight annuity (15)   an annuity contract that provides for a series of payments for the rest of the annuitant's life.

street name (2)   stock certificates issued in the brokerage house's name but held in trust for their customers who actually own them.

strike price (11)   the price contract between the buyer of an option and the writer; it's the stated price at which you can buy a security with a call, or sell a security with a put.

subordinated debentures (8)   unsecured bonds that have a claim that's secondary to other debentures.

suitability rule (15)   a rule excluding investors who cannot bear a high amount of risk from buying limited partnership interests.

supply analysis (14)   study of the competition in real estate by identifying potential competitors and making an inventory of them by price and features.

syndicate (15)   a joint venture—general partnership, corporation, or limited partnership—in which investors pool their resources.

systematic withdrawal plan (13)   a mutual fund service that enables shareholders to automatically receive a predetermined amount of money every month or quarter.

tangible investment (1, 12)   an investment that has an actual form or substance, such as precious metals, stamps, or works of art.

tax avoidance (15)   reducing or eliminating taxes in legal ways that comply with the intent of Congress.

tax credits (15)   tax reductions allowed by the IRS on a dollar-for-dollar basis under certain specified conditions.

tax deferral (15)   the strategy of delaying taxes by shifting income subject to tax into a later period.

tax evasion (15)   illegal activities designed to avoid paying taxes by omitting income or overstating deductions.

tax planning (3, 15)   the formation of strategies that will exclude, reduce, or defer the level of taxes to be paid; the objective is to minimize taxes.

tax risk (4)   the chance that Congress will make unfavorable changes in the tax laws that make certain investments less attractive by driving down their after-tax returns and market values.

tax shelter (1, 15)   an investment vehicle that offers potential reductions of taxable income.

tax swap (9, 15)   selling one security that has experienced a capital loss and replacing it with another similar security in order to partially or fully offset a capital gain that has been realized in another part of the investor's portfolio.

taxable equivalent yield (8)   the return a fully taxable bond would have to provide to match the after-tax return of a lower-yielding, tax-free municipal bond.

taxable income (15)   the income to which tax rates are applied; equals adjusted gross income minus itemized deductions and exemptions.

taxable munis (8)   municipal bonds, used to finance projects considered non-essential, whose interest income is fully taxable by the federal government.

tax-exempt money fund (3) a money market mutual fund that limits its investments to tax-exempt municipal securities with very short maturities.

tax-favored income (15) an investment return that is not taxable, is taxed at a rate less than that on other similar investments, defers the payment of tax to a later period, or trades current income for capital gains.

tax-sheltered annuity (15) an annuity contract available that allows employees of certain institutions and organizations to make a tax-free contribution from current income to purchase a deferred annuity.

technical analysis (7) the study of the various forces at work in the marketplace and their effect on stock prices.

term bond (8) a bond that has a single, fairly lengthy maturity date.

term life insurance (3) form of life insurance in which the insurer agrees to pay a specified amount if the insured dies within the policy period.

term structure of interest rates (9) The relationship between the interest rate or rate of return (yield) and time to maturity.

***The Wall Street Journal* (3)** a daily newspaper, published regionally by Dow Jones; the most popular source of financial news.

theory of contrary opinion (7) a technical indicator that uses the amount and type of odd-lot trading as an indicator of the current state of the market and pending changes.

third market (2) over-the-counter transactions made in securities listed on the NYSE, AMEX, or other organized exchanges.

time premium (11) the amount by which the option price exceeds the option's fundamental value.

time value of money (4) the principle that as long as an opportunity exists to earn interest, the value of money is affected by the point in time when it is expected to be received.

total return (4) the sum of the current income and the capital gains (or losses) earned on an investment over a specified period of time.

total risk (4) the sum of an investment's diversifiable risk and nondiversifiable risk.

traditional portfolio management (16) an approach to portfolio management that emphasizes balancing the portfolio with a variety of stocks and/or bonds from a broad cross-section of industries.

Treasury bonds (8) U.S. Treasury debt securities which are issued with maturities of more than 10 years—usually 20 years or more.

Treasury notes (8) debt securities issued by the U.S. Treasury which are issued with maturities of 10 years or less.

treasury stock (5) shares of stock that have been sold and subsequently repurchased (and held) by the issuing firm.

Treasury STRIPS (STRIP-T's) (8) Zero-coupon bonds issued by the U.S. Treasury.

Treynor's measure (17) a measure of portfolio performance, developed by Jack L. Treynor, that measures the risk premium of a portfolio per unit of diversifiable risk, which is measured by the portfolio's beta.

uncorrelated (16) Describes two series that lack any relationship or interaction and therefore have a *correlation coefficient* close to zero.

underwriting (2) the role of the investment banker in bearing the risk of reselling at a profit the securities purchased from an issuing corporation at an agreed-upon price.

underwriting syndicate (2) a group formed to spread the financial risk associated with the selling of new securities.

unit investment trust (13) a type of investment vehicle whereby the trust sponsors put together a fixed/unmanaged portfolio of securities and then sell ownership units in the portfolio to individual investors.

universal life insurance (3) form of life insurance that combines term insurance with a tax-sheltered savings/investment account that pays interest at competitive rates.

unrealized capital gains (paper profits) (13) a capital gain made only "on paper," that is, not realized until the fund's holdings are sold.

uptick (2) the increase in the price of a stock issue since its last transaction.

U.S. Treasury bills (T-bills) (3) obligations of the U.S. Treasury, sold on a discount basis, and having varying short-term maturities and virtually no risk.

valuation (1, 7) process by which an investor determines the worth of a security using risk and return concepts.

Value Line composite index (3) a stock index published by Value Line, that reflects the percentage changes in share price of about 1,700 stocks traded on the NYSE, AMEX, and OTC market relative to a base of 100.

Value Line Investment Survey (3) a weekly subscription service covering about 1,700 of the most widely held stocks and their industries; popular among individual investors.

variable annuity (15) an annuity contract that adjusts the monthly payment according to the investment experience (and sometimes the mortality experience) of the insurer.

variable life insurance (3) form of life insurance that offers insurance coverage with a savings feature that allows the insured to decide how the cash value is invested; the amount of insurance coverage varies with the policy's investment returns.

variable ratio plan (17) a formula plan for timing investment transactions, in which the ratio of the speculative portion to the total portfolio varies depending on the movement in the value of the speculative securities; when the ratio rises or falls by a predetermined amount, the amount committed to the speculative portion of the portfolio is reduced or increased, respectively.

variable-rate note (8) a specialty bond issue with two unique features: (1) after a specified period of time, the coupon "floats" at a certain amount above T-bill or T-note rates, and (2) every year or so the notes are redeemable at par, at the bondholder's option.

warrant (1, 11) an option for a long period of time to buy one or more shares of common stock in a given company at a price initially above the market price.

warrant premium (11) the difference between the true value of a warrant and its market price.

wash sale (15) the procedure, disallowed under the tax law, of selling securities on which capital losses can be realized and then immediately buying them back.

whipsawing (17) the situation in which a stock drops in price and then bounces back upward.

whole life insurance (3) form of life insurance that provides coverage over the entire life of the insured; offers a savings benefit.

Wilshire 5000 Index (3) measure of the total dollar value of 5,000 actively traded stocks, including all those on the NYSE and the AMEX, plus active OTC stocks.

wrap account (2) an account in which customers with large portfolios pay a brokerage firm a flat annual fee that covers the cost of a money manager's services and the cost of commissions.

Yankee bonds (2, 8) bonds issued by foreign governments or corporations but denominated in dollars, registered with the SEC, and traded in U.S. securities markets.

yield curve (9) A graph that represents the relationship between a bond's term to maturity and its yield at a given point in time.

yield (internal rate of return) (4) the compounded annual rate of return earned by a long-term investment.

yield pickup swap (9) replacement of a low-coupon bond for a comparable higher-coupon bond in order to realize an increase in current yield and yield to maturity.

yield spreads (9) differences in interest rates that exist in various sectors of the market.

yield-to-maturity (YTM) (9) the fully compounded rate of return earned by an investor over the life of a bond, including interest income and price appreciation.

zero-coupon bond (8) a bond with no coupons that's sold at a deep discount from par value.

ACKNOWLEDGMENTS: We wish to thank the following copyright holders who granted permission to reprint the material listed. Box 1.1: Adapted from "How Safety Can Mean Investment Disaster" by Earl C. Gottschalk Jr., THE WALL STREET JOURNAL, September 5, 1991. Copyright © 1991 Dow Jones & Company, Inc. Reprinted by permission of The Wall Street Journal. All Rights Reserved Worldwide. Box 1.2: From "How To Maximize Your Profits" by T. P. Paré, FORTUNE/1992 Investor's Guide. Copyright © 1992 Time Inc. Reprinted by permission. All rights reserved. Box 2.1: From "Why Investors Should Go GLOBAL" by David Carey, FORTUNE/1991 Investor's Guide. Copyright © 1991 Time Inc. Reprinted by permission. All rights reserved. Box 2.2: From "Going for Brokers: Check it Out" by Lisa M. Keefe, THE ORLANDO SENTINEL. Reprinted by permission. Figure 2.2: "An Offering Announcement: F&C International, Inc.," January 7, 1992. Reprinted by permission of Paine Webber Inc. Figure 2.3: From "Investing in a Perilous Market" by Manuel Schiffres, CHANGING TIMES, October 1990, pp. 40–41. Copyright © 1990 The Kiplinger Washington Editors, Inc. and from "Daily Action Stock Charts," TRENDLINE, Standard & Poor's Corporation, November 22, 1991. Reprinted by permission. Table 2.2: Adapted from "Not All Discount Brokers Offer the Same Bargains" by Tom Herman, THE WALL STREET JOURNAL, March 6, 1991. Copyright © 1991 Dow Jones & Company, Inc. Reprinted by permission of The Wall Street Journal. All Rights Reserved Worldwide. Box 3.2: Adapted from "The Life-Insurance Quandary: How Much is Really Enough?" by Karen Slater, THE WALL STREET JOURNAL, July 10, 1990. Copyright © 1990 Dow Jones & Company, Inc. Reprinted by permission of The Wall Street Journal. All Rights Reserved Worldwide. Figure 3.1: "Report on Pepsico, Inc." by Stephen Sanborn, VALUE LINE INVESTMENT SURVEY. Copyright © 1992 by Value Line Publishing, Inc. Reprinted by permission. For subscription information to the Value Line Investment Survey, please call (800)634-3583. Figure 3.2: "Pepsico, Inc.-1990 Stockholder's Report." Reprinted by permission of Pepsico, Inc. Figure 3.3: F&C International, Inc. Prospectus, December 13, 1991. Reprinted by permission of PaineWebber Incorporated. Figure 3.4: "Stock Market Data Bank," THE WALL STREET JOURNAL, January 7, 1992. Copyright © Dow & Company, Inc. Reprinted by permission of The Wall Street Journal. All Rights Reserved Worldwide. Figure 3.5: "The Dow Jones Averages®", THE WALL STREET JOURNAL, January 8, 1992. Copyright © 1992 Dow Jones & Company, Inc. Reprinted by permission of The Wall Street Journal. All Rights Reserved Worldwide. Table 3.2: "Summary of Key Investor Services Available on Dow Jones News/Retrieval," Quick Reference Card, June 1991. Copyright © 1991 Dow Jones & Company. Reprinted by permission. All Rights Reserved Worldwide. Box 4.1: Adapted from "Compounding: It's Boring but a Wonder," by Robert L. Rose, THE WALL STREET JOURNAL, June 17, 1985. Copyright © 1985 Dow Jones & Company, Inc. Reprinted by permission of The Wall Street Journal. All Rights Reserved Worldwide. Box 4.2: From "How Much Risk Can You Take?" by Mary Rowland, THE NEW YORK TIMES, April 8, 1990. Copyright © 1990 by the New York Times Company. Reprinted by permission. Box 5.2: Adapted from "ADRs: Foreign Issues with U.S. Accents" by Tom Herman and M. R. Sesit, THE WALL STREET JOURNAL, February 8, 1990. Copyright © 1990 Dow Jones & Company, Inc. Reprinted by permission of The Wall Street Journal. All Rights Reserved Worldwide. Figure 5.1 "The Stock Market in 1991," THE WALL STREET JOURNAL. Copyright © 1991 Dow Jones & Company, Inc. Reprinted by permission of The Wall Street Journal. All Rights Reserved Worldwide. Figure 5.5: Adapted from "Explanatory Notes" listed daily in THE WALL STREET JOURNAL. Reprinted by permission of The Wall Street Journal. All Rights Reserved Worldwide. Figure 5.7: "Corporate Dividend News," THE WALL STREET JOURNAL, November 5, 1991. Copyright © 1991 Dow Jones & Company, Inc. Reprinted by permission of The Wall Street Journal. All Rights Reserved Worldwide. "Stock Quotes." Reprinted by permission of Standard & Poor's Corp. Box 6.1: From "The Federal Reserve Walks Quietly, But it affects the Economy with a Big Stick" by Manuel Schiffres, CHANGING TIMES, October 1988. Copyright © 1988 The Kiplinger Washington Editors, Inc. Reprinted by permission. Box 6.2: "Ten Commandments of Financial Statement Analysis" by Wm. H. Beaver, FINANCIAL ANALYSIS JOURNAL, Jan./Feb. 1991. Copyright © 1991 by Financial Analysts Journal. Reprinted by permission. Figure 6.1: "Tracking the Economy," THE WALL STREET JOURNAL, January, 27, 1992. Copyright © 1992 Dow Jones & Company, Inc. Reprinted by permission of The Wall Street Journal. All Rights Reserved Worldwide. Figure 6.2: "A Look at the Stock Performance of Key Industry Groups," STANDARD & POOR'S ANALYST's HANDBOOK, 1991. Reprinted by permission. Figure 6.3: "Textiles, Apparel & Home Furnishings-Demand Seen Firming by Late '91," STANDARD & POOR'S INDUSTRY SURVEYS, June 13, 1991. Copyright © 1991 Standard & Poor's Corporation. Reprinted by permission. Figure 6.4: "An Example of a Published Analytical Report with Financial Statistics," Standard & Poor's NYSE STOCK REPORTS, July 18, 1991. Copyright © 1991 Standard & Poor's Corporation. Reprinted by permission. Box 7.1: From "Value Investing Revisited" by Stuart Weiss, INVESTMENT VISION, Aug./Sept. 1991, pp. 67–68. Copyright © 1992 Capital Publishing. Reprinted by permission. Figure 7.2: "Some Market Statistics," THE WALL STREET JOURNAL, December 10, 1991. Copyright © 1991 Dow Jones & Company, Inc. Reprinted by permission of The Wall Street Journal. All Rights Reserved Worldwide. Figure 7.3: "Short Interest Highlights," THE WALL STREET JOURNAL, December 20, 1991. Copyright © 1991 Dow Jones & Company, Inc. Reprinted by permission of The Wall Street Journal. All Rights Reserved Worldwide. Box 8.2: Adapted from "Trading in the Dark: Real Bond Prices Are Hard to Come By" by Edward A. Wyatt, BARRON'S, November 6, 1989. Copyright © 1989 Dow Jones & Company, Inc. Reprinted by permission of Barron's. All Rights Reserved Worldwide. Figure 8.2: "The Announcement of a New Corporate Bond Issue—Coca-Cola Enterprises Inc." Reprinted by permission. Figure 8.5: "The Announcement for a New Municipal Bond Issue—Stanford University," Jan. 8, 1992. Reprinted by permission of Prager, McCarthy & Sealy. Figure 8.6: "Price Quotations of Corporate and Government Bonds," THE WALL STREET JOURNAL, March 18, 1992. Copyright © 1992 Dow Jones & Company, Inc. Reprinted by permission of The Wall Street Journal. All Rights Reserved Worldwide. Box 9.1: Adapted from "Bond Investors Who Fixate Too Much on Yields Risk Missing the Big Picture" by Barbara Donnelly, THE WALL STREET JOURNAL, March 13, 1992. Copyright © 1992 Dow Jones & Company, Inc. Reprinted by permission of The Wall Street Journal. All Rights Reserved Worldwide. Box 9.2: Adapted from "Taking Early Profits on Bonds May

INDEX

THE INVESTMENT
MANAGEMENT DISK (IMD)

SYSTEM REQUIREMENTS

- Any IBM or IBM-compatible PC
- DOS version 2.1 or higher
- 640KB of memory (500 KB free)
- Any of the following disk drive(s):
  - 2 360 KB 5.25″ floppy disk drives
  - 1 1.2 MB 5.25″ floppy disk drive
  - 1 720 KB 3.5″ floppy disk drive
  - 1 fixed disk drive and any floppy disk drive
- Printer recommended, but not required.

USER INSTRUCTIONS

You may run the Investment Management Disk from a fixed disk, from a floppy disk that is large enough to hold the entire system, or from a dual floppy-disk system. It is most satisfactory when run from a fixed disk.

From either a 5.25″ or a 3.5″ floppy disk system:

1. Insert your DOS diskette into drive A: (generally the one on the left or top of a dual disk drive). Always insert disks with the label-side up.

2. Turn on the computer and respond to any date and time requests.

3. The computer will display the A: prompt.

4. Remove the DOS diskette and replace it with the IMD Program diskette. If you are using two floppy disk drives to run the IMD, place the overlay diskette in drive B:.

5. With the computer still at the A: prompt, type START and press the <Enter> key.

To load the IMD program to a fixed disk system:

1. Create a subdirectory called IMD on your fixed disk and copy all of the files from the IMD diskette(s) to that subdirectory. For example, if you are at the C: prompt:

   C:\>**MD IMD**
   C:\>**CD IMD**
   C:\IMD>**COPY A:*.***

2. Rename the START.HD file to START.BAT. (Make this change only if you are running from a fixed disk, not a floppy disk system.)

   C:\IMD>**COPY START.HD START.BAT**

3. From the IMD subdirectory, you may then execute the IMD program by typing START and press the <Enter> key.

   C:\IMD>**START**

The IMD will load and the introductory screen will appear. Follow the instructions from the program. The IMD is menu-driven. Select the chapter and problems you wish to execute by highlighting the menu item or simply type the letter of the menu item. All of the routines in the IMD are keyed to equation numbers or pages in the book for reference. You may choose to enable the printer with the <F9> key to print the results of the calculations.

SEE APPENDIX E FOR COMPLETE LIST OF KEY EQUATIONS
AND DISK ROUTINES.